641.5   c.1
N
Nichols, H.L., Jr.
Cooking with Understanding

DATE DUE

Ehrenhart			
JAN 9 '7?			
Ehrenhart			
Luttrell			
Cloyed			
Ehrenhart			
Cloyed			
Wurst			
Erickson			

COOKING
WITH
UNDERSTANDING

Library of Congress Catalog Card Number: 74-150684
International Standard Book Number: 911040-09-9

Design by Libra Studios and Herbert L. Nichols, Jr.
Typography by Lettick Typografic
Drawings by Joseph A. Romeo
Printing by Rae Publishing Company
Binding by Tapley-Rutter Company

MANUFACTURED IN THE UNITED STATES OF AMERICA

H. L. Nichols, Jr.

COOKING
WITH
UNDERSTANDING

Drawings by Joseph A. Romeo

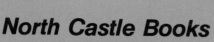
North Castle Books

212 BEDFORD ROAD
GREENWICH, CONN., 06830

ACKNOWLEDGMENTS

I gratefully acknowledge the assistance supplied by growers and processors of food, by their associations, and by friends, housewives and short-order cooks, all of whom have contributed generously of their time and knowledge toward the creation of this book.

I thank the writers and publishers of cookbooks for providing a vast field for research, and for the permissions that they have granted to use parts of their material. My particular thanks to the Avi Publishing Company, whose many books on commercial processing are invaluable sources of food facts.

I am grateful to Joseph Romeo for his patience, understanding and skill in converting my crude sketches and descriptions into finished illustrations.

Above all, my thanks are due to my assistant and fellow-author, Maj-Greth Wegener, for her loyal and efficient operation of my business during the many years I neglected it to write this book, for her help in research, experiment, and editing, and for the recipes and illustrations that she has allowed me to lift from her AMERICAN COOKING FOR FOREIGN LANDS.

The following is a partial list of people, companies, associations and references who have had a part in building COOKING WITH UNDERSTANDING. My apologies for forgetfulness are offered to those whose names should be here, but are not.

American Association for the Advancement of Science, 1515 Massachusetts Avenue, N.W. Washington, D.C. 20005.

American Can Company, American Lane, Greenwich, Connecticut 06830.

American Gas Association, 1515 Wilson Boulevard, Arlington, Virginia 22209.

American Spice Trade Association, 76 Beaver Street, New York 10005.

Svea Andersson, Goteborg, Sweden.

Armonk Hardware Co., Inc., Armonk, New York 10504.

Armour & Company, P.O. Box 9222, Chicago, Illinois 60690.

The Avi Publishing Co., Inc., P.O. Box 670, Westport, Connecticut 06880.

Ball Corporation, Muncie, Indiana 47302.

Bernardin, Inc., 2201 West Maryland Street, Evansville, Indiana 47701.

Bernz-O-Matic Corporation, Rochester, New York 14613.

Best Foods Division, CPC International, Englewood Cliffs, N.J. 07632.

Caloric Corporation, Topton, Pennsylvania 19562.

Canadian Pacific, CP Rail, Windsor Station, Montreal, Quebec, Canada.

Chemical Publishing Co., Inc., 200 Park Avenue, New York 10003.

The Clorox Company, P.O. Box 24305, Oakland, California 94623.

Connecticut Light & Power Company, 330 Railroad Avenue, Greenwich, Connecticut 06830.

The Coffee Brewing Center, 1350 Avenue of the Americas, New York 10019.

The Coleman Company, Inc., Wichita, Kansas 67201.

Consumers Union of U.S., Inc., 256 Washington Street, Mount Vernon, New York 10550.

Continental Can Company, Inc., 1350 West 76th Street, Chicago, Illinois 60620.

Corn Industries Research Foundation, 1001 Connecticut Avenue, Washington, D.C. 20036.

Corning Glass Works, Corning, New York, 14830.

Diamond Crystal Salt Company, St. Clair, Michigan 48079.

John DiGiacinto, Armonk, New York.

Patricia Duncan, Vinalhaven, Maine.

EKCO Housewares Ccompany, 9234 West Belmont Avenue, Franklin Park, Illinois 60131.

W. H. Freeman & Company, 660 Market Street, San Francisco, California 94104.

General Slicing Machine Company, Walden, New York 12586.

Mildred D. Gallik, New York, N.Y.

General Foods Corporation, 250 North Street, White Plains, New York 10605.

Beri Greenwald, New York City.

Harper-Wyman Company, 930 North York Road, Hinsdale, Illinois 60521.

Hershey Foods, Hershey, Pennsylvania 17033.

Lillian Jacobs, Palo Alto, Calif.

Emily Kalba, White Plains, New York.

Norman W. Keller, M.D., Greenwich, Conn.

Kerr Glass Manufacturing Corporation, Sand Springs, Oklahoma 74063.

Kitchenaid Dishwasher Division, The Hobart Manufacturing Co., Troy, Ohio 45373.

Lewis/Neale, Inc., Empire State Building, New York 1001.

Manville Manufacturing Corporation, 342 Rockwell Avenue, Pontiac, Michigan 48053.

Joseph and Marge Marcincuk, Byram, Connecticut.

C. O. Miller, Galion, Ohio.

Nora McMillian, Stamford, Conn.

McGraw-Hill Book Company, 330 West 42nd Street, New York 10036.

Mirro Aluminum Company, Manitowoc, Wisconsin 54220.

National Canners Association, 1133 - 20th Street, N.W., Washington, D.C. 20036.

National Live Stock & Meat Board, 36 South Wabash Avenue, Chicago, Illinois 60603.

National Presto Industries, Inc., Eau Claire, Wisconsin 54701.

National Restaurant Association, 1530 Lake Shore Drive, Chicago, Illinois 60610.

City of New York, Bureau of Water Supply, Municipal Building, New York 10007.

Pan-American Coffee Bureau, 1350 Avenue of the Americas, New York 10019.

Robert Panell, Jr., Norman, Oklahoma.

Robert and Helene Panell, Greenwich, Conn.

Marie Pazona, Greenwich, Conn.

Jean E. Pearsall, Greenwich, Conn.

Chas. Pfizer & Co., Inc., 235 East 42nd Street, New York 10017.

Popeil Brothers, Inc., 2323 Pershing Road, Chicago, Illinois 60609.

Poultry and Egg National Board, 18 South Michigan Avenue, Chicago, Illinois 60603.

Reid Electric Company, 768 North Broadway, White Plains, New York 10603.

Hope Rider, Studio City, California.

Joseph and Ann Romeo, Greenwich, Connecticut.

Aloha Roth, White Plains, New York.

Stefan Salter, Old Greenwich, Connecticut.

Helen Shaw, Charlotte, North Carolina.

Elizabeth Sherwood, Laurel, Maryland.

The Soap and Detergent Association, 475 Park Avenue South, New York 10016.

Standard Brands Incorporated, Test Kitchens, 625 Madison Avenue, New York 10022.

The Sugar Association, Inc., 254 West 31st Street, New York 10001.

Sunbeam Corporation, 5400 West Roosevelt Road, Chicago, Illinois 60650.

Tappan, 250 Wayne Street, Mansfield, Ohio 44902.

Tea Council of the U.S.A., Inc., 10 East 56th Street, New York 10022.

Margareta Thonfors, Goteborg, Sweden.

Otto Troeber, Greenwich, Connecticut.

U.S. Department of Agriculture, Washington, D.C. 20250.

Wear-Ever Aluminum Inc., 1089 Eastern Avenue, Chillicothe, Ohio 45601.

Maj-Greth Wegener, Greenwich, Connecticut.

BIBLIOGRAPHY

The books listed below have been used for reference. Titles marked with an asterisk are recommended for use with COOKING WITH UNDERSTANDING, those marked with two asterisks are strongly recommended.

*AMERICA COOKS, Edited by Ann Seranne. 1967, LC 67-26317, G. P. Putnam's Sons, New York 10016.

**AMERICAN COOKING FOR FOREIGN LANDS, Maj-Greth Wegener. 1969, LC 79-84625, North Castle Books, Greenwich, Conn. 06830.

THE AMERICAN COLLEGE DICTIONARY. 1947-1955, Random House, New York 10022.

THE ART OF FINE BAKING, Paula Peck. 1961, LC 61-12871, Simon & Schuster, New York 10020.

*THE ART OF MAKING GOOD COOKIES PLAIN AND FANCY, Annette Laslett Ross and Jean Adams Disney. 1963, Doubleday & Co., Garden City, N.Y. 11530.

THE ART OF MAKING SAUCES AND GRAVIES, Frederica L. Beinert. 1966, LC 66-20925, Doubleday & Co., Garden City, N.Y. 11530.

*BETTY CROCKER'S COOKBOOK. 1969, LC 69-18834, Golden Press, N.Y. 10022.

*THE BLUE SEA COOKBOOK, Sarah D. Alberson. 1968, LC 67-29995, Hastings House, New York 10016.

BREADS AND COFFEE CAKES, with Homemade Starters, Ada Lou Roberts. 1967, Hearthside Press, New York, 10016.

THE CANNED FOOD REFERENCE MANUAL, American Can Company Research Division. 1949, Third Edition (out of print), American Can Company, Greenwich, Conn. 06830.

*CANDY COOKBOOK, J. H. De Gros. 4th printing, 1967, LC 59-13673, Arco Publishing Company, New York 10003.

The CARLTON FREDERICKS COOK BOOK OF GOOD NUTRITION, Carlton Fredericks. 1960, LC 60-5108, J. B. Lippincott Company, Philadelphia, Pa. 19105

CHAMBER'S TECHNICAL DICTIONARY, edited by C. F. Tweney and L. E. C. Hughes. 1940-1954, The MacMillan Co., New York 10022.

THE CHEESE BOOK, Vivienne Marquis and Patricia Haskell. 1964, 1965, Simon & Schuster, New York 10020.

CHEESE VARIETIES AND DESCRIPTIONS, U.S. Dept. of Agriculture Bulletin No. 54. 1953 and 1969.

CHEMICALS USED IN FOOD PROCESSING, Publication 1274. 1965, 1967, LC 65-60045, National Academy of Sciences, National Research Council, Washington, D.C. 20418.

CHEMISTRY AND PHYSIOLOGY OF FLAVORS, Editor, H. W. Schultz, Ph.D.; Asst. Ed,, E. A. Day, Ph.D., L. M. Libbey, Ph.D. 1967, LC 66-24813, Avi Publishing Co., Westport, Conn. 06880.

COFFEE PROCESSING TECHNOLOGY, Michael Sivetz, M.S. 1963, LC 63-20007, Avi Publishing Co., Westport, Conn. 06880.

*COMMON EDIBLE MUSHROOMS, Clyde M. Christensen. 1943, The University of Minnesota Press, Minneapolis, Minn. 55455.

*THE COMPLETE BOOK OF HOME FREEZING, Ann Seranne. 1953, 1966, Doubleday & Co., Garden City, N.Y. 11530.

THE COMPLETE BOOK OF HOME PRESERVING, Ann Seranne. 1953, 1955, LC 54-7671, Doubleday & Co., Garden City, N.Y. 11530.

THE COMPLETE ROUND THE WORLD MEAT COOKBOOK, Myra Waldo. 1967, LC 67-11158, Doubleday & Co., Garden City, N.Y. 11530.

THE CONSPIRATORS' COOKBOOK, Century Downing. 1967, LC 67-11124, Alfred A. Knopf, New York 10022.

COOKING MADE SIMPLE, (paper), Gertrude Wilkinson. 1962, LC 62-14181, Doubleday & Co., Garden City, N.Y. 11530.

COOKING WITHOUT RECIPES, Helen Worth. 1959, 1960, 1965, Harper & Row, New York 10016

*COOK'S AND DINER'S DICTIONARY, Editor-in-Chief Samuel Davis. Funk & Wagnalls, New York 10017.

**CRAIG CLAIBORNE'S KITCHEN PRIMER, A Basic Cookbook, Craig Claiborne. 1969, LC 68-23951, Alfred A. Knopf, Inc., distributed by Random House, New York 10022.

DICTIONARY OF GASTRONOMY, André L. Simon and Robin Howe. LC 72-89318, McGraw-Hill Book Co., New York 10036.

THE DIET ADJUSTABLE COOKBOOK, Suzy Chapin. 1967, Funk & Wagnalls, New York 10017.

ENCYCLOPEDIA BRITANNICA. 1965, 1971, LC 70-115815, Encyclopedia Britannica, Inc., Chicago, Ill. 60611.

*EXPERIMENTAL COOKERY, Belle Lowe. 1932, 1937, 1943, 1955, Fourth Edition, LC 55-5449, John Wiley & Sons, New York 10016.

*THE FANNIE FARMER COOKBOOK, revised by Wilma Lord Perkins. 11th edition, 1965, Little, Brown & Co., Boston, Mass. 02106.

FARM JOURNAL'S COMPLETE PIE COOKBOOK, Farm Journal, Edited by Nell B. Nichols. 1965, LC 65-16174, Doubleday & Co., Garden City, N.Y. 11530.

FINE PRESERVING, Catherine Plagemann. 1967, LC 67-17888, Simon and Schuster, New York 10020.

FOOD CHEMISTRY, Lillian Hoagland Meyer. 1960, Second Printing Sept. 1961, LC 60-11080, Reinhold Publishing Corp., New York 10001.

FOOD CHEMISTRY AND COOKERY, Evelyn G. Halliday and Isabel T. Noble. 1943, (out of print), University of Chicago Press, Chicago, Ill. 60637.

FOOD ENZYMES, Edited by H. W. Schultz, Ph.D. 1960, Avi Publishing Co., Westport, Conn. 06880.

FOOD FLAVORINGS, Composition, Manufacture and Use, Joseph Merory. 1960, Avi Publishing Co., Westport, Conn. 06880.

FOOD PACKAGING, Stanley Sacharow, B.A., M.A.; Roger C. Griffin, Jr., B.S., M.S. 1970, LC 74-100062, Avi Publishing Co., Westport, Conn. 06880.

FOOD TEXTURE, Samuel A. Matz, Ph.D. 1962, LC 62-17118, Avi Publishing Co., Westport, Conn. 06880.

FOR SERVING 4 (OR EVEN MORE), Louise Pickoff. 1964, LC 64-21362, A. S. Barnes and Co., New York 10016.

THE FREEZING PREPARATION OF FOODS, Donald K. Tressler, Ph.D.; Clifford F. Evers, B.S., M.S. 1957, Third Edition, Avi Publishing Co., Westport, Conn.

FRUIT AND VEGETABLES, R. B. Duckworth. 1966, LC 66-25308, Pergamon Press, London W.1., England.

THE GOURMET IN THE LOW-CALORIE KITCHEN, Helen Belinkie. 1961, David McKay & Co., New York 10017.

**GOURMET'S MENU COOKBOOK, Compiled and Edited by Gourmet, Inc. 1963, Gourmet Distributing Corp., New York 10017.

*THE GREAT SCANDINAVIAN COOK BOOK, Translated and edited by J. Audrey Ellison. 1967, Crown Publishers, New York 10016.

A GUIDE TO THE SELECTION, COMBINATION AND COOKING OF FOODS, Carl A. Rietz. 1961, LC 61-12137, Avi Publishing Co., Westport, Conn. 06880.

HELEN CORBITT'S COOKBOOK, Helen Corbitt. 1957, Houghton Mifflin Co., Boston, Mass. 02107.

THE HIGH ALTITUDE COOKBOOK, Beverly A. Nemiro and Donna M. Hamilton. 1969, LC 67-12738, Random House, New York 10022.

HOMEMADE BREAD, Food Editors of Farm Journal, Edited by Nell B. Nichols. 1969, LC 69-10973, Doubleday & Co., Inc., Garden City, N.Y. 11530.

HOW TO EAT BETTER FOR LESS MONEY, James Beard and Sam Aaron. 1954, 1970, Second edition, Simon & Schuster, New York 10020.

HUMAN NUTRITION AND DIETETICS, Sir Stanley Davidson, R. Passmore. 1959, 1963, Second Edition, The Williams and Wilins Co., Baltimore, Md. 21202.

I HATE TO COOK BOOK, Peg Bracken. 1960, LC 60-10919, Harcourt, Brace & World, New York 10017.

ISRAELI COOKERY, Lilian Cornfeld. 1962, LC 62-10256, Avi Publishing Co., Westport, Conn. 06880.

IT'S NOT ALL IN YOUR MIND, H. J. Berglund, M.D. and H. L. Nichols Jr. 1953, LC 53-7260, North Castle Books, Greenwich, Conn. 06830.

JAMES BEARD'S MENUS FOR ENTERTAINING, James Beard. 1965, Delacorte Press, New York 10017.

*JOY OF COOKING, Irma S. Rombauer and Marion Rombauer Becker. 1967, LC 61-7902, The Bobs-Merrill Co., Indianapolis, Ind. 46268.

KIDS IN THE KITCHEN COOKBOOK, Lois Levine. 1968, The Macmillan Co., New York 10022.

The World Authority, LAROUSSE GASTRONOMIQUE, THE ENCYCLOPEDIA OF FOOD, WINE AND COOKERY, Edited by A. Escoffier and P. H. Gilbert. 1961, (First American Edition), Crown Publishers, New York 10016.

LET'S COOK IT RIGHT, Adelle Davis. 1947, 1962, LC 62-9440, Revised edition, Harcourt, Brace & World, New York 10017.

THE MARGARET RUDKIN PEPPERIDGE FARM COOKBOOK, Margaret Rudkin. 1963, 1965, Grosset & Dunlap, New York 10010.

MEAT HANDBOOK, Albert Levie. 1963, LC 63-17409, Avi Publishing Co., Westport, Conn. 06880.

THE MENU-COOKBOOK FOR ENTERTAINING, Libby Hillman. 1968, LC 68-8524, Hearthside Press, New York 10016.

*META GIVEN'S MODERN ENCYCLOPEDIA OF COOKING, Meta Given. New revised edition 1959, J. G. Ferguson Publishing Co., Chicago, Ill. 60602.

MICROWAVE HEATING, David A. Copson, Ph.D. 1962, LC 62-21391, Avi Publishing Co., Westport, Conn. 06880.

MILESTONES IN NUTRITION, Samuel A. Goldblith, SM. Ph.D.; Maynard A. Joslyn, M.S., Ph.D. 1964, LC 64-13714, Avi Publishing Co., Westport, Conn. 06880.

MILK AND MILK PROCESSING, B. L. Herrington. 1948, McGraw-Hill Book Co., New York 10036.

MILK AND MILK PRODUCTS, Clarence Henry Eckles, Willes Barnes Combs, Harold Macy. 1951, 1957, Fourth Edition, McGraw-Hill Book Co., New York 10036.

MISS BEECHER'S DOMESTIC RECEIPT-BOOK. 1868, Out of print, Harper & Brothers.

MODERN DAIRY PRODUCTS, Lincoln M. Lampert. 1965, Chemical Publishing Co., New York 10003.

THE NEW COOK'S COOKBOOK, Carol Guilford. 1969, LC 74-75904, The Macmillan Co., New York 10022.

*THE NEW GOOD HOUSEKEEPING COOKBOOK, edited by Dorothy B. Marsh. 1963, LC 63-15315, Harcourt, Brace & World, New York 10017.

*THE NEW SETTLEMENT COOKBOOK, Originally compiled by Mrs. Simon Kander. 31st edition, 1954, LC 53-11329, Simon & Schuster, New York 10020.

NEW STANDARD DICTIONARY OF THE ENGLISH LANGUAGE. 1913-1959, Funk & Wagnalls Co., New York 10017.

*NOBODY EVER TELLS YOU THESE THINGS, Helen McCully. 1967, LC 67-12647, Holt, Rinehart and Winston, New York 10017.

PASTA, Evelyn Gendel. 1966, LC 66-24037, Simon & Schuster, New York 10020.

POULTRY PRODUCTS TECHNOLOGY, George J. Mountney, Ph.D. 1966, LC 66-13359, Avi Publishing Co., Westport, Conn. 06880.

PRACTICAL BAKING, William J. Sultan. 1965, LC 65-26190, Avi Publishing Co., Westport, Conn. 06880.

PRACTICAL COOKING AND SERVING, Janet McKenzie Hill. CR 1902 and 1912, Out of Print, Doubleday, Page & Company.

RADIATION TECHNOLOGY, Norman W. Desrosier, Ph.D.; Henry M. Rosenstock, Ph.D. 1960, Avi Publishing Co., Westport, Conn. 06880.

SAVOR OF THE SEA, Dan Morris and Matilda Moore. 1966, The Macmillan Co., New York 10022.

THE SCIENCE OF MEAT AND MEAT PRODUCTS, American Meat Institute Foundation. 1960, LC 59-12057, W. H. Freeman & Co., San Francisco, Calif. 94104.

SERVE IT COLD, June Crosby and Ruth Conrad Bateman. 1968, 1969, Doubleday & Co., Garden City, N.Y. 11530.

THE SHELLFISH COOKBOOK, Marian Tracy. 1965, LC 65-2991, 2nd edition, Bobbs-Merrill Company, Inc., Indianapolis, Ind. 46268.

**THE SPICE COOKBOOK, Avanelle Day and Lillie Stuckey. 1964, LC 64-16339, David White Co., New York 10016.

STANDARD ENCYCLOPEDIC DICTIONARY. 1966, 1968, LC 66-26533, Funk & Wagnalls, New York 10017.

THE STEAK BOOK, Arthur Hawkins. 1966, LC 66-17429, Doubleday & Co., Garden City, N.Y. 11530.

THE SUMMER COOKBOOK, Lousene Rousseau Brunner. 1966, Harper & Row, New York 10016.

SUNSET MENU COOK BOOK, Editors of Sunset Books and Sunset Magazine. 1969, Lane Magazine and Book Co., Menlo Park, Calif. 94025.

SYMPOSIUM ON FOODS: CARBOHYDRATES AND THEIR ROLES, Editor, H. W. Schults, Ph.D.; Asst. Ed., R. F. Cain, Ph.D., R. W. Wrolstad, Ph.D. 1969, LC 70-78606, Avi Publishing Co., Westport, Conn. 06880.

SYMPOSIUM ON FOODS: PROTEINS AND THEIR REACTIONS, Editors, H. W. Schultz, Ph.D.; A. F. Anglemier, Ph.D. 1964, LC 64-18965, Avi Publishing Co., Westport, Conn. 06880.

The TECHNOLOGY OF FOOD PRESERVATION, Norman W. Desrosier, Ph.D. 1959, 1963, 1970 Third Edition, LC 73-94690, Avi Publishing Co., Westport, Conn. 06880.

TOXICANTS OCCURRING NATURALLY IN FOODS, National Academy of Sciences, National Research Council. 1967, LC 66-60059, National Academy of Sciences, Washington, D.C. 20418.

201 NEW WAYS TO COOK GROUND BEEF, Hyla O'Connor. 1966, LC 67-12413, Arco Publishing Co., New York 10003.

THE UNCOMMON COOK BOOK, Ruth Mellinkoff. 1968, The Ward Ritchie Press, Los Angeles, Calif., 90039.

VAN NOSTRAND'S SCIENTIFIC ENCYCLOPEDIA. 1938-1958 Third Edition, Van Nostrand Reinhold Co., New York 10001.

*THE VIENNESE PASTRY COOKBOOK, Lilly Joss Reich. 1970, LC 79-80303, The Macmillan Co., New York 10022.

*A WORLD OF BREADS, Dolores Casella. 1966, David White Co., New York 10022.

A WORLD OF VEGETABLE COOKERY, Alex D. Hawkes. 1968, LC 68-25748, Simon & Schuster, New York 10020.

YOUNG HOMEMAKERS' EQUIPMENT GUIDE, Louise J. Peet. 1958-1963 Revised Second Edition, LC 62-20949, The Iowa State University Press, Ames, Iowa 50010.

TABLE OF CONTENTS

37 ELECTRIC APPLIANCES

38 RANGES (STOVES)

39 REFRIGERATION

PREFACE

It is the purpose of this book to present an extensive coverage of the field of cooking that is simple enough to serve the needs of the student and the beginner, yet thorough enough to enlarge the understanding of the experienced cook. It is primarily explanation and discussion, rather than arbitrary instruction.

The text is divided into five major parts. The first of these is concerned primarily with methods of food handling, preparation and cooking. The second part discusses the characteristics of basic or simple foods, and the third combines them into more complicated dishes. Part Four explains food spoilage and preservation, and some aspects of the relationship between food and health. The last section is concerned with the kitchen, first cleaning it up after a meal, then with the nature of its tools and appliances.

However, the subject does not always divide conveniently or clearly into these classifications. Lemons are rightfully described with Citrus Fruits, but they must also be discussed under Flavoring. When a utensil is concerned with only one food — a waffle baker, for example — it seemed better to describe it with the food than later among the appliances.

Overlapping has resulted in repetition of short bits of information in different sections, to save the nuisance of following cross references. And there is a danger that some subjects may have been lost between sections, so that they are not mentioned at all.

The Table of Contents and the Index are unusually long and detailed, to make scattered (or perhaps misplaced) material easy to find.

Sources of the material in COOKING WITH UNDERSTANDING are very diverse. Work methods and happenings in the ordinary home kitchen are important, and emphasis is given to the problems of the inexperienced cook. Some attention has been paid to procedures and results in test kitchens.

Book references are mostly in two classes. There are the familiar cookbooks, both general and specialty, which tend to present fixed recipes with little or no explanation. There are also technical works, designed chiefly for use of industrial food processors, in which chemical, physical and sometimes psychological aspects of food and cooking are discussed, with limited reference to home cooking.

Many food producers, manufacturers of kitchen equipment and associations of such suppliers have home economics or customer service departments that supply manuals, leaflets and personal letters that contain valuable information.

Other information and viewpoints have been found in scientific and consumer-protection magazines.

There are also traditions (don't leave food in an open can), prejudices (don't eat animals), fads (add milk powder to everything) and oddities (don't stir rice with a spoon), which deserve careful consideration before acceptance or rejection.

Finally, there have been innumerable personal experiments. All the dishes in this book have been tested, most of them according to not only single recipes, but also with combinations of recipes, and recipes that were altered drastically to see what would happen. In addition, various ingredients were cooked singly or in unusual combinations to observe their behavior.

The field of cooking is a confused one, since food substances are extremely complicated and variable, both in themselves and in their responses to processing. As a result, findings in research and experiment are often doubtful and even contradictory.

It has been necessary to use such words as "usually" and "generally", and phrases such as "it is said" and "it seems" with monotonous frequency. And it is probable that they have not been used often enough.

The "authorities" to whom I refer in the text are authors of cookbooks, textbooks, manuals and articles; and personnel of companies and associations. The organizations and books are listed in the Acknowledgments and the Bibliography, with few text references. The parts of their material that have been used without change are in picture or tabular form in illustrations, with credit lines.

I have tried to produce a book with sufficiently wide and basic coverage so that study of it can enable an inexperienced person to cook for a family immediately, without other references or training. But it is also designed to fit in with other helps and means of learning, including classroom instruction, and is particularly intended to increase the interest and value of whatever recipe-type cookbooks are on hand.

Care has been exercised to verify all the material presented, by direct experiment whenever possible, and to keep it accurate and in order during its processing into print. The publisher will appreciate being notified of any mistakes that may be found in spite of these precautions.

COOKING
WITH
UNDERSTANDING

Part One / METHODS

1
HANDLING FOOD

CLEANLINESS

Cleanliness is important in handling food, although it can be overdone. Clean food and clean utensils offer protection for health and reduce rates of spoilage. See Chapter 33, and Index entries under Cleanliness.

In addition, most kinds of dirt are unpleasant or at least unwelcome if they accompany food in noticeable quantities. Nobody likes sand in the spinach, hair in the soup or fingerprints on the apple slices.

Hands. Hands are used to manipulate food both directly and by holding and operating containers and tools. Many cookbooks disapprove of direct contact with food, and will often tell you to use utensils for jobs that are better done by fingers.

Clean hands (washed with soap and water, with finger nails cleaned) are practically as sanitary as any other clean tool. You should not be squeamish about using them whenever it is convenient to do so. But bear in mind that they are delicate, and must be protected from being cut, scraped or bruised, and from touching hot, very cold or corrosive materials. They should be protected by rubber gloves if their skin is irritated by substances being handled, and by gloves, mittens or potholders when dealing with hot utensils.

Hands are likely to need more frequent wiping, rinsing or washing than is required for spoons and other utensils. You have only one pair, so they are used for many different jobs in succession. Also, they handle non-working outside surfaces of tools and containers.

For example, picking up or touching any greasy or oily food (including most raw meat) will leave a film on fingers that will spread to every dry substance that they touch, unless you wipe them on absorbent paper (towel or napkin) or on cloth, or wash them, in between uses.

Utensils. Utensils and containers should be clean and preferably dry at the start of the job. They should be cleaned, usually by rinsing but sometimes by wiping, scraping or washing, if any food sticks to them when they are moved from one food or one stage of preparation to another. If set aside for a future washup, they should be put in water to keep food remnants soft.

Forks and spoons sometimes need cleaning during work. If a recipe tells you to stir

1

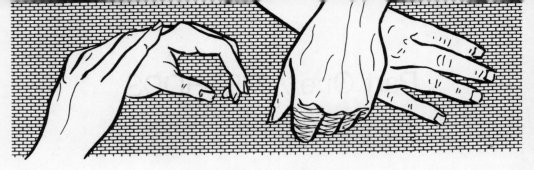

Fig. 1-1. Hands are for handling

or beat with a fork, it is probably because it needs the mixing action caused by flow between the tines. If these slots become clogged, you should open them, usually by wiping from the handle toward the open ends, but sometimes by sliding a thin object like a knife or a toothpick between them.

All food remnants must be thoroughly cleaned out of pans before re-use, as they are likely to cause sticking and burning. Outside deposits should be removed, as they are likely to char into ugly films that are difficult to remove.

Kitchen. It is desirable that the entire kitchen be in good repair, well painted and scrupulously clean. This is good for your morale, makes your food more acceptable to others and reduces chances of accidental contamination.

However, you can get by all right if only the actual working areas are clean, and are re-cleaned as often as necessary during your work. Debris from each process should usually be cleaned up, or at least pushed well to the side, before starting the next phase of the work.

DROPPING AND RETRIEVING

You might have the misfortune to overturn or drop a pan, bowl or platter loaded with cooked or uncooked food. This may create quite a mess if the food is liquid, soft or in many pieces. It may spread and splash over large areas of table, stove and floor; and the prospect of cleaning it up may seem hopeless. However, with a systematic approach it may prove to be a minor job.

There are four steps to be taken: sal-

vage, scraping, wiping and finishing.

Salvage. You should be able to salvage whatever food is on the table. It is to be presumed that it was reasonably clean when you started to work, and it is usually possible to separate bits of other food, and utensils, from the spilled material. The range is much more difficult, and whatever falls on the burners or drains under them may be presumed lost.

The floor is much like the table, but its cleanliness is more in doubt. Your actions here may depend on its condition when it received the food. If it was freshly washed and spotlessly clean it will neither flavor nor contaminate the food. If it was freshly waxed, sandy or just ordinarily dirty the food in direct contact with it should not be used, unless in pieces solid enough to be wiped, washed or trimmed, or deep enough so you can scoop off the top.

It is not necessary to tell your family that part of their dinner was processed on the floor. If you feel like chatting about it, it is tactful to wait until after eating.

If the container was made of glass or china, and it broke, you have a problem of splinters and specks. Both are unpleasant to chew, and glass is dangerous to swallow. If it seems possible that pieces are spread throughout the food, it is wisest to throw all of it away.

Scraping. After you have salvaged as much food as you can or think you should, remove the bulk of the remaining spill by picking up the solid pieces, and pushing or scraping small pieces and soft material.

Scraping usually involves a pusher to

2

move the stuff and a receptacle to receive it. The pusher may be almost anything, including a spatula, a sink brush, cardboard or (except when there is broken glass) the side of your hand. The container for coarse work might be a pan or a bowl, but something with a thin flat edge is better. A dustpan, a sheet of cardboard or even folded paper may be used. In the final stages, or for very small jobs, a pair of file cards or playing cards or even envelopes serves well as both pusher and container.

The container should be emptied whenever it gets full enough to allow its contents to flow back or slop over. It may be dumped in the sink, or put in a plastic bag and then in the garbage, depending on its nature. Or you can empty it into a larger receptacle for later disposal.

If a table has an overhanging edge you can hold a bowl partly under it as you push and scrape off the edge. If there is no overhang, you need a straight sided container or something on the floor to catch spill.

Your disaster area may include the stove top. The upper surface may be scraped and wiped off in the same manner as a table, but working carefully around the burner sockets. If anything has slopped into them and on the burners, you must remove the affected parts, wash them and swab out the remaining surfaces.

Fig. 1-2. It does happen

A range should have a pull-out tray under the burners, or a hinged cooktop that can be raised after unlatching. The lift-top gives access for complete cleaning. The tray can be pulled out, drained and wiped.

Wiping. The spill should now be reduced to a thin layer and small pieces. Take crumpled paper to wipe up most of this remainder. Paper towels are the best material, but a big mess may take an unreasonable number of them. Single sheets of newspaper, well crumpled, make poor but plentiful substitutes for paper towels. A wet cloth is effective if it is rinsed frequently.

If you are going to use both newspaper

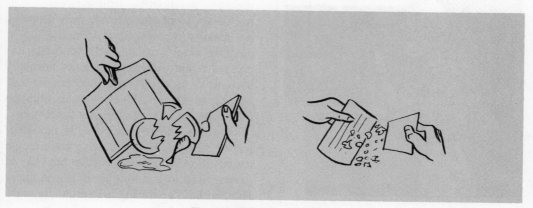

Fig. 1-3. Picking up the pieces

and towels, finish with the towels as they make a cleaner job.

Finishing. The final step is wiping off the whole area, including table top, exposed chairs, chair and table legs, wall surfaces and the floor, with a damp cloth, preferably a dish cloth. Wring it out in the sink and re-wet it at frequent intervals, to avoid leaving a gummy film.

AVOIDING SPOILAGE

The problems of food spoilage are discussed in the chapter on FOOD PRESERVATION and under individual foods. References will be found in the Index under Spoilage.

In general, spoilage is minimized by keeping utensils clean and food wrapped and cold, not opening cans or defrosting frozen food until just before use and frequent picking over of stored fruit and vegetables to remove rotting ones before they cause others to rot also.

FOLLOWING RECIPES

A recipe is a set of instructions for preparing a particular food. It should specify type and quantity of ingredients, sequence of preparation and method of cooking. It is usually rather brief, but is occasionally long and detailed.

Most cookbook recipes are completely arbitrary. They tell you what ingredients you must use, and exactly how much of each except for permitting some occasional liberties in seasoning. The impression is given that the proportions are fixed by natural law, and that any deviation from them makes success unlikely.

But if you read another recipe for the same item, even in the same cookbook, you will find different proportions and often different ingredients, presented in the same positive manner. The tabulation of chocolate sauces in Figure 18-12 gives an idea of the extent of the possible variation.

You will also notice that natural law usually expresses itself conveniently in rather even measurements. Old cookbooks might tell you to use a rounded teaspoon or a scant cup of an ingredient, but it is the present custom to give all measurements in level spoons, cups or definite fractions of cups, in order to protect the cook from having to use her own judgment.

In countries using the metric system, quantities may be given in spoons similar to ours for small quantities, but standard measurements are in grams (one gram equals about .035 ounce) and deciliters (one deciliter is about .42 cup). Here also amounts are conveniently rounded, although the units are incompatible with ours.

It is apparent that a recipe only provides its makers' nearest approximation to a possibly ideal mixture, with amounts expressed simply in measurements normally used. It is probably only occasionally and by chance that the ideal amounts and the quantities in the recipe are just the same.

However, the beginner should nevertheless be scrupulous in following each recipe exactly. She has enough to keep her busy in getting used to handling utensils and materials, without confusing her results by making amateur changes in a good recipe.

Fig. 1-4. Recipes are arbitrary

Variation in Ingredients. Even if recipes were given in correct fine and fractional amounts, and a cook could and would measure the quantities exactly, the ideal mixture would still be hard to obtain. Many ingredients vary from one time to another, and between different areas. Sugar and salt are quite the same everywhere in the country, except perhaps in fineness of particles. But flour in the middle West is likely to be softer than flour of the same brand in New York, and butter is much saltier in the South than in the North.

Eggs vary in weight, even within one size class, and in their proportions of water and other substances. Milk, cream, butter and cheese all vary both in original properties and in their processing and freshness. Flavor and texture of meat are affected by the breed of animal, what it ate, how much it moved around and at what age it was killed; and by the time and conditions of storage and handling.

Most vegetables and fruits vary even more widely in cooking qualities, flavor and texture. Seasonings usually lose strength and may change in flavor during even short storage periods.

The expert cook tends to compensate automatically for such variations. She (or he) has developed a sense of texture, flavor and timing that enable her to make small changes that make the difference between ordinary good food and excellence.

Many cooks do not develop the feeling for food that is required for successful recipe adjustment, or they acquire it only for certain types of food or even just for a few recipes. Such recipes are then likely to become their "show-off" specialities.

With or without special intuition or skill, many experienced cooks do not even try to follow recipes exactly. They read them, decide what the writer intends, and then proceed to use their own quantities and methods, using the recipes as guides or reminders. Results may be either worse or better than would be obtained by following instructions.

Making a Recipe. A great deal of fine cooking is done without benefit of measurements. The cook simply blends ingredients together until the mixture looks right. If she tries to measure them, in order to make up a recipe for a friend, she is likely to get self-conscious and do it wrong.

In such a case, measure out a more-than-sufficient supply of each ingredient before starting work, use them freely during mixing, then measure the remainders and subtract from the original quantities to find the amounts used.

ORGANIZATION

Cooking is often done in a haphazard manner with good results, but effort is usually reduced and the product is often improved by organizing the work.

Thought. The first step is to read the recipe thoughtfully. Will it produce what you want, in nearly the right quantity? Do you have all the ingredients? The necessary

Fig. 1-5. An ingredient may have dete...

pans and tools? Enough time for preparation, cooking and perhaps chilling?

The original choice of the recipe might have been influenced by a desire to use up an over-abundant or aging stock of one or more of the ingredients. This may raise the question whether enough will be used to be worth the trouble, and whether the overstock might have already deteriorated past the point where it will yield a good result.

Setting Up. It is a good plan to start work by getting out all your food materials and tools, and setting them up to check off against the recipe. Make sure that everything is present, and that each food item is not only there but in usable condition.

Most recipes involving baking or roasting call for preheating the oven. It is very easy to forget this in the midst of concocting an unfamiliar dish. You can set a timer to remind you, or you can turn on the oven when you start to mix. The cost of any extra heating time is usually small, and modern ovens do not usually overheat the kitchen, except in very hot weather.

An electric oven should heat to 350° F (medium or medium hot) in 8 minutes, while most gas ovens take around 15. Preheating ovens is standard for most recipes. It is required or at least desirable for some, and serves largely to simplify timing in others. If you forget, and then don't want to wait for heating, add about 2/3 of preheating time to the total time in the oven.

Try to arrange food items in the order in which they will be used, and select a separate place to put the packages after use. This should prevent later worry about whether you have or have not already put in an ingredient.

Timer. Your equipment should include a timer that can be set for a time interval from one to 30 or 60 minutes, and which will buzz or ring at the end of that time. A stop watch, although less common in kitchens, is also desirable.

If you are following a recipe exactly

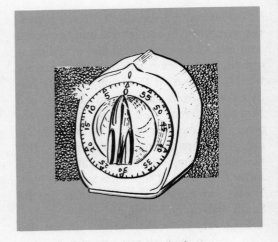

Fig. 1-6. Non-electric timer

(sound procedure for a first try) and are told to beat, stir or allow to stand for a certain number of minutes, it is good to be able to time yourself. The watch is more accurate, but the warning sound from the timer makes it harder to ignore.

You can time yourself with an ordinary clock or watch, but unless you write down the starting time of an operation, you may forget (or worse, remember wrongly) by the time you look at it again.

Re-checking. After you think you have finished combining the ingredients, re-read the recipe to see if you have left something out, either a food or a process. Sometimes it is then too late to do anything about it, sometimes not.

After Cooking. Before starting to cook, or while cooking, make sure that you are ready to handle the food when it is done. You may need pot holders, a wire rack or a serving bowl, tongs or a perforated spoon, a sieve or a colander, a mold or cups, or just space to put something down. Whatever you need, it should be ready at the right time.

MEASURING

A recipe usually tells you how much of each of several ingredients to use, but not always. A few things are left to your judgment, such as "serve on lettuce leaves" or "salt and pepper to taste".

Other directions relate quantity to an effect of some sort — make it thin, thick, smooth and so forth. Most of these assume that you are an experienced cook. The conditions listed are often dependent as much on stirring, heat or other factors as on quantity.

A similar type of instruction is "add water to cover". This is simple enough, unless the food is lighter than the water. Then you use just enough water to float it, and cover the pan.

But most measurements are given in exact quantities.

Units of Measurement. Most American measurement for cooking is done by volume. The basic unit is the fluid ounce, 1/32 of a quart. Fractions of ounces are measured by spoons — a tablespoon for 1/2 ounce, a teaspoon for 1/6. Multiples of ounces may be stated as such (2 ounces, 12 ounces, and so forth) or in 8-ounce cups (1/4 cup, 1-1/2 cups), 16-ounce pints or 2-pint quarts.

Figure 1-7 gives most of the common units of measurement of volume, both American and foreign. Certain staples such as gelatin and yeast may be given by the package (pkg) or by the can. Can sizes are given under Canning, and in the Appendix.

Weight. There are also avoirdupois ounces which are a measure of weight. They are seldom if ever used in our recipes. If weight is intended it is given in pounds (16 avoirdupois ounces) or fractions of pounds.

Any confusion between the two kinds of ounces is usually small enough to be unimportant. A fluid ounce of water weighs about 1-1/20 ounces avoirdupois. Most foods without voids are within 10 or 15 per cent of the weight (specific gravity) of water.

Metric. The metric system of measurement is used in most of the non-English speaking parts of the world and it is expected to gradually displace our method. It

VOLUME					
	Teaspoon (tsp)	Tablespoon (Tb)	Fluid ounce (fl. oz.)	Cup	Deciliter (dl)
Teaspoon	1	⅓	1/6	1/64	.05
Tablespoon	3	1	½	1/16	.15
Fluid ounce	6	2	1	⅛	.30
Cup	48	16	8	1	2.37
Deciliter	20.3	6.76	3.38	.42	1.00

1 pint = 2 cups	1 quart = 2 pints 1 gallon = 4 quarts	1 liter = 10 deciliters

WEIGHT

1 pound = 16 ounces
1 pound = .45 kilogram
1 ounce = 28.35 grams
1 gram = .035 ounce

1 kilogram = 2.20 pounds
1 kilogram = 1000 grams
1 hectogram = 3.52 ounces
1 hectogram = 100 grams

1 avoirdupois ounce water = 1.05 fluid ounces

Fig. 1-7. American and metric measures

is found in very few American cookbooks at present, but an understanding of it is convenient if you ever use foreign recipes. Tablespoon and teaspoon sizes are the same as ours. Other volume measurements for cooking are based on the liter, which is about 33.6 fluid ounces, just a little (5 per cent) larger than a quart. A deciliter is 1/10 of a liter, and equals .42 (say 3/5) of a cup, or 3.36 (say 3-1/3) ounces or almost 8 tablespoons.

Weight measurements are frequently used. They are based on the gram which equals .035 ounces avoirdupois, the hectogram, 3.52 oz. and the kilogram, which equals 2.2 pounds.

Dry volume metric measurements are seldom used in cooking, but are standard in scientific work even here. They are based on the cubic meter, which is big, 1.3 cubic yards, the cubic centimeter (cc) which is .061 cubic inches, or about 2 teaspoons. For precision work (not in kitchens) there is also the cubic millimeter (mm^3) which is 1/1000 of a cubic centimeter.

Imperial. The British imperial ounce is about 5 per cent smaller than the American one (437.5 grains of water instead of 455.6), but the larger measurements — gallons, pints and cups — each hold 25 per cent (1/4) more ounces. A cup holds 10 ounces, a pint 20, and so forth. The net result is that an imperial measure, from a cup up to a gallon, contains about 1/5 more volume of fluid than its American counterpart.

Spoon sizes are also different. Their official tablespoon holds one ounce, about double the American size. There is also an unofficial British tablespoon which holds 2/3 of an ounce, or 1-1/3 American tablespoons. The British teaspoon holds either 1/4 or 1/6 ounce, while the American holds 1/6. If you have unofficial size spoons, the error in using unchanged American directions will be quite small.

Imperial measures are used throughout most of the former British colonial and commonwealth countries, except that cooking in Canada usually is done by American units.

Measuring Tools. Measuring may be done with either ordinary or special utensils.

Tableware teaspoons and tablespoons usually hold very close to their rated capacities (1/6 and 1/2 ounce), but the one you have in your hand might be larger or smaller. It can be checked with a special measuring spoon, or by spooning a measured quantity out of a cup.

Special measuring spoons usually come in sets such as that in Figure 1-8. Capacities may be 1/4, 1/2 and 1 teaspoon and 1 tablespoon. Another of 1-1/2 teaspoons (1/2 tablespoon) would be convenient, but never seems to be present. A soup or dessert spoon often has this capacity.

Fig. 1-8. Measures

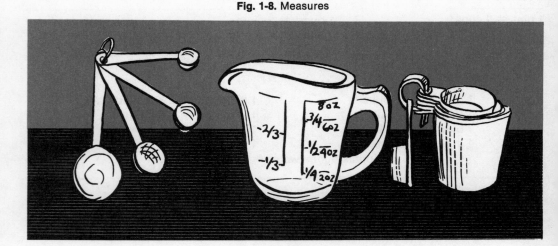

Fig. 1-9. Looking down and looking through

Glass cups are made in 1, 2 and 4 cup sizes. Lines to indicate quantity when filled to their level are engraved on both sides. The Pyrex brand appears to be very accurate, others may be off by as much as 10 per cent. Such cups may also be made of metal, but are more difficult to use. Plastic is pleasingly light, but is likely to be crude and inaccurate.

There are also fractional cups, usually metal or plastic, that are filled to the brim to obtain the rated measurement. They are easy and accurate to use, particularly with solids. Instead of trying to sight across lines and estimate an irregular surface, you can overfill and push off the surplus with any straight edge.

A jelly glass usually holds 8 ounces, the same as a measuring cup, when brim full. A tumbler or water glass should hold 8 ounces if filled to 1/4 inch below the brim, but there are also 7, 9, 10, and 12 ounce sizes, so ordinary glasses are not good for measurement unless checked.

Working utensils such as pans, blender containers, jars in which food is bought, pitchers and sifters are often inscribed with marks or horizontal lines so that they can be used for measurement.

Size measurements may be made with a flat ruler or a metal or cloth tape.

If you are going to use one measuring unit for both a liquid and a powder, in succession, it is efficient to do the powder first, in the dry container, so that it will not stick. It is difficult to dry most surfaces completely so that powder will not stick to them during the next few minutes, although it can be done by rubbing well with a towel and then exposing to gentle heat.

Language. Most recipe measurements are intended to be level — that is, the material is supposed to just fill the space assigned and to be level on top. But occasionally one will call for a measure that is scant, full, rounded or heaping.

Scant means a tiny bit less than level. For a cup, to which it is usually applied, it means to be short a teaspoon or perhaps a tablespoon (1/2 ounce) but usually not as much as an ounce.

Full means a similar extra amount.

Rounded and heaping are usually applied to spoon measures. Both are very approximate, because roundness is a personal concept, and powders vary greatly in the amount that will stand in a column. In a general way, you can assume that a rounded spoon is equal to 1-1/2 level ones, and a heaping spoon twice as much as the level.

Modern recipe writers keep pretty much to level measures, and may make editorial criticisms of any other approach. However, these in-between quantities may be closer to the needs of the recipe than level ones. A cook who believes that a certain proportion is ideal should not be expected to change it by translation into approved level measures. However, since measurement in cooking is an approximation at best, neither side of this argument need be taken seriously.

Liquid. Liquid measures may be transparent glass or plastic with inscribed marks (usually horizontal lines), metal with flush top and stamped lines, or part-cups or spoons that are filled to the brim.

Level may be observed in the filled nontransparent type by looking downward across the near rim to the far side, and adding liquid until it reaches the proper mark. A transparent measure may be used in the same way, or placed at eye level (or the eye lowered to its level), and a sight taken across the surface, through the measuring lines.

Liquid surfaces are usually not quite level, but curve slightly downward (particularly when at the rim) or upward at the

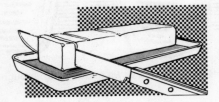

Fig. 1-10. Dividing a stick of butter

edges. The resulting uncertainty in level is too small to matter, except that if you wish to be very precise, you should avoid over-filling spoons.

Very thick liquids may stand in definite mounds, which should be flattened by patting or shaking, or in the case of filled measures, pushed off with a flat edge. They also may stick in the container, from which they must be scraped or pushed to obtain the measured quantity.

Powder. Many important items in recipes are in the form of powder. Finely ground ones include flour, corn starch, baking powder, dry milk, cocoa, gelatin, and powdered and confectioners' sugar.

Coarser powdered or granular substances are granulated sugar, corn meal, bread and cracker crumbs, grated cheese, chopped nuts and dried herbs.

Powder would be very easy to measure if it were not for a problem of density or compaction. It can be shaken or bladed off to a level surface, and it does not spill as easily as liquids do.

But many powders are compressible so that the same measure may hold widely differing quantities (weights) of one, depending on the way in which it has been handled before measurement.

In general, prescribed measurements for powders assume that they are loose or fluffy, as a result of shaking up during spooning or pouring. But brown sugar is often packed measure because it has an inherent tendency to cling in soft lumps. Most baking recipes specify that the flour be sifted before measuring.

Shortening. Solid shortening (also called fat or grease) may be in the form of hard pieces, as in animal fats and cold butter and margarine, or soft and sticky, as room temperature butter and margarine, and hydrogenated oil (Crisco and such) at any temperature.

Butter and margarine are commonly packaged in 1/4-pound sticks that make measurements very easy. Each stick is 4 ounces (both fluid and avoirdupois) or 1/2 of a cup. The wrapper may be marked in 1/4 and 1/8 cups, and/or in tablespoons, and may be cut at the desired line or lines before unwrapping. If such guide lines are lacking, position of cuts can usually be estimated closely. For small divisions, best accuracy is obtained by making marks to first divide the stick in half (wrapped or unwrapped), then at the center point of a half, and again at the center of those halves, as in Figure 1-10. Your last line gives you 4 ounces x 1/2 x 1/2 x 1/2, or 1/2 ounce which is one tablespoon.

If you have hard shortening in irregular shapes, you can usually mash it down until it is plastic. It can then be measured either directly or by displacement, as described below for soft shortening.

Soft or plastic shortening is difficult to measure because it tends to have substantial voids between lumps when put in a measure, and because its stickiness makes it difficult to level the top.

For the first problem, use a glass cup for measuring. Most voids form at the edges, and you can see them and push the grease down into them, or add some to the top to compensate. But to get an accurate top, you should use a measure that holds just the amount you want, 2/3 or 3/4 cup, for example. Then you can smooth the shortening off level with the top with a straight edge. But sets of such measures are almost always made of metal or opaque plastic, so that if you take the benefit of the accurate top surface you must take your chances with subsurface voids. They are hard enough to work out when you can see them, and almost impossible by guess work.

Hard shortening will often come out of a cup cleanly, even when mashed. But it may stick, and soft shortening always will. You can cut it out with a knife or a squeegee while you hold the cup horizontally or upside down. But it is usually easier and cleaner to loosen it by melting.

Put the cup or other measure in hot shallow water, not up to its rim. Hold it there for about 30 seconds, then lift it out and dump the shortening. Use tongs or pliers if the water is too hot for fingers. If the fat does not slide out, heat the cup some more. Or you can hold the cup upside down in a stream of hot water, with your fingers placed to support the lump when it loosens.

Many people find the displacement method to be the easiest and most accurate way to measure shortening. Use a measure at least twice as large as the quantity you need, fill it half full of water, and place pieces or globs of shortening in it until the water level has risen by the amount you want to use. For example, to get 2/3 of a cup of cooking fat, fill a 2-cup measure to the 1-cup line, then put in fat until the water rises to the line for 1-2/3 cups. Pour the water away, holding the shortening in and allowing it to drain thoroughly before use.

You may have to push the top lump down slightly to get it all under water. There is only a small chance of air bubbles confusing measurement, as the water flows around each glob of grease as you put it in.

Shortening seldom requires very exact measurement, but it is advisable to get it near the recommended amount.

Slices. Directions often tell you to slice food, usually vegetables, before cooking. Thickness may be specified, as 1/8 or 1/4 of an inch, or some other dimension.

Slicing may be done to speed up the cooking, for convenience in handling or appearance in serving. Exactness is usually not necessary, but a close approach to it is desirable to assure uniformity of cooking and good appearance when serving.

It is a good idea to measure slices the first few times you make them, until you get used to the appearance of different thicknesses. After that you will probably be able to judge them well enough by eye.

Measuring is done before slicing. You can use any type of rule or tape. It is not easy to read small fractions of an inch. So measure the top surface of the food in inches, making lines on the top surface with knife slits. Then make shorter lines half way in between for 1/2 inches, midway between them for 1/4 and again for 1/8 inch if required. Use the lines as guides in making cuts, which should be as near to parallel as possible.

This is the same principle that is applied to measuring butter in Figure 1-10.

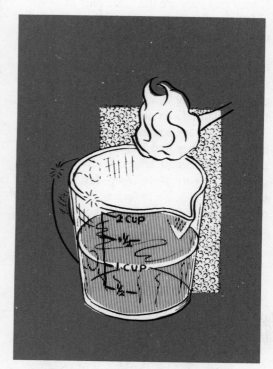

Fig. 1-11. Measuring shortening, displacement method

TEMPERATURE

Temperature is a critical factor in most cooking operations, particularly baking, either in itself or in its effect on the time required.

Fahrenheit and Celsius. Temperature in almost all American cookbooks and kitchens is measured in degrees Fahrenheit (° F). In this scale, plain water freezes at 32° and boils at 212° at sea level. The more convenient Celsius (originally Centigrade) system, according to which water freezes at zero and boils at 100°, is used widely throughout the world and will probably displace our Fahrenheit system eventually. However, that change is still in the future, and all temperatures in this book are given on the Fahrenheit scale with only occasional mention of Celsius.

The Appendix provides figures for conversions between Celsius and Fahrenheit. Notice that they are the same only at −40°.

With either system, a thermometer is used to determine temperature.

Other scales. In addition to these formal and exact temperature descriptions, there are various others that are used in cooking, usually in connection with a particular method, as in roasting or frying. These may vary somewhat from one cookbook to another, but usually not enough to have an important effect. Oven scales are given in Figure 4-4. Deep fat is usually heated to a specific temperature, but speed of browning effect and just-short-of-smoking may be used as standards.

Another set of directions is based on the boiling point of water. There is rapid (or full) boil and slow boil, both at substantially the same 212°, but with differences arising from agitation of the food and the likelihood of sticking and burning. There is simmering, which include important but usually unspecified variations from 210 down to 190° or less. And in pressure cooking (see page 42) boiling water and its steam are confined, and temperature may be measured by steam pressure, or by the rocking of a balanced relief valve.

Color is chiefly an indication of the stage of cooking that has been reached, but it will enable an experienced cook to estimate temperature very closely. Before thermometers, deep fat was at proper heat when it turned a half-inch cube of bread rich brown in 60 seconds. Too quick or deep a brown shows that a pancake griddle is too hot, lack of browning that it is too cool.

A drop of water will evaporate quickly but smoothly from a pan at low heat. At about 400° F such a drop will form into a ball that will move or dance until it is totally evaporated. Temperatures above and below the critical one may be judged by the amount and sound of its activity, and the speed with which it disappears. Frying heat is also indicated by the amount of spattering and smoking that occurs.

For moderate and cold temperatures the sense of touch is a valuable guide. A liquid is lukewarm (about 105°) when it feels just a little warm to the touch of a finger or when a drop is placed on the inside of a wrist. Warm is just a little warmer than that. For hot, or for any doubtful sample, dip a spoon in it and hold the metal against your wrist.

Fingers can be quickly trained to distinguish between room temperature and cool, or cool and refrigerator-cold. But remember that the container often chills long before the contents. Finger nail pressure can usually distinguish between frozen and unfrozen food.

Fig. 1-12. Candy thermometers

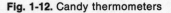

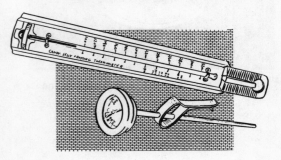

Thermometers. There are three basic types of thermometer used in cooking. One is a glass tube with a bulge or bulb on the bottom. It is partially filled with a colored liquid and air is sucked out of the remaining space to produce a vacuum. The tube is fastened to a backing marked in degrees or, much more rarely, the degrees are marked on the tube itself. Heat causes the liquid to expand and rise in the tube, cold makes it contract and sink. Most of the sensitivity is in the bulb, as it contains much more liquid than the fine hole in the tube.

The glass thermometer is quite liable to breakage if kept in a drawer with other utensils. If dropped, severely shaken or allowed to cool from high heat in a horizontal position, the liquid may separate. If you can't shake it together again, you can estimate the number of degrees of empty space in the column, and subtract that from the reading at the top.

If you get such a thermometer so hot that the liquid rises against the top of the tube it will burst the glass.

The backing piece of an American household thermometer will show degrees Fahrenheit. It may have special markings for certain critical temperatures, such as stages of making sugar syrups, frosting or candy. They are sometimes calibrated in Celsius degrees also.

Another type of bulb thermometer has the fluid encased in metal. Its expansion pushes a diaphragm that moves a hand on a dial marked in degrees and often in critical stage temperatures also.

A third type uses one strip each of two metals that expand differently when heated. They are bonded together. Heat will cause the combined strip to curl away from the one with the greater expansion, cold will bend it oppositely. One end is anchored, the other moves a hand on a dial. This mechanism is more common in thermostats than in thermometers.

Thermometers are made up in several

Fig. 1-13. Labeled temperatures

heat ranges, which are not particularly standardized. Figure 1-14 gives the temperatures covered in the products of one leading manufacturer.

Usefulness. Thermometers are important tools in the modern kitchen, and are generally considered to be essential. However, it is unwise to trust them completely. They are often quite inaccurate, and additional errors can arise through improper use. And some of them are simply not suitable for the use for which they are intended. See Chapter 35.

A candy thermometer can be easily checked. Insert it 2 inches or more into briskly boiling water for 3 or 4 minutes. It should register 212° F. If it does not, make

Thermometer scales, Fahrenheit

Type	Readings	
	Minimum	Maximum
Refrigerator-freezer	−20	60
Household — outdoor	−40	130
— indoor	35	120
Candy and syrup	100	320
Candy, syrup and frying	100	400
Oven	200	500
Meat	130	190

Fig. 1-14. Thermometer scales, F

a note of the error (write it on the thermometer if you can) and adjust any other readings accordingly. Errors are usually in proportion to reading, so that an instrument that is off 4 degrees at 212 would probably be wrong by 6 degrees at 300. But most of the critical points for candy, syrup and simmering are close enough to 212 so that you can simply add or subtract the error. For example, if you want a soft ball candy stage at 234° and your thermometer thinks that water boils at 216°, cook the syrup until the reading is 238°, and you should be about right.

Refrigerator-freezer thermometers should register 32° in a thick mixture of ice in water. Anything higher or lower indicates an error. However, a couple of degrees one way or the other are seldom important in this temperature range.

A meat thermometer can be checked by inserting it in hot water whose temperature is measured by a checked candy thermometer. An error of just a few degrees may not be important, particularly as the dial is usually too small to be read to the exact degree anyhow. But don't heat it above the top of its range on the dial.

Oven thermometers can only be checked against other oven thermometers, or against oven thermostats. In comparing with thermostat-regulated oven heat, remember that many ovens are designed to overheat by 50 or more degrees in the first cycle after starting cold, and that some up and down variation is normal during steady use.

Fig. 1-15. Air lock

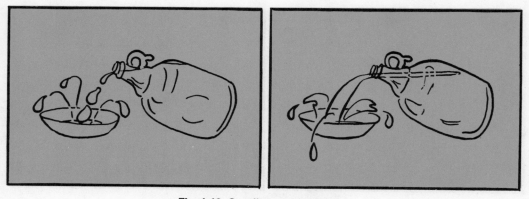

Fig. 1-16. Gurgling and splashing

Frying thermometers that also register for candy can be checked with boiling water, otherwise only against each other or against an automatic fryer thermostat. A fryer does not have extra heat in its first cycle.

POURING FLUIDS

Fluids frequently spill while being poured from one container to another, causing waste of material and slopping the work or serving area. Spillage can usually be avoided by attention to two basic difficulties — vacuum or air lock and adhesion to surfaces.

Air Lock. If fluid is poured out of a container, air must enter the container to fill the space formerly occupied by the liquid. Otherwise a partial vacuum will be created, which would soon prevent liquid from continuing to pour.

Four types of container are shown in Figure 1-15. The pitcher creates no problem, as it has a wide surface open to the air. The tea kettle can take in air around the loose-fitting lid as fluid pours out the spout. But the full soda bottle pours through a single narrow neck, so that air can only reach the up-tilted rear of the bottle by passing through the liquid pouring out of it. The liquid will pour for a moment, then will be stopped by atmospheric pressure pushing toward the vacuum left by removal of liquid. A bubble of air will force its way up the neck, relieving the vacuum, and allowing

another bit of liquid to escape. This process repeats itself very rapidly, causing the pouring to be a succession of gurgles, often accompanied by considerable splashing or splattering.

Maximum interference between air and liquid occurs if the bottle is held vertically, and the least if it is nearly flat. After the bottle is partly empty, it will become possible to hold it so that liquid will fill only about two-thirds of the neck, and it will pour smoothly while air enters above it. An increase in steepness that allows the liquid to block the air will cause the gurgling to resume.

A can whose lid is punctured in only one place will gurgle in the same manner. This can be prevented by making a second hole at the other side or the center. The second hole may be the same size or smaller. It can be made by a second use of an ordinary puncture opener, or a single pressure of an opener with two prongs.

A sudden, forceful spurt of liquid may occur in any air-bound container at the moment when the fluid level falls far enough to allow unobstructed entrance of air. This may cause a splash or surging over the far edge of a cup or a bowl.

Adhesion. Most liquids cling to solid surfaces such as glass, china and metal. They will also often follow such surfaces in defiance of gravity and other forces, so that

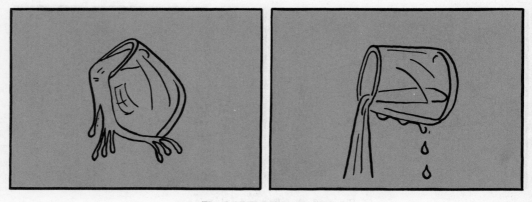

Fig. 1-17. Pouring angles

liquids poured from a pitcher, glass or bowl may dribble and flow down the outside of the utensil instead of moving cleanly through the air to their proper destination. Fortunately, the ability to follow surfaces is limited and can usually be cancelled.

The nature of the surface is important. Water, and water solutions and suspensions, which together make up most of the liquids handled in a kitchen, will follow a water-wet surface much more readily than a dry one, but will not stick to nor follow an oily, greasy or waxy surface. You may therefore be able to pour cleanly out of a container that is dry on the outside, until splash or drip moistens it. And you can almost always prevent dribbling completely by wiping a thin film of butter or other grease or oil onto the surface just below the pouring edge, unless the liquid is oil.

You can often get by without oiling by taking other precautions. The angle of separation between liquid and container is the most important factor, after the character of the surface. This angle is made up of the angle or slope at which the pouring unit is held and the break angle or curve between the surface that carries the fluid and the surface along which you do not want it to flow.

This slope angle depends mostly on the fullness of the container. If it is full, only a slight tip will cause it to spill over, and

there will be a maximum tendency to dribble down the nearly vertical front, or back along the underside of a pouring lip.

If the break between the pouring and lower surfaces is sharp, as in a thin-gauge metal pitcher, the poured fluid usually cannot get around the edge to the underside, and should pour cleanly. With a properly shaped lip, this should be true regardless of the flatness of the angle at which the pitcher is held while pouring. But the thin edge of a can is not equally effective because it does not overhang.

If the pitcher is made of biscuit ware or other thick china, the pouring lip is thick and rounded. If the pitcher is full or nearly so and pouring is slow, the fluid is almost sure to follow the curve of the surface, so that part or perhaps all of it will run down on the front of the pitcher. Even after partial emptying improves the pouring position, the liquid may continue to cling to and follow the wet front.

SELDOM SPILLS   OFTEN SPILLS

Fig. 1-18. Thin edges pour better

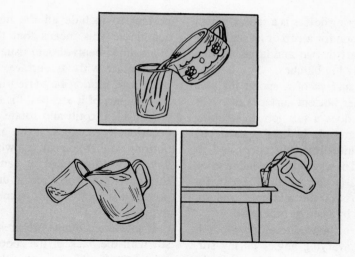

Fig. 1-19. Good pouring methods

Unless you oil it, the only way to pour this pitcher without dribbling when it is full is to tip it suddenly into a steep pouring position. This is practical only if quite a bit can be poured into one container, which is shaped so that it will not permit the liquid to surge or splash over its far side.

Dribbling can often be reduced or caught by overlapping and touching the two containers. This contact is useful for steadying them when an exact amount is being measured.

In any case, the pouring edge should not be far above that of the receiving container. High pouring may lead to poor aim (even a complete miss), splashing and too much frothing of fizzy drinks. If the original container is both tall and full, put the glasses or cups near the edge of the table so that you can hold it at a lower level, off the side. Or you can hold each glass up under the pitcher spout or against the can side as you pour. This last method will allow you to tip the glass so that beer or other foaming liquid will pour onto its side and foaming will be reduced. If you want to reduce it.

COMBINING FOODS

There are a number of ways in which dif-ferent ingredients can be combined. They may be completely or partly mixed together, or perhaps built up in layers or designs. There may be problems in getting certain items to mix with each other, or in preventing them from mixing too thoroughly. Certain combinations benefit by vigorous and prolonged working, others are ruined by it.

It is important to understand what your cookbook means when it tells you to stir, beat, whip, fold, cream, sift, grate, chop, liquefy or blend a mixture, and why certain procedures are appropriate for certain combinations or products.

Stirring. To stir may merely mean to keep in motion by movement of a utensil. But it is done in several ways for a variety of purposes.

Stirring can be used to combine light or heavy liquids and dry ingredients in powder form, separately or together. It is also done to prevent separation of combined materials waiting to be used, and to prevent sticking and burning during cooking and coarse crystallization during cooling. Mixing may be partial or complete. Stirring does not necessarily involve putting air into the mixture. If aeration is a requirement, you are usually told to beat or whip it.

The basic stirring device is a spoon, which may be a teaspoon for a cup or less, a tablespoon for a quart or two and larger special spoons for really big batches.

The curved surface of a spoon fits well into curved inner bottom surfaces of bowls and pans, and does a fair job of scraping along flatter parts. It is hard and strong enough to cut into firm substances and its hollow but solid bowl can be depended upon to move them. It can be used easily for transferring parts of the mixtures, and for testing samples by taste or otherwise.

The concave or bowl side of the spoon is held forward at varying angles during stirring. Mixing action occurs chiefly where the material flows around the edges. Thick or sticky material, particularly such as may be scraped off the surface of a hot pan, tends to accumulate in the bowl. It should be pushed out at frequent intervals, with the back of another spoon, a finger or almost any utensil. If it is much thicker than the rest of a liquid it may be advisable to set it aside and soften it by mixing with a little fluid, before putting it back in the pan.

The stirring motion is ordinarily rotary and horizontal, but may be varied as desired to avoid monotony or to cope with special situations.

Most spoons used for stirring are stainless steel. When scraped repeatedly against the interior of a pan they may wear off Teflon, or scrape enough aluminum oxide to turn a white food grey. Wooden or Teflon spoons are better with such materials.

Wooden spoons, in addition to having a soft, non-abrasive edge, are valued for mixing batter, dough and thick sauce, because of turbulence created by the thick edge. There are also large stirring spoons of plastice or plastic-coated metal, with perforations and/or special shapes.

Stirring may also be done with a whisk, a fork or practically any available utensil, but for average work a spoon is best.

In almost any stirring operation, it is important to include all the material in the container. This means that the spoon (or other implement) should usually be in sliding contact with its surface, and that the pattern of motion be varied in such a way that no part of it escapes this scraping. It is a good idea to tilt and rotate the container occasionally to expose a side and part of the bottom, so that you can see whether there is any unmixed material. It can be very disturbing if you don't see it until you have poured the mixture into some place of no return.

If unwanted lumps are present, you may stir with the back of the spoon against the side of the container, so that they are caught and crushed. Or stir very fast, or change to a whisk and stir fast. Causes and other cures for lumps will be discussed a little later.

Beating and Whipping. The milder forms of beating are the same as the more active types of stirring. It usually involves more vigorous action, which may be needed to combine materials that would rather stay separate, to distribute air through the mixture or just to do the same job in less time. The term is used only in reference to fluids.

Whipping usually means beating that turns a liquid into a thick fluff.

Beating may be done with a spoon, a fork, a whisk or a rotary beater, these tools being named in the order of increasing effectiveness. The first three are usually used with a rotary, somewhat elliptical stroke, one end or one side of which is above the

Fig. 1-20. Spoons may need clearing

surface in order to include low-level splashing and mixing with air. It is often convenient to hold the container at an angle, particularly if the liquid is shallow. Motion is always rapid.

A spoon acts as a blunt instrument, with almost all mixing and beating action at the edge. A fork allows thin or medium liquids to slip between the tines as well as around them, and so produces substantially greater turbulence and finer mixing with each stroke. But it clogs easily in thick or lumpy mixtures. A whisk has a number of wires so arranged that its movement through a liquid sets up a high degree of turbulence with multiple mixing action. The wires are somewhat flexible, and free themselves of clogging material more readily than a fork does. However, under clogging conditions a spoon is likely to be more efficient unless destroying lumps is a major objective.

The rotary beater, shown in Figures 35-36 and 37-29, is a very different proposition. A hand crank or an electric motor turns two 4-vaned beaters in opposite directions in overlapping circles. Their motion, which is usually very rapid, pulls fluid from one side through the overlap, subjecting it to high speed turbulence in the presence of air that feeds downward along their centers of rotation. This action is very effective at mixing, breaking soft lumps and viscous or thready fluids and particularly at incorporating air in the form of very fine bubbles. Being geared for high speed, they usually have little power to cope with thick or heavy fluids, and vanes may be bent by hard lumps. However, a heavy duty model may be able to keep turning in very resistant material.

Thin and medium fluids circulate naturally through the beater, but thick or stiffly beaten ones tend to separate into an inner portion that gets most or all of the beating, and an outer ring that gets little or none. This situation is corrected by frequent or constant changing of the position of the beater in the bowl. In mixers, this is accomplished by locating the beaters off center, and rotating the bowl continuously by power.

Forks, whisks and rotaries are all ineffective at scraping unmixed material clinging to the bottom and sides of a container. The fork does not fit into curves, and is difficult or impossible to hold parallel to the bottom for good contact. Whisks are too springy and yielding to cut into firm substances. Rotaries do not reach thick material a quarter inch beyond their vanes. The only exception to this is of table-mounted electric beaters that have special beaters shaped to almost scrape the sides and bottom of a rotating bowl.

This poor scraping ability makes it advisable and often necessary to stir irregular mixtures with a spoon until they are uniform enough to be handled by the more specialized beating utensils.

Folding. Folding usually means to stir two or more substances together lightly with a spoon, usually with an up and down rather than horizontal motion. They may be entirely mixed at the end of the work, but more often they are meant to keep a little streakiness or other evidence of incomplete blending.

Beaten white of egg is often combined with cake batter or dessert mixes by folding. More thorough stirring results in excessive loss of air, as contact with other substances tends to collapse the fine air bubbles in meringue, and also causes loss of flavor and texture contrasts. The situation is similar with other whipped materials, such as cream and gelatin.

A good technique for folding is to tip the bowl about halfway toward spilling hold it firmly with one hand and stir with a large spoon. Make each stroke follow the bottom or side of the bowl all the way through the mixture at a sloping angle that will make it flow across it. At the end of the stroke raise the spoon horizontally, then bring it back to the beginning just above the

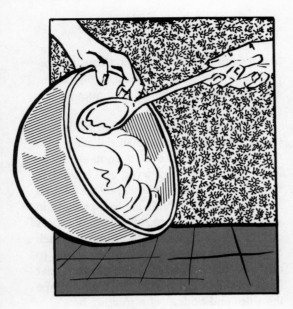

Fig. 1-21a. Folding

surface. Rotate the bowl slightly with each stroke. Avoid slapping the stirrer into the mix, or splashing as you bring it out.

Creaming. Creaming is the process of mashing, stirring or beating shortening (usually butter) so that it absorbs air and becomes more workable (mixable).

The standard or perhaps old fashioned way to cream shortening is to press it repeatedly against the side and bottom of a bowl with the back of a spoon, preferably with a sliding motion. Butter or margarine may be cold from the refrigerator, or softened by standing at room temperature. Work is reduced if it is warm, but some of the structural effect of the creaming may be lost.

The process softens the grease by heat of friction, by breaking down internal structure and as a result of mixing in air. The softening is different in character than that which would be obtained by simply warming it. There is a tendency to lighten in color, probably because of included air.

Creaming prepares shortening to mix more readily and thoroughly with other materials, particularly sugar. These are blended in by adding a little at a time while continuing the process.

Creaming is also done in an electric mixer at low speed. It is easy to do it very thoroughly this way, but it is a nuisance to clean the beater blades unless other processes can follow with the same material.

Many authorities consider thorough creaming a basic necessity in cake making, largely because the air thus introduced into the batter increases lightness. However, creaming done by hand is likely to absorb so little air that it is difficult to measure it. Much more effective aeration may be obtained by using factory-whipped butter, which is about 25 per cent air.

Sifting. Sifting is a process of passing dry material through a sieve. It serves to remove lumps, to combine materials and to fluff up powders to provide a uniform basis for measurement.

You can't sift just by pouring through a sieve, as powders cake so that they bridge over fine holes. You can stir them through with a spoon, but usually it is much more convenient to use a mechanical sifter, that has a lever-operated stirrer on the upper surface of the sieve. Such a sieve may be marked so that it can be used as a measuring cup also.

If two or more different powders are within reach of the stirrers, the combination of their action and the fall from the sieve to the container mixes them together very thoroughly. However, a spoon of baking powder placed on the top of a cup of flour in a sifter will be mixed with only the last quarter of the flour that goes through. Several siftings would be required to produce a

Fig. 1-21b. Creaming

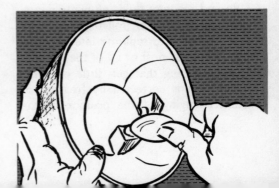

uniform mixture. But if the two powders are roughly stirred together first, one sifting will be enough.

Many American cookbooks and perhaps some American cooks are obsessed with sifting. A cake recipe may call for doing it once before measuring, and then two to four times more for blending. There may be some advantage to doing this, but it is more in the nature of an extra flourish than a necessity.

If you are sifting to measure, place the sifter over or in the measuring utensil, and fill it, usually with flour. Sift until you have the proper amount, refilling the sifter as often as necessary.

When adding a powder to a liquid, as in mixing flour into gravy, the danger of lumps is reduced by making it into a thin sprinkle over the surface, while stirring vigorously. With practice, you can do this by tipping off the edges of a spoon, but a one-hand flour sifter is easier and better.

Grating. Grating involves rubbing a solid food material against a grater that consists of a thin metal sheet with a number of sharp points projecting above holes of proportionate size. The points cut or tear the food into strips or particles that go through the holes and pile up on the other side.

A standard grater has four or five sizes of holes. Coarse ones cut more readily, do not clog easily and have minimum tendency to liquefy food. But their product is often too coarse for your purpose, and they gouge deeply into the material, sometimes taking undesirable deeper layers.

Chopping. Chopping is reduction of a solid food into fine or fairly fine pieces, preferably of rather even size. The product is supposed to be coarser than that obtained by grinding, but the terms overlap. For example, chopped raw meat is almost always ground meat.

Chopping may be done with a curved knife with the food on a cutting board or in a shallow wooden bowl. The board encour-

Fig. 1-22. Sifting may be an obsession

ages pieces to scatter around the work area. The bowl requires that you confine your blows to the center, as one on the edge will upset it with spectacular results.

Chopping may also be done in a glass jar with a chopping knife on a shaft that slides up and down through a hole in the lid. If

Fig. 1-23. Always watch your work

you use one of these, make sure that the bottom pad is fastened down firmly. You can stick it down with a small lump of grease if it is loose in its socket.

Hard food such as nut meats, dry bread and crackers can be chopped in an electric blender, but soft or juicy ones will turn to mush. Stop the blender and check the food every few seconds, as it works rapidly and may make the product too fine.

Grinding. Chopping may be done in a grinder, either hand or electric powered. This will handle hard, dry items and also moderately soft and moist ones such as meat and partially cooked potato. But fruit and cooked vegetables are generally reduced to pulp.

Liquefying. Many solid foods, particularly fruit and vegetables, contain a high percentage of water, and will become thick liquids if their cell structure is broken down. But the liquid is likely to be filled with strings and tatters of the tougher parts.

The electric blender is the ideal tool for liquefying as its high speed and the sharpness of its blades enable it to cut tough parts, even including immature seeds, into very fine pieces, so that it will produce an even textured puree.

Liquefied fruit or vegetables may be used as a beverage, part or all of a soup and as an ingredient in sauces and casseroles.

Blending. To blend is to mix very thoroughly. The means can be any tool, from a spoon to an electric blender. The term is used to indicate that the stirring or beating operation is carried on until the two substances are completely mixed, which may take seconds or minutes, depending on their characteristics and on the mixing method.

Blending usually refers to mixtures of substances that do not dissolve readily in each other. For example, you mix flour and water until they are blended, and sugar and water until the sugar dissolves. In use of an electric blender, the term may include chopping and liquefying.

Dissolving. When one substance (a solute) becomes dissolved in another (its solvent) they become intermingled on a basis of individual molecules or even half-molecules (ions).

It is possible to have solutions of gases, liquids or solids in liquids or solids. Club

Fig. 1-24. Big pieces dissolve slowly

soda is carbon dioxide gas dissolved in water, vanilla extract is a flavoring compound dissolved in alchohol and chocolate candy is sugar dissolved in chocolate. But the vast majority of food solutions made and handled in the kitchen are solids dissolved in water.

Different substances vary widely in their solubility, both in the amount that can be dissolved in a given quantity of water, and the speed with which solution takes place. Both quantity and speed increase (usually) as water is heated, and speed is increased by making the pieces smaller, and/or stirring the mixture.

The molecules in a liquid tear and knock molecules off the surface of a substance that is dissolving in it. Heating increases their speed and energy, and enlarges spaces between them. Making pieces or grains smaller increases the amount of surface exposed to the solvent. Stirring moves filled-up or saturated parts of the solvent away from the solid surface and brings unsaturated parts to replace them.

Many fine powders tend to clump tightly together when placed in water, forming small balls or other shapes that water cannot penetrate. Any dissolving that is done is only at the outer surface, and it may be slowed by a film of air. As a result, special procedures may be necessary to dissolve moderately soluble powder in water or milk.

The first step may be taken by the manufacturer, in processing the powder so it will not clump. One means of doing this is to make a very fine powder, then treat it by slight dampening or other methods so that groups of grains will stick together in open-textured lumps that are readily penetrated by water. These lumps, generally too small to be seen, have rough surfaces so that they either do not stick to each other, or cling very loosely. Powder treated this way may be labeled "instant" or "instantized" to distinguish it from the simple primary product.

Instantized powder usually dissolves without causing trouble. However, until you are used to a particular type or brand, you may be wise to still use the simple precautions described below for ordinary powder.

The simple, sure way to dissolve powder in a liquid is to put the powder in a container, then add the liquid gradually, pre-ferably in a number of very small splashes. After each, stir until it is absorbed, preferably using the back of a spoon with a mashing or creaming motion. In this way, the powder will first become a thick liquid in which any lumps can be readily caught and crushed, then diluted to whatever strength is required.

Another method, less work but somewhat more risky, is to sift the powder onto the top of all or part of the liquid, beating or stirring constantly. If you actually use a sifter, and don't crank it too fast, this should work all right. But heavy sifting, or sprinkling off the side of a spoon, may give the powder a chance to lump.

If you have lumps of fine powder floating in a large quantity of liquid, you may be able to break them up by vigorous action with a whisk or a beater. Or, if there are just a few, you can catch them with the back of a spoon and mash them against the side. If you have lots of time, you might see if they will dissolve by themselves. Sugar, yes. Cocoa probably no.

Thick fluids or soft solids are mixed with thin liquids in the same manner as powders — add the liquid very gradually with mashing and stirring.

Or you can mix the powder with another one that is either more soluble or less fine. If a recipe calls for both cocoa and sugar, or powdered coffee and sugar, stir the two ingredients together before adding liquid. Sugar is both easier to dissolve than the other substances and when it is in the usual granulated form it is coarser as well.

PREPARED (CONVENIENCE) FOODS

Prepared, convenience or ready-mixed foods are those that have been premixed and/or processed so that they require less time, work and/or skill in the kitchen. The terms do not include food whose processing results only in improvement in keeping quality, increase in or loss of nutriments or changes in flavor, nor those whose proces-

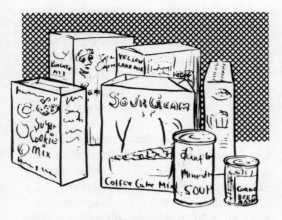

Fig. 1-25. Prepared foods

sing is considered to be standard and expected.

It is not possible to make an absolute distinction between convenience foods and those that are considered basic or standard. Some processing of food before its arrival at the cooking area is probably about as old as cooking. In even the most primitive societies, meat may be butchered where the animal is killed, grain is threshed or pounded in wholesale lots, and some special foods are even pre-chewed.

Prepared foods of one period may become the basic items of another. A hundred years ago most bread was baked in the home, instead of being bought ready-made. The cook used to be expected to prepare her own dry spaghetti, roast and grind coffee, cure hams and do countless other jobs that are now left to the supplier.

There are many possible degrees of stages of preparation. Dry beans may be in their natural state, treated so as not to require pre-soaking or ready-cooked with pork fat and sauce in a can. Dry rice may be obtained in several conditions from one store shelf — as brown rice with the hulls intact, as white rice with the hulls removed, Minute Rice processed to reduce cooking time, converted rice treated to add vitamins and increase cooking time; and mixed or packaged with seasonings and other foods.

A baking mixture may be as simple as self-rising flour, which is flour and baking powder; it may be a cake mix that includes all ingredients except water and perhaps eggs, or be a completely mixed, shaped and ready-to-bake set of biscuits, which are kept refrigerated or frozen until wanted.

Preparation. Convenience foods are obtainable in great variety, and most appropriate cooking processes are used or usable with them. The only general instruction that applies is to follow the directions on the package.

Unfortunately, these directions are not necessarily right, and if you follow them blindly you may get undercooked, overcooked or otherwise disappointing food. The experienced cook will often notice errors, and adjust time or heat almost automatically. Serious trouble during cooking can usually be avoided by watching and testing, and making changes on a common sense basis. A person who is used to preparing regular food can usually do a good job with prepared items on the first try, and almost always on the second.

However, a number of ingredients are in prepared cake and bread mixes which are not available in the kitchen, and their effect on the behavior of batter or dough may not be anticipated. It may be thinner or thicker than you think it should be, without any bad effect on the product.

Prepared mixes can often be improved by being enriched with additional eggs and other ingredients, but any change of this nature should not be tried for the first time when company is coming.

Advantages and Disadvantages. Prepared foods should save time and work, without serious sacrifices. Since their quality is largely fixed by the manufacturer, and preparation usually adds or subtracts only a little, they are likely to benefit the amateur greatly, and help the good cook moderately or not at all.

The beginner is likely to have two principal problems: excessive time taken because of unfamiliarity with the work, and possibility of mistakes in proportioning or in methods of handling. The prepared mix reduces the number of operations, so that less time is used and chances of mistakes are less. Since mistakes impair quality, the mix is likely to give better results than starting from scratch.

The experienced cook saves little time with items such as a cake mix, as she can mix the basic materials rapidly and surely, with only a little more work and a good chance of a superior result. But completely pre-mixed foods such as biscuit dough, pancake flour, frozen waffles or canned hash or stew are a great time saver for her also, which is often more important than the definite loss of quality thas is usually involved.

Frozen foods often offer convenience at the expense of time. Few of them can be defrosted and heated conventionally in less than 20 minutes, and many (TV dinners, for example) take 30 to 40. Conventional refrigerated foods such as eggs, bacon, hamburger, chops and steaks of ordinary one-inch thickness, sausage, liver and most vegetables in thin slices or small pieces cook in much less time than that.

But if you are fortunate enough to have an electronic oven, the time disadvantage of frozen food no longer applies, as defrosting and heating can usually be done in it in 3 to 10 minutes.

After you get familiar with them, you can vary prepared foods in interesting ways, and use some of them as ingredients in more complicated dishes. But their variety is limited, and they take much more shelf and freezer space than the simpler foods that they replace. And too-great reliance on them makes it much harder to learn to cook.

The quality of cake and pancake mixes is usually good. Frozen foods are highly variable, from poor to excellent. At their best,

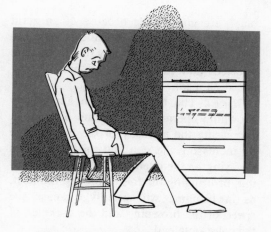

Fig. 1-26. TV dinners take a long time

they may equal freshly prepared or home frozen products. But TV dinners and similar whole-meal preparations seem to be suffering from long term deterioration, particularly in the quantity and quality of the meat and fish portions.

BROWNING

The term browning refers to the darkening of food surfaces when they are exposed to heat. The appearance of brown color on fruit and on some vegetables after peeling or slicing is usually just called discoloration.

Carmelization of sugar (see page 000) is a major factor in browning. Most foods contain at least small quantities of one or more types of sugar. Color is also created in a wide range of other organic substances by heating to a point just below charring.

Browning is a byproduct of cooking with dry heat. It is highly valued in cookery for its appearance, and for the changes in taste and texture that are usually involved with it. It is usually accompanied by the formation of a crust, which at its best is crisp and tender, and at its worst, is thick, tough and tasteless.

Color may be anywhere from deep yellow or pale tan to charcoal black, and may vary greatly on one piece of food. For most tastes and for most foods, black and almost black are undesirable because of an acrid burnt taste. They usually indicate mistakes in cooking. However, if only small areas are affected, they may be cut off bread or ignored on meat.

Rules. The basic factor in almost any browning operation is the rate of heating. Increasing the intensity of the heat source by increasing the pan and oil temperature in frying or the oven temperature in roasting; or bringing the food closer to the heat, as in broiling, will usually increase the speed of the browning and the darkness of the color obtained.

The amount and distribution of moisture in the food is also important. The evaporation of water from the interior to the surface brings dissolved substances which are left when the water evaporates, usually improving both the color and the flavor of the crust that is forming.

Browning of the surface usually occurs while the interior of the food cooks, and the two processes should finish at about the same time. If the heat is low or at a distance, cooking may be complete with little or no development of color. High or close heat may brown and blacken the surface while the interior is still undercooked or even cold, particularly if the food was just out of the refrigerator or freezer. This relationship should be watched, and temperature or distance adjusted when it appears desirable.

Fully cooked but pale food can usually be subjected briefly to very high heat for darkening, without serious effects on the interior. A well-browned but undercooked item can be finished at low heat, or under a protective covering, to avoid an overcooked or burned surface.

High heat for a short period tends to produce a thinner, more tender crust than when lower heat is used to get the same color. If meat is roasted under a cover, the crust is likely to have good color and flavor, but will lack crispness unless it is cooked

Fig. 1-27. It's good to serve it hot

uncovered for 10 to 20 minutes, just before removing it from the oven.

Browning of mixtures such as sauce or gravy may be accomplished by browning one ingredient, usually flour or sugar, and then adding other materials. Or the mixture may be browned by subjecting it, or part of it, to high heat, as for example a shallow layer of gravy being prepared in a roasting pan over a burner.

Additives. It may be possible to brown food at a lower-than-normal heat by applying other materials to the surface. Sugar, flour, butter, paprika and many other substances are sometimes used. The desired color may be obtained, but the flavor is not likely to be as satisfactory as with plain food and proper heat.

HOT FOODS

Except for salads, appetizers and some desserts, most food is intended to be served and eaten hot. Also, most of it tastes best if it is freshly cooked with a minimum of time lapse between cooking and serving. But the cook is limited in the number of her hands, utensils and working space, and she must cope with limited burner and oven space and with variability in cooking time.

Timing. A beginner is very unlikely to get everything to finish cooking at the same time, as it is necessary to develop some knowledge or at least some sense of cooking rates, and get practice in speeding up lagging processes and slowing down those that are too fast.

An example of timing a simple meal is preparation of bacon and eggs (Chapter 10) and toast. If you have two frypans, use one for bacon and the other for eggs. Start the bacon first, start the eggs just after you turn the bacon, put the toaster in action as soon as you turn the eggs, then lift the bacon from the pan and put it on paper to drain. The timing is nicely interdependent. But if you have only one pan you can't do it this way. And if you are cooking a number of batches you may get in trouble trying to tend both eggs and bacon.

Then you simplify your problem by precooking the least sensitive item — the bacon. Get it cooked and out on paper toweling, covered by another piece to keep it warm, before you start your eggs. Then you work to get the eggs and toast finished together, and add the warm-but-not-hot bacon to the plates.

If you have more customers than toaster space, serve half slices first. This is better than either preparing toast earlier to get cold, or making some people wait for it.

Resign yourself to the fact that some things will probably have to wait, at least until you have had a lot of cooking practice. Try to pick the ones which are least sensitive, as bacon rather than eggs, boiled or baked potatoes but not mashed or French fried; usually vegetables rather than meat and carrots rather than peas. This

does not mean that you should serve any of them (except bacon) in any condition except piping hot, just that some can stand holding over in heat, or reheating, better than others.

Most soup improves in flavor if kept on low heat for a while. But this may not help much, as soup gets served first.

HEAT LOSS DURING SERVING

Food that leaves the stove agreeably hot and just on time may still reach the mouth in too cold a condition for enjoyment.

Late Customers. It may take five or ten minutes for people to get to the table after the food is ready and off the range. The worst of this situation is that you usually have to be polite about it.

It is best to announce that the meal is almost ready, or perhaps that it is ready, about five minutes ahead of time. That should get them in, but if you have miscalculated or forgotten something, and have

Fig. 1-28. Announce the meal ahead of time

them sitting hungrily in place before you are ready, it may make you nervous enough to drop a serving dish. However, this is more a personal problem than a kitchen one.

Slow Service. Some American serving and eating traditions seem designed to allow full cooling of food. They are rather pleasing customs, but their interference with good eating is likely to be so severe that they should be scrapped, or at least bypassed frequently. They apply to entertaining at meals rather than to just family feeding.

One of these is carving the roast at the table, after people are seated. An expert carver may go through a simple boneless piece of meat fairly rapidly, but experts are rare and bones are common. It can easily take a minute per helping to slice the meat. If one person adds the vegetables more time is consumed.

But the final disaster is a custom of everybody waiting until everybody has been served, and until the hostess takes the first bite. This is not only bad for food temperature, but may be nerve wracking for the lady, who is probably cook and waitress also. If she has forgotten something important she may have to make an anguished

Fig. 1-29. Carving takes time

choice between leaving it forgotten (the rolls drying in the oven, for example) or delay the eating still further.

From a hot food standpoint, meat should be carved and put on a hot platter immediately before the meal, the vegetables put in serving dishes, and all this bulk food passed around the table. Eating should start just as soon as any plate is filled, or even contains anything to eat.

WARM PLATES

Another important factor in chilling of food is loss of heat into cold (room temperature) dishes. This is usually not serious in regard to deep serving dishes for vegetables, as the bulk of the food is much greater than that of the china, and the dish is heated at first much more than the food is chilled.

Platters and lunch or dinner plates, however, usually carry only a thin layer of food, which can lose a large part of its heat into the china very quickly. This factor alone can reduce a hot-when-served tidbit to an unappetizing lukewarm state before the first bite is taken.

Such an unhappy condition can be avoided or made less severe by heating the plates. This is not an accepted practice, but it is a good one. If you like to serve a good meal nicely, and can stand the strain of one more operation to remember at meal time, you should try it.

A plate begins to feel warm at about 100° F, just above body temperature, and becomes too hot for comfortable handling at 125° or a little higher. These temperatures are below the steady setting capacity of most kitchen heating devices or areas, so dishes are usually left cold or are warmed by makeshift methods.

Ordinary china and glass can be heated to about 180° F, but only if the heat is applied slowly and evenly, and you protect your hands when touching or carrying. It is safer and usually more satisfactory to keep the heat down to around 125°, or 150° at most.

Oven. Many modern ovens with a keep-warm thermostat can be operated at a temperature as low as 150° F, and at that setting will safely warm plates. One takes less than a minute, two may take 1-1/2 minutes to be warm and 3 to be almost hot, but a stack of four will not warm the center dishes for 6 to 10 minutes, unless you shuffle them. No plate seems to get uncomfortably hot, but as with all hot objects, test before you take hold. But there is a serious problem. The oven is likely to be too occupied with cooking food just before a meal to be available for planned and controlled dish heating.

After an oven is turned off when a roast or a casserole is cooked, you may cool it below 200° by leaving the door open, then put in the plates until they are warm or hot.

Range Top. Using an oven will generally make the top of the range hot enough to serve as a warmer. Plates may be put on the top in areas between or beside burners, or on unused and turned-off burners if you have either. The plates will heat only from the bottom up, and may take a long time. Results can be speeded by making two piles instead of one, and by shuffling the top plate to the bottom now and then.

Fig. 1-30. Warming a plate over food

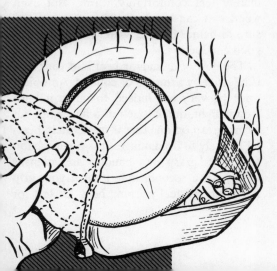

The now almost extinct coal and gas ranges usually had a back corner where dishes would keep warm all day. As a result, dish warming was once a more common practice than it is now.

Late model ranges are beginning to offer a warming shelf on top of the splash guard, which may be used for warming and keeping warm both dishes and food. One of these is shown in Figure 38-1, right.

Dishwasher. A good modern way to heat dishes is to put them in an automatic dishwasher, to be run through part of the drying cycle only. You have to establish your own time by experiment, as it varies widely in different models. The china may get too hot to handle bare handed. It should keep warm for a long time with the door closed. Some machines have a special dish warming setting.

If you have none of these conveniences, you may just soak dishes in hot water in a dishpan for a minute or two, then dry and use them.

Other Methods. Individual plates can be heated quickly by use as lids over pans in which food is being cooked in water or steam. They get too hot for comfortable handling, and will need wiping to remove condensed water on the bottoms. Don't do this with frying food, as the bottoms will be greasy with spatter and they are likely to become so hot that the china will be damaged.

A surface electric burner can be used if given just a short warmup period, perhaps 30 seconds, and is then turned off. This is fine for single plates, but will not work with a stack unless it is shuffled and the heat renewed occasionally.

Don't ever have a dish on a burner while the heat is turned on. It is too easy to forget, leave it on, and ruin the plate. Good china, or plastic, should never be placed on a burner that is too hot to touch with a bare finger.

Fig. 1-31. Warming tray

There are also electrically warmed serving trays, which hold just a few dishes.

BURNS

Burn injuries are very common in the kitchen. The cook handles hot materials of many kinds under widely varying circumstances. Errors, miscalculations and bad luck can result in too-close and damaging contact with them. The number and seriousness of such injuries can be greatly reduced by understanding and avoiding their principal causes. Pain and disablement are minimized by prompt treatment.

Burn damage to skin and flesh varies with the temperature of the substance, the speed with which heat flows from it and time of exposure. Three degrees of severity are recognized — first, in which the skin is reddened, sore and tender but not blistered; second, in which blisters form and the upper and intermediate skin cells are killed; and third, in which the full thickness of the skin and usually some underlying flesh are destroyed.

The seriousness of a burn depends partly on its severity and degree, but even more on the area covered. This is usually expressed as a percentage of the whole body surface. One side of one hand is considered to be one per cent of the skin area. Burns of 15 per cent or more in adults or 8 per cent in infants are likely to cause shock, with pallor and weakness, and need of immediate medical attention. Fortunately, most kitchen burns (except from overturning of a pot of hot grease or water) amount to only a small fraction of a per cent.

Causes. Most burns in the kitchen are caused by picking up hot objects, or by accidental contact with them. The seriousness of the injury to unprotected skin is proportional to the heat of the object, the speed with which its material conducts heat, the firmness of the contact, the size of the contact area and the exposure time.

Heat on burners is much higher than in ovens. You should never touch the body of a pan that is on a burner, or which has recently been on one. Do not place a pan on a burner in such a position that heat can rise directly to the handle, nor so that the handle projects over another burner. Do not leave a spoon or other utensil in a pan on a burner, as the part of the handle that projects over the edge will usually be in a superheated updraft and may become dangerously hot in seconds, long before the food in the pan becomes even warm.

When lifting a lid on a pan containing hot food, tilt it so that steam will not puff toward you, or toward your wrist or arm.

Metal is a good conductor of heat, china and glass are fair and wood and many plastics are poor. At the same heat that would cause metal to burn a finger severely, glass might cause pain without damage and wood merely feel comfortably warm. But even wood can cause a burn after direct exposure to flame. Grease, water and steam are good conductors.

The flow of damaging heat into your skin is affected by firmness of contact. An object must be very hot indeed to inflict a burn from a light, quick touch of a finger tip, but a firm grasp on one that is moderately heated is likely to do damage. It is a good habit to always grasp pan handles and utensils lightly for a second, then tighten your grip if you do not feel warning heat. Or test for heat with a quick touch of a wet fingertip. The moisture gives momentary protection, and its quick evaporation from the surface touched indicates danger.

At any given temperature, burn damage increases in proportion to the skin area involved and usually as the exposure time is lengthened. Snatch your hand away from excessive heat as soon as you are aware of it. Unfortunately, there is normally a time lag between the contact and sensation. Hot water and other liquids, and steam, may cover larger skin areas immediately than solid heat sources will, but steam exposure is usually brief.

Small burns may be caused by spatter from a frying pan, large and serious ones by overturning a container of hot water or grease. Long sleeves, especially on synthetic fabric bathrobes, may be ignited by a gas burner. Steam is dangerous, particularly when under pressure.

Pot holders and other hand protectors are discussed under Handling Devices, Chapter 35.

Treatment. A good immediate treatment for any burn is chilling, by soaking in ice water (with plenty of ice) or applying an ice pack. This may greatly reduce damage to skin and flesh, and also the secondary reactions of shock and illness.

Extensive burns should have medical attention as quickly as possible, while small ones can usually be treated at home or even ignored. Small burns may be dabbed once with tea (see Chapter 26). Butter, grease or

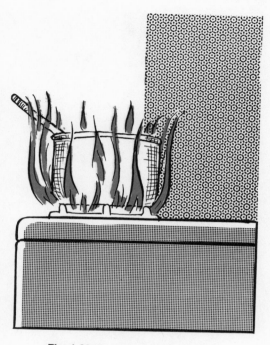

Fig. 1-32. Don't touch the handle

ointment may be smeared over the surface. This has little healing effect, but may reduce pain and prevent skin or scabs from cracking. Infection should be guarded against.

Discomfort and danger of shock from a severe burn can be minimized by lying down and covering up warmly. Contradictions between this and necessity of going out for medical aid, if ambulance or house call service is not available, must be worked out, preferably after a telephone conversation with a doctor.

2
BOILING

BOILING

Boiling is a simple, basic and convenient method of cooking that is under such heavy and largely unjustified attack by modern cookbooks that even use of the word may be in poor taste. Boiling water is used as a medium to transfer heat from a pan into food.

Basic Principle. Plain water boils at 212° Fahrenheit (100° Celsius or Centigrade) at sea level when atmospheric pressure is normal. If it is in a pan heated from below, steam bubbles form on the bottom, rise to the surface and dissipate in the air. The formation of steam from water absorbs a large amount of heat and prevents the temperature of the water from rising much above the boiling point, as long as the steam is free to escape. The rising bubbles keep the water stirred or agitated. The rate of steam formation and agitation of the water is in proportion to the amount of heat coming up through the pan.

Freely boiling water provides the cook with a steady temperature, which will remain about the same until the water is all evaporated. Hot water is a very effective distributor of heat, transferring it into the food at a much faster rate than hot air can. The heat transfer takes place on all surfaces of the food, instead of being concentrated on one side or on a few high spots as in some other methods of cooking.

The temperature of the water is not affected by the rate of boiling. Rapid boiling, with many bubbles and much agitation, might cook the food a tiny bit faster because of more rapid and efficient heat transfer from the pan bottom to the food, but this possible small gain does not justify an increase in the risk of boiling over or going dry, nor the excessive consumption of fuel.

However, production of only a few small air bubbles which tend to stick to the pan bottom usually indicates a simmering temperature, substantially below boiling. If your timing depends on full boiling heat, make sure that at least a few bubbles are breaking steadily at the surface.

Criticisms. The principal criticism of boiling is that the water tends to dissolve varying amounts of minerals, vitamins and flavors out of food. Such substances may be destroyed by the heat of the cooking process, or thrown out with the water when cooking is completed. These losses seem to be moderate unless the food is grossly over-cooked, but no two authorities agree on their extent.

Another objection is that boiling water cooks a number of substances too rapidly so that they become tough. These are chiefly proteins such as are found in egg white, meat and fish. This problem will be discussed under SIMMERING.

Boiling is not as effective as some other cooking methods in developing flavor. Whether this is because it dissolves away flavors already present, or simply fails to point up and enhance them, is dependent on the particular foods being considered, and is something for the technicians to decide. The loss factor is so important in meat that it is only boiled when the water extract is to be saved and served with it as a stew or soup. But many vegetables develop their best flavor when boiled.

Method. The preferred way to boil vegetables is to heat the water to a boil, add the vegetables, keep maximum heat until the water boils again, turn down the burner until bubbling is slow, put a lid over the pan, and cook until tender. You may have to adjust the flame again if the liquid boils over or stops boiling. You should check occasionally to make sure there is still water enough to prevent burning.

The lid is optional. It serves a number of purposes. It slows the boiling away of fluids, may increase cooking temperature and thus reduce cooking time, slightly, provides for steam-cooking of any food projecting above the water and usually reduces cooking smells. But it may cause or increase trouble with boiling over, it interferes with watching the food, and it is accused of contributing to loss of green color in food and to the occasional creation of unpleasant odors.

For open boiling there should be enough water to cover the food, and it should not be allowed to drop much below the top

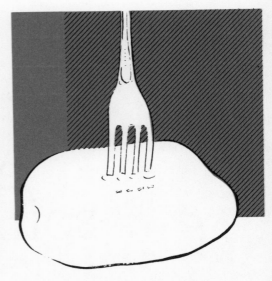

Fig. 2-1. Test for tenderness

pieces. But if covered, you can start with less water, or allow an original high water level to evaporate to a very low level, allowing steam to take care of most of the cooking. In this way you can obtain a concentrated juice for serving with the vegetable, or for use in sauce, gravy or soup. But be sure not to let it go dry, as the food will then scorch and burn and develop unpleasant flavor and smell.

Spaghetti and other pasta products are usually boiled over high heat, so that the rapid production of bubbles will prevent pieces from clumping together. Rice may be cooked in the same manner, or slowly with a minimum quantity of water that will be entirely absorbed. There will be further discussion of boiling methods under particular foods.

Timing. Cooking time varies among different vegetables and among different lots of the same vegetable. It is affected by their type, age and condition, the size and shape of the pieces, and the thoroughness with which you want to cook them.

As an example, white potato slices 1/8 of an inch thick may cook in 5 to 12 minutes, one-inch cubes in 12 to 20 and whole potatoes in 40 to 60 minutes. Differences depend on the characteristics of the potato and the point at which you consider them cooked. Longer cooking periods are chiefly for mashing.

There is also wide variation, due to both natural causes and special processing, in the cooking time of grains such as rice and oats, and pastas such as macaroni and spaghetti. Until you are very familiar with boiling different foods, you will be wise to check up on them with frequent tests.

The test is for tenderness. You can try to push a table fork into large items. If it goes in easily, they are done or nearly done, depending on the effect you want. Remember that the largest pieces take the longest. For small pieces, like peas or grains of rice, take out one or a few, allow them to cool and then chew them. The cooling can be hastened by cold water, or by placing on a cool metal surface.

Boiling Point. The boiling point of water is exactly 212° only under certain standard conditions. The water must be nearly pure,

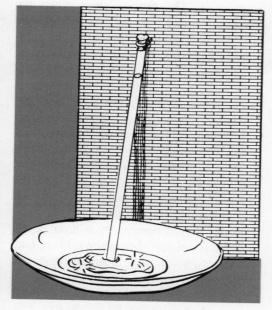

Fig. 2-2. A simplified barometer

the container must be uncovered, the altitude very near sea level and atmospheric pressure normal. In addition, the temperature must be taken at the upper or free surface of the water.

The boiling point is usually raised by dissolved substances, such as salt and sugar. This fact is useful in measuring the proportion of sugar in a boiling syrup by means of its temperature, as indicated in Figure 18-16.

The other factors relate to pressure on the liquid. Water is held together as a liquid by attraction between its molecules and to some extent by gravity, but the most important influence is usually atmospheric pressure. This is the weight of air over the water, which tends to keep its molecules squeezed together and in liquid form.

When water is heated, its molecules are given increased energy, and a temperature will be reached at which they can overcome both attraction and pressure, and expand into gas. This change will require more heat if pressure is high than if it is low.

Atmospheric pressure may be measured by the number of inches of mercury it will support in a tube in a vacuum (a barometer). Normal pressure is considered to be 29.70 inches. Water will then boil at 212°. With the arrival of a storm, the barometer may go down to 29.1 and the boiling point to 211° F. It would take a real expert to detect a difference in time and quality of cooking by boiling, but the consistency of thermometer-regulated candy might show a barely noticeable change.

A rise of 550 feet in elevation would cause the same drop in pressure. This effect of change in altitude is an important problem, and will be considered separately.

Pressure may be increased by depth of water and by tight-fitting pan lids. This does not show much in temperature and cooking time, although it may have a spectacular effect on boil-overs. But a pressure cooker with a sealed lid may be operated with sufficient back pressure (up to 15 pounds per square inch above atmosphere) to speed up cooking greatly.

Parboiling. Parboiling means partial cooking by boiling. If the amount of cooking is quite small, it is called blanching. This is usually a preparation of vegetables for freezing, which destroys enzymes but is supposed to leave the food practically raw.

Otherwise, parboiling is usually done to shorten time needed for another cooking process, or to provide an opportunity to absorb fluids before being mixed with other foods. It may also serve to remove overstrong tastes.

Pasta is frequently parboiled, as elbows for macaroni and cheese, or noodles for lasagne. On the other hand, some people cook them fully anyhow, before putting them in the casserole. Rice may be partly or wholly precooked before combining with other food, either in stuffings or casseroles.

WATCH THE POT

A boiling pot, pan or kettle needs supervision. It should not be allowed to boil over or go dry, and the food should not be allowed to scorch.

Boiling Over. When water changes to steam it increases its bulk many times. Formation of a steam bubble will raise the

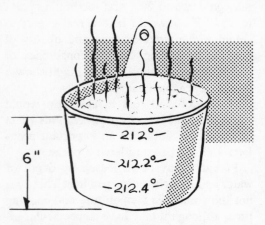

Fig. 2-3. Boiling water is hotter in the bottom of the pan

water level almost as much as if you dropped a pebble of the same size into the water. The bubble has this effect while it is forming and until it has risen to the top and disappeared. If boiling is rapid, many bubbles will be present at the same time, the water level will rise substantially, and if it was previously near the top, it will now spill over. If the pan is a deep one the volume and force of the spill will appear to be out of proportion to the number and size of the steam bubbles existing just before it happened.

This is a pressure situation. If the water is 6 inches deep, the boiling point is about 0.4° F higher at the bottom, where it is carrying the weight of the water over it, than it is at the top. The rising of steam bubbles has heated and mixed the water so that each part of it, from bottom to top, is at the boiling point. When the first bit of water is spilled out by the bubbles its weight is removed, pressure throughout the remaining water is reduced and billions of water molecules are released into steam, creating more and bigger bubbles to spill more water over the top and reduce pressure again. The process stops when the maximum number of bubbles that can be crowded into the water are no longer sufficient to push any more of it over the edge, or when all the overheated water has become steam.

Plain water in ordinary pans does not boil over very violently, and usually does little damage. But if there are dissolved substances that thicken the water so that steam bubbles move slowly up through it, the possible expansion is much greater and the boil-over can be really impressive in action and in the mess that it creates.

Water that is covered by a layer of oil, and that is not disturbed while it heats, may not start to boil until it is superheated, and then foam up very suddenly.

Boil-overs are more likely and often more violent when there is a lid on the pan, particularly if it is heavy and close-fitting. It holds back steam pressure that is added to the weight of the water in restraining creation of steam. When the lid is tipped by the first spilling of the water, this back pressure is released.

The basic cause of boiling over is too much heat. If you make a practice of keeping burners low you will not have this trouble very often. However, burners may change their heat output, fluids usually get thicker as they boil, and it is easy to make a miscalculation. A secondary cause is using too small a pot. Even aside from nearness of the water surface to the edge, a given quantity of water has less potential energy if it is shallow in a wide pot than if it is deep in a narrow one.

Boiling Dry. Boiling dry is an unpleasantness that is at least as common as boiling over, and is ordinarily more destructive. Its causes are too little water, too much heat and/or too little watching.

A pint of water in a wide pan over a vigorous burner might boil away in 15 to 20 minutes, or keep bubbling peacefully for several hours if the setting were medium low. If it were combined with moist food, such as a vegetable or some stew meat, the times would be the same or a little longer. But spaghetti or rice could absorb most of the water so that the balance would evaporate very quickly.

The present popularity of boiling vegetables in a minimum quantity of water has reduced the life expectancy of pots and pans. If you want to boil something while you talk on the phone or weed the garden, use plenty of water. If you must have concentrated juice, boil it down after you have removed the food and while you are making finishing touches on the meal and can stand over it. And if you fail then, all you have lost is the juice and perhaps the pan, but you have saved the food.

It is natural and right to turn a burner on full while you are bringing cooking water to a boil. But once it is boiling, there is no usefulness in a hot flame. Cooking will proceed just about as rapidly at a slow boil, and perhaps rapidly enough at simmer temperature, and chances of a spoiled meal are much less.

If your cooking goes dry and you do not catch it very quickly you will probably spoil the food, a situation which will be considered in the next section. If the dry heat continues long you are likely to ruin the pan also.

A gas flame should be around 3,000° F, and an electric unit on HIGH about 1500°. Aluminum oxidizes rapidly at 800° and starts to melt at 2,200, so it is quite easy to burn a hole through it. In the same situation a stainless steel pan will stay together, but it will probably darken, melt off its wood or plastic handle if it has one, and may warp as well. Aluminum or copper plating on the bottom might burn off. The

Fig. 2-4. Boilovers make a mess

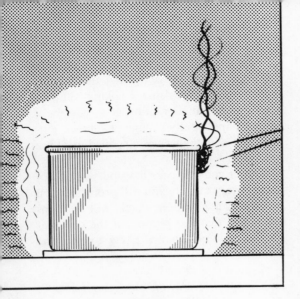

Fig. 2-5. This pan boiled dry

non-stick surface of black iron would be spoiled. Glass might be undamaged, or might melt.

Sticking, Scorching and Burning. The words of this sub-heading make a natural sequence of damages which follows automatically if cooking water is allowed to boil away and the heat continues. But it is more often a problem in cooking or even heating thick liquids or mixtures that do not have any free or separate cooking water. Creamed corn, thick white sauce and mashed turnips are examples of such substances.

The problem arises largely from poor circulation. The water in the mixture that is in contact with the heated pan can boil while the mixture is still cold a fraction of an inch above it. The boiling film passes away as steam or combines with other substances and the thickness of the mixture prevents other water from moving to the hot spot. Without the cooling effect of evaporating water, the temperature rises rapidly, causing the dried food to stick to the pan, then turn brown and finally black. The process gives off gases which cause taste changes, and spread smells through the food and then through the room.

Scorching is not necessarily a bad thing. Under the name of browning, it is important in obtaining desired flavors and crusts on many foods. In general it is desirable as a surface treatment for meat, bread and certain vegetables such as potato and onion. But on pan bottoms and specially in thick liquids it is usually intolerable.

The likelihood and severity of unwanted scorching varies with the intensity of the heat, the nature of the food, the material and condition of the pan and the efficiency of stirring. Intense heat makes the drying-out process much faster. Thick foods, and particularly those containing sugar or starch, are especially prone to trouble. Stirring removes the heated, drying material from the pan surface and replaces it with cooler and moister material. It should be done methodically, so that all danger areas are scraped repeatedly.

Scorching and burning tend to start at a particular point or area, and spread from there. Such a point is apt to be a rough or soiled spot on the bottom, or the side at the upper margin of the liquid, or where food has splashed just above it. The margin is particularly likely to scorch when the flame is wider than the pan bottom, and when the pan sides slope out steeply. Teflon is somewhat scorch-resistant, probably because its very smooth surface does not offer good starting points for the process. Deposits of food from previous use are trouble makers, and many housewives have little trouble with sticking until their children start to help with washing up.

It is possible for one part of a mixture to have reached the burning point while other parts are still bubbling freely. In such a case it is best not to stir, but to remove the pan from the heat and pour the undamaged part into another pan, and resume cooking it more cautiously. You can taste it to see if the flavor has been spoiled.

Lumps. Sticking is usually the start of scorching, but it is also a problem in itself. A thin layer of starchy material drying out against the pan bottom or side may become

38

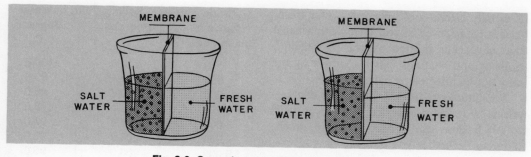

Fig. 2-6. Osmosis moves water into solutions

so firm that it will not re-mix when it is scraped off, and will remain as a lump. Such lumpiness, not followed by scorching, is common when heat is moderately low but stirring is insufficient — either too infrequent or too slow. Lumps are less likely to form if stirring is done with a wire whisk instead of a spoon, and they can often be beaten smooth after forming by vigorous use of a whisk or a rotary beater.

SALT

It is traditional for recipes for boiling almost anything to call for adding salt to the water. The amount of salt is usually one teaspoon, while the water to be salted varies from a cup to a quart. By weight, this is a proportion of salt to water that varies from 1 to 40 down to 1 to 160. For comparison, ocean water averages about 1 to 30, and is very salty.

Cookbooks seldom give any reason for using salt. Cooks usually say either that it brings out the flavor, or that the food tastes flat without it, which comes to about the same thing. Occasionally there are comments (often contradictory) on its effect on color or texture of vegetables.

Addition of salt to cooking water has at least three effects: change in flavor, extraction of juice and slight increase in boiling point.

The flavor change may be fairly definite. People accustomed to rice, spaghetti or vegetables are likely to take unfavorable notice of omission of salt. The dry starches do absorb both water and salt, but most vegetables absorb neither, and merely retain a slight amount of salt on their surfaces. Such vegetables are usually perfectly acceptable when steamed, which is an entirely salt-free cooking process.

Osmosis. Many of the membranes that enclose and separate the cells in vegetables and meat can be penetrated readily by water, but resist crossing by many dissolved substances, including salt and sugar. There is a basic tendency for solutions separated by such a membrane to equalize their strength, by passing water from the less concentrated to the more concentrated side. This process is called osmosis.

Osmosis can be demonstrated by placing dry salt on the cut, dried surface of a vegetable, fruit or meat, or on the thin uninjured skin of a berry. Moisture drawn out of the food will soon dissolve the salt. In solution, this action is weaker, but it is still effective.

Plant and animal cells contain dissolved sugars, salts and many other materials. When heated in plain water they have a tendency to absorb water and dilute their internal solutions, so that they become crisper and slightly weaker in flavor. If the water is salted, this tendency is stopped or reversed, so that juices may bleed through cell walls into the cooking water, making the food more soft and limp in texture, but slightly more concentrated in flavor.

In addition to this more or less one-way movement of water through cell walls, there is usually bleeding of juice into water from spaces between cells, and from within cells that have been injured by peeling, slicing, bruising and heating. This bleeding may or may not be affected by salt.

To summarize, salt in water has definite effects on food being boiled, but they are all small. It does not appear to make much difference whether you add salt or not, except in cooking dry starches, and you can usually suit your own taste in this regard. Except that if you are feeding anyone who is limited to a low-sodium (salt-free) diet, you should never salt cooking water.

SIMMERING

To simmer is to cook in water that is kept below the boiling point, although many cooks use the term for slow boiling at 212° F. To accomplish anything, the temperature must be high enough to have a cooking effect. Eggs will cook in time at 145 or 150° F and most foods at below 190°. But at minimum temperatures both the penetration of heat and the cooking process are so slow that they may not be practical. As a result, low simmering temperature is usually between 175° and 190°.

A simmering pot takes a long time to go dry, and it will not boil over. Keeping temperature below boiling reduces or eliminates the toughening effect that cooking has on some proteins. Sticking and burning is eliminated except in thick or sticky mixtures.

But cooking time is longer, and increases drastically as the temperature is lowered. A potato in 1/8-inch slices that would cook in 8 minutes at 212° might take 10 minutes at 200° and 25 or 30 at 175°. Longer times exaggerate differences between batches. Boiling time for a potato slice at 212° might vary by 1 or 2 minutes either way, depending on its variety and condition, and vary 20 minutes at 175°.

Also, it may be difficult or impossible to keep the water at or very near the desired

Altitude Above Sea in Feet	Boiling Point of Water	
	Degrees, F.	Degrees, C.
0	212.0	100.0
500	211.1	99.6
1,000	210.2	99.0
2,000	208.4	98.0
3,000	206.6	97.0
4,000	204.8	96.0
5,000	203.0	95.0
6,000	201.2	94.0
7,000	199.4	93.0
7,500	198.5	92.5
8,000	197.6	92.0
9,000	195.8	91.0
10,000	194.0	90.0
12,000	190.4	88.0
15,000	185.0	85.0

Fig. 2-7. Effect of altitude on boiling point

simmer temperature. Many electric burners have step controls that prohibit exact regulation of heat, and both variable heat electrics and gas units may fail to maintain a uniform heat output at any one setting. If temperature creeps up, cooking will be speeded, if it drops, cooking will be slowed or even stopped. Fairly frequent thermometer readings, tests of the food and appropriate heat adjustments may be required to assure that the item will be ready on time and that it will not be grossly overcooked.

For most purposes, (but excluding meat) boiling is a more efficient and reliable cooking method than simmering.

Coddling, discussed under EGGS, is a method of obtaining simmer results by cooking in water that is either being heated toward the boiling point, or is being allowed to cool from that temperature.

Altitude. Increase in altitude above sea level lowers the boiling point of water, as shown in Figure 2-7. This is because there is less atmospheric pressure to resist expansion into steam. The high altitude cook is therefore forced to do boiling at simmer temperatures. The automatic temperature control of boiling is retained, cooking time becomes longer, and less toughness develops in sensitive foods.

The reduced pressure and boiling point, together or separately, affect other types of cooking also, particularly baking and pressure cooking. Differences will be discussed under these headings.

STEAMING

Those who have conscientious or other objections to boiling will often settle for no-pressure steaming, also called dry boiling (!), braising, pot roasting and various other names. In its purest form, steaming involves putting food on a rack above a small quantity of water in the bottom of a covered pan, and keeping the water at a slow boil until the food is cooked by the steam rising from the water and held in by the lid.

This process may take about the same time as boiling, or slightly longer. It is not practical for foods such as spaghetti and rice that must absorb a considerable volume of water. It does not dissolve out vitamins. Salt is not used, and could not reach or affect the food if it were, except in causing a slight temperature increase. Flavors are neither dissolved out nor created, and taste of the cooked food may be judged to be superior, inferior or the same as that obtained by boiling, depending on the food and on personal preference.

Steaming may also be done in a double boiler with holes in the upper pan. Heat loss is greater and cooking probably slower than when using a single compartment.

A steaming pan is more likely to go dry than a boiling one if the flame is high and/or the lid is a poor fit. But if this happens the heat will probably damage only the pan at first, not the food. This saves the embarrassment of burned food, and the job of cleaning it from the pan bottom. But the lack of a burning smell to warn you may allow a pan to overheat until it is ruined by warping or by a hole burned through the bottom.

The rack is often omitted. The food is rested directly on the bottom, so that a part of it is boiled in the water and the rest is steamed above it. It may be stirred or manipulated occasionally to change their places. The water level can be high for

Fig. 2-8. Steaming, with and without a rack

Fig. 2-9a. Pressure cooker

safety or low to increase the steam area, as a poor-fitting lid may cause the steamed part to cook more slowly than the other. A low water level offers maximum risk of drying away and allowing the food to burn.

Braising. Low-water steaming with direct contact between food and pan bottom may also be called braising. A rule of thumb distinction is that if the food is intentionally browned by the pan, either by searing beforehand or during the steam cooking, it is being braised. The process is closely related to steaming when the food pieces are large or piled high, but is more like frying when they are in a shallow layer or layers.

Braising will be discussed under FRYING and POT ROAST.

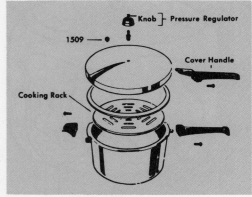

Fig. 2-9b. Pressure cooker parts

PRESSURE STEAMING

In pressure cooking, the steam from boiling water is confined in the cooking vessel, so that pressure and temperature increase, in both the water and the steam confined together. In home cooking a pressure of 15 pounds (about 250° F) is standard, but in canning it may be reduced to 10 pounds (240°) or even 5 pounds.

The pressure makes any given temperature more effective in cooking than it would be if unconfined. In an oven, water boils and evaporates from food, absorbing a large part of the heat. Air is a poor conductor of heat and steam is a good one. High pressure tends to force steam and heat into food. As a result, pressure steam is a very rapid method of cooking.

Cookers. Pressure cookers for the home range in size from 2-quart pans to canners large enough to hold 7 one-quart glass jars. Their general principles of construction and operation are similar, but there are important variations in detail.

Any pressure cooker must be made of metal strong enough to resist internal pressure, and its body and lid must be machined for a locking fit and shaped to hold a steam-tight gasket.

The pan may be steel or stainless steel, but is usually made of heavy aluminum, either cast or sheet. The lid may be of matching material, but may be a thin, flexible metal shaped into a dome which is compressed into place by a clamp-type handle. Rigid lids may be tightened by rotating a fraction of a turn, or on old or large models, by clamp screws and nuts.

The lid is sealed to the pan by a gasket made of rubber or a rubber-like composition. This is the most vulnerable part of the cooker, and is discussed below under Sealing.

A vent or exhaust valve is provided in the lid to permit and control the escape of air or steam. If there is a gauge showing steam pressure, you are supposed to regulate it by increasing or decreasing the heat, and the valve acts only as an emergency relief if you are careless and allow too much pressure to build up.

Pressure may be indicated, and regulated to some extent also, by a vent made of a projecting tube, Figure 2-10. This is closed by a weight resting on it. Sufficient pressure in the cooker, usually 15 pounds, will raise the weight, causing it to rock and to allow the escape of steam. Heat should be regulated so that the weight rocks gently, with regular emission of small puffs of steam. If there is no rocking or steam, pressure is too low. If rocking is rapid, or it stops while a steady jet of steam emerges, pressure is too high.

A single-position weight is usually designed for 15-pound pressure. One with three possible positions can be used for 5, 10 or 15 pounds.

In addition to the regular relief or regulating valve, there should be a safety plug which will melt (if metal) or blow out (if rubber) to release pressure if it should become too high.

Starting. The pressure cooker serves two principal purposes — speed in meal preparation, and safety in canning non-acid food. The canning application will be discussed under FOOD PRESERVATION.

Enough water is placed in the pan to provide steam to fill it, and to provide for replacing whatever part of it leaks out. If the gasket is tight and pressure is regulated by changing burner heat in accordance with pressure reading on a dial, there may be no leakage. But weight-type controls allow almost continuous leakage in small quantities, and gaskets are not always tight. An inch of water may be enough for a quickly cooked item, while a large canner may need two or three inches.

For use, place the food on a rack above the water, put the gasket into position very carefully, put on the lid and tighten it by

Fig. 2-10. Too much heat

twisting or clamping, open the vent, and turn the burner to full heat. Allow steam to escape from the open vent until it is coming out with some pressure, to give it a chance to push out all or most of the air, which is a poor conductor. Then close the valve, setting it at the pressure you want.

Regulating. Leave the heat on full until the desired pressure is reached if it is a gas burner, or a few pounds less if it is an electric, then reduce the heat until you can hold it at or near the pressure you want, without excessive loss of steam. This is more difficult on an ordinary electric range than on gas, as the step-type control may not provide the exact amount of heat you want, and the slower heating and cooling make it difficult to judge effects promptly. The problem of stepped heat may be solved by using the

Courtesy of National Presto Industries

Fig. 2-11. Regulating weight, and pressure gauge

Put 1/2 cup of water in a 4-quart Cooker, and one cup in a 6-quart Cooker, except for potatoes use one cup in the smaller Cooker and 1-1/2 cups in the larger.

Then place rack over the water and set vegetables on the rack. Do not fill Cooker over 2/3 full.

Two or more vegetables can be cooked at the same time, without loss or mixing of flavors, but they must have the same cooking ime.

Older, over-size vegetables require more time than younger, fresher or smaller ones.

Cool the Cooker under running faucet water or in a pan of cold water until steam pressure is completely reduced. If you allow natural cooling, vegetables are likely to be over cooked.

Vegetable	How To Prepare	Cooking Time in Minutes
Artichokes	Wash, trim and score hearts.	10
Asparagus (Tips)	Wash and snap off tough parts. Large ends may be used in soup.	1 - 2
Beans (Green or Wax)	Wash. Remove ends and strings. Cut in one-inch pieces.	3 - 4
Beans (Green Lima)	Shell and wash.	2 - 3
Beets (Whole)	Wash thoroughly. Remove all but three inches of top and leave roots on. After cooking, slip skins off.	10 - 18
Broccoli	Wash, score stems, remove leaves and tough stalk parts.	2 - 3
Brussels Sprouts	Wash. Remove wilted leaves. Leave whole.	3
Cabbage (Quartered)	Remove wilted outside leaves. Wash and cut in quarters.	3 - 4
Carrots	Wash, brush and scrape or peel. Slice or leave whole.	(Sliced) 3 (Whole) 4 - 8
Cauliflower	Wash and hollow out core or separate flowerettes.	(Whole) 5 (Flowerettes) 2
Celery	Separate stalks. Remove tough, stringy fibers. Scrub and wash well. Cut in ½-inch pieces.	2 - 3
Corn (On-the-Cob)	Remove husk and silk. Wash.	3 - 5
Greens (Mild flavored) Beet Greens Spinach Swiss Chard	Select young tender greens. Remove wilted leaves. Wash thoroughly several times and lift from water after each washing.	(Beet Greens) 3 (Spinach) 1 - 3 (Swiss Chard) 2
Kohlrabi	Wash. Peel and cut into cubes or slices.	5 - 6
Onions (Whole)	Wash and peel medium white or Bermuda Onions.	5 - 7
Parsnips	Wash, peel or scrape. Leave whole or cut in halves.	(Halves) 7 (Whole) 10
Peas (Green)	Wash and shell.	(Small) 1 (Large) 2
Potatoes in Jackets (Baking Size)	Wash and scrub thoroughly.	15
Potatoes (for Mashing)	Wash and peel. Leave small potatoes whole and cut large potatoes in half.	10
Potatoes (Small)	Wash and scrub new potatoes thoroughly.	10
Pumpkin	Follow instructions for Hubbard Squash.	10 - 12
Rutabagas	Wash, peel and dice.	3 - 5
Squash - Hubbard	Wash, peel and cut into small pieces.	10 - 12
Sweet Potatoes (Whole)	Wash and scrub thoroughly. Do not peel.	10
Turnips	Follow instructions for rutabagas.	3 - 5

Courtesy of National Presto Industries

Fig. 2-12. Pressure-cooking times

higher heat, and putting an asbestos pad over part of the unit.

If the cooker has a dial gauge you can tell just how much over or under proper pressure you are. With a weight you estimate according to how much it rocks.

In general, if you can keep within a few pounds of proper pressure, and have it over-pressure about as long as under, cooking results will be nearly the same as with steady pressure.

Never leave a pressure cooker unwatched for long. Even though it has operated at a balanced pressure for some time, chance or accident may increase the heat so that pressure will build up dangerously. Food may absorb a great deal of heat early in its cooking, so that when it is hot all the way through, there will be a surplus of heat to build up pressure.

Bad burns may be caused by an unexpected jet of steam from a safety valve or plug. If such devices fail to work, there is a remote possibility that a cooker might blow up. If you have any reason to think that pressure is much too high in a cooker, and that a valve has failed to operate, turn off the heat and go away and leave it alone for a few minutes.

Cooking Time. Figure 2-12 contains a table of cooking times for a number of vegetables. These are figured from the time the pressure is reached to the time you turn off the heat, and include allowances for cooking which occurs while pressure is building up and while it is going down. As with almost every instruction in cooking, these are just an estimate with which to start. In addition to variability in different items of the same food, there is a probability of wide differences in the time that elapses between reaching cooking temperature and reaching the proper pressure. A weak burner and/or a large quantity of water will greatly increase the time between closing the vent and reaching full pressure, and cooking action will occur during this period. The

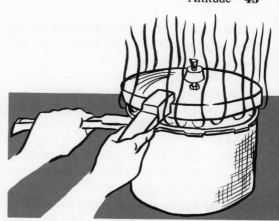

Fig. 2-13. Open cooker cautiously

method and speed of cooling off can also make a difference of minutes during which cooking action is intermediate between that of full pressure and that which occurs at a "simmer" temperature.

Be careful to avoid overcooking. If a vegetable requires 20 minutes of open boiling to be cooked to your taste, the chances are that 2 minutes extra time on the burner will do little harm. But in a pressure cooker with a time of 8 minutes, that same extra 2 minutes might have serious results.

This time chart is only one of several, and all of them are approximate. Unfortunately, you have to depend on such figures, as you can't test for tenderness.

Altitude. All standard pressure cooking instructions are made up for use at sea level. At higher altitudes any given pressure will be reached at a lower temperature, or any given temperature will be represented by a higher gauge pressure.

To keep the same temperature inside the cooker, you would have to increase the pressure by one pound for every 2,000 feet of additional altitude. That is, at an elevation of 4,000 feet you would want to do general pressure cooking at 17 pounds instead of 15, and conventional canning at 12 pounds instead of 10.

For a different approach, you can keep the same pressure, and increase cooking time by 5 per cent for every 1,000 feet over

2,000. That is, at 3,000 feet increase it by 5 per cent, at 4,000 feet by 10 per cent, and so forth.

Cooling. When the time indicated by the chart you are using, or by your experience, is completed, you turn off the heat. If the range is electric, move the cooker off the burner.

The cooling time is part of the cooking time, and you should follow the instructions you have. It is safe to let a unit cool by itself, but this is slow and may cause over-cooking. You cool it faster by wrapping cold wet cloths around it, or by running cold faucet water over it. But some manu-facturers forbid you to do this with their cookers, on the ground that it might warp them. And they may be right. Others tell you to do it, so you should. Some valves may be damaged by cold water, so always avoid letting it run over (or into) the regu-lating valve.

Opening. NEVER turn, adjust or un-lock a pressure cooker lid while there is pressure inside. Usually, pressure will jam the releases, but if it does not, a puff of superheated steam may be released against your skin, and the lid may take off like a shell.

Leave it until pressure has dropped to zero. Test for no-pressure by tipping or raising the valve. If no steam escapes, re-move the weight or lock the valve open, then remove the cover. If you must touch it, use dry pot holders or "warm" gloves, as it will be very hot.

An important precaution is to tilt the lid by raising the side that is away from you. In spite of care, there might still be some pressure there, and even if there is not, enough steam might be present to puff out and burn you, or perhaps startle you into dropping the lid. With it tilted to shield you, you are much safer.

This precaution is valid for raising lids on non-pressure pans, also.

Be careful not to drop the lid, as you might bend it so that it would not make a steam-tight fit.

Most steam valves open automatically when inside pressure drops below that of the atmosphere, so that air can enter. But if one should fail to do so, you might get a vacuum in a cooled cooker that would make it difficult to open. You can then try to let air in by manipulating the valve, or equalize pressure by reheating cautiously until the cover is free.

Sealing. The number one problem of pressure cooking is sealing in the steam. A large number, probably the majority, of pressure cookers are so designed that the pressure of the steam forces the gasket into the space it is supposed to close, so that the higher the pressure, the greater the sealing power. Unfortunately, this also means that as the cooker starts building up from zero pressure, the gasket is at its minimum effec-tiveness. If it has dried out so as to change shape, if it has been damaged or has shrunk, or if it has been carelessly installed, it may allow a substantial amount of steam to leak past it. If this leakage equals the steam-making capacity of the burner, pressure will not build up to force the gasket into a posi-tion where it will stop the leakage. The re-

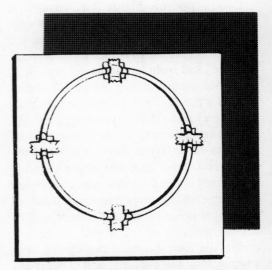

Fig. 2-14. A gasket should be stored with care

sult is no pressure, and therefore no pressure cooking.

You can immediately see that there is trouble by the escaping steam. Sometimes banging the lid with a wood or plastic implement will jar the gasket into a better position, so that the leakage will stop. At other times you have to take the pan off the heat, let it cool a bit (even if steam seems to be escaping freely, enough pressure may have built up to give a powerful puff of scalding steam), and try to rearrange the gasket. Taking it out and putting it in upside down is often effective. If it doesn't work on the second attempt, replace the gasket. If you don't have a gasket, figure that the cooker makes a good steamer anyhow, cook for the longer no-pressure time required, and get a gasket for the next time. But this will not help with canning low-acid food.

A spare gasket is an excellent investment, but unless you store it carefully it may be out of shape and useless by the time you need it. One good way to keep it is to spread it out in its working position on a stiff piece of cardboard, and fasten it there with Scotch tape. Put pieces of paper on the gasket so that the tape will not stick to it, as it might tear when you remove it. Place another piece of cardboard over the gasket, and fasten the cardboards together with rubber bands.

For an extra, very long-term precaution against drying or oxidizing of the gasket material, you will be wise to seal the package in a plastic bag.

3

FRYING

FRYING

In frying, a heated pan or other container transmits heat to food by a layer or bath of oil or melted fat, which may vary from a thin film to a depth of a foot or more. The term is stretched to cover cooking on dry ungreased pans (dry frying), where it overlaps on another dubious term, pan broiling. Neither name is really appropriate, since the essence of frying is the presence of grease, and the distinguishing feature of broiling is direct across-air heating from flame or some other intense source.

In pan frying, also called shallow frying and sautéeing, the food rests on the pan bottom, while in deep frying it either floats in the fat or is supported in a strainer or basket that holds it above the bottom. It follows that use of an inch or two of fat would be shallow frying, provided the food did not float and deep frying if it did. It seems to be the general custom to use either a thin layer or a considerable depth, with no in between stages.

If a small amount of water mixes with or replaces the fat in pan frying, and the pan is covered, the operation is called braising.

Status. Frying is a faster method of cooking than either boiling or roasting. Fat temperature is kept much higher than the boiling point of water, and it conducts heat far more efficiently than the air in an oven. It also can and should produce excellent flavor, blending taste of fast-cooked food with that of the cooking oil, and of various secondary products formed by reactions between food and oil.

On the other hand, fried food can easily become hard and dried-out, and it is usually more or less oily or greasy. Many digestions will not tolerate much or sometimes any grease, so that fried foods have to be avoided partly or entirely. Hardness and greasiness can both be largely controlled by proper cooking and draining.

Frying is a good and much-used cooking method, but its status is much better among people than among their advisors. There are two big cookbooks, covering practically every phase of food preparation, that do not have any index entries for frying. Fortunately, this does not prevent them from including recipes on the subject.

Fat, Grease and Oil. So far as frying is concerned these three terms mean the same thing. Strictly speaking, fat is any white or yellowish adipose tissue of animals, and any

49

Fig. 3-1. Deep, shallow and greaseless frying

chemically similar substance in plants, and it may be solid or liquid. Fat is almost always edible. Grease is any soft fat. It does not include hard fat such as suet or tallow, or substances that are liquid at room temperature. It also includes many inedible lubricants and other substances, but references in this book mean only edible greases. The word oil also has many meanings, but here it will mean only edible fats in a liquid state.

At frying temperatures all of these substances are liquid, and the three names can be used interchangeably.

The fat used in frying serves three important purposes. It prevents, or tends to prevent, the food from sticking to the pan; it provides an efficient medium for conducting heat from the pan bottom to the food and it flavors the food.

Oil (which includes melted fat) forms a slippery film over the metal surface, which holds the food away from it a few molecule-widths, and thus prevents sticking. The film may be reduced by boiling away, or by absorption by the food, so that it must be renewed by more oil creeping into the space, or by moving the food to pick up more oil.

Most fats can be hot enough to brown most food before they reach their boiling point. Breakdowns of their film on hot metal will allow variable degrees of sticking, and additional browning and burning, which can be regulated by scraping with a turner and adjusting burner heat, to produce the color desired. Butter and some margarines turn brown themselves at moderate heat, adding color. Complicated reactions go on inside the fats and in their combinations with the food, to produce the variety of tasty flavors associated with frying.

Temperature. In common with most solids, fats have specific temperatures at which they will freeze or melt, and at which they will boil. But they are such complex chemicals that these temperatures can be somewhat variable for each kind.

Oil or melted fat has another critical temperature, the smoke point. A thin, white smoke comes off the surface when it is still well below the boiling point. This smoke indicates a process of chemical breakdown, with changes in flavor and color.

Smoke is not ordinarily produced in the recommended deep frying range, 350° to 390° F, unless the fat has already deteriorated from over-use. It can serve as a warning of too much heat, before boiling begins.

Deep fat when boiling deteriorates rapidly, is too hot for most cooking and is very dangerous because of splattering, and danger of boiling over and/or catching fire. Shallow frying temperatures are optional, with splattering of grease and burning of food being common penalties for high heat.

In either type of frying, the principal penalties for too-low temperatures are slow cooking, and soaking in grease. Also, the desired crust and fried flavor may not develop.

Hardness. Hardness is usually caused by overcooking, but sometimes just by cooking too fast. Fried foods tend to form a crust at the surface of contact with the hot grease. Hotter grease causes faster crust formation, but may not increase the rate of cooking in proportion. If too much heat is used, this surface will be overcooked, probably hard and possibly burned by the time the inside or the top is cooked. In addition, very rapid cooking tends to toughen some proteins, including white of egg and various meats, even without reference to crusting.

However, it should be remembered that the average family does not need or expect their food to be prepared for the standards of a baby or an invalid. The crisp texture and the taste of slight to moderate crusts are a large part of the reason for frying, broiling and roasting. You don't want to eliminate hardening, just keep it under control.

GREASINESS

Greasiness is a quality that may show in drainage onto plates, appearance and/or flavor in hot food. When the food cools and stands, there may be a strong effect on texture as well. These conditions usually become more noticeable if the food becomes stale, and are the basis for the idea that fried food must be eaten immediately while hot, and not kept for the future.

Greasiness, like crustiness, is not all bad. For many tastes and even for many national tastes it is considered good, particularly if the "grease" is olive oil. And a moderate amount of oiliness in and on the surface of fried foods is an important part of their

Fig. 3-2. Some people enjoy oily eating

special flavor, to be sacrificed only for stern dietary reasons.

Butter is a fat which, because of its unusual qualities of texture, flavor and low melting and browning points, seldom gives a greasy quality to foods fried in it, even when used carelessly or in excessive quantities. The same is true of most margarines, but not of all of them. But these low boiling and browning points prevent the use of either butter or margarine in deep frying.

Potentially unpleasant effects of grease may be considered in three parts: that which soaks into the food beneath the crust during cooking, that which is temporarily held in the crust with possibilities of soaking in later, and a surface layer which may stay where it is, soak in, or move downward.

Prevention. So far as the frying process itself is concerned, the best preventive for soaking-in is high temperature during cooking. Surface crusts are often grease resistant, and form fastest at high heats. Also high temperature speeds the cooking (but as we have said, not in direct proportion) so that the grease will be allowed less time for penetration when it is hot. This prevention of grease soaking must be balanced against the danger of hard crust and dried food when temperature is too high.

There are also characteristics of the food itself that favor or reduce grease soaking. A rich dough containing considerable shortening absorbs more cooking fat than a lean one does. White of egg congeals quickly when heated, and forms a more or less grease-resistant surface.

In the following discussion it will be assumed for the sake of simplicity that the reader does not want fried food to show any noticeable quantity of oil or grease. If this is not your idea, please ignore the suggestions.

The Problem. Drainage of grease onto plates is usually immediate. Any piece of food cooked in a layer of grease, 1/16" or more, will carry some when lifted out of the pan. In addition, fried eggs may have puddles on their upper surface, bacon will be producing it from both surfaces, and sausage will carry considerable quantities on both outside surface and inside. When such an item is put hot on a plate, some of the heat-thinned grease is very likely to drain down onto the plate, producing a puddle whose size is limited by the quantity flowing, its thinness or thickness, and the temperature of the plate. (It will spread wider and thinner on a warm plate).

This puddle, and also greasiness of appearance, can usually be eliminated by pouring off grease, draining and/or blotting the food, and allowing a few minutes for any remaining oil or grease to be absorbed by the food.

Pouring Off. Grease is often poured out of the shallow-fry pan at intervals during cooking. Since it builds up only around foods that are producing it, the general effectiveness of this is doubtful. But it reduces the quantity to be handled at one time, prevents overflow and reduces spilling. When the cooking is finished, it definitely is advantageous to pour off all the grease. This is usually done without removing the food, which is held in the pan by means of a lid (preferably undersize), a turner or any handy object.

Pouring should be into a can or other heat-resistant storage or waste container, which should be dry to avoid boiling and splattering. Steep-sided pans are difficult to drain completely unless you have an undersize lid, as the bottom must be tipped to overhanging to drain the side. If you cannot drain it completely, you can rest the pan on some object that will give a slope to the bottom, and move the food to the high (and dry) side.

You may prefer to leave the grease in the pan if you cannot find a container for it, if the food is too tender to be tipped or you are going to cook another batch in the same pan. In this case you lift the food out of

Fig. 3-3. Hold food while pouring grease

the grease with appropriate tools, usually a slotted turner or tongs.

In deep fat frying you always lift the food instead of pouring away the fluid.

Draining. When you are lifting food directly out of any considerable quantity of hot fat it will carry some of it along. A good part of this will drain off in the first few seconds if you use a basket, a perforated or flat lifter, or tongs. You may hold it over the pan for partial drainage, or put it on a rack immediately. The rack may be any arrangement of wires or thin bars spaced closely enough to support the pieces of food, with some arrangement underneath for catching a small quantity of grease. A colander, or a supported sieve, may be used.

Draining is not very efficient. Drops may cling to the bottom of the food or lodge in narrow spaces between it and the metal. The food tends to cool rather rapidly.

Draining may be just used briefly to dispose of bulk grease before blotting.

Blotting. Food is blotted by placing it on absorbent material, which is usually paper toweling or brown paper, but may be clean scrap cloth, paper napkins, facial or toilet tissue or newspaper. Newspaper absorbs well and is usually available in quantity at no cost, but there is a possibility of some of the print transferring itself to the food. Tissue may have loose lint. Either material may be used for bottom layers, with a protective top of brown paper or towel.

Several layers should be used, as the blotting action is slowed as soon as the paper directly under the food is saturated.

Blotting should be done immediately after cooking, as the grease thickens and soaks back into the food as it cools. It is usually not necessary to turn the food, but you will soak out a little more grease if you do it. The process is nearly complete in a minute. If you are not ready to serve, you can leave it on the paper and cover it with another layer, or with an inverted bowl or plate to keep warm. Or you can wipe out the hot, drained pan and put the blotted food back in it, off the heat or on very low heat, with a cover.

Eggs are difficult to blot. A turned egg can be placed on paper, the plate placed upside down on top, the two turned over, and the paper peeled off. Grease puddles can be taken off the upper surface of either turned or sunny eggs by soaking up with twisted bits of paper. But eggs respond so well to frying with very little grease that this is usually not necessary and it is almost never done.

Fig. 3-4. Draining and blotting

BREADING (DREDGING)

Food that is to be fried is frequently breaded. This usually means that it is coated with flour, crumbs or corn meal, which may be held on by the dampness of the food, or by an added film of water, milk or raw egg.

Breading is used principally to provide a richer fried flavor, and to improve appearance. It may also serve to prevent pieces of food from sticking together. When it includes egg, it is hardened immediately by contact with hot grease, and forms a skin that resists soaking-in and that helps to hold tender food together.

The process of applying the flour or crumbs may be called dredging.

Flour. An entire coating may be made of flour, or it may be applied just as a primer coat, to enable the surface to hold a larger amount of egg.

Plain white flour is generally used, but it may be seasoned. Other types of flour or meal are called for in special recipes. Corn meal provides a slightly gritty texture.

Flouring is appropriate for items that are strong enough to stay together, such as chicken parts, chops and scallops.

Food that is to be floured should be damp, but not wet. Meat usually has sufficient natural dampness, but if it feels dry, wet it and then pat with a towel until drops of water are removed.

The easy way to apply flour is to put it in a paper or plastic bag large enough to permit the pieces to be shaken freely in it. Put in a half cup of flour, more or less, then one or more of the pieces of food. Close the opening of the bag with your hand and shake it up and down a few times. Inspect the resulting coating, re-shake if necessary, and take it out of the bag. Tap lightly to shake off any loose or excess flour.

Coat the rest of the batch in the same way. If there is not enough flour, add more. There should be some left when you finish. It might be usable for other purposes.

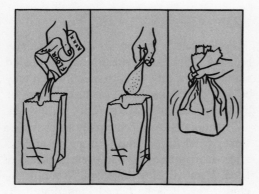

Fig. 3-5. Flouring a chicken leg

Flour may also be put on a large plate, and the food pieces moved around in and turned over several times. You may have to sift some on them also, to get complete coverage.

Flour may be seasoned with up to a teaspoon of salt to the cup (this produces a definite salted flavor) and 1/4 teaspoon of pepper or 1/2 teaspoon of paprika. In addition, you can use very small quantities of nutmeg, powdered ginger or poultry seasoning, and any of a number of dried herbs. If you like it cheesy, add up to 3 tablespoons of very finely grated cheese, preferably Parmesan.

Bread Crumbs. Bread crumbs used for breading food for frying must be dry and usually should not be browned. The bread should be thoroughly stale, or heated in a very slow oven until dry, either on cookie sheets or on the oven grate.

If you use cookie sheets, 250° F is a good oven temperature for drying without browning. Time may be 30 to 60 minutes, depending on the freshness of the bread and the amount of air circulation in the oven. The process is speeded a little by turning the bread occasionally. Test slices by pressing with your finger. They are not done until they have lost all elasticity. The next step is to break a slice. It should be brittle, so that it breaks and crumbles without bending. Even then there may be bits

in a slice that have kept enough moisture to prevent crumbling. Such pieces can be heated some more.

Slices rested on grating bars dry quite a bit faster, but are likely to brown unless temperature is kept down to 225 or even 200°.

Browned bread crumbs change slightly in flavor, but the principal objection to using them where the recipe does not call for them is that they might mislead you about the extent to which the food is cooked. But for non-frying purposes, they may be preferred. They can be obtained by staling bread at higher heat, toasting, or frying (buttering).

Crumbs should be reasonably fine and uniform in order to make a good layer on food, but if they are reduced to flour-like fineness the desired quality of the coating will be lost. To give a general idea, all the crumbs should go through the holes in a colandar easily, and almost none of them should go through a flour sifting screen.

If you are making only a small quantity, you can crumble dried bread in your fingers. For a larger amount, break up the slices and feed them into an electric blender (medium speed for a few seconds), a meat grinder or a rotary grater. Or you can spread them on a board, cover with a cloth to prevent scattering, and crush them with a rolling pin. Or put them in a strong bag and hammer it, or walk on it.

Crumbs are measured loosely by the cup or fraction of a cup. If not used soon, they should be protected from moisture by sealing in a plastic bag or tight container. If you neglect this and they get limp, they can be re-crisped in that 250° oven.

Bread crumbs can often be bought packaged. However, try not to get the type intended for poultry dressing, as they are usually too coarse and soft for frying, and would need to be crushed or ground.

There are also buttered bread crumbs, brown or otherwise, used for topping on casseroles and other oven-baked dishes. For these, you melt 2 tablespoons of butter in a frypan over moderate heat, and add 1/2 cup of dry bread crumbs. Stir until all crumbs are well covered with butter and are thoroughly hot. Continue stirring until they are the color you want. It is best to keep them light if they are to be cooked with the food, or golden brown if they will not. Additional butter may be added during cooking if they appear to be too dry. Salt, up to 1/4 teaspoon, may be used.

Other Crumbs. Cracker crumbs are made in about the same manner as bread crumbs, except that drying in the oven is not necessary except in very soggy weather.

Crackers are chosen for crumbing chiefly on the basis of their flavor. Soda crackers and saltines produce bland crumbs that will not interfere with that of the food they accompany. Graham and Ritz-type crackers have definite flavors which may either improve or take away from the success of the dish. Grahams have a more meal-like texture than the others.

Corn flakes, wheat flakes, potato chips and cake can all be crumbled or crushed to produce crumbs suitable for frying coats.

Egg. Raw egg provides a sticky surface for bare or floured pieces of food, which makes it possible to cover them more or less completely with a layer of crumbs. Whole eggs, whites only or yolks only may be used. It is customary to beat them with about 2 teaspoons of water (or sometimes milk) per egg, to thin them out a little and to smooth out the uneven or ropy texture of the white. The same amount of cooking oil is sometimes beaten in. Beating should be stopped before it creates a froth, as this makes it difficult to apply. A fork may be used instead of a beater.

Applying. The food, which may be damp but not wet, is coated with flour, and any loose particles are shaken off. The diluted egg is put in a shallow bowl or deep plate, and the crumbs in another, or in a bag.

Pieces of food (one if large, several if small) are put in the egg, stirred around and turned over until they are evenly coated. Irregular shapes, like chicken parts, may need touching up with a pastry brush or a baster. The dipped pieces are lifted out, held to drain for a few moments, and then stirred around or shaken in the crumbs. Any bare spots may be touched up by sprinkling crumbs on them with the fingers or a spoon. If they are bare of egg too, the pastry brush is needed again.

Fig. 3-6. Touching up dry spots with watered egg

Coated pieces are tapped gently to shake off crumbs that would fall off during cooking anyhow, then put aside to set. The coating becomes firmer during 10 to 20 minutes standing.

A second layer of egg and crumbs can then be applied in the same manner, if you wish. This makes a deeper, richer coating, but it is somewhat more likely to break off in patches.

Quantity. It is very difficult to estimate the quantity of egg and crumbs that will be

Fig. 3-7. Electric frypan

PAN FRYING

Pan frying is a quick convenient way of cooking. It involves a frypan, skillet or griddle (Chapter 36), usually a small or moderate amount of fat, and a surface burner. Dry frying on Teflon or black iron is similar except that no fat is used.

There are many foods that provide enough grease, or more than enough, for their own cooking. Examples are bacon, sausage, and hamburger with a high fat content. The pan needs no advance oiling, and there is usually an ample and rising grease level during cooking. Sometimes it is allowed to accumulate, at other times it is poured off at intervals, depending on the recipe and the cook's preference.

Other foods tend to soak up grease, leaving the pan dry and themselves over-greasy. For them, the pan should be greased very lightly, and the coating renewed frequently or as necessary. Home fried potatoes take up a lot of fat, but most of it is held between pieces, rather than soaked in. Vegetables, fish and very lean meat take up grease, and breading soaks it in like a sponge.

Recommended pan temperatures are 200 to 250° F with butter, and 250 to 375° with other types of fat, including those that cook out of meat. An electric frypan with a thermostat and a burner-with-a-brain can be set for particular temperatures, and give you a chance to watch the behavior of the fat and the food in different, known ranges.

There are very few foods which cannot be successfully fried at 250°, unless you like a hard crust. The low temperature might cause the food to take up more grease, but it will stay softer and is unlikely to burn.

Splatter. Pan frying may be accompanied by a number of tiny explosions, chiefly caused by water in the food turning explosively to steam when surrounded by hot fat. They throw droplets of fat and sometimes

needed, as variations in stickiness of the food and of both parts of the coating can make a 2 to 1 difference in requirement. For any given quantity of food, small pieces will need more than large ones, and flat or irregular shapes use more than thick and rounded ones.

One watered egg with 3/4 cup of crumbs should provide for 8 croquettes, 1 x 1 x 2-1/2 inches, or for half of a frying chicken. But don't start unless you have more of both ingredients available, as more may be needed. And it is hard to use them down to the last drop or crumb so that an over-supply can save you time and work.

Leftover egg and crumbs can be mixed together, in whatever proportion exists, and fried in butter. The product is usually delicious, although difficult to classify.

Fig. 3-8. Splatter

food particles out of the pan and over sur-rounding areas.

Splatter may be slight or non-existent at low temperature. The number of explosions, and the size and range of the particles, in-crease with added heat. The amount varies with the the type and texture of the food, and with the kind of grease used.

There are special spatter shields that can be arranged to enclose three sides of the pan to catch the splatter. But since a shield must be washed, or at least wiped, the ad-vantage may be small. A cover will keep the particles inside the pan, but enough may escape while you are inspecting the food to make a wipe-up necessary anyhow, and the character of the cooking will probably be changed.

The recommended procedure is to use moderate heat, and wipe off any spattered areas immediately after cooking.

Dry Frying. This term is inaccurate, but it is nevertheless better than its alternative, pan broiling. It is meant to cover the pro-cess of cooking foods that yield little or no grease on an ungreased pan.

At the cost of some sticking, you can cook most foods on a dry pan of any ma-terial, but this is not recommended unless the food is naturally greasy (or oily), or the pan is Teflon coated or is broken-in black iron. Even then, the improved flavor pro-vided by grease is enough reason for its use, unless forbidden or restricted for dietary reasons.

A heavy iron fry pan in which greased or greasy foods have been cooked acquires a non-stick surface, which it will lose if washed thoroughly with detergents or scrubbed with abrasives or steel wool. Tef-lon should be greased (or oiled) before its first use, then it is almost stick proof until part of the Teflon wears off.

Dry-frying on either of these surfaces provides only part of the flavor and appear-ance obtained by genuine pan-frying. The black iron provides a result a little closer

to the real thing, as it does have a grease film in its surface. However, food need not be fried in order to taste and look good, and cooking on a dry pan is kinder to many di-gestions.

Grease-and-Water (Braising). Food is frequently cooked with both grease and water in the pan. The two substances may be supplied deliberately, or one or both of them may be rendered (cooked out) of the food by the heat. The presence of the water prevents the temperature from rising much over 212º F, and it makes it possible to steam the upper parts of the food if the pan is covered.

If, while frying an egg, you add a tea-spoon or two of water to the grease and cover the pan, you will, in effect, steam-poach the top while you fry-poach the bot-tom. The main purpose is to produce an over-lightly effect without having to actually turn the egg. The result is somewhat differ-ent from full-frying, but it is good. Don't do it if the pan is on a high flame, as the spat-tering can be explosive.

Most meats (but not veal) will give out a mixture of water and melted grease as they cook. This serves as a cooking medium and a possible source of gravy. The water asso-ciated with grease is the cause of a large part of the splattering that occurs during frying.

Link sausages may be braised or boiled for a while (like five minutes) in shallow water (1/4 to 1/2 inch) in a covered fry-pan. The water is then poured off, and cook-ing is finished in the additional grease com-

Fig. 3-9. You can add a little water, carefully

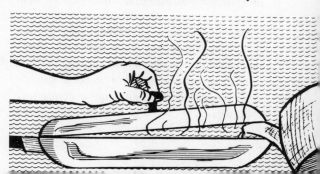

Fig. 3-10. Electric deep fryer

ing out of the sausage, with the pan hot and uncovered to obtain browning. The links should be turned to brown on four sides, or just on two if they are limited to these by being curved.

Liver and hamburger may both be started with a tiny quantity of either grease or water, preferably in an uncovered pan and cooking carried on with whatever the heat brings out of the meat. Additional butter will provide liver with a tasty gravy.

A pot roast is cooked in somewhat the same manner, but since it is usually several pounds, it requires a deep covered pan, takes hours to cook, and heat must be very low to avoid burning or over-crusting the bottom. More details are given in the MEAT section.

Some authorities claim that meat oven-roasted in a covered pan is braised. However, there is an important difference in that the pan cover is kept very hot by the oven, and radiates substantial quantities of heat into the top and sides of the meat.

Most vegetables and meat can be braised in a covered frypan with minimum effort and excellent results. However, the method is best adapted to small or medium quantities, the pot roast being an exception to this rule.

DEEP FAT

In deep frying, there is a considerable depth of oil, or at least enough to cover or float the food. In effect, food is simmered in oil.

Fryer. Most deep frying is done in a deep, straight-sided kettle with a capacity of at least 4 quarts. It may be a simple aluminum pan, looking somewhat like a pail; a special one that can sink down into a stove top on a deep fry burner; or a separate unit that contains a heating unit and a thermostatic control. The last is the most satisfactory, if you have space for it and do enough frying to justify having it.

Deep frying can of course be done in any pan deep enough for the oil, but it may not be safe. Tipping over is a disaster, a mess to clean up and possible severe injury, with fire danger. The pan should have a wide unwarped bottom for stability, there should be no long handle that might cause it to be knocked over and a tight lid should be available to cover it if it catches fire.

Some authorities say that a fryer should not be over 1/2 full of oil, others that 3/4 is proper. There are two questions; stability and boiling over. Thermostatically controlled units are heavy and stable, and can take a high level without being tippy. They are unlikely to boil over by themselves, and reasonable care in lowering food should prevent foaming over. Raising of level by the bulk of food you put in is usually slight. An oil level 3 or 4 inches below the top, before adding food, should be safe.

An electric frypan makes an excellent fryer for small objects, particularly floating ones like doughnuts where you want width rather than depth.

Fat. Most deep frying is done in vegetable fat derived from corn, cottonseed, peanuts or soy beans. It may be purchased either as oil or as semi-solid hydrogenated fat (Crisco, Spry, etc.). These substances are so purified that they have practically no taste except oiliness, and cannot ordinarily be distinguished from each other.

Butter and margarine are almost never used for deep frying, as they break down at temperatures far below the 350 to 390° F customarily used, although their refined fats have good heat resistance.

Other conditions being equal, a frying fat that is solid at room temperature will produce food that seems less greasy or oily that if it is fried in oil.

Temperature. Cookbooks are in general agreement that it is important in deep frying to have the fat at exactly the right temperature. However, they have very diverse ideas about that temperature.

Two of them want practically everything fried at 375° F, which is at least simple. Two others give different and nicely graduated temperatures for various foods, but they seldom agree and often contradict each other. For example, one wants croquettes cooked at the very top of the temperature range, 390°, the other wants to start them at 360 and cook at a steady temperature of 350°. At least, the highest recommendation is comforatbly below the smoke points of frying fats.

When the experts disagree, the layman can only use his own judgment or follow the particular recipe at hand. If there are no instructions, try 375° and change for later batches if it seems advisable.

But the temperature is important. If the fat is too cool, the food is likely to be either pale and undercooked if you take it out at the time when it should be ready; or properly colored but dry, overcooked and probably tough if you leave it in until its surface appearance is right. In either case it is likely to be greasy.

If the fat is too hot, food is likely to come out dark, dry and overcooked at the conclusion of proper cooking time, or rare (or even raw and cold) inside if removed as soon as it has color.

If you have a thermostatically controlled electric fryer you set its control at the temperature you want. These controls are usually quite accurate, but it pays to check with a frying thermometer (or preferably, 2 of them) if things do not work out right.

A fryer that does not contain its own heating heating unit is heated on a burner. If you have a thermostatically controlled burner, set it 5 to 10° higher than the temperature you want, to allow for difference between the bottom of the pan and the fat. Otherwise, you must depend on a frying thermometer. You can check its accuracy by testing it in boiling water. If you are near sea level, it should read very close to 212°. Figure that any error it shows will be about doubled at frying temperatures.

As fat is heated, it reaches a temperature at which smoke rises from the surface. This shows that it is too hot, and its molecules are breaking down into other substances, none of them particularly desirable. If temperature is increased to boiling, the rate of breakdown is greatly increased, and fat goes off into the air as a vapor, which will condense into a greasy film on walls and objects. Hot fat vapor is very flammable, but as long as the fat is not spilled, a fire may be extinguished just by putting a lid over the pan that is producing it.

It should be understood that this instruction is strictly advisory, and conveys information that is apparently acceptable to the majority. If you consider fat expendable, and prefer the flavor and texture obtained, you can, at your own risk, deep fry in smoking or even boiling fat, either as a general practice or to obtain special effects with certain foods.

Bread Test. Before thermometers, the temperature of the hot oil was checked by cooking a piece of bread. This is a good practical test, but the difficulty is that the reaction of different pieces of bread to frying varies even more than the reading of thermometers, so you cannot get an exact reading. But it may be useful to know it.

Take a slice (or a half or quarter slice) of bread, ordinary (1/2-inch) thickness, a day or two old so that it is firm but not at all stale, and put it in the oil. Time it in seconds, preferably with a watch, but in lack of that by counting, "one hippopotamus, two hippopotamus," etc., each of them representing a second. According to two authorities the bread should brown pleasantly in 60 seconds at 375º. Another says that it should have a delicate golden color in 30 seconds. There are other references for 1-inch bread cubes, but unsliced bread is now so rare that this size is unlikely to be available.

Cooling. Temperature of the grease drops when you put food into it. More food, more drop. If you overload it, it may not get back to proper heat until you are finished. It is therefore best to cook in small batches, but there does not seem to be much information on just how small. Moist food that produces a large volume of steam bubbles does more cooling than drier items. As a general rule, do not fill the basket more than 1/4 full. And try to avoid using food straight out of the refrigerator.

The amount of heat loss that occurs immediately depends mostly on the relative volume of food and of fat. Recovery to proper temperature depends on the heat output of the unit or burner. If there are two deep fryers of the same capacity, the one with the higher rating in current consumption (watts or amperes) should recover the fastest.

Always allow time for temperature to return fully to its setting before putting in a new batch of food.

Food Preparation. Food that is to be deep fried should, so far as possible, be in pieces all about the same size and shape, so that they will cook in the same time. This presents just a few little problems when you are cutting big ones into small ones anyhow, as in French frying potatoes, egg plant chunks and similar articles. Fish fillets may vary widely in width and length, but only slightly in thickness, and it is this shortest dimension that counts most.

But cut-up chicken is another story. You are stuck with big pieces and little pieces, and to make it worse, some very thin sections on wings and backs.

The answer is that while it would be easier to fry every piece in a batch the same length of time, it is not necessary. If pieces vary in size, simply assume that the small, and specially the thin ones, will cook sooner. Lift the basket at intervals and look. Take out

Courtesy of Wear-Ever Aluminum

Fig. 3-11. Frying basket on stand

those that look done and put the rest back in.

If food is wet, or very damp, try to dry it by patting with a towel. Water does not improve by frying, it absorbs a lot of heat and causes foaming.

Many, perhaps too many, foods that are deep fried are breaded first. Remember that in the frying they have to be handled very tenderly, to avoid bumping off the coating.

Loading and Cooking. Before you put food in a fryer, figure how you are going to get it out. The fat is too hot to invite you to fish around in it, even with long-handled implements, and you can't just pour it into the sink as you would water.

The majority of foods, from potato strips to chicken, are heavier than the fat and will sink in it. For all these, you want a sieve basket, Figure 3-11. This should be fitted to the fryer, fit closely to the sides and allow a little clearance from the bottom. Most important, it should have a handle or a pair of handles by which you can raise it without getting your fingers uncomfortably close to the hot grease. It is a good idea to keep it in the fryer as a precaution, even if you expect the food to float.

If you don't have a basket, you can get by (but often uncomfortably) with a big per-

Fig. 3-12. Cloth lining in funnel

forated spoon and a long fork of the outdoor grill type. With these you can put food in, and corner or spear it to take it out.

But if you have a basket, you can arrange the food in it at any convenient spot, then lower it into the fat, preheated to proper temperature. You will probably have to take the thermometer out, if you are using one. The water at the food surfaces will turn to steam, foaming up as if the fat were boiling. If this threatens to boil over the top, raise the basket a bit. The bubbling is likely to continue at a slower rate all during the cooking, as additional water is boiled out of deeper layers. You can lift the whole mass of food at any time to check its color and appearance, take out samples for testing, and finally remove it from the cooker.

The basket should have a rack by which you can support it above the fat, so that it can drip into it. Cooked food left here to drain will be kept warmer than if parked elsewhere. However, it should be transferred to paper for blotting very soon after lifting from the grease.

Fried food should be served as soon as possible. If there is a delay, park it in an oven at 250 or 300° F. But if you leave it exposed, it will dry out; if you cover it, the crust will lose crispness.

Food items that float, such as doughnuts and fritters, should be turned when about half done, or whenever you want to check on progress. Turning does them no harm.

RE-USE OF FAT

Deterioration. Fat used for cooking tends to pick up food particles of various sizes, and to undergo decomposition that may make it cloudy, dull or off-flavor.

Loose particles are particularly numerous when frying food that is coated with crumbs, particularly if the coating is loose or poorly applied, and the pieces are handled frequently or roughly. Many of them can be removed during cooking with a spoon, fork or small sieve.

Decomposition is slight at recommended frying temperatures. It becomes serious when fat is heated enough to smoke, and even more so if it boils.

Filtering. Food particles can be removed by putting the liquid grease through a double thickness of cheese cloth, or white paper toweling or facial tissue. This filter material must be supported by a strainer or a funnel, which itself must be securely supported so that it will not move during the work.

The grease is ladled or poured from the fryer into a storage container, often the can in which it was purchased. In order to pour freely and filter rapidly, the grease should be hot, but the hotter it is the more dangerous it is to handle. A fryer used just before dinner should be at a good medium pouring temperature right after the meal.

If there is a drain spout, it is quite safe to use, but you may have a problem arranging the fryer, the strainer and the container efficiently. If there is no spout, it is safer to use a ladle than to pour, particularly when the grease level is high. You may start by ladling down to below the halfway mark, then pour from the fryer.

It is possible but not restful to hold a strainer or a funnel-with-a-handle in one hand and ladle grease with the other. It is more convenient to rest the strainer or funnel in the container being filled, or preferably in a frame above the container. If the grease is to be poured, you need both hands (also pot holders or gloves) for the fryer, and the strainer must be well supported. When it is necessary, filtering can be done into a pan or utility dish, and the product poured into the storage can. A little grease is lost, and an extra item must be washed.

A funnel concentrates the grease flow into a narrow stream, so that slopping is easy to avoid. But a sieve may discharge from any part of its lower surface, and the discharge point or points change. The receptacle underneath should therefore be almost as large as the strainer.

The fryer itself may be used as a storage container for grease. You may put the can or cans of filtered grease in it, or empty them into it.

Clarifying. In addition to picking up particles of food, fat dissolves various chemicals from the food, many of which have noticeable taste, odor, color or flavor. Some of these can sometimes be removed by a process called clarifying.

You do this by letting the fat cool to 110 to 130°, putting in a raw potato, medium size, which has been pared (peeled) and sliced. Reheat the grease slowly, stirring occasionally, to about 300°. Take out the potato and discard it, allow the liquid to cool to a safe temperature, and strain it as previously described.

Most cookbooks recommend this process, but one says it is useless. The problem is that there are so many possible contaminants that a simple potato cannot be expected to cope with all of them. But it works sufficiently often to be worth trying.

Renewal. Even with straining and clarifying, the quality of the fat deteriorates. You will be wise to replace it after four to eight uses. Indications for change are darkening, thickening, smoking at low temperature and odors. And don't use the old fat for cooking, as it is no longer the same fat that it was, in flavor or chemical and physical behavior.

Also, every batch of food soaks in and removes some grease, so each time you use it, either add some or figure that you have less with which to work.

4
ROASTING

OVEN COOKING

An oven is a box in which the walls, door and top, and the air enclosed by them, are heated from its floor, and sometimes from the top also. Food in the oven is surrounded by hot air, and it receives radiant heat from the hot metal surrounding it. Under good conditions, cooking is more uniform than in a pan or under a broiler. It may be slower than the other methods if the pieces or units of food are small, but is efficient when they are large.

The construction and the operating controls of ovens are discussed under RANGES.

Baking and Roasting. These two words both mean cooking in an oven, and the details of their meanings overlap. For simplification, if the food is a single piece of meat or a whole bird, but is not a ham, you roast it in the oven. Anything else cooked in the same manner — bread, cake, fish, vegetables, chops — is baked. However, the term baked goods is limited to substances made from flour dough or batter, and does not cover the other kinds of food that are baked.

Many of the conditions and results of baking are covered in the immediately following sections on ROASTING. Most other important information is very closely related to a particular type of food — cooked flour dough — and can be more usefully discussed in the chapter on BAKED GOODS.

ROASTING

The popular meaning of the word "roast" as a verb is to cook large pieces of meat or poultry in an oven. As a noun, it means such pieces of meat, either before or after cooking. The dictionary gives many other meanings. Many modern cookbooks incorrectly limit the verb to uncovered cooking.

Roasting is called baking when applied to items such as bread, cake, pie, casseroles, meat loaf and, strangely, cured ham.

The roasting process is fairly simple, but discussions of it are often confused and complicated by arguments that may be more closely associated with word meanings than with cooking.

Method. Meat is usually roasted by putting it in either a covered or an open pan, and that into an oven kept at a temperature between 300 and 350° F. The meat may rest directly on the pan bottom, or on a shallow rack, which may be called a trivet.

If the pan is open, hot air and radiation from the oven's inner surfaces heat the upper part of the meat directly, and reach its lower part through the pan and any fluid it may contain. Except for any contact with fluid on the bottom, this is dry heat.

Cover. If there is a cover on the pan, it is heated by air and radiation to nearly the temperature of the oven walls, and re-radiates this heat to the meat. In addition, it holds in part of the steam from the boiling meat juices. This is the feature that many writers find unendurable, apparently on the basis that you may legitimately use either dry heat or moist heat, but never a combination of the two.

The cover will cause faster cooking, to about the same extent as increasing oven temperature by 25°. It is said to increase the rate of loss of moisture from within the meat, but it is not clear whether this is more than would be due just to the faster cooking rate. It changes the character of the crust slightly, perhaps because less of the juice evaporates, and more goes down into the drippings. A crust under cover is likely to be lighter in color than an exposed one (which may be either an advantage or a disadvantage) and to be less crisp. A cover offers an opportunity to adjust these qualities by putting it on or taking it off.

Tests made in experimental kitchens show clearly that the average quality of roasts is

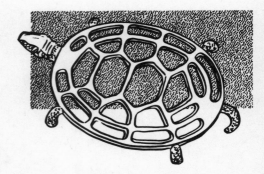

Fig. 4-1. A fancy trivet

better with uncovered than covered cooking. However, home conditions differ from those in the laboratory, and possession and intelligent use of a roasting pan cover may still be recommended.

A roast may also be covered by a sheet of aluminum foil, usually tucked snugly around the upper parts. The effect is generally similar to that of a pan cover, although there are differences in detail.

Water. Many cooks put a half cup to a cup of water in the pan before placing it in the oven. Water may be added from time to time during cooking if the drippings do not keep the pan bottom wet. Most cookbooks denounce this addition of water vigorously, although it is of little importance.

The water will prevent searing of the bottom of the roast, is insurance against its

Fig. 4-2. Roasting pans

developing too heavy a crust and protects drippings against drying out and burning. In a moderate oven it is usually not needed for any of these purposes, but it is difficult to see what harm it does. If a trivet is used, it will not touch the meat. If not, the part of the meat that it touches may be said to be boiled instead of roasted, but it would be very difficult to confuse a piece of it with one taken out of a stew.

If you like to baste a roast, you may need the water to have enough juice to pick up. On the other hand, it will be a little thinner and less advantageous for basting.

Timing. Roasting time is highly variable, so the information in Figure 4-3 should be used only as a rough estimate. Additional information on timing will be given in discussing individual meats, and will usually be found in general cookbooks also. Standard basis is minutes per pound.

Variations arise from the oven temperature used, the type of meat, the degree of cooking (doneness) desired, the size and shape of the cut and the presence or absence of a cover on the pan and of bone in the meat.

Times are usually based on a preheated oven, which is considered a must in the average cookbook. It is convenient and efficient to preheat, but you can start cold if you are in a hurry, and you must do so if the oven is started by a timer when you are out. In this case, just add 2/3 of warmup time, which is about 15 minutes in an ordinary gas oven and 8 minutes in an electric, to the total cooking time.

Meat is usually cooked at between 300 and 350° F, and tables of cooking times are good only in this range. If you want to be independent and use a hotter or a cooler oven, you are on your own.

As a rough basis for figuring different temperature, if you increase it from 350 to 500°, reduce cooking time by one-half. That is, if a chart shows 2-1/2 hours, try 1-1/4 hours, but watch and test it. If you decrease

the oven setting to 200°, the same piece of meat may take about 8 hours, over three times as long as at 350°. But individual roasts will show more time variation at very low than at high temperature.

If you use a covered pan at the temperature in the table, your roasting (or perhaps braising?) time will be 10 to 20 per cent less than shown. Or, if you lower the oven 25°, covered cooking time will be the same as that shown in the table. For part covered, part open, follow your meat thermometer and your judgment.

Timing controls are discussed under RANGES.

Cookbooks usually tell you to have your meat at room temperature before you start to cook it, and base cooking times on the assumption that you do so. But this instruction is not practical. It might take hours for a big piece of meat to get from refrigerator to room temperature all the way through, and by then the outside might start to smell.

Roast	Oven Temperature, F	Minutes per Pound
Beef		
Rare	300 to 350	17 to 21
Medium	300 to 350	20 to 25
Well done	300 to 350	24 to 30
Veal	300 to 350	25 to 40
Fresh pork	325 to 350	30 to 50
Cured ham		
Half	300 to 350	25 to 40
Whole	300 to 350	15 to 20
Chicken		
Up to 5 lbs.	325 to 350	20 to 30
Over 5 lbs.	325 to 350	15 to 20
Duck	325	18 to 20
Goose	325 to 350	25 to 30
Turkey		
Up to 10 lbs.	300 to 350	20 to 30
Over 10 lbs.	300 to 350	15 to 20

Fig. 4-3. Roasting temperatures and times

Degrees Fahrenheit	Description
250	very slow
300	slow
325	medium slow (moderate)
350	medium (moderate)
375	medium hot (moderate)
400	hot (moderately hot)
425	hot
450 to 500	very hot

Fig. 4-4. Oven temperature descriptions

It is standard procedure to either move meat directly from the refrigerator to the oven, or to allow only a short time lapse between them.

Cold meat takes a little longer to cook than warm meat. Most of the timing tables are flexible enough to take care of the difference, and in many of them it will merely correct a tendency to recommend overcooking. But for frozen meat, add about 50 per cent to cooking time. Defrosting procedures are discussed in Chapter 30.

Well done meat may take 50 per cent more time than needed for rare meat. Large pieces of meat usually require less time per pound than smaller ones. Long thin roasts cook faster than short chunky ones of the same weight, as distance from the surface to the center is shorter. Bone conducts heat and speeds up the cooking, while thick fat layers insulate the meat and slow the cooking.

Oven Temperature. The old fashioned way of oven cooking was to superheat it to a temperature of 450 to 500° F before putting the roast in, holding it at that for 20 to 30 minutes, then turning heat down to 350° and covering the pan. The start at high heat sears and crusts the meat, supposedly sealing in its juices so as to reduce their evaporation into the air and dripping into the pan through the rest of the cooking period. Modern researchers state that there is less loss of juice with normal roasting temperature from the start, and no cover at any time. Effects on crust and flavor will be considered below.

It is possible (or even rewarding) to roast meat at 200 or even 165°, taking 6 to 24 hours for the job. Requirements in such low-temperature cooking include long range planning, finding an oven that will throttle down low enough, controls that are reliable enough to keep it there, obtaining a good surface appearance and remembering that you do have something cooking. These are too many problems or perhaps nuisances for the average kitchen, but roasting at low heat is well worth trying when circumstances are favorable. Results can be excellent.

The statement is sometimes made that meat roasted at below 200° will decay before it cooks. This seems highly improbable, unless the meat were in very doubtful condition before cooking started.

Oven temperatures are frequently described as slow, medium or hot. The meaning of the terms varies slightly among various cookbooks, but not sufficiently to create any serious problem. Figure 4-4 gives a fairly standard reference of this type.

Meat Temperature. Temperature of a roast rises steadily during cooking, rapidly near the surface and much more slowly in the center. The interior temperature indicates the extent to which cooking has pro-

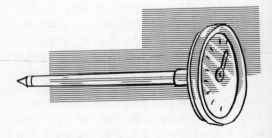

Fig. 4-5. Meat thermometer

	Rare	Medium	Well done
Beef	120* to 140	130* to 160	150* to 170
Veal	—	—	170 to 180
Lamb	140* to 145*	150* to 175	175 to 180
Fresh pork	—	—	170 to 185
Cured pork	—	—	160 to 170
*Figure from Claiborne: KITCHEN PRIMER			

Fig. 4-6. Interior temperature of cooked meat

gressed, and it can be read by means of a meat thermometer, Figure 4-5.

The point of the probe of the thermometer registers the heat, which is shown on the dial. For an accurate reading the point should be as near the center of the meat as possible, but should not be in contact with bone, as this heats more rapidly than meat does, nor in fat that heats more slowly.

If it is difficult to push the probe into the meat, a small hole may be made first with an ice pick or a skewer.

Figure 4-6 shows the interior temperatures of meat for various degrees of cooking. Such figures are subject to argument, of course.

The outer parts of a roast are much hotter than the center. If the roast is removed from the oven and allowed to stand at room temperature, the heat tends to equalize and may increase center temperature of a 6-pound roast by as much as 5° in half an hour. Therefore, if carving is not to be done immediately (and it is easier after some standing time), cooking should be stopped a few degrees before the desired temperature.

A meat thermometer is a very useful tool, and is generally (but not always) more reliable than the cook's judgment in estimating the doneness of meat. It is used to check the progress of the cooking, as well as to determine the moment when it is finished. But it is not absolutely necessary to have one of these thermometers, and many experienced cooks do not bother to use them.

It has been reported that meat cooked at a high oven temperature will be more rare at any internal thermometer reading than when it is cooked in a moderate oven. This indicates that the degree of doneness depends not only on the temperature reached, but to some extent on how rapidly it was reached.

Electronic Roasting. Roasts may be cooked in an electronic or microwave oven, very rapidly and with excellent results. The time ranges from 6 to 9 minutes to the pound, the roasting pan is a glass utility dish and the cover is a paper towel.

The method differs so greatly from ordinary roasting, and is so dependent on the unusual heat source, that it is discussed separately in the next chapter.

CRUST

Roasting is supposed to be done at a fixed temperature for an almost fixed time, with the purpose of getting the whole piece of meat cooked the way you want it. Crust color and texture are important but secondary. Fortunately, you can regulate crust quality with only minor interference with interior cooking.

If other factors remain constant, higher heat means a darker, harder (crispier?) and thicker crust. If there is enough heat to produce crust, lengthening the time will darken and deepen the crust. Hot short heat tends to make it thin and dark, moderate long heat produces one that is lighter in color, thicker and drier.

A hot oven, 400° F or more, may produce a black or burned crust, particularly where there are projections, or bone just beneath the surface that stops outward flow of moisture. In a lower or moderate oven drying out is more likely than burning.

Crust forms and thickens more rapidly toward the end of the cooking period than at the beginning, because its resistance to over-heating decreases as it cooks and dries.

Fat does not ordinarily harden, burn or form a real crust. However, it can acquire an attractive brown frizzled appearance.

For Less Crust If the crust is close to the finish appearance you want long before roasting is complete, you must slow or stop the crust-forming process. It is usually not practical to reduce oven heat because, although this should not hurt the quality of the roast, it will increase the cooking time which is likely to be closely tied in with meal time. Besides, even at much lower heat, an early well-advanced crust might become overdone.

You can slow crust formation and stop its hardening at any point by covering the roast. If you have resisted "New Thought" in cooking and have a lid for your roasting pan, and have room in your oven for it, put

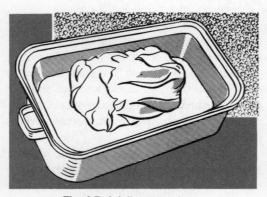

Fig. 4-7. A foil-wrapped roast

it on. The crust will then probably stay the same through the rest of the cooking, or darken and soften slightly. If you remove the cover ten to twenty minutes before finish time it will recover any crispness it might lose while covered.

If you do not have a cover, tear off a sheet of aluminum foil of suitable size, place it over the roast and then press it down around it like a form-fitting garment. The foil will reflect away radiant heat coming from the oven walls. Moisture from inside the meat will invade and soften the crust, keeping it perfect until the last twenty minutes, when you will remove the foil (but not with bare fingers) and allow the crust to re-crisp.

For More Crust. If your problem is not enough crust or crust color as the roasting timer moves into the home stretch, you can turn the heat way up. Twenty minutes at 400 or maybe even 425° F will do about as much cooking as thirty minutes at 325°, and will do much more browning. Don't worry about bad effects on the interior of your roast, it will usually not have any visible or tastable reaction in so short a time; if you remember to shorten cooking time when you increase heat. And NEVER overcook the meat just for the appearance of the outside. You may be the only person who will see it before it is sliced.

There are ways of making a phony brown crust, but the fraud is usually obvious. Rubbing with butter or sprinkling with flour or sugar is just barely allowable, but covering with paprika, which browns readily and is sometimes recommended, may be considered an insult to the flavor of the meat.

Surface Treatment. Surface treatment consists of adding fat or drippings to skin or lean meat surfaces to prevent drying and to provide special qualities of crust. You may rub the meat with oil before roasting, put slices of bacon or pork fat on it, baste it, or do all three.

The oil treatment is harmless and tem-

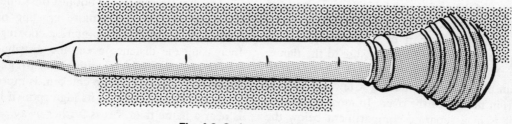

Fig. 4-8. Syringe-type baster

porarily useful. Slices of bacon will fully protect the meat that they cover, and usually the area just below them. However, they introduce an extra flavor that may tend to either obscure or enhance the natural flavor, depending on your taste.

Basting. Many cooks help the development of an attractive, tasty crust by dipping fluid from the bottom of the pan at intervals, and moistening all exposed surfaces. This operation, called basting, may be done with a big spoon or with an oversize medicine dropper, Figure 4-8. With this, you compress the bulb, put the point in the fluid and release pressure on the bulb, thus filling the tube with fluid. You squirt it on the roast by compressing the bulb again.

Basting is usually done at intervals of 20 to 30 minutes, starting when a crust begins to form.

Basting is condemned by modern cookbooks, sometimes because the fluid is supposed to wash fat and flavor off the surface of the meat. You can test its usefulness for yourself by basting half a roast and leaving the other half dry, then balance the result obtained against the trouble of basting.

Bottom Crust. The bottom part of a roast that is resting directly on the pan is heated by direct conduction from the pan, and usually by a pool of drippings. Cooking may be faster than on the upper surfaces, and of a different type. The differences will be greater in an open pan than in a covered one.

If the oven is very hot or the cover is lacking a rather hard thick crust may form

on the bottom. It is particularly likely if the meat is lean, and no water is added to the pan. Under such conditions it may be advisable to put the meat on a rack or trivet that will hold it a half inch to an inch above the floor and clear of any drippings. Rate of cooking would then be only slightly greater than on the sides and top.

Under favorable conditions the bottom of a roast that has been cooked in drippings is the tastiest part of the meat. But it can be dry, tasteless and even burned.

BROILING

Broiling usually means cooking food by direct exposure across air space to open flame or some other source of intense heat. In the kitchen the food is usually under the heat on a special two-level pan, outdoors it is above it on a wire rack. If the article being cooked has no juice, the operation is called toasting. The most frequently broiled foods are meat (steaks and some chops), chicken and fish.

Pan broiling was discussed under its other (and almost equally unsatisfactory) name of dry frying.

Broiling is suited to relatively flat shapes such as steaks, chops, fish and open-face sandwiches. Very thick pieces cooked by the broiling method are usually rotated slowly to distribute the heat on all sides and reduce the run-off of drippings. The apparatus is known as a rotisserie, Rota-Broil or some similar name.

Broilers are usually preheated for about 10 minutes before use. Standard temperature in the compartment is 550° F, but it is really not necessary for it to reach this heat, as the greater part of the cooking is supposed to be done by exposure to the flame.

Compartment. The broiler heat unit in an electric range, and in a few gas ranges, is in the top of the oven. In most gas ranges it is in a separate compartment below the oven floor, and a single large burner serves both to heat the oven over it and broil food below it. In such a unit a fixed high broil position usually makes the oven too hot for most kinds of cooking.

Many modern ranges do not give a choice of broiler heats — they are fully on or turned off. This is unfortunate, as the taste

Fig. 4-9. Broiling

and condition of broiled articles can be affected by changes in burner heat as well as by the differences in distance discussed below.

Rate of Cooking. The speed of the broiling process depends largely on the size and intensity of the heat source and on the distance from it. When the heat is above the food, the food is supported on a broiler rack or pan, the exposed area of which is heated directly by the flame, while the bottom is heated by air in the oven or broiler compartment. The pan contributes an important but variable amount to the cooking.

To achieve the same rate of cooking, food may be near a small flame or further from a

big one, but the effects are not just the same. Nearness usually means more crusting or burning in proportion to interior cooking. Increasing the distance evens the distribution of heat, so that food with a very irregular surface, such as cut-up chicken, is more likely to dry and burn on its high spots if it is near a flame than if it is further away.

Distance between the heat and the food may vary from 1-1/2 inches for a thin steak to be cooked rare to 9 inches for a half chicken. It is selected so as to cook the food to the proper depth in the same time it takes to brown the surface to the right degree. Moving nearer the flame increases the rate of browning, drying and perhaps burning more than it speeds the internal cooking. A thin article or one that is to be served rare inside can therefore be near the flame, a thick and/or well done piece should be further away.

Broiling times will be discussed under the individual foods.

Broiler Pan. In the kitchen, broiler pans are used to hold food under a downward-heating gas flame or electric unit. There are a number of designs, since broiling can be done in any shallow pan or dish that can stand the heat, or any type of grate or open-work metal if provision is made for catching the drippings.

In a flat pan or a dish with a raised rim, juices forced out of the food by the cooking are held in the pan under it and alongside it. Depending on the juiciness of the food, the distance below the heat and the exposed area of pan, such juices may just keep the food moist, may accumulate enough to provide dish gravy, or stock for making a regular gravy; or spill over and mess up the oven. If such juices dry up they will leave a hard residue for the cleanup department.

On the average, food cooked in this manner will be somewhat more juicy than if it is broiled on a rack. The process is the true pan broiling. It may be used for any food, but seems particularly appropriate for fish.

Such a pan may be of pleasing appearance so that it can be used as a serving dish also, with provision for preventing it from scorching the tablecloth or table. If designed for broiler use, it may have a sloped or channeled floor to drain juices into a gutter or sump from which they can be dipped, either during broiling or serving.

Another method is to place a wire grid or rack over a pan to support the food, so that the pan serves only to hold drippings.

Fire. With or without a rack, this pan offers danger of getting on fire. If the flame is too hot or the pan is too close to it, either the food or the boiling grease may catch fire. Once started, the fire tends to increase until both the juice and the food are pretty well consumed. This is a frightening thing to happen to an inexperienced cook, and is embarrassing for an experienced one. It can cause a lot of smoke damage.

If you have a broiler fire, the first thing to do is to turn off the heat. Then, if the flames are small, pull the rack part way out, take out the food with a long fork and cover the burning pan with a cookie tin or any non-burnable material, to cut off the supply of air. If flames are large, leave the pan in place and slide the cookie tin over it.

A fine spray of water, as from a garden hose nozzle, will extinguish the flames almost immediately. Solid water is likely to cause explosive scattering of burning grease, and may cause it to overflow onto the oven and kitchen floors. Fire extinguishers are usually effective, but they ruin the food.

A broiler fire will go out by itself after a while, with little danger of igniting the house but with a probability of smoke damage. This can be limited by opening windows and closing doors.

The safest and in general the most satisfactory broiling equipment is a drippings pan that is entirely covered by a metal tray, which is pierced with enough holes or slots to allow juice to drain freely through it. The tray shields the pan from the heat so that the

Fig. 4-10. A steak is burning

grease in it is unlikely to boil, violently, and the holes are small enough so that fire will not go down through them to the grease. This leaves the meat or other food as the only exposed burnable. It is usually easy to extinguish by pulling the tray out from under the fire and blowing the flame out.

Most ovens come equipped with good broiler pans, but they may be a little large for everyday or light use, and can be a nuisance to take out and clean. A smaller pan, such as the 11-inch round one in Figure 4-12, is more convenient for small meals. But it may be hard to find in the stores.

Turning. Most food is broiled on both sides, the principal exception being fish in the form of halves or fillets. For turning, you wait until the upper side of the steak, chicken or other food looks pleasantly

Fig. 4-11. Broiler pan

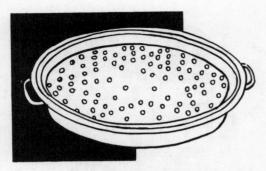

Fig. 4-12. Small broiler pan

browned, then pull the broiler pan part way out of the compartment, being careful not to drop it off its slides. You can then get at it with a turner, forks or whatever your preferred tool may be, and turn each piece over, so the browned side is down.

You should then be 1/2 to 2/3 through the cooking, as the second side often takes only half the time of the first. If you miscalculate, you can always turn it back to the first side, although you may get into complications if you follow a seasoning routine.

Fish is usually not turned if it is broiled in a pan. If broiled on a rack, fillets are usually not turned, but thicker pieces are. Fish is very tender, and is quite likely to stick to the broiler rack. It is advisable to use two turners, with careful manipulation, to loosen and turn or remove it.

Testing. Broiled food is tested mostly by appearance. If it looks done, it usually is, unless you have put it too close to the heat. Steaks are the food most often broiled, and the problem with them may be to see that they do not get cooked, or at least not much.

The only sure test is to pull out the tray part way, make a small cut in an average part of the food, and look. Your cookbook will probably tell you NEVER to do this with a steak, because precious juice will flow out of the cut and be lost, like air from a punctured tire. But this same juice is oozing out all over the heated surface anyway,

and the few extra drops that may escape from a test cut will not make any noticeable difference.

You can test with a meat thermometer. Put it in horizontally, face down, with the point in flesh (not in fat nor against bone) and as nearly half way between the two surfaces as you can get it, before starting to broil. After turning, the thermometer will be face up and you can read it for what you want, rare at 130 to 140° F, 150 to 155° for medium and 160 to 165° for well done. It takes a thick steak or an expert insertion to get accurate results from a thermometer, and it may be damaged by overheating of the exposed head.

Chicken becomes tender as it cooks, so you can test it for doneness with a fork. Small or thin pieces cook most rapidly, and are often removed before the thicker parts. Wings are sometimes protected with foil for the last few minutes.

Seasoning. Food of all kinds can be broiled without seasoning, but many part-time chefs greatly enjoy mixing and applying seasoning, and would not be interested in cooking without it. And results may be excellent, even though natural flavor may be obscured.

Salt should not be put on meat or fish until cooking is almost completed, as it draws an excessive amount of juice, and drippings are often thrown away, particularly when they contain a lot of fat.

Popular seasonings, used individually or in various combinations on steak, are black pepper, mustard, sodium glutamate and prepared barbecue sauces. Most people don't use them, and those that do, generally enjoy making up their own special formulas. They are used much more in outdoor cooking than in the kitchen.

A barbeque sauce may be applied before the start of broiling, and/or spooned over the food at intervals.

5

MICROWAVE (ELECTRONIC) COOKING

MICROWAVES

The microwave or electronic oven provides a unique (but expensive) cooking mechanism. High frequency waves, somewhat similar to those carrying television broadcasts, are generated by a vacuum tube and reflected into an oven, through a wave guide.

These microwaves are absorbed and stopped by water, causing their energy to turn into heat. This raises the temperature of the water, and of any food that is combined or associated with it. The effect is greatest at the surface, where the full energy of the waves is available, but a substantial heating and cooking effect is produced to depths of one to 3 inches. Penetration is least when moisture content is high.

These waves penetrate most dry, nonmetallic materials with little loss of energy and therefore have no heating effect as they go through them. This makes it possible to cook in or on paper, glass, china or plastic. However, because the food becomes hot, only heat-resitant plastic should be used. Unfortunately, this does not include many freezer and refrigerator containers.

Metal reflects microwaves under most circumstances. This makes it possible to bounce them back and forth inside an oven, building them up to very high energy levels.

Two frequencies are assigned for cooking. Most ovens now use 2450 megacycles, over 1,000 times higher in frequency than standard TV bands.

An oven now being introduced uses the other frequency, 925 megacycles. These waves are more efficient at deep penetration, but less effective with thin or small pieces.

They are distributed in the oven by a rotating food shelf, instead of by metal fans (stirrers).

This chapter covers only the cookers using the 2450 wave length, as the other was not available for testing at the time when it was prepared.

Electronic cooking methods are so dependent on special equipment that it will be described here, instead of in PART FIVE with more familiar appliances.

ELECTRONIC OVEN

Models. An electronic oven may be purchased as an oven only, to rest on a counter

REFL TED   GOES THROUGH   ABSORBED
FROM TAL   CHINA-GLASS   BY MOISTURE

Fig. 5-1. Behavior of microwaves

or to be built into a wall, and used as an addition to standard kitchen equipment. But its most pleasing application is as the upper oven of a two oven electric range, as in Figure 5-3. The lower oven and the four surface burners are similar to those described in Chapter 38 under ELECTRIC RANGE, and use the same 240-volt current.

Oven-only models may be portable, and can be used wherever a heavy duty (20 ampere) electric plug-in is available. They may be somewhat lower powered, and therefore somewhat slower in cooking, than built-in units.

Wave Generation. Present microwave models use 120-volt current, while previous models required 240 volts. In either case, it goes through a relay and a transformer to be stepped up to 5,500 volts, and is then converted into microwaves by a magnetron.

The magnetron is the unique and essential feature of the microwave oven. It is a vacuum tube that is about nine inches long and costs over $200.00. As a cooking device

Courtesy of Tappan Co.

Fig. 5-2. Portable electronic oven

it is about as far from a pile of burning sticks as anything science fiction can imagine.

The transformer and magnetron develop heat which is removed by air circulation. In earlier models a small electric powered pump circulates a water-antifreeze mixture through copper tubes that are attached to the units, and are connected to a small fan-cooled radiator in the front bottom of the range.

Radiation. New microwave ovens allow the escape of little or no radiation. However, if they are allowed to get very dirty where the door should fit snugly against the frame, some radiation may get out.

These waves are not ordinarily harmful to people in ordinary amounts of exposure, and they do not have the cumulative effect of atomic radiation. However, microwave repairmen are reported to sometimes suffer from burns or eye cataracts after heavy and repeated exposure.

It is unlikely that a housewife would ever be exposed enough to have bad effects. But it is a good routine precaution, as well as being normal good housekeeping, to keep the unit clean. And never operate it if the door screen is torn or punctured.

Oven. The microwaves generated by the magnetron are directed into the bottom of the oven by reflection along a short tube, called a wave guide. They strike two slowly rotating horizontal metal fans called stirrers, which reflect them at constantly changing angles to distribute them evenly around the interior of the oven.

The oven walls are surfaced with polished nickel-chrome steel, which reflects the waves back and forth until they are absorbed by food. If there is no food, water or other absorbing material in the oven they will build up to such high intensity that they will create undesirable back pressure on the magnetron.

Operation of an empty oven will burn out a watercooled magnetron, sometimes in as short a time as five minutes. Models with air cooling are more rugged, but even these should not be turned on with the timer except when there is food in the oven.

The oven door has a window made of a steel grille with holes about 1/8 inch in diameter. This mesh reflects microwaves, so that they cannot escape through it, and allows a reasonably good view of the food.

In current models, the grille holes may be filled by lamination of a sheet of plastic into the mesh.

There is an overhead 3,100 watt broiler unit, called a browner, which is used to provide browning and/or crusting for foods that cook too rapidly to develop these effects naturally. It can also be used to compensate for irregularities in wave distribution, by supplying an ordinary cooking effect.

The browner may be used with the microwaves, or separately. Its use for ordinary broiling is not recommended.

Cooking is done on two full-width removable shelves or trays made of heat-resistant fiberglas epoxy. There are pairs of supports (glides) that permit moving the upper shelf up and down. The lower tray serves as an oven bottom, a low shelf for cooking and as a safety cover for the stirrers.

Switches and Timers. There are two turn-on switches for the microwaves. The master or on-off switch puts the oven in ready-for-operation condition, by sending a few hundred watts of low voltage current through a heating device which warms up the magnetron in about ten seconds. It also starts the cooling pump and/or fan.

The other turn-on is a timer which directs high voltage current to the magnetron, causing it to produce microwaves as soon as it is warmed up, and shuts it off at the end of a selected time. The timer dial is calibrated from 15 seconds to 30 minutes, with changing proportions so that the first quarter revolution represents less than two minutes, and the last quarter almost 14 minutes. This permits fine adjustments in the short-time

Fig. 5-3. Combination electronic range

range where they are most needed. A warmed-up magnetron produces full cooking effect immediately when it is turned on.

The timer must be turned around to 20 or 30 seconds in order to turn on the current, but can then be put back to as short a time as you need. The timer operates only while the magnetron does, so that you can set it during the warming up period. It will stop if you interrupt the cooking by opening the door, and resume when you close it.

There is a safety switch that shuts off the microwaves whenever the oven door is open, even slightly.

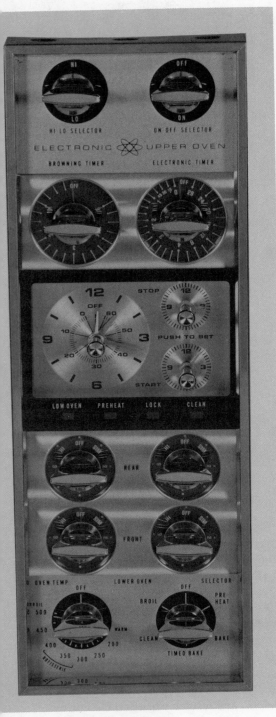

Fig. 5-4. Control, combination range

A high-low switch allows operating the magnetron at either full or two-thirds of full output. Low speed is used chiefly for roasting meat (except turkey) and for a few special effects.

The browner is controlled by a dial timer, with a time range from a few seconds up to six minutes. It can be used whenever the master switch is on, whether the magnetron is operating or not, and it is not interrupted by opening the door. It reaches full heat in 30 to 40 seconds.

CHARACTERISTICS

The principal feature and advantage of microwave cooking is its speed. Food may usually be heated or cooked in a fraction of the minimum time required by conventional methods, chiefly because the heat is applied instantaneously both to the surface of the food and to a considerable depth within it. No time or energy is consumed in heating a pan, grease, air or external water to serve to carry the heat to food.

Since most of the effect is obtained by heating moisture, temperature rarely exceeds that of boiling water. There is therefore no problem of scorching or burning, but drying may produce a hard or tough crust or texture. There may be an opposite problem of trying to produce a crust or a cooked appearance.

Heating and cooking times are of course greatly affected by the temperature of the food when it is put in the oven. For study, the process may be divided into four phases: thawing frozen food, warming cold food to room temperature, heating room-temperature food to cooking temperature, and cooking time.

The speed of heating is determined largely by the relationship between the limited (although large) steady supply of wave energy available and the quantity of moisture present to absorb it. A small amount of moisture will heat very rapidly, a larger quantity more slowly. In the same manner, a little water in a kettle on a surface burner will heat much more rapidly than a larger quantity. In general, doubling the quantity of a food item in the oven will increase the time requirement by 50 per cent.

Small pieces, 1/2 inch or less in diameter, do not provide good absorption of microwaves, and may heat poorly or not at all. But if several of them are piled together to make a larger target, heating should be normal or excellent. Drops of water left on a dish after washing will not be heated or dried by the waves.

Materials that contain less than 10 per cent moisture, or that have moisture only in bound (closely combined) condition, such as flour, crackers and popcorn, may obtain little or no heat from microwaves.

Tough or Tender? There is a general tendency to asume that fast cooking toughens food. Results of super-fast cooking by microwave do not support this assumption except in a few rather puzzling cases. White of egg, some bacon, edges of hamburgers and re-heated yeast-raised coffee cake are sometimes toughened noticeably. But chops, steaks and roasts are usually as tender as when cooked conventionally, and even pot roasts may turn out well.

There is need for research into the cause or causes of observed toughening, but it is evident that speed of cooking is not the answer in itself.

Splatter and Cleanup. Steam often forms in small pockets in food, particularly meat, during microwave cooking and breaks out in a series of tiny explosions that throw juice, grease and sometimes food particles forcefully. Disagreeable splatter can be prevented by covering the food. If the recipe does not call for a covered casserole you can use paper towels or a napkin. If you use plastic, put a pleat in it so it can puff up with steam without pulling in from the edges.

Splattered or spilled food does not burn into hard deposits in this oven. But remov-

ing cold grease from its walls and door grille can be a disagreeable job. First wipe it with paper towels, then with soap and water if necessary. The job can be made easier by heating the oven for a minute with the browning unit, but then you must beware of burns.

The trays and the splatter shield above the browning unit can be taken out and washed. The oven should always be shut off when the lower tray is removed, as this exposes the stirrers. They can be turned by hand if necessary for convenience during cleaning.

Splatter on the browner itself can be burned off by operating it for a minute.

Performance Standard. A microwave oven in proper adjustment should heat eight ounces of water from room temperature (70° F) to boiling in 1-3/4 to 2-1/4 minutes. The water may be in a glass measuring cup, or poured into any glass, china or heat-resistant plastic container, but must not be in metal. The faster time is for models with water-cooled magnetrons.

With this information you can easily test the efficiency of such an oven at any time. You can also use it for guidance in setting the timer, to avoid unwanted boiling. The test may be subject to a five or 10-second question about exactly when the water is really boiling, but this is not important.

Speed of boiling water is comparable to that obtained in a kettle or a wide pan on a good surface burner.

In a water-cooled model, eight ounces of plain water ice at zero Fahrenheit were

Fig. 5-5. Cover food with paper

Fig. 5-6. Cooking may be interrupted for stirring

melted in 3-1/4 minutes and the water boiled at 4-3/4 minutes, indicating that much of the water was hot by the time the last bit of ice melted.

Working with 70-degree water, this oven boiled four ounces in one minute and 16 ounces (one pint) in two minutes 40 seconds.

Heating Action. Microwaves heat water or ice at about the same rate whether it is by itself or combined with food, and the heating time of the food is largely determined by the quantity of water that it contains. For example, if a casserole mixture contained 50 per cent water, a quart of it would include 16 ounces of water, and it might be expected to heat from room temperature to near boiling in three minutes, while a pint of it would take two minutes, both times being only slightly longer than that for the contained water. It would need stirring two or more times to distribute the heat. If the mixture were frozen and at zero temperature the heating time would be almost tripled.

Some mixtures do not absorb the waves readily, and therefore take longer to heat than others with the same water content. However, an estimate of the water is the most reliable basis for figuring heating time.

Cooking is more complicated than just heating, as it includes chemical and physical changes which require both heat and time. In general, pieces or masses two inches in diameter or smaller may be expected to cook in microwaves in about the same time that

very thin slices of the same food would cook in boiling water.

Irregularities. Food in the center of a flat shape heats much more slowly than the edges. The difference is greater than would be expected from the interference with horizontal waves, which are of course partly absorbed by the edges. In addition, the waves may appear to be selective, delivering disproportionate energy to parts that are melted or hot while failing to melt some areas of frost or cold.

To equalize heating, liquids or semiliquids should be stirred several times during heating or cooking. Solids should be in a compact state, so that they can conduct internally from hot to cold spots. Conduction of heat may be assisted by shutting off energy at intervals (opening the door is the easy way) for a few seconds. A flat piece of food may be cut into quarters when partially heated, and each piece rotated so that the former center sections will be at the edges.

The browner can be used effectively to warm up cold areas and help to cook them if the food is thin.

Some foods absorb microwaves much more readily than others. If two different foods are in the oven at the same time they may cook at very different rates. It is therefore recommended that you cook one food at a time. If the first-cooked item cools off, it can usually be reheated in seconds without damage.

Metal in the Oven. In general, the use of metal utensils and objects in the electronic oven is not encouraged, for at least two reasons.

One is that metal is not penetrated by the microwaves. A sealed can, a TV dinner surrounded by foil or a potato wrapped in foil will not cook at all, and the mechanism may be endangered by the build-up of unused energy. Partial shielding, for example when the top is stripped off a TV dinner but it is left in its foil container, has complicated effects. The food receives no cooking energy from the bottom and little from the sides. Most of the waves reach it through the top after multiple reflections from the oven walls and the foil, but their pattern is disturbed and results may be variable.

The heating effect of microwaves may be greatly reduced when they are close to a metal surface, so that food in such a location might heat and cook more slowly than the rest. Even so, the heating is much much faster than in a conventional oven, and could be improved in both speed and uniformity by moving the frozen food to a non-metallic dish.

Sparks. Sparks are a more spectacular effect of the presence of metal in the oven. Reflection of waves may not be complete and pieces of metal may act as antennas, absorbing some of the energy and converting it back to electric charges. These cause heavy sparks to jump between pieces of metal that are close to each other but not touching. Metal decorations on china or glass generate these sparks, which often melt some of the metal and pit and discolor the china. A metal thermometer is likely to be ruined by internal discharges. Sparks may cross gaps more than 1/4 inch wide between pans, pieces of foil or utensils, but damage is unlikely. They may also be seen in a bunch of grapes that is contaminated with metallic-base sprays.

You can produce a vivid demonstration with a twist-seal consisting of one or two fine wires embedded in paper or plastic.

These sometimes come with boxes of plastic bags, and on food wrapped at the factory. Put one around the neck of a plastic bag, twisting it well, put it in the oven and turn on the microwaves. The twisted part will break into flame.

Sparking may also occur in or along greasy or dried-up smears of food left from spillovers, or across pitted insulation above the browning unit. You will seldom see it if you keep the oven clean and don't put metal objects in it. And it is not dangerous, and does no damage except to metal decorations and thermometers.

Increasing the amount of food or moisture in the oven reduces the intensity of sparking.

TV Dinners. Microwaves heat TV dinners efficiently, even in their metal trays.

Take the dinner out of its paper carton, and strip the foil from the top. Cover with plastic wrap, putting a pleat in it to allow for steam.

Because uneven heating of the different foods is likely to occur, it is best to cook it for two minutes, turn off the waves for a resting period of a minute, then finish the heating. Test for cold spots before serving, and if there are any, give it a short rest then another 30 to 60 seconds. Use high range throughout. You can use the browner also for the last minute or two, for color or crispness.

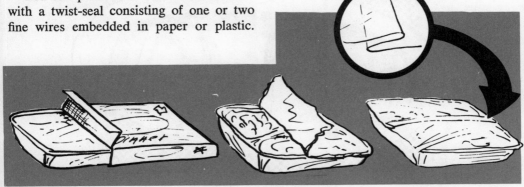

Fig. 5-7a. To heat a TV dinner

One TV dinner with loose material such as scallops, French fries and peas may be thoroughly heated from fully frozen condition in 3 minutes, while a moist compact one of lobster newburg, mashed potatoes and squash may take 5 or 6. Two dinners take half again as long as one, four about twice as long. When you have more than one, arrange them so that they will not shield each other too much — that is, do not have one on a top shelf directly over and close to one on the lower shelf. Electronic ovens do not get on well with metal pans, so you may need to try several arrangements.

If one food in the dinners gets hot well ahead of the others, cover it with foil to protect it from further heating and drying out. Crimp the foil cover firmly to the pan, or you will have a dazzling (but harmless) fireworks display as sparks jump between them.

If a dinner has only one solid, slow heating item such as mashed potatoes, you may obtain more even results if you remove half of it as soon as it thaws, and put it in a special dish.

The tray of the complete-meal TV dinner (the kind that includes soup and dessert) is usually too large to use in this oven. It interferes with proper distribution of the microwaves.

COOKING

The electronic oven is not yet widely enough distributed to justify a detailed discussion of all its special characteristics and uses in a basic text such as this. The purchaser is usually supplied with a special recipe and instruction book.

However, there is some general information about this very different type of cooking that should be of interest to most people, and of value to those who have purchased or might purchase one of the units.

Thin Meat. Thin pieces of meat such as steaks, chops and hamburgers are supposed to be put in a glass utility dish or on a nonmetallic well-and-tree platter on the shelf in its highest position, and cooked with both microwaves and the browner simultaneously. A one-pound steak 1-1/4 inches thick should cook to medium in 3-1/2 minutes without turning.

The same weight of rib or loin lamb chops calls for 3 minutes low speed microwave together with browning for the same time, then turning and using the browning unit only for color and to complete the cooking.

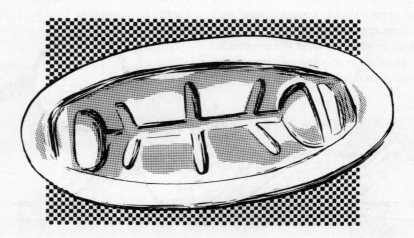

Fig. 5-7b. Well-and-tree platter

Kind of Meat	Cooking Time Minutes per Pound*	Internal Temperature, Degrees F	
		After Cooking	After Standing
Beef (rolled,	Rare, 5 to 6	120	140
standing rib or	Medium, 6 to 7	140	160
rump roast)	Well, 7 to 8	150	170
Veal — all roasts	Medium, 8 to 9	150	170
	Well, 9 to 10	160	180
Pork — all roasts	Well, 9 to 10	165	185
Ham — precooked half	Well, 6 to 7	110	130
— precooked whole	Well, 8 to 9	105	130
Ham — uncooked half**	Well, 9 to 10	165	185
Lamb — leg with bone	Medium, 6 to 7	150	170
	Well, 7 to 8	160	180
— rolled	Medium, 8 to 9	150	170
	Well, 9 to 10	160	180

*The longer times are for roasts of 4 pounds or less
**Recommend using conventional oven for uncooked whole ham

Fig. 5-8. Roasting time with microwaves

A recipe is given for hamburgers (mostly use of the browner) but you will probably do as well to fry or broil them conventionally. The open structure of chopped meat conducts heat poorly, so you might finish with both overcooked and undercooked meat in the same part of the same patty. If you do cook them electronically, push each patty into a compact mass with smooth edges, although this is the wrong thing to do with hamburger ordinarily. Use high speed microwaves and the browner together, for a minute or so. This oven serves very well to heat the rolls (15 or 20 seconds, usually), and to reheat hamburgers cooked and assembled with their rolls ahead of time.

Bacon is cooked 3 or 4 minutes on a crumpled paper towel in a glass utility dish. It must be covered with another towel to stop splatter. Or individual slices may be folded in paper towels. Bacon is occasionally toughened by this method of cooking, and its time advantage is small. But you do not have to watch it, nor clean up after it.

Roasts. The electronic oven usually does a good job with roasting thick pieces of meat — rapid cooking with good flavor and tenderness. The roasting is done in a glass utility dish on a trivet made by inverting a saucer. Cover the top with paper towels or a clean scrap of cloth to prevent splattering. Use low speed unless your recipe specifies high speed, as it will for turkey.

You test for doneness by turning off the microwaves and inserting a thermometer. If the meat is within 20° of the temperature you want, take it out of the oven and park it under some kind of cover for about 20 minutes, by which time the internal temperature should have risen to the proper point. If it is underdone, be sure to take out the thermometer before resuming cooking.

A roast usually acquires a good surface appearance, but you can touch it up with the browner for the last few minutes of cooking if you wish.

A roast cooks most evenly if the length is somewhat greater than the diameter. If it has any part that is particularly small, this may be masked with foil during part of the cooking so that it will not be overdone.

Figure 5-9 gives approximate cooking times for roasts of 4 to 6 pounds. The longer cooking is likely to be needed if weight is above or below these figures, and if the meat is refrigerator-cold.

For roasts over 6 pounds, cook for half the estimated time, then allow to stand for 20 minutes. This allows near-surface heat to move into the center. Then resume cooking.

If the meat is irregular in shape, cover the smaller portion with foil for about half the cooking time.

If a roast has already reached the final temperature you want when you take it out of the oven, you can avoid further cooking and increase in temperature by carving it immediately.

Frozen meat should be defrosted as a separate operation. To do this, put it in the microwave oven, and operate it on the HIGH setting until the surface is hot. Then allow the meat to stand until it has cooled almost to room temperature. Test with a skewer. If it encounters hard frost, repeat the process.

In defrosting a flat piece such as a steak or a patty, you can avoid premature cooking of the edges by placing a smooth strip of aluminum foil around them.

Poultry. Poultry should be of roasting quality. Legs and wings should be tied closely to the body. Thin parts such as ends of wings and legs, and the tail, should be covered with foil for half the cooking time.

A bird should be roasted about equally on all four sides. Start it with the breast up, after 1/4 of the estimated cooking time turn in on a side, then after the same interval to the other side. Finish with breast down.

Cook on a saucer or other non-metallic trivet in an oblong utility dish or on a well-and-tree platter.

Fig. 5-10. Talk lets food get cold

Use HIGH energy setting and the bottom shelf. A chicken is likely to take about 7 minutes to the pound, an 8 or 10-pound turkey 6-1/2 minutes, and a 12 to 16-pound one 5-1/2 minutes. But start testing for tenderness several minutes ahead of schedule.

Cooking time is the same for stuffed or unstuffed birds.

Vegetables. Vegetables are usually cooked with 1/4 to 1/2 cup of salted water in a covered casserole until tender. Cooking time varies widely with the type of vegetable and its quantity, age and condition, but in general it is only moderately faster than ordinary boiling or steaming. At worst, the time is about the same, at best it is about 1/3 of boiling time.

Baked vegetables do better. You can bake one medium potato in 4 to 6 minutes, and 10 of them in 15 to 20. If an Idaho or other baking potato is used an excellent baked flavor and texture is obtained, but skins, although tender, tend to be limp. Other varieties of potato bake to taste more like good boiled potatoes.

Potatoes should be separated by at least one inch while baking, in order to avoid shading each other. They should be punctured by a knife in a few places to let out steam, but if they are not, there will be only a little sputtering.

Eggs. Eggs are somewhat tricky entries for the electronic oven, largely because they cook so rapidly that close watching and split second timing are required. Also, they usually cook a little more after microwaves are shut off, due to adjustments in internal heat.

Eggs in their shells are boiled covered with water in the same time as if the water were over a surface burner. But an egg broken into a custard cup with a little milk or butter will cook in about 20 seconds.

Scrambled eggs, mixed according to whatever formula you like, are put in a glass cake dish or casserole in which some butter (say 3/4 teaspoon for each egg) has been melted. The mixture should be stirred while heating (every 15 seconds for 2 eggs, every 30 seconds for 4) to mix the hotter rim with the cooler center. When it starts to thicken and puff up you can either stir every 10 or 15 seconds to get normal scrambled effect, or leave it alone to get a texture somewhat like baked custard or omelet. It tends to puff up very high while cooking, and go back down most of the way as soon as the microwaves are stopped.

Baking. Baking is the trickiest of the applications of electronic cooking. Cooking time is very short, so that an important difference in results may be obtained by varying time by just a few seconds. And any overcooking and hardening that does occur is not limited to a thin crust that might be scraped or cut off, but is likely to extend all the way through the article.

Baked goods do not ordinarily acquire any surface color from microwaves, but tend to be white or yellow. This is not always important. Many cookies are not supposed to be browned, and many cakes get completely covered with frosting. No difference is noticeable with chocolate flavored doughs. Browning can always be obtained on top at least by use of the browning unit in the top of the oven.

USEFULNESS

Speed. The basis of this oven's high speed cooking was discussed earlier. The question here is the usefulness of this speed.

If a full-time housewife does her cooking on a planned schedule, willingly provides adequate time for the cooking of each menu and seldom has to cope with last minute emergencies; she will probably have little use for this new appliance. But if children's needs (or demands), a job or other activities limit the time for meal preparatin, high speed cooking can be very useful.

For example, if you have an hour to prepare a meal, microwaves will permit you to cook a 6-pound standing rib roast out of the refrigerator; 35 minutes cooking and 20 minutes standing. The 20 minutes gives you time to defrost and cook a frozen vegetable and to bake potatoes. Your range of possible menus is tremendously increased.

On a more humble level of meal preparation the speed may be even more impressive. A pair of TV dinners which would need 40 or more minutes in a hot oven can be ready to eat in 5 to 10 minutes, depending on moisture content of the food. But be sure to strip the foil off the tops, or you will cook nothing but the magnetron.

If dinner is about to be served, and then you find you forgot some essential item, or that extra people have come to be fed, microwaves can usually enable you to correct the error or pad the menu in minutes.

Re-warming. A pleasing feature of the electronic oven is its ability to warm or rewarm cooked food. A portion of coffee cake at room or refrigerator temperature can be made hot in 8 to 15 seconds. If food grows cold on the table because of interruptions or too much talk, or if someone comes late to the meal, the plates and cups may be put in the oven and the food made hot and tasty again in a fraction of a minute, without drying out, dirtying pans or even creating a hot-plate problem.

A meal can be prepared and put on plates in advance, and either set aside or put in the refrigerator, then heated just before serving. It is wise to check the temperature of each item with a finger tip, however, to be sure that everything has heated sufficiently.

Non-stick. Another convenience is the ability to safely heat substances with a strong tendency to stick and burn, which ordinarily call for low heat and frequent or constant stirring. Microwave action does not cause sticking until the food has boiled dry, and burning is practically unknown.

However, some stirring, usually at 15 or 30 second intervals may still be necessary, as material near the edge may boil before the center is thoroughly heated. This is most likely to occur if the container is large and/or the sides slope. Cooking in a straight-sided casserole dish will reduce the need for stirring, and cooking in a highball glass (or a couple of them) may eliminate it.

Timing such mixtures must allow not only for bringing them to a boil, scald, simmer or whatever temperature is desired, but may also have to allow time for cooking or swelling of some of the ingredients. The cookbook that comes with the range should supply exact information on such matters.

Cooking time can be stretched out, if desired, by alternating heating with resting periods, or by using the low intensity setting of the control.

6

OUTDOOR

WHY

Outdoor cooking is a necessity while camping and a desirable feature at a picnic away from home. But most of it is done in back yards and on lawn terraces, within a few feet of kitchens equipped with gas or electric ranges. This move back toward the primitive brings a number of benefits — change of menus, different flavors in the food, a relaxed, informal and even adventurous atmosphere and transfer of some of the burdens of cooking from wife to husband.

The basic outdoor source of cooking heat is a wood fire. But it has been largely replaced in modern practice by charcoal grills in the home yard and by gasoline or propane stoves away from home. They eliminate fuel gathering, reduce the responsibilities of fire tending and almost eliminate the smoke problem.

CHARCOAL GRILL

The basic, portable grill for cooking with charcoal is a wide, shallow metal pan, sometimes called a kettle, that supports the fire under a wire rack that holds the food. The pan is usually supported by a light framework of tubing with a pair of small wheels under one end.

Rack. The rack consists of parallel heavy wires in a frame. It is usually supported on a center stem, and is raised and lowered by a crank or lever beside or below the pan, to regulate the rate of cooking, or perhaps the ratio between cooking and charring. The rack can be lifted off its stem for convenience in fire building and refueling.

Pan. The pan is usually made of rather thin sheet metal. It should be enameled, but is often only painted. Exposure to full heat of burning charcoal tends to destroy paint quickly and enamel slowly, and to cause oxidation of steel. If the grill is left out to become wet with rain or dew after any part of it has lost its protecting surface it will be damaged by rust.

A poor quality pan, or one that is neglected or abused, may burn through before the end of one season, while with better construction or care another may last for many years.

There are alloys such as nichrome steel which are almost completely resistant to such temperatures and to oxidation, but they are expensive and difficult to work, and there seems to be no enthusiasm for their use in these grills.

There are also other types of grill, square or rectangular with a different appearance; and covered, with different control and cooking characteristics.

Charcoal Base. The life of a pan may be lengthened by using a layer of insulating material under the charcoal. These may be perlite granules, usually sold in stores that handle charcoal. These granules have high insulating value, and are light and clean to handle. A layer from 1 to 3 inches thick is placed in the pan, and the charcoal is placed and ignited on top of it. It can be used several times, as it does not burn and most food drippings and particles of charcoal burn out of it. But it should be discarded if it becomes dirty or smelly. If it gets wet, it should be removed from the grill and dried to avoid danger of causing severe rust damage.

Sand or gravel can be used instead of perlite.

A porous insulating layer helps with quick starting of a fire, and may cause it to burn at a higher temperature than on a bare pan, because of circulation of air through it into the bottom of the fire. It also raises the level of the coals, calling for a higher setting of the rack.

CHARCOAL

The charcoal used for outdoor cooking is made chiefly by burning wood with a limited air supply. This causes incomplete combustion which drives off most of the water, creosote, tar, oil, gas, acetic acid and wood alcohol originally present in the wood. The remainder is charcoal, which is a brittle, spongy form of carbon that weighs about 1/3 as much as the wood from which it was made.

Charcoal is an excellent cooking fuel. When it is dry it is reasonably easy to light, burns for a long time with little flame and smoke, radiates intense heat which can be varied by changing the air supply, and usually contributes flavor to food cooked over

Fig. 6-1. Smoke can spoil a picnic

Fig. 6-2. Charcoal grill

it. However, it is dirty to handle, leaving black smudges on things it touches. These are easy to remove from skin (soap and water) but may be more difficult to take out of cloth.

Damp charcoal stored without ventilation may heat up and catch fire spontaneously. This is highly unlikely with the small quantity likely to be kept in a home, but the possibility should be kept in mind.

Charcoal is sold in both a natural or broken form, and in briquets. The natural is obtained by using small pieces of wood, or breaking down large or irregular pieces after charring. Briquets are made of finely ground charcoal mixed with about 5 per cent starch for a binder, compressed into rounded lumps weighing an ounce or more, and dried at a high temperature.

Briquets are denser, so that they provide more heat for the same bulk. They are usually harder to light without artificial helps, tend to burn longer than natural charcoal and give more uniform performance. They are not always pure charcoal, as other fuels such as coke, petroleum coke, coal or lignite may be powdered and mixed into them.

These may be called "mineral char" on the package label. Such mixtures may make excellent briquets, but they often result in difficulty in lighting and/or in bad odor.

A set of briquets may be made up in a sheet by coating and joining them with a more flammable material. Such a sheet, or part of it, may be put in the grill and lighted with a match. This convenience is accompanied by a greatly increased cost per pound, but the difference may not be noticeable when you total all the costs of your cookout.

Smoke for Flavor. Hardwoods make the best charcoal, and hickory is specially valued. However, little of the native characteristics of the wood is present in the charcoal. If hickory-flavored smoke is desired, the surest way to get it is to add hickory chips to the fire just before starting to cook. These are sometimes home made, but are usually bought in bags. They should be soaked in water for at least 20 minutes before use, to avoid too-rapid burning.

Fig. 6-3. Starter fluid

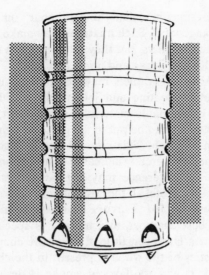

Fig. 6-4. Home made chimney

It seems probable that a large part of the valued charcoal-broil flavor in a steak results from the burning of its own drippings underneath it.

Starting. Natural charcoal may be ignited by building it into an arch or cave, in which you burn a number of twists of paper so as to supply a continuous flame for a couple of minutes. This should start it burning, but it may take a long time to become fully ignited, unless encouraged with a draft made by blowing by mouth or preferably with bellows, or by fanning.

This takes too much time and work or patience for most Sunday chefs, and is not practical with briquets anyhow. The most popular starting method is to sprinkle with a starting fluid (starter), which may be of either the petroleum or the alcohol family, and light that with a match. Best results are obtained if the charcoal is heaped into a cone with the fluid on the bottom layer, or below it in base material. After it is burning well it is spread evenly on the floor of the pan. Even with starters, it is sometimes helpful to create a draft to speed up the ignition process.

Gasoline should not be used as a starter

because it is dangerously explosive, is likely to contain poisonous compounds and has a smell that does not go well with food. Kerosene and fuel oil are safe, but take fire slowly and have a persistent bad smell.

No fluid fuel should ever be poured in a hot grill, or in one in which any charcoal is burning, as there might be an explosion.

Some grills are equipped with an electric heating unit, which can be connected to the house circuit, and becomes hot enough to light charcoal piled on it. A blowtorch, preferably the convenient type attached to a small propane gas tank, will ignite a pile of charcoal quickly if the flame is directed inside the base.

The fire chimney, Figure 6-4, permits kindling charcoal with crumpled newspaper and a match. You can buy one, or make it out of a big (46-ounce) juice can. Cut both ends out, punch a number of holes around one end with a puncture opener, and bend the cut triangles down to form little legs.

This chimney is placed in the bottom of the grill, a sheet of crumpled newspaper goes in the bottom and the charcoal is piled on it, all the way to the top. You can light the newspaper through a bottom hole. The charcoal should be burning well in 15 or 20 minutes. Remove the can (chimney) with tongs or pliers, and spread the burning charcoal. The only drawback is that the amount is rather skimpy.

Fire. Charcoal is usually allowed to burn for 20 or 30 minutes before cooking is started. This time should permit the fire to spread over all the outside surfaces of the fuel, turning its black surface to grey, and driving out most of the small amount of moisture, fluids and gases that may be present. At first it may burn with small flames and noticeable smoke, but it should soon settle down to flameless and almost smokeless combustion, unless worked on by a strong draft.

Temperature rises quickly during the early stages of burning. From then on it

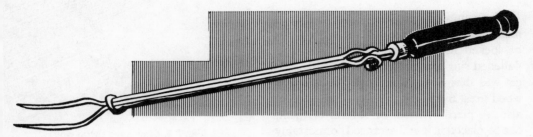

Fig. 6-5. Adjustable-length fork

depends largely on the supply of air and the closeness of pieces to each other. Lowest temperatures are obtained in a deep pan without vent ports; highest if the coals are subjected to a strong draft from bellows.

There should be enough charcoal to cover the cooking area, which is usually the whole bottom of the pan, but may be a spot about half again as big as a piece of food above it. It should be at least one layer deep, with pieces touching or almost touching each other. Additional layers or pieces add only slightly to effective cooking heat, with most of their early energy going wastefully or even destructively through the pan. However, they are valuable in maintaining heat, as the coals shrink as they burn, and a single layer tends to become a set of separated pieces with diminished heat output. An upper layer will settle into spaces as they form, maintaining full heating area and intensity.

The burning time of a briquet varies from 1-1/2 to 5 hours, depending on the amount of air supplied to it, and its closeness to other burning pieces and to reflecting surfaces. Within limits, more air and closer spacing means more intense heat and a shorter burning life. Decrease in volume and surface area of coals, and insulation by ashes greatly reduces effectiveness for the last part of the burning period. In general, the best fire is obtained in the period between a half hour and an hour after starting.

When a fire is to be used for longer than the staying power of the charcoal, more may be added from time to time. This should be done while the coals are still plentiful and hot, so that the new pieces will ignite quickly, with only a brief period in which they might flame or smoke.

If the fire has been allowed to burn out so far that new fuel may ignite slowly or not at all, remove the cooking rack and work somewhat along the lines of making a new fire. Mix the hot coals and the charcoal in a pile, and do not spread it until it is all burning.

If you feel that starting fluid is needed, move the coals to one side, soak the charcoal with it at a distance from the fire, allow it to drain, then put it in the empty side of the pan with a shovel or tongs, and light it by throwing a burning match. After it is burning, mix it with the coals.

It is also possible to light a pile of charcoal somewhere else, then put it in the grill with a shovel or tongs.

Tools. There are various tools other than standard kitchen items which are useful at a cookout. To mention three, a long handled fork is almost a necessity, a clamp-type wire grill may be a convenience and a bellows is a luxury.

The special fork for these occasions has a sliding adjustment in the handle, which enables it to be about 18 inches long for use but only 12 for packing and carrying. It has two tines sharp enough to pierce most solid food (but not corn on the cob) and long enough to get under loose or fragile ones. It permits manipulating food on a charcoal cooker fairly comfortably.

The clamp grill consists of two flat, open mesh rectangles hinged together. They can be locked in closed position by sliding a flattened ring along their handles. This gadget was designed primarily for cooking on wood fires, but it has its uses with charcoal also. A piece of food, or several of them, can be placed in it and arranged comfortably away from the heat, and taken away from it again for inspection, turning or serving. It can be used in addition to the regular grill top, unless a center post interferes, and it can replace it if there are difficulties with the raise-and-lower mechanism.

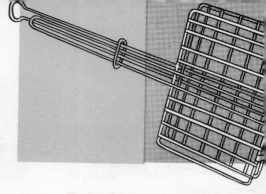

Fig. 6-6. Clamp-type wire grill

The bellows is a fireplace tool, and would not be worth getting for an outdoor cooker only. But if you have one, you can use it to great advantage in stimulating a lagging charcoal fire. By pushing the handles together repeatedly you can generate a concentrated draft that will speed the taking hold of a new fire, revive one that is too cool for its job and bring a normal one up to white heat if you want to put a really deep burn on some of the food, to prove that it is cooked outdoors.

COOKING ON CHARCOAL

The general principles of cooking with charcoal are similar to those for using gas or electricity, except that these factors are important:

> The fire is under the food, not over it
> The food is usually not protected by a pan
> Heat is not easily regulated
> Tolerance for burned and/or raw food is very high

What remains are the basic factors that high heat and/or closeness to heat is most likely to overcook the outside and undercook the inside; and that little heat or excessive distance will cure burning and allow cooking-through, but will increase cooking time and may even fail to provide any cooking.

If necessary a charcoal fire's heat can be reduced sharply by dousing it with water, covering it with aluminum foil, or with more

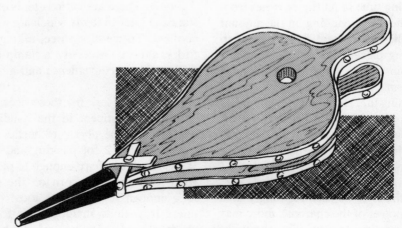

Fig. 6-7. Bellows

90

charcoal, or partly burying it in sand, perlite or other insulating material. Water quickly evaporates, foil is likely to burn through and burying with fuel means a still bigger fire in a few minutes. Sand or perlite will be effective until the coals are raked to allow it to move down under them.

Flame-ups. Flare-ups or flame-ups are a special type of too-hot fire. Grease dripping from food (usually a steak) on the rack boils on the hot coals, and the vapor is likely to catch fire and burn with tall flames, which melt more fat to supply more drippings for more flames. Unless this vicious cycle is interrupted in some way the food will be quickly charred. The flames may be high enough to be frightening.

The master cure for this situation is a fine spray of water. A garden hose nozzle can supply this most effectively. A second or two and the flames are replaced by harmless smoke, without any serious effect on the heat of the coals. Once out, the flames tend to stay out, but if they flare up again they can be squelched again in the same way. If no hose is available, almost any sort of water-loaded spraying device may be used successfully, although a really hot fire would not be controllable with a hand Flit gun. A back pack fire extinguisher, a carbon dioxide extinguisher, or even a soda siphon will usually take care of it. The spray is directed at the base of the flame, on and just above the coals, and perhaps on the meat also. But an extinguisher loaded with carbon tetrachloride will poison the food, and one using soda and acid won't help it any.

The next best method is to remove the steak or other grease-dripper with a long-handled fork, the tip of a carving knife or any available tool. It will usually stop burning while being moved a few feet through the air, but if it flames too persistently to be put on a table, put it down on the grass. It can be brushed or wiped off if necessary before returning to the grill. Flames in the grill will die down quite quickly when deprived of their continuing supply of drippings. If you are really desperate you can overturn the grill, and pick up the coals and steak after the flames go out.

Or, if you just happen to have an asbestos blanket, smother it. Or you can use an old blanket or tarp which will not be a great loss if it gets grease spotted or blackened, or even gets a hole burned through it.

You can practically depend on having at least an occasional flame-up while cooking on charcoal grills, so you should be prepared to handle it efficiently.

Don't ever throw sand on a fire until you have removed the food from the rack. And after you have done that the flames will go out by themselves.

A flame-up looks much more serious than it is. If the grill is outdoors and not under a valuable tree, the worst damage that can result is loss of the food being cooked, and even that is unlikely.

Searing. Meat is usually seared by cooking a minute or two on each side in the lowest position of the rack on a fresh hot fire. This partially seals in juices, and it makes sure that there will be some outdoor-

Fig. 6-8. Flame-up

style crust. The rack is then lifted two or three inches for cooking at a more leisurely rate. Non-meat food is usually started in a medium or high position and kept there.

Steak. Steak is by far the most popular food for outdoor cooking, perhaps equalling double the amount of all other foods cooked in this manner. The most popular cuts are sirloin and chuck. Both have an excellent flavor, and on the average although not in every case, sirloin is more tender and more expensive. Any cut of steak may be used, but round and flank

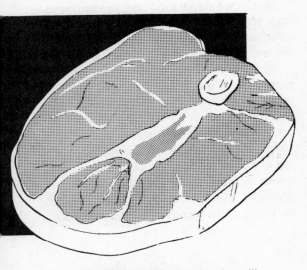

Fig. 6-9. Choice meat for the grill

steaks are probably the least satisfactory because of low fat content.

The best thickness for average use is one inch, but gourmets (show-offs?) may prefer 1-1/2 or 2 inches, which are more impressive. They are likely to be raw in the middle or over-burnt on the outside, or both, but the outdoor enthusiast may relish both these extremes.

The fat around the edges of the steak should be sliced from the outside to the meat every three or four inches, as it has a disagreeable habit of shrinking during cooking, curling up the steak somewhat like a

slice of bacon. Most instruction books tell you to keep the steak out of the fridge or freezer long enough so that it is warm clear through, before starting to cook. The principal and perhaps the only difference is that cold or frozen meat has greater contrast between the doneness of the surface and the interior. A warm steak cooks through more smoothly and readily, showing a color change from brown through pink to red, while a frozen one goes directly from brown to red, and might possibly be even still frozen in the center while burned on the outside. To avoid this, keep the rack higher than usual for slower cooking.

Surface burning and overcooking are most apt to occur where two edges of the meat are slightly separated so that a strong current of hot air rises between them. If you have two steaks, place them so that they either touch or are more than a half inch apart.

Chops. Lamb and pork chops are very good when broiled over charcoal, but they are not nearly as popular as steak. Veal chops have a tendency to be too dry.

Cooking method is the same as with steak, except that fresh pork chops must be cooked through, and must have no rare or raw portions. This means that they must be cooked at a lower temperature (thinner fire and higher rack) than the other meats. If the pork has been frozen at zero Fahrenheit or colder for thirty days it can safely be served rare, but most people will be afraid to eat it.

Hamburgers. Hamburger is usually cooked in sandwich-size patties of 3 to 5 ounces. They may be done directly on the rack, or on sheets or pieces of aluminum foil. Cooking time varies between 4 and 15 minutes, depending on fire heat, distance from the fire and thickness of the meat.

Cooking directly on the grate provides maximum fire flavor, for better or worse, as smoke penetrates even closely packed chopped meat to a greater extent than it does solid meat, and any projections or semi-detached pieces burn more readily. The principal problem is that the patty may fall apart during cooking and handling, with parts falling into the fire. Some chopped meat shapes easily into firm patties, but some tends to fall apart unless it is kneaded and compressed until it has lost part of its character and tenderness.

If there is much falling apart, or fear of it, and you do not have a clamp rack, hamburgers can be cooked on a single layer of heavy foil. A sheet is most convenient, but a separate piece for each patty cooks faster. The draft of heated air around any object on the rack increases cooking (and burning) speed at its edges, particularly where two pieces are placed with a narrow gap between them. You may need to shift patties between edges and center of a sheet. It may need to be held in place with another tool while you lift and turn the food.

The edges of foil may be turned up, pan-fashion, to save juice and melted fat, or may be left flat so that they can drip into the fire.

In a general way, indoor principles apply to outdoor broiling. Some people like hamburgers well done, but most prefer rare or medium rare. Rate of cooking is regulated by raising and lowering the rack. If a lot of cooking must be done the first batch of charcoal may get weak, so that more must be added.

Hamburger rolls are much improved by heating or toasting. If there is space, they can be placed on the rack for the last minute or two. Half a roll may be placed on each patty after it is turned. In this position it will be warmed and also provides a handle to hold the meat on the turner as you lift it off the fire.

Fish. Fish is cooked in about the same way as meat. Whole fish (cleaned) and thick steaks, that are not inclined to fall apart, are cooked like beef steak. But there is a tendency to dry out, so the top should

be dabbed or painted with butter or oil occasionally. Cooking rate is much faster, and overcooking makes it dry and tasteless. Try 3 minutes on a side, and after that keep cooking only about a minute on a side between tests. Tests consist of looking at the general appearance, and specifically of pressing down and sideward with a fork. If the fish cracks (flakes) it is fully cooked.

Fillets, thin steaks and numbers of very small fish are best cooked on foil, in the same manner as falling-apart hamburgers.

Corn. For outdoor cookery, leave the complete husk on each ear, dampen, wrap

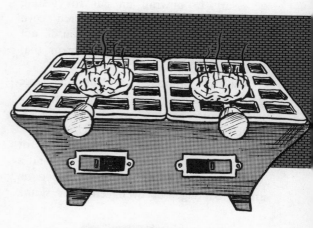

Fig. 6-9. Hamburgers

protectively, cook at maximum distance from the fire, and turn often.

Most cooking takes place in the one third of the circumference of the ear which is toward the fire. The cob seldom conducts enough heat to do much cooking, but steam moving around the ear through and under the husk and wrappings may be very useful, particularly if the outer wrapping does not permit steam to escape easily or at many points.

Heavy aluminum foil is the preferred wrapping for efficient cooking, as it wraps closely and should stay wrapped, restricts escape of steam to its line of overlap, and it also conducts from the hot side to the cool parts. But it is lacking in back-to-nature esthetic appeal, and it adds a little (but very little) to expense, and to garbage.

Frequency of turning and total cooking time are a matter of judgment and testing, because of differences in heat and distance of the fire, and types of wrapping, and even amount of moisture held in the wrapping. The ideal situation would be a slow constant rotation. Failing that, a quarter turn every thirty seconds for a hot fire or every two minutes for a medium one are reasonable. The hot fire might cook the corn in five minutes, the cooler one in ten, but it is necessary to unwrap an ear for testing occasionally. Browned or charred corn kernels are not appreciated, so you do not have the range of permissible error that you have with a steak.

Non-foil wrappings are usually large green leaves. If your cookout happens to be in the tropics, banana leaves are first choice. In the temperate zone you might raid the herbaceous border for elephant ear or castor bean, get burdock leaves from a weed patch, use corn leaves wrapped on like a bandage, or even settle for skunk

cabbage from the swamp. Any leaf that is big enough will do, but some may provide special flavors.

Wet the corn husk and the leaves well. Roll the leaves around the ear in a number of layers, tucking in the ends as well as you can. Place the wrapped ear on the grill so that its weight holds the leaf edge from unwrapping. When you turn it a quarter revolution at a time, as if you were starting to roll it out of the leaf. This frees only a quarter of a wrap, while the other way will loosen an entire wrap.

Another method is to lay the ears of corn, with their husks intact, on aluminum foil on the rack, cover them with another sheet of foil or with wet leaves or grass, and pour on a little water. Turning must be done with the same frequency as when wrapped in foil, with the complication of removing the upper sheet or the foliage to do it. Moisten them each time you turn them, to preserve the semi-steam atmosphere.

Potatoes. Potatoes are more difficult and less rewarding than meat or corn to cook on a grill. They are slower cooking, and contain less protective moisture and practically no fat. If cooked whole directly on a grill they tend to burn on the bottom and stay raw on the top. If cut into chunks or slices they will probably burn on the bottom and dry out on top.

Potatoes may be baked-broiled on the grill by wrapping them closely in heavy aluminum foil, sometimes with a few drops of water and some flavorful greens wrapped with them. Cooking time is two to four times that of a steak. This may be partly compensated by starting them as soon as the fire is lit, as the moderate early heat will give them a good start, and they absorb fresh-charcoal odors only slightly. Another help is to use medium to small potatoes rather than large ones, or to cut the large ones in half. Any additional discrepancy in cooking time may be met either by starting

Fig. 6-11. Corn wrapped in foil

the meat later or eating the potatoes in a partly cooked condition. Or you may bake them in advance, partially or completely, and finish or just heat them on the grill.

Boiled potatoes may be sliced or chunked and home fried on a real pan or a foil pan on the grill, using a little butter or any edible grease. Results are usually excellent. And it is possible, although socially unacceptable, to boil potatoes in a pan on a grill.

Other vegetables. Potatoes are not very common at cookouts, and other vegetables (except corn) are even scarcer. But any vegetable or other food that can be fried, including standard items like onions and eggplant, and non-standards such as sliced tomatoes and squash, can be cooked with a bit of grease on sheets of foil, pie tins or cookie sheets, picking up smoke flavoring from the top. Hubbard squash, acorn squash and turnips can be baked in foil in the same way as potatoes.

COVERED GRILL

A recent and sophisticated development in outdoor cooking is the covered grill, Figure 6-12. In this model the pan is much deeper than in the open type, and has three sets of bottom holes for draft, which can be partly and wholly closed by turning metal discs. The charcoal rests on a rack or grate a few inches above the bottom, and food is supported by another grate. These grates are removable but not adjustable. A domed lid with an adjustable air vent in its top fits closely on the pan.

The pan and lid are made of enameled sheet steel. The pan has a pair of handles, the top has one handle. The pan is supported on a tripod of metal tubing, with wheels on two of the legs. There is a tray to catch ashes falling through the bottom air vents. The bottom of the tripod can be removed, to allow the cooker to be taken indoors and used in a fireplace or on its hearth.

In many ways the principle and use of

this cooker are opposite to that of the standard grills. The only point of entire agreement is that both use charcoal.

The grill fire burns at a fairly even temperature between full ignition and partial burning out, while the cooker fire, resting on a grate with a draft from below, can reach a much higher temperature; and with drafts closed it will go out. Intermediate adjustment of drafts can produce in-between temperatures as desired. On the other hand, it is not possible to raise or lower the food rack to change distance from the fire, although in an emergency the rack can be lifted out temporarily while the fire cools down.

The other basic difference in the covered grill is in the effects of the cover, which make a profound difference in cooking methods. Aside from its fire control status, it reflects fire heat back on the food from above, and imprisons smoke, fumes and odors often so as to produce quite notice-

Fig. 6-12. Covered grill

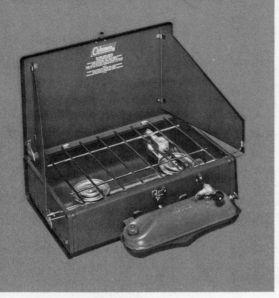

Fig. 6-13. Portable gasoline stove

able changes in the speed and type of cooking and the flavor of the product.

Under similar conditions of fire heat and distance, the cover will probably reduce cooking time by one-sixth to one-third, the greatest difference occurring with slow fire and closed top draft. The amount of charring for any one rate of cooking will be greatly reduced, which may be either good or bad depending on personal taste or the fashion of the moment. But off-flavors comparable to that of charring are produced by the smoke held down by the lid. Smoke flavor can be increased selectively by sprinkling wood chips, herbs, spices and even creosote on the fire. Maximum smoked flavors are produced by closing the upper draft and throttling the lower ones to make a slow fire.

The cover permits cooking of thick pieces of meat such as roasts, whole chickens and other items not suited to an ordinary charcoal grill. Some of the qualities of meat cooked in a covered roasting pan in an oven are obtained, but there is more flavoring from smoke.

It may be important to keep the three bottom drafts at the same adjustment. If one is opened wider than the others the fire

may be hottest directly above it, and cause the food in its area to overcook or burn.

Covered grills are also made with oven-like rack shelves, and in box shapes instead of round.

CAMP STOVES

A stove may be substituted for the charcoal grill. When a cookout is in the immediate vicinity of a house, gas or electric heating units may depend on its pipes or wiring. Elsewhere, the unit must include a supply of its fuel, which is usually either gasoline or propane. Only these free-to-travel types will be discussed here.

A stove is seldom as interesting as a grill or a fire, but it is quick-starting, and efficient if it works properly.

A camp stove may have anywhere from one to 4 burners, but 2-burner models are by far the most popular. They usually fold into a metal case with a carrying handle. Part of the case makes a 3-sided windscreen during cooking. There may be space for two 10-inch pans on the stove with the screen up, and there is almost sure to be room for two 8 or 9-inch pans.

Gasoline. A typical gasoline stove is shown in Figure 6-13. The fuel tank, which is heavily built, has a pump which takes 30 to 40 strokes to build up air pressure to force fuel into the burner, through a valve and a generator. The valve is a simple affair with a turn handle, which can shut off the fuel and usually can also regulate the amount of fuel flow, and therefore the size of the flame.

The generator is simply a portion of the fuel line that is heated by the burner flame, causing the gasoline in it to vaporize and enter the burner as a gas. This gas is mixed with air in a chamber similar to the mixing chambers in regular gas stove burners. It then burns with a hot blue flame. The generator tends to fill with carbon, and a wire for cleaning it, and/or a spare unit, may be packed with the new stove.

Since the burner mechanism depends on its own heat to make the fuel ready to burn, special means are required to provide heat for starting. There are two methods, puddle and choke.

The puddle method is apparently no longer found on new stoves, but there are plenty of old ones around. Underneath the burner there is a shallow cup, which is filled by opening the regular valve slightly (after pumping up the tank pressure) so that liquid gasoline flows through the burner and drips into the cup. When the cup is almost full, shut the valve and light the gasoline with a match. In this small quantity it offers little hazard, as long as you are ready to pull your hand back promptly.

The puddle of gasoline will burn for several minutes, heating the generator until the gasoline in it starts to boil, sending spurts of flame out of the burner. When this flame steadies and turns blue, you blow out any remaining fire in the cup (or let it burn out, if you prefer) and open the valve, to maintain a steady burner flame.

The choke is an air tube running from the top of the tank to the burner. When opened, it permits the flow of air saturated with gasoline vapor into the burner, where you light it. It may ignite quickly, or after some delay. If your match burns short, light another one. When it is lit, open the fuel valve slightly. In a minute or two, the gasoline in the generator will start to vaporize, feeding the burner in the regular way. Then turn off the choke.

Pressure in the tank falls rapidly while the choke is being used, very slowly when only the fuel valve is open. Some stoves need re-pumping every 15 minutes, others can go an hour.

A good gasoline stove should produce a hot, blue flame, but it may have a tendency toward yellow flame tips and sootiness. In still air, at a temperature of 72° F, it should bring 2 quarts of water to a boil in 7 to 12 minutes. In a breeze it would take a little

Courtesy of Bernz-O-Matic Corp.

Fig. 6-14. Portable propane stove

longer for the fast-heating models, and much longer for the slower ones.

Most gasoline stoves will burn only white gasoline or a special Coleman fuel which is more expensive. These fuels can be obtained at some service stations, and at many stores selling hardware, marine supplies or sporting goods. A tank holding a quart will burn 3 to 6 hours, so even the higher priced fuel costs very little.

Gasoline should be handled with care, both because of fire danger and possible contamination of food with its odors. It should be kept in a tight metal container, away from heat and food. The container should have air space at the top and should be kept upright, to minimize fuel being forced past the cap seal by possible heat expansion.

The stove tank should be filled before each use, to avoid running out while cooking. It is usually necessary to use a funnel, and it is a good precaution to put cloth or some other filter material in it, to catch particles that might otherwise clog passages. Do the filling away from any flame or food.

After one burner is going, the other may be turned on and lighted. It is usually supplied from the same line as the main burner, so that you will get no more heat from both of them than from one. But it is divided so that you can conduct two cooking operations at the same time.

Propane. An increasing number of camp stoves use bottled gas as fuel. The supply is usually propane in disposable cylinders holding about 14 ounces each, but hookups for larger and more economical refillable cylinders are possible. One cylinder is used for each burner, and is connected by a hose and fittings.

There are no starting problems with propane. You turn it on, wait a moment and then light the burner with a match. There is no problem of spillage, smell or contamination of food. Fire danger is negligible, although it may be theoretically illegal to transport even one of these cylinders through a vehicle tunnel. Their combined bulk may be less than that of a gasoline can, but in any case the fact that they can be packed anywhere reduces space requirement and packing problems.

On the other hand, the propane burner is usually not as hot nor as easily regulated as that of gasoline, the cost may be ten times as much for the same amount of heat and, most serious of all, there is usually no way to tell how much gas, if any, there is in a cylinder. If you have a scale, you can weigh the cylinder when you get it, mark the weight, and figure that it will be empty when it weighs 14 ounces less. On a time basis, you might get 3-1/2 to 5-1/2 hours with maximum flame on one burner. If the shutoff valve is not tight, it may quietly empty itself while in storage. At least one spare cylinder should always be carried.

A propane stove should have a pressure regulating valve. Many do. Without it, pressure, flow of gas and burner heat will vary with the temperature of the cylinder. It usually cools by evaporation while in use, so that heating rate at the start may be better than it is a little later, and performance at freezing and colder temperatures may be unsatisfactory.

Alcohol. Denatured alcohol is used in a few camp stoves, but because its flame temperature is much lower than that produced by gas and gasoline, it is much less satisfactory. It takes much longer to get water or food to cooking temperature, and it may not be able to do any cooking where it is cold or windy.

Although very flammable, alcohol is not explosive under ordinary conditions, and is safer to carry than gasoline. Its smell is not offensive, but it is very poisonous if drunk or eaten. The flame is usually clean.

Alcohol may be jellied into a soft solid, which is sold in cans, chiefly under the trade name Sterno. It may be used with a light, flat-folding stove, or any arrangement that will support a pan or can just above it. The can is opened by prying up a lid, the contents are lighted with a match, and the flaming can is slid under the object to be heated. It is extinguished by putting the lid back. In a warm, calm place it may take 15 minutes to bring a pint of water to a boil, and it would be useless in a cold wind. But it is so safe and easy to store, transport and use that it definitely has a place in camp supplies, to provide small-scale or emergency heat for warming up or very light cooking. A large can burns for about 1-1/2 hours, a small can for half that long.

Part Two / BASIC FOODS

7
MEAT

MEAT

Meat is the edible parts of animals. In a general sense, the term covers flesh and organs of mammals, birds, fish and reptiles. However, there are important differences among them, and it is customary to discuss them separately. In this chapter, meat will refer only to that obtained from mammals, unless specifically stated to cover other sources.

Most meat is flesh, made up of muscle fiber with associated connective tissue and fat. But the organs are meat also, although liver is the only one that is important in the American diet.

Food Value. Muscle and connective tissue are proteins of the type called complete or high quality. They provide all the amino acids needed to build human protein. In contrast, most vegetable proteins are incomplete. On the other hand, animal fats are mostly of the saturated (polysaturated) type, that is under grave suspicion as a contributing factor in artery hardening and heart failure.

Flesh is usually high in the B vitamins, and low in the others. It contains important amounts of phosphorous and iron, and some calcium and other minerals. Liver and some other organs are excellent sources of most vitamins. Humans apparently can keep good health indefinitely on an all-meat diet, but only if the organs are eaten.

Popularity. Meat represents a substantial part of the American diet. Figure 7-1 shows the average amounts consumed during various years from 1912 to 1969. This is on a pounds-per-person basis. With increase in population, the actual amount consumed has of course increased much more than is shown in these figures.

During this period, pork consumption has remained nearly the same, beef has increased over 70 per cent, and veal and lamb have decreased by half. The net result is an increase of 23 per cent.

The present tendency in chain stores to concentrate selling efforts (including bargain prices) on the most popular foods will probably lead to a continued decline in consumption of veal and lamb.

Tenderness. Tenderness is an important but confusing factor in the popularity of meat. Everyone seems to agree that meat should be tender, and there is endless dis-

(Pounds — Carcass Weight)				
Years	Pork	Beef	Veal	Lamb	Total
1912	66.7	64.6	6.9	**7.7**	145.9
1925	66.8	59.5	8.6	5.2	140.1
1930	67.0	48.9	6.4	6.7	129.0
1935	48.4	53.2	8.5	7.3	117.4
1940	73.5	54.9	7.4	6.6	142.4
1944	**79.5**	55.6	**12.4**	6.7	154.2
1945	66.6	59.4	11.9	7.3	145.2
1950	69.2	63.4	8.0	4.0	144.6
1955	66.8	82.0	9.4	4.6	162.8
1960	64.9	85.0	6.1	4.8	160.8
1965	58.5	99.3	5.2	3.7	166.7
1966	58.0	104.0	4.5	4.0	170.5
1967	63.9	105.9	3.8	3.9	177.5
1968	66.0	109.4	3.6	3.7	182.7
1969	64.8	110.5	3.3	3.4	182.0
1970*	65.4	**113.1**	2.9	3.4	**184.8**

For 50 states beginning 1960.
*USDA estimate
Bold — Record High

Courtesy of National Live Stock & Meat Board

Fig. 7-1. Per capita meat consumption in the United States

cussion of how to make it so, starting with the ancestors of the animal and finishing with complex arguments about manner of cooking, but there is still no certain knowledge about many phases of the problem. The following pages will try to explain the situation as it is understood at this time.

However, tenderness may not be quite as important as it seems. Beef is the most popular meat, and on the average it is the toughest. People will buy the tenderest steak they can afford, and then go out of their way to put a tough, charred crust on it over a grill (see OUTDOOR COOKING). Bakers are encouraged to put the toughest imaginable crusts on certain types of bread and rolls. Faddists who cry out against the toughening effect of quick cooking of protein may regard well-cooked tender vege-

tables as not only inedible but morally offensive.

But regardless of how confused our basic attitudes are on this subject, ability to produce the tenderest possible result from the meat on hand and the cooking methods available is a great asset for a cook to have. But whether this ability should be used under all circumstances may be questionable, particularly when a desired flavor is lost in the tenderizing.

Muscle. The voluntary or striated muscles that make up the bulk of edible meat are mostly bundles of bundles of fine fibers, each bundle being surrounded and supported by a fine sheath of connective and other tissue, as shown in Figure 7-2. In addition, muscle contains fat droplets and granules of glycogen (animal starch) both inside and outside the fibers. These provide a reserve of fuel for muscle activity during life, and this fat provides desirable eating qualities.

Muscle tissue tends to be naturally tender in the freshly killed animal and in meat that has been properly aged, but connective tissue is tough. The tenderizing effect of cooking is mostly in its effect on connective tissue, and unfavorable effects are largely due to bad effects on the muscle.

The involuntary or smooth muscles found in the heart, arteries, veins, lungs and the digestive system are good protein. However, they are not eaten much by Americans, and a description of them is not considered worth-while here.

Color. Muscles contain myoglobin, an iron-rich protein that combines with oxygen to hold it in storage in the tissue. It gives raw meat its characteristic red or pink color. The hemoglobin of the blood, which is also red, is largely drained out of the animal at the time it is killed.

Myoglobin stays red only in the presence of free oxygen, and turns to purple or grey without it. For this reason, meats exhibited in the market may be left exposed, or wrapped in a special transparent plastic that can be penetrated by oxygen but not by the larger water vapor molecules, to preserve color while preventing drying. But the temperature must be kept low, as otherwise the surface may over-oxidize into a brown color (metmyglobin).

Meat which loses much moisture is likely to darken, lose weight and shrivel. Moderate or extreme toughening may occur.

Myoglobin changes color when cooked. It usually stays red up to around 135° F, pink to somewhere between 140 and 150°, and then turns grey or brown, indicating various stages of cooking from raw or rare up through medium and well done. Cured meats such as ham retain their pink color when cooked because myoglobin is converted into a heat-resistant dye by the action of sodium nitrite in the curing solution.

There is another red coloring occasionally present in uncured meat which retains its color in spite of cooking. It has not been identified. If it occurs in pork it makes people nervous, but the shade is dark and quite different from the pale pink of the rare meat. There is also another unknown and presumably harmless substance that may turn well done meat to a reddish hue during refrigerator storage.

Connective Tissue. Connective tissue includes the semi-transparent sheaths around the muscle fiber bundles, which are chiefly a protein called collagen; and tendons that function as non-bony parts of the skeleton. The tendons are tough and usually cannot be tenderized, and should be separated from the meat during carving. The sheaths, although tough in raw meat, may become tender and even dissolve into a semi-liquid gelatin when cooked slowly and thoroughly in the presence of moisture. This moisture may be provided by the natural meat juices, and/or by hot water or steam.

The same cooking process that tenderizes the connective tissue may toughen the meat fiber. The two processes may progress to

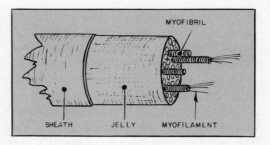

Fig. 7-2. Cutaway of muscle fiber

the point where the meat falls apart into strings.

The proportion of connective tissue increases as the animal ages, and as it exercises.

Fat. In addition to flesh, most meat contains fat, which is white or creamy in color and contrasts with the pink, red or grey of the meat itself. Fat has little structure. It occurs in bands or layers of varying thickness, and also occurs in smaller amounts between or within the meat fibers. It contains little water (perhaps 10 per cent) and provides concentrated nourishment of a kind that is usually acceptable or useful to the human system only in moderate amounts. It is mostly the hard, saturated type.

Thick layers of fat, often on the outer edges of the meat, are useful in protecting meat from drying while it cooks, and in contributing some juiciness. However, there is usually much more of it than is needed for these purposes and for food, and much

Fig. 7-3. Fat distribution in porterhouse steak

Courtesy of National Live Stock & Meat Board

of it may be regarded as an expensive form of waste. In flat pieces such as steaks it should be slashed, as it shrinks during cooking and tends to make the meat curl.

On the other hand, the between-fiber fat, called marbling in beef, is highly valued for a number of reasons. Its presence indicates that the muscles surrounding it have not been working hard during the animal's life, so that it has had no reason to build up more than a minimum of connective tissue. What tissue there is tends to be stretched thin and thus made less strong or tough by the internal pressure of fat droplets.

Fat adds greatly to the juiciness of cooked meat, both by its presence, and by reduction of both the outward drainage and the internal absorption of watery fluids during cooking. And, although solid fat often seems to have very little taste, in combination with the flesh it provides a very important part of the flavor.

Aging. In the living animal muscle is naturally tense and hard, and is kept in the relaxed state by presence of a short-life chemical. After death the supply of this chemical is gradually exhausted so that muscles harden in a half hour to a few hours after death, a condition called rigor mortis. Flesh cooked and eaten while in this condition is likely to be very tough.

After a few more hours or a few days other chemical changes in the muscles cause relaxation and a return to about the original state of tenderness. After this, secondary processes that are not well understood may tenderize either the muscle or connective tissue, or both of them, very gradually over a period of weeks or months. The effect is definite and important in beef, and somewhat disputed for other meats.

During the aging period the meat should be kept quite cold, around 35° F, to avoid damage from mold and bacteria infection. It should not be frozen, as this would interfere with the aging process. In commercial storage plants ultraviolet lamps may be used to keep the air and meat surfaces as nearly sterile as possible.

Curing. Meat curing is basically a process of adding salt (sodium chloride) and/or other chemicals as preservatives. However, it is now used chiefly to change the flavor and color of the meat, and improvement in keeping qualities is secondary. As a result, low concentrations of salt are used, and the salt taste in the meat may be barely perceptible.

The curing solution, called the pickle, contains salt and sodium nitrite as basic materials. In addition, it may contain sugar, sodium nitrate, ascorbic acid, flavorings and other materials. Sometimes the chemicals are rubbed dry on the surface, or dissolved in water that covers the meat in a tub. These surface treatments are for thin cuts such as bacon, or trimmings to be used in sausage. For hams and other large pieces of meat, however, the solution is usually pumped into the artery system or selected interior points, so as to reach all parts of the meat rapidly, before spoilage can occur.

A typical curing brine or pickle for pumping may contain, for 100 gallons of water, 130 pounds of salt, 25 to 50 pounds of sugar, 1.5 pounds sodium nitrite and one pound of sodium nitrate. The nitrate reacts with other substances that change it to nitrite. Less salt may be used in a cover solution. The cured meat contains less than 5 per cent salt in its fluids.

Fig. 7-4. Rigor mortis

Fig. 7-5. A small business

Some bacteria can grow comfortably in salted meat, but they are different species, and fewer species, than can grow in fresh meat. Complete curing thus kills off practically the entire existing crop of microörganisms, and any spoilage occurring would usually have to be from a fresh infection.

The nitrite alters the red pigment of the meat so that it becomes heat-proof, and is not altered by cooking. However, it still may fade if exposed to light and air.

The pumping of curing solution into ham has sometimes been very much overdone, so that the original weight has been greatly increased. Some extra water seems to be useful for tenderizing and juiciness, but beyond that it is an adulterant and a deception.

Home Curing. Home curing of meat is a somewhat hit-or-miss process, which has been largely rendered obsolete by the more efficient and less salty packing house methods. However, it can provide do-it-yourself satisfaction, usually a richer even if saltier flavor, and permits curing of any cut you may wish to try.

For corned beef, try to get either fresh killed or very well refrigerated beef. The brisket is the preferred cut, but you can corn stew meat or a filet mignon if you wish. Get a big crock, made of earthenware,

china or glass (some metal is all right, but some isn't, and beef is high priced merchandise to risk). Put in the beef you want to cure, and put in enough cold water to cover it about 2 inches deep.

Let the meat and water stand in a cool place, preferably around 55° F, for 48 hours. Drain off water, measure it and discard it. Measure the same amount of fresh water (spring water, if possible) and to every gallon, add:

1 to 1½ lb (2¼ to 3½ cups) salt
¼ to ½ cup (2 to 4 Tb) brown sugar
⅓ to ½ oz. (1 to 1½ tsp) saltpeter
   (sodium nitrate, $NaNO_3$)

Depending on the recipe, this may be mixed and used lukewarm; or boiled, skimmed (for spring water contributions?), cooled and then poured over the beef. Then you place a heavy weight on the meat to keep it from floating. Store in a cool place for 10 to 20 days, perhaps turning the meat occasionally. Then drain and refrigerate. The shorter time is for the stronger solution.

You can cook home corned beef directly, or can soak it in cold water for a day or two first to take out some of the salt. Or you can change water while simmering it. Cooking time averages about an hour to the pound, but you can start making tests with a fork in about 2 hours, regardless of total weight.

Smoking. Meat may be cured on its surface by exposure to a heavy concentration of wood smoke. Commercially, this smoke is made by controlled burning of sawdust from hardwoods such as hickory, birch and maple, or by pressing logs against rapidly rotating discs of smooth steel.

The smoke dries out the surface of the meat and deposits various bacteria-killing and flavorful chemicals. Although the altered layer may be quite shallow, it protects against spoilage until the meat is cut or bruised so that un-smoked layers are ex-

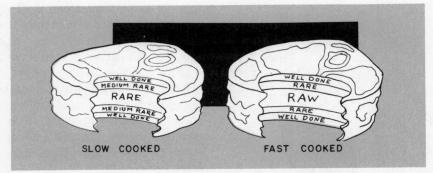

Fig. 7-6. Slow and fast cooking

posed. Flavor changes go deeper than the noticeable physical effect. The smokehouse may be kept hot, so that the meat may become partially or wholly cooked during processing.

Either fresh or cured meat may be smoked.

COOKING

Meat is usually cooked before it is eaten. The purpose is to make it more tender and digestible, to improve flavor, texture and appearance, and/or to kill parasites.

The cooking process, the mechanical side of which is described in PART ONE, involves very complex physical and chemical changes, most of which are not well understood. Some start to act at temperatures as low as 115º F, while others which are usually desirable only in crust, require 4 or 5 times that heat.

An important effect of cooking meat is to change its texture from a rubbery or stiff jelly background to something firmer. This starts to take place at a temperature of 135 to 140º, at the same time that the red of raw beef changes to a pink shade that identifies the meat as being "rare." The temperature and color indication vary among different meats. Continued cooking changes color into the grey-brown of well done beef, or to species-typical colors ranging from white to brown for other meats. A temperature of 185º indicates the well done stage

in any of them. Any higher temperature is likely to be very damaging to all desirable qualities of the meat, except in a thin surface crust.

Internal conditions during cooking may be judged on a basis of heat and time, surface appearance, smell, or test cuts, but in solid chunks can be most easily and usually most accurately read from a meat thermometer, described under ROASTING. Temperature is usually highest at the surface and lowest in the middle, but allowance must be made for the fact that flesh conducts heat more rapidly than fat does, and more slowly than bone. Differences between surface and internal temperatures are greatest when heat is intense, and when the meat is frozen or very cold at the start of cooking.

Muscle fiber does not seem to be affected in tenderness by light cooking, but it may toughen in the medium and well done stages. The effect may or may not be noticeable then, but it may become very pronounced with overcooking, particularly if it is dry. But very long cooking with moisture sometimes makes the muscle tender again.

Heat and moisture first tenderize connective tissue, then dissolve it into a jelly. This cooking process takes time, and unless properly done, may toughen the muscle excessively while tenderizing the tissue.

Tender cuts of meat that contain little connective tissue may be eaten raw, rare or medium with pleasure. Cuts with considerable tissue may have to be well done or overcooked. Slow heat is expected to do less damage to muscle than fast heat will, for the same amount of tenderizing of connective tissue. However, super-fast cooking by microwaves or pressure steam often produces very tender meat.

Dry vs Moist Heat. Cookbooks often make a major issue of choosing between dry heat, represented by broiling, frying and open-pan roasting; and moist heat in the form of braising (any kind of cooking in a covered pan) and stewing. No indecision or compromise is tolerated — you either have a tender cut that must be cooked dry, or a tough one that must be cooked moistly. The reader is told that it is technically wrong to take a middle course by roasting in a covered pan, and there is often an implication that this is morally wrong also.

But there is no clear dividing line between tender and tough cuts, and even experienced cooks may guess wrong. Fortunately, it is practical to cook intermediate pieces either way, with good results.

Dry. Dry cooking usually involves high heat. Broiling involves exposure to flame or metal with a temperature of about 3,000° F (gas) or 1,500 (electric) across a few inches of space, often in an oven heated to 500° or more. Most oven roasting is done at temperatures between 300 and 350° and occasionally higher, although it can be done at simmer temperatures of 185 to 200°. Frying is usually done between 250 and 375°, with the food in direct contact with the heated oil.

A part of dry heat is absorbed by evaporation of moisture from the surface of the meat, so that the amount that penetrates is hard to measure.

Dry cooking processes seldom allow sufficient time to soften connective tissue, so they are usually limited to meat that does not contain much of it, such as prime and choice beef in good cuts, and the young of most animals and birds.

Electronic cooking is dry and is very rapid.

Moist. Moist cooking may be in water (stewing or simmering, rarely referred to as boiling) or in steam (braising). Both operations are supposed to be done at a simmer temperature of 185 to 200° F, which may be difficult to maintain. Recently, the meaning of braising has been extended to cover roasting in a covered pan.

True braising in a heavy covered pan over a surface burner turned low is the standard method of cooking pot roast, and will often produce a very tender result. However, long moist cooking tends to make the meat dry and weak-flavored inside, so that it is important to make gravy from the drippings for good eating.

Pressure-steaming, which is moist and fast, produces results that compare favorably with those obtained by simmering.

Moist heat is a much more effective cooking medium than dry heat, because it conducts heat more readily into the food, and restricts evaporation of its water, which would otherwise have a cooling effect. You can safely put your hand in a 250° oven for a moment, but steam at that temperature would scald it immediately.

Juiciness. Juiciness is a highly desirable characteristic of cooked meat, but it is often lacking. Raw meat is almost always juicy, while meat cooked a long time by any method tends to be dry. However, it very seldom is really dry, it just tastes that way because most of its moisture is in a combined or bound state.

A roast with 70 per cent water content

Fig. 7-7. Indecision

when raw may lose up to 30 per cent of its weight in drippings and evaporation when roasted in a medium oven. The loss would be about the same if it were cooked as a pot roast. Even if the loss were entirely water, the cooked meat would still be over 50 per cent water. The roast would probably taste juicy, and the pot roast dry. No official explanation of the dry feeling and taste is available, and it can only be assumed that the juice can enter into tight combinations with meat proteins from which it cannot be squeezed by either utensils or teeth.

As a general principle, quick and incomplete cooking yields the juiciest meat.

Crust. Overcooking by any method overheats, dries out, toughens and hardens meat. These effects are welcome only if they are confined to a thin surface layer, called a crust. This may be developed on all surfaces of a roast, but specially on non-fat areas, and on the upper and lower surfaces of flat cuts that are normally broiled or fried.

Such a crust may be pleasantly crisp, very tough or anywhere in between. It is usually well flavored because of direct contact with heat, and because juices coming from the interior thicken and evaporate in and on it.

If the drying and hardening process continues too long it goes deeper into the meat, where it usually produces a dry, tough and comparatively flavorless substance that cannot be separated from the crust and spoils it by association. The only good use for such a crust is to put it through the meat grinder and add it to the gravy or use it in hash.

An uncovered roast may develop a more highly flavored crust than a covered one, because more of the juice coming to the surface evaporates, leaving salts and flavoring compounds. The lack of a cover also makes the crust harder and crisper, but it may allow it to become too thick and dry, with resulting toughness.

TENDERIZING

Tough meat may sometimes be made tender by pounding, cutting or treating with an enzyme.

Pounding. Pounding, properly done, breaks up connective tissue and probably the muscle structure as well. It may be done with any hard object. There is division of opinion about whether a smooth surface, such as that of a wooden mallet, or the rough one found on a special tenderizing hammer, Figure 7-8, is more efficient. Many people use the side of a saucer or dish. In any case, the meat should be put on wood or some other surface that will not be injured, and beaten with light hammer blows until its thickness is reduced by about 75 per cent. That is, a 1/2-inch slice should finish with a thickness of 1/8 inch.

The thin sheet of meat cooks very quickly in a frypan, but is more often rolled up with dressing or other foods and baked. A surface treatment of cooking oil may be needed to prevent drying out.

Thoroughly pounded meat is usually tender and it may be tasty, but it retains very little of the character of the original meat. You can take a middle course, by pounding meat only a moderate amount, to produce some surface tenderizing with only slight loss of thickness and other qualities.

Cutting. Butchers often have machines that make a great many closely spaced parallel cuts in the surfaces of a slice of meat, usually a boneless steak. They may be straight down or at an angle, and penetrate 1/4 inch or more. Their tenderizing effect goes no deeper than the cuts, but it seems to make a worthwhile difference to have an easy start for a bite.

Small cube steaks are sometimes both pounded and cut.

Carving can make a big difference in the apparent tenderness of meat. If it is done across the grain, the tough fibers, either connective or muscle, are cut into short

Fig. 7-8. Tenderizing hammer

bits. The thinner the slice, the shorter the bits and the more tender the product. Even if slicing is done with the grain, thinness reduces the number of fibers that must be masticated in a group, and makes chewing easier.

Electric powered rotary slicers are the best tool for very thin slicing of boneless meat.

Enzymes. Meat may be made less tough by treating with enzymes. There are a number of chemicals that act on meat to break down the structure of connective tissue and/or muscle. The most effective of these at present is papain, found in the juice of unripe papaya fruit. It is sold in groceries as a powder, called meat tenderizer, in which it is greatly diluted with salt, and perhaps starch, citric acid, sugar and other substances.

Papain breaks down both muscle and connective tissue. It is ineffective at refrigerator temperature, slow at room temperature and increasingly active up to 150° F, a little below the point at which cooking destroys it. It cannot act on meat cells until it reaches them, and the major problem in its use is diffusing it through the meat.

Instructions on labels may call for warming the meat to room temperature, or moistening it with water. The powder is sprinkled on liberally, and the meat is pierced at half-inch intervals with a fork or a knife point. The meat may then be cooked immediately, cooked after 30 minutes, or stored a while in the refrigerator, depending on what label you are reading.

There is little question about the tenderizing power of papain, but considerable doubt about the effectiveness of the commercial tenderizers when used according to instructions. It has not been shown that the enzyme can penetrate meat with the speed required by instructions, and tenderizing is likely to be limited to thin surface layers and puncture points.

It is worthwhile to remember that most of the tenderizing action takes place during cooking, and it is reasonable to assume it should be better with slow cooking than with fast. The value of time in the refrigerator or on the work table after treatment is chiefly in giving the enzyme time to penetrate more deeply and widely, so that it will be in position to work when it is heated.

Commercial tenderizers are so loaded with salt and other materials that unpleasant taste side effects may occur. Some people dislike the flavor of papain itself, others like it or do not notice it.

In spite of questions and disadvantages, tenderizers are worth trying if you have a problem of tough meat.

Meat packers are experimenting with injection of papain into the animal's blood stream before slaughtering.

CARVING

Carving is the operation by which a chunk or slab of meat or poultry is divided into slices or pieces. It may be all meat, meat and fat, or meat, fat and bone.

Good carving is a highly skilled job. It calls for proper tools, knowledge of meat and lots of practice. A good carver seems to get a greater quantity of meat from a roast than a poor one, and he certainly makes it more attractive and palatable. However, anyone with common sense and a sharp knife can follow a few basic rules and subdivide a piece of meat into edible portions.

Tools. The traditional carving set consists of a knife of high quality with a blade 8 or 9 inches long, a 2-tined fork with a guard to protect the hand, and a steel. The last two items are shown in Figure 7-9. Good knives, although possibly not of the very best quality, can still be obtained readily, but the guarded fork and the steel have become rarities. This is unfortunate. The preferred method of carving rolled roasts is toward the hand, so that a guard on the fork is a useful safety measure.

The steel serves the same function as the barber's razor strop, keeping the knife sharp without repeated and destructive grinding of the edge. If it is used conscientiously on a good knife, and the knife is not abused, it should make other re-sharpening unnecessary. It is customary to strop just before carving, and at any time during carving when the knife does not appear to be cutting satisfactorily.

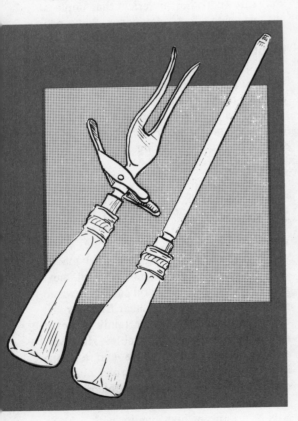

Fig. 7-9. Guarded fork and sharpening steel

Any knife that is long enough to take the widest part of the meat in one cut can be used, provided it is sharp. A dull knife pushes and tears, is hard to guide accurately and will not make thin slices. Sharpening can be done by routine methods described in Chapter 35, but only good steel will take and keep the very keen edge needed for carving. And such an edge is easily spoiled by cutting through the meat onto metal or china, and particularly onto paper; or by allowing the knife to be mixed up with other tools or cutlery in a drawer.

Regular knives are being replaced in carving by electric knives and rotary knives, described in Chapter 37. The amateur will do better with an electric than a standard knife, but the expert will not. The electric rotaries are excellent for boneless meat, but it's size must be within their tray and clamp capacity, which is often quite limited.

Where to Carve. It is traditional that a roast or a steak be carved at the table, after the family and any guests are seated, and usually after the serving dishes of other foods are on the table. It is a pleasant, leisurely custom that gives the carver opportunity to display his expertness, and it provides warm overtones of togetherness in starting the main course. But it involves delay that may be tedious rather than comfortable, and allows too much time for hot food to cool. If the carver is not an expert, a circumstance that is increasingly common, the delay to the meal is greatly increased and the carver may be embarrassed into fumbling and mistakes.

For the sake of the knife, and for stability, carving should be done on a board, preferably on a wet cloth to keep it from sliding. Neither the board nor the cloth have any place on a dinner table. In addition, carving may be quite untidy as a result of spatter of juice and bits of meat, and possible flipping of slices or even the whole roast.

As a result of these factors, carving is

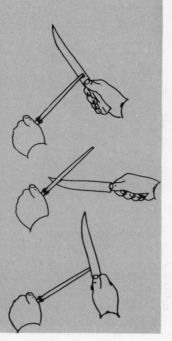

HOW TO STEEL A KNIFE

Hold steel firmly in left hand, thumb on top of handle. Place heel of blade against far side of steel, with steel and blade of knife making a 25-degree angle.

Bring blade down along steel to the left with a swinging motion of right wrist. Entire length of blade should pass lightly over steel.

Bring knife back into starting position, but this time with blade on near side of steel making the 25-degree angle. Repeat stroking motion. Continue alternating strokes until edge is trued.

Courtesy of National Live Stock & Meat Board

Fig. 7-10. How to steel a knife

now most often done in the kitchen, and serving at the table is done from a platter.

If you still prefer to carve at the table, remember that you have the option of doing it either standing or sitting down. Standing is usually more efficient.

Wherever you carve, allow yourself plenty of elbow room. At the table, be particularly careful not to work near filled glasses or vases of flowers.

Firmness. Meat that is fresh out of the oven is usually too flabby to carve well. It should stand 15 to 30 minutes, with the longer time for larger roasts. Some additional cooking, with a rise of as much as 4° in the center, will take place during this period. It may be protected from surface cooling by covering with cloth, or by placing it in the turned-off oven with the door open.

Meat becomes even firmer and easier to carve when it is refrigerator-cold, but that advantage should be postponed to another meal.

Grain. Meat, except for most organs, has a grain — the direction in which the muscle fibers run. These fibers were shown in Figure 7-2. If it is tough it is important to carve across the grain, straight or diagonally, whenever possible. This cuts the muscles and their casing of connective tissue into short bits. But if the meat is tender, or if it is too shallow to make even minimum slices across the grain, it may be cut at any angle, including parallel with grain.

Steak is usually carved with the grain. It has already been sliced across the grain by the butcher, and it is supposed to be tender anyhow.

Bone. Bone structure can be quite confusing. Diagrams showing the best approach to slices are given where particular cuts are discussed, but they may be hard to reconcile with the particular chunk you are trying to carve. Sometimes it helps to probe to locate bone, with the point of the knife or preferably with a narrow tool such as an ice pick.

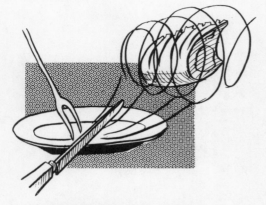

Fig. 7-11. A roast may be evasive

Unless the meat has had very long, moist cooking, it clings to bone. Slices that end at a bone may be freed from it by cutting along the bone before slicing, after each slice or after making a number of slices.

Serving. The carver often has a problem of distribution. Parts of a steak may vary in tenderness and desirability, and it is usually tactful to cut so that the best part is divided to make part of several portions. A roast may be carved so that most of the crust is on a few pieces, or a little of it on many. A chicken or a turkey involves a problem of fair distribution of light and dark meat, and of special parts such as legs and wings. The carver should ask people what they want, and then make an effort to supply it.

Steer — Male unsexed while young
Bull — Fully developed, mature male
Stag — Unsexed after developing secondary physical characteristics of the bull
Heifer — Young female which has not borne a calf
Cow — Female having borne a calf
Veal and calves — Young bovines, either sex

By permission from "Meat Handbook" by Albert Levie, Copyright 1963, Avi Publishing Co.

Fig. 7-12. Classes of beef animals

BEEF

Grading. Beef is the most popular meat in the United States, and in many other parts of the world. It is obtained from cattle, usually specially bred for meat, preferably between the ages of 12 and 18 months. The Federal government grades it according to a series of standards of desirability. The best rating is Prime, then Choice, Good, Standard, Commercial, Utility, Cutter and Canner in descending quality. The last four grades are seldom sold as fresh beef.

Prime is from young, well-fed and little-exercised cattle. It is distinguished by large quantities of fat, including the type that is interspersed with the lean and is called marbling. It is tops in tenderness, juiciness and flavor, but is expensive because it is both highest price per pound, and has the highest percentage of unusable fat.

Choice and Good are good eating meats, with less fat, but often with less tenderness and juiciness. Commercial is from older animals and is likely to be tough unless given long slow cooking.

Classes. Figure 7-12 shows the bovine (cattle) classes. These are not involved in the grading system, but are frequently mentioned. The steer (castrated bull) is generally thought to be preferable to the others for meat quality, but there is not enough definite difference to justify labeling for the consumer. However, stores and restaurants may have strong preferences as to what classes to buy, in anticipation of either better grades or greater percentage yield of desired cuts.

Some buyers have preference for beef from a certain feeding area, as the Corn Belt (Western beef in New York markets, Eastern beef in California). The breed, good pasture when young and good feed-lot practices during fattening are more important than the area of origin or of fattening.

Tenderness in beef is an important consideration chiefly because it is characteris-

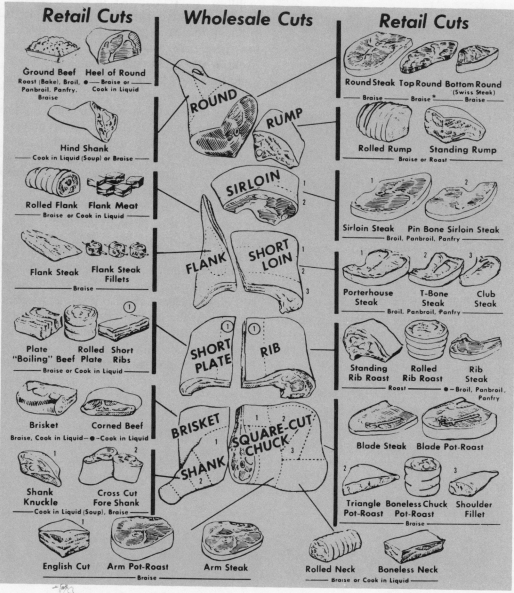

Fig. 7-13. Beef cuts

Courtesy of National Live Stock & Meat Board

tically the toughest of the common meats. The best and tenderest cuts of beef, cooked to perfection, are often not as tender as quite ordinary lamb, pork or poultry.

With occasional striking exceptions, the age of the beef animal at the time of slaugh-tering has an important effect on tenderness (the older the tougher), and can be judged by the color of the meat, which darkens as the animal grows older. Young bones con-tain wide streaks of pink tissue, old ones are almost all bone outside of the marrow.

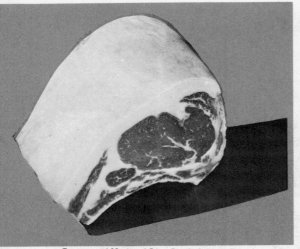

Fig. 7-14. Standing rib roast

Cuts. Figure 7-13 shows the principal cuts used from a beef animal. This illustration is not complete. The carcass can be sliced in a number of different ways, and the same or similar cuts may be known by entirely different names in different areas and different cookbooks. However, this is enough to give a general idea. In addition to these flesh cuts, there is liver, usually sold in slices less than one-half inch thick, and heart and kidneys which are not available in many markets.

The tenderest flesh cuts are usually those from the upper two-thirds of the animal, between but not including the shoulder and hip sections. They include the standing rib and rolled roasts, and porterhouse, T-bone, club and sirloin steaks.

Quantity. In buying solid meat (rolled roast, boneless steak, hamburger) figure about half a pound per person. Steaks and roasts with bone and solid fat masses, get about one pound. People often eat only half these amounts, but you can't count on it. Their capacity is affected not only by their appetites, but by the way the meat is prepared, and by the type and quantity of other food that goes with it.

Leftover meat is seldom wasted. It can

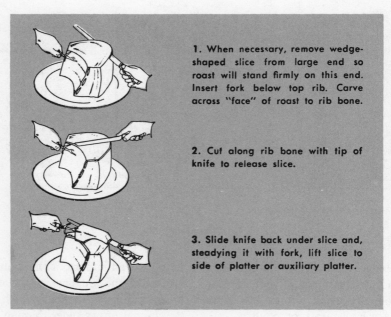

1. When necessary, remove wedge-shaped slice from large end so roast will stand firmly on this end. Insert fork below top rib. Carve across "face" of roast to rib bone.

2. Cut along rib bone with tip of knife to release slice.

3. Slide knife back under slice and, steadying it with fork, lift slice to side of platter or auxiliary platter.

Fig. 7-15a. Carving a rib roast

be served again as solid meat, either cold or reheated, sliced for sandwiches, chopped for hash or used in any of a variety of mixtures.

Roasts. Roasting beef (which is different from pot roast) is most highly valued when taken from the rib or sirloin sections of the animal, but it may also be rump or eye of the round. A rolled roast of any cut is one that has had the bones removed, and the flesh rolled into a cylindrical shape and tied with string.

A rib roast or standing rib roast contains two or more ribs (with the lower or short rib section cut off), and the connecting section of backbone or chine. For ease of carving, the ribs should be sawed through by the butcher where they meet the backbone, so it can be cut away during or just before carving.

Beef is usually roasted uncovered.

If there are ribs, the roast should be rested on their ends. This both serves to make a stand or trivet to keep the meat off the bottom, and keeps the fat side up for self-basting. Rolled roasts are cooked on their sides, also to keep a fat side up. They may rest on a rack or directly on the pan. Addition of a little water to start is optional.

Oven temperature may be slow to medium, 300 to 350° F. Time, in minutes per pound, may be:

Rare — 16 to 21
Medium — 20 to 25
Well done — 24 to 30

Rib roasts cook somewhat more rapidly than rolled ones. It is best to use a meat thermometer. Standard instruction is to take 140 F for rare, 160 as medium and 170 well done. But at least one authority uses a scale that is 20° lower in each category. Take a large roast out when it is a few degrees low, as the center will increase in temperature after it is removed from the oven.

Figure 7-15 gives standard instructions for carving a standing roast. However, they involve the use of a fork with a guard, which you may not have, and cutting toward your left hand, which is dangerous work for an amateur. Until you are used to the tools, it is better to carve with the roast on its ribs or side, even though it is harder to get perfect slices this way.

With the rib roast, it will then be necessary to cut the meat free of the rib (position 2 in the illustration) before slicing, as otherwise the slice will hang over the rib and be difficult to separate from it.

Pot Roast. Pot roast is a chunk of beef, usually 3 pounds or more, taken from parts of the animal that are apt to be tougher than those used for a regular roast. There is some overlapping between the two types, and a cut that would be a good roast in a prime animal might be pot roast in one rated Choice or only Good.

Most pot roasts seem to be de-boned and rolled, except in the blade cut, which is a very thick chuck steak which is braised with the bone in. Shoulder cuts may be prepared with bone or without it.

Pot roast is cooked by braising (steaming) in a very heavy covered pot, which may be a special type called a Dutch oven. It seems to be customary to sear all surfaces of the meat first, which if done conscienti-

Fig. 7-15b. Carving a rib roast

Courtesy of National Live Stock & Meat Board

Steak thickness, inches	Distance below flame, inches	Total cooking time, minutes
1	2	10 to 16
1½	2	15 to 30
	3	20 to 35
2	2	25 to 45
	3	30 to 55

Fig. 7-16. Suggestions for broiling steak

ously will take about half an hour. You put the pot on high or medium heat, grease it lightly with fat from the meat, put the meat in with a flesh surface on the hot pan. Turn or shift it occasionally to avoid burning, and to sear other parts of the surface. Fat does not need to be seared, but some of it should be included to keep the pan greasy. Some recipes call for coating the meat with flour, but others do not.

When searing to a rich brown color is completed, you put a low rack in the pot, pour in about 1/2 cup of liquid, put on the cover tightly and turn the heat low.

The liquid can be plain water, tomato juice, Coca-Cola or anything with water in it. You can put a bit of onion in it at the beginning, and add whole onions, potatoes, carrots and other vegetables about 40 minutes before you expect it to be done.

Cooking time may be 45 to 60 minutes to the pound. You keep it up until the meat is either fork-tender or starts to fall apart, or sometimes just until you are tired of waiting for it. If the liquid boils away, add some more. If it builds up higher than the bottom of the meat you may wish to pour some off (but save it) but is not strictly necessary to keep its level down. Pot roast tends to be drier and less tasty than oven roast, but it provides the makings for a liberal supply of excellent gravy, which is prepared in the same manner as for a roast.

Steak. A steak is a slice of meat that is cut across the grain of the flesh. It is usual-ly one to 2 inches thick, but for special purposes it may be paper thin or a fraction of an inch. The unmodified term usually means beef steak, but they can be made from the meat of any large animal.

The most popular steaks are those that are tender enongh to be broiled. They are usually taken from the loin portions of beef, and include such names as sirloin, porterhouse, T-bone and club. Roasting beef in single-rib slices makes good steak also.

There are numerous other steak cuts that are considered less desirable. They include round, from the rear legs, arm from front legs, flank from the side below the loin and blade or chuck from the upper forequarters. Each of these has its partisans. Flank and round are rather lean meat, do not broil well and flank can be extremely tough. On the other hand, they are high in proportion of flesh to bone and fat.

Chuck includes a pleasing but usually not excessive amount of fat, should be tender enough for cookouts and informal meals, and is apt to have an excellent flavor.

Steak is usually kept 2 or 3 inches below the flame during broiling. Two inches is suitable for a thin or 1-inch steak, and the greater distance for a 2-incher. Figure 7-16 gives a table of approximate distances and cooking times. The shorter times are of course expected to give rarer meat. You slice through fat edges before cooking, to prevent curling because of contraction of the fat. Rub some fat on the broiler pan, after preheating it. Watch the steak. Figure that you will turn it halfway through its cooking time. If it seems to brown too little or too much, change the distance to the flame, or regulate its heat if you are lucky enough to be able to do so.

You can use a meat thermometer if the steak is 1-1/2 inches or thicker. It has to be put in horizontally, the dial may be damaged by heat and it does not give very accurate results in thin meat. Test cuts with a knife are the surest way of checking, and they are well worth the few drops of juice that they may cost.

A steak may be broiled plain, with the addition of salt and pepper on one side or both sides, or treated with a variety of barbecue sauces. The sauces are more often used over charcoal than in a kitchen.

There are two approaches to carving a steak. You may cut and remove the meat in pieces or slices and leave the bone, or you can first cut all around the bone, set it aside, and then carve the meat easily.

A steak is normally carved with the grain, but if it is thick and you think it may be tough, you can make slices with slanting cuts, Figure 7-17, that will shorten the fibers in the cut piece. A steak often looks more attractive, and certainly more like steak, if it is cut straight down into pieces large enough so that there will be no more than 2 or 3 to a portion.

The carver has a problem of fair distribution. In general, the meat in the eye or rounded area of solid meat is the most tender, the narrow-tapering tail is the least tender and the areas very near the bone are the juiciest and tastiest. You may try to give everyone some of each, or leave the tail for seconds, when people might figure that they are lucky to get even that.

Corned Beef. Corned beef is a cured meat, having the same relationship to beef that ham does to fresh pork. The curing solution is usually salt and sodium nitrite or nitrate, which fixes the color so that it remains pink when cooked. However, there are other curing methods that do not affect the color as much, but still produce the typical flavor.

Fig. 7-17. Diagonal slicing

Brisket is the usual cut of corned beef. It is usually somewhat coarse-grained and fatty, and should be tender after stewing.

Standard cooking method is to cover with water and simmer in a covered pan until tender, usually somewhere around an hour for each pound. Home cured beef, or cuts that are exceptionally salty, may be soaked in cold water for a few hours, then cooked in fresh water. Water may also be changed for fresh boiling water during cooking, but this takes away at least as much flavor as it does salt.

Corned beef is served either hot or cold as a main meat dish, often accompanied by horseradish as a seasoning. When hot, it is traditionally eaten with cabbage, which may be cooked in the regular way, or in cooking water poured off the meat. It is the central attraction in the New England Boiled Dinner, Chapter 19.

Corned beef may be difficult to carve neatly when it is hot, as it has a tendency to fall apart. But it may be sliced very thin when cold, and is a popular sandwich filler, particularly with rye bread.

HAMBURGER

Hamburger, known more descriptively as chopped or ground beef, is one of the most popular "cuts" of beef. It can be made from any part of the flesh, but for reasons of economy its quality range is usually from round or chuck steak down to miscellaneous scraps. The best quality is likely to come from chuck, as round does not have as much fat or flavor. It should contain 10 to 20 per cent fat. Less is likely to make it tough and dry, while more (the most common defect) causes excessive loss of weight and bulk in cooking.

Characteristics. General-purpose hamburger is ground once, raw, by the butcher. If it is intended for special fine-grain meat loaf it may be ground again. A butcher shop usually grinds it to order; supermarkets should make it up in fairly small batches several times a day. It can be made at home in a hand grinder, using the fine setting.

Keeping qualities are inferior to those of solid meat. The grinding mixes air and organisms through it, hastening both deterioration and spoilage. It should be kept cold and used within a day or two. For longer storage, make it up into the size and shape in which it will probably be cooked, wrap it well, and freeze it.

Raw hamburger is always tender, because of the grinding. It should also be tender when cooked, but high heat may give it a tough crust and overcooking will toughen it all the way through. Also, both tenderness and taste are likely to suffer if the raw meat is tightly compressed by too-firm handling, or being stored unfrozen under heavy weights. Such mis-handling is probably responsible for the very poor quality often found in hamburgers sold by big roadside restaurants.

Steak. A hamburger steak is almost always an individual portion. Eight ounces is a fairly standard weight, but it can of course be varied upward or downward with ease. It is often composed of two sandwich patties joined side by side.

If made up as a steak, it is usually at least 3/4 of an inch thick. Shape may be oval, round or rectangular.

The meat is preferably plain, but may be mixed with any of a variety of foods and flavorings. Handling and cooking are much the same as for sandwiches, which are described in Chapter 23.

Hamburger steak is usually served as the main course of a meal, with potato and vegetables. It is often topped by fried onions.

As An Ingredient. In addition to being delicious, popular and easy to fix in or near its natural state, hamburger is very valuable as an ingredient in mixes which are usually easy to prepare. These include meat loaf, meat balls of many kinds, chili con carne, stuffed pepper, stuffed cabbage, spaghetti meat sauce and a great many mixtures that have never acquired names.

But it should be understood that it usually can not be substituted in recipes calling for chopped cooked meat, unless you want to press it into very compact patties and cook it first, then grind it. In cooking, the particles of meat tend to become coated with fat, producing a very different texture than meat that has been cooked before it is ground.

VEAL

Veal is generally considered to be the meat of young cattle, from almost newborn (baby or milkfed veal) to about 12 months in age. But one authority limits veal to the zero to 3 months age, and calls the rest of it calf meat.

By any name, veal is strikingly different from the beef of the adult animal. The flesh is usually fine grained, pale or pink when raw and white or light grey when cooked. There may be considerable connective tissue, giving it a tendency toward toughness. The flavor is mild and delicate, and it is often overwhelmed by cooking or serving with highly flavored gravy, sauce or other foods.

The fat is usually firm and white. It occurs mostly in solid masses or rather thick layers, and is not distributed through the lean in fine veins or marbling.

Veal is generally roasted, fried or braised. Its low fat content makes it too dry for broiling, unless it is painted with oil. Cooking temperature is supposed to be slightly lower than for beef, and the meat is always listed for well-done serving only.

Cooked veal can be substituted for either chicken or tuna fish in many recipes.

Roasts. The leg, rump, loin and shoulder of veal are often roasted. Recommended oven temperature is 300° F, or sometimes as high as 350. Time estimates vary from 25 to 40 minutes to the pound, but inside

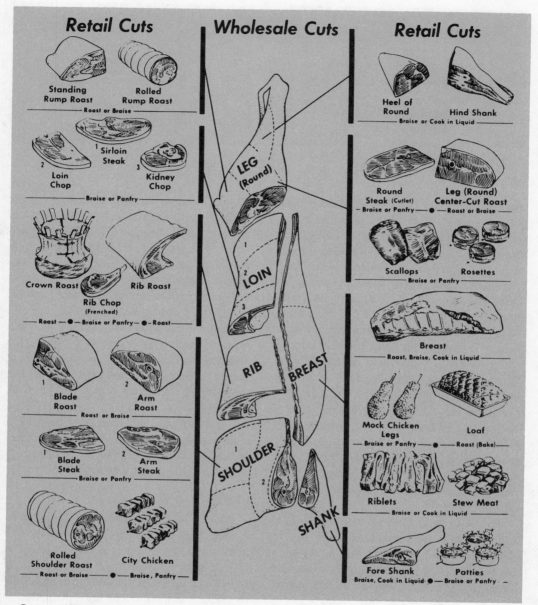

Retail Cuts

Standing Rump Roast
Rolled Rump Roast
— Roast or Braise —

Loin Chop
2
Sirloin Steak
1
Kidney Chop
3
— Braise or Panfry —

Crown Roast
Rib Roast
Rib Chop (Frenched)
— Roast — ● — Braise or Panfry — ● — Roast —

Blade Roast
1
Arm Roast
2
— Roast or Braise —

Blade Steak
1
Arm Steak
2
— Braise or Panfry —

Rolled Shoulder Roast
City Chicken
— Roast or Braise — ● — Braise, Panfry —

Wholesale Cuts

LEG (Round)

LOIN
1
3

RIB

BREAST

SHOULDER
1
2

SHANK

Retail Cuts

Heel of Round
Hind Shank
— Braise or Cook in Liquid —

Round Steak (Cutlet)
— Braise or Panfry — ●
Leg (Round) Center-Cut Roast
— Roast or Braise —

Scallops
Rosettes
— Braise or Panfry —

Breast
— Roast, Braise, Cook in Liquid —

Mock Chicken Legs
— Braise or Panfry — ●
Loaf
— Roast (Bake) —

Riblets
Stew Meat
— Braise or Cook in Liquid —

Fore Shank
Patties
— Braise, Cook in Liquid- ● —Braise or Panfry —

Fig. 7-18. Veal cuts

temperature to finish is agreed upon as 170°. This is plainly a job for your meat thermometer.

In general, best results seem to be obtained by roasting in a covered pan at 300°, with a little water in the bottom to start.

Parts not covered by fat may be moistened occasionally by basting or with cooking oil. The meat may be turned when half done, or left in one position to finish. A rack or trivet is optional.

Cutlet. A veal cutlet is usually a slice of

Courtesy of National Live Stock & Meat Board

Fig. 7-19. Veal chops, rib left, loin right

the leg, but it may be taken from other parts of the animal. It is likely to be 1/2 inch or less in thickness, and may be thinned further by pounding. It is considered to be a great delicacy and commands a very high per-pound price, but is usually given rather brief or second-rate treatment in cook-books.

A standard way to cook a veal cutlet is to coat it lightly with flour, dip it in milk or water-diluted egg and then in crumbs, and fry it. The frying may be done in a little butter or a little grease, or in deep fat. Opinions vary about the pan temperature, some being in favor of very low heat, 250° F or less, while others recommend 350 or more. Deep fat should be about 375°. Cooking time varies from 10 to over 15 minutes, depending on thickness, heat and effect desired.

There are countless variations. On the simple side, leave it unbreaded and fry in butter or braise in butter and water in a covered pan, for 10 to 20 minutes, turning once or more. Or you can do the actual cooking in simmering water, and when it is tender, fry it with or without breading for crispness and color.

In broiling you need to compensate for dryness by repeated oiling or buttering, and by using a non-draining pan as if it were a fish fillet. It can be baked in a pan or utility dish in a little milk, with butter on top, or with tomato or other rich sauce.

A cutlet may be pounded into a very thin sheet to cause or increase tenderness. If the work is thoroughly done, the meat is re-duced to the thickness of weak-kneed card-board, with a considerable increase in area. This may be done before cooking by any method, but it is particularly appropriate to scallopini or other methods that involve rolling the meat up with a filling.

Chops. Veal chops are usually cut about an inch thick. Pan frying is probably the standard way of cooking, with or without breading, but any method may be used. Put some butter or oil on top if you broil or bake them.

It is traditional that veal must be cooked until well done, but both flavor and tender-ness of the chops are likely to be improved if they are slightly underdone.

FRESH PORK

Pork is the flesh of the swine, also known as hog, pig and porker. It is usually both tender and tasty, and it is very popular. It is sold both as fresh meat in the form of roasts and chops, and cured with salt and/or smoked as ham, bacon and specialties.

Figure 7-20 shows some of the more popular pork cuts, with the cooking method or methods recommended.

There are no Federal grades for this meat, as differences in tenderness are small and are difficult to predict. But it should be U.S. Inspected and Approved.

The most popular cuts for roasting are the loin and the leg.

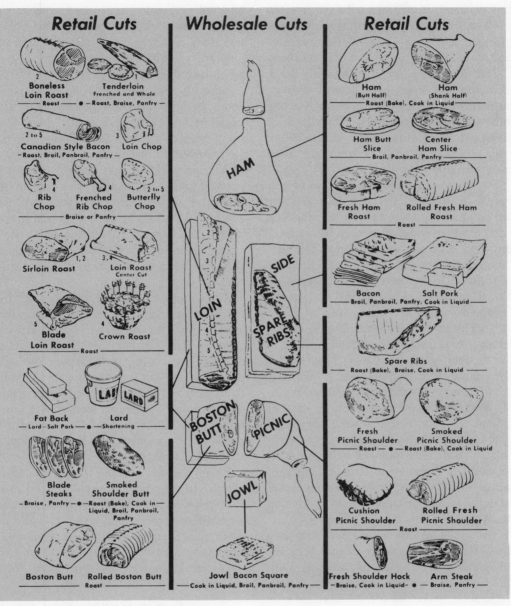

Retail Cuts   Wholesale Cuts   Retail Cuts

Boneless Loin Roast
— Roast —

Tenderloin
Frenched and Whole
● — Roast, Braise, Panfry —

Canadian Style Bacon
— Roast, Broil, Panbroil, Panfry —

Loin Chop

Rib Chop

Frenched Rib Chop

Butterfly Chop
— Braise or Panfry —

Sirloin Roast

Loin Roast
Center Cut

Blade Loin Roast

Crown Roast
— Roast —

Fat Back
— Lard — Salt Pork — ● — Shortening —

Lard

Blade Steaks
— Braise, Panfry — ● — Roast (Bake), Cook in Liquid, Broil, Panbroil, Panfry

Smoked Shoulder Butt

Boston Butt

Rolled Boston Butt
— Roast —

HAM

LOIN

SIDE

SPARE RIBS

BOSTON BUTT

PICNIC

JOWL

Ham
(Butt Half)

Ham
(Shank Half)
— Roast (Bake), Cook in Liquid —

Ham Butt Slice

Center Ham Slice
— Broil, Panbroil, Panfry —

Fresh Ham Roast

Rolled Fresh Ham Roast
— Roast —

Bacon

Salt Pork
— Broil, Panbroil, Panfry, Cook in Liquid —

Spare Ribs
— Roast (Bake), Braise, Cook in Liquid —

Fresh Picnic Shoulder

Smoked Picnic Shoulder
— Roast — ● — Roast (Bake), Cook in Liquid —

Cushion Picnic Shoulder

Rolled Fresh Picnic Shoulder
— Roast —

Fresh Shoulder Hock
— Braise, Cook in Liquid — ● —

Arm Steak
— Braise, Panfry —

Jowl Bacon Square
— Cook in Liquid, Broil, Panbroil, Panfry —

Courtesy of National Live Stock & Meat Board

Fig. 7-20. Pork cuts

Trichinosis. The principal problem with pork is trichinosis infection. The parasite Trichinella spiralis (usually referred to in the plural as trichinae) is a minute worm (nematode) that is born in the intestinal wall, then enters the blood stream and finally the muscles. Here trichinae grow for a while, causing both local inflammation and general poisoning of the system, and then become dormant and are encased in cysts, where they eventually die and are absorbed by the body, or remain as tiny dots of calcified material. If the infected flesh is eaten while they are alive, the worms are released to breed and have young in the intestinal wall of the animal or person that ate them.

Trichinae are widespread in many hosts, including rats, dogs, cats, bears and man, but man usually acquires it through eating infected undercooked pork, either fresh or cured. The porker usually is infected from pork scraps in garbage, or from rodents or rodent droppings in his feed.

For many years about 6 per cent of garbage-fed hogs and one per cent of those fed on grain were infected. Better practices, particularly in cooking garbage before feeding it to hogs are now reducing this percentage. Also, quick tests for the presence of trichinae in the meat are becoming available. It is to be hoped that this disease will become very rare in the near future.

Trichinosis is an unusual disease in that its severity is likely to be directly related to the number of worms eaten. They have a large number of trouble-causing offspring, but these do not ordinarily breed and multiply until they have moved on to another animal. If only a few worms are eaten, symptoms may be so slight that they are not noticed. But if the number is large, either because of ingesting a large quantity of meat, or very heavy infection in a small quantity, symptoms may be very severe and death may result.

The trichinae are also unusual among disease-causing organisms in that they are killed completely by severe freezing. Pork that has been kept at a temperature of zero Fahrenheit or below for 30 days may be considered safe to eat raw or rare, if you want it that way.

Unfrozen pork should always be cooked until it is at least medium-well done. Unfortunately, over-caution often leads to cooking it much too long, until it becomes dry and tasteless. It is only necessary to cook it to 150° F, or, for complete safety, to the 185° recommended by cookbooks or

until all pink color has turned to white or grey. Cured pork stays pink, so the color test does not apply, and temperatures of only 160 to 170° are recommended. In the laboratory, all trichinae are killed by 137° F.

Loin. A complete loin is a row of pork chops in one undivided piece. There are usually 10 or 12 rib chops and 7 loin. The small ends of the ribs (tails of the chops) are trimmed off and used as spareribs.

A complete loin may weigh 10 to 14 pounds, but it is usually sold either as halves, or as 3 pieces: the center, the loin end and the shoulder end. They are given in order of desirability, but the differences among them are often much smaller than between the same cuts from different animals.

The chops are attached to each other by the backbone or plate, which makes the meat almost inaccessible, particularly among the ribs. The butcher should correct this difficulty by sawing or chopping through the backbone between each pair, leaving them attached to each other by the meat; or by sawing lengthwise through the connections to the backbone. Either way the loin is left in one piece, and flesh and bones are roasted together.

Recommended cooking time is 30 to 50 minutes to the refrigerator-cold pound in a 350° oven, uncovered. It is advisable to use a meat thermometer and to get its point in the circular section of solid meat. Well done temperature is 185°. This is a generous 45° above minimum safety temperature. You

Fig. 7-21. Pork loin roast

Courtesy of National Live Stock & Meat Board

Fig. 7-22. Carving a pork loin

would still be safe at 175 or 180°, and the meat might be even tastier.

Keep the fat side up during the whole cooking period, for juice conservation and self-basting. Some recipes tell you to cut the surface of the fat into a pattern of squares, others say to cut most of it off. Neither is necessary.

Pork drippings tend to be very fat, so some of it should be ladled or poured off before making gravy.

Carving. The ease of carving a loin depends mostly on the quality of its preparation by the butcher. If the backbone has been sawed off, there is little opportunity for him to have made a mistake, and you should have no problem. This cut goes only through the bone, a strip of meat being left to hold the two pieces together. After cooking, you continue the butcher's cut through the meat, as close to the backbone as possible, as in Figure 7-22, top. Remove the backbone. This is often done in the kitchen, and only the final carving is done at the table.

Then place the loin on this freshly cut side, with the ribs facing you. Hold it with a fork inserted in the top, and make parallel downward cuts between the ribs. In a large loin you may make two cuts for each rib, one close to each side. This will produce thin slices of meat, alternately with bone and without it. Or you can make single cuts about midway between pairs of ribs, mak-

ing thick slices or chops each of which contains a rib.

If the backbone is chopped or sawed between the ribs instead of being removed, you have to use single cuts and the carved loin will become a platterful of chops. You hold the loin with the fork, with the rib ends up, and slice downward. Your cut in the meat often does not connect exactly with the cut through the bone, so that your slice or chop does not come free.

You can usually break it loose. Hold the loin with the fork, close to where you are working. Insert the knife (which should be a strong one) as far down into the bone at the bottom of your cut as you can, and press it down and twist it at the same time. This tears muscle and ligament and maneuvers the knife around edges of bone.

If the bone was not cut all the way through, it may or may not be broken by this treatment. If not, you can cut it with a butcher's cleaver, a hatchet or a hacksaw. Or you can dodge the issue by serving a double-thick chop.

Leg. The leg, usually referred to as fresh ham or the ham, is a good solid piece of meat, usually weighing 8 to 12 pounds including a large bone. It may be bought and used whole, or in halves called the butt and the shank ends. The butt is usually heavier (about 60 per cent of the whole), has a smaller proportion of meat to bone and provides a wider surface for slicing.

Fresh ham makes a good roast. It can also be partly carved into steaks. In general, it is handled, cooked, carved and used like other leg roasts, and more specifically in the same way as the much more popular cured ham, which will be discussed later.

Recommended oven temperature is 350° F, time 35 to 45 minutes to the pound (longer time for smaller legs) and desired temperature 185°.

Chops. If a pork loin is fully carved by the butcher, it becomes pork chops, which are broiled, fried or baked instead of roasted. They may be from 3/4 to 1-1/2 inches thick, depending on the rib spacing in the animal and eccentricities of slicing them apart. Double-thick chops include two ribs or backbone sections, and therefore have twice the thickness. Some stores now make chops as thin as 1/4 inch by slicing both meat and rib with a band saw.

Frying. You can fry chops on a pan or a griddle, either open or covered. If the chops are thin and/or you use a cover, you can set the burner at medium to medium hot, for a pan heat of 350 to 375° F. But until you are used to cooking them, a temperature of around 300° is safer, with perhaps a last minute finish at high heat if they are not brown enough.

They may be started dry on Teflon, but with other surfaces a light greasing is advisable. You can rub the pan with the fat edge of a chop, or salt it so that it will draw juice out of the meat promptly. Soon afterward you are likely to have too much grease, which you may pour off one or several times during cooking if it gets to be more than 1/8 inch deep.

Unless the pork has been stored at zero Fahrenheit or below for 30 days, you must cook it until it is just well done, with no pink flesh. But you do not want to dry it out and toughen it by cooking beyond that point.

Time in the pan varies with heat, thickness of chops and presence or absence of a pan cover. A one-inch thick chop at 300° ought to cook satisfactorily in 6 or 7 minutes on the first side and 4 or 5 on the second. But it is more usual to give it 10 minutes on each side for safety. Before you take it off to serve it, make a cut or two with a sharp knife, one of them into the circular piece of solid meat. Open the cuts by pulling with the knife and a fork, and check for doneness. If there is pink, turn it over and cook some more, until the color is just gone.

If your chop or chops have been cleared of live trichinae by freezing, you can cut cooking time by about 1/5 and can serve them with a little pink showing, as in medium beef, often with substantial improvement in tenderness and flavor.

Braising. Most cookbooks ignore the very popular custom of frying pork chops, and recommend braising them. The general procedure for plain braising is to salt, sear and brown the chops on both sides in a hot pan, add water from 1/4 inch deep up to sufficient to cover, put on a cover, turn the heat low and simmer for anywhere from 30 to 60 minutes. Differences depend chiefly on what recipe you are reading, but there are necessary variations depending on the thickness of the chops and at what stage you consider them cooked.

Of course, if there is enough water to cover, the chops are being stewed, not braised. But they still taste good.

Gravy may be made from liquid left in the pan after braising, in the same manner as with drippings from a roast.

Fig. 7-23. Shank half of ham

Courtesy of National Live Stock & Meat Board

The water used for braising may be flavored and enriched with a variety of things, including salt, pepper, paprika, garlic, sliced or chopped onions and/or peppers, tomato soup, canned tomatoes, rice or almost anything. The following is a sample of a recipe using such additions.

Pork Chops Creole

6	pork chops
	(about 1½ pounds)
1	medium onion, sliced
1 Tb	green pepper, chopped
1 can	condensed tomato soup
	(about 1¼ cups)
1 cup	water
¼ cup	ketchup
¼ cup	raw rice
2 tsp	tabasco *(optional)*
	salt and pepper to taste

Use a large frying pan, 8 or 10 inch, lightly greased. Brown the chops on both sides over high heat, remove from pan. Brown onions and peppers slightly. Combine all ingredients in the frypan, or in a heavy sauce pan of at least 3 quart capacity. The chops should fit in one layer, but 2 layers can be used.

Simmer in a covered pan on very low heat for about one hour, or until chops are fork-tender. The mixture around the chops should be a thick fluid. If it tends to dry out during cooking, stir in a little hot water.

The rice and other ingredients absorb grease that cooks out of the pork, turning it from a problem into an asset. The ingredients and their proportions may be varied according to whim or materials available.

Ground. Pork may be chopped or ground, either raw or cooked, in the same manner as other meats. It is then used to a small extent in meat loaf and meat balls, but otherwise most of it goes into sausage, which is discussed in a separate section. See Chapter 19, MEAT MIXTURES.

Ground raw pork should be handled with great care, to make sure that not even specks of it get mixed with other foods that might be eaten raw or partly cooked. Hands and utensils should be washed immediately after contact with it.

CURED PORK

Pork is the most popular cured meat, in both salted and smoked types. In solid meats its most widely used forms are ham, bacon and butt. Ground pork is found in the majority of the over 200 varieties of variously cured, smoked and seasoned sausage-type foods, which include many kinds named sausage, and also bologna, frankfurters, luncheon meat, liverwurst and salami.

Ham. The word "ham" means specifically the cured leg of the pig, but it is often used both in reference to uncured pork legs, and to other cuts of cured pork, particularly the butt. Ham is pink in color when in good condition, whether raw or cooked. The color may fade on exposure to air or light. Loss of color may or may not be accompanied by loss of flavor, drying and toughening.

Ham may be slightly or strongly salty. Flavor may be almost lacking, mild or strong, and is affected by the original meat, the type and skill of the curing, aging and the way it is cooked.

A large and increasing proportion of ham is cooked before it is sold to the consumer. To merit the label description "fully cooked" or "ready to eat" it must have reached an internal temperature of 148° F or more during processing. Hams with other labels, even "cook before eating" should have had some cooking, with internal temperature up to 140° or more, in order to kill any trichinae.

Before-sale "full" cooking of ham is done at relatively low temperature, and usually has a favorable effect on both tenderness and flavor. It is sufficient to destroy

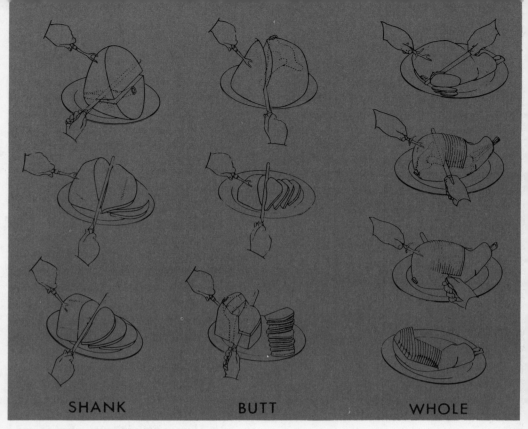

SHANK   BUTT   WHOLE

Fig. 7-24. Carving ham

all trichinae but may not be enough for the average taste. It is intended to be thoroughly heated before serving, after which it will have a cooked texture. This applies to whole and half hams, and to ham steaks.

Virginia hams are cured in a complicated and old fashioned way, and are usually sold raw, and should be soaked and then parboiled before final cooking. This cooking must be thorough.

Cured ham legs may be the same size as fresh hams, or much bigger, up to 24 pounds. One of them will taper from a wide butt to a narrow shank. It may be divided into two pieces near the center. One or both of them may have one or more slices 3/4 to 4 inches thick carved off the cut end, to be sold as center slices.

The butt has thicker meat in proportion to the diameter of the leg bone, but there is additional bone which cuts the proportion of meat below that of the narrower shank. This is not generally understood, and the price per pound for butts is often several cents higher than that for shanks. The best ratio of meat to bone is in the center slices.

A ham is usually roasted (baked) in an oven at 300 to 350° F for 15 to 20 minutes to the pound for a whole ham or 25 to 40 minutes for either half, to an internal temperature of 160 or 170°. But consult any tag or label that comes with it, as cooking time and desired finish temperature are affected by precooking and other special treatment.

A completely precooked ham will take about 10 minutes to the pound to get up to a good serving temperature.

Labeling. The problem of avoiding trichinosis is complicated by the existence of both raw and precooked cured pork and pork products on the market.

124

Cooked and raw ham are similar in color and appearance, except that it may look drier when cooked. Raw ham has a resilient or jelly-like reaction to pressure, while fully cooked ham is firm although soft. But this is not enough of a distinction for an inexperienced person, or even for one who is experienced but careless.

Once pork has been ground and mixed with other substances, there is no easy way to determine whether it is cooked or not. You must know the trade practice, and it may be presumed that it can change. At present, all chopped pork products except fresh sausage appear to have been processed so as to kill all trichinae.

If you cook a cooked ham or pork product instead of just warming it, you are wasting time, heat and energy, and will probably damage the food also. If you do not cook a raw one you are exposing yourself to infection, and it probably won't be good eating either. If you just warm one that is precooked, but you are not sure about it, you may worry too much to enjoy it.

There are so many regulations covering the preparation, labeling and selling of meat that it seems almost unbelievable that processors are not required to label cured pork and pork products as to whether they are cooked, heated enough to kill trichinae, or raw.

BACON

Bacon is a flat cut of meat from the pig's sides, outside the lower (spare) ribs. It consists of alternating layers of fat and lean. It is usually smoked. The original cuts are thin enough so that there is flavor benefit all the way through.

Trimmed slabs are likely to be 1-1/4 inches thick and 9 wide. The slabs are usually sliced to a standard thickness between 1/8 and 1/12 inch. Thick-sliced bacon may be as much as 1/4 inch thick, thin-sliced less than 1/12. Slices are laid together so that they overlap, and packed in 1/2 or 1-pound window boxes, which show only top edges, not full slice.

There is a very large price difference, 100 per cent or more, between different brands of bacon, and there does not seem to be any direct relationship between quality (as indicated by flavor, condition or lean-fat ratio) and price.

Many advisors, both amateur and professional, stress the importance of always selecting the leanest bacon available, because the fat cooks away into waste. This is fine if you like lean bacon, but is not important as an economy. The flesh is about 75 per cent water, which is of no food value whether it stays in the meat or boils off into the air. Even with a 70 per cent loss in fat, you are keeping about as much food value (although not protein) as the lean had in the first place. And it does seem that it is mostly the fat that gives bacon its highly prized flavor.

Bacon is valued both as a minor food and as an ingredient or flavoring. It is seldom used as a main dish, but is an accepted companion to eggs, liver, pancakes, waffles and roe. It is placed on roasting poultry and many baked dishes as a source of fat and flavor and is mixed with spinach and other vegetables to make them taste different. In fact it is probably used a great deal more than it ought to be, as its rather penetrating and distinctive flavor often masks mild and pleasant tastes.

Fig. 7-25. Bacon

Your cookbook will probably recommend broiling or baking for bacon, but most people fry it. Frying is quicker, easier and neater, and results are just as good. Bacon is greasy and splatters badly, and can make a mess of a broiler or an oven.

Bacon may shrink 50 to 85 per cent during cooking, making it a very high priced meat by the time it reaches the table. However, it is usually served in rather small quantities, and its very special flavor and texture are usually well worth its cost.

Frying. For uniform good frying results, use medium heat, around 350°, and put each strip of regular sliced bacon directly on the pan or griddle. However, when the quantity is too great for the space, it is possible to cook several layers at once, but preferably at slightly lower heat. Shrinkage during cooking will allow all of it to reach the pan surface in time for final crisping.

Bacon also cooks well on a hot pan, up to 450°, with increased speed, spatter and danger of burning.

Bacon strips are difficult to separate when they are cold. You can often work them apart with a table knife, but sometimes they just tear into shreds. If you pull on them they stretch. But you can pry off as much as you need in a chunk and put it in the hot frypan. After about 30 seconds turn it over, and with the turner and a fork you can peel off 2 or 3 slices, individually or together. Then turn it again and take off some more.

Or, if you think of it, you can take the bacon out of the refrigerator 30 to 40 minutes ahead of time, and separate the strips without difficulty when you are ready to cook it.

The 9-inch length of a standard strip of bacon is too great for most frypans, although it fits comfortably on a square griddle. You can shorten the strips by cutting the whole package of bacon down the center, if you don't mind the short pieces.

Bacon tends to curl and twist as it cooks,

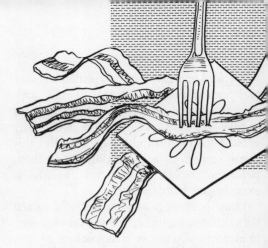

Fig. 7-26. Lifting bacon with two tools

and the parts that are raised above the pan or grease cook much more slowly than the rest. For a uniform result you keep pushing them down firmly with the turner. There are special devices that will hold down a whole panful of bacon, so that it comes out flat without a struggle. But they are a mess to clean, and flat bacon may look a little dull.

Bacon can be turned and manipulated on the pan with just a turner (or spatula) or just a fork, but it is easier and neater if you use both of them. Bacon strips have very little weight and may acquire very irregular shapes, so that control with one tool may be difficult.

Bacon splatters a fine mist of grease over surrounding areas of the stove top. The hotter it is the more it spatters, with bigger drops over a wider range. It may be possible to buy a 3-sided shield to hold part of this in, but it is usually just as easy to wipe off the stove when you are through.

At medium heat standard bacon slices take from 2 to 4 minutes to cook on one side, and the same time or only half that long after turning. There is considerable variation because of differences in the bacon itself, actual heat at a particular pan location, amount of curling and quantity of grease. Slices near the pan edges may be much slower than those in the center, but you can even this up by shifting them around. Deeper grease usually provides faster and more even cooking. You take the bacon off when it is done as much as you wish.

Fat. You usually put bacon in a dry frypan, as it quickly renders out plenty of grease for its own cooking. However, there is no disadvantage to starting with a liberal amount of hot grease from a just-finished batch.

The fat of raw bacon is an opaque white or off-white color. When partly cooked it turns semi-transparent or translucent, and when fully cooked it becomes opaque again, with a chalky to golden-brown color. It is then said to be crisped. The change from translucent to crisp may be abrupt, like a tiny explosion. The lean changes appearance only slightly.

Your cookbook probably tells you to pour off grease one or more times during frying. If you have a large amount in a big pan this is a worthwhile safety precaution, but otherwise it is a poor cooking suggestion. Bacon will never absorb grease as it exudes it at about the same rate whether it is in grease or in air, and a greater or less fat content is of no importance anyhow. Leaving grease in the pan promotes evenness of cooking, as it conducts the heat of the pan bottom to parts of the strips that have curled away from it.

When cooking is finished (or during cooking if you prefer) the grease usually is poured into a can or other container to cool. Many cooks save it for general frying or flavoring. If you just discard it, a can containing solid grease is less troublesome in garbage than the same amount of hot fluid grease.

How Much Cooking? Bacon is supposed to be well done, that is, the fat should be crisped. Health protection is the principal reason with bacon that has not been freezer-stored. It may be that full cooking is not necessary to destroy trichinae, and in any case it would be unusual to get any-

thing worse than a mild infection from a few slices of half-cooked bacon. But it is wise to avoid any unnecessary risk. Another point is that underdone bacon is limp, is inclined to be tough and poor-flavored for the average American taste. However, in some other countries that do not have a trichinosis problem people strongly prefer bacon in the limp stage.

If cooking is continued past the crisping point on medium low heat the color of both fat and lean will darken and the lean will harden. At higher temperatures parts of both fat and lean will burn black, sometimes while other parts are uncooked.

A cook should not be proud of burnt bacon, and it should not be mixed in with other foods. But limited burned spots do not make it unfit to serve as a side dish, with eggs, for example. Some people like or do not object to a little burn, and those who do not like it can cut it out and leave it.

Draining. Cooked bacon is easiest to handle if you pour the grease out of the pan before removing it, but this is not absolutely necessary.

Take the strips out one by one, or several at a time, with a fork and/or a turner, and put it on absorbent paper such as a napkin or towel, to drain. There may be quite a bit of grease, so put newspaper or a plate under the paper. If you are not going to serve it immediately, put another paper towel or any kind of porous cover over it to preserve heat without losing crispness.

Draining, including absorption back into the bacon of grease that did not drain or blot off, should only take a minute or two.

Pre-Cooking. You can interrupt your cooking of bacon without serious harm. It is standard practice in quick-service restaurants to pre-cook a substantial quantity of bacon by either frying or baking, put it on a platter after draining, and cook it another minute or so just before serving. There is seldom any reason to go to this trouble in the home, except perhaps if bacon and eggs are to be served to a number of guests.

Precooking may be partial or complete. Bacon warms up in a few seconds on a hot pan, so that reheating need not overcook it even when it is already well done.

LAMB

Lamb is the flesh of lambs, which are young sheep, usually between 6 and 12 months old. Milk fed lamb may be 3 or 4 months old, and weigh as little as 32 pounds. Special breeds of sheep are used for meat production, others for wool.

After the age of 12 months, sheep are considered to be adult and their meat is called mutton. But one authority says that they are lamb up to 18 months. Mutton is seldom found in American stores.

Lamb and mutton are the only meats that are not banned by any religion (unless vegetarians are considered to be a religious sect), but these meats are not really popular outside of Australia, Britain and New Zealand. Consumption of lamb in the United States is less than 4 pounds per capita.

Figure 7-27 shows some standard cuts of lamb, with suggestions about cooking methods. The meat is usually tender, as is shown by the variety of cuts for which broiling or roasting are recommended.

Lamb has a pleasant and characteristic flavor, which tends to get stronger as the animal ages. The raw ranges from pink to deep red in color, darkening to a variable extent with maturity. It is fine textured and firm, with a moderate amount of marbling. The fat is white and brittle.

Cooking. Many authorities insist that lamb should be medium-well or well done, with an internal temperature of 175 or 180° F. No reason is given, and the cook is left to wonder whether the interdict against rare lamb is due to tradition, taste, texture or parasites. Other cookbooks are more liberal, suggesting 170° for "pink-ish", and one mentions that most Europeans prefer lamb rare, at 160 to 165°. The situation actually seems to be the same as with beef; tenderness is at a maximum, and flavor is best for the average unprejudiced taste in the rare-to-medium bracket, but people who prefer it well done for any reason are certainly entitled to have it that way.

Roasting. Lamb is usually roasted at a temperature of 300 to 325° F, 25 to 35 minutes to the pound. All authorities agree that the pan should be uncovered.

The leg and other lamb cuts often have a thin skin, called a fell. Some cookbooks tell you to take it off before cooking, as it makes the flavor too strong, others tell you to leave it on to conserve moisture and flavor, and to keep it in shape. Obviously, you can take your choice.

If lamb is roasted with the fat side up it does not need turning or basting. Most recipes recommended rubbing with salt and pepper before cooking, which can do little harm. But an equally common instruction to rub it with garlic, or to insert small pieces of garlic in shallow knife cuts, should be disobeyed if you want to be able to enjoy the flavor of the lamb itself.

Broiling. Lamb chops and steaks are usually broiled about 3 inches below the heat, if thickness is 1 to 1-1/2 inches, and 3-1/2 to 4 inches below it if they are 2 inches thick or more. Broiling time varies widely with the thickness, heat and with the thoroughness of cooking. A 1-inch chop may be broiled 5 to 7 minutes on one side, and about a minute less on the other. A 2-inch piece should take about twice as long. It is best to check for color by means of a small knife cut, preferably near a bone.

Before cooking, remove the fell. Either cut off thick fat, or slash through it at 1-inch intervals so that it will not contract and cause the meat to curl.

Frying (Pan Broiling). According to

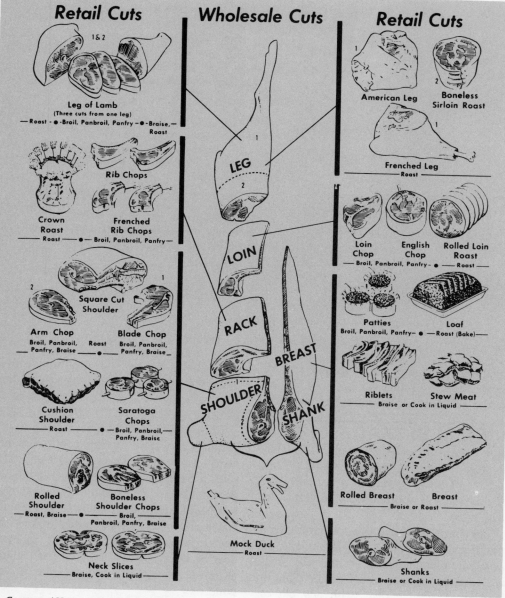

Retail Cuts

Leg of Lamb
(Three cuts from one leg)
—Roast - ● -Broil, Panbroil, Panfry - ● -Braise,—
Roast

Rib Chops

Crown Roast
—Roast —

Frenched Rib Chops
● — Broil, Panbroil, Panfry—

Square Cut Shoulder

Arm Chop
Broil, Panbroil, Panfry, Braise

Roast
●

Blade Chop
Broil, Panbroil, Panfry, Braise

Cushion Shoulder
— Roast —

Saratoga Chops
● —Broil, Panbroil,—
Panfry, Braise

Rolled Shoulder
—Roast, Braise ● —

Boneless Shoulder Chops
Broil, Panbroil, Panfry, Braise

Neck Slices
— Braise, Cook in Liquid —

Wholesale Cuts

LEG

LOIN

RACK

BREAST

SHOULDER

SHANK

Mock Duck
— Roast —

Retail Cuts

American Leg

Boneless Sirloin Roast

Frenched Leg
— Roast —

Loin Chop

English Chop

Rolled Loin Roast
— Broil, Panbroil, Panfry- ● —   — Roast —

Patties
Broil, Panbroil, Panfry- ●

Loaf
—Roast (Bake)—

Riblets

Stew Meat
— Braise or Cook in Liquid —

Rolled Breast

Breast
— Braise or Roast —

Shanks
— Braise or Cook in Liquid —

Courtesy of National Live Stock & Meat Board

Fig. 7-27. Lamb cuts

most cookbooks you don't fry lamb chops or steaks, you pan broil them. As explained elsewhere, to pan broil is to fry with a minimum of fat, starting the process with just a film of grease (often obtained by rubbing a fatty edge of the meat on the pan

as it is heated) or, with Teflon or good black iron, no grease at all. And if any substantial amount of grease renders out of the food, pour it off.

The reason for barring or limiting grease while frying lamb is not clear. It can be

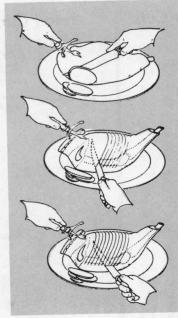

1. With lower leg bone to right, remove two or three lengthwise slices from thin side of leg. This side has the knee cap.

2. Turn roast up on its base and, starting where shank joins the leg, make slices perpendicular to leg bone or lift off cushion similar to method shown for picnic shoulder.

3. Loosen slices by cutting under them, following closely along top of leg bone. Lift slices to platter for serving.

Courtesy of National Live Stock & Meat Board

Fig. 7-28a. Carving a lamb leg

fried very acceptably in a normal amount of grease, as long as it is drained or blotted before serving. The important thing, without grease or with it, is not to overcook it, as it shrinks and toughens rapidly as soon as it passes the well-done stage. It is safest to stop cooking when there is still at least a trace of pink showing in a test cut. This is even more important with mutton than with lamb.

Serving. Lamb has either a natural or a traditional partnership with mint jelly, or as a close second choice, currant jelly. This is served on the side, either on the plate or in a small serving dish, with any cut or preparation of lamb, except possibly stew. A thin gravy may be flavored and decorated with mint.

Roast lamb is carved into slices immediately before the meal. Figure 7-28 shows a recommended cutting procedure, somewhat over-simplified. Gravy is usually served in a boat, rather than poured over the meat.

A rib lamb chop may be fitted with a paper frill around the bone, as a signal that it may be picked up for convenience in gnawing the meat off the bone.

Chopped Lamb. Ground lamb (lamburger?) is widely available, but it is not nearly as popular as chopped beef. It is sold in patties, about hamburger sandwich size; packaged with ground pork and beef for meat loaf or occasionally by the pound. When cooked by itself it seems to lack the tender juiciness found in either chopped beef or whole pieces of lamb, particularly as it is common practice to serve it well done.

ORGANS (VARIETY MEATS)

These edible organs are also called meat specialties and even sundries, as the American public apparently does not want to be reminded of their nature. Each of them has a distinctive flavor and consistency, except that there is a strong resemblance between brains and the two different glands called sweetbreads. In general, there is less variation in the meat of similar organs from different animals than there is in their flesh, and they may lack any characteristic flavor of the animal itself.

The organs are all good protein food, and many of them are very high in vitamins and minerals. Flesh does not provide complete nourishment for humans unless organs are eaten also.

The popularity of the organs for food in the United States suffers from both squeamish and delusion-of-grandeur attitudes. People tend to feel more carnivorous when eating organs than when eating flesh, and also think that organs are inferior parts of the animal and that their consumption involves a lowering of dignity. On the other hand, health and vitamin fads have managed to establish liver, particularly calves' liver, as an esteemed and often very high-priced food.

Liver. The liver, found in all vertebrates, is the largest gland in the body. It has many important functions, including filtering and purifying blood, storing food, production of special proteins and of antibodies and secretion of digestive fluids. At the butcher's it is a lump of smooth, tender and apparently structureless flesh, pale to dark brown in color, surrounded by a membrane and penetrated by a moderate number of tough tubes which carried blood and various products. On the table, it is a tasty protein food that is very rich in vitamins and minerals.

Livers can be bought and cooked whole, but the vast majority of them are cut into slices that average about 1/2 inch in thickness. The slices can be made easier to eat by removal of the tubes before cooking, by cutting with sharp-pointed scissors or a knife while pulling on them. However, it is likely that most liver is served without this servicing.

Raw liver is tender, but has a jelly-like consistency and a raw or undeveloped

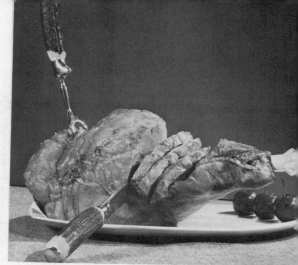

Courtesy of National Live Stock & Meat Board

Fig. 7-28b. Carving a lamb leg

flavor. It cooks very quickly, about 2-1/2 to 4 minutes on a side in a 300° F frypan. It should be slightly pink in the center when served, as it will then retain its original tenderness and have gained a firm texture and best flavor. It may be equally good when just well done, but is likely to dry and toughen in only a few seconds after this stage.

Liver is usually fried or braised, but it may be broiled. Frying is preferably done in a small amount of butter or margarine, with a larger amount added just before removing from the pan. The pan may be either covered or open. The new butter is stirred into the material left in the pan, making a small amount of a particularly tasty gravy that is poured over the liver just as it is served.

Liver is traditionally served with crisp bacon or with pan-fried onions. It may be served as a main dish at any meal. For lunch it may be accompanied by only a simple salad or a small serving of peas or another vegetable, while for dinner there are potatoes also.

For braising, use a couple of tablespoons of water in addition to the butter, cover the pan tightly and cook at a lower temperature. Time may be the same or a minute longer. Addition of more butter for gravy in the same manner is recommended.

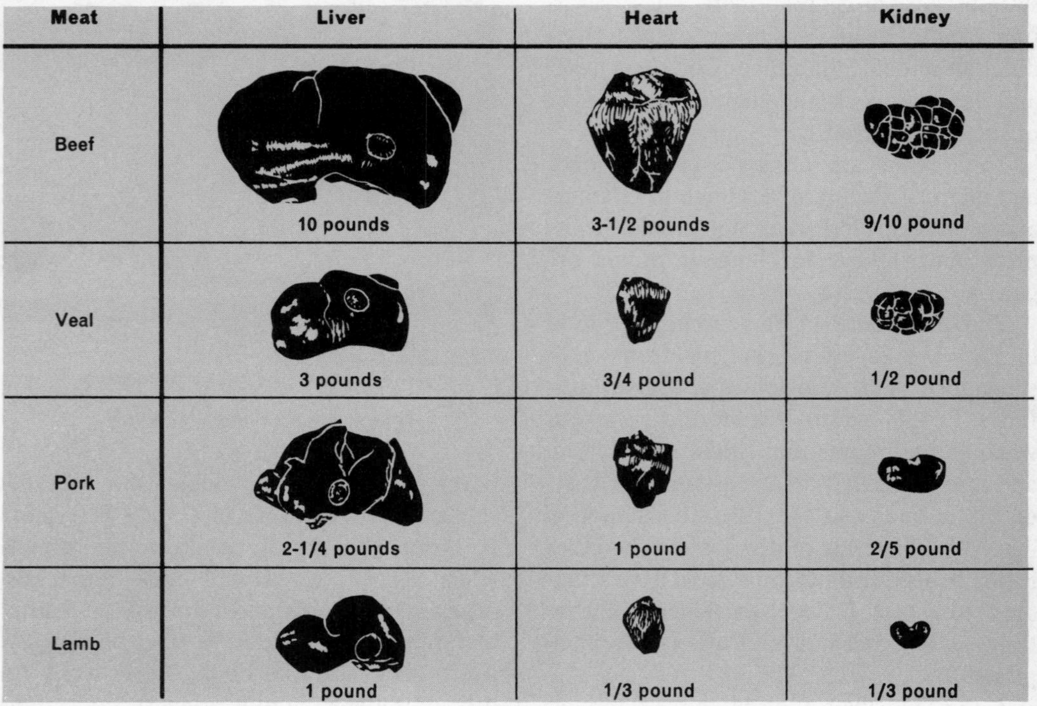

Meat	Liver	Heart	Kidney
Beef	10 pounds	3-1/2 pounds	9/10 pound
Veal	3 pounds	3/4 pound	1/2 pound
Pork	2-1/4 pounds	1 pound	2/5 pound
Lamb	1 pound	1/3 pound	1/3 pound

Courtesy of Armour and Co.

Fig. 7-29. Edible organs (variety meats)

Cooked liver may be chopped or ground for use in paté, for which see the recipe in Chapter 19.

Kidneys. Kidneys are a pair of blood filtering organs that are tender and tasty when taken from young animals, and which are always rich in nourishment. Veal and lamb kidneys are considered to be most desirable for tenderness and flavor, particularly when relatively light in color. The much larger beef kidneys are more economical and still reasonably good and those from pork are considered by many to have too strong a flavor. Beef and pork kidneys are often soaked in cold salt water for two hours, and/or blanched (cooked very briefly) in boiling water containing a tablespoon of vinegar to the pint, allowed to cool, and then cooked in a regular way.

Kidneys are surrounded by a membrane. This should be removed from beef kidneys, and perhaps from large ones of other kinds. Small pointed scissors, especially curved ones, are convenient for this job.

There is a core of tubes and fat which is tender and tasty in small kidneys, but which is usually removed from large ones after slicing the organ in half. There is little waste anyhow. Figure on 4 to 6 ounces uncleaned weight per person.

Young kidneys are usually fried or broiled for 4 to 8 minutes on a side. If sliced 1/4 inch thick, or cubed, they will cook in a minute or two. Overcooking toughens them. Older ones are braised or stewed.

They may be served plain, with butter or with cream gravy, and may be put on toast or nested in rice. They are used in stew, alone or with beef.

Sweetbreads. The most common type of sweetbreads, the ones that come in unequally-sized pairs, are thymus glands. They are located in the upper chest of young mammals, and are often called neck or throat sweetbreads, to distinguish them from the single pancreas gland, sold as the stomach sweetbread. There are sharp differences in preference.

Sweetbreads are soft, tender and delicately flavored. It is standard practice to prepare them in stages. First you simmer them in water to cover for about 20 minutes. This water is made slightly acid by adding a tablespoon of vinegar or lemon juice and a teaspoon of salt for a quart. The cooking loosens the membrane, which you then remove with your fingers under cold running water. The acid keeps them white and firm.

Next you use a knife to cut out veins and dark connective tissue. If you are not ready for the final cooking, put them in the refrigerator.

Sweetbreads may be fried in butter, with or without breading, for 3 to 6 minutes on each side. Or broiled 3 inches below the heat for the same period, after brushing with oil to prevent drying. You can serve them plain, with butter, on toast, with cream gravy or mix them into omelets or other prepared dishes. Three to 5 ounces makes an average serving for one person. There is very little waste.

Brains. The preparation and serving of brains is very similar to that described above for sweetbreads.

Heart. Heart is usually a rather hard, compact meat with a tendency toward toughness. It is economical both because of low price and small amount of waste. You can figure about 1/4 pound undressed weight to a serving. Lamb hearts may weigh only 1/4 pound, beef hearts may be over 3 pounds.

A heart is prepared for cooking by cutting out the coarse fibers and tubes at the top and inside, then rinsing. Some cookbooks recommend soaking a beef heart overnight in a quart of water and 2 tablespoons of vinegar, to tenderize it.

You can slice the heart about 1/2 inch thick, or dice it, and cook it in butter in a frypan over low heat for about 15 minutes, turning at least once. Or cover the pieces with boiling water and simmer until tender.

Tripe. Tripe is the inner lining of the beef stomach. There are three varieties, honeycomb, pocket and plain. Honeycomb is considered to be the best, and it is the type most often found in the market.

Any type may be sold fresh, pickled or canned. Fresh tripe has been partly cooked at the packing house, but its keeping quality is still not supposed to be good. Pickled tripe is fully cooked, but will probably need soaking in fresh water for a while to reduce the pickled taste. Canned tripe is ready to heat and serve.

It is customary to cook fresh tripe by simmering in salted water, covered, for about 1-1/2 hours or until tender. It may then be drained and perhaps blotted, and served in pieces with butter, white sauce or tomato sauce, plus salt and pepper.

Pieces of cooked tripe may be breaded by dipping into an egg beaten with a tablespoon of water, then in bread crumbs, and then fried in butter or hot fat until golden brown. Or it may be fried unbreaded, or brushed with melted butter and broiled 3 inches below the flame, about 5 minutes on a side. It may also be used as a minor ingredient in soup or stew.

Tripe is white or very light in color,

Courtesy of National Live Stock & Meat Board

Fig. 7-30. Slicing pattern for tongue

slightly tough or rubbery in texture and mild in flavor.

Tongue. Tongue is composed mostly of striated muscle, and is therefore similar to the flesh of other parts of the animal. However, it has a distinctive flavor and slightly spongy texture. It may be somewhat stringy at the base and along the sides, but most of the meat is very smooth. There is little waste, only the skin and some gristle and small bones at the root. Allow one pound for 4 to 6 servings. Beef tongues weigh 2 to 5 pounds, veal 1/2 to 2 pounds and lamb about 4 ounces.

Tongue is usually cured, but occasionally is available fresh. It may also be obtained cooked in cans or jars, sliced and packaged for sandwiches, or pickled.

Raw tongue is cooked by simmering in sufficient water to cover until it is tender, which may take 2 to 4 hours. Larger and older tongues take longer. Immediately after cooking, dip in cold water, slit the skin and peel it off from the root end. It may come off easily, like a glove, but sometimes needs help by cutting it free from the meat in spots with a sharp paring knife. Cut out and discard any bone or gristle at the root (thick) end.

Tongue is usually sliced across the grain, starting at the root. A somewhat slanting cut may be required, particularly toward the tip. Slicing is much easier cold than hot. Cold slices may be 1/8 inch thick, hot slices at least twice that.

Tongue may be used like corned beef as the meat part of a boiled dinner, or served sliced either hot or cold or used as a sandwich meat in the same manner as ham. It goes well with horseradish sauce. It is often eaten with mustard or barbecue sauce, or served in salad platters.

8
POULTRY

POULTRY

Poultry is a word that means both a group of domestic birds and the meat of those birds. The important ones are chickens (including rock Cornish hens), turkeys, ducks and geese. There are also less common domestic species such as pigeons (squab), guinea hen; and similar game birds such as pheasant, partridge, grouse and quail.

Poultry is a very important source of human food. The most popular species are well adapted to both being raised in small flocks or as a few individuals, and to mass production under factory-like conditions. Eggs, particularly chicken eggs, are an essential part of man's diet throughout most of the world.

Flesh. Like the meat of mammals, poultry flesh is made up of muscle fiber with associated connective tissue and fat, and the fiber is made up of high qaulity complete protein.

Birds' meat is usually white, grey or brown in color, whether raw or cooked, because it does not contain myoglobin, the oxygen-rich chemical that gives the red color to most raw mammal (red) meat. The fat is creamy yellow in color, soft in texture and is chiefly found immediately under the skin, instead of being distributed through the flesh. It contains a good proportion of unsaturated fats and is said to be low in cholesterol.

In chickens and turkeys the breast and wing meat is usually white, the rest dark. Duck and goose meat is all dark.

The white meat in the breast tends to be somewhat drier, tougher and less flavorful than the dark. But it is so strongly preferred that producers are busy breeding new strains with a larger proportion of white. Even without this development, white meat outweighs the dark.

The white meat has a higher percentage of protein that is found in the dark, or in any red meat. See page 631.

Structure. When considered as food, the most important difference in structure from mammals is the development of the breast muscles, which are the source of power for both up and down motions of the wings. The lower or forward ends of these muscles are anchored to the breastbone. This is enlarged forward and downward by a

135

Fig. 8-1. Roasting a bird

flange, so shaped that the whole bone is frequently called a keel.

More than half of a bird's flesh may be made up of these breast muscles. Although domestic poultry flies very little, the muscles are still there, and have been increased by selective breeding. The fact that they are not used much contributes to their tenderness.

The muscles in the wing itself are used

chiefly for regulating shape and pitch of the wing, and are quite small. Most of the wing area is made up of inedible feathers. The back has no important function in flight, and carries little meat.

Chickens and turkeys are well adapted to walking and running, and have a good development of thigh and leg muscles.

Bird bones are hollow and very light. They are brittle when cooked, and tend to break into sharp splinters. This is the reason why it is unsafe to feed a dog with poultry remnants.

The internal organs resemble those of mammals. There is a heart, lungs, stomach (crop or gullet), intestines, liver, gall bladder and kidneys. There is no bladder for urine, as this is voided through the intestine.

The gizzard is a double-walled sack that contains grits used for grinding hard food, which cannot be chewed or broken effectively in the toothless mouth.

Feathers. Except for the feet and parts of the head and legs, most birds are completely covered by feathers. Body feathers provide covering for warmth, color and general appearance, while the large strong wing and tail feathers make light, extensive and easily adjusted surfaces for flying. Down is a type of small, soft body feather which makes up the covering of very young birds, and is found among the adult feathers, where it serves chiefly for warmth. Pin feathers are young feathers that have broken through the skin, but have not opened up.

Feathers are gripped firmly in sockets in the skin, but will come out if pulled with proper force and direction. All of them are removed, a process called plucking, in preparing a bird for eating.

PREPARATION

Most poultry is now bought in ready-to-cook condition, so that no preparation is necessary. However, the need to convey

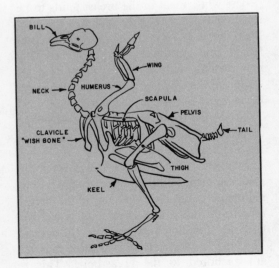

Fig. 8-2. Chicken skeleton

BILL

WING

NECK   HUMERUS

SCAPULA

PELVIS

CLAVICLE "WISH BONE"   TAIL

THIGH

KEEL

a partly prepared or even a live bird into a meal might arise, and a basic cooking text should supply at least minimum information on how to go about it.

For simplicity, the information will be supplied for a chicken, except for leg tendon removal which is usually required only for turkeys, but it can be adapted to any domestic bird.

Selection. If there is any choice among live chickens, the victim should be young, neat and plump, with a bright eye and an alert manner. The comb, if any, should be bright red. If it is possible to plan ahead, it is considered desirable to confine it in a small pen with water but no food for 24 hours before slaughter.

Method of catching the bird is entirely optional.

It is best to avoid tackling a fully developed rooster, as he may fight back effectively, using feet, wings and beak. But like any chicken, he will stop struggling if you can hold him by both legs.

If a chicken has already been killed and plucked, look for plumpness, moist yellow skin, soft legs and feet and a breastbone the lower tip of which bends easily under pressure.

Killing. The approved way of killing a bird is to hang it by its feet, open its mouth, and push a sharp very narrow-bladed knife through its roof into the brain to kill it, and then to cut the two blood vessels in the front of the throat to cause blood to drain. This method is supposed to provide both for relaxation of muscles holding the feathers and for complete drainage of blood, which is desirable.

However, the novice will probably be wiser to confine himself to the simpler operation of cutting off the head, then holding the carcass up by the legs until blood has stopped running.

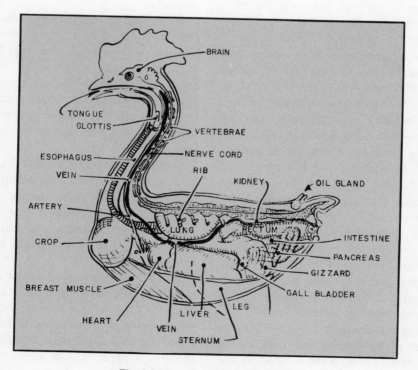

Fig. 8-3. Organs of male chicken

Fig. 8-4. First catch your chicken

Timing. There is a wide range of opinion about the interval that should elapse between killing and eating. It is an old country custom to prepare and cook the bird immediately, with the claim that this gives best results in every way. There seems to be general agreement in other circles that this makes the meat rubbery and flavorless.

Another theory is that the best time to cook is between 8 and 24 hours after killing. And still another says any time after 24 hours, provided refrigeration is used. This last is the condition under which poultry is bought in markets, and it seems to be very satisfactory.

Plucking. Plucking is the process of removing feathers. For greatest efficiency, it should be done immediately after killing. It is most difficult during the rigor mortis period, usually from 4 to 8 hours after death, when the flesh tends to be rigid. It is said that a chilled bird is easier to pluck than one at room temperature.

Plucking may be done dry, or it may be made easier by dipping the bird in hot water, about 140° F. Keep it in water not over 30 seconds, holding it by the legs and moving it up and down a little to get the heat well distributed. This hot water dip, often erroneously called scalding, loosens feathers but it also may cause the skin to deteriorate. It is generally done only with waterfowl (ducks and geese) whose feathers tend to be firmly anchored.

To pluck, you grasp a number of body feathers and move or rub them toward the head (against their natural angle) while pulling lightly. Start near the tail and work toward the head. The problem is to get the feathers out clean without uprooting patches of skin. The rough plucking is not hard and it goes rapidly, but until you are an expert, you will leave a lot of feathers behind and will have to go over it again. The big wing and tail feathers are pulled one by one or a few at a time.

Pin feathers are young, short and unopened. They can be pulled out with tweezers, a strawberry huller or by catching them between your finger or nail and a knife blade.

Down and strays left after the picking may be removed by singeing. You do this by holding the head and the feet and manipulating the carcass over an open flame, usually a gas burner or a candle, closely enough so that loose material will be burned off. You should of course avoid scorching either the skin of the bird or of your hands.

Feather remnants can also be cleaned up by painting the bird with melted paraffin, perhaps combined with several times its bulk of hot water to improve area coverage. When the wax hardens it is pulled off in sheets, and should bring all remaining feathers with it.

Chicken feathers usually have no value, and they can make a mess, particularly outdoors in even a light breeze. Indoors, do the plucking on newspaper which can be rolled up and discarded. Outdoors, stuff them in a paper bag or some other container that is deep and fairly narrow.

Fig. 8-5. Plucking pin feathers

Leg Tendons. The leg muscles of turkeys and large chickens are strengthened by a number of tendons that resemble bone splinters, anchored at the feet and extending up into the drumstick. If well developed they make it difficult to get at the drumstick meat. They should be removed from the raw bird by the butcher, but you might have to do it yourself.

They are easiest to take out when the feet are attached. Cut the skin all the way around the leg a little above the knee, hold the upper leg with the knee projecting over the edge of a table, and break the joint by bending and twisting with the hand. Then pull the foot, slowly but strongly. The tendons should pull out of the flesh, and can be discarded or put into a soup pot with

Fig. 8-6. Removing tendons

other food. If they will not pull free, they can be pried out one by one with a narrow-bladed knife or a skewer.

Drawing (Eviscerating). Taking the innards out of poultry is the messiest part of the preparation. It is a rather simple job once you know how to do it, but it is complicated and unsatisfactory to explain in a book. It is absolutely necessary, as the digestive system produces bad smell and taste if it is cooked inside the bird.

The neck, crop and gullet are removed through an opening or a cut through the neck area. One procedure is to cut the head off (if it has not already been done) leaving the neck as long as possible. Pull the neck skin down, then cut or twist off the spine at the base, where it enters the body. Or you may slit the neck skin down the back to the shoulder, then cut and remove the spine at the shoulder.

You then put a finger in through the hole where the neck bone was and loosen the tubes, crop and gullet from their weak attachment to surrounding membranes, pull them out of the body and cut the connections immediately below them.

The rest of the innards are reached by making a slit from just below the end of the breastbone to just below and then around the vent. This should be deep enough to slice cleanly through the body wall, but should not cut into any of the organs.

The digestive system has now been cut loose at the upper end by removal of the tubes and at the bottom by cutting around the vent end of the intestine. You can therefore remove them by putting a hand in the cavity and pulling them out. The best grip is the gizzard, if you can locate it in the center right. The heart should come out with the other entrails. Also remove the kidneys in hollows near the base of the backbone, and the spongy red lungs toward the front.

Check with your fingers to make certain

that you have removed everything. If there is fat in the cavity you should probably take it out and discard it, as it is often too strongly flavored, and it may make the bird too greasy.

You should also cut out the small oil sac at the base of the tail, which supplied the bird with material for preening its feathers.

If the bird is a hen of laying age, there may be a number of eggs in various stages of development. They are all edible. Those that have shells or shell membranes can be used as regular eggs. Less developed ones are mostly yolk, and are often orange in color. These can be used in any recipe calling for yolks, with adjustment for smaller size.

The final step in drawing is to rinse the body cavity with cold water, also cleaning off any smeared outside parts, then wiping dry. Or you can do the cleaning up without water, just using a damp cloth.

Giblets. You now separate the edible or usable organs from the waste. The liver, the heart and the outer part of the gizzard are known collectively as the giblets. The liver may be included with the two other organs in being chopped fine for mixing with gravy or dressing, or may be saved for other uses discussed later.

The liver is attached to the gall bladder, which is a rather frail sac containing bile, an extremely bitter digestive juice. This must be carefully cut or pulled away without releasing any of the liquid. If part of the liver is discolored, leakage has probably occurred already, and the discoloration must be removed with the bladder. It is much better to lose part of the liver than to risk spoiling all of it with the taste of gall. It is carelessness in this regard that is the cause of the bad taste too frequently found in packaged chicken livers.

The heart is very firm meat. You simply trim off any blood vessels coming out of it.

The gizzard consists of an inner and an outer envelope, the outer one being con-

sidered the gizzard proper. The inner one contains gravel, and must be discarded. You cut into one of the thick sides but not into the inner envelope, put your thumbs in opposite sides of the cut, and peel the gizzard away, turning it inside out.

Disjointing. A chicken is usually divided into 2 (but occasionally 4 to 8) pieces for broiling, or into 6 or 8 parts for frying. Small pieces are good for small children, and cutting is much easier when raw than after cooking.

A broiler should weigh between 1 and 2-1/2 pounds, dressed (cleaned) weight. It is split, or divided into halves, by cutting through the flesh over the backbone and the breastbone, and in a line between them, then cutting lengthwise through or directly beside these bones. Use poultry shears, a strong sharp knife (some people prefer it saw-toothed) or a hacksaw. Break the backbone joints in several places by snapping the cartilage, so that the half will not curl up during cooking.

A frozen chicken can be cut into neat halves with an electric skill saw.

A fryer is in the next size bracket, 2-1/2 to 3-1/2 pounds. It may first be cut in halves in the same manner, or cut through the breast but not the back; then divided into smaller sections with shears or a knife. With the knife, you cut through the flesh at the joint, then wiggle it to get it between the bones to pry them apart.

Frying pieces may be: 2 drumsticks, 2 thighs, 2 wings, 2 pieces of breast and 2 of the back, which may be either the sides or the front and the back. The neck makes an additional piece, which is not highly esteemed. The skin should be left attached to each piece.

ROAST CHICKEN

A roasting chicken or roaster may be from 2-1/2 pounds to over 7, and should be less than 10 months old. In the bottom range it overlaps on the fryer. If over 5 pounds, it is probably a capon (desexed male).

A roaster is a dressed, drawn, but not disjointed bird. Weight should be from 3/4 to 1 pound per person. The chest (gut) and neck cavities are usually stuffed.

Stuffing. Stuffing or dressing, which is used chiefly in poultry but sometimes in fish or meat, is usually a mixture of bread crumbs with seasoning and binders or en-richers. No two cookbooks give just the same ingredients and proportions, and they even disagree hopelessly on the quantity to make.

Stuffing is put mostly in the chest or abdominal cavity of the chicken, but a smaller amount will also go in the front cavity, above the breast. It should be put in loosely rather than firmly, as it tends to swell. You may use from 1/2 to 1 cup per pound of ready-to-cook bird weight. It is safer to make the larger amount. Any surplus can be baked in a greased dish.

Bread crumbs are preferably made from dry white bread with the crusts removed. Sliced bread that is left loosely piled at room temperature should dry enough in about a day. The same result can be obtained in a slow oven or over any source of heat in a few minutes. The bread should be only dry enough to pull apart or crumble readily, but not completely dried out, hard or toasted except for special recipes. The crumbs should be coarse and may be small cubes, as pulverizing them would make the dressing too heavy.

A cooked stuffing may be soggy wet, damp or dry, depending on the preference of the cook or of the locality. This can usually be controlled in the mixing, although occasionally moisture will be absorbed from the bird, or the ingredients may contain or give up an unexpectedly large amount of water.

A simplified recipe for poultry stuffing is:

Bread Stuffing

4 cps	coarse bread crumbs
½ cup	melted butter
⅓ cup	minced onion
½ tsp	salt *(optional)*
⅛ tsp	pepper *(optional)*

Put the crumbs in a bowl and scatter the salt, pepper and onion over them, stirring them with a fork as you do it. Then sprinkle the butter on slowly, still mixing lightly with the fork.

Additional seasonings are usual. You can buy a poultry seasoning that is specially mixed for stuffing. This quantity would take from 1/2 to 1 teaspoon of it. Or you can work up your own combination. Nutmeg and paprika are used among the ground spices, and thyme, tarragon, basil, bay leaf, parsley and sage are candidates among the herbs. But here, as always, experimental seasoning is risky, and if it is done at all it should be with the greatest caution. For a moist, compact dressing, add up to 1/3 cup of condensed chicken bouillon or hot water.

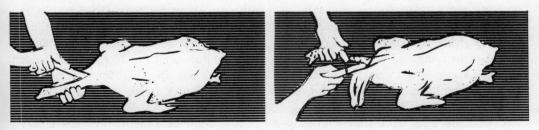

Fig. 8-7. Neck cut

The quantity of minced onion may be doubled, and matched in quantity by chopped celery and/or green pepper.

You can convert this mix into a specialty dressing by adding 1 cup of any one of the following:

Cooked and browned sausage meat
Browned sliced mushrooms
Fried onions
Cooked or half-cooked oysters, chopped
Cooked, chopped shrimp
Cooked, whole baby shrimp
Cooked chestnuts, chopped

There is a question of adding eggs. With this basic mix, and with any of the additives suggested, you can use 1, 2 or 3 eggs, lightly beaten so that they will mix well.

If you make more dressing than you can put in the cavities, you may cook it separately in a pan. It will probably take only about 2/3 as long and be drier, as it will not be protected by the bird's flesh. It may develop an unpleasantly hard crust unless the pan is covered. Flavor is likely to be inferior because of lack of contact with the juices and odors of the poultry during cooking.

Trussing. Trussing is the operation of tying, pinning and/or sewing a roaster bird together to prevent it from falling apart in the oven, and to reduce the danger of overcooking its extremities. You may get satisfactory results without doing it, but it is a safety measure and a pleasant piece of good workmanship.

A loose, dry dressing tends to fall out of the body slits. You can prevent this by coarse sewing, using a darning needle and thin white string, by fastening the sides with skewers or by tying.

If you know how to sew, this method presents no problem. If you don't, it is too complicated to explain here.

Skewers are long thick pins with loop-type heads. To use them, you hold the slit

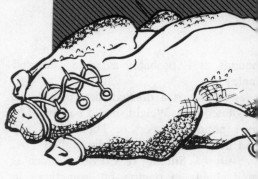

Fig. 8-8. A trussed roaster

closed or nearly closed with one hand, and insert several skewers with the other. They should be about an inch apart and parallel, going through the skin on one side of the slit, then through the dressing and finally through the skin on the opposite side. There should be enough friction between the raw meat and the pins to hold against opening and spillage. As the meat becomes tender with cooking the grip is less secure, but by then the dressing is likely to have become firm enough to stay in place.

The skewers can be made more secure by winding light string or strong thread around them and across the opening, as in Figure 8-8. This also provides an anchor for tying in the legs. They are pulled close in to the body, and string is tied around them, around the tail and laced among the skewers.

Wings may be held in place by a long skewer through both of them and the body, or by wrapping string around them and around the body. Both legs and wings can also be fastened in by sewing.

Roasting. Cookbooks generally recommend roasting chicken uncovered in a moderate oven, 325 to 350° F, but disagree seriously about the time. Good results can usually be obtained with 20 to 30 minutes to the pound for a small bird (under 5 pounds) but only 15 to 20 should be needed for a large one. But there are recipes calling for 40 minutes to the pound for a big chicken.

It is common practice to roast chicken in a covered pan, in spite of official disapproval. This allows using a 25° cooler oven for the same time, or a hot oven for a shorter time. The cover should be left off for the last 10 minutes to crisp the crust. A cover may be made out of a large piece of foil, which may be either form-fitted or loose.

You check a trussed chicken for doneness by pushing a fork into thigh or breast. If it is tender, it is cooked. Or you can wiggle a drumstick of an untrussed bird. If it is loose in its socket it is done.

The meat will carve best if it stands for about 20 minutes after cooking is finished. Put it on a platter in a warm place away from drafts, and cover it with a towel. You need to get it out of the pan to make the gravy anyhow.

The particular problem in roasting poultry is the fact that it is not a solid chunk of meat, so internal circulation of juices is poor and exposed portions tend to dry out. The wings are most sensitive, then the small ends of the drumsticks. In each case there is thin meat directly over bone, with all-around exposure to heat and evaporation. The breast may also be a problem because its meat may be very dry naturally.

The problem is met in a number of ways. Trussing greatly reduces the exposure of wings and legs. A cover on the pan or on the bird reduces the rate of evaporation. Quick-cooking areas may be protected individually by fitting them with little foil

Fig. 8-9. Roast chickens

Courtesy of Poultry and Egg National Board

jackets about halfway through the roasting time. Or use pads of a few layers of cheesecloth under brown paper, tied on with string and kept moist by basting.

Basting, which is the lifting of juices from the pan with a spoon or a syringe and running them over the meat, serves to moisten and cool the exposed surfaces, and provides a taste-promoting circulation of drippings. It is said that in test kitchens it has the unfavorable effect of washing off protective fat, but results in the home seem to be good. You may baste just once or twice, or every 15 to 20 minutes.

Instead of basting, you may paint the surface with oil or melted butter occasionally.

When a chicken is roasted with the breast up, it may be decorated with strips of fat bacon, which protect it directly and by means of the fat rendered out of them. This mixes the flavors in a way that some people like, and others don't.

The position of the bird in the pan is important, particularly if there is no cover. The upper surface dries out most, and the characteristic position on its back with the breast up is the worst possible one.

If you do not have a rack in the pan, and in poultry roasting it is optional, the condition of the bottom will depend on the accumulation of drippings. If there are plenty they will protect it, but the purist may object that this section is being stewed rather than roasted. If the pan goes dry, overcooking will occur at points of contact. If there is a rack, the bottom will cook in the same manner as the sides. In any case, it will get the most benefit from flavorful juices from the stuffing.

Good results can usually be obtained by starting the roasting on one side, shifting it to the other side when almost half done, and using the breast-up position only for a few minutes final browning. This can be done in addition to taking other precautions.

OTHER METHODS

Broiling. Use very young chicken, one to 2-1/2 pounds, split (halved) or quartered for broiling. Put in one layer on a broiling rack, skin side down, in a preheated oven or broiler compartment with the top of the chicken about 4 inches below the heat. Seasoning with salt and pepper and brushing with cooking oil or butter are optional, and may be done either before cooking or during it.

Total broiling time is likely to be between 30 and 40 minutes, with variation depending chiefly on the distance and intensity of the heat, but partly on the heat conducted to the food through the pan. Large chickens will cook more slowly than small ones. Also, if the chicken pieces cover most of the surface of the pan they tend to cook more slowly than if a large part of its area is exposed to the heat. An old fashioned open wire rack will cook them slowest of all, as it absorbs and conducts very little heat.

The upper surface of the chicken is subject to intense drying, while the lower surface keeps moist because of less exposure to heat, and poor air circulation. It is there-fore advisable to turn the pieces over occasionally, perhaps at 10 minute intervals, to equalize these conditions. They may be oiled or buttered at this time if they seem to be drying too much.

There may be one or two high spots which show early symptoms of overcooking or burning. You may ignore this situation as being unimportant, or correct it by rearrangement, or by fitting foil caps over the affected areas when they are up. If there is a general tendency toward over-browning you may lower the pan, or reduce the heat if it is adjustable. If too little color develops, check the heat to make sure it is on full, and if it is, raise the pan to bring the chicken nearer the heat.

Broiled chicken is usually served as is, except that the drippings in the pan may be poured over it.

Breading. Most fried and some baked chicken is breaded, usually with egg and cracker crumbs or with plain flour. But bread crumbs or fritter batter can be used.

General instructions on breading are given on page 53.

A medium size fryer, weighing 3 pounds, may require from 1 to 2 cups of crumbs, with 1 or 2 eggs — perhaps 2 medium or 1

Fig. 8-10. Turning breaded chicken

jumbo — beaten lightly with 2 tablespoons of milk or water.

Either crumbs or flour may be seasoned with salt or pepper, or left plain.

Pan Frying. Cooking is done in a frypan wide enough to cook a number of pieces in a single layer. For a deluxe dish with finest flavor, fry in butter. Many people like margarine as well. It is more common to use cooking oil, for its combination of low price and stability, sometimes mixed with a little butter for flavor. Breaded chicken soaks up a lot of grease, so it will probably have to be replenished frequently during cooking. Start with a depth of about 1/4 inch and keep it near that, or at least do not allow any part of the pan to go dry. The pan may or may not be covered at first, but is usually uncovered for the last half of the cooking time, to promote crispness.

Cooking temperature may be medium low to medium high, anywhere from 250 to 375°. Butter and margarine should be used only in the lower part of this range. For the same thoroughness or stage of cooking higher temperature will produce a darker and perhaps drier product, offer greater risk of burning, consume more oil and take less time. Small pieces and parts with thin flesh cook most rapidly, sometimes in 10 minutes. Larger ones may take as long as 30 minutes. When the meat is fork-tender, it is done.

The chicken must be turned at least once, and may be turned several times. The breading is fragile, and may be very loosely attached to the meat, because of water brought to its surface by the heat. You therefore want to handle the pieces as little as possible, and as gently as possible. It is practically necessary to use two utensils, one in each hand, to avoid knocking them around. You may use two forks, a fork and a turner or spatula, or tongs with either a fork or a turner. Cut under each piece before you pick it up, as the breading may be stuck to the pan, and leaving it there would

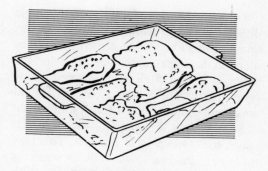

Fig. 8-11. Baked chicken

both deprive the piece of its coating, or skin, and leave a spot on the pan which would conduct heat poorly and would be likely to burn.

Deep Frying. Chicken for deep frying may be breaded with flour, egg-and-crumbs or fritter batter, according to taste.

The fat should be preheated to about 350°. Cooking time should be about 15 minutes, but smaller pieces may cook more quickly. The surface should be golden brown, and pieces should be removed before they become a full brown. The color indicates the progress of the cooking fairly well, and some undercooking is much to be preferred to even slight overcooking, as chicken hardens and toughens very quickly in deep fat.

Serving. If the meal is informal you may serve at least part of the fried chicken from the pan or draining basket directly onto the plates. Blotting is usually not necessary.

If serving will be delayed just a few minutes, pile the pieces on a platter and cover them with paper towels or a cloth. If the wait may be longer, put it in a very low-temperature oven. A glass or metal cover is good for keeping it warm and preventing drying, but it may cause the breading to get soft or even soggy.

Baking. Chicken may be baked in many different ways, both simple and complicated. The baking may also be only part of the cooking, being either preceded or followed by frying or broiling.

Use a well-greased utility or casserole dish, of a size to allow one to two layers. Some people like the greater crust development in a single layer, others prefer the softer skin and flesh of a covered lower layer. Parts of a 3-pound chicken should make one layer in a 9 x 13 inch utility dish.

Start with a little liquid — from a teaspoon to 1/4 cup — in the dish. This may be butter, chicken stock, milk or water as long as the pieces are not breaded. With breading, which is unusual, only butter or margarine should be used.

Keep the oven at 350° F, or start it at 400° and cut down to 350° after about 15 minutes. Either turn the pieces occasionally or baste with the drippings or with additional butter. Cook until a golden brown and fork-tender, 25 to 35 minutes.

Either pan fried or deep fried chicken may be half cooked, then transferred to a dish in the oven to continue cooking. Or baked chicken may be put close under a broiler for some last minute crust-darkening.

Stewed, Boiled or Poached. You may stew a chicken because you think that it is so old (in the chicken world old age comes on at 10 months) and tough that you can't do anything else with it, or because you want to cut it up for use in dishes where hardened crusty bits would be unwelcome; in salad, creamed chicken or chop suey, for example. Or you may prefer the method because it is easy. Stewed chicken is said to be less dry than a roast, but this not always so.

Chicken may be boiled in one piece and come out looking like a bleached roast, or be cut up into pieces first. The pieces fit into a smaller pot and are easier to handle when you are taking the meat off. If you leave it whole you may wish to truss it, that is, tie the legs and wings to the body to keep it in a compact package.

Start with enough boiling water to cover pieces, or to at least half cover a whole bird. Cover, and simmer until tender, that is, until a table fork will push through a drumstick to the bone without undue effort. A whole bird should be turned over occasionally to equalize cooking time in and out of the water. Pieces may be rearranged, or if entirely covered, left where they are. A 5-pound chicken may cook in 2 hours, usually takes 3 and might take 4. If meat starts to fall off the bones without having passed the tenderness test, you will have to figure you have a real tough one that should be ground up for croquettes, or for specially designed salad or hash.

Fricassee. In this discussion, fricassee is taken to mean stewed (or poached, if you prefer) chicken in a cream gravy.

One procedure is to cut the chicken into sections as for frying, and stew it in simmering water until tender, as above. Keep the pan covered, and allow the liquid to evaporate down to make a concentrated broth. Pour the liquid off, keep the chicken warm. Allow the broth to cool, or hurry it up in the fridge or the freezer. When the fat hardens on the surface, peel it off.

Melt 1/4 cup of this chicken fat (if there isn't enough, bring it up to measure with butter or margarine) and blend it with 1/4 cup of flour in a pan over medium heat. Add one cup of the broth and one of cream or milk, stirring constantly, until it almost boils. If it is thick it is done, if it isn't turn the heat low and stir until it is done. Add salt and pepper to taste, and possibly mix in a few green peas for appearance. Put the chicken on a serving platter, pour some of the gravy over it and put the rest in a bowl.

A possible improvement in both color and texture may be obtained by mixing an egg yolk with the gravy. Beat the yolk lightly. When the gravy is thick, add a few tablespoons of it to the yolk, mix well, and stir the mixture into the rest of the gravy.

This can also be made into a pleasing chicken cream stew by cooking a few carrots, small potatoes (or large ones cut in halves or quarters) and an onion or two with the chicken. Put them in late or take them out early to avoid overcooking. Put them with the chicken on the platter and cover with gravy.

Many cookbooks recommend that you fry the chicken a bit before poaching in water, to give a brown color to it and therefore to the gravy. There is no harm in this if you like your food brown, but it may take away from the distinctive appearance and flavor of the original dish.

COOKED CHICKEN

Creamed. Cooked chicken, either specially prepared or leftovers, can be used to advantage in a wide variety of dishes. Creamed chicken is excellent in itself, and serves as a base or a starter for a number of combinations.

Creamed Chicken (Serves 4)

2 Tb	chicken fat or butter
3 Tb	flour
1 cup	chicken broth, milk or half of each
⅓ cup	medium or light cream
1½ cps	cooked chicken, cut small salt and pepper to taste

Melt the butter in a pan over low heat, stir in the flour until well blended, then add the broth and/or milk slowly, stirring steadily. Turn the heat up to medium, bring almost to a boil, turn heat down and cook for 2 minutes. Stir in the cream, broth and seasoning and keep over low heat for another 2 minutes. It is then ready, but it might be improved by a half hour in a double boiler top, over simmering water.

Serve on toast or waffles, or in a ring of rice.

Another approach is to use only 2 tablespoons of flour, and stir in one lightly beaten egg 2 minutes before serving. A half cup of

coarsely cut hard boiled egg may be added, or substituted for an equal amount of chicken. Optional seasonings include 1/4 teaspoon of nutmeg, 1/4 teaspoon of prepared mustard and/or a tablespoon of sherry. Decorations may include parsley or watercress, whole or chopped, a strip of pimiento, and paprika.

Curried. Use the above recipe, but add 1 to 3 teaspoons of curry powder.

A la King. Use the creamed chicken recipe, adding 1/2 cup of cooked mushrooms and 1/4 cup of cooked pimientos, each cut into small pieces.

LIVERS

The chicken liver is a tender and tasty tidbit. But one or even two or three livers are not enough to serve for a meal, and they may be more of a problem than an asset. If you are preparing roast chicken, you can cook the liver briefly with the other giblets, chop all of them finely and mix with the gravy, the stuffing or both. For fried chicken, bread the liver in the same way as other pieces, but put it in last so that it will not cook more than 3 minutes in deep fat or 5 minutes on a pan. For broilers, put livers in available space on the pan about 5 minutes before the chicken is cooked.

If you are going to make a main or side dish of chicken livers, the simplest and possibly the best way to fix them is to pan fry them at about 300° F in a little butter or margarine. Cook until only slightly pink in the middle, making occasional test cuts. About 4 minutes on one side and 3 on the other should do it. Add a tablespoon or two of additional butter just before they are done. Put the livers on a platter or on the plates, either by themselves or on toast fingers, stir the butter in the pan to combine it with old butter, juice and coagulated juice, and pour it over the livers.

Your cookbook is likely to tell you to cut them in halves or quarters, to season

Weight, pounds	Minutes per pound	Total cooking time, hours
4 to 6	30 to 25	1½ to 2½
6 to 8	25 to 22	2½ to 3
8 to 10	22 to 20	3 to 3½
10 to 12	20	3½ to 4
12 to 16	20 to 18	4 to 4½
16 to 20	18 to 15	4½ to 5
20 to 24	15 to 13	5 to 5½

Fig. 8-12. Turkey roasting times

them with salt and pepper, to bread them with flour or crumbs, or to fry in bacon fat. There is no great harm in these procedures, but they are extra work and tend to detract a little from the delicate flavor of the livers themselves.

Bacon makes an excellent accompaniment to any liver. It may be worth while to cook it in a separate pan, so the two contrasting flavors will be intact until they reach the mouth.

TURKEY

For both cooking and serving, turkey can usually be regarded as just a great big chicken. This is not to say that there is no difference in flavor, but the two flavors are in the same class, so that they respond similarly to both cooking methods and combinations with other foods. In general, chicken is regarded as more delicate in flavor and as a superior ingredient. Except in small quantities, it is considerably more work to prepare, a fact that may influence its higher rating.

Size. Turkeys are obtainable in a wide variety of sizes, generally from 7 to 20 pounds, dressed. Half-turkeys may be available also. Much larger turkeys, up to 40 or even 50 pounds, can sometimes be obtained on special order.

Turkey is traditionally a holiday bird, although it is now obtainable in most markets in either fresh or frozen form throughout the year. An allowance of one pound per person is adequate, but 1-1/2 or 2 pounds is more customary, partly to offer an atmosphere of generous supply, and partly because cooked turkey is a very handy substance to have on hand and in the freezer. It is almost always roasted, partly because the bulk of its parts tend to make broiling and frying difficult.

An apartment-size oven, 15 inches wide, 18 deep and 12 high, will hold a 12-pound bird. The oven that is standard in American ranges, about 24 x 20 x 14 inches, should take up to 22 pounds. Several

Fig. 8-13. Turkey for dinner

pounds might be added to these figures if a turkey is unusually short and compact.

Roasting. A turkey is prepared for roasting in the same manner as a chicken. The processes of killing, plucking and drawing differ chiefly in scale, except that the removal of leg tendons, which is usually unnecessary with a chicken, is almost essential with a turkey. Stuffing and trussing are done in the same manner, but require much bigger skewers and stronger string.

Any of the stuffing recipes can be followed for turkey. There should be a little less than a cup of it for each pound of dressed weight.

Recommended oven temperature up to 14 pounds is 325 to 350° F, and 25° less for bigger birds. This is for uncovered roasting. Covered times are no longer available, but the general rule applies, that time can be kept the same by reducing temperature 25°.

The problem of preventing overcooking of exposed parts is about the same as with a chicken, and can be handled in the same ways.

Full cooking is indicated by appearance, and by tenderness as indicated by penetration with a fork or easy twisting of a drumstick. Or you can use a thermometer, and aim for a 190° temperature in the thigh.

DUCK

Ducks show much less variation in size and uses than chickens do. The average duck in the market is of the Pekin (white) variety, weighs 4 to 6 pounds dressed, and is intended to be roasted. The meat is all dark, it is usually tender and well-flavored, but may have a strong or gamy taste. The quantity is small in relation to the total weight of the bird, which has a great deal of fat. Allow about 1-1/2 pounds dressed weight per serving.

Duck is sometimes not stuffed, on the ground that the stuffing may taste too gamy or pick up too much fat. This effect is usually very small, and if you like duck you probably also like duck dressing. Use any stuffing mixture, but the addition of chopped celery may be in order, as it goes well with this bird. The amount of butter in the dressing may be reduced.

You may cook it, trussed or untrussed, in either an open or covered pan in a 325° F oven, allow 20 or 18 minutes respectively to the pound. No basting is needed, as it practically oozes grease. It may be advisable to remove fat from the pan a couple of times, pouring it out or using a baster. Some people esteem the fat highly for miscellaneous pan frying, others discard it.

Duck may be fried or broiled, but roasting is much more usual. Differences in handling are chiefly regulated by the greater fat content.

GOOSE

In the kitchen, goose bears the same relationship to duck that turkey does to chicken. It has the same general type of build, flesh and high fat content. Allow one to 1-1/4 pounds per serving.

Goose is usually roasted in a moderate oven, 325 to 350° F. Time is 25 or 30 minutes to the pound.

9

SEAFOOD

FOOD FROM THE SEA

Seafood can be divided into two major classifications, fish and shellfish.

For food purposes, a fish may be defined as an animal that lives in water, which may be salt or fresh; breathes by means of gills, has a vertebrate (jointed) internal backbone, is cold blooded and has fins. This definition includes eels and sharks.

Shellfish are from two different animal families, the crustaceans and the mollusks. Crustaceans, which include lobsters, crayfish, crabs and shrimp, have many legs, a tough outside skeleton with joints to permit bending, and active habits.

Mollusks, which include oysters, clams, scallops, mussels and snails, usually have an outside heavy skeleton or shell in one piece or in two pieces hinged together. The body is differently organized than ours, and its parts are difficult to recognize.

Mollusks are free swimming when very young, but most of them settle down to a life of no movement (oysters and mussels) or very limited movement (snails and clams). Scallops, however, swim freely by clapping their shells together.

Squid and octopus are also mollusks, but are active and do not have shells. They are good to eat, but are not popular as food in this country.

Dietary Value. The edible portions of fish and shellfish average about 10 per cent protein. This is complete protein, of the same high quality found in meat. The fat content ranges from less than one per cent in very lean fish up to about 20 per cent in fat fish. But unlike meat fat, this is polyunsaturated, and is as harmless to the arteries as safflower oil.

Seafood is rich in minerals, particularly iodine. Fat fish provide good supplies of vitamins, while lean ones may be only fair in this respect, as their vitamins and fat tend to be concentrated in the liver and other organs, which are usually not eaten.

Oysters, clams and very small fish, particularly the young of larger fish, may be eaten whole, and provide a complete and reasonably balanced diet. The vitamin C deficiency disease, scurvy, which was the principal ailment of sailors for centuries, and which was combatted by lime and lemon juice, could have been readily prevented and cured by straining sea water

151

Fig. 9-1a. Shark, eel and fish

A fishy smell is so commonly associated with sea food that it is properly accepted without comment. However, it should be avoided and limited as much as possible. Seafood should be cooked as soon as possible after catching or buying it. No scraps, cleaning water or other residues from its preparation should be left around. Dishes, pans and utensils that have been in contact with sea food should be washed promptly. If the smell persists, rub them with salt or very salty water, rinse, and then wash in the usual way.

Fish should be wrapped carefully in plastic before being put in the refrigerator, and should not be cooked long or at a high temperature.

through cloth, and eating the small organisms (plankton) that would not go through it.

Smell. Fish and most sea food tends to develop a distinctive odor, that is, to smell fishy. This odor is usually not found in perfectly fresh clean fish, but it develops rapidly in warm temperatures, slowly in the cold. It presumably is a smell of aging and/or decomposition, but it appears long before any other signs of deterioration are present. It may be noticed while cooking fish that were odorless when raw.

FISH

True fish range in length from half an inch to 10 or more feet in length, with weight up to a ton. The sharks, which are a related but more primitive family, have a minimum adult weight of several pounds, and the largest of them weigh many tons.

Flesh. The flesh or meat of raw fish is usually white or near-white, often with a slightly translucent quality. But it may be grey, pink or red. Grey meat, which may be quite dark, often appears in certain parts of some fish that otherwise have white flesh. The dark parts often appear to be more juicy and flavorful.

Fish may be classified as fat or lean, depending on the percentage of fat in their flesh. This is supposed to be helpful in determining how to cook them. In a general way, fat fish are most suitable for broiling, lean ones for frying, but you can cook either kind either way.

Figure 9-2 gives the fat-lean classification of a number of fish. It is a combination of data from a number of sources. The center column lists fish about which references disagreed, those that are variable in fat content, and some that are partly fat and partly lean. For example, both halibut and

Lean	Doubtful or Variable	Fat
Carp	Barracuda	Bluefish
Catfish	Eel	Butterfish
Cod	Halibut	Mackerel
Flounder	Herring	Mullet
Haddock	Salmon	Pompano
Pickerel	Smelt	Rosefish
Red snapper		Shad
Swordfish		Tilefish
Weakfish		Trout
Whiting		Tuna
		Whitefish

Fig. 9-1b. Fat and lean fish

Fig. 9-2. Fish skeleton

almon are fat, but the steaks that we buy are lean.

Bones. Bones are a major problem in serving and enjoying fish. They are usually rather small in diameter, round, sharp at one end and white or near-white. Their arrangement is very different from that found in land animals, and both placing and number of bones varies from one species to another. As a result, people often fail to detect their presence until they have started to swallow them. Such bones may lodge in the back of the mouth or in the throat, where they can be a painful and sometimes dangerous nuisance.

If the fish is very small the bones may be chewed and swallowed. Sardines and small smelts are examples. If it is very large it is easy to carve around bones, as in cod and swordfish. Otherwise, bones may be removed before serving, as in filleting and boning, or the fish eater picks his way cautiously among them. Both the cook and the consumer benefit by knowing the basic arrangement of the skeleton.

Figure 9-3 shows a typical fish skeleton. There is a skull, a spine or backbone rather similar to ours, and a rib cage that encloses the viscera, that is, the heart, stomach, intestines, liver and so forth. These ribs curve out from the spine in pairs, then curve in toward the bottom. Behind the viscera there is a single row of ribs pointing down and usually somewhat backward, and another single row of ribs, shorter ones, projecting upward from the spine for most of its length.

There are also sets of parallel bones attached to the fins.

Fins. A fish usually has five sets of fins: the tail or caudal, the back or dorsal, the belly or anal, the pelvic or ventral and the front or pectoral. They vary greatly in different species in development and placement. The tail supplies most of the swimming power, but the others are essential for balance and maneuvering.

Fins are made up chiefly of bone, gristle and skin. They are ordinarily not edible, although they may be boiled to extract flavorful substances and gelatin for soup or sauce.

The tail fin bones are attached to the last segment (segments?) of backbone. The others are anchored by bones extending down into the flesh, where muscles fasten them to the main skeleton.

Catfish have needle-sharp spines in some of their fins, so that it is dangerous to handle them when they are alive, and caution must be used even when they are dead. These spines are sometimes poisoned to produce intense irritation, in addition to the pain of punctures and cuts.

Fig. 9-4. Scaling and finning

PREPARATION

Wiping and Washing. You will usually rinse or wipe off a whole fish before you start to work on it, but if it looks and smells clean you may not. It should be wiped or rinsed after scaling, and wiped inside after cleaning.

Your cookbook will probably tell you to wash or dip cut pieces again before cooking, probably in salted water. You may be sternly warned against washing long before cooking or letting it stay wet because water causes rapid deterioration of the flesh. However, no reason is given for washing these clean pieces of fish, and unless you know of one, you might as well skip it.

Scales. Most of the true fish have scales. These are small, hard plates that may be compared to tiny fingernails, fastened to the surface of the skin at their forward ends and overlapping like shingles. They are very gritty and unpleasant to eat, and should always be removed before serving.

Since the skin is otherwise usually thin, tender and tasty, it is customary to scrape the scales off the skin, a process called scaling. This is necessary only if the skin is to be eaten, but it is often done as a matter of habit or routine even if the skin itself will be taken off later.

Scaling is done by scraping from the tail toward the head with a special serrated scaling tool, a dull knife or even a spoon. You wet the fish, put it down on a cleaning board or a table, and hold it by the head; or pin the tail to the board with an ice pick and hold its handle. If you scale with a knife, hold it at right angles to the skin so as not to dig in.

Use either short or long strokes, and be sure to work close to the fins. Until you are used to the job, it is well to check your results by running your finger along the cleaned surface, from tail to head, to feel if any have been left. You should be able to scale completely with the fish on one side and then the other.

Wipe or rinse the fish after scaling, to remove any loose ones that have been left behind by the knife.

Scaling should be the first operation in preparing a fish for eating. It is helpful to be able to hold onto the head and fins. More important, loosened scales are apt to enter any cuts made by cleaning and finning, and remain with the flesh. But since scaling is not as important as cleaning (removing the organs), it may be either done afterward if time is short, or avoided by removing the skin.

A delicate uncleaned fish such as a flounder should not be grasped tightly

Courtesy of U.S. Dept. of Agriculture

Fig. 9-5. Beheading

around the middle while scaling, as this may rupture the gall bladder and make it too bitter to eat.

Finning. Fins are removed by cutting around them to the full depth of the bones with slightly converging cuts, after which the fin may be pulled out with its complete bone structure. The bones are often delicate, and you have to be careful to cut alongside and not through them.

The dorsal fin often requires a pair of parallel cuts almost all the way from head to tail. The others usually call for more or less oval cutting.

Finning is best done with a fillet knife, which has a narrow blade and should be kept very sharp. The narrow blade allows cutting on a curve, and the sharpness not only makes cutting easier, but helps you to distinguish between flesh and bone. But any sharp knife with a point can be used.

Finning is sometimes done by cutting the external parts off with a knife or heavy scissors. This leaves the bones to complicate eating. They would be easier to find and remove if the whole fin were left intact.

The tail is cut off by cutting through it just forward of its fins. This is easy in small fish, but in larger ones may require care in getting the knife between the vertebrae, or using other tools as in cutting off the head. The tail is frequently left on, and

definitely should remain if the head does.

Cleaning (Eviscerating). Cleaning may be used as a general term for the whole preparation of a fish for cooking, but it more often covers removal of the innards — mostly the digestive system — from the belly. Most of these are not edible, and decomposition of food in the stomach and intestine may give the flesh off-tastes and odors within a few hours in warm weather.

The time that a fish can be left uncleaned without damage is subject to many variables, beside that of temperature. The best policy is to do it as soon as possible after death, and to keep the fish as cold as possible in the meantime. The job can be postponed without risk if you can keep the fish alive on a line, or in a basket or tank.

A fish that is to be filleted need not be cleaned, but the fillets must be cut off it as soon as possible. If it is cleaned, filleting can be postponed until cooking time, if necessary.

If the fish is to be kept whole, you put it on its side, cut the throat just behind the gill covers from the bottom up to backbone, then slit the belly from the hole or anus forward to the first cut, deeply enough to sever the body wall but not to cut into the organs. Pull them out with your fingers or with a knife. They should come out in a single mass except for the kidney and a blood line, which you may have to scrape loose from the spine separately. Scrape away blood flecks or other bits with the knife, and wipe out the interior with a paper towel or a cloth.

A female fish may contain a mass of small eggs enclosed in a membrane. This is called roe. A male may contain a similar although smaller sack of sperm, which is creamy in consistency and is known as milt. These are the most highly prized portions of a few fish, and they are excellent food.

The liver is the only other part of the innards that is considered edible. It is sometimes quite large in proportion to the size of the fish. It should be easy to recognize and to separate from the other parts. You cook it in the same manner as chicken liver, as described on page 147.

Another cleaning method is to remove the head by cutting through the body behind the pectoral (front) fins, then slit the belly. This wastes a little flesh, and may put some rib splinters in the front portion of the flesh. But it is quick and easy.

Head. The head of the fish is mostly the bony structure of the skull, with the eyes, mouth, gills and gill covers. The gills correspond in function to the lungs of a land animal. Water is taken in through the mouth and pumped through the gills by motion of the covers. Blood vessels extract oxygen from the water as it goes past. In stringing or fastening a fish to keep it alive, it is essential that the fastening of the line not interfere with this water circulation.

Some large fish have edible meat in the cheeks and/or in the tongue. Otherwise the head is considered to be waste. It may be removed either before or after cooking, or left on. Removal makes the fish shorter, to fit in a smaller pan, and prevents it from seeming to direct an accusing glare at a sensitive cook. If you leave it on it will improve appearance for less sensitive people, and will protect the front end of the body

from overcooking. And if you are going to cut fillets or steaks, its removal is not necessary and it gives you something extra to hold onto while you are carving.

If you do remove the head before cooking you can best do it as part of the eviscerating, after you make the belly cut and before you remove the innards. A fish has no distinguishable neck, but you can cut just behind the gill covers, following their vee shape, and then straight up. A good knife will usually cut through the spine, but you may wiggle it a bit to get between the vertebrae. If you can't cut through, cut all the flesh, place the fish with its head projecting beyond a table edge, and pull the head down sharply. This should break the backbone so that a little trim cutting will separate head and body. The bone may also be cut with poultry scissors, a saw, a cleaver or bolt cutters.

Courtesy of U.S. Dept. of Agriculture

Fig. 9-6. Trimmed, filleted and steaked

CARVING

Even very small fish are customarily cleaned and scaled before cooking, but fins, head and tail may be left on, and they are cooked whole. Larger ones may be more thoroughly trimmed, and may be cut into pieces for easier cooking, special treatment or convenience in eating. The cutting up of raw fish will be discussed under the headings of filleting, splitting, steaking and chunking.

Filleting. Filleting is the process of converting a fish into two supposedly bone-free slices, one from each side. The basic technique is to lay the fish on its side, cut down to the backbone just behind the pectoral (front) fins, turn the knife on its side and cut diagonally toward the other end of the fish with a gentle sawing motion, keeping it at proper depth by sliding it along the

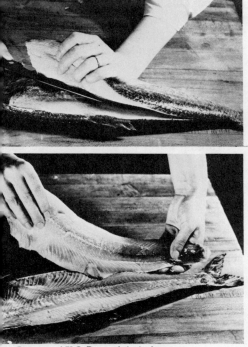

Fig. 9-7. Cutting a fillet

backbone and ribs. But of course there are details.

The fillet-maker has two objectives. One is to get the largest possible part of the fish into the fillets and off the skeleton. The other is to avoid including any bones in the fillets. Unless the fish supply is very limited, bonelessness is the most important objective. Efficiency in getting most of the meat comes with practice.

A fish may be filleted most easily without being cleaned, but it must be done soon after catching. The head, fins, skeleton and innards can then be discarded in one piece, and the firm body makes cutting easier. But it should be scaled, even if you intend to skin the fillets, as the knife is likely to push scales down into the flesh. The beginner will be wise to cut out the fins before he starts, as otherwise it is very easy for the knife to wander enough to include fin bones in the fillets.

A good procedure for your first few fillets is to work on an uncleaned fish, cut out the fins and their root bones, start the fillet at the base of the tail and cut the upper part ahead of the lower. At first it is desirable or perhaps necessary to pull the flesh gently upward as the knife cuts it free of the bones. This puts the flesh under gentle tension, so that it will cut readily, and permits you to see how you are doing. If the knife rides up and leaves a substantial bit of meat, go back and cut closer to the bones. A hacked surface is almost unavoidable on first tries, and it does not hurt the flavor.

The knife should be very sharp. Raw fish, and particularly its skin, has a rubbery quality that encourages a dull knife to tear rather than cut it. Even the sharpest knife will, if gently operated, be stopped by a bone, so that you will feel its presence, but a dull knife might encounter enough ordinary resistance so that you would exert enough force to crush and break small bones. An expert prefers to use a very narrow-bladed special fillet knife, but the amateur is better off with a normal wide blade that will keep the edge headed in one direction.

You may also cut fillets from the top down, either straight or diagonally. With this method, an uncleaned fish and a nice touch, you can make a butterfly fillet consisting of the two regular side fillets joined across the belly by a wide strip of uncut flesh.

A fillet may be cooked and served with the skin on or off. It may be removed either before or after it is cut out of the flesh. If done before, it eliminates the need for scaling.

The size of the fish used for filleting varies with the species and the cook. Generally, if a fish weighs less than 1-1/2 pounds it is more trouble than it is worth (but not always). If weight is over 4 pounds, steaks may be more efficient.

If filleting is roughly done, there will be a considerable amount of flesh left sticking to the ribs. In addition, there is usually good flesh in front of the fins, and a little in the base of the tail. All this may be salvaged by cutting off the head and frying the skeleton, for 2 or 3 minutes on each side in a moderate (275-300°) pan in a little grease, with or without sprinkled bread crumbs. These remnants of flesh are often more tender and tasty than the larger pieces, and are easy to scrape off the bones.

Splitting. A split fish is usually filleted on one side only. The fillet may be lifted off, or left connected at the bottom, as for a butterfly fillet. There seems to be general agreement that the skeleton should be left attached to the lower piece, along with head and tail, during cooking, for maximum juiciness and flavor. There is also the practical advantage that the backbone and attached skeleton can be easily lifted off the flesh after cooking, but usually has to be cut off when raw.

Splitting reduces the thickness of the fish to be cooked by one-half, and cooking time by one-third. It makes a fillet out of one side, and exposes the bones for easier removal on the other side. But if carelessly done it may detract from appearance and embed broken bone splinters in unexpected places.

Steaking and Chunking. If your fish is over 4 pounds you may wish to cut it into steaks instead of fillets. If it is over 6 pounds you surely will.

For steaks, take your scaled, cleaned, finned and possibly skinned fish and cut it into cross slices, at right angles or at least at a steep angle to the backbone, as in Figure 9-8. Such slices should be at least half an inch thick and probably not more than an inch. Each cut will go through the backbone (not difficult with a sharp, heavy knife) and will include one or more ribs or rib-sets, or parts of them.

To make chunks, you cut the fish into extra thick steaks, then cut them into squares. This is a first step toward a fish stew.

Skinning. Skin, when cooked with the fish, is usually tender and wholesome, but it is not universally liked. It is often removed for plain cooking, and must be left out of mixtures such as chowder, where it would separate from the flesh and make soggy tatters and lumps.

Skinning a fish presents about the same problems as peeling a peach. There is considerable variation in strength of skin and in the tightness of its attachment, both among species of fish and individuals of one species. The general rule is to make a cut through the skin at either the tail or the head end, and pull the skin while you hold the fish. The pulling is done by holding the loosened skin flap against the blade of a knife. If resistance is encountered, cut and pull gently until you get through the difficult spot. If the fish is large and the skin is thick you may want to grip it with pliers while you pull.

Eels and catfish have very tough skins, which should be removed from the neck down. If you hook the jaw on a nail in some fixed object, and have pliers at hand if you need them, you should have no trouble. But be very careful in handling a catfish, as it may have spines in the fins that can easily make painful cuts in your fingers.

To skin a fillet, put it on a board with the skin side down, slice through the flesh at one end, grasp the exposed end of skin between thumb and finger, turn the knife flat and cut gently with it away from your fingers, while you pull on the skin. Don't just hold the skin, the pulling action is im-

Courtesy of U.S. Dept. of Agriculture

Fig. 9-8. Cutting steaks

portant in making it separate from the flesh.

COOKING

Raw fish is slightly translucent in appearance and will not come apart without cutting or pulling. Cooked fish is opaque, and will split or flake apart under gentle pressure. The function of cooking is to make these changes in texture and appearance, and to enhance the flavor.

Fish cooks rather quickly, and at a low temperature. An internal reading of 140° on a meat thermometer indicates full cooking. However, few people use thermometers, as the flaking characteristic is easily

tested and just as dependable. A gentle sideward pressure on the surface of cooked fish will make it split, even if it is covered by skin. Overcooking, by heating above 140° or by holding it at that temperature, causes drying, toughening and loss of flavor.

Your cookbook may tell you that all fish is naturally tender, and that the only cause of toughness is overcooking. Unfortunately, this is not so. Some species of fish, such as mackerel, are frequently tough; halibut may be both dry and tough and even swordfish is not always tender. However, tender fish are often made tough by overcooking, and tough ones are made tougher the same way.

Fish may be cooked by almost any method. Frying and broiling are probably the most popular.

Pan Frying. Fish may be pan-fried whole (after cleaning), without heads and tails, or in the form of fillets or steaks. Recipes usually call for breading, but bare frying appears to be more common.

The pan may be dry if it is Teflon or black iron, but it is better for it to have 1/8 to 1/4 inch of some kind of grease. Use medium heat, 300 to 350° F, or lower temperature if you prefer. The pan may be either open or covered.

Heat the pan, but do not let the grease bubble or boil unless it is butter or margarine. Put in a single layer of fish or fish parts. Cook for 5 or 6 minutes or until brown on the bottom, turn and cook for 2/3 this time on the other side. Test for flaking, and remove from the pan if done. Serve immediately.

Average open cooking time for fillets 1/2 inch thick is 8 or 10 minutes, including both sides. Whole fish or steaks an inch thick might take 12 to 15. But testing is more important than timing.

For breading, take 1/4 cup of flour, fine cracker crumbs, corn meal or mixtures of these or similar materials to the pound of fish. Mix with a half teaspoon of salt if you wish. Have the fish pieces damp but

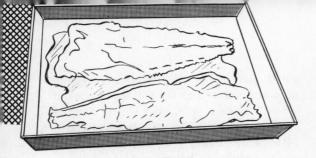

Fig. 9-9. Fillets for baking

not wet, roll them in the crumbs on wax paper or shake them together in a bag. You can use egg and crumbs, but this is more usual for deep frying. Fry in the same manner as bare fish, but be more careful about loosening from the pan before turning.

If the grease disappears during frying, add more. If the fish browns too fast or the pan smokes, reduce heat; if no browning occurs increase the heat.

Deep Frying. Fish may be deep fried whole or in fillets, or less often in steaks or chunks. It is usually breaded. The preferred temperature is 350 to 375° F, with a number of recipes specifying exactly 370°.

Breading may be just flour or crumbs on damp fish, or the fish may be dried and given a three layer coating by dipping first in flour, then in lightly beaten egg and finally in crumbs.

Cook until golden brown, lift out in the basket, drain well and serve.

Broiling. Fish may be broiled in the same manner as steaks and chops, but it is likely to fall apart while being turned over. It is therefore usual to broil it on one side only, in thicknesses from 3/4 inch to 2 inches. Thinner pieces are too fragile to cook on a rack, thicker ones may not cook evenly.

The fish may be whole, split, filleted or in steaks. If it is lean it should be painted with oil, and perhaps repainted halfway through the broiling.

You can use a preheated broiler pan with a standard rack, greased. Split fish should have the skin side down. If the fish is two

inches thick, place the rack so that the top of the fish will be about 4 inches below the broiler. Thinner fish can be closer.

A broiled fish may be difficult to remove from the pan. If it is properly cooked it is tender and fragile, and it is likely to be stuck. You may have to first pull the broiler out of the oven, then use two turners, and some careful undercutting, to lift a fillet or steak in one piece and get it to a platter. Or you may take a safer and easier course of cutting it on the pan, and putting the pieces directly on the plates.

The juices of the fish drain through the broiler slots into the lower pan, from which they can be poured over the fish as it is served.

Fish may also be broiled in a heat resistant dish or platter that will hold its juices around it and that can be used as a serving dish. Such a utensil is likely to be extremely hot, so precautions should be taken to protect your fingers and the table top.

Baking. Baking is highly recommended by many cookbooks as the easy way to prepare fish, but there is general disagreement about the way to do it, and particularly in regard to correct oven temperature.

You use a greased baking pan or ovenproof platter. It is a good idea to line it with foil, partly to reduce the cleanup job required to remove baked-on fish juices and partly to simplify handling the fish itself. A tender fish firmly stuck to a pan can easily become a mess before it reaches a serving platter or the dishes.

Baking is best adapted to whole fish, but is also used for steaks and fillets. While you can bake a small fish or a single fillet, less than a 2-pound weight hardly justifies the use of the oven.

There is danger of drying out. The skin and the head are partial protections for whole fish. Fillets should be put in a small enough pan so that they can be piled in two or more layers. As a further precaution, all surfaces may be painted with oil or dotted with butter, and this protection renewed by basting or fresh applications at 10-minute intervals during cooking.

Seasoning may be done before cooking or may be omitted. A light sprinkling of salt and pepper is usual. Dried herbs of one or several varieties may be sprinkled on top.

Oven heat may be anywhere from 350 to 500° F. As usual, the hot oven cooks faster, makes a harder crust and is more likely to burn both crust and food. For a first try, select some temperature in the lower range, say between 350 and 400°, and modify it next time according to experience. Or change it during cooking to get more or less crust.

Cooking time may be expected to be 6 to 12 minutes per pound, most of the variations being for temperature but some of it for the particular fish. A fish will not fall like a cake if you open the oven door, so you can safely start testing for flaking early in the cooking. If you like to use a meat thermometer, consider it done at 140°.

Frozen fish takes from 50 to 80 per cent longer to cook than if it is at refrigerator or room temperature.

Stuffing. Baked fish may be stuffed. You can use any poultry dressing such as is described on Page 141. For a whole fish, fill the belly cavity loosely, close with skewers or toothpicks, and then lace it with string. This is recommended because both flesh and skin are so tender that the fastenings tend to come out.

Stuffing may be put between two layers of fillets, or even packed under or around a steak.

Fish may also be baked on a layer of mixed finely cut vegetables such as carrots, onions, celery and string beans, which become richly flavored with fish drippings.

Simmering. Simmering, also called poaching and often developing into boiling, is a simple and reliable cooking method. It is preferred if the fish is to be flaked

Fig. 9-10. Fish may be simmered

or broken up for use in salads and canapes, as there is no crust to complicate it with differences in texture and color. It is very suitable for any fish that will be served with a thick sauce that would hide and soften crust produced by other methods.

The basic fluid for simmering is plain water. If you are not satisfied with this you can add salt or any seasoning you like, acidulate it by adding up to 3 tablespoons of lemon juice or vinegar to the quart of water, with half that quantity of salt, or replace water with milk, cream, wine or even beer.

Another procedure is to cook up a special liquid, court bouillon, in which to simmer the fish. This may be almost any kind of a thin soup flavored with vegetables and seasoning. There does not seem to be any agreement on materials, cooking time or other details, and its preparation is more in the line of gourmet elaboration than basic cooking.

Whatever liquid you use, you will get best results by keeping its temperature in the simmer range, between 180 and 210° F. This is most important with cuts of fish, which are likely to break up into shreds if boiled vigorously.

The liquid remaining after you remove the cooked fish may be kept as a fish stock, for cooking the next batch of fish or for use in soup or sauce. It may be strengthened by boiling to concentrate it, or by cooking a batch of fish trimmings — head, bones, unused skin and tail — in it before discarding them.

Simmering time, from a cold start, is 5 to 9 minutes to the pound, based on the weight of the individual fish or pieces, rather than their total weight. But start testing for flakiness at 3 or 4 minutes.

Cut fish may lose its cohesion when simmered so that it will be difficult to get it out of the pan in presentable condition. You can guard against this problem by cooking it in a deep fryer basket, or by lining the pan with a piece of cheesecloth long enough so that you can pick up the ends with tongs and use it as a sort of sling to lift the fish onto a platter where you can deal with it more comfortably. If you don't have cheesecloth, you can use a clean dishcloth or white rag.

Steaming. Fish may be cooked on a rack or a steamer pan, covered, above gently boiling water. Or it may be simmered in a covered pan without enough water to cover it, so that the top will be steamed and the bottom water-cooked.

Cooking time and general results are similar to those obtained by simmering. If you use the partly-in-water method for whole fish, turn them over when about half cooked, as the bottom may cook faster than the top.

Sauce. Fish cooked in any manner can be served without sauce, but the bland taste and texture of water-cooked fish blends excellently with some of the white sauces, and many people prefer to have a seasoned sauce on fried or broiled fish. It is customary to serve slices of lemon with fish, and butter, salt and pepper should be on the table.

A medium white or cream sauce may be used by itself on boiled or steamed fish, with pleasing results. It can be made special for fish by adding sliced or diced hard boiled eggs, in the proportion of one or two eggs to a cup of sauce to a pound of fish.

Butter may be seasoned for use with fish. You can cream a quarter pound of butter with finely chopped parsley and chives, and add some capers. Use a tablespoon of each if they are fresh, a teaspoon if they are dried.

Lean fish are more likely to be served with elaborate sauces than fat ones, but results may be good either way.

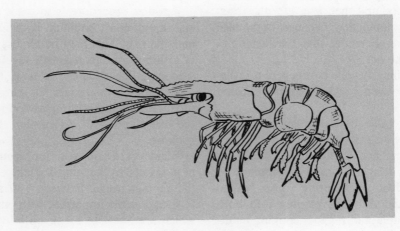

Fig. 9-11. Shrimp

SHELLFISH

Shellfish are totally different classes of animal than the vertebrate fish, but they resemble them rather closely for food purposes. The shellfish are also rich in minerals and vitamins, naturally tender so that brief cooking or no cooking is required and they provide a good variety of textures and tastes.

SHRIMP

The shrimp is a small crustacean that is usually dull green but occasionally brown or pink when raw and is pink or pink and white when cooked. It comes in a number of varieties and sizes. The smaller ones are usually superior in flavor, while the biggest ones, called jumbo, are tops in convenience and in cost.

Shrimp may be bought raw, either whole or with their heads cut off, or precooked with shells removed.

The shell is quite easy to shuck, either before or after cooking. Cut it with a knife or tear it with fingernails at the front bottom, forward of the legs, then tear it off. For ordinary cooking you break or pull the tail off, but for fancy dishes you leave the tail part of the shell attached. Very small shrimp are often served with the shells on, and shucked one by one by the customer.

The shrimp has an intestinal canal running along the base of a groove in his back. This is called a vein or a sand vein. Almost every cookbook will tell you to remove it. This can be done fairly easily by scraping with a beer can opener, a toothpick or almost anything.

While it might occasionally be gritty, this vein is usually removed only for appearance or in respect to convention when serving guests. If we were similarly fussy about cleaning clams and oysters we would have nothing much left to eat.

Shrimp are most easily cooked in simmering water, from 3 to 5 minutes or until they turn pink. This method is good either before or after shelling.

The other principal cooking method is to roll shucked shrimp in batter (any kind that you like) and deep fry them for two or three minutes at a temperature of 350 to 375° F. There is no damage done if they are slightly undercooked, but they get very tough when overcooked.

They can also be pan fried, preferably in butter with or without breading.

LOBSTER

The lobster is a large and highly valued crustacean. There are two distinct types, the northern Maine or homard species, and the distantly related rock or spiny lobster, often called crayfish. The Maine lobster is valued partly for its big, meaty claws; the southern variety chiefly for its tail.

Maine Lobster. The weight range is from the minimum legal size of one pound, called chicken lobster, to 5 or more pounds. Those weighing over 3 pounds are likely to be tough but are sometimes very good eating.

Lobster is sold either alive or cooked. Alive, they are dark green, sometimes with red markings, and cooked they are always some shade of red. A live one is frightening and somewhat dangerous if you don't know how to handle it, as the big claws can give

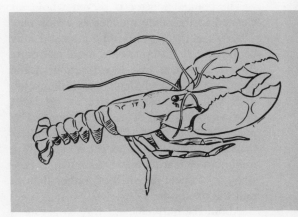

Fig. 9-12. Northern lobster

a nasty nip. They can be made safe by jamming them with plugs of wood.

A lobster that is to be broiled should be cleaned before cooking. You kill it by cutting the spinal cord between the body and tail sections with a heavy sharp knife. Then turn it on its back and slit it down the center. Remove the stomach or lady, which is immediately behind the eyes, and perhaps the dark vein that runs back through the tail. Cut or break the shell so that the flesh of the halves is turned up. Do not remove the greyish liver (tomalley) or the reddish eggs (coral) if there are any.

Preheat the broiler, put the lobster halves on the rack with shell side down, butter the flesh, and broil 10 to 15 minutes, about 3 inches below the flame or heat unit, occasionally basting with melted butter.

Broiled lobster should be accompanied by a fasten-at-the-neck napkin, a nutcracker or a pair of pliers for the claws, a regular fork and an oyster fork, a saucer of melted butter, a slice of lemon and salt and pepper.

Boiling. For boiled lobster, use either fresh water with a tablespoon of salt to the quart, or sea water. Use a pot big enough to hold the lobster (or lobsters) and put in enough water to cover. You put the live lobster headfirst into the boiling water, cover the pot, reduce the heat and simmer it 4 minutes to the pound.

The cooked lobster is served whole, or cleaned in the same manner as a raw one.

Extracting Meat. Boiling a lobster may be only the first step toward more elaborate dishes. The next one is extraction of the meat, which is a difficult and tedious job until you have had practice at it. Twist claws and legs off with your hands. Use pliers freely to break the shell, and pull at the tender flesh gently to get it out with a minimum of tearing apart. As much as possible, try to peel the shell off rather than to pull the meat out.

About the only efficient way to get meat out of the small claws is to break them at both ends and suck the meat out. Then you swallow it, so it is no gain for your pile of meat.

You should get about 3/4 of a cup of cut-up lobster meat for each pound of live lobster.

Lobster Meat. Cooked lobster meat is a great delicacy, both on its own and as an ingredient. It is at its best when just out of a fresh-cooked lobster, but is almost as good frozen and can be used with enjoyment from a can.

You can put bits of lobster meat on toothpicks or on crackers and serve them for canapes, pour sauce on it and offer it for cocktails, put lettuce under it and mayonnaise or some simple dressing over it for salad or panfry it in plenty of butter for a snack or a main course. In each case you will be delivering top quality.

And if you want to be more elaborate, there is Lobster Newburg. The following recipe is averaged from eight different ones, and is of course subject to whatever changes you or the state of your supplies consider advisable.

Lobster Newburg *(for 4 people)*

2 cps	cooked lobster meat
4 Tb	butter
1 cup	medium or light cream
3	egg yolks, lightly beaten
1 Tb	sherry
1 Tb	brandy
⅓ tsp	nutmeg or paprika

• • •

2 cps	cooked rice, hot *(use about ¾ cup of raw rice)*

or

4 slcs	toast

Cook the lobster and butter together for 3 minutes over low heat, stirring several times. Add the sherry and brandy, cook another minute, then add the cream, egg yolks and seasoning. Stir (still over low heat) until slightly thickened.

Serve on hot rice, or on toast cut into triangles or strips.

Rock Lobster. A whole rock lobster is cooked and served in about the same manner as a Maine lobster. The difference is that most of the meat is in the tail, which therefore receives special attention. In fact, the tail is so important that it is usually the only part that is shipped any distance.

Tails usually range from 1/4 to 1/2 pound each. There are much larger ones, but they are not always available. Those in American markets are usually frozen.

The back or upper side of the tail is covered by fairly heavy, jointed shell and the underside by a thin, flexible membrane. The tail has a tendency to curl downward when handled and particularly while cooking. You can straighten it by occasionally bending it forcibly upward, or keep it straight by running a skewer lengthwise through the flesh.

An intestinal vein runs the length of the center of the tail, near the lower surface. This is usually not removed unless the meat is being cut or broken up for a casserole or salad.

Tails are cooked by boiling (simmering or poaching), by broiling or by a combination of the two methods.

It is desirable but not necessary to thaw frozen lobster tails before cooking. Use sufficient salted water (a tablespoon of salt to a quart) to cover, bring it to a boil, put in the tails, turn heat down after boiling resumes, and simmer about one minute for each ounce in the largest tail if thawed, or 1-1/2 minutes if frozen.

A portion may consist of one large tail or two small ones. You can serve them hot with melted butter and lemon wedges, or allow them to cool and then use the meat in any recipe calling for cooked lobster.

Fig. 9-13. Southern lobster

The meat is easily removed after cutting the lower membrane with kitchen scissors or a sharp heavy knife. You can cut it full length along one edge, and fold it back, or cut both edges and remove it.

To broil a lobster tail, you cut the bottom membrane along both sides and remove it, bend the tail backward until it cracks or at least assumes a somewhat backward curve, dab butter on the meat and broil about 3 inches below the heat for about 5 minutes.

Another method is to put the tails in boiling water, take them out as soon as the water boils again, and broil only until the surface starts to brown.

CRAB

Crab is second only to shrimp as America's favorite shellfish. A number of different species are eaten, and they vary in size from a few inches to several feet across the spread legs. There are important variations, but the basic flavor and tender, filamented structure are similar.

Crabs are naturally hard-shelled. Occasionally they shed the shell in order to grow a bigger one. They are known as soft-shelled crabs after shedding, and before the new shell has formed and hardened.

Crabs that are sold live sometimes have their legs cut off to prevent them from

165

Fig. 9-14. Crab

running away. They are cooked in boiling or simmering salted water, preferably sea water if you have it, for about 20 minutes. This is a long time compared with other shellfish. Hard-shells are cooked live, then cleaned, but soft-shells are cleaned first.

The cleaning of a crab is a complex operation that cannot be covered adequately in a book, even with illustrations. It is killed by cutting off the head, well behind the eyes. The shell, if there is one, can be pulled off, the big top one first, the much smaller pointed lower one afterward. The digestive system and a large spongy pair of gills are inedible. The legs and claws must be de-shelled. In addition, there are many thin bone-like plates and needles called tendons mixed in with the flesh, which must be found and removed. They are often found in prepared meat.

The big legs of the Alaskan king crab are cut into sections and sold frozen. They are handled in the same manner as lobster tails. In addition, solid crab meat, which may be in chunks or in shreds, and from any one of a variety of crabs, may be available fresh packed, frozen or canned. It is

expensive but filling, and you can serve 4 people well on a pound.

Crab meat may be served cold by itself or in salad, or hot after frying in butter, and substituted for lobster in the Newburg recipe.

BIVALVES

Bivalves are the shellfish that have a pair of shells hinged together. They include the best eating among the mollusks — scallops, oysters, clams and mussels.

Their muscular and nervous system is organized so that the shells are open when the animal is relaxed, and are kept in their usual closed position only by muscular effort. As a result, if the animal is dead or sick, the shell usually opens, so that even the amateur can tell at a glance if they are in good condition.

Except for the scallop, the edible bivalves are sedentary, that is, after a brief free-swimming childhood they settle down in one place. They feed by pumping water through themselves, and extracting organic matter, both alive and dead, from it. As a result, they are very subject to contamination from sewage, and may be carriers of a number of diseases, including hepatitis. We are likely to get whatever they have, because we eat the entire animal including the digestive system, usually raw or after only brief cooking.

Bivalves should never be gathered near septic or sewer outlets, or in any water that is not approved for swimming.

SCALLOPS

Scallops are two-shelled mollusks that swim briskly by clapping their shells together, having developed a large muscle for this purpose. This muscle is the only part of the animal that reaches our markets, the rest being discarded for lack of demand.

There are two species, the small, bay scallops whose muscle has a diameter of a half-inch or less, and the sea scallop which may be two inches across. The bay species is better flavored and more tender, and has been harvested so extensively that it has become scarce.

Both varieties have firm flesh, are tender and have a slightly sweet taste. They are so good that about the only way you can spoil them is to overcook them, but this is frequently done. It is advisable to thaw them before cooking. If frozen, add at least 50 per cent to cooking times.

At home they are usually pan fried in butter, with or without breading; deep fried with breading, or poached. Deep fry time is 2 or 3 minutes, and poaching or pan frying at medium heat takes about twice as long. When they are heated through, and are browned or crusted, they are done.

Scallops may also be eaten raw.

OYSTERS

Oysters combine the characteristics of being a simple food that can be gathered by hand at the right (unpolluted) bit of seashore and eaten raw, and being a gourmet's delight also. Unfortunately, a combination of too-great popularity on land and under-

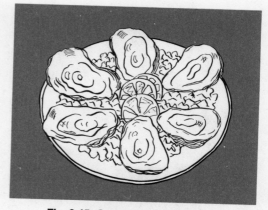

Fig. 9-15. Oysters on the half shell

water attack by pollution and pests such as starfish has resulted in almost complete loss of the original oyster beds, and the oysters we buy have to be artificially planted and raised.

There are a number of varieties of oyster, each with its special characteristic and flavor. In addition, one variety of oyster may have several different tastes, depending on where it grew. The subject is too complicated to be dealt with in a book of this type.

Oysters are sold raw in the shells, or by the pint without shells. A pint should contain about 12 oysters if they are a good size and plump, but the number is quite variable.

Shucking (Opening). The first step in dealing with an oyster may be to rinse it in cold water, scrubbing with a brush if it looks as if sand or debris were clinging to it. Many oysters are cleaned off before marketing. Then place it on a table, flat side up.

To the inexperienced, the shell looks like an impenetrable defense. The two halves are closely fitted together, and held tightly by a strong muscle. However, it is possible to push a knife blade through the crack between them at the thin end, push it along the inside surface of the flat side to the hinge, and cut the muscle. The shell should then open completely without resistance.

Fig. 9-16. Clams

Remove the upper shell, then cut the remnant of muscle free of the bottom shell, which holds the loosened oyster as if in a small saucer. You can serve it just this way, chilled, or tip it into a container with other shucked oysters for cooking.

This job can be made easier by smashing the thin edge of the shells with a hammer, or with strong pliers, widening the crack to insert the knife. Don't wreck the whole shell, just the edge.

Serving. Oysters are most popular served raw and very cold in half the shell. The animal is picked out with a special small fork, and eaten whole. The bit of salty and tasty juice remaining in the shell should be drunk. They are considered to be self-salted, and many prefer to have them with no seasoning at all. Others like a squirt of lemon juice, and/or a bit of pepper. There is an increasing tendency to supply a highly spiced cocktail sauce in which they may be dipped.

The next most popular serving method is pan fried or deep fried. They are usually breaded. For a dozen oysters, lightly beat two eggs with two tablespoons of cream, dip each oyster in the mix and then in freshly rolled cracker crumbs. Put aside for a few minutes on a plate or on waxed paper.

For pan frying, use 1/4 to 1/2 inch depth of butter, or a half and half mixture of butter and cooking oil, hot enough to bubble. Fry about one minute on each side, just enough to brown them a bit. They are done when the edges curl.

For deep frying, have the fat at about 370° F and cook about two minutes, or until light or golden brown. If you get a full brown color, parts of them are pretty sure to be overcooked.

Oyster stew is a rich cream soup. A typical recipe is:

Oyster Stew

1 pt	shucked oysters
¼ cup	butter or margarine
1 qt	half and half, or 1 pint each of milk and light cream
½ tsp	salt, or to taste
	pepper to taste
	paprika for decoration

There are at least two ways to put this together. One is to melt the butter in a pan, add the oysters and cook slowly until their edges curl. Add the milk and cream slowly, stirring, heat just short of boiling, simmer a couple of minutes and serve. The other is to put the milk/cream and the oysters in the pan first, heat just short of boiling and simmer until the oysters curl. Stir in butter and serve.

With either way you may put a dab of the butter, or other butter, in the bowls before pouring. Scatter the paprika very thinly on individual portions.

CLAMS

On the east coast there are two principal varieties of clam: the soft-shelled or long neck type found chiefly north of Cape Cod, and the hard-shelled or round clam to the south. The two shells of a pair are almost identical in both species. The hardshells are subdivided into littlenecks (small), cherrystones (medium) and quahogs or chowder (large). The Pacific coast has the razor and Pismo varieties, and several others.

Clams are likely to be sandy or muddy when dug, and may take several washings in cold water. Those at the store are usually thoroughly clean. There is also a question of sand inside them. It is said that clams will clean themselves of internal sand if left overnight in cool salt water. A liberal supply of cornmeal is said to help, as they can take the corn meal in as they put the sand out. I have not been able to test this because my clams never seem to be that sandy inside.

Clams may be eaten whole, and used whole or in pieces in chowder and other dishes.

Shucking. The process of taking clams out of their shells is usually known as shucking.

One method is to hold a hard shelled clam (Figure 9-17), in the palm of your left hand with the hinge toward you. With the right hand, insert a thin paring knife in the widest part of the crack between the shells, which is usually away from you and toward your fingers.

Continue to hold the knife to steady it, and squeeze it into the crack by closing your left hand, so that the fingers press on the back of the blade. You may rock the knife slightly with the right hand if necessary. Once it has penetrated, pull it to the right until the point is just inside the shell. Then move the point toward yourself to cut

Fig. 9-17. Opening a clam

the left hand muscle, then draw the base of knife in to cut the other muscle. You now can raise the upper shell easily.

The clam is attached lightly to both shells by membranes. Free these by running the knife point under them, cutting close to the shell to get as much of the muscles as possible. You may then dump the clam into a container for further processing, or twist off the upper shell and serve the meat raw (on the half shell) in the lower portion.

The clam's body is surrounded by a salty, clam-flavored juice which is highly valued by some and despised by others. If you want to save it, do your shucking over a bowl or pan which will catch spills and avoid wasting it.

If a clam opens easily, without cutting the muscles, it is probably dead and unfit to eat.

Clams that are to be cooked can be opened by putting them in a hot oven or boiling water. When the heat kills the animal its muscles relax and the shells open automatically. But this bit of cooking may affect the flavor of clams to be served raw, and it constitutes an admission of failure to separate the shells the regular way.

Soft shell clams are almost always steamed, a process that causes them to open.

Clams may be eaten on the half shell raw in the same manner as oysters. In addition, they may be cooked in about 10 minutes in a 400° F oven, or in 5 to 8 minutes under a broiler. A bit of butter and some bread crumbs may be added before cooking.

Fried. For frying, clams should be shucked and drained.

There are differences of opinion about the neck, which is very tough. You can leave it on complete, remove just its black skin, or cut the whole part off and discard.

Clams are usually breaded, pages 53 to 56. For a pint of shucked clams, use one egg with water. Have a cup or more of crumbs available.

Fry in deep fat, 365 to 375° F, until golden brown, probably for 2 or 3 minutes. Drain well, and serve immediately. A pint of clams should take care of 3 or 4 people.

Steamed. Steamed clams, usually of the softshell variety, are popular and easy to prepare. The shells are checked for firm closure to make sure the animals are alive but are not opened, and are cleaned by rinsing and by light scrubbing if necessary. Put in a deep kettle with a little water, only a few tablespoons to the quart, cover closely, and cook over low heat for about 15 minutes, or until shells have opened.

Serve in large soup plates, or any kind of dishes. Pour or strain the broth from the kettle into glasses. Serve these and saucers of melted butter with the clams.

Softshell clams are picked out of their open shells by the end of the neck, dipped in the broth and in the butter, or in one or neither of them according to taste, and eaten. The tough neck end is discarded. Hardshell steamed clams may be eaten with an oyster fork, or any available utensil.

Figure at least a quart of steamed clams in their shells for each customer. Some will eat much more, but others less.

10

EGGS

GENERAL DESCRIPTION

In cooking, the word "egg" means the egg of a female (hen) chicken unless some other bird is specifically mentioned. But it is often possible to get duck eggs after a little searching, and turkey and goose eggs may be available locally. These other eggs are of interest chiefly because many people are allergic to chicken eggs, and some of them are able to eat the eggs of other birds without difficulty.

Turkey eggs taste very much like chicken eggs. Those from ducks and geese have a slightly different flavor, but it is not noticeable in baked products or other mixtures, although the color might be a little deeper or more golden.

Turtle and other reptile eggs are rare specialties. Fish eggs are small and are attached together in masses, and are called roe or caviar.

All bird eggs are basically similar. They are made up of a hard but brittle shell, a white, a yolk and several membranes. See Figure 10-1. They are round in cross section and oval lengthwise. One end may be smaller (thinner or more pointed) than the other, a feature that is quite noticeable in chicken eggs.

Value. The white and yolk are concentrated solutions or colloids that together contain all the food materials necessary for the growth and development of a bird before hatching. They supply most dietary requirements for humans.

In addition to being a concentrated and healthful food source, eggs have the advantage of convenient size, agreeable taste, individual sanitary wrapping and extraordinary usefulness in blending and mixing with a wide variety of other foods, to which they may contribute thickening, stabilizing, flavor and color. They are a very important part of our diet.

Their approximate composition is shown in Figure 10-2.

Shell. Egg shells are hard but brittle and weak. They are composed chiefly of calcium carbonate, the principal mineral in bones. Shells are too difficult to eat and to digest, to have much dietary value. It is important to keep even the smallest pieces of them out of food, to avoid grittiness.

Shells may be white, or various shades of brown. Color depends chiefly on the

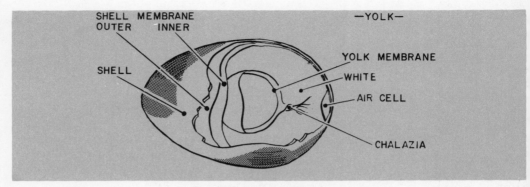

Fig. 10-1. Structure of an egg

breed of hen. It is of some importance in classifying eggs, but it provides little indication of flavor and none of nutrition.

The shell is porous, particularly at the large end. It has a thin outer covering called the cuticle, and two inside membranes. One of these sticks to the shell, the other forms an envelope for the white. They allow slow passage of water vapor and air. Many, perhaps most, of the eggs in the stores have had a surface treatment of mineral oil which reduces the porosity of the shell.

Even wtihout this help, the shell provides an effective barrier against organisms, and will usually prevent spoilage of the egg except when it is kept wet, dirty and/or warm.

A crushed area or a crack in the shell does not damage an egg unless the membranes are torn, so that the white can leak out and infection can enter.

Both shells and membranes are weak, so eggs have to be handled with extreme care to avoid damaging them.

White. The white in a fresh egg is a transparent liquid made up of thin inner and outer layers, and a thick middle part. As an egg ages, the thick part tends to get thin, and the thin parts watery. There is wide variability both in the original firmness and the rate at which it degenerates, and the differences are important in gradings eggs for quality.

It includes a pair of fibrous thickenings at the ends, called chalazae or chalazias, which hold the yolk centered as long as the white is thick.

The white makes up 55 to 60 per cent of the weight of the egg. It is about 87 per cent water and 12 per cent protein. This protein is a type called albumin. When heated over 140 to 149° F it jells permanently into a whice solid. Hardness increases moderately with higher cooking heats.

White of egg takes in large quantities of air when it is whipped or beaten, forming a stiff mass of fine bubbles that may be called either beaten whites or meringue.

It takes 8 or 10 whites from standard (large) eggs to fill an 8-ounce cup.

Yolk. The yolk is a thick liquid, enclosed by a membrane, and consisting of alternating layers that may differ very slightly in color. It's average color ranges from pale yellow to orange, and depends both on the breed of chicken and its diet. It makes up about one-third of the weight of the egg, and averages 49 per cent water, 32 per cent fat and 17 per cent protein. It is rich in vitamins. A big egg sometimes has two yolks.

Yolk has a high sulfur content, which causes it to tarnish silver rapidly.

In a high quality fresh-laid egg the yolk material is thick and the enclosing membrane is fairly strong. As a result, the yolk is not apt to break when the egg is opened and poured, unless it is punctured or roughly handled. As the egg ages its liquid thins and the membrane weakens, so that it becomes very difficult to use the egg without breaking the yolk. But it is possible for a perfectly fresh egg to have a weak yolk.

Yolks thicken and harden when cooked at 149 to 158° F and higher, and contribute to the stabilizing influence of eggs in mixtures. In addition, the yolk acts as an emulsifying agent in binding oil-and-water mixtures together.

There are 12 to 14 yolks to the cup, using the conventional large eggs.

Yolks do not beat up well, and even small quantities mixed with whites prevent them from becoming meringue. However, a well beaten whole egg contains considerable air in small bubbles, although it is not stiff. Its lightness can be increased by separating the white and yolk, and beating the whites before beating the two together. An even lighter mixture is obtained by beating the two separately and then stirring them together lightly with an up and down motion with a spoon, an operation called folding.

Air Cell. Since an egg's shell and membranes are slightly porous, air, water vapor and other gases can pass through them slowly. There may or may not be some air in an egg when it is laid, but if it is

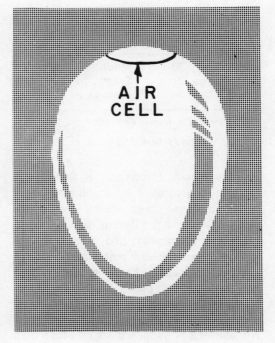

Fig. 10-3. Air cell

cooled its contents will shrink and air will enter to fill the empty space, usually in the more porous large end. It penetrates the outer shell membrane, which is held in place by sticking to the shell, but pushes the inner membrane inward, forming a bubble or air cell between them.

The cell tends to form in the center of the large end, where it is held in position by the force needed to separate the membranes, by the stiffness of the white and usually by the fact that eggs are packed for shipment or storage with the large end up.

As the egg ages, water tends to evaporate from it and pass through both membranes and the shell in the form of vapor, causing additional air to enter and enlarge the bubble. Evaporation is slowed by moderately high humidity, low temperature and treatment of shells with mineral oil. An enlarged bubble tends to make the egg float.

The air cell is one of the indicators of egg quality (large cell, old or low-grade egg) but it does not prove anything by itself.

	Whole Egg %	Yolk, %	White, %
Moisture	73.0	50.0	86.0
Protein	73.0	17.0	12.0
Fat	12.0	31.0	0.2
Sugar (as glucose)	0.0	0.2	0.4
Ash	1.0	1.5	1.0

By permission from "Practical Baking" by William Sultan, Copyright 1965, Avi Publishing Co.

Fig. 10-2. Average composition of eggs

Minimum Net Weight in Ounces for Dozen Eggs			
Jumbo	30	Medium	21
Extra large	27	Small	18
Large	24	Peewee or pullet	15

Courtesy of University of Connecticut

Fig. 10-4. Egg sizes

Its only specific importance is that if it is large, it may cause a boiling egg to crack.

Sizing. Eggs are graded by size (on the basis of weight-per-dozen) and by their conditions when newly laid. Standards vary somewhat among different states, but the Connecticut ratings given in Figure 10-4 may be taken as typical. Weights are calculated on the per-dozen standards to avoid use of fractions of ounces and fine scales. No one egg is supposed to be more than 1/12 ounce under the average weight for the dozen, and there should not be a difference of more than 1/4 ounce between the largest and smallest eggs in a dozen.

The choice of egg size is an individual matter. The best buy can be figured approximately by comparing prices with weights. For example, extra large at 81 cents a dozen would be about the same price per ounce of egg as large eggs at 72 or small at 54 cents. But if you serve two eggs as a portion, very large eggs will cost you more and feed your customers better than smaller ones.

Jumbos are the only class that can be greatly overweight, and are sometimes a bargain for that reason. Chicken eggs often weigh 3 or more ounces, and in such very large sizes often have double yolks. The record size recorded to date is 320 grams, about 11 ounces.

In recipes calling for eggs, assume that the large (24 ounce per dozen) size is meant unless something else is specified. This is the standard egg in many areas at present, where the medium size is considered to be small, and smaller sizes may be hard to find.

Grading. Eggs may be graded in any of the following classes: AA, A, B, C or rejects. A basic requirement for acceptability is good shape and clean and uncracked shells. After that, judging is on the basis of air cell, yolk, and white.

Eggs are inspected by a process called candling. This involves holding them against a small source of light in a dark room, first still and then with a slight spin. An expert can judge the internal condition accurately in this manner. It is usual to also break and inspect sample eggs from a batch for rating purposes.

The air cell should be as small as possible and have minimum side-to-side movement when the egg is tilted. In an AA egg it should be not over 1/8 inch deep, in a B not over 3/8 inch. Movement in AA is 1/4 inch or less, in B it is not limited.

The yolk should be round, firm and ap-

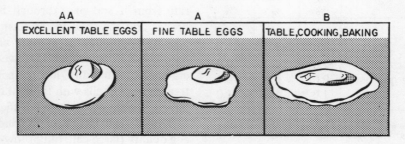

Fig. 10-5. Appearance of egg grades

proximately centered in the egg, with little change in shape or position when rotated. It should be free of dark spots and indication of any development of a fertilized germ cell.

The white should be reasonably firm. This is indicated by its keeping the yolk centered in the egg. Thinner white allows more yolk movement. The white should be free of blood clots or spots for grading purposes, but these do not interfere with food value nor do they usually affect taste.

The cook can roughly grade eggs after they are opened. On a flat surface a fresh AA egg will have an upstanding yolk, perhaps one-third of a globe, with a thick white close around it, with no white thin enough to run away. With decline in grade or increase in age the yolk becomes wider and lower, and an increasing proportion of white is thin enough to flow away from the egg. An egg that is tired but still edible may have such a weak yolk membrane that it will break no matter how carefully it is handled, and a white that is almost all as thin as soapy water.

The differences between grades are mostly a matter of appearance and firmness. Flavor differences are moderate, usually less than would develop during a week of storage. Lower grade eggs are almost always the better value for baking use, if they can be obtained. But they are more popular with bakers than with housewives, and are seldom seen in stores.

Flavor. It is generally agreed that an egg has its best flavor within a few hours of being laid, and tends to suffer a gradual decline from then on. The rate of the decline seems to be affected somewhat by the breed and individual characteristics of the egg, but more importantly by storage conditions. In the shell it keeps best at a temperature of about 30° F and high humidity. Higher temperatures accelerate degenerative changes and evaporation, low humidity increases evaporation only. The exact re-

Fig. 10-6. Roosters are not needed for egg production

lationship between these changes and loss of flavor is variable.

Consumers maintain that there are differences in flavor between brown and white-shelled eggs, egg marketers claim that flavor is identical. Without being in a position to make the very delicate tests required, it would seem reasonable to assume that eggs produced by different breeds of hen (as indicated by variation in shell color) might also have differences in flavor. However, they are not noticeable to the average person.

Fertilization. Commercial eggs are usually unfertilized (infertile). A hen lays at about the same rate, rooster or no rooster, and a fertile egg is subject to the danger of spoilage by growth.

If an egg has been fertilized, the living embryo will be found on one side of the yolk in the form of a lump or knot. If such an egg is kept warm, ideally at 101° F for 21 days, it will probably develop into a chick. A person opening it after a week of development is likely to have a very unpleasant surprise.

No growth occurs in embryos below

40° F so that modern refrigeration keeps even fertile eggs as just eggs.

STORAGE

The supply of eggs is subject to wide fluctuation, while both home and commercial demand for them is fairly steady. The areas of egg production are often not those of maximum consumption, and considerable time may elapse during collection, cleaning and grading, shipping and distribution. Fortunately, their keeping quality is excellent when they are properly treated.

The term "fresh" as applied to eggs has different meaning in different areas, and there may be places where it has no meaning at all. But it usually can be taken as an indication that the eggs have not been sidetracked to long term storage during their trip from hen to consumer.

Decay. The inside of an infertile egg is usually sterile when it is laid. Although porous, the shell and membranes provide fair protection against penetration by organisms. But if the egg is washed, the process may force mold spores or bacteria into it. And under warm moist conditions, such organisms may grow vigorously enough on the outside of an unwashed shell to penetrate it.

Egg is a good growth medium, so decay may proceed quite rapidly. Refrigeration will usually prevent it from starting, but will only slow it down after it gets going. The first result is often destruction of the yolk membrance with development of a bad taste. This may be followed soon by color changes and anything from a musty to an extremely offensive smell. Since there are many different types of infection, there is no dependable pattern.

It is wise to be mildly suspicious of every egg, although bad ones are extremely rare in stores. The basic precaution is to break each egg into an empty cup, instead of into other eggs or a food mixture.

Fig. 10-7. A very tired egg

Refrigeration. Refrigeration is the standard method of preserving eggs in their shells. In commercial storage a temperature of 29 to 31° F (eggs freeze at 28°) with humidity of 80 to 92 per cent is used. Under these conditions eggs may stay in good condition for six months or more.

In the home, any normal refrigerator temperature is satisfactory, even up to 45°. Keeping quality is better than average for refrigerator items. Quality should not decline noticeably (to the average person) for several weeks, particularly if temperature is toward the low side.

Shell Coatings. The shelf life of eggs under any storage conditions can be extended by coating the shell with some substance that will prevent moisture from getting out and infections from getting in.

Water glass (sodium silicate solution) was widely used for this purpose before refrigerators were plentiful. These dipped eggs might keep for months in a cellar with a temperature of 50 to 55° F.

Eggs are now coated with edible mineral oil to prolong their life in cold storage.

Freezing. Eggs cannot be frozen conveniently in the shell because the shells break, often making both freezing and thawing messy operations. Whole eggs, frozen out of their shells, keep their flavor and usefulness but may undergo considerable changes in texture. Yolks of frozen and then thawed eggs tend to be thicker and the whites thinner.

For home freezing, shelled eggs may be placed in plastic bags closed against evaporation (see FREEZING) which can then be placed in any type of container. Each bag may contain one egg, two, or more, depending on the expected use. Or the eggs may be separated, and yolks frozen in one set of bags, whites in another.

Eggs that have been lightly beaten together preserve texture much better than those in which yolks and whites are uncombined.

Commercial Freezing. Eggs are frozen in large volume for bakeries and other manufacturers who use eggs in their products. They are made up as whole eggs, yolks only and whites only.

Whole eggs are thoroughly mixed (or lightly beaten) before freezing. Largest production is in the spring, when egg laying exceeds demand. Freezing is done, usually in 30 pound cans, at −10 to −25° F for storage at about zero for up to a year.

Plain yolks tend to jell and separate when frozen, stored and then thawed. In addition, a gummy or a lumpy consistency may appear. These changes in texture may be prevented by mixing in about ten per cent of salt, sugar or glycerin before freezing. Processors use salt in preparing eggs for manufacturers of mayonnaise and salad dressings, and sugar for bakers, confectioners and ice cream makers. Glycerin is a specialty for bakers, because of an improvement in keeping qualities and volume of cakes.

Powder. Eggs are dried by spraying into a heated chamber, so that practically all their moisture is removed. The resulting powder has good keeping qualities, does not need refrigeration, and is said to be as satisfactory as fresh eggs in baking. It can be used to make scrambled eggs.

Dried eggs are reconstituted by adding water. For one part of the powder, use three parts of water for whole eggs, 2-1/2 for yolks, or eight parts for whites. It is recommended that the powder and water be mixed thoroughly to prevent lumping, and then allowed to stand an hour for absorption.

Fig. 10-8. One-handed egg cracking

In cake doughs it may be possible to mix the egg powder with the flour and add the water to the liquids, to avoid a separate mixing operation.

BREAKING EGGS

Boiled eggs are cooked in their shells. For any other use, the shell must be broken and the contents poured out. This should be done without mixing with pieces of egg shell. If the whites and yolks are to be separated, it is important not to break a yolk.

A nimble-fingered short order cook may open an egg with one hand, striking it briskly, midway between the ends, on the edge of a fry pan or bowl, and opening it by finger pressure. Less skilled or showy people strike the egg on the pan in the same way, or hit it with the edge of a knife or other utensil, and open it with two

Fig. 10-9. Two-handed egg cracking

Fig. 10-10. Holding back the yolk

hands, usually putting thumbs or thumbnails in the crack, then pulling it apart.

The beginner will have difficulty regulating the strength of the blow. Too hard will mean penetrating far enough to break the yolk, and even to open the shell so that the egg will slip out of the back. Too weak a blow will not crack the shell around the sides, so that the attempt to pull it apart is likely to crush the shell so as to mix pieces of it into the egg, and perhaps will put a thumb through the yolk as well.

The amateur's safest approach is to crack the egg all the way around with a series of 3 to 5 light blows. Then sink thumbnails

Fig. 10-11. Lifting a boiled egg

slightly into any part of the crack and pull it open. The additional blows take an extra second or two, but avoidance of a mess with even a few of the first eggs is well worth the time.

Yolk Breakage. A yolk may break without being touched or roughly handled. This may or may not be significant. It usually means that the egg is old, that is, that it has been either improperly stored or stored for too long. But a fresh egg sometimes has a weak yolk membrane, probably due to dietary or inherited deficiency in the hen. It is good policy to sniff at an egg whose yolk has broken easily, as this can be a sign of spoilage.

Separating. It is often necessary to separate the whites and the yolks. To do this you crack the egg in the same manner, but hold the crack horizontal or only slightly tipped, with the large end of the egg down, as you open it over a cup. The yolk will settle in the lower half, and most of the white will spill out. The remainder will usually follow if you tip and rotate the lower shell slowly, being careful not to dump out the yolk or puncture it on the edge of the shell.

If stringy parts of the white are only partly free you can pull them out by squeezing against the outside of the shell with the other piece, or with any utensil, and pulling downward. The yolk in the shell and the white in the cup are then tipped into containers. Any additional eggs needing separation are broken over the cup, one at a time, in the same manner.

Using a Cup. There are several reasons for breaking eggs into a cup, and then transferring them to the mixing bowl, pan or other larger container. The most important one applies when the whites are to be beaten. Even a tiny amount of yolk will prevent whites from whipping up stiff. If a yolk breaks into a cup only one white is put out of action, but if it breaks into a bowl the whole batch may have to be replaced.

Even without the need of separating, there is always a small chance that an egg may be bad, so that it might spoil a number of others if broken into a container with them.

Eggs that are to be poached can be put into the water more gently and safely from a cup than directly from the shell. And one with a broken yolk can be set aside, to avoid marring the appearance of the batch.

Pieces of Shell. Broken pieces of shell sometimes have to be removed from white of egg, which is clinging and elastic. You can get them out quite easily with tweezers. Otherwise, use the tip of a spoon or a table knife to work each piece against the side of the container, then slide it up. You may need patience and several tries to get it free.

Shell is tasteless and harmless, but it is hard and gritty, and can spoil the pleasure of eating food that contains it.

BOILED EGGS

Eggs are boiled in their shells. The unopened egg can be put in sufficient boiling or simmering water to cover.

Cooking time varies with the result wanted, the eggs' size and temperature and the water temperature. In any given time a large egg will cook less thoroughly than a small one, and a cold egg less than a warmer one. For example, an egg taken from a 35° refrigerator would need to be cooked 5 minutes to reach the consistency of a room-temperature one cooked 4 minutes. Instructions usually seem to assume that eggs are taken out of the fridge far enough in advance to warm up, but they almost never are.

There is no noticeable difference in speed of cooking between rapidly and slowly boiling water. Simmering near the boiling point makes a little difference, and keeping water temperature under 200° F both slows the cooking rate and gives the white a different, softer consistency.

If the water is boiling or very near boil-

ing, a 2 to 2-1/2 minute egg should have a half-congealed white and a liquid yolk. A medium or 3 to 3-1/2 minute egg has a mostly-cooked white and a fluid yolk. Four to 5 minutes provide a cooked white and a thickened yolk. All of these are rated as soft boiled, or in the modern phrase, soft-cooked.

If cooking is continued to 8 or 9 minutes, the egg will be firm all the way through, but the yolk will be moist and very slightly rubbery. By 15 minutes most or all of the yolk will be fully cooked, making it lighter in color and more tender. At 20 minutes you are sure of having the yolk fully cooked, but a grey or greenish dis-

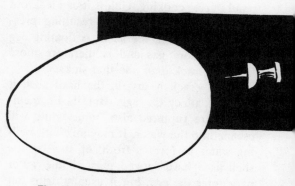

Fig. 10-12. A push-pin to let out air

coloration may appear where the white and yolk are in contact. This is harmless, but definitely undesirable because of its appearance. The white may or may not become slightly harder with the longer cooking times.

Eggs should be removed from the water as soon as the desired stage or time is reached. You can dip them out one by one with a large spoon, or hold them in the pan with a lid while you pour the water out.

Simmering. Some cookbooks will tell you NEVER to boil eggs, as it makes them tough. They recommend simmering. For most people, boiling is better. You don't need a thermometer or long experience to tell the temperature, so that timing is simplified, and fussing with the heat is not a problem.

The boiled egg is firmer in the white than a simmered one. Many people prefer it that way, and in any case, even the hardest soft boiled egg can hardly be considered unpleasantly hard or tough except from the standpoint of invalid diet or baby food.

Shells crack almost as frequently when eggs are simmered as when they are boiled.

Cracked Shells. A freshly laid egg should have only a very small amount of air or gas in it, and will usually sink in fresh water, while a stale one with its enlarged air cell will float.

The air or gas inside the shell will expand during cooking. Unless it can leak out fast enough to relieve the resulting pressure, it will crack the shell. A floating egg contains more gas and is therefore more likely to crack than one that sinks.

If the crack is just in the hard shell it will not affect the egg. But if the membranes are ruptured also, some white will escape into the water. It may mix with boiling water to form a froth, or stay on the shell as a hard-cooked mass. Some water may enter the egg, but it usually drips out when the egg is taken out of the water, or when it is opened.

Cracking can usually be prevented by making a pin hole in the air cell. This may be in the center of the large end of the egg, or in the part that is above water as it floats. A glass-headed push pin is good for this purpose, as it is very sharp and the head prevents it from penetrating deeply. You may want to mark the hole with a pencil so you can see what it does. If it is not in the air cell, it may let out a little white instead of a lot of air.

Cracking of the shell can usually be prevented by starting the cooking in cold water, a method called coddling.

Coddling. According to the dictionary, to coddle means to boil gently. In regard to eggs, however, it usually means to put them in warm or cold water, then heat it to a boil. This may prevent cracking of shells, as expanding air is given more time to ooze out before developing pressure enough to break out. Cooking is started at a lower temperature, causing the white to have a softer texture. The main difficulty is in obtaining accurate timing.

Egg white starts to coagulate (harden) at 140 to 147° F. This is a little more than half way between room temperature and boiling. You will not go far wrong in timing if you count half the time between turning on the heat and starting to boil as cooking time. For example, if it takes 6 minutes to bring the water to a boil, figure that the eggs have cooked 3 minutes. If you are trying to get 4-minute eggs, cook them another minute.

Allow a difference in cooking time for the starting temperature of the eggs, in the same manner as when boiling them.

Another cooking method is to put the eggs in boiling water, turn off the heat, and let them stand in the water until they are done. In general, figure twice normal boiling time, although results will be affected by the amount of water in the pot (a large

Fig. 10-13. Egg cups

Fig. 10-14. Egg slicer

Hard eggs may be boiled 10 to 20 minutes, depending on whether you want the yolk moist or tender; or simmered for a somewhat longer time. They may be served whole either in or out of their shells, or shelled and quartered or sliced. The shell is crushed on one side by hitting it against some flat surface, and it is then peeled, pushed or pulled off together with the soft membrane under it. It usually comes off more easily when the egg is hot than after it is cooled. As with most non-dissolving hot objects, pain of handling can be eliminated by chilling it with cool water before or during peeling.

Occasionally hard eggs are very difficult to peel, whether hot or cold, because the shell membranes stick to the white. There does not seem to be an explanation of this, nor any remedy except patient work, but fortunately it is a rare occurrence.

The egg may be too crumbly for satisfactory slicing when it is hot or warm, but will become firmer when chilled. An egg slicer will make the work easier and improve results. This is a slotted socket that holds the egg, and a hinged arm with fine wires that slice the whole egg when they are pushed down on it.

The surface of the egg may be too tough for the wires to penetrate. You then open the cutter and rub the egg along them lightly. This will start the cuts, so that when you next close the slicer they should penetrate the rest of the way easily. And this difficulty does not imply that the egg is too hard to eat with pleasure.

Hard boiled eggs may be served hot with butter and salt, or cold with salt. They make attractive additions to most lunch boxes. You can slice them for use in sandwiches and salads, and slice or chunk them for regular egg salad, sauces and casseroles.

POACHED

A poached egg is simmered without its shell.

volume stays hotter longer than a small one) and by the temperature of the room.

Serving. Soft boiled eggs are often served whole in the shells, and broken into a saucer or the large end of an egg cup by the person who eats them. The shell is cracked all the way around, the egg broken in half, and the contents poured or spooned into the cup. Since they should be very hot, it is really better if the hostess does the breaking, as she can chill them under a faucet just before handling.

Eggs that have been cooked 4 minutes or more may be firm enough so that there is a choice of cutting them into pieces and stirring, or eating them off the solid with a spoon. Butter, salt and pepper are commonly used.

A firm soft boiled egg may also have shell removed from about half of it, usually the small end, and then be placed shell down in the small part of an egg cup. It is eaten from the top down. Seasoning may be added after every couple of bites.

Hard Boiled. It has become fashionable to refer to hard boiled eggs as hard cooked eggs, because of the current prejudice in favor of simmering them. But simmering is practically the same process as boiling, and an egg can also be hard cooked out of its shell in a frypan or an oven.

Fig. 10-15. Egg poacher

The eggs are usually broken into a shallow pan of slowly boiling water, or broken into a cup and tipped into the water one by one. The first method is more direct, but offers a risk of scalding fingers if the egg is held low enough to let them touch the water, or high enough to make the water splash. And there is always the off chance of a tired egg that might spoil the looks of a whole batch. Putting them in one by one makes it easier to separate them when they are cooked.

When the eggs are in, turn the heat down so that the water will not boil energetically, as the bubbles tend to pull off parts of the uncooked white and turn them into a froth. Below this point, slower cooking by lower temperatures makes the white softer-textured, but since a poached egg can hardly be tough, this is usually just a matter of taste.

Water usually is just deep enough to cover the tops of the yolks. More water is wasteful, less may require splashing water over the tops to avoid leaving a raw-looking yellow spot where the yolk is not covered.

Eggs may also be steam poached by cooking them gently in about a quarter inch of water in a covered frypan. This is a little slower than the standard method, and taste and consistency are slightly different.

Eggs are usually poached about 3-1/2 to 5 minutes, until the whites are firm and the yolks thickened. Their consistency can be checked by pushing the yolk gently with a spoon.

When cooked, the eggs may be lifted out of the water, one or two at a time, on a large perforated spoon or turner. There is a possibility of parts of them sticking to the bottom of the pan, so the lifter should be slid under them carefully, making sure that any sticking spots are cut through, before trying to lift them. A Teflon lined pan in good condition practically eliminates the danger of sticking.

Poached eggs are usually served on toast (any kind), 1 or 2 eggs to a slice. It may be buttered or dry. Try to free the eggs of water first, to avoid making it soggy. If you take them out one at a time you can hold each one over the pan a moment to let it drip, but if there are two on the lifter one of them may slide off. Another way to get rid of water is to hold the eggs in place with an undersize pan lid while you tip the pan to pour the water out. You can then lift the eggs out in the regular way, or slide them out.

An egg poacher is one to four shallow aluminum cups or hollows on a stand. It is placed in a pan of boiling or simmering water, and the egg or eggs are deposited in the hollows. This keeps the eggs separated and formed during cooking. The frame is lifted when cooking is complete, and the eggs tipped out with a spoon.

FRIED

Fried eggs are very popular, and may be prepared in a number of different ways. "Sunny", "sunnyside up," or "looking up" means cooked on one side only, while "over" means cooking on both sides, although not necessarily by turning them over. An egg fried for a sandwich is usually "wrecked and over" meaning that the yolk is deliberately broken at the beginning, and the egg is cooked on both sides, but usually not enough to make the yolk solid.

Except for sandwiches and scrambled eggs, you are usually not supposed to break yolks while frying them. But don't feel too badly if you do it accidentally, just make the cooking time a little shorter. Some yolks break very easily, few of them are rugged, and even the most experienced cooks mess them up now and then. The flavor remains the same.

The consistency, taste and appearance of fried eggs varies with the amount and kind of fat, the rate of cooking, and how long they are cooked.

Grease. Any edible fat, oil or grease may be used. Butter is the most expensive, gives an excellent flavor, is rarely "greasy" and requires low heat. Margarine behaves similarly. Eggs are frequently fried in the grease of bacon or sausage cooked just before them or with them in the same pan.

Any depth of grease may be used, from enough to cover them down to a thin film wiped on with a paper towel. Frying may be greaseless in Teflon-coated pans, or well used black iron. Technically, this is not frying, but there is no better word for it.

Deep grease, 1/4 inch or more, provides security against sticking, but is extravagant, causes splattering during cooking and turning and may produce eggs that are too oily. However, excellent flavor, appearance and texture are often obtained.

If a small amount of fat is used, it may be put in the pan as it warms up, and pushed around as it melts to cover the whole bottom surface. Oil or melted grease can also be distributed by tipping the pan

Fig. 10-16. Sunny egg

back and forth. A more plentiful supply will spread itself naturally. Or you can drop the egg in the middle of a grease puddle, which it will spread around itself.

The grease should be hot but short of boiling when the egg or eggs are dropped or poured into it except butter and margarine which can be allowed to boil. From then on the temperature may be kept down for tenderness, and to reduce splatter; or kept high for fast cooking and good browning. Temperature range is low to hot, 250 to 400° F for normal cooking, but some people like to do them patiently in butter at 180°, or less.

Sunny. Sunny (unturned) eggs are usually cooked at moderate temperature, 250 to 300°, to allow the white to cook completely or almost completely and the yolks to thicken before the bottom hardens or burns. If served with a substantial amount of uncooked white showing, it is likely to be called a snotty egg. A few people ask for them. Cooking time ranges from a normal 1-1/2 to 5 minutes, or up to 9 if you follow one book. During cooking you may turn up an edge occasionally to check up on browning or burning. A fried egg is benefited for the average taste by light browning. But dark brown bottoms are usually tough, and burnt ones are for the charcoal eaters. If the bottom is overcooking, turn down the heat; if it is not browning enough for your taste, turn it up.

When you decide that your eggs are cooked, turn off the heat and remove them with a clean turner or a spatula. One at a time is recommended unless they cooked into one piece. Cut or pull apart connections between eggs that you will not pick up together, using a fork to hold and the turner to cut. Slide the turner around under the eggs to make sure they are free of the bottom. Even a small thread of white stuck to the bottom or another egg or a lump of food stuck to the turner, can cause a mess.

Have a plate, preferably a warm one,

right next to the frypan. Raise the egg (or eggs) clear of any grease, hold it for a moment if necessary to allow it to drain, then lower it gently onto the plate and slide the turner out. Repeat for the next one.

Fried eggs are both fragile and slippery, and attempts to carry them on a utensil from a stove to a table, or any other distance more than a few inches, should be postponed at least until you are accustomed to handling them.

Over. If eggs are to be "over" you turn them when the white is half to two-thirds cooked. You free them from the pan and from other eggs as carefully as if you were going to pick them up, raise them (preferably one at a time if they can be readily separated) and turn the spatula so that they will land gently and upside down. The direction of turn may be away from you or to either side, but never toward you, as you may splash a gob of hot grease, or even egg, out of the pan, and it is better if it does not hit your skin or clothes.

It is also possible and satisfying to turn eggs by flipping the pan, but this is for the experts. If you want to try it, practice first with a thoroughly fried egg or some other object that will not make a mess when you miss. And use a pan with sloping sides.

Cooking time is much shorter on the second side, particularly if you have broken the yolk. Unless you have orders to the contrary, try to finish with the whites solid but soft and the yolks thickened but not solid. Color is optional, and is regulated by the intensity of the heat. Light or golden brown is often preferred. Serve with the most attractive side up.

Covering. An egg may be cooked on both sides without being turned. You may get the effect by covering the pan from the beginning, or you may make it sure by putting in a teaspoon of water when the bottom is half cooked and then covering. Splattering from this small quantity of water is mild unless you are frying in a lot of very hot grease. Appearance and flavor from this steam cooking on one side are slightly different than that from frying on both sides.

You can also get your "over" effect by finishing one-side cooking under a broiler, either in the frypan or after sliding the eggs out onto a pan without a handle, or onto a heat-resistant dish.

SCRAMBLED

To scramble eggs, you mix the whites and yolks together more or less thoroughly, either before or during cooking. They are often mixed with milk, water or cream; and occasionally with other foods. The crudest scramblers are little more than fried eggs that have been very roughly treated, and the finest resemble custard. All types are good eating.

The differences depend on the type and thoroughness of mixing, the quantity of milk used and the intensity of heat.

Simple (Wrecked). The simplest and quickest way to cook eggs is to break them into a hot pan with some butter, and immediately start stirring them with a turner or a fork, either slowly or briskly. You remove films of cooked egg from the bottom, where it is replaced with less cooked material. The job takes only a minute, or 2 at the most. White and yolk preserve their color, but they are so mixed that they must be eaten together. Slow stirring gives a coarse mixture, briskness makes it finer.

Such eggs may be soft and moist, or dry, the difference being only a few extra seconds in the pan. They can easily absorb a tablespoon of milk or water per egg, if it is added at the beginning.

Many people maintain that pan mixing does not give true scrambled eggs, others that they are the only type that deserve the name. It is not possible to quote an authority, as these eggs are too easy to make to have found a place in cookbooks.

Milk, Cream or Water. Scrambled eggs

Fig. 10-17. Milk is a tenderizer for eggs

are made tender by adding milk; water or cream may be substituted with good results, with slight differences in flavor that are matters of personal preference. For each "large" egg you can use no milk, or up to 1/3 of a cup. More milk means eggs that are fluffier and more tender, reaching a custard consistency at maximum amount. But if you use 1/4 cup or more there is a strong possibility of some of the milk separating, so that a little water will drain out of the cooked eggs onto the pan or the plate. This does not affect the flavor or consistency of the eggs, but may annoy the eaters and embarrass the cook. Drainage is greater with hard cooked eggs than with moist ones, and when the plate is cold rather than warm. It can be concealed by serving the eggs on toast.

Mixing. Eggs can be just stirred to mix white, yolk and milk, or they can be thoroughly beaten. The beaten eggs are usually somewhat lighter, although most of the beaten-in air is lost during cooking. If you want to try for maximum effect, beat the whites stiff first, then beat in the yolks and milk briefly and cook immediately.

Cooking. Heat a buttered, greased or Teflon lined pan to medium or medium

high heat, 250 to 350° F, then pour the eggs into it. Almost immediately, start scraping the bottom of the pan gently with a turner or a tablespoon. Soon each stroke will remove a layer of cooked egg and allow raw egg to replace it on the hot surface. If heat is moderate and scraping rapid and constant the eggs will have a smooth consistency and even color. With the same heat, slow or interrupted scraping will work on thicker layers, and will produce a soft lumpy consistency that is generally liked. High heat produces firmer lumps, and streaks of brown crust that will mix in for a different but pleasant appearance and flavor. If you miss any pan surface, high heat can quickly produce burnt spots, the bad flavor of which will go through the whole batch.

If the eggs have been beaten thoroughly they will separate into two layers in the pan, liquid below and foam on top. At first only the liquid cooks, so there is no effect from the beating. As the mixture stiffens and leaves bare spots, foam can be pushed onto them. But it cooks poorly because of the insulating effect of the air in it, and it is hard to predict how much of the beaten-in air will be present in the cooked eggs. Fortunately the egg and milk react during cooking to lighten even an unbeaten mixture or one that has lost its air.

Consistency. Some people like their scramblers very thoroughly cooked, until they are dry and crumbly. Others like them a bit moist or even semi-liquid. Whatever you want, turn off the burner or lift the pan off an electric unit a few seconds ahead of time, as the heat in the eggs and in the pan continues the cooking.

The eggs are scraped out onto the plate or plates, and served immediately. Scrambled eggs tend to harden and loose flavor while standing.

Mixtures. Scrambled eggs may be mixed with a wide variety of seasonings and flavorful foods. Salt (not over 1/8 teaspoon to an egg) may be beaten into them, pepper should be only put on top when serving. Chopped or grated food, such as ham, sausage, bacon, mushrooms, raw or cooked onion, green peppers, or cheese may be added at any time after beating. If put in before cooking they make the eggs heavier, and are likely to prevent part of them from cooking. If added at the end they will not be heated and will cause the eggs to cool rapidly. The best method, if you want to take the trouble, is to heat your additions (except cheese) in a separate pan, and mix them with the eggs just before taking them off the fire.

BACON AND EGGS

Bacon is such a standard combination with fried or scrambled eggs that this is an appropriate place to mention cooking them together.

It takes from 3 to 8 minutes to cook bacon, and from 1-1/2 to 5 minutes to cook eggs. Bacon is not hurt by waiting a few minutes after cooking, while eggs are. Cooking of bacon should therefore start before the eggs, so that it will be finished at the same time or before. You have fewest complications if you finish it first, particularly if you have only one frypan.

Fry the bacon as described on page 126, and put it on absorbent paper. If you cover it, use paper or cloth, as a solid cover might un-crisp it.

You can cook the eggs in the same pan. You can use all the bacon grease, part of it, or pour and wipe it out of the pan and add butter. The wiped-out pan is best for scramblers, to avoid making them greasy and marring their appearance with specks of bacon.

Turn the burner low or out while removing the bacon. When the pan is ready, put the heat at medium. Break the eggs into the pan, holding them high if you have kept enough grease to spatter on your fingers. Space them as evenly as possible, and

don't worry if some of them run together a bit. Or pour in the scramble mixture and cook as just described.

OMELETS

There may be as many ways to make omelets as there are cooks to make them At their best they are a superb delicacy and at their worst they are still nourishing.

Basic Mix. Omelets are made from the same basic mix as scrambled eggs. The important difference is that they are no stirred during cooking enough to break up the structure.

Simple Omelet

4		eggs
6	Tb	milk or light cream
¼	tsp	salt
		pepper *(optional)*
1	Tb	butter

Beat the eggs lightly with a fork or a whisk, just enough to mix whites and yolks Stir in the milk. Put a 6 or 8-inch frypan on medium heat, melt the butter in it and pour in the egg-milk mixture. The pan should have a non-stick surface of Teflon or broken-in iron.

Cook at medium or medium-low heat on an electric unit, or in a pan of boiling water or over an insulating pad on a gas burner until it congeals or sets. It can be left alone for the whole cooking time if the heat is low, or checked at 6 and at 8 minutes for crust, by pushing an edge gently away from the pan.

Cooking can be speeded slightly, and a variety of texture introduced, by a small amount of scraping, starting when it has cooked about 7 minutes. Hold a table knife at an angle of about 30° to the surface, and push it gently along the bottom an inch or two in a number of places. This will bring cooked egg and forming crust up into the body of the omelet, and allow still-liquid egg to reach the pan for quicker cooking.

Cooking time should be about 10 minutes. This omelet should be puffed up into a souffle-like texture by small gas bubbles formed by the milk-egg-heat reaction.

To serve in the simplest way, loosen it from the pan with a table knife or spatula and slide it out on a plate, right side up. Cut it in halves or quarters, and eat it with butter, seasoned with salt and pepper.

Filling. If you don't want to be that simple, turn the omelet out on a large plate, and heap one half with about a cup of filling. This may be hot creamed chicken, crab meat, mushrooms, asparagus or almost anything creamed; chopped crisp bacon, coarsely grated cheese — anything that sounds good. Then fold the bare half over the heaped half, or cut it and lay it on top. If you have been properly generous with any semi-liquid filling, some of it will flow out over the plate. Cut with a knife and serve with a turner or tablespoon.

An omelet can also make an excellent dessert. Sweeten it with a half teaspoon of sugar per egg, and give it a filling of jam, jelly or finely cut sweetened fruit.

Folding Pan. Another way to cook the same basic mixture is in a special hinged omelet pan, Figure 10-18. It should be well buttered, and can be used in several ways. One, put all the mix in one side, fold the other side over as a lid, cook it until you figure it is two-thirds done, then turn it up-

Fig. 10-18. Hinged omelet pan

Courtesy of Mirro Aluminum Co.

side down. The omelet should fall neatly from the upper part into the lower, and resume cooking, getting (you hope) a golden crust on both sides. Even with Teflon, it pays to check after the turnover to make sure it is not clinging or perhaps half-clinging to the top.

Or you can use the pan opened, with half the mix in each side. When it is nearly done (these thinner layers will cook more quickly) put a moderate amount of some filling on one side, fold the other side over it, check to make sure the upper part came down, and cook about another minute. It is very helpful to heat the filling separately, as this will improve both the temperature and the texture of the omelet.

Fluffy Mix. Omelet may also be beaten before cooking. There are three general ways, rated by the amount of air you manage to get in. One, you beat the eggs with a rotary beater until the bubbles are fine, add the milk and beat for about 15 seconds. Two, beat the whites until they are stiff, then beat in the yolks and milk. Three, beat the whites stiff in one bowl, beat the yolks in another, add milk to the yolks and beat lightly, then fold (stir lightly) the whites and yolks together. None of these air mixtures are stable, so cooking should be started in a preheated pan immediately.

A fluffy omelet mix may be cooked in any of the ways appropriate to a stirred mix. But there is also a technique of cooking it on a flat griddle or a large frypan.

The griddle or pan should be well greased, preferably with butter, and should be medium hot, about 300° F. The eggs are poured on it immediately after beating, and will spread out over a large area. As a bottom crust starts to form, you fold the edges up and toward the center, until you have reduced it to a little less than twice the size of the finished omelet you want. If liquid egg runs past a fold out onto the pan, leave it long enough to thicken on the bottom, then fold it in.

Turning. Continue cooking until the bottom crust is strong enough for turning, usually from 1-1/2 to 3 minutes after cooking starts. The top will still be raw. Slide a long spatula under one side, free it from the pan, and fold it over on top of the other side, with the bend as near the center as you can get it.

This is a tricky operation. If you do it before the crust is strong enough, if part is stuck to the pan, or you are clumsy, the section you are turning may break up. If it does, patch it up as well as you can by pushing or lifting the pieces into an upside down position on the other section. You can put the wrecked side on the bottom when you serve it.

Decrease the heat if the part you turned over was brown, increase heat if it was pale yellow. Continue cooking about a minute, then turn the whole omelet over with a spatula or a pair of turners. Continue cooking until the center is moist but not wet. The mixture will have separated somewhat, so that the light frothy part is in the center, and as it provides its own air-foam insulation, it will cook slowly. You can usually open the edge opposite the fold with the

spatula or a fork to take a look. If the bottom threatens to get too dark, reduce the heat and turn the whole omelet over to cook it some more on the other side.

The difficulty of handling a large omelet may be avoided by cutting it into strips about the width of the turner, and folding it one section at a time. Some running together occurs, but you can cut the sections apart each time you move them. Each section can be one portion when you serve it.

Oven. An omelet may also be cooked without turning in an oven. Pour the mix into a pie pan or a shallow cake pan. Temperature should be about 325° F for bright metal and 275 to 300° for glass, with dull metal somewhere between.

Special Mixes. Some of the fillings used in fancy omelets, and a number of other foods, can be mixed in with the egg either before or during cooking. These additions are usually rather finely chopped or cut, but may be coarse. They may consist of bits of cooked ham, bacon, asparagus or peas; or raw onion, pepper or hearts of lettuce. Undiluted condensed vegetable soup makes a good omelet mix, using a 10-1/2 ounce can for about 6 eggs.

Fig. 10-19. Egg whites beat up stiffly

These items may be used alone, or in various combinations. The recipe given on page 478 for western sandwiches is equally good in omelets, using a tablespoon of milk per egg, and minimum quantities of the other ingredients.

Omelets mixed with other foods cook more slowly and are usually heavier than the plain variety. They are also more likely to break when being turned. It is a good plan to get some practice with ordinary and filled omelets before trying a mixture.

MERINGUE (BEATEN WHITES)

Egg whites can usually be beaten or whipped to a stiff consistency. They are then called meringue when they are used by themselves or as a topping for desserts. Meringue usually includes added sugar.

Whites may also be beaten more or less stiffly before mixing with yolks, flour and other ingredients, usually to obtain a smoother mixture and/or include air in the product. Occasionally, the purpose may be to break up the chalazas, so that they will not show up as unmixed white in some cooked mixture.

To beat well, whites must be free of any trace of egg yolk or other fatty material. Commercial bakers have found that as little as a half of a per cent yolk will affect whipping quality seriously. The eggs should be fresh, and they beat most readily and stiffly if they are at room temperature, rather than refrigerator-cold.

At home, beating is usually done in a bowl. It should not be so large that the whites spread out on the bottom too thinly for picking up by the beater, nor too small to hold the fluffed-up whites and any other ingredients that you will add to them.

An 8-ounce measuring cup holds 8 or 10 whites from "large" eggs. They usually increase their bulk by 4 to 6 times when beaten stiff.

Eggs are usually whipped by a double-rotating beater, which may be hand or electric powered. You crank the hand type at any convenient speed through the whole operation, but an electric is usually started slowly and then speeded up.

Texture. The whites start puffing up almost immediately, but at first they have a coarse wet appearance and a limp texture, with relatively large, thick-walled bubbles. The bubbles get smaller, harder and more numerous with continued beating.

Two stages are mentioned in recipes. "Standing in wet peaks" means that the appearance is wet and shiny, and that if you stop the beater and raise it, the material will cling and try to follow it upward, and it is left standing in a sharp peak where the beater had been.

"Stiffly beaten" is a later stage, when they are so firm that the egg inside the beater will be raised with it, and the part around it will not slump into the hole it leaves. They are very white and look dry.

Sweetening. If the meringue is to be sweetened, add granulated or extra fine sugar at the stand-in-peaks stage. You may then beat just enough to mix it in well or go on to make it firm.

A half teaspoon of sugar to the white will make it barely sweet, and a quarter cup will make it very sweet, like an icing. For most purposes, one tablespoon for each white may be used, unless your recipe or your taste calls for a different amount.

Sugar dissolves rather slowly in meringue. Fine sugar makes it sweeter at first than granulated, but the difference may disappear after a few hours. The coarse sugar is said to make meringue slightly more vulnerable to weeping when it is cooked.

Some cooks and cookbooks add up to 1/3 teaspoon lemon juice or vinegar, or 1/8 teaspoon cream of tartar, for each egg. This may serve to point up the flavor and to give stability, but it does not appear to be absolutely necessary.

Kisses. Meringue kisses are somewhere between desserts and baked goods in use,

Fig. 10-20. Eggs are an ingredient

but since they are just white of egg and sugar, they can reasonably be described here.

Meringue Kisses

3		egg whites, room temperature
¾	cup	sugar
1	tsp	vanilla *(optional)*
1	tsp	vinegar *(optional)*

Beat the whites until they stand in peaks. Then add the sugar a little at a time, perhaps in 4 to 6 portions, and beat for 2 minutes each time. Vanilla and vinegar, if used, are beaten in after the last of the sugar. Some recipes recommend continued beating for another half hour.

Meringue with this much sugar in it is a very stiff mixture, very difficult to beat by hand and a strain on an old or poor quality electric mixer.

Baking is done on cookie sheets covered with paper. Most recipes bar waxed paper and insist on brown, but one specifies waxed. There is little difference in results, but the brown may be slightly preferable.

The oven is preheated. Recommendations range from 225 to 275° (cool oven) with 250 a good middle point. The higher

temperature tends to produce a chewy center, the lower range a crisp one. Cooking time is 50 to 80 minutes, or until the outside looks slightly creamy instead of pure white. If it is important to have the center cooked crisply, you have to break one open for a test.

Another cooking method that is excellent if you have the time, is to preheat the oven to 450° F if it is modern and well insulated, or 475° if it is an older model. Put in the meringues, turn off the heat, and leave for 4 or 5 hours, until the oven is cool. After that, they can be taken out at any convenient time, even the next morning.

Meringue may be measured in heaping teaspoons (one to measure, another to push it out), or put in a pastry bag and squeezed out. The bag is necessary if you are going to make particular shapes, as the beaten mixture is sticky and hard to work.

When done, peel them off the paper (or peel the paper off them) and put on a rack to cool. Keeping quality is usually excellent.

Meringues may be served plain, or with ice cream (meringue glacée), crushed fruit or berries, or almost any sauce.

EGGS AS INGREDIENTS

Eggs are an extremely important food in themselves, but they are probably even more valuable as an ingredient in other foods.

Eggs emulsify oil, and bind together mixtures that would be unstable without them. For example, when oil and vinegar are shaken or even beaten together to make a salad dressing they stay together just for a moment, then separate. But if they are beaten with egg yolk at high speed in a blender, it coats the fine droplets of oil formed by the beating so that they cannot re-combine, and thickens the mixture so that the droplets cannot work their way up through it. Mayonnaise is an example of an egg-stabilized mixture.

When eggs are cooked, their fluids change to solids. In so doing they thicken liquids or cause them to become solids, also. Stirred and baked custards are examples.

Eggs are a leavening agent — that is, they may react with other parts of a mix during cooking to create air or gas bubbles that give lightness, and by their thickening and solidifying characteristics they prevent the bubbles from escaping. In many mixtures they keep the setting of colloids from becoming too firm. Good omelets and souffles are examples of the air entraining function, and a popover (see page 423) is an extreme one. However, most raised baked products need other leavening agents, in addition to eggs.

In addition to these valuable chemical and physical characteristics, eggs provide excellent nourishment, flavor and color. It is not surprising that many foods are judged for quality largely on the basis of the number of eggs used in them.

11

MILK AND
MILK PRODUCTS

Milk is a fluid food produced by all mammals for the nourishment of their young. It is made by the mammary glands, a process called lactation, and is usually removed from them by suction. Production starts shortly after birth of offspring and continues until the end of the normal nursing period for the species, the start of the next pregnancy or stoppage by failure to remove the milk as it is formed.

Milk normally forms a complete food for the infant of the species that produces it, and a complete or nearly complete food for other mammalian babies. Almost all the milk used in the United States, and most of that used throughout the world, is produced by cows. Goat's milk is probably second in general importance. Milk from sheep, buffalo, camels and reindeer is important in many localities.

Figure 11-1 gives the approximate composition of milk from humans and a number of animals.

In this country, the unmodified word "milk" when used in connection with food means whole, sweet cow's milk. Whole milk contains either the full natural amount of cream (fat) or enough of it to meet legal standards for whole milk. The adjective "sweet" means that it is in a natural, fresh or unsoured condition.

If the cream is taken out, it is called skim milk. Sour whole milk is simply called sour milk, but sour skim milk is buttermilk. There are also special sour milks, skim or otherwise, such as yogurt and kumiss.

Milk is usually pasteurized to reduce the number and kinds of organisms living in it. This prevents spread of disease and improves its keeping qualities for short-term storage. It may be sterilized or powdered for long-term storage.

Evaporated milk is concentrated, sterilized and canned. Condensed milk is pasteurized, concentrated and mixed with a large amount of sugar. Concentrated milk is pasteurized, then reduced in bulk for convenience in storage and shipping.

Powdered or dried whole milk is a powder containing all milk substances except water. The fat in it limits its storage life at present, so most of our powdered milk is non-fat or skim milk. It has become one of our important foods.

	Water %	Protein %	Fat %	Lactose %	As
Cow	87.29	3.42	3.66	4.92	0
Human	87.60	1.20	3.80	7.0	0
Ass	89.88	1.98	1.45	6.24	0
Buffalo	82.44	4.74	7.40	4.64	0
Camel	87.67	3.45	3.02	5.15	0
Cat	83.05	7.00	4.50	4.85	0
Dog	74.55	3.15	10.20	11.30	0
Elephant	85.63	3.20	3.12	7.42	0
Ewe	80.60	5.44	8.28	4.78	0
Goat	87.37	4.00	3.00	4.84	0
Llama	86.55	3.90	3.15	5.60	0
Mare	89.86	2.00	1.59	6.14	0
Porpoise	41.28	11.20	45.80	1.15(?)	0
Rabbit	68.50	12.95	13.60	2.40	2
Reindeer	66.10	10.15	19.80	2.50	1
Sow	80.63	6.15	7.60	4.70	0
Vixen	81.86	6.35	6.25	4.23	1
Whale	69.80	9.43	19.40	?	0
Zebu	86.20	3.0	4.8	5.3	0

* Compiled from various published analyses.

By permission from "Modern Milk Products" by Lincoln Lampert, Copyright 1965. Chemical Publishing Co.

Fig. 11-1. Milk composition

These various milk forms will be discussed below.

There are also an increasing number of synthetic foods closely resembling milk, cream or milk products. These usually carry a label specifying that they are "non-dairy" foods, but the name often tries to imply a dairy-association. Dairy and non-dairy products may be mixed in a prepared food.

Importance. Milk is an extremely important food, both in its liquid state and in processed foods. It is almost essential for young children, highly desirable for all children and a pleasing and nourishing part of adult diets. As of 1960, the average consumption of milk and milk products in the United States was 653 pounds per person. But this is a substantially smaller amount than in most countries inhabited by North

Europeans. The high figure was for land, 1,448 pounds per person.

Uses. Almost two-thirds of our mil consumed as fluid milk, or is used in c mercial or home cooking. This incl evaporated, powdered and condensed r and ice cream.

As a drink, milk is highly nourish usually easy to digest, pleasant in taste moderately thirst-quenching. It is often vored with chocolate, and occasionally fruit syrups or other flavorings.

Milk for infants is usually diluted sc what with water, and other substances be added to it in accordance with a forr which may be changed a number of ti until one is found that suits the partic baby.

Milk is used in a variety of cooked tures, both for food value and advant

Product	Pounds of Milk Required
Butter	23
Cheddar Cheese	10
Evaporated Milk	2.5
Sweetened Condensed Milk	2.5
Nonfat Dry Milk	11.0
Ice Cream (per gallon)	14
Dry Milk	7.8
Dry Cream	19
Malted Milk	2.3
Cottage Cheese (skim milk)	6.25

By permission from "Modern Milk Products" by Lincoln Lampert, Copyright 1965. Chemical Publishing Co.

Fig. 11-2. Milk equivalents

in texture and taste. It is also the basic material in a variety of foods carrying the general classification of milk products. Figure 11-2 gives the pounds of whole milk used in preparing a pound of these, and of each of several forms of concentrated milk.

COMPOSITION

The average general composition of cow's milk, along with that of other animals, was given in Figure 11-1. It can be seen that all milk contains water, protein, fat, lactose and ash. The proportions vary greatly among different species, largely in accordance with special needs which we shall not consider here. There are also wide variations among individuals of a species, and the milk of one individual may vary because of food, season, length of lactation or nervous condition.

Milk from Jersey cows has a much higher fat content than that from Holsteins. This is averaged in the table. The difference amounts to about a half ounce of butter per quart of milk, and can be ignored in general cooking.

Grades and Classes. Milk is graded for sale under various regulations, most of which have more to do with sanitation and bacterial count than quality. Particular attention is paid to market milk, which is supplied to consumers in its fluid state.

Certified Milk differs from other milks in the extreme care that is taken to assure sanitary conditions of production and handling. It is held to a maximum bacterial count of 10,000 per milliliter (about 1,000th of a quart) before pasteurizing and 500 afterward. Frequent analyses are taken to determine the nature of the bacteria. Guaranteed Milk is very similar to Certified Milk.

Increasingly stringent standards for the regular milk for the home, Grade A, have greatly reduced the importance of Certified Milk. Its bacterial allowance is or was recently 200,000 per milliliter before pasteurization, and not over 30,000 at the time of delivery.

Grade B milk may have a count of 1,000,000 before pasteurization and 50,-000 at delivery. Its retail sale is prohibited in many localities. Grade C is even more alive.

Some localities have an AA grade. This may mean that it is up to Certified standards, that it has a higher than standard fat content, or both.

Class I milk is any fluid market milk sold directly to consumers. Class II and III, also called manufacturing milk, are used in preparing evaporated and powdered milk, butter, cheese, ice cream and chemicals, and commands a lower price.

Fat. Milk fat, more often but less correctly called butterfat, consists of very tiny droplets or globules distributed throughout the milk. Each globule is surrounded by a layer or frail membrane of protein and other material, which prevents it from combining with other globules to form larger globules or masses of fat. It is thought that Vitamin A, pigments and some enzymes are in the membrane rather than in the fat itself.

When milk is churned it is subjected to mechanical beating or agitation that breaks the films enclosing the fat globules, so that they are released to combine with each other to form more or less solid masses of fat (butter) which separate from the fluid remainder (buttermilk).

Milk fat is made up of a great number of different fats, combined in rather definite and uniform proportions, so that one batch of butter is likely to be very similar to any other.

The fat globules are lighter than other parts of the milk, and will move gradually upward to form a layer of cream, if they are undisturbed. In goat's milk the globules are so small that they have little power to rise, and are kept from doing so by the

Fig. 11-3. Skim and whole milk

random battering of other molecules. In homogenized milk the size of the globules is reduced mechanically in order to prevent cream separation.

Skim Milk. Skim milk, which may be called non-fat milk, is what is left of whole milk after the cream is removed. It has lost all or most of its fat and its vitamin A, the amount remaining decreasing with the efficiency of the separation. It also loses the film of phosphorous-rich protein that surrounds the fat particles, and prevents them from combining with each other.

The yellow tint of milk is in the cream, so skim milk has a chalk-white or bluish appearance. It is thinner in body and in taste but is more thirst-quenching.

Skim milk is used instead of whole milk chiefly by people who wish to limit their intake of either fat in general or saturated fat in particular. There are also some who prefer its taste.

Skim milk may be used in almost any cooking recipe calling for whole milk if you add about 2 teaspoons of butter to each cup or 2-1/2 tablespoons (1-1/4 ounces in weight) to the quart.

Protein. Milk proteins are good for human nourishment, and also serve as the raw material for the manufacture of useful inedible substances such as paper, paint, glue and plastic. They are very complex, both in chemical composition and in their behavior.

Casein makes up 2 to 4 per cent of milk, and lactalbumin about 1/2 per cent. There is also lactoglobulin, but its amount and purpose are subjects for argument.

Casein. Casein is a complete protein. It contains all the dietary-essential amino acids although it is a little low in cystine. Casein occurs only in milk and in chemicals made from milk. It is usually in combination with calcium, and occurs in a number of slightly different forms in the milk of different animals. Its particles in solution are too fine to be seen with a microscope, but they are large enough to catch and scatter light rays, giving skim milk its white or bluish-white opaque appearance.

Curd. Casein is the principal factor in the formation of milk curd, the very weak solid that appears when milk turns sour, or when it is curdled by mixing with acid or is jelled by rennet (Junket). Curd quality is important in the digestibility of milk and in the manufacture of cheese and other milk products. It is described in terms of hardness (firmness) and softness.

Soft curd is more quickly and easily digested than hard curd, and is therefore considered desirable for infants, invalids and people with digestive problems. Whole milk and especially homogenized whole milk make softer curds than skim milk, because of mixing of fat with the casein. Rennet, yogurt and cottage cheese curds are soft. Curds may be softened before forming by diluting the milk with a little water, or by boiling it.

In general, cow's milk produces harder curds than that of other mammals.

Whey. Whey is the thin, almost-clear fluid that may separate from the casein and most of the fat when they form into curd. It contains all the rest of the milk, including water, albumin, lactose and minerals. It may separate naturally, as during the souring process; or be temporarily jelled into it, as in a rennet dessert.

Commercially, whey is a byproduct of the manufacture of cheese and casein. It is condensed or dried for use in infant formulas, and may be used in some varieties of cheese and cheese spreads, and in condensed soup. It contains some fat, which may be made into butter. It is seldom used directly in home cooking.

Although whey is a good food substance, normal demand has not equalled the supply, and disposal of it has been a pollution problem in many areas.

Albumin. Albumin, or lactalbumin, is a minor part of cow's milk, although it makes up half the protein in human milk. It is coagulated by heat, and helps to form a soft rubbery layer on the surface of milk that is heated.

Lactose. Lactose, or milk sugar, makes up about 5 per cent of milk, is its principal solid ingredient and is practically its only carbohydrate. It is not nearly as sweet as cane sugar, and is only 1/14 as soluble in cold water. It is not useful for ordinary sweetening or cooking.

Lactose is digested by a special enzyme, lactase. Some adults, usually among those who have not had milk for many years, are incapable of producing this enzyme and therefore find milk to be indigestible.

The poor solubility of lactose causes problems in the preparation and storage of some milk products. So much water is evaporated out of sweetened condensed milk that there is not enough left to always keep the lactose in solution. Some of it may crystallize, and if the crystals are large enough to be noticeable, the customer may believe that there is sand or possibly ground glass in his can of milk. Available water in ice cream is reduced by freezing, so that lactose may crystallize in this also. Fortunately, crystallization is usually very slow, so that it becomes noticeable only in old stock. The manufacturer usually cannot prevent the crystals from forming, but he can treat the substance in such a way that

Fig. 11-4. Curds and whey

the crystals should be very small and therefore inoffensive.

Lactose crystals may be described as a harmless nuisance. Those in condensed milk will disappear if it is either heated or diluted, but in ice cream they can be eliminated only by melting, beating and refreezing with agitation, an operation that is not practical in most homes. Ice cream with lactose crystals usually has larger and softer ice crystals also.

Lecithin. Lecithin is a fat-like substance that shares with soap and detergent the ability to dissolve one end of its molecules in fat and the other in water. It forms a very thin layer on the surface of fat globules, preventing them from combining with each other. This layer is broken during beating or churning, allowing the fat to separate and form butter.

Lecithin may oxidize to form compounds with a variety of non-milk flavors, and is chiefly responsible for off-flavors other than sour ones. At worst, it may cause a fishy taste and smell.

Vitamins. In general, milk contains an adequate supply of vitamins when fresh from the cow, and after normal processing and storage. The amounts, however, are both disputed and variable.

Carotene, which can be converted into Vitamin A in our bodies, varies from 1.5 to 25 milligrams per liter of fat, the difference depending mostly on the amount in the feed. In May and June cows usually eat a great deal of fresh grass, and the resulting high carotene content of the milk fat gives a richer or yellower appearance to milk, cream and undyed butter at that season. However, the lack of yellow color does not necessarily indicate that milk is low in this vitamin, as it also occurs in colorless forms.

The amount of Vitamin D is affected both by feed and sunlight. The supply will be good if the cow's food is rich in the vitamin, or if the cow is exposed to plenty of sunlight. An increasing proportion of

Fig. 11-5. Sunlight builds Vitamin D

milk is treated by ultraviolet light irradiation or by additives to bring the Vitamin D content up to a standard of 400 International Units per quart.

Minerals. Milk contains practically all the mineral elements present in the soil or which the cow's feed is grown, some in slight traces, others in easily measurable quantities. Most or all of them are essential in human nutrition, and many of them are important in the secretion of milk, and in its behavior and uses.

Calcium is the most obviously important of the elements in milk, partly because it offers a more generous supply of a usable form than our other ordinary foodstuffs. Calcium is essential for building of bones and teeth, and is therefore very important to the young and growing child. The amount of it in milk stays remarkably constant, because if the cow does not get enough in her diet she will transfer it from her bones to the milk.

CREAM

Cream is the fat-rich portion that rises to the top while milk is standing, or is discharged from the inner ports of a centrifugal separator. This tendency of fat to separate is a special characteristic of cow's milk.

Cream is classified according to its fat content. According to Federal standards, light, coffee or table cream must have 18 to 20 per cent fat, light whipping cream 30 to 36 and heavy whipping or pastry cream, 36 per cent or more. There are also a number of state standards.

A simple approximation that is easy to remember is that heavy cream may be 40 per cent fat, medium cream 30, light cream 20 and half and half, a mixture of milk and light cream, about 10 per cent. The terms heavy and light refer to thick and thin viscosity, and are opposite to the real weight differences. Whole milk is 3-1/2 to 5 per cent fat, say an average of 4.

The rise of cream to the top of standing milk is called gravity separation. The process is more active at room temperature than in the refrigerator, and is more rapid and more complete in a wide shallow pan than in a deep narrow bottle. Warm temperature and a wide surface both favor the more complete separation of fat from other milk substances, so that the cream will be thicker. But to avoid rapid souring, temperature is usually kept below 55° F.

The initial separation may take 8 to 24 hours. After that there may be a continuing rearrangement of fat globules, often forming a very thick or semi-solid plug in the top of a milk bottle, or a skin on a pan.

Gravity-separated cream on a milk bottle may contain from 18 to 30 per cent fat in its liquid portion, and up to 60 per cent in a plug. In a pan it is likely to be 30 to 40 per cent, but may be 80 if semi-solid. Very thick cream can sometimes be pulled or lifted in a single piece off a pan, but a delicate operation of removing it in a liquid state with a spoon, called skimming, is usually required.

Gravity separation has been replaced in the dairy by the centrifugal separator, and homogenizing is making separation impossible in the home.

Whipping Cream. Whipped cream is a very highly prized ingredient, topping and/ or decoration for a wide variety of desserts.

Cream's whipping quality depends largely on its fat content, which should be at least 30 per cent for a reasonable assurance of success. It is believed that the fat globules, their membranes and accompanying milk proteins combine to make a stable structure that holds air introduced into it by beating. Under favorable conditions and with good luck, a somewhat thinner cream might whip, but this cannot be depended upon.

Heavy cream makes a denser, stronger and longer-lasting whip than medium cream, but the medium is often preferred because it is softer, more delicate and less fattening. If fat content is over 38 or 40 per cent there is no gain in whipping characteristics, and the product may seem too buttery.

Cream whips best when it is cold. It is said that the critical temperature is 50° F, but for surest results both the cream and the bowl, and possibly the beater too, should be refrigerator-cold. This is less important with really thick whipping cream than with marginal types.

Whipped cream is usually sweetened with granulated or powdered sugar. Using granulated, a slightly sweet taste may be produced by one tablespoon to the cup of liquid cream, and dessert sweetness with 2 to 4 tablespoons. For general purpose dessert topping, try 2 and add more if necessary. You can use slightly less powdered sugar, as the finer particles mix more thoroughly.

Do not add sugar until the cream is nearly as stiff as you want it. It may be made as stiff as meringue, but it can be more pleasing in appearance and taste if it is a little bit sloppy.

The principal hazard in whipping cream is to over-whip it so that it turns to butter.

This can happen to any cream, but it is most likely if the cream is heavy, stale or warm. It usually warns you of coming disaster by developing a slightly rough or grainy appearance. If you see this, stop beating immediately, as a few more beats may turn it into a mass of lumps. If sugar must be added, stir it in gently with a spoon.

The standard tool for whipping cream is a hand egg beater, but it is done equally well and possibly with less work by an electric beater or mixer. At the other extreme, you can whip it with a whisk or even (if old tales are true) with a silver table fork. The bowl should be small enough to provide a working depth of an inch or more.

Cream increases from 1-3/4 to 2 times

Fig. 11-6. Skimming cream from bottled milk

when it is whipped. This is much less than the 4 or 6 times that white of egg fluffs up. Heavy cream holds maximum expansion and shape rather well, while medium cream tends to shrink somewhat, and may develop a slight separation of whey. But any of it should be good for at least an hour at room temperature or several hours in the refrigerator and usable for a much longer time. But it must be tightly covered to avoid absorbing other flavors, and drying out.

The cream on the top of a bottle of non-homogenized milk is usually rich enough to whip, if you can get it off without mixing it with the milk below. Start by tipping the bottle and pouring until you see the milk-cream line approach the pouring lip. The rest you can dip out with a deep-bowled

measuring spoon, a plastic spoon after heating and bending the handle, or an iced tea spoon with the bottle held at an angle.

For whipped evaporated milk, see page 207.

Aerated Cream. Sterilized cream placed in a properly designed container with gas under high pressure can produce a very fluffy aerated or aerosol unsweetened whipped cream at the pressure of a button. Stiffness and stability are good, and volume is six or eight times that of the original cream.

The product is too fluffy and unsubstantial to replace home-whipped cream in first class desserts. It offers a quick and convenient way to improve both the taste and appearance of casual desserts such as ice cream sundaes and pre-mixed puddings.

There are also synthetic aerated cream preparations that are used in the same manner. Flavor and texture are very similar, and keeping quality is better.

PROCESSING

Milk provides good living for a wide variety of micro-organisms, which may be from the cow, people, the air or handling equipment. A few of these cause serious disease — tuberculosis, diphtheria, scarlet fever and food poisoning, for example — and modern methods of combining milk from many sources could lead to widespread epidemics unless precautions were taken.

The precautions start in the barn. Farmers who sell milk, and in many states, even those who produce for their own use must keep barns, milk cows and milk equipment in a sanitary condition. Use of certain insecticides and types of feed are regulated or prohibited. Cows are inspected and tested, and milk from diseased individuals or herds cannot be used.

Regulations and inspections are particularly thorough if the milk is to be sold raw (unpasteurized). Raw milk is now found only in home use, very small scale operations and in a special form called certified milk. Its use is diminishing.

Sanitary regulations and inspections continue through all handling and processing of milk until it reaches the consumer. However, all of these precautions together are not adequate to protect the consumer against possible infections. It is necessary to treat the milk just before bottling to kill any dangerous organisms that may be present in it.

Pasteurization. Pasteurization may be described as a mild heat treatment or as incomplete sterilization. It consists of heating a foodstuff for a definite time at a definite temperature, and then cooling it immediately. It is regulated to kill all the disease organisms, 90 to 95 per cent of other bacteria and most yeasts and molds.

Complete sterilization would require heating the milk for the time and to the temperatures used for evaporated milk. This would create an undesirable flavor that would greatly reduce its popularity, and would change some of its cooking characteristics. It is not considered necessary, because it is possible to kill all disease-causers (except for anthrax, which is practically unknown in this country) with much milder treatment.

It is also desirable to keep pasteurization at a low enough time-temperature level to permit survival of some of the lactic acid bacteria which cause souring. This process, while usually not welcome, is at least a normal and healthy one. Without the acid it makes, other and more heat resistant bacteria would attack the protein and the milk would rot — a much more disagreeable condition.

A highly desirable side effect of pasteurization is improvement in keeping qualities. This was the original reason for its introduction in this country. The health advantages were realized later. The improvement results from the great reduction in the number of organisms that cause souring and

Fig. 11-7. Inspection standards are rigid

spoiling. Also, enzymes such as lipase and amylase which cause off-flavors are destroyed. However, when it finally does spoil, it is more likely to do it in an unpleasant manner than when raw.

At present there are two recommended methods of pasteurizing milk. The standard process it to keep the milk at 145° for 30 minutes. The H.T.S.T. (high-temperature short-time) formula calls for 161° F for 15 seconds. Milk products with a very high fat content require an extra 5° of heat in either method.

Proper pasteurization has little or no effect on the flavor of milk, but occasional overheating due to error will cause a cooked taste and a slight darkening in color.

Homogenization. The fat globules in milk range in diameter from 1/10 micron to 20 microns (a micron is about 1/25,000 of an inch), with an average above two and three. They are lighter than the other substances in the milk, and if the diameter is 4 microns or more they will tend to rise to the surface to form a layer of cream. Those with a smaller diameter will be so knocked around by the random movement of other molecules that they will not rise.

Homogenizing is a process of reducing

Fig. 11-8. Cream line

the diameter of fat globules below this critical point. It involves forcing the milk under high pressure, usually 2,000 to 3,000 pounds per square inch, through a narrow opening and then a ninety degree change in direction. Increasing pressure decreases the size of the globules. The mechanics of this process are not understood, or at least are the subject of argument.

The primary purpose is to prevent separation of cream. This separation used to be a valued feature of milk, as it made some cream available in the home without the necessity of buying it separately. Bottled milk is often judged for quality on the basis of the location of the line between cream and milk — the lower the richer the better. This may be a nuisance to the dairy, as both the amount of cream and the way it separates are variables that are difficult to control.

Also, if the bottle stands undisturbed for several days, the cream rising to the top may thicken to the point where some of it does not mix back into the milk readily, so that it forms lumps, or even a semi-solid plug that has to be dug out with a spoon.

The use of paper containers for a large share of milk used in the home has taken away the advantage of being able to see the cream line, without reducing the disadvantages of its existence.

Side Effects. Homogenizing usually makes milk thicker and more opaque, providing a more cream-like appearance that makes it more acceptable as a coffee additive. It is more easily coagulated by heat or acid, which means that it is more apt to curdle in coffee, soup, gravy and cooked dishes if it is not fresh. On the other hand, home made custards may require longer cooking when it is used. Its whole-milk curd is made softer and more digestible, but skim milk curd is not affected.

A layer of sediment may sometimes be found on the bottom of a bottle of homogenized milk. It consists of minor impurities, including dead cells, which would remain suspended in ordinary milk or would rise with the cream. It does not indicate anything wrong with the milk, but the tactful producer can remove such particles by a process called clarification.

Since a large and increasing proportion of our milk is homogenized, it is apparent that consumers feel that advantages outweigh disadvantages.

Homogenized Cream. Homogenizing makes cream thicker and smoother, but difficult or impossible to whip, or to churn

Fig. 11-9. No way to tell fresh from stale

into butter. It is likely to curdle in hot coffee. It is tricky and unrewarding to use, and is not generally available.

KEEPING QUALITIES

Milk is very perishable. Fresh raw milk may turn sour in a few hours at a temperature of 80° F or in a few days at 35°. Sour milk is an excellent food, but most people do not like it and will not use it unless the souring is done in some special way. In most discussions of milk's perishability and storage time it is assumed that sour milk is spoiled milk.

The souring process is discussed in the next section.

Pasteurized milk and cream stay sweet for a week or more (industry spokesmen may say two weeks) if kept well refrigerated, although there may be a noticeable decline in flavor and an increased tendency for cream to separate or curdle when heated, during that period. Their containers usually do not give the date of pasteurizing, except in code, but they should.

Fig. 11-10. An off flavor?

In many sections of the country, there is no way that a consumer can assure himself of getting fresh milk, or especially cream, whether purchased at little store, big store or from a milkman. Stale packages get mixed up with fresh ones, sometimes by accident and sometimes deliberately. This uncertainty is added to the danger of souring due to possible improper refrigeration.

It is surprising that the dairy industry does not date its containers openly, even in the hard-to-justify lack of a legal need to do so. Increased consumer satisfaction should more than outweigh the cost and nuisance involved, especially in view of the increasing popularity of synthetic cream substitutes.

Off-Flavors. An off-flavor is any taste which is not considered to be natural to a food and which is unpleasant to some of the people who eat the food. Milk is moderately subject to them, partly because its natural flavor is so mild that it cannot disguise anything else. A sour taste is not an off-flavor, nor is it even considered a stale flavor, but is just part of the natural aging of milk.

The most common cause of off-flavors in milk is enzymes. One of these is lipase. Under certain conditions it breaks down milk fat, liberating some fatty acids with a rancid taste and smell. These are valued in certain cheeses, but are most unwelcome in milk. This enzyme is fortunately destroyed by pasteurization, and is made inactive by refrigeration. It would be very active in homogenized milk, except that all of that which reaches the home is pasteurized.

There are several other enzymes that cause milk to acquire peculiar flavors. They may accomplish this alone, in combination with each other or with the help of bacteria and other organisms. However, pasteurizing destroys most enzymes and bacteria, and reasonably prompt use prevents development of those that survive.

It should be born firmly in mind that the

development of a mild unusual flavor in milk does not imply that it is not good to drink or use for cooking if you don't mind the taste. It does not indicate danger.

Exposure to direct sunlight will change the flavor of milk, particularly if it is homogenized. Contact with even minute quantities of copper in the processing machinery produces or rather speeds up the development of an oxidized flavor, but this particular influence is counteracted by homogenization. It is all very complicated, and is of little importance to those who buy milk and cream from regular commercial sources and use it within a few days.

Freezing. The storage life of fresh milk can be increased to months and perhaps years by freezing, particularly if it can be kept at -10 or $-15°$ F. Flavor is not much affected, but there is a tendency for the solids to separate from the water in very fine curds when it is thawed, which gives it an unattractive grainy appearance.

Such separation is less likely and less severe if the milk is homogenized and/or if thawing is done slowly, as in a refrigerator. If these two good influences are combined there may be no noticeable effect of the freezing, except that the milk may have a greater tendency to develop oxidized flavors.

Concentrated milk is said to freeze and thaw more satisfactorily than whole milk.

Freezing must be quick for good results. It is interesting that the freezing point for all cow's milk, whether it is rich or lean, is very close to $-0.545°$ C, or about $31°$ F. Freezing point is a sensitive test for watered milk, as even one per cent of added water will make a measurable increase in it.

SOUR MILK

Souring. Fresh milk is almost neutral in acid-base reaction (pH 6.4 to 6.9), and has a slightly sweet taste because of its lactose sugar. It almost always contains various varieties of bacteria which feed on the lac-

tose, converting it to lactic acid, and causing the milk or cream to become sour. The reaction usually stops at about one per cent acid and a pH of 4.2, but sometimes will continue to 2 per cent acid and a pH of 3.5, which is down in the lemon juice class.

Souring of fresh raw milk can take place in a few hours at room temperature, and in two to four days in a refrigerator, the time varying widely with the number and types of bacteria present and with the temperature. Pasteurized milk has a much lower bacteria content, and may stay fresh a week or even longer at $35°$ F.

Acid causes separation of milk into curd, a soft solid, and whey, a thin liquid. If milk is slightly sour but has not separated, it will separate very readily if heated or mixed with even very mild acid. Stale milk or cream is therefore a risky substance in coffee or on fruit.

Milk that has turned sour is spoiled only to the extent that it cannot be used as fresh milk, due to both chemical and physical changes. It remains an excellent food, as it retains and may even increase its nutritional value, and many people like its flavor in a limited way. It is usually marketed and

Fig. 11-11. Sunlight changes flavors

Fig. 11-12. Milk may rot instead of souring

used in special forms, such as buttermilk and yogurt.

Lactic acid slows or stops the growth of many species of bacteria which would otherwise attack casein and other substances, causing the milk to rot and producing very disagreeable flavors and odors. This type of spoilage can occur in milk that is over-pasteurized so that the lactic acid bacteria are killed, and in evaporated milk after the can is opened. It is often prevented by natural infection with souring-type bacteria from the air.

If sour milk is infected by certain molds, they will consume the acid and restore conditions under which the acid-intolerant bacteria can grow. The molds and bacteria then combine to create an inedible, bad smelling mess. For this reason, sour milk, buttermilk and sour milk products should be kept refrigerated as carefully as fresh milk.

A small amount of alcohol, up to one per cent, may be present at some stages in the souring of milk.

Flavor. When milk sours and separates, most of the sour taste goes into the whey.

If curd and whey remain combined in a custard-like jell, as in yogurt, the flavor will be more sour than in cottage cheese, which is separated curd from which the whey is drained and rinsed.

Buttermilk. Genuine buttermilk is the liquid that remains after milk or cream, usually sour, is churned until the fat separates from it in the form of butter. It is similar to skim milk, except that it contains lecithin and some phosphorous-rich materials, originally on the surface of the fat globules, which are separated from them by churning. It also contains some fine particles of butter.

But commercial buttermilk is now apt to be a substitute material, which is often called cultured buttermilk to distinguish it. It is made by almost sterilizing skim milk by high and continued pasturization temperature (185° F for 30 minutes), then adding a mixture of selected bacteria that will produce a standard amount of acid and the desired flavor and consistency. The milk is allowed to stand at 72° F until sufficient acid has developed, is stirred to break up the curd, and then bottled. A small amount of milk fat may be added to improve flavor, and tiny particles of butter may be added for appearance.

Cultured buttermilk is reasonably uniform in texture and flavor, and is a pleasant summer beverage for those who like a sour drink. But it is a poor substitute for genuine buttermilk, as it lacks some of its flavor and nutritive ingredients, and it does not have the variety of beneficial organisms needed by some digestive systems.

Acidophilus milk is made by inoculating sterilized milk with Lactobacillus acidophilus organisms. It is more acid than buttermilk.

Yogurt. Yogurt, or yoghurt, is a soured milk with a custard-like consistency. Two organisms are used, Streptococcus thermophilus and Loctobacillus bulgaricus. They may be grown separately, then added to

pasteurized homogenized milk kept at 110°
F. Fermentation takes about three hours.
The stable custard or jell texture is obtained partly by adding 3 to 5 per cent of
non-fat milk powder before pasteurizing.
For liquid yogurt this powder is omitted,
and the product is beaten or agitated to
break up the curd.

Yogurt is sold plain, and also with added
fruit or chocolate flavor and/or 3 to 5 per
cent sugar.

CONCENTRATED MILK

Since fresh milk is about 87 per cent
water, shipping and storage costs may be
greatly reduced if some of the water can
be removed to reduce its bulk and weight.
Usually concentration is combined with preservative treatment to prevent spoilage.

Fresh. Fresh concentrated milk is whole
milk that is pasteurized, homogenized and
then evaporated under vacuum until its bulk
is reduced by 1/2 to 2/3. The evaporation
costs little, as it is done together with the
other processes. The savings in bulk and
weight should reduce storage and shipping
costs substantially.

If processing is done at a central plant,
the product may be shipped by tanker to a
local distributor, who may then re-pasteurize it before putting it in bottles and containers.

The consumer may use the concentrated
milk directly as coffee cream or in cooking,
and for regular milk she can reconstitute

it by adding one to two parts of water, as
directed on the container. The product
should be identical with whole milk in consistency and flavor, and often is. However,
it may have a harsh flavor for a day after
mixing due to the crystallizing of calcium
salts or other materials in the concentrate,
which take a while to dissolve when water
is added.

Concentrated fresh milk should be cheaper than whole fresh milk, and it has certain
side advantages, such as use instead of
cream in coffee or on cereal, or in making
a richer milk by not adding the full quantity
of water. However, most consumers do not
want to bother with mixing, and may feel,
that the flavor is not just the same. Sales
are not very satisfactory, and it is not available at all in many areas. As a result, this
very advanced and quite useful product
may be a casualty of our affluent society,
at least temporarily.

Evaporated. Regular evaporated milk is
whole milk, minus about 60 per cent of its
water, sterilized and canned. It is the most
widely used form of concentrated milk. According to Federal standards, it must contain not less than 7.9 per cent of milk fat
and not less than 25.9 per cent of total milk
solids. In addition, it may contain up to a
tenth of a per cent of stabilizer salts and be
fortified with Vitamin D. There is also
evaporated skim milk, which differs only in
its much lower fat content.

The whole milk is usually a mixture from

Fig. 11-13. Milk is big business

a number of dairies. It is graded carefully, passed through a clarifier to remove any foreign material, and then brought to the desired percentage of milk fat by adding either cream or skim milk. It is heated to just below boiling (forewarming), concentrated by evaporation of its water in a vacuum pan, homogenized at high pressure, and forced into cans through small holes in the top covers. Standard cans for home use hold 6 or 14.5 ounces.

The filled cans go through a sterilizer, where they are subjected to 235 to 262° F for 15 to 20 minutes. This heat is necessary to destroy all organisms. It changes the milk in various ways, particularly in a slight darkening of color and changes of flavor which are probably due to caramelization by heat reactions between lactose and protein.

Canned milk has a tendency to jell just after processing. This can usually be prevented at the cannery, by adding small amounts of salts such as sodium citrate or calcium chloride to the milk before sterilizing, and by vigorous shaking of the cans as they cool. Once in a while it will congeal anyhow, so you may open a can that looks more like custard than milk. It will return to normal consistency if you remove the lid and stir vigorously. Unfortunately, the cans are usually a rimless type that cannot be gripped by a rotary opener, so you would have to use a lever opener or a knife.

Milk almost never spoils in the can, but it may deteriorate slowly. Cream may separate in spite of the homogenization, but it can be stirred back in. The milk may lose its brownish tint and become yellow or greenish and become thinner. Small crystals of calcium citrate may appear after long storage in a warm place. None of these changes affect its safety or food value, and there are only minor changes in flavor.

Evaporated milk, either diluted or in its original stage, will spoil or sour after the can is opened, so it should be kept cold in the same manner as fresh milk.

Fig. 11-14. Armored cows

Uses. Evaporated milk may be used directly from the can (armored cow) in coffee, on cereal and in general as a cream substitute. However, except for those who have developed a fondness for it, it is not a good substitute, as the flavor is different and the texture is often syrupy.

It may be diluted (reconstituted) to the food value and approximate consistency of whole milk by adding an equal volume of water. Its cooked flavor seems to prevent much use as a beverage, but it is usually satisfactory as an ingredient in cooking. It is preferred to fresh milk in infant formulas because it has a much softer and more digestible curd.

Evaporated milk may be whipped if the milk, the bowl and the beater are all thoroughly chilled. A good consistency, similar to that of whipped medium cream, may be obtained with a rotary beater in about a minute, with an expansion that may be better than 3 to 1. One to 3 tablespoons of sugar may be used to a 6-ounce can.

This whipped milk starts to go flat quite quickly, and should be used within 15 minutes of whipping. However, it re-whips readily, even after sugar is added. The air and sweetening make the canned flavor less noticeable.

Condensed. Sweetened condensed milk is the original concentrated milk, and had extensive use during the Civil War. It is preserved with sugar, and does not have to

Fig. 11-15. Long before the K ration

be sterilized. It is usually made of pasteurized whole milk, mixed with a 65 per cent sugar syrup (sucrose, or a mixture of sucrose and corn sugar), then evaporated under vacuum to reduce its bulk. It is put in cans for home use or in drums for bakeries.

The added sugar stays in solution, but some of the less soluble lactose crystallizes out of this too-concentrated mixture. The processor "seeds" the milk just before canning with a little of an older batch of condensed milk, powdered lactose or dry skim milk powder, to provide a large number of nuclei upon which lactose crystals will form. If there are enough separate crystals they will all be too small to be noticeable, or will at least not be objectionable. Large crystals make the milk gritty, but do no harm otherwise.

This product must contain not less than 28 per cent of milk solids and not less than 8.5 per cent milk fat, so that it is somewhat richer or more concentrated than evaporated milk. In addition, it carries a heavy load of sugar, 42 to 44 per cent. Two varieties with slightly different formulas are on the market, "Eagle" in 15-ounce cans and "Household" in 14-ounce cans. Eagle contains slightly less sugar and more milk solids.

Product	Water	Protein	Fat	Lactose	Ash	Citric Acid	Maltose and Dextrose
Nonfat Dry Milk	3.0	36.0	0.7	51.0	8.0	1.3	—
Dry Whole Milk	2.3	26.0	26.7	38.0	6.0	1.0	—
Dry Buttermilk	3.0	36.0	5.0	48.0	8.0	—	—
Dry Cream	0.6	11.0	72.0	14.0	2.4	—	—
Malted Milk	3.0	14.0	8.0	21.5	3.3	—	50.2
Dry Whey	4.0	12.0	0.6	72.4	11.0	—	—

By permission from "Modern Milk Products" by Lincoln Lampert, Copyright 1965, Chemical Publishing Co.

Fig. 11-16. Average composition of dry milk products

The concentration of sugar in condensed milk prevents growth of bacteria. Lack of air in the cans prevents growth of molds. Certain yeasts are able to grow under these conditions, but they are almost always destroyed during pasteurization. However, the milk deteriorates slowly in storage unless it is cool. It may set to form a soft jelly, suffer some separation of an oily cream or even develop a cheesy flavor. However, these processes are very slow, and seldom cause problems in the home.

Condensed milk is used in cooking, as an infant food and occasionally as coffee cream or a spread on crackers. Special recipes are provided by the manufacturer. It has a pleasant, uncooked taste, but can only be used where heavy sweetening is required or at least tolerated.

DRY (POWDERED) MILK

Milk may be concentrated even further by removing all the water, and processing the solid remainder into a soluble powder. Dried milk was known in Asia before the thirteenth century, malted milk has been available since 1887, and an excellent quality whole milk powder (Klim) was obtainable in 1931. However, milk powders did not become an important consumer item until after 1946.

Dry milk products include powders made from whole milk, skim milk, buttermilk, malted milk and cream. Of these, the dried skim milk, now officially known as nonfat dry-milk solids, is by far the most important, chiefly because of its excellent keeping qualities, and ease of dissolving and mixing.

Whole milk, nonfat milk and cream powders for home use are made by pasteurizing (prewarming) the fluid, concentrating it by boiling in vacuum pans and spraying it into a current of hot, dry air. Vacuum lowers the boiling point below flavor-damaging temperature. Low heat processes favor solubility of the powder.

Individual particles of milk powder made in this manner are soluble, but they tend to pack together closely so that water cannot penetrate them. The mass dissolves rather slowly and lumps are likely to persist a long time. The instant type of powder now in general use is made up of loose clusters of the fine particles. This is discussed on pages 23 and 210.

Dry Whole Milk. Dry whole milk must contain at least 26 per cent milk fat and not more than 5 per cent water. If properly made and used within a reasonable time it can be mixed with 6 to 7 times its weight in water to make a product very similar to fresh milk, although a processed flavor may be noticeable.

Unfortunately, its keeping quality is limited by the deterioration of its fat in storage. It is usually good for two months at room temperature and somewhat longer in the cool. After that, off flavors which may be stale, tallowy, musty, fishy or rancid may develop. A number of methods are being tried to increase its shelf life. These include mixing with anti-oxidants and packing in vacuum or in nitrogen or carbon dioxide gas. It is important to keep it dry.

Most dry whole milk is used commercially by bakers and candy manufacturers,

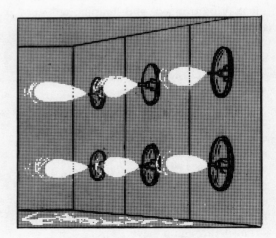

Fig. 11-17. Inside a milk drying room

but it may be rarely available in small packages at the grocery for home use. If it is in good condition it can be mixed with water and used in the same manner as milk, as a beverage, and in cooking. If it is used to replace nonfat dry milk in cooking, allowance must be made for its additional fat content.

Nonfat Dry Milk. Powdered skim milk is known as nonfat dry milk, presumably because the manufacturers believe that nonfat avoids sales resistance to the term "skim" and that dry is more acceptable than powdered. Fortunately, the new terms are equally descriptive.

This powder can be reconstituted into skim milk by mixing with water, one cup of powder to 3 to 3-3/4 cups of water, or 4 tablespoons to one cup. The larger quantity of water gives the same proportion as fresh skim milk, the smaller quantity makes it a bit richer. Whole fresh milk can be substituted for part of the water, or added to the finished mixture, for richness and a fresher taste.

Most milk powder, including all of it that is meant for home consumption, is made by spraying concentrated milk into a stream of hot, dry air. Quick evaporation of water leaves a powder that includes air bubbles, which improve solubility. More air may be trapped, and lumping tendency reduced, by treating the powder grains so that they will clump together loosely in small clusters that can be penetrated by water. The clustered powder may be called "instant" or "instantized".

Such powder dissolves or disperses readily in cold water if properly handled, but can become gummy or lumpy. It should be mixed in a bowl rather than a glass, first with 1/3 to 1/2 the water and then with the rest of the water, and a whisk or rotary beater should be used instead of a spoon. If the liquid should turn out to be lumpy, strain it through a sieve.

Milk powder has a tendency to absorb moisture from the air, forming lumps that may become quite hard. It should be kept in its original sealed packages until used. Bacteria content is usually very low, so that milk made from it should have good keeping quality.

This reconstituted milk has a slightly processed flavor, but its greatest weaknesses are its lack of cream and the likelihood of its containing lumps for a while after mixing. It has considerable use as a beverage, however. It can be substituted for skim milk in cooking, or for whole milk if you add 1-1/2 to 2 tablespoons of butter for each cup. The powder can be mixed with the dry ingredients, and the water added separately.

Nonfat dry milk is also used (and sometimes over-used) as an additive or substitution to increase nutriment, develop crust color and make changes in texture. Six per cent of the flour in bread may be replaced by the milk powder, without change in other ingredients.

Malted Milk. Malt is a food material prepared from cereal grain by causing it to start to germinate. This modifies the seeds' natural food substances and produces enzymes (particularly diastase) which have the power to convert starch to sugar.

The process is one of keeping the barley or other grain damp, warm and ventilated until the desired condition is obtained, then stopping growth by drying it. If the malt is wanted for enzyme activity the drying temperature is kept low, but for maximum flavor it is heated to 200° F or more.

In preparation of malted milk, dried malt is crushed and mixed with wheat flour and hot water. Enzymes convert the cereal starch into the sugars maltose and dextrin, after which the mixture is filtered. The filtrate or extract is mixed with whole milk, one pound of milk to 1-1/4 pounds of extract, with added salt and sodium bicarbonate. The resulting liquid is concentrated and dried. It is available as ordinary and instant powders, and as tablets in plain and chocolate flavored form.

Malted milk is a concentrated, vitamin-rich and easily digested food. Its principal uses are in beverages and candy, and in food for babies and invalids. It is not much used in cooking.

Powdered Cream. Light cream may be dried by the spray process, producing a flaky, light, cream-colored powder. Its keeping qualities are only fair, and production is not on a large scale.

Dry cream may be used in coffee. However, many of the powdered "coffee cream" products contain no milk or cream at all, being made up of other materials with better long-term keeping properties and generally similar flavor.

COLD MILK DRINKS

Milk is an excellent beverage in itself, and is very popular as whole milk, skim milk and buttermilk. It is also a base for many mixtures, such as chocolate milk, eggnog and various varieties of shakes (or milk shakes) and malteds. All of these have in common that they are usually served cold and often very cold with inclusion of ice cream or cracked ice, that they are so nourishing that they are as much a food as a beverage, and that they should be drunk rather slowly, in sips, to avoid the formation of coarse, hard-to-digest curds in the stomach.

These drinks are discussed under BEVERAGES.

Milk is also an ingredient in ice cream sodas and some other fizzy drinks.

COOKING WITH MILK

Milk is a major or minor ingredient in a vast number of recipes. It is somewhat tricky to work with, and a knowledge of its peculiarities will help to prevent difficulties and disappointments.

Curdling. Milk tends to curdle — separate into numerous small lumps — when it is mixed with acid or heated. This is especially true of homogenized milk. The probability of curdling varies widely with the condition of the milk and with the circumstances.

Acid is a stronger curdling agent than heat, and a substantial amount of it may be present in the milk. The souring process is gradual, and it may create an acid condition before there is a casually noticeable change in either flavor or odor. Milk in this condition will curdle much more readily from other causes than that which is absolutely fresh and sweet. Since you have no convenient test for acidity, and since you can seldom be sure of the time the milk took to reach you, it is best to take precautions at all times.

When you are adding milk to a hot or a mildly acid liquid you should pour it in slowly or a little at a time, and stir vigorously. This either prevents curdling or causes the curds to form in such small sizes that they are not noticeable. Even if lumps do form, vigorous beating may cause them to disappear.

Sticking and Burning. Milk tends to stick and harden on a heated surface in a non-conducting film that soon scorches and burns. You combat this by low heat, shortest practical heating time, stirring, pan selection and mixing.

The first two suggestions are somewhat contradictory, as low heat takes more time than high heat. But the idea is to avoid continuing heating or cooking any longer than is absolutely necessary. Especially, if the recipe says scald milk (heat it until a few bubbles appear at the edge) don't keep on heating it until it boils.

Stirring is not as effective as it is with thicker liquids, as the film is removed only at the line of contact between stirrer and pan; not dragged off a wider strip by friction of the liquid.

Pan selection may be very important. Scorching tends to start at a spot where

Fig. 11-18. Skin on hot milk

Skin. A soft skin usually forms on the surface of milk or a milk mixture when it is heated above 140° F unless it is stirred frequently or perhaps constantly. The skin or film is probably composed chiefly of casein and albumin. Its formation is speeded by increasing heat. It seems to form more readily on stale milk than on fresh and on whole milk rather than skim.

This skin is a disagreeable complication in cooking with milk. It can be prevented by stirring or beating. After skin forms it can often be dissolved by vigorous stirring. At other times it will not dissolve, but will wrap around the spoon or sink out of sight. If not destroyed by stirring, or skimmed off and discarded, it may make sauces lumpy and hot milk drinks unpalatable.

heat is concentrated. If pan metal is very thin and/or a poor conductor of heat, a burner hot spot will create a hot spot inside the pan directly above it. If a pan is dented, cracked or pitted, and particularly if it has even the tiniest remnant of burned or even dried food sticking to it from a previous use, scorching will start there. A careful housewife may have no trouble until her children become old enough to wash the dishes. Minimum danger is with a heavy cast aluminum pan with a Teflon lining. But if you stir in this, try to use a wood or plastic utensil to avoid scratching or wearing away the surface.

You can avoid all danger of scorching by using a double boiler, with water in the bottom, but this takes an extra pan and a lot of extra time.

BUTTER

Butter is concentrated milk fat. It is considered to be the premium quality fat throughout a large part of the world. It is valued for its excellent nutritive quality, flavor, digestibility and compatibility with other foods. In primitive areas its ease of manufacture is an important asset.

It is the highest priced common fat.

Description. The best butter has a fine flavor, a solid waxy body, a uniform color, any salt is entirely dissolved, appearance is bright rather than dull or greasy and any drops of water on a cut surface are small and clear. Average composition is shown in Figure 11-19. In addition, it may contain up to 4 per cent of air by volume.

Type	Fat	Moisture	Salt	Curd
Salted	80.47	16.54	2.15	0.84
Sweet	81.00	18.05	—	0.95

By permission from "Modern Dairy Products" by Lincoln Lampert. Copyright 1965, Chemical Publishing Co.

Fig. 11-19. Butter composition

Butter has no definite melting or freezing point. It is composed of a mixture of different fats, each of which has its own separate softening point, and it is 1/5 water. Melting point may be affected by the diet of the cows and by details of handling during manufacture. Most samples of butter melt between 82 and 96° F, with an average around 85°.

Butter becomes comparatively hard at refrigerator and freezer temperatures, but small pieces can always be cut by a sharp heavy knife, with pressure. It softens enough to spread on fresh bread somewhere between 65 and 72°. Soft butter, at room temperature, is a great convenience because of easy handling, but its taste may be improved when it is somewhat colder. It keeps well for at least several days and usually for weeks at 72°.

The boiling point is somewhere around 250° F, much lower than most other fats. At and above the boiling temperature it tends to brown, producing a color and flavor that are highly esteemed. With a little more heat it will scorch and burn, so frying with butter is tricky. But these characteristics depend partly on the presence of a small percentage of non-fat milk solids, and water and salt. Pure, clarified milk fat is much more stable.

Cream. Butter is made by churning or agitating cream until the protective coating on the fat globules breaks down, permitting them to combine into granules that separate from the fluid called buttermilk. The cream may be thick, thin or in the form of whole milk, and it may be either sweet or sour. If it is sour it is said to be ripened.

Medium cream, with a fat content of 30 to 33 per cent, is preferred for butter making. Heavier cream may cause extensive sticking to the paddles and churn, and thinner cream and milk take more time and work. Loss of fat due to failure to form granules is also at a minimum with the medium cream. All cream should be pas-

Fig. 11-20. Old butter churn

teurized for health reasons. This process improves the flavor and keeping quality of sweet cream butter.

Temperature of the cream is important. Commercially, churning is done at about 50° F, while on the farm slightly higher temperature, 52 to 62°, is recommended. Cream from pasture-fed cows should be cooler than that from cows on dry feed. The cream must be held at proper temperature for several hours before starting to churn, as the fat globules respond very slowly to temperature changes. Too high a temperature may make butter that is soft and greasy with poor keeping quality, while too low a temperature prolongs the work and produces brittle or tallowy texture.

The souring process in cream and milk is chiefly one of changing of lactose to lactic acid, and it does not affect the milk fat at all. The difference between butters made with sweet and sour cream lies entirely in the small residue of buttermilk that remains in them.

Butter made from pasteurized sweet cream usually has a good flavor and keeps well. The flavor of sour cream butter depends largely on the nature of the organisms that multiplied in the cream during souring. At its best it has a superior taste and smell, but it may also have a variety of off-flavors. It does not keep as well as the sweet cream product.

Manufacture. With proper temperature and fat content, cream takes 30 to 40 minutes to churn. But an egg beater and a bowl may make whipping cream into unwanted butter in less than 5 minutes.

Most butter is now made in creameries (butter factories) which obtain their cream from a number of dairies. Each batch is graded for quality. If it is too sour it is neutralized with some alkaline compound such as sodium bicarbonate. It is then thinned with skim milk or thickened with heavier cream to bring the fat content to 30 to 33 per cent. The standardized cream, which may now be one batch or a mixture of many, is filtered, pasteurized and cooled to 50° F.

The conventional churn is a rotating cylinder fitted with side shelves which lift and splash the cream. There is a window so that the operator can watch the process. It may be big enough to process tons of cream at a time. When butter separates into granules the size of wheat grains, the churning is stopped and the buttermilk is drained away.

The butter is usually washed with cool water to remove most of the buttermilk that remains after draining. The washing also removes various trace substances and contaminants that produce off-flavor. It is very important with ripened cream, less so with sweet cream. The water is usually chlorinated or pasteurized before use, to avoid possible contamination of the butter.

After washing the butter is worked. This is a kneading process by which the butter granules are forced into a compact mass. At this time the fat-water content is balanced to meet the legal requirement of 80 per cent milk fat (and to exceed the requirement as little as possible) by squeezing water or buttermilk out or by working extra water in. If salt is used, it is added at the beginning of the working process.

The worked butter is molded and cut into print shapes, usually quarter-pound and one pound, wrapped in an odor-repelling parchment paper, and put in one pound cardboard boxes for home use. Or it may be cut into pats or chiplets for restaurants, or packed in tubs holding 63 or 64 pounds for bakeries. Quarter-pound sticks often have wrappers marked in tablespoons and fractions of cups, for convenience in measuring.

The standard butter stick is 4-3/4 inches long, 1-5/16 wide and 1-3/16 high. It weighs 1/4 pound and has a bulk of 4 fluid ounces (1/2 cup).

Whipped Butter. Butter may be whipped so as to include about 25 per cent air. This increases its bulk by 1/3, makes it lighter in color and softer in consistency and changes the flavor. It may be salted but is more likely to be unsalted.

Whipped butter may be substituted for ordinary butter for any purpose, if allowance is made for its increased bulk, and for possible lack of salt. For each tablespoon in the recipe, use one tablespoon plus one teaspoon, for one cup use 1-1/3 cups, and so forth.

With this allowance, the whipped variety is to be preferred in any recipe calling for creaming butter, as it is already creamed

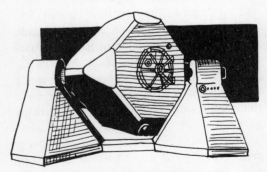

Fig. 11-21. Industrial butter churn

more thoroughly than you could hope to do it. It is often preferred for putting on top of pancakes, vegetables and other hot foods.

Whipped butter may be sold in round containers, or in half-pound cartons of wrapped sticks 1-5/16 inches square and 4-3/4 inches long. These are the same diameter as standard butter sticks, are a half inch longer and weigh 2-2/3 ounces instead of 4 ounces.

Salt. Salt is added to butter to improve keeping quality and flavor. However, butter made from good sweet cream keeps well without salt. A minority of people prefer the unsalted flavor, and another minority must avoid any salt because of low-sodium diets.

Unsalted butter is called sweet butter, and is therefore easy to confuse with salted butter which advertises on the package that it is made from sweet cream.

The amount of salt varies with the region. The most common proportion is 1-1/2 to 2 per cent, but 3 per cent may be used in the South. Salt does not dissolve in or mix with fat, and is carried by the water portion of the butter, where it may have a concentration of 8 to 16 per cent. This is a strong enough solution to hold most bacteria and flavor-altering reactions in check. But because of the blandness of the fat, salted butter seldom has a genuinely salty flavor, atlhough it can be immediately distinguished from the unsalted type.

Coloring. The natural color of butter varies from almost white when cows eat feed that is low in carotene to deep yellow, almost orange, when they are in fresh pasture during the spring. Some breeds, particularly the Jersey and Guernsey, transfer a higher proportion of the carotene in the feed to the cream than other breeds. Although little change in flavor is associated with these differences, they are objectionable to consumers, and the dairy industry has been adding fat-soluble color when it is desirable for many years, with the approval of the government, in order to keep a more uniform color throughout the year.

Butter is chiefly colored with one of two dyes: beta-carotene, obtained from carrots or made synthetically; and annatto, which is obtained from the seeds of a tropical tree of the same name.

Nutrition. Butter is mostly fat, with almost negligible amounts of protein and carbohydrate. It is among the most digestible fats (digestibility is stated to be 97.8 per cent), and is the only one that can be tolerated by some people.

Butter fats are largely of the saturated type, which means that they are under suspicion of causing or at least contributing to high cholesterol levels in the blood, with resulting tendency toward arteriosclerosis.

It is a high-energy food, producing about 3,400 calories per pound, or a bit over 100 to the tablespoon. This last figure compares with vegetable cooking fat at 110, American cheese 60 and granulated sugar 45.

Butter is an excellent source of Vitamin A, but the quantity varies with the cow's diet and therefore with the season. As an average, butter made between June and September may contain 18,000 international units to the pound, while in March there may be less than 10,000. But it is never without a good supply. Vitamin D content is variable, and other vitamins go largely into the buttermilk.

Uses. Butter is used for a wide variety of

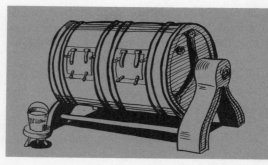

Fig. 11-22. Butter may be touched up with a little color

purposes. It is a spread for bread, a sauce for vegetables, a medium for pan frying, a flavoring, a decoration and an ingredient used for improving flavor, texture and/or color.

It is the most acceptable grease for the majority of people, both as a matter of custom and taste and on the basis of digestibility. But it is also the most expensive, so it is widely replaced with margarine, hydrogenated oil and other fats. There is also the problem of its chloresterol content, mentioned above.

Of course butter has its limitations also. It has a low boiling and browning temperature, which makes it useful in producing colorful crusts on pan fried food, but practically prohibits its use in deep frying (even if you could afford it). It contains 20 per cent water, which means that if you substitute it for a pure grease in a recipe, you should use 25 per cent more than the measurement given, and probably make allowance for the extra water in the mixture. It is not a pure fat, and the trace of milk proteins and other solids might complicate cooking.

Clarified Butter. Clarified butter is almost pure butter fat, made by removing water, salt and nonfat milk solids. It is made by melting ordinary butter over low heat, then chilling the resulting liquid. The product is a layer or mass of butter-colored grease, with a film or scattering of light-colored material on the top, and a thicker layer of salty, whitish liquid in the bottom. Remove the grease from the container, cut the film from the top and wipe off the bottom, and you have clarified butter.

Clarified butter usually has a poor flavor and a grainy consistency when solid. Its behavior in the frying pan (including heat resistance) is similar to that of vegetable oil, and it largely lacks the special foaming, browning and burning characteristics of butter. It is sometimes called for in sauce recipes.

MARGARINE

Margarine, usually pronounced "margerin" or "margerine" is not a dairy product, but since it is used chiefly as a synthetic butter, and does contain some milk solids, it fits in this chapter better than it would elsewhere.

Composition. Maragarine is an emulsified fatty product composed wholly or in part of fat other than milk fat, together with water, skim milk, salt, coloring and sometimes flavoring and added vitamins. A minute amount of sodium benzoate or other preservative may be added. Minimum fat content is the same as in butter, 80 per cent, except in diet margarines where a large part of it is replaced by water.

The principal fats and oils used in margarine are corn, soybean, cottonseed, coconut, safflower seed and oleo oils; and lard. Oleo oil is the liquid portion of beef fat. It is not used to a great extent now, but was once a major ingredient, and gave the product its original name of oleomargarine. Lard is used in increasing amounts, in the soft form called neutral lard. Small amounts of butter (usually less than 5 per cent) may be added for flavor. No animal fats are present in vegetable or nut margarines. The relative quantity of different fats may be largely dependent on their prices. They are all wholesome, and only a very discriminating sense of taste can detect differences between them.

The average composition of margarine in percentage by weight is said to be fat 80.52, water 15.43, salt 2.40 and milk curd 1.65. Some skim milk is substituted for water in working basic oils into a desired consistency, and diluting them to the 80 per cent basis which is both required legally and preferred by consumers.

Additives. Margarine may contain a small amount of preservative, which may be greatly to the consumer's advantage if it has been over-long in the store or in his

Fig. 11-23. Ice cream is highly esteemed

refrigerator. If it is fortified with vitamins A and D it is likely to equal and often exceed butter in the amount supplied.

A synthetic butter flavor, biacetyl, may be added. Like most use of artificial flavors, this may do more harm than good. Margarines have perfectly good flavors of their own, which may be spoiled by clumsy attempts to imitate butter.

Diet or soft margarine has less fat and more water than the standard type. It is not recommended for cooking, and it may separate or weep after freezing.

Comparison. In general, margarine is a butter substitute that owes most of its popularity to its much lower price, which may be 10 to 80 per cent below that of butter. Butter is generally but not unanimously considered to be superior in flavoring and cooking characteristics, but there is great similarity.

Butter is made of only one material — milk fat — and its range in quality is fairly narrow except where it has been abused either in manufacture or in storage. Margarines are made of different fats in varying proportions, with different methods and objectives in processing and may be doctored with artificial flavors. It is probable that there is a much narrower gap between butter and the best margarines than between the best and worst margarines. Here, the words "best" and "worst" are used to indicate butter-like qualities, a scale that is not entirely fair but that is the best available, and that seems to have no relation whatever to price.

Many people who have eaten margarine for many years, particularly during childhood, have a strong preference for margarine over butter on a basis of flavor and texture alone.

The texture is usually softer than butter, particularly when cold. This was originally a matter of design to obtain easier spreading, but is now due at least partly to inclusion of the maximum possible proportion of polyunsaturated fats. The texture is a strong argument in favor of margarine, and the unsaturation may be one also.

The behavior of butter and margarine in baking is practically identical, and they can usually be substituted for each other in any recipe, except that margarine might not be appreciated where the primary purpose of butter is for flavoring. In this book, butter and margarine are considered to be equivalent to each other. Mention of margarine is omitted from most recipes and instructions involving butter, but only to avoid repeating the long and monotonous phrase "butter or margarine."

ICE CREAM

Ice cream is an ancient and highly esteemed dessert, formerly made in the home but now largely a factory product. Its basic ingredients are sweet cream and flavoring, but it usually contains milk and stabilizing substances, or a milk-and-egg custard without cream. Air is an important ingredient, which may account for more than half the bulk of the cheaper commercial varieties.

Two principal problems in preparation of frozen mixtures that include milk or cream are the tendency of milk sugar and water to crystallize coarsely, and the possibility of the milk curdling or separating if the mixture melts.

True ice cream is definitely a dairy product, but it will be discussed under DESSERTS because there is no reasonable way to separate it from frozen non-dairy gelatin and sherbet frozen desserts in which milk and cream are unimportant or lacking.

1. **Very hard** (grating):
   a. Ripened by bacteria: Asiago old, Parmesan, Romano, Sapsago, Spalen.
2. **Hard:**
   a. Ripened by bacteria, without eyes: Cheddar, Granular or Stirred-curd, and Caciocavallo.
   b. Ripened by bacteria, with eyes: Swiss, Emmentaler, and Gruyère.
3. **Semisoft:**
   a. Ripened principally by bacteria: Brick and Münster.
   b. Ripened by bacteria and surface micro-organisms: Limburger, Port du Salut, and Trappist.
   c. Ripened principally by blue mold in the interior: Roquefort, Gorgonzola, Blue, Stilton, and Wensleydale.
4. **Soft:**
   a. Ripened: Bel Paese, Brie, Camembert, Cooked, Hand, and Neufchâtel (as made in France).
   b. Unripened: Cottage, Pot, Bakers', Cream, Neufchâtel (as made in the United States), Mysost, Primost, and fresh Ricotta.

Courtesy of U.S. Dept. of Agriculture

Fig. 11-24. Cheese classifications

CHEESE

Cheese is a high-protein milk concentrate, available in great variety. Its manufacture may be a complex matter. During processing it is acted upon by curd-forming substances, enzymes and bacteria which may have been present in the milk or added to it, by influences of moisture or dryness, heat or cold, presence or absence of molds and sometimes by added material, color and flavor. Slight variations in any of these processes may make a substantial difference in flavor and texture of the cheese.

It is not the place of a basic work on cooking to go into the delicate and sometimes very complicated methods by which

cheese is produced. Figure 11-24 gives a classification of some of the principal varieties of cheese on the basis of hardness. There are said to be about eighteen basic kinds of cheese subdivided into 400 varieties with a total of 800 names.

Soft cheese contains over 45 per cent water, hard and semi hard cheeses 30 to 45 percent, and hard cheeses less, the proportion diminishing with hardness. Very soft cheeses with high water content, such as cottage cheese, are perishable with a refrigerator life as short as a week. The hard cheeses may keep a year or more if they are cool and are protected from drying out, while semisoft varieties are intermediate and variable in life. These approximate times are figured after ripening, which ranges from two weeks for cottage cheese to two years for some hard varieties, and after normal distribution and selling time.

Cottage cheese spoils by developing off-flavors and becoming moldy and rotten. Other cheeses may develop off-flavors, but more often suffer from an over-development of their own characteristic flavor to such a degree that it is no longer desirable. Loss of moisture causes excessive hardness and often a loss of flavor, usually in a gradually deepening surface layer.

Some specialty cheeses have foul odors, so that opening one may cause people in the room to look at each other with suspicion and reproach. Such smells do not indicate spoilage, and are often accompanied by mild and pleasant flavor.

Storage. In general, cheese keeps in best condition for the longest time if it is cold. At room temperature Cheddar and several others of the fairly hard cheeses suffer minor internal change rather quickly. This results in a film of oil forming on all surfaces, making it somewhat unpleasant and messy to handle, but doing no other apparent damage. If it is left in warm storage it will resume the ripening process, becoming sharper and possibly developing off flavors. Oiliness will not develop in a refrigerator, and any ripening is extremely slow.

Most cheese can be frozen and thawed, once or several times, without any important change in flavor. Texture may or may not become crumbly. Freezing increases its good-condition shelf life by at least ten times.

Cheese is usually benefited in both flavor and texture by warming to room temperature before serving. This is specially true of process cheese.

Cheddar. The most important cheese in cooking and for general family consumption in America is Cheddar. It is called American cheese in the United States, Canadian cheese in Canada and Cheddar in England. It is a firm or hard cheese which is usually yellow, but may be either white or orange in color. It is slightly salty. Flavor ranges from bland to very sharp, largely as a result of differences in curing time. Medium sharp has the highest rating.

Cheddar has a low and somewhat variable melting point. It may be put on casseroles and open face sandwiches for melting under a broiler, mixed into casseroles in small chunks or dissolved in hot white sauce. The sauce may be mixed with things, with or without further cooking, or just poured over them. It may be grated and

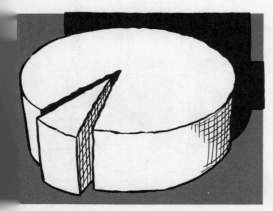

Fig. 11-25. A round and a wedge of cheese

sprinkled on surfaces, but in this use it is often second choice to Parmesan.

In addition to its uses in cooking, Cheddar is very popular sliced in cold sandwiches, alone or with other fillings. It is served with crackers as a snack, and in cubes with toothpicks to accompany cocktails.

These uses are shared by a number of other cheeses, particularly in the firm varieties.

Swiss. Swiss cheese is another "hard" cheese. It is probably second only to Cheddar in popularity. It is typically off-white in color, slightly sweet and is distinguished by the presence of holes up to 5/8 inch in diameter, and spaced one to 3 inches apart. The sweetness and the holes are both produced by cultured bacteria.

Swiss cheese has been made in Switzerland for hundreds of years. It is now made in other countries, but differences in texture and flavor have enabled Switzerland to maintain a substantial export sale of their own product.

The flavor is quite different from that of Cheddar. It has about the same uses as a raw cheese, but is not used as much in cooking. A cheese dish that has lost its appeal through repetition can often have its popularity restored by changing to Swiss.

Process Cheese. Process cheese is made by melting or grinding together a number of different batches of cheese of one variety with addition of very small amounts of emulsifier, edible acid, cream, color and water. Processing must include keeping at 150° F or more for 30 seconds or more, so that the product is effectively pasteurized. Water content may not be more than one per cent more than that permitted in the cheese from which it is made.

Processing makes use of cheese that may be too sharp or too bland, off-color or off-flavor, too old, in broken pieces and with various other defects that make it hard to handle or sell in its natural state. The cheeses that go into each batch are selected and balanced so that the product sold under a particular brand name will always have just about the same flavor and texture.

The softened or melted cheese is pressed or poured into plastic or foil containers, or into a strip of rectangular cross section which is cut into desired sizes and wrapped. In either case, the packaging or wrapping is so close that no air is left in contact with the cheese.

An increasing amount is factory-sliced for sandwiches. The slices are sometimes wrapped individually in plastic and then in packages, but more often are packed together, with or without thin paper separators. Standard thickness is about 1/8 inch, which is on the stingy side, so that at least two are needed in a picnic-type sandwich.

The texture is more solid and rubbery than that of natural cheese. It may be quite difficult to handle when chilled. Slices stick to each other and to the knife, and tend to break or pull apart. But at room temperature things go much better, so it is a good idea to take it out of the refrigerator ahead of time if you can.

Most process cheese is either American (yellow or white) or Swiss. It is very popular, although cheese-lovers seldom like it. It offers a dependably mild or medium flavor, uniform color and texture in any one brand and excellent keeping qualities. You know what you have before you open the package.

Most natural cheese varies quite a bit from batch to batch, and therefore usually from piece to piece, and provides a touch of adventure rather than security.

The two types of cheese are practically identical in nutrition. Process is usually cheaper, sometimes much cheaper.

Cheese Food. Process cheese food is prepared in the same general way as process cheese, but up to 49 per cent of other products may be included. These may be cream, milk, fruit, vegetables and meat flavoring. The finished food must contain not less than 23 per cent fat nor more than 44 per cent moisture.

Cheese spread is usually a process food with more water, plus gelatin, gum and sometimes sweetening.

Cottage Cheese. Cottage cheese is probably the most popular variety of natural cheese. It is classified as a lactic acid, unripe, soft curd cheese. It may be made at home from milk allowed to sour naturally, or curdled by adding rennet. The whey is drained out thorough several thicknesses of cheesecloth. The product may be called pot cheese or Dutch cheese.

Cottage cheese is made commercially from pasteurized skim milk. It is usually sweet, and is curdled by rennin or other enzymes. If made from sour milk it may be labeled "tangy." The curd is cut into cubes, 7/8-inch or smaller, to be labeled large curd or small curd, depending on size. It is drained, and washed several times in cold water.

The curd is usually cured at about 35° F for two weeks, then mixed with a small quantity of cream. To earn the name of creamed cottage cheese it must contain at least 4 per cent fat. The plain variety contains about 22 calories per ounce, the

Fig. 11-26. In a cheese shop

creamed 28 calories. Either type may contain up to 80 per cent water.

Most cottage cheese is eaten raw. In salad it may be served on lettuce plain, garnished or mixed with fruit or vegetables, either loosely or in a gelatin mold. It may be eaten plain, salted, sugared or with fruit, or with milk or cream as a cereal.

Its use in cooking is limited. It may be mixed with noodles and other food in casseroles, and it is a good substitute for Ricotta in lasagna.

Cream Cheese. Cream cheese is prepared in the same general way as cottage cheese, but it is made from light cream instead of skim milk. It must contain at least 33 per cent of milk fat and not more than 55 per cent water. It may contain a small amount of added gum or stabilizer. Its keeping qualities are fairly good.

Cream cheese is firmer, richer and more expensive than the cottage variety. Its use in salads is largely confined to special bits, such as small cheese balls rolled in chopped nuts, or thin slices on the side. It has important use as a spread on bread and as a sandwich filler, etiher plain or mixed with chopped nuts, chopped stuffed olives or similar items.

In cooking it is the major ingredient of cheese cake, is used in lasagna-type casseroles and is a substitute for butter in some cookies. It is also used in dips and spreads and in coffee cake fillings.

Cream cheese makes an excellent base for dips. It is diluted with the juice of the flavoring material (for example, anchovies or stuffed olives) or with milk to a consistency slightly thicker than heavy cream. The other material is then cut very fine, grated or made into a puree with a blender, then mixed with the cheese. If any acid is present the mixing should be immediate and thorough to avoid any tendency to curdle.

Italian Cheeses. There are a number of specialty cheeses developed in Italy which are widely used in this country, either as genuine-article imports or as similar varieties manufactured here. The imports are usually superior or at least truer in flavor, as much of the processing involves detailed knowledge and skilled craftsmen, and an amount of hand work which would be uneconomic here.

Parmesan is a very hard cheese made from partly skimmed milk, and cured in several stages for two or three years. Its major use is in grated form as a garnish and flavoring, particularly on spaghetti and other pastas. It is included in many Italian dishes, and rivals Cheddar as an ingredient in cheese sauce.

Parmesan can be obtained in grated form in shaker-type boxes. It is reasonably satisfactory, but for full flavor it is better to buy it in solid form and grate it just before use.

Mozzarella is a soft, white unripened cheese with a rubbery consistency and a bland flavor. Its principal use is in pizza.

Cociocavallo and Provolone are tough, stringy cheeses when medium cured, and so hard as to be usable only by grating when fully cured. The stringiness is obtained by heat treatment and stretching of milk curd. Both are salted and dried, Provolone is smoked also.

Ricotta is made from fresh milk whey, after the curd has been removed for cheese making. About 10 per cent milk or skim milk may be added. The albumin in the whey is coagulated by boiling, then dipped out and drained. When fresh it is very similar to cottage cheese, when thoroughly cured it is hard enough to grate.

12

VEGETABLES

GENERAL DESCRIPTION

In a broad sense, vegetables include all edible parts of plants. But both by popular usage and Department of Agriculture standards, the fruits which are not customarily served as part of the main course of a meal are called fruits or berries, not vegetables. They include apples, peaches, cherries, melons, grapes and most berries. But tomatoes, egg plant, squash, beans and similar fruits are classified as vegetables.

Ripe grains, such as wheat and rice, are also not considered to be vegetables.

In general usage there are further complications. The word vegetable may be used both for the whole class of non-fruit non-grain plant food, or in a narrower sense to distinguish cooked and low-starch from raw and high-starch. For example, spinach and boiled cucumbers are vegetables, but lettuce and raw cucumbers are salad greens. Potatoes are listed separately from other vegetables on a menu, and they may be bracketed with rice or grits. The emphasis and exact meaning of these distinctions vary from place to place and time to time,

but fortunately it is seldom essential to use just the right word.

Most vegetables other than ripe seeds have a very high water content, 70 to 90 per cent, and are high in vitamins and low in food energy.

Boiling is the most popular cooking method. After that comes steam, including pressure steam. Baking is less used, except perhaps for potatoes, and broiling is uncommon.

CLASSIFICATION

Vegetables may be classified in a number of different ways. Color is an important basis, as it can be readily distinguished, and it is often an indication of characteristics that affect method of preparation. They may be green, yellow, red or white, or various mixtures and off-tints of these colors.

Another classification is according to the part or parts of the plant that we eat. There are roots (including bulbs and tubers), stalks or stems, buds, leaves, flowers and fruit. The fruit may be used when it is immature (green), when it is ripe or in both

223

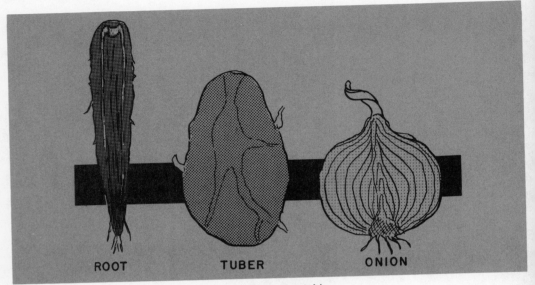

Fig. 12-1. Root vegetables

conditions. Some vegetables are mixtures of two or more of these parts, others may have two edible parts which are usually prepared separately.

Botanists classify on the basis of plant families. Scientifically, this is essential, and knowledge of this type is usually very helpful to the farmer and the gardener, but of rather less importance to the cook. Some of the relationships are a little surprising, as for example the family Solanaceae, which supplies us with tomatoes, peppers, egg plants and potatoes for the table, and also produces in other species tobacco and even more poisonous substances.

Roots. Root vegetables are generally enlarged sections of root where food materials are stored by the plant for future use. Many of them are not roots in structure, but are parts of the stem growing underground. Botanically this is an important difference, but it has only background interest for the cook. However, some cookbooks are quite firm about making the distinction, so a brief explanation is in order.

The carrot, radish, turnip and parsnip are true roots. They have structural division from the stems above and grade more or less smoothly into the feeding roots below. If the root is sliced lengthwise, it will be seen to have at least two different structures, an inner and usually coarse part connecting the stem base with the lower end, and a finer flesh around it.

The white potato is the most important example of a tuber. It differs from a root chiefly in having a number of small scale leaves and buds set in its surface. These are called eyes. Each of them has the possibility of developing into a plant. The potato also lacks a center axis for transport of nutrients, as the feeding roots are on separate groups of stems.

Bulbs, such as the onion, are a sort of underground bud. There is a section of compressed (but tender) stem surrounded by overlapping leaf bases, roots at the base and a connection to the regular stem at the top.

COLOR AND COOKING

Green. The green coloring in vegetable leaves, stems and unripe fruit is chlorophyll the substance that uses the energy of sunlight to manufacture plant carbohydrate from air and water. Although it is the basi for most life on the earth, it does not have any special nutritive value.

Chlorophyll does not dissolve readily in water. It tends to fade and acquire a brownish tint when cooked in water that contains acid or certain minerals. This undesirable effect increases with the length of cooking, and may be caused by overcooking even in the absence of acid.

Acidity in water can be caused or increased by acid in the vegetable, which may be leached out of it as it cooks. Your cookbook may tell you not to cover vegetables while they cook, because volatile acids will be caught and condensed by the lid, to drip back into the pot. However, it is very difficult to demonstrate the existence of any acid in such drippings. And a cover has the good effect of increasing the rate of cooking slightly.

Substitution of steaming for boiling will make harmless any acidity in the water, but may accentuate the concentration and effect of any that is present in the food. Pressure steam, however, is so fast that color is little affected by it.

Water that is slightly alkaline (hard) retains good color in green vegetables. If it is very hard it may accentuate the color, making it too bright to look natural. This is easy to counteract with a few drops of vinegar or lemon juice. Attempts to make acid water alkaline by added baking soda are likely to produce an artificial shade of green with an almost poisonous appearance, and may produce an unpleasant surface mushiness or sliminess as well, unless the amount used is tiny.

Water may be tested for acidity or alkalinity with litmus paper, obtainable in drug stores. It is red in the presence of acid, and blue if the water contains free alkali. To a certain extent, the intensity of color indicates the strength of the acid or basic reaction.

With any type of water, it is a good idea to heat it to a boil before you put a vegetable in it, get it back to boiling as soon as possible, and keep boiling during the whole cooking period. The quick start not only shortens cooking time, but also puts possibly harmful enzymes out of action immediately.

Yellow. Yellow and orange vegetables, such as carrots, sweet potatoes and some varieties of squash and corn, get their color chiefly from a pigment named carotene or carotin. Carotin is little affected by mild alkali or acid and does not dissolve readily in water. Its losses in cooking are small, usually about 10 per cent. However, if you overcook a vegetable so that its cells break down and become mushy, the pigment will escape from them and color the water. Also, yellow vegetables may acquire a brown or dirty tinge if allowed to stand for long periods while warm or hot.

Fig. 12-2. Neutralizing alkalinity

Carotin can be converted into Vitamin A in our livers, and it is usually our principal source of this vitamin. This fact has caused an over-emphasis on the importance of eating lots of yellow vegetables. Roots seem to be the only vegetables of this color that are really rich in carotin, and equal amounts are found in green fruits and leaves, particularly when the leaves are dark green and the yellow tint can be masked by chlorophyll.

Vitamin A is destroyed by light, and cooking and serving instructions are sometimes based on a mistaken assumption that carotin is similarly sensitive, in spite of the obvious fact that nature creates and stores it in the presence of light. Carotin is not damaged to any important extent by normal exposure to light during either storage or cooking.

Carotin is the principal pigment in the yellow leaves that are so plentiful in Autumn. The color becomes apparent when the chlorophyll dies and fades away. However, tree leaves are not digestible and are therefore not nourishing.

Red. Red coloring may be produced by pigments in the carotin family, as in tomatoes and some carrots. But in garden beets, red cabbage and autumn leaves it is caused chiefly by a different family of chemicals called anthocyanin.

Anthocyanin has no nutritional value, but like chlorophyll, its color is important in the attractiveness of the foods in which it occurs. This color is preserved by mildly acid cooking water, but tends to become purple or even blue in hard water or in the presence of any alkali. For this reason a little vinegar or lemon juice is often added to the water. Since beets are sweet and cabbage is bland, many cooks feel that acid improves the flavor in addition to keeping the color.

Unlike chlorophyll and carotin, this red pigment dissolves in cooking water, sometimes leaving the vegetable quite pale. There are two very different methods of avoiding this color loss. One is to leave the vegetable in one piece and uninjured. Beets may be cooked whole, unpeeled and unbruised with the root and an inch or two of stalk still attached. The opposite system is to trim and peel them, then slice them so that they will cook quickly and not have time to lose too much color. In the same manner, red cabbage may be cooked whole or in large chunks to resist color loss, or shredded to cook quickly.

White. White vegetables should stay white during cooking. But they often contain flavones, substances related to the red dyes, which tend to turn them slightly brown or grey if the water contains dissolved iron or certain other minerals, or if cooking goes on too long.

Different batches of the same vegetable may vary widely in this tendency to change color. In general, specimens that are very white when you buy or pick them are less likely to turn than those that are already somewhat murky. This may be another way

Fig. 12-3. White vegetables should be very white

of saying that young and fresh-picked vegetables keep their appearance best, but there are probably factors of soil chemicals and weather that influence this also.

If dripping water leaves rusty stains in your house, you have probably enough iron in the water to cause poor appearance when you boil white vegetables. If this is the case, you can either bring cooking water from elsewhere, or steam them.

OTHER COOKING CHANGES

Flavor. Neither flavor nor nourishment are dependent on keeping good color, but they often go together.

The amount of cooking is often a critical matter in flavor. Raw vegetables tend to be crisp, hard and tough, and the hardness and toughness increase with maturity. Flavors may be weak or strong, but tend to be of a "raw" type which most Americans enjoy only in salads. Such flavors are changed by cooking into forms that are generally more acceptable, and remain characteristic of the vegetable. If cooking is continued until a general breakdown of cell walls occurs, other and usually unpleasant flavors and smells are likely to be released.

Texture. The cooking process breaks down and tenderizes the vegetable, except for mature cellulose fiber, which remains tough.

In a majority of vegetables there is an early cooking period with no apparent effect, then a more or less steady change from toughness to tenderness to mushiness, at a rate varying with the temperature, and the type and maturity of the vegetable. The cook's object is to stop this process at the point where texture is most agreeable to the consumer or in agreement with the prevailing fashion.

The present trend in the literature is to recommend a semi-raw condition. Instructions warn against cooking too much, but never against cooking too little. The proper procedure for the average person is to cook until tender, testing with fork or teeth as necessary. A small amount of overcooking usually does less damage than the same amount of undercooking. Flavor is of course a matter of taste, but it can usually be enjoyed most thoroughly if a vegetable is tender enough to be masticated completely without excessive effort.

Vitamins. Vitamin content usually (but not always) has a downward trend all the way from harvesting to eating. A substantial loss of Vitamin C as a result of heating is a major argument in favor of undercooking. This subject is discussed under NUTRITION. Here we will simply repeat that the cook's preoccupation should be with flavor, texture and appearance. If she does well with these, vitamins can be safely left to take care of themselves.

Minerals are usually not affected by cooking, except to the extent that they may be leached out in cooking water and discarded. Chemical changes that make them available or unavailable are rather rare and not well understood.

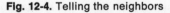

Fig. 12-4. Telling the neighbors

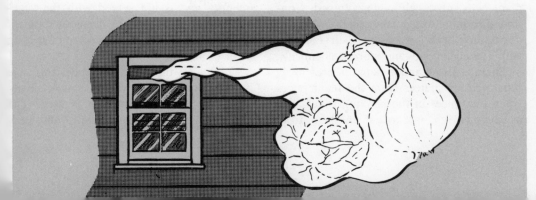

Fig. 12-5. A partitioned plate

Smell. Foods tend to give off characteristic odors while they are being cooked. These smells are sometimes quite strong and rank, and may be evident throughout the house and even the neighborhood. Such vegetables are usually classed by cookbooks as either strong-juiced or strong-flavored, although they are neither. They are just strong-smelling unless they are handled tactfully. Or to put it another way, they are likely to stink.

Most of these belong to the cabbage family. They include cabbage (green or red), cauliflower, brussel sprouts, broccoli and kohlrabi. There are also turnips and onions. In onions there may be a distinction, as their smell while boiling is ordinarily considered to be rank, while almost the same smell produced by frying is supposed to be appetizing.

At the moment, vegetable smells are undesirable, so cookbooks are full of advice about how to reduce or eliminate them. They differ sharply on such details as using much or little water and whether there should or should not be a lid on the pan. But they do agree, correctly, that the major cause of cooking smells is overcooking. Cooking to tenderness leaves most of the plant cells intact, although softened. Continued cooking to a mushy condition breaks down their walls, releasing their contents with any accompanying odorous chemicals.

There is also reaction between previously separated substances from the plant juices when they meet in the cooking water, and as chemical changes occur in them from heat. This factor may be greatly emphasized in cooking instructions. However, since rank smells result from bruising the living plants in the garden, it seems likely that most of the odor is already there, and is simply released by the cooking.

Cooking Liquid. The water in which vegetables are cooked is called by many names, including cooking water, cooking liquid, juice, pot liquor and even vegetable consomme. Its qualities vary with the type, condition and age of vegetable, and with the quantity at the start and particularly at the finish of cooking. It contains a share, which may be small or large, of the flavor and nutrients of its vegetable. Some authorities give the impression that it contains practically all of the "good" of the food, so that saving and using it becomes one of their main objectives in cooking.

In spite of wide recognition of the liquid's health-giving virtues, it seldom occurs to the authors of cookbooks that it can be served with the vegetable. The usual instruction is to drain and serve, unless it is to be concentrated and mixed into a sauce.

The reason may be that food served out of liquid tends to drip and drain some of it onto the plate, where it may soak into the mashed potatoes or dilute the gravy. This difficulty may be avoided by serving the vegetable in a saucer, or less elegantly in a partitioned plate section, with a liberal amount of its juice.

A vegetable is likely to benefit by being wet with its own juice when it reaches the mouth. Draining before serving may sacrifice much of the flavor-advantage of boiling.

If the liquid is really tasty, is small in quantity and is not served with the vegetable, it is very likely to be drunk or spooned up by the cook, either at the time of serving or of cleaning up.

Otherwise, the cook is supposed to save it for making soup, gravy or sauce, saving it in the refrigerator until it is used. The flavor and vitamin content deteriorate steadily and sometimes rapidly during storage, and the average housewife is likely to find the liquid with fur on top by the time she gets to use it. But there is a solution — freeze it into cubes, and store them in a labeled plastic bag or closed jar in the freezer. This will preserve the liquid's virtues almost intact, and keep it readily available for partial or complete use. If the quantity is small, individual cube-cups are more convenient than a tray.

Since freezer space is limited, you may wish to concentrate the liquid by boiling it. This should be done in a partly covered pan to exclude vitamin-destroying oxygen, and over high heat to save time and fuel.

Fig. 12-6. Some vegetable juice tastes good

But if you don't want to drink the stuff, serve it, save it or bother with it, turn your cookbooks' faces to the wall, and pour it down the drain.

Milk. Vegetables are sometimes boiled in milk, or milk is added to the cooking water, to improve or change color or flavor. The remaining liquid is usually treated with more respect than plain water, but it is subject to the same basic set of choices. It often serves as the inspiration for making cream soup.

Cooking in milk is complicated by skin forming on the top, and by its tendency to build deposits around the edge that scorch and burn easily.

SELECTION

Vegetables may be selected on the basis of age, (maturity), age (length of time in storage), color, firmness, crispness and price. These are in addition to the basic factors of whether you want fresh vegetables, want this particular vegetable and think it will fit in any of your menus for the near future.

Maturity. In your own garden the principal basis of selection is maturity. Most vegetables have a period of several days during which they are near their best eating condition. This period is much shorter in hot weather than in cool weather, and may vary from a day for corn in August to a month for a pumpkin in October.

A garden is likely to dictate both your choice of vegetables and their maturity, as you can only pick what is ready.

There are differences of opinion about the stage of development in which a vegetable should be eaten. Some people like everything young and tiny for delicate flavor and maximum tenderness. Others like vegetables so mature that they are almost over-age, feeling that the resulting hardness or toughness is either desirable, or a small price to pay for full flavor and large yields. Most people choose their vegetables in an

Fig. 12-7. Selection of vegetables may be limited

intermediate condition, and many have no particular preference, or vary in their preference from time to time.

In any one market there is usually a very limited choice of degree of maturity in any one day. In small-unit items such as peas or spinach you pretty much have to take run-of-the-counter, but larger pieces such as eggplant or heads of lettuce allow choice for apparent age, as well as for size and condition.

Texture. Vegetables have a wide range of texture, according to the kind and whether they are ready to eat. But in general they should be hard, firm or crisp; not soft, limp or squashy. These standards are comparative, and some experience is necessary with each vegetable before it can be easily selected as being in its best condition. Spinach can hardly be expected to be as crisp as iceberg lettuce, and a tomato should not be as hard as a potato.

Excessive limpness in leaves is chiefly a result of loss of water, and can sometimes be corrected by soaking in cold unsalted water, rinsing and then wrapping in plastic, or by storing in a dampened compartment in a refrigerator. In a head of lettuce or cabbage it may affect only the outer leaves, which can be stripped off and discarded.

Slight widespread softness in a fruit or a root that is accompanied by a wrinkling of

the skin is usually a result of drying also. It usually indicates a too-long storage period, or storage under poor conditions, and it can be expected to go with reduced flavor and poorer texture at the table. Softening in spots that is associated with changes in color, particularly to brown, is usually a sign of decay. Sometimes the bad spots are on the surface and can be peeled off, at other times they go through much or all of the center. Rotting material may get very soft and even liquefy.

The inner condition of a melon in regard to maturity and possible spoilage may sometimes be discovered by tapping it with a knuckle. It is possible to distinguish among the dull sound of greenness, the resonant "plunk" of a ripe one, and the quietness of over-ripeness.

Color. Color is a very important factor in judging the quality and probable flavor of vegetables and fruits. However, it is not practical to give much useful information in regard to it on the printed page. Tints of colors do not lend themselves well to black and white descriptions nor even to color photography.

More importantly, color is basically determined by the variety of the article and its maturity, but is also subject to other influences such as weather, the health of the plant and substances in (or not in) the soil

230

which may influence it strongly, without corresponding effects on flavor or other qualities.

Varieties offer sufficient confusion. Potato skins may be brown, tan or red; corn kernels may be yellow or white; apples may be green, yellow, red, brown or combinations of these colors; tomatoes may be red or yellow, squash yellow, plain green, striped green or brown, and cabbage green, white or red. Colors generally give some indication of taste or cooking qualities, but plant breeders are producing so many new varieties that the most experienced shopper may be led astray.

When sunlight is less than normal during the ripening period, full color often does not develop. Minute traces of certain minerals in soil may increase, decrease or change the appearance of parts of plants grown in them. Lack of water may cause early appearance of mature coloring on unripe fruits.

However, there is generally a pleasing quality about the color of a plant and its parts when it is in good eating condition. This quality can be recognized by an observant person after only a little experience, and is very helpful in distinguishing ripe from unripe, and relatively fresh from too-long-picked. But many off-color and off-condition vegetables are still good to eat.

PREPARATION

Preparation of a vegetable may include washing, soaking, trimming, peeling, husking or shelling, removing bad spots or blemishes and/or cutting into smaller pieces.

Washing. A vegetable should be washed and possibly scrubbed if it is dirty, or you think that it is either dirty or tainted with chemical sprays. Home picked vegetables usually carry soil. However, many vegetables bought in the modern market have already been very thoroughly cleaned, and are so packaged or handled that there is no need of any further cleaning. But it does no

Fig. 12-8. Wash them if they are dirty

harm to wash them again if it makes you feel better.

Solid vegetables are usually simply rinsed under running water while rubbing with the fingers. If resistant pockets of dirt are detected, as is often the case with roots, they may be taken off with a small scrubbing brush or the back of a knife, still under running water.

Leafy vegetables such as spinach and open-growth lettuce may be rinsed and perhaps rubbed gently one leaf at a time, or a number of leaves may be swished around in a basin of cold water. A surprising amount of sand and other earth particles may be present. Washing leaf by leaf is tedious and is not usually done unless the batch is small. But swishing may have to be kept up through several changes of water. A few gritty pieces may stay through either method.

Many vegetables have particular places where dirt is likely to lodge, and to stay during casual washing. Examples are deep-set eyes in potatoes, the slits behind artichoke leaves and any sockets where stems are attached. Individual attention to these spots with a brush or water spray should take care of them.

An increasingly important reason for washing vegetables is the desire to remove spray chemicals. These are usually poisonous, often extremely so. There is a wide range, from a comparatively harmless rotenone group through poisons like nicotine and arsenic that are deadly in quantities but almost harmless when in minute doses, to synthetics such as DDT which accumulate in the human or animal body, and can build up to dangerous levels if even tiny quantities are eaten repeatedly. These poisons are discussed under NUTRITION.

Unfortunately, poison sprays are usually made up to stick on plant surfaces in spite of rain, and are unlikely to be removed completely by washing. Also, they generally penetrate the surface of the plant a small distance. Peeling is a much more important precaution than washing in such cases.

Soaking. Soaking is usually done in cold water, which may be either fresh or salted, depending on what cookbook you are reading. Fresh water has a crisping effect, but it is noticeable only in leaf vegetables. Salt water tends to make vegetables limp, but the change is slight.

No reason ever seems to be assigned for firm instructions to soak certain solid vegetables such as cauliflower. On the basis of results it may be assumed that the purpose is to induce worms to come out of hiding. But if they are there they will come out anyhow early in the cooking and can be

Fig. 12-9. Soaking out the worms

skimmed off the water then. The cook can decide for herself whether the separate treatment is worth 20 or 30 minutes.

Dried vegetables such as beans, peas and lentils are usually soaked for periods ranging from one hour to 12 or more, before cooking. This greatly shortens the cooking time, and also appears to have a favorable effect on the flavor and texture of the cooked product.

Soak water can be used for cooking the vegetable, unless it has acquired an off taste or undesirable material.

Trimming. Trimming and discarding of inedible or unwanted parts of the plant may be done before, during or after peeling. Preliminary work may include cutting off tops and fine roots of root vegetables, pulling off outer leaves that are tough, dirty or wilted; cutting out large spoiled or under-ripe areas or breaking or cutting off stems, flowers and leaves.

These operations are so mixed up with peeling or husking that they are best included under those headings.

Paring and Peeling. To pare means to remove a very thin layer, usually skin, by cutting. The specific meaning of peel is to pull, rub or break skin off. In ordinary usage and in this book peeling may be used to include paring, but paring is limited to cutting.

Paring knives are the smallest of the kitchen knives, with blades 3 to 3-1/2 inches long. Paring tools, Figure 35-5 are easier to use on many surfaces and have the advantage of automatically making very shallow cuts, so that a minimum of edible material is removed with the skin.

Roots and fruit have skins which may or may not be removed before eating. Whether it is necessary or desirable to peel them depends on the local custom, the variety of vegetable, the way it is being cooked and served, and sometimes on its age. Skins of young vegetables are usually tender enough to be chewed without difficulty, and their flavor does not differ greatly from that of the flesh under them. They may be eaten with pleasure if the item is served whole or sliced, when either raw or cooked. Examples of this type are summer squash, cucumbers, carrots, tomatoes, new potatoes and eggplant. However, if such a vegetable is to be mashed and/or mixed with other foods the skins may then seem too tough and stringy, differing unpleasantly in texture from the rest of the mix.

The skin on mature and old vegetables is likely to be tough, hard or tasteless enough so that peeling is advisable unless the skin is to be used for a cooking container, as in baked potato or stuffed eggplant.

Skins may be taken off to remove discoloration or other blemishes, or because of a possibility that they may be tainted with chemical sprays.

A vegetable should be washed if it needs it, whether it is to be peeled or not, as some of the dirt on a skin is almost sure to get on the peeled surface. The hands should be freshly washed also, as some freshly exposed surfaces (white potato, for example) can pick up dirty smudges from fingers that look perfectly clean.

It is a very good idea to pare vegetables under cold water running from the faucet. This eliminates any need for a separate washing operation before peeling, and you do not need to rinse afterward. Pieces of skin are removed as fast as they are cut loose, so they cannot remain and confuse you about what you have and have not pared. Smudging from fingers and discoloring from contact with air are avoided. As a result, blemishes are easily seen and can be entirely removed as part of the peeling operation. Smell is carried away by the water also, a very great advantage in peeling onions.

There are three general classes of skins found on the fruits and roots that make up the bulk of peelable vegetables. They are the hard-and-firmly-attached, the soft-loose-and-rubbery and the tender-and-firmly-attached. The best known example of the first type is on a true fruit, the apple. A hard crisp skin is firmly bonded to firm crisp flesh. It is easily removed in strips by a sharp knife or parer, with most of the cutting done in the flesh immediately beneath the skin. Most squash, cucumber and eggplant skins are of this type.

The peach and the tomato have soft rubbery skin more or less loosely attached to the flesh. If the fruit is fully ripe, it is possible to peel many varieties by pulling strips of skin off with the fingers, or by making a small knife cut, then holding the edge of the skin against the side of the knife with a finger, and pulling. If the fruit is not fully ripe, or is a hard-to-peel variety, the loosened skin tends to tear, so that new grips must be obtained again and again, putting nicks in the peeled surface and making the process slow and frustrating.

Such skin is almost impossible to remove with a parer, and is difficult with a knife, as

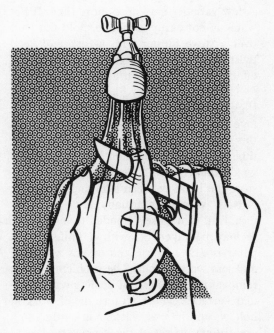

Fig. 12-10. There are advantages to paring under running water

Fig. 12-11. Cut pieces

it tends to bunch up ahead of the blade without cutting. If you must pare, try to have the knife razor sharp and cut deeply with a sawing motion. A toothed or scalloped blade may be helpful.

These soft skins can usually be separated from the flesh by heat. Dipping in boiling water for 30 to 60 seconds should loosen them so that they can be easily pulled off. A few varieties may need more time. If hot water is not easily available, hold the fruit over a stove burner with a fork and keep twisting it so as to singe all surfaces. The effect is not as uniform as with water heat.

The surface under the skin might get slightly cooked, which may be a disadvantage if it is to be eaten raw. You can keep this effect to a minimum by a short dipping time, and putting the item in or under cold water immediately. Cooling does not restore the bond between skin and flesh.

Root vegetables usually have a rather thin, frail skin closely bonded to hard flesh. It may be taken off with a knife, but a parer is easier to use and makes a thinner and less wasteful cut. The problem of skin removal is mostly one of dealing with irregular surfaces, which require detail work in hollows and pits, or wastage in cutting high areas down to get at the hollows.

Root skins are softened and loosened by boiling, but the effect is slow. Just dipping for a few seconds or even a minute may have no effect. The skin should be loose enough to be easily rubbed off by the time it is cooked. This peeling should be done under the cold water faucet, as the vegetable is then very hot all the way through. And the skin may stick again if you allow it to cool fully.

Onions have a special type of skin, which will be discussed under ONIONS.

Husking and Shelling. Some vegetables have protective coverings which cannot rea-

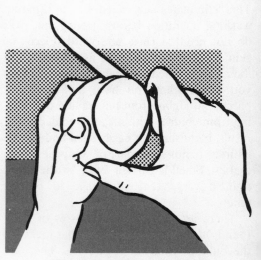

Fig. 12-12. Slicing in the hand

sonably be called skins, and which are removed by pulling, tearing and breaking, with little or no use of knives or other cutting tools.

Examples are inedible bean and pea pods, corn husks, and unwanted outer leaves of head lettuce and cabbage.

These will be discussed under the individual vegetables.

Blemishes. In view of the many diseases and pests that attack vegetables, the more or less rough handling they suffer during harvesting and transportation and the time that may elapse before they reach your kitchen table, it is surprising that so many of them need only routine treatment to prepare them for cooking. But you must always be alert for various defects which might offend you or those at your table or which might merely make the food a little less attractive or desirable when you serve it.

Defects include discoloration, which may arise from age, disease scars, decay, insects present in the vegetable or their residual damage in the form of burrows, droppings and stains; bruises which may affect color and/or texture, over-ripe and usually over-soft spots and under-ripe sections which are apt to be both hard and flavorless.

CUTTING UP

There are many ways of dividing vegetables into pieces, before cooking or serving. Sometimes they are broken (green beans) or pulled apart (cauliflower and broccoli), but they are usually cut.

The cut pieces may be halves, quarters, slices of various thicknesses and shapes, strips, cubes, balls, random pieces or fine shreds. See Figure 12-11.

Most of this cutting is or at least should be done on a cutting board, which is basically a piece of wood that prevents the knife edge from touching the table, a contact that is likely to damage one or both of them. The board can be replaced by several thicknesses of paper (although paper dulls

a knife quickly) or by layers of peelings from the vegetable.

If the quantity is small, slicing or random hacking may be done holding the piece in the left hand and cutting with the right hand (of course, reverse this if you are left handed). Hold the knife (preferably one with a short blade) at the base of your fingers and pull it toward your thumb, Figure 12-12. This is not as safe or as accurate as cutting on a board, but it is often more convenient.

Texture. Some vegetables, such as the white potato, are of firm and regular texture throughout and can be cut in any convenient direction. Winter squash and pumpkin have regular texture for only a short distance inside the skin, within which there is a hollow containing unwanted seeds and fibers.

The tomato has a regular pattern of outer flesh running into inner braces around spaces filled with juice and edible seeds. It has a different appearance when sliced across (the usual way) and when sliced parallel with the core. The sweet pepper is somewhat the same construction, but center flesh is often reduced to a few strips, juice is lacking and air spaces are so expanded that the centers are left poorly supported and often fall out of slices.

Firm crisp vegetables such as the potato and egg plant can be sliced by direct pressure of a reasonably sharp knife. If the knife is dull, a back and forth or sawing

Fig. 12-13. Slicing on a board

motion aids cutting. A soft juicy vegetable such as a ripe tomato calls for a really sharp knife, with light pressure to avoid squeezing out semi-liquid pulp and a sawing motion. It may be necessary to use the point of the knife to start the cut. Air filling such as is found in the sweet pepper also calls for light sawing with a sharp edge.

Such characteristics as toughness or tenderness and solidity or juice or air space should be kept in mind when planning and doing a cutting job.

Slicing. To slice a simple solid, such as a potato, you hold it on a cutting board with one hand and make parallel cuts with a knife held in the other hand, as in Figure 12-13. If it is hard to hold steady, take a slice off one side and rest it on the resulting flat spot.

Depending on their use, slices can be anywhere from as thin as you can cut up to 1/2 inch or more thick. They are usually cut across (that is, on the short dimension), or at right angles to the core or stem if there is one, but for special purposes they may be lengthwise or diagonal.

When repeated cuts bring the knife near the fingers with which you are holding the vegetable, you may make the last few cuts without holding, you may span the length with thumb and finger and cut with the knife under your hand, or turn the end piece over on its flat cut side.

If you have a lot of slicing to do, and/or you want to do it very neatly, use a slicing board or an electric rotary meat slicer.

If the vegetable is made up of many layers (for example, onion or cabbage) the slices may tend to fall apart into curved or circular strips. If you want to avoid this, you can try making the slices thicker, sharpen the knife or handle them more gently. Even if you intend to cut them into strips, it may be worthwhile to keep the slices together.

Some vegetables of proper size can be handled by an egg slicer.

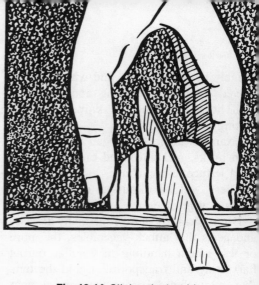

Fig. 12-14. Slicing the last bit

Strips. If the vegetable is to be cut into strips, you first slice it as described above, then slice the slices. If you can hold it together as you slice it, or reassemble it, take just one slice off the end to give it a flat spot and stand the stack of slices on that spot. Then repeat the slicing process, Figure 12-15. Strips are usually square, 1/4 inch in diameter and up, but they can also be very fine, and/or wider than they are thick.

There are pressure cutters, such as that in Figure 35-10, that have a grid or grids of fine knives or strong wires mounted in a substantial frame, and can make a set of slices or strips in a single pass.

There are also scalloped knives or cutters which can be used to give a wavy finish to two or four sides of the pieces.

Fig. 12-15. Cutting strips

Leaf vegetables such as spinach are often cut into strips from 1/2 to one inch wide.

Onion, cabbage and similar vegetables which tend to fall apart when sliced will disintegrate when cross sliced into strips. You will get quite long strips at each edge, and very short bits at the center. The only way such items can be kept in strip form is to pull the slices apart, and settle for curves instead of straight lines.

Cubes. For dicing (cutting into cubes) you hold strips together, set them on their sides and make another series of parallel downward cuts. Strips are more difficult to hold together than slices particularly if you try to cut with a sawing motion. Sometimes you have to cut them one or a few at a time if you want them to look like cubes.

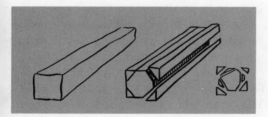

Fig. 12-16. Making shreds with a knife

Random and Shaped Pieces. Slices may have a disadvantage of sticking so closely together that they act like still-solid pieces, with results such as irregular cooking and difficulty of handling and mixing with sauces or other foods. If regular slices are not needed for structure or appearance, you may cut up the vegetable irregularly by making knife cuts that are not parallel. Most of the pieces will then be more or less wedge-shaped, they will usually slide or fall out of contact with each other, reducing these difficulties.

Separation of pieces is made more positive by cutting with a curved knife or with a spoon.

Smooth-textured vegetables and fruit may be cut into balls by using a scoop,

which is a round spoon with a deep bowl. Two common sizes are 7/8 and 1-1/4 inches in diameter. It is pressed into the vegetable and moved through it on a curve, with some side-to-side motion. By allowing small flat or irregular places on the surface of the ball, cuts can be made close enough together to use most of the material. Remaining scraps can generally be utilized in some way.

Shredding. Shreds are very fine strips, usually less than 1/8 inch in diameter. They are sometimes made in the same manner as ordinary strips but this requires time and patience. They may also be made by cutting a vegetable into coarse strips, then paring the strips with constant change of cutting area so that the shreds tend to be triangular in cross section rather than flat. Those that are too wide can be individually slit afterward.

But most shredding is done in a grater, of perforated metal, using a coarse section. When you rub a chunk downward the projecting lower lip of each hole gouges into it and directs a fine strip or shred through the hole. Since there are a large number of holes the work goes rather rapidly. It may be necessary to remove the pile of shreds several times during the job.

Some substances are too brittle to stand this cutting and still stay together, and crumble into powder or fine pieces. If soft or juicy food turns to mush, try using coarser holes. Shreds may form properly, but break up if handled roughly.

Shredding tenderizes the food, particularly when the cut is fine.

ARTICHOKES (FRENCH)

The French or globe artichoke is a flower bud of a variety of thistle plant. It is a series of sets of overlapping petals on a relatively small, cone-shaped heart. The tips of the petals may taper into thorns, and most of their bulk is tough and fibrous. But toward the base, where they are behind other petals, they are increasingly filled and covered with a material that is soft and bland when it is cooked.

An artichoke should preferably be young, weigh 1/4 pound or less, be green or bright green with little or no brown at tips, and folded more or less tightly together. However, failure to pass these tests does not necessarily mean that a specimen is undesirable.

The thorny petal tips may or may not be trimmed off with scissors before cooking. If there is a stem, cut it off flush with the bottom of the bud. You may want to wear gloves when you handle them. The petals can be pulled outward to allow more uni-

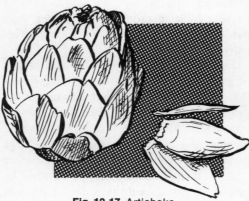

Fig. 12-17. Artichoke

form cooking, and for possible removal of dirt behind them. You get it out by swishing the artichoke, stem side up, in warm water; or by spraying it from the bottom.

Artichokes are supposed to be boiled upside down in a wide kettle in two inches of water spiked with salt and lemon juice. But they won't stand on their heads unless you have just enough to fill the kettle from side to side. Fortunately they can also be cooked on their sides like common vegetables in a covered pan in either deep or shallow water, or they can be steamed. Cooking time ranges from 20 to 40 minutes, depending on size and method. In a

pressure cooker, about 10 minutes. You test for doneness by pulling back a petal and probing the white material as its base with a fork. It should be as tender as jelly.

Eating. To eat an artichoke, place its large end on a plate and peel the petals off one by one, starting at the base, dip in melted butter, Hollandaise sauce or any similar preparation, and pull the petal between your teeth to scrape off the soft material. Scraped petals are piled at the side, or in another dish.

When all the petals are off you are left with a white cone covered with a fibrous mat. The upper fibers can be scraped off with a fork or a spoon. The remainder is called the heart. It can be cut in pieces with the fork and dipped in butter or sauce. It is the nearest thing to solid food found in this vegetable.

An artichoke with its sauce is usually served as a special course, and is most often one to a customer regardless of size.

Artichoke hearts, usually slightly acidified with vinegar, can be bought in cans. They are often served as appetizers, whole or cut up, with toothpicks.

ASPARAGUS

The underground part of asparagus is a long lived perennial plant of the lily family. Its above-ground parts die in the autumn and are renewed in the spring. This renewal takes the form of rapid growth of a stem bud from underground. Our table asparagus consists of these stems, cut before their buds can open. They are called spears.

The bud parts or tip are almost always tender, and are sometimes used raw in salads. The stem immediately below the tip is tender when cooked, further down it is tough no matter what you do with it. Flavor is best in the tip, and declines about in proportion to increasing toughness. The edible section is usually 3 to 6 inches long. The toughness is referred to as woodiness.

Preparation. There are three basic ways to serve the spears. Retain more than the edible part, trimming them perhaps 8 inches long. The consumer may pick such spears up in his fingers, and eat down from the tip until it becomes too tough to be interesting. The remaining stalk, with a chewed end, is put back on the plate. This is an efficient system, as it allows the consumer to exactly suit his own ideas about how tough it can be and still be edible. But it is messy, and it is no longer much used.

The cook is generally expected to guess the spot in each spear where it passes from edible to inedible, and to serve only the former in a full size spear. It is said that bending the stalk will cause it to break with a snap at just this point. This seems to assure you of taking only tender material, but may waste some also. Another test is to push the point of a sharp paring knife against the surface of the stalk. If it indents it, it is likely to be tough, if it penetrates smoothly, it should be tender.

If the stalk is broken off short, some of a delicious and usually expensive vegetable is wasted. If it is too long, the stringy toughness of the extra stalk may spoil eating pleasure, unless it is courageously cut off and left on the plate.

The third method is to trim off the inedible portion, then cut the approved part into pieces one or 1-1/2 inches long. This procedure should be limited to asparagus that is ill-shapen or otherwise unfit for serving as whole spears, or that is to be served in dishes such as casseroles or salad mixes. Pieces are not as attractive as whole stalks, and to some extent they prevent the consumer from telling just what part of the stalk he is eating and adjusting his bite for it. If you are careless enough to include some really tough pieces you will probably embarrass both yourself and your guests.

There are two extra precautions to keep tough sections of stalk out of mixtures. One is to cook the asparagus whole or in halves, and do the final cutting after it has been cooked and is easily tested. The other is to cook in two pans, one for the completely safe tips and upper stalks, the other for doubtful stalks. Cook the stalk sections longer and test them individually with a fork.

There may be paper-like scales on blanched stalks that will remain hard when cooked. If they are found they can be peeled off with a paring knife. Commercial asparagus has usually been washed, and since it is fresh out of the ground it is unlikely to have been sprayed. But if it is dirty or you think that it is, you may rinse it and even scrub it with a brush.

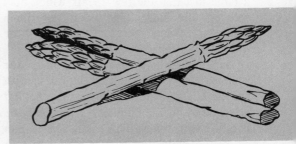

Fig. 12-18. Asparagus spears

Cooking. Asparagus is usually boiled, semi-steamed or steamed for about fifteen minutes. If it is not fully covered with water the pan should be covered. Cooking time is less with thin and tender spears, longer with fat or old ones. The tip may be fork-tender in a little more than half the cooking time. The tenderized area increases down along the stalk until it gets to the fibrous material which is permanently tough. There may be an inch or two which some people can chew or at least swallow, but is inedible to others.

In the preferred method of boiling whole spears, their length and their fragility when cooked offer a problem. The best utensil is a large frypan, which offers an ample bottom surface for laying the spears flat, and low sides to simplify removal. But don't use someone else's black iron pan, as the boiling water may remove its oily surface.

Side-grasping tongs, or two turners, can get them out intact. With the tongs, carry them by the stalks with the tips somewhat down as shown. This both avoids pressure on the tender tips, and danger of breaking off from their own weight. Tip the plate as you lower them onto it.

If you must use a deep pan, take a lid small enough to fit inside it. When cooking is finished, lower it onto the asparagus and hold it while you pour off the liquid. Then turn the pan upside down and raise it away from the lid. Most of the asparagus should then rest intact on the lid. But do this over a table to catch the few spears which may roll off the side. This operation offers plenty of chance for getting scalded or burned, so proceed very carefully.

Asparagus may also be boiled (or steamed) vertically in tied bundles, with the stalk ends down. Strings may be left attached to lift the bundles, or they may be handled with tongs. This takes a deep pan or kettle, which is usually wide also, so that covering the spears would require too

much water. So use an inch or two, or as little as you like, in the bottom and cover the top of the pan to steam them.

Juice. Asparagus produces about the finest flavored vegetable cooking liquid. It can be used to moisten the spears on the plate, or instead of water in the cream sauce or casserole recipe. If it is to be used in soup, extra quantity with some loss of quality can be obtained by boiling the discarded ends of the stalks separately. And you might find yourself some tender eating among them at the same time.

Serving. Hot asparagus may be served plain, with its own juice, with melted butter, or white, cheese or Hollandaise sauce. Spears are often served on toast, which is usually trimmed of crusts and cut in fingers or diagonals. It may be plain or buttered.

Cold cooked asparagus may be served plain or with melted butter, mayonnaise or almost any salad dressing, usually in full length spears.

When raw, only the tips are used. They are sliced thin or broken into flowerets, and mixed with fine-sliced onions, radishes, cucumbers or almost anything.

Mixtures. Asparagus is sometimes served with sauces that are complicated

Fig. 12-19. Asparagus with salad

mixtures, including such items as hard-cooked eggs, parsley, cheese, bread crumbs, mushrooms and onions. Or it may be cooked with the same or similar ingredients in a casserole.

A reasonably simple and usually satisfactory casserole for 4 people may be made as follows:

Asparagus Egg Casserole

1¼ lb	asparagus, tender parts only, cooked in one-inch pieces
4	hard-boiled eggs, sliced
1½ cps	thin white sauce
¼ cup	buttered bread crumbs

In a buttered 1-1/2 or 2-quart casserole, arrange asparagus and egg in alternate layers. Cover with crumbs. Bake in a moderately hot oven, 400° F, for 20 minutes or until hot.

BANANAS

Bananas are used principally as fruit, and are described under that heading. They are rarely prepared as vegetables, but can be served cold as a vegetable-and-potato substitute, or fried as a breakfast dish or snack.

For frying, a banana can be anywhere from half green to full ripe. Peel it, slice it in half or thirds lengthwise, and fry in butter over medium heat until lightly browned, probably 6 to 8 minutes on a side. The flesh becomes translucent, so tender that it is almost sloppy, and sweeter than it was when raw. Serve hot with fried eggs, with or without ham, bacon or sausage.

Plantain. The plantain is a large, unsweet banana that is widely used as a starchy vegetable in the tropics. It is appearing in many of our markets. They usually must be cooked to be eaten. They may be used when green, ripe or over-ripe, with differences in flavor and cooking time.

Plantains may be fried, in the manner described for bananas except that enough slices should be made to keep them down to 3/8 inch thickness, or heat should be lower. But a basic method of cooking is to peel, cut in one to two-inch chunks and boil them until tender.

GREEN BEANS

Green beans, sometimes called string beans, stringless beans, snap beans or round beans, are immature fruits in which both young bean seeds and their protective pods are eaten.

Very small beans, shorter than 2 or 3 inches, are not harvested because of small yield. When the pods start to turn yellow the beans are too old for eating whole. Between these two extremes any age or size will do. The younger beans are more tender and have a more delicate flavor than larger ones, but yield less per plant and are more work per pound to prepare. Home gardeners tend to use smaller beans than are ordinarily found in the markets.

In general, good beans are a fairly bright green, and are crisp and tender enough to break with a snap when bent sharply, and can be easily pierced with a thumb nail. A tired, long-stored bean may change shape without breaking, and be rubbery enough to yield to the thumb nail without being pierced.

Preparation. Many varieties of green beans have a fine surface fuzz, which may pick up dust and which certainly tends to hold any dirt which may get on it. You may therefore wish to wash them, preferably by agitating in warm water. If the water gets dirty, pour it off and repeat the process.

The beans sometimes have brown or rusty spots from fungus or insect damage. They are said to be particularly likely to form if the beans are picked wet, or are washed and set aside in a heap without drying. The spots are harmless and may be eaten, but the fussy cook is likely to take the time to cut them off (they are very shallow) with a sharp knife.

From 1/8 to 1/4 inch is either broken or cut off the stem end of the bean, to get rid of the stem. The original green bean variety (the true string bean) had a tough thread running from the stem along the upper or rib surface to the opposite end. Getting rid of this was a plant breeder's triumph, but there are still some of them around. If you happen to get a batch, you break the bean at the stem end from the bottom, and pull the stem upward and along the bean, pulling the thread out.

There is a very widespread custom of breaking or cutting off the tail end also, and discarding it. This makes no sense, as the tail is just as good as the rest of the pod in tenderness and nourishment. But people who are accustomed to discarding tails may never be comfortable while eating them.

The stemless bean may be left whole, broken (or cut) into pieces about an inch long (cut beans) or sliced lengthwise into very thin strips (French style). The slicing is usually done with a special bean cutter that may be found in the handle of a paring tool, Figure 12-20. Each bean is pushed and then pulled through a slot crossed by fine wires that cut the strips with very little effort. However, the very fat beans that need fine slicing the most may not fit in the slot. In this case, or if you do not have a

Fig. 12-20. Bean slicer

slicer, use a paring tool or a very sharp small knife.

Cooking. In common with most vegetables, green beans may be boiled with plenty of water, half-boiled, half-steamed, with less water, or steamed or pressure cooked. The water may be fresh or salted. If the water does not cover, the pan should have a lid. Non-pressure time for whole or cut beans is 20 to 30 minutes, for French style 10 to 15 minutes, the differences depending on coarseness and maturtiy. Pressure cooker time at the usual 15 pounds is 3 to 4 minutes, with French style at the shorter time.

Beans are sometimes cooked in milk or in part milk or water to preserve a better green color and for a slight change in flavor. Cream or milk may be mixed with a little concentrated cooking liquid before serving.

Serving. Most green beans are served hot and plain. The consumer can touch them up with butter, salt and/or pepper if he wishes. Cookbooks recommend draining them, then reheating with melted butter and a little sugar, or with white or brown sauce. These special touches may produce a pleasing variety, as will also mixing in a little fine-cut raw onion, or adding a sprinkling of Parmesan cheese after serving, but most of the time beans will be enjoyed most when they are plain.

Both cooked and raw beans are used to a limited extent in salads. When raw they should be very young and tender, or as a poor second choice, sliced thin.

YELLOW BEANS

Yellow beans, also known as wax beans (because of their smooth, waxy skin in contrast with the fuzz of green beans) or butter beans, are close relatives of green beans, and are handled similarly. These beans are green when they start to grow but turn yellow when still quite small. They may be picked and eaten as soon as they are mostly yellow, or left until just short of maturity.

Fig. 12-21. Lima bean(s)

a stage indicated by prominent bulges at each seed.

Yellow beans are easier to wash than the green varieties, but otherwise methods of preparing, cooking and eating them are too similar to justify a separate discussion.

FRESH LIMA BEANS

The edible part of lima beans is usually just the bean seeds. There are a few exceptions. Some varieties have sweet tender pods that can and should be eaten whole. And wastefully young beans from other varieties may (or may not) be used in the same way.

The bean seeds, now to be called beans for simplicity, should be large enough to justify the expense of buying or growing them and the labor of shelling them. The smallest commercial size, baby limas, are most dependable for tenderness and flavor, but are sometimes equalled by very much larger fresh beans. As they reach maximum size, they become harder and more starchy with change in flavor.

The pod is usually flat, with its opposite sides in contact. As the beans grow they push the sides out, forming bulges, whose size is a good indicator of the seed's size. When maturity is reached the bulges are usually in contact with each other, and the pod starts to turn yellow. The bean is then entering a twilight zone in which it is too old to be a good new or fresh lima, and too young to be a good dried one. But some people still like them when prepared as fresh limas.

There is about a four-to-one difference in the yield of shelled limas from a pound of whole pods between the baby and maximum edible sizes, in the same variety of bean. Because of the amount of waste in the pods, fresh limas must be figured as one of the higher priced vegetables.

Fresh limas may sometimes be bought already shelled. This gives you the advantage of knowing just what you are getting, but flavor may deteriorate quite rapidly after the pods are removed. The shelling may be done at some central point where there is enough volume to justify using machinery for the purpose, so they may be pretty stale by the time you get them. It is a good idea to try them, but bear in mind that frozen ones may taste better.

Lima beans that are both fresh and young are likely to have a pleasant bright green color. But this color may fade quite soon, either in the pod or while cooking, to a neutral or greenish straw color. Although less attractive, the faded beans may still be sweet and tender.

Preparation. Shelling lima beans is a bit tricky. The pod will usually open at the rib line, if the rib and the opposite side of the pod are squeezed together. The beans are fastened at the rib by delicate stalks, and can be removed by running a finger or thumb the length of the inside of the opened pod. Unless some special effect is desired, all the beans should be used, including any smaller-than-baby-size runts and also nearly ripened giants with a yellowish color. If you want to be especially

Fig. 12-22. Dry beans

careful, and there are a lot of big ones, cook them separately and combine with the others only if you consider them good enough when cooked.

If the pods do not snap open readily, either because they are a difficult-to-shell variety or because your fingers are clumsy, place them one by one on a cutting board and slice the rib off with a sharp knife. Most of the beans will then fall out of the pod when you pick it up.

Cooked cold limas are welcome in salads if they have good crispness, flavor and color. If they do not, they are better left out, as a mushy or faded bean that might get by all right as a vegetable is dreary on a salad plate.

Cooking and serving. Lima beans should be cooked until tender by boiling or steaming 20 to 30 minutes, depending on size and initial tenderness. Pressure cooking about 2 or 3 minutes. Limas are more sensitive to overcooking than most other vegetables, and will turn mushy if you leave them on too long.

Juice from water-cooked limas usually has an excellent flavor, particularly if it is allowed to boil down to a concentrate. It should be served with the beans, even if it means using saucers. It can be pointed up

by adding butter, salt and even pepper to taste, if you wish.

Succotash. Succotash is a mixture of lima beans and corn. Because of their different characteristics, the two vegetables are usually cooked separately, and combined shortly before serving. The corn may be either kernel or cream style.

The standard proportion is equal quantities of both, but you can vary this to any extent you wish. Taste is usually good, but for pleasing appearance the beans should have a definite green color.

Succotash may be pointed up by addition of chopped raw onion and/or pimiento, from 1 teaspoon to 1 tablespoon to the cup of mixture, and a little milk or cream. Butter may be added when serving, or while eating.

DRIED BEANS

If beans of almost any variety are allowed to ripen fully on the vine, the seeds harden and the pods become brittle, so that shelling is easily done by hand or by machinery. The ripe beans contain little water, and are mostly starch and protein, so they are an excellent and concentrated form of nourishment. Price is usually low.

Dry beans do not make good flour, as they are entirely lacking in the gluten needed in baking. They are usually made edible by cooking with water to soften them. Their flavor is then very bland, and they are often flavored or used in mixtures to overcome this defect.

Cooked dry beans have a well earned reputation for creating large quantities of intestinal gas. This might sometimes be a factor in deciding whether or not to serve them as a main dish.

Preparation. Most dry beans now come neatly packaged in paper or plastic bags. They can be assumed to be clean and ready to use unless evidence appears to the contrary. Such evidence might be off-color or mis-shapen beans, a musty smell, or the presence of fine powder or webs indicating insect work, or sticks, leaves or incidental trash indicating careless cleaning. In such cases, wash thoroughly, pick them over, and then smell and inspect to determine if they are usable. They won't be poisonous, but they may be disagreeable.

Dried beans do not absorb water readily. The most efficient way to start them is to soak them in cold water for about 12 hours, which usually means overnight. In a general way, this cold water soak is equivalent in softening effect to two or three hours simmering, and is usually much less trouble.

Cooking. Beans swell as they soak and cook, to about double their bulk, and most recipe measurements are based on dry beans. So measure them before starting either process.

If you just want to cook the beans without fancy business, use two cups of water for each cup of beans, dry measure, plus a half teaspoon of salt per cup of water if you wish. Put in a pan of ample size to allow for possible boiling up. Heat to boiling, reduce heat, cover, and simmer until the beans are soft, perhaps 30 to 40 minutes. The water should become a thin gravy, well below the top of the beans. If it is very thin, cook a little longer. If it gets low and thick before the beans are cooked it may allow sticking and burning, so you should add a little water, preferably boiling water.

Add about a tablespoon of butter per cup (still dry measure) of beans, and salt and seasoning if you wish. Depending on your taste buds, pepper, paprika, chopped parsley or strips of pimiento may be used, the last three being as much for color as for flavor.

Baked Beans. Baked beans are a standard Saturday night meal in many parts of New England. The following is a sample recipe, which is altered in some way or other by almost everyone who uses it.

New England Baked Beans
(5 or 6 portions)

1	lb	brown beans, navy beans or other
½	lb	salt pork, cut in thick slices
1		medium onion, sliced
¼	cup	molasses
¼	cup	brown sugar
4	cps	boiling water
1	tsp	salt
1	tsp	dry mustard
		pepper to taste

Rinse the beans, check them over and remove any bad ones, then soak overnight in cold water. When ready to cook them, pour off the water and put them in a heavy pan. Add all the remaining ingredients and the boiling water. Heat until boiling resumes.

Pour into a 2-quart casserole, cover, and place in a very slow (250° F) oven. Cook for 6 to 8 hours, until tender. Uncover for last hour, to permit formation of a crust. Add a little water any time that beans appear to be getting dry.

You may not want to keep an oven going for this length of time. You can get results that are practically as good by keeping them in the heavy pan, and simmering them on a surface burner for about the same time. Heat must be very gentle — the lowest setting on an electric unit, or a low flame and a heat-distributing pad on a gas burner. Stir slowly now and then with a wooden spoon. Add a little boiling water if they get too dry to stir easily.

BEETS

The red garden beet plant, which is the subject of this discussion, gives us two quite different vegetables. The root, which is usually meant when the word "beet" is mentioned, is the most important. It is bland or sweet in flavor and very bright in color. The tops provide a leafy vegetable similar to spinach, which will be discussed separately.

The beet root is usually fat and almost heart-shaped in cross section. It tends to be fairly smooth-surfaced, is covered by a thin skin, and is dark red in color. The red tinge extends through the flesh of the beet and upward into the top stalks and the ribs of the green leaves. There is a non-edible (or at least not-eaten) tap root extending below the bottom point, and there may be groups of smaller roots anywhere on the surface.

Beets are usually sold with the tops attached. The extent of leaf wilting is one indication of the length of storage, or sometimes of bad conditions of storage. The skin should preferably not be bruised or damaged.

Very small beets, an inch or less in diameter, can be harvested in the home garden as a thinning-out process. Similar sizes are sold in cans. But the beets in the market are usually 2 or 3-inch, or even larger. As with most vegetables larger sizes usually mean less tenderness and a coarser flavor, and in beets they cause certain cooking problems as well.

Preparation. There are two separate ways of preparing beets, the choice between them depending largely on the color question discussed on Page 226.

If your beets are small, or you are primarily interested in preserving color, you will cook them whole. Cut off the tops, leaving at least one inch and possibly three inches of the stems. Do not trim roots. Wash lightly if they are dirty. Do not use a brush or rub hard, and avoid nicking or bruising the tender skin. Prepared in this way, the beets should suffer minimum loss of their bright red juice during cooking. They are skinned and trimmed after they are cooked.

If the beets are too large to cook whole conveniently (over 3 inches), if you are not specially interested in the color or you believe that these precautions are not worth while, trim the stalks and roots off flush, remove the skin with a parer or a sharp knife, and slice the beets. Slices are usually 1/8 to 1/4 inch thick and are cut across the stem line, but there is no firm rule about this. Or if your object is only a moderate reduction in size for faster cooking, you may just cut them in halves or quarters.

If your recipe calls for diced or cubed beets, hold the beet together as you slice it, then turn it to rest on its top and slice twice again, straight down, with all cuts at right angles to each other and spaced about 3/8 inch apart. It may be easier if you set aside the top slice, to give the remainder a flat base for steadiness while making the second and third cuts. Such slices, together with any uncut sections that slide out while you work, can be cubed separately at the end of the job.

If you cook them whole, you finish preparation afterward. Drain off the liquid and leave them in the hot pan, alongside the sink. Run a medium or strong stream of cold water from the faucet, and hold each beet in the water as you work on it, to avoid overheating your fingers. Cut the top and roots off flush and slide the skin off with your fingers. You may then serve them whole, or go on to slicing, cubing or dicing according to your recipe or your taste.

Cooking. The standard way to cook beets is by boiling in a covered pan. They

Fig. 12-23. Beets

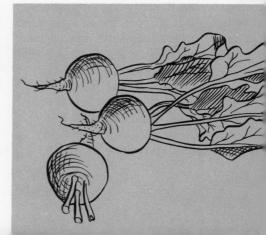

re started with enough boiling water to over or float them, brought back to a boil nd kept at a slow boil until tender with ccasional checking. This may take any- here from 25 to 60 minutes, depending ostly on size, but somewhat on variety nd age. The water usually boils down to /4 or less of the original quantity, and oiling water should be added if necessary ▸ prevent going dry. If less starting water used, the water level must be checked arlier and more frequently.

Steaming gives good results and takes out the same time. Presure cooking, for 2 to 18 minutes, is good if you guess the me right. Otherwise it is inconvenient be- ause you can't test for tenderness.

If the cooking water is hard, the beets ay turn to an unattractive, or at least un- onventional, tint of purple or blue. You an prevent this by adding vinegar or lemon ice, a teaspoon or more per quart, be- re cooking.

Serving. Hot beets may be served plain nd dry, or with a very little juice, on din- er plates, or in more juice in saucers. If eir diameter is one inch or less they hould be whole, if two inches or more ey should be sliced or cubed. In-between izes are optional.

Beets may be topped with butter in the an, serving dish or on the plate. Vinegar r lemon juice should be available, as any people like to add a touch of tartness. hopped chives, parsley or mint may be dded for appearance and flavor. Sour auces or horseradish may be combined ith them in the last minutes of cooking, or oured over them at the table.

Hot beets do not mix well with other ods, as the color tends to run, and it is ften unattractive in watered-down shades.

Cold beets are widely used in salads, here both their color and flavor is attrac- ve. Tiny ones may be whole, but usually ey are sliced, cubed or shredded.

Harvard Beets. Harvard beets are boiled

beets served in a thickened sweet-and-sour sauce. The amount of acid can be varied from just a touch to definitely sour, to suit individual tastes. The recipe below is only slightly acid.

Harvard Beets *(for 6 people)*

2 lb	small beets, boiled and peeled *(or larger beets, cubed or sliced)*
1 Tb	cornstarch
¼ cup	vinegar *(or more for increased sourness)*
3 Tb	butter, melted
2 Tb	sugar
2 Tb	water
1 tsp	grated onion
	salt and pepper to taste

Mix cornstarch with water and stir in melted butter. Add vinegar and heat, stir- ring constantly until mixture comes to a boil and thickens. Add all other ingredients and keep over low heat until beets are thoroughly hot, stirring occasionally.

Beet tops. Edible beet tops are the stems and leaves of young garden beets, or of a special variety of beet that has been bred for quality (or quantity) of top rather than of root. They usually have green leaves with red veins and stems. Although the flavor is different, it is similar to spinach and other greens in most characteristics

Fig. 12-24. Diced beets

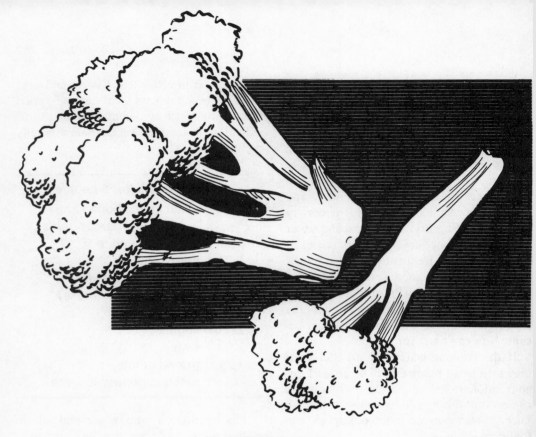

Fig. 12-25. Broccoli

and it is prepared, cooked and served in much the same manner as is described on page 264.

Beets in the garden usually require thinning one or more times. If the plants are pulled when the root bulges are small, the whole plant may be washed and cooked in the same manner as tops alone.

BROCCOLI

Broccoli is made up of tight bunches or heads of green unopened flower buds, with stems. The plant is a member of the cabbage family, and it may have a rank smell when fresh and raw. The smell tends to disappear during moderate cooking, and to reappear if it is overcooked.

Broccoli is supposed to be in rather large heads. Smaller heads and sprigs have equally good flavor, but they are not in style, and are usually acceptable only from the home garden. The head should be all green, as it

may undergo some change in flavor and cooking quality when the buds start to open into tiny yellow flowers.

Preparation. Your cookbook may tell you to soak broccoli, heads down, in cold salted water for a half hour or an hour. It is not apparent whether this serves any purpose, except perhaps to bring worms out of hiding, but it can do no harm except perhaps cause slight wilting.

With or without a bath, you strip off the leaves. The stems may be left intact, or trimmed back to within three inches of the buds, or to just below the point where they start to split into smaller stems. Long stems may have a woody surface layer, which you strip off in strips by catching it at the bottom between a paring knife and you thumb, and pulling upward.

Stalks that are 3/8 inches or more in diameter should be slashed into halves or quarters lengthwise, cutting from the bot

248

tom up to but not into the head. Otherwise, the solid stalk might not cook as rapidly as the porous head, and would still be semi-raw and tough when the buds were tender.

Cooking. Broccoli is usually boiled with enough starting water to cover it. A cookbook is equally likely to tell you that you must put a lid on the pan or that you must not put a lid on the pan. As always, the lid makes the operation more efficient. The water is usually salted, but this is optional.

Cooking time varies from 12 to 20 minutes, the difference being mostly in size and tightness of the heads. Steaming takes about the same time, pressure cooking 1-1/2 to 2 minutes.

As a member of the cabbage family, broccoli can produce strong and penetrating cooking odors. The most important precaution is not to overcook. This does not mean you must eat it semi-raw, just don't let it keep cooking until it is mushy. And other things being equal, there should be less smell with a lid on the pan than without it.

Serving. Broccoli may be served as a pile of individual flowerets, or as part or all of a larger head. The head itself can be separated by breaking, but the stalk has to be cut. The two parts should be equally tender, but the head is supposed to be more tasty and desirable, so all portions should share the two parts.

While broccoli is often or perhaps usually served plain or with butter, it has a natural affinity for a number of additives. You can cover it with white sauce, white sauce with chopped or sliced hard-cooked egg, Hollandaise or cheese sauce, with excellent results.

Cold broccoli occasionally appears in mixed vegetable salads, but it is not generally regarded as good salad material, either cooked or raw.

BRUSSEL SPROUTS

This is another member of the cabbage

Fig. 12-26. Brussels sprouts

family. The sprouts are somewhat like tiny heads of cabbage, and grow thickly along the vertical plant stalk. They are a late crop and are highly frost-resistant. They can sometimes be dug out of early winter snow drifts without apparent damage from exposure.

Size range, depending largely on age, is from about 1/2 to nearly 2 inches in diameter. Color may be light or dark green. Smaller sprouts may be picked in the home garden, but they do not appear in the stores. Very large ones may be too strong flavored. Sprouts may be very hard, with leaves packed together closely like cabbage, or a little loose and floppy like Boston lettuce. There is not much difference in flavor, but the tight wrapping gives less waste, a more attractive appearance and better texture.

They are often sold in quart boxes. One should be enough for four servings to people who like them, or eight to an average group. They are not universally popular.

Preparation. The outer leaves of the sprouts may be discolored or worm-eaten. The small stub of stalk may be tough. A good procedure is to cut the stalk end with a sharp knife, far enough into the sprout to remove the bases of the outer layer or two of leaves. These leaves may then fall off, or can be easily rubbed off. Inspect the remainder to see if it looks all right. If it does not, peel leaves until it does.

Large, tight sprouts may benefit by a pair of crossed slices 1/4 or 3/8 inches deep at the stem end, to shorten cooking time and to make it easy to cut them with a fork after they are served.

Cooking and Serving. Brussel sprouts may be boiled with deep or shallow water, salted or unsalted. Time varies from 8 to 10 minutes for tender specimens that are small or have been cut up, to 15 or even 20 minutes for tough ones and uncut big ones. Overcooking should be avoided because of probable smell, in addition to the usual consideration of loss of crispness and flavor. Pressure cooking takes from 2 to 4 minutes, but is of doubtful value because of the problem of timing.

Brussel sprouts may be served plain, with butter or with any of the sauces recommended for broccoli.

CABBAGE

A cabbage consists of a mass of leaves curled and overlapped into a very tight, heavy ball. The surface is usually green and the interior white, but there is also a red or purple variety. Cabbage harvested in the spring and summer has a much greater proportion of green leaves than is found in those picked in the late fall, which are often called winter cabbage. There is some difference of taste among varieties, and of course among individual specimens of any one variety.

The diameter of the sound or solid part of a mature cabbage varies from 4 to 10

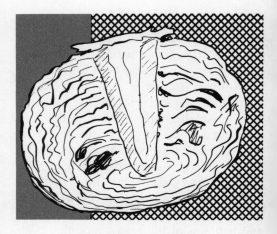

Fig. 12-27. Half a cabbage

inches, with weights from less than 2 to more than 8 pounds. Quality may be good in any size. When it matures too far, it changes texture and shape, pushes a stalk up through the middle and ceases to be an accepted food item.

Preparation. The cabbage head usually has a few loose leaves around it, which should be pulled off. The stem should be cut flush with the bottom. Any leaves or spots that are discolored or worm-eaten should be removed, or the bad spots cut out. Cutting is usually easier, as the close overlapping of leaves at the top makes them difficult to tear off.

The head is then rested on the bottom or stem end, and cut in halves, quarters or pie-slices so that no part is more than 1-1/2 or 2 inches thick. The inner or woody part of the core can then be cut out of each slice. This is in preparation for plain old-fashioned boiled cabbage.

If your taste or your recipe calls for shredding before cooking, cut the head into quarters, remove the hard part of the stalk then cut the quarters into slices about 1/4 of an inch thick, working parallel to one o the cut surfaces. These slices should fall apart into shreds during handling or cooking. If not, you can pull or crumble them apart.

For cole slaw, slices should be as thin as you can manage, for maximum tenderness and best appearance. It is discussed on page 491.

Cooking. Cabbage is usually boiled in enough water to cover it. A lid on the pan is recommended but is optional. Cooking time for slices is 5 to 10 minutes, and for shreds, 3 to 6 minutes. Test slices for tenderness at the thick end. To test shreds, take one or two out with a fork, rest them for a few moments to cool, and test with the teeth. Drain it thoroughly as soon as it is cooked. You may add butter and salt to it while it is waiting in the pan to be served.

Cabbage is strong-smelling, and under modern standards it is desirable to prevent it from announcing itself to the neighbors, particularly as its low price makes it an anti-status symbol. This problem was discussed on page 228 under Smell.

Serving. Cooked cabbage is a tender and tasty vegetable when served plain, or with the addition of butter and salt and pepper to taste. It is more interesting to eat when in slices than in a pile of shreds. It is corned beef's traditional companion, but otherwise cannot be said to be particularly popular.

It is sometimes served with white or cheese sauce, but it is not as well suited to them as its cousins, broccoli and brussel sprouts.

Red Cabbage. Red cabbage is generally similar to the green-white varieties. But to preserve its color, you might reasonably add a little vinegar to its cooking water, and shred it instead of slicing it to shorten cooking time.

Hot red cabbage is usually dosed within vinegar before serving, but this is not necessary for the average taste.

Cole Slaw. Raw cabbage is served mostly in the form of cole slaw. This is basically finely sliced cabbage coated with mayonnaise and seasonings. But there are so many ways to make it that the only item that can

be regarded as almost fixed is the cabbage. Except that it can be made after a fashion from iceberg lettuce.

A standard procedure is to shred or chop the cabbage finely, chill it, and then mix with mayonnaise, boiled dressing or sour cream, in the proportion of 1/4 cup of dressing to each cup of cabbage, for 2 people. From 1/3 to 1/2 of the cabbage can be replaced by finely cut celery, apple or drained crushed pineapple.

CARROTS

The edible part of a carrot is a root which has a bright yellow or orange skin and flesh. There are many varieties on the market, varying in shape from the long and thin to the short and fat, and from pale yellow to deep orange. There are definite differences in flavor, cooking time and probably other characteristics, but there is no clear overall advantage of one type over another.

Carrots are edible from the time they become yellow, when they are only slightly enlarged rootlets. They tend to get stronger in flavor and harder in raw texture as they get older. As they reach maturity they become coarse and woody, and it may not be possible to adequately tenderize them by cooking.

Most carrots are sold in bunches with the tops on, but very large ones may be trimmed and sold by the pound. They keep quite well as long as the tops are on, but if exposed to dryness or heat, the tops will wilt and the roots soften. The tops have a rank flavor, and are not considered to be edible.

Fig. 12-28. Carrots vary in shape

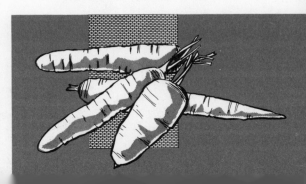

Preparation. To prepare whole carrots for cooking, wash them if they are dirty, cut off the tops flush, or even cut into the top of the carrot slightly. Trim off the tap root, and any other roots. Young carrots cooked whole may not need to have the skins removed. Older carrots may be peeled either before or after cooking. But if you are going to slice, dice or grate the raw carrot, peel it first. Use a paring tool or a sharp knife. The knife may be used either to slice off the skin, with a strip of flesh underneath; or may be turned at right angles to the surface and used to scrape, back and forth. The skin is almost always thin and delicate. It is difficult to remove only if the surface of the flesh is irregular.

The skin becomes soft and loose during cooking, and can then be rubbed off with thumb and fingers. Discomfort from the hot carrot can be avoided by doing the work under the faucet, in a moderate stream of cold water.

The raw carrot should be rinsed during or after peeling, to remove shreds of skin and possibly to show up unpeeled areas. It is then ready to be boiled or steamed whole; or to be sliced, diced, made into strips or shredded. Slices are made crosswise, straight for circles or diagonally for oval pieces. They may be anywhere from 1/8 to 3/8 inch thick, with 1/4 inch being usual. A few thick carrots in a bunch of thin ones may be sliced lengthwise into halves or quarters to equalize cooking time.

For dicing or cubing, you hold the carrot together during the first slicing, then make two additional sets of slices at right angles. This is sometimes difficult because of the shape. You may have to do several section of a carrot separately.

Very thin lengthwise strips for salad may be made with a parer, a sharp knife o a medium coarse grater. They are usuall 1/16 to 1/32 inch thick. The thinner yo can make them, the more tender (or the les tough) the result.

Raw carrots may also be put in a blende to make a thick pulpy juice favored b health enthusiasts.

Cooking. Carrots may be boiled in fres salted water, covered or uncovered, o steamed. Cooking time is very irregula varying not only with age and tendernes: but also with variety. Young carrots o pieces of large ones should cook in 10 t 20 minutes, but it is possible for them t take 30. Pressure cooking at 15 pounds i scheduled for 2-1/2 to 4 minutes, but re sults are somewhat uncertain because c the impossibility of testing.

Serving. Hot carrots are an excellen vegetable served plain, with a little of thei own juice, or with butter, or served in saucer with a lot of their juice. The juic may be concentrated, and enriched wit cream. Or a white sauce may be poure over the drained vegetable.

Sliced carrots may be mixed with similar quantity of peas, either while cook ing or just before serving.

Cold raw carrots, except in the ver small product-of-thinning-the-row sizes, ar too hard to be used whole or sliced in ap petizers or salads. But when they are pare into very fine strips, they are eaten happil by strong-jawed people, and their color i very pleasing.

13
MORE VEGETABLES

CAULIFLOWER

Cauliflower is similar to broccoli in that is made up of tight heads of unopened ower buds, and it is a member of the cabage family. However, the buds are white instead of green, and they are more tightly acked in the head, which is usually shalower than that of broccoli.

Head width ranges from 4 to over 7 inches. The head is preferably one solid iece. This is important if you are going to erve it intact or in large sections, but not you are going to break it up into small lumps (flowerets) for cooking.

Color should be creamy white. It tends darken when bruised, and when the buds art to open into flowers. The second cause more serious, as it indicates over-maturity nd possible change in flavor. Dark areas ay be trimmed off with a knife, but the apearance is then spoiled in a different way.

Preparation. The stem is usually cut ff just below the point where it starts to ranch out. Large leaves surrounding the ead are removed, but small ones growing ut of branch stems may remain. If the ead is to be cooked whole, a slot or a pair of crossed slots should be cut up into the stem to promote even cooking. A single knife cut may close up in this firm material and have no effect, but two parallel cuts 1/16 inch apart, more or less, with the slice between them removed by twisting the knife at the end of the second cut, will allow water or steam to penetrate freely.

If you are going to break the head up, you may separate the flowerets from the main stem by breaking them off individually or in chunks with your fingers, or by cutting them off with a knife. The stem may be sliced into pieces of similar thickness, either lengthwise or across.

Cooking. Cauliflower may be boiled, steamed or pressure-cooked. The special white-vegetable problems were discussed earlier. A large head of cauliflower, 7 inches across, may take 30 minutes to cook. Cutting it into quarters will reduce time to 15 to 20 minutes. Breaking it into flowerets cuts the time down to 6 to 10 minutes. Presumably, the reduction in cooking time will lead to a whiter product, but certainly the broken-up parts are less attractive than the whole.

The amount of cooking is more impor-

253

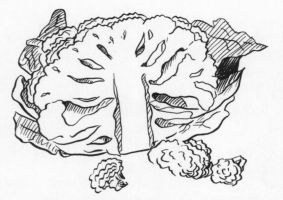

Fig. 13-1. A half cauliflower, and flowerets

tant than the method. It used to be that cauliflower was cooked too long, leading to mushiness, off-color and smells. Now it is often cooked too little so that it is too hard and still has a raw taste, and much of the pleasure of eating it is lost.

Flowerets may be dipped in egg, rolled in bread crumbs and deep fried at 350 to 370° F. They should be done when golden brown. Or they may be combined with thin white sauce in a casserole and baked.

Serving. Hot cauliflower is a tasty vegetable served plain or with butter. It also takes well to most sauces, particularly to white sauce and cheese sauce. You can hardly go wrong with it, provided it is reasonably well cooked and drained.

Cold flowerets, which may be raw, half-cooked or cooked, are popular in salads and are occasionally used as appetizers.

CELERY

Commercial celery is the stalks and just-sprouting leaves of the celery plant. Its nat-ural outer color is pale green, but it is fre-quently shaded during growth so that it i white, with pale yellow leaves. It is slightl fibrous, has a crisp, crunchy texture whe raw and is tender when cooked.

A bunch of celery consists of a numbe of stalks growing from a single large-toppe root. They are more or less crescent-shape in cross section, and are easily broken awa from each other. The lower sections of th inner stalks, and particularly the undevel oped stalks sprouting among them, ar called hearts of celery. Lower parts of al stalks are trimmed away from the uppe parts and are eaten raw. They may be plain salted or act as carriers for dabs of chees spread and similar delicacies.

The bases of the stalks make good lodg ing places for dirt. This is readily remove by washing if you separate the stalks.

The easiest way to prepare and cool celery is to cut all stalks into one to tw inch lengths, and boil or steam until tender about 10 or 15 minutes. They may also b sliced lengthwise, if desired. Serve hot with butter, white sauce or cheese sauce.

Celery is good in soup. Pieces are mad much smaller for this.

CORN

Sweet corn, also known as green or mil corn, is probably the most popular Amer ican vegetable, but it is neither liked no eaten in most parts of the world.

Corn grows in the form of kernels on a enlarged central stalk called a cob. The col

Fig. 13-2. Celery

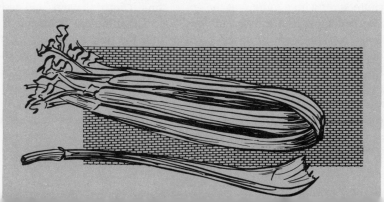

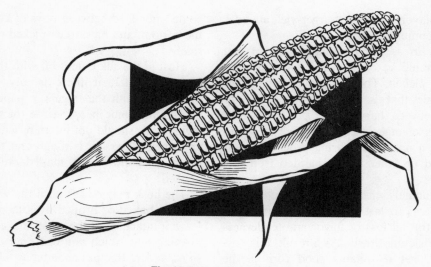

Fig. 13-3. An ear of corn

is hard and inedible. In commercial varieties it averages about 8 inches in length, but may be longer or shorter. Cob and kernels are surrounded and protected by a many-layered husk. There are fine strands called corn silk or silks that extend from each of the kernels through the top of the husk. They served for fertilization, each carrying a pollen grain from the plant's tassel to the developing grain. The lower parts are sometimes absorbed as the ear matures, but some silk is always present.

The cob, silk and husk are generally inedible, and make up most of the bulk of the ear.

Development. The kernels grow from points on the cob. They are generally in parallel rows, except in the Country Gentlemen varieties. They may be immature or poorly developed toward the tip. Best flavor and texture for all eating purposes are usually reached when the kernels have grown large enough to touch those in the next row, and have attained full yellow color in the yellow varieties. Black corn may still be almost white. They are then juicy, with a high sugar content and have a shiny appearance. This is called the "milk" stage. Continued maturing causes

the kernels to pack closely together, flatten and lose luster. Sugar is converted into starch, there is less and thicker juice, and skins become thicker and tougher. This advanced milk stage may be too tough for enjoyable eating from the cob or as kernel corn, but may provide a fair grade and large quantities of creamed corn.

In cool autumn weather, corn may retain sugar and tenderness much further into maturity than it does in the summer.

After reaching maximum size the kernels dry out and become very hard. Then the corn has ceased to be a vegetable and has become a grain. It is in this final stage that most corn is used; for cattle food, milling into corn meal and cereals, and for seed. However, the commercial ripe corn is usually of different varieties than the sweet corn, as it is grown for a large yield of dry grain, rather than good flavor and texture in the milk stage.

Varieties. There are also many varieties of sweet corn, each with its individual flavor and growth characteristics. Most of them are yellow. New hybrids are constantly being developed to combat insect and disease damage and improve yields. Varieties grown in home gardens are often better-flavored than the larger-yielding ones grown commercially.

Freshness. For best flavor and texture, corn should be cooked and eaten as soon as it is picked. There is probably no other vegetable that is as quickly sensitive to time between harvest and pot. The most obvious change is converting of sugar to starch, a normal maturing process that is speeded up when it is separated from the plant.

Fortunately, the rapid rate of deterioration seems to last only a few hours, after which further loss of flavor and tenderness proceeds quite slowly. As a result, it is possible to get reasonably good corn in the markets that is from a day to several days old. Even winter corn from farms a thousand miles away is sometimes quite tasty. Young corn endures storage better than mature ears.

Fresh corn keeps best when cold, so in spite of its bulk, it has a claim on your refrigerator space. It keeps better in its husk than without it, so don't open it until you are ready to cook it. If you do husk it, and cooking is delayed, wrap it in plastic such as Saran Wrap, as exposure to air not only dries it out but speeds up the sugar-to-starch change.

Dents in the kernels in table varieties usually indicate drying out due to too long or improper storage. This change may affect only a small area that has been partially exposed by stripping back part of the husk for inspection.

Husking. The husk is removed by tearing it down from the top or silk end. A section is grasped between finger and thumb and pulled down to the bottom. From 1/4 to almost 1/2 of the circumference may be stripped at a pull. A wider piece is difficult to pull, a narrower one may fail to remove the inner layer. Each strip may be pulled off the bottom separately, or they may all be broken off with the stalk at one time.

Pieces of the inner husk sometimes become embedded between rows of kernels at the bottom, and have to be picked off separately.

Most of the silk comes off with the husk. The remainder, if there is any, can be rubbed off with the fingers, a paper towel or a cloth. Some people rinse them off. A few strands should not interfere with eating enjoyment. The silk is tough and tasteless, but it is harmless. It may darken when cooked.

The husk may be left on if the whole ear is to be baked or broiled. It is then best to leave it intact, or at the most, make a small opening into which you can pour or inject some water. Recipes sometimes tell you to strip back the husk, remove the silk, then replace the husk. But the torn husk will not hold moisture nor protect the kernels as well as a whole one, and silk removal can be postponed until the ear is husked for serving.

Trimming. There is often from 1 to 4 inches of stalk projecting from the bottom of the cob. It may be broken off during husking. It is worth keeping if you are going to cut or scrape the corn off the ear as it can serve as a handle. Otherwise, it just adds extra length to an item that is already awkwardly long. You can break it off, cut it just below the cob or cut it off with the bottom of the cob. Cobs vary in hardness, but can usually be cut easily with a sharp heavy knife used with a rocking motion, with a serrated knife, a saw or even kitchen scissors.

Inner husk lodged between rows of kernels can often be removed most easily by cutting off the bottom of the cob, then lifting the cut ends of the husk.

Part of the upper end of the ear may be thin with undeveloped kernels. Such a portion may be cut or broken off. Areas that have been eaten or discolored by worms, birds or animals should be cut off or cut out and discarded.

Trimming the ends may serve both t

make the corn more attractive and to fit it into a pan of limited size.

Corn does not need to be washed, unless you get it dirty after husking.

Boiling. The standard method of cooking corn is to use a large enough pan to hold the ears, put in enough water to cover them, heat it to a full boil, put in the corn and cook covered at full burner heat for 3 to 5 minutes, remove from the water and serve.

The first problem is pan size. At the moment, full grown ears of sweet corn are usually between 7 and 9 inches long, with 8 inches very usual. Diameter ranges from 1-1/2 to 2 inches. Only two 8-inch ears will fit in the bottom of an 8-inch pan, but a third ear could be fitted at the sides if it were broken in half. If this pan had ordinary dimensions it would hold 3 of these layers. A 10-inch pan would hold 5 or 6 full ears to a layer, plus a couple of shorts or halves. An oval roasting pan 9 by 13 inches would hold a large number, perhaps 10.

If water is boiling over high heat when room-temperature corn is put in it, it will retain sufficient heat to start cooking it immediately. You time it from then, as it may be fully cooked before boiling resumes. This is true when there is enough water to cover or float the corn. If any corn is only partly covered, turn it once if there is a lid on the pan or several times if it is open.

Good varieties of corn of proper age are tender when picked, but have a raw taste. Three minutes of cooking may or may not leave a trace of this in a batch of 6 or 8 ears, while 5 minutes will eliminate it. Longer cooking tends to cause gradual darkening, limpness and toughening, but many cooks allow it to boil for 10 minutes or more and like the result.

Increase the recommended short cooking time by about 1 minute if the corn is cold from the refrigerator. If the quantity of corn is large, reheating of the water on an ordinary burner may be quite slow. You can compensate for this by adding 1-1/2 minutes cooking time for each 6 ears more than the original 6.

The corn should be separated promptly from the water at the end of the cooking period. The water can be used to cook successive batches of corn, but otherwise is not good for much, and can be discarded unless you want to save it until you are sure the corn is fully cooked.

The safe way to get the corn out is to lift it with tongs, an ear at a time. You can serve it directly onto plates, or pile it on a platter and cover it with a napkin. Try to schedule it so that you can serve it at once. If there are to be two or more batches, the first can be eaten while the next one cooks.

If you pour the water off the corn, a good method is to rest a corner of the pan in the sink, and tilt it by a heat-shielded hand (glove or pot holder) under the opposite side. Pour until there is danger of

Fig. 13-4. Lifting corn with tongs

Fig. 13-5. The lid will slip

dumping the corn, then hold the lid firmly over the pan, leaving a narrow space at the lower side for water to pour out.

Steaming. The main problem in steaming corn is to have a large enough steamer. If you don't, you may break the ears in half to fit in a smaller one, or improvise a rack in a canning kettle.

The procedure is to have water in the bottom boiling vigorously, put the corn in its tray or rack above the water, cover, and cook three to five minutes. Some people like to leave the inner layer of husk on the ears, and cook a minute longer. The benefit is supposed to be an improved flavor because no water touches the kernels, the obvious disadvantage is the necessity of taking off the hot husk.

Baking and Broiling. Slightly different flavor can be obtained by baking (roasting?)

Fig. 13-6. Pouring water off corn

corn on the cob in the oven, or cooking it under the broiler. It needs protection against drying out, which may be provided by part or all of its own husk, or by a wrapping of aluminum foil. If the husk is opened to remove the silk, or is taken off in favor of the foil, the corn may be buttered or watered before cooking.

Recommended roasting time is 10 to 12 minutes in a 400° oven, broiling 3 to 5 minutes on a side, three to four inches below heat. Results are much less certain than with boiling or steaming.

Eating on (off?) the Cob. Corn on the cob is eaten by chewing off two or three rows at a time, usually after spreading them with butter and sprinkling with salt. This is messy work, and calls for frequent use of a napkin. Sometimes the ear is rolled in melted butter, which makes it even messier. It may be held by means of small handles equipped with pairs of needle spikes for pressing into the ends of the cob, Figure 13-6, thus limiting the smearing to the face.

Tender corn is easy to eat on the cob, tough old corn may be a problem. A sure sign of over-age or overcooking is kernels that pull out of the cob rather than being cut off by the teeth.

Corn on the cob may be difficult for, or forbidden to, people with new or poorly fitting dentures, sore mouths or braces on front teeth. But they can eat the same corn if it is cut off the cob.

Cut Kernel Corn. Cooked corn may be cut off the cob by holding the ear vertically on a plate and slicing downward with a knife, preferably one that is neither very sharp nor very dull. A sharp knife is likely to cut into the tough roots of the kernels and into the cob itself, making the product unnecessarily tough and gritty. A dull knife is tiresome to use, and the heavy pressure it requires may cause accidents, such as sliding and/or a broken plate.

Keep each slice just off from the cob at the center. You will probably get almost all the corn from two rows, and a slice off two more. Overlap cuts as much or as little as you please. Make a second series of cuts when you have been once around. If the corn is tender you can use the back of the knife with downward strokes to scrape off the rest of the pulp, leaving the bases of the skins. If it is too hard for this, use the edge again, with extra care not to cut into the cob, until you have most of the corn down on the dish. Then take the next ear.

If you expect to do much stripping of cobs, either in cutting off kernels or in creaming them, it is worth while to prepare a holder-board. Take a regular cutting board, preferably a small size, or a piece of 3/8 or 1/2-inch plywood, 4 x 4 inches

Fig. 13-7. Corn handles

or larger, and put a small nail through it so that the point projects at least 1/4 inch on the other side. It is best if this is a snug fit, as for example a 4-penny common nail in a hole made with a 3/32 inch drill. You can hammer a nail through plywood, but a cutting board is apt to split, and in any case the nail would be hard to remove when not needed.

Put the board on the table, nail point up, and press either the trimmed top or the bottom of each ear onto the nail, before you start to work on it. This will prevent the ear from sliding around as you scrape it, reducing effort and avoiding accidents. If the board itself tends to slide, put wet cloth or paper under it.

Scrape the corn off the board into a bowl

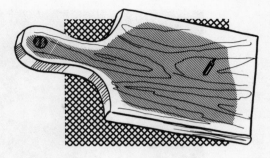

Fig. 13-8. Cutting board, with nail to hold corn

or pan after each ear or two. The nail can be taken out when you use the board for other work and for storage, but the empty nail hole may need special cleaning.

Raw corn may be cut in the same manner. It is much more juicy, and will make a product intermediate between kernel and cream corn.

In cooked corn, this cutting job, which is quite easy once you get the knack of it and not too difficult at any time, serves not only to provide access to delicious corn for mouth-handicapped people, but it is also the basis for the best possible frozen corn. In both raw and cooked corn it is the first step toward obtaining delicious flavor in a number of recipes that specify canned corn, because they think nobody is going to take the trouble to process fresh corn for the purpose.

Whole-kernel corn can be obtained by using a two part circular knife such as that shown in Figure 13-8. It is spread over the small end of the ear and twisted down on it with one hand while the ear is twisted oppositely with the other. Unfortunately, the

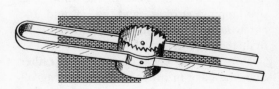

Fig. 13-9a. Corn kernel stripper

Fig. 13-9b. Cutting kernels with a knife

only home model we could obtain was so tight and sharp that it cut too deep, so that the product was inferior to that obtained with a regular knife.

Creaming. Creamed corn consists mostly of the insides of kernels, extracted from them when raw. It may also contain a certain amount of kernel skins, and some whole or part-kernels may be mixed with it, either deliberately or accidentally. Too sharp a tool may include bits of the cob. It is best when made from the same tender quality of corn you eat on the cob, but it is also the best use for older and tougher ears, which yield a larger quantity with somewhat less flavor.

To cream corn you slice each row of kernels with a sharp knife, then hold the ear vertically and push the slit kernels downward with the back of the knife. Use overlapping strokes, and go around the ear twice, pushing off the bulk of the corn first, then salvaging what was missed.

You use the back of the blade rather than the edge in order to avoid cutting off the kernel skins and parts of the cob. The skins are not noticeable when part of the whole corn, but may be unpleasant when too many of them float around independently. Cob parts are all tough and tasteless, and may be gritty.

The special creaming tool shown in Figure 13-10 is cheap (if you can find one to buy) and reduces the work greatly. The little teeth on one side will slit several rows of corn at once, and the curved ridge on the other side pushes a wider strip than a knife blade can.

For creaming, leave any stalks on the ears to provide comparatively dry and convenient handles. The nail board described earlier should be used if possible. If the corn is thin and watery you may put the board in a platter, or use a platter only, in order to conserve the juice.

Corn prepared this way has a very smooth creamy texture. If you like it a little rougher, you can slice fine or coarse pieces off some un-slit kernels, or even include some whole kernels. These pieces should be from reasonably young and tender ears, to avoid any suggestion of toughness when they are eaten.

Cooking Creamed Corn. Creamed

corn sometimes separates into a thin fluid and stiffer solids, which are comparatively easy to cook. But it is more often a thick liquid with a high starch content, which sticks to everything, conducts heat poorly and scorches easily. It cooks quickly, in 3 to 5 minutes at 180° F or higher, but it can be mean stuff to get to and hold at such a temperature.

You can cook directly over an electric burner turned to LOW if you stir and scrape almost constantly, preferably with a soft rubber or plastic squeegee instead of a spoon. If a ball or line of thickened material scrapes from the pan and accumulates on the stirrer, scrape it off and throw it away. Its consistency is likely to be something like chewing gum, and it won't mix back in with the rest. By the time the corn starts to boil with big slow bubbles it is probably cooked and ready to serve.

A gas burner, even when turned very low, supplies too intense a heat in a small area for direct cooking of creamed corn. It can be used safely only if a heat diffuser or insulator is placed between flame and pan.

You can cook creamed corn in a double boiler with little attention and no risk, but this will take at least 20 minutes for one cup, and longer for more. You can reduce this time by starting it over direct heat, then putting it over boiling water when it starts to stick. Once over water it will not give any trouble sticking, but it may develop a weak crust that should be stirred in

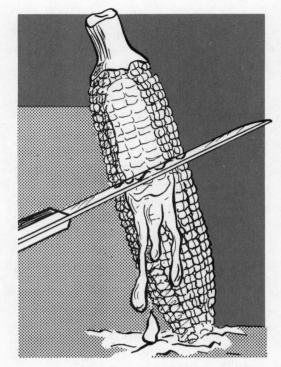

Fig. 13-10a. Creaming corn with a knife

occasionally, to preserve a smooth texture.

Thick creamed corn may be thinned by adding cream, milk or water in the proportion of 1 or 2 tablespoons to a cup, but it may then become too thin when it is heated, so that you will have to serve it in saucers.

Canned creamed corn is slightly inclined to stick and burn, but not nearly as severely as the fresh, raw variety.

If you have an electronic oven, you can put the raw corn, mixed with a teaspoon of

Fig. 13-10b. Corn creaming tool

milk for each cup, into a covered non-metallic casserole, cook on high heat for 2 minutes, stir once and then cook a minute for each cup, or to taste. Let stand for 2 minutes before serving.

Souffle. Home creamed corn forms the basis for excellent souffles. Or you can use it out of a can. For example:

Corn Souffle *(for 4)*

2	cps	creamed corn, preferably raw
2		eggs, slightly beaten
1	tsp	flour
		salt and pepper to taste

Stir all ingredients together. Put in the top of a double boiler, over boiling water, and cook 10 or 15 minutes, or until just firm. Or cook in a casserole dish in a moderately slow oven, 300 or 325° F until firm and lightly browned. Tradition says that the dish should not be greased.

One-half teaspoon of baking powder would probably make this souffle even lighter, but the flavor would be slightly impaired.

Fritters. Fritters can be made with kernel or creamed corn, or with a mixture of them. For kernel corn prepare the batter given for dessert fritters on Page 557, but omit the sugar. For a batch made with one cup of flour you can use anywhere between 3/4 and 2 cups of kernel corn. This may be canned, but will taste much better if it is fresh or home-frozen, prepared by first cooking on the cob and then cutting off. It should be well drained, so as not to thin the batter.

Cooking procedure is the same as for the dessert fritters.

Cream-style corn is mixed directly with egg and thickener to make a fritter mix. For most delicate flavor and texture, mix one cup of cream corn (preferably home made) with half of a well beaten egg. Add a dash of salt, if you like, and fry in butter at medium heat, turning as soon as the underside is brown. This batter will probably be quite thin, and spread into a thick pancake. Cooking time should not be over two minutes to a side, and the inside should be slightly moist when served.

You can use a whole egg if you prefer, and you can stiffen either mix with bread crumbs, possibly 1/4 cup, if you want to deep fry them or perhaps just like them thick. Or you can puff them a little with 1/4 teaspoon of baking powder. These additions make the fritters a little less flavorful.

Serve hot with butter, or with butter and syrup.

Freezing. It is not practical to can corn at home even with a pressure cooker. It is non-acid and requires a high temperature, 240° F (10 pounds pressure) for over an hour even in that, so it is greatly overcooked. But it is easy and safe to freeze, and results are excellent.

The simplest procedure is to boil or steam more corn on the cob than the family can eat. After the meal, slice the surplus off the cobs with a knife, seal it in labeled bags or boxes and keep it in the freezer until needed. Its flavor will probably be superior to that of commercially frozen corn.

Creamed corn also freezes well. It is best if it is blanched by a minute in boiling water before cutting, or cooked or half cooked, after creaming, but it may be satisfactory (although somewhat gooey to cook) even if it is frozen raw. But the freezing should be done immediately after creaming.

Cooked corn may be left on the cob, wrapped in plastic, and frozen. But it is seldom as good as when cut off the cob before freezing. Both flavor and texture are often damaged by the presence of the cob.

CUCUMBER

The cucumber is a faintly striped green immature fruit of a vine of the squash family. In the market the length varies from 6 to 12 inches, and weight from 5 to 12

Fig. 13-11. Cucumber and egg plant

ounces. A cradle-snatching gardener may pick them smaller, and they sometimes grow to a weight of several pounds before becoming tough.

The primary uses are in salads, sandwiches and as pickles.

Both the skins and seeds are tender and edible, so preparation often consists only of washing and slicing them. Slices may be paper thin up to about a quarter inch. The flavor is good but not strong, and the principal attraction is the crisp, crunchy texture. They go well with almost all salad ingredients and dressings.

Cucumber may be prepared as a cooked vegetable in the same manner as summer squash, or put through a blender to make soup.

EGGPLANT

The American eggplant is a relative of the tomato. It is a rather large fruit, pear-shaped or egg-shaped, varying from 5 to 10 inches in length, and in weight from 1/2 to 2 pounds. The shiny skin is dark purple in color regardless of age. There are eggplants of other colors also.

Eggplant has a firm, heavy flesh when picked. If it is stored too long, or under hot or dry conditions, it tends to lose water and

to shrink, soon acquiring a wrinkled appearance that may cover the whole fruit, or just a few spots. This wilting is often, but not always, accompanied by a toughening of its texture. So if you can get your eggplants with smooth skin, do so.

The flesh is moist but not juicy, is full of edible seeds and is not considered palatable until it is cooked. It has a distinctive flavor which is enjoyed by many, but for others, needs to be modified or disguised by mixing with other foods.

Preparation. Eggplant skin is sometimes tender enough to be edible when it is cooked, and sometimes not. If you are cooking it in slices, it may be reasonable to leave the skin on, and it can be easily be removed during eating if it proves to be tough. But for mixtures and most uses, it is safest to take it off. It can be peeled with a parer or a sharp knife.

Slices may be 3/8 to 3/4 inch thick, and are made straight across the stem line. No part of the flesh need be removed, as both the center stalk and the seeds are tender unless it is badly over age. To dice it or make cubes you put the slices back together, except for the slice on the stem end, stand them on that end, and make downward parallel knife cuts a half inch apart. Then make another set of downward cuts at right angles to the first ones. At some point in this process the vegetable will start to fall apart. Any pieces that escape must be cubed separately.

Omitting the third set of cuts leaves you with sticks or fingers which can be fried, either bare or after breading. They are inclined to break, so handle them with care.

If your recipe calls for mashed eggplant, cook thoroughly and then use a potato masher or a grinder on its coarse setting.

Cooking. Eggplant is cooked in a number of different ways. The easiest is to simply fry the slices at medium heat, preferably in butter on a griddle. A slice 3/8 inch thick should take about 4 minutes on one

Fig. 13-12. Greens usually need washing

side, 3 on the other. It may be helpful to put a small dab of butter on top of each slice immediately after turning. You can dampen the slices with a slightly beaten egg, and cover them with bread crumbs or flour before frying.

Half-inch cubes of eggplant may be deep fried, either plain or preferably with an egg-and-crumbs coating. Fat temperature may be between .365 and 375° F.

Eggplant is very successfully cooked in casseroles, plain or in combination with other foods.

Serving. Eggplant is only occasionally served by itself as a boiled vegetable. It may be in the mashed or cubed form, with butter, salt and/or pepper to taste, but usually without sauce. Fried eggplant is more popular, in the form of either slices or sticks, breaded or unbreaded.

GREENS

Greens are leaf vegetables. In this section we will consider only the ones that are normally cooked before eating. This leaves out lettuce, chicory and endive, which are mostly used raw in salad and which are discussed separately.

Cooking greens include some plants grown, or picked wild, for this purpose only; such as spinach, kale, collard, mustard and dandelion; and tops of root vegetables such as beets and turnips.

Greens are best when picked young, except that spinach preserves its good qualities to maturity, largely because its stalk and vein structure has less tendency to become coarse. The quality of greens may be greatly affected by weather, as they may become tough in dry weather or tasteless when it is very hot and wet. For that reason the crops harvested in the Spring and the Fall are considered to be the best.

Greens tend to carry considerable quantities of dirt and sand, as it splatters or blows on them while they are growing, and the upward reach of the leaves provides pockets in which it stays. You have a choice of separating the leaves and rinsing them one by one, or swishing bunches of them around in a pan of water. You keep washing as long as the dirt keeps coming out, as even a little sand may take away the pleasure of eating.

Very young beet tops do not need trimming. As they get older the red stalks get thick and prominent, and spoil the appearance if not the flavor of the completed dish if they are allowed to remain. You remove them by laying the leaves one at a time on a board, and cutting them out with a sharp knife.

264

All greens need to be inspected for bad spots. This is part of washing the leaves individually, but is a separate job if you swish them. The spots may be places that are discolored by fungus, possibly a result of picking and piling them when they are wet. You also cut or tear out patterns of insect feeding and crushed, wilted or encrusted areas.

Greens are sometimes boiled whole, but it is more usual to cut them into strips or to chop them. For strips you take a fistful and cut them with scissors, about 1/2 inch wide, or hold them down on a cutting board and slice with a knife. Cut close to your hand and keep backing it away. For chopping, make the strips very narrow, then cross cut them. If this is not fine enough, you can finish up with a chopper in a wooden bowl or with a meat grinder.

To make a puree, put the cooked greens through a blender.

Greens are boiled rather than steamed, as steam does not circulate readily through them and may leave some parts almost raw while others are fully cooked. Boiling water keeps the leaves stirred up so that heat is well distributed. However, they have a tendency to float, and may need to be pushed down now and then. They also need stirring to prevent sticking to the bottom.

Cooking time is extremely variable, from 5 to 10 minutes for young spinach to well over an hour for kale and mustard.

Most recipes call for cooking with bacon or other pork, and pepper or other flavorings. This is all right if you like it, but you should try them plain first.

The cooking water may be drained off greens for tidiness in serving, or left with whole or strip ones to keep them moist. In dishing them out wet, you can remove most of the juice by pressing each heaping spoonful against the side of the pan before moving it to the plate. Chopped greens stay sufficiently moist without standing in juice.

Greens are usually served with butter, and salt and perhaps pepper to individual taste. They may be benefited by white sauce (in which case they should be well drained), by mixing with pieces of hard cooked eggs, topping with the same eggs cut up fine, or sprinkled with grated cheese.

Spinach. Spinach has special characteristics of fine texture, flavor and public acceptance that have promoted a greater variety of uses for it than for the others. It is the only one that appears to be widely available in frozen and canned form.

Spinach goes particularly well with hard-boiled eggs, as in the casserole on page 400. It is occasionally served raw as a replacement for lettuce.

KOHLRABI

Kohlrabi is a plant of the cabbage family that grows a tasty bulge in the stem just above the ground. It is white, with a white or white-and-purple skin. Quality is variable, some plants being very tender, others tough and woody. Tenderness is favored by cool weather, plenty of moisture, and immaturity. Size range is from 2 to 4 inches, with the best prospects for tenderness 3 inches or less. A tender skin that can be

Fig. 13-13. Kohlrabi

easily pierced with a thumbnail is an indication of good condition.

Kohlrabi may be prepared by stripping off stems and leaves, washing, removing a thin slice from the lower or root end, then peeling it like an orange with the fingers.

Cross-slices 1/4 inch thick, put in boiling water, should cook tender in 6 to 10 minutes. It is served plain, with possible addition of butter and salt. It also goes well with white or cheese sauce.

LEEKS

The leek is a relative of the onion, and has a milder variation of its flavor. It is shaped like a big immature onion (scallion) with a long narrow white bulb dividing into a crown of green leaves.

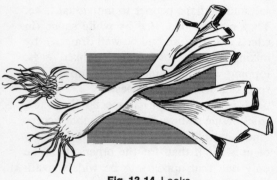

Fig. 13-14. Leeks

There are differences of opinion about how much of a leek is usable. Some people use only the white part, others add a varying amount of green, from 1/4 inch to most of the plant. The leaves have a tendency to be tough, particularly on the outside and in older plants.

The cleavage between leaves and groups of leaves may reach down a short distance into the white bulb, and may be expected to contain dirt. Most of this can be washed out under a strong stream of faucet water, but complete removal may require splitting or pulling it apart.

There is no distinct skin like an onion's,

but the surface is likely to be somewhat hardened or coarse. If so, peel it thinly with a knife or paring tool. Cut off the bottom tip to remove the roots.

Leeks can be cut into chunks and boiled, 10 to 15 minutes or until tender, and served as a vegetable. They are good hot, plain or with butter, or may be eaten hot or cold with sliced hard boiled eggs and decorated with parsley. The chunks are sometimes half cooked by boiling, then breaded and deep fried.

Leeks are better known in combinations with other foods, often as seasoning rather than a bulk item. They are particularly esteemed in French cooking. Vichysoisse soup, for example, is a puree of one part of leek to two parts of potato in chicken broth, plus seasoning.

In some localities, a variety of wild onion is known as a leek, but it is closer to garlic in strength of flavor and persistence of smell, and cannot be used in recipes calling for leeks.

LETTUCE

Lettuce is a leaf plant which forms the basic ingredient of salads, and it is discussed in that section. It is only occasionally cooked and served as a vegetable.

There is a recipe for braised iceberg lettuce, which calls for slicing it into wedges, frying them in butter until brown, then adding a little water and simmering under cover for 20 minutes. These wedges may be very fragile, and must be handled with care.

MUSHROOMS

Mushrooms are the edible fruit of fungus plants. The fungus family does not have chlorophyll, so that it cannot build up its own substance from inorganic material and sunlight, as green plants do. It lives on organic matter, and in the case of most of those that we use for food, this material is dead or dying.

Most of the fungus plant is made up of a

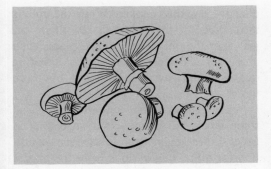

Fig. 13-15. Mushrooms

mass of root-like fibers called mycelium, which is spread through its food material. At intervals the plant produces a fruiting body which pushes out into the air, then forms a great number of tiny seeds called spores. The growth and ripening of the fruits may be very rapid, usually taking a few days, but sometimes only a few hours. They are eaten in the bud or immature fruit stage, after which they become unattractive.

There is a great variety of edible mushrooms. Unfortunately, there are also a number of kinds that are poisonous, and some of these are deadly. For this reason, most

people confine their use of mushrooms to commercially grown ones that are entirely safe and are sold in stores, although flavor is unlikely to be as good as when they are field grown.

Most commercial mushrooms are one variety, *Agaricus bisporus*, and any recipe calling for mushrooms refers to it. When mature it is shaped like a pudgy little umbrella, is an off-white color, has an easily removed but tender skin on its upper surface, has pink or grey gills, and grey spores. The spore color can be determined by removing the stem, and putting the upper part, with its gills down, on a piece of white paper with black printing. After a few minutes or perhaps a few hours, enough spores will have fallen to be visible as a fine powder.

The most poisonous mushroom (toadstool) is the Amanita, which includes a number of varieties which resemble the edible type superficially. But it is a cleaner white in color, the upper skin usually does not peel as readily, and both the gills and the spores are white. It is easy to distinguish when the umbrella has opened, but in the bud stage only an expert can be sure.

There are many varieties of fungus fruits which can be easily and safely distinguished, and whose flavor, texture and cooking qualities vary from passable to excellent. They include the puff balls, ink caps, bracket fungi and (best of all) morelos. Study of a book on fungi, such as COMMON EDIBLE MUSHROOMS by C. M. Christensen (University of Minnesota Press) may be very rewarding to those who live or vacation in the country.

OKRA (GUMBO)

Okra, or gumbo, is a small green fruit or seed pod that is popular as a vegetable in the South, where it grows best. It has only marginal acceptance elsewhere. The pods are tapering, ten-angled, and may be from three to ten inches long when mature.

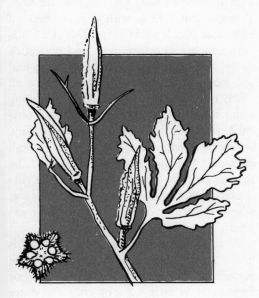

Fig. 13-16. Okra

Fig. 13-17. Onions

Mature pods are coarse and woody, so the vegetable must be picked young. It is then bright green, crisp and brittle. Yellow or brown color usually indicates maturity and toughness. Dull color or limpness shows over-long storage.

Okra has a distinctive flavor. It may be eaten by itself as a vegetable, served in combination with tomatoes or onions, or used as a thickening material in soups. It contains a mucilage or thickening agent, and must be handled tenderly and briefly during preparation and cooking to avoid a slimy texture.

It is usually washed, not peeled, and cut into cross slices about 1/4 inch thick. It may be cooked in boiling water, steam or butter for 4 to 8 minutes.

ONIONS

Onions are highly flavored, pungent-smelling bulbs made up of concentric layers of leaf bases. A tissue-like skin covers the outside and may also occur between layers. Size varies from slightly oversize marbles to 5-inch diameter monsters weighing over a pound. Color may be white, yellow, red or purple. The light colors and small sizes are usually preferred for cooking. The shape is basically that of a globe, usually flattened somewhat on top and bottom, but sometimes extended into a slender oval.

Onions are widely used as a vegetable, but their principal value is in flavoring or seasoning. For this purpose they are more effective raw than cooked. While the bulb is most used for this purpose, raw finely cut leaves of the onion and related plants such as chives and leeks have similar flavoring qualities. The leaves are grass-like, but more fleshy.

While garden-fresh onions may have some flavor advantages as a vegetable, in general these bulbs keep in excellent condition for quite long periods, with the harder northern onions being somewhat superior to the larger and softer varieties such as the Bermuda. Best temperature is just above freezing, but fairly long storage at temperatures up to 55° F is practical, and a week or two at room temperature may do little damage. Deterioration, when it occurs, is indicated by a loss of firmness and finally by brown rot.

Flavor varies greatly among different varieties. It tends to get stronger with maturity. Texture remains good until sprouting occurs, but then becomes woody.

Preparation. Almost all uses of an onion start with peeling it. There are different ideas about how this should be done. If the onion is very small and tender you may wish to remove only the outer tissue skin. You can cut into it with a sharp-pointed knife and peel it off in strips. But since it is both tender and transparent, and may stick to the flesh, this may be difficult to do and you may not be sure whether you got it all off. If the onion is soaked briefly in boiling water the skin will be toughened and loosened, so that it will come off more readily.

Another factor is that the layer of flesh immediately under the outer skin, and the skin inside that, may be tough. This is particularly common on the upper surface, where a green or dark color may show exposure to air while growing.

A safer and easier method of peeling is to cut a thin slice off both the top and the bottom of the onion, then use a knife or fingernails to strip off not only the outer skin but one or two outer layers of flesh,

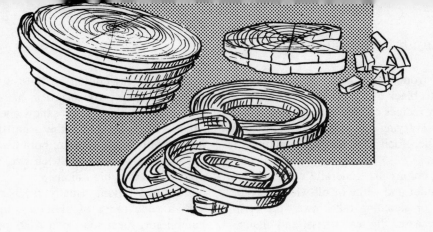

Fig. 13-18. Onion rings and pieces

along with the skins under them. You may take off up to three layers in a darkened area, and only one over the rest of the surface.

Cutting or tearing an onion releases large quantities of its pungent odor cells into the air. They react strongly with eye tissues, causing smarting, reddening and tears. This unpleasantness can be avoided by doing the peeling under a stream of cold water from the faucet, which will wash away almost all of the odorous substances, preventing them from getting into the air. Or you can work underneath the surface of water in a bowl, but this is usually less convenient.

If an onion is to be cooked whole it should be pierced several times from the sides through the center with a pin, ice pick or skewer. This should prevent any trapped and expanding fluid from pushing inner sections out through the ends, making the vegetable less attractive.

Small and medium onions are usually boiled whole, large ones may be cut in half or quarters for faster and more uniform cooking. The outer skin should be removed, as it may give the water a bad color and flavor.

If the peeled onion is sliced across, the slices will be made up of a series of rings diminishing in size from the outside in. These rings readily separate from each other if the slice is bent or handled roughly. If finer pieces are needed, parallel or radial cuts are made in the slice, or in a stack of slices, in one or two directions. Thickness of slices, and spacing of other cuts, is optional but 1/8 to 1/4 inch are usual. This operation will release some tear-forming gas, but not as much as peeling. It is difficult to do under water.

Whole peeled onions, or large pieces of onion, can be reduced to a pulp on a medium coarse grater, or in a blender.

Cooking. Onions are usually boiled or fried. For boiling whole, they should be pierced to prevent pushing apart. Instructions may tell you to use huge quantities of salted water and leave uncovered, but results should be equally good with just enough fresh water to float or cover them, and a cover on the pan. Cook until fork-tender, an operation that may take from 15 to 30 or more minutes, depending on size and variety. Then drain them, and perhaps add some butter while they are standing in the pan waiting to be served.

Sliced onions will cook by boiling in as little as 5 minutes, but they lack the attractiveness of the whole or quartered unit.

Onions are sliced and sometimes crosscut as well before frying. Butter is a favorite medium, as it combines with the onion to produce a special flavor, and it favors quick browning. However, any cooking grease or oil may be used. Medium or low heat produces even cooking and color; high heat usually produces a variation in pieces or strands from very lightly cooked through brown to black and a crisper texture.

Many recipes call for half-cooking onions by either frying or boiling, mixing them with other food and then completing the cooking.

Raw onions are generally crisp, moderately tender and white or off-white in color. Boiling or steaming takes away the crispness, increases the tenderness, and changes the flesh to a translucent appearance, with color ranging from white to buff depending on the variety of onion, its age and the length of cooking. The raw onion is much more strongly flavored and pungent in smell than it is after cooking. The slight value for nutrition is not changed much. Therefore, in cooking, half-cooking or not cooking onions you do not have any important problem aside from obtaining the exact flavor and appearance that you want.

Onion rings are dipped in thin batter, then deep fried a few at a time at about 375° F until golden brown, usually a minute or two. It is important that the batter should be cooked, but the onion may be raw without damage. Test the first batch. If you want them cooked more, reduce the heat by 25° and increase the time.

The rings may be dried on absorbent paper, lightly salted and kept in a warm oven until served.

Serving. Boiled onions are usually served plain or buttered, or with white sauce. White onions, on account of small size, attractive appearance and possibly flavor differences, are considered to be the best. They are often served with white sauce. Cheese sauce is also good, but seems to be seldom used.

Fried onions are usually served in rather small quantities on top of or along side of meat, particularly steak or hamburger. If well fried, they lose as much as 2/3 of their raw bulk, but since they are usually inexpensive the small portions are probably due to their moderately strong flavor rather than their cost.

Slices of raw onion, 1/8 to 1/4 inch thick, are frequently served in hamburgers and sometimes in other sandwiches or in salads. These are preferably from the Bermuda or other large onion, both because of the slices being near sandwich size, and the milder flavor of big onions.

Chopped onion, usually raw, is mixed with a wide range of materials, including hamburger, meat loaf, pan fried potatoes, peas, gravy, casseroles and salads.

Onion is excellent and popular for seasoning or flavoring other foods. However, it has the disadvantage of smell, which may remain in the breath of people eating it for an hour or more. It is also to some extent habit forming, in that a cook may use it so much that she no longer tastes small quantities, then use continually larger amounts to get the same effect, eventually providing much more onion than her customers can enjoy.

PARSNIPS

The parsnip is a large, tapering fleshy root of a plant belonging to the parsley family. It has a mild but distinctive flavor, which is usually either very much liked or violently disliked. The flesh is white or pale yellow, is fine in texture under the skin and coarse in the core. The skin is very thin, and may be scraped off with a knife held at right angles, or taken off with a paring tool.

The young parsnip, picked in late spring or summer, is starchy and, aside from its special flavor, rather bland. As the weather gets cold some of the starch changes to sugar, making it sweet. Freezing is said to improve its flavor, but at least it does it no harm, and harvesting may be done in the middle of the winter with pneumatic drills if you like them that much.

To cook, you cut off the top, remove the skin and any blemishes, and boil for 20 to 30 minutes. Short time is for small roots, or those that have been sliced in halves or quarters lengthwise.

Boiled parsnips are eaten with butter, and may be heavily seasoned or just touched up with lemon juice. They may be fried in butter until brown, with frequent turning because they scorch easily. Or dip them in egg and crumbs and deep fry them.

PEAS

Green Peas. Green peas are the globular, unripe seeds of a legume closely related to the beans. Five to ten seeds grow in a pod, which is split between the fingers in order to remove them.

There are many varieties of peas. A few of them, more popular in Europe than here, have edible pods when young. Other varieties must be shelled, and the pods are discarded. The principal distinction between them for the cook is the size of the peas, which may be as small as a 3/16 to 1/4 inch diameter for early, small or petit peas up to double size for giants. Almost any variety can produce tasty small peas when picked young, but only a few can grow big without getting dry and tough.

Pea pods should be bright green. Any yellow or brown tint is likely to indicate over-maturity or too long a time since picking, except for little bruise marks or fungus spots which have less significance.

An under-age pea pod is quite flat. As the peas grow they bulge the sides, and at maturity the pod may be almost round. The size of the peas can therefore be judged fairly well by inspection of the pods. Small peas are usually tender with a delicate flavor. Larger ones may or may not be tender and have a stronger flavor, but have the definite advantage of giving you more food per pound of whole peas.

The flavor of peas tends to deteriorate sharply in the first few hours after picking, and again if there is a delay between shelling and cooking them. Peas bought in the market have already lost their garden freshness, but the flavor they have left holds up fairly well until the pods are removed.

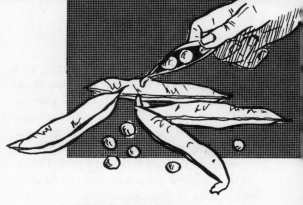

Fig 13-19. Peas and pods

Preparation. Pea pods have seams along opposite edges. They usually split readily if the two edges are squeezed toward each other. If a pod does not split, it can usually be twisted or pulled apart easily. Some of the peas are loosened from their tiny stalks by opening the pod, the others can be pulled or pushed out with a finger or thumb.

Getting the peas out of one pod is quick and easy as soon as you have had a little practice. But getting them out of a big pile of pods (about 1/2 pound, before shelling, makes an individual serving) is work.

If practical, peas should not be shelled until it is time to cook them, as they may then lose flavor rapidly. If you must shell them in advance, keep them in a plastic bag or a plastic-covered bowl with a few drops of water until you use them.

Peas are often washed before shelling, because of a possibility that dirt or contamination on the outside of the pods will be transferred to the peas.

Cooking. Peas may be boiled, simmered, steamed, or pressure-steamed, with a normal cooking time of 10 to 20 minutes, and a pressure time as low as 2. Large peas and old peas need the most time, in fact, on a cook-until-tender basis, they may never make the grade, but go directly from semi-hard to mush.

The best test is to remove a pea, cool it and chew it, although something of their condition can be judged by the way they feel against a spoon if you stir them.

Their cooking juice rates high in flavor.

271

If you boil in a covered pan, starting with just enough water to cover, you should finish with a fair quantity of a very pleasing fluid. This should be served with the vegetable, drunk by the cook or used in something if it is at all possible.

Serving. Garden-fresh peas probably fulfill their highest purpose when served plain with a little of their cooking juice, plus butter, salt and possibly pepper to taste. Peas from the freezer, the market and the can may be served in the same manner, also with pleasing results.

Peas are also excellent in a wide variety of combinations. They may be mixed half and half, or in any desired proportion, with diced carrots. The carrot pieces should be about the same size as the peas, and preferably not more than twice as large. Or peas may be mixed with a small quantity of onion, either extremely small whole onions, or less-than-pea-size pieces. These may be cooked with the peas for their whole cooking time, half of it or even left raw, depending on your taste. Or you can combine peas with cooked mushrooms, cauliflower or celery, or with fine cut raw celery.

Peas may be cooked in milk, or milk may be added to them in the last few minutes of cooking. They also do well in a thin white sauce, but lose their flavor in cheese sauce.

Because of their convenient size, their good color and texture and their flavor, cooked green peas serve well as either a minor or a major ingredient in gravy, white sauce, salads and salad jellies, casserole mixes and other foods. A pea salad is described on page 491.

Dried Peas. Dried peas come in two varieties, whole and split, and in two colors, green and tan. The whole pea includes a skin that retains its form even after cooking has reduced the seed parts (cotyledons) to mush, and which many people find disagreeable to eat because of its texture. The skin or shell has been removed from the split peas. Skins can be removed from whole

peas after thorough cooking by putting them through a strainer.

It is not clear whether the color is a question of plant variety or of method of processing. The green split peas are favored for soup because the color is more appetizing.

Dried peas are highly nourishing, concentrated food. In a general way they are used in the same ways as dried beans, but are sweeter and smoother in texture (if skinned), and are more used for soup and less in baked form.

Dried peas may be washed and picked over to remove possible undeveloped pieces and trash. They are usually soaked several hours or overnight to reduce cooking time, but this is not strictly necessary. Some peas are processed in the factory to shorten preparation time, in which case directions on the label should be followed.

SWEET PEPPERS

Garden peppers of all colors are produced by plants related to the tomato, with a completely different ancestry than the vine which gives us black pepper. Most of these peppers are very highly flavored, and some are used in hot mixtures, others to make red pepper and similar seasonings. Most of the hot peppers are long and thin.

The sweet or bell pepper, generally known as the green pepper, is fat and short, with a mild flavor. This is the only member of the family that is widely accepted as a vegetable in the United States, and it will be the subject of this discussion.

These peppers have good flavor and a crisp, tender texture, from the time of first

Fig. 13-20. Sweet (bell) peppers

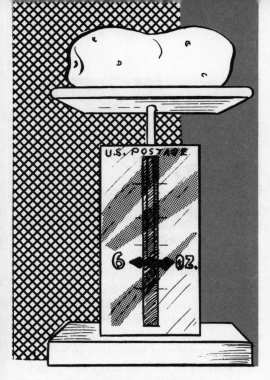

Fig. 13-21. A medium potato

frying them alone in halves, or in chopped condition with onions. They may be cut in halves, quarters, slices, strips or cubes for mixing, usually in small proportions, in stews or casseroles.

For salads, peppers may be sliced across, about 1/8 inch thick. In small peppers the centers are used, in large ones they may be either used or discarded. Slices may be cross sliced for small pieces to sprinkle as a garnish, or to be mixed into such items as potato salad or tossed salad.

The most distinctive cooking use for them is to serve as the container part of stuffed peppers, described on page 385.

POTATOES (WHITE)

White potatoes are root tubers. The plant that produces them is a relative of the tomato and eggplant, and also of the deadly nightshade and other unwholesome species. Sweet potatoes and yams are not closely related to them, and will be discussed separately.

There are many varieties of potatoes. All of them have white or off-white flesh, a thin brown or red skin and a number of "eyes," each of which can sprout and grow into a new plant. There is great variation in mature size, with a range in weight of 4 to 18 ounces, and in longest dimension, 2-1/2 to 6 inches. In addition, some varieties are picked before they are mature, and there are usually very small sprouts or secondary tubers associated with a mature crop. When a recipe calls for a medium weight or size potato, it usually means one weighing about 5 or 6 ounces for boiling or mixing, but sometimes 10 ounces for baking.

Potatoes are classified principally on the basis of texture and use. A baking potato tends to become mealy and fragile when cooked, and is favored for both baking and deep frying. The general purpose potato is smoother in cooked texture, and might sometimes be said to be waxy. Although it can be equally tender, it does not fall apart as readily. It is best used for boiling and

development through maturity. The skin is glossy green (red when mature) and is edible. Most of the flesh lies immediately under the skin. The interior, made up of fibrous walls and seeds, is also tender and edible but is often discarded.

The keeping quality of peppers is only fair. They are crushed out of shape if piled too high in the market, and they tend to lose moisture, shrivel and wrinkle.

Preparation. Peppers should be peeled only when they are going to be cooked in mixtures with other food, where the texture of the skin might be disagreeable. The best way to get it off is to put the pepper in boiling water for 30 to 60 seconds, cool it under the faucet, then strip the skin off with the fingers. Without this hot dunking, the skin is difficult to remove, and it is likely to take away some of the small amount of flesh available.

Peppers are seldom boiled, except as cut-up pieces in mixtures. There are recipes for broiling them whole, after painting them with oil (keep 3 inches under flame, turn several times, cook about 8 minutes), and for home-frying, and for all dishes in which slices or chunks of potato are mixed with other foods or cooked or served with sauce. They are generally used for mashed potatoes.

These distinctions are ignored by many cooks, who simply buy potatoes on the basis of price and appearance, and cook them any way they want, with reasonably good results.

If you do become curious, you can test. On a commercial basis the two types are tested by putting them in a solution of 8 or 9 tablespoons of salt to a quart of water. If the raw potato floats, it is a general purpose type, if it sinks it is for baking. Because of individual variations among potatoes this test is not 100 per cent accurate, but it is a good general guide. The salt solution, which is about 12 per cent, may have to be strengthened with a little more salt, or weakened by adding a little water in order to make the distinction.

Immature potatoes, harvested in the spring or early summer, are called new potatoes. They are usually small, and have very thin fragile skin, a firm flesh and a special and delicate flavor. They are particularly good boiled and as salad, and are seldom baked.

Preparation. Market potatoes have usually been very thoroughly washed. Home grown ones should be washed immediately after picking, allowed to dry separately from each other and then stored. It is usually not necessary to wash potatoes as you prepare them for cooking, unless they look or feel dirty.

Potato skins are edible but are usually not eaten, except on boiled new potatoes and occasionally on baked potatoes. They are always left on baked potatoes until they are served, and also on boiled new potatoes. For most other uses they are removed, either before or after cooking.

The skin of a raw potato is firmly fastened to the flesh, and requires a knife or a

Fig. 13-22. Baked potatoes

paring tool for removal. The parer is easier to use, and much more economical of potato, a particularly desirable feature since there is a theory that nutriments are concentrated just under the skin. Raw potato peeling is somewhat tedious because the surface is irregular, so that many short strokes are needed, and the eyes are usually in little hollows, and are dug out individually with a special tip on the parer, or by the point of a knife. This job will show up any trace of dirt on your fingers as conspicuous grey smudges on the freshly exposed potato flesh.

If potatoes are to be boiled you can profitably postpone peeling until they are cooked. The skin can then be easily rubbed off with the fingers, preferably under the cooling influence of a stream of cold water from the faucet. The eyes still must be cut out, unless you figure you can get away with leaving them in. Peeling may become difficult again after they cool.

A peeled raw potato may be roasted with meat or boiled whole, cut into halves, quarters or slices to boil more quickly, cut into strips for French (deep) fries, or into slices, strips, cubes or chunks for a great variety of uses.

Basic procedure in slicing potatoes was described on page 236. Slices are usually 1/8 to 1/4 inch thick, but may be much thicker if they are a starting point for other shapes.

French fry strips may be 3/8 to 1/2 inch square. They are sometimes rectangular in cross section, or scallopped. Two inches is a good length, but this is dependent on potato size. Extra long pieces are likely to break, and small ones may fall through the basket.

Cooked peeled potatoes are often cut in irregular shapes for home fries or for salad. You hold the potato in the same way as for slicing, but the cuts should be at different angles and directions. If the pieces look too coarse after you have finished, cut the pile at random by pushing the knife straight down on it, as pulling or pushing will simply pull the pile apart. If the pieces are too fine, cut the next one more coarsely. There is no rule about piece size for either product, but remember that if the potatoes are tender, they will break up somewhat during the frying or mixing.

Cut surfaces of potato turn brown, but rather slowly, so that you need take no special precautions during preparation if they are to be cooked promptly. If they have to be held over more than 20 minutes, however, put them in water, preferably with lemon juice or ascorbic acid.

Baking. Potatoes are usually baked in an oven kept between 350 and 450° F. Time varies with the variety and personality of the potato and the heat of the oven. A medium size (8 oz) potato may take from 40 to 60 minutes at 400°. You should stab it a couple of times with a fork before putting it in, as the skin is sometimes steam-tight, and enough pressure may build up inside to break open the potato or even cause it to explode.

You also test for doneness with a fork, and cook until it slides into the potato easily. Or you may follow cookbook advice and squeeze the potato through a folded towel. But you cannot usually judge by appearance or by cooking time.

Potatoes are sometimes wrapped in aluminum foil before baking. This insulates them, so that you need a hotter oven or a longer time for the same degree of cooking.

It also holds in moisture, so that the skin is softer and the texture is somewhat different — purists will deny that it can be a "true" baked potato. The most important effect of the foil is that it makes it possible to keep the cooked potato hot, tasty and ready to eat for a long time. This is the reason that this method of cooking is used by most restaurants.

The electronic oven does top quality potato-baking in a very brief time. One medium potato takes 4 to 8 minutes, six of them 15 to 20 minutes.

Boiling. Potatoes may be boiled in much or little fresh or salted water, or steamed with about the same results. Whole potatoes may be cooked with or without their skins. Their condition is determined by testing with a fork. Time varies considerably with size, and an effort should be made to have all the potatoes in the pot about the same size, so they will be done at the same time. Medium size whole potatoes may take 20 to 40 minutes to be fully cooked.

Amount of cooking desired is affected by individual taste in hardness and softness, and also by the way the potatoes are to be

Fig. 13-23. Test for tenderness with a fork

used. If they are to be mashed they must be thoroughly cooked to avoid lumpiness; if they are to be salad they should be firm enough not to break up when mixed with dressing. If they are intended for further cooking, as in home frying or baking in a casserole, they may be anywhere from half to fully cooked, depending on the recipe and the result wanted.

Cooking time may be reduced to as little as 6 or 8 minutes by making slices 1/8 to 1/4 inch thick, arranging them loosely in the pan, and boiling vigorously so that water will circulate between the slices.

Boiling is often just a first step toward using potatoes. They are the basis for mashed, most home fried and many casserole potatoes, and for potato salad. In addition they are delicious eaten hot with butter. There are further discussions under these various headings.

Deep Frying. Deep fried strips of potato, generally known as French fries, are very popular. The principal problem in preparing them is getting the deep frying equipment set up, which may be a nuisance if it is seldom used. An electric frying kettle with automatic heat control is the best, in fact almost the only kind of fryer that should be used by an amateur. General construction and method of use are discussed on page 58 and in Chapter 37.

Strips of potato, 3/8 to 1/2 inch square, or sometimes 3/8 by 1/2, are fairly standard for French fries. They are placed in a wire basket and lowered into fat heated to around 300 to 330° F, and kept there until they have turned a golden brown color. The basket is lifted and held over the fryer to drip a few moments, then the potatoes are served to individual plates with tongs, spread on paper for grease removal, or dumped into a serving dish. If there will be any delay in serving they should be covered by a cloth.

For the average taste a French fry should be tender all the way through, but still crisp and firm. The surface color should be somewhere between yellow and medium brown. The appearance should not be greasy. If the grease is too hot the surface tends to turn dark brown before the centers are cooked, if it is too cool the color will be too light, and grease may soak in deeply. Cooking too long hardens them, starting at thin ends and corners. They tend to become limp if serving is delayed.

Pan (Home) Frying. Pan or home frying may be done with either raw or cooked potatoes. If raw they should be thinly sliced, cut in fine strips, or made into strings with a coarse grater. The same shapes are possible with cooked or semi-cooked potato, and in addition thick slices or random chunks may be used.

If the potatoes are cooked, you need to get them heated through (which is easy) and develop a pleasing color and texture, which may be more difficult. A particular problem is that cooked potatoes absorb grease too readily. No matter how much you put in the pan, short of floating the food, you will soon find it dry. The best way to manage this is to put in a little grease often, directly on the pan surface, then tilt the pan or move the food to distribute it.

If you are using random size and shape chunks, or slices, you will probably both stir and turn them. If heat is low (on an electric frypan 225 to 250° F) they will need little attention, and stirring may be omitted, but they will develop little color. At the opposite extreme, about 400 or 450°, you will be kept very busy both stirring and turning, will burn a few surfaces and small pieces, and may raise quite a bit of smoke. If you are frying in butter, don't go above 250 or at the most 300°.

Raw potatoes are fried at low or medium temperature, 225 to 275°, to give them time to cook while surface color is developing. They absorb less grease than precooked ones. The pan should be covered for uniform cooking, and you might put in a couple of teaspoons of water for a short steaming effect. When they are almost cooked, according to fork tests for tenderness, turn the heat high to brown them.

Grated potatoes, whether raw or cooked, are shaped into a patty or several patties about half an inch thick after pressing down firmly on the pan with a turner. Heat should be low if they are raw, medium if they are cooked, but in either case you may want to turn the heat high for the last minutes before turning or serving, to develop more color.

Pushing down the patty serves both to bring the upper surface nearer the heat for better cooking, and to compact the mass so that it will be less likely to fall apart when you turn it.

Mashed. Mashed potatoes are made from fully cooked boiled or steamed potatoes without skins. General purpose potatoes give somewhat better results than the baking type. New potatoes do not mash well.

The mashing operation consists of reducing the potatoes to a smooth consistency, while mixing in milk and butter. The product should be white, fluffy and free from lumps, but it often falls short of one or more of these goals.

The first requirement is that the potatoes be evenly soft so that they will react uniformly to the mashing process. For this result, all potatoes in the batch should be the same kind, age and condition. The size of the potatoes, or of the pieces into which they are cut, should all be about the same, so that they will cook evenly. The cooking should be thorough. Then drain them completely, and allow to stand covered for a few minutes to absorb any remaining water.

Hard potatoes tend to resist crushing, and to remain in lumps. This is particularly true when there are both hard and soft potatoes together, which is the reason for the preceding paragraph. Lumping can be reduced by thorough mashing, or eliminated by putting through a ricer.

The two tools in Figure 13-24 are specifically designed for mashing potatoes and similar foods. With either tool you should scrape the sides and bottom of the pan or bowl several times with a big spoon, to make sure that no unmashed potato remains.

The mashers are used chiefly with a short-stroke up and down motion on the sections that need it the most, with occasional rotary sweeps for mixing and for checking for concealed lumps. Mashing time may be as short as 2 minutes or as long as 10.

Mashing of a small quantity may be done with a big spoon. You can start by pressing straight down on the mass of potato, and finish by stirring with the back of the spoon almost touching the side of the container, so that pieces of potato are squeezed against it.

A heavy duty electric mixer running at low speed does an excellent job of mashing potatoes, provided they are adequately cooked. There should be enough of them to at least half fill the bowl, in order to give the beaters something to bite into. Also, it is usually easier to mash a small batch by hand than to get out the mixer, use it, clean it and return it to storage. The mixer actually mashes more rapidly, but because no manual effort is required the process is

Fig 13-24. Potato mashers

Fig. 13-25. Mashed potato: good, too thick, and too thin

generally continued longer. Small quantities may be done in a blender.

It is usually recommended that you preheat the bowl, beaters and milk in order to keep the potatoes hot. This is a good idea, but if you start with hot potatoes and serve them very soon after mashing, they will probably be hot enough without this extra trouble.

The amount of milk and butter to be added varies with the type and condition of the potatoes. For six medium size potatoes, about 5 ounces each, try 1/2 cup of milk and 2 tablespoons of butter. Add them a little at a time during the mashing, mixing in thoroughly each time before adding more. Butter, aside from an excellent effect on flavor, adds to smoothness and lightness. It continues to have this effect even in many times the recommended amount, as the ability of cooked potatoes to absorb butter seems almost unlimited. The milk produces the same effect up to a point. Then additional milk thins out the mixture too much for the average taste, and seems to take away from the fluffiness which is the ambition of the cook and the pleasure of the customer.

You probably have an idea of the proper consistency of mashed potatoes from eating them, if not preparing them. But if you do not, take a heaping tablespoonful — almost globular — and place it carefully on a flat surface. If the texture falls in the most approved range, the shape will be something like that shown in Figure 13-25, left — flat bottom, bulging sides and peaked top. If it is hunky it needs more milk, if flattened it has had too much milk already.

The white color is highly valued in mashed potatoes. It is produced by good potatoes, milk and plenty of beating or whipping. Never do the beating in an aluminum pan, as enough oxide may come off the pan to turn the potatoes grey. They are then all right to eat but not to look at.

SWEET POTATOES AND YAMS

The sweet potato and yam plants are not related to each other, nor to the white potato. However, the resemblance among their edible roots is close enough so that they can be treated as one class of vegetable.

Both the sweet potato and the yam exist in a large number of varieties. Those grown for food in the United States are usually yellow or orange in color and moderate in size (4 to 12 ounces). The principal differences are that the sweet potato is long, narrow and tapering while the yam is thicker and blunt, and that the yam is much more moist, and darker in color. There are moist sweet potatoes and orange sweet potatoes, that are usually sold as yams because they go against these distinctions. In a general way, the two are interchangeable, but the drier and firmer flesh of the sweet potato makes it more adaptable to combinations. However, over the past 30 years yams have increased in use at the expense of the sweet potato.

Through the rest of this discussion, any reference to sweet potatoes will include yams unless a specific difference is stated.

Preparation. Most varieties of these roots are difficult and annoying to peel. There is a delicate outer skin attached to a soft but knife-resistant fibrous layer over the flesh. Skin and fiber are usually edible when cooked being more tender and tasty than the skin of white potato. But since they are not as tender as the flesh they are usually discarded. If the skin can be removed, the fiber layer is acceptable, being considered part of the flesh.

Sweet potatoes should be left whole and unpeeled for baking. For boiling or steaming they should wear their skins, but they may be sliced into two or more pieces lengthwise for faster cooking. It does no harm to peel them first, in fact they may look a little better. But the skin can be rubbed or pulled off so easily after cooking (under a stream of cold water) that it is wasted work to struggle with it beforehand.

Peeling is required or is advisable if the potatoes are to be sliced or diced before cooking. The best tool is a sharp paring knife. Make the cuts as shallow as possible. A slight sawing motion is helpful, particularly if the blade has small teeth. Wide scallop teeth make the edges of the cut irregular, but cut more effectively.

Cooking. Sweet potatoes and yams may be boiled in salted or unsalted water with or without a lid, or steamed or semi-steamed with a lid. Cooking time ranges from 15 to 30 minutes, depending on size and variety. Accurate testing may be done with a table fork — when it slides into the potato easily, cooking is complete.

Baking may be done in a 400° F oven, or 50° hotter or cooler. Time for a medium sweet potato or yam, say 6 inches long and 2 inches in diameter, and weighing 8 ounces may be about 40 minutes at 400°. If the skins are to be eaten they may be brushed with oil halfway through the cooking, or if they show signs of peeling or blackening.

It is important to puncture these potatoes in at least two places before baking, as the fiber and skin may be sufficiently strong and vapor-resistant to hold in steam pressure, so there is a possibility of an explosion that will make a mess of the oven and a nearly total loss of the potato.

Candied sweet potatoes are most easily prepared by baking or broiling slices of cooked potatoes with butter and granulated sugar. Margarine can of course be substituted for the butter. Some recipes replace the white sugar with brown sugar or even (regrettably) with corn syrup. The potatoes may be sliced thinly, 1/8 to 1/4 inch, buttered and put in layers, or sliced thickly, 1/2 inch or a little more, and set side by side. Light colored, dry-fleshed potatoes are as greedy for butter as white potatoes, and may need two or more tablespoons to the pound, with an equal amount of water, to avoid drying. Most yams may get by on half the butter and with no water. Sprinkle sugar on top to taste, perhaps 1/2 cup for 6 potatoes in a 6 x 10-inch pan.

Since the food should already have been cooked by boiling, its re-cooking need only make it hot and provide crispness and perhaps color. The best effect is to have the sugar about half melted. A half-inch depth in a glass utility dish might take 20 to 30 minutes in a medium (350° F) oven.

Serving. Boiled sweet potatoes are easily peeled under cold running water by rubbing or scraping away the thin brown skin,

Fig. 13-26. Sweet potatoes and yams

Fig. 13-27. Radish rosettes

leaving the fibrous layer. They may then be served plain or with a dab of butter on top. Or the peeled potatoes may be sliced, usually 1/4 inch or thicker, before serving.

Sweets may be mashed in the same manner as white potatoes, with much the same effect, although they may be somewhat fibrous. But mashed yams, with their moist texture, may not be very different than before the mashing.

Mashed sweets or yams, while still hot, may be put in a casserole or utility dish with marshmallow on top, and put in a hot oven or about 5 inches below a broiler until the marshmallows turn brown. The number of marshmallows is optional, ranging from two or four as decoration up to half or even solid coverage. The heat will cause them to melt down and join each other if they are at all close. This makes a very sweet vegetable dish, but it is well liked.

Sweet potatoes seem to be seldom used in salad, but that does not mean you cannot try them if you wish.

RADISH

The radish is a crisp root with a peppery taste. The most popular variety in the United States is a quick-growing Spring variety with white flesh and red skin, almost round in shape. There is also a type with white or near-white skin and a more elongated shape, and varieties with purple or black skins that are found in some markets.

Radishes are used chiefly for decorations and very light eating, on relish trays and salads. They may be made into rosettes by cutting strips of skin from the top down along the sides, leaving them attached at the base and bending them outward. They may also be sliced thinly, either across or vertically, and scattered on other foods. The white flesh and bright red skin make an excellent contrast. Very young leaves may be used sparingly among the salad greens.

Radishes can also be boiled and eaten hot, but they do not seem to be popular in this way. In other countries, radishes may weigh up to 2 pounds, and may be quite important as vegetables. And there is a variety that is raised for its large seed pods, which are eaten fresh or pickled.

SALSIFY (OYSTER PLANT)

Salsify, which is called oyster plant or vegetable oyster because that is the way it tastes, is a long slender root with white

Fig. 13-28. Salsify

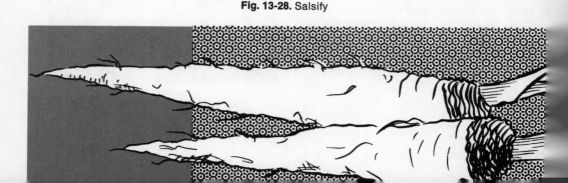

flesh that is tender and rather bland when cooked. It matures in late autumn, and is not injured by freezing as long as it is in the ground. It is not a popular vegetable, and may not be obtainable in many localities.

The tops and any thin roots are cut off and discarded. The skin is thin and firmly attached to the flesh. It is removed by paring, a simple operation if the surface is smooth and a tedious job if it is rough. Peeled pieces should be put immediately in water, or water plus a little vinegar, as they may discolor quite rapidly in air.

These roots may be as much as a foot long, so they are seldom boiled whole. You may cut them in pieces to fit the pot, or slice them in any thickness from 1/8 inch up. Boil slowly, steam or simmer them 15 to 20 minutes, until tender.

Boiled salsify may be served plain or with butter, in either chunks or slices. It is more usual to cover it with white sauce. Variations include boiling it with a small amount of chopped celery, and putting a chicken bouillon cube in the sauce.

SUMMER SQUASH

There are a number of varieties of squash that start to mature in early summer, and then continue to be available until frost. They are closely related to the later maturing winter squash, but are very different in keeping qualities, method of preparation and flavor, so they will be considered separately.

Summer squash includes the yellow crookneck and straight varieties, and zucchini. They are edible from the smallest size that is worth picking until just short of maturity. When in prime condition the yellow squashes have a fairly even, pale color and a smooth skin. With approaching maturity the surface becomes rough and knobby, and the color deepens toward orange. The zucchini tends to develop a dull or grainy appearance.

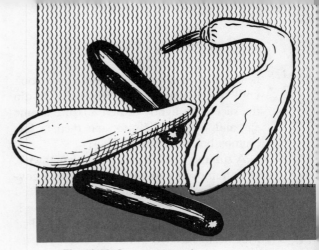

Fig. 13-29. Summer squashes

The young squash are completely edible — flesh, skin and seeds. At maturity both skin and seeds become too hard to be good food, and the flesh acquires the taste and texture of poor winter squash.

Preparation. Squash usually grow on the ground under the protection of large leaves. They may have some dirt sticking to their undersides, but can be assumed to be free of poison sprays. Rinse under the faucet, and rub off any remaining dirt spots.

This type of squash is usually cut crosswise into slices 1/4 to 1/2 inch thick, but there is no objection to diagonal or lengthwise slicing if you prefer. Very small ones may be left whole, larger ones may be cut lengthwise into halves.

Young and medium ages do not need peeling, older ones do. The knobs on the older ones make paring difficult and wasteful. If in doubt, leave the skin. If it is tough after cooking, you can remove it with a knife while holding the slice with a fork.

Young seeds are tender and good to eat, old ones are hard or tough and should be removed before cooking.

Cooking. Squash is usually boiled or steamed in a covered pan. It takes about 6 minutes if it is young, tender and in 1/4-inch slices, and up to 15 minutes if it is old and in 1/2-inch slices. Test with a fork for tenderness.

It may also be fried in half-inch slices in butter or other grease over low to medium

281

heat. Turn in about 4 minutes, then cook until tender and slightly browned. Or dip the slices in a lightly beaten mixture of one egg and 1/4 cup of milk and then in fine crumbs before frying.

A summer squash may be cut lengthwise, seeds removed and cooking done in a covered frypan over a burner, or a covered casserole dish in the oven. You can serve it plain, with butter, or filled or partly filled with hash, mashed potatoes, diced vegetables, or even the drained solids from canned minestrone soup.

Fried squash slices are served just as they come from the pan, except that if they are very greasy they may be rested briefly on absorbent paper first.

Serving. Boiled sliced squash is excellent served plain or with a little of its own juice, plus butter, salt and/or pepper to taste. Or the slices may be mashed and put through a ricer to remove the seeds and skin. The result is mashed squash or squash puree. It was once the standard way of serving, but has lost ground to the simpler and more inclusive slices.

WINTER SQUASH

Winter squash ordinarily does not mature until near the end of the growing season. The fruit is reasonably frost resistant, although the vines are not, and keeping qualities are good. Varieties include acorn, Hubbard, butternut, and the closely related pumpkin.

The flesh is much firmer than that of summer squash, the skin is likely to be tough and inedible and the seeds are hard. Part of the difference arises from the fact that these are mature. However, a mature summer squash does not compare with a winter squash in flavor and usefulness, and immature winter squash are not popular.

Preparation and Cooking. Rinse and scrub sufficiently to remove any dust and dirt, and cut out any bad spots.

The usual cooking method is baking. For this purpose you may cut small squash in half, large ones into quarters or whatever size is appropriate for individual servings. Use a heavy knife, a saw or a cleaver. Leave the skin on, but scrape out the seeds and the fibrous material mixed with them. A few threads clinging to the flesh do no harm. A large spoon is the best tool for this job. If you use a knife, hold it at right angles to the surface you are cleaning, so as not to dig into it.

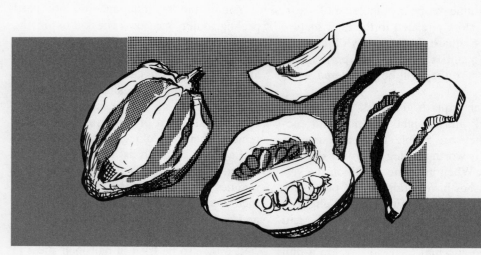

Fig. 13-30. Winter squash

Fig. 13-31. Carved pumpkin

It is customary to butter the cut surfaces to reduce or prevent drying. You can bake them on a cookie sheet or in glass utility dishes, skin side down, in a moderately hot oven, around 400° F. Tender squash in small pieces may be fork-tender in a half hour, while a big tough half may take over an hour. If surfaces seem to dry excessively or turn dark while the flesh is still hard, reduce the oven temperature. Or if they are tender but don't have a satisfactory cooked appearance, turn the oven all the way up for a few minutes.

Baked squash is usually served just as it comes from the oven, with the skin side down, and butter melting in the hollow inside. The flesh is readily cut with a fork, and the skin is left. But if you want to do extra work, you can scoop out the flesh, mash it with butter and salt until smooth, then serve it either in the skins or from a serving dish. If a masher doesn't make it smooth enough, put it through a food mill or ricer, then stir vigorously to get rid of any stringiness in texture.

Mashed squash may also be put in a buttered casserole dish, covered with marshmallows, and placed in a hot (425° F) oven until the marshmallows melt and develop a lightly brown crust. The number of marshmallows is optional. If the surface is about half covered when the marshmallows are old you should get a good coverage. This is a very sweet dish, in the same class as candied or marshmallow-topped sweet potatoes.

You can boil or steam the squash instead of baking it. You can start the same way, with cleaned halves or slices. Then take the skin off with a sharp knife or parer, cut the flesh into half or 3/4 inch cubes, and boil or steam until tender, 7 to 10 minutes. Flavor is not quite as rich as with buttered and baked preparation, but is still very good. If you mash it, you avoid trouble with heat-formed surface films.

Pumpkin. The pumpkin is closely related to the winter squashes, differing chiefly in its much larger size. Weight varies from a few pounds up to 75 or more in show specimens.

Pumpkin can be prepared and cooked in the same manner as winter squash.

In addition, it has two special uses. One is as a carved and candle-lighted Halloween symbol and decoration. The other is as a pie ingredient.

TOMATO

A tomato is considered to be a vegetable,

Fig. 13-32. Tomatoes

although it is actually a fruit with berry-type seed arrangements, and is used more for salad and seasoning than as a regular vegetable. It grows on frost-tender vines, varies in size from little cherry tomatoes to one-pound monsters 4 or more inches in diameter. Color is usually red, but some varieties are yellow.

This fruit is soft, juicy and acid. It is well supplied with A and C vitamins. Sugar content is so low that it has practically no use in desserts.

Green tomatoes that have reached full size will ripen after picking, preferably on a sunny window sill. But flavor, texture and vitamin content are best in vine-ripened fruit. Tomatoes for the market are usually picked green or partially ripe to reduce spoilage during shipment. Since ripe tomatoes may stay in good condition only a few days after picking, those in markets are usually picked while partially green, the degree of greenness being in proportion to the expected time of traveling and handling,

so that they will be ripe when they reach the grocer's shelves. Also, tomatoes with the best resistance to spoilage during transportation are usually not the varieties with the best flavor. As a result, tomatoes that must be shipped long distances are likely to be inferior to those grown locally.

Machine-harvesting of tomatoes has had an effect on the quality obtainable in the market. To make this operation efficient, tomatoes must all ripen at the same time and have skins tough enough to protect them during rather rough handling. New varieties were developed with these characteristics, with some sacrifice of flavor and texture.

Preparation. Tomatoes may carry dirt, dust and insecticide on their surfaces. It is therefore reassuring, although possibly not necessary or effective, to wash them before use. If they are not to be used immediately, be sure to allow them time to dry before putting them away.

The whole tomato is usually edible —

Fig. 13-33. Harvesting tomatoes

lesh, seeds and skin — even the tough machine-resistant skins. The skin is left on if the tomato is to be baked or broiled whole or in halves, stuffed, or sliced for eating raw. It may or may not be left on slices put in mixtures with okra, peppers and other vegetables. It is definitely removed before preparation of stewed tomatoes, sauces and flavorings. The peeling process was described earlier, under PARING AND PEELING. The stem, if present, should pull out easily.

It is customary to slice tomatoes across, at right angles to the core. In this way each slice except the top and the bottom ones gets a reasonable share of each of its rather different parts. Thickness of 1/4 inch is usual.

Tomatoes should be inspected before use, and any blemishes cut out. These may be discolored or rotten spots, over-ripe or under-ripe sections, or scars from insect or disease damage. An otherwise ripe and perfect tomato sometimes has a section of hard green core near the stem. Brown or tan streaks on the skin are usually growth cracks. Appearance is their chief fault.

When in prime condition a tomato is likely to be so soft and juicy that care in slicing is required to avoid squeezing out the pulp around the seeds. A peeled tomato slices even more easily than it squashes, but it is slippery to hold. If the first penetration of skin is difficult, start the cut with a sawing motion or by inserting the point of the knife.

If a tomato is to be stuffed it should be of such shape that it can stand on its bottom or blossom end. Start by cutting a slice off the stem end. Then scoop out the core, seeds and semi-liquid pulp, leaving the flesh of the walls and bottom intact. Fill the resulting hollow with any one of a variety of cooked or half-cooked stuffings. Any sort of meat or vegetable hash may be used. It is usual to mix the removed tomato pulp with the stuffing.

Cooking. Tomatoes may be baked plain, baked stuffed, boiled, fried or cooked in a casserole alone or with a variety of other foods. A whole tomato may break open or even explode if heated in an oven. This mess can be prevented by cutting out a cone around and below the stem (a part that is quite likely to be tough anyhow), or by piercing it deeply in a few places with a fork, toothpick or narrow-bladed knife.

Recommended baking temperature is 350° F (moderate oven) and time 15 to 20 minutes. But large tomatoes with moist stuffing might take up to 35 minutes for thorough heating.

Tomatoes are boiled in a covered pan with a moderate amount of water, for 5 to 20 minutes or until soupy. They should first be peeled and quartered or sliced for quick and even cooking. The result is a rather lumpy, strong-flavored stew. It may be eaten directly as a vegetable, but more often is used as an ingredient in mixtures.

When used in spaghetti sauce and other smooth products, the seeds and stringy parts of the pulp are removed in a food mill or ricer.

Tomatoes may be sliced and fried plain, but most cooks prefer to coat them. They may be dredged with flour mixed with sugar in a proportion of about 4 to 1. To get a thick coating, make the pieces bleed by sprinkling them with sugar and a little salt. Let them stand until moist, dip in the flour mixture, let them stand until moist again and dip once more. Frying may be in bacon fat or any other shortening. Cook at about 350° F until thoroughly browned, then turn to brown on the other side. Total time in the pan may be only 3 or 4 minutes, for a half-inch thickness.

Sliced green tomatoes can be fried in the same way.

Boiled tomatoes, or raw ones that have been diced or sliced, may be heated or cooked in a buttered casserole in a moderate oven. They are usually covered with bread crumbs, and may be pointed up by mixing with small amounts of chopped onion, carrots or celery, plus mustard or pepper for seasoning. Or tomato may be placed in alternate layers with egg plant.

Serving. Baked or stuffed tomatoes are served one to a person, just as they come from the oven. If there is juice in the pan, ladle some over the tops.

Fried tomatoes can also be taken directly from the pan to the plate if they are not greasy. If there is grease standing in the pan, pour it off just before finishing cooking. Greasiness may be reduced by a few minutes on absorbent paper or on a rack before serving, but heat will be lost.

Boiled tomatoes are usually too soft to put on a plate with other food, and are therefore served in a saucer. Casseroles are usually stiff enough for plate service.

Slices of tomato about 1/4 inch thick placed on lettuce and topped with mayonnaise or any salad dressing make a simple and excellent salad by themselves, or the nucleus for a more elaborate buildup. For use in tossed salads or mixtures the slices are cut in smaller pieces, or the tomato is cut into small wedges and pieces of wedges.

TURNIPS AND RUTABAGAS

The turnip is primarily a root vegetable. It includes the "American" turnip which probably originated in Asia, and the Swedish turnip which is commonly called rutabaga. These are different species of plants, but for cooking purposes are sufficiently alike to be discussed together. Preference between them, and among the many varieties of each, are matters of local custom and personal preference.

They both are found in both yellow and white varieties. Those with yellow flesh are generally considered to be better in flavor, firmness, nutrition and keeping qualities to the white. But at least one cookbook states that the white ones are completely superior. There is probably as much difference be-

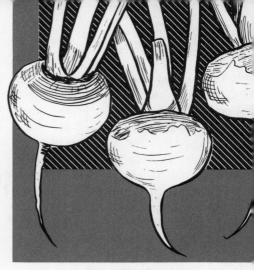

Fig 13-34. Turnips

tween varieties in one color as there i between colors. The yellow color range from yellowish-white to orange.

Turnips may also be classified on the basis of shape. They vary from long ones with a length three times as great as width to flats that are wider than they are high Skin color is variable, particularly in the upper part which projects above the ground and it may give some clues about the quality of the flesh.

Turnip leaves (turnip greens) are edible and are prepared in the same way as other greens. They may be obtained from regular turnips growing in the home garden, bu the commercial supply is chiefly from special varieties which are strong on leaves bu do not develop a usable root.

Turnips have excellent keeping qualities which may be further improved commercially by dipping in wax after harvesting trimming and washing. A waxed turnip with the stalks and leaves removed should keep several months in a cool or cold place.

Turnips range from an inch or less in diameter to seven inches or more, and may weigh less than an ounce or more than six pounds. Size depends on variety, growing conditions and maturity.

Preparation. The turnip root skin is often tender when cooked, but it is usually not eaten. It is cut off raw with a paring tool or knife. There may be a 4 to 1 difference in time required for a turnip with a rough surface, as compared with a smooth one. The skin may be rubbed off after cooking, but it falls apart and may take more time and trouble than when it is raw. Any wax on the skin should melt and float to the surface during cooking.

Small, young turnips, usually 1-1/2 inches in diameter or less, may be eaten raw like apples by strong-toothed youths. The flavor may resemble that of a mild radish. With increasing age the flesh becomes very hard, and with old age (or should we say maturity?) may develop a woody grain. The hardness disappears with enough cooking, but the woodiness may persist and make the cooked root too coarse and stringy.

Depending on size, turnips may be prepared for boiling by just paring, or by quartering, slicing or dicing. Cooking time is reduced by thin cutting. Since a turnip may be both big and hard, a sharp thick-bladed knife or a saw-tooth type is best. The knife may be pushed down with a rocking motion and heavy pressure.

Cooking. Turnips are usually boiled, but may also be steamed, pressure-steamed or baked. Boiling time may be from 9 to 15 minutes for 1/4-inch slices or pieces, 15 to 25 minutes for 1/2-inch thicknesses and much more for big chunks and whole turnips. Test for tenderness with a fork, pushing it to the center. If the turnips are to be served in pieces they may be left crisp or slightly underdone, but if they are to be mashed they must be soft.

Small turnips, up to 8 ounces, may be baked in the same manner as potatoes, in their skins, or peeled and cooked in the pan with a roast. Time is about the same as for a potato, or slightly longer. Test with a fork.

Serving. Boiled or steamed turnips may be served plain or with butter, with salt and perhaps pepper to taste. White turnips may have a white sauce added, but this is seldom done with yellow varieties.

Turnips are mashed in the same manner as potatoes. However, their texture is not injured by being put through a ricer or food mill, and this is usually the easiest way to prepare them. The ricer has an added advantage in that it will hold back the fibers in old turnips. If present, such fibers must be cleaned out of the basket after each squeeze, so that they will not block the holes.

Mashed turnips may be served plain, or may be mixed with butter, salt and pepper or other seasoning. Heavy cream is sometimes substituted for butter. Use at least a tablespoon of either to the pound or pint of turnips.

14
FRUIT

FRUIT

Botanically, a fruit is any developed ovary of a seed plant, with its contents and accessory parts. This definition includes not only the fruit and berries discussed in this section, but also nuts, grain and many vegetables.

In the cookbook, fruit is limited to the members of this class that have more or less soft, fleshy material (flesh or pulp) usually surrounding a seed or seeds, that are usually ripe or nearly ripe when eaten and that are most often eaten as dessert or snacks. This is a very vague definition or perhaps understanding, but it serves well enough.

Berries are small fruits containing many small seeds, usually close to the surface. They differ from other fruits chiefly in the size of the seeds, which are small enough to be eaten and which cannot be removed without breaking down the structure of the fruit. They also tend to have a higher acid content. They may or may not be included when the word "fruit" is used.

Uses. Most fruit can be eaten raw, and served either whole or sliced for breakfast, snacks or dessert. Lemons and limes are exceptions, as they are used only for flavoring or in sweetened drinks. The majority of fruits can be cooked for use as dessert, either by themselves or as parts of mixes or structures, and are discussed further in that chapter.

The major reference for uses in cooking starts on Page 547. Other references will be found in the Index.

Seasons. All fresh fruits are seasonal products, but because of the different climates in which they can be grown, and the adaptability of many of them to storage, the majority of them can be found in at least some markets through most of the year. Figure 14-1 shows the months during which a large number of fruits and berries might be available. Many of these are not mentioned in the text.

Canned and frozen fruit should be always available, but supplies are sometimes used up so that particular items are scarce or unobtainable.

APPLE

The apple is probably the most popular and widely cultivated fruit in the world.

COMMODITY	% Jan	% Feb	% Mar	% Apr	% May	% June	% July	% Aug	% Sept	% Oct	% Nov	% Dec
Apples	11	10	10	8	6	3	2	3	10	15	11	11
Apricots					5	62	31	2				
Avocados	11	11	11	11	9	7	6	6	5	6	8	9
Bananas	7	8	9	9	10	10	8	8	7	8	8	8
Blackberries					13	56	19	12				
Blueberries					2	32	39	23	4			
Cantaloupes	*	1	1	3	8	24	24	22	12	4	1	
Casabas						1	5	16	29	29	18	2
Cherries	*				14	39	42	4				1
Coconuts	8	6	8	5	3	3	4	4	11	14	18	16
Cranberries	1	1							6	21	49	22
Figs, Fresh					1	15	8	29	24	19	4	*
Grapefruit	12	12	13	12	10	6	3	2	2	8	10	10
Grapes	3	3	3	3	2	6	10	18	19	15	11	7
Honeydews	2	5	7	6	3	7	14	22	21	12	1	*
Lemons	7	6	7	8	10	11	11	10	8	7	7	8
Limes	6	4	4	4	6	15	16	13	10	7	6	9
Mangoes			2		19	39	29	10	1			
Nectarines	2	5				16	35	34	8			
Oranges, West	9	9	10	10	9	7	7	7	7	8	6	11
Oranges, Fla.	15	15	14	11	10	6	2	1	*	3	10	13
Peaches	*	*	*		2	26	31	27	13	1		
Pears	6	6	7	6	4	1	6	15	16	15	10	8
Persimmons	1								2	41	39	17
Pineapples	8	9	12	14	15	17	7	4	2	3	4	5
Plums-Prunes	1	1	1		2	18	25	25	24	3		
Pomegranates									20	63	15	2
Raspberries					1	21	55	5	6	7	4	1
Strawberries	1	2	5	15	31	26	10	5	3	1	*	*
Tangerines	24	8	3	1							20	44
Watermelons		*	1	2	11	27	33	21	5	*		

*Less than 0.5 of 1 % of annual total.
The table is based on unloads of fresh fruits in 41 cities as reported by the U. S. Department of Agriculture, and on import figures.

Courtesy U.S. Department of Agriculture

Fig. 14-2. Availability of fruit

It grows in the temperate zones, and in some tropical highlands. There are hundreds of varieties, only a few of which are likely to be available in any one place.

Apples may be classified in several different ways. Summer apples, maturing in July and August, tend to have poor keeping quality, and should be used within a few weeks. Fall and winter apples are usually harder-fleshed, and will keep for months under proper conditions.

Rating may be according to sweetness,

but this is limited mostly to cider-making, as individual apples may be much sweeter or less sweet than the average of their variety. These differences average out when they are used by the ton. Extremes in this characteristic are represented by the tree-ripened Delicious and the crab apple.

Apples may also be classified as eating, cooking and cider varieties. Eating apples should be sweet or only mildly acid and tender and tasty enough to be munched with pleasure just as they come off the tree. This class is the best to use whole for dessert or snacks, and sliced in salads. Cooking apples may be more acid, but most importantly should preserve flavor and the desired texture when cooked. There is a subdivision according to cooked texture, as pie and most desserts are best if the apples or their slices preserve at least some of their shape while becoming more tender, while apple sauce is best with apples that collapse into mush. Cider is outside of our field of interest.

Cooking apples should almost always be "tart". Tartness is almost equivalent to acidity or sourness, but not quite. It is the characteristic of having the right amount of both acid and sweetness to point up and intensify the apple flavor, and is somewhat on the acid side in the raw apple. A bland apple lacking tartness may make an excellent eating apple but it will be disappointing when cooked. Such a deficiency may be partly remedied by adding lemon juice, about a teaspoon to the pound.

Eating. Raw eating quality is greatly affected by individual taste, method of ripening and ripeness. Some people can eat crabapples from the tree and enjoy them, others cannot tolerate a raw apple unless it is sweet, bland and completely lacking in acid flavor. Some apples seem to develop best flavor and fragance only if fully tree ipened, others are good when not quite ripe or when ripened in storage.

For average taste and under average con-

Fig. 14-1. Most fruit grows on trees

ditions, the red Delicious and the Golden Delicious are the finest eating apples. But the McIntosh and many other cooking apples, under ideal conditions, can excel the average Delicious in raw quality.

People who really like raw apples usually like to eat the skin. Many others eat it because there is no other easy way of disposing of it when munching a whole apple. But the skin is likely to be made mildly poisonous by insecticides, and it is safer to discard it if many apples will be eaten. The apple tree is sprayed as many as 20 times during the growing season, and residues of the spray are almost sure to be on or in the skin. They are very unlikely to be concentrated enough to cause any problem if the skin is eaten only occasionally.

Ripeness for Cooking. Ripeness is desirable in cooking apples, but may not be essential. A great many physical and chemical changes occur during the final ripening stage, including a tenderizing of flesh, reduction of acid and increase in sugar, increase in flavor and fragrance, increase in and then loss of pectin and development of skin color. When some of these changes progress to their maximum, the apple may become too bland for best results in cooking, although it may be just right for eating.

Apples that are naturally somewhat sour give best flavor in cooking if fully ripe, while sweet ones may be better a little before maturity. Most apples, ripe or otherwise, become sufficiently tender when cooked, acidity can be counteracted with sugar and skins are either discarded or lose much of their color in cooking.

Pectin content is a delicate matter that will be discussed under JELLY.

Flesh. A ripe apple has firm, crisp flesh that is usually white or near-white. The first sign of over-ripeness may be loss of crispness or occasionally slight darkening in color. This is usually accompanied by loss of fragance and dulling of flavor.

Enzymes cause apple flesh to darken rapidly on exposure to air, turning it to a rather unattractive brown after peeling or slicing. Darkening can be delayed by wetting, as described below under Peeling.

If you use only part of an apple, leave the balance unpeeled, and put a piece of plastic wrap over the cut surface, rubbing it with your finger to make it adhere. There should be only thin surface discoloration during several days storage in the vegetable drawer in a refrigerator, and that much can be cut off easily at time of use.

Skin. The skin is thin, strong but not tough, and firmly fastened to the flesh. It may be red, yellow or green, or spots or mixtures of these colors. The russet apple, which unfortunately has become very rare, is as brown as a potato.

Fig. 14-4. One-piece peeling

Skin has a strong apple flavor, but it is usually discarded because of its toughness and the probability that it contains residues of poisonous sprays which cannot be removed by washing. It may be waxed by the grower or wholesaler to improve appearance and keeping qualities. Such wax is harmless.

Core. A stringy core extends through the apple from the stem to the lower or blossom end. A number of hard, dark seeds are located in slightly hardened pockets in the flesh in or close to the core. The core and seeds are usually cut out and discarded before cooking, except in preparing apple sauce or juice.

Spoilage. Apples are very sensitive to rough handling, although the damage often is not apparent for several days. Impacts or pressure cause the skin and surface flesh to lose their resistance to penetration by organisms, and decay is likely to start in such places and spread through the apple, and often through other apples in contact with it. The speed and extent of such rotting vary widely with the variety, condition and temperature of the apples, and the nature of the organisms.

Windfalls — apples that have fallen to the ground — are usually bruised, and are poor investments at any price unless they will be eaten, or at least cooked, very soon. Storage life of apples may also be shortened by the common practice in roadside markets of pouring them from a display basket into a bag.

A brown spot at the surface is usually

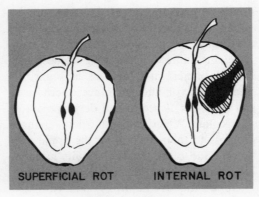

SUPERFICIAL ROT   INTERNAL ROT

Fig. 14-3. Decay in fruit

shallow and can be removed while peeling, but it sometimes extends through the entire apple. Don't use any brown parts, particularly if they are soft. They are likely to have a bad flavor, and tend to spoil the texture of cooked desserts also.

The presence of any substantial amount of rot makes apples unusable for cider. In addition to giving an off taste and causing rapid spoiling, their semi-liquid pulp bursts the filter cloths in which they are pressed.

Apples are subject to attack by a legion of insects, birds and molds. You are unlikely to find damaged apples for sale, as commercial growers try to protect them while growing by frequent spraying and by orchard sanitation, and then use only intact and unmarred fruit for sale as whole apples. The others, called culls, are used for cider or animal food.

But if you raise your own apples, or get them from neighbors or as roadside windfalls, you are likely to have apples with worms, worm holes, parts eaten away, hard lumps, skin thickening and discoloration and other defects. Fortunately, in a raw apple damage extends no further than its visible signs. If you cut out and discard defects, the rest of the fruit should be as good as if there had been no blemishes. But do it soon, as any kind of break in the skin is an opening for decay.

Peeling. Apple skin is hard and firmly anchored to the surface, so it must be cut off. A paring tool is most convenient, but a sharp knife will do just about as well if you are used to it. Peeling is done most rapidly and easily with wide cuts, but these waste more of the flesh than narrow ones because of the curve of the surface. The amount wasted is usually trivial, but it can be disturbing to the thrifty.

Peeled apples are usually cored and sliced also. If you want to peel before slicing, and your hand is steady, you may remove the entire skin in one spiral strip, starting at either the stem or blossom end.

Or you may take off a ring at each end, and peel the rest in parallel strips.

Or you may cut the apple first, into quarters, eighths or other slices, and peel them individually, cutting the long way. This is likely to be faster but less interesting.

Unless your fingers are freshly washed you will leave embarrassing smudges on the freshly exposed surfaces of the fruit. Also, cut apple discolors rather rapidly on exposure to air. Pieces should be put in a bowl of water as they are finished. If they will be in it more than a few minutes, add lemon juice, up to a tablespoon to the cup. Or use 1/4 to 1/2 teaspoon of ascorbic acid.

Coring. The apple core and seeds are almost always discarded, and are usually cut out before cooking. There are four general methods. You may remove them from the uncut apple with a rotary corer, slice the apple and cut out the core with one push of a slicer-corer, or cut the apple into 4 to 8 wedge slices, then cut the core parts out of each slice individually. Or the apple may be sliced or eaten inward from the outside, and the core thrown away when all usable material has been removed.

The cylinder cut out by a mechanical corer contains some edible apple at the top and bottom, and may not remove the whole core structure in the middle. If the apple is to be cut up anyhow, trimming the individual slices is more accurate and thrifty. Display slices, as in the top layer of a salad,

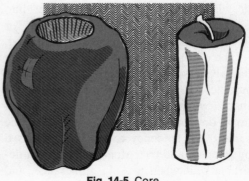

Fig. 14-5. Core

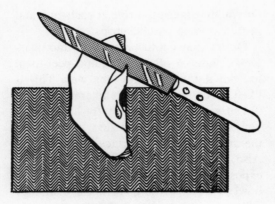

Fig. 14-6. De-coring a section

should be hand-trimmed even if a corer has been used.

Sections of core are cut out with a curving stroke, as in Figure 14-6. Turning the knife in the cut is likely to break the slice, which is undesirable if it is to be used partly for appearance. Breaking is less likely if you use a narrow-bladed knife, lift the edge instead of pressing down on the back as you twist it, and do the coring before peeling. A wire cutter will not break the slice, but it is hard to control and may make a very irregular cut until you have practiced with it.

A trimmed apple or an apple slice may be cut into slices or pieces of any desired thickness, thinness or shape to suit the recipe being followed. It takes about 1-1/2 pounds of apples to make a quart of small pieces, or 6 ounces to make one cup.

Cooking. Apples may be baked whole or with just the core removed, cut into pieces and baked with just seasoning or in combination with other foods, or stewed.

The effect of cooking is usually to make the apple softer and more tender. Some varieties keep some or all of their original shape when thoroughly cooked, others break down into mush or sauce. In any one variety, the tendency to mush is increased by ripeness and over-ripeness. This is a desirable trait when making applesauce, and when baking whole apples with their skins

on. It may be considered either unimportant or undesirable in making other desserts. Usually, sufficient shape for most purposes can be retained if cooking is stopped as soon as they are tender, but accurate selection of the stopping point is more important with some apples than with others.

In general, an apple that is specially recommended for applesauce and for baking has a tendency to mush, and those that are recommended for "all purposes" will mush only when cooked a long time.

Juiciness affects cooking quality, either favorably or unfavorably, but is difficult to estimate without experience. Very juicy apples make thin applesauce, and will make a runny pie unless extra thickener is added.

Details of cooking apples will be found in various dessert recipes. Consult the Index.

PEAR

The pear is a very close relative of the apple. It is third in importance among the temperate zone fruits.

Most pears are small at the stem, and thick at the blossom end. In short, they are pear-shaped. The flesh contains clusters of hard cells, called grit cells. These may

Fig 14-7. Pears

not be noticeable raw, but contrast sharply with the soft cooked texture. Grittiness varies and is greatest in Oriental varieties known as sand pears. Their coarseness is tolerated partly because they are resistant to fire blight, a very serious disease of the trees.

Pear flesh is white or nearly so.

The most popular variety is called Bartlett in the United States and Williams in Europe. It is medium to large in size, has soft, sweet juicy flesh, a tender skin that is usually yellow with touches of red and a minimum amount of core. It is harvested in late July and in August. Picking is done when it has attained full size, but is still green, as it tends to turn brown in the center if left on the tree to ripen. It can then be held in cold storage for a month, or ripened at any time by keeping at a temperature of 65 to 70° F for a week or so. Eating-grade pears are often individually wrapped in paper, or packed in coarse sawdust or other protective material. Ripeness is judged on the basis of color and slight softness to the touch.

There are a number of varieties which have more slender and regular shape, with brown or green skin. Their flesh is somewhat firmer than that of the Bartlett, and keeping quality may be much better. Flavor varies from the best imaginable to insipid.

Properly ripened pears of good varieties are among the finest fruits for eating raw. The skin is usually eaten, because it is tender and good, but it is safer to remove it because of the possible presence of spray residues. Most of the core is edible, only a few strings and seeds needing to be discarded. The principal problem in eating them from the hand is excessive juiciness.

Most pears are used as fresh, raw fruit, but a substantial number are canned commercially, or stewed in the home. Lack of tartness makes them less popular than apples in desserts. There is a limited market for dried, preserved and pickled pears.

Special varieties of juice pears are raised in Europe to make perry, an alcholic drink.

Preparation. A pear may be peeled in any of the ways described for apples. But the skin is more tender and the flesh under it is softer, so the paring tool is recommended rather than the knife. If a knife is used, it can sometimes be held at right angles to the surface, and used as a scraper rather than a cutter.

A coring tool is seldom used, as it would waste too large a proportion of the slender end. The preferred method is to slice the pear lengthwise into quarters or halves, then cut out seeds and any core strings with a paring knife or a spoon.

Pears do not darken as rapidly as apples on exposure to air, but cut slices may become limp in addition to darkening. Try to avoid peeling and slicing until immediately before use. If storage is necessary, cover the pieces with water and ascorbic acid or lemon juice, and keep them cold.

Fig. 14-8. Pears are juicy

This works well with some varieties, and less satisfactorily with others.

Pears are popular in salads, as halves or slices, either raw or cooked. A half on lettuce with mayonnaise is a simple but attractive side dish or dessert. Cottage cheese, or any mild cheese, goes well with pear.

Cooking. Pears may be used in pies and a few specialty desserts, but the standard method of cooking is stewing. For this purpose they hold their shape best if they are not fully ripe.

The fruit should be pared, cored and cut into halves, quarters or slices. Cook in a covered pan over moderate heat in a medium sugar syrup (see page 000), enough to just cover or float the pieces. Time may be 8 to 15 minutes, depending on variety and size of the pieces. When they are fork-tender, they are done.

Stewed pears may be served warm or cold, either in their syrup or drained and with cream. They may be sprinkled lightly with nutmeg or cinnamon.

PEACH

The peach is second only to the apple in importance among temperate zone fruits, although production is much smaller. It has a rather large pit or stone at the center, containing a single nut-like seed. It is related to the apricot, plum and cherry. The whole group may be referred to as the stone fruits.

Peach flesh may be either yellow or white (yellow in most commercial varieties) and is usually sweet, soft and juicy when ripe. There are wide variations in all characteristics.

The skin is soft, should be loose on the flesh and may be slightly tough and rubbery. It is usually covered with a soft down or fuzz, but the nectarine variety (often thought to be a peach-plum hybrid) is smooth-skinned. Color is red, yellow or combinations of these tints. Some varieties retain a bit of green even when fully ripe.

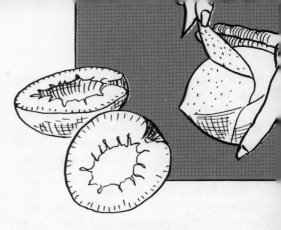

Fig. 14-9. Freestone peach

The pit is a hard rough shell enclosing an inner nut. The nut should not be eaten, as it may contain a little prussic acid, which is very poisonous. In freestone peaches the flesh pulls away from the pit easily, in cling varieties it must be cut away. Cling peaches have firmer flesh after cooking, are usually less tasty and are generally sold canned. Freestones, often the Elberta variety, are more popular in fresh and frozen form.

Peaches have a definite, distinctive flavor that is generally liked. The principal drawbacks to the fruit are that it must be tree-ripened for best taste and texture, and its keeping qualities are only fair after ripening. These characteristics do not fit well with modern methods of harvesting, storing and transporting fruit. As a result, the average fresh peach in the market is quite inferior to those that are locally grown, and often to those that are frozen or canned.

Peaches vary widely in size. Medium peaches, about 2-1/2 inches in diameter, weigh about 5 ounces and are figured 3 to the pound or 7 or 8 to the quart basket, which is customarily heaped. One to 1-1/2 of these make a single serving of raw peach slices, and 8 or 9 of them should make a quart of stewed peaches including juice.

Uses. Peaches have a very wide range of usefulness. They are excellent raw, either whole or sliced, plain or with sugar and cream; fresh-stewed or canned, in desserts such as pie and cobbler and in ice cream. They can be substituted for apples in most recipes except apple sauce (peach sauce seems to be unheard of except as jam), and can be used instead of strawberries almost anywhere.

Preparation. A good ripe peach tastes best eaten from the hand, skin and all, although there is a serious problem of juice running off your chin, and probably a poison hazard from spray residues. But many people do not like the skin because of its fuzzy outer coat, and it is limp and unattractive when cooked. Any kitchen preparation of peaches is likely to start with peeling them.

Many peaches can be peeled easily and completely by pulling the skin off. You pinch a bit of it between a knife or a finger nail and your thumb, and pull. You may get off anything from a little triangular piece to half the skin. You grasp an edge of the remaining skin in the same manner, pull again, and repeat until finished.

However, some varieties of peach do not part with their skins readily, and none of

Fig. 14-10. Peach skins are loosened by heat

them will unless they are quite ripe. You cannot pare the skin as you would an apple, as even if it is too tight to pull off, it is likely to be too loose to resist the knife enough to cut well. And some parts are likely to be tight and others loose. You can just struggle with this, with some pulling and some cutting, but it is better to dip the peach in boiling water for a minute or maybe two, or singe it briefly over a burner, then dip it in cold water. The skin should then come off like a glove.

If your peach is a freestone (and it probably is, unless you raised it yourself) you then make a cut down to the pit, starting at the stem end and going all the way around, through the blossom end. You should then be able to pull it into halves, by twisting the knife in the cut, or putting your thumbs in the stem end and pulling it apart. Pick the pit out and discard it. You may use the peach in halves, or you may cut it into thin or thick slices, according to your recipe or preference.

You need special tools and experience to make halves from a cling peach. In the ordinary kitchen, you peel it and cut slices from it in a random manner until there is nothing left but the pit.

Peach flesh deteriorates rapidly on exposure to air, darkening and becoming limp. Either prepare them immediately before use, or put the pieces in water spiked with two tablespoons of lemon juice to the pint.

APRICOT

The apricot is closely related to the peach and resembles it in a general way. But it is smaller, has a strong and distinctive flavor and is smooth-skinned. A large part of the apricot crop is dried, and most of the rest is canned. The fresh fruit appears in the average market for only short periods.

An apricot is peeled and prepared in the same manner as a freestone peach. Slices or halves may be eaten plain, with sugar or with sugar and cream; or used in fruit salads. They may be used in desserts in about the same manner as peaches, but are not as popular. It is more common to use the dried or canned fruit in cooking.

Dried apricots are usually stewed before using. The procedure is to sort and trim them with scissors if necessary to remove dark spots, soak them in cold water (6 cups to the pound) for an hour or two, bring the water to a boil and then simmer until the fruit is swollen and tender, about 15 minutes. Add one cup of sugar, and simmer for about 5 minutes. These should be the equivalent of canned or fresh-stewed apricots, except that the flavor is more pronounced.

PLUM

This is another stone fruit, closely related to the peach and the apricot. It is extremely variable. Color when ripe may

Fig 14-11. Prunes and plums

be purple, red, yellow or green. Weight ranges from less than an ounce to almost 4 ounces. They may be very sweet to very sour, with some mild or bland varieties. There are different combinations, such as flesh that is sweet generally, but very acid against the pit and/or the skin.

Most plums are served raw, but they can be included in cooked desserts in the same manner as peaches or apricots.

Prunes. Prunes are dried plums. They are made from varieties that contain

Fig. 14-12. Cherries

enough sugar to assist preservation, and that have a firm flesh that gives up and then regains its moisture with little damage. One of these, which is small, oval and purple-skinned, is also sold fresh under the name of "fresh prune".

Prunes are black and wrinkled in appearance. The pits are usually present, but may have been removed. Whole prunes vary greatly in size, the larger ones being more expensive. They are usually re-combined with water before use, by cold soaking overnight, or simmering for 30 or 40 minutes. Flavor is definitely different from that of fresh plums. It is usually improved by adding 1/4 cup of sugar for each pound of prunes, while simmering.

Prunes may be served in their own syrup as a breakfast fruit or as dessert. They are used as an ingredient in some salads, and in a moderate number of desserts.

CHERRY

The cherry is the smallest of the stone fruits. It is popular in a number of varieties, particularly the sweet Bing (black) and Royal Ann and the sour Montmerency.

Bing cherries may be medium to large in size. They have a firm, sweet, dark-colored flesh, and are mostly marketed as fresh fruit and eaten raw. Royal Ann, a red or yellow-red variety, averages somewhat smaller. It is used as fresh fruit, canned fruit and as artificially colored and flavored maraschino cherries. Most sour cherries are canned or frozen for use in pie.

Sweet cherries may be served whole and raw, as dessert or snacks. Or they may be cut in half, and the pit removed. Or the pit may be removed by pulling off the stem and inserting a special pitting tool, the end of a paper clip, or a strong hairpin, which is maneuvered to cut the pit free and pull it out. Pitting in this way is likely to spoil the appearance until you have become quite skillful.

Sour cherries should be both pitted and sugared before use. For fresh ones, try a cup of sugar to the quart of whole cherries, which should come to about 3 cups of pitted cherries. But some will need quite a bit more sugar. Sugared sour cherries may be eaten raw or stewed, but they are usually put in a pie.

CITRUS FRUITS

The citrus fruits are a popular and distinctive group that are grown in most subtropical and tropical regions. Their flesh or pulp is made up of hundreds of small juice sacs or vesicles, which are packed into crescent-shaped segments which are surrounded and separated by membranes. The abundant juice contains sugar and citric acid in highly variable proportions, a gratifying amount of Vitamin C, pectin and other nutrients, vitamins and minerals.

The skin or rind is composed of a thin, oily and usually colorful outer layer, and a white inner layer. It is soft enough to be torn by the fingers, and is often easy to separate from the flesh segments. It is rich in vitamins and other nutrients, but is usually bitter, so that its use in human food is very limited.

There may be many seeds, few or none. If present, they are of moderate size and

Fig. 14-13. Citrus fruits

are in the segments, along the inner edge.

Keeping qualities are generally good or excellent as long as the outer skin is not punctured, but there are considerable differences in this regard among various species and varieties.

Rind. Recipes will frequently tell you to use the grated rind of a lemon, lime or orange, or less frequently, a teaspoon or some other quantity of the grated rind, for flavoring. This is a particular type of flavor; usually strong, pungent and bitter but not

Fig. 14-14. Grating lemon peel

sour. It is agreeable in small quantities in many combinations, but can be distasteful in the wrong place or in too great quantity. The rind is usually accompanied by juice or pulp of the same fruit.

The flavorful part of the rind is the thin outer surface, the part that carries the color. If your grater cuts much below that it will take white material that has little, if any, of the desired taste. However, it merely dilutes the good part, and does not spoil it.

Grating citrus rind is quite difficult until you are used to it. A fine grater tends to produce a tiny quantity of semi-liquid mush; a medium one will cut deeply into the white layer while leaving some of the surface. The fine grater requires quite heavy pressure to cut at all. If you are lucky enough to be able to obtain a medium-fine grater (they do exist), you should be able to get a reasonable quantity (say a teaspoonful from a lemon) that is neither wet with punctured oil sacs nor loaded with white scrapings. Without this, you can alternate the coarser and finer graters for reasonably good results.

Grated peel dries out and loses flavor rapidly. It should not be prepared until you are ready to use it. If you must keep it,

Fig 14-15. Glass juicer

dampen it and wrap it carefully in plastic.

Juice. In spite of the convenience of bottled and frozen juice, many oranges, lemons and limes and some grapefruit are "squeezed" at home for juice. The simplest is to cut the fruit in half, across the segments, and press and rotate (ream) each half on a hand squeezer such as that in Figure 14-15. A few half-turns should cause practically all of the juice to run into the bottom, from which it can be poured into a container. Seeds and membranes can be pulled or strained out by a fork. A sieve should not be used, as it would hold back desirable sacs of juice.

Fig. 14-16. Two ways into an orange

Some hand squeezers rest on top of a glass or container, and have small holes that allow juice to drain down, but hold coarse pieces back. An electric squeezer, which is usually an attachment on some other unit, rotates the protruding center so that you need only hold the half-fruit against it until the juice is out.

Freshly squeezed juice usually has somewhat better flavor and texture than the prepared types. Frozen concentrated juice tastes better than canned.

ORANGE

The orange is the most popular and widely distributed of the citrus fruits. There are two principal commercial types: sweet and mandarin. Each has a number of varieties. In addition, there are sour oranges used chiefly for marmalade.

Sweet. The sweet orange is by far the most important in commercial production. Varieties include the Washington Navel, mostly known merely as navel, which is a seedless winter variety, and Valencia Late, a summer orange. Both of these are grown in dry areas such as southern California with the help of irrigation. Florida, with a moister climate, produces a number of different varieties which are marketed together as Florida oranges.

About half this country's orange production goes into juice, a large part of which is concentrated and frozen. The skins are used as a source of pectin, and as cattle food. Fresh oranges are eaten as snacks, for desserts and in salad, and many of them are squeezed for juice at home.

Preparation. A simple method of preparing an orange for eating is to cut it in half at right angles to the line between stem and blossom ends. This cuts all segments in half, so that their flesh can be taken out with a spoon and eaten directly. Additional knife work may be done, as will be described under GRAPEFRUIT.

Or you may peel the orange and then separate the sections. The usual way is to dig a thumb nail or a dull object such as a spoon handle into the skin, penetrating to the membrane that protects the flesh, then run the peeler under the skin, lifting and breaking it. If it separates easily a few passes will finish the job. Otherwise, the peeler may have to be moved from side to side as well as forward, and care must be exercised not to cut or tear the membrane. It may help to cut the rind into strips with

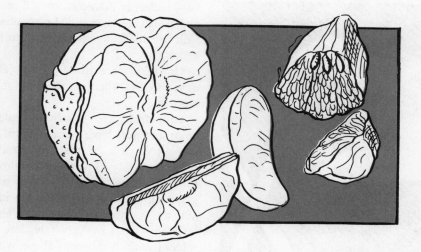

Fig. 14-17. Sections of an orange

a knife, and push or pull them off one at a time. Or you can peel it like an apple.

There are strings of white material similar to the inner rind, between the segments. They may come off with the skin, or be pulled off separately. Or you can leave them.

After peeling, insert both thumbs into the hollow at the stem end, or any other hollow or split, and pull the orange apart gently, first in half and then into individual sections. If membrane starts to tear away from the pulp, start separation from another part. Some oranges almost fall apart into sections, others stick together. Sections are used raw and usually chilled in desserts and salads, and are rarely cooked at home.

If there are seeds, they are a nuisance. You remove them by slitting the membrane at the inner edge with a sharp knife, and pushing them out by sliding the knife along the outside of the membrane. The segment does not look as good afterward, but it is much easier to eat.

The segment membranes of oranges may be tender, but they are often tough enough to chew up to a small unpleasant ball of fiber, which must either be swallowed with

Fig. 14-18. Slitting a section to remove seeds

difficulty or returned to the plate with embarrassment. If you find that you have such oranges, you can change them into tender morsels by skinning the sections. This is quite a bit of work, and may be impractical if the membranes cling to the pulp. The best way, usually, is to slit the core edge full length with scissors or knife, then strip the membrane off in pieces with your fingers.

Mandarin. The mandarin is a representative of a different group of oranges, of which the tangerine and the Temple are also well known. These varieties usually have a rough loose, tender skin that is easily removed, sections that separate easily from each other and pulp that is sweeter and more reddish that than of the sweet orange. They are less juicy, and spoil more readily during shipment and storage.

A large part of the mandarin orange crop is canned in sections, which are used to advantage in fruit cocktails and salads.

GRAPEFRUIT

The grapefruit is the largest of the commercially grown citrus fruits. It is believed that it originated in Jamaica as a mutation of the shaddock or pummelo, a similar but smaller fruit that is chiefly popular in the East Indies. A medium-size grapefruit may be 4 inches in diameter, over 3 inches high and weigh 14 ounces. The smallest grapefruit are likely to be bigger than large oranges.

Grapefruit are usually more acid than oranges, but there is considerable overlapping.

Grapefruit are usually a pale yellow color, but may have a pink flush if the flesh is pink or red, or may be turned partly brown or rusty by certain harmless organisms. The flesh is light yellow, sometimes greenish, pink or red, while the inner skin and the membranes are white. There may be many seeds or very few, but they are seldom entirely absent. Those with just a few seeds are often said to be seedless.

There are about 20 commercial varieties with yellow or normal flesh grown in the United States, and 4 or more with pink or reddish pulp. The yellow varieties range from extremely acid to barely sweet, the pinks and reds from mildly acid to barely sweet. All of them have the very distinctive grapefruit flavor.

About half of our grapefruit crop is eaten raw, the other half is either pressed for juice or divided into segments and canned, usually in sugar syrup.

Serving. The usual way to prepare grapefruit is to cut it in half, at right angles to the center line between the stem and blossom ends, and serve the halves in saucers, one per person. You may wish to go further, and remove seeds (pry them out with a narrow-bladed knife), put on sugar and perhaps even set a maraschino cherry at the center.

The grapefruit segments have been cut in half. The eating procedure is to dig the pulp out of each half-segment in turn with a teaspoon or a narrow-bowl grapefruit spoon. This is a little bit of work, and may involve squirting juice into the eye or elsewhere. Eating can be made easier by cutting around the pulp in each section with a knife, before serving. Unfortunately, the busy meal-preparer is likely to cut down on her work by slashing with the knife, without cutting the pieces free. This is likely to make eating much more difficult, or perhaps less agreeable, than leaving the half-grapefruit intact. It may make it almost impossible to spoon up the flesh without including sections of tough and flavorless membrane.

If you want to do a real job serving easy-to-eat grapefruit, take the seeds out of the halves, cut the flesh free from the dividing or side membranes in all sections, then cut both membranes and flesh free from the inner surface of the skin. You do this by running a sharp (but preferably not sharp-pointed) knife around the outside, and then

underneath until the membranes are all free and can be lifted out, in one octopus-like chunk if your cutting has been thorough. The pieces of flesh remain in the skin as in a cup. You can then add sugar, a cherry, or even little pieces of orange. This is a nuisance to prepare, but makes a really deluxe breakfast dish or dessert.

You may also peel a whole grapefruit, separate the sections, and serve them with sugar as a fruit (this is unusual) or plain as a part of fruit salad. Break or cut them into pieces to mix into fruit cocktail. If there are seeds, it is best to remove them by slitting the inner edges, and pushing them out.

LEMON

Commercial lemons are so acid that they are hardly ever eaten, but their flavor is so distinctive and excellent that they are grown in enormous quantities (over a million and a half tons a year) for use in flavoring and in lemonade.

There are many varieties of lemon, ranging from quite small to as big as grapefruit, and from very acid to bland, with flesh that

Fig. 14-19. Fixing a grapefruit

Fig. 14-20. A lemon and segments (wedges)

may be yellow-green, yellow or pink. But commercial production is standardized on varieties that yield a rather small fruit, about 2 inches in diameter and 2-1/2 long, with a nipple-like projection at one or both ends. Weight is between 2 and 3 ounces. The outer skin is yellow, the inner skin and membranes white and the flesh is pale yellow. The citric acid content of the juice is about 5 per cent. The resulting sourness is slightly offset by a variable sugar content.

Lemons may be tree-ripened, or picked when fully grown but green and then ripened in storage. The trees bear all year, so there is no problem of seasonal supply. However, greatest consumption is in the summer. About half the crop is sold fresh in the markets, the other half is made into juice which is bottled or canned, or concentrated and frozen.

It is customary to serve lemon wedges or slices with seafood, salads and beverages that might be benefited by the lemon flavor and the acid. Wedges are greatly to be preferred, as they permit squeezing the juice without getting so much of it on the fingers. Slices are sometimes cooked with fish, but the result is too highly acid for general acceptance.

Lemon juice is diluted with water to make lemonade. It is usually an important ingredient in iced tea and is very widely used in small quantities in cooking to bring out or intensify flavor of foods, or to increase acidity of cooking water. It is obtained from the fresh fruit by reaming, in the same manner as from an orange. A medium size lemon should yield 3 or 4 tablespoons of juice. The fresh juice is considered to be superior to the bottled and frozen products, but only by a narrow margin.

Lemon juice has a high content of Vitamin C (ascorbic acid). This adds to its value in the diet (from a nutrition standpoint, it is its principal or only dietetic value), and it also gives it the property of preventing fruit from darkening. A tablespoon of lemon juice in a cup of water provides a bath in which sliced apples, pears, peaches or potatoes can be held for several hours without noticeable deterioration.

LIME

The lime is another very acid citrus fruit, valued for its juice. There are two somewhat different types grown commercially. The Tahiti group resembles a lemon in size, weight and juice content, but it has a different taste and both flesh and skin are green or yellowish green instead of yellow. The Mexican varieties are smaller, and may have the lemon shape, be globular or anything in between. Flavor is just about the same. There are also a number of non-commercial varieties and hybrids, including some so low in acid that they are known as sweet limes.

Limes, their pieces and their juice, can be substituted for lemon in almost any recipe, provided you like their taste, which is definitely different. In general, limes are scarcer and more expensive than lemons, are less popular but are more valued as a special treat. They are sometimes used for flavoring largely as an excuse to color food green.

BANANA

The banana is the most important of the tropical fruits, both as a local food and as an export industry. It is very nourishing, has good flavor and texture, is easy to eat or prepare and is available all year.

The most important commercial variety, Gros Michel, is usually from 7 to 9 inches long, 1-3/8 to 1-3/4 thick and weighs 5 to 9 ounces. Its flesh is creamy white in color, with a streak of tiny, brown, infertile seeds through its center. The skin is green in the unripe fruit, yellow when moderately ripe and usually yellow with small brown spots when fully ripe. It is thick and soft, and has the convenient characteristic of tearing lengthwise into strips which separate easily from the flesh. A banana can therefore be readily peeled with the fingers, starting at either end. Part can be left unpeeled to serve as a holder when eating it from the hand.

Some soft strings from the peel may stick to the flesh, so that they may be peeled off separately. The surface of the peeled fruit is slightly fuzzy, and there is a widespread but unverified belief that this fuzz is indigestible and should be scraped off by light strokes of the back of a knife or some other utensil before eating or using the fruit.

The peeled banana may be eaten whole, cut into chunks or sliced thinly or thickly, either across or lengthwise. Slices tend to stick together, so irregular chunks may be better for some purposes.

Bananas are good with sugar and cream or milk, in or on salads and for decoration on icing or meringue. They are featured in a number of desserts, including gelatins, pie and cake.

There are many varieties of bananas besides our standard commercial one. There are short thick ones with red skin, and others whose skin is green even when ripe. There are dozens of varieties of small or finger bananas, which are favorites where they grow but which are kept out of our markets by poor shipping and storage characteristics. And there are big bananas, called plantains, which contain starch instead of sugar and which should be cooked before eating.

Bananas contain about 22 per cent carbohydrate, mostly in the form of sugar, have a fair assortment of vitamins and are rich in minerals. This means that they are good nourishing food.

Storage. Bananas usually keep very well until they are fully ripe. The thick, tough skin offers reasonably good protection against bruising and entrance of organisms. If decay does occur, the flesh becomes brown and soft and soon causes the skin to turn brown or black on the affected spots.

Fig. 14-21. Bananas peel easily

Any unpleasant flavor or consistency that accompanies spoilage is limited to the part that turns color, and if it is cut out, the rest of the fruit can be used.

Fully ripe bananas soon become overripe, with soft translucent flesh and loss of flavor. This deterioration can be slowed or prevented by putting ripe fruit in the refrigerator, where it should stay in good eating condition for at least several days and often for a week or more. But the skin turns brown or black, so as to make the fruit look rotten. Refrigerated bananas are unattractive to eat from the hand, but are excellent when peeled and sliced before serving. This statement is apparently in contradiction to all official utterances, but it is easy to verify.

Fig. 14-22. Pineapple

PINEAPPLE

The pineapple is a tropical fruit with many distinctive characteristics. The fruits are big — 1-1/2 to 4 pounds or more — but they grow on low bushes which are almost entirely made up of big leaf spikes. The flesh and juice are heavily loaded with sugar, acid and enzymes, with sugar increasing at the expense of acid in the final stage of ripening. Flavor and fragrance are strong, different and delicious.

The fruit has the general shape of a bulged cone, with a spray of leaves on top. The surface has a pattern of knobs that, together with its shape, gives it a resemblance to a gigantic pine cone. The color when ripe is yellow or brownish yellow. There is a center core which is inedible except in the best and ripest fruit. The flesh has a distinct grain, radiating out from the center.

Full sweetness develops only when ripen-

ing is completed on the bush. Once ripened, a pineapple spoils quickly, so those in the markets are necessarily picked while green. In any one shipment, those that are the ripest when they are sold were probably the least green when picked, and are to be preferred.

A ripe pineapple has a rich yellow color, yields slightly to pressure and has good fragrance. The surest indication, however, is that the center leaves in its topknot pull out easily. Decay usually starts at the bottom, and is indicated by softness, browning and perhaps weeping of liquid.

Once picked, pineapple ripens best at room temperature in the dark. It should be refrigerated as soon as it is fully ripe, unless it can be eaten immediately.

A 2-pound pineapple is called medium size, although it is near the low end of the range of weights. It should produce 2-1/2 to 3 cups of diced fruit, enough for 4 to 6 people when served with sugar.

Because of distance to principal markets and the perishability of fresh pineapple, a very large part of the crop is canned or frozen. Canned pineapple, packed and cooked in syrup, is available in slices, bits or chunks and shredded (called crushed). Frozen pineapple, which is considerably less common, may be in slices, fingers or chunks.

Pineapple juice is canned and frozen for use as a drink by itself, but it is more important as an ingredient in many mixed fruit drinks.

Preparation. There are a number of ways to attack a pineapple. If you are going to slice it, which is the usual procedure, you can peel it before or after. If before, hold it by its leaves, and cut away the skin with a sharp knife in a series of strokes from top to bottom. Cut deeply enough to remove all the skin except that in the eyes, which are deep depressions between the knobs. Cut these out after peeling, with the point of a paring knife or a paring tool. Then turn the fruit on its side, cut off the top and bottom, and slice the remainder 1/2 to 3/4 inch thick, unless special uses or taste call for thicker or thinner slices.

Or you may find it easier to slice the whole fruit, then cut off the peel and cut out little triangles for the eyes, doing each slice separately. This takes longer only if you are used to peeling whole prineapples, and there is likely to be less wastage.

Unless you have a very ripe, fresh-picked pineapple (most unlikely in the temperate zone) you should remove the core from each slice. If you are going to use whole slices, cut out a round piece with a biscuit cutter or a sharp knife. If you intend to dice or mash the fruit, make a number of straight cuts through the flesh along the edge of the core, as illustrated. Discard any hard or woody parts.

For dicing, you can divide the cleaned slice, or several slices on top of each other, with two sets of cuts at right angles to each other in the usual way, or you may cut only across the grain and break the pieces along the grain with your fingers.

A pineapple may also be sliced length-wise, with or without peeling. You cut it in halves, quarters or eighths from the leaves down to the base, then cut the core out of the sections. If you did not peel the whole fruit, you can peel each section now. Or you can make a careful single cut, or a cut from each side of each section, to re-move the peel in one piece, after which it can be used as a boat or dish for serving the flesh, which may be left whole, or cut into bite-size chunks.

Most of our raw pineapple is quite sour,

so it is customary to sugar it after prepara-tion, then put it in the refrigerator (or just on a side table, if you don't like it chilled) for an hour or more before serving. In ad-dition to sweetening it, sugaring greatly in-creases its apparent juiciness.

Use - raw. Fresh pineapple is almost al-ways used raw, as the canned product is more economical and less work, and is usually of good enough quality for any cooking purpose.

Raw pineapple is tricky to handle. It contains enzymes which curdle milk and cream almost on sight, prevent gelatin from jelling and attack proteins in egg white and meat. This enzyme is destroyed by cooking, so you can avoid complications by using canned pineapple instead of fresh in mix-tures.

Fresh pineapple is used chiefly as a des-sert or in salad. As a dessert, it is sliced, chunked or put in a boat. Unless it is quite sweet, it is usually sugared in advance. Even when very sweet, have sugar available on the table. Pineapple is usually not sugared for salad. If it is sweet you can use a lot of it in a fruit mixture, but if it is acid use less and make the pieces smaller.

Use - cooked. Almost all cooked pine-apple is canned. You use the slices for or-namental effects, or sometimes for direct serving in their syrup as dessert. Chunks and crushed, which are cheaper, are also more convenient for all routine work.

Pineapple has a very wide range of use-fulness as a principal ingredient and as a flavoring in desserts and in salads. It can be substituted for apple in most recipes, except for sauce, but crushed rather than chunked

Fig. 14-23. Cutting up a pineapple slice

pineapple must be used whenever a soft or pulpy product is desired, as pineapple tends to retain its shape and crispness in spite of cooking.

Pineapple slices are used to decorate and flavor baked ham. Crushed, it is used for flavor and texture in gravy, sauce and ice cream.

GRAPE

The grape is a very important fruit. Most of the crop is used for commercial production of wine, juice, jelly and raisins. But liberal quantities are to be found fresh in most markets. Some varieties keep well during storage and shipping, and are available most of the year, while others are seasonal. Fresh grapes are usually eaten as snacks or dessert, but they are also good in salads.

Grapes are berries, but are almost always classed as fruits. Shape varies from globular to long ovals. Very large ones may weigh half an ounce, medium ones 1/5 ounce. They grow and are marketed in dense clusters. Most varieties have several small seeds near the center, but a few are practically seedless. It is possible to swallow the seeds whole or to chew them to powder, but most people would rather not. Skin may be tender, tough or anything in between.

The most popular eating grape is probably the Thompson Seedless. It has the great advantage of being seedless or nearly so, has tender skin and is sweet when properly ripened. It is smaller than other table grapes. Its greatest disadvantage is a trade custom of picking it when too green for best flavor, to improve its shipping and storing qualities. It is yellow in color when fully ripe, but most of those in the market are green, or at best, yellowish green.

Flavor and sweetness are quite variable in any variety of grape, being affected not only by ripeness, but also by temperature and moisture during the growing season. Color of ripe grapes may be clear green,

Fig. 14-24. A bunch of grapes

yellow-green, yellow, amber, russet, red, purple or black, depending on the variety. They often have a whitish bloom on the skin that resembles mold but is harmless and often attractive.

Seedless grapes are preferred for salads, or for inclusion in any mixture such as fruit cocktail. For special effects, laboriously achieved, you can cut big grapes in half lengthwise and remove the seeds. If the skins are tough, as they are specially likely to be in the red Tokay variety, you can peel them. Skins pull off easily, but you have to peel a lot of them to make much of a showing. Canned grapes are usually whole seedless grapes, peeled.

Raisins. Raisins are dried grapes. They are important in cooking, and are found in hundreds of dessert recipes. They are made from a limited number of grape varieties.

The most popular type is the seedless raisin made from the Thompson Seedless grape, usually by drying in the sun. The natural grapes are grey or brown to black in color, wrinkled, and are separate and loose in the package. Golden raisins are treated with lye and sulfur fumes and then dried artificially, to produce a slightly different flavor and an attractive yellow or amber color.

Other types of raisins seem to be getting rare. There are large grapes, sun-dried whole and sometimes on the stems, served with fresh fruits for dessert. Similar big raisins may have the seeds removed (seeded raisins), after which they are packed solidly. They are particularly good in bread and plum puddings, but may be difficult to obtain. They should be loosened up before measuring.

Currants may be either imported raisins made from a small black seedless grape, or a fresh berry not related to grapes or raisins.

Raisins have a special sharp, sweet flavor and chewy texture. If cooked with sufficient water they swell and become tender, and are found in this condition in puddings. In baked goods they are likely to keep a little of their natural texture. They are widely used in muffins, cakes, desserts and salads. Seedless raisins are usually put in whole, but may be chopped for special effects.

BERRIES

Technically, a berry may be any soft fruit with many seeds. But in the kitchen and the market it is called a berry only if it is small and is not a grape.

There are a great many berries, but only a few are widely used. The best known ones are the strawberry, blueberry, raspberry, blackberry (with its cousins, loganberry and boysenberry) and cranberry. Gooseberries and currants are plentiful in some areas, rare in others.

One solid working difference between fruit and berries is that a berry is almost never peeled. Such an operation is impossible with most of them and impractical with all. Washing is often done, but it is inefficient except in removing loose dirt and floating away trash. Regulations on timing, amounts and types of spray are usually much more stringent with berries than with other fruits, because of the impossibility of removing the residues.

Berries are usually more acid than fruit, but the difference is often masked by a high sugar content. They tend to get very sour when cooked, unless considerable sugar (say 3/4 cup to the quart of berries) is added. Dry sugar is used rather than syrup, as juice is pulled through the thin skins easily, and there is so much of it that extra water would not be welcome.

Berries often require picking over to remove extra stems, leaves, and green or over-ripe specimens.

Strawberry. The strawberry can be the largest of the berries, but its taste is just as good when it is small. Giant strawberries may weigh as much as 2 ounces each, while an ordinary specimen might be around 1/2 ounce. Shape may be conical, globular or irregular. The flesh is usually white or pink, the skin red. There are considerable variations in flavor and in sweetness. Both are best when the berries are ripened on the plant, and are eaten soon after picking. However, reasonably good results are obtained from ripening them in a warm room, and even long-distance shipping does not destroy their unique and delicious flavor, although it certainly dulls it.

Strawberries have a slightly rough skin, and they grow close to the ground or even lie on it. As a result they are likely to be dirty or dusty. The best way to clean them is rinsing with high pressure water. The wet berries tend to spoil rapidly, and water clinging to them will dilute cream or other added substances. It is therefore best to spread the washed berries in a single layer on absorbent material and leave them until dry, a matter of a few minutes on a dry day or half an hour or more on a humid one.

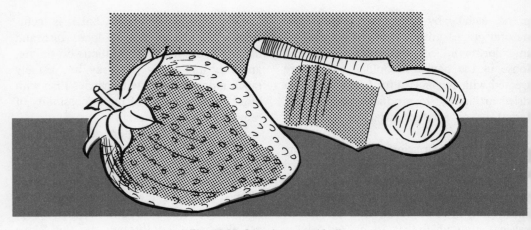

Fig. 14-25. Strawberry and huller

Keeping qualities are rather poor. Unripe berries usually stay in good condition until ripening is complete, if they are kept separated from each other and temperature is moderate. Ripe berries tend to get soft and mushy, and to develop decayed spots; or will sometimes dry out, losing attractiveness and flavor. Decay spreads quickly from one berry to others in contact. Try to use ripe berries as quickly as you can, and if you can't, keep them in the refrigerator in a plastic bag with a few small ventilation holes punched in it.

The stem is attached to the berry at a group of very small leaves, usually in a hollow. The process of removing the stems-and-leaflets is calling hulling. It is done by pushing thumb and/or finger nails into the flesh alongside the hull, then pulling it out with a pinching, twisting or tearing motion. Or you can use a special hulling device, as illustrated, which is pushed in on each side of the stem, tightened and pulled out.

Strawberries keep best with their hulls in place, so their removal should be the last step before serving or cooking.

Use. Strawberries are excellent eating both raw and cooked. They may be held by the stem or in the fingers and eaten plain, or dipped in sugar after each bite. They are served with cream (anything from light to medium, depending on your taste) and sugar for both breakfast and dessert. Strawberry shortcake (page 555) is one of the most highly prized American desserts.

Stewed strawberries are tasty and easily prepared. The berries should be rinsed, hulled and soft, hard or discolored spots should be removed. They may be sliced, halved or left whole. Mix sugar with them, 1 to 1-1/4 cups to the quart for fairly acid berries, half that for very sweet ones. Let stand about half an hour in a saucepan, by which time there should be a layer of juice in the bottom. Cover, and cook over low heat, stirring occasionally, until the berries are soft and tender. This should take about 8 or 10 minutes. Serve warm or cold, plain,

Fig. 14-26. Blueberries

or with sponge cake. Whipped cream may be added.

Other popular uses for strawberries are in pie and in ice cream, both of which are discussed under the appropriate headings.

Blueberry. The blueberry is a firm fruit somewhat similar to the grape in structure, but much smaller. It is marketed in two sizes, the large cultivated and the smaller native or wild variety. The small ones have more flavor, may be accompanied by stems and trash and are becoming difficult to get, probably because of higher labor costs associated with them. Blueberries are sometimes called huckleberries. It is not clear whether the difference is one of locality or variety. There is a considerable color range, from light blue to almost black, without any consistent relationship to flavor. There are high-bush and low-bush varieties.

Blueberries can be distinguished from other wild berries by a fringe around a hollow in the blossom end, Figure 14-26.

Blueberries may be eaten raw, plain, with sugar or with sugar and cream. They are also good when stewed, and as a pie filling, but their special use is in rather sparse mixtures with baked goods and other foods, in which they serve somewhat the same purpose as raisins, although the flavor is entirely different. Examples are blueberry pancakes and blueberry muffins.

Blueberries can be frozen raw without any special treatment. Pick them over, wash them if necessary and allow to dry. They can be frozen in shallow layers on trays, or packaged and then frozen. The wrapping must be moisture-vapor proof. A few drops of water may be added to the package as an extra precaution against drying.

Raspberry. A raspberry is composed of a cap or thimble-shaped formation of globular seed-and-juice cells, separate from a hard core, which remains on the plant after picking. There are a number of different colors; black, blue, red, orange and yellow. Red and black are the chief com-

mercial varieties, with strong preference for one or the other in different areas. Acid content is very high, but may be masked by natural sugar.

Raspberries should be picked ripe, have poor keeping qualities, and should be used as soon as possible after picking or purchase. Black ones, particularly the small wild varieties, are firmer and last somewhat longer than the red.

Raspberry seeds are too small to be removed without destroying the structure of the fruit, but they are large enough to be a nuisance or a disadvantage at times, particularly after cooking.

Most raspberries are probably eaten raw, with sugar and cream. They become very acid and juicy when cooked, so may require more sugar and more thickening than other fruit when made into pie. Raspberry puree or juice is an excellent flavoring for sauce. Jam, and to a less extent jelly, are important commercially and are often made at home.

Blackberry. The blackberry is a cylindrical berry composed of a number of globular cells containing juicy pulp and a coarse seed, surrounding a core which should be tender and juicy but which is often tough or stringy. The ripe fruit is usually jet black, although there are purple

Fig. 14-27. Raspberries

varieties. Unripe berries are green, almost-ripe ones are red. A few red cells may be present in an otherwise black berry. Such berries are usually discarded if the fruit is to be eaten raw, and used if they are to be cooked.

There are a number of varieties of black-berry, both native stocks and selected or hybridized types. Most of them are quite sweet (but only when fully ripe), and are so tender and juicy that keeping qualities are poor. They are available fresh only in the localities in which they are grown. They grow over a large part of the country. Wild vines can bear good, abundant fruit, but crowding and various diseases usually damage the crop without reducing the nuisance value of their thorns.

Boysenberries and loganberries are large, sweet varieties of blackberries that are extensively cultivated for canning, and which are occasionally available fresh.

Blackberries are eaten fresh, plain or with sugar or cream and sugar. The seeds may be a problem for people with dentures, but otherwise high-quality blackberries can be substituted for raspberries and strawberries in most recipes. They make excellent jelly and jam.

MELON

Melons are members of the same family as cucumbers, gourds pumpkin and squash. They grow on trailing vines. There are two quite different species, the muskmelon and the watermelon.

Muskmelon. The muskmelon, more often called just melon, includes all varieties except the watermelon. They are large fruits, composed of a skin of variable texture, beneath which is a continuous layer of flesh which is usually of highest quality on its inner side, and becomes harder, less tasty and paler or greener next to the skin. The interior is a hollow more or less filled with a mass of seeds and fibers, some of which may be loosely attached to the flesh.

They are usually scraped out with a large spoon, and discarded.

The cantaloupe, Figure 14-28, is the most common American melon. It varies in shape from round to oval, weighs two to four pounds, and has a ribbed skin with a netted finish. It attains best flavor if it is not picked until fully ripe (the test is softness to pressure at the blossom end) and is then eaten immediately. Ripe cantaloupe spoils quickly and should be kept refrigerated.

It is very difficult to pre-judge the flavor of a cantaloupe at the market. A few of them are almost as good as those raised at home, some are practically tasteless and the rest are somewhere between these extremes. Both the variety and the time of picking are important. Commercial growers may raise a poor-flavored melon because of good growing, picking and shipping qualities; and they may pick better varieties too green for good flavor to reduce spoilage during shipping and marketing.

The honeydew melon is larger than the cantaloupe, has a smooth white or greenish-white skin, with similar flesh coloring. It is sweeter and lacks the musky flavor. Honeydews are less damaged by picking before full ripening, and have rather good shipping and storing characteristics. Ripeness may be indicated by softness at the blossom end, by general appearance, and by hollow-sounding resonance when tapped with the knuckles. But any melon is a bit of a gamble, and you can't be sure of its flavor and tenderness until you have tasted it.

There are a number of excellent melons that are generally similar to the honeydew, except in the appearance of their skin. Each has its own special flavor. They include the Persian, Spanish and casaba varieties.

Melon is usually chilled before serving, but many people prefer to eat it at room temperature.

Fig. 14-28. Cantaloupe

Uses. Melons are almost always eaten raw, as breakfast fruit or as dessert. The cantaloupe variety is usually prepared to blossom end, scooping out the seeds and then cutting it, still lengthwise, into serving pieces. The customer eats the flesh out with a spoon, or occasionally with a fork. The flesh may be cut free of the skin with a knife before or after serving, but left in place. However, there is some guesswork in deciding how near the skin you can cut without getting into hard and tasteless material, so this is better worked out one bite at a time.

Depending on the quality and sweetness of the melon, and personal taste, it may be touched up with lemon, salt or sugar. is eaten.

Melon may also be diced, or cut into balls with a special deep-bowled spoon, for mixing into fruit cocktail or fruit salad.

Watermelon. The watermelon is the largest commercial fruit (its rival in size, the pumpkin, is classified as a vegetable). The small globular or picnic watermelon averages 3 or 4 pounds, while the more common cylindrical variety ranges from 15 to 30 in the market, and specimens as heavy as 50 pounds have been reported. The skin is usually deep green except for a patch of lighter color where it rested on the ground while it grew. The flesh is pink or red, solid except for encased seeds, and is crisp in texture with a delicate, sweet flavor. The percentage of water is very high, but the price per pound is low.

Watermelons may be picked before they are fully ripe, and ripen and stand up well during short-term shipping and storage. Ripeness may be judged by resonance when thumped, by slight yielding under pressure on the skin, particularly at the blossom end, and by general appearance. But no test except sampling is conclusive, so "plugging" may be used. A hole about an inch in diameter is cut through the skin and about two inches into the flesh, and the resulting plug is pried out, inspected and tasted.

Plugging is rather frowned upon in markets, as the melon's principal defense against rot is an unbroken skin. But most markets sell melons cut in halves or smaller pieces, and those with a rich color are practically sure to be ripe and tasty.

Watermelon is eaten raw. It may be served in slices an inch or more thick, in chunks or in wedges. Customers usually remove their own seeds, which are arranged in a pattern in the middle and outer flesh. The inner flesh is seed-free, and may be sweeter than other parts.

Watermelon serves as a light dessert, a thirst-quenching snack or (when cut into fine slices, cubes or balls) as a salad ingredient. It is preferably refrigerated, but does keep itself comfortably cool at room temperature by surface evaporation.

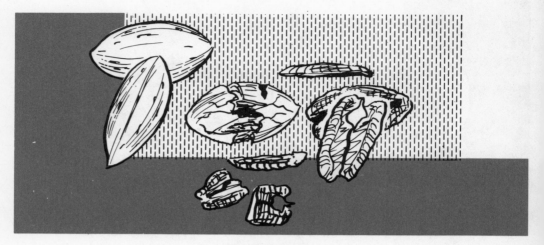

Fig. 14-29. Pecans

TREE NUTS

The true nuts are tree fruits, with hard shells and firm meat. The chestnut is mostly carbohydrate, but almost all others are low in carbohydrate and high in fat, with fair but variable amounts of protein. Vitamin content ranges from fair to poor.

Water content is very low, except in chestnuts.

Nuts are a highly concentrated food. They are usually high in price, but may be a better value than meat from a nourishment standpoint. They are eaten by themselves as snacks, but in meals usually appear only as flavorings, adornments and

Fig. 14-30. Peanut plant

suppliers of crunchiness. In this capacity they provide an effect of luxury at modest cost in money and work.

Whole nuts may be bought in single varieties or in assortments. They are often served after dessert during the Thanksgiving to New Year holiday season. Shelled nuts are more convenient for use in the kitchen, but may have less flavor and are inclined to spoil more quickly. Broken or chopped nuts lose flavor more rapidly than unbroken meats, but may be a little more convenient to use.

Almonds may be bought in sliced or slivered form, for convenience in adding to sauce or scattering on coffee cake.

Nut paste is good for flavoring, but it does not provide the crunchy texture that is usually wanted with nuts.

The oil in nuts may go off-taste and then rancid rather easily, particularly after shelling. They should be kept in original packages or in plastic bags, and used rather soon. You should sample nuts before using them, because if the flavor is bad it can be very very bad.

PEANUTS

Peanuts resemble tree nuts in many characteristics, but they are produced by annual bushes or vines related to peas and beans. Flowers are produced on branches above ground in normal legume fashion, but when fertilized they grow downward-reaching stalks called pegs. These penetrate the earth and produce the nuts underneath the surface.

Peanuts enter our kitchens mostly in ground form, as peanut butter. This is a protein and oil-rich food that is used as a sandwich and cracker spread that is prized by most children. It is obtainable in finely ground or smooth form, or coarse and crunchy. Salted peanuts are eaten in large quantities as snacks. Salted or unsalted, they can be used to enhance flavor and texture in the same manner as tree nuts, but their lower price deprives them of glamour.

15
GRAIN, CEREAL AND PASTA

GRAIN

True grains or cereals are the dry fruits of grasses. They are grown primarily for their starch content, although they may have important secondary amounts of protein. The leading grains are wheat, rice and corn. Oats, rye, barley, millet and sorghum are of secondary general interest, but may be important locally. Wheat, rice and rye are raised chiefly for human consumption, while the larger part of the others are used for animal food. Unripe corn is eaten in large quantities as a vegetable.

Kernel. Each grain kernel is a complete seed, made up of three structures. The endosperm contains most of the starch and the protein, which is called gluten, and is usually light in color. The germ, which is the living part, contains most of the fat or oil and vitamins, and is darker in color. The coat or skin, often called bran, may be hard or tough, dark in color, composed largely of somewhat indigestible cellulose and is often rich in flavor and vitamins. Figure 15-2 shows these divisions in a corn kernel. A diagram of a wheat kernel will be found on Page 404.

Most wheat, rye and dry corn intended for human consumption is ground into flour and then cooked into bread. Rice and barley are usually cooked without grinding, and oats may be either ground or rolled thin. Any grain may be processed into cereal to be eaten with milk or cream.

WHEAT

Wheat is used mostly in making flour, which is discussed under that heading in the chapters on THICKENERS and BAKED GOODS.

It is also used to make cereals, of which the best known are probably farina, puffed wheat, shredded wheat and wheat flakes. The last three will be discussed below under COLD CEREAL.

Farina. Farina is tiny pieces of wheat endosperm called middlings. They are removed from flour processing after the bran and germ have been removed, and before reduction to the fineness of flour. Only hard wheat can be used, as soft wheat would become pasty when cooked.

Farina is sometimes flavored with malt or cocoa, or blended with some of the germ and bran of the wheat. Most of it, however, is plain white endosperm, en-

317

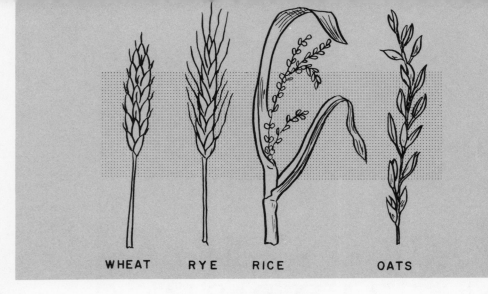

Fig. 15-1. Grains

RICE

riched with added vitamins. In quick cooking varieties, it may be partly or wholly precooked or gelantinized.

RICE

Rice is the staple food for more than half the world's population. The intact kernel is usually pale brown in color, but the more common de-hulled or polished kernels are white. Most rice is boiled and then eaten alone or in various mixtures. Some of it is made into rice flour, rice starch or cold cereal. The starch and flour are little used in the United States.

Rice may be classified on the basis of grain length, as long, medium, or short. The long-grain varieties tend to cook into a dry and fluffy condition and are favored for direct eating, while short grains may be more inclined to be firm and sticky, and may be preferred in puddings and soup. However, this distinction is not absolute, as there are differences among varieties in each grain class. Recipes usually do not specify any particular kind.

Rice always means white or hulled rice unless some other kind is mentioned. Brown rice kernels are complete with their inner skin, only the outer hull having been removed. They have a different taste, provide vitamins missing in white rice and have

inferior keeping quality because of th presence of oil in the germ.

There are three ways in which whit rice may be worked over before being pack aged for the market. It may be polished which means being brushed and the coated with a thin layer of talc and glucose The coating comes off when it is cooked and offers no advantage. Processed or con verted rice is partly cooked before the ski is removed, causing some of its vitamin to soak into the endosperm. Precooked o Minute rice has been fully cooked, the dried. Either of these prepared varietie may have added vitamins.

Cooking. Cooking time in boiling wate for ordinary white rice is 12 to 15 minutes for brown rice and processed rice about 25 and for precooked only 5 minutes. Under cooked rice is hard and gritty, when over cooked it becomes soft and sticky. Occa sionally you may get rice that can stay gritt on the inside even after it is gluey on th outside. The only remedy is to switch t another brand or variety until the inferio crop has been used up.

There is a standard formula for cookin white rice that appears on many packages It is:

"Combine 1 cup rice, 2 cups cold water 1 teaspoon salt and 1 tablespoon butter o

318

margarine in heavy 3-quart saucepan. Turn heat high until it boils, then reduce to medium low. Stir once with fork (don't use spoon). Cover pan tightly and simmer 12 to 14 minutes or until all liquid is absorbed."

You can get excellent rice by following these instructions exactly, but a number of modifications are allowable and may even be advisable.

Rice varies in its ability to absorb water, and people's taste in the doneness of the grains is not uniform. If you have rice that is unusually thirsty and/or customers who like soft rice, you are likely to have a dry pan before cooking is complete. And very soon after that scorched food. This is particularly likely if you cut the recipe in half. You should check your pan of rice several times toward the end of the cooking period, and have boiling water available to add if it is needed.

The salt is for flavor, and is recommended for most tastes. But it can be omitted for dietary reasons, without any penalty.

The butter reduces a variable tendency of cooked grains to clump together, and it also has flavor value. If part of the rice is to be kept for future use, it may remain more easily workable if you double the proportion of fat.

A 3-quart saucepan is huge and is certainly not necessary. It may be left over from an older recipe, in which a cup of

Fig. 15-3. A big pan for a small job

rice was cooked in 10 cups of water, which were drained off through a sieve. It is possible, although not comfortable, to cook this batch (about 22 fluid ounces, when mixed) in a 3-cup pan, and a 1-quart size should be ample unless you are in the habit of letting things boil up vigorously.

Stirring scrapes the rice grains against each other, rubbing off starch and making the water thick. It should be kept to a minimum, but a spoon is just as usable as a fork.

About 10 minutes after turning down the heat, start testing. Take out two or 3 grains, cool them and chew. When they are soft enough, the rice is cooked. If any water remains in the bottom it will be absorbed in a few minutes while standing, or can be poured off while you hold the rice in the pan with the lid, if you are in a hurry. Rice tends to dry and fluff while standing briefly in the pan, with or without a cover.

In cooking brown or processed rice it is best to follow the directions on the package.

White rice expands to 2-1/2 to 3 times its dry bulk when cooked. Brown rice and processed rice expand somewhat more, so will require a larger amount of water. Precooked grains double their volume.

Rice that is to be used in further cooking may be either fully or partly cooked, depending on the recipe. For part cooking, use the same quantity of water or only slightly less, as rice may not cook properly

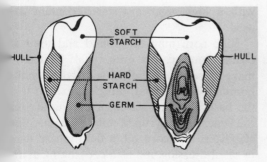

Fig. 15-2. Cross sections of corn kernel

Fig. 15-4. Corn

unless every grain is in contact with water during the early stages. You can pour off any surplus water when it has reached the condition you want.

Serving. Rice may be served hot at any meal, instead of potatoes. It may be eaten plain, but more often is moistened with butter or gravy. If it has been standing and has formed lumps, they should be broken up gently and prevented from re-forming by mixing with butter while heating. Rice may also be served as a breakfast cereal, either hot or cold, with cream or milk and sugar.

The texture of good rice is that of soft, non-sticky separate grains. It is excellently suited to forming a base for a wide variety of meat, fish and vegetables in sauce or gravy. The rice may be put first on the plate in the form of a ring, a flat layer or a mound and the other food poured over it. In a general way, it is interchangeable with toast in this use. Chicken a la king, lobster newburg, beef stroganoff and most curries are examples of such dishes.

Rice may also be mixed with such semi-fluid foods, before, during or after cooking.

Rice is an excellent ingredient for stuffed pepper or cabbage, and croquettes, which will be discussed under MEAT MIXTURES.

CORN

Corn (called maize in Europe) is most important in the American diet in an un-ripe or milk stage, and this use for it is discussed under VEGETABLES. Special varieties with a high-sugar low-starch content are used.

Ripe corn may be ground and used a coarse flour, called corn meal; heated to make popcorn, de-hulled with lye to make hominy or processed into dry cereals. It is the basis for corn starch, widely used as a thickener; corn syrup, a mild sweetener and stabilizer; and corn oil, a fluid grease used in salad dressing and as a cooking medium

Corn is the most important animal fee

crop in the United States, and its products are important for many industrial uses.

Corn Meal. The endosperm of corn contains two types of starch, hard and soft. The gluten is inferior in both quality and quantity to that found in wheat.

There is limited demand for fine flour made from corn, but a coarser grade known as corn meal is sold widely, and is a principal food in many Latin American countries. The soft parts contribute fineness and smoothness, the hard parts a slight but definite grittiness.

There are two types of corn meal. Milled corn meal is usually yellow, is rather finely ground and is made and sold in large quantities, mostly in the form of prepared mixes for corn muffins and bread. Water-ground meal is made by old-fashioned grinding between stone wheels, is usually made from white corn, is coarser and more gritty, is supposed to retain nutrients lost by processing in big mills and may have poor keeping quality. The two can be used interchangeably in most recipes, but the coarser type is widely regarded as superior.

Corn meal may be used unmixed, but in baking it is more usual to mix it with white flour, which may vary from 20 to 60 per cent of the mixture, depending on the recipe and type of product.

Corn bread and muffins have a distinctive and excellent flavor and a pleasing consistency when they are hot, but tend to become dry, flat and flavorless when cold. They gain back most of their good qualities when reheated, once.

Corn meal is the principal material in tortillas, a staple and highly valued food in Mexico and many other countries.

Hominy. Whole or pearl hominy consists of whole grains of white corn from which hulls and germ have been removed. It may be prepared in a mill, and sold canned or as dry pellets. It is less popular than hominy grits, which are made by breaking the hulled grains up into particles

that are larger than those in farina, and very much coarser than meal.

These grits are used as a hot cereal, as a replacement for potatoes or rice, as a side dish with meat and in mixtures such as croquettes. They are very bland in flavor and usually pure white in color.

Cooking time and method vary with fineness of grind and with local custom. Follow the directions on the package. If you don't have directions, try:

Hominy Grits

1 cup grits
4 cps boiling water
1 tsp salt
1 Tb   butter *(optional)*

Bring the water to a boil in the top section of a double boiler. Add the grits while stirring over medium heat. Cook over same burner for 5 minutes, stirring occasionally. Add the butter, if used. Have other water boiling in bottom of double boiler, put the top containing the hominy on it and cook covered for 15 minutes, or perhaps much longer, until it is moderately thick and the grains do not taste sharp or raw. Avoid excessive stirring or overcooking, as either will make it pasty.

The butter is useful for flavor, and reduces any tendency of the grits to become pasty or lumpy.

Cooked grits can be substituted for cooked rice or mashed potato in a number of recipes, but as it is finer and smoother than rice and coarser than the potatoes, results are not the same, and the product may be less flavorful.

Popcorn. Popcorn is a type of corn whose kernels expand almost explosively when heated, creating a fluffy, crisp, tender morsel. The amount of expansion varies from 30 to 40 times the bulk of the original grain, but may be much less if the kernels are in poor condition.

The popping is the result of steam pressure. Other grains can be popped also, mostly to produce dry cereals, but this is possible only under extreme and controlled conditions. The ease and thoroughness of this action in popcorn is not understood.

Popping may be done in a wire basket heated at an open fire or over a stove burner, or in a thin layer of butter or other oil in a heavily covered frypan. Open fire gives a better flavor, the frypan gives more even results. The hot popcorn should be sprinkled liberally with melted butter and with salt to taste and served immediately while hot. The corn should be turned over several times while these items are added, for even distribution.

Popcorn hulls are very tough. They tend to fold back in a rosette at the base, where they may be hidden by overlapping puffs. If a kernel does not pop, or pops only partly open, it should be picked out and discarded, as it is uncomfortable to bite. In fully popped kernels the hull is usually weakened sufficiently to make it tender and edible.

RYE

Rye is a grain that has superficial resemblance to wheat, but which has a distinctive flavor, and is usually richer in nutrients. Its gluten is of poor quality, however, so that rye flour must be mixed with white in order to produce a raised bread. Pumpernickel bread is made without white flour.

Rye is ground into products with various degrees of fineness. It is sold as rye meal, similar in particle size to corn meal, and more commonly as much finer grained flour. The flour may be one of three grades — white, medium and dark. The white is the purest and least flavorful, the dark includes a good bit of bran, and both its color and taste are more desirable for those wanting real rye flavor.

Rye bread may be made by substituting rye flour for half the white flour in any standard recipe, but the French bread type seems to produce best results. Brown sugar may be substituted for white sugar.

Rye is of little general importance in American home cooking, but rye bread is a popular bakery item.

OATS

Oats are the third most important grain crop in the United States, but here as well as throughout the rest of the world, most of the crop is used as animal feed. The small part prepared for human consumption is processed as rolled oats, which are used to make a hot cereal, oatmeal, and baked goods.

In processing, the oat grains are roasted at 212° for about an hour, to reduce moisture and weaken the hulls. They are then dehulled (an oat grain without a hull is called a groat). Groats are rolled into thin flakes, either whole or after being cut into pieces. Whole-groat flakes make the traditional oatmeal, which takes about 15 minutes to cook. Thinner and smaller flakes allow cooking in 5 minutes. Oatmeal made of the larger flakes has better keeping qualities, if it is necessary to keep it hot for more than a few minutes.

Fig. 15-5. Popcorn

HOT CEREAL

Hot cereals are usually made from grain kernels to which little or nothing is added, except that some kinds are restored or fortified by the addition of vitamins. Cooking consists of boiling or simmering in water for varying periods. They are usually eaten for breakfast with milk or cream and sugar, but are also used in other ways. In general, they are economical, easy to prepare and very nourishing. Their warmth has a very favorable start-of-the-day effect for many people.

Most cereal has a slight grainy or irregular consistency, resulting from the swelling of the starchy granules or pieces from which it is made. Incomplete cooking is likely to leave these particles gritty and the liquid between them too thin; too much cooking may create a smooth and rather disagreeable paste.

There is a very wide range in the cooking time of cereals. Some starches cook at lower temperatures and in shorter time than others. Larger pieces or grains take more time than smaller ones. Some people like cereal semi-raw, others want it like paste. In addition to these more or less natural differences, we now have many cereals that are partly or entirely pre-cooked, so that cooking time is very short, sometimes so short that it is done in the saucer instead of the pan.

A cookbook can therefore offer only general instructions, subject to modification and contradiction by the directions on the cereal box. But even these are not the final word. For if you find that following them gives you a cereal that is too thick or too thin, too gritty or pasty or objectionable in any way, you can use your own judgment in varying the procedure to get something you like better. Both the amount of water used and the cooking time are quite flexible. For one thing, short cooking time is considered to be a good sales point, and a

Fig. 15-6. Have plenty of boiling water, but be stingy in using it

longer cooking time than directed on the package often produces a better result. But it is likely to require additional water to avoid over-thickening.

The rule of thumb with a strange cereal is to use four times its volume of water, but in package directions the proportion varies from 1-1/2 to 1 up to 6 to 1 in different cereals. When in doubt, have an ample supply of boiling water but be stingy about using it. Start with a bit less than twice as much water as cereal, then add as needed during cooking. If you put in too much so that it seems too thin, cook it longer. You run a risk of pastiness, but may simply obtain a more fully cooked and pleasing product.

The standard method of combining is to have the water boiling over maximum heat in a rather large pan, then sift in pre-measured cereal gradually while stirring. When boiling resumes, turn heat low and cook for the required length of time (for modern cereals, usually about 5 minutes). Stir occasionally at first, then frequently and carefully after it starts to thicken and danger of scorching increases.

The cereal and water mixture tends to foam up as it is first mixed and when it starts to boil. This is the reason for the large pan.

Package directions call for a measured quantity of water and a specific cooking time, which usually work out very well for average taste. If you like a thinner cereal, increase the water either slightly at the beginning, or by adding boiling water slowly when the recommended time is finished. If you want it thicker, cook it a little longer or turn off the heat, cover the pan and let it stand for 3 to 5 minutes.

There are also instant products that are prepared by mixing measured quantities of cereal and boiling water in the saucer in which you eat. You are likely to find both flavor and consistency different from regular cereal, and the product is not nearly as hot as if the mixing were done in a pan over a burner.

Sometimes an instant cereal will take more time and work than one that is just quick-cooking. There is one that is prepared in a pan and is supposed to boil for just 10 seconds. Then put it to the side until it is as thick as you like it. This thickening seems to taken 5 or more minutes, may be incomplete and allows so much cooling that you have to heat it again, both to make it hot and to improve consistency. When all this has been done you have an excellent cereal, but "instant" is not quite the word for it.

Old fashioned cereals may take from 15 minutes to an hour or more to cook. It is a nuisance to watch and stir them, so they are best cooked in the top of a double boiler, or over very low heat. If you use an ordinary pan over a gas burner, use a metal or asbestos mat to spread the heat evenly over the bottom.

COLD CEREAL

Grain kernels can be treated in a variety of ways to make cold cereal. The most common are flaking, shredding and puffing.

The acceptability of cold cereals depends very largely on crispness, which requires a very low moisture content, usually around 2 or 3 per cent. They tend to absorb moisture in humid weather and become tough and/or flabby. They are well protected in the original package, but after that is opened they may need to be protected by a plastic bag. Crispness can be fully restored by heating to drive off the extra moisture. Spread in a pan and heat for a few minutes in a low oven, or stir over a low burner.

They are usually served for breakfast, with added milk or cream and sugar, but some of them can also be crushed and used for cooking crumbs.

Flakes. Corn flakes are made by removing the hull and germ, and breaking the rest of the kernel into very coarse grits, usually representing half a kernel. They are cooked in pressure steam, 15 to 23 pounds, with a flavoring syrup of sugar, malt, salt and water for 1 or 2 hours, until they are translucent. They are partially dried in warm air, set aside to "temper" for several hours, then flattened or flaked by steel rollers under very heavy pressure. They are then toasted in rotating drums, to reduce moisture content to about 3 per cent, to brown, dextrinize and caramelize part of the starch for flavor, and to make them blister for lightness and appearance.

Wheat flakes are made in the same general way, but the details of processing are different because of the nature of the grain.

Puffs. Puffs are whole or polished grain kernels that are subjected to moist heat under pressure, then blown into a vacuum chamber. This results in a very light, crisp texture with great increase in size.

Shreds. Shredded wheat is the best known member of this class. Whole wheat grains are made into a mash that is forced through fine holes to make shreds, which are shaped into biscuits and baked.

MACARONI PRODUCTS

Macaroni products, also known as pasta or as alimentary pastes, include macaroni, spaghetti and egg noodles, and a wide range of other products that vary mostly in shape, but may also contain special ingredients.

The basic raw materials are water and durum wheat, a very hard type whose gluten is not elastic enough for good bread-making, but which makes dough that can be formed readily by extruding (pressing through small holes). The preferred size is a fine meal called semolina, which passes through a #20 sieve, but is 97 per cent held on a #100 sieve. Flour, all of which passes through the finer sieve, makes a dough which is more difficult to process and a product that is more easily damaged by overcooking.

Macaroni and its relatives can be made from farina or flour from regular hard wheat instead of durum, but appearance, cooking qualities and flavor are generally held to be inferior.

Optional ingredients are egg white solids to improve resistance to overcooking, extra gluten, salt and flavorings or seasonings.

Noodles must contain egg, and are formed in flattened or ribbon shape. The same dough in tube shape would be egg macaroni.

These products are made of de-hulled and de-germed flour, and may be vitamin-enriched to increase dietary value. Such enrichment is usually higher than that used in

Fig. 15-7. Shredded wheat

bread flour, to compensate for expected losses in cooking water.

Durum wheat imparts a faint yellowish or cream color to the product. Even though it is ordinarily considered to be white, this slight tinting is considered important to consumer acceptance, as its occasional absence is noted unfavorably. In noodles, egg yolk may be used instead of whole egg largely for color effect, and considerable trouble may be taken to get yolks from hens whose diet gives yolks a deep color.

Shapes. According to industry definitions, macaroni consists of hollow tube-shapes between 0.11 and 0.27 inch in diameter. Spaghetti is cord-shaped, not hollow, and between 0.06 and 0.11 inch, and vermicelli is less than 0.06 in diameter. All measurements are dry.

Figure 15-8 shows some, but by no

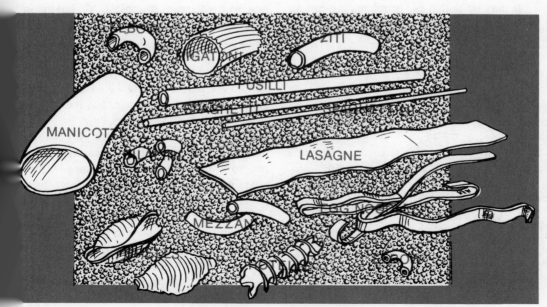

Fig. 15-8. Some varieties of pasta

means all, of the shapes and names that are available in pasta. Even if all these were made of exactly the same dough, they would have important differences in eating qualities, as size and shape affect the texture and acceptability noticeably.

Cooking. Most pasta is cooked in ample quantities of rapidly boiling water. Instructions on 8-ounce and 1-pound packages often call for 6 quarts of it. This appears to be excessive, both in relation to the amount actually needed by the pasta, and the equipment of the average kitchen. You would probably need an 8-quart kettle, to allow a margin for spill or boiling over. Got one? Perhaps the turkey roasting pan?

Such instructions are sometimes carelessness in printing instructions meant for a large package on smaller ones also. But the reason for wanting plenty of water is that during cooking some starch granules detach themselves from the surface of the pieces. If the quantity of water were small, it might be thickened so much that it would be pasty, pieces would clump together and it would drain poorly. The rapid boiling tends to prevent clumping.

It may be that these problems are not as severe with modern spaghetti, macaroni

and noodles as they were when the instructions were written. In any case, a pound of spaghetti will cook satisfactorily in 2 quarts of water to which 2 tablespoons of butter or oil have been added. But the additional water does no harm, just calls for a bigger pot and longer preheating. And it completely eliminates any danger of boiling dry.

The standard recommendation for salt is one teaspoon for each quart of water, which is about 1/5 of the saltiness of sea water. This is mostly for flavor, as it serves to point up a rather faint and bland natural taste. It may have some value in the cooking also, but do not hesitate to leave it out for a salt-free diet.

Grease in the cooking water, one tablespoon or more to the quart, reduces any tendency of the strands to stick together during or after cooking. Extra butter, up to 2 tablespoons to the dry pound, may be mixed in after draining, both for flavor and to reduce or prevent sticking during standing or refrigeration.

Cooking time varies from less than 5 to over 25 minutes, depending chiefly on the size and shape of the pieces, but also on how well you want it cooked. Variations in the makeup of the dough may change softening characteristics. Fine vermicelli is the quickest, and coarse macaroni or shells the slowest. For the most used forms, spaghetti and elbow macaroni, try 10 to 15 minutes or the time on the package, but make tests during the last 1/3 of the boiling.

Raw pasta is hard and brittle. It becomes flexible and tough almost immediately when put in boiling water. The toughness disappears gradually during cooking. Some people like it quite tough, and some prefer it as soft as well-boiled potato. The majority like it with enough toughness to give it some individuality, but not enough to cause any difficulty in cutting or chewing.

When you think it might be cooked, take out a strand or two for testing. They are hard to get out unless you use two tools, so

Fig. 15-9. Separating spaghetti from water

that you can catch them between. Strands laid on a cool part of the stove top will chill enough for a chewing test immediately.

If it will have further cooking, as in a casserole, you can regard it as done when it is still quite tough, if it seems to have absorbed nearly its full quantity of water.

When cooking is complete you pour off the water. This is most easily done by dumping the contents of the pot into a colander. Your recipe will probably tell you to rinse it at this point. Old ones call for cold water, newer ones for hot water. Cold water is expected to harden any sticky film of starch on the outside of the pieces, hot water should wash it off. Cold water chills the food, and it is awkward stuff to reheat, so this practice is bad unless it is going into a salad or storage. Ordinary hot faucet water will cool it just a little. Rinsing is usually not necessary with present-day pasta, particularly if you have cooked it with butter or other fat, and stir in some more immediately upon returning it to the cooking pan or putting it in the serving bowl.

Serving Spaghetti. Spaghetti may be served hot as an appetizer, as a side dish instead of potato or as a main course. As a side dish it may be plain, with butter added or with butter and grated cheese available. As an appetizer or main dish it is almost always served with sauce, which may be mixed in, heaped on top and/or available in a serving dish.

Spaghetti sauces are a whole field of cookery in themselves. They tend to be rich, thick and highly seasoned. Most of them have some sort of tomato sauce as a base. Several examples are given under SAUCES, pages 366 to 368. Grated cheese is usually served in a shaker or side dish.

Spaghetti with sauce seems to make a natural combination with meat balls, which are often cooked in or at least served in the sauce. They are usually small, 1-1/4 to 1-3/4 inches in diameter.

The traditional, approved or Italian way

Fig. 15-10. Wind up a mouthful

is to serve spaghetti in full-length (10-inch) strands, and to expect that they will be eaten without cutting. This is difficult to do in a civilized manner. The expert seems to spear some with a fork, put the end of the fork in the bowl of a spoon (preferably tablespoon or dessert spoon) and twist the fork until the speared spaghetti is wound up in a ball. This ball, which may be either large or small, is then stuffed into the mouth.

A more rational but less inner-circle method is to cut the spaghetti with the fork or with a knife and fork into pieces that can be picked up on the flat of a fork in the usual manner. Unless your customers

Fig. 15-11. Then cram it in

are spaghetti specialists, you can simplify their eating by breaking it up before you cook it.

Spaghetti is used only occasionally in casseroles and rarely in salad, although it can be substituted for elbow macaroni in any of them, so far as cooking procedures and flavor are concerned.

Macaroni. Macaroni comes in both long straight tubes and in short bent ones. The second type, called elbow macaroni or often just elbows, seems to be the more popular.

Macaroni is seldom served spaghetti-style with sauce, but this is more a matter of custom than of failure to go well with it. The special combination for macaroni is cheese. They are usually baked in casserole fashion as described on page 396, but are occasionally just stirred together in a pan.

Noodles. Noodles, often referred to more fully as egg noodles, differ from most of the macaroni family in having egg mixed in the dough, and in being shaped in flattened ribbons instead of rods, tubes and other shapes.

To justify their name, egg noodles must contain at least 5.5 per cent of egg solids.

Noodles are marketed mostly in two sizes, fine and wide. When packaged, they seem to have a random and rather tangled arrangement, with a great deal of air space. They may occasionally be seen unpackaged, in which case parallel strands are made into bunches and looped or knotted together before hardening.

Noodles are seldom or never served as appetizers or main dishes or with spaghetti sauce. They may be used hot with butter as a potato substitute, but more often are combined with other foods in casseroles.

Noodles are cooked in the same manner as the other pastas.

Part Three / COMBINED FOODS

16
FLAVORINGS

FLAVOR

In this chapter we are concerned with substances that are added to food primarily to improve or at least change their flavor. Some of them, like sugar and chocolate, are foods in themselves. Others, like pepper and vanilla extract, are taste with practically no nourishment.

Sense of Taste. We sense flavor through taste buds and smell receptors. The taste buds are located chiefly on the tongue and nearby areas of the throat. They respond only to salt, sour, sweet and bitter flavors, and to their combinations. Smell is responsible for the rest of the tasting mechanism. But what we taste is also closely linked with chemical sensitivity, texture, color, temperature, our inherited peculiarities and our training and experience.

Flavor is difficult to analyze and classify. A pure chemical should always taste the same, but different people will react to it and describe it very differently. One bitter chemical, PTC (phenyl thio caramide) that is used for testing, is tasteless to about 1/3 of the people who try it. Most foods are complicated compounds, no two lots of which are likely to taste exactly the same. With variation in both sense of taste and actual flavor, there is ample room for disagreement.

The human sense of taste (including smell) may be very delicate and precise. An experienced taster can often tell on the basis of a sip or two of wine what part of the world grew the grapes that went into it, and may be able to tell the year of the harvest as well. Sterilization of certain foods by radiation changes about one molecule in 40,000, and the resulting flavor differences are noticeable enough to be a problem.

Differences in sense of taste of individuals are in part inherited, part training or habit, and part associations, all of them subjects too complicated for this book. Their net result is that some people will eat and enjoy most anything, others hardly like anything (children especially) and the majority struggle with at least a few unreasonably strong likes or dislikes.

Seasoning. Seasoning is a term that includes most flavoring that is not naturally in the food itself. The major exception is in regard to desserts, where even spices are seldom referred to as seasoning.

Specifically, seasoning includes salt, spices, herbs, flavorful extracts of ordinary foods (onion salt and tomato paste, for example), acidifiers such as lemon juice and vinegar, and chemicals such as monosodium glutamate. It does not usually include sugar, chocolate or most fruits or fruit extracts.

There is a great deal of disagreement about the use of seasonings, and attitudes are usually based on differences of taste that cannot be reconciled by argument. Extremists on one side maintain that none of them are necessary, as each food has its own natural and proper flavors, which can be best utilized by proper preparation, cooking and blending with other non-seasoned foods. The other side considers that few foods are worth eating unless they are fully seasoned, preferably with mixtures or blends of seasonings.

There are people who have delicate senses of taste that they have trained to distinguish each item in a complex flavoring structure, and who take real pleasure in savoring and identifying the different items. These include the gourmets who invent, broadcast and enjoy recipes that include, or are even mostly made up of, elaborate seasoning and cooking methods.

Seasonings tend to be habit forming. A pleasing taste sensation may get dulled by repetition, but brought back to nearly its original charm by increasing the dose, or by combining with an additional herb or spice. This may happen again and again. It is sometimes questionable whether a person insisting on and getting highly spiced food is really tasting anything more than his neighbor who does not even bother to salt the original plain food.

It is generally admitted that it is worse to use the wrong seasoning or too much of the right seasoning than to use none. The amateur cook has sufficient problems with the handling of the food itself, without going into problems of seasoning. If she is using a general cookbook, she can probably follow its directions fairly safely, but if she has a specialty book, it is best to either omit the seasonings completely or arbitrarily cut the quantities in half.

However, one book is available that combines simple recipes with expert seasoning. This is Craig Claiborne's "KITCHEN PRIMER." It is recommended as a companion volume to this, for those who find my advice and recipes too bland.

Seasoning for the Family. A question of particular importance in adapting recipes to your own family is whether they like food simple or complicated, bland or spiced. In general, simple food tends to be bland and complex food more highly flavored, but this is not always so.

Americans are quite largely eaters of comparatively bland and simple food, but writers of cookbooks tend to like it complicated and highly seasoned. This is partly because a person interested enough in cooking to write a book about it usually enjoys working with seasonings; and partly because to attract attention, a new recipe must differ from a standard one, and the easiest way to make a difference is to spice it up.

The result of this schism is that good plain cooking is being driven underground. Its recipes are passed around by word of mouth, or obtained by experimental omission of seasonings from book instructions. Too often, however, book or magazine directions are followed literally, and a habit is built up of eating food that is too elaborate for maximum enjoyment.

Seasoning is and should be done on a basis of individual flavor preference. The cook tends to flavor or not flavor according to her or his own judgment, tempered by the expressed or suspected preferences of the customers. If amounts used are moderate and there are no special diet restrictions, there is no question of health involved, nor can anyone reasonably say that use or not-use of seasonings in home meals is a mark of either good or bad cooking. It is said, however, loudly and clearly by many authorities. For example, Adelle Davis, in "LET'S COOK IT RIGHT," states: "The greatest weakness of American cookery is the failure to season food interestingly.

Effect of Cooking. The flavor of cooked unseasoned food depends only partly on its raw taste, which may be improved, degraded or even lost in preparation and cooking. It is the fashion among health-oriented writers to imply that raw food has the flavor, and the best we can hope for in cooking is to lose as little of it as possible. This is usually not so. The flavors of many uncooked natural foods are not acceptable to the majority of civilized people, just as the foods themselves are unacceptable to their stomachs.

Cooking serves to make food digestible and to change flavors or create new ones. Each cooking process produces a different result, but this is seldom because one saves the original flavor and another does not. Flavor may be created by the interaction of the food, the cooking medium and the heat. Even the material and texture of the container may be a factor in flavor.

An egg may be fried in any one of a dozen different fats, in a mixture of fat and water, on a dry Teflon pan, covered or uncovered, or on a hollowed piece of toast in an electronic oven. It may be cooked very rapidly over a high flame or very slowly over a low one, with a time range from 1-1/2 to 10 minutes.

Each change in method produces differences in flavor and texture, some important, some very slight. You can choose among them, and if you choose the one that is easiest, that is your privilege.

Smell. It is often said that the good smell of cooking indicates that the food is losing flavor. It might, but more often these good odors are a byproduct of flavor being created, as in the browning of the surface of a roast or the combining of different substances in a stew.

Such smells usually indicate that the cooking method is a good one, and often that the process is nearly complete. But smells of burning and charring, except possibly in outdoor cooking, do indicate damage or at least a danger of it.

SALT

In chemistry, salt may be any substance that can be produced by reaction between

Fig. 16-1. Inside a salt mine

Courtesy of Diamond Crystal Salt Co.

an acid and a base, and that will separate into oppositely charged parts (ions) in solution. In medicine it is a laxative. But in cooking it is always one particular salt, sodium chloride. This is the most universally used and appreciated flavoring, an essential mineral in the diet and a chemical that affects food in a number of ways. It also has the characteristic of producing subfreezing temperatures when mixed with ice.

Need for salt as a mineral is discussed under NUTRITION, and some of its chemical and physical activity under BOILING, PRESERVING and VEGETABLES.

Salt is a very common and easily obtainable mineral. It is extracted from ocean water by evaporation, and mined or dissolved out of rock-like deposits left in the beds of former seas and salt lakes. Many salt formations are enormously thick.

Salt has its own strong and distinctive flavor, which can be sensed directly by the taste buds. Almost everybody likes a few items of food that taste salty, and there are some who like almost everything that way. But the average recipe and the average cook use it in amounts small enough so that the food seldom has any salt taste at all. Yet if the salt were not there, the food would probably taste flat to those who were accustomed to its presence. It appears as if the principal flavor-function of salt is as an intensifier or sharpener of other flavors.

Too much salt will overwhelm the other tastes, and make food unpleasant or impossible to eat. But how much is too much depends on the salt-tolerance or salt-hunger of the person eating it, the nature of the food (especially its flavor-strength) and the quantity to be eaten. Hors d'oeuvres such as anchovies and caviar can be enjoyed even if they are so extremely salty that they would not be acceptable to most as a main course.

The effect of salt may be somewhat different when it is mixed with food than when it is sprinkled on top. This is part of a gen-

eral difference between blended and contrasting flavors, and preference between them is largely a personal matter. It is safest when in doubt to mix in a minimum amount of salt or none, as it can't be taken out, and salt added at the table is at least a tolerable substitute.

People in normal health can eat as much salt as they like without ill effects. In very hot weather it is often recommended that extra salt be eaten on food or taken in the form of pills, to replace the considerable amount lost in sweat. But those who suffer from retention of too much fluid in their tissues must limit their intake of salt severely, and should not have it added to any food that they eat.

Salt occurs naturally in meat and in a few other foods, but only in small quantities.

Table Salt. Table salt is purified so that only traces of substances other than sodium chloride remain. It is usually sold in moisture-resistant one pound boxes with metal pouring spouts. A small quantity of potassium iodide may be added, in which case the package must be labeled "Iodized". This treated salt is intended for use in areas where natural iodine supplies are deficient, and serves no special purpose elsewhere.

Salt is hygroscopic, that is, it tends to ab-

Fig. 16-2. Found on almost every table

sorb moisture from the atmosphere when relative humidity is over 75 per cent. This moisture forms a brine on the surface of the crystals, which causes them to stick together. The depth of penetration of the brine depends on the humidity, the exposure to the moist air and the length of time. In extreme cases it will liquefy the salt.

When humidity drops below 75 per cent the water evaporates, leaving the dissolved salt in the form of bridges between the crystals. If there has been just a little brine these bonds are weak and the resulting lumps are easily crumbled. But if dampening has been severe, lumps will be so hard that they will be difficult to restore by crushing or grating.

Water absorption can be a major nuisance, as damp salt will not go through the holes in a shaker or even pour from a box, and it stands up on a spoon so as to be difficult to measure. The trouble usually occurs only on hot humid days, and in shakers rather than in original packages, whether they are opened or not. Shakers may be kept dry by keeping them in a plastic bag while not in use, or on a warm surface such as a stove top over a pilot light, or on a water heater.

Partial relief may be obtained by using a tall shaker with only a small amount of salt

Fig. 16-3. Infinite brine

in the bottom, or by adding a few grains of raw rice to the salt. The tall shaker delays the movement of moisture down to the salt, and the rice tends to break up weak lumps in the salt when it is shaken, and may absorb some water also.

The manufacturer may add a small quantity of small chemical such as tricalcium phosphate to the salt to reduce water absorption. Such salt is usually labeled and advertised as free-running, but the protection is limited and precautions against lumping under extreme conditions should still be taken.

An old-fashioned method of avoiding trouble with clogged shakers is to serve salt at the table in little dishes, called salt cellars, instead of in shakers. There may be tiny spoons for dipping the salt out, but it is more usual to pick it up with thumb and finger. With these containers, salt remains usable (although not pleasantly so) no matter how sticky it gets.

Rock Salt. Rock salt is very coarse, and is usually not as purified as table salt. It is used in home freezing of ice cream, melting ice on sidewalks and is an important industrial chemical.

Rock salt has the same tendency to absorb moisture, but its larger crystals are not so closely packed, and are not fused together as readily. However, if left for a long time in a damp place and then dried, it may become as hard as the rock for which it is named, and might need to be broken up with a hammer. For this reason, any opened bags should be protected by wrapping in plastic.

Brine. Brine is a solution of salt in water, strong enough to taste salty. Cooking or preserving brines are usually made with table-quality salt, but natural brines may contain many chemicals in addition to this sodium chloride.

Sea water is a natural brine, which contains from 2.9 per cent salt in the polar oceans to 3.5 per cent or more in the trop-

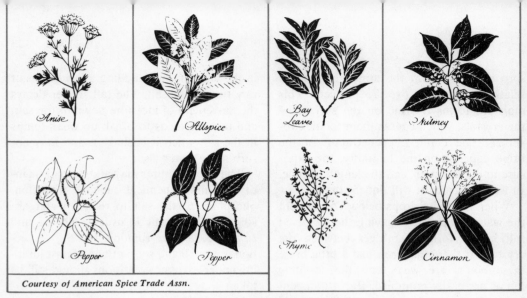

Anise

Allspice

Bay Leaves

Nutmeg

Pepper

Pepper

Thyme

Cinnamon

Courtesy of American Spice Trade Assn.

Fig. 16-4. A few spices and herbs

ics. It averages about 3.0 per cent, or a bit under 6 teaspoons to the quart. Inland bodies of water without drainage may become saturated brines, containing more than 25 per cent of salt and associated minerals. Strong natural brines are obtained from wells in some areas.

Sea water is too salty to be palatable.

Salt-curing. Salt-preserved meats such

Fig. 16-5. Table-size pepper grinder

as corned beef and ham are very salty if made by old recipes, and may require several changes of water during boiling to make them palatable. But modern packing plants have reduced the salt content of such meat so far that you may not even notice it.

SPICES AND HERBS

According to the dictionary, a spice is any aromatic or pungent vegetable substance used to flavor food, and a herb (you may say an herb if you wish) is any plant without a woody stem, which dies back to the ground after bearing seed.

In cooking talk, spice is often limited to products of tropical or subtropical plants. The term herb is used for plants which are used in food for flavoring rather than nourishment. Flavor is generally milder than that of spices.

Both spices and herbs are used because of their distinctive flavors, and any food value that they may have is of secondary interest. Many of them are credited with useful medical properties.

A description of the commercial forms of the most-used spices and herbs will be found in the Appendix. In addition to these dried forms, many of the temperate zone herbs can be obtained fresh, and used for garnishes as well as for flavoring.

Two seasonings are particularly important in American cookery.

Pepper. Black pepper is the most popular spice in American food. It is used frequently although not liberally in the kitchen, and is usually present at the table, in a shaker which is a companion piece to the salt. It has a pungent, pleasing taste and a strong aromatic odor, goes well with almost any non-sweet food that can stand spice and it keeps its flavor well.

It is produced in the form of small, hard black peppercorns, which are immature berries. They are usually ground to a powder before using; either by the producer or at home. There are small hand-cranked mills which grind the peppercorns at the table, dropping the resulting flakes or powder directly on food.

The pepper has a special flavor when fresh ground, but it retains an excellent and characteristic flavor for months and even years after grinding, even if left in an uncovered shaker.

White pepper is made by grinding peppercorns from which the black hulls have been removed. It is light yellowish-grey in color. Taste and odor are similar to that of black pepper, but it is somewhat milder. It is particularly favored for light-colored sauces.

Garlic. Garlic is the powerfully flavored bulb of a plant in the onion family. Its smell is even stronger than its taste. The flavor is sometimes pleasant, particularly when the quantity present is very small. In certain combinations it is repulsive, although still popular. The flavor of meat cooked with bits of garlic embedded in it can sometimes be distinguished from that of rotten meat only by an expert. However, the admirers of garlic are numerous and vocal enough so that any complaint about its presence is likely to be socially unacceptable.

As a flavoring, garlic might have won only moderate acceptance and had few enemies, if it were not for its odor. It has a very strong and long lasting smell, which is offensive to most people who do not eat it. A good strong dose of garlic may leave its odor in the breath for three days and in the sweat for two or three more. The only defense in close association with a garlic-eater is to eat some yourself, after which you no longer notice. But then your friends will.

Garlic is firmly established in American cookery and life. You can't fight it, but you can limit your use of it severely. You may be able to provide enough of the taste by rubbing a cut clove of garlic on the bowl or pan in which food is being prepared, or by sprinkling garlic salt.

ACIDS

Acids are usually sour, and are therefore the taste-opposites of sugars, although there is no chemical antagonism or relationship between the two groups. Acids occur naturally in most fruits and particularly in berries, and it is common practice to offset them by adding sugar, often a great deal of it.

Sweet and acid mask or cancel each other to some extent, but it is usually possible to tell that both are present unless one is much stronger than the other. And sugar does not ordinarily interfere with the fruit flavor — it may even accentuate it by free-

Fig. 16-6. Garlic cloves

ing it from competition with too much acid.

A small amount of acid often sharpens and brings out flavors in food that are too bland or too sweet without it. Or perhaps the acid taste is pleasing in itself.

The two acids most used in the kitchen are lemon and vinegar. Cream of tartar is another acid that appears in a number of recipes, but it is usually for chemical effect rather than for flavoring.

Lemon. Lemons are described in the section on FRUIT. Their juice is strongly acid, and has a distinctive and pleasing taste. The rind is less acid, and has a somewhat different flavor which may be strong

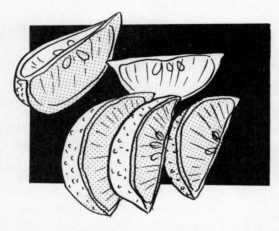

Fig. 16-7. Lemon wedges

or weak. Lemon extract carries the flavor of lemon, but is non-acid.

Lemon juice is part of a great number and variety of recipes, in amounts ranging from a few drops to a tablespoon or more. Like many other flavorings, it is slightly habit forming, and continuous use dulls the ability to taste it. Some cooks add it as a matter of habit to fruit pies and puddings, to sharpen the taste of the fruit. But it may serve to mask a distinctive but delicate flavor. It is safest not to use it for this purpose unless the fruit's taste is definitely too bland or below normal.

A medium size lemon should yield 3 to

4 tablespoons of juice. You obtain it by cutting the fruit crosswise and squeezing it in the same manner described earlier for citrus fruits.

Slices of lemon are commonly served with sea food, tea and various bland substances, permitting the customer to either use the juice for flavoring or let them alone, an ideal way to allow for individual taste preference. The slices should be wedge-shaped for convenience in squeezing.

The rind is often used in addition to the juice. You prepare it freshly at the time of use by rubbing the lemon on a medium grater, taking mostly the yellow surface. A medium sized lemon (about 2-1/2 ounces) should furnish a teaspoon of rind, perhaps more if you are an expert with a grater.

Lemon juice may be bought in bottles. It keeps well at room temperature until it is opened, and then should be refrigerated. It can be substituted for fresh juice in recipes (but with some loss in flavor), but it cannot provide rind.

Vinegar. Vinegar is a dilute solution of acetic acid, which is formed by the action of bacteria on alcohol. Natural vinegar results from the fermentation of fruit juices, and carries characteristic flavor derived from the fruit. Cider vinegar is the commonest of these, and wine vinegar can be bought in some localities. The acetic acid content ranges from 4 to 6 per cent. It should be stated on the bottle, as it is a measure of the acid strength.

Most of our vinegar is white vinegar, made from fermenting grain, and distilled to remove color and side flavors. Distillation also sterilizes it, so that it keeps indefinitely in the unopened bottle, and for long periods after opening. Acetic acid content is usually 6 per cent, but it may be 5.

White vinegar is just acid, without any other flavor. If you have no lemon, or do not like it, you can substitute vinegar for lemon juice in the proportion of 2 parts of vinegar to 3 of juice, but you will just get acid, not flavor. Cider vinegar replaces lemon juice in equal amounts, with a similar disadvantage.

Miracle Fruit. Within the next few years we may be able to obtain an extract or a synthetic principle of miracle fruit (Synsepalum dulcificum), a recently studied West African berry whose juice contains a taste-modifying protein that makes sour things taste sweet. It is not sweet itself. It must be taken a minute or two before the acid, not mixed with it.

EXTRACTS

Extracts are concentrated solutions of flavoring substances, which may be either natural or artificial. Only natural ones are generally recommended for home use.

Extracts are often preserved in alcohol, which evaporates readily and may take most of the flavor with it. They should be kept tightly corked when not in use, and preferably stored in a dark or dim place at moderate temperature. Even under the best conditions they lose strength gradually. Except in baked goods, they are added as a final touch after cooking is completed, to avoid loss by evaporation.

Vanilla. Vanilla is probably the most popular flavoring in American cookery. If used in moderate amounts (and most recipes are reasonable about this) it adds a very delicate flavor, or sharpens other flavors without becoming noticeable itself. But in too-large amounts it has a sharp or acrid taste which may be unpleasant.

Vanilla is a bean grown in the tropics. We use it chiefly in the form of an alcohol-base extract. But some people prefer the dried bean (both pod and seeds) ground or grated into tiny bits, or powder. It is sold in other countries as sugar exposed to vanilla. In flavoring strength, a teaspoon of the extract is approximately equal to 2 or 3 teaspoons of vanilla sugar.

Almond. This is the strongest of the extracts, and recipes seldom call for more

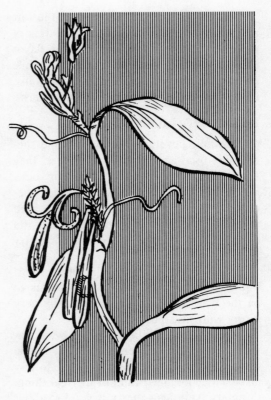

Fig. 16-8. Vanilla vine

than 1/4 or occasionally 1/2 teaspoon. It may be combined with other flavorings for special effects. For example, one or two drops of it with a teaspoon of vanilla extract produce a quite passable pistachio flavor.

Other Flavors. Quite a variety of flavoring extracts may be available in specialty stores. These include lemon, orange, wintergreen, rose, clove and maple. In general, it is safest to stay away from them until you are very sure of what you are doing in the kitchen.

Meat. A true meat extract consists of juice or clear gravy from the meat, with fluid evaporated until it becomes a thick or solid concentrate. They may be preserved by a canning process, or by mixing with a very large quantity of salt, as in bouillon cubes.

Unfortunately, the high price of the raw material has caused most manufacturers of the extracts to add synthetic meat flavor and/or vegetable protein. The result, while pleasing to many people, seldom tastes like meat, and therefore has limited usefulness.

WINE AND LIQUOR

Alcoholic beverages are widely and successfully used as flavorings. However, they are seldom found in plain or amateur cooking, being chiefly valued in gourmet specialties. But since they are less risky than many of the concentrated flavorings in everyday use, there is no reason not to try them if you wish.

Brandy is the most popular of the hard liquors for flavoring, and sherry seems to be the favorite wine. You can get by very nicely with just these two.

Avoid non-alcoholic liquor or wine flavorings, as most of them taste as synthetic as they are. And don't feel you have to buy a special "cooking" brand of the real thing. Ordinary American sherry is good at about fifty cents a pint, and even a fine grade of brandy (cognac, if it is imported) should not cost more than five or six cents a teaspoon.

All of the alcohol and most of the flavor evaporates quickly during cooking. So your wine or liquor is usually added as the last touch, in the same way as vanilla extract. Even with this precaution, the alcohol content of the flavored food is usally negligible, and eating it does not count as drinking anyhow.

SAUCES

There are a number of flavoring sauces, such as Worcestershire and A-1, which are used to sharpen or alter the flavor of sauces and gravies, and sometimes for direct addition to meat and sea food.

The quantity used in mixtures may be as small as a drop or two to a quart, or as large as one part in four. In very small quantities they usually point up the taste without changing it, but in large doses they dominate the mixture.

Most people like or at least do not object strongly to these flavorings. But to play safe, you might start by using 1/4 to 1/2 of the amount called for by the recipe, and use your judgment from then on.

CHOCOLATE

Chocolate is both a highly popular flavoring and a nourishing food. It is made from cacao beans, which are the fruit of a tree grown in equatorial regions. The beans are extensively processed to produce commercial chocolate. Differences in flavor depend somewhat on the locality in which the beans were grown, but mostly on the processing methods. The most noticeable difference is in the amount of sugar that is added.

Chocolate itself is made up about half and half of the bitter, flavorful chocolate substance and of cocoa butter. This butter is a delicate, almost tasteless fat that melts at a slightly higher temperature than dairy butter, about 92º F. Just below melting temperature it is soft and plastic, and it becomes moderately hard and brittle when cold. Chocolate hardens, softens and melts along with its butter, although the other substances are relatively insensitive to temperature.

Types. Chocolate is sold as cooking, bitter, unsweetened or unsweet chocolate in the form of one-ounce squares; as bittersweet or semi-sweet in bars and in small pieces called bits, chips or morsels; as sweet or milk chocolate in bars and shapes, and also as syrups.

The bitter chocolate is used only in cooking, the bitter-sweet serves both as an ingredient and as a candy. The others are eaten mostly as candy, in solid form, mixed with almonds or peanuts or as coating on candy and crackers. Syrups are used on desserts, particularly ice cream, and in beverages.

	per cent sugar	per cent milk solids
Bitter (unsweet)	0 to 20	—
Bitter-sweet (semi-sweet)	20 to 40	—
Sweet	40 to 65	—
Milk	35 to 50	12 to 25

Courtesy of Hershey Foods

Fig. 16-9. Sugar in chocolate

Bitter chocolate may or may not contain sugar; other classes always do. The amount varies with the sweetness classification, and also with the batch or brand. General ranges of sugar content are shown in Figure 16-9.

The amount of sweetness desired in chocolate flavored foods is also variable, among writers of cookbooks as well as among other people. A study of recipes for chocolate syrups shows that the amount of sugar suggested for each one-ounce square of bitter chocolate ranges from 2-1/2 to 8 tablespoons, with additional corn syrup in some of the sweeter ones.

You may need to substitute one kind of chocolate for another in a recipe. You should take in account not only the changed amount needed for chocolate flavor, but also the adjustment of the amount of sugar in the recipe, if you are trying to follow it exactly.

For example, to replace 2 ounces (squares) of bitter chocolate, you would need approximately 3 ounces of semi-sweet chocolate, but should use one ounce (2 tablespoons) less sugar. If you went on to sweet chocolate, you would use 4 ounces, with a reduction of 2 ounces (4 tablespoons or 1/4 cup) in sugar.

These amounts are approximate, but since you don't really know just what the proportion of ingredients is in any particular piece of chocolate, there is little use in trying to figure it out more closely.

Cocoa. Cocoa is made by removing half the cocoa butter from bitter chocolate, and grinding the resulting hard cake into powder. Dutch process cocoa has further treatment to make it somewhat darker, richer and more readily soluble.

Cocoa has a full chocolate flavor, but it is less rich because of the lower fat content.

Three level tablespoons of cocoa are generally accepted as providing a chocolate flavor equivalent to that from one ounce of bitter chocolate. You can simply interchange these amounts in recipes, except in baking. Then it may be desirable to allow for the difference in fat content.

If you are substituting cocoa for chocolate, add one tablespoon of shortening for every ounce of chocolate. If you are substituting chocolate for cocoa, reduce the other shortening in the recipe in the same proportion.

Storage. If chocolate is stored where the temperature is 80° F or higher, its butter may melt and some of it will then separate and move to the surface. When cooled again, the chocolate will probably have a grey or white surface appearance, it will be more fragile and there may be a change in flavor. This may be found agreeable or otherwise in eating chocolate, and can affect results in cooking slightly. But the color returns to normal when it is melted.

Mixing. Chocolate does not dissolve in or mix well with other substances unless it is melted. This may be done before or after mixing.

Fig. 16-10. Cups and instant coffee

Chocolate will melt safely if you put it in the top of a small double boiler over hot water, or in a container in a very slow oven, for a few minutes. It is likely to boil and burn on direct heat, even turned low. Melted chocolate is a thick sticky liquid, and there is likely to be waste or tedious scraping getting it from a pan into the mixture where it is used.

It may be easier to melt the chocolate in water or milk over low heat. This can be done with chunks, but it is much faster and easier if you first shave the chunks into 1/8-inch slices, which will crumble, or grate it coarsely. First heat a small quantity of fluid, perhaps 1/4 to 1/2 cup for each ounce, add the chocolate and stir over low heat for a minute or two. If it is milk chocolate, use a double boiler.

Using 1/4 cup will give you a very thick liquid that may be difficult to blend with other substances, while 1/2 cup makes it more manageable. But don't use much more, as then sections of chocolate may tend to float around independently, and be difficult to corner and mix in.

Cocoa seldom offers a mixing problem, as you can sift or stir it into dry ingredients, or into a small part of the wet ingredients until smooth and liquid enough to blend with the rest of the batch. Or you can dissolve it more rapidly in hot liquid in the same manner as chocolate.

COFFEE

Coffee is important chiefly as a beverage, and is discussed in that section. But it is also used as a flavoring in jelly, frosting, milk drinks and a wide variety of desserts. Ground coffee beans must be brewed into a beverage before use as a flavoring, since they include residues with unpleasant tastes, but instant coffee can be used directly. Its brewing was done at the factory.

Coffee measurement is uncertain. Recent recipes may give quantities in terms of spoons of instant coffee powder, which is definite. Older ones tell you about cups or perhaps spoons of strong coffee, which raises two questions. Strong coffee is an individual concept, meaning one thing to someone who likes espresso and quite another to someone who is nervous about insomnia. A measuring cup holds 8 ounces, a coffee cup 5 or 6.

A reasonable standard of coffee strength is that 5-1/2 ounces of hot water mixed with a slightly rounded teaspoon (1-1/3 to 1-1/2 level teaspoons) of instant coffee powder will produce coffee beverage of ordinary strength. This would be 2 teaspoons to the 8-ounce measuring cup. Fifty per cent more coffee (or 1/3 less water) should produce strong coffee. You can use these proportions for the recipe, and for comparing with brewed coffee.

Instant coffee powder can be mixed with dry ingredients or carefully with liquids. It dissolves readily in hot water and with moderate difficulty in cold. But like other fine powders, it is capable of forming little balls that resist solution for quite a while. If it is poorly mixed with water and then stirred in with non-liquid ingredients, such balls might persist and upset the flavor balance. Make sure they are eliminated, by crushing them with a spoon or by vigorous stirring.

Freeze-dried coffee particles are coarse and irregular in size, so they do not mix thoroughly with dry materials. But they dissolve easily in either hot or cold water, without forming lumps.

Coffee is very bitter. A recipe should provide some sweetening to offset it, unless the amount is small.

As a general guide (to be ignored if you have more specific information), for each 8-ounce measuring cup of more or less neutral flavored food, such as gelatin, milk shake, custard, or ice cream, use instant coffee at the rate of 1/2 teaspoon for mild, a teaspoon for moderate and 2 teaspoons for strong flavor.

SUGAR

Chemically, there are many different kinds of sugar. They are carbohydrates closely related to starch, with a tendency to have a sweet taste and to be soluble in cold water. One of these, sucrose, is of much more importance in cookery than all the rest together.

Other sugars include lactose, found chiefly in milk; fructose (levulose) in fruit; dextrose (glucose) which is a basic substance in plant and animal metabolism and is the principal ingredient of corn syrup; and maltose, which is obtained by fermenting grain. Figure 16-11 indicates the official ratings of relative sweetness of these sugars, using sucrose at 100 as a standard. However, many people do not find that dextrose tastes sweet at all.

Sugar is a very popular flavoring and food, and is a good source of energy. Use of it is generally considered to be excessive, however, as it contains no vitamins, displaces more nourishing food from the diet and causes tooth decay.

Sucrose (White Sugar). In a cookbook and in ordinary speech, the unmodified word "sugar" means granulated white sugar, a highly refined sucrose (99.9 per cent pure) in small crystals. It is obtained from the juice of either sugar cane or sugar beets, and may be referred to as cane sugar in either case.

Sugar	Sweetness Value
Sucrose	100
Levulose	140 - 175
Invert	100 - 130
Dextrose (Glucose)	60 - 75
Corn syrup	30 - 60
Maltose	30
Lactose (Milk sugar)	15

Fig. 16-11. Sweetness of sugar

Sugar is very important in the human diet and in cooking processes. It is primarily a sweetener, but it may also be used partly or wholly for nourishment, as the principal substance in candy, and as a preservative, tenderizer, stabilizer, juice extractor, coloring agent or decoration. It is marketed in several forms which differ chiefly in fineness of particles.

The coarsest of these forms is rock candy, formed by the gradual growth of crystals on strings suspended in a supersaturated solution. These crystals may be an inch or more in diameter, are transparent and are eaten as candy to a very limited extent. They may be crushed into fine pieces for scattering on top of cookies.

Next come very small cubes and other coarse crystals, sometimes dyed different colors, that are used as decorations. They may be known as sanding sugar.

Granulated is the coarsest sugar in common use. Its largest crystals are about 1/32 inch in length. Verifine or superfine consists of smaller crystals, which have much greater surface area in proportion to their bulk, which permits them to dissolve faster. This is an advantage when sugar is used to sweeten drinks, particularly cold ones, as less waiting and stirring is needed.

Verifine sometimes seems to be markedly sweeter than granulated. A sample placed on the tongue will dissolve more rapidly,

Fig. 16-12. Softening brown sugar

supplying more sugar molecules to the saliva and therefore more sweetness. If sugar is beaten into cream or white of egg, there may not be enough water in the bubble films in contact with each crystal to dissolve it fully.

The greater number of small crystals will provide more locally sweetened areas, and therefore a greater sensation of sweetness, than larger ones. This difference reduces as the whipped product stands, as the granulated size crystals gradually dissolve and become dispersed in the fluff.

Powdered sugar is much finer than verifine, averaging about 1/5 the particle size. It is usually made by grinding ordinary crystals, and then screening to a particular size. It dissolves faster than verifine, and therefore may seem sweeter.

Powdered sugar is used in making icings in which any graininess would be undesirable, in dusting over sweet baked goods such as doughnuts, cookies or plain cake and as a substitute for flour in preventing cookie dough from sticking as it is rolled. It is also convenient for sweetening drinks.

The finest ground sugar is confectioners'. It has a tendency to form lumps, which is sometimes counteracted by mixing with up to 3 per cent of starch. It is used chiefly in icing and candy.

Uses. Most of the uses of sugar are discussed in other parts of the book, but this is a good place to review them together, briefly.

The sweetening characteristic is of course used to make food sweet, and it makes sugar the principal ingredient in candy, and

an important one in most desserts. In the same connection, it may be used to point up, modify or overcome an acid taste.

In addition, small amounts may be used in gravy to enrich the flavor, in leftover vegetables to freshen them and to improve batches of carrots, peas or other sweet vegetables that for some reason lack their natural sweetness.

In strong concentrations it kills microorganisms by absorbing water out of their cells.

Small to moderate amounts of sugar tend to tenderize wheat and egg proteins, and to improve texture of cake and custard. Moderate to large amounts of sugar stabilize beaten white of egg or cream, reducing or eliminating tendency to shrink and weep. Larger amounts react with pectin and acid to make jelly.

Sugar mixed with or sprinkled on fruit or berries draws juice out of them by osmosis, providing syrup in which they may be eaten or cooked. It turns brown (caramellizes) when heated, a subject discussed below under Caramel. Both the ordinary and special sugars may enhance the appearance of desserts or candy when sprinkled on top of them.

Brown Sugar. Brown sugar consists of fine crystals of cane sugar with molasses syrup adhering to them. The color depends on that of the molasses. The darker variety has a more pronounced flavor.

If this sugar is exposed to dry air, moisture evaporates from the molasses, causing it to thicken and cement the grains into a hard lump. The original brown sugar package is carefully wrapped to avoid loss of moisture. Once opened, you should keep it in a plastic bag.

If exposed to humid air, the sugar will slowly absorb moisture and the lumps will disappear. An easy method is to put the sugar and a small container of water in a plastic bag or a box. Softening may take a few hours or a day or more.

If you don't have that much time, you can pound or crush the lumps with a hammer or a rolling pin, or pulverize them by rubbing on a grater. If the pieces are small, you can spread them on a pan, add a wet cloth and place in a warm oven for a few minutes. Re-dampen the cloth if it dries.

Brown sugar fluffs up into a loose structure when disturbed. It should be pushed down into a measuring cup firmly enough so that it will keep its shape when dumped out. You use about 1/5 more of it than white sugar for the same sweetening effect.

Brown sugar is used to give special flavor to a variety of desserts, and in making syrup. The flavor is not as generally acceptable as that of white sugar. It is chemically more acid, and may contain traces of minerals and vitamins.

Two grades, or perhaps colors, are manufactured for home use; light brown or #8 and dark brown, #13. The lighter color is more widely available, and is probably indicated in a recipe unless the dark kind is specified. You can match the light sugar fairly closely by mixing the dark half and half with granulated.

There is also a granulated brown sugar (Brownulated®) which has the handling characteristics of granulated white sugar in that it pours freely under ordinary conditions and does not change bulk appreciably when packed down. It is between light and dark brown sugars in flavor. In substituting for packed measures of either regular brown sugar, increase the measurement by about 1/3.

Invert Sugar. Sucrose or cane sugar is a disaccharide, meaning that it is a chemical combination of two simpler sugars. When heated in a solution in the presence of acid, or when treated with enzymes, it combines with a little water and separates into the two sugars, dextrose and fructose. The mixture is called invert sugar.

After this change it resists crystallization and has an increased tendency to absorb and retain moisture. Invert sugar is used in food manufacture, and is created in some foods — dark chocolate cake, for example — as an incident in the cooking process.

Other Sugars. There are some non-sucrose sugars that are sometimes used in the home, but usually in small quantities.

Dextrose (glucose) is supposed to be about 3/5 as sweet as cane sugar, but many people find it almost tasteless. It can sometimes be bought in packages, and is the principal ingredient in corn syrup. Other sugars and starch are largely converted to glucose during digestion and assimilation.

Maple sugar, consisting mostly of sucrose, is very sweet, with a unique and highly esteemed flavor. It can be obtained in hard blocks, as soft candy and as a residue when maple syrup evaporates. It is used as a flavoring, and is dissolved in water to make syrup.

Maple syrup, honey and molasses are described under SYRUP, page 375.

Caramel. Sugar changes in color, taste, and chemistry when it is heated. If you put granulated sugar in a dry frypan or heavy saucepan over moderate heat and stir or shake it constantly, it will darken in color. When it turns light amber color it is called caramel, and is used in making caramel syrup or sauce.

If you continue to heat it until it is medium or dark brown it will be almost flavorless, and is suitable for coloring gravy or stew. If allowed to blacken it will acquire an acrid or disagreeable taste, and will melt, boil and char on the pan.

These changes in color and flavor are not

Fig. 16-13. Synthetic flavors are being studied suspiciously

confined to plain sugar heated in a pan, but tend to happen to any kind of sugar, anywhere, that is heated sufficiently and is not dominated by other chemicals.

Sugar in some form is present in small quantities in most foods, or can be formed in them by natural alteration of starch. Caramelization of sugar is a major factor in the formation of crisp, brown and tasty crusts on food that is cooked with dry heat. It is often influenced by the presence of other substances in the food.

SYNTHETIC FLAVORS

A synthetic flavoring may be an artificial non-organic copy of a natural flavoring, or a wholly or partly new flavor.

Copies. A natural flavor is likely to be a mixture of a number of substances, each of them with a very complicated molecular structure. Analyzing and then building such molecules in the laboratory may be difficult and tedious, and commercial production

might be more expensive than harvesting and processing the natural substance.

Synthetic flavorings are therefore seldom an exact duplicate of the whole original. It may copy one molecule with the characteristic taste and/or smell and fail to imitate the rest of the compound; or it may be a quite different chemical that happens to have a similar taste.

As a result, most synthetic flavors are not good imitations. They are usually much cheaper to make than the natural products, but the cost difference in home cooking is negligible, and there is no reason for using most of them, as long as the genuine ones are available.

If it is necessary to flavor artificially, the amount should be kept to a minimum, as differences may not be noticeable in a faint flavor, but become unpleasantly apparent when it is strong.

It is said that there are new and very accurate synthetic flavors that have been developed in laboratories but they have not been successfully marketed.

Substitutes. An expensive flavoring substance may be replaced by another natural flavor, or a compound of natural flavors, that is similar but not identical to the original. As an example, beef extract is partly or wholly replaced by an extract of vegetable protein in a number of beef concentrates. There may be a synthetic beef extract in the compound also.

The flavor of vegetable protein is in the same class as that of beef, but distinctly different. A person expecting a beef taste might be annoyed or even nauseated by it, while tolerating or even enjoying it if it were introduced as an entirely different flavor.

The sales of products containing it show that it has a wide acceptance, but it tends to be associated with cheap restaurants and canned food, so that it should be used with caution in the home.

Non-sugar Sweeteners. They are synthetic sweetening compounds which are

Fig. 16-14. Start mixing food coloring on the side

cheaper than sugar, but whose wide use is based on diet and health advantages, rather than on economy. They supply sweetness without calories and with very little bulk.

The traditional synthetic sweetener is saccharin. It is powerful but uneven in its effect. There is a bitter component that most people can sense as an aftertaste, particularly in strong dosages. And there are some who taste the bitterness rather than the sweetness right away.

Sodium cyclamate is much more satisfactory. Most people can appreciate its sweetness without disagreeable side tastes. It has enjoyed wide popularity in foods and drinks for reducing and sugar-free diets, and in other places where the bulk, cost or some chemical activity of sugar were undesirable. There is no evidence that it is harmful to humans, although some discomfort may follow excessive use.

Unfortunately, it has been shown that massive doses of it may cause bladder cancers in rats. According to law, this prevents it from being used in human food. It has been withdrawn from the general market, so that its use is largely restricted to doctor-

supervised diets. It will probably be replaced by other chemicals of similar type.

Synthetic sweeteners are unsatisfactory, or at least very tricky, to use in cooking at home. They provide none of sugar's expected and generally useful side effects. They are good for sweetening either hot or cold beverages only when people like them. Their disadavantage is that they do not supply sugar to raise its level in the blood, and may therefore not give the lift that is often the reason for drinking the beverage.

Monosodium Glutamate. Monosodium glutamate is a non-food chemical that has the characteristics of sharpening or accentuating natural flavors, although it has no distinct flavor of its own. It seems to be harmless in the amounts recommended on packages (Accent, for example), but in heavy doses it causes headache and other unpleasant symptoms in sensitive people, and it is said to have caused brain damage in experimental animals.

Some people feel that the flavor benefits provided by this chemical are a necessary part of good living, while others cannot detect any difference from its use. In general, it might be assumed that it is not needed with good food that is properly prepared, but that anyone who wishes to use it is certainly entitled to do so.

COLORING

A variety of artificial colorings are made for use in food. They are very strong dyes, soluble in water and readily mixed with or soaked into most kinds of food. They are flavorless and safe to eat, but quite risky to use.

The palatability of food is greatly affected by color. We associate certain colors with certain foods, and discrepancies may be confusing and disturbing. A lack of color, or dull, muddy or confusing colors, tends to make food unappetizing, but colors that are too brilliant or just unexpected may awake an alarm reaction that will destroy appetite completely. Bright colors in food are usually thought to have a poisonous appearance, and must be avoided.

Colors are often added to cake icing, to go with a flavoring, as green for mint or red for strawberry, or just for decoration. Ice cream or sherbet is dyed for flavor indication, but seldom for decoration alone. The attractiveness of the food can be improved in this way, but only if great restraint is used. The colors should be kept down to delicate tints.

Colorings may be bought in either liquid or paste form. The liquid should be used only one drop at a time, each mixed in to observe the effect before adding the next drop. Paste is usually more potent, and it is safest to dilute a little of it in water, and put the solution in drop by drop. For safety, mix either one with a small quantity of the food, then mix that with the rest, a little at a time.

TEMPERATURE

Temperature is not ordinarily discussed as a flavoring, but it is one of the most important of them. A moderate change in it

Fig. 16-15. Ice may be a flavoring

can alter the taste and acceptability of food and beverages drastically. The effect is partly that of emphasizing or dulling existing flavors, and partly a matter of custom and association.

Flavors tend to be most distinct at medium temperature. Below 40 or even 50° they tend to become progressively weaker, both because of the effect of chilling on the taste mechanism and the reduction in activity of the flavor substances. But many foods and drinks require chilling to make them pleasing to the majority taste. This effect of cooling is usually counteracted by increasing the quantity or strength of the flavoring.

Cold. Substances ordinarily served cold, that is, below 40°, include many beverages such as water, fruit juice, fruit-flavored and carbonated drinks, beer, highballs and many cocktails, milk and milk mixtures and iced tea and coffee. It is usual to chill white wine but to serve red wine at room temperature

Ice cream, sherbet and a variety of frozen desserts may be served at anywhere from 32° down to below zero, with a resultant wide range in taste and texture. They are seldom served at very low temperatures from choice, but simply because they keep best when very cold, and are served directly from storage.

There is considerable difference of opinion about proper temperature for serving fruit, particularly melons. The flavor is undoubtedly best, or at least strongest and most characteristic, at or near room temperature, but coolness is desirable in itself, and to many is more than worth any loss of flavor that it causes.

Frozen food, or sometimes even chilled food, may cause numbing of the mouth and unpleasant and even painful digestive reactions. This is a highly individual matter, as some people will suffer severely and others will never be bothered at all.

Chilled food warms rather gradually after serving, unless speeded up by very hot atmosphere. An exception is any beverage containing ice, which will stay at about 32° until most of the ice is melted.

Hot. Hot food usually leaves the cooking process at temperatures between 180 and 212°, but cools considerably during serving and before eating. The average person may tolerate a temperature as high as 160° in a slow-conducting or low-specific-heat substance such as a muffin, if taken in small bites, but be limited to 140° or less in a moist food such as mashed potato or a beverage.

Other people have much higher or lower tolerances. Cocoa may taste painfully hot at a temperature at which coffee can be enjoyed.

The effect of extreme heat is to almost destroy flavor, but most foods that are served hot taste best when they are just below an uncomfortable temperature. Cooling to a lukewarm condition may (or may not) take away much of its taste appeal. This may be due to changes in flavor, to physical alterations such as solidifying of grease, or be a matter of the attitude of the consumer.

Mixed. A special taste sensation may be obtained by having food of two or more temperatures in the mouth at the same time. A good example is Baked Alaska, described under DESSERTS. When this is fresh from the oven, you can eat hot meringue, cold ice cream and neutral-temperature cake at one bite.

An easier way to relish variety in heat is to pour a room-temperature drink into a glass filled with ice cubes, let it stand for 30 seconds to a minute and then drink it. Some parts of the liquid will be ice cold, others seemingly warm, and they will be mixed but not blended on your tongue.

TEXTURE

Texture is another non-flavor item with important flavor influence. Texture is the characteristic of being smooth, grainy, lumpy or ropy; tender, firm, chewy, gluey or tough; crisp, flaky or soggy; heavy or light, and so forth. Some of these words may evoke taste sensations just from reading them, usually because of association

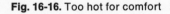

Fig. 16-16. Too hot for comfort

with foods of which they are characteristic.

A change in texture may seem to either improve or spoil a flavor. Undoubtedly, some combinations are good and others are not. But this is often a matter of training. Grainy fudge is called "sandy" and is generally unacceptable, because fudge is smooth when properly made. But the grainy structure of a bran cooky or muffin is enjoyed.

In general, the most desirable texture in a food is that which the customers expect. If changes are to be made, it is likely to be safer to make them in the direction of smoothness, tenderness, flakiness or lightness rather than their opposites.

ANTI-FLAVORS

Flavors may be weakened or cancelled by other substances in a mixture. The balancing of sugar and acid, one working against the other, has already been mentioned.

A flavor is of course weakened by being diluted. If you keep adding small quantities of water to a good-tasting beverage, you will weaken the flavor, and it is possible that you will create a different taste which might well be an unpleasant one.

In a food, vanilla can be diluted until it disappears without becoming unpleasant at any time, but an increase in its strength will quickly create a disagreeable taste. On the other hand, very weak coffee flavor may seem to be an off-taste, but it can be extremely strong without change in its basic character.

Thickeners such as gelatin and starch weaken flavor by building its chemicals into their own molecules, so that they cannot dissolve in the mouth as readily.

17
THICKENERS

THICKENERS AND GELS

This is a very important group of materials in food preparation. It includes a number of widely different substances that can cause liquids to thicken and/or solidify. The principal types are found in eggs, pectin, gelatin, starch and rennin.

Their discussion involves a few special words. Gelatinization is the change that occurs when a molecule starts to absorb large quantities of water into its structure. This results in thickening the liquid as water is withdrawn from it and as the molecules enlarge and soften.

Gel when used as a verb means to change to a jelly, or to set, or sometimes just to thicken. The usual meaning is the same as jell, and the words are used interchangeably. When used as a noun it means any structureless solid or colloid made up chiefly of water. Jelly, Jell-O, baked custard, junket, cornstarch pudding and cold consomme are gels. The first two and the last one are also jellies.

A gel or a gelling process is said to be reversible when the substance can be returned to its original liquid or thin state by some simple method, such as reheating.

Eggs. Egg proteins solidify when they are cooked. If raw egg is included in a mixture that is heated, its change from liquid to solid will thicken the mixture, changing a thin fluid to a thick one, or perhaps to a solid. Both white and yolk have this property, but it is more strongly developed in the white. Gelatinization starts at 140 to 150° F.

If eggs or an egg mixture are added suddenly to a hot fluid, parts of the egg may harden immediately into lumps that will be of no use in the thickening process and then become a nuisance in the completed food.

This difficulty is avoided by adding some of the hot fluid to the eggs with immediate stirring, thus warming and diluting them so that they will not form lumps as readily or at all when stirred vigorously into the remainder of the heated material.

Gelatin. Gelatin is a protein that is obtained by processing collagen and similar substances in the connective tissue in animal skins and bones. Extraction may be done by hot water, but is aided by the presence of either acid or alkali.

Some gelatin is extracted as a side effect

Fig. 17-1. Some thickeners

of cooking meat. The amount varies with the collagen in the meat, and with the cooking method. As a result of this, unprocessed pan gravy may be expected to separate when cold into an upper layer of fat and a lower one of jelly. The jelly usually has a delicate texture and a rich meat flavor.

Gelatin does not dissolve in cold water, but it absorbs some of it, and softens and swells. It dissolves readily if the water is heated to 120° F. However, the powder must be dissolved in two stages. First it is mixed with cold water (about 1/4 cup to the tablespoon of gelatin) and allowed to soften for a minute. Then the water is heated, usually by adding hot liquid.

If the gelatin is put directly in heated water the powder clumps together and becomes difficult to dissolve, and builds a varnish-like deposit on the sides of the container. Mixing with another powder, such as sugar, may make possible direct dissolving in warm water.

When the solution cools, it sets or solidifies to a gel or jelly, the firmness of which is determined largely by the proportion of gelatin, but is affected by the temperature and the presence of other substances. The product, which is also called gelatin, ranges from the softness of semi-liquid desserts to the hardness of medicine capsules.

Under favorable conditions, it can form a gel when it is only 1/2 of one per cent of the fluid. For household use, a proportion of one tablespoon to one pint (1 to 22, or about 5 per cent) is usual.

Prepared gelatin is widely sold in packages of envelopes that each contain one scant tablespoon. It is the basic material for molded salads and desserts. In addition, it is used in smaller quantities as a stabilizer to prevent separation and crystallization of mixtures, particularly ones that are to be frozen, or stored for a long time.

A jelly made of gelatin and water will soften if warmed and liquefy if heated, and will usually re-gel if cooled. The reaction can be reversed this way a number of times. The temperature at which changes take place is affected by the percentage of gelatin — the more gelatin, the higher the temperature. A weak mixture may be firm in the refrigerator and sloppy at room temperature, while a strong one might be stable but too firm and rubbery for eating pleasure.

An exposed surface of gelatin tends to dry out slowly, forming a tough skin with changes in color and shape. It should be covered if it is to stand for more than a few hours.

Jell-O is the trade name for a very popular brand of gelatin-plus-flavoring. But the same name is also used for other dessert

Fig. 17-2. A tablespoon of gelatin gels a pint of water

Fig. 17-3. Seaweed is a source of thickeners

roducts, which are distinguished by additional specific names.

Pectin. Pectin is a complicated carbohyrate found naturally in most fruits. The ommercial variety, which may be in either quid or powder form, is a concentrate made hiefly from waste material such as citrus kins, apple pulp left after cider extraction nd beet chips after processing for sugar.

Pectin is a moderately effective thickening agent, but only when it is mixed with oth acid and sugar. It may then be able to orm a jelly even when it is only one per ent of the mixture. Most fruit contains oth acid and pectin, so that if it is cooked ith sugar and cooled it should set into jam coarse parts are included, or into jelly if nly the juice is used.

The quantity of both pectin and acid in uit is variable. The pectin in unripe fruit largely in an insoluble form, and the extent of its conversion into the active form is ffected by conditions of ripening. It may eteriorate or disappear with full ripening, pe fruit may not contain sufficient acid, nd it may be so sweet that not enough ugar is added.

An experienced jelly maker will usually clude both ripe and not-quite-ripe fruit in very batch, thus making sure of the presnce of both acid and pectin. He will also avoid a too-high temperature or too long a cooking time, as they can destroy pectin.

As a result of these complications, jelly that depends on natural pectin may fail to set, and need to be re-cooked.

Commercial pectin may be added to make sure that jelly will set. If the natural conditions are favorable for jelling, this addition can make the product too hard. However, this is a smaller risk than not having it jell at all.

This subject is discussed further under JELLY, page 621.

Vegetable Gums. There are a number of vegetable gums and mucilages that are used as thickeners and gelling or smoothing agents in commercially prepared foods. They include agar and Irish moss (carrageenin), both prepared from seaweed or algae; gum arabic, karaya and tragacanth.

They have valuable properties, but are complicated in application and should not be used in the home except by very experienced cooks.

STARCH

Starch is one of mankind's principal foods. It is also the most important and versatile of the thickeners for both food preparation and industry. It is present in most plants, and is the major substance in grain

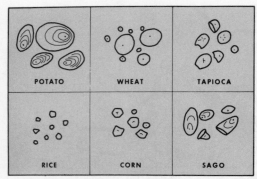

Fig. 17-4b. Layers in potato starch granules

and in most root vegetables. Here we are interested in its behavior as a thickener.

Starch is a very complex substance, and each plant builds it in a slightly different structure. But it is all made up in two ways from molecules of dextrose, a natural, simple and not-particularly-sweet sugar, which in turn is manufactured in green leaves and sunlight from water and carbon dioxide. Several hundred dextrose molecules may be attached to each other in an end-to-end chain. The starch formed in this way is called the linear chain or amylose fraction.

Or the chain may branch after about a dozen molecules, and the branch chains split

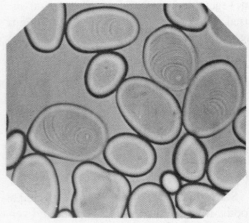

Fig. 17-4a. Microscopic appearance of common starch granules

into branches in turn, until a tree-like structure of several thousand molecules is built up. This starch fraction is called branched chain or amylopectin. Each plant produces starch that has a fixed proportion of these two fractions, and no two species of plants have the same proportion.

Iodine reacts with the linear fraction to form an intense blue, and with the branched molecules to form a red or plum color. This type of coloring is a sure indicator of the presence of starch, and the shade indicates the relative proportions.

The branched molecules, under proper conditions, cause a smooth thickening of liquids. The straight ones are less efficient thickeners, but cause gelling when the mixture cools. The behavior of any particular starch is determined by the proportions of the fractions, and by details in the construction of the molecules.

Molecules are combined into tiny granules, which may be built up in layers.

Photography in polarized light and in special wave lengths is used to study differences in starch structure.

In the plant, starch serves as a reserve supply of food, stored chiefly for use by germinating seeds or for next-season growth of the plant itself. Starch is insoluble in cold water, but is readily changed back to dextrose by a number of enzymes, one of which is found in our saliva, and by some chemicals.

The table opposite shows the approximate proportions of fractions in some of the more common starches.

Tapioca contains about 16 per cent of linear chains, potato starch 22 and cornstarch 27 per cent. From a practical standpoint, this means that tapioca will not form a solid jelly, potato starch might and cornstarch will. But there is also a special cornstarch made from waxy maize that is entirely the branched fraction, and which will not gel at all.

Sources. Starch may be present in smal

amounts throughout a plant, but it tends to be concentrated in specific storage areas, usually seeds or roots. It makes up the larger part of the bulk and the food value of grain seeds such as wheat, corn and rice; other seeds including beans, peas and peanuts (but these last three are also high in protein), and chestnuts and breadfruit. It is also the chief food in edible roots such as potatoes, yams and parsnips. All of these are sources of human food, and some of them are of dominating importance.

The starch that is most used as a thickener is white flour. This is not a pure starch, as it contains up to 15 per cent protein.

Almost pure starch for cooking purposes is extracted from corn, potatoes, arrowroot, rice, tapioca (cassava) and sago. Corn is the most important of these sources, and its starch has wide industrial use also.

General Properties. While each starch behaves in an individual manner, the similarities among them are more important than their differences. They are insoluble in cold water, but will soak up varying quantities of it, swelling and softening as they do.

If heated in water to a critical heat, called the gelatinizing temperature, starch dissolves in or combines with the water to produce a thickened liquid. This temperature

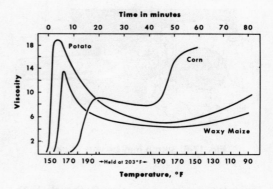

Fig. 17-5b. Cooking and cooling curves

is not a point, but is a range, and in any batch of starch, some of the granules will gelatinize at lower temperatures than others.

The gelatinizing process may take from 3 to 20 minutes, depending on the variety, purity and fineness of the starch, the temperature, presence of other substances and other factors.

If the mixture is heated to a higher temperature, if it is held for a long time in the gelatinizing range or if it is stirred vigorously, the greatly extended starch molecules start to break up, releasing the trapped water and allowing the viscosity of the solution to decrease.

Figure 17-5 shows changes in thickness of solutions of 3 starches in water, as they are heated through gelatinization to 203° F, held there and then allowed to cool. In all cases, the holding period caused some thinning, which would have been more severe if the solutions had been stirred. The recovery of the corn starch was due to its ability to form a gel, which is lacking in potato and waxy maize starches.

Refined starch is usually bought in the form of a fine powder, or in small pellets. Powder has a tendency to absorb moisture and become lumpy. Lumps should be mashed or pressed through a sieve before using.

More importantly, it will also form lumps when mixed with hot liquid, which may be

Type of Starch	Per cent of Amylose (linear fraction)	Gelatinizing Temperature, Fahrenheit
Arrowroot	23	154 - 167
Corn	27	144 - 162
Waxy corn (amioca)	0	144 - 162
Potato	22	136 - 155
Rice	18	147 - 167
Sago	25	158
Tapioca	17	126 - 147
Wheat	25	136 - 147

Courtesy of Corn Industries Research Foundation

Fig. 17-5a. Starch characteristics

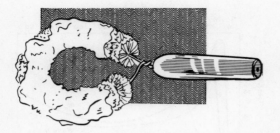

Fig. 17-6. Starch may be very sticky

difficult to break up by stirring. Starch, both purified and in the form of white flour, is usually mixed in advance with a little cold water, to avoid lumps or to deal with them before they are distributed through a mixture.

Pure starch is almost tasteless. It is a good carrier for the flavor of some foods associated with it, either by nature or in cooking, but in general tends to have a diluting or blurring effect on them.

Anti-gels. A heavy concentration of sugar will delay or prevent proper gelatinization of some starches. If starch is to be used in any mixture containing a large amount of sugar, some of the sugar should be kept back until the mixture has thickened, after which the sugar will do no harm.

For example, a pie filling might call for 7 times as much sugar as corn starch. If it is all put together at once the starch will not gelatinize completely even though normal cooking time is extended, and the product may be dull, mushy and thin. But if the sugar is originally limited to 3 times the amount of starch, the granules will swell almost completely, the balance of the sugar can then be added, and the filling should be clear, glossy and heavy bodied.

Acid also affects starch behavior. A weak acid will speed up the original thickening of a mixture, but also will cause it to break down and thin out abnormally. A strongly acid or alkaline material may delay or prevent thickening, and will cause rapid thinning of any good body that is obtained.

Undercooked starch tends to bleed, that is, water will separate from it leaving a lumpy liquid or a shrunken gel. This tendency is increased by refrigeration or freezing.

Paste. Starch makes excellent paste, and it is the prime raw material in the making of industrial adhesives. Anyone cooking with starch, or any material rich in starch, should always keep this in mind, because it can turn to paste in a kitchen as easily as in a factory.

Even uncooked starch can become somewhat sticky when wet. Cooked starch is very sticky, and overcooked starch is worse. Unless in a dilute solution, it sticks to pans and utensils, builds up in crevices, clots on brushes and even on knives used for cleaning and it dries into a hard solid firmly bonded to surfaces beneath.

Any tools or utensils used for starchy foods such as mashed potatoes, creamed corn or blanc mange should be cleaned immediately after use, preferably with a forceful spray of cold water. Hot water can be used, but it may continue its cooking and increase its stickiness. After thick deposits have been rinsed off, the remainder can be handled by normal methods.

Cold-Water-Swelling. If starch is cooked and then dried on heated rolls and drums, the product will swell and become viscous when it next comes in contact with either hot or cold water. This type of starch is used extensively in packaged instant puddings.

White Flour. General purpose white flour contains about 88 per cent wheat starch. It is the standard material for starch-thickening sauce and gravy. Its wide use may be partly due to its availability in practically every kitchen, but its stability, appearance and texture are good also. Its solutions are white and cloudy or opaque, giving a "cream" effect, and they solidify only if the concentration is very high.

The standard white or cream sauce described on page 357, which is simply a heated mixture of butter, flour and water, is the basis for a wide variety of more complicated sauces.

Ordinary flour tends to lump annoyingly when mixed with water. It is best to start by adding a little water to it in a small dish or shaker, to permit thorough mixing, and the crushing or straining out of any lumps.

Such lumps usually have a dry center surrounded by a water-resistant skin of wet flour. Lumps will not form again, once every grain of flour is wet.

If too much liquid has been added, so that the lumps cannot be caught to crush them, the mixture should be put in a sieve and drained and pushed through it. Or beat it in an electric blender.

Lumping is reduced in a flour-grease-water preparation by mixing the flour with the melted grease first, as in preparation of a roux for cream sauce.

There are specially processed instant-type flours (Gold Medal's Wondra for example) that mix very readily with water and almost eliminate the problem of formation of lumps.

Sauce or gravy thickened with flour will thin out seriously if heated too hot or too long, or stirred vigorously.

Arrowroot. Arrowroot is starch extracted from any one of a group of roots or tubers, most of which grow in the tropics. It is made up of very small granules, which may group together in balls. When heated with water it produces a fine, transparent thick liquid, which gels when cold if in sufficient strength.

Arrowroot is used chiefly in dessert and and salad mixtures where its fine texture and transparency are an advantage, and not in gravy where these same characteristics are usually unwanted.

In substituting for flour in a recipe, use 2-1/2 times as much arrowroot to obtain the same thickening.

Cornstarch (Corn Starch). Next to

Fig. 17-7. Crushing lumps through a sieve

white flour, cornstarch is the most used starch for food thickening. It is stronger — one spoonful of it does the thickening of 2 spoons of flour. It has a higher than average gelatinizing temperature and produces

Fig. 17-8. Cassava plant

a thickened liquid that is semi-transparent, smooth in texture and has good resistance to heat thinning. It tends to gel when its mixtures are cooled to room temperature.

Cornstarch is used rather often in sauces and occasionally in gravy where a smoother texture than that provided by flour is wanted. It is sometimes used instead of eggs, or in addition to them, in desserts where a thickener or gelling agent is wanted. It is used alone with water to make a dessert, cornstarch pudding or blanc mange. It is popular for thickening the filling in fruit pies.

Amioca is starch from a special variety of corn, waxy maize. This has been hybridized from Chinese plants, and gets its name from the appearance of cut kernels. It consists entirely of the branched fraction, and cannot be used in cornstarch pudding or any other gel. It is very effective as a thickener, but thins out quickly if overcooked.

Potato Starch. Potato starch gelatinizes quickly at a fairly low temperature. Its solutions are relatively transparent, and tend to be stringy or cohesive in texture. It breaks down seriously if overcooked. It is not very widely used at present.

Tapioca. Tapioca is made of refined starch from the root of the cassava, a widely cultivated tropical plant. The root is treated to remove bitter and poisonous chemicals, and finely ground into a flour which is very rich in starch. This is moistened, then heated with continuous stirring, so that the flour particles form small lumps, which are the tapioca of commerce.

The granules may be coarse (pearls) or fine. The fine type, sold as minute or quick-cooking tapioca, is the most common and is often the only size available.

The tapioca granules swell and soften during cooking, and part of their material dissolves in the water to thicken it. However, it usually does not quite lose its granular consistency, and the presence of small, soft translucent lumps is the distinguishing characteristic of tapioca, and of similarly processed sago.

Tapioca seldom forms big lumps, either in storage or in the mixing and cooking process. Its principal use is in desserts, particularly in tapioca pudding (see page 535) and as a thickener in fruit pies.

Sago. Sago is a starch obtained chiefly from the trunks of sago palms native to Indonesia. It is pulverized and then made up into granules similar to those of tapioca, and it is used in the same general way as tapioca. It is more widely used in northern Europe than in the United States.

18
SAUCE, GRAVY AND SYRUP

SAUCE

Sauce is usually a liquid that is added to a food when it is served, to improve its flavor, appearance and/or nutritive value. Hard sauce, however, is a solid. The liquid may be thin, so that it flows easily and soaks into the food, thick enough so that it will neither soak in nor flow away, or in any intermediate state. It is often thin when hot and thick when cold.

Milk and either plain or whipped cream are often used as sauce on cereals and desserts, but they are never given the name unless they are mixed with other ingredients. Sauce prepared from the cooking juices of meat is called gravy, not sauce, but it will be included in this chapter anyhow. Syrups are discussed after the sweet dessert sauces, although the greatest use for those made from cane sugar is in preserving food.

Salad dressings are really sauces.

The non-sweet sauces, aside from these dressings, are mostly variations on a basic white sauce made up of liquid, butter and flour. There is also the Hollandaise group, made up of butter, egg yolks and lemon juice. Melted butter, with or without sea-soning, is an excellent sauce. Those based on vinegar and oil belong in the salad group.

A dip is a very thick sauce that is served in a small dish, and scooped out with bite-size pieces of food such as potato chips, crackers or cold shrimp.

WHITE (CREAM) SAUCE

This basic sauce is made in four standard proportions, from light or thin to extra heavy. Thin sauce is made when further cooking is needed, as in casseroles. Medium is used directly on vegetables and fish, either alone or in combination with other foods such as cheese or egg. Heavy may be an ingredient in souffles, and extra heavy is a binder in croquette and other mixtures.

These four weights of sauce are made up in proportions given on the next page.

Mixing and Cooking. Procedure is the same for any of these. Melt the butter in a small saucepan, preferably a heavy one, over moderate heat, add flour and salt and stir until smooth. At this point the mixture is known as roux.

Turn the heat low, then add milk slowly, stirring constantly. The milk will cause the roux to stiffen and ball up, and the stirring must mix this paste smoothly with the milk. This is one of the many times a cook (particularly a new one) feels the need of three hands. One is needed to pour the milk, one to stir and one to hold the pan steady.

The third hand would not be needed if the pan were heavy enough to stay in place against the moderate disturbance of the stirring. A large pan would take care of it, but the greater bottom area will multiply your problem with stiffening and lumping. A small iron frypan would be excellent, but it is likely to have food film or particles that would spoil the appearance of the sauce, unless you cleaned it thoroughly enough to spoil its non-stick surface.

So you have to do the best you can, using one hand continuously for stirring, and dividing the time of the other between pouring and holding. Stir lightly while you are not holding.

Stirring may be done with a spoon, is better with a fork and best with a whisk, provided it is shaped to reach into the angle between the bottom and the sides of the pan. If it is not, you might still use it, and scrape out the angle occasionally with a spoon.

Continue stirring until sauce boils, and then for about 2 minutes until it becomes thick and smooth. If if contains lumps you can probably smooth them out by vigorous churning with a whisk or a rotary beater. Or you can pour it through a sieve into another pan, pushing any lumps through with the back of a spoon.

Fig. 18-1. All you need is three hands

Instant-type flour almost never forms lumps.

Longer Cooking. For the average user, the white sauce is now complete. But there are people and cookbooks who want it cooked another 20 minutes, in a 350° oven or in the top of a double boiler, covered, although this may cause overcooking of the starch with thinning of the sauce, and formation of a thick upper layer that will form lumps unless beaten back in, or sieved. Never leave this sauce standing over direct heat without stirring, as it sticks and

	White (Cream) Sauce (makes one cup)			
Ingredients	Quantities			
	Thin	Medium	Heavy	Extra Heavy
Milk	1 cup	1 cup	1 cup	1 cup
Butter	1 Tb	2 Tb	3 Tb	4 Tb
Flour	1 Tb	2 Tb	3 Tb	4 Tb
Salt (optional)	⅛ tsp	⅛ tsp	⅛ tsp	⅛ tsp

scorches easily, particularly in the thicker types.

Any of these white sauces can be slightly enriched, thickened and tinted by stirring in a lightly beaten egg yolk just before taking it off the heat.

Uses. Plain white sauce is a pleasant addition to a wide variety of foods, either as a regular custom, or occasionally for variety. The list includes asparagus, broccoli, brussel sprouts, carrots, cauliflower, mushrooms, okra, boiled potatoes and fish.

It is also used in the final cooking of some of these items, and in a variety of casserole dishes.

A number of sauces with special names are made by mixing small quantities of other foods with white sauce, or by simple changes in ingredients.

OTHER FLOUR-THICKENED SAUCES

Make either thin or medium white sauce (or halfway between them), cut two hard boiled eggs into either fine or coarse pieces, and stir into the sauce as soon as it has thickened. You can flavor it slightly with a dash of pepper, a drop or two of Worcestershire sauce and/or 1/4 to 1/2 teaspoon of lemon juice, but it is good enough without them.

Egg sauce is particularly good with boiled fish.

Cheese. For a cheese sauce, make thin or medium white sauce and add 1/4 to 1 cup of grated cheese, preferably sharp Cheddar. The amount depends on how cheesy you like it. Add it after the sauce has thickened, and stir over heat until the cheese has entirely melted.

You can also get a reasonably good cheese sauce by heating concentrated Cheddar soup, or you can use this soup to flavor your white sauce.

Other Additions. You can make a horseradish sauce by simply adding 3 or 4 teaspoons of prepared horseradish to a one-

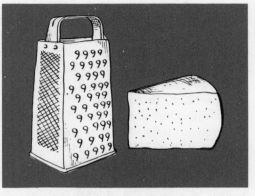

Fig. 18-2. Grate cheese for easy mixing into sauce

cup batch of thin or medium white sauce. This is not the only way, or even the best way to make it, but it is the simplest.

Another method is to whip 1/2 cup of cream, add 1/4 teaspoon of salt and 2 or 3 tablespoons of horseradish. A dash of red pepper can be added to either of these to increase the bite. Horseradish is considered appropriate for beef, corned beef, and ham, and sometimes for hamburgers or croquettes.

Velouté. This is a heavy white sauce in which the milk is replaced by chicken broth or concentrated chicken soup, strained to remove any rice and meat. After it has thickened, remove from the heat and thin it with about 1/4 cup of light cream. It is used chiefly with chicken and veal, and can be considered either a sauce or a cream gravy.

Béchamel. For this fancy name, you get a sauce halfway between white and velouté. Use half chicken broth and half milk or cream in any of the white sauce recipes. It is often enriched with a slightly beaten egg yolk, stirred into the sauce just after cooking.

Brown Sauce. Brown sauce, which might be said to be a meatless gravy, is a cream sauce in which the butter, the flour or both have been scorched. There are three different ways to do this.

You can brown the flour ahead of time. Spread white flour about 1/4 inch deep on the bottom of a clean frypan. Place over moderate heat and stir frequently until the flour takes on an even tan color. If not for immediate use you can store it in any moisture-proof bag or container.

Browning develops a special flavor, and the browned flour will color gravy or sauce in which it is used. But its thickening power is reduced by half. In any recipe calling for flour as a thickening agent (the white sauce recipes, for example), double the quantity if the flour is light brown. It becomes almost useless except for color if it is dark.

The next approach is to brown the butter in the pan, before you add plain white flour. Stir it so the browning will be even, and add the flour as soon as you have the color you want.

Finally, you can brown flour and butter together. Just keep stirring them on the heat until they have color, then add the milk. The problem here is deciding how much extra flour to use, as part of the color is from the butter. You will be safest to use double quantity, for if you are wrong it is easier to thin the sauce with milk than to thicken it with more flour.

There are no particular advantages to brown sauce, but it is good to know how to make it in case it is called for in a recipe. And if you substitue concentrated broth or consomme for the milk, it makes a passable gravy.

HOLLANDAISE

Hollandaise is a rich, highly esteemed sauce consisting basically of butter, egg yolks and lemon juice. Recipes and special instructions are highly variable, and it is considered risky to make because the butter and yolks are an uneasy combination that will separate or curdle at the slightest excuse. Fortunately, curdling does not harm the flavor, and it can usually be easily corrected after it occurs.

The following is a typical recipe:

Hollandaise Sauce

½ cup	butter *(¼ pound)*
3	egg yolks
3 Tb	hot water
1 Tb	lemon juice
¼ tsp	salt *(optional)*
	cayenne or black pepper *(optional)*

Put water in the bottom of a double boiler, but not enough to reach the upper pan. Bring to boil, turn down heat until it simmers. Put on top pan and melt the butter in it. Beat egg yolks thoroughly in a small bowl, then slowly pour melted butter into them while stirring steadily, preferably with a whisk. Return the empty pan to the double boiler to keep hot.

Add the hot (many recipes say boiling) water slowly to the egg-butter mixture, still stirring. Then pour it from the bowl into the pan, and stir it steadily and thoroughly until it thickens, probably in 2 to 5 minutes. The thickness will be only that of medium cream, and it is unlikely to increase with further cooking. Take pan away from its under section immediately, and stir lemon juice and any seasoning into the sauce.

The sauce may thicken on the bottom and in the edges of the pan, so that the spoon will scrape up lumps. If this happens, lift the pan away from the water for a few seconds to cool it, still stirring and scraping. Discard the lumps into a saucer, as they may fail to dissolve if put back in the sauce, and would then make it lumpy.

This sauce tends to curdle, that is, separate into fine semisolid flakes or granules surrounded by oil. This is mostly likely to occur if it is cooked at too high a heat or for too long (that is why you take it off the heat at once when it is thickened), or if it is not stirred enough.

It usually will not curdle if you follow directions, but occasionally it will for no apparent reason. This hazard adds to the interest in making the sauce, and to the triumph if it stays together.

If it separates or starts to separate, you can almost always smooth it out again by adding a tablespoon of boiling water or of heavy cream, then beating it vigorously with a whisk or a rotary beater.

Hollandaise is served warm or hot over eggs, fish or vegetables. It is particularly good on asparagus.

If there is delay in serving, keep it warm and covered, then reheat over hot water with frequent stirring, just before use. It may develop a surface skin while waiting, but this dissolves when stirred in. It may also be kept covered in the fridge for a day or two, then reheated in the same manner. But each extra process increases the danger of curdling or of re-curdling.

Mock Hollandaise. A mock Hollandaise sauce is supposed to resemble the real thing and be somewhat easier or at least safer to make. It is likely to call for cornstarch or flour as a thickener and as a stabilizer against curdling, but it may not. Some of the "mock" recipes are more complicated to follow than the real thing.

One method is to make a medium white sauce, described a few pages earlier. When it has thickened, remove it from the heat, add a tablespoon of lemon juice, pour a little of it into two lightly beaten egg yolks, mixing well, then pour them in the sauce in the pan. Cook over low heat with constant stirring for about 2 minutes, or until smooth and thickened again.

TARTAR

Tartar sauce is designed especially for serving with seafood. It is usually thick and coarse in texture, and is served on the side rather than being poured or heaped on the fish.

Recipes for this sauce vary greatly. The following includes the main elements, in average proportions. Quantities can be varied to taste, and substitution of similar ingredients should do no harm.

Tartar (Tartare) Sauce

1 cup	mayonnaise
1 Tb	onion or chives, finely chopped
1 Tb	fresh parsley, chopped
1 Tb	dill or sweet pickle, finely chopped
1 tsp	capers, finely chopped

optional additions

1 tsp	prepared mustard
½ tsp	lemon juice or vinegar
1 Tb	chopped celery
2 dps	tabasco sauce
1	egg, hard boiled and chopped
	salt
	pepper

Mix ingredients together thoroughly. The consistency should be slightly thicker than mayonnaise. If you want it thinner, dilute with lemon juice or water.

GRAVY

Gravy is usually a meat flavored sauce, prepared from juice, fat and particles remaining in a pan after cooking meat or

Fig. 18-3. Makings of tartar sauce

poultry. Fish and vegetable sauces may be prepared in the same manner, but are much less popular. They may or may not be called gravy.

Gravy is served hot. This is particularly important when it contains fat and/or flour. It is a good plan to fill the gravy serving pitcher (gravy boat) with hot water a few minutes ahead, then empty it and put in gravy that is boiling hot. It takes an exceptionally good gravy to be still palatable when it is cold or even lukewarm.

An exception is natural gravy, which may still be tolerable when partly cooled, and delicious when chilled into a jelly.

Most gravy is made from oven roasts. The same procedure is followed with pot roast. For stew, an already existing gravy is used as it is, or more often thickened by stirring in flour that has been blended with a little cold water.

Drippings. Meat that is being cooked exudes juice more or less continuously, and shrinks and becomes lighter as a result. The juice is composed of variable proportions of water, melted fat, with much smaller quantities of flavorful salts, natural flavoring compounds and bits of protein.

Part of the water and volatile compounds evaporate directly from the surface of the meat, and part moves downward into the pan bottom, where additional evaporation takes place. There is little loss of fat by evaporation unless the heat is very high.

The juice and other material in the pan bottom is called the drippings. It may be increased by small quantities of water poured into the pan at the start and occasionally during roasting, although this practice is criticized by many authorities.

A hot oven or a covered pan will increase the loss of juice from the meat. High heat increases the rate of evaporation, but a cover slows it. A high evaporation rate decreases the proportion of water to fat. Fat meat produces more drippings, including both fat and water, than lean meat.

There are large individual differences in the juiciness of roasts.

As a result of these and other variables, you generally do not know in advance just how big your pool of drippings will be, nor exactly what will be in it. You may use it just as it is, adjusting the materials you add to it on a basis of your judgment and of results obtained.

You may take out part of the pool, usually the fat part, and use the rest. Or you may pour it all out, separate it into juice and fat, and use measured parts of each according to a recipe.

First Steps. Gravy making starts with lifting the meat out of the pan and putting it in the cover or on a platter, then putting it in the turned-off oven or covering it to keep it warm while it firms up and other work goes on.

The most tasty part of the drippings is the solid or semi-solid brown part, made up of flakes of crust and finely divided solids brought out of the meat by the juices. Some or most of this material may be stuck to the pan, and scraping it free is an important part of gravy-making.

A wooden spoon is the preferred tool. It will not dig unwanted metal or enamel out of the pan, nor scrape off burned areas. If some spots are too hard for it, but not burnt, you can scrape them carefully with a steel spoon, a knife or a spatula. Burned material should not be used. If possible, scrape it loose and wipe it out with paper. If a considerable area is charred, transfer the good material to another pan.

The rack or trivet, if any, is usually difficult to scrape with any tool, and this is the principal objection to using it. You can wash it in another container with a few tablespoons of plain hot water and a clean brush, and put the enriched water back in the pan.

Gravies made from roast drippings may be roughly divided into three classes: pan (natural), thickened and cream. There is

Fig. 18-4. Pouring grease off gravy

also dish gravy, but this is juice that comes out of the meat as it is carved, and it is ordinarily not cooked or processed.

Pan Gravy. Pan or natural gravy may be all of the drippings and nothing more, it may be the drippings with an excess amount of fat removed or the drippings extended with water, bouillon or consomme.

For a completely natural gravy, you scrape off all residues with a spoon, preferably wooden, then stir or beat them into the liquid, preferably with a whisk, until the resulting fluid is reasonably smooth. If there is too little of it and it is thick, add hot water.

You can extend it with condensed bouillon or consomme soup if the meat is beef, chicken bouillon or broth, or the liquid strained from condensed chicken-and-rice soup if it is chicken. You can use chicken for veal, but stick to hot water thinning for lamb and pork. If there is a lot of gravy and it is thin, boil it until it is thicker.

The proper thickness for gravy is entirely a matter of local custom, and you must use your own judgment or ask for advice about it.

Free grease in or on gravy is not usually liked. You can remove it from the surface by delicate dipping with a spoon, by soak-

ing it up with a blotter or by putting it into a wide shallow pan and that in the freezer, picking out the hardened fat after a few minutes, and reheating.

Thickened. Thickened gravy, which comes close to being a standard American type, is made by mixing flour (or occasionally some substitute such as cornstarch) with the drippings, and cooking the result for 3 minutes or more until it thickens.

A rule of thumb for gravy proportions in a batch for 2 people is:

2 Tb	flour *(or 1 Tb of cornstarch)*	
2 Tb	fat	
1 cup	non-fat liquid	
¼ tsp	salt *(optional)*	

These proportions govern the consistency, and are subject to change from a variety of causes. Flavor depends mostly on the quality and quantity of the meat substances in the drippings. A gravy made with drippings only, should be more tasty than one to which you add water. But if the drippings obtained their volume from water added during cooking, or from restriction of evaporation of water, there might be no difference.

If you want to make gravy in exact proportions, lift out the roast, scrape the pan to loosen the brown deposits, then pour and scrape everything into a clean container, preferably one of transparent, heat-resistant glass. Then separate the fat and other substances.

If there is a lot of fat you can pour some of it off. A glass container allows you to see what you are doing. The melted fat is on the top. Tilt the container an increasing amount, pouring until the lower liquid comes up to the edge, as in Figure 18-4.

The remainder can be dipped off, preferably with a ladle or a spoon whose handle has been bent to make nearly a right angle with the bowl. If there were lots of time, which is seldom the case, you could allow it to cool and lift it off in a slab. A small quantity can be cooled in the fridge or freezer, but hardened fat has to be re-melted to make gravy.

Put fat back into the roasting pan, 2 tablespoons for each cup of gravy you want, and heat slowly. Put the same quantity of flour in a screw-top jar with 4 times its bulk in cold water, cover, and shake vigorously.

Pour the flour-water mixture slowly into the fat, stirring constantly. When the two have combined, pour the non-fat drippings in slowly, still stirring. Use a cup for each 2 tablespoons of flour, extending them with water if necessary. Turn up the heat to medium, and cook from 3 to 5 minutes, until thick and smooth, and colored the way you want it.

Coloring. You can regulate the color of the gravy while you cook it. Chicken gravy should be yellow to light brown, all other gravies medium to dark brown, with the medium shades usually preferred. The drippings may be brown or colorless. The flour starts out white, is yellowed by grease and browned by heat.

A roasting pan is usually much larger than a burner, so you have a hot spot where gravy boils and browns, and cooler parts where it is inactive. Keep the heat low while you are preoccupied with combining the ingredients, then turn it up moderately. Stir almost constantly, shifting material between the hot spot and cooler places, with every stroke scraping the bottom to prevent sticking and burning. To increase the rate of darkening, turn up the heat; to check it turn the burner down or out. Thin films darken much more rapidly than deep layers.

Gravy can also be darkened more or less artifically with browned flour, caramelized sugar or dark meat extracts. It can be increased in quantity by using any of the materials mentioned under PAN GRAVY.

Dry Flour Lumps. Most gravy-makers

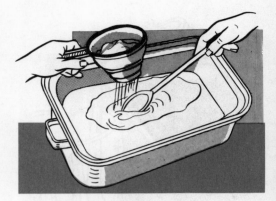

Fig. 18-5. Add flour through a sifter

add flour directly to the fat for gravy, instead of pre-mixing it with water. This is perfectly practical, but it involves possible trouble with lumps.

The best way to put it in is with a one-hand sifter, which you load with the correct quantity of flour before starting. You manipulate it so as to produce a steady, gentle fall of flour into the pan, while you stir vigorously. Or you can shake it off the edge of a tablespoon or a cup, but you have to be expert to do this smoothly.

If the flour falls too thickly, some of it may cling together in lumps that become coated with grease, which holds them together and makes them difficult to break up. Such lumps are the major curse of home gravy, yet they can be readily avoided by pre-mixing the flour with water, by putting the flour down in thin "dusting" layers from a sifter, or by vigorous stirring with a whisk instead of a spoon.

Once formed, lumps cannot be broken up by ordinary stirring and may resist vigorous churning with a whisk or a rotary beater. But you can destroy them by pouring the gravy into a sieve and pushing it through with the back and then the side of a spoon. Any residue left in the sieve will probably be meat particles, which you scrape off and return to the gravy after checking them for lumpiness. Unfortunately recovery is usually incomplete.

Fig. 18-6. A cure for lumps in gravy

There is "instantized" flour, which seldom forms lumps. Its use is recommended for gravy and sauce making. Even if you do not find lumps much of a problem, it may be pleasanter not to have to guard against them.

Cream Gravy. Cream gravy is a thickened gravy in which at least half of the nonfat liquid is milk or sometimes light cream. The same procedures are used as for regular gravy.

Casual Method. Few experienced cooks bother to measure gravy ingredients. The drippings are kept in the pan, although if they are very fat some of that may be ladled off. Flour is added with vigorous stirring until the liquid has the consistency of heavy cream, then water or broth until it is like thin cream, and it is then cooked slowly back to thick cream or ordinary gravy appearance.

Proportions may or may not come out near the ideal, but the gravy is usually excellent.

Success with this depends on recognizing appearances that are difficult to describe. The chief problem is that flour makes a paste with grease that thickens when water is first added, then thins, then thickens again with cooking. These changes may confuse and discourage the amateur who has no guide to the quantity of flour needed.

If you want to try it, use a tablespoon of flour for each pound of roast, unless it looks very greasy, in which case make it 1-1/2 tablespoons per pound. Add water sparingly, if at all, until the gravy is cooked and then thin it until it looks right.

Additions. Poultry gravy is often given extra body and flavor by adding the giblets — heart, liver and outer gizzard — from the bird. You get most benefit from them if you cook and fine-chop them, then add them after the blending in of flour is complete. If you put them in earlier you will not be able to tell whether you have lumps.

This and other gravies can also be benefited by adding a little of the crust of the meat, after grinding or chopping it. You can even use bits from a previous roast of the same type, if they are not dried out.

Many other things are put in gravy, for better or worse. Salt, 1/8 to 1/4 teaspoon per cup, is fairly standard, and pepper is common. You may also add finely chopped onion and/or parsley or herbs. Possible flavorings include paprika, sherry, Worcestershire, chili sauce, lemon juice and catsup, but any noticeable quantities of these are likely to be a mistake.

There is also sodium glutamate, if you believe in it. But avoid imitation beef extracts, vegetable protein and similar material, as they are likely to give gravy a canned flavor.

Quantity. It is generally accepted that the amount of gravy you will get from a roast is uncertain. There are also wide differences in local and individual appetites for gravy. But in a general way, you should be able to work up a cup of gravy for each 2 pounds of a roast, and this should take care of 4 people.

If it looks as if the natural gravy will fall short, or you want extra quantities for any reason, you can extend it indefinitely if you have the simple supplies mentioned under Pan Gravy for increasing the amount of juice, and butter or any shortening to provide more fat.

Fig. 18-7. Spaghetti sauce often separates

Substitutes. A passable gravy can be made without cooking any meat at all. You use butter or any shortening for fat, and concentrated bouillon, broth or consomme soup for juice. Shake up the flour with some of the soup, blend with the fat over low heat, add more soup and cook for 3 to 5 minutes. The proportions are the same as for real gravy; 1 tablespoon each of fat and flour with one (measuring) cup of soup.

You can buy fair canned or dried gravy. However, it is likely to taste of vegetable or yeast protein, it is widely used in the cheaper restaurants and, if recognized, it will reduce appreciation of your cooking. Home made gravy almost always tastes better, it salvages excellent meat drippings which might otherwise be wasted, and it is good cooking experience.

SPAGHETTI SAUCE

Almost any non-sweet sauce can be used on spaghetti and other pasta. It may be cooked with it in a casserole, mixed with it just before serving, or served on the side. It often has cheese as an ingredient, or depends on having grated cheese sprinkled over the top, on a serving platter or on individual portions.

However, the most widely used type of pasta sauce consists partly or mostly of tomato, is well seasoned and is thick in consistency.

Many of these sauces tend to separate when poured over the top of spaghetti. A rather watery fluid goes to the bottom and thicker and usually more flavorful parts stay on top. Wateriness may be greatly increased if the spaghetti is wet, so it should be allowed to stand in the hot, covered pan for a few minutes after draining, until surface water is absorbed.

Separation detracts somewhat from the attractiveness of the dish, but remedies for it may be even less desirable. It is reduced if the sauce is mixed with the pasta before serving, and eliminated if the mixture is not served for several hours. This may be one of the reasons that many consider spaghetti-and-sauce to be at their best the day after cooking.

Fine texture, such as is found in most canned pasta sauces, will usually prevent separation. Put your sauce through a blender and it will stay together. But you lose the roughness or variety of texture which is one of the most pleasing features of home made or good restaurant sauces.

Tomato Base. The tomatoes are usually canned (whole and/or in smooth concentrates) but may be fresh. They must be peeled. The Italian or plum tomato is usually considered to be superior, but good sauces can be made from other varieties.

These sauces are often cooked a long time, 4 hours or more, so that whole tomatoes cook down to a soft pulp, most of which mixes smoothly with the other ingredients, but some small pieces of pulp are likely to remain. There will also be seeds. This roughness or coarseness is considered to be a necessary characteristic of good sauce by many. Those who prefer it smooth can put it through a sieve or a blender, use tomato paste or concentrated soup instead of whole tomatoes.

The traditionally long cooking time for spaghetti sauce helps to blend the various ingredients into a single composite flavor. The most resistant material to such blending, in both taste and texture, is the flesh of whole tomatoes. If you substitute concentrates, the cooking time can be and usually should be shortened considerably. On the other hand, cooking time should be 15 to 30 minutes longer than directed when tomatoes are raw, as recipes generally assume the use of canned ones which are of course precooked.

Almost everybody who makes spaghetti sauce has his or her own particular recipe or method. There are variations in type of tomato, in presence of other food ingredients, cooking time and particularly in type and amount of seasoning.

Two sample recipes, one for long-cooked and the other for quick-type, will be given along with a few of the possible variations that may be made in them.

Basic. The following recipe shows one of dozens of ways in which this sauce can be made. Proportions can be varied moderately without making an important difference, or changed greatly to produce different flavors or textures, without changing the basic operation.

Fig. 18-8. Scorching is indicated by smell of scrapings

Spaghetti Sauce

3 or 4	cps	canned tomatoes *(1 can)*
½	cup	tomato paste *(1 small can)*
1	Tb	olive oil or bacon grease
½	cup	onion, minced
1	tsp	oregano
1	tsp	minced parsley *(or ½ tsp parsley flakes)*
2	Tb	sugar
½	tsp	garlic salt
2	tsp	salt

Fry onion in oil or grease until wilted. Mix with all the other ingredients, bring to a boil with frequent stirring, then turn heat as low as possible and simmer slowly for 4 hours, or longer. Check it occasionally to make sure the heat is low, and that it is not sticking and burning on the bottom.

Test for sticking is to scrape the spoon across the bottom and then up along the side. If it gathers some thick or hard material, sticking has occurred, and if it is brown or black it is scorching or burning. In this case, taste the sauce. If it is all right, pour it into another pot or pots without scraping, and continue cooking on lower heat. If it tastes scorched, you may have to discard it. Careful cleaning of the pot before use is a basic precaution against this disaster.

The amount of sugar, onion, salt and parsley may be doubled or halved. Garlic salt may be omitted, doubled or replaced by a crushed clove of fresh garlic. A basil leaf may be used instead of oregano or in addition to it. A medium size green pepper, finely chopped, may be included. A quartered carrot and a split large bone (marrow bone) may be cooked with it, but fished out and set aside before serving.

Quick. A quick spaghetti sauce may be made by replacing the tomatoes in the previous recipe with about the same amount of tomato puree or paste, with concentrated tomato soup or with mixtures of these ingredients, adding 1-1/2 to 2 cups of water and reducing the simmering time to 1/2 hour.

Part of the tomato base stock may also be replaced with a commercial spaghetti sauce such as marinara, to take advantage of its special seasonings.

Meat. Meat spaghetti sauce is usually one of the tomato-based mixtures, plus ground meat. In the recipe just given, use 3/4 to one pound of hamburger. After heating the onions, remove them from the pan, leaving the oil over medium high heat. Crumble the meat into it, stirring briskly until it is brown and in small pieces. Then add it to the other sauce ingredients.

Sausage meat may be used in about the same manner, but because of the stronger flavor, quantity might be limited to a half pound. Link sausage may be cut into very small pieces and used in the same way. Browning may be done in a dry pan, and grease from the sausage may be either added to the sauce or discarded.

One excellent recipe calls for thoroughly mixing 2 eggs with the raw hamburger, together with 2 teaspoons of bread crumbs and all the seasoning for the sauce.

Cheese. Any spaghetti sauce may have cheese added to it. For our basic recipe, use up to half a pound, grated or diced to make about 2 cups. This is ordinarily Parmesan or American (cheddar), but may be mozzarella or Swiss. It can be put in at the beginning and cooked with the other ingredients, or stirred in a few minutes before serving.

A regular cheese sauce, page 359, is often served on or with macaroni, but seldom with spaghetti although it is very good on it.

Cheese is used as a sauce topping more often than as an ingredient. A shaker or small serving bowl of grated Parmesan is a standard accompaniment to pasta dishes.

Romano cheese may be used in the same way. Cheddar may be served in grated form, or in somewhat coarser crumbles.

Any of these may be scattered either thinly or thickly over the top of the sauce on top of the pasta, and sometimes are put directly on dry or buttered pasta, without sauce.

Sea Food. Finely chopped seafood, usually clams, are a popular addition. About half a pound is sufficient to give a good flavor of the sea to basic sauces.

SALAD DRESSING

Salad dressing in the widest sense is any cold sauce served on or with a salad. Some authorities prefer to limit it to uncooked sauces of the oil-and-vinegar family, excluding boiled dressing, but the first definition is best for our purposes.

Oil and Vinegar — Unmixed. The simplest salad dressing is oil and vinegar, placed on the table in two bottles, called cruets, which may have restricted openings, so that fluid pours in a very thin stream, or must be shaken out in drops. Pairs of such bottles, in special shapes and nested in a stand, used to be standard table accessories, but are now less common.

The oil may be either olive oil or a neutral-flavored salad oil, processed from corn, peanuts, cottonseed, soy beans or other

Fig. 18-9. Nested cruets

seeds. The vinegar may be distilled white vinegar, either plain or flavored with salt, and tarragon, garlic, capers or similar seasonings. Or cider, malt, wine or other special vinegar can be used.

This arrangement deprives the hostess of opportunity to show off mixed dressing, but it gives the salad-eater the privilege of working out his own proportions.

Mixed. The oil and vinegar may be pre-mixed, or at least put on the table in the same bottle or dispenser. A usual proportion is two parts of oil to one of distilled vinegar, or equal amounts of oil and cider or wine vinegar, but you will have to work this out by taste. The same oil varieties and vinegar seasonings can be used. However, you can also add pepper, finely chopped herbs, paprika or other solids in tiny bits.

Oil and vinegar do not stay mixed. You can combine them by shaking the bottle vigorously, but they will separate quickly, the oil rising to the top. The harder you shake, the slower the separation, but it is not worth while to work too hard, as the best time you can get can be measured in seconds. It is customary to shake this type of dressing lightly just before pouring, each time.

Stabilizer. The mixture can be stabilized so that it will separate more slowly, or stay permanently mixed, by an emulsifier, which is a substance that coats oil droplets so that they cannot combine with each other. If the droplets are made moderately fine by shaking or beating, and kept that way by an emulsifier, they will rise very slowly, as cream rises in milk. If they are made very fine, or the mixture is also thickened, they will not rise at all, or will take days or months to do so.

The simplest stabilizer is egg. One teaspoon of either white or yolk to a cup of oil and vinegar will slow its separation time to several minutes if shaken by hand, or to hours or even days if beaten in a blender. The appearance will be cloudy or milky.

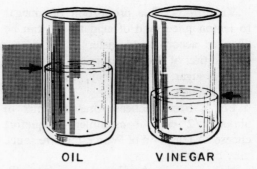

OIL   VINEGAR

Fig. 18-10. Base for standard salad dressings

Most home made non-mayonnaise dressings are not stabilized, although store-bought ones with the same names often are.

Oil and vinegar, with but more usually without stabilizers, may be flavored, colored and thickened with any of a vast number of substances, including catsup, chili sauce, sugar, cheese, soured cream, pureed fruit or vegetables and even peanut butter. Each type of mix is likely to carry its own name, which may vary among different localities or cookbooks.

French Dressing. The French dressing in this recipe is an oil-vinegar mix, with half the vinegar replaced by lemon juice, and seasoning added. It is only one of a number of mixtures bearing the name. Those that are made commercially are often stabilized so that they do not ever separate under normal conditions of storage and use.

French Dressing

1 cup	salad oil
¼ cup	vinegar
¼ cup	lemon juice
1 tsp	salt
1 tsp	dry mustard
1 tsp	paprika

Put all ingredients in a bowl and beat vigorously until they are well blended. Pour into a glass jar or bottle with a tight top, and shake well before each use. This makes about 1-1/2 cups of dressing.

Variations. The proportion of vinegar to lemon juice, and of acid to oil, can be changed according to taste.

Addition of 3 or 4 teaspoons of confectioners sugar, or of honey, will produce sweet French dressing.

For a French cheese dressing, mix in about 1/2 cup of crumbled Roquefort cheese. A teaspoon of Worcestershire sauce may be added.

You can mix the French dressing with up to an equal quantity of ketchup.

Mayonnaise. Most mayonnaise is made commercially, and can be found in every grocery in glass jars in a wide range of sizes. But it tastes better when made at home. The ingredients are simple and so is the preparation. The only problem — and it is serious one — is that it has a tendency to separate or curdle, so that you can seldom feel relaxed when making it.

No two recipes are exactly alike. The following will serve as a good sample.

Mayonnaise *(1½ cups)*

1	cup	salad oil
1	Tb	lemon juice or vinegar
1		egg yolk
1	tsp	confectioners' sugar
1	tsp	dry mustard
¼	tsp	salt

Mix all ingredients except the oil. Then beat vigorously while adding the oil, first drop by drop, then evenly poured in a thin stream. Beat with a whisk or a rotary beater until mixture has thickened. If it shows a tendency to separate, beat faster, adding a little boiling water or cream if necessary. Refrigerate it until used.

For a stronger flavor, you can double the amount of lemon juice or vinegar. For an even lighter texture, fold in half a cup of whipped cream just before serving.

Mayonnaise, either home made or bought, is the base for many dressings. For example:

Russian Dressing

¼	cup	ketchup
1	tsp	chili sauce
2	Tb	grated onion
½	cup	mayonnaise

A more elaborate mix, with an interestingly lumpy texture, is:

Thousand Islands

1	Tb	chili sauce
1	Tb	chopped green olives
1	tsp	chopped chives
1		hard boiled egg, chopped
⅔	cup	mayonnaise
¼	tsp	paprika
		salt and pepper to taste

Stir dressings until well blended.

Boiled. Boiled salad dressing is used in the same general way as mayonnaise. It is not as rich, but has its own flavor.

Boiled Salad Dressing *(1½ cups)*

2		eggs
2	Tb	flour
½	cup	sugar
⅓	cup	vinegar
½	cup	evaporated milk or cream
2	Tb	butter
½	tsp	salt
½	tsp	dry mustard *(optional)*

Beat eggs until foamy. Mix dry ingredients together, then mix thoroughly with eggs. Put in top of double boiler over boiling water, or over a heat pad on a low or medium burner. Add vinegar slowly, stirring constantly.

Continue stirring until mixture thickens, then remove from heat immediately and stir in the butter and evaporated milk or cream. Cool, then chill, and keep cold.

MARINADE

A marinade is usually a thin sauce that contains acid or wine, and that is mixed with meat, fish or vegetables before they are cooked. It is likely to be highly seasoned.

A marinade is basically for flavor, but it may serve a more important function in tenderizing meat. For flavor, the mixed-together or steeping period may be as short as a half hour, but for tenderizing it should be at least 5 hours, usually overnight, and sometimes for as long as 2 or 3 days. For short periods, the food should be cut into pieces, perhaps 1/2 inch cubes. It is most effective at room temperature or warmer, but there is a danger of spoilage that usually makes it advisable to do the steeping in a refrigerator. Pieces should be rearranged occasionally to distribute the effects evenly.

The desirability of the flavor change is a matter of taste. Long steeping alters the original flavor of the basic food, and may eliminate it in time, but substitutes its own set of flavors, usually sour and spicy.

There is no uniformity among marinade mixtures. Those intended to just acidify (point up) a basic flavor may be simply oil and acid, perhaps with salt and mild seasoning. But a barbecue marinade is likely to be very strongly seasoned.

Fig. 18-11. Check sweet sauce by tasting

Food may be cooked in a marinade, full strength or diluted, or the sauce may be painted or dribbled on it during cooking. Left over marinade may be used in preparing a more complicated sauce to be poured over the same food after cooking.

A simple uncooked marinade, which can be used on meat, fish or vegetable, is:

Marinade
(for one pound of cut up meat)

2	Tb	lemon juice or vinegar
¼	cup	olive or salad oil
½	tsp	salt

This may be used as is, or seasoned with one or more of the following:

⅛	tsp	pepper
1	tsp	chopped parsley
½	tsp	basil
1		clove garlic, crushed
¼	cup	dry wine
1	tsp	sugar

or with any other seasonings that happen to appeal to you.

SWEET SAUCES

There is a considerable variety of sweet or dessert sauces in cookbooks, and even more kinds are improvised at home. Anything that is sweet and will flow might be used, although there are types that are popular, and others that are not.

Vanilla. This is a general purpose pudding sauce that is easy to make and satisfactory to eat.

Vanilla Sauce

½	cup	sugar
1	Tb	cornstarch *(or 2 of flour)*
1	cup	boiling water
3	Tb	butter
1	tsp	vanilla

Ingredient	Number of recipes in which found
Chocolate, unsweet	15
Chocölate, bittersweet	6
Sugar	12
Marshmallows	1
Honey	1
Corn syrup	7
Water	7
Milk	4
Milk, condensed	1
Milk, evaporated	4
Cream	6
Butter	6
Other shortening	1
Flour	1
Cornstarch	2
Egg	3
Salt	9
Almonds	2
Vanilla	18
Instant coffee	1
Rum	3

Fig. 18-12. Ingredients used in 20 recipes for chocolate sauce

Mix the sugar and starch well, to avoid lumps. Put in saucepan over moderate heat, add boiling water gradually while stirring. Cook and stir for 3 or 4 minutes, or until thick and smooth. Remove from heat, stir in butter and then vanilla. Best when served hot or warm, over bread pudding or any fruit-and-cake dessert.

This sauce can be made richer by stirring in 1/4 to 1/2 cup of light cream, after cooking is completed. Or it can be made leaner by using less butter.

Fruit Sauce. A fruit sauce can be made in the same manner as vanilla sauce. Omit the vanilla, and replace the water with fruit juice. Use extra sugar if necessary to counteract the acidity.

Or you can flavor the basic sauce with a tablespoon of lemon juice, and/or 1/2 teaspoon of grated lemon rind.

Custard. Custard sauce is usually an extra-rich stirred custard, or a normal custard thickened with flour. A basic recipe is:

Custard Sauce I

2 cps	milk or light cream
3	eggs *(or 6 yolks)*
⅓ cup	sugar
½ tsp	vanilla
⅛ tsp	salt *(optional)*

This is mixed and cooked in the manner described for stirred custard for dessert, page 528.

Another way to do it is:

Custard Sauce II

2 cps	milk
2	eggs *(or 4 yolks)*
⅓ cup	sugar
1½ tsp	flour
1 tsp	vanilla
¼ tsp	salt *(optional)*

The flour is mixed thoroughly with the sugar before mixing with the milk and egg. Otherwise the preparation is the same as for regular custard. The texture is changed, and the flavor is less rich.

Chocolate. Chocolate sauce is used on cake-type puddings and ice cream, and is diluted to make beverages. It may be thin, thick or even solid. There are a great many recipes for it, no two the same, which range from the very simple (dissolve a 6-ounce package of bittersweet chocolate in a tall can of evaporated milk) to quite complicated procedures.

Figure 18-12 lists the ingredients used in 20 chocolate sauce recipes taken at random from cookbooks. The proportions given are widely variable also. An ounce of bitter chocolate may be accompanied by 1/4 to 3/4 cup of sugar, causing differences in sweetness that do not show in the recipe names. Corn syrup may be the only liquid ingredient.

None of these recipes call for cocoa, although it is much easier to use than chocolate, and just as flavorful. The recipe below features cocoa, but if you want to go along with the crowd you can replace it with 2 ounces of bitter chocolate. The extra fat will just make the sauce a little richer.

Fig. 18-13. Fudge sauce may be tested by dripping on ice.

Chocolate Sauce

½	cup	cocoa
½	cup	sugar *(or to taste)*
½	cup	water
1	Tb	butter *(optional)*
1	Tb	light corn syrup
½	tsp	vanilla *(optional)*

Mix the sugar and cocoa thoroughly. Put in pan with water and corn syrup, bring to boil over moderately high heat, with frequent stirring. As soon as it boils, turn heat low, add the butter if you use it, and simmer for 2 minutes, stirring just enough to mix in the butter as it melts. Add vanilla, if you use it, and serve.

This recipe makes a scant cup of a rich, sweet or semi-sweet sauce that has the consistency of medium cream when it is hot, and of heavy cream when cold. It makes a good dessert sauce at either temperature. The butter makes the sauce richer, but it is a question of taste whether this is an advantage.

You can make cocoa or chocolate milk by using 1-1/2 to 3 tablespoons of this sauce to a cup of milk. This is good for a cold drink, but it is usually easier and more satisfactory to make the hot beverage directly from cocoa.

The sauce will keep a week or two in the refrigerator. It should be closely covered. Some separation may occur, with thickening at the top, but stirring or possibly stirring with some heating, should smooth it out again.

Fudge. Chocolate fudge sauce is simply a chocolate sauce thick enough so that it must be hot or at least warm to be poured, and/or will set to a more or less hard and chewy state when put on ice cream. Judging from the recipes, it is important that it should not turn to or resemble fudge, as they contain enough extra corn syrup to make sure that it cannot possibly crystallize.

The chocolate sauce in the recipe just given, or almost any chocolate sauce, becomes fudge sauce if boiled over medium high heat for 4 to 10 minutes, after adding the butter. You can test it for the consistency you want by dripping it on an ice cube. Or reduce the water to 1/3 cup, increase the corn syrup to 2 tablespoons, and test in the same manner.

Brown Sugar and Butterscotch. There are a number of sweet sauces and syrups made with brown sugar as both the sweetening ingredient and the flavoring. Some of these are called brown sugar and others butterscotch, without any consistent distinction between them. Except that most butterscotch sauces contain corn syrup, and most brown sugar ones do not.

Some of these preparations are very simple, while others are fairly complicated. The following will serve as a basic cooked formula:

Butterscotch Sauce

½ cup brown sugar
          (dark preferred)
½ cup white corn syrup
0 to 4 Tb water
2 Tb butter
⅛ tsp salt *(optional)*
½ tsp vanilla *(optional)*

Cook the first 2 or 3 ingredients over moderate heat for about 10 minutes. This will probably mean about 6 minutes heating up and 4 minutes boiling. Then add the last 3 ingredients, stir well and check consistency.

Without water, you will have a very

Fig. 18-14. Worker in a honey factory

thick sauce which will solidify on an ice cube. Two tablespoons of water reduce it to moderate thickness, 4 to medium. You can add water to get the consistency you want. The sauce becomes somewhat thicker when it cools.

For creamy butterscotch, thin it with heavy or medium cream instead of water. At least twice as much will be needed for the same reduction in viscosity. This mixture can be thinned out with water also.

Another brown sugar mixture will be discussed under SYRUP.

Caramel. Caramel sauce is usually a water solution of caramelized (scorched) white sugar. The simplest way to prepare it is:

Caramel Sauce

1 cup sugar
1 cup boiling water

Put the sugar in a small, moderately heavy pan over medium heat. Stir it almost constantly, keeping the bottom and sides scraped clean. As soon as the sugar starts to get sticky or to show a yellowish color, turn the heat as low as possible.

According to standard instructions, you continue with low heat and constant stirring until the sugar has melted to a pale amber liquid. However, even on the lowest heat setting of a standard electric burner, the first scrapings may remain as undissolved white or barely off-white lumps until the liquid darkens to brown, perhaps with a bitter or scorched taste.

It is best to remove the pan from the heat as soon as the average color is what you want, figuring that the dissolving of the lumps will lighten the liquid only a little.

Measure a cup of boiling water, and pour it very slowly into the hot sugar, stirring vigorously. It will steam violently. When the water is all in, put on moderate heat, stir until the sugar dissolves, then boil for about 5 minutes.

The result is a rather thin sauce, which will be sweet and mild if light colored or unsweet and acrid if dark. If it is too sweet you can put in a few drops of vinegar, if not sweet enough add sugar, a teaspoon at a time.

Caramel sauce is a traditional accompaniment to baked custard in many countries, and is used chiefly on desserts whose own flavor is rather bland.

For a thicker sauce, blend 2 to 4 teaspoons of cornstarch with 2 tablespoons of water, and stir into the mixture as soon as the browned sugar has dissolved. It can be enriched with a tablespoon or more of butter, and pointed up with up to 1/2 teaspoon of vanilla.

Hard Sauce. Hard sauce is a mixture of confectioners' sugar with butter or heavy cream or both. The proportion is usually around one cup of sugar to 1/3 to 1/2 cup of butter and/or cream. There may also be flavoring, such as a half teaspoon of vanilla or a teaspoon of brandy.

Lemon hard sauce requires a teaspoon each of lemon juice and grated lemon rind, or more if you like your lemon strong. Nutmeg or cinnamon may be sprinkled on top of the completed sauce for decoration.

All ingredients should be at room temperature. The sugar should be absolutely free of lumps, as they would spoil the texture. Sift it to be sure. Pack it firmly while measuring.

Cream the butter thoroughly, then blend in some of the sugar, then the flavoring, then the rest of the sugar. Beat it on the low speed of a mixer, or use a lot of energy getting it well mixed with a spoon, as thorough working improves its texture.

Hard sauce may have a consistency as relaxed as soft ice cream or almost as firm as fudge, depending on your preference or perhaps just on the way it comes out. If it has much butter in it, it will become much firmer if chilled. Cream is less affected by temperature, but hardens more when it is kept a day or two. If it is too stiff at room temperature you can mix in a little cream, milk or brandy; if it is too soft it needs more confectioners' sugar, sifted.

Hard sauce is particularly appropriate for steamed pudding (plum pudding, for example) and mince pie, but it is used on a wide variety of desserts, preferably hot ones.

If brown sugar is substituted for confectioners', you have Sterling hard sauce.

SYRUP

Syrup, which is also spelled sirup, is not clearly distinguished from other sweet sauces. It is usually made of quite simple ingredients, with some type of sugar as a major item. Chocolate, butterscotch and caramel sauces are frequently called syrups.

Honey is a natural syrup, molasses is a by-product of sugar refining and corn syrup is a solution of a natural sugar, dextrose, produced by factory methods from corn. Maple and brown sugar syrups are water solutions of their respective sugars, and white sugar syrups are made from granulated sugar chiefly for use in preserving food.

Honey. Honey is a thick, very sweet liquid made by bees. It is a concentrate of nectar and other substances found in flowers, and it varies in color and flavor with the variety from which it is extracted. Bees keep different strains of honey separate, when there is enough to enable them to do so. The principal sugars are dextrose and fructose (levulose).

Bees store honey in small wax compartments, a group of which make a comb or honeycomb. For commercial production, beehives are fitted with removable racks and frames. Some of the honey is sold in intact combs in the small wood frames where the bees stored it, but most of it is removed from combs in centrifugal separators, strained and sold in liquid form.

Fig. 18-15. Maple syrup is from trees

Honey has excellent keeping qualities. But if it is stored in a cool place and/or for a long time it is likely to crystallize into a soft moist sugar, with some change in flavor. This form is sometimes more convenient, as for example in spreading on bread or crackers, but it is not generally considered to be desirable. It can be remade into liquid of the original quality by

moderate heat. But heating over 140° F is likely to darken it and cause deterioration of flavor.

Honey is used as a syrup for pancakes and waffles, as a spread for crackers and biscuits and as a sweetener to partly replace sugar in some baked desserts. In spite of its sweetness it is chemically acid, so that it will not fit in every recipe. It has a mild tendency to absorb water, so that it helps to keep cake moist and fresh.

Molasses. Molasses is a by-product of the refining of cane sugar. It contains most of the cane sap materials except for the sugar and water that have been removed. It is manufactured in a number of grades, ranging from a light sweet syrup with a high sugar content to a dark, almost bitter "blackstrap" residue.

Light or medium molasses may be used as a pancake syrup, although its distinctive flavor is not enjoyed by everyone. In cooking it is valuable as a flavoring in many medium or dark-colored breads and cakes. It has a water-absorbing characteristic that keeps baked goods fresh, and an acid reaction that allows the replacement of baking powder by soda.

Corn Syrup. Corn syrup is a solution of dextrose (glucose) in water. The dextrose is produced by treating corn starch with acids and/or enzymes that break its long and complicated chains of molecules down into the simple sugar structure of dextrose. White corn syrup may contain up to 10 per cent of cane sugar (for sweetness) and the dark variety may include the same proportions of molasses, for flavor.

Either type may be used as pancake syrup, but it is not particularly popular this way. Its chief value is as an ingredient. It is a mild sweetener, and a powerful smoothing agent. When mixed with white sugar or sugar syrups it will prevent or greatly reduce formation of crystals in candy and frozen fruits, it cures oversweetness in certain all-sugar candies and

Name	Type, per cent	Sugar, cups	Water, cups	Yield of syrup, cups	Boiling point, F
Light or thin	30	2	4	5	213.8
Medium	40	3	4	5⅓	214.7
Heavy	50	4¾	4	6½	215.5
Extra heavy	60	7	4	7¾	217.5

Fig. 18-16. White sugar syrups

icings, and in general produces smoother texture even in smooth foods. It is an economical extender for maple and other special syrups.

It may have a favorable effect on browning of baked goods, sheen of canned fruit, cohesiveness of frostings and moisture retention in stored foods. But is should be used with caution. Some people are used to and prefer the conditions that the corn syrup corrects. Also, if you use too much you may get over-soft, smooth and even gooey textures that are undesirable.

In general, you are safe in using corn syrup if a recipe tells you to, but don't increase the quantity recklessly. The need for rather exact control of proportions is the reason that corn syrup is much more widely used in commercial cooking than in the home.

Maple. This is the most highly regarded and highly priced of the syrups. It is produced by boiling down the thin, almost tasteless sap of the hard or sugar maple tree. Drains are inserted in the trees in the late winter, when sap is flowing freely. It drips from these into pails, which are emptied at intervals into larger containers that are taken to a concentration plant which is usually both small and crude.

The basic material (sap) is free or nearly so, as the trees grow wild and are little damaged by the draining, but labor costs are very high.

Commercial maple syrup is concentrated directly from the sap, and should be 64 per cent sugar, with a weight of 11 pounds to the gallon. It has a pleasant consistency, a unique and delicate flavor and is very sweet. It is considered to be the best syrup for pancakes, waffles, French toast and similar items. It is used for flavoring custards, candies and icings, either in syrup or sugar form.

The syrup will turn into sugar if it is allowed to evaporate, and the sugar can be made back into syrup by adding water and heating moderately. In areas where it is produced, people often use a thicker, much more concentrated syrup than the commercial standard. Their's is partly sugar when it is cold, so that it must be served hot. This is the finest way to enjoy it.

Maple syrup or maple sugar may be added to other pancake syrups for flavor. The effect is usually good, but this is a matter of taste. Some people prefer to avoid the maple flavor unless they can have it unadulterated. In any case, avoid the use of synthetic maple flavor.

Brown Sugar. A simple and tasty pancake syrup can be made from brown sugar, white sugar and water. The brown sugar may be either dark or light, and the proportions of the sugars can be varied to taste.

If you should use all dark brown sugar the result would be a medium molasses; if all white you would have clear, very sweet unflavored syrup more suitable for canning fruit than for eating.

For a first try, combine in a saucepan:

Brown Sugar Syrup

1 cup dark brown sugar
1 cup granulated sugar
1 cup water

Stir over low heat until the sugar is dissolved, then cool and use.

If it is too thin for your taste, you can either boil it down or add more sugar. The flavor can be changed by adding only one of the sugars. You can spike it with maple sugar, maple syrup or vinegar. For a strong molasses flavor, add dark molasses.

White Sugar. White sugar syrups are used primarily for packing fruits or berries that are to be canned or frozen. They may be made with water, with the juice of the fruit being preserved or with a mixture of the two. The sweetness and viscosity (thickness) of the syrup are determined by the proportion of sugar.

It may be classified by weight (really viscosity) as light, medium or heavy; or according to percentage of sugar. This last is called percentage in cookbooks, but in texts for commercial processors it is called Brix degrees.

Figure 18-16 shows the makeup of syrups that are ordinarily used. There are some differences among cookbooks and preserving instructions. They are not very large, and in case of doubt you can always follow the recipe you are using. Some instructions give different proportions for syrups of the same weight, depending on whether it will be used in freezing or in canning.

Use of these syrups will be discussed under FOOD PRESERVATION.

19

MEAT MIXTURES

SAUSAGE

By definition, sausage is finely chopped meat, or a combination of finely and coarsely chopped meats, blended with seasonings and spices, and sometimes with small amounts of other food materials. It is usually stuffed into a casing or container, which may be made of animal entrails or of synthetic material. In a general way the term may be held to include over 200 different meat products, including frankfurters, bologna and salami.

Specifically, however, the unmodified word sausage means pork sausage to most people.

Pork. The common American pork sausages are supposed to be made entirely of ground pork and seasonings. They are sold in the form of links that weigh an ounce or more each (except cocktail sausages, which may be 1/4 ounce or less), in patties and in cylindrical 1-pound packages of sausage meat that are sliced into patties for cooking. It is raw unless the label says it is cooked.

Only a few brands of sausage are sold nationally, but there are a great many of local manufacture. Those that are sold interstate are subject to supervision as to contents and sanitation, while local ones may not be. There is wide variation in type and strength of seasoning, and in texture both before and after cooking.

Sausage should always be fully cooked because of possible trichinosis organisms. But it should not be overcooked, as this causes it to lose tenderness and flavor.

Sausages are usually fried, but are sometimes baked or broiled. A recommended cooking method for links is to start them in a covered frypan containing 1/4 to 3/8 inch of boiling water over medium high heat. Cook for 5 minutes, pour off the water, then fry them in the same pan over medium heat, with several turnings, until they are golden brown. Total cooking time should be 8 to 12 minutes for 1-ounce links or patties.

Or you can just start them cold in an open pan or griddle on medium or low medium heat, 300 to 350° F, and cook with occasional turning until done. Total cooking time is about the same. This is the preferred method for patties, as they might disintegrate in water. Grease may be poured

379

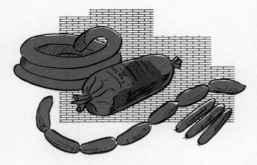

Fig. 19-1. Sausages

off occasionally, or allowed to accumulate in the pan.

Fried sausage can be served directly from the pan, but will be more attractive if it is parked on absorbent paper or a rack for a minute, so that grease on its surface will be either blotted off or absorbed.

Sausages can be baked on a rack in a shallow pan, preferably in a single layer, and may be turned one or more times if necessary to equalize their color. Heat should be 325 to 350°, and time about 25 minutes. A good color is desirable, but they can be eaten any time after they have cooked through. The test for doneness is to break one in half and look at it. If the center is pink or has a different texture than the outer part, it needs more cooking.

Sausage may also be broiled, about 6 inches below the flame or electric unit, with at least one turn.

Pork sausage is usually raw, but it can be bought cooked in patty form. If cooked, subject it to enough heat of any kind to brown it on both sides.

There is an old prejudice in the meat industry against freezing cured pork products, but results with present-day sausage are usually excellent. It retains good flavor and texture for months in the freezer, and becomes trichinosis-safe in 30 days at 0° F. The good keeping quality is presumably due to inclusion of anti-oxidant chemicals which protect it against rancidity.

Sausage is popular as a breakfast and

lunch meat, and is often served with eggs or pancakes. It is also used, but less commonly, as a dinner entree. It is frequently accompanied by apple sauce, or apple in some other form.

Sausage meat is also an ingredient in some recipes for poultry stuffing. Unless it has been freezer-stored for a month, it should be cooked and then chopped back to the degree of fineness required. Without this precaution, it is not safe to use in dressing which may not be heated enough for safety.

Frankfurters. Frankfurters are also known as franks, hot dogs, hots, Texas hots and wieners. The standard type contains about 40 per cent pork and 60 per cent beef, both meats cured and finely chopped. There are also all-beef frankfurters. Regular frankfurters are enclosed in a thin membrane, skinless ones are held together by a hardened surface.

Franks are supposed to be pre-cooked, but seem to always be cooked again, at least briefly, before serving. They have a basically reddish color, which is not changed by heat. Many of them are surface-dyed to a bright, poisonous-appearing red, or are sold in packages of transparent red plastic to produce the same effect.

The standard formula for cooking, or perhaps heating, frankfurters is to put them

Fig. 19-2. Skinless franks may curl after being split

in boiling water, turn off the heat and leave them for 5 to 8 minutes. But you can boil them for 4 minutes or simmer them for 5 or 6 to obtain the same effect. This may be total cooking, or a first step before broiling or frying.

Cold franks are broiled about 3 inches below or 5 inches above a fire, turning frequently to get even browning and crisping. They may take 4 to 10 minutes to heat through and get a good appearance. If they are already hot they can be placed closer to the heat, watched more closely and be ready to eat in a minute or two.

Frying is done on a buttered or lightly greased pan, covered or uncovered, at 300 to 325° if they are cold, or 400° if they are hot and need surface finishing only.

Flavor and attractiveness are increased by slitting lengthwise before broiling or frying, but many of the skinless ones tend to curl up, and make this refinement impractical.

Most frankfurters are eaten as sandwiches, in special long narrow hot dog rolls slit lengthwise. It is a good idea to toast or at least heat the roll first, and it may be buttered.

The hot dog and roll may be eaten plain, but it is usual to add liberal amounts of mustard, relish, catsup, chili sauce, sauerkraut, chopped onion or combinations of these substances.

In addition, frankfurters are often the main dish in informal meals. They may be boiled (or broiled or fried) and served with baked beans, sauerkraut or potatoes. Cream gravy or cheese sauce may be added to them. In addition, they may be cut up and mixed into a variety of casseroles or salads.

HASH

The American College Dictionary has two definitions of hash that relate to food. They are: 1. A dish of chopped meat and potatoes, usually sautéed in a frying pan. 2. Any preparation of old material worked

Fig. 19-3. Dictionaries are for definitions

over. And that is about as close as we can get it.

In the home, hash is usually a mixture of cooked meat that has been cut small or ground, potatoes and a moistener or binder such as gravy, broth, sauce or just water. It usually contains onions, and may include almost any vegetable and even hard boiled eggs. Seasoning may be lacking, simple or complicated.

There is no standard recipe or method. Proportions often depend chiefly on the quantities of various ingredients that are available. If not limited in this way, they are determined by widely varying tastes and local customs.

Meat. Meat is the essential ingredient of hash, unless it is fish hash. The recommended kinds are corned beef, roast beef, pot roast, lamb, turkey and chicken, usually in that order. No mention ever seems to be made of veal or pork, but they make excellent hash also.

The meat is supposed to be leftover portions of a roast, or as a poor second choice, canned meat opened for the purpose. However, steaks, chops and trimmings can be used. They usually do not have enough bulk for a good batch of hash, except when a steak turns out to be so tough it is inedible, but they can be used with other meat.

Hash meat is supposed to be lean, but you will get best flavor and texture if you can include 5 to 10 per cent fat if the meat is ground or cut very fine. But if the cut is coarse, most fat should be trimmed away.

The meat may be put through a grinder, preferably at the medium or coarse setting, or cut with a knife into fine pieces, cubes or chunks. The grinder has a special advantage in that it permits you to use crust (the tastiest part of most meat) even if parts of it are quite hard, and would have to be cut away before dicing, as grinder-size pieces are too small to present much of a problem in texture or chewing. Tough meat should be ground also. But many hash-eaters have been brought up on rough-cut meat, and will not be happy with anything finer. Poultry is seldom ground.

Moisteners and Binders. Hash containing only meat, cut or chopped potatoes and other solids is composed of separate bits that do not stick to each other at all. This condition is acceptable or even desired by many, but the majority prefer a more cohesive product, particularly one that can be shaped into cakes that will stay together during final cooking and serving. Also, the meat may not be tasty enough or in sufficient quantity to flavor the hash fully.

A liquid added to the hash mixture will act as a binder. Even plain water will soften the potato surfaces so that they will stick slightly to each other and to the meat. It may be useful during heating in drawing out or activating some of the flavor of the

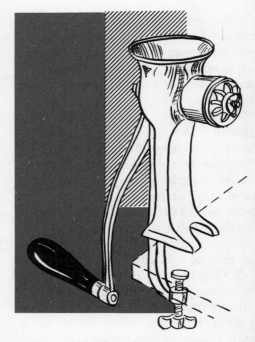

Fig. 19-4. Hand meat grinder

meat. But water is a weak last resort for such purposes.

The best moistener is home made flour-thickened gravy, preferably prepared from the hash meat when it was cooked originally. If it has solidified it can be restored to a thick liquid by stirring in a little hot water in a pan over low heat if necessary. The gravy provides flavor, sometimes more than the meat does, together with moistening and binding qualities.

If you don't have gravy, you may take it out of a can or prepare it from a powdered mix. But remember that while some of these gravies are good, others are awful. If you don't think it is good enough to use with freshly cooked meat, you shouldn't use it in hash. Except that if the gravy's only bad feature is that it is over-seasoned, the hash will dilute it and make it more palatable.

Or you can use home made broth or soup stock, canned concentrated bouillon or consomme soup or (as a last resort bouillon cubes dissolved in hot water. You can use up to 1/2 cup of these liquids to a cup of chopped meat as a water-type moistener, or you can put in a cup or more of it and boil it down.

The larger quantity adds more flavor, but takes more time and is likely to cause overcooking of the already-cooked ingredients.

Gravy may also be made from neutral grease or butter, flour and condensed meat-soup, as discussed on page 366.

Hash made with mashed potatoes, or with potatoes cooked until soft enough to be self-mashing during mixing, does not require gravy as a binder and may become somewhat mushy if it is added. But it will benefit greatly by the flavor, and it should firm up in a few extra minutes heating on the pan.

Corned beef usually has no gravy, so its hash is generally made without binder.

There are also milk, cream and cream sauce thickeners. You may replace water with milk or cream, or gravy with cream (white) sauce. These do nothing for the basic hash flavor, and in fact may interfere with it, but they function well in moistening and binding it. Condensed mushroom soup has the same general characteristics.

Those who like tomato flavor can use condensed soup instead of gravy, or add a tablespoon or two of catsup to any of the moisteners. Again, the distinctive flavor of hash is changed or lost but things work out well otherwise.

Potatoes. Potatoes are probably present in most of the hash made in this country. They are usually boiled, then diced or cut fine. If they are to hold their shape, a little undercooking is advisable, especially if your recipe calls for long cooking of the hash. But many people deliberately crush or grind them, or substitute mashed potatoes, to get smooth texture.

Baked potatoes usually disintegrate during stirring because of their crumbly consistency. But peeling them by removing the brown skin may leave an under-skin that will stay together in rags and pieces that may be objectionable. You can cut or grind such pieces with the meat, or avoid them by deep paring, or by spooning the potato out of its skin instead of peeling it.

Some recipes call for raw potatoes, which may be grated, cubed or cubed and then ground with the meat. They avoid the overcooked condition which follows using fully cooked potatoes and then cooking the hash for extended periods.

However, if potatoes are raw, the hash must be heated long enough to cook them. If the potato is grated or ground, the pan is hot and covered and the hash is moist and compact, this may take as little as 10 minutes. But a loose hash in an open pan may need 30 minutes or more. Cubed raw potatoes may need cooking under a cover for an hour.

Raw potatoes supply some free moisture, and have a greater binding effect than cooked ones.

The proportion between meat and potatoes is important in deciding the character of the hash. The no-potato variety is strong on meat flavor and protein content, but there are many who do not consider it to be real hash. Many recipes call for potatoes ranging from 1/4 of the meat to double its quantity, and some people will use up to 4 times as much potato as meat.

Increasing the proportion of potato past the equal-the-meat mark tends to diminish flavor and food value as well as cost. However, moistening with good gravy and some skillful seasoning can sharpen and improve flavor in any proportions.

Rice. Boiled rice can be substituted for cooked potato in any hash recipe. It changes the character of the product greatly. Although texture and flavor may be excellent, it is generally not popular, except when it is used as a stuffing. Stuffed peppers, for example.

Onion. Onions are in more than half the recipes. When mentioned, quantity per cup of meat ranges from 2 teaspoons to 1/2 cup. They always start raw, and may be described as minced, cut coarsely or sliced. Small doses of minced onion are just mixed in, while larger quantities and coarser cuts are sautéed in butter or drippings before adding the hash mixture to them and stirring.

The quantity of onion, like the seasoning, is entirely a matter of individual preference.

Seasoning. Hash is usually lightly salted by the cook, unless the meat is corned beef or ham. Pepper is frequently used, but in small quantity. Each of the following is mentioned in at least one recipe: basil, garlic, paprika, chopped parsley, chopped sweet pickle, sugar, thyme and Worcestershire sauce. Cheese may be recommended as a top dressing for hash baked in a casserole, but it tends to overwhelm the hash flavor.

Other Ingredients. Other things that you might be told to put in hash are: diced or sliced hard boiled eggs, chopped or diced green pepper, mushrooms, chopped celery and beets or diced turnips, beets or carrots.

Poultry hash may be expected to include poultry dressing, but this is usually a mistake unless both the hash and the dressing are loose and dry.

Recipe. The proportions given below are suitable for a first try for average tastes. They are based on a single cup of chopped meat. This is a small batch, enough for 2 to 4 people, depending on how much they like hash and how much other food is served with it. For more people or larger quantities of leftovers, simply increase all quantities in proportion.

Meat Hash

1 cup	cooked meat, coarsely ground or finely cut
1 cup	cooked potato, diced or finely cut
½ cup	gravy or condensed broth
1 tsp	minced raw onion
1 tsp	salt
1 Tb	butter or grease for frying

You can add almost anything to this, or take away anything but the meat, and it will probably still be hash.

Mix the meat, potatoes, onion and salt, lightly if you want to avoid mashing pieces of cooked potatoes. Stir in the gravy, and it is ready for heating (which you can call cooking if you wish).

Fig. 19-5. Most hash recipes include onions

Hash may be heated in individual patties, in a sheet or shapelessly, on a griddle or in a large frypan. The first two forms are attractive if it sticks together well enough to be turned. Thickness may be from 1/2 to one inch. Use medium temperature for a light crust, high temperature and close watching for a brown, heavy crust. Check by lifting an edge.

Patties are usually turned and browned on both sides, while a sheet is folded half over like an omelet, using two turners.

You can just dump the hash into the pan, and mix it occasionally by running a turner under it, lifting and turning, to bring the crusting parts to the top. Make enough passes to cover the whole bottom of the pan. Frequent turning provides an even mix, fewer turns or high temperature means more crusty bits and greater risk of burning.

Heating and crusting time will be 5 to 10 minutes. It does not matter whether this much onion cooks or not, or rather, it will taste good either way. If you use raw grated potato, or have extra broth to boil down, cook about 25 minutes, using low or low medium heat after the first two minutes.

Raw potato cubes may take an hour to cook, and you will be safer to bake that hash in a casserole, covered for 45 minutes and open for the last 15, in a medium hot 375° oven.

STUFFED PEPPERS

The peppers that get stuffed are the large, sweet bell peppers. They are usually green, but ripe red ones are good too. It is best if you can get medium or large ones, both to reduce the work and to increase the proportion of filling to skin.

A pepper may be stuffed whole, or in halves. For whole stuffing, cut off the small end far enough below the stem for a nearly full-width slice. Remove the insides by grasping and pulling with thumb and finger, and/or cutting resistant fibers free of the shell with scissors, a knife or even a spoon. These parts may be cut small, along with the slice from the top, and mixed with the stuffing; or may be discarded.

For halves, trim off the stem, cut the pepper lengthwise from top to bottom and remove the insides more easily.

About half the recipes tell you to blanch the trimmed peppers by boiling for 5 to 10 minutes. This is to destroy enzymes that might cause limpness and loss of color as they are heated in the oven. The advantage is doubtful, as the heating takes little time and the blanching causes or adds to overcooking. This is an extra operation that can just as well be skipped, unless you feel strongly for it.

Stuffing. The definite requirements for

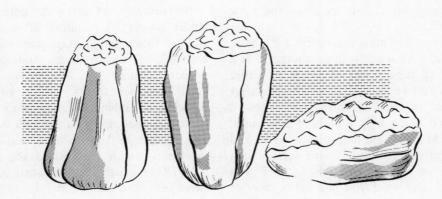

Fig. 19-6. Stuffed peppers

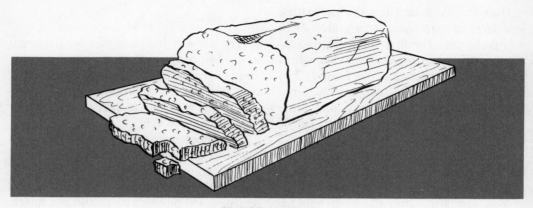

Fig. 19-7. Meat loaf

pepper stuffing are that the mixture be fine enough to fit with reasonable solidity in the space provided, that it be cooked sufficiently so that it will safely finish inside a moist, protective covering in 20 minutes in a moderate oven. The rest is a matter of taste, and there is probably no matter on which cookbooks are more permissive than this. In particular localities and particular families, however, there are likely to be strong preferences, or occasionally a strong aversion to the whole idea.

Peppers may be stuffed with hash — home made, canned or frozen. It may be zipped up a bit by addition of chopped pepper (that stem slice that was cut off, and possibly insides) or onion. If home made, try a special hash in which cooked rice is substituted for potato, in about the same proportion.

If no cooked meat is available for a hash, you can work it out with hamburger. Put a couple of tablespoons of grease or butter or olive oil or equivalent in a frypan over medium or medium high heat, cook a chopped onion in it for about 2 minutes, then add a half-and-half mixture of cooked rice and raw hamburger, stir for about a minute or until the meat looks as if it is cooked, add what you like in the way of salt, pepper and other seasonings, and put it in the pepper shells. Or you can substi-

tute baked beans or finely cut potato for the rice.

For a somewhat more elaborate recipe, try:

Stuffed Peppers *(for 5 or 6)*

6 or 8	green peppers *(depending on size)*
⅔ cup	raw rice *(or 1½ cups cooked rice)*
1 lb	chopped beef
1	egg
1 cup	water
1 can	tomato paste *(about 4 oz)* salt and pepper to taste

Boil raw rice in salted water until almost tender (about 10 minutes), allow to cool and mix thoroughly with chopped meat, egg and half of tomato paste. Add salt and pepper if desired.

The pepper shells, whole or half, blanched or unblanched, are filled with a stuffing pressed down lightly with a spoon. The top may be flat or peaked, and may be touched up with the rest of the tomato paste (if you use this recipe), some chopped sweet pepper, a slice or sprinkle of cheese, or just a bit of butter or paprika.

Not every pepper is shaped to stand upright on a flat surface, so it is helpful to have whole ones fit snugly in a baking dish, so that they can support each other. The dish should be greased.

Bake in a preheated moderate (350° F) oven for 50 to 60 minutes if the filling includes raw meat, or 20 to 30 minutes if it is entirely precooked. If the tops do not brown satisfactorily, turn the heat way up for the last few minutes. If they should start to dry out, put a little hot water in the baking dish.

MEAT LOAF

Meat loaf is usually made by mixing together chopped raw meat, egg, liquid, and cracker or bread crumbs, together with various embellishments and seasoning. It should be cohesive enough to hold together if it is cooked on a flat surface without side support, and to permit it to be sliced without falling apart.

The loaf usually has no difficulty satisfying these requirements, and is often too dense and heavy, and even tough.

Meat. The meat may be one kind or several. A time-honored recipe calls for equal quantities of beef, veal and pork. Other combinations are: one pound of beef with 1/2 pound of veal, 1-1/2 pounds beef with 1/2 pound of pork, and 2 pounds of veal with one pound of ham or sausage. But most recipes settle for just beef, perhaps because this simplifies the shopping.

Meat is usually ground at the store, but you can do it at home. A butcher might not want to clean out his machine to grind a small quantity of pork or veal. You can buy the meat whole, preferably scraps or a cheap cut, and grind it yourself. Fat should be kept down to about 10 per cent.

Recipe. A recipe for one large meat loaf or two small ones, is:

Meat Loaf *(for 6 people)*

1	lb	ground beef
½	lb	ground pork
½	lb	ground veal
1		egg, not beaten
1	cup	dry bread crumbs
¼	cup	water, broth or milk
1	Tb	salt, about
¼	tsp	pepper *(optional)*
2	Tb	finely cut raw onion *(optional)*

Mix the ingredients in a large bowl, preferably with a wooden spoon. Thorough mixing gives evenness of texture and taste, slight mixing provides some variability. A strong electric mixer might be used, but there is not enough stirring here to justify the trouble of setting up and cleaning up.

The loaf (or loaves) may be shaped by hand as desired and baked on a broiling rack and pan, or in the bottom of a large casserole or roasting pan. Or the mixture may be used to fill a utility dish or loaf-cake pan. The rack and the larger containers allow melted fat to drain away, for minimum greasiness of the product.

Baking time is about one hour at 350° F, which makes ample allowance for safe cooking of the pork. Cooking is usually done uncovered without attention, but it may be basted with its own drippings, and/or broth or butter. Slices of bacon may be laid on top.

This recipe can be changed in almost any way to suit available supplies, or taste or whim. The proportions of the three

Fig. 19-8. Meat balls

meats may be equal, or one or two of them may be left out. Two eggs may be used. The bread crumbs and/or onion may be doubled or omitted.

Additions. Other foods may be mixed in. Green pepper, pimiento, onion in small quantity and any of a variety of seasonings may be added. You can use up to a cup of mashed potato or cooked rice to either replace the crumbs, or to supplement them. Tomato ketchup may replace part or all of the water.

Sliced hard boiled egg, carrots, or large pieces of pepper may be folded into the center of the loaf as it is being shaped.

Meat loaf may be eaten hot or cold; plain, with gravy or in a sandwich.

MEAT BALLS

Meat balls are very similar to meat loaf in composition, but are shaped into balls or very thick patties which are usually between 3/4 inch and 1-1/2 inches in diameter. They may be cooked by frying, braising or simmering in spaghetti sauce.

There is unlimited variety in ways to make up meat balls. Thirteen recipes were studied in 8 cookbooks. All but one contain beef, 6 contain pork (one of them pork only) and only 3 call for veal. Three do not call for egg, one has whites only. Seven include dry crumbs, 3 wet bread and 3 have neither. Six call for butter, 4 for cheese, 9 for onions, 9 for salt, 5 for milk or water and one for a can of ham spread.

Seasonings include allspice, caraway, garlic, green pepper, lemon juice and rind, nutmeg, oregano, paprika, parsley, pepper, sugar, wine and Worcestershire. Pepper is in 8 recipes, nutmeg in 4 and the others in 3 or less.

Meat balls are frequently named according to supposed national origin. Swedish and Italian are supposed to be quite different types, but no consistent difference between them appears in the recipes, not even in seasoning. But the Italian ones are likely to be cooked in spaghetti sauce, while the Swedish are more likely to be fried.

The recipe below shows the range of proportions of the more common ingredients in the 13 recipes, and offers a suggestion for a first try for your own.

Sauté onions in butter until golden brown. Soak bread crumbs in milk, then add ground meat, onions, egg and seasonings. Mix until smooth. For main meal use, shape meat balls with hands to about 1-1/2″ in diameter and brown in more butter on all sides.

Meat Balls			
Ingredients	Minimum	Maximum	Try
Raw chopped meat	1 pound	1 pound	1 pound
Dry bread crumbs	none	1 cup	½ cup
(or wet bread)	none	5 slices	none
Water or milk	none	1½ cup	½ cup milk
Egg	none	1⅓	1
Butter	none	4 Tb	2 Tb
Cheese, grated	none	¼ cup	none
Onions, minced	none	2 Tb	2 Tb
Salt	none	2 Tb	¼ tsp
Pepper	none	¼ tsp	optional
Other seasonings			optional

Shake pan continuously to keep round shape of meat balls.

If used with spaghetti sauce, add meat balls to sauce and cook for about 10-15 minutes. If used by themselves, sauté meat balls in frying pan the same amount of time, then remove them and add a little water to pan to get all pan juice out, which is served with meat balls. For "smorgasbord" or for serving on tooth picks with cocktails, shape into very small balls, 3/4″ in diameter and proceed in the same manner as described for larger meat balls.

CROQUETTES

Croquettes are usually prepared from minced or ground cooked meat mixed with thick white sauce and seasonings, shaped into cones or rolls, breaded and deep fried. One or 2 eggs or egg yolks may be included. Mashed potatoes may be substituted for some or all of the sauce.

Boiled rice may be used in considerable quantities, and in rice croquettes, may be the only solid ingredient. Fish (particularly canned fish), shellfish, cheese or mushrooms may be substituted for meat.

Meat is always cooked and is usually a leftover. It may be of any kind, although chicken (and often, turkey masquerading as chicken) and veal are favorites, and beef is seldom mentioned.

Instructions usually call for mincing, that is, cutting very fine. While this may have technical advantages, it is tedious work, and the coarse or even the fine setting on a meat grinder (if you have one) provides for an equal or superior croquette with much less work.

The white sauce provides a binder to hold the meat particles and any other ingredients together during shaping and frying, and provides moisture, richness and flavor. A plain thick sauce is satisfactory, but you get best flavor by making it with an appropriate meat broth instead of water.

Recipe. Croquettes are almost as variable as hash in their possibilities. However, the following is a good representative recipe for a first batch.

Meat Croquettes *(4 servings)*

2 cps	cooked meat, ground or finely cut	
1 cup	extra heavy white sauce, Page 358	
1	egg yolk	
	salt and pepper *(optional)*	

Crust

3 Tb	flour
⅓ cup	cracker crumbs
1	egg
1 Tb	water

Beat the egg yolk lightly, add some hot white sauce, stir, pour mixture back into sauce and stir for one minute. Add the full amount of sauce to the meat if it is dry, but hold back a couple of tablespoons if it is moist. Spread in a thin sheet on a pan or break up into small pieces. Chill thoroughly.

The cold mixture should be firm enough to be molded and keep its shape, but moist enough so that the shapes do not break apart readily. If it is too thin, mix in cracker crumbs (probably only a tablespoon or two) until it has a good consistency. If it is too thick, mix in sauce, milk, broth or water a little at a time.

Fig. 19-9. Croquettes

Fig. 19-10. Middle-of-the-road is all right for recipes

Shape the chilled mixture into cones, cylinders or balls. Cones are the standard or typical shape. They may be from an inch to 2 inches in diameter at the bottom and 2-1/2 or 3 inches high. Cylinders vary from one to 1-1/2 inches in diameter and may be 2 to 3 inches long. Balls are anything from one inch up.

In any shape, increasing the size will increase the ratio of insides to crust, and will of course diminish the number of croquettes obtained from one batch.

A good way to settle the size is to divide your mix fairly evenly into as many parts as you want croquettes. Then shape them.

Crust. The crust is an important part of a croquette, and should be carefully made. Beat the egg and water together lightly, and put in a shallow dish. Spread the flour on a piece of wax paper, a plate or on the table.

Roll each croquette in the flour, pat and shake off any surplus, roll it in the beaten egg and water, making sure the entire surface has been coated by it, raise it and give it a few moments for any surplus to drip off; then roll thoroughly in crumbs. If any bare surfaces show, put them down against the crumbs, or pick up some crumbs and sprinkle and pat them on.

Frying. Croquettes are usually fried in deep fat, at 350 to 375° F, for 3 to 5 minutes or until golden brown. If they float or the fat is not deep enough to cover, they are turned once during the cooking. Since all ingredients are already cooked, the frying serves only to heat them and provide a good crust, so the exact length of cooking is not important.

They are generally put in two to four at a time. When any are done, lift the basket out of the grease, pick the croquettes out one at a time with tongs or with two spoons or other utensils (a large one underneath to lift, a smaller one to steady it) and place on a rack or absorbent paper to drain. Serve hot, plain or with medium white sauce.

Croquettes may also be fried in very shallow fat, or buttered and then baked in an oven. They are good either way, but usually not as good as when deep fried, and there is some question about whether they are still genuine croquettes.

STEW

The traditional stew is a whole meal made in one pot, with meat, potatoes, vegetables and gravy simmered together, contributing their flavors to the cooking liquid and to each other. In the old days, everything was put in right at the beginning and cooked for hours on the back of the stove. The vegetables were usually grossly overcooked.

The newer way is to start with the meat, and add the vegetables when there is just enough remaining time to cook them properly. And there are even pople who are so far away from the original idea that they cook each item separately, only combining them when serving.

Meat. Any kind of raw meat can be stewed, but fat should be trimmed off to reduce greasiness and simplify eating. Most recipes call for beef, a few for veal or lamb, and none for pork.

Stew is a good use for cuts of animals that are likely to be tough, as the long wet cooking breaks down connective tissue. The particular cuts vary with the section of the country. It is usually safe to ask for stew meat, or pick up a package with that label. And there is no law against stewing a tender cut, if that is what you want to do.

Stew meat may be bought with or without bones. If there are bones, they should be sawed (or chopped, but this may make splinters) into 1 or 1-1/2-inch pieces. They complicate the handling and serving, but add flavor and interest. The weight of bone varies with the cut, but is usually between 25 and 50 per cent of the combined weight. If bones are removed, large sinews should be taken out also.

Bony or boneless, the meat should be cut into cubes or pieces 1 or 1-1/2 inches in longest dimension. Large pieces interfere with stirring and are difficult to serve from beneath gravy.

Fig. 19-11. Serving stew

Vegetables. The traditional stew vegetables are carrots and potatoes, with onions and turnip frequently present. Recipes occasionally call for parsnips, peas, whole green beans, cauliflower or mushrooms.

Recipe. It is easier to talk in a general way about stew than offer a specific recipe, as there are many different ways to make it, most of them good. The following is a middle-of-the-road recipe. It will be followed a little later by one for a special kind of stew, New England boiled dinner.

Meat Stew (for 4 to 6 people)

2 lb	lean boneless stew meat *(or 3 pounds with bones in)*
1 lb	carrots *(about 4 large or 12 small)*
8	onions, small or medium
2½ lb	potatoes *(about 8 medium)*
1	small turnip, cubed *(optional)*
1 qt	boiling water
2 tsp	salt *(optional)*
⅛ tsp	pepper *(optional)*
2 Tb	fat trimming or shortening *(optional)*

For Gravy *(optional)*

2 Tb	flour
⅓ cup	cold water

Cooking. This size stew fits comfortably in a 3-quart saucepan, pot, deep-bottom Dutch oven or a deep fryer, with some space to contain possible boil-ups.

Stew meat may be seared, to give it and gravy a brown color and (hopefully) a like-roasted flavor. Searing is entirely optional. It is usually done in the stew pot, but if this is not made of heavy metal or you are afraid of burning your hands on the sides, you can sear on a griddle or frypan just as well. Put the fat or shortening in it, push it around to cover all surfaces, heat to sizzling and put in the meat. It may be either bare or dredged in flour.

Keeping the heat medium high, push the meat around to keep it at least partly in the fat, and turn it frequently with a long-handled fork or turner, or both. When pieces are medium brown on all (or most) fleshy sides, this operation is complete. It is likely to take 1/2 hour in your cookbook, but may take only 5 minutes in the kitchen.

You should have a quart of boiling water ready. Combine the water and the meat in your stewing pot, keep over high heat until it boils, then turn it down until it is just simmering and cover it. Check occasionally, and add water (preferably hot) if necessary to keep the level high. Cooking time should be 1-1/2 to 2 hours. The meat is cooked when it is fork-tender, or when it starts to fall off the bones or separate into strings.

If floating scum appears during the cooking, skim it off and discard it.

The vegetables are added 1/2 to 3/4 of an hour before serving. Scrape the carrots, and cut them in thick slices if they are big or in pieces 1 or 2 inches long if they are small. Peel the potatoes and cut them in quarters or in thick (1/2 or 3/8 of an inch) slices. Peel the onions, and pierce them with a knife from side to center to reduce squeezing out of centers. Add boiling water to cover.

The cooking time of the meat is always a question, and it may run over the 2-hour limit given above. Vegetables are highly variable in this respect also. In the opinion of people who really like stew, overcooking of some of the ingredients does no damage, and may improve matters.

To please others with more exact ideas, you can fish out any item, meat or vegetable, that is fully cooked, and keep it on the side while the rest of the pot catches up. Keep it warm, and put it back at the end for last-minute heating.

Many people avoid this problem by cooking the meat and vegetables separately, and combining them when serving. But in this way they do not get the special blend of flavors that gives stew its character. Also, fussing with a number of pans may be more trouble than timing several foods in one pot.

Gravy. To many, gravy is the most important part of the stew. It may be left natural but more often is thickened with flour, and it is sometimes flavored and/or colored with various additives, including meat extract, tomato paste, glutamate and/or browned flour or sugar.

For an adequate supply of gravy, keep the level of the liquid at the top of the food. If you thicken it, blend the flour and cold water (use a whisk in a saucer, or shake together in a narrow glass), push the food aside with a big spoon or turner, pour the flour and water into the liquid and stir to mix well. Turn heat up to boiling for a few minutes, stirring the stew gently to mix the thickening throughout.

Serving. Stew may be served directly from the pot, or from a large serving bowl, preferably with a big ladle. It is important that it be hot, and it may even be worth while to heat the plates, as stew loses much of its appeal when it is lukewarm. However, it keeps well in the fridge or the freezer, and often tastes better the second day than the first.

Be sure to have bread on the table. Stew addicts use it to soak up gravy, making bits of mush which they may consider the best part of the meal.

Meat Pie. Meat pie, often called pot pie when small, is a stew with a pie-type crust on top. Pieces are cut smaller, with a maximum size of about 1/2 inch. A pie pan may be used, but a casserole or baking dish is more usual.

NEW ENGLAND BOILED DINNER

A boiled dinner consists of a chunk of meat, usually cured, which is cooked in water and is accompanied by vegetables cooked in the same water. It differs from corned beef and cabbage by including other vegetables, and from stew in having its meat in one large piece and in not including gravy.

The meat is usually corned beef, but may be ham or ham shoulder, ham hocks or other cured meat. And it is perfectly possible to make it with uncured meat, but the flavor will be different and you will then want to make gravy, which will change its character.

The quantities in this recipe are all approximate, and can be varied according to preference or availability.

New England Boiled Dinner

4 to 6 lb	corned beef, smoked pork shoulder or ham
8	carrots, whole or thick-sliced
8	small onions, pierced
4	medium potatoes, quartered
2	small turnips, quartered
3	small parsnips *(optional)*
1	small head of cabbage, cut in 8 wedges

If the meat is very salty, put it in cold water to soak for 6 or 8 hours, then rinse it. Put it in a large pan with cold water, bring to a boil and skim. Turn down heat and simmer for 3 to 4 hours, or until it is fork-tender. Then lift it out and keep it covered in a warm place.

Skim off grease or froth from the top of the cooking water. Put in the carrots, onions, potatoes and turnips, bring to a boil and then simmer for 20 minutes. Add the cabbage and cook an additional 20 or 25 minutes, or until all the vegetables are tender. Put the meat back during the last few minutes to warm it.

Lift meat and vegetables out with strainer-type spoon and arrange on a large platter.

CHOPPED LIVER

Cooked liver may be chopped or ground to make liver paté, which is usually served cold as an appetizer, probably on a bit of lettuce. The paté may contain nothing but liver, or be mixed with any of a variety of seasoning or texture-changing ingredients.

The chopping or grinding, which is usually done after frying, braising or simmering, but may be done before baking, may be coarse, exceedingly fine, in between or a mixture of several finenesses, according to your recipe or your preference. An electric blender will produce a very smooth product.

Pork liver seems to make the best paté, with chicken a close second. But the pork is way down on the consumer acceptance scale, so if you use it don't say so, except

Fig. 19-12. New England boiled dinner

to those who might be allergic to pork. Any liver can be used with good results.

Chopped Chicken Livers

½ lb   chicken livers
1   small onion, finely chopped
1 Tb   butter or margarine
1   hard boiled egg, chopped
1 Tb   sherry
       salt and pepper to taste
1 Tb   mayonnaise

The liver is cooked until the pink color has just gone, and then taken off the heat before drying and crusting can start. Some liver can stand long cooking, but it is safer not to risk it.

Sauté onion in butter or margarine, add chicken livers and simmer over low heat about 10 minutes. Grind liver, onion, and egg in a meat grinder, or chop it up finely with a fork. The mixture should be somewhat crumbly. Stir with sherry, salt, pepper and 1 tablespoon mayonnaise.

Serve on crackers as a cocktail snack, or put on a leaf of lettuce, decorate with a tomato wedge and slice of cucumber and serve as appetizer.

20
CASSEROLES

CASSEROLE

A casserole is a container, pot or baking dish, and it is also the food combination that is baked in it.

Container. The container is usually made of glass, but it may be china, soft biscuit ware or metal. The metal may be bare or enameled. The surface may be plain, pleasantly finished or beautifully decorated. It usually has or at least may be fitted with a close-fitting cover.

Casserole dishes vary somewhat in proportions. A typical 2-quart model may be round, 8-1/2 inches in top inside diameter and 2-3/4 deep. The sides are vertical or very slightly sloped outward, and curve smoothly into the bottom. A pair of small projecting ears on opposite sides give a grip (but a very hot one) for handling. The cover is likely to have similar ears.

Contents. There are many differences of opinion about the nature of a "real" casserole. One authority says that it must contain either rice or pasta, another that it really applies only to raw food cooked in a covered casserole dish in a moderate oven.

In the present general meaning, a casserole may be any combination of two or more foods cooked in a casserole dish, whether it is covered or uncovered. Even this very flexible definition can be extended to food combinations baked in a square or rectangular baking dish or loaf pan. But if it contains enough sugar to make it sweet, it becomes a pudding instead.

In any case, the casserole has become a highly valued part of American cooking. It is usually (although not always) easy to prepare, can provide a whole meal out of one dish, is usually flexible about time and temperature of cooking and time of serving, and provides food that is likely to be both delicious and nourishing.

Casseroles are extremely difficult to narrow down to a few recipes, as practically anything goes. I made an attempt to make up a table showing ordinary combinations, but it spread off the paper in both directions because of the great variety of ingredients.

A few types of casserole will be discussed for purpose of illustration, but it should not be assumed that these are necessarily better than the many for which there is no space.

Some casseroles are mixed before plac-

Fig. 20-1. Casserole dish and cover

ing in the dish, and can be stirred. These are usually the fastest to put together, and they are good for electronic cooking. Others are mixed except for a crust of special materials placed on top, which should not be disturbed. Such a crust is sometimes added late in the cooking or heating.

Still other casseroles are carefully built up in layers, and would lose much of their character if they were mixed up.

PASTA

Pasta products, particularly macaroni, spaghetti and noodles, are widely used in casseroles. They provide bulk, nourishment and a pleasing irregularity in texture.

Macaroni and Cheese. Macaroni and cheese is probably the simplest and most popular of all casseroles. The same ingredients can be stirred up in a pan, but the effect is not as satisfactory.

Macaroni and Cheese
(for 4 to 8 people)

½ lb	elbow macaroni, raw (about 2 cups)
2 Tb	butter
1 Tb	flour
1 tsp	salt
2 cps	milk
½ lb	Cheddar cheese, grated roughly or thinly sliced
¼ tsp	dry mustard *(optional)*

Cook macaroni in salted water until tender, and drain. Melt butter in a heavy pan, mix in flour, stirring constantly, then add milk a little at a time, still stirring. Add salt, pepper and 3/4 of the cheese, stirring until cheese is all melted.

Add the drained macaroni and mix well, then put mixture into a greased baking dish, sprinkle with the remaining cheese and bake in a medium hot oven, 400° F, for about 20 minutes, or until slightly browned on top.

Fig. 20-2. Casseroles may be poured or built up

If this is the whole meal, it will serve 4 people. If used as a substitute for potatoes, it should take care of 6 or 8.

Many variations are possible. The cheese for the top can be grated and mixed with the same bulk of dry cracker crumbs. Cubed boiled ham or frankfurters, or coarsely broken tuna or other sea food can be mixed in before baking. Either spaghetti or noodles can be substituted for macaroni.

Macaroni, Meat and Sauce. This is another one that goes together very quickly, if you have the ingredients.

Courtesy of Corning Glass Works

Fig. 20-4. Oval casseroles

Macaroni Hamburger Casserole
(4 portions)

1	cup	raw elbow macaroni *(¼ lb)*
1	tsp	salt
½	lb	chopped meat
1	Tb	butter
1½	cps	spaghetti sauce *(home made or canned)*
¼	cup	*(or more)* grated cheese

Cook macaroni 10 or 12 minutes in boiling salted water, or until softened but not tender. Melt butter in frying pan, add chopped meat, break it apart with a fork and stir over moderate heat until it is crumbly.

Mix the macaroni, meat and spaghetti sauce thoroughly, put into a greased baking dish (1 or 1-1/2-quart size), and sprinkle cheese on top. Bake in 350° oven for 20 minutes, or until top is lightly browned and macaroni is tender.

Courtesy of Corning Glass Works

Fig. 20-3. Square casseroles

Lasagne. Lasagne is a casserole built in layers in a wide, shallow baking dish. Recipes vary in proportions, but the following should serve as a fair sample.

Lasagne *(for 4 to 8 people)*

1 lb	Lasagne noodles
1 lb	Ricotta *(Italian cottage cheese)*
½ lb	Mozzarella *(diced or sliced)*
4 Tb	Parmesan, cheese, grated
1 batch	Meat spaghetti sauce, page 368

These noodles are very wide, and may be either flat or crinkled. Cook in 3 to 6 quarts (see page 326) of rapidly boiling water, with a tablespoon of salt and a tablespoon of olive oil or other shortening, until tender, about 12 minutes. Drain, and keep moistened.

Take a large baking dish, about 9 x 13 inches. Cover bottom lightly with meat sauce, and add a layer of noodles. Cover them with mozzarella and ricotta, and add a layer of sauce. Repeat process to top of dish, ending with noodles. Spread top with sauce and sprinkle with grated cheese.

Cover dish with aluminum foil and place in an oven preheated to 375° F. Bake for 20 minutes, then remove foil and bake for an additional 5 minutes.

Liver and Bacon. Here is a casserole that has a number of ingredients, but is still fairly simple to make, and makes an excellent meal. The origin of the name is unknown.

Columbus Casserole *(Serves 5)*

1 cup	elbow macaroni, raw
4 slcs	bacon
1 lb	beef liver, cubed
3 Tb	flour
1 tsp	salt *(optional)*
½ cup	chopped onion
1 can	condensed mushroom soup *(10¾ oz)*
1 cup	milk
1 Tb	soy sauce
1 cup	whole kernel corn
	minced parsley
	pepper to taste

Boil macaroni in salted water until almost tender, about 10 minutes. Rinse and drain.

Fry bacon lightly and set aside. Roll liver cubes in a mixture of the salt (if used) and flour, and brown in bacon grease. Remove from pan.

Brown the onion in the same pan. Put liver back in pan and simmer with onion for about 15 minutes. Pour mushroom soup

Fig. 20-5. Columbus had a casserole named for him

in a casserole or baking dish, about 2-quart capacity. Stir in milk and soy sauce, add the macaroni and the liver mixture, then the corn, and mix well. Place bacon slices on top.

Bake in a medium oven, 350° F, for about 40 minutes. Sprinkle with parsley just before serving.

Fig. 20-6. Macaroni and cheese

SEAFOOD

Both fish and shellfish are good in casseroles, which are most often made with canned or smoked varieties, both for convenience and because the mixture can both absorb and benefit by the stronger or less-true flavors.

Tuna. Canned tuna is a principal or important ingredient in many popular casseroles. It is a natural for the purpose, as it is economical, cooked, tasty, tender and easily stored. Salmon can be substituted for it in most casseroles, but at a higher cost.

The following is only a sample of many possible combinations.

Tuna and Rice Casserole

1 can tuna, broken in small pieces
    (7-oz)
1 can condensed mushroom soup
    (10½-oz)
2 cps cooked rice
1 cup milk
2 Tb butter or margarine
¼ cup chopped green pepper
¼ cup minced raw onion

Topping
¼ cup bread crumbs
½ cup grated Cheddar cheese

Fry the onions and pepper in the butter until tender, add the mushroom soup (or the same amount of medium white sauce), milk, rice and tuna, stir well and pour into a greased 1-1/2 or 2 quart casserole dish.

Mix bread crumbs and cheese and sprinkle over the top. Bake in a medium oven, 350° F, about 20 minutes or until cheese is melted and the top has a golden color.

This makes a reasonably simple, satisfying meal for 4 people. It can be lightened by serving a green salad or vegetable on the side, if you wish.

Smoked Salmon. Smoked salmon has a strong and special flavor that enables a small amount of it to give character to a much larger quantity of bland food such as potatoes, as in the following recipe.

Smoked Salmon and Potato Scallop
(6 portions)

3 oz smoked salmon *(one can)*
3 cps raw potatoes, thinly sliced
2 eggs
1¼ cps half and half or light cream
¼ cup butter or margarine
1 Tb flour
½ cup minced onion
¼ cup chopped green pepper
1 tsp salt *(optional)*
¼ tsp pepper *(optional)*
    paprika

Fry onion and green pepper in butter until wilted, 8 or 10 minutes, but do not allow them to brown. Remove from heat and mix in the flour. Boil potatoes about 10 minutes, then drain. Cut salmon into 1/4 to 1/2-inch pieces.

Fig. 20-7. The start of a tuna and rice casserole

In a greased baking dish, about 1-1/2 quart capacity, put 1/3 of the potatoes, a little pepper if used, then half on the onion mixture and half of salmon. Continue with these layers, and the top one will be potatoes.

Beat eggs slightly with salt, then with cream, pour over mixture in baking dish and sprinkle lightly with paprika. Bake in medium oven, 350° F, covered with foil for about 15 minutes and then without foil for an additional 30 minutes.

Shellfish. Shellfish such as shrimp, lobster or crab are admirably adapted to casserole cooking, but because of cost are usually reserved for luxury occasions. The following is good with any of these three, or with mixtures of them.

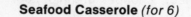

Seafood Casserole *(for 6)*

2	eggs, slightly beaten
1 cup	milk
2 Tb	melted butter
1 cup	bread crumbs
1½ cps	shrimp, lobster meat or crabmeat, or a mixture
1 Tb	lemon juice
½ tsp	dry mustard *(optional)*
	salt and pepper to taste

Blend eggs, milk and butter, add salt and pepper, then the dry mustard if you like it. Add bread crumbs, lemon juice and then the shellfish, mixing well. Pour into a greased 1 or 1-1/2 quart casserole, and bake in a medium 350° F oven for about 40 minutes, until browned and bubbly.

Serve with melted butter and a fresh green salad, or cole slaw.

EGGPLANT

Not everyone likes eggplant. But those who like it at all usually appreciate it in casseroles, for which it seems to have a special quality. It is good just sliced and baked by itself with a little water, plus some butter or olive oil. Its slices can be alternated with slices of zucchini and/or tomato.

Alone, or in these combinations, it may be accompanied by layers of crumbled and browned chopped meat, minced or sliced onion that has been partly cooked, or by grated cheese alone or mixed with bread crumbs.

SPINACH

Spinach goes particularly well with hard boiled eggs. The following recipe is an example of their combination.

Spinach and Egg Casserole *(for 4 or 5)*

1 lb	fresh spinach *(or a 10-oz frozen package)*
3	hard boiled eggs, sliced
1 Tb	lemon juice
2 Tb	butter
2 cps	thin white sauce *(see page 358*
¼ cup	grated Swiss-type cheese
½ cup	grated Parmesan-type cheese

Rinse and clean spinach. Without drying, and without adding water, put in a covered pan over very low heat until wilted, about

5 minutes. Pour off any liquid and put spinach in a greased baking dish, sprinkle with lemon juice and arrange egg slices on top.

Make a white sauce using 2 cups of milk, add the Swiss cheese and half of the Parmesan. Pour over the spinach and eggs and sprinkle with the remaining Parmesan cheese. Bake without cover in medium hot oven, 375° F, for about 20 minutes or until top is golden in color.

SOUFFLE

A soufflé has just a few simple ingredients, but since one of these is air, it is a bit tricky to make and to serve.

Soufflé is the French word for "puffed up" and it is an excellent description of what you should get. The basic soufflé is a medium white sauce with egg yolks added, and stiffly beaten egg whites folded in. Some other food, usually finely chopped, is likely to be mixed in at the same time as the egg yolk, to give the dish its flavor and name. If enough sugar is used to make it sweet, it becomes a dessert.

It is usual to make the white sauce freshly, as part of the soufflé-creating process. The following recipe is fairly standard, but you can substitute heating ready made white sauce for the first part.

Fig. 20-8. Seafood is delicious

When the sauce has thickened, add the cheese, cover, stir occasionally until melted and mixed in. Beat egg yolks until pale in color, add the hot cheese sauce to them gradually while stirring.

Allow to cool slightly, while you beat the egg whites until they form shiny peaks. Fold the whites gently into the cheese mixture, then turn into a 2-quart casserole, or a soufflé dish (it has fluted sides) of similar capacity.

Cheese Souffle *(4 portions)*

2	Tb	butter
2	Tb	flour
1	tsp	salt
⅛	tsp	prepared mustard *(optional)*
1½	cps	milk
½	lb	sharp American cheese, grated or thinly sliced
6		eggs *(separated)*

Combine butter, flour, seasoning and milk over low heat as described under WHITE SAUCE (or use previously made sauce).

Fig. 20-9. Cheese souffle

Your recipe is likely to tell you not to grease or butter the dish, on the ground that a soufflé must be able to grip the sides in order to climb. Or it may tell you to butter it, then sprinkle it thinly with flour or grated cheese.

Informal home tests have shown no difference in speed or height of rising between buttered and unbuttered side sections of the same dish, but the soufflé separated much more readily from the buttered parts, avoiding waste of its good-looking and good-tasting crust. When you make a soufflé, butter half of the dish, side and bottom, and compare results for yourself. Or if you want to be really thorough, have 1/3 dry, 1/3 buttered and 1/3 buttered and floured.

Put in a preheated slow oven, 300° F, and cook for about an hour, until it is puffed high and is any shade from golden to light brown on top. There are two ideas about when a soufflé is done. The conventional idea is that it should be cooked all the way through, so that a test knife comes out clean. But some people like it when it is still semi-liquid in the center.

People should be already sitting at the table with their eating tools in front of them when you take a soufflé from the oven, as it shrinks and loses crispness and flavor as it cools. It is still good to eat when cold, but is not nearly as good.

Other Soufflés. A wide variety of other foods may be added to a cheese soufflé, or used to replace the cheese. Instead of cheese, you can use a cup of minced vegetables, chopped celery, kernel corn, chopped cooked meat or chicken, or any other finely divided substance you fancy. Or you can put the same ingredients, but in larger pieces, in the bottom of the dish and cook the soufflé on top of them.

But anything you use must be well drained, as water or vegetable juice is likely to flatten the soufflé even before it gets in the oven.

21
BAKED GOODS

BAKING AND BAKED GOODS

The term baking originally applied specifically to oven-cooking of bread and cake, but it is now extended to include pie, casseroles, potatoes and even ham. If you cook it in the oven, are not broiling, and it isn't a solid chunk of uncured meat, you are baking it.

However, "baked goods" are still limited to cooked flour doughs and batters. It is their preparation and cooking that will be considered in this section.

INGREDIENTS

The most important substances generally used in baked goods are flour, eggs, leavening, fat, sugar, water, milk, salt and flavoring. These, or some of them, are mixed together in various proportions to form dough or batter. This is usually but not always baked in ovens.

Dough and batter are terms with meanings that may overlap. Dough is usually thicker, and may be made with either yeast or baking powder. Batter apparently never contains yeast, at least not as an active ingredient.

Altitude. High altitude affects baking in complicated ways which are not well understood. The texture and flavor of bread and rolls is affected, and some practice may be required to bring them back to lowland results.

As a basis for trials, alter recipes for each increase of 3,000 feet in altitude above sea level by reducing baking powder by 1/8 and increasing liquid by 1/8. A very slight reduction in sugar is sometimes beneficial, and less shortening is needed in rich cakes. The amount of egg may be kept the same or increased slightly.

FLOUR

Flour may be any finely ground grain. In a broader sense, it may be any finely powdered loose material.

Most of the flour used in baking is white flour made by removing the non-white parts from wheat grains, and grinding the remainder, a process that is called milling. Not all white flour is suitable for use in baking, the principal exception being that made from durum wheat, which is used almost entirely in macaroni and similar products.

All flour is very finely ground, and must

403

pass through a U.S. Standard 100 sieve (100 holes to the inch).

Wheat Grain. For milling purposes, the wheat grain or kernel may be considered to consist of three parts. One is the endosperm, or food storage part, which consists of starch cells in a network of protein (gluten) and small amounts of other substances. This makes up about 85 per cent of the grain, is white or near-white in color, and is the source of white flour.

The protective coatings of the seed, known as bran, are darker in color. Bran contains considerable nourishment, but its color and distinctive flavor make it necessary to remove it as completely as possible from white flour.

Wheat germ is the embryo or living part of the wheat. It contains most of its fat and vitamins. The fat tends to turn rancid in storage. The germ is removed in making flour, but its vitamins may be replaced artificially in enriched flour.

There are two major types of flour-producing wheats, called hard and soft. Hard wheat contains more and tougher protein and is most suitable for bread and rolls, while soft wheat is preferred for cake and

pastries, because of differences in the behavior of their gluten. The general purpose flour on the store shelves is usually a blend of the two.

Starch. Starch, which was described earlier in the chapter on THICKENERS, is a carbohydrate found in all types of grain, and to a certain extent in all plants. Figure 21-2 gives the percentage found in a few representative foods. Pure starch is a fine white powder, without taste or odor. It is insoluble in cold water, but when finely ground it mixes with it readily. It combines with hot water to make a paste or gel.

Starch is chemically similar to sugar, and is readily converted into glucose and other semi-sweet sugars, usually by the action of enzymes. It is somewhat different in structure in each plant, and is found combined with other substances which often give it characteristic flavors.

Starch is unpleasant to eat and difficult to digest when it is raw, but is well-liked and nourishing when cooked. In general, it is cooked with sufficient water and for sufficient time to soften it, without permitting degeneration into paste with water or into hard lumps or crusts without it. Water may be supplied from the plant structure, as in a potato, or added to it as in baking and in cooking rice or macaroni. Added water may be in the form of other foods such as milk and eggs.

Gluten. Gluten is a combination of proteins which make up from 5 to 15 per cent of white flour. It combines with water to form an elastic substance that holds gas bubbles (mostly supplied by leavening, described below) from escaping, and also provides a framework for starch cells. The gluten in wheat is superior in both quantity and quality to that found in any other grain and it is responsible for the superior baking performance of white flour.

Light mixing of water with flour cause gluten to form a very delicate network through the starch. Continued mixing cause

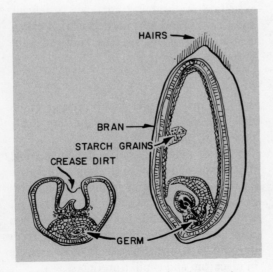

Fig. 21-1. Cross sections of a wheat grain

it to become stronger and coarser, and it is said that the gluten is being developed. If mixing is continued after maximum strength has been reached, the dough reaches a let down or slack stage in which its elasticity is reduced.

Development of the gluten is greatly affected by its proportion to the starch and other ingredients in the dough, and by special characteristics of the wheat variety or of the season in which it is grown.

Flour with a high gluten (protein) content is called strong flour, and favors the development of a strong or elastic dough, suitable for bread or hard rolls, while a lower proportion (weak flour) is better for cake and cookies. A strong flour from hard wheat will have 15 per cent or more gluten, a weak (cake) flour 5 to 10 per cent, with general purpose flour between the two.

Almost any home baked products can be made satisfactorily with general purpose flour, and it is used automatically in any recipe that just says "flour". If cake flour is wanted it is specified. But cake flour is becoming rare in the stores, possibly because most of it goes into cake mixes. You can substitute 7/8 of a cup of general purpose flour for one cup of cake flour, in any recipe.

If flour is kneaded under gently running water, the starch will be gradually washed out of it, leaving the gluten. Such gluten is used in vegetarian diets in preparing meat substitutes.

Treatments. Flour from wheat of different varieties is blended to make a product that is as nearly uniform from year to year as is practical. This work is so skillfully done that variations may not be noticed by the average cook or baker, in spite of extreme changes in the wheat supplies. However, flour sold in one area may differ noticeably from that in another, even if the label is the same. It is usually softer in the South than in other parts of the country.

After blending, the flour is bleached and matured. Bleaching, usually done with chlorine dioxide, intensifies the whiteness of the flour by oxidizing a yellow pigment, carotene, present in small quantities.

Maturing, which improves quality for baking purposes, mostly by strengthening the gluten, occurs naturally if flour is stored for 6 to 9 months under proper conditions, or almost immediately if bleach or special chemicals are used. Flour for commercial bakers may contain potassium bromate, added to improve baking quality.

These bleaching and artificial maturing processes are strongly criticized by health crusaders, but there does not seem to be

Food	Average starch content, per cent
Corn	55 - 65
Oats	35 - 38
Peas	37 - 42
Potato	12 - 20
Rice	70 - 80
Rye	44 - 46
Wheat	55 - 70
Yams	25 - 35

Courtesy of Corn Industries Research Foundation

Fig. 21-2. Starch content of various foods

evidence of any important loss or damage resulting from them.

However, the removal of wheat germ during milling causes almost total loss of the vitamins in the wheat kernel. This loss is remedied by enriching each pound of flour with 2.0 to 2.5 milligrams of thiamine (vitamin B_1), between 1.2 and 1.5 mg of riboflavin (vitamin B_2), 16.0 to 20.0 mg of niacin (nicotinic acid) and some iron and calcium.

Flour enriched in this manner is returned to whole wheat values of nutrition, except for fat, trace elements and the doubtful value of bran.

Fig. 21-3. Whole wheat does not rise well

Self rising white flour is usually general purpose flour to which not over 4-1/2 per cent of baking powder has been added. It may be enriched in the same manner as regular flour. Special precautions must be taken to guard it from moisture, which would weaken the baking powder.

Whole Wheat. Whole wheat flour, also called entire wheat or graham flour, is made by grinding the whole grain, including husk and germ. It is pale brown in color. Although the proportion of gluten is only moderately lower than in white flour, the effect of the bran and the germ is to interfere with baking qualities, so that bread made from whole wheat flour tends to be heavy. A good bread may be obtained by using a half and half mixture of white and whole wheat flour.

Whole wheat flour makes up less than 2 per cent of flour production in the United States, and it is sold almost entirely to bakeries.

Sifting. Flour packs down during transportation, storage and handling to a variable extent, so that a cup of it from one package may weigh more, and therefore contain more flour, than the same measurement from another. These differences are largely eliminated if flour is fluffed up by being put through a sifter, as described on page 20.

Receipt amounts are therefore usually in quantities of sifted flour. First you sift it, then you measure it. This is of course a nuisance. There are several ways of doing it, of which the most accurate is to place a measuring container under the sifter, and keep sifting, adding more if necessary, until the container is full to the proper level. Or you can sift an unmeasured batch of flour, and dip it out with a measuring spoon or cup. But it will be packed a little by the dipping, perhaps 1/16 loss of bulk. Or, when you are used to the way flour acts, you can measure it shaken-up but unsifted, and allow for a difference of 1/8 from the recipe measurement.

In the long run, it is much easier and safer to sift, if your recipe tells you to. If you have a sifter. Sifting is recommended for the recipes in this book.

It is probable that additional sifting, which is demanded by many cookbooks, has some effect on the baking process, but since excellent results can be obtained without it, it should be regarded as an extra flourish rather than a necessity.

LEAVENING

Leavening is any substance that causes dough or batter to rise, either before or during cooking, by introducing or forming bubbles of air or gas. Beaten eggs, creamed shortening and sifted flour include air that mixes into dough. Yeast produces gas bubbles by fermentation, baking powder and baking soda make them by chemical reaction.

Yeast. Yeast is a microscopic one-celled organism of the fungus type, which lives on sugar. The varieties used for raising bread live on sugar in dough, changing it first to simpler compounds and finally into carbon dioxide and alcohol. If there is no sugar, the yeast can manufacture it from starch by means of the enzyme diastase, which is

Fig. 21-4. Sifting increases the bulk of flour

usually present in flour and which can be secreted by the yeast. But this extra process takes longer.

The carbon dioxide gas is held in the dough by the gluten, and causes it to rise or swell. It will rise further during baking because of the expansion of gas bubbles as they are heated. The alcohol also changes to gas, at about 175° F, causing more expansion, but it then escapes and is not found in the finished product. It can sometimes be smelt in underdone bread.

Yeast is prepared commercially in large quantities in special cultures, and may be in either moist or dry form. Moist or compressed yeast, once the standard type for household use but now difficult to obtain, keeps best at 32 to 34°, at little colder than average refrigerator temperature. It loses strength in storage and may become moldy, so that it should be used when fresh if possible. It is mixed into a slurry (thin paste) with lukewarm water before using.

The more popular and available dry or granular yeast has a low moisture content and its cells are dormant. It is re-activated by mixing with at least 5 times its weight of warm (105 to 115° F) water and allowing it to stand for 10 minutes. One-quarter cup of water is enough for one package, but a cupful is often used. Milk may be replaced by water, or sugar may be added.

Granular yeast is sometimes mixed with the dry ingredients, and allowed to find its own moisture in the dough. This is easier, and may be done whenever the recipe so directs. Its action may be slower and less sure, however. Mixing may not be as complete, and any direct contact with concentrated salt will kill the yeast.

In standard sizes, an envelope package of dry yeast, which contains a scant tablespoon, is equal to a cake of moist yeast.

Dry yeast has reasonably good keeping qualities. Packages are stamped with an expiration date at the time they are filled, and are expected to be usable for a year.

This yeast is supposed to be kept in a cool place (meaning around 55° F), but this cannot be found in an average house. It is better to put it on a pantry shelf at room temperature than in the refrigerator, but avoid storing it near a stove or a water heater.

The rate of yeast fermentation in dough is affected by a number of conditions. Its speed increases with temperature up to about 110°, but it dies at 120°. More yeast means faster-starting action, but not necessarily more action. It is slowed by the presence of more sugar than it can use readily. For this reason, a lean (sugarless) dough such as is used in regular bread needs less

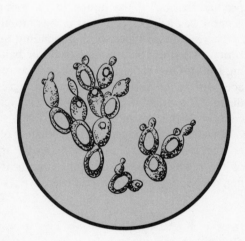

Fig. 21-5. Yeast cells

yeast than a richer (sweeter) one for coffee cake.

Because of these variables, there is no definite rule for the amount of yeast to use. But generally, in the absence of instructions, one package of yeast to each cup of liquid, or to each 3 cups of flour, will be enough to give reasonably quick results. Less yeast will give slower action, but should produce the same amount of rising if it is given time.

A dough may also be supplied with yeast

by mixing in a little uncooked yeast-raised dough (sour dough) saved from a previous but recent baking. This was once a standard practice, but is unusual now.

The preparation of really good yeast doughs and baked products requires experience, luck or intuition, but a passable product may be achieved at the first attempt by keeping in mind the nature of the process, which will be discussed under DOUGH.

There are also special "Coolrise" recipes in which dough is put in the refrigerator to rise.

Chemical Leavening. Leavening may also be done by use of chemicals which, when in contact with each other and with water, give off carbon dioxide gas, which produces rising of the dough in the same general way as gas from yeast fermentation.

There are two types, both depending on action of sodium bicarbonate (soda or baking soda). One is the soda itself, which reacts with acids and moisture in the ingredients. The other is baking powder, which contains both soda and a dry acid.

Powder may produce gas immediately on contact with water, act slowly or have part of the reaction take place only after heating, depending on the formula used.

Fig. 21-6. Baking powder produces gas

Baking Powder. There are a number of different formulas for baking powder. All of them contain bicarbonate of soda as the gas-forming part, but they differ in the acid and in the filler.

A tartrate powder contains cream of tartar, and usually tartaric acid also. These are fast-acting powders, as they start to evolve gas as soon as they are moistened. This means that mixing should be completed promptly, as stirring liberates gas from the batter, nullifying the leavening effect.

There are two types of phosphate powder, one that is made with acid phosphate of calcium, which is very fast acting, and another that is made with a heat-treated and protective-coated anhydrous form of the same chemical, which is very slow acting.

Then there are double acting powders, which contain both the fast acting acid phosphate and an inactive-until-heated sodium aluminum sulphate. They may be labeled D.A. for double-acting, or S.A.S. for the sulphate compound. This type releases some gas during mixing, and then another batch after cooking has started.

The D.A. and S.A.S. powders are supposed to be 25 per cent stronger than the tartrate and phosphate types, which equal each other in strength. The recipes in this book are based on the D.A. type, so that if your baking powder label says neither D.A. nor S.A.S., use 25 per cent more of it to get the same result. No warning of this will be given on the label of either type.

The situation is not even that simple. If you work very rapidly, your batter with tartrate powder will lose less gas and will rise more than if you worked slowly, and will be more nearly equal to D.A. performance. A batter leavened with D.A. is much less affected by speed of mixing.

Some texts on cooking recommend different starting temperatures in baking batters containing different types of baking powder, with the lower temperature for D.A.

Baking powder contains a filler, which

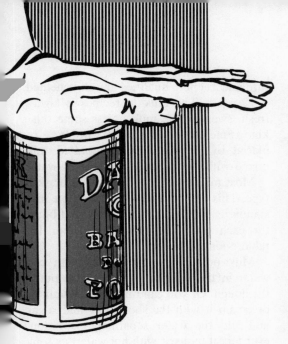

Fig. 21-7. Close baking powder tins tightly

serves to equalize its strength with others in its class, retard absorption of moisture and keep it free-flowing. This is usually starch, but may be calcium carbonate (lime) which tends to neutralize acid in mixes.

If you use one of these lime-filled powders, and know what is in it, you do not have to change from baking powder to soda when you use buttermilk, as this filler will neutralize the lactic acid.

The only part of this you need to remember is that the D.A. - S.A.S. powders are stronger, so you use more of other kinds in order to stick to a recipe. But plenty of housewives have cooked happily and successfully for many years with both types of powder without realizing that there was any difference.

This discussion has been made rather detailed to give an idea of the great complexity that underlies cooking, and that makes it impossible to reduce it to an exact science, or even to positive instructions.

Baking powder must be kept dry. If it absorbs moisture from the air it loses strength, and may eventually become useless. This deterioration is usually accompanied by caking or hardening. Caked or very old baking powder, or any that has been left open and exposed to moist air, should be discarded. Replacement is inexpensive, and may save a baking project.

Always keep the lid of your baking powder can pressed firmly in place, to seal out moisture.

Baking Soda. When you bake with an acid, such as buttermilk, sour cream, molasses or chocolate, you may replace part of the baking powder with baking soda. One measure of soda equals two measures of powder in leavening effect. A half teaspoon reacts with and neutralizes one cup of buttermilk. Too much soda causes a harsh, unpleasant taste.

Baking soda reacts more quickly than most baking powders, so that dough prepared with it should be mixed and put in the pan quickly.

While the powders react in the presence of water alone, the soda must meet both water and acid before it becomes active.

EGGS

The handling and most of the uses of eggs are discussed in Chapter 10. Only their applications to baking will be considered here. One of them, leavening, is so important that there was some question of putting eggs under that heading.

Beaten eggs contain air bubbles, most or at least many of which are included in the dough after proper mixing. They therefore lighten or leaven it. In addition, the bubbles expand when heat is applied, both by air expansion and by addition of steam from nearby moisture.

The white (and possibly the yolk as well) changes and usually improves the ability of the gluten to retain bubbles of air or carbon dioxide during baking. The effectiveness of eggs is indicated by the fact that they are the only leavening in popovers, which are mostly crust surrounding empty space.

Eggs also give a flavor to cake which

most people consider desirable and many consider essential. The yolk provides a yellow color that distinguishes between two types of cake. The fat and other solids of the eggs provide a hard to define but important quality best known as richness.

Eggs are about 75 per cent water. This should be considered in adding or subtracting eggs from a recipe. In fact, the chemical and physical effects of eggs on a dough — leavening, flavor, richness and water content, are so extensive that an inexperienced cook will do well not to make any changes in this item.

When a recipe calls for beaten whites, they usually should be in a stage called wet peaks. Then a withdrawn beater pulls them into a steep peak or peaks, leaving little or no depression. The egg stands in this shape, and has a wet, shiny appearance.

Longer beating produces a stiff mixture wtih a dry appearance, which does not move into the hole left by the beater. In this condition it does not blend as smoothly or easily with dough.

MILK

The general characteristics of milk as a food and beverage were discussed in an earlier chapter. It is an important ingredient of almost all baked products except hard-type bread and rolls.

Whole milk is about 88 per cent water, which is in itself a very important item in proportioning dough mixes. However, milk increases the absorptive qualities of dough, so some of this water is used up.

A bread dough containing milk should be made slacker (softer or thinner) than one that includes only water, as the milk's casein causes stiffening during fermentation, particularly with high-gluten flour. On the other hand, if a soft cake flour is used, milk tends to make the dough firmer at mixing time.

Milk enriches cakes because of its fat and lactose sugar content. Crust color, texture and keeping qualities are all benefited.

Powder. The milk in recipes is always fresh, sweet whole milk unless some other kind is mentioned. But it can always be replaced by powdered or evaporated milk mixed with the required quantity of water.

Most milk powder is the nonfat or skim type. This can be brought up to whole milk standards by adding 1-1/8 ounces of butter for each quart, or a bit more than 1/2 tablespoon to the cup.

Milk powder may be mixed with cool water in the regular way and then put in the dough. Or you can mix it with the flour, or cream it with the shortening and sugar, and add the water separately. But don't ever mix it by itself with hot water, as some of its casein may congeal into lumps that could be removed only by a sieve.

Evaporated milk mixes easily with an equal quantity of water. Its special taste, and that of the powder, are very seldom noticeable after cooking.

Sour. Sour milk is chemically similar to fresh whole milk, except that it is strongly acid. It is usually bad-tasting but wholesome. It is seldom mentioned in recipes, but it is fairly common in the home as a result of keeping fresh milk too long.

Souring can take place in a few hours in a warm room, or in 3 to 10 days in a refrigerator. Differences depend on temperature and the number of bacteria present at the beginning.

Home-soured pasteurized milk is likely to be good in cooking if it has turned rather rapidly at or near room temperature. Under good refrigeration it may rot before or during souring, with production of unwanted compounds.

Buttermilk is sour skim milk, usually cultured, and stabilized at about one per cent acid. It is satisfactory for baking, is featured in many recipes, and can be used in many more.

Sour milk, or buttermilk plus fat, can be substituted for fresh whole milk in recipes

Fig. 21-8. Standing in wet peaks

for yeast-raised doughs without any other changes. However, yeast thrives on the acid, so the dough will rise faster and must be used sooner. There is a difference in flavor, which may be preferred occasionally but is usually not liked as a steady diet.

When substituting sour for fresh milk in chemically leavened doughs or batters, baking soda (bicarbonate) is substituted for part or all of the baking powder. For each cup of buttermilk or sour milk used to replace fresh milk, add 1/2 teaspoon of baking soda and leave out one teaspoon of baking powder. The basis of this is that the powder is about half acid-forming chemicals, and that half is replaced by the soured milk. But the half that is soda is still needed.

SHORTENING (FAT)

Any edible fat or oil may be used as an ingredient in dough. Those most commonly and successfully used are butter, hydrogenated vegetable oil, margarine and lard. When so used, they are called shortening. Shortening is also contributed by egg yolks, chocolate and some other ingredients.

Shortening contributes "shortness", richness, tenderness and flavor to baked products. Mechanically, it assists in the aeration and resulting leavening, lubricates the gluten in yeast-raised doughs, acts as an emulsifier in holding liquids and preventing separation, and provides for development of flakiness in pastry.

Shortening should be at room temperature, about 70 or 72° F when you start to work with it, so that it will be soft enough to mix and blend readily. The best way to manage this is to take it out of the refrigerator (if that is where you keep it) a half hour or more ahead of time. Putting it over heat is likely to melt parts of it, which should be avoided unless the recipe calls for it.

Cold butter or any hard grease will soften quickly if cut or shaved into very thin slices, or if it is mashed or pushed around. The mashing process may be much like the important operation of creaming.

Creaming. Creaming is a process of kneading butter or other shortening. The first stage of the job is to give it a smooth consistency and work some air into it. This is described on Page 20.

When the butter (or whatever) has been worked until it offers almost no resistance to the spoon, you add sugar, often mixed with other dry materials, in small batches. Work each of them in thoroughly before adding the next. Continue to use the back of the spoon.

You may avoid the first stage by buying whipped butter. Increase quantity about 1/3 over the amount of regular butter, to allow for the included air.

YEAST DOUGH

Dough is the mixed raw material from which bread and similar products are made. It is classified in various ways, one of which is the method of leavening, whether by yeast, by chemicals or by other means.

In yeast doughs the standard sequence

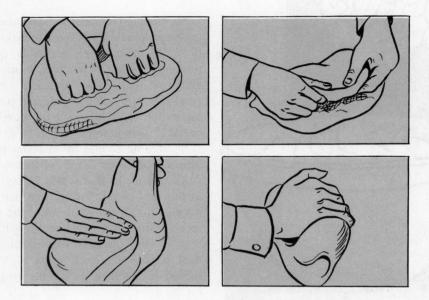

Fig. 21-9. Kneading dough

of operations includes activating the yeast, then mixing it and the other materials together in proper proportions. Quantities are basically those given in the recipe, but it is customary to hold out some of the flour (or more rarely, some of the liquid) until mixing is nearly complete. This enables you to control the final consistency, by adding or withholding as needed.

After mixing, the dough goes through a succession of kneading or working operations, each followed by a resting or proofing period in which the yeast produces gas to make it swell. Work must be started several hours before cooking.

The general process of making and cooking dough will be explained first, followed by more specific instructions for particular types.

Most bread, rolls, sweet rolls and raised doughnuts are raised by yeast.

Mixing. By the standard method, the first step in mixing yeast dough is to sprinkle the dry yeast in 1/4 cup or more of warm water, 105 to 115° F, in a warm bowl, and stir until it is dissolved. Have other liquids in the recipe lukewarm, and add to the yeast solution. Then add the shortening, and the flour a little at a time, beating to combine smoothly.

Your recipe may tell you to scald the milk. This is not necessary with pasteurized or homogenized milk, as the anti-yeast enzyme in it has already been destroyed.

An electric mixer on low or medium speed can mix dough as you add flour until it gets too heavy. Then stop it, clean off

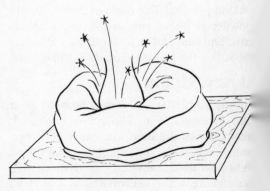

Fig. 21-10. Punching down

the blades, and finish mixing with a big wooden spoon. Or you can use the spoon from the beginning.

Add flour until you have a dough that does not stick to the sides of the bowl, but pulls away from it into a ball as you stir.

First you dust a bread board or table top lightly with flour. Turn the dough out on it, scraping out any that may have stuck, and turn the bowl upside down over it. Leave it for 10 minutes to rest and become stiffer and more workable. Rub your hands lightly with melted shortening.

Kneading. Kneading is required for yeast-raised doughs. Its purpose is to strengthen or develop the gluten in the flour, so that it will be able to retain the carbon dioxide formed by the yeast, and will give the cooked product the proper consistency.

You knead dough by pushing it away with the heels of your hands, drawing it back with your finger tips, giving the dough ball a part turn, and then repeating the process. If it spreads out to the sides, fold them back over the center.

Keep kneading and turning until the surface of the dough is smooth and elastic. You should be able to hold the palm of your hand on it for 30 seconds without sticking to it.

Kneading takes from 5 to 15 minutes. A small batch, energetic work and skill favor a short time.

Proofing. Round up the dough in a smooth ball. Smear its surface completely but thinly with shortening, to prevent formation of a raw crust which might streak the bread. Grease a bowl, put the dough in it, and cover with a damp towel or a tight lid.

Put the bowl in a warm place, 80 to 85° F until the dough ball doubles in size, which should take 1-1/2 to 2 hours. The process of increasing the bulk of dough by standing it in a warm place is known as proofing.

The doubling in size is not an end in it-

Fig. 21-11. Put dough in a warm place

self, but an indication of a desired stage of development. Sometimes it may not quite double, other times it may overdo it a bit. Also, bulk may be difficult to judge.

The test is to poke two fingers quickly into the dough to a depth of 1/2 inch, then pull them out. If the dent stays, the dough is in a doubled condition and is ready for the next step.

When the dough has risen you punch it down. Push your fist down through the center of the ball. Fold the edges into the resulting hole and punch it again. This releases or splits up coarse bubbles of carbon dioxide. Then cover and let rise again until it doubles, an increase that will take less time (but we can't say exactly how much less) than before.

Then take the dough out, put it on the floured table, and divide it into the number of loaves or rolls you want. The easiest way to divide it is to cut it with a knife, but some people feel that it should be cut only with the side of the hand, or pulled apart.

Let the pieces rest 10 minutes or so, covered, then shape them. Loaves should be put in the baking pan, but other shapes need not be. Cover them again, put them in the warm box, and leave until they have doubled in size. This is the third doubling. There will be little rising in the oven.

Warm Box. It may be difficult to find a place with the desired 80 to 85° temperature. In summer Nature often supplies it everywhere, but at such times you are unlikely to feel like baking bread. You may have a utility room containing a water heater, an area near the furnace or a small room that you can warm up with an electric heater.

If you have a gas oven, the pilot light (if any) will keep it warm. If it is too warm, you can leave the door partly or fully open. Or warm a pilotless oven with pans of hot water. There should be a pan of water in any dry enclosure, as air around the dough should be kept moist.

While 80 to 85° is considered the best temperature for dough development, it is not the only one. Yeast will grow and even flourish over a very wide range of temperature, but with differences in texture and flavor of the dough, and in the speed of rising.

If the temperature is above 85 or perhaps 90°, rising is rapid, texture is coarse and the bread is likely to have a raw or too-yeasty taste. At 70° there is a tendency to develop a slightly sour taste. But many, many housewives do proof their bread at ordinary room temperature, often with excellent results.

Even if you have a recipe for proofing in the refrigerator, you may have problems. At present these specify a narrow temperature range, 38 to 41°, which is warmer than the usual setting. But you can probably just turn up the control for the occasion, and back down again when you are finished.

QUICK DOUGH (BATTER)

Baking powder, or baking soda with acid, starts to produce gas as soon as it touches the moisture in the mixture. The dough or batter starts to rise. Part of the gas will be lost while you finish mixing, and transfer the dough or batter to pans. The longer you take for these operations, the more of the gas will be lost.

The proportion of loss will be higher with quick-acting than with slow-acting powder, and highest when there are unreasonable mixing and handling delays. However, recipes allow for ordinary losses, and no harm should result even if you take somewhat longer than an experienced cook would. And once the batter is in its final position in a pan, it can be left a while without damage.

It is because of the early start of leavening action that recipes try to impress on the reader that the pans should be greased and ready and (but a little less importantly) that the oven should be lit before the dough is mixed. Or more specifically, before the liquid and baking powder are combined.

BAKING

In the baking process, conditions must be regulated to allow cooking all the way through and to allow full raising, without causing burning or hard crusting on the outside. It is also important that the surface acquire whatever degree of coloring is appropriate.

The two principal factors are the oven temperature and the bulk and shape of the individual loaves or pieces being baked. Important secondary factors are the moisture content of the dough, the reflecting qualities of the pans and the distribution of heat in the oven.

Temperature. Baking is usually done at moderate to hot temperatures, 350 to 450° F. The proper temperature should be supplied by the recipe. If it is not, try 400°

as a base point, and modify it up or down in accordance with the factors being discussed and results obtained. Recipe temperatures may also be adjusted.

The length of the cooking period depends both on the time needed to accomplish the necessary chemical and physical changes at a given temperature, and that needed to heat the food to that point. These are added together to obtain cooking time.

The surface of dough starts to heat as soon as it is in a hot oven, but the temperature rise may be slow at first because of cooling by evaporation, reflection of heat by the pan and inward movement of surface heat.

Heating of the interior will be later than at the surface in proportion to the distance and to the amount of moisture in the dough. The important distance is the shortest one — cookies 1/4 inch thick will bake in almost the same time whether their width is one inch or four.

A very wet dough may take much longer, perhaps twice as long to cook as a relatively dry one, because of the time and heat needed to evaporate and/or combine the extra moisture.

Unless the oven is too hot, movement of moisture from the interior to the surface will prevent excessive drying out, crust formation or burning until the surface has cooked enough to block easy travel of the moisture. Recipes and pan sizes are usually balanced so that interior cooking is completed very soon after that of the surface. But if you have a problem of wet insides and cooked outsides, turn the oven down to 300 or even 250° F and/or brush exposed surfaces lightly with milk or water.

Pans. Baking pans are discussed in the PANS AND POTS chapter. The chief item of interest here is the reflecting qualities of the material. Radiant heat rays from burners and oven walls penetrate readily through clear glass, are retarded by china and dull metal, and are stopped and reflected back by bright metal.

A bright new aluminum pan will therefore transmit less heat to the food than the other materials.

The result is that cooking is slower, and a larger share of the total heat enters the food through the top. At any one temperature, the bright pan causes more crusting and browning to occur on the top than on the sides and requires a longer cooking time.

If your pans are dull you should use a temperature about 15° lower than you would for bright pans, or you should make the cooking period a few minutes shorter.

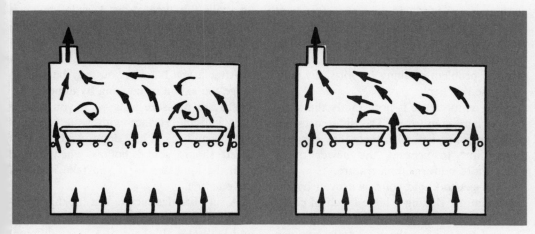

Fig. 21-12. Air circulation in an oven

With a glass pan, use 10° cooler than for dull metal.

Heat Patterns. The typical oven is heated from below for baking. The burners may be in a separate broiler compartment underneath or in the floor of the oven. There is a steady circulation because air heated at the bottom rises, transfers part of its heat to oven walls and roof and to the food, and then either goes out a vent or goes back to the bottom to be re-heated.

In this type of oven there is always upward movement of hot air, and there may or may not be a return downward movement of not-quite-so-hot air.

If two pans are placed in contact with each other, the rising air will curl around their outer edges, heating them more than other parts and causing faster cooking. If they are left with a very small gap between them, or there is a narrow gap between a pan and an oven wall, the restricted air space will act like a flue, speeding up circulation and overheating those edges.

With this in mind, keep a gap of at least an inch between pans, and 1-1/2 inches between a pan and an oven wall.

If pans fill an entire shelf the heat will be trapped underneath them, and very uneven and probably unsatisfactory baking will result.

In addition to absorbing heat from circulating air, the food and pans absorb radiant heat from the burner and from the hot metal around them. This factor is helpful in producing more uniform cooking, except for the problem of shiny or not-shiny pans discussed earlier.

The temperature is not exactly the same everywhere in an oven. The differences are slight in some, while in others they are very important. In general, the newer ovens have more uniform temperature.

You get to know your own oven by experimenting. Baking a large batch of cookies is a good test. By putting small pans in several locations at the same time, you can find where the heat is and how it acts. Then you can make allowances not only for cookies, but other kinds of food also.

Color. Color is a critical problem with baked goods. They must be removed from the oven very soon after they are cooked through, as otherwise they will dry out. If the oven is not hot enough the outside may still be white or pale yellow, which gives an unappetizing look to most items. If the oven is too hot they may be brown and ready to burn while the center is still uncooked.

You can often correct poor color by checking about five minutes before cooking is completed. Color may be increased by making the oven hotter, or sometimes by painting or scattering on a small amount of milk or sugar. Browning may be checked by reducing the temperature, and/or putting aluminum foil over the dark parts if they are exposed.

Testing. The most elementary test for doneness in bread and cake made from chemically leavened dough is to insert a broom straw, toothpick, testing wire or any other thin object into the center of the piece. If any fragment of dough sticks to it, bake a while longer. If it comes out clean, cooking is complete.

A wooden toothpick is probably the most accurate of these indicators. One recent text calls this type of test "crude" but it is the simplest and surest one for the inexperienced cook, and for many with experience also.

After a few batches you may be able to judge the extent of cooking by appearance. There are pressure tests — if you push a dent into the surface with your finger, it will spring back if it is done. And a loaf of bread should sound hollow when tapped with the knuckles — if you take it out of the pan first.

A sure but destructive test for thin cookies is to take out a sample, break it in half, and look at it. If the center looks different from the upper and lower parts, it is not fully cooked. Except some cookies are supposed to be a little raw in the center to make them chewy, but in this case the recipe should tell you so.

WHITE BREAD

Bread is usually made in larger quantities than other baked goods. Home made bread is troublesome to make. It is usually eaten very quickly, in any amount. Either the dough or the finished bread keeps well in the freezer if properly wrapped. All of which is in favor of large batches.

This recipe is for a milk bread that is intermediate between the hard-crusted water mix that produces French bread and hard rolls, and the roll mixes that include egg, with more sugar and shortening. It will make 3 or 4 loaves, weighing from 1 to 1-1/2 pounds each. Or you can make only part into bread, and the rest into rolls. It is heavy work, but worth it.

Fig. 21-13. The toothpick test for cake

Basic White Bread

9 cps	flour
2 pkgs	yeast
1 cup	lukewarm water *(105 to 110° F)*
1 tsp	sugar
2 cps	milk *(or 1 cup of milk and 1 cup cold water)*
4 tsp	salt
¼ cup	sugar
¼ cup	melted butter or shortening

Sift flour, measure and set aside. Dissolve sugar in lukewarm water, pour or crumble yeast into it, stir and set aside for 10 minutes.

Heat milk or milk-and-water to almost boiling, pour into 5-quart mixing bowl with salt and 1/4 cup of sugar, and allow to cool to lukewarm. Then stir in the yeast-water mixture. Add about half the flour

and the cooled melted shortening. A strong electric mixer can take the work through here, but no further.

Add and stir in flour with a big wooden spoon until you have a smooth soft dough that has thickened just past the sticky stage. If you don't put in enough flour, the dough will be unmanageable, and if there is too much you toughen the bread.

On a first batch you might figure on just using the full 9 cups of flour, and risking a bit of toughness. But if you work it out carefully, you might have 1/2 to 3/4 of a cup left over.

Then follow the instructions under YEAST DOUGH.

Baking. Bread or loaf pans come in several sizes, of which 9 x 5 inches, and 3 inches high, is good for average loaves. These pans may be glass, but are more often aluminum.

Bake in a moderately hot oven, about 400° F, for 30 minutes, or a shorter time for small loaves. The bread should be done when it is well risen, preferably above the sides of the pan so that there is a bulge or "spring". The crust should be golden brown and crisp. As mentioned earlier, you can test it for a hollow sound by tapping the bottom after it is out of the pan.

Turn the loaves out on a rack or racks. They will sweat and get soggy where they are in contact with a solid surface. Allow to cool gradually, preferably in a warm place, free of drafts.

Bread that is sliced and buttered when it is fresh and hot from the oven is delicious. You may feel that a small sacrifice of quality in the remnant of one loaf is not too high a price to pay for it. Use a sharp or toothed knife. And don't eat too much of it, as some people find it hard to digest.

FRENCH BREAD

French bread is made from a water yeast

Fig. 21-14. Bread should rise above the sides of the pan

dough, shaped into long thin loaves and baked on cookie sheets. The same dough makes excellent hard rolls, and can be used also in making English muffins or pizza crust.

There are deep differences of opinion about what constitutes a real French bread dough. Purists claim it should contain no milk, sugar or shortening, but most recipes sneak two of them in. The strong and often tough crust that is characteristic of this bread results to a considerable extent from the way it is baked.

French Bread

4	cps	flour, about
1	pkg	yeast
1	cup	lukewarm water *(105 to 110° F)*
2	tsp	sugar
1	Tb	shortening
2		egg whites, unbeaten
1½	tsp	salt
1	Tb	corn meal *(optional)*

Sift and measure the flour. Soak yeast in 1/4 of the cup of water for 10 minutes. Put remaining water in 4-quart bowl, mix in sugar, salt, shortening and one cup of flour and beat until smooth.

Stir in the yeast mixture, then one egg white. Add flour gradually, beating and stirring until the dough is stiff. Put it on a lightly floured board, and knead, proof and punch it down in the manner described earlier for YEAST DOUGH.

You can make all this dough into one loaf, about 14 inches long and tapered at the ends; a somewhat smaller loaf and a few rolls, 2 or 3 small loaves, or 15 or 20 rolls.

Place them on a greased baking sheet sprinkled with corn meal, which both prevents sticking and gives a special gritty texture to the bottom crust. Make five or six diagonal slashes about 1/8 inch deep across the top of the loaf or loaves.

Beat the remaining egg white with a tablespoon of water (and a teaspoon of salt if you like a salty crust) and brush it over the loaf or pieces. Cover with a damp cloth and leave in a warm place until they double in size. Bake at 425° F to start and reduce to 350 after 10 minutes. Keep a shallow tin of boiling water on the lower shelf to produce crustiness.

Baking time should be about 45 minutes for a single loaf, 20 or 25 minutes for smaller portions. Take the bread out once

Fig. 21-15. French bread

or twice during baking to brush again with egg white mixture. When done, the crust should be golden brown. After turning out of the pan, a loaf should sound hollow when you thump it.

ROLLS

Rolls are made with dough that is basically similar to bread dough, but which is usually made richer by moderate increase in shortening. Eggs are often added.

Soft Rolls

2½	cps	flour
1	pkg	yeast
2	Tb	soft butter
1	Tb	sugar
¼	cup	warm water
¾	cup	lukewarm milk
1	tsp	salt
1		egg, lightly beaten *(optional)*

Put the water in a warm mixing bowl, stir in the yeast, let stand for 10 minutes, then stir in the milk. Add butter, sugar and salt and mix in 2 cups of flour, gradually. Beat with a wooden spoon for 5 minutes, or with an electric beater on slow speed for 2.

Blend in enough more flour to make the dough just firm enough to handle. Follow general instructions for kneading, allowing to rise, then punching down, given under YEAST DOUGH. It is not necessary to allow it to rise again after punching, but you will get finer texture if you do.

You can manipulate the dough to get rolls of almost any shape. If you roll it out about 1/3 inch thick you can cut round rolls 2 or 2-1/2 inches across with a biscuit cutter or a glass. If you make them smaller size, with a juice or shot glass, and place them in the pan in groups of 3, you get cloverleaves.

For Parkerhouse, cut ovals or roll out rounds to oval shape, crease the short way across the center with a floured knife handle, paint the upper surface with melted butter and fold at the crease. Bowknots are obtained by cutting the dough into strips, or rolling it between the hands into a rope, then tying knots in it. Paint surfaces with butter, both during and after shaping, to prevent re-combining.

Place shaped rolls on greased cookie tins or shallow baking pans, cover with cloth and allow to rise for an hour. Bake at 425° F until well browned. If you are in doubt about the inside, test with a toothpick.

Hard Rolls. Use the same recipe as for

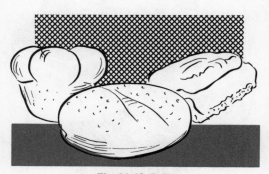

Fig. 21-16. Rolls

Soft Rolls, with an additional egg white, or the French Bread recipe unchanged. The dough is handled the same way, but it is unusual to make fancy shapes. Shape into balls or cylinders about 1/3 of the size you want for the rolls. Put aside, preferably in a warm spot, for an hour. Bake at 400° F, with a pan of boiling water in the oven to keep the air moist. Paint with egg white diluted with water before putting in the oven.

For seeded rolls, sift sesame or poppy seed onto the tops just after applying the egg white.

BISCUITS

Plain biscuits are the simplest of the quick (chemically leavened) breads. They contain just flour, baking powder, shortening and a bit of salt. Once you get the knack they are quickly and easily mixed, and even this slight trouble can be reduced by buying ready-mixed ingredients in a package, or even rolls of dough that need only be sliced and put in the oven.

Biscuits do not contain as much shortening as pie crust does, but the principal difference is in the use of baking powder. They differ from muffins in their lack of eggs.

In general, baked goods taste better when

Fig. 21-17. Tall biscuits

they are hot or warm than when they are cold. This is particularly the case with biscuits, which should be baked immediately before eating time and served from the hot pan, whenever possible. They are good with butter, and/or jam, jelly or honey.

Plain. Biscuit recipes are usually similar to each other, but no two are likely to be exactly the same. The proportions given below are in the center of the range, and minor variations one way or another should have little noticeable effect. As with pie crust, minimum handling of the dough is the most important factor in good results.

Plain Biscuits

2	cps	flour
3	tsp	baking powder
½ to 1	tsp	salt
⅓	cup	shortening
¾	cup	milk

Sift and measure all the flour, and then sift with baking powder and salt into a bowl. The second sifting is advisable here, as a lump or clump of baking powder shows up as a brown spot on the crust.

Add shortening, and cut it in with a pastry blender or two knives until the mixture is crumbly, as described under PIE CRUST, page 451. Then add the milk all at once, and mix quickly with a wooden spoon until dough leaves the sides of the bowl, and can be gathered into a ball. This should not take over a minute of stirring.

Put the dough ball on a floured board, wax paper or pastry cloth and knead briefly, 6 or 8 strokes or for about 30 seconds. Then roll and/or pat out (be sure to have flour on rolling pin and hands, as this dough can be really sticky) until it is about 1/2 inch thick. Cut out circles with straight-down pushes of round cutter or glass, dipped in flour for each cut. Put remnants together, and cut or mold into similar size.

Arrange rounds on a cookie sheet. If you

Fig. 21-18. Muffins

like biscuits crusty all over, place them an inch apart, otherwise make spaces only 1/2 inch. Bake in a pre-heated 450° oven until they are golden brown and can pass a toothpick test, about 10 or 12 minutes.

These biscuits should be about one inch thick. If you like them thinner and mostly crust you can roll the dough 3/8 or even 1/4 inch thick. For tall biscuits, make it 5/8 or 3/4 inches thick.

Stir-and-Roll. This is practically the same recipe, with salad oil substituted for the solid shortening. You can hold back a tablespoon of the milk. You do not need to blend in the oil — just add it and the milk at the same time and stir briefly, until the dough leaves the side of the bowl and can be formed into a ball. Rolling, cutting and baking are the same.

Buttermilk. You can make buttermilk biscuits by just substituting buttermilk for milk in either of these recipes. But it is more usual to then replace half (1-1/2 teaspoons) of the baking powder with 3/4 teaspoon of baking soda.

Variations. A great many variations on these basic recipes are possible.

For drop biscuits, use an extra tablespoon of shortening or oil, and an extra 1/4 cup of milk. Stir together in the bowl, then transfer directly to baking sheet or into muffin pans by heaping tablespoons. Cooking takes 3 or 4 minutes longer.

Bacon biscuits call for addition of 1/4 to 1/2 cup of drained, crisp crumbled bacon when stirring in the liquid. Or use the same quantity of chopped chives — for chives biscuits, of course.

For cheese biscuits add 1/2 cup of grated cheddar cheese to the flour mixture, after sifting.

A recipe for sweetened biscuit for shortcake and other desserts is given on page 556.

MUFFINS

Muffins are another easily made and popular type of bread, somewhat more elegant in appearance than biscuits. They are best when eaten fresh and hot from the oven, but can also be eaten cold.

Standard muffins differ from standard biscuits chiefly in containing egg and sugar, with somewhat less shortening, and in being cooked in individual tins or cups instead of on a sheet. Mixing time is shorter, but cooking is longer. Various recipes show only a moderate amount of difference in ingredients. The most important requirement in all recipes is light, almost incomplete mixing of the batter. Over-mixing causes poor texture and toughness.

Pans. Muffin pans, also called tins or cups, contain a number of slightly tapered depressions, each of which holds one muffin. They are also used for cup cakes. These may be 6, 8 or 12 in a single sheet, or be individual units. The multiple ones are usually sheet aluminum, but may be foil. Individual units may be made of the same materials, but more often are of glass or pleated paper.

The cups are only approximately standardized. The medium size, which is the most popular, is about 2-5/8 inches across the top, 2 inches at the bottom and 1-1/8 inch deep. Your cookbook may call it a 2-inch cup. It holds between 1/4 and 1/3 cup, level measure. Somewhat larger cups that hold 1/2 cup are called medium in some cookbooks.

There are also small cups and tiny cups (minicups?), down to less than 1/8 measuring cup. Any of these should be only 2/3 filled with batter, to allow for expansion.

Muffin cups require greasing, unless Teflon-lined. Greasing with butter seems to improve flavor and texture of the crust, and

Fig. 21-19. Muffin texture

it is often used even with Teflon. The greasing should be done before mixing the batter, as it takes a little time.

If you do not have enough batter for all the cups in a multiple pan, it is a good idea to put 1/4 to 3/8 inch of water in the empties. Otherwise their extra heat-absorbing capacity may cause the muffins next to them to cook too rapidly.

Plain Muffins
(about 12 medium muffins)

2	cps	flour
3	tsp	baking powder
½	tsp	salt *(optional)*
3	Tb	sugar
1		egg
1	cup	milk
3	Tb	melted butter

Sift and measure flour. Resift or mix well with baking powder, salt and sugar, put in large bowl. Beat egg in small bowl, add milk and melted butter. Make a well (central hollow) in the flour mixture and pour in the other ingredients, all at once. Stir quickly until the flour is just dampened, continue stirring for only 4 or 5 strokes.

The batter should be lumpy, not smooth. Spoon the batter into prepared pans (greased unless Teflon or paper), filling cups about 2/3 full. The batter should drop cleanly from the spoon. If it does not, you have probably overmixed it.

Put in an oven preheated to about 425° F, and cook until they are golden brown and a test toothpick comes out clean, about 20 minutes. Take out of the oven, loosen by passing a dull knife around the edge, then pry slightly to lift the muffin.

Serve immediately, uncovered, preferably on a hot plate. Surplus muffins may be loosened, turned on their sides for ventilation and put on a rack to cool.

There are many variations. The basic recipe may be altered by doubling the butter and the egg, tripling the sugar and cutting the milk down to 3/4 cup. The resulting muffin is often called Twin Mountain, and is sweeter and somewhat lighter than the plain variety.

In either case, you may cream the butter, add the sugar to it and mix it with the flour mixture, rather than melting the butter and putting it in with the milk.

Texture. Cooks and cookbooks make a major issue of muffin texture, perhaps because results tend to be poor if you work hard. If mixing of the liquid and the flour is just sufficient to dampen all the flour, a job an expert can do in 15 to 30 seconds, depending on her energy level, and the batter is spooned into the cups promptly, the muffins should be the lightest and best, with small air holes evenly distributed in a tender structure.

Too little stirring results in larger, irregular holes, and perhaps some dry spots, but this situation seldom arises. Overstirring is the error most often committed. It results in a less tender (but not necessarily tough) texture, and the combining of numbers of air holes into long strings called tunnels. To a muffin fancier, these tunnels are a disgrace.

The tunneled muffin is likely to have a knob on top. This is caused by a firm crust forming before expansion of the dough is complete, so that pressure builds up to a breakthrough of some still-liquid batter, that cooks over the original surface.

A couple of generations ago such knobs were regarded as a sign of top-quality muffins, now they indicate failure. But these muffins do still taste good, and the knob usually has an attractive appearance.

ENGLISH MUFFINS

English muffins are not at all like any other muffins, and very little like any other popular food. They are small, flat, rather tough rounds of bread made with yeast dough and "baked" on a griddle or frypan on the top of the stove.

Fig. 21-20. English muffin, broken open

English Muffins

4	cps	flour
4	Tb	melted butter
2	Tb	sugar
1¼	cps	milk, lukewarm
½	cup	water, warm
1	pkg	yeast
2	tsp	salt *(optional)*

Dissolve yeast and sugar in lukewarm water, and allow to stand 10 minutes. Heat milk to lukewarm, add to yeast with butter, salt and a little flour and blend. Add the rest of the flour, stirring with a large spoon (preferably wooden) until well mixed. Turn dough out on lightly floured board and knead until it is smooth and elastic.

Then place it in a greased bowl, cover and let rise in a warm place until double in bulk, possibly 2 hours.

Roll out dough to be about 3/4 inch thick and cut round cakes, about 3 or 4 inches in diameter, with a cutter or a glass. Combine and cut the scraps. Let rise in a warm place for about 45 minutes.

Fry the muffins on a lightly greased griddle at about 300° (moderately hot, or over a burner set at medium) for 15 or 20 minutes, turning occasionally.

Serving. English muffins are almost always split and toasted before serving. Appearance and flavor are most interesting if they are torn apart rather than cut. There is a soft ring or depression running around the muffin, between the crusts. Insert fingers in this and pull apart.

To avoid chance of tearing the crust, make small tears in several adjoining places before pulling it fully apart. Or slice them with a knife, if you would rather.

You can use a pop-up toaster, but you may have some trouble with high spots causing them to stick down. Or heat them under a broiler. Serve hot with butter on them or beside them, and jam or jelly on the side.

These muffins (either your own or bought ones) can be used to make individual pizzas. Spread the filling on the broken or cut surfaces, and heat in a hot oven or under a broiler.

POPOVERS

Popovers are a special sort of muffin, made without any leavening except egg. They increase their bulk by 4 or 5 times while cooking, and consist mostly of crust and large voids.

Popovers

1	cup	flour
1	cup	milk
2		eggs, beaten
1	Tb	melted butter
1	tsp	sugar
½	tsp	salt

Preheat oven to 475° F. Use 10 custard cups, supported on a cookie sheet, or muffin pan (preferably deep) with medium size cups. Grease them thoroughly, and preheat in the oven for a couple of minutes before using.

Mix flour, sugar and salt in a mixing bowl. Beat eggs in another bowl, first by themselves, then with butter and milk, and add to flour. Beat thoroughly with a rotary beater for a minute or two to develop the gluten. This batter is thin and easy to beat.

Pour into hot pan (or cups), half filling the cups, and place in hot oven. Cook for 12 minutes, then reduce heat to 350° and bake for 12 minutes longer. Puncture with a skewer or an ice pick, and cook 3 to 5 minutes more.

Popovers start to rise as soon as they are in the oven, and may be showing some color even before you turn the oven down. They rise high above their containers, and may slump to one or all sides. The irregular shape is characteristic.

The popover consists of an outer browned crust, a few inner partitions, and a soft or moist inner lining on the crust. Puncturing while cooking lets out some steam and should prevent the lining from being soggy.

Lift them out of their cups with tongs or quick fingers, and serve immediately with butter and possibly jam. Leftovers can be reheated for another meal or snack, but not in an electronic oven, which toughens them.

COFFEE CAKE

The term coffee cake is flexible enough to include almost any bread or cake customarily eaten as a breakfast, snack or light meal, with coffee, tea or milk. One of its specific meanings is a group of rolls and pastries made of a sweetened yeast dough, sometimes called kuchen, with or without extra flavorings, ingredients and/or topping.

There are also a number of coffee cakes made with baking powder. They are distinguished from dessert cakes chiefly by a smaller sugar content.

Sweet Rolls. These sweet rolls are leavened with yeast, and are handled according to the general procedures discussed earlier under YEAST DOUGH. Recipes vary greatly in the size of the batch, and may call for 1-1/2 to 8 cups of flour.

In order to compare the proportions, these have been reduced to a 2-cup basis below. The unusable fractions (1/3 of an egg, for example) are for comparison only. Both the range of variation in the recipes and a recommendation for a first try are given.

Heat the milk to lukewarm, add to the yeast in a mixing bowl and allow to stand for 10 minutes. Add the eggs, butter, sugar

Sweet Rolls *(Two-cup batch)*			
Ingredients	Minimum	Maximum	Try
Flour	2 cps	2 cps	2 cps
Yeast	¼ pkg	1⅓ pkg	1 pkg
Eggs	⅓	2⅔	1 or 2
Butter	2 Tb	6 Tb	4 Tb
Sugar	1½ Tb	6 Tb	4 Tb
Milk	2½ Tb	22 Tb	12 Tb *(¾ cup)*
Salt	¼ tsp	1⅓ tsp	optional
Spice	none	1/10 tsp	none
Lemon rind	none	1/5 tsp	none

and salt and mix thoroughly with a strong rotary beater. Add about half the flour while continuing to beat. Remove and clean the beater, and let the dough rise at room temperature about 45 minutes.

Mix in more flour, using a heavy spoon. Use just enough to make the dough just barely firm enough to handle. Cover with a damp cloth, and chill in the refrigerator for a half hour.

Knead the dough for 8 or 10 minutes, then make into shapes and arrange on buttered pan, leaving room for expansion. Brush with melted butter, cover with a clean towel and let rise for about an hour, or until bulk is doubled. Bake in a preheated oven at 400° F until golden brown, which should take 10 to 20 minutes, depending on thickness of the pieces.

Shaping. This dough holds its shape fairly well during rising and cooking, although straight lines bulge into curves, so that most shapes remain recognizable. Painting with butter prevents features of design from melting into each other, so they will separate easily even if they overlap.

Round coffee cakes (often mis-called Danish) may be made by shaping the dough into a rope about 3/8 inch in diameter, and arranging it in a flat spiral. Or you can shape it into rings, or into squares or triangles, or even cook it in a pan-width flat sheet, to be cut up later.

Sweet rolls are usually embellished in some way. They may be frosted just before or just after taking out of the oven with a little confectioners' sugar dampened with water, or sprinkled with granulated sugar a few minutes before cooking is complete. A quarter of a cup, more or less, of raisins may be mixed with the dough. They may be whole or cut into small pieces.

The rope of dough from which you form a spiral cake may be painted with butter and dusted with cinnamon and sugar, and raisins inserted between the loops. The top may be sprinkled with finely sliced nuts, or

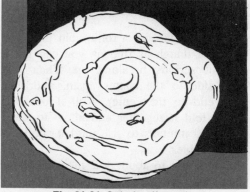

Fig. 21-21. Spiral coffee cake

with any one of a number of crumb and similar toppings.

Danish. Danish pastry may be prepared from sweet roll dough by rolling it into thin plates separated by films of butter. To do this you knead it, then roll it on a floured board or table into an oblong, about 1/4 inch thick. Slice 2 quarter-pound sticks of medium-cold butter into squares about 1/8 inch thick, and arrange half of them along the center third of the dough.

Fold one of the side thirds of dough over the buttered center, and put the remaining butter slices on it. Then fold over the other side. Press the edges firmly together, dampening them if necessary to make them stick. If the butter has had time to soften, put the dough into the refrigerator to harden it slightly. A temperature of about 40 or 45° F is ideal for this job.

Figure 21-22 shows the dough after the

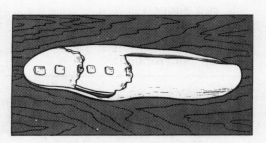

Fig. 21-22. Folding dough over butter, for Danish pastry

third fold. The resemblance to a space ship is unintentional.

Pat and roll with a rolling pin until you have the dough as thin as you can get it without serious breaking up. Then fold each side to the center again, and then each end to the center. Roll it out thin again, fold it together and allow to stand 20 or 30 minutes to rise until its bulk almost doubles.

Roll it out to about 1/2 inch thickness, then shape into crescents, spirals, circles or anything you wish, and put on cooky sheets greased or covered with oiled brown paper. Brush with butter, allow to rise again, and then bake at 375 or 400° F for 20 or 25 minutes, or until done. You can sprinkle with chopped nuts and/or sugar.

With Baking Powder. There are also a number of coffee cakes prepared with baking powder instead of yeast. Since preparation of the dough or batter involves less fussing, recommended quantities in the batch are usually smaller, calling for only one or two cups of flour, instead of two to eight. Proportions are only moderately variable. They can be used as dessert cakes also.

The following is a conventional type of recipe that should give good results.

Plain Coffee Cake

1½	cps	flour
1		egg
3	Tb	butter
¾	cup	sugar
½	cup	milk
2½	tsp	baking powder
½	tsp	salt *(optional)*

Cream the butter, first alone, then with sugar, and mix thoroughly with the egg. Stir in the milk. Sift the flour, baking powder and salt together and stir in. Spread batter in greased and floured 9 x 9 inch baking pan. Bake in medium oven, 375° F, for 25 to 35 minutes, or until a test wooden toothpick comes out clean from the center.

This basic cake can be embellished by adding to the batter a half cup of raisins, or the same amount of unsweetened or semisweet chocolate that has been coarsely grated. This would be the last operation before putting the mixture in the pan.

Coffee cake may be served plain, but it is more usual to put a topping of some kind on it, such as those mentioned on page 441. Or it can be spread with marmalade or jam.

CAKE

There are two principal types of cake, distinguished chiefly by the presence of shortening (butter cakes) or its absence (sponge and angel food). There is an intermediate type called butter-sponge or chiffon cake.

Butter cakes may be subdivided into yellow, white, one-egg, two-egg, chocolate, spice and pound cakes, or classified in other ways. A distinction can also be made between "old-time" and "quick mix" cakes.

Most of this discussion of butter cakes will concern start-from-scratch cakes cooked out of the basic ingredients of flour, sugar, egg, milk, baking powder, shortening and flavoring.

There are cake mixes, many of them of high quality, which eliminate some of the mixing steps, and which can be made according to directions on the packages. You will get better results with these, if you have had practice with the full proportioning and mixing operation. But you can do it the other way also, and practice with mixes before tackling the whole job.

Falling. There is a special hazard overhanging anyone who makes a cake — it may fall. That is, a large part of the carbon dioxide and/or air in the dough may leak out of it during baking, leaving a thin or misshapen super-cooky that is likely to be heavy, soggy and tough.

This disaster was once very common, is now rather rare, and its causes are obscure. It usually follows some major mistake in proportions, mixing or oven temperature, but may be caused or assisted by jarring of the oven by slamming doors, people running or a nearby explosion.

Ingredients. The basic cake ingredients are flour, shortening, baking powder, milk, sugar and flavoring.

Most cookbooks recommend using cake flour, which is a soft-wheat, low-gluten variety especially compounded for cake. But this is scarce and difficult to buy in many areas, and the advantage in using it is small and even doubtful.

Recipes here are based on ordinary or general purpose flour. If you use cake flour, use two additional tablespoons for each cup, without changing other ingredients.

Butter is highly esteemed as a cake ingredient, for its effect on flavor and on crust color. Margarine or hydrogenated fat may be substituted in the same quantities. Reduce the quantity about 10 per cent if you use solid fat (lard, for example) or oil, as these are not diluted with either water or air.

The nearly hopeless confusion in regard to baking powder has been discussed earlier. These recipes are based on the double-acting type. If you use another kind you can use the same quantity, or up to one-third more.

Milk is whole sweet milk, unless buttermilk is specified. Powdered non-fat milk mixed with water may be substituted if shortening is added, in the amount of 1/2 tablespoon to the cup.

A cup of buttermilk contains about the same amount of acid as is contained in a teaspoon of baking powder. To substitute buttermilk for milk in a recipe, reduce the baking powder by one teaspoon and add a half teaspoon of baking soda and a teaspoon of shortening, for each cup.

Sugar is ordinary granulated sugar, un-less something else is specified. If a recipe asks for fine granulated sugar (this is most likely in the no-shortening cakes) use veri-fine or similar sugar, or pulverize the regular sugar with a rolling pin.

Vanilla extract is a standard flavoring in white and yellow cakes, but it may be replaced with half or two-thirds the quantity of a half-and-half mixture of almond and lemon extracts or lemon only. This is a background or point-up type of flavoring.

In addition, there are many especially flavored cakes; chocolate, spice, orange and so forth, many of which involve adjustment in other ingredients and/or mixing methods.

Preparations. It is even more important in cake making than in most types of cooking to assemble all ingredients and utensils in advance, for several reasons. One is that the ingredients should be at room temperature before mixing. This involves getting butter, eggs and milk out of the fridge at least half an hour in advance.

Also, a cake depends almost absolutely on the presence of all its ingredients and accessories. If the cat drank the last of the milk or a neighbor borrowed the cake pan, the fact should be discovered before operations have started, not when they are past the point of no return.

Since baking powder is involved, there should be little delay between the time it is moistened and the batter is spread in the pan.

Each item should be placed in your work area, then checked off against the recipe. The beginner will find that the work will go more smoothly if everything is measured, the oven is turned on to pre-heat and that any necessary greasing or paper lining is placed in pans, in advance of any mixing.

Measuring. The ingredients should be carefully measured, as otherwise you will not know whether to blame the recipe or yourself for anything that goes wrong, nor will you be able to use it again with confidence in having the same success.

The flour should be sifted once, then measured, mixed with the baking powder and salt or other dry ingredients, then possibly sifted again to assure complete combining. If you use butter or margarine divided into the usual quarter-pound sticks, you can measure it in sticks or fractions of sticks, on the basis that each equals one-half cup or 8 tablespoons.

Other types of shortening may be measured either by packing solidly into cup or cup-fraction measures, or by sinking it in water in a two-cup measure, until the water has risen by the required amount. These measurements are discussed in the first chapter.

Baking powder is measured in teaspoons, struck off level with any straight surface, held perpendicular so that it will not push the powder down and compact it.

Fractions of spoons of baking powder (rarely used) or of soda are best measured level in the correct sizes of fractional spoons.

Granulated sugar and flavorings usually offer no special problems in measurement. Brown and confectioners sugar are usually packed tightly into the measure, to overcome a tendency to fluff up.

MIXING BY HAND

Conventional Way. The standard method of mixing cake batter involves the following steps.

First all ingredients are assembled in time to allow them to warm up to room

temperature. The pan or pans are usually prepared for use by greasing and/or papering.

Fat is creamed by mashing it against the side of a bowl (a wooden spoon is generally recommended for this job) until it has a creamy consistency. If it is butter or margarine, it becomes lighter in color. Then sugar is added and creamed in a little at a time.

Egg yolks, with or without whites as directed by the recipe, are beaten and mixed into the butter and sugar. If the eggs are to be separated, you beat the whites first, until they stand in soft peaks.

You can help them to stay in good condition while they are waiting to be used, by holding out part of the sugar from the creaming process and beating it into the whites, about a tablespoon to the cup. Then tap or wipe off meringue clinging to the beater, which can be used to beat the yolks, without cleaning it. Well beaten yolks become light in color and smooth in texture.

The flour is sifted, measured, mixed with baking powder and any other dry ingredients. Mix the milk (after measuring) with flavoring or other liquids.

Put about 1/3 of the flour in the bowl with the butter and sugar, and mix them thoroughly, using the same wooden spoon. Add 1/2 of the milk and mix, perhaps not quite so thoroughly. Add another batch of flour with thorough mixing, then stir in the rest of the milk, and finally the balance of the flour.

Pour and scrape the batter into your prepared pan or pans, and bake for the time and at the heat given in your recipe. In general, cakes are baked at moderate heat, about 350° F for 20 to 30 minutes, but loaf cakes and those containing fruit take longer.

Muffin Mix. Cake ingredients may be mixed in the same manner as muffins. Beat the eggs, either together or separated as directed by the recipe, mix with milk, cooled

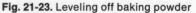

Fig. 21-23. Leveling off baking powder

melted butter and any other liquid; put the mixed dry ingredients in a large bowl, make a well or crater in the center, pour in the liquid mix and stir as vigorously as you can without splashing. Don't stop when the flour is all dampened, keep going for another 30 to 60 seconds, to produce a smoother batter. Pour or scrape it into the prepared pan or pans promptly. Muffin-mix cake is most often baked in muffin tins, to produce cup cakes.

Quick Mix. The quick mix method is also known as one-bowl and modified-bakers methods. Somewhat more sugar is used, to improve the workability of the batter, and it cannot be used safely with just any recipe.

Sift and pour the dry ingredients into a 2-quart mixing bowl, add the shortening, the unbeaten eggs and half the milk. Stir slowly with a wooden spoon until the flour is dampened, then vigorously for 2 minutes, stopping occasionally to scrape down the sides of the bowl and rub the spoon carefully over the bottom, to avoid having any material escape mixing. Add the rest of the milk, and the vanilla or other flavoring, and stir for another 2 minutes.

MIXING BY MACHINE

The "machine" in this section is a conventional rotary mixer that includes a double beater and a rotating support for the bowl. It should be strong enough to keep plugging when the mixture is thick, and be able to be set at very low speed for the final mixing.

Electric beating can be done in a variety of ways, and no two sets of instructions are likely to agree entirely. Those given here are offered only as workable suggestions.

Conventional Method. If egg whites are to be beaten separately, do them first at medium speed, adding a tablespoon of sugar for each. When they reach the soft-peak stage, stop the beater and scrape them into another container.

Fig. 21-24. A machine for mixing

Do not wash beater. Put in the fat and beat for about a minute on high speed or 2 minutes on medium, until it is creamy or fluffy. Beat in the rest of the sugar, using a rubber scraper to reclaim material that has moved out of reach of the beater.

Add whole eggs or egg yolks and beat at high speed for one minute, stop the beater and scrape things together. Set beater at its slowest speed, and add flour and milk alternately in small quantities and then the beaten white of egg, if any, until all materials are thoroughly blended. Stop as soon as this result is obtained, as the greatest fault of electric mixing is the danger of over-mixing and resulting toughness.

Many cooks use the mixer only through the stage of mixing in yolks, then transfer the bowl to a table and blend in the flour, milk and whites by hand. They feel that this is the only way to be sure that the cake will be properly tender.

Machine Quick-mix. This method is only for recipes adapted to it. They are called either quick-mix or one-bowl cakes in most books.

Put sugar, sifted and measured flour, salt and baking powder in mixing bowl. Add the shortening and half the milk, then beat at medium speed for 2 minutes. Add the rest of the milk, the eggs or egg fractions and the flavoring and beat 2 minutes longer. These batters are usually smooth and thin. Pour into pans immediately.

PANS AND BAKING

Pans. There are four types of cake pans — round shallow ones for layers, low-sided squares or rectangles, called baking, utility or loaf pans, high-sided rectangles usually called loaf pans, and ring or tube pans, used mostly for sponge and angel food.

Any of these pans may be made of aluminum or tinned steel. Non-ring pans may be glass. Metal pans may be lined with Teflon.

Most layer pans are 8 or 9 inches in diameter, with vertical or nearly vertical sides one to 1-1/2 inches high. Pan materials were discussed earlier in this chapter. Two 8-inch pans are considered to have about the same capacity as one 6 x 10 x 3 inch loaf pan.

Sticking. Sticking is a problem with cake, as it is so tender that it breaks and tears easily, and it tends to develop a pleasantly colored and tasty crust that is likely to be injured if it is necessary to cut the cake loose from the pan. On the other hand, there is a theory that a cake will not rise properly unless it can stick to the sides of the pan. Casual tests made by greasing only half a cake pan did not indicate any such effect, but perhaps with other mixes or other pans there might be a difference.

There are layer cake pans that have a cutter hinged to the center of the bottom, that can be rotated to cut the cake clear of

Fig. 21-25. Layer pan with a cutter

the pan whether it is greased or not. This will free you from danger of breaking the cake, but does not necessarily save the crust from injury. Or the bottom may be removable by pushing it up, allowing the cake to be separated from it by a knife.

A recipe may tell you to grease or oil (meaning cooking, not lubricating oil) the whole inside of the pan, or the bottom only. An extra precaution is to dust the greased surface with flour. Since a cake may stick even to a greased surface (the grease is absorbed by the crust as it cooks), it may further recommend that you put a piece of oiled paper in the pan bottom.

You can use any type of clean, unprinted firm paper — wax, brown or typewriter — place the pan on it, draw a pencil line

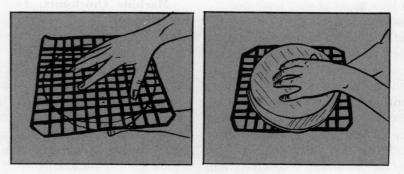

Fig. 21-26. Turning a cake onto a rack

around the bottom, then cut with scissors
a little inside the line. Oil or grease the inside bottom of the pan, put the disc of
paper on it and oil the paper.

If you also grease the sides, you should
be able to turn this cake right out of the
pan onto a rack. If the sides are dry, you
cut around the cake with a knife, turning
the edge slightly toward the pan to prevent
it from removing the crust, then turn the
cake out.

Incidentally, the turning procedure is to
put the rack upside down on top of the
cake pan, then turn rack and pan over together. This way the cake will have a short
fall or none.

The paper will probably stick to the bottom of the cake. It is best removed by taking it by the edge and bending it back 180
degrees, then pulling parallel with the bottom, as illustrated. This is much less likely
to uproot parts of the crust than an upward
pull would.

As an extra precaution, follow the paper
with a knife, ready to cut free any part of
the cake that seems to be sticking.

Filling Pans. A butter cake may be expected to increase in volume 50 to 100 per
cent, from raw batter to fully baked condition. If you want the edge of the cake to
be even with the edge of the pan (a usual
objective) you should fill a pan 1/2 to 2/3
full.

The center rises much more than the
sides, which are restrained by friction with
the pan, drag of the forming crust and by
firming up before there has been time for
full development of carbon dioxide from
the baking powder. This center bulge is
harmless or agreeable in a loaf cake, but is
an embarrassment and a problem in a layer
cake.

A cake surface can be made less rounded
or even entirely flat if the batter can be distributed in the pans so that it is deeper near
the edge than at the center. But many cake
batters are too thin to stay where they are

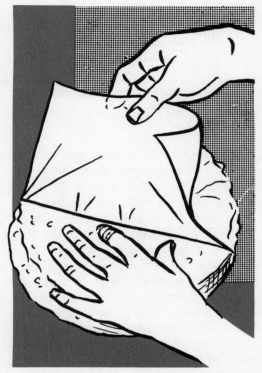

Fig. 21-27. Bend paper back sharply when
pulling it off a cake

put; while others can be arranged nicely
but will slump to flatness as oven heat lique-
fies their fat and growing gas bubbles push
them around.

The proportions in many recipes are
such that following them faithfully is apt
to produce a batter thin enough to level
out in spite of efforts to pile it at the edges.
This condition may exist in one batch and
not in another, because of differences in
type of flour, size and quality of eggs and
differences in measurement. One-bowl batters are often quite liquid.

If the matter is important to you, hold
back part of the milk until the end of mixing, and use only enough of it to produce
a satisfactorily thick batter. This is something the experienced cook does automatically, but it takes a little resolution on the
part of the amateur.

Arranging Layers. If the cooked layers

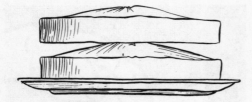

Fig. 21-28. A poor fit

for a two-level cake bulge on top, the situation is serious in regard to the lower one, as it will make contact with the bottom of the top layer only at the center, and a ridiculous amount of thick frosting might be required to fill between them at the edge.

If the bulge is moderate you can hide it by turning this bottom piece upside down, and placing it on a plate of such size that it will be supported by the raised edges. If there is too much bulge for this, you must trim it off with a long sharp knife. The cut surface is best put on the bottom, as it is likely to be too fragile for easy spreading of a thick icing, and too absorbent for a thin one.

Standing. It is most efficient to put the cake pans into the preheated oven as soon as they are filled. But it is not necessary, as the undisturbed batter can stand for a half hour, or perhaps even as long as three hours, with little damage. But it must not be stirred or pushed around, as the motion would release many of the gas bubbles evolved by the baking powder and liquid, causing the cake to become heavy.

Baking. Cake is usually baked in a mod-

Fig. 21-29. The bottom layer is installed upside down

erate or moderately hot oven, between 350 and 400° F, although sponge and angel food may call for only 300°. Recipe temperatures and times always are figured on a preheated oven, and are usually for bright aluminum pans.

The oven should be level, or at least the rack should be. If you don't have a carpenters' level, put about 1/4 inch of water in your widest glass pan, put the pan on the shelf you will use, and notice whether the water is the same depth in all parts. Methods of leveling an oven are discussed in the chapter on RANGES.

Cake should be placed in a central location — rack halfway between top and bottom, cake in the center of the rack. If there are two cakes, place them on each side of the center, with at least one inch space between pans and 1-1/2 inches between them and the oven sides.

If there is not enough space on one rack for the cakes, use two racks, above and below center with just enough space so a high-rising cake on the bottom won't touch the upper one, and arrange the pans so that one is not directly over another.

Some authorities recommend cooking the first few minutes at 25 to 50 degrees lower temperature to give the baking powder a good chance to work. Both time and temperature vary with the type of powder and the size of the pan, and adjustments get a little too complicated for home use.

Cooking time should be given in each recipe. In general, cup cakes may cook in 15 to 20 minutes, layers in 20 to 25 and loaves in 20 to 30. Baking time is greatly affected by the amount and kind of moisture in the mix, so it is best to refer to the time given in the recipe.

Tests. At best, cooking time for baked goods are approximate. It is wise to start to test for doneness about 5 minutes before schedule, or even earlier if a glance through the oven window (if you are fortunate enough to have one) makes you suspicious.

Three general tests for doneness were described earlier. Another indication for cakes is in the nature of a final warning. A cake starts to shrink when it is fully cooked or perhaps as it starts to overcook, and will pull away from the sides of the pan.

If shrinkage occurs in the oven, take the cake out immediately, and make any other tests outside. But do not be concerned if your cake starts to separate from the pan after you have taken it out of the oven, as this is just normal loss of bulk due to cooling.

Color. The ideal outside color for white and yellow cakes is golden brown, and the cake may be acceptable or even praiseworthy through a wide color range, from creamy yellow to milk chocolate. Lighter and darker shades may indicate under or overcooking, and in any case are less appealing.

Color is greatly affected by the makeup of the batter, but the controlling influence is usually oven heat. For any one pan of cake, increasing oven heat will start coloring earlier and produce a darker product. You can often adjust color by increasing or decreasing the heat near the end of the cooking time.

Very dark brown and black are colors that are seldom permissible, as they bring a charred or burnt taste that is prized only in outdoor cooking. It is caused by too hot an oven, uneven temperature in the oven and by pans of uneven shape and color. It often occurs when glass pans are used at brightware temperature.

Burning is usually very shallow, and can be scraped or cut off. Hold the cake so that the affected part is vertical or overhanging, and rub or scrape lightly with a knife held at right angles to the surface.

The dark crumbs dislodged in this way should fall free of the cake, and you should quickly get down to a surface of more pleasing taste and appearance. If the area is large, you can use a small grater instead

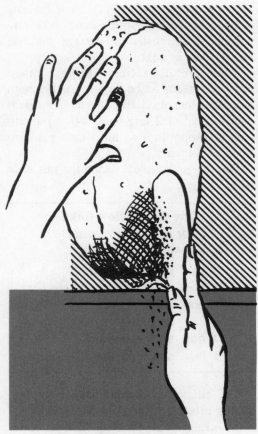

Fig. 21-30. Scraping off a burn

of the knife. If it is deep, cut it off and cover the scar with icing.

YELLOW (WHOLE EGG) CAKE

Yellow cake contains egg yolks and gets its color from them. Most recipes call for whole eggs, but there is a type, gold cake, that uses yolks without whites. An option of substituting extra yolks for whites is offered in some other recipes.

Many cookbooks have recipes for two types, one-egg and two-egg. Choice between them is largely a matter of taste, as the cost of the extra egg is seldom a deciding factor.

Two-egg is richer in taste, color and nourishment, and is likely to be first choice for layer cake, but only a runner-up for loaf and cup cakes. One-egg is a clear favorite in puddings such as upside-down cake, and may be found listed as cottage pudding rather than as cake.

There are also recipes for 3-egg cakes, but these seem to be two-egg cakes with quantities increased 30 per cent (3 medium eggs instead of 2 large, and other ingredients in proportion) to fill 9-inch pans instead of 8-inch.

One-Egg. A typical recipe for this cake is:

One-Egg Yellow Cake
(for two 8-inch layers)

1½	cps	flour
2	tsp	baking powder
½	cup	milk
½ to ¾	cup	sugar
1		egg, beaten
¼	cup	butter, melted
¼	tsp	salt *(optional)*

Use either the conventional or muffin-mixing procedures described earlier.

Two-Egg. The two-egg yellow butter cake is very popular for layer cakes and makes good cup cakes. Different recipes for it are very similar. Here is one of them.

Two-Egg Yellow Cake
(for two 8-inch layers)

1¾	cps	flour
2		eggs
⅓	cup	butter
1 to 1½	cps	sugar
¾	cup	milk
2	tsp	baking powder
¼	tsp	salt *(optional)*
½	tsp	vanilla *(optional)*

This is an old time recipe, in which conventional mixing starts with creaming the butter, page 20.

Egg Yolk. These cakes, usually called gold or golden, can be made from special recipes, or by slight tampering with whole-egg recipes. To convert a one-egg cake, replace the egg with three yolks and add 1/2 teaspoon baking powder (making 2-1/2 teaspoons in all).

Two whole eggs may be replaced with 5 yolks, along with increasing the baking powder to 3 teaspoons.

WHITE CAKE

White cakes are made with whites of egg, without the yolks. White cake tends to be slightly drier and less rich than yellow cake, but the difference in these qualities may be slight or non-existent. There is always a slight difference in taste and a definite one in color.

As a general rule, a whole-egg recipe can be converted to one for white cake by substituting 2 or 3 whites for each egg, and increasing the shortening by one tablespoon for each missing yolk. But it is much better to use a recipe made especially for white cake if you have it.

The following is a fair example.

White Cake

2	cps	flour
3		egg whites
½	cup	butter
1¼	cps	sugar
⅔	cup	milk
3	tsp	baking powder
½	tsp	vanilla

Follow the procedures given earlier under conventional hand mixing. The whites are beaten to soft peaks, and folded in just before baking. For a loaf, use a buttered and floured pan 12 x 8 inches and bake at 350° F for about an hour. Or make two 9-inch layers, cooked at 375° for 25 or 30 minutes.

CHOCOLATE CAKE

Chocolate cake is an inclusive name for any cake flavored with chocolate or cocoa, including the very dark devils' food type.

Chocolate is a strong and distinctive flavoring that is very bitter, and has an acid reaction chemically. It is also a food that is about half cocoa butter, a delicate fat with a slightly higher melting point than dairy butter.

Cocoa is a processed chocolate from which half the fat has been removed. As explained under Flavorings, it can be substituted for chocolate in any recipe, provided fat is added to make up its deficiency.

Recipes for chocolate cake vary widely. Many of them avoid the use of sweet milk, substituting buttermilk, coffee or just water. Some compensate for the acidity of the chocolate by substituting soda for part of the baking powder, but many do not.

There is no profit in pursuing these complications here. The subject is too complicated for discussion in a basic text, so we will dismiss it with just one sample recipe, a cake so dark that it has acquired the name of Mississipi Mud. It is quite easy to prepare, and is often a favorite for children learning to cook.

Mississippi Mud

2 cps	flour
4 sqs	bitter chocolate, shaved
2 cps	water
2 cps	sugar
1 cup	butter or margarine
1 tsp	baking soda
2	eggs, slightly beaten
1 tsp	salt *(optional)*

Fig. 21-31. Chocolate layer cake

Bring the water to a boil, add chocolate, bring back to a boil and then cook for about one minute. Add sugar and butter, and allow to cool. Sift flour, measure it, sift with soda and salt. Stir into chocolate mixture, add the two slightly beaten eggs and mix well.

Bake in greased and floured loaf pan, 6 by 10 by 3, or in two 8-inch layer pans in slow oven, about 300° F for about 1-1/2 hours, or until a test toothpick comes out clean.

This cake may be eaten plain in loaf form, but it goes well with either white or chocolate icing. In common with most chocolate cakes, it holds moisture and retains freshness very well.

SPONGE CAKE

A "true" sponge cake contains neither leavening nor shortening except for eggs, and can be the lightest and most delicate of cakes. However, it can be a little tricky to make, and it is safer to start with the fluffy type, which contains baking powder (but still no shortening).

Sponge cake is leavened chiefly by fine air bubbles in stiffly beaten whites of egg, which are carefully mixed into the batter just before putting it in the pan. The principal problem in making it is that of blending beaten white of eggs with flour finely enough to produce an even-textured cake, without losing the beaten-in air which is necessary for lightness.

Fig. 21-33. Folding in the whites

Fluffy Sponge Cake

6		eggs, separated
1½	cps	flour
1½	cps	sugar
½	cup	*(scant)* cold water
2	tsp	baking powder
1	Tb	lemon juice
1	tsp	vanilla
1	tsp	salt *(optional)*

Put yolks in large bowl, beat with rotary beater while adding half the sugar for about 5 minutes, until the beater is stiff to turn. Remove beater, wiping material on it back into the bowl, and clean beater thoroughly. Stir in flavorings with a wooden spoon. Add flour and water in several portions alternately to yolk mixture, beating vigorously each time.

Put egg whites in another bowl, add salt, and beat partially. Add the rest of the sugar gradually and beat until soft, shiny peaks are formed when you lift the beater. Fold whites into the yolk mixture with a wooden spoon, a rubber scraper or a whisk.

This folding is the critical operation, and the success of the cake may depend on it. The mixture should be smooth, but some air and lightness is lost with every unnecessary stroke. A good technique is to tip the bowl about halfway toward spilling and hold it firmly with one hand while you stir with the other.

Fig. 21-32. Sponges

Make each stroke follow the bottom or side of the bowl all the way through the batter at a sloping angle that will make the batter flow across it. At the end of the stroke raise it horizontally, then bring it back to the beginning just above the surface. Rotate the bowl slightly with each stroke. Avoid slapping the stirrer into the batter, or splashing as you bring it out.

As soon as the mixture is smooth pour and scrape it into a 10-inch ungreased ring (tube) pan. Put it an oven preheated to about 325° F, and cook for about an hour. You test it by pressing it lightly with your finger or a spoon. If it springs back it is done.

Remove the pan from the oven and put it upside down on a rack or table. The pan may have a projecting tube or side pieces on which it can stand so that air can circulate under it. If it does not, use a funnel or a bottle to support it. When it is cool, disassemble the pan if it is that type, or free the cake by cutting along its edges with a knife.

A deep sponge cake should be cooled upside down to prevent its own weight from squeezing it into a compact mass while its structure is still warm and plastic. The need of hanging the cake is of course an excellent

Fig. 21-34. Ring sponge cake, cooling upside down over a bottle

reason for not greasing the pan, as it could then fall out.

Or you may bake the cake from this recipe in round layer tins (it makes two 8-inch) or in muffin tins to make about 30 medium cup cakes. These should be buttered or greased.

Sponge cake does not cut well with a knife. You will do better if you use a special cutter that looks like a comb with long, slender metal teeth, or use two forks to tear it apart.

Sponge cake is eaten plain, with butter, frosting (preferably light-textured) or sauce. It can be used in desserts such as shortcake.

FROSTING AND FILLING

Frosting, or icing, is usually put on cakes to make them sweeter or moister and to give them a more attractive appearance. Filling, which is put between layers of cake, may be identical with frosting used on the top or sides, or quite different. If it is different it is likely to be less sweet.

The distinction between frosting and icing is complicated and obscure, and varies locally. The two words will be used interchangeably here.

Frosting may be classified as to whether it is cooked or uncooked, fluffy or solid, thin or thick, sweet or unsweet, or perishable or otherwise.

As might be expected from the varieties suggested, almost anything goes. It is best to follow standard recipes for your first few batches, but after that you can compound your own. But avoid having a grainy texture. For raw icing use confectioners' sugar, preferably sifted to remove lumps. Granulated is suitable only if it has been cooked to dissolve it thoroughly.

Only a few basic varieties will be described here.

Plain Icing. Plain icing, also called confectioners' icing, is simply confectioners' sugar dissolved in boiling water. The ratio is about one cup of the sugar, packed, to

Fig. 21-35. Liqueurs make good flavorings

2 tablespoons of water. You stir them together until smooth, then add an additional amount of one or the other to obtain the consistency you want.

For a layer cake it should be thick enough to stay in place, while for loaf and coffee cakes where it may be applied sparingly it can be quite thin.

Plain icing can be made less plain by flavoring with a half teaspoon of vanilla, substituting hot lemon, orange or strawberry juice for the water, mixing in 2 tablespoons of cocoa with an extra tablespoon of hot water or substituting a liqueur for part of the water. You can enrich it a little by using milk instead of water, and/or putting in 1/2 to one teaspoon of butter per cup of sugar.

This last change takes us into the next section, on butter frostings.

Basic Butter Frosting. Butter frosting

is comparatively simple to make, but you have to work fairly hard unless you use a mixer. Its consistency is easily adjusted, and it is readily adapted to a wide variety of flavors.

There is a rule of thumb that says one cup of confectioners' sugar produces enough frosting for one layer of an 8-inch cake. But if you like your frosting thick, allow 1-1/2 cups. The following is for an 8-inch 2-layer cake.

Basic Butter Frosting

⅓ cup butter or margarine
3 cps confectioners' sugar
¼ cup light cream, or milk
1 tsp vanilla extract

Put the vanilla in the milk. Have the butter at room temperature, and cream it until it is fluffy. Mix in sugar until it is hard to work, then milk, and sugar again, adding them in small amounts and mixing thoroughly.

The mixture should be easy to spread with a knife. If it is too thick, stir in a few drops more cream; if too thin, dust a little more of the sugar over it and work it in.

With Egg. You can replace part or all of the cream in the above recipe with egg yolks, preferably beaten until thick for ease of handling and texture. One approach would be to use a tablespoon of milk or cream with two egg yolks, then add additional milk as needed to get proper consistency. The icing will have a richer flavor, and a yellow tint.

Or you can use two stiffly beaten whites to mix with vanilla and sugar, then thin it down with cream or milk as and if required. Medium or heavy cream supplements the egg white better than milk.

Flavor Variations. Butter frosting is easily made in a variety of flavors, by substituting other liquids or materials for the cream or milk. The vanilla may be either omitted as unnecessary or retained to point up the other flavor, according to the judgment of the cook.

For orange icing, replace the cream with the same quantity of orange juice. Add a teaspoon of grated orange rind for color and flavor. Or use lemon juice and lemon rind for lemon icing.

For strawberry icing, replace the milk with 1/4 cup of juice from frozen strawberries, or 1/3 cup of mashed strawberries.

For mocha flavor, replace the cream with 1/4 cup of cocoa and 1/4 cup of strong coffee. For chocolate flavor, put in 1/2 cup of cocoa and replace the cream with 2 egg yolks, unbeaten.

Liqueur frosting needs 1/4 cup of your favorite liqueur, or of one you want to use up, instead of cream.

There are of course many other possibilities.

Coloring. It is occasionally desirable to add coloring to frosting. This might be to make it look like it tastes, as a green tint for lime flavor or a pink one for strawberry, which are not provided sufficiently by the flavoring substance itself. Or you might want to write in color, Happy Birthday or some other message.

The food colors sold in markets are safe to eat, but are so very potent that they are not artististically safe to use. Bright colors in food look unnatural and even poisonous, so you should keep your tinting moderate, except in small areas such as letters or designs. The best way is to put a little of the icing in a saucer, and mix in a tiny amount of coloring.

Then stir this colored icing into the rest of it, a little at a time, until you have the shade you want. If there is any surplus in the saucer, you might be able to use it as lettering or a design. Or you can eat it with a spoon.

Basic Boiled Frosting. This is an example of the frostings that are based on cooked sugar syrup and meringue. Because it includes a considerable amount of air, you get a greater bulk of icing in proportion to the sugar used. The point of this is usually in the reduction in calories.

In addition, such icings usually have a pleasing texture and appearance.

Boiled Frosting

1¼	cps	sugar *(granulated)*
⅓	cup	water
3		egg whites
1	tsp	vanilla

Mix sugar, salt and water in a heavy pan and stir over low heat until the sugar is dissolved. Cook the mixture until it reaches 240° F, when a drop of it will form a hard ball in cold water. Remove from heat.

Beat egg whites until stiff, and pour sugar syrup into them in a thin stream, beating constantly. Continue to beat until the mixture stands in stiff peaks. Spread immediately on cake. This recipe should frost two 8-inch cake layers.

The top may be left plain, or decorated with chopped nuts, shredded coconut or colored sugar.

Seven-Minute Frosting. This is one of the most popular of the cooked frostings. It requires less cooking but more beating than the boiled type.

Seven Minute Frosting
(for 2-layer, 8-inch cake)

1		egg white, unbeaten
3	Tb	cold water
⅞	cup	sugar
¼	tsp	cream of tartar
½	tsp	vanilla
1	tsp	white corn syrup *(optional)*

Put all ingredients except vanilla in top

Fig. 21-36. Arrangements of paper to catch cake frosting

pan of a double boiler. Beat with rotary beater until mixed, then put over boiling water and beat steadily until it stands in peaks. This should take about 7 minutes with a hand beater, or 4 with an electric.

Remove upper pan from heat, placing it on a pad on a table or in a pan of cold water, add vanilla and continue to beat it until cool. Spread on the cake immediately, as it soon becomes too stiff to handle.

This icing tends to form a delicate crust after standing a while. If you don't want this, use the the corn syrup to prevent it.

Putting It On. Frosting should be applied with a knife or a spatula on freshly-baked, just-cooled cake. It should be cool so as not to cause the frosting to melt or thin, with problems of soaking in and running off, although you can often get quite special effects with a thin layer applied to hot cake. The cake should not stand around bare after cooling, as the icing should seal in its aroma and moisture. Any broken pieces should be fitted tightly in place, and all loose crumbs should be brushed off.

A loaf cake may be iced on the top only, or on top and sides. The sides are supposed to be done first, probably because they are the real test of the frosting's consistency, and because the quantity that they can hold is more nearly fixed than it is on top, where you can either pile it on thick or spread it out thin, depending on quantity available.

It is convenient to ice a cake on the plate on which it will be served, to avoid damage in handling. You can avoid slopping up the plate by covering it with paper, cut in strips or other shapes so that it can be easily pulled out from under the edges when you are finished.

To apply frosting to the sides, you take a pile of it on the knife, near the end, push it against the bottom of the cake and move the knife upward, either straight or diagonally. You should have enough on the knife to cover to the top and overlap on it a quarter or half inch. If this is not practical you can make two or more passes to reach the top. Work your way around the cake with overlapping strokes.

The frosting should be thin enough so that it will glide under the edge of the knife without pulling on the cake, and without balling up again behind the knife. Otherwise it may lift crumbs or even patches of surface off a tender crust, which will mix it and spoil its appearance.

Uncooked frosting can be easily thinned. Cooked frosting will probably be getting thicker, so you can only try putting it on more heavily, or changing your work angle.

If the frosting is too thin it will creep down and form piles at the base. If it does this immediately, you can thicken the rest of a batch of uncooked icing by stirring in some confectioners' sugar.

If you do not notice it until you have

Fig. 21-37. Finished with swirls

done a large part of the cake you are faced with the need to repeatedly push it back up with knife until time, working through evaporation and crystallization, thickens it enough to stay. If you live that long.

After the sides are done, you can scrape the rest of the icing, or as much as you intend to use, onto the top of the cake and spread it around until you have complete coverage and a reasonably even depth.

The question of the final finish now comes up. Some frostings have a tendency to spread smoothly, while others are oppositely inclined. It is not at all necessary to produce a smooth finish, but a fussy, patched-up look is undesirable.

After you have the cake completely covered to a more or less even depth, and are reasonably assured that the frosting is not creeping down the sides, go over the whole surface with a few bold strokes. Try a spiral for the top and a circular motion around the sides. Then don't fuss with it.

Icing may be decorated with a scattering of cubed or crystal sugar, plain or in color, with chopped or sliced nuts, or with lettering or candles.

Layer Cake. In icing a layer cake do the top of the bottom layer first. If you use the same frosting that will go on the top and sides, spread it right out to the edges. If it is filling of a different type, keep it back 1/4 inch or more, to avoid getting the two mixed on the surface.

You should have a perfectly flat surface to work on, if you have turned this layer upside down. But if for any reason you are using the top, place the frosting somewhat deeper on the low areas than the high ones.

Place the next layer on the iced one, right side up. This is usually the top layer. If it is not, it may be necessary to slice its top surface to remove a center dome, which is likely to be too high for correction by extra icing around the edges, when you put on another layer.

When the top layer is in place, the sides can be iced. This may be done in the approved way, from the bottom up, or the easy way from the center of the top outward and downward.

Fillings. Layer cakes often have a filling between layers, which is different from that on the top and sides.

A filling may be jelly or jam, plain or flavored custard stiffened with cornstarch or flour, or marshmallows softened by melting wtih a little cream.

TOPPINGS

Toppings are upper surfacings for cake, coffee cake and puddings that are less sweet and smooth than icings. There are many different kinds. The simplest consist of whole, chopped or sliced nuts, poppy seeds or shredded coconut. They may be applied before, during or after baking.

Plain icing, page 437, is excellent on coffee cakes. It should be put on quite thinly, preferably when the cake is warm.

Streusel. Streusel is an excellent, general purpose topping that in its simplest form consists of equal parts of sugar, flour and butter. For an average coffee cake (an 8-inch round or a 10-inch ring) use 1/3 cup of each.

Mix the sugar and flour thoroughly, then work in the butter until the mixture is crumbly. Spread on top of the cake before baking. For yeast doughs, you can put it on after shaping and before the second rising pressing it in slightly with your fingers.

This may also be used as a coffee cake filling. Put the dough or batter in the pan in two or more layers, with streusel in between.

There are many recipes for streusel with different proportions, and with added materials. For a sweeter mixture, use 1/2 cup of sugar, and 1/4 cup each of flour and butter. For less sweetness, increase the flour to 1/2 cup, and reduce the other two ingredients to 1/4 cup each.

If you put the topping on after the cake is baked, put it under a broiler for 3 or 4 minutes, far enough away (say 4 inches) so that it will melt slightly but not burn. The cake should be warmed first, to decrease the possibility of the topping coming loose when the cake is sliced.

COOKIES

Cookies are small, thin cakes, which are usually cooked on flat metal sheets. The batter or dough is thick.

They may be paper-thin, or up to a half inch in thickness. Diameter is often between 1-1/2 and 2-1/2 inches. Shape can be round, irregular or fancy.

Most cookie recipes are good, and they are generally easy to follow. The proportions of ingredients and work methods vary widely, however.

Sugar Cookies. The simplest type is called a sugar, plain or basic cookie. The following is a good recipe that has the advantage of easily remembered amounts.

Sugar Cookies		
2 cps	flour
1 cup	sugar
½ cup	butter
1	egg
1 tsp	baking powder
1 tsp	vanilla

Cream the butter, then add sugar gradually, mixing in with back of spoon. Beat the egg and vanilla lightly, and combine with butter and sugar.

Sift the flour, measure, then add baking powder and mix well by sifting or stirring. Then mix with the other ingredients with stirring, creaming and/or slicing motions.

If the mixture is too dry to combine easily into dough, add up to one tablespoon of milk or water.

Shaping. This dough may be rolled out, piecrust fashion (page 454), either at once or after an hour in the refrigerator to make it less sticky.

You can avoid floury taste and toughening, by dusting with confectioners' sugar instead of flour. Apply it with a sifter to avoid formation of fine lumps.

Roll to 1/8 to 1/4 inch thickness, which will almost double during baking. Cut into shapes with cookie cutters, into rounds with a glass, or into squares or triangles with a cutting wheel or a knife.

If the dough is sticky, coat the cutters with grease and/or flour.

Drop Cookies. You can cut or tear off small pieces of dough and roll them into one-inch balls. They slump and spread while baking. Or thin the dough by mixing in a few teaspoons of milk, and drop it on the pan by the teaspoonful.

Baking. Bake on cookie tins, sheets of foil, or pans turned upside down. Greasing may be unneeded when there is this much butter in the mix, but it is a safety precaution.

Handle rolled and shaped cookies with a pancake turner, and balls with your fingers. Space shaped cookies 1/2 to one inch apart, drop cookies about 2-1/2 inches, center to center.

Bake for 8 to 12 minutes in a 375 or 400° F oven, until slightly browned and cooked through. Remove a sample and break it in half for inspection. Take out individual cookies if they are done ahead of others.

Take them off the pan with a turner, and put them on racks to cool.

Variations. You can change recipe proportions drastically. For example, cut the flour in half, to one cup. This will make the dough stickier, so it won't roll unless cold, and cookies will slump and flow on the pan, becoming very thin and crisp. Cooking time will be shorter, perhaps 5 to 7 minutes.

With either amount of flour, you can add a cup of semi-sweet chocolate bits, and/or 1/2 cup of coarsely chopped nuts.

In the basic recipe, you can double the butter and/or the egg. Each such change produces a very different type of cookie.

You can also sprinkle tops with either granulated or colored topping sugar, before or during baking.

DOUGHNUTS

Doughnuts are "baked goods" that are fried in deep fat instead of being baked. There are two distinct types, doughnuts and raised doughnuts. The first is made with baking powder or soda, the second with yeast. They are quite different in character, but they are equally entitled to their name.

The challenge of doughnut-making is to fry dough without getting it greasy. If the grease soaks in no deeper than the brown crust, you win. You may still have an excellent doughnut even if the grease penetrates much more deeply, but it is technically less desirable.

It is important to have the fat at the right temperature, 360 to 365° F for plain doughnuts, 370° for raised ones. If it is cooler it tends to soak in and to produce a pale crust; if hotter it may make too dark and hard a crust before the interior is fully cooked. Penetration of grease is also affected by the materials in the recipe and the manner in which they are mixed, but

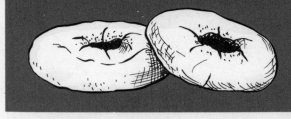

Fig. 21-38. A home made delicacy

these relationships are not always too clear.

Doughnuts are traditionally made in the shape of hollow rings, but they may also be solid circles, balls or any uncomplicated shapes you prefer.

Plain. Doughnut recipes generally resemble those for coffee cake prepared with baking powder, except that they contain less butter. But more than half of them use buttermilk instead of milk, or sour cream instead of milk and butter. This may be a matter of flavor, or it may affect the grease resistance of the dough.

Aside from this, there is not enough variability to justify analysis. The following is a fairly standard recipe:

Plain Doughnuts

2	cps	flour
1		egg
2	Tb	butter, melted
½	cup	sugar
½	cup	buttermilk*
2	tsp	baking powder*
½	tsp	baking soda*
½	tsp	salt *(optional)*
¼	tsp	nutmeg *(optional)*

* If you do not have buttermilk, use the same quantity of sweet milk, 3 teaspoons of baking powder and no baking soda.

Sift and measure the flour, re-sift 1-3/4 cups of it with other dry ingredients. In a bowl, mix thoroughly the egg, butter and milk, add the flour mixture and stir well. Then add enough flour to make the dough almost firm enough to handle, but still soft.

Chill for 2 or 3 hours, to make it workable. In this way you can get by with less

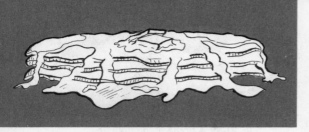

Fig. 21-39. Pancakes, syrup and butter

flour than would be needed if the mixture were to be shaped when warm, and thus get a more tender product.

In order to keep the dough firm, you may divide it in thirds, taking out only one part. Put on a floured board, and roll out to a thickness of 1/4 inch or slightly more.

With a floured doughnut cutter, or another shape if you prefer, cut out as many doughnuts as you can, and set them aside on a floured piece of waxed paper. Pile the trimmings, including as little flour as you can, and roll them out again, either by themselves or with the next batch out of the refrigerator. Until you are used to cooking them, it is advisable to finish cutting before you start frying.

Have the fat heated to 360 or 365° F. Lift the doughnuts with a turner or any suitable tool, and lower them gently into the fat, one by one. Fry only 3 or 4 at a time to avoid cooling the fat. They will sink, then float. When the underside is brown, about 2 minutes, turn them and cook for another minute or two until they are an even brown color all over.

Lift with a fork or tongs, without piercing them, and put on absorbent paper to cool.

Doughnuts are delicious plain and as soon as they are cool enough to bite, but they may be difficult to digest at this time. If so, allow them to cool, then eat them either cold or reheated.

If you like them sugared, put some powdered sugar in a paper bag, then add doughnuts 2 or 3 at a time, and shake them gently until well covered. They will pick up more sugar if you do this while they are hot.

Raised. Raised doughnuts are made from Sweet Roll dough, described earlier. After the first rising, put on a lightly floured board, cut in two pieces, shape them into balls, cover and let stand about 10 minutes.

Then roll out 3/8 to 1/2 inch thick, cut out doughnuts, and set aside on a floured surface to rise, about 45 minutes. If they are not covered they will develop a slight crust that makes them easy to handle.

The fat should be slightly hotter than for plain doughnuts, about 370° F. Cook them on one side and then on the other, for a total of about 3 minutes until golden brown all over. Drain on absorbent paper, and shake up with sugar in a bag if you wish.

PANCAKES (GRIDDLE CAKES)

Like English muffins, pancakes are fitted

Plain Pancakes			
Ingredients	*Minimum*	*Maximum*	*Try*
Flour	1 cup	1 cup	1 cup
Baking powder	½ tsp	2 tsp	1 tsp
Eggs	1	1	1
Butter, melted	1 tsp	5 Tb	3 Tb
Sugar	none	4 Tb	2 Tb
Milk	½ cup	1 cup	1 cup
Salt	¼ tsp	½ tsp	¼ tsp

into a section of this book where they do not belong, only because there seems to be no better place for them. They are not baked, but fried. On the other hand, they certainly are a flour-and-baking-powder product more closely related to baked goods than to anything else.

Cookbooks usually call them griddle cakes, while people call them pancakes. The pancake designation seems good enough. After all, isn't a griddle a kind of a pan?

Most prepared pancake mixes are highly satisfactory, and account for most pancakes that are served. But it is a good idea to know how to make them out of basic materials also.

Recipes vary widely in the size of batch recommended, starting with anywhere from one to 3 cups of flour. A number of sweet-milk pancake directions, adjusted to go with one cup of flour, are given at the bottom of the page, with suggested proportions for a first try.

One cup of flour produces 5 or 8 pancakes, to serve 2 or 3 people. If more are needed, double the recipe. On account of the widely-agreed-on egg, it is hard to increase the batch by one-half.

Beat egg, milk and melted butter until well blended, then mix in the dry ingredients just enough to wet them thoroughly. Consistency should be similar to that of heavy cream, but may be a bit lumpy. If it is too thick, stir in more milk.

Grease or butter a griddle lightly, and have medium hot, 300 to 325° F. Pour batter on it, using 3 or 4 tablespoons for each cake. For convenience and even measure, use a 1/4-cup measure, and dip it out of the bowl. The batter should spread out in a rough circle, about 4 or 5 inches across.

Cook until the top is covered with bubbles and the bottom is golden brown. These two things should happen together, in about a minute. If the whole top is bubbly and the bottom is pale, turn up the heat. If the

Fig. 21-40. Wrong amounts of batter

bottom is dark, or is splotched with dark and white, lower the heat. Turn cakes with a turner, and cook the other side until it has a good color.

Serve at once with butter and maple or other pancake syrup or honey. They are usually served in stacks, with two or three piled on top of each other, but may be served singly to start everyone eating at the same time. A 10-inch square griddle should cook four at a time.

Buttermilk. For buttermilk pancakes, simply replace the milk with buttermilk, and one teaspoon of the baking powder with a half teaspoon of baking soda.

WAFFLES

Waffles are made from batter very similar or identical to that used for pancakes, but the method of cooking gives them an entirely different appearance and taste.

No cookbook offered exactly the same recipe for pancakes and waffles, although all of the recipes fell within the limits of the pancake batters in the same group of books. However, the smallest amount of butter in a waffle mix is 2 tablespoons, and none of them are totally without sugar.

The only significant difference is that several waffle recipes called for separating the eggs, beating the whites stiffly and folding them into the batter after other mixing was complete, to make the waffle lighter and crisper. With this change in procedure,

445

the pancake recipe given earlier becomes a waffle recipe.

Waffle Baker. Waffles are totally dependent for their character on the appliance used to cook them, the waffle baker or waffle iron. It consists of upper and lower electric heating units with grid surfaces, hinged together. This hinge should be sloppy, so as to allow the upper lid to lie snugly on the lower one at the start of cooking, and to rise without tipping as the batter expands.

Sticking is a very critical problem in making waffles, as the shape of the surfaces makes it impossible to slide them out with a turner or any other tool, although a screwdriver can be used, very gently, to loosen a few stuck spots. The original iron grids, and the more modern cast aluminum ones, should be seasoned the first time they are used by painting liberally with oil.

The first waffle after oiling will be too greasy to be edible. After this, waffles should not stick as long as they contain a minimum of 2 tablespoons of butter to the cup of flour, as this is enough fat to renew the oily seal in the pores of the metal.

But if a waffle does stick for any reason, clean out the ruins gently. Possible tools include a screwdriver, a paring knife, a matchstick and a stiff brush. When it is clean, re-season it with oil and a sacrificial waffle.

Waffle irons treated with silicone or coated with Teflon should also be broken in with oil unless instuctions with them specifically forbid it.

Waffle bakers come with a variety of controls. For full convenience there should be an adjustable thermostatic control, with a light to indicate whether working temperature has been reached. It is usually part of the heating circuit, and goes out when the baker is hot enough to turn itself off. This should be an indication that an empty unit is ready for some batter, or that a loaded one has finished the cooking process.

If your waffle baker does not have automatic controls, or if you do not trust them, you have only to remember that when a waffle stops steaming, it is cooked.

High cooking temperature provides a browner and crisper (or harder) product than a low temperature. Cooking too long increases brownness and hardness. High, closely spaced knobs tend to produce a crisp waffle, while low widely spaced ones give you a softer, moister product.

Waffle bakers come in different sizes and shapes, and will take between 1/4 and 1/2 cup of batter. You have to experiment to determine the proper amount.

You can ladle the batter into one with a spoon, but it is more efficient to pour it out of a small pitcher, preferably a measuring cup. You do not have to spread it evenly, as the upper mold will push down high spots and the batter flows as it starts to cook.

Too little batter will produce a waffle that is not fully formed on the top, but you can serve it upside down. Still less batter will not fill the bottom fully, and it will lack edges. In each case, appearance is affected but flavor probably remains good.

Too much batter will cause overflowing, sometimes to a spectacular extent. There should be a built-in trough to catch this, and it is a good plan to have a platter or paper underneath anyhow. The spilled batter hardens quite quickly on the outside of the cooker, and is then easy to remove — usually.

Other batters may be cooked in a waffle baker. They should have at least 2 tablespoons of shortening to the cup of flour and 3 is safer, to avoid sticking.

22

PIE

PASTRY

Pastry is a general term covering several classes of baked goods which have (or at least, may have) a flaky consistency. The word may refer only to the cooked-dough portion, as the crust of a pie, or to its combination with fillings or toppings.

The most important American pastry is pie. Pies usually have pastry crusts with more or less sweet fillings and are eaten for dessert or for snacks, but there are also meat pies that may be served as the main courses of meals.

Danish pastry is a type of coffee cake, which has caused the term pastry to be extended to other coffee cakes and sweet rolls that have no claim to flakiness. It is described under COFFEE CAKE.

Puff pastry — Napoleons, cream puffs and patty shells — is the flakiest type. Its preparation in the home is rather limited, and it will not be covered in this book.

PIE CRUST

Pie crust is a thin layer of pastry which may form a bottom layer, a top layer, or both. It is usually made from basic materials, but packaged mixes of varying quality are obtainable. There is also another type of crust, made of crumbs, which will be described separately.

A cook's first pie crust usually involves a lot of fussing and uncertainty, but results are often excellent and practice builds a good technique quite rapidly. Most large general cookbooks are quite thorough in instructions.

In general, tenderness and flakiness are considered to be the most highly desirable qualities in pie crust. But not everyone agrees. Recipes calling for minimum shortening (1/2 cup or less with 2 cups of flour) aim for strength rather than tenderness. Some cooks will deliberately continue to knead crust dough until it is tough, because they believe that it then has more character and flavor.

Pie Pans. The standard pie pan is round, with sloped sides and flat rim or flange, as in Figure 22-2. It is usually made of thin aluminum sheet, aluminum foil or heavy glass. Glass or dull metal allows slightly faster cooking, and more browning of the bottom crust, than shiny metal does.

Pans are measured across the top of the

Fig. 22-1. Pies

opening. The standard size is 9-inch, and it is figured to provide 6 to 8 servings. An 8-inch pan holds 20 to 25 per cent less, and 10-inch about 25 per cent more. The 8-inch size is losing popularity, with manufacturers at least, and is becoming difficult to buy.

The next smaller size is a 5-1/2-inch tart pan made of foil, for one or 2 servings.

The proportion of filling to crust usually decreases when smaller pans are used, unless it is heaped much higher.

A standard 9-inch aluminum pie pan has

a bottom diameter of about 7 inches, a depth of 1-1/4 inches and a rim or flange width of about 1/4 inch. Fluid capacity is about one quart. A glass pan is similar, but 1/2 inch wider on the bottom, so that it holds a few ounces more.

Ingredients. The ingredients of pie crust are just four: flour, shortening, water and salt.

Flour supplies the bulk and strength of the pastry. It should be the general purpose type, sifted before measuring.

Shortening supplies the tender-and-flaky factor. Hydrogenated vegetable oil such as Crisco or Spry is generally used, and is most satisfactory for the amateur. Experienced pastry makers often prefer lard, or may use chicken fat or butter to get special flavor or consistency.

The presence of water and a small quantity of milk solids in butter and margarine may interfere with tenderness, but they are favorable for good browning.

Cooking oil may be used instead of solid shortening, but it is not as popular. The

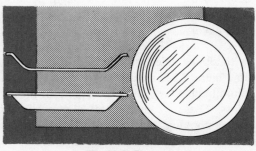

Fig. 22-2. Pie pan

448

product tends to be tender but crumbly rather than flaky. Mixing is easier but handling is more difficult.

Salt is considered an essential ingredient because the other materials are very bland. It gives an edge or a taste to what might otherwise be considered to be almost flavorless. However, the crust does have a delicate flavor of flour and shortening cooked together, and is strongly flavored by the filling. For many tastes, little or no damage will be done if you forget the salt or leave it out for dietary reasons.

Water serves as a binder to hold the flour-shortening combination together for shaping and rolling, and combines with the flour to make the structure of the crust during cooking.

Too little water will not keep dough together properly while rolling, so that it frays or cracks. Too much makes it wet and sticky, and slows down the baking process so that it might not cook on schedule, and remain rare and soggy in the finished pie.

Proportions of Flour and Shortening. The usual proportion recommended for pie crust is 2 cups of fluffed-up (sifted) flour to 2/3 or 3/4 of a cup of solid shortening. This is 4 to 1 or 8 to 3. But you may find a recipe calling for a full cup of shortening (2 to 1) or only 3/8 of a cup (over 5 to 1). If the shortening is oil, you can get by nicely with a half cup.

If you use butter or margarine, increase the quantity by 1/5, to adjust for the water they contain.

As the proportion of flour is increased or

Fig. 22-3. Too much shortening (or too little flour)

the shortening decreased, the pastry tends to become more firm and tractable in handling, but harder or tougher when cooked. Too little flour (or too much shortening) makes a dough that is likely to be sticky and greasy, and therefore difficult and unpleasant to handle, but a crust that should be flaky and tender.

An excessive amount of shortening may be partly corrected by its stickiness, as it will pick up more than the normal quantity of flour during rolling.

Recipes. Although recipes agree very well on the nature of the ingredients in plain pie crust, they differ greatly in the amounts. The recipe below shows the spread in recommendations for materials for a double crust for a 9-inch pie, together with a recommendation for a first try.

While this recipe is intended for a 9-inch pie, the beginner will be wise to use it for an 8-inch size the first time. If you should roll the crust too thick, or have other difficulties, you would still have enough for a neat full size pair of crusts. Any surplus crust can be used to advantage in a tart, or as plain bits of baked crust.

Two-Crust Pie Shell			
Ingredients	Minimum	Maximum	Try
Flour (sifted)	2 cps	2½ cps	2 cps
Solid shortening	⅜ cup	1 cup	¾ cup
Water	⅛ cup	¼ cup	¼ cup
Salt	½ tsp	1 tsp	1 tsp

There are a number of factors involved in making up this recipe, which will be discussed in several following sections.

Measurement. In any general instructions on preparing pie crust you are likely to be told that exact proportioning and measurement of the ingredients is absolutely essential. But since the proportions vary widely from cookbook to cookbook, it seems unlikely that failure must follow neglect of exact measurement.

On the other hand, a person (and particularly an amateur) using a recipe should follow it with reasonable faithfulness, as otherwise there is little purpose in using it and no way to fix the blame for possible disappointments.

Both flour and solid shortening have characteristics that often lead to grossly inaccurate measurement.

Regular flour tends to pack together during packaging, transportation and storage, and can be fluffed up again by sifting. A cup of flour taken from a bag that has been at the bottom of a heap may yield 1-1/2 cups sifted. A cup of the same flour taken from a bag that had carried less weight might yield less than 1-1/4 cups sifted.

Since there is no easy way of measuring the compactness of flour in the bag or canister, recipe amounts are almost always in sifted flour. Fortunately, sifting is easy. You scoop up batches of the flour in a one-cup one-hand sifter and sift it into a 2-cup measure. Or into a one-cup measure twice.

If you do not have a sifter, stir the flour with a whisk, or, in spooning it from storage shake it lightly off the spoon edges into the measuring cup. The whisk is almost as effective as sifting. For spooned flour, use 7/8 of a cup where a full cup is listed.

A cup of sifted flour weighs about 6 ounces, while the same amount of unsifted and unstirred flour may weigh up to 9 ounces.

Measurement of shortening is discussed on page 10.

MIXING

Temperature. Many pie crust recipes stress the great importance of keeping the dough cold, both to make it workable and to insure proper blending of the ingredients. They say that the materials should be cold, water must be ice water, and the dough must be frequently put back in the fridge to chill. But there are other recipes that demand that you have materials at room temperature, and some even want the fat pre-mixed with boiling water.

Cold usually makes dough more workable, particularly while you are combining the shortening and the flour. A more manageable mix may yield a better crust simply because you don't have to handle it as much.

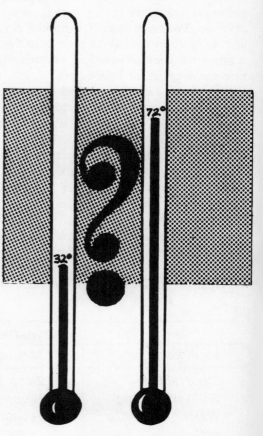

Fig 22-4. The experts disagree

But it is possible to make excellent crust without keeping the dough cold or even cool.

Handling. The way in which the dough is mixed and handled is a very important factor in the quality of crust. It is much safer to mix it too little than too much. Most pie crust failures are due to over-handling.

Flakiness depends primarily on the existence in the rolled dough of tiny flat plates of nearly pure shortening separated by films of moistened flour. Too-thorough blending of flour and shortening reduces the size of the bits of fat below that required for rolling out into the desired plate structure. However, this by itself would not interfere with tenderness.

Excessive kneading, mixing or rolling of dough after water has been added is likely to work the gluten in the flour into a tough structure, which is needed in bread and must be avoided in pastry. This is discussed under Gluten, page 404. The working and damage can occur both while mixing water into the dough, and while rolling the dough into sheets.

Another form of damage occurs during rolling — too much of the flour used to prevent sticking is worked into the dough, changing its proportions and making it harder.

Flour and Shortening. These two ingredients should be blended in such a way that the shortening is in small pieces, the size of corn meal or of small peas, depending on whose recipe you are reading. Each of these should be completely coated with flour. When the dough is rolled into a thin sheet, the pieces of fat will squeeze out to be very thin and flat, and will still be separated from each other by flour, which is moist and flattens out into sheets. This is the structure of flakiness.

The mixing process is called "cutting in". It goes best if the fat is moderately stiff, as cuts made in it will then stay open long enough for flour to follow the cutter into

Fig. 22-5. Don't bang the blender — it splatters

them. This may be most of the reason for the insistence of many cookbooks on keeping the whole operation cold. But cutting in can be done, even if less efficiently, with soft fat or even with oil.

Put about 1/3 of the flour in a bowl, cover it with all the shortening and put the rest of the flour on top. Take a pastry blender, or dough blender, Figure 35-35, push it down through the layers, raise it and lower it again and again, varying your work point and pushing loose flour around as necessary to get it in the action.

The mixture is supposed to spill off the sides of the blender as you raise it, but it may not. You can tip the blender and perhaps dump or shake it off. If not, scrape it off with a knife or another tool. Don't bang the blender on anything to shake dough off it, as the wires are likely to vibrate and send it in a shower over a wide area.

After a minute or two you will see the mixture beginning to separate into soft pieces. These should get smaller as you work, until the small-pea size is reached. But after getting down to the size of very large peas or even marbles, they may start to stick together, increase in size and ball up on the top of the wires. If you have been conscientious about working the whole batch evenly, and the loose flour is all combined, you can stop now.

Further work should do no harm, as flour does not get sensitive to mauling until it is mixed with water, but it is unlikely to do much good either.

An experienced cook is likely to take 2 to 4 minutes to do the cutting in.

If you do not have a pastry blender, you can do the cutting in with two knives, holding them at an angle of about 45° from vertical and moving them through the material close together and in opposite directions. This will take longer than the blender would, but results should be just as good.

Pie crust may also be made by a strong electric mixer at low speed. Its use is tolerated with regular flour, and recommended with instant-type flour. You may have to use a large spoon to scrape material from the sides of the bowl back within reach of the beaters.

Mixer cutting-in time is about a half minute, but you regulate it by appearance of the product rather than time.

Oil Pastry. Most people use one of the solid shortenings in pie crust. These can produce the flakiest pastry, because of the way they preserve some of their structure while being rolled out thin. But delicious,

Fig. 22-6. This dough is resting

tender crusts can be made with salad or cooking oil. Flakiness is often obtained if mixing is not too thorough, and the mixing process is much easier.

You use about 25 per cent less oil than you would shortening, so that a half-cup of oil should be enough for mixing with two cups of flour. You put the sifted (or well shaken up) flour and salt in a bowl, and pour in the oil.

You can mix it with a big spoon, a fork, a pastry blender or even with your fingers if you prefer. It blends quite rapidly, producing the same coarsely granular appearance as with solid shortening. You stop when the pieces are the size of small peas, or before that if large pieces start to clump together.

Water. There are at least three entirely different systems for combining water with the mixture of flour and shortening. You can sprinkle it on the mixture and work it in, mix it first with a portion of the flour that is not mixed with shortening and knead the two batches together, or boil it and mix it with the shortening and then combine it with the flour.

These methods might be classified as regular or sprinkle, paste, and boiling water methods.

Sprinkle. Sprinkling is done after the cutting in of flour and shortening is complete. It may be done from the fingers, a tablespoon, a salt shaker or a clothes sprinkler. The first is easiest for the experienced; one of the others is recommended for the amateur. You dampen the upper surface of the dough, mix it in with fingers or a spoon, sprinkle and mix again, and continue until the dough is willing to pull away from the sides of the bowl and cling together in a ball.

This mixing should be done as quickly and lightly as possible. It is not necessary to get an absolutely even dampness and texture through the batch, and if you try for perfection in this regard you will probably be over-working the dough and toughening the crust.

The right quantity of water varies, but is usually 3 to 5 tablespoons. You work toward a texture of dough, rather than to use up a specified quantity of water. Using more water makes the mixing quicker and easier, and within reasonable limits will not interfere with crust quality in itself. But a wet dough is particularly sticky and mean to handle, and you will probably use too much flour rolling it, and might get it tough that way.

Three out of four recipes will tell you to use ice water, and cooks who follow this instruction may tell you that success cannot be obtained without this chill. However, the temperature effect of this small quantity of cold water on ten times its bulk in dough must be very small, and good crust can unquestionably be made with room-temperature water. But there is certainly no argument against using ice water if you wish.

Paste. Put 1/4 to 1/3 of the flour in a small bowl or large dish, and stir it with a tablespoon while you slowly pour in 1/4 cup of water. Keep stirring until all the flour is dampened. You will have to clean out the bowl of the spoon several times, with the back of a teaspoon or with a finger. This operation should be done with a minimum of stirring, as working a flour-water combination toughens the flour.

If you cannot wet all the flour with a reasonable amount of work, sprinkle on another tablespoon of water.

Cut together the shortening and the remaining flour until it separates into fairly uniform particles. Then mix in the flour-water paste, using your fingers, a strong spoon, a pastry blender or any other tool that appeals to you.

Try to get a fairly even blend of the two materials, but do not try for a perfect one, as the effort will tire both you and the dough.

Boiling Water. For this method, the water is heated to boiling and thoroughly mixed with the shortening, which is then allowed to cool. The resulting emulsion is mixed with the flour by stirring, in the same manner as oil. This crust should be tender, but is likely to be mealy rather than flaky.

It has a tendency toward heaviness, against which most recipes recommend mixing 1/2 teaspoon of baking powder with the 2 cups of flour. This requires that rolling out be done promptly, or its effect will be lost.

Resting. When you are finished, roll the dough up in a ball or a cylinder. Many cooks seem to feel that it should then rest for 15 to 30 minutes before rolling. If it is very sticky let it rest in the fridge, as cold should make it more workable.

Even if you do not feel that the dough

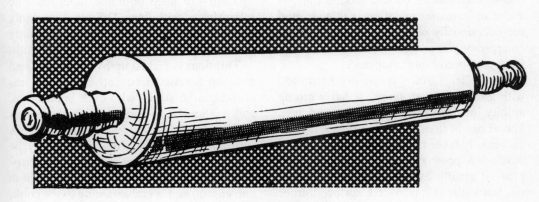

Fig. 22-7. Rolling pin

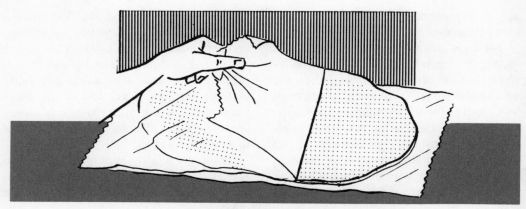

Fig. 22-8. Pulling off wax paper

needs a rest, its siesta gives you an appropriate time in which to prepare the pie filling, or at least to clean up the utensils dirtied in making the dough.

Pie crust dough should always be protected against drying out, by moisture proof wrapping. If this is done, and it does not contain baking powder, it will stay in good condition for at least several days in the refrigerator, and for weeks or months in the freezer.

ROLLING

Rolling Pin. Dough is usually spread into a sheet with a rolling pin, Figure 22-7. A standard size has a working width of 9-1/2 inches and a diameter of about 2. It turns freely, often on bearings, on handles one at each side. Different models may be wider or narrower or fatter or thinner, and are occasionally of a different shape. In an emergency you can use a round bottle or a food can, preferably unopened.

The roller surface is usually hardwood with a fairly smooth finish. It has a strong affinity for dough when it is new, and even liberal use of flour may not prevent it from sticking. It takes months or years of use to develop a good surface, but you can improve it greatly by rubbing it with cooking oil, heating it evenly over a surface burner until it is too hot to hold but not too hot to

touch, then applying more oil and allowing it to soak in.

This process may be repeated several times. Wipe the roller with paper toweling before use. The treated surface is not noticeably oily, but it does not stick to dough as readily and holds flour better. It should never be washed with soap or detergent, just cleaned off with paper or a dry rag after use.

Teflon does not appear to be a satisfactory finish for rolling pins.

Where to Roll. Rolling can be done on any flat washable surface. You can use a large bread board, but a plastic, enamel or marble top on a work table is perfectly satisfactory.

Flouring. Pastry dough is sticky, so it is necessary to keep both the table and the roller dusted with flour. Dribble it on thinly with a sifter or a spoon, then rub it lightly with your hand or with an open-mesh cloth.

This flour is picked up by the dough, and must be renewed frequently. But it is important to be stingy with each application, and it is unwise to sprinkle it on the dough itself, as it tends to toughen the crust. A very thin skin of such toughening may be harmless or even agreeable in adding crispness, but if it gets at all thick or strong it is unpleasant, and is embarrassing to the cook.

When the dough sticks to any surface,

scrape or slice it off with the back of a knife, a finger nail or anything, wipe the area with a paper towel, and dust it with flour.

The amount of flour used and trouble with sticking can both be greatly reduced by wax paper or pastry cloth, which will be discussed below. However, it appears that most pie crust is rolled without either of these aids, chiefly because with a little practice you can avoid sticking, without the nuisance of using them.

Wax Paper. Dough may be rolled between two sheets of wax paper, to reduce or eliminate flouring. The wax surface does not stick easily, and if it does, it can often be freed from the dough by bending back at a sharp angle, Figure 22-8, and pulling. If the dough still sticks to it, it can be taken off with a knife as the paper is pulled.

Wax paper has the further advantage that it reinforces the thin sheet of rolled-out dough. If you peel off the top layer of paper, you can then safely pick up the bottom paper with the dough, turn it upside down on the pie pan, and then peel off the paper. The risk of breaking a crust handled in this manner is slight.

Oil crust is almost always rolled between wax papers, as it is very tender and is more likely to fall apart than other types.

It is a good extra precaution to rub wax paper lightly with flour before using it, unless you have already assured yourself that this particular dough does not stick to it.

Wet the table before putting the bottom sheet down, so that it will not slide around. It is best to use fresh paper for each crust. But if the supply is short, turn the original paper over to do the second crust.

Pastry Cloth. A pastry cloth is a piece of specially treated canvas that provides a surface on which to roll pie crust, cookies and biscuits. It is paired with a light, elastic cloth (stockinette) that is pulled over the rolling pin. Both cloths are supposed to be liberally spread with flour the first time they

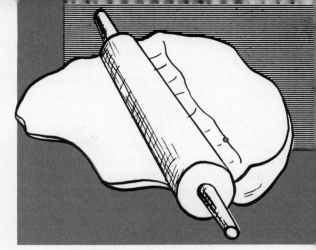

Fig. 22-9. First roll one way

are used, or after washing. This is rubbed into the pores of the cloth, so that there is no longer any on the surface. Any surplus is scraped off with the side of a spatula.

The cloth tends to slide around on a table until you learn how to control it. The edges can be tucked under a bread board, but it is too small (usually 18 x 24 inches) to be fastened over table edges. You can fold it over the near edge, lean against it, and do most of the rolling away from you.

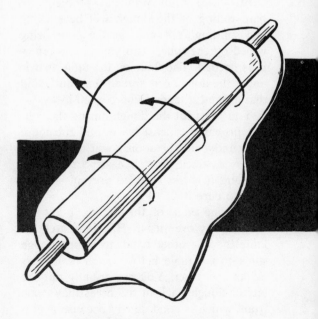

Fig. 22-10. Then roll across

If dough sticks to either cloth, scrape and wipe it off, and rub more flour into the offending spot. When you are through, scrape off any excess flour, roll the covered pin into the canvas, then put in a plastic bag until you need it again. It needs less flour and rubbing after the first time.

This method ordinarily gives you the least trouble with sticking. But the cloth is troublesome to prepare, you need practice in using it and it may be a nuisance to have around. If you are going to use it often it is probably worth while.

Rolling. If you are making a 2-crust pie, divide the dough into two portions, either equal or slightly unequal. The lower crust is slightly larger, and is made first.

Roll out from the center in all directions. Use medium to light pressure, so that the edge of the dough will move out from 1/2 to 1 inch with each stroke at first, and decreasing amounts as it becomes wider. Lift the roller clear to return it to center.

You can produce a nearly circular shape after a little practice by always rolling toward the shortest part.

Sticking. Your principal problems in bare rolling of the dough will be sticking and splitting. You can see the flour being wiped off the roller, and you should renew it as needed. The flour on the table that is under the dough gets spread too thinly, and that around it tends to be pushed away.

You must lift the dough during the rolling, probably at least twice, and rub more flour under it. The sooner you do this, the easier, as thick crust is easier to lift than thin and it is less work to prevent sticking than to cure it.

Lift one edge of the dough, pulling it back slowly over itself. Have a spatula or knife in your other hand, to loosen dough stuck to the table before much of it tears out of the sheet. You can usually put the bits of dough back in the holes they came from, which is good chiefly because it prevents them from filling with flour.

When you have lifted slightly more than half the dough sheet, spread flour very thinly on the table where it was, and put it back in place. Then lift the opposite side in the same manner, cut it free where necessary, put flour under it and replace it. You can then resume rolling. This can be done more quickly than it can be described.

Sticking is most severe when the dough contains a high proportion of shortening or water. Splitting is usually a symptom of shortage of one or the other. As the sheet is widened it splits into sections near the edges.

You can patch each gap by moistening the edges slightly and adding a little dough, either fresh or taken off a projection on the edge, and rolling it in. Such patches seldom show in the cooked crust, and don't really matter anyhow.

FINISHING

Trimming. The finished dough sheet should be approximately round, 1/8 inch or less in thickness, and at least 2 inches wider than the pie pan size in any direction. The flat flange around the pan edge may be about 1/4 inch wide, and it takes 1 to 1-1/2 inches to go up and down the side slopes. You may need an extra bit, in case it shrinks after measuring, if it is irregular in shape or you don't get it right on the center of the pan.

Put the pie pan upside down on the sheet of dough as a pattern, and cut a circle that is at least an inch out from it, with a pastry wheel or a knife. Pick up the trimmings and set them aside, and take up the pan and put it upright.

Picking Up. There are at least two good ways of transferring your thin, fragile dough sheet to the pan. One is to pick up an edge, fold the sheet in half and then pick it up. Doubling its thickness and halving its area makes it much easier to handle. Or you can fold it twice, into quarters, before picking it up.

Fig. 22-11. Bottom crust — cutting and lifting

Another method is to place the rolling pin near one edge, pull the edge up around the pin and roll lightly away from it. The dough will wrap around the pin, and can be unwrapped onto the pan by turning it the other way over it.

Placing Bottom Crust. Center the raw crust on the pan as accurately as you can, and very gently pat or push it down into the hollow where the sides meet the bottom. Do not stretch it — move extra material down from the edge if it does not slide down naturally. It should fit the pan smoothly, without any air spaces under it.

The pan does not need to be greased, but it is sometimes rubbed with butter for browning effect and flavor.

Pushing the crust down may cause the part extending upward along the sides to bulge in several folds. You can flatten each fold by bending it to one side or the other, then squeeze it against the pan side to reduce its thickness. Or you can cut out the surplus material, wet the edges of the cut and press them together, to keep the crust thickness uniform. But this is seldom done.

Next you press the crust lightly down onto the level flange around the edge of the pan, and cut off any overhang with scissors or a knife, so the dough is even with the pan edge.

If it is a one-crust pie, or you are going to bake it empty as a shell, you can get a fancier appearance by trimming with pinking shears or a grooved pastry cutter (Figure 22-11), or by pressing down the edge with a fork or making designs in some other way, 22-12.

Fig. 22-12. Decorating edge with a fork, or by pinching

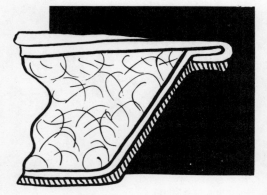

Fig. 22-13. Turned-under edge

The crust is allowed to relax for five or ten minutes before filling or putting it in the oven. If it shrinks so as to pull out of shape you can reshape it.

Pie Shells. The bottom crust of a pie is often baked before filling it. It is then called a pie shell or a pastry shell. This is standard practice when the filling requires a short cooking time, or is cooked separately for some reason.

The main problem in baking a pie shell is the formation of steam under the crust, which may push it out of shape. This can be prevented by making a number of holes in the raw dough after it is placed in the pan, using a fork or a pointed knife. The tool should be twisted a little in the holes, to make sure that they are open.

Holes should prevent bubbling, but a very liquid filling such as custard might go through such holes afterward and lift up the crust.

You can prevent heaving without puncturing the crust by loading it with clean pebbles, dry beans or some other weight. Or you can put a pie pan inside it — the same size if aluminum, the next smaller if glass.

Upper Crust. The upper crust is sometimes made about 1/2 inch smaller than the bottom one, as it does not have to extend down into the hollow of the pan. It is

rolled in the same manner and to the same thinness. Trimming to size may be done on the board, or after putting it on the pie.

You should cut a design into the center, with several open holes 1/8 to 1/4 inch in diameter, to allow steam to escape during cooking.

You usually roll the upper crust immediately after installing the lower one. Then fold it in half or in quarters, and leave it while you make or finish the filling. If this is a long process, cover both crusts with wax paper, plastic or slightly dampened cloth, to prevent drying.

Preparation of fillings will be discussed separately.

You pour or spoon the filling into the lower crust in the pan. It should be almost as high as the edge at the sides, and mounded upward in the center. Put the folded top crust on it, so that the holes will come at the center, spread it out, and pat it down lightly to conform to the filling. Then press it down firmly around the rim, so that it will stick a little to the lower crust.

Edging. There are a number of different techniques for finishing off the rim of a pie. You can simply cut the crust flush with the outer rim, then use a fork or some other design-making tool to press the two crusts firmly together all around. Or you can trim the lower crust flush and the upper one 1/2 inch out from the edge, turn the upper edge under the lower, Figure 22-13, and then press down with the tool, making adjoining or overlapping prints all the way around.

You want to create a juice-proof seal, good appearance and good texture. Many fruit and berry pies become very juicy during cooking, the juice is good if you can keep it in and bad if it boils out onto the oven floor.

A well-sealed edge and an un-cracked or well-patched crust, combined with top vent holes in the center will usually (but alas, not always!) hold it in. The folded-under upper crust makes the best seal. It also

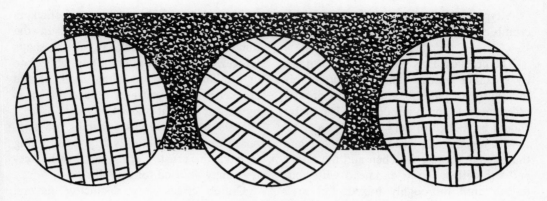

Fig. 22-14. Lattices

makes a thicker rim of crust, that will tend to cook faster and brown more deeply than the rest of the surface.

Appearance is a matter of individual judgment. You may prefer either the simple overlap or tucked-under; or you may like either the old fashioned appearance of edges pressed together with a fork, or the more formal designs made with a pastry cutter. There are no rules that you must follow.

If the crust turns out very well you can't have too much of it. If it is second-rate and this shows up most clearly in a triple-thick edge, your customers have the privilege of leaving that edge without implying a criticism of the pie itself.

Lattice. A top crust may be cut or formed into a lattice, Figure 22-14. This gives an attractive appearance, and is midway between a full crust and no crust in protecting the filling.

A lattice may be a little trouble or a lot of trouble to make. In general, its attractiveness increases in proportion to the difficulty of the method.

There are plastic dies that will cut a full set of square holes in a crust in one operation. Put the cutter on the table with cutting edges upward, lay the crust on it, and make a few passes with a rolling pin. Then lift the dough gently, starting at one side

and pulling it over on itself. You should then have a lattice top. But if it sticks to the cutter anywhere, or any of the holes are not fully cut, you may have to do some detail work with a knife.

It is more usual to roll crust out a bit thicker than the usual 1/8 inch, then cut it in strips 3/8 to 1/2 inch wide. Lay some of them on top of the filling, parallel and about 1/2 inch apart. Then put on another set of parallel strips at right angles for squares or some other angle for diamond-shaped holes. Trim the ends flush with the edges of the lower crust, and push them down firmly to attach them. If you wish, you can put an extra strip around the top of the edge to conceal the ends of the cross strips.

The prettiest and most time-consuming lattice is woven. This is a little beyond our "basic" approach to cooking, but you can work it out with a little patience. It is shown at the right side.

CRUMB CRUST

Crumb crust is a substitute for pastry that is sometimes used with gelatin, custard or meringue pies. It is a mixture of cracker crumbs, sugar and butter or margarine, with occasionally some added cinnamon or nutmeg, and may be served either raw or cooked.

A typical range of recipes for one 9-inch crumb crust is shown below.

The crackers may be reduced to crumbs by crushing with a rolling pin, preferably in a plastic or paper bag, by a meat grinder set at medium, or in a food mill. The butter should be melted or very soft.

Mix together the crumbs, the sugar and the spice if you use it. Then add the butter and stir with a spoon or knead with your fingers until thoroughly mixed. Put in a buttered pie pan, distribute evenly over bottom and sides to the top, and make compact and smooth by tamping and rolling with glass tumbler, or by pressing down and turning another pie pan of the same size.

If you wish to sprinkle some of the same mixture on the top, reserve about 1/4 of it for the purpose. This will make the crust thinner. Or mix an additional amount.

The crust is made firm before it is filled by chilling in the refrigerator for several hours (butter sets up better than margarine) or by baking and then cooling. You may put it in a 375° F oven for 8 or 10 minutes, or in 300° for 15. Indication of doneness is a slight browning of the edges.

For a meringue pie, you put a pre-cooked filling in a chilled raw crust, prepare and spread the beaten egg whites (see page 189), and bake in a moderate (350° F) oven until the meringue is lightly browned, about 15 minutes.

A number of different kinds of crackers may be substituted for grahams, in the same quantity. Zwieback, any of the snaps (ginger, chocolate or lemon) or chocolate or vanilla wafers are often used. If the cracker is sweet you may reduce the sugar by half or leave it out entirely.

Stale bread and cake crumbs are supposed to be suitable only if you are going to bake the crust. Cornflakes or other cereals may be used for crumbs.

Crumb crusts have distinctive flavors, which may either supplement or detract from the flavor of the filling. They are good for variety, but lack the steady appeal of the pastry crust.

BAKING

Pies with pastry crust are baked in a hot oven, 425 to 450° F. Time varies from 30 minutes to over 50. Crust and filling may be tested for tenderness with a table fork. But moderate resistance may be offered by a fully cooked crust if it is tough, or if it includes a thin, flour-hardened skin.

Pies are often removed from the oven just on a basis of cooking time and/or appearance. The crust should be golden or light brown in color, and it often develops a slightly blistery or mealy appearance.

Pie shells cook much more quickly, usually in about 20 minutes. Color is a reasonably safe indicator of doneness.

Juice. Fruit and berry pies often develop

Graham Cracker Crust			
Ingredients	Minimum	Maximum	Try
Fine crumbs of graham crackers	1⅓ cps	2 cps	1½ cps (18 or 20 crackers)
Butter or margarine	¼ cup	½ cup	¼ cup
Sugar, confectioners preferred	¼ cup	½ cup	¼ cup
Cinnamon	none	1 tsp	none
Nutmeg	none	¼ tsp	none

too much juice, so that they boil over. You can reduce the likelihood of this happening by making sure that there are vents in the top crust near the center, and that the top and bottom crust are firmly pressed together all around. Sometimes you can use a less juicy recipe.

The best precaution is to place a sheet of foil with upturned edges, or a cookie tin, on the oven bottom or a lower rack. If you have it at least 4 inches below the pie it should not interfere with its cooking, but it should not rest directly on an electric heating unit.

There may also be a problem of juice soaking into the crust, although it will often not do so even if no precautions are taken. Raw crust is almost waterproof, but as it cooks it tends to become porous. If you have used a thickener with the fruit, the juice should be thickened by this time so that it has little tendency to penetrate the crust. You can increase this protection by scattering part of the thickener and sugar mixture on the bottom crust, so it will be right where it is needed to slow down the juice.

Some cooks brush the lower crust with white of egg, beaten slightly to make it manageable. When heated, this congeals to make a film which should seal the pores in the crust, and makes it more resistant to soaking.

The upper crust does not have juice-soaking problems except when it is a lattice, parts of which sink into the filling, or when quantities of juice boil up through the vents (or more often, through breaks in unvented crust) and pour over the top. In both cases, the soaking might slow cooking of the crust slightly, but it is more likely to improve flavor than to damage it.

FRUIT FILLINGS

Fruit and berries appear to be the most popular pie fillings. Only three examples, apple, peach and strawberry, will be dis-cussed. The same general procedures can be followed for other types.

The sweetness and juiciness of fruit is variable, and the taste of consumers in regard to sweetness and juice varies also. As a result, the recommended quantities of sugar and thickeners are only middle-of-the-road suggestions, and can be varied up or down according to the judgment or previous experience of the cook.

Bear in mind that increase in thickeners (flour and corn starch particularly) tends to deaden flavor, so that sugar may be increased to compensate, and lemon juice (see page 291) may be added sparingly. If corn starch is used, best results will be obtained if it can be allowed to thicken before the full amount of sugar is mixed with it.

Apple. Apple is by far the most popular of the pies, and is also one of the safest to make. It seldom turns out wrong, as long as good cooking apples are used. Avoid the Delicious variety, which is excellent only when raw.

The best cooking apples have a definite apple flavor and odor and are slightly sour (tart). For pie and pudding you are safe with Baldwin, McIntosh, Greening, Rome and Winesap, to name just a few.

A standard recipe for a 9-inch apple pie follows. If you want a 10-inch pie, increase quantities by about 1/4 (25 per cent).

Apple Pie
pastry for two 9-inch crusts
(see page 449)

2 to 2½	lbs	cooking apples *(5 or 6 cps of slices)*
⅔ to 1	cup	sugar
2	Tb	flour
2	Tb	butter *(optional)*
1	Tb	lemon juice *(optional)*
¼	tsp	salt *(optional)*
½	tsp	cinnamon *(optional)*
¼	tsp	nutmeg *(optional)*

Prepare pastry, put bottom crust in 9-inch pie pan, preferably glass. Roll top crust, fold and set aside. Protect crusts from drying with wax paper or plastic. Peel and core the apples, and slice about 1/4 inch thick. Blend the sugar, flour and salt together, scatter 1/4 of the mixture on the bottom crust, then stir the rest lightly through the apples, trying to coat them completely without breaking many slices.

Put the apples into the pan, arranging them to fit against sides of the crust compactly, to be slightly below the level of the top of the pan and to mound up in the center. Sprinkle on lemon juice and then seasonings, if used, and add any butter in small pieces.

Put on the top crust, cut vents near the center for escape of steam, trim the edges and seal to the bottom crust. Bake in preheated 425° F oven for 35 to 50 minutes, until apples are fork-tender and crust is tender and golden or light brown.

If you have really first class apples you can get by very well without seasoning for many people, but there are others who are not content without spices. Use lemon juice only if the apples seem tasteless. If in doubt you can use half the quantity, or only a few drops. Butter makes the pie a little richer.

The flour is used to thicken the juice and protect the lower crust against being soaked. The amount is a guess, and is right for average apples. Very juicy ones might take more, dry ones less. But until you are quite experienced you cannot judge juiciness, and are best sticking to the average. But if you make several pies in succession from the same batch of apples you can adjust the quantity.

This is not an important problem. Many apple pies are made without thickening because people like the thin natural juice. If it takes two days to eat a pie, the unthickened one is likely to have better texture and flavor the second day than the thickened one. In any case, there is always a slight loss of flavor when thickening is used.

Two tablespoons of flour can be replaced by one tablespoon of corn starch or one to 1-1/2 of tapioca. However, flour is generally believed to be most suitable for apples.

The full upper crust can be replaced by a lattice crust, page 459.

Fig. 22-15. Apple pie

Fig. 22-16. Pints of strawberries

Apple pie is good hot, warm or cold. It is usually served plain, but is also popular with vanilla ice cream on top (a la mode) or with plain or whipped cream. Slices of cheddar cheese may be served on the side.

Peach. Peach pie may be made in almost exactly the same way as apple, just substituting an equal weight of peaches for apples, but increasing the sugar to 1 or 1-1/8 cups. Omit the cinnamon and preferably the nutmeg. If you feel you need extra flavoring, use a very few drops of almond extract.

Fresh peaches in prime condition are available for a much shorter season than apples, but good quality canned peaches can almost always be obtained. Here is a recipe for using them in pie. Directions apply to either cling or freestone varieties, but freestone are more like fresh ones.

Canned Peach Pie
pastry for two 9-inch crusts

1 can *(#2½, 29 ozs)* peaches in
    heavy syrup
½ cup sugar
3 Tb flour
1 Tb butter *(optional)*
    dash of nutmeg or almond
    extract *(optional)*
⅛ tsp salt *(optional)*

Drain peaches, saving syrup, and slice them. You should have about two cups. Roll out half of the pastry dough, make and install lower crust. Blend sugar, flour and salt, sprinkle 2 tablespoons over bottom crust, and the rest over peaches, stirring in

carefully, so as not to break many slices. Add 1/2 cup of the syrup and stir in gently.

Dot with butter and sprinkle with nutmeg if you wish. Put on full top crust or a lattice crust, as described earlier.

Bake in preheated moderately hot oven, 425° F, for 30 to 40 minutes, or until crust is tender and brown. Juice should be bubbling below vents or between lattice strips. Put on a cake rack to cool, or serve immediately. Can be eaten hot, warm or cold; plain, with ice cream or cream.

If frozen peaches are obtainable, they may be used in the same manner as the frozen strawberries discussed below.

Fresh Strawberry. Simple berry pies are all made in about the same way. Strawberry is the most popular (with good reason) and will be used as an example. Quantities are given for a 9-inch pie, but are approximate because berries vary greatly in sweetness and juiciness. For a 10-inch pie, increase them by 1/4.

Fresh Strawberry Pie
pastry for a 2-crust, 9-inch pie

1 qt ripe strawberries
¾ cup sugar
2 Tb flour
¼ tsp salt *(optional)*
1 egg white, lightly beaten
    (optional)

Line a 9-inch pan with bottom crust. If you want to try making it juice-proof, brush it liberally with the egg white.

Clean and slice the berries. Mix sugar, flour and salt together, sprinkle two tablespoons on the pie crust, mix the rest gently with the berries, until most surfaces are coated. Put berries in crust. There should be enough to fill just below the edge, rising to a mound in the center.

Roll out top crust, make center vents, spread over pie and seal to edges. Or make a lattice top. Bake in a moderately hot oven (425° F) for 35 to 50 minutes, or until crust is golden or light brown and tender.

This pie is usually served cold, but it is good warm also. You can eat it plain, or with any kind of cream (ice-, liquid or whipped).

Frozen Strawberry. Frozen strawberries are usually available all year, while fresh ones are likely to be scarce and high priced for considerable periods. For a pie almost equal in quality to the fresh-berry product, take:

Frozen-Strawberry Pie

pastry for a 2-crust,
9-inch pie

2 pkgs sliced, sweetened, frozen strawberries, thawed (16-oz, each)

¼ cup sugar *(optional)*

2 Tb flour *(optional)*

1 egg white, lightly beaten *(optional)*

These two packages of strawberries should contain together, about 2 cups of berries and 1-1/3 cups of juice, a total of 26 fluid ounces. Separate the juice from the berries. Mix the flour and sugar together, and then add a little of the juice. When smooth, add the rest of the juice, and heat until thickened, preferably without boiling.

Allow to cool, mix with the berries and pour into pastry-lined 9-inch pan, mounding slightly in the center. Add a vented top crust or a lattice crust. The bottom crust may be painted with white of egg.

Bake in a medium hot oven, 425° F for 30 to 50 minutes, or until crust is pleasantly browned. This pie should be quite juicy. If you don't want any flowing juice, use up to 3 tablespoons of flour, or substitute a

tablespoon of quick-cooking tapioca and one of corn starch.

With the larger amount of thickening, you may add a teaspoon of lemon juice to offset the resultant deadening of flavor.

For a very juicy and very tasty pie, use the thawed strawberries just as they are, without either sugar or thickening. You may either paint the bottom crust with white of egg, or leave it alone.

Deep Dish. If you use a top crust or lattice, and no bottom crust, you have a deep dish pie. It is usually baked in a casserole or utility pan of smaller size, so that the fruit filling is 1-1/2 inches or more in depth. A one-quart casserole is all right

Fig. 22-17. Custard pie

but snug for deep-dishing the filling for a 9-inch pie, while a 1-1/2-quart size has ample space but may make it a little shallow.

A deep dish pie usually has a standard upper crust with vents, but you can use a lattice instead.

Baking temperature and time are about the same as with a regular pie. The only item that requires much cooking is the upper crust. Watch this, and take the pie out when it is done.

Open Face. An open face or one-crust pie has a bottom crust only. This is unusual construction for a fruit or berry pie, but there is nothing against it. If you use raw fruit, you can follow the procedures given for a 2-crust pie, but simply do not put on a top crust.

If you use canned fruit, or prefer to cook the filling separately, you can use a pre-cooked pie shell and limit baking to whatever time is needed to heat crust and filling together.

DESSERT FILLINGS

This heading includes all the non-fruit dessert pies. A wide variety of puddings, both home made and ready-mix, can be used for fillings, but only a few examples will be given. In many cases, a pre-cooked bottom crust is used, and there is usually no top crust. Mince pie is an exception, as it is baked between two raw crusts, in the same manner as standard fruit pies.

Custard. Custard pie is a baked custard in a single pie shell. It is likely to be a richer-than-average custard. A typical recipe is:

Fig. 22-18. A risky maneuver

Custard Pie
pastry for 1-crust, 9-inch pie

3		eggs
½	cup	sugar *(or to taste)*
2	cps	milk
1	Tb	egg white, lightly beaten *(optional)*
¼	tsp	salt *(optional)*
⅛	tsp	nutmeg *(optional)*

Line a 9-inch pie pan with rolled-out crust. You may paint its inside with the slightly beaten white of egg, to prevent soaking in. Unless you have a separate supply, you can obtain this by separating one of your custard eggs, beating the white, taking out the amount needed for painting, then adding the yolk and the other eggs.

Beat the eggs just enough to mix them thoroughly, add the sugar and salt, and stir. Then add the milk (or milk and cream) and stir until well blended. Put the pie pan and crust in a preheated hot 450° F oven, pour the custard into it carefully, sprinkle the nutmeg on top and close the door. After 10 minutes, turn the heat down to 300°.

Bake for 50 minutes, or until a knife put in the custard 1/3 of the way out from the center comes out clean. The center may still be liquid, but heat from the rest of the pie should finish cooking it, outside the oven on a rack. The surface should be lightly browned.

Unfortunately, the bottom of the crust is often soggy. This may be due to under-cooking because of the cooling influence of the custard, because of liquid soaking into it, or a combination. It is least likely to happen in a glass pan, because the crust receives the maximum amount of direct (radiant) heat through that.

Custard is often baked in pre-cooked pie shells, or poured into a pie shell that has been partly baked (say for 10 minutes) and is still hot and in the oven. The shelf can be pulled out, and the pouring done without removing the pan. For a fully pre-cooked shell, the filling may be partly cooked as a boiled custard, to shorten the baking and soaking-in time for the already-baked crust.

Another system is to bake the pie shell and the custard in separate pie pans of the same size. The custard pan, which should be greased, may be put in shallow water, and cooked at 375º F, or just on the oven rack with temperature at 250º. It is allowed to cool, and shortly before serving, is loosened from the pan slopes by a knife and from the bottom by jiggling it, and it is then slid into the pie shell.

This method prevents any danger of soggy crust at the first serving, but it risks disaster. If you try this and the filling breaks up, or if it sticks and you have to spoon it into the shell, you can make it attractive again with a layer of whipped cream. If you have cream.

Pumpkin. Pumpkin pie is a traditional Thanksgiving dessert, and in some areas is a year-round favorite as well.

It is made from a puree made by peeling dicing, boiling and mashing pumpkin. Or it can be taken out of a can. The pie is usually the custard, open face type described here, but it may also be made by the chiffon method.

Pumpkin Pie

1		single 9-inch pie crust, raw
2		eggs
¾	cup	sugar
1¼	cps	hot milk
2	cps	mashed pumpkin
1	tsp	cinnamon
½	tsp	nutmeg
¼	tsp	ginger *(optional)*

Prepare the crust as described for Custard Pie, above.

Beat the eggs slightly, and mix in the sugar and spices. Add the pumpkin and milk alternately in moderate amounts, stirring each time until smooth.

Pour and scrape the mixture into the pastry-lined pie pan. Place in a preheated 450º oven. After 15 minutes, turn the heat down to 350º, and bake for about 45 min-

utes longer, or until done. Test in the same manner as the Custard Pie.

Pumpkin pie is served bare in some sections of the country, and is heavily covered with sweetened whipped cream in others. In either case, it is usually at room temperature.

A very similar pie can be made from winter squash, or from sweet potatoes.

Chiffon. Chiffon fillings are light-textured gelatin puddings, which are put in baked and cooled pie shells or crumb shells and served cold. The flavoring is usually fruit puree or one of the more acid fruit juices.

This is a sample recipe:

Lemon Chiffon Pie

1		baked single pie crust, 9-inch
4		eggs, separated
1	Tb	gelatin powder
1	cup	sugar
¾	cup	water
⅓	cup	lemon juice
1	Tb	grated lemon peel *(optional)*
½	cup	whipping cream *(optional)*

Soak the gelatin in the water for 5 minutes. Then add the lemon juice, egg yolks and half the sugar, and mix together thoroughly. Put in a heavy saucepan over low heat, stir constantly and take it off before it boils. This is important, as otherwise this mixture will usually curdle.

Then stir in grated peel (if you have it you certainly should use it, as it improves the flavor) and put pan in cold water. Cool until the mixture mounds slightly if dropped from a spoon.

Meanwhile, beat the egg whites until they are fairly stiff, then add the rest of the sugar gradually and continue to beat until stiff and dry. Then add the cooled gelatin mix and stir with a spoon until well blended. Pour or spoon the mixture into the pie shell, swirling it against the edges and into a low mound toward the center, leaving the rotary marks made by the spoon as decoration. Chill for several hours before serving in order to allow it to become firm.

You may wish to enrich the pie with a half cup of cream, beaten until stiff. You may either fold it into the filling just before putting it in the shell, or serve it on top of the completed pie.

Cream. Cream pie filling is usually an egg-plus-flour custard, cooked in a saucepan or double boiler and poured into a baked pastry shell. There is no further cooking unless the pie is to have a meringue top. It may be served cold or at room temperature.

A standard recipe is:

Cream Pie

1		9-inch pie shell, baked
3		egg yolks, slightly beaten
3	cps	milk
1	cup	sugar
½	cup	flour
½	tsp	vanilla *(or to taste)*
¼	tsp	salt *(optional)*

Heat milk without boiling it. Mix sugar, flour and salt in a heavy saucepan or in the top of a double boiler, pour in the hot milk a little at a time and stir vigorously until the mixture is smooth. Bring to a boil, then turn down heat and simmer until it thickens.

Pour a little of it into slightly beaten egg yolks, mix, and return to pan. Simmer for a little while without boiling (which might make it curdle), stir in vanilla and remove from heat. Allow to cool a few minutes, then pour the cream filling into the baked pie shell in its pan. The pie can be served at room temperature or chilled.

The same mixture can be served without the pie shell as a pudding or used as a filling for custard "cream" puffs and various pastries. It can also be elaborated upon by meringue or whipped cream, either mixed in or used as top dressing.

For meringue, use the 3 egg whites you separated from the yolks and about 5 tablespoons of sugar. Beat the whites until fluffy, add the sugar gradually while beating, and keep beating until they are stiff and glossy. The meringue is usually spread over the top of the pie, and then browned about 5 minutes in a hot (425° F) oven. But you can also fold part or all of it into the filling just before pouring it into the crust.

Whipped cream may be made by beating 1/2 cup of heavy or medium cream until smooth but not stiff, then beating in 1/2 to 1-1/2 tablespoons of sugar. The whipped cream may be used in the same ways as

Fig. 22-19. Meringue-topped pie

Fig. 22-20. Swirl finish

meringue, that is, as topping, last minute fold-in, or both.

Cream pie may be flavored in a number of ways. Some of the possibilities are replacement of white sugar with 1-1/4 cups of brown, to make butterscotch pie; or to add 2 squares (ounces) of bitter chocolate, melted in some of the milk, and 4 tablespoons of sugar to make a chocolate pie.

Bananas provide both flavoring and substance.

Banana Cream Pie

This calls for a special recipe, to avoid overflowing the pan. Use:

1		9-inch pie shell, baked
2		egg yolks, slightly beaten
2	cps	milk
1	cup	sugar
⅓	cup	flour
1	tsp	vanilla *(or to taste)*
¼	tsp	salt *(optional)*
2		large or 3 medium well-ripened bananas

Prepare the filling in the same manner as for regular cream pie. Slice the bananas about 1/4 inch thick. You have an option of placing them in the pie shell before pouring in the filling, mixing them gently with the filling, or arranging them on top after it is poured. Or you can pour some filling, make a layer of the bananas, then add the rest of the filling. A whipped cream topping goes very well with this.

Serve at room temperature or chilled.

Lemon Meringue. A lemon meringue pie consists of a single pie shell, a lemon-flavored filling and a meringue topping. The filling may be made in the same manner as that for cream pie, with the addition of 3 to 5 tablespoons of lemon juice (and perhaps some grated rind) instead of vanilla, but there is danger of curdling.

It may be made with gelatin, but will lack richness. The usual formula is a special cornstarch custard.

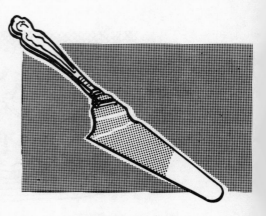

Fig. 22-21. Pie server

The recipes are basically similar, with some variation in proportions, particularly of lemon juice and of sugar, which is to be expected. Some call for cornstarch only, others use part cornstarch and part flour. The difference is that a cornstarch mixture may set into a jelly, but if flour is included it will not.

The tabulation below gives the spread of ingredients in various recipes, and a suggestion for a first try.

Mix the cornstarch and 1/3 of the sugar thoroughly, combine with water in a saucepan over medium heat, and bring to a boil, stirring constantly. Boil for one minute, then pour about half the mixture into the slightly beaten egg yolks, stir and return the mixture to the saucepan. Add the rest of the sugar, and simmer for a minute, taking care not to let it boil. Stir in remaining ingredients for the filling and pour into baked pie crust in pan.

Make the meringue by beating the egg whites until they are stiff but still have a wet appearance. Add sugar, a little at a time, and continue to beat until sugar has dissolved. Spread meringue over hot filling, scraping it quickly out of the bowl and swirling it around so that it is in full contact with the crust edge all the way around to prevent shrinking. The spoon marks make an attractive finish.

Bake in a hot oven, 400 to 425° F for 8 or 10 minutes, until the meringue is lightly browned. Put on rack in a warm

Lemon Meringue Pie			
Ingredients — Filling	Minimum	Maximum	Try
Baked pie shell, 9-inch	1	1	1
Egg yolks	2	4	2
Cornstarch	4 Tb	8 Tb	4 Tb
Flour*	2 Tb	4 Tb	none
Sugar	¾ cup	1½ cps	1¼ cps
Water	1 cup	2 cps	1¼ cps
Milk**	none	2 cps	none
Butter	1 Tb	3 Tb	2 Tb
Lemon juice	1 Tb	8 Tb	3 Tb
Grated lemon rind	½ tsp	3 tsp	2 tsp
Salt	none	½ tsp	¼ tsp (opt'l.)
Ingredients — Meringue			
Egg whites	2	4	3
Sugar	3 Tb	8 Tb	5 Tb
Cream of tartar	none	¼ tsp	none
Lemon juice	none	1 tsp	none
Vanilla	none	½ tsp	none
Salt	none	¼ tsp	none

* Substituted for cornstarch
** Substituted for water

room away from drafts, and serve as soon as it has cooled.

SERVING

Pie is almost always sliced into wedge-shaped pieces in the pan. There may be 4, 6 or 8 of them, all the same size; or they may be made different sizes according to the wants or needs of each person.

Same-size pieces may require a bit of practice. For any even number, first make a middle cut all the way across with a knife or pie server. For 4 pieces make another center cut at right angles, dividing the pie in quarters. Two additional cuts, halfway between the first pair, will give you 8 pieces.

For 6 pieces, make the center cut, then cut each side into thirds, estimating as accurately as you can.

Be careful to make all cuts all the way through the crust to the pan, to avoid stick-ing, tearing or breaking and even overturning as you lift the slices. It may require considerable care to make a clean cut where the bottom meets the edge.

Slices may be lifted out with a special triangular pie server, or a spatula, with two knives or a knife and a fork. This may be quite easy with a cold, dry pie that sticks together, and very difficult with a hot, tender, juicy one.

The first slice is the hardest, as you have to move the server down the side, then level along the bottom. If its front is wide enough to make a good lift it will not get the center of the edge because of the curve of the pan, and it will be too wide to go far toward the center of the pie. You may have to figure on breaking and then patching the first piece. The others can be undercut and lifted from the side, and are much easier to get out.

23

SANDWICHES

TWO-SLICE

The most common type of sandwich in the United States is made up of two slices of bread or roll, separated by a filling made up of a layer or layers of non-bread food. Other types will be discussed later.

Bread. Bread is usually white, but rye and whole wheat are often used, particularly with certain types of filling. Rye is considered to be a natural carrier for corned beef, for example.

Almost all store bread is sold sliced. The standard type has slices about 1/2 inch thick. Thin-sliced is likely to be 3/8 inch. There is also Melba bread with 1/4-inch slices, but this may be difficult to obtain.

Crusts are left on the bread in preparing sandwiches of a hearty, lunch-box or outdoor type, but may be cut off for daintier appearance and easier eating when they will be served at luncheons, teas and catered affairs.

French and Italian bread are less often used. They are usually not pre-sliced, so you can choose your own thickness. A loaf may be sliced lengthwise like an oversize roll, and filled to create a monster sandwich.

A roll may be sliced horizontally and used instead of two slices of bread. Round soft rolls, sold as hamburger rolls or barbecue buns, are standard for hamburgers, and are occasionally used with other fillings. Hot dog or frankfurter rolls, long and thin, are pretty much limited to frankfurters.

Hard rolls, sometimes very hard, are the distinctive feature of wedges and hero sandwiches, with a variety of fillings.

Very fresh bread may be too tender for sandwiches, as it tends to crush into a doughy mass during spreading of butter or filling, or because of weight resting on it while being carelessly stored or transported. Stale bread is dry and lacking in flavor. Somewhere in between is best for sandwich making.

Toast. Sandwich bread may be toasted before or after putting in the filling. Toasting firms or hardens the bread and heats it and sometimes the filling as well. It is most useful when done immediately before serving.

Toasting-before-filling is done in any type of toaster. The filling materials should be ready to put in the sandwiches, and the customers should be ready to eat them.

471

Toasting may be to any desired color. In general, it should be lighter with a dry filling than with a moist one.

A filled sandwich may be toasted under a broiler, on a dry or buttered frypan or griddle or in a two-unit griddle with a hinged top. With a high temperature the surfaces brown with little heating of the filling, with slower heat the filling is warmed too. The sandwich is usually turned so as to brown both sides, except in a hinged griddle that does both sides at once.

A sandwich may be opened before putting under the broiler, to heat the filling directly.

Sliced rolls may be toasted, or heated in the oven or in the pan in which a hot filling is being prepared. Details will be discussed under individual sandwiches.

Spreads. A spread may be a moistener, moisture barrier, lubricant and/or flavoring applied thinly to one or both bread (or roll) slices before adding the filling. Butter and margarine are the most used, but mayonnaise is also popular.

A spread may also be a whole filling that is soft and uniform enough to be spooned onto the bread and spread with a knife. Spread fillings include peanut butter, jelly, jam, cream cheese, chopped liver and applesauce.

Many spreads, including butter, peanut butter and cream cheese, are too stiff to spread readily when chilled, particularly if the bread is fresh. They tend to crush the bread and then roll up with it over the back of the knife. If there is not enough time to let them warm up, they can be softened by creaming (kneading with the back of a spoon), preferably in a slightly warmed bowl or saucer. Or they can be cut into very thin slices or small chunks and scattered over the bread, then spread after a few minutes.

Lettuce. Lettuce is a deservedly popular sandwich material. It adds bulk, crispness and variety of texture to other fillings, and

Fig. 23-1. A popular sandwich

will reduce or prevent soaking of oil or moisture into the bread.

Lettuce and tomato, Figure 23-2, is a popular sandwich combination. It may be the whole filling, be supplemented by half-slices of bacon or make up an extra layer in a hamburger or other meat sandwich. Tomato slices are slippery, and it is a good precaution to pin together sandwiches that contain them. Toothpicks are the usual fastening.

Soft Mixtures. Many sandwich fillers are of soft material that is too irregular in texture to be considered a spread. Egg, chicken and tuna salads, chopped hard boiled egg and chopped ham are examples. They may be a little sloppy to eat, as bits of filling tend to squeeze and fall out of them.

Such mixtures may be moist enough to dampen the bread, making it soggy and disagreeable. Partial protection may be obtained by spreading butter carefully on the inner surfaces of the bread, and by putting the filling between lettuce leaves. However, it is good policy to eat them soon after preparation.

Salad mixes easily become contaminated

during preparation, and provide a favorable medium for multiplication of bacteria. None of these are desirable, and a few of them in the salmonella and streptococcus family have been responsible for group illness after picnics.

Precautions to take include using clean hands, utensils and materials, keeping materials cold before and after mixing, keeping the sandwiches as cool as possible and arranging for the shortest reasonable time between making them and eating them. Which is standard advice for most other picnic food, too.

Slices. Food that can be sliced is usually convenient for sandwich preparation. Most meat and cheese fall in this classification. In addition, there are salad vegetables such as tomato and cucumber. Iceberg lettuce is occasionally sliced instead of unfolded, to avoid struggles to make it lie flat.

In preparing the slices and putting them into sandwiches, it must be kept in mind that any defects are hidden by the bread, and that bread is soft and fragile.

Meat should be trimmed free of any pieces of fat large enough to be disagreeable to eat, and of all bone, gristle, tendons or hard crust that might be unchewable and which would tend to pull the sandwich apart. Tough skins should be removed from sausage meat such as liverwurst, from wrapped or waxed cheese and sometimes from tomato and cucumber. Rotten or disagreeably soft spots should be cut out of the vegetables.

If the filling is even slightly tough, it can be made easier to eat by slicing very thin. A single slice of beef 1/4 inch thick is likely to be difficult to bite cleanly in a sandwich, which would be pulled apart by teeth pulling out an incompletely detached piece. But the same beef in four 1/16-inch slices would be easier to bite, and any unbitten shreds would be much weaker and less likely to damage the sandwich.

Only the most expert or lucky carver can

Fig. 23-2. Tomatoes are slippery

produce such thin slices with a regular knife. It is easier with an electric knife, and no problem for an electric rotary slicer. Packaged sliced meat for sandwiches is usually 1/16-inch or thinner.

Proportions. There is a wide range of proportion between bread and filling. At the worst, there is the item sarcastically called a jam sandwich (two slices of bread jammed together) where the filling is almost invisible. The bread is the least expensive part of the sandwich and is filling, but it is short on both flavor and balanced nourishment.

There is no standard to quote. Many people are perfectly satisfied with a single 1/8-inch slice of meat or cheese between 1/2-inch slices of bread. Others want half an inch or more of filling between thin slices.

Fig. 23-3. Tough meat can wreck a sandwich

Fig. 23-4. You can be stingy or generous

Even with high priced sliced meat, and butter on all the bread, a sandwich is still quite an economical form of food, and you should be inclined to be generous with fillings unless you are actually running out of material. A tentative standard might be a minimum thickness of 1/4 of an inch for meat and cheese fillings, and 3/8 inch for egg salad and similar material. Butter, peanut butter, jam and jelly are often preferred in very thin layers.

Seasoning. A sandwich eaten away from home is usually supposed to be a complete unit, containing whatever salt, pepper and other seasoning is desirable for its full enjoyment. The maker of sandwiches must use his or her judgment in adding them, or can supply them in small paper or other packages packed in the same bag.

Salt is likely to be expected with uncured meat, tomato and cucumber, but not with cheese. It is usually included in salad mixtures and meat loaf, but extra might be wanted to offset the blandness of the bread.

Fig. 23-5. Complete meal service

Liking for pepper is an individual matter, but few people are annoyed by it if the quantity is small or moderate. Like salt, it is dry and does not cause damage during storage or transportation.

Pickles or pickle slices should be wrapped in plastic and packed on the side, as they may be moist enough to make bread unpleasantly soggy.

Catsup and prepared mustard are popular sandwich condiments, and either may contain enough water to make bread soggy. For advance packing, they should be applied in very thin films, and/or the bread should be protected by intact leaves of lettuce or by buttering.

Trimming. It is likely that the majority of sandwiches are served and eaten whole. But appearance and comfort in eating can be improved by trimming.

A sandwich is easier to hold and eat, and less likely to drip filling, if it is cut in half. The cut may be straight across, from top to bottom, or diagonal. However, if sandwiches with thick or sloppy fillings are to be piled on a plate, it is better not to cut them, as it increases likelihood of them falling apart.

Trimming of crusts is a personal matter. Some people like crusts, others don't. In general, hearty sandwiches for lunches and picnics are not trimmed, unless there is a problem of crusts being burnt or particularly tough.

Wrapping. Sandwiches may become stale very rapidly, so it is best to wrap them in plastic as soon as they are made. Individual bags are most convenient, but you may pack several in a larger bag, wrapping them individually in napkins if they are inclined to fall apart.

CLUB

The club sandwich is usually three slices of toasted bread with two layers of filling, sliced into four triangular or square pieces. Fillings may include lettuce and tomato, plus some meat such as bacon or turkey. Fillings are usually generous, so that it is necessary to pin the pieces together with toothpicks, preferably before you cut them.

HOT FILLINGS

Many of the most popular sandwiches are hot inside. They include frankfurter, hamburger, cheeseburger, egg and egg combinations and grilled cheese. In addition, sliced meat and meat loaf may be hot when assembled, either because of being cut off a heated chunk or as a result of special heating.

These are not usually considered to be hot sandwiches, as this name has become restricted to an open face sandwich with gravy, which will be described later. However, the sliced meat fillings are the only members of the hot-inside group that do not lose most of their attractiveness if allowed to get cold.

These sandwiches are improved by hav-

Fig. 23-7. Hamburger

ing the bread or rolls heated also, by toasting or otherwise.

Hamburger. Hamburger is one of the most popular, nourishing and easily prepared of the hot fillings. It is made up in patties weighing from 2 to 6 ounces (but less than 4 is stingy). The best way to prepare these is also the easiest, but it can seldom be found in a cookbook. Cut or break the original lump into the size pieces you want, weighing them on a postage scale if you crave accuracy. Shape them into patties by putting on any clean surface, then pulling and pressing lightly into shape. They may be 3 to 4-1/2 inches in diameter and 3/8 to 1 inch thick. If you want to season before serving, wait until they are nearly cooked, then sprinkle with salt and/or pepper.

Hamburger is fried or broiled on both sides, and may be rare, medium, well done or burned up, depending on the wishes of the customer and on errors in satisfying them.

Frying, for which this meat normally provides its own grease, may be done between 200 and 400° F, with a preference for the 300 to 350° range. A 3/8-inch thickness should cook to medium rare in about 1-1/2 minutes on a side at 300°, while a 1-inch patty will take at least twice as long. But results vary, and unless you are used to cooking them, it is recommended that you test visually by making and opening up cuts.

If the meat is very loosely packed it will develop little chimneys that carry heated

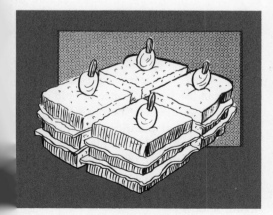

Fig. 23-6. Club sandwich

air upward from the bottom, cooking the meat close to them right through the center. This looseness produces a pleasantly varied texture, but makes it hard to test for doneness.

High pan temperature produces a harder and darker crust, and a sharper difference between inside and surface cooking. Even with medium heat, a thick rare hamburger may be barely warm in the middle. A covered pan makes cooking somewhat faster and more uniform, with poor crust development. Effect on taste is variable, and may be unimportant.

Hamburgers may be broiled 2 inches be-

Fig. 23-8. Cheeseburger

low the flame for crispness, or 4 inches for ordinary cooking.

Hamburger may also be mixed before cooking with a variety of substances. Cookbooks often insist on this. For a pound of chopped meat, it is usual to ask for 2 tablespoons of minced raw onion, a teaspoon of salt and a dash of pepper. This is fine if you and your family are tired of the taste of straight hamburger.

You can get a change of texture by mixing in up to 4 level tablespoons of bread crumbs. But for the long pull, plain unadulterated chopped beef is hard to improve.

The cooked hamburger may have almost anything added to it. Many people like to add from small to large quantities of one or more of the following: salt, pepper, raw onion (in slices), butter cheese, catsup, mustard, pickle, relish, Worcestershire, lettuce and/or tomato.

These sandwiches are usually made up with special soft round rolls. There seem to be two sizes at present, with the smaller ones more expensive than the large.

Small rolls make a tastier sandwich because of the larger proportion of meat, but the others are better for filling people up economically.

Ordinary bread slices make good hamburger covers too.

The sandwich may be improved by heating the roll. This may be done in the oven, under the broiler or in spare space on the griddle. It is usually pre-sliced, but in any case should be sliced horizontally and opened up before heating.

Cheeseburger. A cheeseburger is usually a hamburger plus a slice of cheese. The cheese is likely to be cheddar or cheddar-type, but may be Swiss. The slice is about the size of the hamburger patty or a little larger, and 1/16 to 1/4 inch thick. It is preferably but not necessarily one piece.

Slices of appropriate size but minimum thickness can often be bought ready made in packages, and may be either square or round. Since they are very thin, two or more may be used in a sandwich. Otherwise, a block of cheese may be sliced for the purpose.

The simplest cheeseburger is a hamburger sandwich with a slice of cold cheese put on top of the meat before serving. But both taste and popularity are improved if the cheese is melted. This may be done by putting it on top of the frying hamburger immediately after turning it, or on a broiling hamburger 15 to 30 seconds before taking it out.

For a deluxe treatment, place the cheese

Fig. 23-9. Fixing a bacon-and-egg

on the upside-down top half of the roll, and put it under a broiler for 15 to 30 seconds, just long enough to melt the cheese. Then put the meat patty on the lower half of the roll, and serve the two open-face.

The consumer may fold them together, after applying any flavoring or additions to the meat that he make like, or he may eat the two halves separately.

Some cookbooks think that a cheeseburger is made by mixing grated cheese with the raw chopped meat, 1/4 to 3/4 of a cup to the pound, together with onions and flavorings. The resulting sandwich is good enough to eat, but a restaurant could never sell it for a cheeseburger.

Egg. For a plain egg sandwich, put an egg in a hot buttered or greased pan in the same manner as for frying. Break the yolk by tapping it once or twice with the turner. Flattening the yolk in this way makes cooking time shorter.

When the egg is firm on the bottom, probably in 1-1/2 to 2 minutes, turn it over and cook it from 30 seconds to a little over a minute, so that the white is cooked and the yolk soft enough to flow just a little when cut or bitten.

Put the cooked egg on a slice of but-

tered bread, put another slice on top, put it on a plate and cut it in half. The cutting not only makes it more convenient to eat; it gives you a final check on how well you did.

With Bacon or Ham. A bacon and egg sandwich may be made by putting four half-slices of cooked or almost cooked bacon on top of an egg being fried for a sandwich, just before turning it. It is not practical to use raw bacon because its cooking time is longer than that of the egg.

You can use more bacon if you feel generous, or you can use whole slices of bacon and bend them.

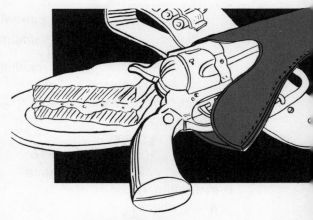

Fig. 23-10. Western

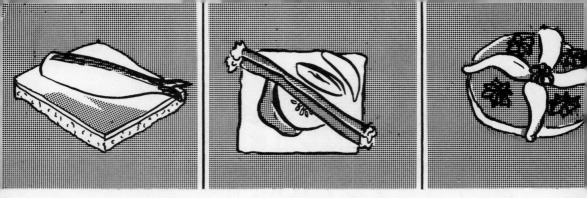

Fig. 23-11. Open face sandwiches, Swedish style

The cooked bacon may be put on the pan first, and the egg broken over it.

For a ham and egg, use at least two thicknesses of conventional sliced cooked ham, placed on top of the egg just before turning.

The western sandwich is a standard item in low priced and quick service restaurants in most parts of the country, but I cannot find a complete recipe for it in any cookbook. The data below is from conversations with short order cooks, and personal experiments.

The ham, onion and green pepper are supposed to be equal in quantity, but can be varied according to taste or availability.

Beat the egg lightly with a fork, stir in the other ingredients, and fry.

A single sandwich may be best cooked in a very small (5-inch) frypan which will keep it from spreading. On a larger surface, turn the edge back toward the center after partial cooking, to keep it down to sandwich size. Cut apart two or more cooking on one griddle in the same manner.

Moderate heat of 300 to 325° F gives good results, but either very slow or maximum heat may be used. Cooking time (2/3 for first side, 1/3 for other) ranges from 3 minutes for high heat and a rare (gooey) result, to 8 or 10 minutes for low heat and well done.

High heat requires close watching to avoid unwanted scorching and burning. You usually turn it when the thin edges have cooked through, but earlier if lifting an edge shows it is getting too brown.

Adding milk to the egg thins it so that it will be inclined to flow out of the mixture

Western Sandwich (one serving)			
Ingredients	Minimum	Maximum	Try
Egg	1 medium	1 jumbo	1 large
Milk, cream or water	none	1 Tb	none
Finely cut cooked ham	1 Tb	⅓ cup	3 Tb (or 1/6 cup)
Chopped raw onion	1 Tb	⅓ cup	3 Tb (or 1/6 cup)
Chopped raw green pepper	1 Tb	⅓ cup	3 Tb (or 1/6 cup)
Salt	none	¼ tsp	none
Bread, white, rye or whole wheat	1 slice	2 slices	2 slices, white

Fig. 23-12. Hot beef sandwich

at first, so that you have to keep turning it back in. Cooked texture is lighter.

The single cookbook recipe found for a western sandwich advised minimum quantities of ham and onion, no green pepper, and required frying of the onion five minutes before mixing with the rest.

OPEN FACE

The open face sandwich uses only one slice of bread, with the filling lying on top of it. Except for the hot sandwich, it is rather rare in the United States, but is the standard type in some other countries.

The filling is often arranged in patterns, and very attractive effects can be arranged after a little practice. Any type of sandwich material can be used.

Hot Sandwich. A hot sandwich is made by putting a layer of bread on a plate, nearly covering it with sliced meat and pouring hot gravy over both. Only the gravy has to be hot, but results are better if the plate and meat are heated also.

The bread should be slightly stale, as it is subjected to pressure when the meat is cut, and is softened by gravy soaking in. If one slice of bread is used it may be just a snack, but if there are two slices, it is the main course of a meal.

Beef is the most popular meat for a hot sandwich, but lamb and pork are used also. There may be a single thickness (although with some overlapping of pieces) of 1/4 inch or more, or several layers of very thin slices.

24

SOUP

SOUP

Soup is a liquid, semi-liquid or jellied food. It is served as an early course in a meal, as a whole informal meal or occasionally as a beverage. There are so many kinds that it is difficult to classify them.

Prepared. A great variety of canned soups of fair to excellent quality are available in stores. Some of them are ready to heat and serve as they come from the can, others are condensed and are meant to be diluted with an equal quantity of water or milk. There are also frozen and dried soups, many of them of superior quality.

The existence of these soups, and the disappearance of the coal and wood ranges which supplied simmering facilities as a no-cost side benefit from regular cooking, have greatly reduced the amount and importance of soup in home cooking.

However, you can still make a better soup than you can buy. Also, you can change and enliven the bought soup, sometimes using it just as a base for an elaborate concoction of your own, as in using a canned consomme as a soup-stock base for your own vegetable soup.

At others times, flavoring or minor additions will improve or at least change the ready made soup so that you can feel that it is something of your own.

Prepared soups are also valuable materials for general non-soup cooking. Consomme and bouillon can be used to enrich or even make gravy, condensed mushroom soup serves well as a white sauce in many dishes and cheddar soup can be used for cheese sauce.

Kinds of Soup. Soups are divided into several classes, with many varieties in each class. But the divisions are usually not clear, because of overlapping of both ingredients and method of preparation.

Major divisions are clear soup, which is usually a meat broth called consomme or bouillon, but which may be made from vegetables; cream soup, in which milk or cream is used as part or all of the liquid; chowder, which is usually a cream soup containing chunks of salt pork, seafood and vegetables; purees; and non-cream soups containing chunks of vegetables and/or meat.

Clear Soup (Meat Broth). Clear soups are usually meat broths, obtained from

Fig. 24-1. There was more soup in those days

Fig. 24-2. Bones make good soup

stewing meat and/or bones for several hours, to transfer their flavor and a little of their nutriment to the cooking water. The bones should be cracked or cut so that the marrow can be reached by the water. The meat may be stew meat or scraps, either cooked or raw. Some recipes call for browning the meat first, as in a stew, and some do not. Trim as much fat off it as you can.

Put the bones and/or meat in a deep pan and add water to cover an inch or two deep. Bring to a boil, then simmer for one or two hours, preferably two. Add water if the level goes down below the top of the bones. Take out the meat or pour off the broth when you think it has extracted all the flavor it can.

Even with trimmed meat, you are likely to have a disagreeable amount of melted fat floating on the surface. If you are in a hurry, you can skim most of it off with a spoon, and blot off some more by delicately dipping an edge or fold of paper towel into the grease spots. But it is more efficient to let it cool, then lift the hardened grease off

in a slab, if it is thick, or skim it off with a turner if it is thin and delicate.

Grease on soup is considered undesirable and an indication of poor cooking. But it is not really that bad, and many people will especially enjoy soup with a bit of grease on it.

Clear soup may be cloudy because of very finely divided particles suspended in it. It can be cleared up or clarified by a little extra cooking with white of egg and egg shell. For each quart of soup, use the white and shell of one egg. Break up the white by mixing it with a teaspoon or two of water, and crumble the shell. Stir these into the soup, boil it for two minutes and then let it stand for 20.

The very small particles should clump together into larger ones, which settle out, or which you can strain out by pouring it through two layers of cheese cloth, or some other kind of filter.

Vegetable Broth. The most common type of clear vegetable soup or broth is the water in which vegetables have been boiled. Some vegetables, for example asparagus and fresh peas, produce a broth that the selfish cook will drink herself, before it gets any further. Many others yield fluids that have a strong characteristic flavor and taste good, but which are not of great interest until they are combined with other fluids or foods. Water from string or wax beans, carrots and squash usually fall in this class.

Then there are vegetables such as cabbage and onions whose cooking water is likely to be strong-flavored, unsuitable for use by itself and to be handled with caution in blending with other foods.

For a given quantity of vegetables, the less cooking water you have the better (or at least, stronger) it tastes. But it is likely that using a large quantity of water for boiling gives you more flavor in the water than when you use a little, but it may be too diluted to be of top quality. Such juice can be concentrated by boiling after the vegetable is removed.

Vegetable broth can be used as the basis for cream or non-cream soup, either alone or in combination with meat broth. It can be used as a superior substitute for water in making gravy, and for making white sauce for the same or a compatible vegetable. If strong enough, it can be made directly into a cream soup by adding flour, in the amount of 2 to 3 teaspoons for a cup of broth, but it will be improved by working in the same quantity of butter also.

Cream Soup. At its simplest, a cream soup is simply a thin white sauce, made in multiples of a cup of milk, a tablespoon each of butter and flour, and a little salt and pepper. Procedure is standard: melt the butter, add the flour and salt, mix well, stir in milk gradually and cook until smooth. This operation produces a milk soup, which can be eaten as is, but is usually the base for something else. At least, it rates garnishing with parsley, croutons, grated cheese or something.

This can be turned into a cream of vegetable soup by adding 1/4 to 1/2 cup of vegetables, single or mixed. These may be diced, chopped, mashed or made into a paste, or can be partly coarse and partly fine.

Vegetables that can be used, alone or in combinations, include potatoes, carrots, peas, mushrooms, beans (lima, wax or green), onions, turnips and spinach. The quantity depends on whether you want to stress the soup or the vegetables.

A meat background can be given to this by substituting a meat broth, yours or canned, for up to half the milk. If you want to keep up its milk-richness, substitute evaporated for whole milk.

Another and very different approach to a cream soup is to take, for example, 2 cups of milk, 3/4 of a cup of mashed vegetable(s) and a slice of onion, put them in a double boiler or in a saucepan over low heat and cook for 20 minutes, stirring occasionally.

You can stir in a couple of bouillon cubes, or slip in a little broth to get a near-meat flavor. If the vegetables seem too coarse, take them out and put them through another chopping or a food mill. Season with salt and pepper to taste.

This soup may be too thin. It can be thickened by longer cooking, a slow process; by making a puree of the vegetables in a blender, which may make the soup too thick, or by thickening it with flour, a process called binding. For each two cups of soup, take a tablespoon of flour and a table-

Fig. 24-3. Vegetables make good broth

Fig. 23-4. Serve it right from the pot

spoon of butter, blend them over slow heat, mix in a little soup and pour back into the soup. Reheat, stirring constantly (or just frequently, if heat is low) for about 5 minutes.

Chowder. Chowders seems to have three things in common: they are soup, they usually contain salt pork and they do not contain other meat. Most of them are cream soups, the outstanding exception being Manhattan clam chowder, which is a water-based clam-potato-tomato recipe.

New England clam chowder is typical of this group of soups, and is excellent either as a first course (in a cup) or as a main course (in a bowl). The recipes vary, but the following one is representative:

New England Clam Chowder

1 to 2	pts	shucked clams
3 to 4	ozs	salt pork, cut into small cubes
2		medium onions, thinly sliced
4		medium potatoes, cubed
1	cup	chopped celery
3	cps	water
1	qt	milk
2	Tb	butter
1	tsp	salt
½	tsp	pepper *(optional)*

Fry pork cubes until they are crisp, remove from pan. Fry onion lightly in pork fat, pour into a large saucepan and add potatoes, celery and the 3 cups of boiling water. Simmer for about 15 minutes, then add the clams and their juice.

Bring to a boil, add milk and butter and heat until almost boiling. It can be served immediately, or simmered for another 15 minutes if convenient. Just before serving, remove any skin that may have formed on surface, and add the pork cubes.

For a fish chowder, replace the clams with 1 or 2 pounds of fresh or thawed frozen fish such as cod or haddock. Simmer it in 2 cups of water for about 15 minutes. Use this cooking liquid as part of the 3 cups of boiling water in the recipe. Break the fish up into bite-size pieces, and add it to the soup pan after simmering the vegetables.

Puree. Vegetable puree soups are becoming very popular, since the electric blender makes it easy to make them well. They are cream soups, made either with milk or with flour (or both) plus a vegetable (usually cooked) that has been pulverized in a blender. Excellent results can be obtained from unlikely sources. For example, either cucumber or Zucchini squash makes first class soup.

A puree need not be all smooth if you don't wish. Small pieces of the same cooked vegetable can be added after the blending. Tips of asparagus, flowerets of cauliflower or just very small pieces of the vegetable add variety in texture and appearance.

Chunk Soups. There are many soup recipes that provide a sort of mini-stew, consisting of meat and vegetables in small pieces, in a broth that may be thick and limited in quantity, like a moderately thinned-out gravy, or that may be nearly as thin and clear as water, and abundant. The solid food in an 8-ounce serving of vegetable-beef soup may be as little as two tablespoons, or as much as 5 ounces.

The meat is usually beef or poultry, occasionally lamb but apparently never pork. But pork makes good soup too. Being a fat meat, it gives you a skimming job, but the other meats are likely to be greasy, also.

Chicken. Chicken soup, with noodles or rice, is very popular in both home made and canned form. Traditionally, it is made with stewing chicken, but fryers or broilers are often just as cheap, require less cooking and are likely to have more tender meat.

Chicken Noodle Soup

4 to 6	lbs	chicken, cut into large pieces
1		small onion, whole
6		peppercorns
4		tops of celery stalks
1	Tb	salt
8	oz	fine noodles, raw

Fig. 24-5. An excellent puree-maker

Put chicken and next 4 ingredients in a large pot with 2 to 2-1/2 quarts of water. Heat to boiling, skim froth, put on cover and simmer until the meat is fork-tender. Broilers may be done in 45 minutes, while stewing chicken (fowl) may take up to 2-1/2 or even 3-1/2 hours.

Lift chicken pieces out of broth, remove skin and cut the meat into pieces of variable size, with none over 3/8 inch long or wide. Strain the broth into a saucepan, add the noodles, heat to boiling and simmer until the noodles are almost tender,·add the chicken and simmer a few more minutes.

Scatter parsley over the top, and serve.

This should yield 3 to 3-1/2 quarts of soup.

The noodles may be replaced with one or 2 cups of cooked rice, put in the broth 5 or 10 minutes before serving.

The quantity of either noodles or rice may be greatly increased over these directions. Some families like this soup as a chicken-noodle or chicken-rice stew, with only a little broth.

25

SALAD

SALAD

A salad is usually a combination of lettuce (or similar raw greens) served cold in combination with other food or foods, and a sauce which is always called a dressing.

This does not cover all the possibilities, as there are popular salads (potato, for example) that are often served without greens, some that are just lettuce and dressing, others that are lettuce and food without dressing, and there are even hot salads. But the first description still holds for the majority.

Use. Salads are eaten to some extent all year, but their greatest popularity is during hot weather, when cold food and light food both have their greatest appeal. By fortunate coincidence, that is also the season when salad ingredients are likely to be at their best, in quality, variety and economy.

Most salad is eaten as a minor course or a side dish at a hot meal. But it can also be an entire meal, with plenty of nourishment and variety. The emphasis is generally on vegetables and fruit, but meat or sea food is often featured.

There is no limit and no restriction on what you can put in a salad. All a cookbook can do is give some basic principles, some exceptions to those principles and then a short or a long list of suggestions about good combinations.

Salad may be served in a bowl, on a platter or in individual portions which may be on separate small bowls or plates or with other food on a dinner plate. The bowl is preferably a special one made of wood, with matching large wooden spoon and fork-type server. Individual bowls are usually wood also, but may be plastic.

Dressings. There are a great many varieties of salad dressing. Most of them include vinegar, few of them are cooked and all of them are served either chilled or at room temperature. They are in Chapter 18.

GREENS

There are a number of varieties of leaf that are used as a principal ingredient of salad. Aside from head lettuce, to be discussed below, they include romaine, escarole, endive, chicory, dandelion, spinach and watercress. Except for romaine and watercress, it is usually important to use only tender young leaves, as mature ones

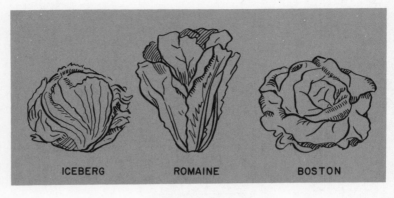

Fig. 25-1. Three lettuces

are likely to be both tough and bitter.

Greens usually need washing. Except for heads, you separate them leaf by leaf under running water. Hard or discolored parts should be removed, often by tearing or by cutting with scissors.

It is desirable, although not always strictly necessary, that the leaves should be crisp when served. They are often limp when you get them, but can usually be revived by soaking in cold, unsalted water for 1/2 to 2 hours, or by putting in a plastic bag with a little water in the refrigerator for a somewhat longer time.

Some of these leaves are large, others small. They may be left whole (unless too large for the salad plates) or cut or torn into smaller sizes. Large leaves or pieces have the best appearance, but they may be a nuisance to serve and to eat.

Head Lettuce. There are two principal varieties of head lettuce, iceberg and Boston.

In iceberg, sometimes called cabbage lettuce, the leaves of the head are curled around each other, somewhat like cabbage but usually not quite so tightly. The outer leaves are green and thin with a slight toughness, and are sometimes limp. The inner ones are white or pale green, thick, tender and crisp.

This lettuce is very bland. Its considerable popularity may be more because of its texture than its flavor. It is usually bought rather than raised at home, as the art of persuading it to form good heads is a difficult one to master.

Boston lettuce usually grows with a more open head. The leaves are usually greener, slightly less crisp and more flavorful. However, the two lettuces are sometimes very much alike.

Either variety is likely to have damaged or discolored outer leaves which should be stripped off and discarded. However, all leaves that are in good condition should be used.

The leaves can be loosened for stripping by cutting through their bases and the stem, Figure 25-2, left. If you are just going to take off a few, you can break and tear them with your fingers, starting at the stem end. But if you want to separate the whole head, remove the stem with a cone-shaped cut, and run water forcefully into the hole. It pushes its way between the leaves and loosens them so that they can be peeled off more easily.

Iceberg lettuce is often sliced or shredded, instead of being taken apart. You can strip leaves first, to form a base for the salad, then shred the rest. You do this by making parallel knife cuts, 1/8 to 1/4 inches apart. Then you may slice the slices, pull them apart into irregular shreds, or combine the two methods.

Fig. 25-2. Separating lettuce leaves with water

Cut leaves wilt sooner than torn ones because the veins are opened in more places. These lettuces are crisped in the same manner as other greens. Undisturbed heads or hearts can be kept in the refrigerator for a week or more with little deterioration, if put in a plastic bag with a little water, folding the bag over to make it almost but not quite airtight.

Serving. A leaf, or usually several leaves of lettuce, selected or trimmed to fill the proper area, makes the foundation for most salads made up in individual portions, and for many that are in serving dishes. Lettuce is also put in sandwiches in addition to the regular filling, to add crispness and moisture.

Raw lettuce is not welcomed by many people with troublesome dentures, nor by a large number of hearty, outdoor-type men who refer to it, as well as to most salad ingredients, as "rabbit food". With these exceptions, lettuce is very popular, and can be served freely whenever it seems to fit in.

Etiquette permits cutting salad into pieces with a knife. This is sometimes a necessity and often a convenience, as large pieces are frequently served to improve appearance. However, many people are shy about using a knife for a salad, as it used to be bad form. Also, if you are eating from a bowl with a curved bottom, you have to be careful about spilling.

SIMPLE SALADS

There are salads that contain only a few simple, easily prepared ingredients, yet make very satisfactory introductory courses or side dishes.

Lettuce. Lettuce, either in the form of chunks from an iceberg head, or leaves from it or other greens, is often served with just oil and vinegar dressing. There is at least one country that takes great pride in its cuisine, in which this seems to be considered to be the only possible salad, so that our more sophisticated concoctions are looked at with wonder and dismay.

Lettuce and Tomato. A leaf or two of lettuce, with one or more slices of tomato on top, with or without dressing, is a standard accompaniment to light meals in many parts of the country.

Fig. 25-3. Wrap lettuce loosely

The tomatoes are washed or wiped off if they need it, and sliced or cut into chunks. It is usual to cut them at right angles to the core, in slices about 1/4 inch thick. But you can also cut them in wedges (except for sandwiches) or in slices parallel with the core.

When served as a salad, tomato and lettuce may be plain, or have either oil and vinegar or a thickened dressing.

Lettuce and tomato is often put inside a sandwich.

Cucumber. Cucumber and salad are almost as closely identified as lettuce and salad. Its pale green color, crispness and flavor are a good combination with other raw foods, and with dressings.

The lettuce and tomato combination is often supplemented by thin slices of cucumber. Salad dressing — still almost any kind — is then much more likely to be added. Or you may serve just cucumber and lettuce, most often with just oil and vinegar.

Tossed. This is a little less simple. The ingredients are usually lettuce — often of two or more kinds — torn or cut into bite-size pieces, crisp vegetables cut or chopped to be bite-size or smaller, oil and vinegar and seasoning. It is primarily a lettuce salad, and the lettuce is usually greater in bulk than all the other ingredients combined.

The following will serve as a sample.

Radishes, cucumbers, cherry tomatoes and other vegetables may be substituted for the celery, pepper and tomato, or used in addition to them. Ordinary salad oil may be used instead of olive. Seasoning is a matter of individual taste.

Trim away any discolored outer portions of the lettuce, then pull off the outer green leaves and tear them into bite-sizes pieces. Put them in a wooden salad bowl, add the cut-up vegetables, sprinkle with oil and vinegar and then with seasoning. Use a large wooden spoon and fork to mix lightly by picking up sections of the salad from the bottom, raising them a few inches and then dropping them, often upside down. All surfaces should be well coated with the dressing.

This mixing process, or tossing, gives the salad its name. Many people who are otherwise only mildly interested in cookery take pride in their selection of ingredients and preparation of dressing, and in their technique of tossing them together.

OTHER VEGETABLE SALADS

Almost any chilled vegetable can be put in a salad, either raw or cooked. If it is hard or tough when raw, like carrots and cabbage, simply shred it finely enough so that it will be tender, or if it is on the borderline (like cauliflower) break it into small

---

Tossed Salad *(6 portions)*

1	medium head of lettuce
2 stlks	celery, chopped
½	medium green pepper, sliced
1	medium tomato, in small wedges
2 Tb	olive oil
1 Tb	vinegar
½ tsp	oregano
⅛ tsp	garlic powder *(optional)*

Fig. 25-4. Tossed salad

enough pieces so it can be crunched without too much discomfort.

Salad vegetables are usually cut into at least bite-size pieces, or into slender fingers such as carrots quartered lengthwise, celery with tops cut off or cucumbers in long wedges.

Vegetables are generally arranged on a bed of lettuce with careful regard to appearance. The size, shape and color affect the placing of each item. Also, pieces that may require special care in dishing out or in eating with the most enjoyment, such as spears of asparagus, are not buried or obscured by other items.

Dressing may be chosen for color as well as for flavor, and be placed in a pattern. The arrangement may have a planned and formal look, or be very informal.

If the salad is served in a bowl the fixing may involve only the top layer.

Green Bean. This salad does not require the usual fresh ingredients, and is usually served without lettuce. It is excellent with cold meats, particularly ham, and can be substituted for a hot vegetable in an ordinary meal.

Green Bean Salad *(4 to 6 portions)*

1	can	string beans *(about 2 cps)* or similar amount of fresh ones
½		medium onion
2 or 3	Tb	French dressing, home made or commercial

If canned beans are used, heat them. Fresh ones should be boiled or steamed until tender. Drain, and put in a salad bowl. Pour dressing over them, mix it in lightly, and let stand a few hours in the fridge. Just before serving, slice the onion thinly, add it and mix carefully.

Pea. This is a different way to make a vegetable salad. It may be served either with or without lettuce.

Pea Salad *(4 to 6 portions)*

2	cps	small green peas, cooked
1	Tb	lemon juice
1		egg, hard-cooked and finely chopped
2 or 3	Tb	mayonnaise
1	Tb	whipped cream *(optional)* chopped parsley

You can start with fresh, frozen or canned peas. If they are raw, cook them until tender. Drain well, and allow to cool to room temperature. Mix the mayonnaise, (cream), egg and lemon juice in a bowl, add the peas and stir together carefully. Chill in the refrigerator for at least 3 hours.

Stir gently again just before serving. Sprinkle with chopped parsley.

Cole Slaw. Cole slaw is shredded cabbage plus a dressing, which is usually mayonnaise.

It is difficult to advise as to quantity. Cole slaw may be served in liberal portions as a cold vegetable or (with a lettuce leaf) as a salad. Or it may be served by the teaspoon, or in portions anywhere between these extremes. To be on the liberal side, figure about 1/2 to 3/4 cup of shredded cabbage (weight 3 or 4 ounces) per person.

Cole Slaw *(5 to 8 portions)*

4	cps	shredded cabbage *(1 medium head)*
3	Tb	mayonnaise
1	Tb	sugar
1	Tb	vinegar
1	tsp	grated onion *(optional)*
2	Tb	whipped cream *(optional)* salt and pepper to taste

Trim the cabbage head, and place it on a cutting board with the stem side down. Make close parallel cuts as long as you can hold it, then turn the cut face down and

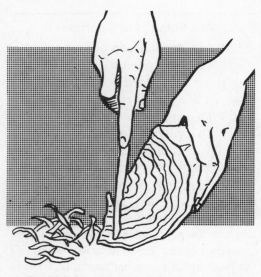

Fig. 25-5. Shredding cabbage for cole slaw

slice the rest. Cut the pile of slices in the same manner. Because of the curve of the leaves, some parts will be more finely cut than others. You can leave it this way, or go over at least some of the coarser parts individually.

The thinner you slice it, down to 1/32-inch shreds, the more tender it will be. Press it down in the cup when you measure it.

If you use cream, mix it thoroughly with the mayonnaise. Then combine with the sugar and vinegar. Thorough beating with a whisk will reduce danger of the cream, if any, being curdled by the vinegar. Pour this dressing over the cabbage just before serving, and toss lightly to mix.

Cole slaw can also be made with commercial sour cream instead of mayonnaise.

If you don't have cabbage, you can make a reasonably good imitation slaw with shredded iceberg lettuce. If you have lettuce.

One-half to 1 cup of shredded pineapple added to this recipe will produce Hawaiian cole slaw.

Potato. Potato salad is basically a mixture of cut boiled potatoes, mayonnaise or similar dressing and small quantities of other foods added for seasoning, texture and appearance.

Potato Salad

2	lbs	potatoes
3	Tb	salad oil *(amount optional)*
3	Tb	vinegar *(amount optional)*
4	Tb	mayonnaise
3	Tb	minced onion *(optional)*
2		hard boiled eggs *(optional)*
		salt and pepper to taste

The potatoes are preferably new or general purpose type, with a firm or waxy texture, cooked just short of full tenderness, so that the pieces will not break and crumble excessively during preparation. But any potatoes can be used. In fact, salad is one of the uses for tired end-of-the-season specimens that have little flavor of their own.

But for best results it is necessary to use freshly boiled potatoes, still hot or at least warm. The skins are peeled or rubbed off under running water, and the potatoes cut into small pieces. These are usually of random and irregular shape, with the largest dimension an inch or less, and greatest thickness 3/8 inch or less. But sometimes the cutting is in regular shapes, such as slices, square-trimmed slices or cubes.

The freshly cut pieces should be sprinkled, lightly or heavily according to taste, with vinegar and oil mixed about half and half, or with any colorless dressing containing vinegar. The ingredients for adding flavor and/or color may be added at this time.

For most tastes, the minimum addition is finely cut or grated raw onion, scallion or leek. But if you don't like onions, you may leave them out. In addition to, or instead of, onion, raw fine-cut or grated sweet pepper (green or red), celery or cucumber may be used, preferably in small amounts, and seldom over two tablespoons to the pound of potato.

Hard boiled egg in random size pieces, from mashed up to thin slices or small chunks, improves both flavor and texture. It can be added either to the potatoes or to the dressing.

The basic dressing for the salad is mayonnaise. If you use the store type, you may improve its mixing quality by adding not more than one part of water, milk, cream or vinegar to 4 of mayonnaise, stirring together well. Add whatever seasonings you want — some people like to add a bit of dry mustard and even cayenne, in addition to the salt and pepper — and then mix with the potatoes.

Every surface should be coated, but stirring should be kept to a minimum, particularly if the pieces tend to break up.

There is a recipe for home made mayonnaise on page 370, and one or more will be found in any general cookbook. In addition, there are many recipes for similar dressings made specifically for potato salad. Or you may replace it with a simple oil and lemon juice or vinegar mixture, anywhere from three parts of oil (olive or salad) to one of acid, up to equal quantities of each.

Regular mayonnaise and many other dressings contain eggs, and sometimes milk or cream as well. These mixtures provide excellent food for bacteria, which multiply rapidly in them under favorable conditions. A salad made with them might be contaminated accidentally while being mixed, and if left at room temperature for a considerable time might become dangerous to eat.

It is therefore important to be clean and quick about making the salad, to refrigerate it as soon as possible, and pack it to stay cool if it must be transported. A further precaution when long unchilled periods are expected is to make it without eggs or mayonnaise, using oil and vinegar.

EGGS

Eggs appear in a great many salads of the more nourishing type. They seem to be always hard cooked, usually by boiling but occasionally by scrambling and then frying into a firm pancake. Sometimes they supply most of the food and flavor, while in other recipes they are secondary although often important.

The true egg salads are in the first class, while the recipes given earlier for potato and chicken salads are in the second.

Egg salad usually consists of hard boiled eggs with mayonnaise and seasoning, usually with some chopped vegetable to lighten it. The following recipe may be considered typical, although many will consider it to be over-simplified.

Fig. 25-6. For nourishing salads

Egg Salad

3		hard boiled eggs
⅔	cup	chopped celery or cucumber
3	Tb	mayonnaise
½	tsp	dry mustard *(optional)*
		salt and pepper to taste
		paprika

Fig. 25-7. Meat salad

Chop the eggs into pieces of variable size, some quite fine, others coarse. Add the remaining ingredients except paprika, and stir carefully but thoroughly, until all pieces are coated. Serve on lettuce leaves, with a little paprika sprinkled on top.

This salad is an excellent sandwich filler, except that it makes the bread soggy quite quickly. This effect can be reduced by buttering bread thoroughly, and putting lettuce both above and below the filling. Do not keep this salad long without refrigeration, as unfriendly organisms can multiply rapidly in it.

Almost anything else can be put in egg salad. The list includes tomato pieces, seedless grapes, and chopped onion, chives, nuts or sweet peppers (green or red).

FRUIT

Fruit salads are somewhat like vegetable salads in the general rules — or perhaps lack of rules — in selection and arrangement of materials. Fruit should rest on a bed of lettuce, and it should be cold, tasty and colorful. But fruit is really much better suited to salad than are most of the "other vegetables". Good flavor and color comes naturally to them.

Most fruit is either naturally sweet, or reacts well to sweetening. As a result fruit salads are not only good salads, but often good desserts also.

Apples. Raw apples are probably the most useful salad fruit. They are crisp, reasonably tender and usually tasty. They are also almost always available. For tł˙ purpose you do not have to limit yourself to tart cooking apples, but can include a Delicious variety to great advantage. Cooked apples are poor salad material because of their softness.

There is one serious drawback to apple in a salad — the tendency of cut surfaces to darken unattractively. This can usually be overcome by coating the pieces with salad dressing immediately after cutting. If the pieces are to be served bare, try to postpone cutting them until the last possible moment, or as a poor second choice, keep them in cold water liberally laced with lemon juice or ascorbic acid (see page 293), and put them in the salad just before serving.

Peaches. Peaches are highly satisfactory in salads. But raw ones darken in air even more rapidly than apples, and may acquire a disagreeable limpness as well. The same precautions can be used, but results are usually better if you use cooked peaches, or blanch raw pieces by putting them in boiling water for about 3 minutes.

Waldorf. This is an example of a salad that is easy to make and very sophisticated in taste and appearance. It is particularly pleasing with pork or ham.

Waldorf Salad *(6 portions)*

2	cps	apple pieces *(about 3 medium apples, unpeeled)*
1	cup	chopped celery
½	cup	chopped walnuts or pecans
3	Tb	mayonnaise
3	Tb	whipped cream *(optional)*
		lettuce

The apples may be any good eating variety with a colorful skin. Cut them in small chunks rather than slices.

The quantity of nuts is very flexible. You can get by with 1/4 cup, but some people put in a cup or more, making it almost a nut salad with apples. Whipped cream improves both appearance and flavor, and is recommended if you have it. Without it, you may have to use an additional tablespoon of mayonnaise to get full coverage.

Mix ingredients together carefully, making sure that all surfaces of the apples are coated. Serve on crisp lettuce leaves.

MEAT, POULTRY AND FISH

Meat salad may be a plate of assorted sliced cold meat with a few lettuce leaves around the edge, a mixed salad in which pieces or strips of meat are found among the vegetables and fruit, or a mixture of diced meat with dressing and other foods, as in the chicken salad discussed below.

Chicken. Chicken salad is very popular as a summer food. It is often the main dish of cold suppers at home, and the special feature at picnics. Recipes vary greatly, and it is likely that no two people prepare it in exactly the same way. The following is a representative sample.

Chicken Salad *(6 portions)*

2 cps	cooked chicken, cut into cubes
1 cup	chopped celery
1 Tb	lemon juice
4 to 5 Tb	mayonnaise
2 to 3	hard boiled eggs, cut in rather large slices
	salt and pepper to taste

Mix together all the ingredients except the eggs. Then add eggs, and mix in carefully to avoid breaking the pieces. Chill for several hours. Can be served plain, on lettuce or in sandwiches.

For a meatier salad, omit the eggs.

Mock Chicken. Mock chicken salad is prepared in the same way, but the chicken

Fig. 25-8. Chef's salad

Fig. 25-9. Tuna is a sport fish, also

is replaced by veal, or by white tuna with the oil rinsed away.

Chef's Salad. This is a deluxe salad, involving a number of ingredients. It is often served as a luncheon dish, both at home and in restaurants. It is satisfying to eat, and like so many salads, is light in calories.

Chef's Salad *(5 or 6 portions)*

1	medium head of lettuce, cut in thin strips
½ cup	cold chicken, in thin strips
½ cup	boiled ham, in thin strips
½ cup	cheese, Swiss type, in thin strips
2	hard boiled eggs, quartered
1	large *(or 2 small)* tomatoes, cut into wedges

Dressing

1 Tb minced chives
2 Tb chopped pickles, dill or sweet
3 Tb mayonnaise
2 Tb vinegar
3 Tb salad oil
1 Tb Worcestershire sauce

Put lettuce in the bottom of a large salad bowl. On top of it put piles of chicken, ham and cheese, each by itself, arrange egg and tomato wedges on top, and chill.

When ready to eat, bring the bowl to the table for display, keeping the dressing separate. Just before serving, pour dressing evenly over salad and toss lightly to get everything mixed.

Wide variations are of course possible, both in selection and in proportions of ingredients.

Bacon and Cheese. Make up the Tossed Salad on page 490, or use your own recipe, but leave out the oil and vinegar.

Add 6 slices of crisp cooked bacon crumbled into small pieces, and 1/2 cup of Cheddar cheese cut into 1/4-inch cubes.

Use 3 or 4 tablespoons of a creamy type dressing, such as Thousand Islands or Russian. Mix well just before serving. The bacon may lose crispness if it stands long after mixing.

Sea Food. Many sea food salads are prepared according to a simple formula. The meat, which may be canned or fresh cooked, is usually tuna for economy or crab, shrimp or lobster for luxury, but most kinds of fish can be used. It may be in small pieces, cubed or mashed.

This is mixed with from 1/2 of its bulk to an equal amount of chopped celery, cucumber and/or apple, and with enough mayonnaise to coat all the ingredients. The mayonnaise may be very slightly diluted with cream, milk or water for easier mixing.

The taste may be pointed up by mixing in a moderate quantity of minced raw onion and some lemon juice or vinegar.

Fig. 25-10. Individual salad mold

The tuna recipe given below is typical.

Tuna Salad *(4 portions)*

1	can	tuna *(about 7 oz)*
¾	cup	chopped celery, cucumber or apple
4	Tb	mayonnaise
1	Tb	grated onion *(optional)*
1	Tb	lemon juice or vinegar *(optional)*

Break up the tuna with a fork and mash it, so that part is fine and part is left slightly coarse. Mix in celery, then the mayonnaise. Use more mayonnaise, or mayonnaise and a thinner, for a softer consistency. Less is required for crab meat. Chill in refrigerator for an hour or more.

Serve with crisp lettuce leaves if possible, either as a salad or in sandwiches.

Shrimp, and freshly cooked fish, are usually broken into small pieces instead of being mashed.

JELLIES AND MOLDS

An increasing number of salads include gelatin mixes. They may consist of a simple flavored gelatin, such as tomato aspic, or be complicated constructions of different fruits or vegetables held in jelly.

Jelly. The behavior of gelatin was described under THICKENERS. For salads, one cup of liquid may be mixed with one tablespoon (ounce package) if a firm jelly is wanted, or 3/4 ounce if a soft consistency is preferred. In summer the firmer gel is safer, as considerable warming and softening may occur after serving.

The liquid may be water if a clear jelly is wanted to hold and show off the other ingredients. For plain aspic use clear soup — stock, broth or consommé and for tomato aspic use tomato juice, or sometimes stewed tomatoes. For flavored jelly, use fruit juice instead of water, or flavored gelatin instead of plain.

The proportions between jelly and other ingredients is highly variable. You can serve just a flavored jelly — tomato aspic, for example — on some greens. Or additional ingredients may be separate from the aspic. On the other hand, there are salads that call for almost a solid mass of other ingredients, just held together by jelly.

Between these extremes, precautions should usually be taken to keep the ingredients properly distributed in the jelly. This may mean fixing only the top and sides for attractive appearance, or careful arrangement of materials all the way through.

Molding. Jelly mixtures can be set in a bowl, serving dish or pan, and spooned out onto a salad platter or plates. In this case, the top appearance is the important one.

A more pleasing appearance can usually be obtained, however, by loosening the jelly in its container, and turning it out upside

Fig. 25-11. A mold for jelly salad

down, a process called unmolding. This may be done from an ordinary bowl, or pan or custard cup, but a mold that gives it a special shape will add to its attractiveness.

Such molds, Figure 25-11, may have almost any shape, and may have either plain or elaborately formed surfaces. The fancy ones give a deluxe touch to the salad, but it may be more difficult to get out of the mold in perfect condition.

The bottom of the mold is the top of the salad, and the sides will also be on display, so the items you want to show should be arranged against them. Your first step is to make your gelatin mix, and cool it to room temperature. Paint the mold very lightly with salad or cooking oil, then put it in the refrigerator.

When chilled, take it out, pour in a thin layer of the gelatin, and put it back for a few minutes until the gelatin is about as thick as white of egg. Then tip, spoon or brush it over the sides, and arrange your show layer of materials. This may be sprigs of parsley, egg slices, orange sections, bright bits of jelly or any appropriate substances. Put the mold back in the fridge until the gelatin is firm enough to hold them.

It is possible to put the decorations against the bare sides of the container, but the appearance is unlikely to be as good.

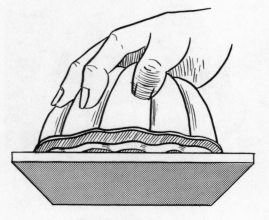

Fig. 25-12. Unmolding

The different textures break up the smooth jelly surface.

Once you have the surface set up, you can either just pour in the rest of the material, or build it up in layers. For pouring, the gelatin should be chilled until it is thick enough to hold the other materials from either floating or sinking. A consistency like firm raw white of egg is usually good.

Fruit and vegetables should be drained of any juice or rinse water before combining, to avoid diluting the gelatin.

To build up in layers, pour cool gelatin to make a layer in the bottom of the mold, arrange the other ingredients in it, chill until it has set, put in more gelatin and more mix, and so forth until the mold is filled or your materials are used up.

Layers can also be built up of two or more colors of gelatin, some of which may be clear if you wish.

You can vary the thickness (viscosity) of the gelatin at any time. If it is too hard, warm it; if it is too thin, chill it.

Unmolding. Gelatin sticks like glue to a mold, but thanks to its low melting or liquefying temperature, you can get it out fairly easily.

The first step, if the shape of the mold allows it, is to cut around the edge with a thin, sharp knife, about a half inch or maybe an inch deep. This takes care of the part of the container that is difficult to heat.

Then dip the mold in warm water, preferably not over 110° F. At this temperature, a metal mold should stay in about 30 seconds, a glass one about 90. At 100° or body temperature, the time for metal will be about 45 seconds, but glass may take three minutes or more. You can test for results by shaking the mold. If the jelly quivers away from the sides, it is ready.

Raise the mold, dry it, and arrange lettuce leaves on its top, if you wish. Put the serving platter upside down over the mold, then turn the two of them over, holding them together.

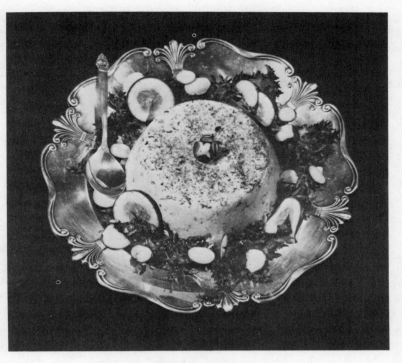

Fig. 25-13. Cucumber jelly

With luck the jelly will separate cleanly from the mold and reach the platter intact. If it sticks in it, soak a cloth in hot water, wring it out and wrap it around the mold. Repeat if necessary until the jelly is free.

Tomato Aspic. Tomato aspic is apparently any tomato-flavored jelly used in salad. The recipes for it are very diverse. The basic material may be either tomato juice or stewed tomatoes. Since the mixture is usually strained anyhow, there is little practical difference except that the whole tomatoes are a little more work than the juice. Aspic is always cloudy anyhow.

Gelatin is necessary and a thick onion slice seems to be almost standard, as is a bay leaf. Some acid in addition to the tomato is expected. This may be lemon juice or vinegar, or a larger quantity of unsweetened grapefruit juice. Such acid is usually balanced with a little sugar. Whole or solid spices such as peppercorns or cloves may

be safely added, as they are removed by the straining process.

Aspic can be served in the summer without lettuce as a vegetable or with lettuce as a salad. It is commonly accompanied by other types of salad mix. It is often molded

Fig. 25-14. A salad can be lettuce and dressing, and anything else

into a ring, whose center may be filled with seafood, chicken or potato salad.

A typical recipe is:

Tomato Aspic *(6 portions)*

2	cps	canned tomato juice
¼	cup	cold water
2	Tb	gelatin powder
¼	cup	lemon juice
2	tsp	sugar
1	slc	onion, ¼ inch or more thick
½	tsp	Worcestershire sauce *(optional)*
6		peppercorns *(optional)*

Dissolve the gelatin in cold water. Mix the rest of the ingredients in a pan, bring almost to a boil and then simmer for about 5 minutes. Remove from heat, add gelatin solution, stir well until thoroughly mixed. Strain through a sieve, then pour into ring mold, any mold of suitable size or individual molds. Chill until completely firm, probably 2 hours. Unmold carefully, preferably on crisp lettuce leaves.

Cucumber Jelly. This gelatin salad is rather easy to make and most attractive in appearance. Its pale green color and crisp texture are specially appreciated on hot days.

Cucumber Mold *(8 portions)*

2	cps	fresh cucumber, cut into small cubes
1	pkg	Jell-O, lime flavor
1	cup	boiling water
1	cup	sour cream
2	Tb	sugar
		paprika

Dissolve Jell-O in boiling water, mix well and let cool until somewhat thickened. Stir vigorously and add the other ingredients, except the paprika.

Pour the mixture into an oiled mold and chill until completely firm. Then unmold carefully, decorate according to taste with greens, cucumber slices and lime or lemon wedges. Sprinkle with a little paprika for color contrast.

If lime Jell-O is not available, you can use lemon flavor, plus green food coloring, added cautiously a drop at a time, before cooling.

26
BEVERAGES

BEVERAGES

A beverage is anything that can be drunk, a definition which covers quite a bit of ground. It may be hot, cold, thick, thin, carbonated, alcoholic, sweet, bitter, sour, tasteless and/or nourishing or non-nourishing. Its primary purposes may be to quench thirst and to make eating easier, but there are many other uses, many of them social. Stimulating, relaxing or sleep-inducing effects are often important.

Beverages usually consist chiefly of water. Water itself is one of the best and most widely used drinks, although its popularity is not high.

Many cold drinks are purchased in bottles or other containers, and poured and drunk without any processing except chilling. These include milk, soda, beer and many fruit juices and fruit-flavored preparations. Concentrated juices need only mixing with water, and Soup has its own little chapter. Alcoholic drinks are a specialty out of the field of this book.

This leaves us with coffee, tea, cocoa and mixed milk and ice cream drinks as cooking or processing problems.

COFFEE

Coffee is made from the roasted beans of a tropical plant of the same name. They are bitter, flavorful and aromatic. It seems to be the most popular single beverage, both in this country and throughout much of the world. It is also highly valued as a flavoring.

Coffee is sold as whole roasted beans which may be ground in the store or at home, as ground coffee with various degrees of fineness and as water-soluble dried extracts called instant or freeze-dried, depending on the method of preparation.

Caffeine. Coffee beans contain .75 to 1.5 per cent of caffeine, a chemical which in moderate quantities acts as a stimulant and a diuretic (kidney stimulant). These effects are usually beneficial, but in too-large amounts or in people who cannot tolerate it, caffeine produces nervousness, rapid heart beat and insomnia.

The presence of this drug is responsible for part of coffee's popularity and most of its unpopularity. It is generally considered to be an unsuitable beverage for children, and it is forbidden to adults who belong to

501

various religions and health groups, or who suffer from certain diseases.

There are varying amounts of caffeine in coffee. It is often estimated at 60 to 100 milligrams for a 6-ounce cup of ordinary (arabica bush) coffees, and double that for the African or robusta variety. The No-Doz keep-awake tablet contains 100 milligrams, Empirin Compound 75 milligrams (1/2 grain), a 6-ounce cup of tea 60 to 80 and cola beverages about 30. A one-ounce sweet chocolate bar contains 60 to 80 milligrams of caffeine, also.

The above figures are from one source. Other sources, possibly equally reliable, report very different amounts, particularly twice as much in tea. Their test beverages are probably stronger. The exact amounts are of little importance.

Caffeine dissolves readily in hot water, so it is one of the first substances extracted in brewing, and the amount in the beverage is little affected by the length of the brewing time.

Reaction to caffeine is a personal matter. Some people can consume unreasonable quantities of it in beverages and still remain relaxed and sleep well, while others may be given the jitters and insomnia by a single cup. Effects usually do not last more than a few hours.

Most of the caffeine can be removed from coffee without serious effect on its flavor. De-caffeinated coffee is widely available in both ground and instant form.

Water. Coffee can be made with any drinkable water, but if you want to follow approved directions to make really good coffee to satisfy discriminating tastes, there are various rules to follow in selecting and handling it. Some of them appear to be reasonable, others not.

You are counseled to avoid water that has an off-taste because of the presence of sulfur or organic compounds, that contains chlorine (which is used in treating almost all public water supplies) or that contains

rust or mud because of recent disturbance in pipes or mains. Water with any of these afflictions can be brought up to standard by means of an activated charcoal filter.

Hard water is said to be harmful only in that it forms scale in the coffee-making equipment, which is a problem in restaurants but not usually in homes. Methods of removing scale by treating it with acid are discussed under CLEANING UP.

Artificially softened water, in which calcium compounds are replaced by more soluble sodium combinations, is said to be unfit for brewing coffee.

Although water used in brewing coffee is subjected to much higher temperature than is used in pasteurizing, it is not supposed to make contaminated water safe. But thorough boiling before making the coffee, a precaution that is little extra trouble when using the drip method, can make any water safe although not necessarily good-flavored.

You are always supposed to start with cold water. The starting temperature af-

Fig. 26-1a. Water is the basic beverage

fects operation of a percolator, although lukewarm is really as good as cold. For the drip method, in which water is brought to a boil or a near boil before contact with the coffee, the starting temperature should not affect the brew noticeably unless your hot faucet water has an off taste not present in the cold supply.

Flavor. Coffee flavor is highly variable, as it is affected by the species and variety of the plant, the area, altitude and climate in which it is grown, the method and thoroughness of roasting and the method of preparation and serving.

In general, it is considered that coffee grown at high altitudes is less bitter and more aromatic than that from low altitudes. But preference in this regard, as well as in other details of grown-in flavor, is a question of taste and custom, rather than of absolute and measurable quality.

There are deliberate differences in the degree of roasting. Coffee for the United States usually has a mild roasting process,

Fig. 26-1b. But other kinds may be more appreciated

producing beans of a brown color and medium pungency. Increased cooking produces a darker color and more acrid flavor which is favored in many parts of the world. Undercooking leaves an unpleasantly astringent (puckery) taste and does not develop the full flavor.

Most of our ground and instant coffee consists of blends which are made up of three or more varieties. Proportions may be changed from year to year to maintain a certain flavor, or more rarely to produce a new flavor that is expected to be more popular. Both the blends and the degree of roasting may be varied to suit regional preferences within the States.

Roasted coffee contains a number of different flavoring substances, which are extracted in various proportions, depending on method of brewing. Recommendations for coffee-making are based on experience in extracting a maximum of those that people like, and a minimum of those that they don't. Water that is not hot enough will not be efficient at obtaining desirable flavors. Too long a brewing time will extract additional substances whose flavor the majority find unpleasant. For this reason, in making coffee stronger you usually use more coffee, rather than longer brewing time.

Coffee that is kept hot for extended periods, or that is allowed to cool and is then reheated, declines in quality and often develops off flavors. However, deterioration is less rapid and severe when it is not in contact with the grounds from which it is made. Flavor can be preserved a long time by freezing.

A pound of coffee (16 ounces) is said to contain 5.5 ounces of soluble material, of which the first 2.9 to 3.5 ounces are considered desirable for extraction in preparing a beverage. The balance, obtainable by longer brewing, is considered too bitter and astringent for American tastes. Practically all directions for coffee making are based on this idea.

TEMPERANCE DRINKS.

pound of sugar to each pint of juice. Put it into bottles, cork and seal it, and keep it in a cool, dry place. When wanted, mix it with ice water for a drink. Or put water with it, make it *very* sweet, and freeze it. Freezing always takes away much of the sweetness.

The juices of other acid fruits can be used in the same way.

Sarsaparilla Mead.

One pound of Spanish sarsaparilla. Boil it in four gallons of water five hours, and add enough water to have two gallons. Add sixteen pounds of sugar, and ten ounces of tartaric acid.

a tumbler of it, take half a wine-glass of the water, and put in half a tea-

From "Miss Beecher's Domestic Receipt-Book," Fifth Edition, Harper & Brothers, Copyright 1846

TEMPERANCE DRINKS

COFFEE

Mocha and Old Java are the best, and time improves all kinds. Dry it a long time before roasting. Roast it quick, stirring constantly, or it will taste raw and bitter. When roasted put in a bit of butter the size of a chestnut. Keep it shut up close, or it loses its strength and flavor. Never grind it till you want to use it, as it loses flavor by standing.

To prepare it, put two great spoonfuls to each pint of water, mix it with the white, yolk, and shell of an egg, pour on hot, but no boiling water, and boil it not over ten minutes. Take it off, pour in half a teacup of cold water, and in five minutes pour it off without shaking. When eggs are scarce, clear with fish skin, as below. Boiled milk improves both tea and coffee, but must be boiled separately. Much coffee is spoiled by being burned unequally, some too much and some too little. Constant care and stirring are indispensable.

FISH SKIN FOR COFFEE

Take the skin of a mild codfish which has not been soaked, rinse and then dry it in a warm oven, after bread is drawn. Cut it in inch squares. One of these serves for two quarts of coffee, and is put in the first thing.

Fig. 26-2. Coffee, 19th century

TEA AND TEA MAK...

COMPOSITION OF AVERAGE BLACK TEA (CHURCH)

In 100 parts there are: water 8.0, albuminoids 17.5, theine 3.2, tannin 17.5 chlorophyl and resin 4.5, essential oil 0.4, minor extractives 8.6, cellulose, etc. 34.0, mineral matter 6.3.

A cup of tea infusion has little or no nutritive value, but it increases respiratory action and incites the brain to greater activity. The stimulating effects of tea upon the nervous system are due to the essential oil and theine: the tannin produces astringency. Tea was at first used medicinally, and was not indulged in as a beverage until the close of the seventeenth century. "The first brewers of tea sat down to eat the leaves with butter and salt." The only ... in the United States are at Pinehurst, S. C. Here tea ... carried on. ... The tea is shipped in closely ... pounds, or fractions there- ... plants, ... to

From "Practical Cooking and Serving" by Janet McKenzie Hill, Doubleday, Page & Company, Copyrights 1902 and 1912

BOILED COFFEE

In a coffee-pot that has been well-aired and well-scalded put twice as many level tablespoonfuls of ground coffee as there are cups to be served, add as many egg-shells, washed before the eggs were broken, as there are cups to be served; or the white of an egg may be used, that of one egg being sufficient to clear about seven tablespoonfuls of ground coffee. Add a tablespoonful of cold water for each cup of liquid desired, and mix thoroughly; add the requisite number of cups of freshly boiling water and let *boil* five minutes after boiling begins. Pour a little cold water — from a quarter to half a cup — down the spout, stir in one tablespoonful of fresh coffee, and set the pot where it will simmer fifteen minutes. The quick bringing to a boil is what gives the bright, fresh flavor. The long simmering gives the mellowness. For the first reason, we make it with the hottest water possible. Just as good coffee can be made with cold water, if you have, as on a picnic, a hot flame and wide-bottomed, shallow receptacle for the coffee. But made in the ordinary cylindrical coffee-pot, over the ordinary heat of the stove, you will have "dead" coffee, if a cold or lukewarm mixture works its slow way to a boiling point. And it will have a "sharp" taste, if not given the proper amount of simmering.

FILTERED COFFEE

After-dinner, or black coffee, is usually made in a "drip" coffee-pot, in which the boiling water drips through the fine-ground coffee that is held in a filter. To prepare: put a cup of fine-ground coffee in the filter, or strainer, of the coffee-pot, and set the pot in a dish of boiling water, if the means of keeping the liquid hot be not otherwise provided; pour into the strainer a quart of water, freshly drawn and heated just to the boiling point; after the water filters through the coffee into the lower receptacle, pour off and return a second, and, sometimes, a third time to the filter. When the infusion is of the required strength, pour from the receptacle into a hot coffee-pot, and serve without delay, preferably with cream and sugar.

Fig. 26-3. Coffee, early 20th century

Fig. 26-4. Two tablespoons of ground coffee to six ounces of water

However, there are a number of people who brew coffee for much longer than the recommended times, and are apparently happy with the results. And there are also many who find ordinary coffee lacking in bitter and off-taste substances, so that they strengthen it by roasting the beans almost to the point of charring, and/or add substances such as chicory.

Strength. The taste acceptability of coffee may depend more on the strength and the temperature than on the flavor quality. Ordinary drinking coffee is rated as weak, medium (or ideal) and strong. As a rough standard, use 5-1/2 ounces of hot water, and add one level teaspoon of any instant powdered coffee for a weak brew, a rounded teaspoon for medium and one heaping or two level teaspoons for strong.

The general American preference is for medium or strong, and those preferring medium can usually adjust to strong more readily than to weak. If it is necessary to cut down to weak coffee for medical reasons, sometimes a change in brand will be helpful, as some keep their flavor under dilution better than others do, or decaffeinated coffee may be used full strength.

The Coffee Brewing Center recommends for the ideal-tasting coffee a proportion of 2 tablespoons of ground coffee to 6 ounces of water. There are official measures, which are plastic spoons that hold 2 tablespoons. This proportion is not affected by fineness of grind, which is compensated by differences in brewing time.

There are many coffee drinkers who do not go along with this. In some areas one tablespoon to the cup, plus one "for the pot" was long considered standard. Excellent (by amateur standards) coffee may be made in a percolator with only 2 teaspoons to the cup, plus one for the pot, but it does not have the richness of the ideal brew.

The Center's recommendation for coffee brewed in restaurants is 2 to 2-1/2 gallons of water to the pound of coffee. This works out to 7 to 9 ounces of water to each 2 tablespoons of coffee, somewhat weaker than the home recipe. Restaurants often go further, and use 3 or 4 gallons of water to the pound, with an extended brewing time.

Demitasse coffee, served after dinner in small cups, calls for a 1/3 reduction in the quantity of water, to produce a stronger brew.

As an indication of the extent of differences of opinion that have existed in regard to proper brewing of coffee, Figures 26-2 and 26-3 give (without recommendation) recipes taken from two cookbooks, one published in 1868, the other in 1912.

Temperature. Most coffee is drunk hot. Many coffee drinkers have a preference (which may sometimes amount to an obsession) that it be very hot, or at least, too hot for drinking when served. The Coffee Brewing Center recommends that coffee be made with water at about 200° F, and that the coffee brew not be kept any higher nor much lower than 190°. Electric percolaters seem to produce and hold it at about 160°, which is satisfactory to most people, or as low as 140° if there is a WEAK setting and it is used.

A substantial part of coffee's heat is lost

in cooling by the cup, mixing with cream or milk and sugar, and in various serving and waiting delays. An actual drinking temperature of 140° is about as hot as most people can manage, although there are some, who seemingly have asbestos linings in mouth and throat, who demand it quite a bit hotter.

According to authorities, coffee should never be brewed with boiling water. However, percolators are very popular and they do just that. Each spurt of water spread over the ground coffee is boiling, although the solution in the pot below should not and seldom does get nearly that hot.

There are two objections to the use of boiling or almost-boiling water on coffee grounds. One is that the very hot water tends to dissolve a higher proportion of bitter substances, the other is that desirable substances already dissolved are often vaporized and lost. Also, if coffee is kept standing at very high temperature it is likely to have normal staling or deterioration processes speeded up greatly.

Instant coffee dissolves completely in the water, so its temperature does not affect proportions in the drink, nor does it greatly affect solubility. And the volatile substances are seldom present.

Boiling water is generally used, chiefly because boiling is the sure and simple indicator of thorough heating. As a result, the coffee is likely to be very hot, and to require prolonged waiting or other treatment before drinking.

If coffee is too hot, and there is not enough time to let it cool naturally, you can speed the process by adding ice or water from a water glass, using extra milk or cream, vigorous stirring or (most inelegantly) by pouring into the saucer and back into the cup.

Grinding. Although 1/4 to 1/3 of the coffee bean is soluble in hot water, its structure is such that very little can be dissolved out of the whole roasted bean. It is necessary to grind it into particles to make it accessible. The fineness of the grind regulates the speed with which solution takes place, and to a less extent, affects the nature of the chemicals extracted.

There are three standard grades of fineness: regular (percolator), drip and fine (filter). Small particles are often measured by the size of hole in a screen that they will or will not go through. A 14-mesh screen has 14 holes to the inch, a 28-mesh 28 holes, and so forth. Figure 26-6 shows the size distribution in these grades. There is also an all-purpose grade which can supposedly be used for any purpose.

Coarse and medium particles can be supported in metal sieve baskets with fine holes. These are used in percolators and non-filter drip pots. However, there are always some fine particles with the larger ones, and some of these go through the holes and create a sediment in the beverage. Most of this will be trapped in the bottom of the pot and will stay there if you don't use the last half-cup.

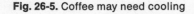

Fig. 26-5. Coffee may need cooling

Name	Coarse, held on 14-mesh screen	Medium, held on 28-mesh screen	Fine, passes 28-mesh screen
Regular	33%	55%	12%
Drip	7	73	20
Fine (filter)	0	70	30

Fig. 26-6. Coffee grinds

Many people don't mind a little sediment anyhow, and the only real disadvantage is that if the coffee stands a while, these particles of bean will cause it to become stale and ill-flavored quite rapidly.

Fine grind should be held on a fine-meshed filter of paper or cloth to avoid excessive washing through. Ordinarily a filter will keep the coffee completely free of sediment, and the paper kind may go further and strip it of valued colloid particles. Such colloids are found chiefly in coffee made from fine grounds, as the water can pick them up only from surfaces.

Coffee may be ground at home in special coffee mills, either hand or electrically powered. It is said to be important to keep them clean, as a few grains of old, tired bean may give an off flavor to a fresh batch. But the construction of most of the mills makes it practically impossible to clean them.

Electric blenders may be used as coffee grinders, following directions that come with the machine. One model at hand calls for medium speed for 20 to 30 seconds for regular grind, 35 to 40 for drip and 50 to 60 for filter. Blenders are much easier to clean, and this is usually done routinely after each use.

Keeping Quality. Roast coffee deteriorates, suffering loss and alteration of volatile aroma substances and developing a stale taste, when exposed to moisture and/or oxygen. An expert taster will find whole beans stale in a week to 3 weeks after roasting, can detect staleness in ground coffee spread on a tray for an hour, or in a freshly opened vacuum can after a day. The average person's taste is far less sensitive, but there is no question but that the quality of coffee goes down steadily in storage.

Vacuum-packed coffee is free of both free moisture and oxygen, and it keeps in perfect condition for long periods. But the vacuum required (and provided) must be as complete as industrial machinery can create, as even a trace of oxygen can cause a stale and objectionable flavor.

If you want to keep your coffee up to top quality standards, it is best to buy whole roasted beans in small quantities and grind them daily at home. If you use ready ground coffee, get it in vacuum cans or small amounts. Either beans or grounds not under vacuum benefit by being tightly covered and kept in a cool or cold place (preferably your refrigerator), and by being used as promptly as possible.

However, the basic coffee flavor is so good, the attainment of perfection so rare and the average coffee drinker either so tolerant or so undiscerning that you can usually get by very well if you handle coffee in the same general way as other grocery staples.

COFFEE MAKERS

In spite of the increasing popularity of instant coffee, much of the beverage is still

Fig. 26-7. Stove-top percolators

prepared directly from ground roasted coffee beans. There are four types of pot or coffee maker commonly used: percolator, drip, filter and vacuum. Drip and vacuum are usually both called drip, but there are distinct differences between them in use and type of beverage produced.

All of them use the same formula, 2 tablespoons (or one Official Coffee Measure) of grounds to 6 ounces of water. This is not an absolute rule, but is strongly recommended by all authorities, and should at least be used for a starting point.

Pots may be made of aluminum, stainless steel or glass, or combinations of them. Aluminum is probably the most popular, but many people feel that it gives a taste to the coffee, particularly if it stands in it. Stainless steel is more expensive. It may be used for the whole utensil, or as a lining in an aluminum one.

Authorities on coffee insist on the absolute necessity of keeping coffee makers clean. However, most of the metal units, whether plain or electric, are so constructed that thorough cleaning is practically impossible.

A brown stain or deposit builds up with use. This is moderately difficult to remove in exposed places, and a coffee maker usually has a number of areas where it is well protected.

However, the harmfulness of this deposit to coffee flavor is open to question.

Glass may be either transparent or decorated. It cannot affect flavor, is pleasing in appearance and in the transparent models, allows watching the coffee-making process. But it is subject to breakage. It is easeir to clean than the metal.

Percolator. A non-electric percolator, Figure 26-7, consists of a pot with a handle and pour spout, a lid with a domed glass center, a pump or stack and a sieve basket with a perforated cover. The pot is usually marked with lines indicating the number of cups, but the cups may be 5-ounce instead of the conventional 6-ounce.

Fig. 26-8. Parts of percolator

You pre-measure the water you want to use, or fill the pot to a line or some known level. Be sure the water surface is below the basket. Put regular grind coffee in the basket, two level tablespoons (or your own individual variation of this) to the 6-ounce cup. To prevent some of the smaller particles from going through the sieve into the water, wet the basket. Fill the basket away from the pot to avoid spillage. Assemble the parts, put on the lid and put the whole percolator on a burner, turned high.

The bottom flange of the pump covers a

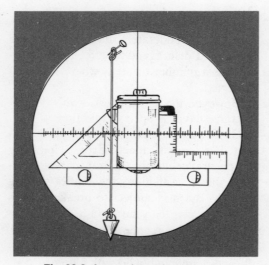

Fig. 26-9. A percolator should be level

large part of the bottom of the pot, and holds a flattened cone of water under it. This water, being immediately over the burner, heats more quickly than that in the rest of the pot. When it boils, the steam tends to go up the pump tube, pushing water ahead of it with a gurgling noise. The water strikes the dome in the lid, is distributed in a spray over the basket top, goes through holes, drips into the coffee grounds and eventually soaks through them and the basket sieve, and drips into the water in the pot.

Meanwhile, water flows from the pot

under the flange edges into the pump and up into the tube, to replace the water forced into the top.

The pump works slowly and uncertainly at first, as much of its heat is lost into the surrounding water. As it heats up its action becomes very rapid. You should then turn down the heat until it pumps briskly but not frantically, and let it perk 6 or 8 minutes. You can form an opinion as to its readiness by looking at the color through the glass top, if you lose track of the time.

A percolator is most efficient when it is filled to just under the basket.

If there is less water it will not stand as high in the tube, and less will be moved with each steam bubble. And if the level is quite low, steam tends to escape under the edges of the flange instead of going up the tube. This may also happen if the heat is too high.

When perking is completed, either on a time or color judgment basis, you shut off the heat and pour the coffee directly from the pot into cups. The basket and pump can be left in place until cleanup time, except that if you reheat the coffee you should remove the basket or at least the grounds, so that it will not resume perking and become black and bitter.

Percolator coffee ordinarily has a little sediment, consisting of fine particles of grounds. These can be reduced by wetting the basket before filling it, but you may expect some anyhow. They do no harm unless the coffee stands quite a while, but will then tend to make it bitter. You can shake up the pot between cups and deliver a few grains in each cup, or let them settle to pour into the last cup, or to be mostly left in the pot with a half cup of unpoured coffee.

Grounds in the coffee can be eliminated by putting a paper filter in the basket. This is an extra operation, and a tight-mesh filter will remove some of the agreeable colloids along with the fine sediment.

Non-electric percolators range in capacity from 2 to about 6 cups.

It is important that a percolator be level. Otherwise, most of the water will go through the grounds on one side, over-extracting them and getting little benefit from the other side.

You can see this happening in a glass utensil, but might never know in others. If you think yours may be off level, give it a half turn when the perking time is half over. That should even things up.

The percolator is a cheery, talkative and companionable coffee pot. It fills the surrounding air with delicious, appetite-stimulating coffee fragrance, as no other coffee maker can. Unfortunately, it does not leave much of the aroma to be smelled and tasted in the poured cup of beverage. But as long as the perking is done in the same room as the drinking, the gain may be greater than the loss.

A stove-top percolator allows great flexibility in proportions. Its user can suit his personal preference, not only in the proportion of grounds and water, but also in how long the brewing continues.

Electric Percolator. Electric percolators with automatic controls are very satis-

Courtesy of Sunbeam Corp.

Fig. 26-10a. Electric percolator

factory coffee makers. They have become an almost standard piece of kitchen or dining room equipment, in spite of the fact that many people who own them ordinarily use one of the drip pots part of the time. They cost from $7.00 to $30.00 in sizes up to 8 cups, and only a little more for 30-cup party types.

Structure, shown in Figure 26-10, is similar to that of the stove-top percolator described earlier, except that the pump is located in a small well below the floor of

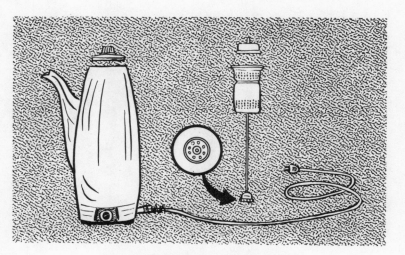

Fig. 26-10b. Parts of electric percolator

the pot. This well is heated electrically. Water flows into it through a valve around the tube, is partly vaporized, and forced in a jet up through the tube, bouncing off the cap and dripping back down through the grounds.

When the coffee brewing is complete, the heat in the well is automatically shut off and percolating stops. But the control doesn't know anything about the strength of the coffee; it is merely a thermostat in the base. The pot is so designed that when the right proportions of cool water and ground coffee are used, the coffee will be at proper strength when the water reaches a temperature of 140 to 160° F, differences depending on the make of the percolator and the setting of the thermostat. If you forgot to put in the coffee, the pot would put the water through the same cycle in about the same time, and shut off at the set temperature.

If the thermostat is adjustable for mild, medium and strong coffee, the MILD (weak) setting will shut off the electricity at a lower temperature than if it is set at STRONG. The mild temperature is usually a bit too cool for good coffee, if there is any delay between pouring and serving. But you get the mild coffee more quickly, and you can use extra grounds for more strength.

If you like hot coffee, and/or want to get the most out of your investment in ground coffee, put the adjustment on STRONG and leave it there. You can keep the heat and reduce the strength by putting less grounds in the basket.

The automatics will keep coffee hot indefinitely after it is perked. If its temperature drops more than a few degrees below the turn-off point of the thermostat, the heat will come on again and in most models perking will resume for a few moments.

Unless you take the basket or at least the grounds out this will make the coffee much stronger and probably ranker. Coffee tends to get stronger and blacker anyhow if it stands heated for long, and this occasional re-perking it through the tired grounds is likely to make it undrinkable for many people.

There is usually a light to indicate that the pot is connected and turned on. In some models it lights whenever the pot is plugged

in, in others only while the heating unit is turned off by the thermostat.

An electric coffee pot might or might not be damaged by boiling dry, depending on how the thermostat is arranged. But it can't do it any good, and you should be careful not to let it happen.

Deposits may build up inside the well, insulating it and interfering with proper performance. A special cleaning tool may be provided. If not, you can use steel wool and detergent. Form the wool into a cylinder, or put it on a spoon handle, and twist it around and around with pressure.

Drip. The drip coffee maker, Figure 26-11, has an upper section with a few fine holes in the bottom, a central sieve-basket for drip-grind coffee, and a lower section with a handle and pouring spout. It is usually made of aluminum or of glass. Other types of drip pot are described below under Filter and Vacuum.

The procedure of use is to put the proper amount of coffee (presumably 2 level tablespoons per 6-ounce cup of water) in the basket, insert the basket in the top of the lower section or pot, insert the upper section in the basket, pour boiling water (premeasured, or to fill to an indicator line) into the upper section, put on the lid, and wait for the water to drip into and through the coffee into the pot. This may take 4 to 6 minutes.

The passage of this much time and contact with the grounds and various parts of the pot cool the water quite a bit. The coffee should be hot enough to please most people, but it might not. You can make it hotter by pre-heating the lower section with hot water, by standing it in a dish of hot water, or by putting it over a burner turned very low.

When dripping is complete (a few seconds after all water is gone from the top) you remove the top and the basket, transfer the lid to the bottom, and serve by pouring from the pot directly into cups. Or, if you want to be elegant, transfer the coffee to a glass carafe for serving.

Size range in drip pots is from one cup up to 6 or 8. Using the full capacity is not as critical as with a percolator, but it helps. If you give it only a part load the coffee may turn out both cool and weak. It is then advisable to use some method of heating the pot, and to use a slightly higher proportion of coffee.

A one-cup size may have a stand instead of a bottom pan, so that it can drip directly into a cup.

There are people who pour their drip coffee back in the top, for an extra passage through the grounds. This may be to compensate for stinginess in measuring out the ground coffee, a desire for extra strong coffee or a liking for the bitter compounds that single dripping carefully avoids.

Filter. The filter pot is similar in principle to the drip pot, to the extent that a measured quantity of hot water moves from an upper position through ground coffee into a lower section. But there is no detachable upper section, all the water and ground coffee are in contact in a single compartment until the coffee has dripped through into the lower section, and a fine-mesh filter of paper or cloth is used instead of a sieve-basket. One style is shown in Figure 26-12.

The filter usually screens out all coffee grounds, no matter how fine, so a fine grind may be used and the beverage should always be free of sediment. But filters are a nuisance. Cloth ones must be properly installed, washed well after each use (a slightly disagreeable job), and replaced at intervals. Paper filters must usually be folded into shape and are discarded after each use, making an extra item to buy and to worry about having on hand.

The hot water may be just poured into the top of a filter pot, but it is advisable to first put in just enough to wet the grounds, then add the rest. Otherwise a variable part

Courtesy of Corning Glass Works

Fig. 26-12. Filter coffee maker

of the coffee may float, supported by air trapped between particles and by the surface tension of the water, so that they partly or wholly avoid contributing to the brew.

Instructions with the pot may tell you that you must not only wet the grounds first, but that the rest of the water should be added slowly, with stirring. Flavor may be affected slightly by this procedure, but it is a nuisance and may tear up the filter if carelessly done.

There is no top section or basket to remove, but you will probably want to lift out the filter and grounds before pouring the coffee.

Vacuum. The vacuum coffee pot, often called a Silex, is a special kind of a filter pot. It has two glass sections or bowls, a filter and sometimes a cap or cover.

The upper bowl has a soft gasket that makes an airtight seal when it is placed in the neck of the lower one, and has a tube that extends almost to the bottom. A filter, which may be either cloth or paper, is held snugly over the top of the tube by a clip at the bottom. The cap, if present, is used mostly to keep dust out of the upper bowl when it is not in use.

Put water in the bottom bowl, about 6 ounces for each cup of coffee you want. There may be measurement marks on the bowl that you can use, but they seem to be 5 ounces or less to a cup. Secure a filter (new if paper, clean if cloth), over the tube, place the upper bowl on the lower, and twist slightly to get a good seal. Put fine-ground coffee in the upper bowl, using 2 tablespoons to the cup unless you have a definite preference for a stronger or weaker brew.

Place the pot on strong heat and bring the water to a boil. Steam pressure building up above the water will start to force the water up the tube into the upper bowl, where it will mix with the ground coffee. Reduce the heat to simmer if it is gas, or turn it off if it is electric. Stir the fluid in the upper bowl a few times, and remove the pot from heat after a minute.

The lower bowl will now be filled with steam except for a shallow layer of water below the tube. As it cools, the steam will condense, creating a vacuum that will assist gravity in pulling the liquid back down from the upper bowl. This should take about 2 minutes.

Using pot holders or gloves, remove the upper bowl by gentle twisting and pulling, and set it aside. Serve coffee directly from the lower bowl.

A cloth filter should be washed thoroughly after each use.

Directions with a vacuum pot, and instructions in other references, make this operation a little more complicated. You are supposed to put the lower bowl on the heat first, and bring it to a boil. Then you put the filter and ground coffee in the up-

Fig. 26-13. Vacuum coffee maker

per bowl, remove the lower one from the heat, and insert the upper part in it. Return the pot to reduced heat, and carry on with the steeping.

This system of making a delayed coupling of the two sections, after the bottom one is hot, is probably a gourmet touch. I have never seen it done by anyone accustomed to using these coffee makers.

Boiled. Boiled coffee, which is sometimes more accurately called pan coffee, is probably the oldest brewing method, and the product can be excellent. However it no longer has either popularity or social acceptability, and is seldom made except under primitive camping conditions. But since it is the really basic method, it is described here for the record.

A coarse or regular grind is preferred. Proportion is the same as by other methods, with two tablespoons to the cup as a good starting place. Put the water into a pan, bring it to a boil, add the ground coffee and stir until all of it is wet. Let it come to a boil again, but be prepared to move the pan or turn down the heat quickly, as it foams up and is likely to overflow the pan.

Simmer or boil very slowly on reduced heat for 3 to 5 minutes (2 to 4 minutes if you use drip grind). Take off heat and allow it to stand for 2 or 3 minutes to settle, then serve.

There should be little sediment except in the last cup. But if you want to pour it immediately after brewing, or want to keep even the last cup without grounds, pour it through a strainer.

This is only one of many possible methods. Others range from actually boiling grounds to up to five minutes down to care-

Fig. 26-14. Boiled coffee

Fig. 26-15. Coffee cups

fully avoiding bringing the brew to a boil at all. Many people like to include eggshell to cause the finer suspended particles to clump together and settle out. If you feel adventurous, you might try the recipes in Figures 26-2 and 26-3.

INSTANT (SOLUBLE) COFFEE

Instant coffee has been available for a long time, but its popularity is recent. It is manufactured by brewing coffee in a more or less conventional manner, then evaporating the water away to leave a soluble powder. The standard type is a very fine powder obtained by moderate-temperature boiling under vacuum, then grinding the residue.

To make the newer freeze dried coffee, the coffee beverage is frozen and the water evaporated (or, more accurately, sublimed) away while frozen, in a high vacuum. The product includes some powder, but it may consist mostly of small flakes with a porous structure.

In either case, the volatile aromatic substances that give fresh coffee its characteristic and appealing odor tend to be lost. However, there are also processes for catching these substances, concentrating them and returning them to the powder. This process can give instant coffee at least part of the aroma of fresh coffee, but it is a mixed blessing, as it lowers its stability and keeping qualities.

Powdered coffee usually dissolves quickly and easily in boiling water, and in warm or cold water after some stirring. It may be made either in individual cups, or in a pot, pitcher or carafe. But like other fine soluble powders, it has a tendency to form lumps or cakes in the water if handled incorrectly. These may require crushing against the side of the cup, or vigorous stirring. They are formed of a core of dry powder, surrounded by a skin of dampened grains. They will seldom be troublesome, or even appear, if the powder is kept dry, and if it is put in a dry cup and boiling water added. Damp powder, or powder added to water, has maximum tendency to lump.

The flakes of freeze-dried coffee do not clump together under most circumstances, so they seldom form lumps.

There are substantial differences between brewed and instant coffee in both chemistry and taste. Instant usually lacks the volatile and aromatic substances, the colloidal oils that may account for up to 10 per cent of the flavor-basis of fresh brew, and it is usually more acid. On the other hand, it is highly resistant to development of stale or off tastes, and does not deteriorate seriously during normal storage after being opened. Beverages made with it have good keeping qualities.

Since there is no water lost in brewing, instant coffee proportions are usually figured on 5-1/2 instead of 6 ounces to the cup. A level teaspoon of powder makes weak coffee, a rounded teaspoon medium or "ideal" and a heaped one, strong. A freeze-dried product may need about 1/4 less for the same result.

Powdered instant coffee may be used as a spice. It offers good taste and appearance when sprinkled on the top of custard, junket and similar desserts, in the same manner as cinnamon and nutmeg.

SERVING COFFEE

American coffee is usually served hot directly from the coffee maker into the cup. However, it is sometimes poured into a glass carafe or a pitcher, then dispensed into the cups. Some heat is usually lost in the process, together with most or all of any coffee-grounds sediment. Coffee in a carafe may be kept hot over a very low burner, with less damage to color and flavor than if kept in a percolator.

Cups are variable in size and shape. Brim-full capacity may be between 6 and 8 fluid ounces. There are also super-size cups, usually acquired as gifts or souvenirs. A cup of coffee is usually figured to be 5-1/2 ounces. Except with instant coffee, this means starting with 6 ounces of water, to make up for water held by the grounds and lost by evaporation.

Unfortunately, coffee makers are often advertised and marked for cups of other sizes, 5-ounce being common even in the water container, and marking by 4-ounce cups is not unknown. A good first step with a new coffee pot is to check its capacity with measured water, so that you will know what you have.

It is said that 2/3 of American coffee drinkers add sugar to the beverage, and about 2/3 add milk or cream. Since many people add sugar (or sugar substitute) only, and others add milk or cream only, the percentage who drink it plain may be quite small. But these figures are not particularly reliable.

Cream and Milk. If you add milk, cream or equivalents to coffee (which may or may not be sweetened) you get a somewhat different, smoother taste; added nourishment, a cooling effect which may be important for those with tender mouths who must drink in haste, and an increase in the ceremonial aspect of coffee drinking. But according to coffee specialists, you lose a true taste and enjoyment that can be obtained only by drinking it black.

Cream may be anything from heavy whipping cream to half-and-half, with richness and flavor being generally favored by the thicker creams, and diet and economy calling for the thinner varieties. There are special coffee creams, which differ among various localities, but are usually light or very light.

Use in coffee is a severe test of the condition of cream. If it is even in the first stages of turning sour it may embarrass you in one of two ways. It may curdle, producing a number of floating whitish lumps that are most unwelcome. They can sometimes be eliminated by vigorous stirring, or by crushing them against the cup with the back of a spoon, but they may be indestructible.

The other unpleasantness is to have the cream mix in smoothly, but release colorless butterfat which floats in droplets in the top of the coffee. In general, the thicker cream is more likely to cause this trouble, but even whole milk and evaporated milk may do it.

The amount of milk or cream varies widely with personal taste. The individual coffee creamers in Figure 26-16 hold a little less than an ounce, brim full. This is enough or more than enough for most people, but two are sometimes used in a single 5-1/2 ounce cup of coffee.

Cheap eating places and economical housewives customarily serve plain milk, and sometimes even skim milk, instead of cream. Some people strongly prefer milk to cream, and most coffee drinkers can put up with the substitution cheerfully.

Evaporated milk is widely used in coffee, particularly in the military, on small ships and under other conditions where refrigeration of supplies is a problem. It is rich and smooth, but gives coffee a special flavor, which is sometimes liked but more often disliked. It is often served direct from the can, and may be known as armored cow. Condensed milk has a more natural flavor, but is usable only by those who like considerable sugar.

There are also powdered additives made of powdered cream, or of synthetic material with better keeping quality, which are usually more satisfactory than the canned varieties as substitutes for liquid cream.

Iced Coffee. Hot coffee should usually be very hot. Cold coffee should contain a liberal number of ice cubes. Intermediate temperatures for this beverage are not popular.

There are at least three different ways to prepare iced coffee from brewed coffee. You can make coffee double strength, and pour it hot into a pitcher or into tall glasses filled with ice cubes. But be prepared to add more ice. Or you can make it ordinary strength, cool it to room or fridge temperature, then serve it with a few ice cubes.

Or you can make a regular strength brew, freeze it into cubes, use them to fill glasses, then pour fresh hot regular-strength coffee to fill. Again, be ready with more ice, whether coffee or plain.

You can make cold coffee directly with water and instant coffee, but it may be diffi-

cult to dissolve. It is safer to make it into a syrup first with a little water, preferably hot, then dilute it with cold water and pour over ice cubes.

Cream and sugar are sometimes added in the pitcher or carafe, before pouring into glasses, but this is practical only when everyone likes these additives. It is safer to provide them on the side, and let people mix to their own taste. Verifine sugar dissolves better than ordinary granulated. But be sure to provide iced-tea spoons, long and slender, for stirring.

With Ice Cream. A coffee float may be made by putting one or two balls of vanilla or coffee ice cream in a tall glass of cold coffee, usually premixed with sugar and cream.

A coffee soda may be a half and half mixture of regular or double strength coffee and club soda, both cold, to which two balls of ice cream (vanilla, coffee or chocolate) have been added. A shake or malt is made in the regular way (see page 522), with a teaspoon or possibly two teaspoons of instant coffee used for flavoring. Or it may be made with regular coffee, cream, sugar and ice cream.

TEA

The word tea means a number of things, all of them closely related. It is a bush that

Fig. 26-16. Individual creamers

grows in the tropics and subtropics, the new leaves and leaf buds of the bush (particularly after drying); a beverage made from these leaves and an afternoon meal at which the drink might be served.

As a drink, tea is second only to coffee among the non-soda beverages in world wide popularity. It is very popular in Britain and in countries under British influence, where its consumption is greater than that of coffee.

Varieties. There are a number of varieties of tea bushes, which vary in their preferences as to soil and climate, and in their taste. However, the maturity of the leaves and buds that are picked, and the manner of preparation, are more important, or at least more easily recognized, in the prepared beverage.

The three principal classes of tea are black, green and oolong. All of these involve preliminary withering of the leaf in the sun or indoors, rolling it to change the structure and release juices, and sifting and sorting. Black tea is then dampened and fermented, oolong is partly fermented and green tea is steamed without fermenting.

Fermenting is claimed to reduce the astringency of the leaf and to develop the color and aroma of the beverage. After processing, the leaves are dried in ovens (fired), then put through cutting, sifting and sorting machines.

Most tea used in the United States is the black variety.

Sorting grades are usually broken pekoe, consisting mostly of terminal buds with some fine leaf fragments; orange pekoe containing some terminal buds but being largely fine leaves, pekoe and pekoe Souchong containing coarser leaves and a remainder of pekoe dust or broken tea.

The tea bush sprouts new stems and leaves several times a year. Each set of new growth is called a flush, picking or crop. First and second pickings are often more highly valued than the later ones.

Fig. 26-17. Pouring tea

Caffeine. Tea is usually less valued and feared than coffee as a keep-awake drug, but it may contain twice as much caffeine — 2 to 4-1/2 per cent if brewed in a teapot in standard fashion (5-minute infusion). But there is less liquid in the average cup of tea than of coffee, as smaller cups may be used and underfilling, or diluting with cold water, are more common.

The caffeine content of a cup of tea is variously estimated from 0.6 to 1.0 or more grains.

Tannin. Tannin is a more or less bitter-tasting chemical that is produced in slightly different forms in a wide variety of plants. Tea contains from 2 to 4 times as much of it as it does of caffeine, and obtains a large part of its body and characteristic flavor from it. Tannin is mildly medicinal, as an astringent that can reduce certain types of internal bleeding and as an antidote to certain poisons.

Tea is an excellent soothing and healing medicine for burns, such as are all too common in kitchen work. But it must be limited to small burns, and should be applied only once, briefly, as a quantity of tannin may have serious side effects if absorbed into the body by any route other than the digestive system.

519

Fig. 26-18. Tea bag

Brewing (Steeping). Tea is usually made by combining boiling water and tea leaves, then leaving them together for a limited period, a process that may be called steeping or infusion.

In the traditional method, the tea leaves, about a rounded teaspoon to the cup, are placed in a china, silver or glass pot, boiling water is added and the mixture is allowed to stand 3 to 6 minutes, with or without stirring. The fluid is then poured into another container or into cups through a strainer, which may be set in the base of the spout, or be a separate unit. It removes some or all of the fine fragments of tea leaves which otherwise would accompany the beverage.

Tea is now sold commonly in paper or muslin bags, each containing a slightly rounded teaspoon of finely divided tea leaves, enough for one cup of tea of average strength. The cloth permits free circulation of hot water but prevents pieces from getting into the fluid. A number of tea bags may be placed in a pot for brewing in the standard manner, or one bag may be placed in each cup, and the boiling-hot water poured onto it. The bag may be left in the cup for one to 4 minutes, according to taste, and may be allowed to rest undisturbed, or hurried by stirring and pressing with a spoon.

When brewing is complete (it is usually judged by color) the bag is lifted out by an attached string, and some fluid may be squeezed out of it by pressing it against the cup inner rim with a spoon. It may be parked in the saucer, but a tactful hostess will provide some other receptacle for it.

Like coffee, tea provides a large number of water-soluble substances, which are dissolved successively during steeping. Tea that is steeped for 6 minutes will not only be stronger than that which is brewed for only 3, but it will have a different flavor and chemical content.

It is the fashion now to keep brewing to a short time, and to enjoy only those substances that are quickly extracted. But there are probably some people who still enjoy the old fashioned tea made by keeping leaves and water simmering in a kettle on the back of the stove all day.

There are also their opposite numbers who like their tea weak, and will pass a tea bag around to make two or even three cups in succession.

When tea is brewed in a pot, strength can be adjusted to individual tastes by making it quite strong, and providing a pitcher of hot water with it. Each person can then pour tea first, estimate its strength by its appearance, and add hot water to dilute it to taste. The only problem here is variability in color of various tea blends.

Water. Water quality has an important effect on the taste of tea. In general, a neutral or soft water with a minimum of dissolved minerals is best. However, reasonably good tea can be made with almost any drinkable water, if a variety and grade of tea that will counteract its defects can be found. But there are about 2,000 possible blends of tea, so experimenting might take a long time. And only a few are widely available.

Temperature is probably more important than quality, as only water that is boiling or nearly boiling seems to be able to extract full value from the leaves. As a result, freshly prepared tea should be much too hot to drink, and waiting for it to cool may be a nuisance.

If the cup is only 2/3 or 3/4 filled with strong hot tea, cold water may be added to dilute it to normal strength and a safer temperature. Such water may be served in a pitcher or a glass, in addition to or instead of the hot water pitcher provided for dilution only.

Instructions for making tea usually specify that the water be cold and fresh, that it be heated to boiling and used immediately, and that previously heated water should not be used, as it will make the tea flat in taste. It is likely that there are taste differences between freshly boiled cold water and other boiling water, but it is very doubtful if the average tea drinker is capable of detecting them in his beverage.

Serving. Tea is served in many different ways. When hot, it may be drunk plain, with sugar, with milk or cream or with lemon. When cold, it is usually liberally iced, and served with lemon and sugar.

The serving of hot tea is often a special ceremony with its own protocol, which is somewhat out of the field of cooking.

MILK DRINKS

Fresh sweet whole milk is an excellent beverage in itself. Flavor and consistency are pleasing, and nutritive values are excellent. Sweet fresh skim milk is also good, but it has less body and flavor. Reconstituted dry skim milk usually has a more or less processed taste but most people can get used to it. It may be made thicker and more nourishing by using less water (or more powder).

Diluted evaporated and condensed milk are seldom used as beverages, because one has a cooked taste and the other is too sweet.

Buttermilk is a popular drink among those who like a sour flavor, and those who

Fig. 26-19. Milk is both food and beverage

are convinced that it has special health building qualities. Sour whole milk is seldom used as a beverage.

Milk may be flavored and fortified in a number of ways. Chocolate flavoring is popular, and fruit syrups are sometimes mixed with fresh milk. Eggs, malted milk and milk powder may be mixed or beaten with either whole or skim milk.

Shakes, Frosteds and Malteds. In a cookbook a shake is almost any mixture of milk, flavoring and other liquids or semi-liquids. It sometimes includes cracked ice either as part of the mixture or as a partial filler for the glass in which the beverage is to be poured. Each variety seems to have a few friends, but none of them appear to be really popular.

At a soda fountain, the basic milk shake is likely to be a mixture of 1/3 syrup (chocolate, fruit or other) and 2/3 milk, beaten in a special blender with a long shaft and short vanes. It may include ice cream, and is then called a frosted milk shake, or just frosted for short.

The frosted milk shake is becoming increasingly popular in the home as a result of widespread ownership of blenders and high speed beaters. One recipe is:

Fig. 26-20. Soda fountain blender

Chocolate Frosted *(1 portion)*

⅔ cup vanilla ice cream
⅓ cup chocolate syrup
1 cup milk

The ice cream should be soft enough so that it can be cut with a spoon, or it may not blend properly.

Combine the three ingredients in a blender jar. If you have the type used by soda fountains, beat for about one minute. In a home blender, beat until smooth and fluffy. This might be for only 3 seconds on high speed or 10 on medium.

The mixture might increase in bulk as much as 75 per cent, depending mostly on the quantity and quality of the ice cream. Short beating time may leave lumps (not necessarily a disadvantage if they are very small), long beating warms and melts the ice cream.

For a thick shake, use up to double the amount of ice cream, with or without a corresponding reduction in milk. It is not truly thick unless a spoon will stand up in it. For a stronger flavor, use chocolate ice cream instead of vanilla.

For other flavors, replace the chocolate with other syrup, such as vanilla, coffee or fruit. Or increase the milk, and use direct flavorings such as vanilla extract, instant coffee or fruit jam instead of syrup.

A malted is a milk shake (usually frosted) of any flavor, plus one to 3 teaspoons of unflavored malted milk powder.

A float is any type of milk shake or frosted, plus one or two balls of ice cream added after mixing is complete.

Eggnog. The basic eggnog is an egg beaten into a glass of milk, usually a tall one. It is a part of many invalid, convalescent and weight-gaining diets. It is more nourishing than milk and may be easier to eat (drink) than egg in other forms.

The flavor is mildly pleasant, but most people prefer it if it is slightly sweetened or flavored. A half to 2 teaspoons of sugar may be used in an 8 to 12-ounce glass. Cinnamon or nutmeg may be dusted over the top, or chocolate or fruit syrup may be added.

An egg may be added to milkshake ingredients before beating (blending). The product is more often called eggnog than milkshake.

A more elaborate eggnog is used as a holiday drink, usually with added rye and rum.

Bottled eggnog may be bought from dairies during holiday seasons. It is a rich smooth drink, but it lacks the froth and is often gummy because of added stabilizers.

COCOA AND CHOCOLATE

Cocoa and chocolate, which were discussed a while ago under FLAVORINGS, are used both as a principal ingredient and as a flavoring in beverages. They are not as

Fig. 26-21. Popular flavorings

popular as coffee and tea, from which they differ in having a lower caffeine content and a higher food value.

A hot drink made with cocoa, sugar and milk or water is called cocoa. If chocolate or chocolate syrup is substituted for cocoa, the drink is usually called hot chocolate.

Chocolate makes a richer, fatter drink than cocoa, and is more trouble to dissolve. Syrup usually contains additives that make the drink dull-flavored and too smooth. Otherwise, the three make beverages that are very similar and that are used in the same way. They are particularly favored for young people who have not yet developed a liking for coffee or tea, or who are not permitted to drink them.

Cocoa and hot chocolate are somewhat more festive drinks than coffee and tea. Although the basic bitterness is no greater than that of coffee, sugar is almost always added during cooking. Whipped cream or marshmallow is very commonly added, to further increase sweetness and richness.

Recipes. Recipes for hot chocolate and cocoa seem to be different in every household and almost every cookbook. There are fundamental differences, in taste, habit and local custom, in almost every detail of their preparation. They start with the strength, or perhaps weakness.

An ounce of bitter chocolate is expected to flavor 16 to 21 ounces (2 to 2.6 measuring cups) of water and milk, but its flavor equivalent in cocoa is used with 3 to 9 cups of liquid. The liquid may be anything from straight milk to equal quantities of milk and water.

Naturally, there are differences in sweetness. Two to 2.6 tablespoons of sugar are used for each ounce of chocolate (except for a recipe for French chocolate that has 6 tablespoons), but for 3 tablespoons of cocoa you may be told to use anywhere from 1-1/2 to 4 tablespoons of sugar.

Most of the recipes call for salt in such tiny quantities that it should make little difference to leave it out. Vanilla is usual, but ranges from a few drops to one teaspoon to a quart or more of liquid, and is usually too little to be tasted by any but the most discriminating. One recipe asks for a little butter, two call for cinnamon and one for cornstarch.

Liquid is usually specified in terms of 8-ounce measuring cups or 4-cup quarts. Cocoa is ordinarily served in coffee cups, which have a practical capacity of 5-1/2 to 6 ounces. Losses in liquid during heating and handling are usually less than the added bulk of cocoa and sugar.

You can figure that a quart of milk and/ or water will yield 5 full cups or 6 skimpy ones. Circumstances and appetite will determine the need for seconds, but it is usual to figure that half the customers will want another cup.

Milk may be whole, skim or made from powder, according to taste or availability of supplies.

Hot Cocoa. The following indicates ordinary variables in recipes for one quart of cocoa, or about 6 coffee cups.

In each strength there is the same quantity of liquid, with different proportions of milk and water. The principal variable is the quantity of cocoa. You can also add a few grains of salt or drops of vanilla, or a tiny bit of cinnamon or nutmeg.

Cocoa can be made in individual cups, but is less work to mix if you do the whole batch at once. In either case, you mix the sugar and cocoa thoroughly to prevent the cocoa from forming solid lumps. Add just a little of the boiling water, or if you do not use it, milk heated to just below boiling (scalded).

There should be enough liquid so that you can stir the cocoa into a smooth paste, but not enough to float any of it away from the sugar. Then add and stir in the balance of the water, if any, and then the milk.

The cocoa can be drunk immediately, but if made in a pan, it may be improved by simmering for a couple of minutes. The heat must be kept low to avoid sticking on the bottom and boiling over at the top.

It is said that the boiling water is necessary to dissolve the cocoa thoroughly and prevent a grainy texture, but this does not seem to be true. Milk should not be boiled, as it has a strong tendency to stick and burn, it changes flavor and its tendency to form a skin on the top is greatly increased.

The surface skin that forms on hot milk and milk mixtures is a disagreeable feature of cocoa. It can be reduced by keeping heat moderate, by stirring or by covering the surface. It can also be lifted off and discarded. See page 212.

A surface covering of froth can be made by beating the cocoa vigorously with a whisk or rotary beater, preferably in the pan just before pouring. Or give it a few seconds in a blender at high speed, between

Ingredients	Strength Minimum	Maximum	Medium
Cocoa	3 Tb	6 Tb	4 Tb
Sugar	1½ Tb	8 Tb	4 Tb
Boiling water	none	1 cup	½ cup
Hot milk	4 cps	3 cps	3½ cps
Salt	none	¼ tsp	none
Vanilla	none	1 tsp	none

Hot Cocoa (for 4 people)

the pan and the cups. The skin can be suppressed and the drink enriched by adding whipped cream or marshmallow.

A heaping teaspoon of whipped cream, which may be either sweetened or unsweetened, is ample to protect and embellish a cup of cocoa. The heat will flatten it out quite quickly, after which it might be renewed. You will therefore need to whip only 2 teaspoons of cream for each cup of cocoa, and will probably have to prepare too much, just to have enough to beat. A blender can whip a very small quantity.

An aerosol container of whipped cream, real or artificial, is excellent for this purpose as you need only use as much of it as you want.

One marshmallow (there are about 45 average-size ones in a pound) both decorates and sweetens cocoa. You might reduce the sugar by 1/3 or more if you intend to use them.

A quart or more of hot liquid may be difficult to pour without slopping, particularly if the pan is nearly full. It may be advisable to use a ladle for part or almost all of it.

Hot Chocolate. Hot chocolate is a richer and usually stronger drink than cocoa. It may be somewhat harder to prepare because of extra care needed to melt and dissolve the chocolate. Typical recipes have the range of ingredients below.

Shave the chocolate (cut into thin slices

Fig. 26-22. You can add a marshmallow

which crumble) put it in a pan over low heat, add about half the boiling water, stir until well mixed, then add the rest of the boiling water, stirring until smooth. Add the hot milk, gradually at first and then rapidly, continuing to stir. Turn up burner and heat mixture until it bubbles at the edges.

This is only one of several possible procedures. Your recipe may tell you to bring the mixture of chocolate and water to a high boil twice, removing it from the heat in between until bubbling stops. This is

Hot Chocolate (for 4 people)			
Ingredients	Minimum	Maximum	Try
Unsweetened chocolate	1½ oz	2 oz	2 oz
Boiling water	½ cup	1 cup	1 cup
Hot milk	2 cps	4 cps	3 cps
Sugar	3 Tb	5 Tb	4 Tb
Vanilla	¼ tsp	1 tsp	½ tsp
Salt	none	¼ tsp	none

probably to insure that blending is complete. But it is likely to cause over-thickening, particularly on the sides of the pan, so that combining with the milk is made difficult. Thorough stirring without boiling is safer.

Chocolate can be dissolved in a cup of very hot milk in the same manner as in boiling water. But do not mix the chocolate directly with a large quantity of milk, as they will blend slowly and uncertainly.

Hot chocolate is served in the same manner as cocoa, including precautions to avoid or remove surface skin, and possible topping with whipped cream or marshmallow.

Chocolate Milk. Chocolate milk (or chocolate flavored milk) is an important dairy product. It usually consists of whole sweet milk plus about one per cent of cocoa and 5 to 7 per cent of sugar, with vegetable gum or starch added as a stabilizer to prevent separation or settling out.

This amount of cocoa is able to supply only a weak or bland chocolate flavor. The stabilizer thickens the liquid and creates an over-smooth, somewhat synthetic texture. This does not prevent the product from enjoying wide popularity, particularly among the young.

Chocolate flavored skim milk is sometimes offered in stores. The only difference is the lack of milk fat, with its flavor and nourishment. There are also chocolate drinks of similar character which contain little or no milk.

If you want a rich chocolate drink without excessive sweetness, you may have to use cocoa, or unsweetened or semi-sweet chocolate. It is advisable to make it into a syrup with hot water or milk first, then add cold milk gradually as you stir. If the product is not sufficiently cold, chill it. If you are in a hurry, pour it into glasses or freezer trays, and put them in the freezer for a few minutes or in the refrigerator for about 30. A rich mixture can stand some dilution with ice cubes.

For a quart of milk, try about 2 ounces of bitter chocolate or 1/3 cup of cocoa, with 1/4 to 1/2 cup of sugar. Or use 3 ounces of semisweet chocolate. You may use no sugar with this, or up to 1/4 cup, depending on the sweetness wanted. Or use the sauce recipe on page 373. If in doubt, use less sugar, as it is easy to add even after pouring into glasses.

Dietetically, chocolate milk is considered to be inferior to whole milk. The chocolate seems to combine with the milk calcium to greatly reduce its availability to the body, particularly when the diet is otherwise low in calcium. This cancels out one of the principal advantages of milk as a food for children.

Syrup. Both hot and cold chocolate drinks can be prepared from chocolate syrup, which may be homemade, but is usually bought in a bottle or a can. Syrup blends with milk or water at any temperature, requiring only a moderate amount of stirring. But it will mix more easily if you thin it with a little milk before adding all of it.

Bought syrups are mixed with sugar, which is of course a convenience. But if you want a strong chocolate flavor, and obtain it by increasing the proportion of syrup, you will probably make the drink too sweet. They also usually contain stabilizers to prevent separation, which make the drink over-smooth for many people.

Syrups and carbonated water, dispensed from faucets, are the basic materials for soda fountain drinks.

27

DESSERTS

GENERAL DESCRIPTION

Definition. A dessert is any food that is served at the end of a meal. The term includes pie, cake, pudding, raw fruit and cheese, in all their varieties, in addition to such middle-of-the-meal items as fritters and souffles if they are served at the correct time. It sometimes even covers after dinner coffee and cordials.

In cookbooks, however, it is customary to put cake and pie in other sections, and to limit the dessert section to a variety of puddings and prepared fruits. Except for a few general remarks, this arrangement will be followed here.

Sweetness and Richness. In the broad meaning of the term, most but not all desserts are sweet. Cheese is not a sweet at all, and raw fruit is often acid. Among sweetened desserts there is a wide range from gelatins and some custards and pies that contain little sugar to mousses and puddings that are loaded with it.

There is a similarly wide range in richness, from the stiffened water in simple Jell-O to custard bread pudding and strawberry shortcake. Choice of degree of sweetness and richness is primarily a matter of individual and family taste, but considerable juggling can be done. A rich nourishing meal can get by with a lean dessert, and a weak meal can be enhanced by a rich and nutritious finish.

Groupings. The desserts in this chapter are grouped as custards, gelatins, frozen, and fruit combinations. Some of them do not fit well under their headings, except perhaps by association, but I could not find better places for them.

Many desserts and classes of dessert are omitted because full explanations of them would take more research and space than is justified by their importance.

CUSTARD

A custard is a cooked mixture of milk and egg, usually with sugar and flavoring. The egg or eggs may be whole, or the yolks only. The egg thickens the milk, which becomes a thick liquid if it is stirred during cooking, or sets it to a weak delicate gel if it is baked undisturbed.

This is a simple type of dessert, but timing is very important in preparing it, as it can be injured by being either undercooked or overcooked just a little. If you stay with it you are all right, as tests for doneness are simple. A stirred custard will just begin coating a spoon, a baked one will just stop coating a knife.

Custard may be eaten plain or with a sauce or topping. It may be used as a sauce, or as a base or ingredient in other sauces and cooked dishes. It is closely related to omelets, scrambled eggs and souffles.

Custards are likely to be injured by rapid or high-heat cooking. The liquid or stirred type may therefore be most safely cooked in a double boiler over simmering water, and dishes for baked custard are often set in a pan of water in the oven.

Stirred Custard. Stirred custard is often called boiled custard, but it should not be boiled, as this greatly increases risk of curdling. Stirred or liquid custard are therefore better names for it.

Stirred Custard *(4 portions)*

2	cps	milk
2		eggs *(or 4 yolks)*
¼	cup	sugar
¼	tsp	salt *(optional)*
½	tsp	vanilla *(optional)*

The eggs can be increased to 3 or even 4 if you wish, to obtain a richer and thicker custard, for either dessert or sauce.

Fig. 27-1. Testing custards

If it is to be used as a sauce the quantity of sugar and vanilla can be increased, and if it is to be frozen they can be doubled.

Replacing eggs with double the number of yolks gives custard a deeper color, and makes slight differences in texture and flavor.

It is standard practice to scald or at least heat milk before mixing it with the eggs. This shortens cooking time. If the milk should be unpasteurized, it would also serve to destroy enzymes that might interfere with thickening of the custard.

Eggs are usually beaten slightly, enough to thoroughly mix white and yolk, but usually not enough to break up the stringy part of the white (chalazia). If the eggs are beaten sufficiently to eliminate them, the resulting froth may not mix properly with the milk nor get full advantage of the cooking. If you are sensitive about a few small white streaks in the custard, you can remove them by pouring the egg-milk mixture through a sieve after beating.

Put the eggs or yolks in a 1- or 2-quart bowl and beat or stir them to a smooth, non-frothy liquid. Heat the milk to just short of boiling, when small bubbles appear at the edges, then add it slowly to the eggs, stirring constantly. Then mix in the sugar and salt, until dissolved.

Pour the mixture into the top part of a double boiler, with a low level of simmering water in the bottom pan. Cook and stir until the custard just starts to make a smooth coat on a metal spoon, perhaps in 12 to 15 minutes. Then remove the upper pan from the heat immediately, and stir in the vanilla. If you suspect that you have overcooked it, set the pan in a container of cold water.

It is also possible, although more risky, to cook a custard over direct heat, either an electric burner at its LOW setting, or on an insulating pad over a gas burner. But you run the risk of subjecting it to too much heat, with possible curdling, or stick-

Fig. 27-2. Floating island

ing and scorching on the bottom. In stirring, scrape the bottom lightly and then look at the spoon. If it has picked up some thickened material, the bottom is too hot. Move the pan immediately to a cool spot, leave it there for half a minute, then return it to a reduced heat. Discard thick scrapings.

If you have cooked it a little too long, or on too high heat, have used stale milk or had bad luck, the custard may curdle, separating into fine lumps or grains. If this happens, chill it by setting the pan in cold water or by pouring it back into the mixing bowl, and beat it vigorously with a whisk or rotary beater. This should fix it unless the condition is very bad.

Stirred custard may be used as a sauce, or chilled and served plain for dessert, as a thick smooth liquid that is eaten with a spoon. It is sometimes embellished with a sprinkling of nutmeg or cinnamon, or by adding fruit jelly in small lumps, but its highest and best use is as the bottom part of Floating Island.

Floating Island. For this excellent old time dessert you make a liquid custard in the way just described, using 4 yolks instead of 2 whole eggs. While it is chilling, make the islands by beating the 4 egg whites until they are fluffy, then adding 4

tablespoons of sugar gradually while beating until shiny and stiff. Spoon this meringue in individual separted lumps onto the top of the custard, and serve.

You can put the custard in individual saucers first and put one portion of meringue on each, or put all the custard in a wide serving bowl, dot the meringue on it in separate islands, and serve into saucers at the table with a ladle or an oversize spoon.

Some recipes recommend poaching the meringue. Simmer water in a wide frypan (like 10-inch), and spoon the meringue onto its surface, not letting the portions touch each other. Cover and cook for two minutes, then lift out with a slotted spoon or a turner, and put on the custard. Be sure not to let the water boil, as it will break up the meringue.

Poaching cooks the surface of the meringue so that it will not tend to dissolve in or mix with the custard. The advantage is negligible unless the dessert, or part of it, is to be held for another meal.

The islands (plain or poached) may also be put on wax paper under a broiler very briefly, to brown the surface. The gain in appearance may be outweighed by toughness of the brown areas if serving is not done immediately.

Islands are sometimes ornamented with dots of bright colored jelly, shaved chocolate or caramel syrup. But the basic white-on-yellow color combination can hardly be improved.

Baked Custard. Baked custard uses the same basic formula and ordinary variations as stirred custard. Procedure is the same until you have finished mixing the hot milk into the eggs. Then, instead of pouring the mixture into a double boiler, you put it in a baking or casserole dish, or into a number of custard cups whose capacity is usually about 4 ounces or 1/2 cup each.

These containers are baked in an oven at low temperature. This temperature may be obtained by throttling the oven down to a few degrees below 200° F, or by keeping it at 300 or 350° and putting the custard containers in a pan of hot water. Theoretically this should reach up almost to their rims, but this makes handling them difficult and dangerous, so that you may settle for only 1/2 inch of water.

If the mixture in the cups is hot when it goes into the oven, cooking time should be 20 to 35 minutes. The time varies widely with the starting temperature of the mix, the oven temperature and details of the mix. Homogenized milk may cook more slowly than regular milk. Doneness is determined by testing, rather than timing.

A preliminary test is appearance. A skin forms on the surface, which may remain almost colorless in a low temperature oven, but otherwise should turn yellow or brown when cooking. The positive test is to insert a sharp-pointed knife (a knife with a round end would be more likely to make a scar) into the custard. It will come out clean and dry if it is done, but wet with custard if it is not.

Two places to test a large dish are at the center and halfway from it to the edge. It should be done at the halfway point and slightly underdone in the center, as cooking continues for a short while after removal from the oven. A cup is tested at the center only, and should be fully cooked.

Another test, good for a large dish only, is to shake it gently. If there is only a small area of quivery liquid in the center, under the skin, it is done.

Remove the custard or custards from the oven and place on a rack to cool, then in the fridge to chill. But if you think they are overcooked, set them in a pan of ice water.

If baked custard is overcooked, or cooked at too high a temperature, it may fill with air holes, and tend to "weep" or exude whey. There is no remedy for this, but unless the condition is extreme, more damage is done to the pride of the cook than to the taste of the dessert.

This custard is scooped out of a baking dish with a large spoon or a turner, eaten directly from cups, or unmolded from cups to be eaten upside down. For unmolding, the cups should be buttered before filling. It is usually served plain, but may have caramel or fruit sauce added, or cinnamon or nutmeg sprinkled on top.

Individual custards unmolded from cups and served with thin caramel sauce are a favorite Latin American dessert, called flan.

Bread Pudding. If you soak a bowl full of bread and raisins with raw custard, add a bit of spice and bake it, you have bread pudding. Here is a recipe:

Bread Pudding

5 slcs*	stale white bread
3 cps	milk
3	eggs
½ cup	sugar
2 Tb	butter or margarine
½ cup	raisins, large ones preferred
½ tsp	vanilla
½ tsp	cinnamon
½ tsp	salt *(optional)*

* Standard 5/8-inch thickness, about 4 x 4-1/4 inches, weight about one ounce. If you have thinner slices, use more of them.

Butter a 1-1/2 or 2-quart casserole or a 10 x 6 by 1-3/4-inch glass baking dish. Spread the rest of the butter on the bread, cut in quarters and/or strips and pack lightly and neatly into the dish, with the raisins

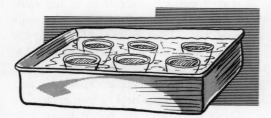

Fig. 27-3. Individual baked custards

scattered between layers but not on top.

Some recipes tell you to use toast instead of bread. This provides a firmer texture, with a different taste.

Mix the custard in the same way as for STIRRED CUSTARD, but hold out 2 tablespoons of sugar. Pour the uncooked mix over the bread and let stand 5 to 10 minutes, pressing the bread down lightly from time to time. Mix the remaining sugar with the cinnamon and sprinkle it over the top.

Bake on an open rack in a preheated 325° F oven for 25 to 35 minutes, or until a knife inserted in the center comes out clean and the top is brown.

Bread pudding may be served hot, warm or cold; and plain or with cream or any of several sauces, such as vanilla or fruit.

French Toast. French toast is better known as a breakfast delicacy than as a dessert, but since it can be a dessert and it is definitely a custard product, here it is. It is a dish somewhere between fried bread and custard bread pudding, served with butter and syrup or jam.

No two cookbooks and possibly no two cooks agree on just how French toast should be made, but each recipe is very positive. They agree on the need for slightly stale bread, egg, salt and either milk or cream, but not on proportions or cooking time.

The following covers most of the variations:

If this is all you are serving, it will feed one person or possibly two, but as a side dish it is enough for 4. You can multiply the recipe as necessary.

Fig. 27-4. Dipping French toast

All the recipes studied for this discussion specify that the bread be given a quick dip in the liquid, or that it be held in it for a few seconds at the most. Dipping is easiest if it is done in a soup plate or other wide flat vessel, rather than in a mixing bowl. The bread can be handled directly with the fingers, or with tongs or a turner and a fork.

The amount of liquid taken up by the bread varies not only with the dipping time but also with the staleness of the bread and the thickness of the mixture. Penetration is fastest with dry bread and a thin mixture.

If you dip only for a fixed length of time, a thick mixture will coat more slices than a thin one will. But a very thick mixture of cream and egg well beaten will cling to the surface of the bread in a thick layer, even if it does not soak in at all.

If you want really rich French toast, soak the bread all the way through. This will take 3 to 5 minutes working from both sides, in a mixture of a half cup of milk with one egg. If you are impatient, soak it a minute and then spoon more custard on its uncooked side as it fries. Such toast has the consistency of good bread pudding.

French Toast			
Ingredients	Minimum	*Maximum*	*Try*
Egg, slightly beaten	1	1	1
Milk or cream	1 Tb	1 cup	½ cup
Sugar	none	1 Tb	none
Salt	none	¼ tsp	none
Bread	2 slcs	6 slcs	4 slcs

531

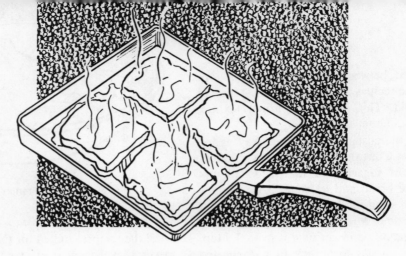

Fig. 27-5. Four slices on a griddle

The more usual quick-dip toast is fried in butter at medium heat, 300° F, for about a minute on each side. The wetted part cooks so quickly that it is mostly a heating operation, so you can regulate cooking time by color. The slices are not harmed by repeated turning, so the easiest way to check on the bottom is to put it on the top.

Soaked bread takes much longer, 4 or 5 minutes on each side. Heat should be low except right at the start, to avoid burning. It should have a consistency like baked custard throughout when it is done.

The most convenient cooking utensil is a flat griddle that will hold four slices. A waffle iron fitted with flat plates instead of a grid may be used to cook both sides at once.

Some restaurants prepare French toast from chunks of bread instead of slices. They are dipped in a rich egg-milk mixture and deep fried.

French toast that includes sugar may be eaten with butter alone, or with added powdered sugar or cinnamon. But most of it, whether sweetened or not, is served with maple or similar syrup, or with jam, jelly or fruit sauce.

CORNSTARCH

Cornstarch, described under THICKEN-ERS, is a widely used thickening and smoothing agent. When heated with water, or with water solutions or mixtures such as milk, it swells and forms a smooth gel.

In small amounts cornstarch makes liquids thicker, smoother and more stable; and in larger amounts causes them to set to a firm solid. In still larger amounts it makes gels that are tough, rubbery and unpleasant.

Cornstarch has acquired a somewhat dubious reputation for dessert use. It is a more effective and dependable thickening agent than egg, but lacks its flavor and food value. It is often substituted for the sake of economy, possibly producing an inferior product and therefore becoming known as a cheapening agent. Also, it is so effective that if too much is used, the food may become stiff and tasteless.

But if you use cornstarch properly, it is useful to the cook and pleasing to the consumer. You will find it in many dessert recipes as a thickener, and there is one pudding in which it is the principal ingredient. However, this cornstarch pudding is no longer popular, perhaps because of competition of ready-mix desserts that are somewhat similar.

RENNET

Rennet is an enzyme obtained from the stomachs of young calves, where it serves to help in the digestion of milk. It is useful in making desserts, in softening milk curd,

532

in controlled curdling of milk for cheese making, and in various other ways. It is available in most groceries in tablet form, usually with the trade name "Junket."

A light, pleasant dessert, resembling a thin, pale baked custard, can be made by following the recipe in the box, approximately as follows:

Basic Junket

2 cps	milk *(not canned)*
3 Tb	sugar
1 tblt	Junket rennet
1 Tb	cold water
1 tsp	vanilla

Set out 4 or 5 dessert dishes or custard cups. Combine milk, sugar and flavoring, and heat to lukewarm (110° F). Crush tablet into the tablespoon of water, mix well, and add to warm milk mixture. Stir for only a few seconds, and pour immediately into dishes. Allow to stand undisturbed for 10 minutes, then chill in refrigerator.

The dessert can be given a custard appearance by adding two drops of yellow food color. The vanilla can be reduced to a half teaspoon, or for a very bland dessert, omitted entirely. A half cup of the milk can be replaced by cream.

A half teaspoon of almond, lemon or other extract can be added, or used to replace the same amount of vanilla. Fruit slices may be put in the dishes before pouring in the mixture.

RICE PUDDING

Rice pudding is a popular dessert that can be made in several ways, the relative merits of which are the subject of much argument. There are two basic kinds — custard and creamy — either of which may be made with or without raisins. And consistency varies, from nearly solid blocks of rice with just enough pudding mix to glue them together, to those that are so fluid that they could be used for sauces.

Regular rice, either long or short grain, should be used for pudding. Quick-cooking rice may not soften and expand enough to give the accepted consistency, and converted rice may react differently enough to need special treatment.

Baked Rice Custard. For this you use a standard custard recipe, increase the sugar and flavoring slightly, and mix with about half its bulk of cooked rice, plus raisins if you like them. Baking is done in the same manner as for plain custard in a casserole dish in a pan of water in a 300° oven, time is similar and so is the clean knife test for doneness.

A complication is that the rice tends to settle to the bottom, particularly right at the beginning. This sometimes causes the pudding to consist of a compact or even solid layer of rice topped by a layer of plain custard.

This separation can usually be reduced by stirring the mixture when it is about half cooked. This can be done with only minor disturbance of surface film or decorations by sliding the spoon in near the edge, and stirring the bottom without breaking through to the top. By now the rice grains have expanded and become slightly less inclined to sink and the custard has thickened to support them better. But you cannot stir after the custard has started to set, without spoiling its texture.

A working recipe for baked rice custard pudding for 4 to 6 people is:

Rice Custard Pudding

2 cps	milk
2	eggs *(or 4 yolks)*
⅓ cup	sugar
¾ cup	cooked rice *(represents ¼ cup raw rice)*
¼ cup	raisins *(optional)*
¼ tsp	salt *(optional)*

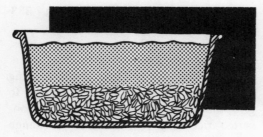

Fig. 27-6. Rice may settle out

These ingredients are subject to variations, as discussed under CUSTARDS. The rice may be increased to a cup for a thick pudding, or decreased to a half for a larger proportion of custard. Separation into layers is less noticeable when the amount of rice is increased.

Sugar may be increased to a half cup or more, if you like it sweet.

Stirred Rice Custard. This may be a standard custard mixed with cooked rice and frequent stirring in a double boiler. The test for doneness is thickening. The custard picks up some starch from the rice, both causing it to thicken and to be less likely to curdle.

A recommended proportion is two cups of custard (or of the milk that goes into it) to a cup of cooked rice. More rice might lead to too stiff or cereal-like consistency, less might cause custard to flow out of it. A too-stiff pudding can be thinned without damage by stirring in cream, one that is too thin can be thickened by stirring in a lightly beaten egg and recooking very briefly.

Texture can be made lighter by making the custard with the yolks only, beating the whites stiffly and folding them into the rice-custard after it is cooked.

Raisins may be added with the rice. Use about 1/4 to 1/2 cupful for each cup of cooked rice.

Old Fashioned. The old fashioned or milk rice pudding uses no eggs, and depends on long cooking to move starch from the rice grains into the milk, to thicken it. It is supposed to be soft and creamy. If it is thick and hard you have either used too little milk (or too much rice) or cooked it too long.

Old Fashioned Rice Pudding

1	qt	milk
¼	cup	raw rice *(not instant)*
½	cup	sugar *(vary to taste)*
1	tsp	butter
¼ to ½	cup	raisins *(optional)*
⅛	tsp	nutmeg
½	tsp	salt *(optional)*

Mix all the ingredients except raisins and nutmeg in a 1-1/2-quart casserole. Bake uncovered in a moderate oven, about 325° F, until almost firm. Stir often to distribute rice in fluid. Add raisins, if any, after about an hour. Sprinkle nutmeg on top a few minutes before taking out of oven.

Cooking time should be 2-1/2 to 3 hours. The rice should be cooked much sooner, but there is a question of consistency. If the fluid drains out of a spoonful of rice lifted out of the casserole, it is not cooked enough. Try to estimate its progress so that you can leave it undisturbed for the last 15 minutes to acquire a browned skin or crust, which may be accelerated or created by a broiler unit if necessary.

Do not stir after adding the nutmeg, as more than half its value is as top decoration.

The rice in this recipe — one-quarter cup — seems very small, but it is entirely adequate.

TAPIOCA

Tapioca consists of balls of starch granules made from cassava root. It is made in two sizes, the large pearls and the small minute variety. The minute cooks more quickly, provides a smoother product and in general is so superior that the pearls are seldom seen in stores.

Tapioca is used as a thickener, and will be mentioned in some dessert recipes. It can also be used as the main ingredient of an excellent dessert. This can be made in several ways. The one given here is almost straight from the back of the box.

Fluffy Tapioca Pudding

2 cps	milk
3 Tb	minute tapioca
5 Tb	sugar
1	egg, separated
⅛ tsp	salt *(optional)*
¾ tsp	vanilla

Mix the tapioca, salt, 3 tablespoons of the sugar, milk and the egg yolk in a saucepan. Let stand 5 minutes. Beat the egg white, then gradually add 2 tablespoons of sugar, beating until it stands in soft peaks. Set aside.

Cook tapioca mixture to a full boil, stirring constantly. According to the basic recipe, this should take 6 to 8 minutes on medium heat, but it takes me 20. It is probably worth some risk of sticking to use high heat, at least until the mixture thickens.

Then take off the heat and add the white, stirring sufficiently to blend, and the vanilla. Allow to cool and thicken for 10 minutes. It can be eaten warm or cold, plain or with cream.

It is also possible to beat the white with the yolk, and cook them with the tapioca from the beginning. It simplifies preparation, but it is not as light and is in greater danger of being sticky if overcooked.

Tapioca goes well with fruit. You can pour it over sliced cooked peaches, or add one or two cups of them at the same time as the beaten white. Raw fruit may be sliced thin and cooked in the tapioca from the beginning, with enough extra sugar to keep it sweet.

GELATIN

Gelatin, which is described under THICK-ENERS, can be used to make a number of types of dessert, including jelly (or Jell-O), jelly with fruit in it, whipped or snow concoctions and Bavarian cream. Either plain or fruit flavored gelatin can be used for the first two, the others are better with plain only.

Gelatin sets and keeps set best if it is chilled. As a general guide, figure that plain gelatin will jell in a refrigerator in about 2 hours, but if it is mixed with fruit it will take 4. A large bowl will take longer than a small one, a mix containing only a little gelatin is slower than one that contains a higher proportion and acid in the mix may delay or even prevent setting.

Fig. 27-7. Gelatin mold

You can serve gelatin desserts in any kind of a serving dish, preferably the one in which it jelled, or standing on a platter or individual plate after being taken out of a mold. The mold may be a fancy one, with special shape, fluting or ornamentation; or it may be a casserole dish or a custard cup.

Plain Jelly. Gelatin can be bought unflavored, either in packages of envelopes that each contain one tablespoon (1/4 ounce) that will gel one pint of water, or in small bulk packages from which you measure it with a spoon. It is sometimes available in sheets, that weigh a little more than an ounce for each 100 square inches.

One sheet, 5 x 5 or 2-3/4 x 9 inches, equals about one tablespoon.

Gelatin is also sold ready mixed with a wide variety of flavors and sugar (and/or sugar substitutes), usually in 3-ounce packages, and most often under the trade name Jell-O. These will make an adequate dessert by simply being mixed with a cup of boiling water, then with a cup of cold water, and chilling until set, probably in 2 to 4 hours.

Differences in time depend on other ingredients in the mix, the temperature of your fridge and the hardness that you want. Quicker setting, perhaps in as little as 30 minutes, can be obtained by replacing the cup of cold water with 10 ice cubes, stirring until slightly thick, and then removing any unmelted ice.

You can make a simple jelly of the same type with unflavored gelatin, mixing with juice from fresh, frozen or canned fruit. The product may be superior or inferior to the package, depending on your choice of materials.

Jell-O and other plain gelatin-and-flavor desserts may be served plain, or with cream, milk or evaporated milk, sugar, fruit or berries, or plain cake. They become salads if they are put on lettuce.

Fruit in Jelly. A fruit flavored gelatin can be given more body and class by putting solid fruit in it. Almost any fruit or berry can be used except raw pineapple, which contains an enzyme that may prevent jelling.

It may or may not be important to get the fruit smoothly distributed through the jelly. It is of minimum importance if it will be served out of the dish in which it jells, of more interest if it is in a mold from which you will detach it and it can be very important if this molded jelly is to be served to guests.

Fruit varies in specific gravity. In general, raw fruit floats and cooked fruit sinks, but there are exceptions. If you put the fruit in fresh-mixed gelatin solution it will

Fig. 27-8. Fruit may move into a layer

go to either the top or the bottom, and will leave a layer of clear jelly above or below it. If you use both floaters and sinkers, you may have two fruit layers with clear in between.

You can get around this, if it matters. Chill the gelatin mix, the mold and the fruit. When the gelatin has thickened a little, to the consistency of raw egg white, put some in the bottom of the mold and smear or paint some on the walls of the mold. Put it back in the refrigerator. The thin layer should set enough to support fruit pieces quite quickly.

Then take everything out of the fridge, dip fruit pieces in gelatin and place them in the mold where you think they will look good. Spoon gelatin into the spaces between. Keep building. If it gets sloppy, you should chill everything again.

If you are using several different kinds and shapes of fruit and are artistically inclined, you can make a nice looking dessert. You can point it up with nuts, pieces of marshmallows or other oddments if you wish. This operation is described under SALADS, page 498.

Whipped. Gelatin can be whipped like white of egg when it has cooled and partially set so that it is of the consistency of the white of a Grade A egg — that is, it will make a low mound if put unsupported on a flat surface. If it is thinner than that it may still whip, but after you are through, it might settle back to a clear jelly.

It also can be beaten with white of egg, both giving it stability against bleeding and slumping, and increasing its volume.

Marshmallow pudding is a good example of whipped gelatin and egg.

Marshmallow Pudding *(6 to 8 servings)*

1½ Tb	gelatin powder
1 cup	sugar
½ cup	cold water
½ cup	boiling water
4	egg whites

Soak the gelatin in the cold water 5 minutes, then mix with the boiling water and stir until dissolved. Allow to cool.

Whip the egg whites with a rotary beater until stiff. Add the gelatin slowly while beating. Then add the sugar gradually, still whipping. Add the vanilla and whip until it thickens.

Chill 4 hours and serve plain, with cream or with custard sauce. The sauce may be beefed up with a little Cointreau or sherry, a teaspoon to a tablespoon to each cup.

Bavarian. There is a variety of pudding, and also some other dishes, called Bavarian cream. Most of them are composed of a beaten mixture of gelatin and egg lightly mixed with whipped cream, often with added flavor, fruit, berries, nuts or other appropriate substances. The egg yolks are sometimes omitted. In general, they are rich and light, and are sometimes referred to as cold souffles.

This is an area in which you can almost write your own recipe, as the variations in the published ones are endless. The following gives the general idea:

Bavarian Cream

1 Tb	plain gelatin *(1 envelope)*
½ cup	sugar
2	eggs, separated
1¼ cps	milk
½ pt	heavy or medium cream
½ tsp	vanilla

Mix the gelatin with half the sugar in a saucepan. Beat the yolks and the milk together thoroughly with a whisk or a rotary beater, and add to the gelatin and sugar. Stir over low heat for about 5 minutes, until the gelatin dissolves. Stir in the vanilla, then chill in the fridge until it starts to stiffen, about 20 to 40 minutes.

Beat the egg whites to soft peaks, gradually beat in the rest of the sugar. In another bowl, beat the cream until stiff. Stir the beaten whites into the gelatin, then fold in the cream.

Put in one big mold or in individual molds (you should have about 4 cups of Bavarian) and put in fridge until firm. Unmold, and serve with cream, custard or fruit sauce, or whatever appeals to you.

You can enrich this recipe further by using up to 4 egg yolks, or cut it down by omitting them entirely. You can use more sugar or less sugar to taste, or distribute the sugar differently among the three ingredients. The vanilla may be omitted or doubled; you can add 1/4 teaspoon of almond extract to it or put in 1/2 teaspoon of almond and omit the vanilla. Some or all of the milk can be replaced by fruit juice, coffee or sherry.

In any of these versions, Bavarian cream may be too much on the smooth-and-sweet side for some tastes. You can provide a change of texture by adding up to 3/4 of a cup of chopped hazel or cashew nuts, or make it an almost-Nesselrode pudding with a cup or more of cooked chopped chestnuts. A cup or more of sweetened berries or cut-up fruit can be folded in after the cream, but if you do this, use an extra teaspoon (1/3 envelope) of gelatin, to overcome interference with setting by the acid.

Or you can stick to the smooth cream, and line the mold with macaroons or lady fingers. The macaroons should be cut in strips unless they are very small. Lady fingers should be slightly stale.

ICE CREAM

Ice cream is a frozen dessert made with cream and/or milk, sugar and flavoring, or with a stirred custard. A substantial amount of air is usually included in the cheaper commercial varieties. Factory-made ice cream almost always contains small quantities of stabilizers to prevent or reduce crystallizing.

If an ice cream carton is returned to the freezer after removing part of its contents, the part that remains is likely to develop an undesirably waxy surface layer. Its formation can be prevented by fitting a layer of thin plastic wrap snugly over all exposed surfaces. Or it can be cut or scraped off before serving.

Ice cream can be bought in a very wide variety in both quality and flavor. At its best it is very very good, and at its worst it is still cold and refreshing. But there is still room for the home freezer, as its product is usually quite different from any that can be found in a store.

Home Made — Uncooked. Home made ice cream is a superb dessert or snack, but the best varieties require the use of a cranked ice cream freezer, which is a very specialized piece of kitchen or household equipment.

Ice cream can be made in a number of

Fig. 27-9. Ingredients for simple ice cream

different ways. They are difficult to classify because of confusion in the names used for them, and because there are many recipes that are partly one type and partly another.

A basic home variety, originally called Philadelphia ice cream, is excellent for immediate eating, but tends to crystallize badly during freezer storage.

Uncooked Ice Cream

1 qt   cream
1 cup sugar
1 tsp vanilla

The cream may be medium, light or half and half, depending on taste and budget. If medium, it can be beaten to soft peaks and the sugar beaten in. Any cream can be used as an unbeaten liquid, with sugar added to all of it and dissolved by stirring. Or you can heat one cup in a pan, dissolve the sugar in that, and then add it to the balance. Vanilla is added toward the end of mixing.

Whipping increases the bulk of ice cream substantially, perhaps by 30 per cent, and changes its texture.

This recipe can be juggled freely. A pint of medium cream plus a pint of milk is almost the same as a quart of light cream. Light cream cut with an equal quantity of milk is half and half. You can use more milk, or all milk, if you wish, moving from ice cream to milk sherbet. If you really like vanilla you can use up to a tablespoon of the extract with no harm. Sugar can be either decreased or increased according to taste.

Milk and cream should be as fresh as possible, to minimize a tendency toward fine-grained curdling during freezing and thawing.

It is important to remember that freezing reduces the intensity of practically all flavors, so for ice cream use 20 to 100 per cent extra sugar and flavoring, in comparison to a dessert to be served at room or refrigerator temperature. This applies also to fruit or berries that may be added.

The freezing process will be described after a review of some other types of ice cream mixes.

Adding Eggs. The next kind of ice cream is made from thin cream or whole milk enriched and stabilized with eggs or egg yolks, up to six to a quart. The eggs add richness and greatly reduce any tendency to separate or crystallize. They combine most smoothly if beaten only until whites and yolks are thoroughly blended.

If you wish to prevent the chalazia (lumpy strings of white) from appearing in the ice cream, you can put the beaten eggs through a sieve.

This enriched mix is sometimes called custard ice cream, but most people reserve the name for cooked mixtures.

Custard. In the home, custard ice cream is prepared from a cooked mixture of milk and eggs. At roadside stands it is a soft, super-smooth ice cream that is quite unlikely to contain an egg.

An ice cream custard is prepared in the same manner as a dessert custard, except that it is more likely to contain a thickener such as flour, cornstarch or gelatin. They are good insurance against separation, but they may take a little away from the distinctively home made quality of the ice cream.

A basic recipe, for use with a churn freezer, is:

Custard Ice Cream *(for 6 to 8 people)*

1	qt	milk *(or light cream)*
4		eggs *(or 8 yolks)*
1	cup	sugar
1	tsp	vanilla *(optional)*
2	Tb	cornstarch *(optional)*

This is made in the same manner as the Stirred Custard on Page 528 unless you use cornstarch. In that case, mix the cornstarch

with half the sugar, and add to the milk before mixing with the eggs. Mix in the balance of the sugar about 3 minutes after the cornstarch. This prevents excess sugar from slowing its thickening.

It is also possible to make the custard in the same manner but using only half the milk or cream, then mixing with the unheated other half when cooked. This produces faster cooling on the way to freezing.

Both ice and energy can be saved by thoroughly chilling the custard in the refrigerator before freezing it.

Chocolate. Next to vanilla, chocolate is the most popular single ice cream flavoring. It may be used instead of vanilla, or in addition to it, in any basic mix.

For standard strength, use 1-1/2 to 2 ounces of unsweetened chocolate to a quart of cream or milk. For a rich strong flavor, double the larger amount. Shave the chocolate and blend it with 1/2 cup of hot milk or water over low direct heat, or in a double boiler. It may be mixed with the other ingredients any time before freezing.

You may wish to add 2 to 4 tablespoons of sugar to the ounce of chocolate to offset its bitterness.

Fig. 27-10. Smoothing out some fruit

Three tablespoons of cocoa may be substituted for an ounce of chocolate. This is easy in a custard, where you can mix it with the sugar and allow it to dissolve during cooking. Otherwise, dissolve it like shaved chocolate, but you are likely to need twice as much liquid.

Chocolate Chip. Chocolate chip ice cream is the basic vanilla ice cream mix, plus tiny bits of semisweet chocolate, 3 to 6 ounces to the quart. Use a medium coarse grater for chocolate bars, or crush cookie-type chocolate chips with a rolling pin or a wooden potato masher. The chocolate must be cold to prevent it from flowing and sticking.

Coffee. Coffee ice cream can be made by adding 2 to 5 teaspoons of instant coffee to any basic ice cream. Coffee can also be added to chocolate ice cream, with the result called either coffee or mocha.

Powdered coffee should be thoroughly mixed with sugar, or dissolved thoroughly in half a cup or so of the mix, before stirring it, to prevent possible formation of non-dissolving lumps.

The quantity of coffee may be increased according to taste, but there is more danger of over-flavoring than there is with chocolate.

Fruit. Fruits, especially peaches, and berries, especially strawberries, make excellent ingredients for ice cream, as they supply pleasing flavor, color and texture, in addition to increasing the bulk. They may be used as a rough mashed pulp, a puree or strained juice. Sugar should be added until they are somewhat sweeter than would be desirable if they were served plain as a dessert.

Many cooks also add lemon juice, up to two tablespoons to a quart of fruit, to sharpen the taste against the loss that will occur in freezing. But this changes the natural flavor, usually to its disadvantage.

The quantity may vary widely, according to the availability and price of the fruit and the wishes of the cook. If fruit is naturally bland in flavor, has lost taste during storage or is canned, larger quantities may be needed than if it is top quality.

In general, a pint of mashed and sweetened fruit or puree will make a good combination with a quart of cream or custard. One to 1-1/2 quarts of whole fruit, plus a cup or more of sugar, should produce this amount, with peaches and apricots more likely to run over and strawberries under.

Mashing. For mashing, the fruit is peeled and pits are removed, and berries are hulled. They are washed first if they are dirty. Any hard, over-soft or discolored spots are cut out. If the flesh is hard or firm, cut it into small pieces; if it is soft you can either cut it up or leave it whole. Crush with a potato masher, the back of a very heavy spoon or any convenient blunt instrument against the sides and bottom of a bowl until the desired consistency is reached.

Fairly coarse pieces can be left if the ice cream is to be eaten soon after it is frozen, as they remain soft and tasty. But in zero storage they freeze hard, lose taste and become difficult to eat.

Puree. A puree may be made of fruits or berries by pushing them through a food mill, a sieve or a colander, or by grating them. The smaller the holes, the finer the product. Hard or tough parts will be left behind on the sieves, and they should be discarded rather than pushed through with extra pressure. The grater cuts most such particles into fine pieces, but lets some strings through.

A blender usually cuts up everything that is fed to it, the fineness depending largely on its speed and the time it works. As with many blender operations, you must be sure that the whole containerful is being treated, by pushing down repeatedly on the sides with some sort of wood or plastic tool. Otherwise, pieces of fruit may arch over the cutters and remain intact.

A puree retains the full flavor of the fruit,

and gives it to the ice cream. However, it does not provide the interesting variety in appearance, texture and taste offered by the shreds and pieces of mashed fruit. If it is made on a fine sieve it will hold back most berry seeds, an effect which may be considered desirable for raspberries and blackberries, but unnecessary or undesirable with good strawberries.

Sugar. Sugar is almost always mixed with fruit before adding it to ice cream. The sugar in the cream or custard just about takes care of that part of the mix, and has no surplus sweetness. Most fruit requires at least 3/4 of a cup of sugar to a quart of whole fruit; berries may get by with the same if very sweet, or need twice as much if they are really sour.

Peaches turn brown very quickly after peeling and cutting unless kept under water, or immediately protected with sugar and ascorbic acid, as described on page 590.

Juice. A mash or puree of fruit or berries may be hung in a bag of cloth — muslin is traditional for fruits, but several layers of cheesecloth will do — over a container. If mashing has been thorough, the juice will drain out leaving the pulp. The juice, usually with added sugar, is used to flavor the ice cream. It provides less color, flavor and interest than either mash or puree.

Fig. 27-11. Ice cream freezer

More fruit is needed as a substantial part of it is left in the cloth.

The increasingly high price of fruit and berries, and the general availability of bottled fruit juices and concentrates, has made home preparation of non-citrus fruit juices rather uncommon.

Mixing In. Fruit or fruit juice is often not added to ice cream until it is almost frozen, for two reasons.

The acid in fruit may curdle fluid milk and cream, a danger that is reduced by chilling and practically eliminated by partial freezing, Also, fruit has a lower freezing temperature than milk, and its anti-freeze properties greatly prolong the dull period of cranking before freezing starts. On the other hand, it is a nuisance to open the freezer, and the dasher may freeze in place while you do it.

In unstirred refrigerator tray mixtures, early adding of' the fruit may provide too much time for separation between various liquids and solids.

ICE CREAM FREEZER

A hand-cranked ice cream freezer is shown in Figure 27-11. An electric model is similar, except that the crank is replaced by a motor. This is a two-quart model, which will make about 1-1/2 quarts of ice cream, which should serve from 6 to 10 people, depending on their appetites.

Construction. The ice pail is usually wood. It must be watertight except for drain holes high in the sides. If it has not been used for some time, soak it in water overnight to close up leaks. The ice-salt mixture cannot chill the can properly unless its voids are filled with water.

Brackets on the top of the pail hold the cross frame and gear box, with a latch to provide for releasing them.

The gear box unit includes a crank and handle, a shaft and a set of gears which drive inner and outer sockets which rotate in opposite directions. The outer one turns the freezing can, the inner one the dasher.

The gears are usually run dry because of fear that any lubricant put on them might work its way down into the can along the dasher shaft. As a result there may be a great deal of friction and some annoying squeaking. If the freezer is left in a damp place they may rust, increasing friction and possibly producing flakes of rust.

The gear box usually has a cover which can be removed for inspection and cleaning of the gears. A wire brush will remove rust. You can lubricate them with very small risk of drip by rubbing cooking oil on them with a cloth, or using a solid lubricant such as water pump grease very sparingly.

The can is round, tall and is usually made of cast aluminum. It has a center bottom socket or extension that fits a round projection or socket in the bottom of the pail. The cover has a raised square at the center with a hole through it. The square meshes with the outer gear drive, and the dasher shaft goes through the hole. Can and cover are slotted so that they cannot turn separately, but the cover can be lifted off easily.

Operation. The procedure is to place the filled and covered can in the pail, fitting it into the bottom socket; pack the space between can and pail, with layers or a mixture of ice and salt, place and clamp the gear box and turn the handle in the right direction.

The salt forces the ice to melt. In melting it takes heat out of the can, causing the mixture in it to first chill and then freeze. The turning of the can stirs the ice-salt mixture and distributes the cold. The dasher blades remove the chilled and then frozen layer or film from the inner surface of the can as it forms. It mixes with the liquid to form a mush of steadily increasing thickness. When the combined work of scraping the can and stirring the mush becomes too great to permit normal turning of the crank, the ice cream is frozen.

Fig. 27-12. Ice crusher

The general program is simple, but there are details.

Ice. The ice should be rather fine in size. Coarse pieces melt and absorb heat slowly, prolonging the freezing operation. They may turn into positions where they jam against the can, causing hard turning. Longest dimension may be between 1/4 and one inch, but there is no lower limit in size except in your energy in reducing the ice.

It was formerly the custom to get a block of ice from the ice truck, or perhaps to cut it out of the pond, and either shave it with a special tool, or put it in a burlap bag and smash it with a heavy hammer. There is no ice truck now, but in winter you might gather snow, or chop ice from a swimming pool. Snow is mostly air, so a

Fig. 27-13. Freezer can and dasher, cutaway

surprisingly large volume of it is required.

The chances are that you will have to use ice cubes, 10 to 15 pounds of them. You can make them in trays and accumulate them in plastic bags in the freezer, or buy them. An ordinary ice cube weighs a bit less than an ounce, a filled tray 14 ounces. Unless you have a high powered ice grinder, your best method of reducing them to freezer size is to put them in a bag and pound them.

The bag should be burlap, or some other strong and expendable cloth. An old seed or animal feed bag is good. If you don't have a bag, wrap the ice in cloth, with enough overlap to stop its pieces from flying. Then pound it.

A sledgehammer with the handle held vertically, with short up and down strokes of moderate force, is excellent. With patience you can do the job with anything that is heavy and hard enough to break ice under cloth.

Salt. You should use coarse rock salt, of the type used to de-ice walks and driveways. You can use table salt if you must, but the cost is greater and results are poor, as it tends to wash down to the bottom of the pail rapidly. Don't use calcium chloride — it makes the mixture too cold and too quick-acting.

Various quantities and proportions of ice and salt are recommended by cookbooks and in freezer directions. The quantities vary with the space in the freezer, and with the temperatures of the room and ice cream mix. Increasing the proportion of salt presumably increases the speed of the freezing, but results of tests are confusing.

Anyhow, the recommended ratios of crushed ice to salt, on a weight basis, range from 6 to 1 to 24 to 1, the first figure being the ice. If you take a generous proportion of 8 to 1, have at least 10 pounds of ice (8 quarts, chipped) and 1-1/4 pounds (2-1/4 cups) of salt ready for a 2-quart freezer. It is safest to have at least a 50 per cent over-supply.

For a larger freezer, increase quantities about in proportion to capacity. That is, for a 3-quart freezer, expect to use 50 per cent more ice and salt.

Packing. Make sure the hole or holes high in the side of the pail are open. They are your protection against a rising tide of salt water that might overflow into the top of the can. Install the dasher in the can, pour in the mix (preferably chilled), put on the cover, place the can in the pail and center it, put on the cover and clamp on the gear box. Turn the handle to make sure that the can turns.

Put a layer of ice in the bucket around the can, about 3 inches deep. Press it down to a thickness of 2 inches with a wooden spoon or any suitable tool. Add a layer of salt to cover the ice. Turn the crank a couple of times to make sure you have not jammed the can by pressing in the ice.

Then add another layer of ice and one of salt in the same manner, and crank again. Build up the ice and salt in alternate layers until you have buried the can, except for the center of the cover. Adding a quart or two of cold salty water will speed up the action.

One or more additional layers of ice and salt are likely to be needed during freezing.

Cranking. Start cranking as soon as packing is complete. You can go slowly at first, 20 to 40 turns a minute. Freezing will start when the whole mixture is well chilled, causing a resistance that you will be able to feel. Then turn the handle faster, 60 turns a minute at first and finally 100, until it is very difficult to turn.

Cranking should be nearly continuous. If you get tired, or need time off to pack in more ice, ask for a volunteer.

The crank must be turned so that the can will revolve against the cutting edge of the dasher scrapers, Figure 27-13. This allows the scraper edges to cut a layer of frozen cream off the can on each revolution. If rotation were the other way, the scrapers would stir the liquid, but could not scrape and mix in the frozen material.

In a side cranked freezer, the crank usually moves away from you in the top part of its circle. The less convenient horizontal crank may go either way. You should check on this by inspecting the dasher and noting the correct direction for it, before putting on the cover.

The ice mixture shrinks during cranking, and supplies of both ice and salt should be available to build it up. It probably will not be necessary to cover the top after the first packing. Salt water from the melted ice should accumulate in the pail, and may rise high enough to spill out the drain holes. If the appearance of the floor is of any importance, it should be protected.

Finishing. When freezing is complete, remove any ice mixture that may be on the cover of the can or within an inch of it. Wipe the cover off carefully to make sure no ice or salt (specially salt) can fall into the can. Then take off the gear box and the cover. Grasp the dasher shaft and pull it up slowly, scraping the ice cream off it with a spoon, and finally placing it in a bowl. Enough ice cream will stick to it to make it interesting to scrape, particularly for children.

Storage. Replace the cover and put a cork in it, or plug or protect it in some positive way. Build up the ice-salt layers, or plain ice only, to the top of the pail, burying the can. Check the drain holes to make sure they are open, cover the freezer with cloth or newspapers and leave it until it is ready to serve. If the time is long, check the ice level every hour (or oftener in a warm room) and renew it as necessary.

Ice cream can be removed from the can to trays and put in deep freeze but there it will freeze very hard rapidly, and the pleasant home made softness will be lost.

Fig. 27-14. Scraping down the dasher

You can use an insulated container, for example one of the foam pails used for carrying ice cubes. Chill it in the deep freeze beforehand, put the ice cream in it, cover it, and return it to the freezer. This will provide safety from melting and entrance of salt, and hardening will be very slow.

ICES AND SHERBETS

These two words are often used for the same mixture. There is a simple distinction that can be made, but it is often ignored. An ice is a frozen sweetened fruit juice, or mashed or pureed fruit, which is generally diluted with water. A sherbet differs in having milk or cream added to the other

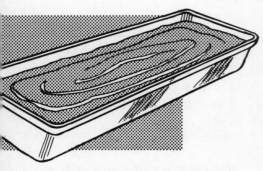

Fig. 27-15. Or make it in a freezer tray

ingredients. But you may have to call it a water ice or a milk sherbet to make the distinction absolutely clear.

While both of these are desserts, they can be served as appetizers or as side dishes also. For this purpose they may be made with a little less than the regular amount of sugar.

Best results are obtained by using a crank freezer, but you can make them in freezer trays. If you remember to stir them every 20 to 30 minutes, carefully scraping all frozen parts off the tray and then stirring vigorously, you can usually obtain passable results, although texture will probably be coarse. Those without milk are safer, as

milk and cream tend to separate if coarse crystals form.

Addition of gelatin stabilizes and smooths these mixtures, so that they may freeze satisfactorily in a tray with only one stirring. It also provides better keeping qualities, thickens liquid melting from them and is likely to reduce sharpness of flavor. Use up to one teaspoon per pint.

Ices. Ices are the simplest and lightest of the frozen desserts. They can be made from juices and concentrates such as lemon, lime, orange and grape that are likely to be in the kitchen and are available in every store. Synthetic mixtures for cold drinks may also be sweetened and frozen.

Use at normal strength or concentration for drinking, but with extra sugar. Or dilute with up to 1/3 water.

Ices tend to be harder than ice cream.

Sherbet. Sherbet can be almost as thin as an ice or just as rich as some of the thinner ice creams, or anything in between. It is easy, almost automatic, to make good sherbet if you have an ice cream freezer and don't mind preparing and cranking it. But when you freeze it in trays, results are not so certain, and you may have to choose between two disadvantages.

If you use just the simple materials — fruit, milk and sugar — you get clear flavor and a thin melt-down liquid that proves you didn't get it at the store. But the texture will be more or less rough, depending on just what is in it, how cold the freezer and how often you remember to stir it.

With gelatin you get relative freedom from crystals, at the price of a slightly blurred flavor and a smoothness that might be considered excessive.

MOUSSE

A mousse is a simple but rich mixture that can be served as ice cream when frozen, or as a pudding when chilled or at room temperature. It usually does not crystallize nor acquire a rough texture during

By permission from "American Cooking for Foreign lands" by Maj-Greth Wegener

Fig. 27-16. Baked Alaska

freezing, even when not stirred. It may separate or weep a little when allowed to stand unfrozen, or while thawing.

All the recipes include whipped cream. This is one of the uses where heavy whipping cream may be a little better than medium cream, as it is more secure or perhaps entirely secure against crystallizing as it freezes, and it has less tendency to weep.

Whipped evaporated milk may be used if flavoring is strong enough to disguise its taste. There may be some loss in stability.

The whipped cream is folded into a mixture that gives body and flavor. Preferably this is white of egg, sugar and flavoring. Whole eggs may be used, with loss in bulk and lightness, and with changes in color and flavor.

Egg may be partly or wholly replaced by gelatin, dissolved in water, coffee or fruit juice. A teaspoon of gelatin with a cup of liquid is equivalent to 2 egg whites. See page 536 for method of whipping gelatin.

Egg white mixtures tend to deteriorate during refrigerator storage, but gelatin improves for several days if protected from drying.

Vanilla Mousse *(4 or 5 cups)*

2	egg whites
½ cup	sugar, preferably fine
1 pt	heavy or medium cream
½ tsp	vanilla

Beat the egg whites until stiff, add and beat in half the sugar. Beat the cream until it is thick but not stiff, then beat in the rest of the sugar and the vanilla. Fold the two together. For ice cream, put in refrigerator trays or fancy molds, and put in the freezer for a few hours. Dip the tray or mold briefly in warm water to loosen it for unmolding or serving.

As a pudding, it may be served immediately, or after chilling for several hours. It is sometimes eaten plain, but is better with cream (liquid or whipped), custard sauce or fresh or stewed fruit. It can be used as a sauce as is, or after softening by stirring in some cream or other liquid.

Variations. If you put in a tablespoon of sherry and most of a half cup of finely crushed dried macaroons (the almond kind) and freeze it in little paper cups with a bit of the crushed macaroon sprinkled on top, you have Biscuit Tortoni.

For coffee mousse, increase the sugar to 3/4 of a cup and stir in 2 tablespoons of instant coffee dissolved in 1/4 cup of hot water, then cool. For chestnut, put in 1/2 cup of chopped chestnuts or marrons. A cup of small pieces of crisp baked meringue kisses makes it Chantilly mousse. It is also adapted to chocolate flavor, and to mixing with puree of almost any fruit or berry.

For a gelatin mix, replace the egg whites with one teaspoon of gelatin dissolved in a cup of liquid — water, coffee or fruit juice, for example — with whatever extra sugar the flavoring may require. Flavor and texture will be inferior for the first day, at least equal the second day and probably superior from then on. There is less likelihood of separation or weeping when thawing.

BAKED ALASKA

This dessert is valued chiefly for its surprise effect, serving ice cream out of a hot oven. But it is also a pleasing combination of materials, enhanced by temperature differences. It relies for success on the insulating power of the fine air bubbles in meringue.

Baked Alaska *(6 or 8 portions)*

1	small loaf or single-layer cake
1 qt	ice cream *(usually vanilla)*
3	egg whites, room temperature
⅔ cup	sugar

Place the cake layer on a large serving platter, and cover it with the ice cream. Put in the freezing compartment until just before serving. Beat the egg whites until fluffy, then add sugar gradually, continuing to beat until stiff and shiny.

Cover the ice cream and cake completely with this meringue, and put in a very hot oven, 475° F, for 2 or 3 minutes, until the top turns golden brown. Serve immediately.

FRUIT

Raw — Whole. There are those who maintain that fresh fruit is the best dessert. It is unquestionable that top quality raw fresh fruit equals or surpasses anything that a chef can prepare. But such fruit is only rarely obtainable.

Our generation has access to a previously unheard of variety of fruit. But the largest part of it is of varieties selected for keeping and shipping qualities rather than flavor and tenderness, that have been picked before proper ripening to avoid spoilage on the way to the consumer. The fruit has probably spent a long time in transit and storage, and still may not have reached the best condition still possible for it by the time it is eaten.

It is a rare home that has a good assortment of fruit in prime condition on its own trees ready to be picked. It is also unusual to be able to buy an assortment of attractive, sweet fruit in the ·market just when you need it. Often, substandard fruit may be bought in advance and ripened, for serving during the day or three that it is at its prime.

A bowl of fresh fruit, pointed up with a few nuts and perhaps discreetly backed up

Fig. 27-17. Raw fruit for dessert

by some open saucers of sugar, makes a nice looking dessert. But it is often not of a good enough quality to live up to its appearance and provide diners with a satisfying finish to their meal.

Fruit is frequently accompanied by a platter of cheese, allowing the diners to eat either one, or both.

Raw — Sliced. Sliced raw fruit or whole berries, usually served with sugar and (except for apple and pineapple) cream, is excellent breakfast dish, snack or dessert. They may be equally acceptable when cut immediately before serving, or sliced hours in advance and sugared in order to draw out the juice.

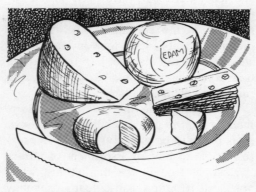

Fig. 27-18. Cheese may be dessert

But advance sugaring should be light, as there are great differences in liking for sugar, and it is easier to add it while eating than to take it away. A drawback is browning of surfaces of cut apples, peaches and some other fruits.

Cream is usually sweet, and may be anything from half and half to a heavy whipping cream. If you serve a pitcher of medium cream and one of milk you will enable most people to have what they want, taking it either straight or mixed.

Canned. Commercially canned fruit has a good standard of quality, excellent keeping characteristics and wide availability. It is likely to be accepted as an occasional simple dessert on any but the most sophisticated levels of eating, and may be frequently enjoyed by many families. Home-canned fruit is usually much better in taste, and is likely to be highly valued as dessert by a family and its guests.

Frozen. Frozen fruit is usually better flavored than canned, is available in not quite so extensive variety and has good keeping quality as long as the freezer works. However, it is often in a twilight zone between being raw and cooked, defrosting is a nuisance and use as a simple dessert seems to be more limited. This is true of both commercial and home products.

Stewed. In principle, fresh stewed fruits and berries differ little from their canned and frozen counterparts. But they are the best in freshness and flavor, and they usually represent some timely triumph in raising or finding and picking the berries, in getting a fruit tree to bear usefully in spite of insects, fungi and birds, or perhaps just striking a shrewd bargain with an overstocked produce man.

It is regrettable that recipes for preparing them have practically vanished from the modern cookbook. Many people are still able to get fresh berries at no cost or little cost, either picking in their gardens, on wild land or in pick-your-own farms where the price is low. A trip to the country may result in a car full of apples or peaches at prices that are only a fraction of home market costs.

It used to be that berries and fruit were stewed for eating in the same manner as for canning. But complications like cold packing and packing in syrup have destroyed this old relationship, so stewing (or boiling or poaching if you prefer) berries and fruit for dessert is a project that must stand on its own feet. Except: what you don't eat, you can freeze or can.

Cooking fruit brings out or accentuates both its flavor and its acidity. Berries that are just slightly tart or even bland when raw are likely to be unpleasantly acid if cooked without sugar.

The rule of thumb for stewing berries is to add 3/4 of a cup of sugar for each quart, but if you have a sweet tooth one cup is likely to be better. Start with about 1/4 cup less for fruit. Taste while cooking, and add sugar to taste. But of course you can't take sugar out. If you have more of the same fruit you can cook up another batch with less sugar or none, and mix them.

You may mix sugar with berries or sliced fruit several hours in advance, and cook them in their own juice. Since this might cause some loss of flavor, it may be better to start with enough water to cover the bottom of the pan, say 1/4 cup to the quart of fruit, add the berries and sugar, cover the pan and cook over low heat, checking against sticking and scorching several times in the first few minutes.

Cooking time may be as little as 5 minutes, or as long as 20. Usually, 10 or 12 is about right. The berries should be tender and they may be limp, and juice should be abundant and tasty.

Blueberries hold their shape very well when stewed, strawberries may almost lose theirs, and other berries are intermediate. Limpness, when it occurs, is usually more than offset by excellent flavor. Fruit usually holds its shape well, unless it is overcooked. Overcooking may be accidental, or deliberate in order to make a sauce.

Unless you want a sauce in which the individual berries or slices are indistinguishable, it is important that sugar be present as soon as cooking begins. Water will go through cell membranes toward the most concentrated solution, as discussed under OSMOSIS. This process will tend to cause fruit cells to absorb too much water, swell and burst, disintegrating the fruit, unless the sugar in the cells is balanced by sugar in the cooking water.

Stewed fruit is best served plain, a saucer for each person at the table, and a bowl with a ladle for seconds. You can add ladyfingers or pound cake, on the side or in the saucer under the berries. Whipped cream is sometimes a welcome addition.

Applesauce (Apple Sauce). Any stewed fruit served as a dessert or a side dish is called a sauce in some parts of the country. Here we call it that only if it has been cooked or processed so that the individual pieces are softened and blurred so that they cannot be clearly distinguished from the syrup around them. There are

Fig. 27-19. A roadside bargain

coarse or home style sauces in which you can tell that there are separate pieces, and puree or strained ones that have a smooth, even consistency.

Apple sauce, equally well known as applesauce, is the most popular of the fruit sauces. Most of it is purchased in cans and jars and it is usually good. But it has a special fine flavor when made at home.

You can make sauce from any cooking apple. A few varieties, mostly summer like the Greening, are particularly good for sauce because they tend to cook down to a mush, which is just what you want.

There are almost complete differences of opinion about the way in which apples should be prepared. Your cookbook may tell you to just quarter them, to core and slice but not peel or to core, peel and slice.

The seeds and skin provide extra flavor or at least a difference in flavor, but they are a nuisance during processing. The skins are almost certain to carry some traces of undesirable insecticides, but they do supply flavor which you can't get in any other way.

Don't use apples or parts of apples that give evidence of spoiling by brown color, unnatural softness or both. Rot sometimes (although not always) causes off flavors strong enough so that part of one apple might spoil a whole batch.

Apples are usually measured by the pound, as they do not fit well into quart baskets. In comparing recipes with berries, you can assume that 1-1/2 pounds of apples will make about a quart of cut pieces.

Applesauce

2	lbs	tart apples
½	cup	sugar, or to taste
1	cup	water
⅛	tsp	salt *(optional)*
1	tsp	lemon juice *(optional)*
1	tsp	butter *(optional)*
⅛	tsp	cinnamon *(optional)*

Cut the apples down through the core into 4 to 8 pieces, cut out the sections of core and stem, peel, and cut the pieces into slices about 1/8 inch thick. Put them in a pan with the water, sugar and salt, stir them together, cover tightly and cook with occasional stirring until the apples are mushy. Time will vary widely with the apple variety, from less than 5 to more than 20 minutes.

Applesauce can be served in just the condition they come out of the pan, still showing more or less of the original shape of the pieces, and with (usually) some thick but separate juice. If you stir and beat them vigorously with a big spoon, you get a pleasantly lumpy fluid, showing little or none of the original pieces.

You can reduce them to a really smooth sauce by pressing them through a food mill or a colandar or coarse sieve, or by beating them in a blender.

Or you can slice up whole apples, including skins and cores. Cook them in the same way, but without the sugar. Put the product through a coarse sieve with considerable stirring, and repeated taking out and discarding of skins and seeds. Then mix the sugar into the sauce, let it stand a few minutes to dissolve, and stir again.

Still another option is to remove the cores but leave the skins, slice and cook the apples with the sugar, and use an electric blender for sauce that includes skins.

Lemon juice is recommended only if the flavor of the apple sauce seems flat. If the juice makes it too acid, add more sugar.

The value of the butter is questionable, but it can do no harm. The cinnamon pleases most people but not all. It is usually dusted over the top of the sauce in the serving dish.

Applesauce is usually eaten plain as a side dish (vegetable?) with pork, as dessert, as a spread on bread and as a breakfast fruit. When a dessert, it may qualify for a whipped cream topping.

BAKED APPLES

There are at least two ways to bake almost-whole apples, and many methods to bake them after slicing and other preparation. Any good cooking apples can be used.

Plain. The simplest method is to take the cores out with a rotary corer, stand the apples with stem ends up in very shallow water in a wide casserole or utility dish, and cook in a 350° F oven until tender enough to be pierced easily with a toothpick, which will probably be 45 to 60 minutes.

Serve plain, with cream and sugar on the side. They are likely to be quite sour.

Stuffed. These baked apples may be stuffed, by filling the core hole with white or brown sugar, with sugar and raisins or even with sausage meat. It is helpful if you can stop the corer just before it cuts through the bottom of the apple, and twist the core out, as otherwise some types of stuffing will tend to leak out the bottom.

If cores won't pull out naturally, you can cut them loose from the side with a knife. The knife slit is not apt to cause trouble, and without it it is quite easy to break an apple in half as you struggle to pull out part of a core.

You can glaze baked apples by putting sugar on top, or by standing them in a sugar syrup instead of plain water, and basting them with it as they cook.

Scalloped. Scalloping apples means to slice them and bake them in a dish. A recipe is:

Scalloped Apples

2 lbs	cooking apples
¾ cup	sugar
3 Tb	butter
½ tsp	cinnamon

Core and peel the apples, and slice them about 1/4 inch thick. Arrange the slices in layers in a 2-quart baking dish or casserole, sugaring each layer and dotting it with butter. The top layer gets a dusting of cinnamon also.

Cover the casserole, and cook at 350° F for 30 to 40 minutes, or until tender. Serve as is, or with plain or whipped cream.

Brown Betty. This fine dessert is usually made with apples, but it is also successful when featuring peaches, apricots or even prunes. A typical recipe is:

Apple Brown Betty *(for 6 people)*

4 cps	peeled sliced apples
2 cps	stale bread crumbs
½ cup	sugar *(or ¾ cup brown sugar)*
¼ cup	melted butter
¼ cup	hot water *(or cider)*
½ tsp	cinnamon
¼ cup	raisins *(optional)*
1 Tb	lemon juice *(optional)*
¼ tsp	salt *(optional)*

The apples as always, should be firm, tart and free of rot. If there is to be any delay between slicing and use, park them in water to which a little lemon juice or ascorbic acid has been added. The crumbs may be bought in a package, or made from stale or otherwise dried bread that has been toasted, preferably light or medium brown.

Seasoning is adjusted to taste. Lemon juice may be omitted or even increased, according to the acidity of the apples and your liking for lemon. If you like raisins, put them in with the apples. Spice and salt may be mixed with the sugar, or sprinkled on top. The cinnamon may be replaced with 1/4 teaspoon each of powdered nutmeg and cloves.

Sprinkle the butter over the crumbs, mixing it in lightly. Use 1/3 of the crumbs to make a layer in the bottom of the dish, spread half the apples over them, then half the sugar, another third of the crumbs, and the rest of the apples, sugar and all the remaining crumbs on top.

Cover the dish, bake in a preheated moderately hot (400° F) oven for 30 minutes. Remove cover, continue baking until the top is brown and crusty and the apples are easily pierced with a toothpick, maybe 10 minutes more.

Serve hot, warm or at room temperature with cream or whipped cream.

For peach, apricot or plum brown betty, follow this recipe but use only half the quantity of fruit. Raw fruit is preferable, but drained canned or a frozen product may be used.

Crunch. This is the next in a series that takes us by easy stages from plain or dressed-up fruit to cake-with-fruit combinations. It is basically the same arrangement of sliced apples (or other fruit) as in dish-baked apples, but the sugar is included in a topping, instead of being mixed with the fruit.

Apple Crunch *(5 servings)*

4 cps	apple slices *(about 1½ lbs apples)*
⅔ cup	flour
¾ cup	sugar *(or 1 cup brown sugar)*
⅓ cup	butter
1 tsp	lemon juice *(optional)*
½ tsp	cinnamon *(optional)*

Stir flour, sugar and any spice together in mixing bowl, add butter and cut together with a pastry blender or two knives (as described for pie crust, page 000) until it is all crumbly in texture.

Pare and core apples, slice them 1/4 inch or thinner, and place in a 1-1/2 quart baking dish (about 10 by 6 inches) or a 2-quart casserole, making one layer with leveled top. If they are flat-tasting, sprinkle them with lemon juice. Cover with the flour-sugar-butter mixture.

Fig. 27-20. Loosening a core

Bake in a preheated moderate (375° F) oven for 20 or 30 minutes, until apples are tender and top is golden brown. If the top browns before the apples are done, continue to cook with a cover or foil over the dish. If the top is pale when the apples are cooked, put it under the broiler until it colors. This may take only a few seconds, and you should be alert to pull it out as soon as ready, as crumb toppings burn very easily.

Serve (preferably hot) plain, with cream or whipped cream, or with any sauce you like.

Other fruit — peaches, apricots, plums or even strawberries — may be substituted for the apples. They may be either raw, or cooked and drained. The proportion of fruit may be increased if desired.

FRUIT WITH CAKE

There are a number of desserts which involve baking fruit with or in cake, or occasionally with muffin or biscuit dough. There is a general lack of agreement among cookbooks and among people in different areas as to the meaning of their names.

Pandowdy or upside-down cake usually consists of a layer of cake cooked on top of a layer of fruit or berries. Cottage pudding is usually plain cake served with a sauce, but some fruit may be cooked in it.

A cobbler may be a pandowdy with a tablespoon of flour mixed with the fruit, or a deep dish pie in which biscuit is used instead of pie crust. The top of the filling may be only partly covered.

Dumplings are made up of single pieces or small piles of fruit, with biscuit or pastry folded completely around them. Fritters are made by encasing the fruit in soft dough and frying, usually in deep fat.

Shortcakes are usually a combination of cake or biscuit with raw, sugared fruit or berries and whipped cream.

Pandowdy (Upside-Down Cake). Pandowdy consists of a bottom layer of fruit and a top layer of cake, or less frequently, muffin or biscuit. It is often called upside-down cake, but some people contend that this name really applies only if the fruit is pineapple. Apple is the fruit most often used, but peaches, apricots, plums, berries and of course pineapple are all satisfactory.

The cake part is usually a one-egg cake, cottage pudding or a plain muffin recipe. The problem is that this is more cake than you need for an ordinary one-meal size pandowdy, particularly as the average recipe is stingy with the fruit. These recipes cannot be made in fractions very well, as an egg is a nuisance to divide in half, or into any fractions.

The best procedure is to make a full recipe for one-egg cake, page 000, use 1/2 or 3/4 of it in the pudding and make cup cakes with the rest. For the fruit part we will use apples for a sample, as follows:

Apple Pandowdy *(5 to 6 servings)*

2 lbs	cooking apples *(about 5 cps of slices)*
½ cup	sugar *(or ¾ cup of brown sugar)*
¼ tsp	nutmeg or cinnamon
¼ tsp	salt *(optional)*
1	one-egg batter, page 434

Preheat oven to moderate temperature, 350° F. Butter or grease a shallow baking or utility pan, 8 x 8 or 7 x 11 x 2, or equivalent.

It is safest to pare the apples, but if the skins seem tender you can leave them on. It is traditional with this dessert to slice the apples very thin, to cut them into fine strips, or put them through a coarse grater. If you use the skins, arrange the slicing or grating to cut them small, not in strips.

Fine cutting has the advantage of making it easy to smooth off the upper surface so that the cake batter added to it can have an even thickness.

Pack the apple slices or strips smoothly into the pan, scatter the salt and then the sugar over them, and put the pan in the oven for 10 minutes. This will start the cooking, and give you time to mix the cake batter if you are experienced, or if you

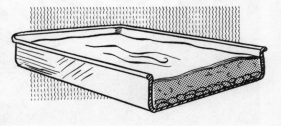

Fig. 27-21. Pandowdy

have measured out the ingredients ahead of time. But don't mix the batter until you are ready to use it, as the baking powder starts to work as soon as it touches liquid.

Spread batter over the apples, all of it if you want a thick cake, part of it if you would rather emphasize the apples. Bake 30 to 35 minutes, or until a toothpick inserted in the cake comes out clean. Cup cakes, if any, will bake a little more quickly.

Allow to cool on a cake rack for a few minutes, then loosen the sides from the pan with a knife, and invert onto a serving plate. Or you can cut and serve it directly from the pan, inverting each slice as you put it on the plate.

Pandowdy may be served plain, with whipped cream or with vanilla or other sauce. It is best when it is hot, but still good when it is cold.

Pandowdy may be made with any fruit, raw or cooked, with peaches, apricots and pineapple being popular, but rating below apple. If the fruit is cooked (usually canned) you omit the precooking, and if it is in large pieces, such as peach halves or pineapple slices, you use only a single layer of them.

The amount of sugar can be increased if the fruit is particularly sour, or if you like it sweet. Sugar can be decreased with naturally sweet fruit, and is sometimes omitted with canned fruit. You can substitute brown sugar of any shade for the white sugar, using 30 to 50 per cent more.

Dutch Apple Cake. For Dutch apple cake, you prepare the same cake mix (but usually not muffin) as for pandowdy, spread it in a large shallow buttered pan, 8 x 8 or 7 x 11-inch. Pare and core the apples, cut them into eighths, and press them lightly into the surface of the dough, core side down. Sprinkle with sugar and cinnamon mixed, and bake at about 375° until both the apples and the cake test done, about 30 minutes.

Remove from pan to a cake rack to cool slightly, or serve directly onto plates. Eat it warm or hot, plain or with any sauce. Hard sauce or lemon sauce is usually recommended.

Grunt. The main part of this dish is the same as pandowdy, except that the fruit or berries are usually mixed with the dough, instead of being placed in a separate layer. But they sometimes settle into a bottom layer anyhow.

There is also a topping, which may be:

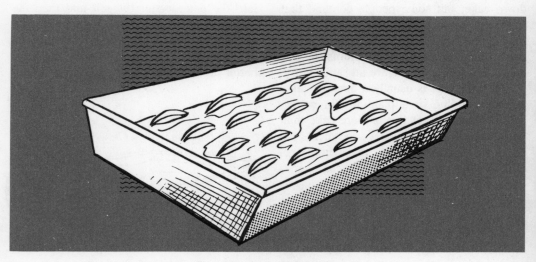

Fig. 27-22. Dutch apple cake

Topping for Grunt

½ cup brown sugar, packed
1½ Tb flour
3 Tb firm butter
½ tsp cinnamon

Put these ingredients into a 1-quart bowl, and mix by cutting in with a pastry blender or a pair of knives until crumbly, with pieces the size of small peas. Sprinkle over the cake before putting it in the oven.

Cobbler. For one type of cobbler, make in the same way as pandowdy, except that you mix a tablespoon of flour with the sugar, and stir this in with the apples instead of sprinkling it on top. Minute tapioca may be substituted for the flour. If you use corn starch, mix it separately with the apples, and sprinkle the sugar on top as with pandowdy.

For a right-side-up cobbler, make 1/2 the recipe for sweetened (shortcake) biscuit dough, below, roll it out to be about 18 inches across and more or less round. Put it in a greased 8 x 8 or 7 x 11-inch utility dish, or some similar pan, smooth it into the corners and against the sides, and let the surplus hang out.

This dough may be sticky and very difficut to roll. Sprinkle it liberally with flour while you work.

It may be easier to spread it into shape by patting and pressing it with your hands, instead of with a rolling pin. Coat them with oil and/or flour.

Prepare any fruit pie filling, heat it separately, spread it in the pan, fold in the rest of the dough. It does not matter whether it meets or not, as cobblers often have part of the filling exposed. Bake for about 1/2 hour in a preheated hot (425°) oven.

Or you can put the hot filling in the pan first, roll the dough just enough to cover the top, and bake.

Shortcake. Shortcake is usually a sponge cake or biscuit in two layers, with crushed berries or fruit between them, and crushed, sliced or whole berries or fruit on top, served with plain or whipped cream on top and/or on the side. It should be one of the finest American desserts, but frequently suffers from preparation with too little fruit and too much cake. This mistake, or perhaps misplaced economy, is more serious with biscuit than with cake.

For a big, old fashioned strawberry shortcake to serve 6 to 12 people, try:

By permission from "American Cooking for Foreign Lands" by Maj-Greth Wegener

Fig. 27-23. Strawberry shortcake

Strawberry Shortcake

Biscuit

2	cps	flour
⅓	cup	vegetable shortening
2	Tb	sugar
1	cup	milk
4	tsp	baking powder
1	tsp	salt *(optional)*

Berries and Cream

2	qts	strawberries
½	cup	sugar *(or more)*
1½	cps	medium or heavy cream
1	Tb	sugar

Fig. 27-24. Taking out a fritter

Sift together flour, sugar, baking powder and salt, then cut in shortening with two knives or a pastry blender until all the flour is taken up into a crumbly mixture. Mix in milk quickly, stirring as little as possible.

Spread batter in two round baking pans, 8 inches in diameter. Greasing is not necessary, but you may butter them for flavor. This batter is soft, sticky and difficult to smooth. Your hand, rubbed with grease and then flour, is a satisfactory tool for flattening it.

Dot a little butter on top and bake in a hot oven, 450° F, for 12 to 15 minutes until a test toothpick comes out clean. Take out of the oven, and allow to cool for a few minutes.

Wash the berries if they are dirty, remove their hulls and set aside a few of the best looking ones for decoration. Slice most of the remaining berries or cut them into chunks. If some of them are small and soft, you can leave them whole. If any are hard, cut them into very fine pieces, or mash them coarsely.

Stir in the 1/2 cup of sugar, and allow them to stand for a few minutes to become juicy.

Whip the cream until it is soft, and beat in the tablespoon of sugar. Shortcake looks and tastes best if the whipped cream is a little sloppy, rather than beaten stiff.

Turn one of the biscuit-cakes upside down on a platter, put about half the cut or mashed berries on it, add the other cake right side up, and spread on the rest of the berries. You may either pile the whipped cream on top, or put it in a bowl with a spoon for self service. If there will be a delay in serving (avoid this if possible) the cream should be kept separate.

The whole berries should be put on top or alongside, wherever they look best. If the cream is on the cake, some of these berries should be on top of it.

If you don't have enough strawberries, you can get by with one quart, but the result won't be as fine or rich. It would be better to use one biscuit only, cutting it either into two layers or two half-rounds. Or you could cook only half of the biscuit recipe, but finding proper size pans (30 or 35 square inches each) might be difficult.

Cutting a single biscuit in half horizontally to make two layers is a delicate job. But mistakes will be well covered by strawberries.

You may also bake the batter as a number of separate biscuits, which you slice horizontally and fix with berries for individual servings.

The biscuit may be replaced with sponge cake, preferably the recipe given on page 436, baked in two 9-inch pans. But you can use bought cake, either in large rounds or in individual cakes with hollow tops.

Ripe peaches can be substituted for the strawberries, with excellent results. They may be fresh, or freshly thawed frozen ones, with canned freestones as a third choice. Handle them in the same manner as berries.

FRITTERS

Fritters are fried delicacies made of soft dough which surrounds or is mixed with other food. Most of them are sweetened, contain fruit and are used for dessert. Others contain corn or other vegetables, or occasionally meat, with the corn being the most popular.

There is the usual wide variation between different recipes for fritters. A middle-of-the-road recipe for the batter is:

Fritter Batter

1	cup	flour, sifted
1	tsp	baking powder
1		egg *(2 eggs optional)*
2	tsp	melted butter
½	cup	milk
½	tsp	salt *(optional)*

for dessert fritters only, add

3	Tb	sugar

Mix the flour with the other dry ingredients. Beat the egg thoroughly, stir in the milk and butter, and the flour mixture, and stir or beat until smooth, but no longer.

A test for a good mixture is to pour some slowly off the side of a large spoon. It should drop in successive long triangular globs. If it runs smoothly it is thin and

should have a little more flour, if it falls in irregular lumps, it is too thick and you should add milk, a teaspoon at a time.

Some cooks separate the egg, mix in the yolk at the beginning, and fold in the stiffly beaten white just before frying.

Fruit. Fruit fritters may be of either the mixed or the coated type.

To mix, you take about a cup of grated cooking apples, or of diced peaches, apricots or bananas, or 1/2 cup of blueberries, mix with the batter, and fry. The smaller quantity of blueberries is to reduce difficulty with the mix falling apart while cooking, as the batter clings poorly to them. They are usually shallow-fried.

For coating, you cut the same fruit into thick slices or coarse pieces, dip and roll them in the batter until they are thoroughly covered, then cook.

Frying. For deep frying the fat should be 360° F and should not be allowed to go below 350. Drop mixed batter a heaping teaspoon at a time, coated pieces one by one. Try to get about 5 frying at a time. More might cool the grease too much.

Fritters float, so you don't need a basket. Turn them in about 2 minutes, or when they are brown on the underside. Total cooking time should be 4 or 5 minutes, to cook them through and get a golden brown color.

When done, lift out with slotted spoon onto absorbent paper and let them drain and absorb for a minute. You can sprinkle them with powdered sugar at this point, or leave them plain. Serve hot like pancakes, with syrup.

For pan frying, have the skillet medium hot, about 350°. If grease is about 1/2 inch deep the process is about the same as deep frying. If you use just a film of grease (or preferably, butter), the batter should be thin enough so they will spread a bit on the pan. Use lower heat, about 300°, and cook 3 or 4 minutes, or until browned, on each side.

28

CANDY

CANDY

A great many different kinds of candy can be made in the home, including fudge, taffy, peanut brittle, fondant and even dipped chocolates. However, only fudge seems to be made frequently at present, and it will be the only one considered in this discussion. Recipes for most of the others are in many general cookbooks.

An extensive discussion of home candy-making, full of details for both amateur and specialist, will be found in the CANDY COOKBOOK by J. H. Gros.

Fudge. Fudge is a candy composed of soft, finely crystallized sugar with flavoring. The flavoring is usually chocolate, but may be maple or molasses. Nuts are often included.

The fine crystallization is obtained by cooking granulated sugar (or, occasionally, brown or maple sugar) with water or milk, and preferably with a stabilizer such as corn syrup, to the soft ball stage, at a boiling temperature of about 234° F. The liquid is cooled undisturbed until lukewarm, then beaten vigorously and poured into a buttered pan.

The problems to be solved are to reach but not pass the correct temperature while cooking, and to prevent development of coarse sugar crystals which would give it a sandy texture.

Crystallization. A hot dense (supersaturated) solution of sugar will usually cool without crystallizing if it is not disturbed, and if it is not in contact with sugar crystals. But if it is stirred the whole mass will tend to crystallize.

It is important to most consumers that the crystals in fudge be so small that they are not noticeable, so that the candy has a smooth feeling in the mouth. They must be small not only when the candy is made, but also through any period of time until it is eaten.

Since the amount of sugar is limited, increasing the number of crystals will decrease their size. Vigorous stirring or beating has this effect. For best results, beating should not be started until the mix has cooled to lukewarm, about 110 or even 105° F, when it has become unstable so that thousands (or perhaps millions) of crystals will form at almost the same time. If it is allowed to cool much below this point, it will become too thick for efficient stirring.

Reasonably smooth fudge can be made with just sugar, water and flavoring. But it is not quite stable, and over a period of days or weeks the larger crystals will grow by absorbing sugar from smaller ones, until an originally smooth candy becomes quite sandy. Addition of a small quantity of stabilizer will usually give a smoother product, and will keep it that way.

Stabilizers. There are a number of substances that interfere with the crystallization of sugar. In proper quantities they can keep crystals small during cooling and stirring, and prevent them from growing bigger afterward. These include corn syrup, butter (or cream) and cream of tartar.

Corn syrup consists chiefly of glucose (dextrose). This sugar seldom crystallizes, and it interferes with the building of ordinary (sucrose) sugar crystals. Its presence in the fudge mixture delays crystallization well into the cooling stage, and limits the growth rate and therefore the size of the crystals when they do form. It makes fudge smoother, and will compensate for some mistakes in cooking and beating.

However, if you use too much corn syrup, the candy will either not crystallize at all, or will require very long and tiresome beating (say 30 minutes instead of 5).

The effect of this syrup continues after cooling and during storage, so that candy that includes a proper proportion of it should not turn sandy.

But some people prefer the slightly rough texture of plain fudge to the smoothness of the stabilized variety. And candy that includes much of the syrup may have a tendency to be slightly viscous and sticky. For these reasons, the amount of it in the mix should be carefully limited.

Cream of tartar causes part of the sugar to turn into crystal-retarding invert sugar. The proper quantity varies with the hardness of the water you use, and with cooking

and beating time, and in any case is so small (perhaps 1/40 of a teaspoon to a cup of sugar) that it is difficult to measure. Corn syrup is safer and easier to use.

Butter and cream are only partly effective as stabilizers, but soften the candy and improve its keeping quality. They are used chiefly for flavor and richness.

Chocolate Fudge. Chocolate fudge is the favorite among home made candies, as it is reasonably easy to make and chocolate flavor is popular. There is wide variation in recipes and procedures, but any of them should produce good candy. The one given here is about the simplest, but results are usually excellent. Yield is about one pound.

Chocolate Fudge

2 cps	sugar
6 Tb	cocoa *(or 2 oz shaved bitter chocolate)*
½ cup	water
2 Tb	corn syrup, either kind
2 Tb	butter *(optional)*

Put all ingredients except butter in a 4 to 6-cup saucepan, and stir to combine over medium heat. Cook until a candy thermometer shows 234° F and/or a drop of syrup forms a soft ball when dropped in cold water. Details of these important tests will be discussed below.

The cooking process is chiefly one of boiling off excess water. Unfortunately, this mixture is very bubbly, and you may have to reduce heat to LOW to prevent boiling over, particularly in the 4-cup pan. But the larger pan may not provide enough depth of liquid to give a useful reading on the thermometer.

Cooking time should be about 8 to 10 minutes. Many recipes call for double the quantity of water or milk, which would require over 20 minutes or a higher flame.

The mixture must be watched to make sure it does not boil over, but it needs little stirring. Heat must never be high enough to dry out or burn the upper fringe of the liquid on the pan sides.

When your tests indicate that it is done, take the pan off the heat, stir in the butter and allow the mixture to cool to lukewarm, undisturbed. This may take 15 minutes or more, but can be speeded up by putting the pan in a container of cold water and changing it occasionally.

While it cools, butter a 9-inch pie pan, or any low-sided pan or dish of similar area, to have it ready to receive the fudge after beating.

Cleaning Pan. There is a small chance that the film or streaks of syrup on the pan sides may crystallize, and cause part or all of the batch to crystallize prematurely and coarsely while cooling. This has not happened to me, but candy specialists warn against it. They recommend that the pan sides be swabbed clean with a wet pastry brush or cloth.

This is difficult to do, and for the amateur a better precaution is to pour the whole batch into a clean pan to cool. Just move the part that will pour, as scraping will start crystallization. You can scrape out the rest

and make a ball of candy of it, but keep it separate from the main part.

Amount of Cooking. The proper amount of cooking is rather critical for fudge. If overcooked, it tends to harden very suddenly during beating, so that it congeals in the pan and around the spoon, and may be impossible to pour into the pan in which it should set. Or if poured in time, it sets so hard that it crumbles as it is cut, and may be, or soon become, too hard to eat comfortably.

If it is not cooked enough it takes an excessive amount of beating to produce crystallization, perhaps 20 minutes or more as contrasted with a normal time of 2 to 6 minutes. If badly undercooked, it may not harden at all.

Fudge that is the wrong consistency can be mixed with water and re-cooked. But smash or grind hard pieces first, as otherwise they can take half an hour or more to dissolve in hot water, with constant danger of boiling over.

Testing. There are at least three methods of determining when fudge is cooked — reading a thermometer, observing stringiness and chilling drops in water.

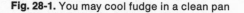

Fig. 28-1. You may cool fudge in a clean pan

Fig. 28-2. A soft ball test

Since the invention of the candy thermometer, cookbooks have been unanimous in relying on it. However, until you know how to test a thermometer (see page 13) and have become familiar with the behavior of the one you are using, it offers a wide margin of error.

The desired temperature is 234° F (although one authority says 236) and that is the bottom of the "soft-ball" range. This is at sea level, and becomes lower with altitude. You can compensate for altitude and for thermometer errors by checking the instrument in boiling water, and adding 22° to its reading. The result is your the-fudge-is-cooked point.

The thermometer may register improperly because of insufficient depth of syrup, or contact with the pan bottom or side. Markings may be too fine or light may be too dim for you to read it exactly. But you can have a flashlight and your glasses handy.

With all its faults, the thermometer is the best indicator for the beginner. If you make tests also, you will soon be familiar enough with them to judge the condition of the syrup very accurately.

As it approaches the soft ball point, it will form strings when poured slowly off the edge of a spoon. These strings usually start to form at 230 or 232° and disappear below 238°. They should be distinctively long and thin at 234. This is a preliminary test, to be confirmed by dropping into water.

Put 3 or 4 inches of water, preferably chilled, in a glass. When the syrup has started to make strings, drop a little of it in the water. When not cooked enough, the drop will break up and part or all of it will disperse.

At the desired stage it will stay together and form a more or less round, flattened blob on the bottom. If you lift this out you can roll it into a soft ball between thumb and finger. Since this test takes a bit of time, take the pan off the heat while you do it.

Beating. The usual way of beating fudge is to stir it vigorously with a spoon while holding the pan in a tipped position, as in Figure 28-3. A tablespoon is satisfactory, but a wooden spoon is preferable if the pan is Teflon-lined. A whisk does a better beating job, but may be very difficult to disentangle if the fudge hardens unexpectedly. Rotary beaters, either hand or electric, are inadvisable for the same reason.

Recommended starting temperature is 105 to 110° F, which is lukewarm or just barely warm to the hand. However, the beginner may do better to be a bit impatient, and start beating at 115 or 120°, or a little bit hot to the touch. This is because the fudge may set up too hard for effective beating at the lower temperature if you have overcooked it slightly, or if you are inattentive and let it get a bit too cool.

These temperatures can be determined accurately enough by feel. If you want to use the thermometer anyhow, and it registers in a low enough range, wash it off first and then put it back in the pan, as otherwise fudge sticking to it may cause premature crystallization.

The fudge offers a moderate resistance to beating, which increases slightly as it cools. When it starts to crystallize, its temperature rises a few degrees, resistance decreases and it may become a bit lighter in color. When this happens it should be poured into the pan immediately, as it will then harden very quickly. Normal beating time is 2 to 6 minutes, but longer times are not at all unusual.

These changes are not always obvious, and you may not realize its condition until the fudge is hardening around the spoon. Then you scrape it into the buttered pan or dish as rapidly as possible, moving the beating pan around as you do so to distribute it as well as possible, to avoid having it pile up in an over-thick lump.

After pouring and pushing as much out as you can, scrape the rest, which may be semi-solid and ball up in the spoon, from which you detach it with another spoon.

The best effect is obtained when the fudge is liquid enough to spread out in the pan, but thick enough so that the final bits poured stand up in low ridges or swirls on the surface.

Cut the fudge into squares with a sharp knife as soon as it is firm enough not to close the cuts. If cooking time has been just right, you can cut it at any time, but if it is a bit overdone and is allowed to cool and harden completely, it is likely to chip along the knife cuts, spoiling its appearance.

Variations. The half cup (4 ounces) of water may be doubled, if you don't mind a long cooking time, or may be replaced by 5 or more ounces of milk or 6 or more of cream. The corn syrup can be reduced or eliminated if a sandy texture is desired or can be tolerated. Or you can increase it up to 4 tablespoons, subject to the possible disadvantages listed earlier.

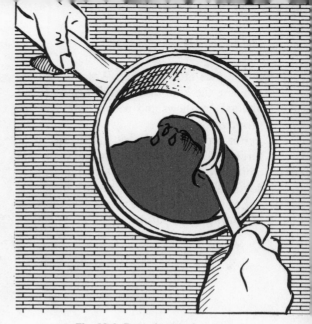

Fig. 28-3. Beat vigorously

The quantity of cocoa or chocolate may be increased by 1/2 for a very strong flavor, or reduced by about 1/3 for a mild one. Brown sugar may be substituted for white. Vanilla may be added just before beating, 1/2 to 1 teaspoon.

For nut fudge, add 1/2 to 1 cup of unsalted nut meats, which are usually coarsely chopped, but may be whole or halved. They should be mixed in, as the candy should set too rapidly to allow sticking them in

Fig. 28-4. Pour quickly

the surface after pouring. Walnuts and pecans are the kind most frequently used, but almonds, cashews and peanuts are also appropriate.

For brown sugar fudge, use brown sugar (preferably dark) instead of white sugar and omit the cocoa or chocolate. For a stronger flavor, add 2 tablespoons of dark molasses.

For maple fudge, use maple sugar instead of brown, or use part brown and part maple.

Storage. Fudge usually dries out and hardens if left uncovered a few days. If it contains a large amount of stabilizer, it may become soft and sticky on the surface, with or without hardening inside. It should be kept in moisture proof wrapping, and preferably in the refrigerator.

Well-wrapped fudge will keep for months in the freezer, usually without any deterioration in either texture or flavor.

29

SPOILAGE AND PROTECTION

DETERIORATION

Most food has a tendency to deteriorate, particularly if it is exposed to unfavorable conditions, and much of it needs to be handled and stored in ways that counteract its weaknesses.

There are many different standards by which the condition of a food may be judged. In this section it is assumed that nobody wants to eat food that will make him sick, and that decay, pronounced change in taste and strong odors are usually unwelcome, unless they follow certain customary and accepted patterns, such as are found in the souring of yogurt and ripening of certain cheeses.

In general, the term spoilage is limited to breaking down of food structure and development of unwanted and often offensive changes. Change in water content with hardening and loss of flavor is also an important source of food loss. Depending on the food and method of losing or absorbing moisture, these changes may be called staling, drying, dehydration, freezer burn, lumping, caking, liquefying or deliquescing.

SPOILAGE

Each food or food substance has its own characteristic way or ways of deteriorating, and of responding to favorable or unfavorable conditions.

Some spoilage processes are steps in the natural growth or maturing of the food, others are the effect of outside influences. A few, such as caking of salt or sugar because of water absorption, are reversible, but most of them have permanent results.

Causes. Most food deterioration (aside from bad cooking) is caused by one or more of the following:

1. Bruising, crushing and breaking
2. Over-ripening
3. Alteration by enzymes
4. Attack by organisms
5. Changes in fat
6. Changes in water content

Bruising. Most food can be damaged by too-rough handling. Some fruits and berries are very delicate, and become increasingly so as they ripen, while root vegetables are fairly rugged. Hard rolls

565

Fig. 29-1. Fruit is often handled roughly

may be very resistant to impact, fresh bread is easily crushed so as to lose shape and texture and a cake with soft icing cannot even be touched by anything without damage. The serious damage from bruising is usually not in the injury itself, but in the admission or encouragement of organisms causing rotting, and in starting of enzyme action.

Bruising and similar damage may result not only from rough treatment, but from piling too high so that lower pieces are crushed. Separation by cardboard packing, or even wrapping each piece in paper, may avoid or reduce damage by weight.

Fruit is often protected from bruising by being picked and shipped while unripe. This reduces losses greatly, but it usually has a flavor penalty.

Over-ripening. Most fruits and vegetables are considered most desirable as food at one stage, or sometimes during several stages of maturing. In a general way, fruit is hard and acid when unripe or green, soft but firm and with at least some sweetness when ripe, and mushy and less flavorful when over-ripe. Vegetables are small, crisp and tender-when-cooked when young, but large and woody when old. Many of them change character completely.

The selection of the state of development at which any particular specimen may be considered ripe for the purpose for which it is to be used, varies tremendously according to custom and individual taste. But whatever stage is wanted is the one at which it should be at the time when it is eaten.

The most important elements in ripeness are the stage of development at picking, and the time before use. Some varieties continue to mature after harvesting, others do not. Room-temperature storage favors continued development, while chilling slows or stops it.

Enzymes. Enzymes are organic substances that cause or hasten chemical changes in organic matter. They are particularly active in fruit and vegetables, and most of the changes that they cause are considered to be undesirable. They are destroyed by heat, so that they offer no problem if food is canned, or is cooked before freezing. But their action is only slowed, not stopped, by cold; and may be expected to resume at full speed as soon as food is defrosted. Precautions must therefore be taken against their action in freezing raw foods.

The action of enzymes is very complex,

and is not worth a detailed description here. One example will be sufficient. Raw peaches contain phenolic substances and an enzyme, peridoxase, which will oxidize them in the presence of air, causing them to turn brown. Over very long periods, some of the oxygen required for the browning might be obtained from other substances inside the peach.

As a result of this enzyme reaction, cut surfaces of peach exposed to air will turn brown rather quickly. Too-long-frozen peaches may be slightly off color when opened, and way off soon after thawing. Nobody wants to eat brown peaches, even if they still taste good. And the same reaction, or another occurring at the same time, is likely to make the flesh limp.

The action of this enzyme, and enzymes in general, is retarded by salt, sugar, citric acid, ascorbic acid (Vitamin C), coatings that temporarily exclude air, extreme cold, and various preservatives. The preferred methods for short-term protection are keep-in water laced with lemon juice or ascorbic acid, or coating with salad dressing or other sauce. For longer periods, and in preparation for freezing, fruit may be packed with sugar or sugar syrup, and vegetables may be cooked or partly cooked (blanched).

A primary precaution against enzyme damage is not to peel, cut or bruise the fruit or vegetable until you are ready to process it.

Trimming. Fresh fruits and vegetables are alive, and are usually capable of carrying on a certain number of organic processes, even though they are separated from the rest of the plant. They retain, to a varying but often considerable degree, ability to mature or ripen, build up or destroy chemicals such as sugar, starch or pectin; and to prevent action of enzymes and attack by organisms. Tubers can sometimes repair damage from cuts and bruises.

Life processes are often changed or

Fig. 29-2. Destructive organisms come in many sizes

stopped by trimming. Corn keeps best if the husks are intact, peas if they are in their pods and parsley if it is on its stems. And obviously, removal of skin exposes fruit to rapid deterioration.

In some cases (corn, for example), natural protection can be replaced effectively by good packaging. There is a question whether tops left on carrots and beets are useful enough to compensate for the moisture they use.

In general, trimming should be kept to a minimum until the food is being prepared for eating or cooking.

Organisms. Organisms are of all kinds and sizes. Big ones, from bears down through rats and mice to ants, usually work from outside the food, although certain moths and mites may lay eggs that develop inside it. These raiders are controlled primarily by direct counterattack, killing all of them in the home, neighborhood or factory; and secondarily by storing food in tightly closed containers of materials such as metal, glass or china.

Very small and microscopic organisms such as molds (fungi), yeasts and bacteria live in (or sometimes on) the food and are

567

part of it. They get to it by being carried by air or occasionally by water, and from containers, utensils, hands and clothing. Any food that is exposed to the air, even briefly, is almost sure to acquire them. However, much heavier and faster-working infections may be caused by contact with contaminated hands, utensils or food remainders.

Some of these organisms, particularly yeasts, are very useful to us. They may convert sugar in fruit juice to alcohol (and carbon dioxide) to change the juice to wine, or convert sugar in dough to carbon dioxide (and alcohol) to raise bread. The bacteria that sour milk by changing lactose sugar to lactic acid are mostly a nuisance in the home but essential workers in a cheese factory.

Each of these organisms is likely to be limited to a particular food substance and a rather narrow range of conditions under which it can utilize it. However, there are so many varieties that any food item is likely to support dozens or perhaps hundreds of kinds, each of them represented by thousands or more likely by millions of individuals. Their uncontrolled growth and multiplication changes the flavor, texture and chemical characteristics of food, eventually making it undesirable or even poisonous as food for humans.

The rate of spoiling is greatly affected by the number of organisms originally present. Bacteria multiply by division, each individual becoming two which in turn grow and then divide.

Under very favorable conditions this cycle may take 20 minutes, but under poorer conditions may take hours or days. An original infection might consist of just one airborne individual of a certain species, or of a few million of them scraped off a container. It would take the individual some 23 cycles, or at least 7 hours, to build up to the million mark.

This difference in possible spoilage time is why it is important to keep food preparation on as sanitary a basis as possible. While you can't prevent this type of spoilage by such care alone, you can certainly slow it down. Millions, or perhaps billions, of ordinary spoilage bacteria may be needed to produce noticeable effects.

The growth and multiplication of yeast and fungus follows the same principles, although they are not as easily demonstrated mathematically. Yeast multiplies chiefly by a type of cell division called budding, while fungus spreads both by root-like extensions and by spores that separate and start new colonies. Fungus is aided by dampness, darkness and poor ventilation.

When microorganisms are few in number they generally flourish best when they are in groups, but when the groups get too large they interfere with the growth of those in the inside.

Colonies on the surface are often subject to unfavorable conditions. If they are broken up and mixed through the food, as in chopping meat or stirring custard, their rate of increase and the speed of spoilage is greatly increased. Freezing and thawing usually changes the structure of food so as to make it more easily penetrated.

Like enzymes, most microorganisms are favored by warmth and slowed by chilling, made inactive by deep freezing and destroyed by sufficient heat. They differ greatly in their temperature requirements and tolerances. Most of them prosper at temperatures between 70 and 100° F, multiply very slowly below 40°, not at all at 15°, and die if heated to 180 to 250°.

But one group of bacteria, called thermophilic (heat-loving), is inactive below 80 to 110° and grows vigorously at 150° or higher.

Control of microorganisms starts with keeping the food as free of infections as is reasonably possible, keeping it chilled for short term storage and processing it for storing for longer periods.

Processing may consist of freezing to inactivate them, drying so that there will be no water to support them, adding sugar or salt to absorb water away from them, pickling to make fluids too acid for them, or killing them by heat or radiation and sealing the food so that it cannot be re-infected.

Poisoning. Most spoilage organisms eventually cause bad taste, smell or texture that makes food unpleasant to the point of being inedible. There are also some that cause disease, that are poisonous, or that secrete poisons, so as to cause severe illness and death. They will be discussed in the chapter on ILLNESS FROM FOOD.

Changes in Fat. Fat deteriorates by two kinds of chemical change. The more important one is reaction with oxygen in the air and from other sources to become rancid. Rancid fat has a very unpleasant taste and smell.

If no oxygen is present, the fat can break down more slowly in a somewhat different manner, a process called hydrolyzing. Changes in flavor and odor may be equally unpleasant. On a practical basis, there is no objection to the general custom of referring to all such changes as rancidity.

In the presence of air at a temperature of 80° F, fat may start to turn rancid in a few hours. In plastic wrapping at zero degrees the process is so slow that it may not be perceptible for a year in pork and for longer periods in beef and lamb. Baked goods containing fat have a long useful life at room temperature, and seldom turn rancid when frozen.

Rancidity at first detracts only slightly from flavor, but when well advanced makes the food offensive and inedible to the average American. However, it never creates deadly poisons.

Rancidity is controlled first by keeping fatty food cold and not keeping any to-be-frozen food long enough to start to deteriorate. For long storage, wrap to exclude air

and keep the temperature as low as possible. In the freezer, keep temperature at zero or colder, limit storage to a reasonable time and use the food promptly after thawing.

CHANGES IN WATER CONTENT

Loss of Water (Drying or Dehydration). All food contains some water, and its amount and distribution are usually quite important to its texture, flavor and usability. Problems arise when its quantity changes.

The most common change arises from water evaporating from the food surface into the air. This is the major cause of the staling and hardening of baked goods, brown sugar and many other foods, and the formation of crusts or skins (not resulting from cooking) on still others.

Maximum evaporation occurs when air is warm, dry and in movement. Warmth increases the activity of water molecules, so they can leave food more readily. Dryness (low humidity) means that the air has space to accommodate them when they arrive, and circulation moves them away quickly to make space for more.

The best defense against drying by evaporation is to place or wrap the food so that it is exposed to little or no air, and that any air present cannot circulate. This is accomplished most readily by wrapping or packaging.

Combination. We are aware only of the free or lightly combined water in food that makes it juicy, moist or soft. Food may also contain a variable amount of water that has entered into combinations with other substances that are firm enough so that moisture is no longer in evidence. Dry grains such as wheat usually contain about 8 to 14 per cent moisture, as do dry cereals. An extreme example is gelatin desserts, which may contain up to 97 per cent water and yet not be even moist.

Combination is a secondary cause of the

staling and hardening of bread. The process occurs most rapidly at low but above-freezing temperatures, in the thirties. This is why bread in the refrigerator becomes stale more rapidly than at room temperature, if both are wrapped to prevent evaporation. However spoilage from mold is much more likely to occur when the bread is warm.

This locking up of water may be partly or wholly reversible. Bread is freshened temporarily by toasting or by heating in an oven, and gelatin mixtures turn to slightly thickened water between 100 and 120° F, then back to solids at room or refrigerator temperature. But some of the water in grain cannot be freed without heating it until it chars.

In general, it can be assumed that our digestive systems can set free and utilize practically all water present in food, no matter how firmly it is bound.

Absorption. Another problem is that some food materials are hygroscopic, meaning that they tend to absorb moisture. Their absorption depends on the humidity, and each has a critical point below which it is inactive. Activity is affected by temperature, perhaps because at any given percentage of humidity, warm or hot air holds more moisture than cold air.

Common table salt is a familiar example of a hygroscopic substance. At ordinary temperature and humidity it is a free flowing mass of crystals. On a hot humid day it will first consolidate into a sticky mass and then liquefy, a process called deliquescing. This action is reduced but not eliminated by additives that, according to labels, make it free-flowing. Granulated sugar becomes sticky under the same conditions, but ordinarily will not liquefy.

When humidity drops, moisture moves from the salt or sugar back into the air, leaving the partly dissolved crystals sticking together in lumps. They will be soft enough to crumble at a touch if only a little

Fig. 29-3. Bread gets stale

moisture was absorbed, or almost as hard as rock if there was a lot of it.

Lumps may be broken up by pressure, rubbing them together, enclosing in cloth and pounding with a hammer or by grating. Or sugar may be used in syrup or candy, and to sweeten drinks, and either sugar or salt lumps may be used in cooking and in other food preparation where they can be dissolved directly.

Absorption of water can be prevented by packaging, using the same materials and methods that are effective against drying. But these are seldom helpful with salt shakers which normally stand exposed on tables or shelves, particularly in areas where exposure to high humidity is only occasional.

WRAPPING AND PACKAGING

Wrapping and packaging have become essential features of food marketing and use. They provide protection against bruising and crushing, attack by microorganisms, loss or gain of water, and oxidation;

and offer convenience in measurement, recognition and storage.

Commercial packaging is generally of good quality. With certain exceptions which will be mentioned, food can be left in the original wrapper until used, unless it is to be stored in different quantities, or put through preliminary processing.

Home wrapping materials may be roughly classified as flexible materials such as plastic, foil or paper in the form of sheets or bags; and rigid and semi-rigid containers.

FLEXIBLE WRAPPINGS

General purpose wrapping material for food should be convenient to use, sanitary, almost impermeable by water and water vapor, easily sealed and of good appearance.

Thin plastic. Several kinds of thin, transparent plastic for wrapping or bagging food can be bought in markets. There are also plastics of similar appearance for other purposes — garbage bags and wrappers for non-food items — which may or may not have the high moisture-vapor resistance that is essential in food wrapping.

Examples of the preferred types are Saran Wrap in sheet form and Baggies and Kordite shaped into bags.

Sheets. Sheet, film or roll plastic is sold in a standard width of 11-1/2 inches in 50 and 100-foot lengths. It is very thin, about .0015 of an inch, and has a soft and clinging texture.

This material can be used on any food or object that is firm enough to keep its shape during wrapping. It is also used for covering food on plates, and for making temporary lids for cans and jars. It often carries a mild electrostatic charge, which adds to its tendency to cling closely to food and dishes.

It has the disadvantage of clinging to itself, and care must be exercised to prevent it from folding over on itself during handling. Its thinness and transparency

Fig. 29-4. Salt absorbs water from humid air

make it difficult to see well enough to separate it.

You obtain a sheet by pulling the desired length off the roll while it remains in the package, then tearing it against a metal edge. Place the article to be wrapped in the center of the sheet. Fold the two shorter sides over the food toward each other, then fold in the other two sides. Press out any excess air trapped with the food as you work. One approach to this rather standard procedure is shown in Figure 29-5.

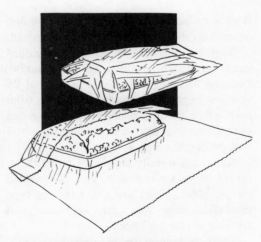

Fig. 29-5. Plastic makes good wrapping

Fastening may be by means of tape or one or two rubber bands. The clinging characteristic of the film usually results in a good seal at all edges.

For short-term protection, fastening may be omitted, and the package held together by resting it upside down, so that its weight prevents the edge from unfolding. But this should not be done for freezer use, as it may get loosened or even unwrapped during handling.

Bags. Bags are likely to be made of plastic that is about the same thickness (or thinness) as that in the rolls, but it has a firmer, less clinging body, so that it feels

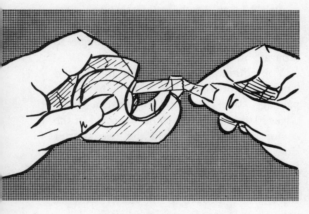

Fig. 29-6. Tape is a good sealer

thicker or heavier. This plastic may be flat, or embossed in a waffle or alligator pattern.

Bags are made in 3 not-quite-standard sizes, sandwich, food-wrap and jumbo, fastened together end to end in rolls of 25 or more bags. They can be torn loose from each other readily, usually by pulling one out of the package, then holding the roll and pulling the bag at one edge.

Such bags usually consist of a flat sheet, folded to make one side, and heat-sealed on two sides. There are also envelope-type sandwich bags that are separate, and stacked in the package.

Twist fasteners, to be described later,

are usually provided in packages of bags.

To load a plastic bag fully, place or pack food into the bag until it is not more than 3/4 full. Press it against the food to eliminate large air pockets, then twist the empty upper part a half or full turn, creating a tight, narrow neck just above the food. This is held shut by a twist fastener, a rubber band or tape.

Or the top of the bag may be folded over one side, with or without twisting, and secured with tape or rubber bands.

For a part load, the food is placed in a lower corner and the bag is flattened, air is worked out of it, and it is folded sideward. The top may then be twisted and/or folded and fastened in the same manner as a full bag.

The bag is somewhat simpler to use than sheet plastic, the three factory-sealed sides help in forming a non-leaking package and it can often be re-used if its load is not sticky. But the sheet usually fits more closely to the food and makes a more shapely package.

Either kind of plastic makes rather shapeless packages of soft or loose food. For neat stacking they should be put in boxes, usually of waxed paper or cardboard. The boxes also serve to protect the fragile plastic against tearing or puncturing.

Plastic sheets and bags can be re-used if they are clean and clear. But if they are cloudy they are likely to have lost vapor resistance. They are then also more likely to have holes which spoil their effectiveness.

Foil. Aluminum foil consists of very thin sheet aluminum, usually sold in rolls with widths of 12 or 18 inches and lengths of 200 or 75 feet. If free of holes it has excellent water and vapor resistance, it is easily shaped into a neat package and has an excellent appearance.

But it does not cling to itself at all, and since it is somewhat stiff, its overlaps on packages are usually not vapor tight unless carefully sealed with tape. Foil imprinted with a pattern that roughens it may fit more closely.

Foil is an insulator, as it reflects heat away. Freezing and defrosting are both much slower inside a foil cover than a plastic one. It should therefore be removed for any kind of rapid defrosting, and it must come off if the food is to be put in an electronic oven.

Paper. Waxed paper is an old favorite among wrapping materials. It is water repellent, smooth surfaced, translucent in appearance and somewhat stiff in texture. It usually does not have resistance to water vapor, water soaks into it after a while and its packages do not seal well. It is convenient for neat wrapping of food items such as sandwiches, when they will be eaten quite soon.

Waxed paper is useful in the kitchen at providing clean, disposable, non-stick surfaces on which to work dough, shape hamburger, catch crumbs and bake cookies.

Freezer paper is usually a light brown, slightly stiff paper with one side treated for moisture vapor resistance. It is not snugfitting, and it does not seem to have any advantage over plastic, except perhaps in greater puncture resistance. Its packages are harder to seal.

Butcher paper is a light brown paper widely used by butchers in wrapping freshly cut or ground meat. It has only moderate moisture resistance, and tends to absorb juice and sticks to meat. It should be removed soon after bringing the meat home.

Newspaper is an old standby for wrapping everything. However, it has no water resistance, and its print may come off onto damp food. It is a fair insulator, and may be used outside plastic or foil packages to help keep the contents hot or cold.

CLOSURES AND SEALERS

The efficiency of a package is greatly increased if it is closed and/or sealed. This serves to prevent unwrapping, spilling of contents and movement of air and vapor. It is not required if the package is to be kept intact for only a short time, will not be disturbed until it is ready to be opened, and results of spillage will not be severe.

Most closing devices also seal, but may then take a little extra care in applying them.

Tape. Tape used in sealing food packages is usually the pressure-sensitive or "Scotch" type, in which one side is sticky as it comes off a roll, and no moistening is necessary. It adheres well when pressed onto almost any dry surface, including glass and plastic, but not on oily, wet or damp materials. In the presence of a little oil, such tape may stick at first, but come off later. For this reason it is not entirely trustworthy.

Freezer tape is made of strong paper, usually tan but sometimes brightly colored. It is similar to the masking tape used by painters, but the adhesive may be specially processed to keep its grip when very cold. You can write on it with pencil, pen or crayon, and can use it for labeling as well as sealing. It is cheaper than other types.

There are two varieties of transparent tape, one of which is made of cellophane and is clearly transparent with a very faint yellow tinge. This is the cheaper variety. Its disadvantages are that you cannot write on it, and it tends to turn yellow, curl at the edges and become brittle. The other kind, a polyethylene plastic, usually available as 3M's Magic Transparent Tape, is translucent or cloudy in appearance, but is harder to see on the package. You can write on it, and it seems to have a longer life.

Some kinds, or perhaps just some batches of some kinds of tape, lose their grip after months in a freezer and curl up at the ends, gradually releasing the package. If you find this happening, just slip on rubber bands to hold the curling tape, or better yet, take the food out and eat it.

To seal a package, tape across the final

overlapping fold, as in Figure 29-7. This is effective only with thin plastic that is closely wrapped around the food, as loose wrapping will allow air to enter at other overlaps. Foil may need complete sealing of edges.

Tape may be used to seal a bag, by running it all the way along the mouth, or by twisting the bag and putting the tape around its neck. Bend a short piece of the tape into a U with the sticky side in, put it around the neck and press sides together. The piece should preferably be 2 to 4 inches long and not over 1/2 inch wide. It will be much easier to get off if you turn in about 1/4 inch of each end and press it, to make tabs that you can grip to pull it apart.

A bag may also be closed, its upper part folded down along its side, and then stuck

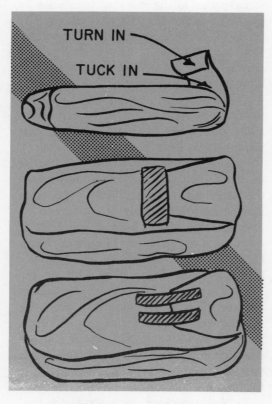

Fig. 29-7. Folding and fastening a bag

down more or less thoroughly with tape. The two sides of the bag should be held together just over the contents when you fold it, or the inner side will hang down too far and make a sloppy package.

It is also good practice to fold-in a triangle at each side, and/or the last half inch of the top, for appearance and to improve the efficiency of the seal.

Twists. A twist fastener is a thin wire or pair of wires surrounded by soft material. They were originally made like pipe cleaners — a double twisted wire holding some fuzz. Now they are mostly straight single wires, embedded in a strip of paper or soft plastic about 3-1/2 inches long and 1/5 inch wide. A twist can be bent into any shape, and will stay in it.

To use this fastener, close the bag over the food, pushing out as much air as possible, twist the top part until there is a narrow neck just above the food. Put the fastener around the bottom of the neck in a U-shaped loop, take the two ends between thumb and finger, and twist them until the fastening is tight. A half turn may hold it, a full turn surely will.

The extra several-turn twists you find on store packages are simply a result of exuberance on the part of the wrapping machine, and serve no purpose.

Twists are re-usable until they fall apart, because of separation of wire from coating, after which the wire(s) is too hard to see. Plastic is good for many, many uses; paper for two or three. Incidentally, this wire is just the right diameter to clean plugged nozzle openings in the current models of windshield washers.

Tabs. Bread and other foods may be sold in plastic bags twisted to close, and held with a tab of plastic or stiff paper, Figure 29-9. You get it off by twisting sharply, wiggling and pulling; the twist is the important part of the technique. It may tear the bag as it comes off, but it slips back on easily.

Fig. 29-8. Using a twist sealer

A tab provides a reasonably tight seal, but possibly not good enough for long-term freezer storage. It can be re-used a number of times.

Rubber band. A rubber band, preferably a short one, can be used instead of a twist fastener. It is put on in as many loops as are needed to make it tight.

First, pull the band down over the top of the bag to the bottom of the twist you have previously put in the neck. Hold the band on the neck and pull it away with the other hand until it is under tension. Twist it a half turn, put the resulting loop over the top and onto the first part of the band, again pull tight and twist a half turn, and repeat the process until you have used up the slack in the band.

If the bag is not too full, you can simplify this job by bending the neck over double, then put on the rubber band far enough below the bend so that it won't slip off. This makes the neck thicker, so you will need fewer loops, and the loops are more easily made without interference from a loose top.

Or you may fold the bag over to the side, in the same manner as for tape, and put one or preferably two rubber bands around the package, at right angles to the fold.

Bands should be rather thin, and long enough to be snug without squeezing into the package. A loose band may be tightened by means of a half-turn loop, as described above.

Heat. Heat sealing is the standard commercial method of sealing plastic. Two dry, clean sheets can be welded together by the right amount of heat with moderate pressure. Too little heat will not cause sealing, too much will melt a hole.

In general, this method is more work and less reliable in the home than the others. But if you do it right, it makes a very neat package.

Fig. 29-9. Tab sealer (size exaggerated)

Fig. 29-10. Or you can use rubber bands

CONTAINERS

Containers include cans, bottles, jars and tubes. They may be made of metal, glass, plastic or cardboard. The metal can is of dominant importance in the canned food industry, but is of little importance in home packaging. Glass is important in commercial canning, and makes up the containers for most home canning and jelly making, but has only incidental use for short term storage. Plastic and cardboard are useful both for the short term and for freezing.

Most containers are supplied with some sort of lid. This may be a loose fit, as in an old fashioned jelly glass, a loose fit that can be made into a tight, complete seal with a gasket, as a mason jar; or a press fit that can be assumed to make a seal for a few days, but which may not be reliable in frozen storage.

Provided the container itself is water-vapor proof, a satisfactory seal can be made by fastening a piece of plastic film over the top with a rubber band, Figure 29-11. If the container is not full, the plastic may be oversize, be pushed down into a snug fit with the food surface to reduce the volume of air in contact with it, and then sealed to the outside with the rubber band.

The use of containers in home canning, jelly-making and freezing are discussed in following chapters.

Cans. Cans are available in the average kitchen in a variety of sizes, they cost nothing (unless you buy the food just to get the can) and they are rugged. A good rotary opener will remove the tops cleanly. A sharp splinter of metal may be left where the cut finishes, but it can be pressed down with the back of a spoon or squeezed flat with pliers.

There is a widespread prejudice against re-using cans, because of a belief that when in contact with air the metal either poisons food, or gives it a bad taste or color. There is no basis in fact for the first idea and taste and color effects are rare.

In general, it is good practice to keep leftover canned food in the can in the refrigerator, as it is likely to be both sterile and inert. Make a tight lid for it with plastic film and a rubber band if there is not enough liquid to cover the food.

If your prejudice against food-to-metal contact is strong enough to make you uncomfortable, or the can is rusty, you can put a plastic bag in the can and the food in that.

Some cans, vacuum coffee and salted nuts, for example, have a close fitting push-on plastic lid that can be used as a tight cover after the metal lid has been cut or pulled out.

It is difficult to seal a used can completely enough to make it safe for long-time storage in a freezer. But you can use it as a protective container for a twist-sealed plastic bag.

Glass. Glass containers are made in a variety of sizes and shapes. Jelly glasses will be discussed under JELLY, and Ball jars and other gasket-sealed types under

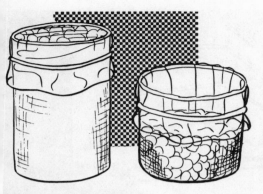

Fig. 29-11. Plastic closures, straight across and tucked in

CANNING. There are tumblers of various sizes, and special freezer jars.

Glass does not react perceptibly with any food at any temperature, and its transparency usually enables you to check the kind, quantity and condition of food without opening it. But it is brittle, so that it may break from a sharp blow or sudden change of temperature, and its splinters are sharp and dangerous. There are many foods that deteriorate on exposure to light (applesauce, wine, beer, milk and vanilla extract, for example), and these should be stored in the dark if in untinted glass.

There is danger that the expansion of freezing food that contains liquid will break a glass container. However, those with slightly tapered sides very seldom give this trouble, and have the advantage that the frozen block of food will slide out readily if the glass is heated a little.

Pyrex or Corning Ware glass casseroles with lids can be used for refrigerator or short period freezer storage, but the tops may not seal well enough to protect the food for long periods.

For freezing, depth of solid or liquid food should be limited to less than 1/3 of the width, as otherwise there might possibly be enough side thrust to break the glass. The food surface is likely to bulge in the center during the last stage of freezing.

Vacuum. The more important use of vacuum in preserving the flavor of certain canned foods will be discussed under CANNING.

The vacuum or Thermos bottle uses vacuum as an insulator. As shown in Figure 29-12, it consists of a double-walled glass bottle protected by a metal casing. The glass is silvered like a mirror, except in the inside where food is kept, in order to reflect heat. The space between the walls is a high vacuum, that is, it contains almost no air or other gas, so that only a little heat can be carried across it by the motion of molecules.

The top opening is closed by a cork, or by an adjustable plug of rubber and metal which is less efficient as a heat seal. The metal casing has a screw-on cap which serves both for protection and as a drinking cup. Other cups may be nested inside it.

A wide mouth Thermos has a much larger top opening, closed by a threaded cap. It is more convenient for thick liquids and for food, but is less efficient as a heat barrier.

A vacuum bottle will keep coffee hot for

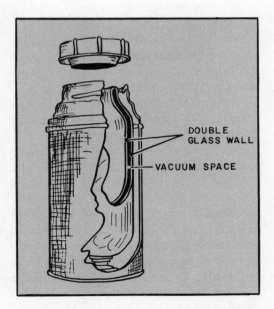

DOUBLE GLASS WALL

VACUUM SPACE

Fig. 29-12. Cutaway wide-mouth vacuum bottle

Fig. 29-13. Twist and press tops

several hours, and preserve the chill of a cold drink with plenty of ice in it for 12 or more hours. It is good practice to overheat or overchill the food just before putting it in, for maximum temperature endurance.

This device is very helpful, but also very fragile. It must always be handled with care.

Bottles and jugs that depend on insulation such as plastic foam are good and useful, but not nearly as effective in heat conservation.

Maintenance of hot or cold temperature may depend more on the bulk of the liquid (or other food) than on the quality of insulation. Loss or absorption of heat is directly related to the surface area, but its effect is dependent on the volume of the food and its specific heat.

The proportion of surface to volume decreases as bulk is increased. A pint vacuum bottle of coffee will cool many times faster than a quart vacuum. Foam-insulated jugs are usually of one gallon capacity, and the advantage of bulk is such that temperature maintenance may be comparable to that in a one-pint vacuum flask.

Plastic. The plastic discussed here is the rigid or semi-rigid transparent or translucent type.

Formulas and preferences are in a state of change. It has comparatively little use in the commercial packaging industry so far, being largely confined to bottles for liquids and cups for candy and specialties, but it probably makes up the bulk of containers made for home use. The most popular one holds about a pint, but there are one-cup and other sizes also.

Containers with press-on lids, such as the one in Figure 29-13, right, are widely used. The container itself, which may be round or square, is slightly tapered, a convenience in stacking with tops off and in dumping out food. The lid has a deep groove that should grip both the inside and outside of the container's rim or in the round type may have a flange that fits snugly around the outside only.

In either case, a slight pressure should be required to put the rim in place, and again to remove it. The seal between lid and container is usually vapor tight in a new unit of good quality, but is likely to leak otherwise. In cheaper grades they are often such a poor fit that they are hardly worth the struggle to install.

There is a wide range in quality. For full usefulness, the plastic should not lose shape when boiled nor crack when chilled. If these qualities are not mentioned on the label, they are probably lacking. In any case, there is a general tendency to lose shape and/or crack with repeated use.

Cracks spoil vapor-tightness, but do not damage food unless there are splinters. They can be patched with Scotch tape. These problems with plastics will probably be reduced as better ones become more common.

Jars may also have twist caps, Figure 29-13, left. Container and lid are usually thicker and stronger than the push-on type. Lids are much less likely to come off, and although more expensive, are to be preferred for liquids and for conditions in which they may not remain upright, as in a lunch box or picnic basket.

Such jars sometimes have double walls separated by insulation, which help to keep food either hot or cold, although they are not nearly as efficient as vacuum construction.

Plastic is also used for measurement cups, pitchers and shakers. These are cheaper and lighter than those made of glass, but the measuring indications are less often accurate. They may deteriorate, even if not abused.

Cardboard. Cardboard appears in home packaging principally in two forms. One is re-use of containers in which cottage cheese, sour cream, yogurt and similar products are purchased. These are usually round, tapered and fitted with press-on lids. The cardboard is waxed or plastic-treated to be waterproof and usually vapor proof also. They can be used several times for refrigerator storage, if washed immediately after each use.

When they become limp, or the inner surface becomes discolored or smelly, they should be discarded.

Cardboard boxes may also be purchased flat, and folded into box form. These are intended to be used in freezer storage, with a plastic bag inside.

30

FREEZING AND DRYING

FREEZING

Quick freezing usually does less damage to the flavor and texture of properly prepared food than any other method of preservation. It can be applied to a very wide variety of foods, and it is the easiest home method.

Freezing to 0° F (about −18° C) and below stops or almost stops most processes that tend to make food deteriorate. But it may damage or even ruin the food by formation of ice crystals.

Ice formation. When water freezes, its molecules arrange themselves in crystals. A growing crystal has the characteristic of drawing to itself molecules of water, separating them from other substances with which they were combined. It can damage the cell structure of food by puncturing or tearing the cell walls and/or pulling water out through them.

Crystallization may also damage some of the non-cell structures called colloids, such as cooked starch and egg white, by separating the water and other substances.

Fast freezing creates many fine crystals, slower freezing produces fewer but bigger ones. Small ice crystals do less damage. Because they are small, they are less apt to puncture and tear, and because they form quickly there is less time for molecules to be moved out of their proper places. For both reasons, the movement of molecules that does occur is for shorter distances.

If a food that may be damaged by freezing is to be frozen, the process should be completed as rapidly as possible.

Quick freeze. There are a number of opinions about what constitutes quick freezing. One standard is that the whole process be completed in 90 minutes, another that freezing should progress inward at .3 centimeters (about 1/8 inch) per minute or faster. Another authority considers only the most critical temperature range for forming ice crystals, from 32° F down to 25, through which the food should pass in not over 30 minutes.

From a household standpoint, any food can be considered to be quick frozen if it has been placed in a freezer that maintained temperature at or near zero Fahrenheit during the freezing period. In commercial plants, freezing temperature may

Fig. 30-1. Freezing stops many kinds of spoilage

be anything from zero to 40 below, and freezing is often accelerated by circulating air by means of fans, or putting the food in pre-cooled brine or syrup. In laboratories, temperatures as low as minus 500° F are used.

Placement of food may be important in getting it frozen quickly. Packages should not be put in the door compartments, as they are usually several degrees warmer than the interior. If there are several packages, they should be separated, and put in different areas if possible. If there are cooling tubes in the shelves, put the packages directly on the shelves.

Small packages freeze faster than large ones, so from this standpoint pints are preferable to quarts. Packages larger than a quart are usually not advisable, but roasts are frozen whole, regardless of size. Wrapping in foil slows freezing somewhat.

Quantity. In order to take advantage of the degree of cold that is offered by your freezer, or the way it is set, you must be careful to limit the amount of new, unfrozen food that you put in it at one time. Too much will contain enough heat to make it freeze too slowly for best results, and to warm up other articles in the freezer at the same time.

Since most freezers are set just at zero, they cannot afford to get warmer by more than a few degrees. Overloading may warm them enough to produce excessive crystallization in the food being processed, and softening and recrystallization of previously frozen stored food, with damage in quality to both.

The instruction book for your freezer should tell you how many pounds of fresh material it can freeze in one batch. If it does not, assume that you can freeze about twice as many pounds as its rated capacity in cubic feet. That is, if your freezer holds 8 cubic feet, it should be able to freeze about 16 pounds of room-temperature food at one time. With larger freezers, over 12 cubic feet, the proportion is usually lower, about 1-1/2 pounds to the cubic foot.

Whenever possible, play safe by keeping below the maximum amount.

If the food is hot, reduce the quantity by 1/4 to 1/3. If it is refrigerator cold, keep the difference as a safety margin.

VEGETABLES

Vegetables must be partially cooked (blanched or scalded) before freezing, to destroy enzymes, and thus prevent the deterioration which so quickly shows itself after a heavy frost in the garden.

Blanching is the preferred method of eliminating enzymes, and will be discussed in some detail. Comparable results can be obtained by cooking vegetables fully before freezing, but this takes too much time if any considerable quantity is prepared.

Preparation. Vegetables are cleaned, trimmed and either cut or left whole in the

Vegetable	Size	Time in boiling water, minutes*	Time in steam, minutes*
Asparagus	Small	2 to 4	3 to 5
	Large	3 to 5	5
Beans, green	Frenched	2	2½
	Cut or whole	3	4
Beets, whole	Small	1½ to 2	2½
	Medium	2 to 3	3½
sliced		nr	2½
Brussels sprouts	Small	3 to 4	4 to 5
	Large	4 to 5	5 to 6
Carrots	Whole	2 to 5	3 to 5
	Sliced	2 to 3	2½ to 3
Corn, whole kernel		2	4
creamed		1	2
on-the-cob		5	6
Greens, all kinds		1 to 2	nr
Peas	Small	¾ to 1	1 to 2
	Large	1 to 2	2 to 3

nr — not recommended
* — at sea level. Increase by about 10 per cent for each 1,000 feet of altitude

Fig. 30-2. Vegetable blanching times

same general manner as when they are to be cooked for immediate serving. Suggestions will be found at the beginning of Chapter 12, and under individual vegetables which are in alphabetical order in Chapters 12 and 13.

Blanching. Part-cooking before freezing is called blanching. It is the same process as parboiling (see page 36), but is usually for a shorter period.

Most enzymes are destroyed by keeping food at 212° F for a period varying from 50 seconds to 2 minutes, depending on the vegetable. However, cooking periods up to 5 minutes may be required, as time is needed for the heat to penetrate. But it is always quicker than to cook the vegetable for serving.

Blanching may be done either in boiling water or in live steam in a closed (but not sealed or pressurized) container above boiling water.

In general, water blanching is preferred for leaf vegetables such as spinach which steam penetrates poorly, and steam is better when the vegetables are finely cut, so that water could remove too high a proportion of their juices and nutrients. Steam is faster, theoretically at least, and is less likely to damage food, but is more dangerous to the operator.

Figure 30-2 shows recommended blanching periods for some vegetables. In water, this is the actual boiling time, and does not include the time it takes for the water to resume boiling, after the food is in it. For steam, it is timed from the moment you put the lid over the food.

The times given are necessarily variable, because of differences in size, shape and maturity. If in doubt, use the longer times. More complete lists will be found in manuals on freezing food.

Water-blanching. The standard recommendation for water-blanching vegetables at home is to use a 6 to 12 quart open kettle of boiling water, and a smaller, long-handled wire basket, sieve or other strainer.

You load the basket with not more than a pound of vegetables, lower it into the boiling water, wait until the water boils again, keep track of time, agitate the vegetables enough so that heat will be evenly distributed through them, and lift the basket out of the water when a specified time is reached.

Checking with a second hand or even a stop watch is usually recommended because accurate timing is said to be essential. Too short a blanching time permits spoilage. Too long blanching is said to cause loss in quality of color, flavor and nutrients, even though fully cooked vegetables freeze very well.

Instructions on this operation seem to take no account of an important variable — the blanching that occurs between the time the vegetable is put in the water and the resumption of boiling. Since many enzymes are destroyed by temperatures well below 212° F, the blanching process might be complete when you start to time it.

This critical waiting time does not depend on the quantity of boiling water, as is frequently assumed, but by the relationship between the heat input of the burner, and the movement of this heat into the vegetable and into the room from the water surface and from the outside of the kettle. The time will be shortest if the burner is big and hot and the quantity of vegetable is small. A cold vegetable will take more time than a warm one, and a big kettle will lose more heat than a small one.

A large quantity of water will be cooled by fewer degrees than a small quantity when a given amount of vegetable is added, but it will take longer to regain each degree, so the amount of waiting or waste time remains the same. Either amount of water will boil faster if there are fewer vegetables in a batch, but that means more batches. The only way to really speed up the job is to increase burner heat output.

It is sometimes possible to have a gas burner altered to produce a super size flame, and there are some double-quick electric units. Either of these would be helpful both to blanching and to hurry-up cooking. But there is a simpler method.

Instead of using a cumbersome 6 to 12 quart kettle on one burner, use two 3 to 6 quart kettles on two burners, with two dunking sieves each holding only a half pound of food. With a little practice you will be able to manipulate two strainers almost as readily as one, and your waiting time will be cut just about in half.

In smaller sizes, a pan and strainer combination can be replaced by two pans. Have

Fig. 30-3. Two burners heat faster than one

one of them part-filled with boiling water on a burner. Put the food in it, in the same way as for ordinary cooking. After proper blanching time, put the other pan on the burner and pour the water into it, holding back the food with the lid or catching it in a sieve. Boiling will resume in the second pan almost immediately, and you can put in the next batch.

Steam-blanching. For steam blanching you need a kettle with a capacity of 4 or more quarts, with a closely fitting cover and a bottom rack that will hold a strainer load of vegetables above the top of an inch or so of water. A heavy, close fitting lid around which the steam escapes rather evenly is best.

A pressure cooker or canner of the right size is ideal, but be sure not to lock the lid in place. For extra security against unwanted pressure, you may remove the valve, the gasket or both.

The strainer should have a detachable or hinged handle, so that it will not interfere with closing the lid. You should wear insulating gloves to protect your hands and wrists while handling the lid and getting the strainer out. Pliers, a long fork or some other tool may be needed to fish for the strainer or its handle.

Put about an inch of water in the kettle or cooker, put it on your hottest burner turned on full, and bring to a boil. Put a strainer with vegetables in the kettle, put on the top, and allow to steam for the recommended time.

If the food is matted together so that steam may not penetrate it readily, remove the cover and shake it up one or more times during the blanching.

Working time begins the moment the cover is on, as placing the strainer on the rack does not interfere with the boiling. But add 10 or 15 seconds to the steaming period each time you take the lid off.

Chilling. Most instructions seem to recommend or even insist that the blanched food be chilled immediately after lifting out of the boiling water. This is done by holding the loaded strainer under the cold water faucet, where temperature should be 60° F or lower, or by sloshing it around in ice water.

This operation is supposed to retain flavor by shortening the time between blanching and freezing, and to reduce the multiplication of bacteria that takes place in warm food.

These factors are important enough to make chilling a standard part of commercial food freezing. But its use in casual home freezing operations seems very doubtful except as a way of saving waiting time.

If you do cool, the most efficient method is to put a colander or extra basket in a large pan under the cold water faucet, with the pan full and the water running briskly. Dump your blanching basket into the colander. You can then fill that basket with fresh food immediately, and resume blanching.

All pieces of the load in the colander will be chilled quickly and equally, as they are immersed in water that is kept chilled and circulating by the stream from the faucet. You do not have to hold up a basket or keep renewing a supply of ice.

Not-Chilling. Water will drain back into the kettle as you lift the basket out. If you leave the vegetable in the basket, or dump it in another one, it will lose most of its heat almost immediately if it is loose pieces (green beans, for example) or within five or

Fig. 30-4. Chill in a colander in a pan

ten minutes if it is closely packed, like spinach. The remaining heat is likely to disappear during packing. The surfaces have been fairly well sterilized by the blanching, so that microbe population is very low.

The few extra minutes of natural as against water cooling are not going to result in either spoilage or noticeable change of flavor. And you avoid the probable loss of nutriments and addition of organisms involved in water cooling.

Theoretically, it is possible to pack and wrap the vegetables while they are hot, and freeze them immediately. The extra burden on the freezer would be moderate. Freezing food at 150° F and chilling it to zero takes about half again the amount of energy required if the food had been cooled to 72°.

But there is a question whether the packaging material is designed to remain leakproof in contact with hot food. And there is also a problem of burned fingers.

Full Cooking. Preparing vegetables for freezing in the way just described may be quite a project, particularly the first time. It requires or at least asks for a big kettle or kettles, long-handled strainers and a bit of organization. If you just want to try your hand at freezing a small surplus, the trouble is likely to be out of proportion to the results.

A simplified method which is usually satisfactory is to cook vegetables for eating in your usual way, serve part, and pack the rest for freezing. In packing, you may cover them with the liquid in which they were cooked (or half-cover them, if that is all the liquid you have), or drain and dry-pack them. Or, as a compromise measure, you can scoop the to-be-frozen part of the vegetable out of the pot any time after blanching should have taken place and before full cooking.

After defrosting, blanched vegetables need to be cooked almost as long as raw ones. Fully cooked ones need only be

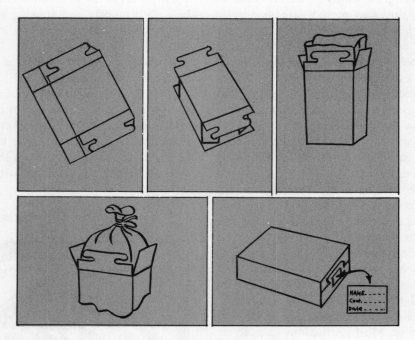

Fig. 30-5. Packing in a bag in a box

warmed up, in the same manner as canned produce. Intermediate amounts of pre-cooking require part time cooking after defrosting, with doneness judged by tests for tenderness.

As an average, vegetables that are fully cooked before home freezing are likely to be slightly less colorful and tasty than those which were blanched. But they are so nearly equal that you may not be able to tell the difference, and they should be clearly superior to all canned and most commercially frozen food.

PACKING VEGETABLES

Food for the freezer can be wrapped or packed in plastic, foil or almost any type of container. But it is very important that the packaging be carefully done, so that both the material used and the sealing of openings will prevent the passage of water vapor. Freezing slows evaporation but does not stop it.

Vegetables may be packed dry, loose, in their own juice, or in brine.

Dry. For dry packing you fill containers to the top with drained vegetable, sometimes shaking or pressing the pieces down to get more in the package. Then seal, label, and put in the freezer.

Asparagus should be cut short enough to fit. It should be handled carefully to avoid breakage, particularly if it is fully cooked. Sections of cauliflower or broccoli should be arranged to fit as well as possible, without pressure which would break them up and make them less appetizing.

The combination of a sealed plastic bag for holding in moisture, and a cardboard box for protection and convenience, in labeling and stacking, is strongly recommended for vegetables and fruit. The best, or perhaps the only way of filling the bags efficiently is to place each one in its box first, then put in the food. You will probably have to lift the bag slightly in order to seal it.

If the food is semi-liquid, it may bulge the sides of the box during packing, and be hard to get back in shape afterward. This can be prevented by putting the box in a supporting frame, or perhaps just by bracing the wide sides with a couple of heavy bookends.

Loose. Loose packing is a true fast-freeze method. You spread pieces of the vegetable thinly on pans, trays or foil, and put them in the freezer. Medium size peas will freeze hard in a few minutes this way. But leave them in at least half an hour, to assure full freezing all the way through. Allow up to an hour for larger pieces, like fat green beans.

Pack the frozen pieces in bags or containers in the same way as for dry pack, but because they are hard, they will not pack down and you may get only about 3/4 as much in a package. Seal, label and put right back into the freezer.

If there is juice that you want to save to serve with the vegetable, freeze it separately in ice cube trays, and pack the cubes in the same containers with the vegetable. A tray with compartments for very small cubes (minicubes) will be convenient, as you may have to break up larger cubes to distribute the juice evenly among the packages.

Fig. 30-6. Hold the box in shape with bookends

Fig. 30-7. Probably good, but what is it?

Wet Pack. Wet pack is used chiefly for fully cooked vegetables, which are frozen in their own juice. Packages are only 7/8 filled, to allow space for expansion.

If there is not enough juice, you may either divide it evenly among the packages, or dilute it with water to come to the top. You can cook down the extra water a little when you are heating to serve, but the partial filling is better from a flavor standpoint.

This is the slowest freezing method, and some loss of flavor and texture may occur. But it is the most convenient way to handle small amounts, and it has the advantage of high resistance to drying out, which may damage dry or loose pack if a seal is not perfect or the storage period is very long.

Brine. In brine or salt water pack, a salt solution of about one teaspoon to the cup is used instead of vegetable juice. Some flavor advantage may be obtained by using water in which the vegetable has been blanched.

This is a fairly strong solution, about 2 per cent or 2/3 the strength of sea water. It is usually drained and discarded after defrosting.

Brine pack is slow in freezing. The vege-

table may freeze before the water because of the salt, but full freezing with stoppage of ice crystal formation does not occur until after the solution is frozen hard.

There does not seem to be any particular advantage to this method of freezing.

Labeling. Every freezer package should be identifiable. Some labeling can be avoided without creating problems, if the wrapping is transparent, the shape of the package is distinctive and packing in the freezer is systematic.

Transparent plastic not placed in boxes is very helpful, but it may become obscured by frost, either inside or outside, so that you either make a wrong guess in a quick grab at a package, or even cannot tell by close examintaion. Packaged appearance cannot be depended on to reveal whether you have a pork chop or a veal chop, but until badly frosted, you can distinguish between a chop and hamburger.

Frosting usually indicates that the package has been in the freezer too long, but doubt as to the contents may result in leaving it there again and again, while younger and more recognizable items are used.

A few items have such distinctive shapes — ears of corn, for example — that you can safely assume that you will know what they are.

If you have the time and interest, it is a good idea to label every freezer package, even if the wrapping is transparent. Aside from packages that are clearly self-labeled by shape, anything wrapped in foil or freezer paper must be labeled if you are going to be at all efficient in using it. And food in boxes looks like all other foods in boxes.

Unlabeled packages of any sort do not give the date of freezing. Since you should use oldest stock first, this is important. They also cannot be safely stored in commercial lockers.

Minimum information for a label is the name and description of the contents and the date of freezing. If you share the freezer with anyone else (even it if is your freezer) put your name on it also. If you use a freezer locker, add your locker number.

The description may be only the name of the food, such as peas or string beans, or white corn or yellow corn. You may want to add information about whether it is from your garden, a roadside stand or a market. If the variety is known and you consider it of interest, add that. You probably should distinguish between sliced and mashed squash.

Markers that have a brush or sponge tip saturated with ink (Magic Marker, for example) will usually write on any surface, although the color may be a little faint on waxed or oiled surfaces, and on some smooth plastics. No pressure is needed.

It may be difficult to mark wrapped packages with other writing tools. A porcelain pencil, designed to write on glass and china, usually makes a readable mark, but at least light pressure may be required. Ordinary pencils and ball point pens will not write on wax, although you may be able to scratch the information faintly into the surface.

Freezer tape provides a good surface. You can write on a strip used for sealing, or on a separate piece stuck on as a label.

Good labels can be made out of stiff paper or thin easy-to-write-on cardboard. If you have no suitable scrap you can buy 3 x 5 inch index cards cheaply at stationery counters. Each card can be cut to make several labels. You can fasten them to the package with tape or a rubber band, or by puncturing a corner and stringing it on a twist fastener that has been tightened on the food bag.

FRUIT

Fruit contains the same types of enzymes found in vegetables. They cause rapid spoiling after fruit is peeled, cut up or otherwise

Fig. 30-8. Sugar preserves fruit

killed. The enzymes could be destroyed by blanching, but since fruit is often preferred raw, it is usually packed with preservative instead.

As the enzyme-caused damage is largely a process of oxidation, the substances used to prevent it are called anti-oxidants. The most important of these are sugar, ascorbic acid (vitamin C) and citric acid. Salt is effective, but it is not used with fruit. Sulphur dioxide and other sulphur compounds are not suitable for home use.

Sugar. Sugar is the standard preservative for fruit. It serves not only to check enzyme damage, but it is desirable and often essential for counteracting acid flavor.

In the dry method the fruit is peeled and cored if necessary, cut into pieces, slices, quarters or halves, and sugar is added and mixed lightly until it covers all its surfaces. The proportion is generally between a half cup and a cup of sugar to a pint (pound) of fruit. The amount of sugar is varied in accordance with the acidity of the fruit and the taste preferences of the family.

The sugar draws juice from the fruit and dissolves into a thick syrup, which may or may not have enough volume to cover the slices. If it does not, water can be added to bring it to the top.

Syrup. More often, sugar is dissolved separately in water to make a syrup which is poured over the freshly cut fruit pieces. This makes the product more juicy, with more flavor in the fruit and less in the syrup. If the fruit is very juicy the dry sugar method is preferable.

The percentage of sugar in syrup may be anything from 10 to 60, and the names may range either from thin to thick or from light to extra heavy.

Cookbook instructions may be in proportions, as for example one part of sugar to 3 of water. In American publications, it can usually be assumed that quantities are in bulk measurement rather than by weight, so there would be one cup of sugar to 3 of water. This particular solution would be 25 per cent sugar, a rather light syrup.

The recipe may give proportions in cups of sugar to a quart of water, which are easy to follow, or in percentages, which are difficult. In addition, commercial freezers and canners designate syrups by a numbering system, and by Brix degrees, which are merely percentages of sugar.

The candy section in your cookbook may classify them by their boiling points, the higher the temperature the thicker or heavier the syrup. See Figure 18-16.

Fortunately, it is seldom important (outside of candy making) to have an exact proportion of sugar in syrup. If you get somewhere near, that is good enough.

To prepare a sugar syrup, mix the desired amounts of sugar and water (cold, warm or faucet-hot) in a pan, apply medium burner heat with constant watching and occasional stirring until it starts to boil, then remove it from the heat to cool. If you use it very hot it will have a cooking effect on the fruit.

In general, thick or heavy syrups are used with the more acid fruits and thin ones with those lower in acid. For the average taste, the thicker syrups are preferred, as the acid content of fruit seems to be emphasized by thin ones.

If you are experimenting, start with a medium syrup and change it as you wish for later batches. A thin syrup may be thickened either by adding sugar or by boiling.

Up to half the sugar in a syrup may be replaced by corn syrup. This reduces sweetness while maintaining thickness.

Ascorbic Acid. Ascorbic acid is considered here as an antioxidant used in preserving quality of frozen fruit. But it is also Vitamin C, an essential part of our diet.

This vitamin may be purchased in drug stores, and occasionally in groceries in powder form. It may be pure, or mixed with citric acid and sugar.

Ascorbic acid is added to sugar in the proportion of about 1/4 teaspoon to the cup and mixed well before putting on fruit. In syrup, some authorities recommend using the same proportion to the sugar, others that one teaspoon be used to the quart of syrup. In the mixed preparations, follow directions on the label. Four times as much may be needed. Do not put it in syrup until after it has cooked and cooled, and preferably not until you are ready to use the syrup.

Keeping Quality. The books give frozen raw fruit a maximum freezer life of about 6 months, as it deteriorates slowly in spite of freezing, sugar and additives. However, I have eaten home-frozen peaches that were still excellent, although a little soft, after three years.

Sound procedure in freezing fruit is to use plenty of sugar, add ascorbic acid, date it plainly, plan to use it within a year, keep oldest stock in front and never throw it away on account of age without trying it.

Cooked Fruit. You can also freeze cooked fruit and berries, with no complications. Simply prepare and stew them as if for canning or serving for dessert (see Page

548), pour them into suitable containers or bag-box combinations, allowing space for expansion, and freeze. Flavor and general quality are excellent, and might be maintained for years.

MEAT

Meat is usually easier to freeze than vegetables and fruit. There is no important problem of spoiling by enzyme action, so it can be frozen raw. It can also be frozen cooked or half cooked, if this is more convenient.

Preparation. Before freezing, meat should be cut or shaped into the size portions you will use. Frozen flesh is very difficult to carve, and with the presence of bones may be impossible. So if you have a six pound piece of meat that you want to use as two three-pound roasts, carve it and wrap the pieces separately. You also have the advantage of faster freezing and thawing in the smaller pieces.

Roasts and other large pieces of meat do not fit well into any package. It is sufficient to wrap the meat in plastic, which should be pressed against the surface everywhere so as not to leave air pockets. Sealing can be done with freezer tape or Scotch tape, with the extra precaution of rubber bands if you do not trust it.

You can also double wrap by putting the wrapped meat in a plastic bag.

You might be able to buy stockinette. This is an elastic open-mesh cloth made in cylinders that can be stretched over the outside of the plastic. It prevents unsealing, and also holds the plastic snugly against the meat.

Pre-wrapped meat at the supermarket may be wrapped and sealed in plastic, but at present it usually rests on a cardboard tray. It is a major nuisance to have to scrape frozen cardboard off frozen meat, and many people feel that the cardboard affects the flavor of meat if it is frozen with it. So it is best practice to open the butcher's

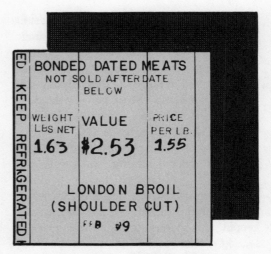

Fig. 30-9. A complete meat label

package, take out the cardboard and re-wrap. But you can use the label, just adding your date.

If enough cooks complain to enough butchers about this re-wrapping, all-plastic meat packages may become standard.

When you are freezing a number of similar units of meat together, such as chops or hamburger patties, the pieces should be separated by two thicknesses of plastic, which usually means wrapping each piece separately.

Plastic will not stick strongly to plastic, but it will stick to frozen meat. The two layers allow you to separate the pieces more readily, to permit using only the number you want; with faster defrosting, and easier cooking when frozen.

Follow the general rule (on page 582) about putting the unfrozen meat in places where it will freeze fastest, and in regard to not overloading the freezing capacity.

Each package should be labeled with name and cut of the meat, its weight and the date of freezing.

Pork. Any type of meat may be frozen successfully. There is an old tradition, or perhaps a superstition, in the meat industry that smoked pork products such as ham, bacon and sausage are ruined if frozen.

This is simply not so. There may occasionally be some deterioration in frozen storage, for reasons to be discussed below, but a series of tests show no important difference in flavor and texture in the freezing and defrosting process, even when repeated.

Frozen storage can eliminate trichinosis infection in pork. See page 120.

Frozen Storage. Frozen meat must be protected against drying, oxidation, and rancidity.

Thorough wrapping with moisture-vapor proof material guards against drying, and keeping this material close to the meat and sealing it takes care of the oxidation. Rancidity, discussed elsewhere, is a degenerative change in the chemistry of fat.

Time is one of the principal factors, but the process is slowed by excluding oxygen, and by extreme cold. It varies with the type of fat, and among meats is relatively rapid in pork and slow in beef. When properly wrapped and kept at a steady 0° F, pork may be expected to keep well for 8 to 18 months, beef from 2 to 3 years. If you could keep the temperature down to −30° both meats might last your lifetime. But that is not the purpose of a freezer.

POULTRY

Poultry and poultry parts are frozen in the same manner as meat.

Whole birds should have legs and wings fastened as closely to the body as possible, as they are particularly subject to drying out and, if allowed to project, they take extra space and may puncture the wrapping.

The fastening may be done by pinning in place with skewers or tying with string before wrapping, or compressing with rubber bands or string after wrapping.

Dressing is supposed to be taken out of the bird, and frozen in a separate package of packages. This is because it does not always get heated to sterilizing temperature during cooking, and it is regarded as too good a multiplication place for organisms

Fig. 30-10. A well-packed freezer

to be trusted to freeze slowly inside the body cavity.

FISH

Fish should always be scaled and cleaned before freezing. Otherwise, you may freeze whole fish, but it is more convenient to process them for cooking first. That is, if they are small and are to be eaten whole, keep them that way. But fillets and steaks should be cut first.

The pieces freeze faster for possibly better flavor and texture, and if wrapped separately, can be cooked without defrosting or hacking.

Fresh fish is usually little damaged by freezing, although there may be a little separation of juice, and slight toughening is

sometimes noticed or perhaps only suspected. But tired fish seems to get much
more tired.

BAKED GOODS

Baked goods of the bread family, including rolls, cake, coffee cake, cookies and pie
crust are almost ideal foods for freezing.
They require only moisture-vapor proof
wrapping. Neither texture nor flavor are
often affected by freezing or defrosting.

However, they may suffer from movement of moisture while in frozen storage,
and so require special treatment in thawing
if they have been in the freezer more than
a few weeks. See Chapter 30.

When freezing items such as hot dog or
hamburger rolls, or English muffins, you
should cut or split them first, if it was not
done by the bakery, even if it involves the
nuisance of opening the store package and
rewrapping. The two halves of a frozen
sliced roll are fairly easy to break or pry
apart, and will then take less than a third
of the defrosting time of a whole one. Also,
slices are easy to put in a toaster or grill
for immediate thawing.

It is also a good plan to wrap rolls and
similar items in the quantities that you
normally use at one time. If you expect to
use English muffins two to a meal, wrap
them in pairs after splitting them. It is a
nuisance to take a package of 5 or 8 out of
the freezer, remove a pair, then repair the
package and put it back. On the other
hand, it is little extra trouble to take out
two or three small packages if they are
needed.

STORAGE

Packing the Freezer. The usefulness of
a freezer can be greatly increased by arranging the food in it in a definite pattern.
Almost any arrangement will do as long as
you can remember what it is and can keep
it that way.

The primary requirement is to arrange
the stored food in classifications and sub-
classifications. One area for meat, one for
fish, one for vegetables, and so forth. Then
subdivide — roasts in the back, hamburger
to the left, chops to the right and poultry
sections in the middle, for example — so
that you will not have to rummage through
a whole section for an item.

You may have to pile several different
things on top of each other for lack of
space, so the three meat items mentioned
would be on top of each other, but you can
still always put the chops on the bottom.

Another approach to arrangement may
be on the basis of stability. If your freezer
is usually well loaded, and some items are
in boxes and others just wrapped, you may
work out an arrangement that gets a maximum of boxes on the bottom on each shelf,
with slippery sliding things in thinner layers
on the top.

Or you might have a policy of keeping
roasts in front, as a dam to hold back small
irregular packages which might otherwise
spill out in an avalanche when you open
the door.

There are many advantages to orderly
arrangement. The first is speed in finding
things. If you have an upright freezer you
should limit the time you hold the door
open, as its cold air flows wastefully out
on the floor while you search and the food
warms. If you have a chest, you are likely
to find it a burden to lift racks out while
you search for what you hope you have
somewhere.

A more important factor is ease in keeping track of what you have, to avoid both
running out of stock and buyings things
that you have and don't need because you
think you are out of them.

The chief enemy of orderly arrangement
is overloading. When the freezer gets too
full, a shelf or area may over-fill without
room to expand, and items that belong
there get into spaces where they do not
belong. Also, you should have a little

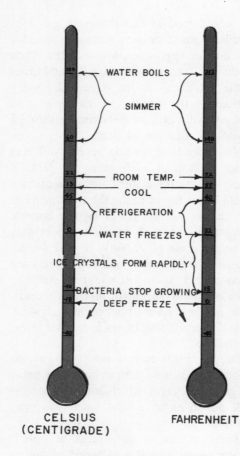

CELSIUS (CENTIGRADE)   **FAHRENHEIT**

Fig. 30-11a. Two temperature scales

empty shelf space reserved for two purposes, quick-freezing of new material and for temporary piling of purchases for later sorting and placing.

If you return from the market with frozen food and find you have urgent jobs to do immediately, you will naturally just shove things in the freezer without taking

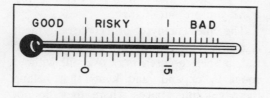

Fig. 30-11b. Freezer temperatures

time for proper sorting. If they are all in one place you can easily sort them later, but if they have been put in at random into different areas you may not find some of them for a long time.

Temperature. The approved storage temperature in home freezers is zero Fahrenheit. This is true of both separate freezers, and freezer-refrigerator combinations. Most (but perhaps not all) foods would keep longer and in better condition at lower temperatures. But after the zero point each degree of drop provides a smaller amount of benefit, and the cost of obtaining it rises. Therefore, colder temperatures are not considered to be worth their cost at home at present.

Freezing compartments inside refrigerators (with no separate outside door) may stay anywhere between zero and 30° depending on the model and condition of the machine, and the setting of its controls. Only a few provide quick freezing, and most of them do not keep frozen foods well for more than a few days.

Water in food does not freeze to any great extent at 32° F. because of dissolved substances. Ordinary food may be frozen completely at 25°, but parts of it may be on the edge of thawing, and ice crystals are likely to grow. Most crystal formation and all bacterial growth seem to stop at around 15°, but strong salt or sugar solutions may retain some liquid down below zero.

Up-and-down changes in freezer temperature, caused by opening doors, putting in unfrozen food, and the normal off-on cycle of the pump may promote growth of ice crystals and unfavorable changes in texture and flavor. Such effects are important above 15°, and very slight at zero and colder.

Drying. Drying of food is slowed but not stopped by freezing. Ice can change directly from its solid state to water vapor, a process called sublimation. Freezing-then-drying is an excellent commercial process for preservation of a variety of foods, but its effects at home are almost always bad.

The drying process is officially called dehydration, dessication or freezer burn. Its effect is usually to make the food hard or tough, and there are often changes in color.

The best defense against drying is proper wrapping, which was discussed in the preceding chapter. The need for it varies somewhat with the type of food and the length of storage. Open-textured materials such as bread and hamburger tend to be damaged by dehydration quite rapidly, while solid meat and wet-pack vegetables take longer. But it is good to form the habit of carefully protecting each item put in the freezer, as it is easily done, and the food may not be used as soon as you expect.

Drying is more severe in frost-free freezers than in models that allow ice crystals to build up in their interiors.

Glazing. Bare food may be protected temporarily by coating with ice, a process called glazing. If a frozen object is sprayed with cold water, or dipped in it, a coating of ice (glaze) will form on it. Repeated applications will continue to build an ice layer on it until they warm the surface too much, at which time it can be put back in the freezer to be re-chilled.

A piece of food completely coated in ice cannot dry out. But porous, absorbent materials such as bread would become too wet when defrosted, putting on the ice is tedious work and the food must be checked occasionally to make sure its coating is still there and complete. Glazing is at best a temporary or emergency substitute for wrapping, or as an extra precaution when placed inside of wrapping.

The same effect is not usually obtained from a layer of frost deposited during storage. Frost is likely to have pores through which water can continue to move outward from the food, and its crystals may draw out moisture themselves.

Movement of Moisture. Food may be damaged by movement of moisture within

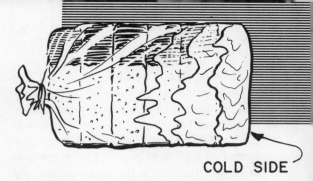

COLD SIDE

Fig. 30-12. Frost may build up inside a package

a sealed package. In porous materials such as bread and cake it has a tendency to vaporize from the food and condense as frost crystals on the inside of the moisture-proof wrapping, or on the nearby surface of the food. If there are temperature differences of even a fraction of a degree, the crystals will tend to grow most at the coldest side or spot.

This process is usually slow, but it is continuous, and in months or years may draw almost all of the water out of the bread.

A small amount of out-of-place moisture will usually redistribute itself if the food package is not opened for a few minutes after thawing is completed. Larger amounts require leaving it wrapped for as much as a day afterward, to avoid staleness in one part and sogginess in another.

This problem may be reduced by shaking the package, and knocking it around a little, right after taking it out of the freezer, to distribute the frost crystals more evenly.

Moisture movement in the package is greatest with open-textured baked goods such as bread and cinnamon buns, and least with compact materials like pound cake and French crumb cake.

DEFROSTING

Most frozen foods require un-freezing, a process called defrosting, or thawing. This may be done very slowly in a refrigerator, slowly at room temperature, rapidly over a burner or in an oven, very rapidly in a microwave oven, or by combinations of these methods.

Thawing time is variable, as foods differ in their insulating qualities and water content. In general, the higher the percentage of water and the thicker the unit, the slower the melting. A pint of loose frozen peas spread on a piece of paper at room temperature will thaw in a few minutes, but the same quantity frozen in a block of their own juice may take an hour or more.

Any sort of wrapping on frozen food will slow the defrosting process. This effect is least with transparent plastic and greatest with aluminum foil. The foil can be used to advantage in covering legs, wings and other projections during room-thawing of poultry, to prevent damage by too much warming and drying.

Meat. Chunks of meat take a long time to defrost. For roasts figure 1-1/2 to 2-1/2 hours to the pound at room temperature, and 3 to 5 hours in the refrigerator. But flat cuts such as one-inch steaks thaw rather quickly.

Cookbooks often tell you that you should never thaw any thick piece of meat at room temperature, as the outside may get warm enough to spoil before the ice is gone from the center. This might happen, but it is very unlikely. Heat is carried to the meat surface mostly by conduction through air, which is an insulator. The moisture-filled meat is a good heat conductor, and tends to transfer its slowly gathered surface heat into the inside quite rapidly.

As a result, the surface usually stays refrigerator-cold during the whole thawing

Fig. 30-13. Foil prevents drying out during thawing

process. But don't get absent minded and leave it out after it is fully thawed.

Defrosting at room temperature usually allows a more convenient time schedule than the refrigerator method. A Sunday dinner roast can be taken out of the freezer late Saturday evening, and a roast for the evening meal may start its defrosting early the same morning.

Watery fluid may leak out of the meat as it defrosts. This is almost sure to occur with beef, and may or may not with lamb and pork. Take the precaution of putting the meat on a platter or shallow pan that will hold a few ounces of fluid, to prevent it from running around.

Cooking Frozen Food. It takes from 20 to 100 per cent longer to cook a frozen food than the same item at room temperature. The most important variable is solidity. A solid block, frozen creamed spinach for example, thaws very slowly in boiling water, while dry-pack frozen peas thaw almost instantly.

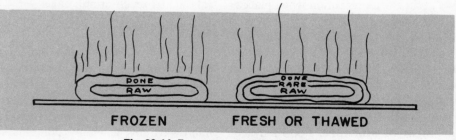

Fig. 30-14. Frozen meat cooks differently

Any open structure that allows hot water or steam to penetrate the block speeds thawing. Breaking a block up with a strong knife or a screwdriver before or during heating opens it up with the same effect. But don't do this in a good pan, and specially not in Teflon.

A vegetable in small pieces frozen together may break apart quickly under a thin stream of hot water from a faucet. Put the pan underneath, and use the water for finishing the melting and doing the cooking over a burner.

A steak, hamburger or roast shows a different pattern when cooked frozen. The change from the cooked surface to the raw inside is abrupt, with little of the grading through pink found in fresh or thawed meat. And rare cooking may leave it still very cold in the middle.

A lower cooking temperature in a pan or oven, or more distance from a broiler flame, will reduce the frost effects.

REFREEZING

On the subject of refreezing, most publications for the consumer, as well as labels on frozen food, simply say "DON'T" or "NEVER." Commercial sources and research institutions generally find little reason not to refreeze, as long as precautions are taken against spoilage.

So far as texture and flavor are concerned, damage from refreezing is usually of the same type that occurred in the original freezing, but is much less extensive if conditions are the same. Twice-frozen lamb, bacon, green peas or spinach, for example, can seldom be distinguished from once-frozen items. But cauliflower may be a little more limp.

Spoilage. The critical matter is spoilage. Commercially packed frozen food seems to be frequently loaded with bacteria — not enough to cause any unpleasantness if it is immediately cooked and eaten, but enough to provide a running start for multiplication in the weakened food structure if it is left at room temperature, and to a less extent under average refrigeration.

The packers of the food have no control over the handling of their products in homes, and their surest way to avoid possible criticism and even lawsuits is to forbid refreezing. In this way, they cannot reasonably be held responsible for food left out long enough to spoil, and then refrozen.

Frozen and thawed vegetables are dead, and their structure has been more or less damaged by ice crystals. As a result, they spoil rapidly, sometimes in less than 3 hours after complete thawing, at 70° F, and occasionally in as little as 3 days at 35°. This is assuming a fairly heavy contamination at the time thawing started. Home frozen products should last longer.

Seafood is damaged easily and thoroughly by standing after thawing. Fortunately, it usually gives warning of poor condition by a strong smell.

Meat. Most cookbooks are particularly emphatic in forbidding the refreezing of meat. It is curious that this should be so, as meat suffers even less from refreezing than vegetables and fruit do. There is minor

Fig. 30-15. Not for refreezing

Fig. 30-16. For over-stock and for emergencies

structural damage, and a number of small chemical changes take place, but there are no important differences in either nourishment or taste.

Meat usually freezes faster the second time than the first — beef round that originally becomes only 20 per cent frozen at 27° may become 60 per cent frozen at the same temperature during refreezing.

Meat that has been frozen and thawed spoils somewhat more rapidly than fresh meat does, but it is difficult to set up a definite time schedule for it. The above suggestions on vegetables should cover it. If it looks and smells good enough to eat, it should be good enough to freeze or refreeze. Penetration of spoilage, however, is more rapid than before freezing and thawing.

You have to be specially careful with pot roast, rolled roast and other de-boned cuts, as bacteria are usually folded inside them during processing. If in doubt in regard to one of these, open it up for inspection.

Chopped meat usually spoils rather rapidly and uniformly, and any decay inside it will be evident at the surface at least by smell.

If you are doubtful about refreezing meat, you can cook it, then freeze it as soon as it cools off. The cooking will usually sterilize or at least pasteurize it for safety, and it is sometimes convenient to have cooked meat that is ready to eat as soon as it is defrosted. It is most quickly available if sliced before freezing. Slices should be dampened with water or gravy before wrapping.

Freezer Breakdown. A freezer may stop freezing because of mechanical breakdown, being disconnected, or power failure. The ordinarily unobservant householder may have no warning of the first two until considerable warming has occurred. Some freezers show a small green light whenever power is on, and if such a light is not on, immediate investigation should be made.

A battery-powered warning light, perhaps with a bell or buzzer also, that would go on if freezer temperature rose more than a few degrees above its setting, would be highly desirable but is apparently not available at present.

In a properly insulated and well-filled freezer most foods can remain 2 to 4 days before they thaw fully. A nearly empty freezer would defrost in 1/4 that time. There is usually time for the repairman to call, or the power to come back on, before substantial damage is done.

So far as spoilage is concerned, it is safe

to refreeze any food that still contains ice, and a package that still feels very cold is all right. Borderline or doubtful items should be inspected. In general, standards for refreezing given above can be followed.

The principal problem is that a freezer cannot quick-freeze its entire contents. The refreezing process will be slow in a well-loaded cabinet, ice crystals will form, and texture and flavor of many foods will suffer. The load can be reduced slightly by moving all soon-to-be-eaten foods to the refrigerator.

If there is a freezer-locker plant in the vicinity, arrangements might be made to take most of the food there, for quick refreezing after damage has been discovered, and for storage while the home freezer is not operating.

If a rotten smell develops during a freezer breakdown, you should wash and dry all inside surfaces of the cabinet, and wash (or wipe thoroughly) any packages that you salvage. Otherwise, the smell may persist for months.

Dry Ice. Dry ice is one of several names for solidified carbon dioxide. It is a white, snow-like material that sublimes (changes directly to vapor) at around $-110°$ F. Whenever it is left unconfined, as when resting on a freezer shelf, it will maintain its surface at this very low temperature until it disappears.

Dry ice has many commercial uses, and can be obtained in or near most cities.

This substance is almost as harmful to the bare hands as hot metal, as its extreme cold produces painful frostbite. Always wear gloves or use padded pot holders when picking it up or moving it.

Exposed dry ice vaporizes much more rapidly than is usually necessary to provide enough chill for food protection. The process can be slowed by wrapping it loosely in several layers of aluminum foil, newspaper or any insulating material. A freezer thermometer can tell you whether you are

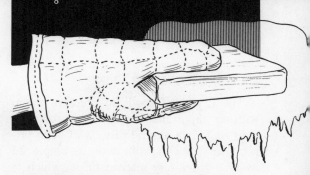
Fig. 30-17. Protect your hands from dry ice

slowing the heat absorption too much or too little.

Gas evolving from dry ice builds up pressure which must be allowed to escape, so that it is important in non-vented freezers to leave the door open slightly while using it. You can reduce the resulting inefficiency of cooling by blocking the door firmly in a just-open position, then packing some sort of insulating material between the door and the jamb, except for a vent hole near the top.

Dry ice should not be used in an unventilated room, as there is a small chance that the carbon dioxide gas might build up to a dangerous level.

Open Door. If a door on a cabinet freezer is left partly open, cold air from inside it will flow out near the bottom and warm air from the room will enter near the top. If the cooling lines are in the shelves or elsewhere in the box, parts will stay quite cold while others thaw, and considerable time may elapse before total thawing occurs.

In a frost free freezer there will be immediate and almost total loss of freezing action. The cooling lines are not in contact with any food, and they do not have the capacity to reduce warm air from the room to subfreezing temperature in a single cycle. The air that has been cooled by passing over them will be discharged on the floor, to be replaced by more air from the room.

Unless such a freezer is very solidly packed, an open door will permit rapid thawing and spoilage.

DRYING (DEHYDRATING)

The drying of foods to preserve them, with an important side benefit in reducing their bulk, is a natural process of great importance. It is also artificial means employed by man from very ancient times, which is now being expanded and diversified.

Grains, nuts, legumes and some fruits mature and remain on the plant to dry in the air and sun. Such drying may be aided in wet seasons by heating gently with fires, either outdoors or indoors.

A number of kinds of fruit, including apricots, grapes and plums, may be harvested and then dried in the sun. Fish and thinly sliced meat may be dried on racks, often in climates offering little sunshine. Application of preservatives, or special care in turning or other handling, may be necessary to reduce or prevent damage from action of enzymes and organisms during the drying process.

A large and increasing proportion of food drying is now done in factories. They compete vigorously with the sun-driers on many of the old standby products, and offer a number of new items.

It is customary to reserve the term "drying" for outdoor and primitive methods, and to call the factory processes "dehydration", but the terms are used interchangeably in this discussion. There are two other words, evaporation and desiccation, that may be used for either. But an evaporated product is usually still liquid, while a desiccated one is solid or powdered.

At its best, sun drying produces top quality results, particularly with fruit. But there are problems of unsuitable weather, insect attack and dust, and it is likely that on the average the factory dehydrated products are more reliable.

Keeping Qualities. Dried foods keep very well under ordinary household conditions. This is because they contain so little water that they do not support life. Even their enzymes are slowed or stopped by the dryness, if they have not already been destroyed during processing by blanching or by sulfide chemicals to make sure.

The lack of moisture has two effects on organisms. One is simply to deprive them of a source of water for their life processes. The other is a tendency to suck any moisture that they may already have out through their cell walls by osmosis, a process described on page 39.

The moisture percentage in dried foods ranges from 3 to 25 per cent. The higher amounts can be tolerated in fruit which contains enough sugar to bind some of the water, so as to prevent it from being used by cells.

Low moisture content does not always stop organisms that can obtain water elsewhere. In humid weather molds may be able to get enough from the air for growth, and insects can walk or fly to other sources. Also, many of these foods will absorb water from humid air, building up at least a damp surface layer which not only encourages organisms but also may make the surface

Fig. 30-18. Many foods are sun-dried

Product	Fresh	Dehydrated	Canned or Frozen
Fruit	50-55	3-7	50-60
Vegetables	50-85	5-25	50-85
Meats	50-85	15-20	50-60
Eggs	85-90	10-15	35-40
Fish	50-75	20-40	30-75

Fig. 30-19. Bulk of fresh and processed foods

slimy and unpleasant. Or if the food is powdered, absorbed water will make it lumpy or even form a solid cake which is difficult to use.

It is therefore often necessary and always desirable to pack dried or dehydrated foods with moisture proof wrapping, plus whatever packaging is needed to protect the wrapping and make it easy to label, handle and store.

Drying does not have any direct effect on the degeneration of fat, which limits the useful life of foods that contain it. This is probably the principal reason for the acceptance of powdered skim milk in preference to the whole milk product. Fatty foods may include antioxidants to slow or possibly prevent development of rancidity.

Concentration. There is a very wide range in the amount that foods are concentrated by drying or dehydrating. Evaporated milk is reduced in bulk and weight to about 50 per cent, powdered skim milk to 10 per cent of the original fluid. Figure 30-19 indicates reduction in space requirements for some other classes of foods.

Such concentration makes dried food economical to ship, store and handle. Conversion from liquid to solid (powdered) state reduces cost and weight of containers, and loss from breakage and leakage. Refrigeration is not needed, and long shelf life reduces spoilage problems.

The principal problem is one of consumer acceptance, which is based largely on the nuisance of recombining with water and on questions of taste and texture. Very few dried or dehydrated foods are eaten directly from the package, unless you want to include dry cereals in this class.

Too-fast drying, or use of food that is in poor condition, may result in the formation of hard crusts that will not absorb water. Such parts are not edible unless they are ground or cut very finely, and they may prevent water from reaching uninjured parts. This is one of the main problems with acceptance of dried foods.

Rehydration. Rehydration is a word that has not yet been made official by dictionaries. It is an informal but useful term used in industry and laboratories to cover restoration of water that has been removed from any substance. It is both more descriptive than the term reconstitution, and more general than dissolving, soaking and plumping.

Methods vary with the nature of the substance. Solids such as dry prunes, apricots, beans and peas are soaked for a long time, often overnight, in cool or warm water, or for shorter times in hot water. This is usually a separate operation, before cooking.

Powders are usually dissolved in water or milk, to reproduce the original liquid from which the concentrate was made. Improved manufacturing processes are making this a much easier job than it was a few years ago. Problems and methods are discussed under Dissolving, page 22.

Liquids can be easily and quickly mixed with the full quantity of water unless they are very thick. In that case, start adding water slowly with thorough mixing, then add it more rapidly as the concentrate becomes thinner.

The process of adding water to a concentrated fruit juice, particularly if it is or has been frozen, is known as reconstitution. Bottles of unconcentrated fruit juice often state on the label that they contain reconstituted juice.

The concentration costs little extra when the juice is being pasteurized, and it offers worth while economies in shipping and storage. Quality can be maintained at a high level, but on the average is below that of fresh juice.

Methods of Dehydration. Dehydration is usually done in a current of warm, dry air. Pieces that are larger than powder are rested on trays, racks, a slotted floor, movable trucks or conveyor belts. In a cabinet dryer the food is stationary, in a tunnel it is moved slowly through the drying area and in a kiln it is stirred and turned on a slotted floor through which hot air rises.

Many problems exist. Very slow drying is uneconomic and risks spoilage. Fast drying may cause surface crust to form which prevents further evaporation. Either method may cause, or fail to prevent, undesirable changes in taste, color and texture. Processes have to be worked out separately for each food.

In most foods, better results are obtained by using moderate temperature with a vacuum to speed evaporation, than by the same rate of drying at normal pressure with warmer air. But cost is usually higher. The most advanced application of this technique is freeze drying.

Liquids, even quite thick ones, may be dried in sprays or on drums. They are forced through a nozzle that disperses them as small droplets in the drying air, or are deposited in a thin film on heated, rotating drums. Powder formed from the spray falls or is blown into ducts, and is collected. The dried film is removed from the drum by a scraper blade, and then ground. In general, a spray drier produces a better product.

If liquid is to have only part of the water removed, the operation is called concentration rather than dehydration. Evaporated milk is probably the best known product of this type. Fruit juices that are to be frozen are usually concentrated first.

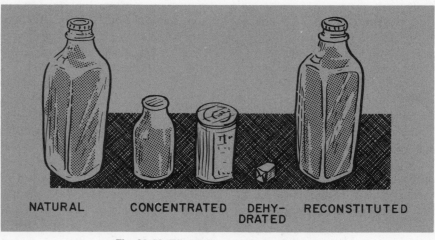

NATURAL   CONCENTRATED   DEHY-   RECONSTITUTED
                                       DRATED

Fig. 30-20. Effect of concentration on bulk

FREEZE DRYING
(FREEZE-DEHYDRATION)

In freeze drying, the food is first frozen, and then the ice is evaporated (sublimed) out of it, leaving the dried food as a porous structure that is about the same size as before processing. Rehydration is usually quick, easy and thorough, as water can soak through it as if it were a blotter, instead of being held out by shrunken, compact material. Soluble powders dissolve without lumping.

Drying is usually done under high vacuum, only 15 per cent or less of atmospheric pressure, with a steady supply of dry thin air. The change from ice to water vapor absorbs heat and chills the food so that the process is slowed. This is counteracted by resting the food on shelves heated to 110° F or even more, or by using microwaves, so that the chill of evaporation is counteracted enough to keep the food just below freezing temperature. When the ice is all gone, temperature rises over 32°.

In meat, this removal of the ice takes out about 94 per cent of the moisture. The balance may be evaporated at above-freezing temperature, without injuring the porosity.

Freeze drying usually produces a high quality product. At present, costs may be several times higher than for conventional dehydration. It can be expected that improved techniques will reduce this cost difference, and that an increasing variety of foods will be processed in this way.

Canned fruit concentrates that liquefy when thawed are not considered to be freeze concentrated, as the excess water is usually removed first by evaporation, and the thickened juice is frozen as a second process.

31
CANNING AND PRESERVING

CANNING

Canning is of importance to the homemaker both because of the wide use of commercially canned food in preparing meals, and the lesser possibility of canning fresh garden produce for future use.

Canning dates from the French "Appertizing" process invented in 1795, and English patents of 1810 which included using tin-plated canisters, from which the word "can" was probably abbreviated. The causes of food spoilage were not known at that time, but reasonably effective processes were worked out on a trial and error basis.

Successful canning requires heating food hot enough and long enough to kill the bacteria that cause that particular food to spoil, and hermetically (absolutely) sealing the sterilized food so that new organisms cannot get into it, and air, other gases and moisture cannot get out.

Canned food is not necessarily sterile, as some organisms that are highly heat resistant may survive the processing. However, it kills all poisonous or poison-forming species, and all varieties that multiply at ordinary storage temperatures.

Since the heat process used to prevent spoilage cooks at the same time, most commercial canned vegetables, meat and fruit are cooked and ready to eat. Those that are served hot need merely to be heated, without attention to any cooking requirement. Others can be used directly from the cold can or container.

Canning has a variable but usually undesirable effect on flavor and texture of foods, largely because of the necessity of overcooking them. Some products, such as soda and beer, often seem unaffected.

Containers. Food is usually canned in cans of tin-plated steel (which may also be lacquered or enameled inside), or in glass. There is increasing use of aluminum cans and of steel cans with aluminum tops that have tabs and scoring to permit opening by pulling on a ring. There is limited or experimental use of tinless steel cans, tin plated glass and flexible containers.

Figure 31-2 shows some specialty cans which open by means of rings or keys.

Metal and glass containers are mostly interchangeable for canning. Traditionally, glass is used for jams, jellies, pickles and beverages; and metal for vegetables, meat,

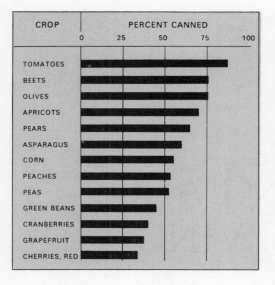

CROP	PERCENT CANNED				
	0	25	50	75	100
TOMATOES					
BEETS					
OLIVES					
APRICOTS					
PEARS					
ASPARAGUS					
CORN					
PEACHES					
PEAS					
GREEN BEANS					
CRANBERRIES					
GRAPEFRUIT					
CHERRIES, RED					

Fig. 31-1. Much of our food is canned

fish, fruit and soup. However, each material repeatedly invades the field of the other, and you can often choose between them on the store shelf in selecting a variety of items.

Metal is light-proof. It does not break, although it can be punctured by impact or by rusting. There is a much-argued question about whether the tin plate, and possible minute exposures of steel, affect the flavor and quality of various foods, and how much. Tin does bleach some highly colored foods, but the canners should and usually do use lacquered cans for these, that prevent contact with the tin.

Glass is likely to break if dropped, banged or handled roughly. Clear glass permits some food to be damaged by light, while protective brown or green glass is usually unattractive. The glass itself is absolutely inert, and does not react with food, or affect its taste or color in any way.

Either container may be used for keeping unused portions of the food in the refrigerator. The unfounded prejudice against using metal in this manner is discussed on page 576.

A glass container permits you to see

how much is in it, and its condition.

Sizes. Can sizes, proportions and names are complicated and confusing. There are many approved or standard types and sizes, and others that are not listed but are nevertheless found on market shelves.

Most but not all of the standard sizes are cylindrical — that is, they are round with flat tops and bottoms. The proportion between diameter and height varies greatly. Choice of shapes and sizes is largely traditional, but is often affected by efficiency in processing. There is a trend toward use of smaller sizes.

The canner has two designations for cans. One is informal, such as No. 2 or No. 303, the other is a code for the actual size. For example, a condensed soup can, informally known as a No. 1 Picnic, is a 211 x 400. The first digit in each number is inches, the next two are for 16ths of inches. This can has an outside diameter of 2-11/16 inches and a height of 4 inches even (4-00/16 inches).

A recipe may tell you to use a can of a certain size, such as No. 2 or No. 300, of one of the ingredients. Can size is not usually stamped in the can or printed on the label, so a large element of guess work is introduced. And there may be two or more cans with one number. In addition, you may want to substitute fresh or home

Fig. 31-2. Cans with ring or key openers

canned food, and would need to know how much the can holds.

Figure 31-3 supplies information on a few popular size cans. A more detailed listing will be found in the Appendix.

Glass containers have equal variety in size, and a great number of different shapes. A few of them that correspond in capacity and general shape to popular can sizes are known by the same informal name, such as 303. The majority of them, however, may not have numbers and are described simply by capacity in fluid ounces and by a general description of shape.

Juice. Vegetables are ordinarily packed with their own cooking water. This is usually rich in the flavor and nutriments of the vegetable, and should be used in heating it. It can be eaten with the food, used in soup or gravy, or discarded afterward. There is no basis for a widespread belief that canning juice should not be used.

If you wish to serve the food with a small amount of concentrated juice, drain the can into a pan, boil the juice until it is reduced in quantity and/or strengthened in flavor to your taste, then add the vegetable. Cover the pan, and keep over high heat for about a minute, or until boiling resumes.

Fruit and berries are canned in sugar syrup, which is discussed in page 378.

Acidity. The acidity of a food is very important in deciding the method and particularly the amount of heat to be used in processing it.

Acidity is measured on a scale of pH values, the "pH" standing for a reversed measurement of the percentage of free hydrogen ions. More ions mean more acid. A pH of 7.0 is neutral, higher values are alkaline and lower figures are increasingly acid.

An acid flavor may be masked or counteracted by adding sugar, but this has no effect on pH rating.

Very few foods are alkaline. Those with a pH range of 5.0 to 6.8, which include

CONTAINER Consumer description		
Industry term	Approximate Net Weight (check label)	Approximate Cups
8 ounce	8 oz.	1
Picnic	10½ to 12 oz.	1¼
12 oz. (vacuum)	12 oz.	1½
No. 300	14 to 16 oz.	1¾
No. 303	16 to 17 oz.	2
No. 2	1 lb. 4 oz. or 1 pt. 2 fl. oz.	2½
No. 2½	1 lb. 13 oz.	3½
No. 3 Cyl.	3 lb. 3 oz. or 1 qt. 14 fl. oz.	5¾
No. 10	6½ lb. to 7 lb. 5 oz.	12-13

Courtesy of National Canners Assn.

Fig. 31-3. Capacity of some cans

meat, fish, poultry, dairy products and most vegetables are called low-acid or sometimes non-acid foods. Manufactured food items such as soup and spaghetti-with-sauce often have a pH of 4.5 to 5.0, and are called medium acid.

The pH of 4.5 is the important dividing line for the canner. The most deadly and the most resistant of food poisoning organisms, a bacterium called Clostridium botulinum, cannot grow in foods with a pH of 4.5 or lower, and can be disregarded in processing them. But any food in the medium or low-acid groups must be assumed to be infected with it, and treated to destroy it. And as we shall see, it is a difficult organism to eliminate.

Acid foods, with pH between 4.5 and 3.7 include peaches, pears, oranges, apricots and tomatoes. High-acid foods, from 3.7 down to 2.3, include most berries and pickled and fermented foods. All bacteria

Harvesting

Receiving raw product

Soaking and Washing

Sorting and grading

Blanching

Peeling and Coring

Filling

Exhausting

Sealing

Processing

Cooling

Labeling

Warehousing and Packing

Courtesy of American Can Co.

Fig. 31-4. Commercial canning

that are active in these two groups are easily killed by boiling at 212° F. However, there are a few very tough enzymes that may partly survive such cooking, and cause some deterioration during storage.

Processing. Figure 31-4 shows the sequence of events in the canning process. The blanching, which was described under FREEZING, kills the majority of microorganisms left by the washing, and protects

the food against deterioration until the cooking heat reaches it. It is used selectively, just on the foods that will tolerate it and will benefit from it.

Containers, either cans or glass jars, are filled with blanched or raw food that is in final condition, piece size, etc., except for cooking, together with water, salt and any other additives. Air is exhausted from the container by displacing it with steam, heat

Product	Can Size*	Process-Agitated at 260° F		Conventional	
		Time, Min.	Temp., °F	Time, Min.	Temp., °F
Peas	307 × 409	4.90	260	35	240
Carrots	307 × 409	3.40	260	30	240
Beets — sliced	307 × 409	4.10	260	30	240
Asparagus spears		4.50	270	16	248
Asparagus cuts and tips	307 × 409	4.00	270	15	248
Cabbage	307 × 409	2.75	270	40	240
Asparagus spears					
brine packed	307 × 409	5.20	260	50	240
brine packed	603 × 700	10.00	260	80	240
vacuum packed	307 × 306	5.00	260	35	250
Evaporated milk	300 × 314	2.25	200	18	240

*First digit in each number is inches, the next two are sixteenths.

By permission from "Technology of Food Preservation", 3rd Edition, Copyright 1970, Avi Publishing Co.

Fig. 31-5. Shortening cooking time by process-agitation

expansion before sealing, or with pumps, and covers are placed and sealed.

The sterilizing or cooking process varies with the nature of the food — the degree of acidity, the type of organisms commonly found in it, the size of pieces, the thickness (viscosity) of any fluid, the heat tolerance and the size of the container.

The problem is that complete sterilization will often overcook food so that it becomes unpalatable and loses nutritive value. The process is often regulated to kill everything except the spores of certain thermophilic (heat-loving) bacteria, which have very high survival temperatures, which flourish at temperatures of 120 to 170° F and that are inactive below 80 or even 110°, depending on the species.

Since canned foods are not normally this hot while in storage, such bacteria have no chance to multiply and spoil the food. Their possible presence is the reason that canned foods should not be stored in hot places.

Heat and Time. Ordinary boiling temperature, 212° F, is not sufficient to sterilize low or medium acid foods. C. botulinium can survive 5 hours of such boiling. Temperatures of 240 to 250° are required to kill this organism, if the cooking time is to be kept within reasonable limits. The 240° corresponds to that of steam under 10 pounds pressure.

The heat resistance of organisms seems to increase in proportion to their number of concentration. Sterilization of a can of corn inoculated with 10,000 spores of an organism may take 15 minutes longer cooking at 240° than a similar can inoculated with 10 spores. For this reason it is very important that everything about a canning operation be kept as clean as possible, whether in the factory or the home, to avoid heavy infections from tools or utensils.

The organism will not be killed unless the heat reaches it. The heating of a can in the cooker occurs by conduction through its walls and into the food, and by convection currents inside the can which mix heated fluid at the edges with cooler material in the center.

If the pack is solid (tuna, for example) there is no convection and heating to the center will take longer. If the fluid is thick and slow moving, as in some condensed soup, convection is slow and inefficient.

Delicate instruments (thermocouples) are used to find the slowest-heating spots in sample cans, and such "cold spots" are used in calculations of sterilizing time necessary.

Vegetables and some other products can be sterilized in a fraction of conventional time by using much higher heat, and continuously shaking or agitating the containers so that the food circulates rapidly during the process.

This agitation process usually results in better flavor, color and nutrient retention, in addition to saving the canner's time. Agitation will probably find increasing use.

Figure 31-5 shows comparison between still and agitated cooking.

Keeping Qualities. Canned food that is completely sterilized in containers that do not leak should keep indefinitely. But metal cans and lids are subject to attack by corrosion by certain food combinations and by defects of manufacture from inside, and attack of moisture, chemicals and impact from the outside. If a leak develops the contents will probably spoil before you have noticed it.

If the food is not completely sterilized, but there are only surviving spores of the heat loving bacteria, it will keep as well as if it were completely sterilized if you store it in a cool or not-over-75° F place. If it is kept in a hot place, or if normal temperature bacteria are present in it, it will spoil.

There are flat-sour organisms that make canned food go sour without creating gas, but most spoilage gives off carbon dioxide and other gases which cause the can to bulge. It is best to assume that any can with an end bulged contains spoiled food, and it can be thrown away without opening. But not into an incinerator, where it would probably explode.

Never taste canned food that you think may be spoiled, unless it is acid or high acid. That is, unless you want to take the precaution of boiling it vigorously for 15 minutes first. This destroys the botulism toxin, which may not produce any warning appearance or odor, but is so incredibly poisonous that a millionth of a gram may kill a man.

Spoilage in the very acid foods may produce unpleasant and unexpected appearance or taste, but it does not create poisons.

Under normal conditions of use and storage you might never have a case of spoilage of commercially canned food. If your storage closet is hot, and/or you keep some cans for years before you use them, you are likely to have an occasional one spoil. But your chance of getting one loaded with botulism is less than one in billions.

Food loses some of its good qualities in the canning process, as it is often necessary to more or less overcook it to sterilize it. And conventional canned foods are always cooked foods — they cannot be raw as frozen or dried ones may be.

It is likely that there will be marked improvement in the quality of premium brands within a few years, and in most canned goods shortly afterward, as the high temperature agitator cookers come into use.

Deterioration. Unfortunately, there is often a very gradual deterioration in flavor and texture as the can stands on the shelf. Solids tend to soften and lose some of their substance, flavors may become less definite or mix together. Such changes are unlikely to be noticeable for a few months or even a year, but they do occur, and they involve a definite loss in quality.

Try to put new cans of food at the back of the shelf, so you will automatically use the oldest ones first.

GLASS LID

RUBBER

SEALS HERE

Fig. 31-6. Clamp jar

HOME CANNING

Canning was formerly the only way in which a housewife could preserve low cost or over-abundant food for future use. Its usefulness as a home process has decreased owing to the greater ease, convenience and safety of freezing.

However, canned food does not require frozen storage with its space limitations, expense and dependence on uninterrupted electric power.

Home canning involves clean containers that can be easily and completely sealed, cooking food in such containers until all (or practically all) organisms are killed, and sealing the containers.

CONTAINERS

Clamp Jars. Home canning is almost always done in glass jars with gasket seals with clamp or screw fasteners.

The original canning jar, Figure 31-6, is available in quart, pint and half-pint sizes. It may be called wire-clamp, Ideal or Light-

ning. Both the bottle and the cap are clear glass. The gasket between them is soft rubber. A pair of wire loops or bails are double hinged to sockets in the jar so that one passes over the cap where it is held by a center notch, and the other locks it there with pressure when pulled down against the side of the jar.

This design is simple and has given good service for generations. But there are a few requirements for good results, or even any results.

The rubber in the gasket must be soft, flexible and without cracks. A test is to bend it double and pinch the bend between finger and thumb. If it pinches flat without showing any cracks, it is all right.

The bail with a nearly flat cross piece goes on top, and must be in the notch on the top ridge, while the curved bail moves down against the side of the jar.

To open a sealed jar, first move the lower (curved) bail or locking loop up, then pull the upper bail toward it and down. This leaves the cover free to be lifted or pried off.

There should be vacuum in the jar because of contraction of food and vapor as it cooled. This holds the lid down, which usually does not and should not lift off with just finger pressure. You release it by making an opening through which air can enter.

The gasket ring has a projecting tab. This is sometimes constructed so that pulling its sides away from each other will cause it to tear, so that the gasket is pulled apart and allows air to move in. If the tab is not made to split, or you cannot get a good enough grip on it, release the vacuum by putting a table knife or any other thin utensil between the gasket and the top, forcing it in to the back of the gasket and twisting.

This should allow air to leak in along the knife, breaking the vacuum and usually allowing the lid to come off without further resistance. But if the gasket is stuck top and bottom with spilled juice, you may have to pry at several places, or use a heavier tool such as a screwdriver, to release it.

Be suspicious of the contents of any jar if the lid lifts off without resistance. Where there is no vacuum, there has been either poor canning procedure or a leak, either of which is likely to allow spoilage.

Pressure in the jar, that lifts the lid or puffs out, is a sure sign that the food is spoiled.

Screw Top — One-Piece. The majority of glass canning jars are now threaded, with screw-type caps which may be made in one piece or in the more popular two-piece construction.

The one-piece cap, Figure 31-7, may be made of zinc with a porcelain lining in the top. It seals with a separate soft rubber ring, similar to that used with clamp lids. The seal may be on the jar top or more commonly on a shoulder below the threads.

After the jar is filled, the cap is turned down tight to seat the gasket, then loosened slightly to allow escape of heated air and steam during processing. It is tightened again immediately after the cooking is finished.

If the jar is over-filled, or tipped while the top was loose, juice or food may get on the threads, and cause difficulty in removing the cap when the food is to be used. Very hot water on the cap will usually expand it away from the glass, making it easier to loosen. Or you may hold the jar upside down in the hot water, to permit it to penetrate along the threads and dissolve or soften the substance that makes it stick.

Tapping the center of the cap may also be helpful. A twist-type clamp (see Chapter 35) will give you extra leverage to force it off.

Screw Top — Two-Piece. Vacuum in a jar may be a more powerful sealing force than clamps or threads. The two-piece

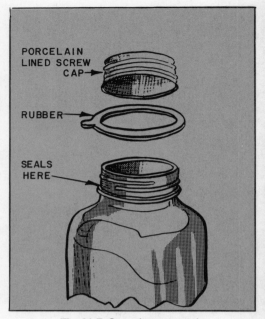

Fig. 31-7. One-piece screw top

metal jar top, Figure 31-8, takes fullest advantage of vacuum.

There is a flat or slightly domed lid, usually made of thin metal, with a built-in rubber or possibly plastic ring gasket that covers the jar top, and a separate threaded ring or band which screws down on the threaded jar. The band has a flange that overlaps the lid, above the gasket, and that can pull the lid down into tight contact with the jar.

The jars, lids and rings are kept in hot but not necessarily boiling water just before use. A jar is emptied of water, and filled with food. The lid is placed on the top, then the ring is placed and tightened, but without much force. It is not re-tightened after processing.

This sealing device allows pressure from inside the jar to escape between the gasket and the glass during cooking, but as soon as the jar and its contents cool, internal pressure drops to a partial vacuum, so that the lid is forced down tightly by atmospheric pressure and becomes a complete seal.

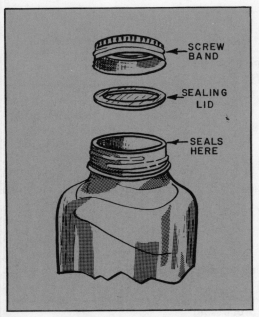

Fig. 31-8. Two-piece screw top

If the lid is of flexible metal it will probably change shape, from domed to flat or from flat to concave, depending on its design, after thorough cooling. If it does not, press the center with your finger. If it does not bend down then, there is probably no vacuum and therefore no seal, and the jar should reprocessed, or its contents should be eaten.

But if the lid is made of rigid metal or of glass, this test does not apply.

Instructions usually call for removing bands after 12 hours, and storing without them. This permits use of the same bands in sealing more jars, and avoids possible struggles with stuck threads later when you want to open them. But the bands are inexpensive, and while in place they protect the tops against being accidentally dislodged. Many housewives leave them on until the food is used.

If the band sticks, it can be removed in the same ways as the one-piece top. It is usually easier to soak off, as water can often penetrate the threads from both top and bottom. Once the band is off, the top is very easily loosened by pushing a sharp knife point between glass and gasket.

You can also pound on the lid to change its shape, or puncture it to destroy the vacuum. These tops should not be re-used anyhow, even if they appear to be in perfect condition.

General Precautions. Whatever type of jar and top you use, there are similarities in handling. Always inspect the top (or the shoulder) of the glass where the ring or gasket will contact it. If it is cracked, nicked or chipped, discard the jar as it will probably not seal. Check gaskets, seals and tops. Make sure that you have the right tops and the right gaskets for the jars you are using.

Jars, tops and rings should be washed in hot soapy water. Do not use a wire brush, steel wool or abrasives as they might cloud the glass. Rinse thoroughly, and place in hot water until you are ready to fill them.

It is usually not necessary for this water to be boiling, or for the jar to be sterilized, as the processing takes care of this. But if you are following instructions that call for boiling water, use it. It can do no harm to the canning, and if you are careful, it should not hurt you either.

Avoid subjecting jars to sudden changes of temperature. Don't put a hot jar on a cold surface, particularly a metal one, and don't stand it in a draft that will cool one side rapidly. Don't pour boiling water in a cold jar. There is only a small chance of cracking a jar by doing these things, but it is better to play safe.

Any jar, whether sealed by pressure or vacuum or both, may be tested by turning it upside down and shaking it. Any appearance of froth or liquid on the outside shows that it is not properly sealed, and will spoil. Lack of evident leakage does not guarantee that the seal is perfect, but it is a good enough indication to justify putting the jar on the shelf.

pH Value	Food Item	Food Groups	Spoilage Agents
	High temperature processing 240°-250° F		
Low acid			
7.0	Lye hominy	Meat	Mesophilic spore-forming an-
	Ripe olives, crabmeat, eggs,	Fish	aerobic bacteria
	oysters, milk, corn, duck,	Milk	
	chicken, codfish, beef, sar-	Poultry	
	dines		Thermophiles
6.0	Corned beef, lima beans,	Vegetables	Naturally occurring enzymes
	peas, carrots, beets, aspar-		in certain processes
	agus, potatoes		
5.0	Figs, tomato soup	Soup	
Medium acid			
4.5	Ravioli, pimientos	Manufactured foods	Lower limit for growth of *Cl. botulinum*
	Boiling water processing (212° F)		
Acid			
	Potato salad		Non-spore forming aciduric
	Tomatoes, pears, apricots,	Fruits	bacteria
	peaches, oranges		
			Acidic spore-forming bacteria
3.7	Sauerkraut, pineapple, apple,		
	strawberry, grapefruit	Berries	Natural occurring enzymes
High acid			
3.0	Pickles	High acid foods	Yeasts
	Relish	(pickles)	Molds
	Cranberry juice	High acid-high solids	
	Lemon juice	foods, (jam-jelly)	
	Lime juice		
2.0		Very acid foods	

By permission from "Technology of Food Preservation" by Norman W. Desrosier, 3rd Edition, Copyright 1970. Avi Publishing Co.

Fig. 31-9. Foods grouped according to acidity

BASIC APPROACHES

There are two basic methods of preparing food for processing, cold pack and hot pack. In cold pack, also known as raw pack, the jars are filled with uncooked, unheated food and hot liquid, after which they are capped and exposed to heat long enough to accomplish cooking and destruction of organisms.

In hot pack, the food is cooked or partly cooked before being put into the jars, and the processing time in the jar is shorter. Hot pack is more efficient, but there are certain vegetables — tomatoes are the outstanding example — which usually have better texture and flavor if they are cold packed.

Processing of either type may be done by heating the filled jars in boiling water in an open kettle (water bath method) or by steam in a pressure cooker. Pressure treatment is required for ALL low-acid foods, on account of possibility of infection with the botulism organism, discussed earlier.

Water bath is used with either cold or hot pack, pressure is usually only with hot pack, although there are exceptions.

Food that is to be canned should always be thoroughly rinsed, washed, and freed of decayed, over-soft, hard or discolored parts. You should be more careful than in preparing food for immediate eating for at least two reasons.

The important one is that most or perhaps all of the organisms that might cause spoilage are in dirt or films on the outside, so cleaning gets rid of them. The other is that you do not know when you will be serving your canned goods, nor to whom, and there might be circumstances under which dirt or discoloration would be particularly embarrassing.

BOILING WATER BATH

This method is limited to berries, fruit and vegetables which are in the acid or high-acid groups, Figure 31-9. It is probably used most frequently with tomatoes, where its advantages in preserving flavor and texture are easily noticed.

The first step is to study the recipe you are using, and the manufacturer's instructions for the jars. Clean and inspect the jars as suggested under General Precautions.

Get out all the equipment you need, and check it. The most important item is the water-bath canner, a very large pot or kettle usually containing a wire basket, and designed to hold from 6 to 9 one-quart jars on a rack with their tops under two

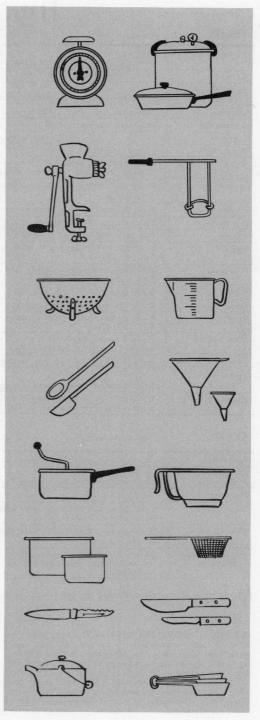

Courtesy of Ball Corporation

Fig. 31-10. Canning equipment and utensils

Fig. 31-11. CANNING TIME TABLES

FRUITS	(See footnotes below)	Boiling Water Bath Minutes Pints	Boiling Water Bath Minutes Quarts	Pressure Cooker Pts. & Qts. (Minutes)	Pressure Cooker Pounds
Apples	Wash, pare, core, cut in pieces. Drop in slightly salted water. Drain. Boil 3 to 5 minutes in syrup. Pack. Add syrup or water.	20	25	10	5
Apricots	Wash, halve and pit. Pack. Add syrup or water.	20	25	10	5
Berries (except Strawberries and Cranberries)	Wash, stem, pack. Add syrup or water.	15	20	8	5
Cherries	Wash, stem, pit. Pack. Add syrup or water.	20	20	10	5
Cranberries	Wash, remove stems. Boil 3 minutes in heavy syrup. Pack.	10	10	....	....
Currants	Wash, stem, pack. Add syrup or water.	20	20	10	5
Dried Fruits	Soak in cold water overnight. Boil 10 minutes in same water. Pack.	15	15	....	....
Figs	Cover with fresh water, boil 2 minutes. Drain and use this water to make syrup. Boil 5 minutes in syrup. Pack, add syrup.	30	30	10	5
Fruit Juices	Crush fruit, heat slowly, strain. Heat juice according to recipe. Pour into jars.	10	10		
Grapes	Wash, stem, pack. Add syrup or water.	20	20	8	5
Nut Meats	Pack into jar. Process in oven at 225° for 45 minutes.	....	....	....	....
Peaches	Peel, pack, add syrup, or boil 3 minutes in syrup, pack, add syrup.	20	25	10	5
Pears	Select not overripe pears, pare, halve, boil 3 to 5 minutes in syrup. Pack. Add syrup.	25	30	10	5
Pineapple	Slice, peel, remove eyes and core. Boil in syrup 5 to 10 minutes. Pack. Add syrup.	30	30	15	5
Plums	Wash, prick skins. Pack. Add syrup.	20	25	10	5
Preserves	Prepare as per recipe. Cook until thick. Pack. Process in water bath.	20	20 (180° – simmering)		
Rhubarb	Wash, cut into pieces. Pack. Add syrup. Or bake until tender. Pack. Add syrup.	10	10	5	5
Strawberries	Wash, stem, boil gently for 3 minutes in syrup. Cover the kettle and let stand for several hours. Pack.	15	15	....	....
Tomatoes	Scald ½ minute, cold dip, peel, core, quarter. Pack.	35	45	10	5
Tomatoes (Low Acid)	Scald ½ minute, cold dip, peel, core, quarter. Pack.	45	55	15	5
Tomato Juice	Wash, peel, cut in pieces. Simmer until soft, press thru fine sieve. Bring to boil. Pour to within ¼ inch of top of jar.	10	10	....	....

SOUPS	(See footnotes below)	Boiling Water Bath Minutes	Pressure Cooker Minutes	Pressure Cooker Pounds
Asparagus	Use tough part, boil. Press through sieve, pour into jars.	180	40	10
Clam or Fish Chowder	Mix ingredients. Boil ten minutes. Pack into jars.	240	90	10
Pea Soup	Boil peas until soft, press thru sieve. Pour into jars.	180	60	10
Soup Stock	Cover bones and trimmings with water. Season. Cook 2 hours. Remove bones. Pour into jars.	180	45	10
Tomato Soup	Mix vegetables. Cook tender; sieve. Add flour and butter; bring to boil; pour into jars.	15	....	....
Vegetable Soup Mixtures	Use any vegetable combinations. Boil 5 minutes or pack raw. Pack into jars. Process time necessary for vegetable requiring longest processing.	....	....	....

A pressure cooker is recommended for processing low-acid foods as it gives a greater degree of safety.

notes

ALTITUDES ABOVE SEA LEVEL—The time given in the time tables in this book is for the half pint, one-pint or one-quart pack, (for half gallon jars see following note). For all size jars the time must be increased when the boiling water bath is used at an altitude of 1,000 feet or more. For each 1,000 feet above sea level, add 1 minute to processing time if the time called for is 20 minutes or less. If the processing time called for is more than 20 minutes, add 2 minutes for each 1,000 feet.

When the pressure cooker is used at an altitude of 2,000 feet or more, the pressure must be increased by 1 pound for each 2,000 feet altitude.

ALL VEGETABLES EXCEPT TOMATOES, ALSO ALL MEATS, POULTRY AND FISH CANNED AT HOME MUST BE BOILED IN AN OPEN VESSEL TEN TO FIFTEEN MINUTES BEFORE TASTING OR USING.

Time for Different Size Jars — The time in these tables for water bath canning applies to half pint, pint and quart jars. If canning fruit in water bath with half gallon jars add 10 minutes to processing time; for pressure cooker add 5 minutes to processing time. When canning vegetables and meats, for half gallons in pressure cooker or water bath, increase time 20% over time for quarts. For half pints, use time for pints.

Fig. 31-12. Canning time tables, continued

VEGETABLES

		Pressure Cooker			Boiling Water Bath
		Minutes			Pts. & Qts. Minutes
		Pints	Quarts	Pounds	
Asparagus	Wash, pack raw or boil 3 minutes and pack.	25	30	10	180
Beans (String or Wax)	Wash, string, cut, pack raw or boil 5 minutes and pack.	20	·25	.10	180
Beets	Wash, leave roots and tops long, boil 15 minutes. Skin. Pack.	30	40	10	120
Brussels Sprouts or Cabbage	Remove outer leaves, wash, cut, boil 5 minutes, pack.	45	55	10	120
Carrots	Wash, peel, slice or leave whole. Pack raw or boil 3 minutes.	25	30	10	120
Cauliflower or Broccoli	Remove outside leaves, wash, cut. Pack raw or boil 3 minutes.	25	40	10	150
Corn (Whole Grain)	Remove shucks. Cut from cob. Pack raw or bring to boil. Pack loosely to within 1 inch of top of jar.	55	85	10	210
Greens (All Kinds)	Wash thoroughly. Steam or boil to wilt. Pack loosely.	70	90	10	180
Hominy	Boil 3 minutes. Pack loosely.	60	70	10	120
Mushrooms	Clean, wash, cut large ones, boil 3 minutes. Pack loosely.	30	35	10	180
Okra	Wash, boil 1 minute. Pack.	25	40	10	180
Onions	Peel, wash, boil 5 minutes. Pack.	40	40	10	180
Parsnips or Turnips	Wash, peel, slice or cube. Pack raw or boil 3 minutes.	20	25	10	90
Peas	Shell, wash and grade tender peas. Pack raw or bring to boil. Pack loosely to within 1 inch of top of jar.	40	40	10	180
Peppers (Green, Sweet)	Wash, remove seed pod, boil 3 minutes. Pack.	35	35	10	120
Potatoes Irish	Wash, and scrape small, new potatoes. Pack raw or boil 3 minutes. Add boiling water.	40	40	10	180
Pumpkin	Cut in pieces. Peel. Steam, boil or bake tender. Pack.	60	80	10	180
Rutabagas	Wash, peel, slice or cube, boil 5 minutes. Pack.	35	35	10	90
Sauerkraut	After curing, pack, add kraut juice or weak brine.			....	15
Spinach	Wash, steam or boil to wilt. Pack loosely, within 1 inch of top of jar.	70	90	10	180
Squash (Summer, Scalloped Zucchini)	Cut in uniform pieces. Pack raw or bring to boil and pack.	25	30	10	180
Squash (Acorn, Crookneck, Hubbard or Banana)	Cut in pieces. Peel. Steam, boil or bake tender. Pack.	60	80	10	180
Sweet Potatoes (Dry)	Wash, boil or steam 20 minutes, remove skins. Pack.	65	95	10	180
Sweet Potatoes (Wet)	Wash, boil or steam 20 minutes, remove skins. Pack. Add liquid.	55	90	10	180
Tomatoes	(SEE UNDER FRUITS)			(SEE UNDER FRUITS)	

MEATS

		Pints	Quarts	Pounds	Minutes
Lamb, Veal, Beef, Steak	Bleed well. Cool thoroughly. Pack raw without liquid or precook and add 3 to 4 tablespoons liquid.	75	90	10	210
Pork	Bleed well. Cool thoroughly. Pack raw without liquid or precook, pack, add salt 1 teaspoon to quart, add 3 or 4 tablespoons liquid.	75	90	10	210
Tenderloin, Ham, Pork Chops	Sear until lightly browned. Pack. Add 3 to 4 tablespoons water or broth. Or pack raw without liquid.	75	90	10	210
Sausage	Fry or bake cakes until brown. Pack. Add 3 to 4 tablespoons liquid.	75	90	10	210
Chicken, Rabbit, Duck, Turkey	Bleed well. Cool thoroughly. Pack raw without liquid or precook and add 3 to 4 tablespoons liquid.	75	90	10	210
Venison, Wild Birds, Geese	Bleed well, cool thoroughly, soak in brine 30 minutes or parboil. Precook, pack, add salt 1 teaspoon to quart, add 3 or 4 tablespoons liquid. Or pack raw without liquid.	75	90	10	210
Fish, All Kinds	Use only firm, fresh fish. Bleed well. Wash. Pack raw without liquid.	100	100	10	240

NOTE: **A pressure cooker is recommended for processing all meats as it gives a greater degree of safety. DO NOT add liquids to meat packed raw. Pack meats loosely and only to within 1 inch of top of jar.**

Courtesy of Kerr Glass Manufacturing Corp.

inches of water. An 8-jar unit at hand is round, 14 inches wide and 9 deep. Test to see how many of your jars your kettle will hold, as it is considered good practice to prepare only enough food for one set of jars at a time, preparing the next batch while the first is cooking.

Other equipment varies with the food and your circumstances. You will probably need, or at least benefit from having, paring knife or tool, a jar-lifting tongs, a big bowl, a narrow scraper and a large funnel. A number of items are shown in Figure 31-10. No one project will require all of these, and it is probable that some essentials are left out.

The first step is to fill the canner half full of water, and put it on a burner turned on full, so that it can heat while you prepare the food. It should be hot but not quite boiling when you put the jars in it. Also prepare extra hot water in another kettle or pan, for filling over jar tops, and for replacing any part that has boiled away.

Use only good quality, sound fruits or vegetables. Wash and drain them to remove both dirt and organisms. Remove hulls, cores, pits seeds and/or skins, depending on what food you are processing, and cut out all soft, unnaturally hard or discolored spots. Leave whole, or slice or dice them according to directions or your preference.

Raw Pack (Cold Pack). If you are using the raw pack method, put the prepared food directly into the jars, pressing down firmly, and leave about 1/2 inch of free space at the top.

The spaces between the pieces may fill with juice, or may not. Add water, juice or other syrup to fill spaces, so that the top of the liquid will be 1/2 inch under the cap level. Have the extra liquid boiling hot if possible.

Remove any air bubbles that are against the glass by running a narrow plastic or rubber bottle scraper, or a knife, around the inside edge. Such bubbles will delay heating if they stay down, causing local cool spots where organisms might survive, and if they rise they will increase the air space. If releasing the bubbles lowers the liquid, add more to bring it back to the 1/2 inch line.

Hot Pack. This process is similar to the cold pack, with the important exception that the food is thoroughly heated, and therefore partly or fully cooked, before it is poured into the jars. This shortens the processing time, but causes a variable increase in the total amount of cooking.

Since most canned food tends to be overcooked, this is likely to be a slight taste-and-texture disadvantage, as compared with cold pack.

There is no sharp line of distinction between methods, as pre-cooking periods in hot pack may be very brief, and have little more effect than adding hot liquid in cold pack. There is a general preference for the hot method, except for tomatoes which are generally processed from the raw state.

Boiling. Wipe top and threads of jars with clean damp cloth. Put on caps, as directed in instruction book or in previous discussion here. Put the jars in the canner (you may do this one at a time as they are filled and capped, or all at once.) Add hot water to cover tops about 2 inches deep. Heat canner until water boils, turn down heat to a gentle boil.

Processing time starts when boiling does.

Boil the time recommended in your recipe, or in Figure 31-11 or 31-12. Add more boiling water if necessary to keep jar tops covered. When done, turn heat down or off, remove the jars with tongs (unless they are in a removable basket) and stand them on cloth or wood, out of drafts, until cool.

Test for seal after 12 hours, or earlier if you are suspicious.

To repeat, this method should not be used for any non-acid or low-acid foods.

PRESSURE CANNING

In pressure canning, food is processed at higher-than-boiling temperature in order to kill the botulism organism. In addition, it often produces a higher quality canned product because of the shortened cooking time.

Cooker. A pressure cooker, which is discussed in Chapter Two, consists of a heavily built pot or kettle, equipped with a gasketed, lock-on lid, a pressure gauge or control and a safety valve.

While cooking for immediate serving is usually done at 15 pounds pressure, recommended canning pressure for most foods is 10 pounds of steam, which is produced by a temperature of about 240° F. This often results in a long cooking time that would be considered to be excessive in commercial practice.

There are two standard sizes of canner. The small one, called a 12-quart, holds 4 one-quart or 5 one-pint jars. The larger one, rated at 18 to 21 quarts (water capacity, probably) holds 5 to 7 jars. Either size should be equipped with a rack that holds the jars off the bottom of the cooker, and that has handles that enable you to lift rack and jars out of the cooker together.

Processing. Preparation of the food is usually done by the hot pack method just described. Put 2 or 3 inches of water in the pressure cooker and install the rack. Place filled and closed jars on the rack so that there will be space between them for circulation of steam.

Put on the cover and adjust or clamp it as directed by the manufacturer. Open the petcock, to allow air to escape. Close the safety valve unless it serves also as a petcock. Place over high heat.

Leave the petcock open for 7 minutes for a small cooker, 10 minutes for a large one, counting time after steam begins to escape in a steady stream. This is to insure full release of air. Then close the petcock.

Pressure will rise gradually. When it is within 2 or 3 pounds of working pressure, lower the heat so as to reach full pressure gradually and avoid overshooting. Processing times, given in Figures 31-11 and 12, do not start until full pressure has been reached.

Stay near the cooker and check the gauge frequently. Proper adjustment of heat can be tricky, particularly over an electric burner with step-type controls. Also, the jars will absorb considerable heat at first, requiring a higher burner setting than will be needed after they are hot.

You probably will not be able to keep the pressure exactly at 10 pounds, but if you average the times it is a little above or a little below it will work out the same. If there is a weight instead of a gauge, adjust heat so that it rocks slowly.

At the end of the processing time, turn off the heat, and/or remove the cooker from the fire. Allow it to cool until the gauge shows zero. Then open the petcock slowly, with a gloved or cloth-protected hand. If no steam escapes, or after it stops coming out, release and remove the lid, lifting it at a tilt so that any steam will escape at the back, away from you.

As the rack of jars is very heavy, it is best to remove them individually, with tongs or gloved hands. Put them on cloth or paper, away from drafts, to cool.

Tighten jar lids if they are clamp or one-piece screw type, do not touch them if they are two-piece. Test for seal in the same way as in open-bath processing.

JELLY

There are at least two kinds of jelly. One is made with gelatin. This may be present naturally, as in meat juice, or be added in powdered form from a package. Gelatin jellies were discussed under SALADS and DESSERTS. The other kind has pectin for the jelling agent, and will be the subject of this discussion.

Fig. 31-13. Jelly jars

In addition, there are weak solids with similar characteristics that can be made with rennet, corn starch and other agents. These are described briefly under DESSERTS.

Pectin jelly is basically fruit juice cooked with sugar. It is usually expected to be firm enough to hold its shape (with only moderate bulging) when turned out of its jar, yet to be soft enough to be spread with a knife. It should quiver when disturbed.

However, it may be made as a thick or a medium liquid or as a quite hard solid, either by mistake or for some special purpose. It was formerly supposed to be clear, but may now be considered to be acceptable whether clear or cloudy.

Jelly is used primarily as a spread, on bread or in sandwiches. It has many other uses in sweet breads and on desserts, of which jelly filling in doughnuts is probably the best known.

Good jelly made in the standard way is likely to contain 60 to 65 per cent sugar, making it highly resistant to microorganisms. A thin layer of mold may develop on exposed surfaces, but this can be scraped off. But for flavor reasons, it should be kept sealed and preferably stored in a cool dark place.

Glasses and Jars. Jelly is traditionally cooled and stored in special jelly glasses holding barely 8 ounces when full to the brim. Useful capacity is 6-1/2 to 7-1/2 ounces. These glasses have a curved taper from top to bottom to make it relatively easy to empty the contents in one streamlined chunk. A thin metal cap is a snug fit around the top of the glass. It is not tight enough to keep the contents sterile, as the jelly is supposed to be topped by a layer of paraffin.

If lids are missing, or you are using lidless glasses, you can make tops out of plastic film held by rubber bands around the outside tops of the glasses.

You can also use ordinary drinking glasses (water tumblers) and emptied wide mouthed glass containers in which baby food, asparagus or other foods were purchased. They can be lidded with plastic film, held with rubber bands, as in Figure 29-11.

An increasing amount of jelly is put in tapered, wide mouth jars with two-piece screw caps. The standard jelly size is rated at 8 ounces, but may hold only 7 or 7-1/2. They are also made in larger sizes, and are used both for jelly and for freezing. They do not require paraffin seals.

Regular mason or canning jars can be used, but because of the narrow neck openings jelly must be spooned out of them.

It is advisable to boil glasses of any type before use. Put them in hot water, heat it until it boils, turn off the heat and leave them in the water for use while still hot.

The boiling serves two purposes. Jelly is resistant to spoilage, but is often not immune to it, so the heat sterilization of the jars serves to protect it. And a hot jar should not crack when hot jelly is poured into it. A cold one might.

Paraffin. Most jelly is sealed in its jars with paraffin.

In the United States, paraffin is a synthetic wax derived from petroleum. It is sold in food stores, usually in one-pound packages containing 4 pieces. It is white or colorless, semi-transparent, tasteless and odorless. It does not react with food, and produces no changes in taste. It melts at around 135° F and boils at under 200°. It burns readily, and is almost explosively flammable when boiling.

In other countries, paraffin (or paraffin oil) may mean a liquid fuel similar to kerosene.

Our paraffin is melted in a pan over low heat or hot water. High heat is dangerous, as part of it can liquefy and boil violently while most of it is still solid. Thin white vapor shows dangerous overheating.

Melted paraffin is poured over hot liquid jelly immediately after it is put in glasses. If this is done gently, it will spread over the surface without making a pit in it. A good method is to pour enough to make a layer about 1/8 inch thick, allow it to harden, add the same amount again, then tip the glass slightly and rotate it so that the paraffin touches and seals to the glass all the way around. But you can get by with the first 1/8-inch layer, or put in a full 1/4 inch all at once.

People who make jelly often, may have a special pan for paraffin, in which they keep whatever is left over. Such a pan should be kept carefully covered, as dust or trash would spoil the appearance of the topping on the next batch of jelly.

If a food pan is used, wash it afterward twice in very hot water with detergent, as otherwise some might be left to float up to make a harmless but unattractive film on the next food you cooked in it.

Pectin. Pectin was described under THICKENERS, page 351. It occurs naturally in most fruit and berries, to a varying and not entirely predictable extent. It may be in an unfinished and useless form in green fruit, and may deteriorate and disappear with over-ripeness or even full ripeness.

Figure 31-14 gives ratings of a number of fruits in regard to expected pectin content.

Pectin jellies are usually more delicate in texture than those made with gelatin, and they are not liquefied by warmth or much hardened by cold.

Rich in acid and pectin	Rich in pectin but poor in acid	Rich in acid but poor in pectin	Poor in both acid and pectin
Sour apples	Sweet apples	Apricots	Elderberries
Sour blackberries	Quinces	Sour cherries	Peaches
Crab apples		Pineapples	Most over-ripe fruits
Cranberries		Raspberries	
Red currants		Strawberries	
Gooseberries			
Grapefruit			
Concord grapes			
Guavas			
Lemons			
Sour oranges			
Plums			
Most almost-ripe fruit			

Fig. 31-14. Pectin and acid content

Pectin will thicken a liquid only if both acid and sugar are present. Since most fruits are acid and it is customary to add considerable sugar for jelly making, these requirements are usually easy to meet. But if the fruit is non-acid because of its variety or by reason of over-ripeness, it is necessary to add acid, probably in the form of a tablespoon or less of lemon juice to a cup of fruit juice.

This addition can usually be avoided in cases of ripeness by substituting about 1/4 or 1/3 of not-quite-ripe fruit (if available) for that much of the ripe batch.

You can make a simple test for pectin quantity or perhaps quality in fruit juice. Mix equal parts (say a tablespoon each) of the cooked unsweetened juice and denatured (rubbing) alcohol. If the pectin content is good you will get a large clump of jelly, if it is just adequate there will be a few smaller clots and if it is poor the

Fruit	Preparation*	Water to add, per quart	Cooking fruit	Sugar for each quart of juice
Apple	Slice thin	To barely cover	Boil gently until soft	3 cups
Blackberries	Crush (optional)	0 to ¼ cup	Cook gently until berries swim in juice, 10 to 15 minutes	3 cups
Crab Apple	Slice or chop	To barely cover	Boil gently until soft	4 cups
Cranberry	——	To barely cover	Boil gently 5 or 10 minutes, or until some berries burst	3 cups
Red Currant	——	¼ cup	Cook about 10 minutes or until soft	3 to 4 cups
Concord Grape	Crush (optional)	¼ cup	Cook 15 minutes, or until grapes swim in own juice	3 cups
Sour Orange	Peel, seed and chop	4 cups	Boil until mushy	4 cups
Plum	——	¼ to 1 cup	Boil gently until juice flows freely	3 to 4 cups
Quince	Core and slice	To barely cover	Boil gently for 45 minutes or until soft	3 to 4 cups
Raspberry	Crush (optional)	¼ cup	Boil gently until berries swim in own juice	3 cups

*After washing and removing stems

Fig. 31-15. Jelly-making suggestions

result will be a thin flaky sediment, or the liquid may even remain perfectly clear.

Denatured alcohol is poisonous, so do not taste the product. You can perform the same test with non-poisonous grain alcohol, but it may be difficult to get. Alcoholic drinks are too dilute for reliable results.

The quantity of pectin determines to a considerable extent the amount of sugar that should be used. If pectin is deficient, it can be concentrated by boiling down the juice. But if a normal amount of sugar is used, this will carry it way above the jellying point and result in crystalline, glazed or otherwise second-rate jelly. Less sugar permits greater concentration.

These problems can be bypassed by adding a commercial pectin concentrate in liquid or powder form. With this, you are almost sure the mixture will jell. You can use all-ripe fruit without worrying about its pectin content, adding lemon juice if it is needed for acidity. And you can use from 20 to 150 per cent more sugar, substantially increasing the quantity of jelly at little cost, and without paying the penalty in oversweetness that you would expect. But the consistency may be too firm for many tastes.

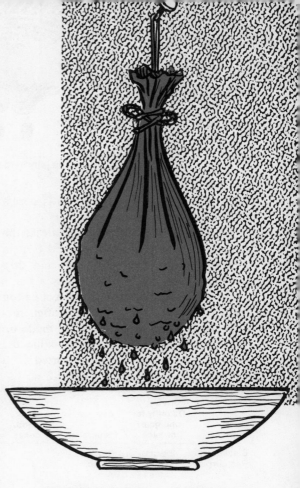

Fig. 31-16. Dripping from a jelly bag

PREPARATION

Fruit. Fruit for jelly can be imperfect and irregular in shape and color without affecting results.

Rinse or wash the fruit gently. Remove soft spots. Follow the recipe you are using, and your own judgment, about removing hulls, caps, stems, pits or seeds. You usually leave them in, and leave the skins on. Small berries may be left whole, other fruit is generally sliced or chopped. Crush the fruit if the recipe says so, or if you have no recipe. Crushing may be done with a potato masher, an electric mixer or a blender.

Measure the processed fruit. A 2-cup glass measuring cup is convenient. Then add water according to your recipe, or the table in Figure 31-15. You will notice that the amount of water for a quart of fruit ranges from 1/4 cup to 4 cups. Cook the fruit in the water 5 or 10 minutes, or until soft, unless otherwise directed. The heat extracts juice and pectin from the cells.

If you intend to add pectin, follow the recipe that comes with it. It may call for crushing the fruit thoroughly and heating it without adding any water. In this case, you may have to start on low heat to avoid scorching the pulp and thick juice. Directions may call for crushing and straining without cooking.

For the clearest jelly, you are supposed not to stir the fruit, but just shake the pan occasionally. This is a refinement that it is better to avoid for the first few tries at

Fig. 31-17. The jelly in the right-hand spoon is cooked

least. Stir gently, but as often as is necessary to prevent sticking.

Juice. The standard way to extract the juice is to put the crushed, cooked fruit in a wet jelly bag and let it run and drip through. You may be able to buy a ready made bag. If not, use a wide piece of cotton flannel, or several layers (4 are often recommended) of cheese cloth. The made up bag may be hung over a pan, while the cloth usually needs to be supported in a colander or perhaps a deep fry basket in a pan or bowl.

If you do not disturb the fruit, you will get the clearest juice and therefore the most transparent jelly available from that particular fruit. If you squeeze the bag you will get more juice and get it much more quickly, but it will be cloudy. A middle course is to squeeze the bag by twisting both ends or by pressing with a potato masher, then re-strain the juice through the

Fruit	Quantity for one quart of juice	Preparation*	Water to add, cups	Cooking fruit	Liquid pectin to add, fluid ounces	Lemon juice to add	Sugar to add (cups per quart of juice)
Blackberry	2½ qts.	Crush	0	Use raw	7	—	7½
Red currant	3 qts. (4 lbs.)	Crush	1	Bring to boil, then simmer 10 minutes	3½	—	7
Concord Grape	3 lbs.	Crush thoroughly	½	Bring to boil, simmer, covered, 10 minutes	3½	—	7
Peach	3½ lbs.	Pit, do not peel, crush thoroughly	½	Bring to boil, simmer, covered, 5 minutes	7	¼ cup	7½
Plum	4 lbs.	Pit and crush	1	Bring to boil, simmer, covered, 10 minutes	3½	—	6½
Quince	3 lbs.	Remove core and stem and blossom ends, do not peel	4½	Bring to boil, simmer, covered, 15 minutes	3½	¼ cup	7½
Sour Cherry	3 lbs.	Pit, crush thoroughly	½	Bring to boil, simmer, covered, 10 minutes	7	—	7

*In addition to washing and removing stems

Courtesy of General Foods Corp.

Fig. 31-18. Jelly-making with added pectin

washed bag or through similar cloth. It should regain most of its clarity.

Taste the juice. It should have a tart or sour taste, somewhat like a mixture of one part of lemon juice with 3 parts of water. If it has not, add up to a tablespoon of lemon juice for each cup. Then add sugar, usually about 3 cups to the quart, but vary this according to recipe, taste or experience. The finished jelly will be somewhat less sweet than the juice.

Cooking The Juice. You should have a large heavy pan or kettle. Juice and sugar boil violently and spatter, so its capacity should be at least 3 times the load that you put in it. A wide bottom is desirable to make the layer of liquid thin, so that it can boil freely. Jelly is prepared in medium or small batches, often 4 and seldom more than 6 cups at a time.

If no pectin has been added, boil the sugar-juice mixture rapidly, without stirring, to the jellying point which is 7 to 11° F above boiling, or between 219 and 223 on a candy thermometer at sea level, if it is accurate.

Because of differences in jellying temperature, you need another test. With a large metal spoon, dip up some of the boiling syrup, then tilt the spoon to pour it slowly off the side. If it is not cooked enough, the liquid will form a stream or one or two sets of drops. At the jelly point it forms flakes or sheets at the edge of the spoon as illustrated.

Boiling time is supposed to be 12 to 20 minutes, but you should start to make tests after 5 minutes.

Remove the jelly from the heat as soon as you get a satisfactory test. Skim off any foam that has appeared on top, as it has a poor appearance and is the last refuge of heat-resistant organisms. Take glasses or jars out of the hot water, drain and fill them.

Cooking With Added Pectin. Use a large pan, as the problem of boiling and splattering remains the same. If possible, follow a recipe for the particular fruit, either in a cookbook or from the pectin package. Otherwise, follow Figure 31-18. Incidentally, the Certo brand of liquid pectin at present is sold with a useful recipe book wrapped around the bottle, under the label, where you might miss it if you didn't read the label carefully.

Measure the juice into the pan, add sugar in the proper proportion, usually 1-1/2 to 2 cups of sugar to one of juice, and mix well. Place over high heat and bring to a boil, stirring constantly. Add the quantity of pectin recommended on its label, bring to a fully rolling boil and then boil hard for one minute.

Remove from heat, skim off foam, and pour into prepared jars or glasses.

Liquid pectin recipes give quantities in bottles and half bottles. A bottle holds about 7 ounces. Calculations on part batches would be easier if the manufacturer diluted the product with an ounce of water and sold it in 8-ounce (one cup) containers.

Filling Glasses. If the glasses do not have a sealing screw-type lid, fill all of them to within a half to quarter inch of the top. Have some paraffin melted in a small pan, and put in a layer or layers of it on each glass immediately, as described on page 621.

Allow glasses to cool away from drafts, resting on a cloth or a rack. Then store, preferably in a cool, dark place. Jelly may keep indefinitely, but there is likely to be a gradual loss of flavor.

With screw-top jars, fill them one at a time to within 1/8 inch of the top. Using gloves or pot holders, put the lid or disc on the jar, with the gasket side down, and screw band down tightly. Turn the jar upside down for about 30 seconds, so that the hot jelly can destroy any mold or yeast that might have settled on the lid. Stand the jar upright and go on to the next one. Allow to cool in the same manner as glasses.

You may remove the screw bands or leave them on, as you prefer.

Failure to Jell. Jelly may set rapidly, or very slowly. But if it is still liquid after 24 hours, you may assume that it is very unlikely to jell.

The difficulty may be insufficiency in any of the three vital ingredients; pectin, acid or sugar. Check back over the instructions to see if you left out or short-measured anything. If the juice tasted tart and you remembered to put in the sugar, the fault is likely to be lack of pectin.

But is also possible that you did not cook it enough. Even if both temperature and sheeting off a spoon appeared to be right, this particular batch may have needed more concentration. The cure is to re-cook it. Add a small quantity of water, perhaps a half cup to the quart, and put in a large pan over high heat, with constant stirring.

Cook it a little past the point at which you took it off before, remove from heat, skim and pour into clean, prepared glasses.

Or you can add the same quantity of water to the nonjelly, and use it as sweetened fruit juice, add pectin and cook it accordling to added-pectin directions. You certainly should do this if it fails to jell after the second attempt.

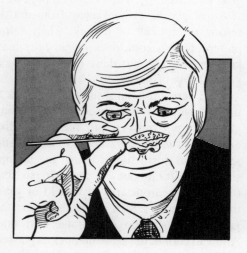

Fig. 31-19. Jam should mound on a spoon when done

FREEZER JELLY

Freezer jelly is made with uncooked juice and added pectin. It is not sterilized, but should have fair keeping qualities because of the high sugar content. Recommendations are for storing it in a refrigerator for up to 3 weeks, or in the freezer for indefinite periods.

The fruit is rinsed and trimmed in the same manner as for regular jelly, and is then very thoroughly mashed or crushed. Grapes and some other fruits may be heated slightly, but most are left cold. Then you place it in a dampened jelly bag or cloth, and squeeze and press it to extract all the juice. Raw fruit is likely to give a poor yield if allowed to drip by itself. As a result, freezer jelly is supposed to be cloudy, but there is no law against filtering the juice again if you wish to do so.

Measure the juice into a bowl or a pan, add the sugar required by the recipe (usually about 7-1/2 cups of sugar to 4 of juice) and mix well. In a separate small bowl, mix the pectin with about one tablespoon of water or lemon juice for each cup of fruit juice. Add to fruit juice, and stir for 3 minutes.

Pour or ladle into glasses or jars, and cover with tight lids or plastic film. Allow to stand at room temperature for 24 hours to set. Then keep in the refrigerator for early use, or in the freezer for storage.

JAM

The principal difference between jam and jelly is that jam uses most of the edible parts of the fruit, while jelly includes only the juice.

Fruit selection is somewhat the same as for jelly, except that riper specimens are usually preferred. Fruit, or parts of fruit, that cannot be mashed readily should be discarded.

Fruits for jam are usually peeled, but if you have a blender you can pulverize the skins in it and put them back with the fruit. Cores, stems and coarse seeds are removed, either in advance preparation or by putting the mashed fruit through a food mill.

Seeds may be kept in berry jam, or discarded. They clearly identify the product, and may offer a pleasant variety of texture and appearance. But, they may have a disagreeable effect if they are coarse or very numerous. You will therefore find some recipes telling you to get them out, with a food mill or sieve, and others telling you to leave them in. A good compromise is to divide the batch, de-seed part of it, and then recombine for further processing.

The trimmed and possibly de-seeded fruit is sliced, chopped, or mashed and then mixed with sugar, 3 or 4 parts of sugar to 4 of fruit. The mixture is put in an oversize pot, and stirred over low heat until the sugar dissolves. Heat is then turned up to a maximum, as this favors a bright clear color. Unlike jelly juice, this fruit paste must be stirred more or less constantly.

For a firm jam, the cooked or jellying point is about 9 or 10° F above the boiling point of water, or 221 or 222° at sea level. It can be tested by sheeting some liquid off a spoon, but results are obscured by the solids.

The accepted test is that if the hot mixture rounds up in a spoon, it is done. But if pectin is to be added, full boiling is limited to one minute, after which the pan is removed from the fire, and the pectin is stirred in.

Jelling is not as critical with jam as with jelly, as jam is usually acceptable and is often preferred if it is softer than jelly from the same fruit. It of course becomes thicker and firmer as it cools and jells.

The cooked mixture is poured into glasses or jars, and is covered and protected in the same manner as jelly. However, there is an extra complication in possible separation of juice and solids because of floating or sinking, particularly if the solids have been left coarse.

Instructions with pectin recommend stirring and cooling in the pan for a few minutes until thick enough to hold the fruit in suspension. Instructions with jars tell you to pour as soon as cooking is finished, and then turn the jar over after a few minutes to redistribute the fruit. If thickening is slow, this may have to be done several times.

RADIATION

Food may be treated by ionizing radiation to improve keeping qualities, and for some other purposes. This technique has not yet been approved for commercial processing of human food, but it is of great interest for the future, perhaps the very near future.

Gamma rays appear to be the most promising type. These are a short wave magnetic radiation, somewhat like X-rays. They have good penetrating power, are fatal to all organisms if doses are large enough and they do not cause or increase radioactivity to a measurable extent. Sources include spent fuel from atomic reactors,

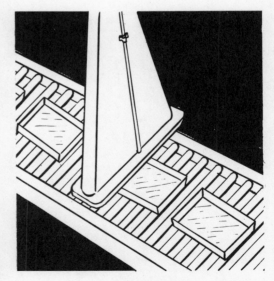

Fig. 31-20. Radiation-sterilizer

special radioactive isotopes and/or particle accelerators.

This radiation (and many other types also) separates some electrons from atoms in the material being treated, creating pairs of new units, called ions, that have opposite electrical charges. This change results in the breakdown and rearrangement of molecules containing the atoms. If the molecules are part of living cells, the cells are injured or killed. Sufficiently intense radiation will kill all organisms in its path.

However, the molecules of the food and perhaps of the package in which the food is sealed may also be broken down and changed. This may result in alteration in taste, smell, color and texture, and may make wrapping materials porous and brittle. In general, increased intensity increases probability of noticeable bad effects, but results can be affected by temperature, presence of water and other chemicals and the length of time of exposure to the radiation.

The general problem is one of working out ways in which to obtain desired results without bad effects.

There are a number of areas of possible use. First, strong radiation can sterilize food so that it can be kept indefinitely in a sealed container at room temperature. Such food need not be cooked, but it often must be blanched to destroy enzymes.

Second, in limited doses radiation can perform some of the functions of pasteurization, to prolong the storage life of perishable foods such as fresh meat, fish, vegetables and fruit.

Other potential uses are destroying insects inside of containers to protect stocks of food, preventing or delaying sprouting of potatoes and other vegetables, killing parasites in meat, tenderizing meat and even aging wine.

32

NUTRITION

NOURISHMENT

Basically, we eat to obtain nourishment. The pleasures of eating, our refinements of taste, our preferences and even our dislikes, are nature's usually successful methods of changing eating from a mere necessity to an interesting occupation.

We need many kinds of nourishment. The three basic types of food are protein, carbohydrate and fat. They will be discussed only briefly, as they are covered in detail in many books.

We also need smaller quantities of a great number of substances that are not exactly nourishment, but which must be included in our diet. They are classified as vitamins and minerals.

There seems to be general agreement in principle about human needs for proper nourishment, but equally general disagreement about the ways in which these needs should be met. The subject is very complicated and parts of it are not well understood. Since it involves health, almost everyone is interested.

The result is a variety of advice, much of it from apparently reliable sources and backed by appealing arguments, on how to select, prepare and eat food. Conflict of opinion is so extreme that a housewife may become convinced that she will be wrong, whatever she does.

The purpose of this chapter is to examine the problem and some of the weaknesses in the prevailing arguments about it. It is hoped that the total effect will be relaxing.

Water. Water is not ordinarily considered under the heading of nourishment, but it is the most urgently needed material that we put in our mouths. Every body process depends on it, and we die very soon if we cannot obtain it.

However, because water is so universally needed and is usually available in ample supply, it is quite properly taken for granted in most dietary discussions.

Water may be taken straight, or in any of an infinite variety of flavorings and combinations. Most people prefer it cool or cold. Its taste, if any, usually depends on tiny quantities of dissolved chemicals, of which chlorine has unfortunately become the most familiar. In some areas the drinking water is slightly salty (brackish).

The average daily requirement for water

Fig. 32-1. Diet is a subject for disagreement

is said to be 2 quarts a day. A substantial part of this can be obtained from solid food, which often has a very high water content.

Various characteristics of water are discussed elsewhere in this book. References will be found in the Index.

Protein. Proteins are organic compounds that contain nitrogen. They are made only by living cells.

Proteins are made up of various combinations of basic substances called amino acids, of which 22 are known. Most of these can be manufactured in the human body if they are not in the diet, using nitrogen, carbon and oxygen from other sources. But there are 8 of them that cannot be made in the body, and each of them is necessary in its building and repair.

A complete protein is one that contains all 8, and it is almost always of animal origin — meat, organs, poultry, fish, milk and eggs, for example. Most vegetable proteins lack one or more of the acids, and are called incomplete.

The body ordinarily does not store any incomplete protein from one meal to the next. It does not wait for a missing amino acid in order to build the particular protein it needs. It may break down another protein in its tissue to obtain it, or destroy the incomplete set, excreting the nitrogen. The carbon-oxygen remainder may be oxidized to provide energy, combined with hydrogen from water to make fat or excreted in the feces.

If plant material is used as a source of protein, it is therefore important that animal food be eaten at the same meal, or that there be two or more types of vegetable protein eaten together, so that one may make up the deficiencies of the other.

Protein body substances are being continuously broken down and replaced, so an intake of fresh proteins for rebuilding work is essential for health. Proteins can also be oxidized to obtain energy, if both carbohydrates and fats are in short supply. This process is leisurely, so high protein foods are not satisfactory for a quick pickup of energy, but are excellent for maintaining it over long periods.

Carbohydrates. Carbohydrates are organic compounds of carbon, hydrogen and oxygen that we eat as starch, sugar and cellulose. They make up more than half of the average diet, as they are produced easily and abundantly by plants, keep well and are generally pleasant to eat.

Carbohydrates are generally not used directly by the body. They may be oxidized to provide energy, stored temporarily in the liver and muscles in the form of glycogen (animal starch), or converted into fat. A substantial amount may not be absorbed by the digestive system at all, but pass through the intestines, where they are useful in providing bulk.

Sugar and starch are readily broken down by digestive enzymes to glucose, which circulates in the blood and can be used directly by cells for fuel. They are often called quick energy foods. They also make ideal raw material for building fat.

Fat. Fat, grease, oil and shortening are various names for the edible organic fat compounds that are an important part of our diet. They consist of a great many combinations of a single alcohol-like substance called glycerol with various hydrocarbons (compounds of hydrogen and carbon) called fatty acids. Their chemistry is very complex.

Organic chemists tend to talk about fatty acids instead of fats. This may be because their differences are in the acids rather than the glycerol, because the acids often get separated to exist as part-fats or because four syllables sound better than one. For the lay reader, fatty acid can be read as fat without serious error.

Dietetically, fats are placed in two classes, unsaturated (polyunsaturated) and saturated. A fat is unsaturated if it is possible to add hydrogen atoms to its molecules, and is saturated if it carries all the hydrogen that can be combined with it. Unsaturated fats

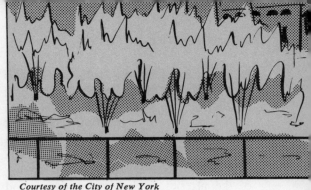

Fig. 32-2. Water is improved by aeration

tend to be soft or liquid at room temperature, saturated ones solid.

Most animal fats are partly or fully saturated, while those from vegetables and fish tend to be unsaturated. Margarine and shortenings such as Crisco consist largely or wholly of vegetable oils that have been solidified and partly saturated by a process called hydrogenation, in which hydrogen

Meat	Protein, %	Fat, %	Moisture, %	Food Energy Calories per Lb.	Riboflavin (B_2) % of Daily Needs For an Av. Adult Found in 1 Lb.
Turkey (roasted)					
White meat	34.3	7.5	58	923	15
Dark meat	30.5	11.6	57	1022	33
Chicken (roasted)					
White meat	31.5	1.3	68	621	11
Dark meat	25.4	7.3	67	754	22
Beef (cooked)					
Round steak	27.0	13.0	59	1049	8
Porterhouse steak	23.0	27.0	49	1539	7
Rump roast	21.0	32.0	46	1701	6
Hamburger	22.0	30.0	47	1648	7
Pork (cooked)					
Ham	24.0	33.0	42	1800	9
Loin chops	23.0	26.0	50	1499	9
Lamb (cooked)					
Rib chops	24.0	35.0	40	1871	10
Shoulder roast	21.0	28.0	50	1539	8
Eggs (boiled) 8 = 1 lb.	13.4	10.5	74	648	56

Compiled from data of Scott (1956) and Poultry and Egg National Board by Chick Master Incubator Co. Anon. (1958).

By permission from "Poultry Products Technology" by George J. Mountney, Copyright 1966, Avi Publishing Co.

Fig. 32-3. Protein in animal foods

is artificially combined with them. This change improves both texture and keeping quality.

The importance of the distinction is that a large quantity of saturated fat in the diet seems to promote the deposit of cholesterol inside the arteries, causing hardening of the arteries, high blood pressure and heart strain. It also appears that either eating an increased amount of unsaturated fat, or taking exercise reduces this effect.

Fat of both kinds is unpopular in reducing diets. However, our bodies have more difficulty building new fat from it

CARBOHYDRATE   PROTEIN

Fig. 32-4. One for a quick start, the other for a long pull

than from carbohydrates, so its weight-adding effect may not be in proportion to its very high calorie value.

Fats make up about 40 per cent of the average American diet. This is up from about 32 per cent in 1915. Consumption of fat is reduced in war time or during economic depressions.

Fat is seldom eaten as a complete unit of food, in the way that we take mostly-protein in meat and mostly-starch in bread. It enters our diet in natural and kitchen mixtures, as a spread, sauce or topping and as a cooking medium in frying.

VITAMINS AND MINERALS

Vitamins. Vitamins are substances that make possible the chemical reactions inside our bodies. They act as catalysts taking part in the reactions but not being directly used up or changed in them. A dramatic example of a catalyst is metallic platinum, which, without the application of any heat, will cause a mixture of cooking gas and air to ignite.

Catalysts are needed in the body because many of the necessary chemical changes are ones that do not occur in non-organic chemistry, and others ordinarily take place only at high temperatures. Sugar will combine with oxygen in the open air only near flame temperature, but it does it in our bodies at 98° F.

Since a vitamin may perform its job many times before breaking down, only small quantites are needed to maintain our supply.

Vitamin requirements are rather similar throughout the animal kingdom but there is wide variety in the ability of different species to manufacture them internally. For example, Vitamin D is formed in liberal quantities in human skin that is exposed to sunlight, but it is not present in most natural foods. Since our exposure to sunlight is not dependable, this vitamin is prepared synthetically and added to milk, margarine and some other foods.

We obtain Vitamin A chiefly by working over a food substance, carotene, which is found in many yellow, orange and dark green foods.

Our vitamin requirement is dependent to some extent on how much we eat. This is reasonable, as more food requires more processing work. A person who has little to eat may have an adequate vitamin supply, but suffer from a deficiency if given additional vitamin-poor food.

At least 15 vitamins have been identified, isolated and purified. It has not been defi-

Fig. 32-5. Foods rich in starch

nitely established that the human body needs all of them. There are just good reasons for suspecting that it may.

There may also be additional vitamins that we need but which have not yet been found or isolated. But they would be of less importance than those that are known, as it has been demonstrated that people can stay healthy on limited, highly refined diets if known vitamins are added to them.

Supplements. There are certain processed foods or food wastes which are particularly rich in one or more vitamins, and which are added to the diet chiefly for their vitamin content or other health-giving qualities, with nourishment or taste being secondary. There is no absolute distinction between these and regular foods, but substances such as black-strap molasses, brewers' yeast and wheat germ are clearly supplements.

Pills. All known vitamins can be manufactured, and these synthetic vitamins are available in pure form and in mixtures as pills. Pure vitamins may be prescribed by a doctor for special reasons. The mixtures, called multiple vitamins, may be taken either on doctor's recommendation or independently for assurance that full vitamin requirements will be met, regardless of possible lack of any of them in the diet.

There are two classes of multiple vitamin pill. One simply supplies the minimum daily adult requirement (MDAR) of each. The other, known as a therapeutic pill,

supplies more than the minimum requirement of some or all of them, and in addition may contain a daily requirement of most minerals also.

Minerals. There are a number of minerals that are essential to body processes. It cannot be said that one is more important than another, as an absolute lack of almost any one of them would make life impossible. However, comparison may be made either on the basis of the bulk required or in regard to the likelihood of a deficiency.

On a life-long basis the metallic element sodium is probably the greatest in quantity, but it is easily obtained from common salt, which is naturally present in meat, added to many foods during cooking and available in a shaker on most tables.

Potassium, a very similar element, is needed to keep sodium in balance in nerve action and in other electro-chemical processes, but the quantity required is much smaller. It is present in most foods, and very seldom becomes a deficiency item, except among people taking diuretic medication.

Calcium and magnesium, a closely associated pair of elements, are needed in considerable quantities during childhood, youth and pregnancy, as they supply most

SATURATED   UNSATURATED

Fig. 32-6. Extent of polysaturation may be indicated by hardness

Fig. 32-7. Human skin cannot make Vitamin D here

of the hard material in bones. Calcium is the more important of the two. During adult life only small quantities are needed for replacement purposes.

These two substances are abundantly present in many vegetables and in solution in hard water. But the body cannot use much of this supply, and the principal usable source is milk.

These four elements, sodium, potassium, calcium and magnesium, are usually not included in therapeutic vitamin-mineral pills because of bulk and other factors.

Other minerals of known importance are iron for use in red blood cells, phosphorous for supplementing calcium-magnesium in building of bones and teeth and iodine for the use of the thyroid gland. In addition, manganese, cobalt, fluorine, silicon, zinc, nickel and aluminum are found in the body. They are all presumed to be needed, although functions of some are unknown.

The average American diet is so varied that it supplies ample quantities of all these minerals, and of vitamins too.

PROBLEMS

Vitamins may be partly or wholly destroyed by light, heat, cold and time, may be leached out of our food in cooking water, or may be refused by our bodies because of the presence or absence of other chemi-

cals. Our mineral requirements are elements which cannot be destroyed, but they can enter into compounds which our bodies cannot use, or go down the drain with cooking water.

Vitamins and minerals often tend to be present in largest quantities in the less appetizing parts of our food. In the wheat grain they are mostly in the germ and in the bran coating, both of which are removed in making white flour. In rice they are also in the outer coating, which is taken off in preparing commercial white rice.

In animals they are concentrated in the organs, most of which are poorly valued. As a result, much of our best food material does not reach our kitchens at all.

Anti-vitamins. There is an enzyme, thiaminase, which seems to have been created just for the purpose of destroying Vitamin B-1. It is present in some fish: whitefish, carp, catfish and herring; and in a few shellfish: clams, lobsters, mussels and shrimp.

If any of these are eaten raw for extended periods, a vitamin deficiency may de-

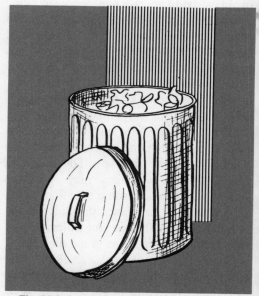

Fig. 32-8. Some of our most nourishing food goes here

velop. Occasional indulgence should do no harm. The enzyme is destroyed if the food containing it is cooked.

There are other substances that destroy or cripple vitamins, or lock them into compounds that make them unavailable. However, in the general field of nutrition, this anti-vitamin activity is a small and usually not-important factor.

Refining. The rejection and wasting of vitamin-rich parts of food is not a perverse behavior limited to modern civilization. The milling of wheat and rice to get white grains is about as widespread as the culture of the plants, and probably reaches thousands of years into the past.

Fig. 32-9. Its vitamins and minerals will be lost

Man apparently has an innate tendency to select bland, white and refined carbohydrate food. When none is available, he will eat the cruder grains and like them. But given a choice, the majority will take the refined types.

This taste preference has been continually reinforced by the fact that highly refined grains keep better. Grain coats and germ contain fats that are likely to become rancid in storage in a few months, and they attract vermin. Husked, de-germed grains and flour made from them will keep almost indefinitely if they are dry, and fewer precautions are needed to keep out mice, insects and other pests.

Now good keeping qualities are chiefly a matter of convenience and economy, but in the past they were often a matter of life or death.

The long experience of man has been that by refining his grain to obtain a whiter, purer foodstuff, he has obtained more pleasing taste and important improvement in keeping qualities. He did not know that in the refining, vital substances essential to good health were lost. However, there was some realization of the inadequacy of grain alone as a diet, and it has usually been supplemented with meat, fish, vegetables or at least rich sauces.

Sugar has followed the same path to purity. The sap of sugar cane is not only rich in sugar, but also contains vitamins and minerals. In order to obtain white color and true, unmixed flavor these valuable substances are removed by crystallizing and bleaching. White sugar is therefore a plain energy food, without more than a trace of either vitamins or minerals.

However, a source of pure energy is not to be despised, and sugar's chemical purity assures a uniform uncomplicated taste on which a cook can depend for accurate sweetening.

Meat. Many peoples have lived chiefly on meat, from necessity or choice. Where necessity ruled, they ate practically the whole animal, and were well nourished. But when meat has been plentiful, or was in competition with other foods, the tendency has been, as now, to eat the flesh (muscle fiber) and discard the rest.

The flesh is generally considered to be poor in vitamins, which are found chiefly in the organs. This is also a type of refining which can contribute to malnutrition.

It has been determined experimentally that man can live on meat alone, provided he eats both the flesh and the viscera. This is presumably true of an all-fish diet also, for shellfish and other invertebrates.

There appears to be an association between eating large quantities of meat, and particularly of meat fats, and hardening of the arteries with accompanying increase of danger of heart attacks and strokes. But it is sufficient precaution to limit intake, as it is very seldom necessary to stop eating meat entirely.

Poultry and sea food do not appear to involve any such health danger.

Vegetarians. Vegetarians are people who do not eat meat, poultry or fish. Many of them will not eat food of animal origin, such as milk or eggs. Such abstinence is sometimes a matter of genuine preference, but more often it is an expression of a belief or principle, which may be religious, health-seeking or moral.

To the outsider, the religious base seems unconvincing.

On the health front, man's internal structure, particularly in regard to the length of the intestine, appears to indicate that he was designed to eat both meat and vegetable food. Since no plants supply protein that is complete for our needs, exclusion of animals and their products from diet makes it more complicated to take care of protein requirements, as mentioned on page 630.

The popular conception is that a vegetarian diet includes lots of vegetables and fruit, fresh and appetizing. But this is not necessarily so. A substantial part of it may be made up of imitation meat — steaks, chops and cutlets — compounded of vegetable proteins such as wheat gluten, ground nuts and soy flour, and flavored with various vegetable extracts.

At their best they can be mistaken for meat loaf or compact poultry dressing, but they are very often heavy or soggy, unique in flavor and difficult to digest.

Such diets may also depend heavily on legume seeds and cereals.

On the moral side, a hard core vegetarian does not believe that it is right for man to kill animals for food, nor to keep them in servitude to produce his food. There is much sympathy for these viewpoints among many who continue to eat animal food anyhow. But if the extreme vegetarian concept were adopted by everyone, it would mean the almost complete extinction of many species of animals including hundreds of millions of individuals.

Fig. 32-10. Vegetarian dream

Denial of birth and existence to our domestic animals to save them from exploitation and death would be a very doubtful service to them.

In general, our health would probably benefit by increasing the proportion of vegetables and fruit in our diet, and there are many who would benefit by reducing intake of meat and/or cereal food. But the real vegetarian diet is only for those who believe in it strongly enough to overlook its inconveniences.

DIET — FOR NOURISHMENT

Now we understand the damage that we can do to the nutritive value of our diet by refining and selecting foods or parts of foods. Our processing industries are capable of giving us whatever we want, in refined, half-refined or natural foods. We can store even the most delicate of foodstuffs for months or years if we are willing to pay a small to moderate price in inconvenience and money.

We can also select from a variety of cooking processes those that cause the least loss of vitamins and minerals. We can make concentrates of vitamin-rich natural substances, and manufacture pure synthetic vitamins.

Choices. There are at least three ways in which we can handle the problem of inclusion of enough nourishment in our diet.

First, we can ignore it, and eat just what we like within bounds of common sense, our taste, our pocketbook and perhaps our physician's specific personal advice. Second, we can devote ourselves partly or wholly to eating "healthy", unprocessed or partly processed, vitamin-rich foods, and preparing and supplementing them in such ways as to preserve their nutritive value. Third, we can eat what we like and also take multiple vitamin pills as supplement or medicine. Or, of course, we can mix up parts of all three systems according to our individual whims.

Eating What We Like. The vast majority takes the first course. The average American housewife has a general knowledge of the principles of nourishment, but does not bother herself much with the details. She simply tries to provide a variety of food, generous in quantity, cooked and served in a manner to please her own tastes and those of her family.

Results seem to be good. We grow bigger and live longer. There are even faintly disturbing side effects of abundant nutrition, such as the increasing size of children's feet.

Recognizable vitamin deficiency diseases are largely limited to those who are very poor, or who do not have anything near an average diet. It is often said that increasing tendency to fail military physicals in one age group, and to have heart attacks in another, are the fault of our diet. It is more reasonable to blame them on lack of vigorous work and play. A dairy cow has a much more complete and scientific diet than her sister out on the range, but she is way behind her when it comes to jumping fences.

Health Diet. The second choice is to fuss scientifically over a diet, balancing its

Fig. 32-11. Does good nutrition grow big feet?

ingredients, choosing those that are richest in nutrients and reinforcing them whenever possible, then handling and cooking them with special care. The net result is usually increase in protein and roughage, and reduction in carbohydrate.

For those who are interested in this approach, a good reference is "LET'S COOK IT RIGHT" by Adelle Davis.

This book is by an authority in the field, it gives strong arguments for unrefined food and for enriched diets, and offers a variety of recipes that make it easy to put the ideas into practice.

There are also many books and pamphlets that appear and disappear, which offer information on health-oriented eating.

Unfortunately, most healthful principles make it necessary to substitute whole wheat flour for white, brown rice for white rice and brown sugar, molasses or honey for white sugar (or, very often, just leave out the sugar). In just those three items you will run head-on into the taste barrier; the almost instinctive preference of man for refined food as demonstrated by his behavior in a whole series of civilizations.

To narrow this attitude to our own culture, for over 50 years doctors, dieticians and food faddists have been urging wider

acceptance of unrefined foods. There has been little organized opposition — millers and manufacturers can make just as much money out of unrefined or half refined products, and they usually advertise whatever sells the best.

Yet, in spite of great pressure, and passive acceptance of the principle by the average American, the sales of "healthful" foods remains at a low, low level. For example, only 2 per cent of American flour is whole wheat.

Health crusaders often seem to feel that this non-acceptance is the result of a vast concealed conspiracy between food processors and government officials, but it rests solidly on taste preferences that are very old and deeply rooted.

Policy. The question is, can you, as a cook for yourself and others, afford to buck this non-acceptance? The answer is "yes" only if you and yours are members of the minority who either prefer unrefined foods or don't care one way or the other.

Otherwise, remember that cooking is a lot of work and responsibility, and it should be rewarded with appreciation. If you insist on giving people what is good for them even if they don't want it, they will not be grateful. If you limit yourself to sneaking in an occasional unwanted whole wheat or fortified item, you will probably get away with it and may even be thanked, but only a family autocrat can make a steady thing of it.

An individual may be willing or even anxious to eat a health diet, but his health may not permit it. For example, the bran covering of the whole wheat grain is too harsh for many 20th century digestive systems, and if eaten in any quantity may cause distress and even damage.

Also, at least 10 per cent of the population has allergies which cause discomfort and illness, and unrefined products contain many more allergens, and in stronger doses, than the refined ones do.

Fig. 32-12. A health diet must be enforced

Fig. 32-13. Wolves of malnutrition

Nervous Strain. A health diet depends not only on its raw materials, but on cooking and handling and methods also. It demands special attention to preventing loss of vitamins by the action of heat, light, time and cooking water. It calls for saving cooking water poured off vegetables, spaghetti and rice, and using them in soup and baked products. It may call for enriching almost everything with powdered milk, in regard to which see page 641.

There are endless precautions required. Don't get milk in transparent bottles — light destroys Vitamin B-2. For the same reason, handle cheese in the dark and cook eggs in a covered pan. Keep oxygen away from raw fruits and vegetables while preparing and serving — it destroys Vitamins A, C and E. Rush all vegetables from garden, market or refrigerator through washing, peeling and cutting to the cooking, as the food value is going down with every second that passes.

Books full of these instructions communicate a feeling of harried pessimism. In them, cooking is not a dignified I-am-my-own-boss occupation, but resembles whipping a dog team across Arctic wastes while wolves threaten to drag passengers off the rear of the sled.

Or, on a less facetious note, they express a feeling of desperate poverty, which can only be relieved from moment to moment by salvaging every possible vanishing scrap and drop of nutriment, regardless of the work involved.

Supplements. A housewife who is uncertain about the adequacy of the food that she is providing, and is disinclined to get into the complications of health-oriented diet, can supplement her cooking with vitamin pills.

The use of these pills is criticized by a number of authorities. They seem to feel that sufficient vitamins can and should be provided by food, that if a cook doesn't worry about vitamins, she will lose all interest in proper selection and cooking of food, and that regular consumption of multiple pills carries the probability of dangerous and perhaps fatal overdoses.

The first point is certainly valid, but it does not constitute an argument against adding a harmless margin of safety. The other two objections are hopelessly weak. Vitamins are a rather recent discovery that did not noticeably improve the quality of home cooking, which finds its excellence largely in desire to please and in pride of accomplishment.

The vitamins chiefly concerned in danger of overdosing are A and D. Either of these can poison the system if taken in large

Fig. 32-14. Trying to take an overdose of multiple vitamin pills

daily doses over a long period, and results can be fatal. But in Vitamin A the danger point is not reached until the daily ration exceeds 200,000 units, while multiple pills contain only 5,000 to 8,000 units.

The situation is more confused in regard to Vitamin D. In general, adverse effects will show at dosage of 150,000 units a day, but there is an isolated report of 2 deaths following taking of 20,000 to 40,000 units a day for several months. In multiple vitamins you get 400 units a day, the same amount that is added to a quart of milk.

In order to get vitamin poisoning from these pills you would have to eat them by the handful, day after day and week after week. And it takes only one a day to provide assurance that normal requirements are met, and even one a week can provide a no-worry backing for ordinary cooking.

33
ILLNESS FROM FOOD

INDIGESTION AND POISONING

Food is usually nourishing and agreeable, but there are various circumstances under which it can cause discomfort, illness and even death.

Indigestion. Eating too much at a meal, or exercising immediately after a normally heavy meal, will make most people uncomfortable. Also, most people can be made at least mildly sick by eating even moderate quantities of certain foods or combinations of foods, which differ from person to person.

Aside from allergy, which will be discussed separately, such difficulties may arise from structural, nervous or chemical peculiarities or diseases of the digestive and assimilation systems.

Freshly baked or soggy bread, and food that is greasy, acid, soggy or highly spiced, are common causes of indigestion, particularly when associated with over-eating. However, this is a highly individual matter which each person must work out for himself, preferably with the help of his doctor if the condition is severe or increasing.

The primary preventive and treatment for indigestion is to relax after a meal.

Intolerance. A person may not be able to digest a particular food or group of foods because his digestive system fails to produce a special chemical needed to handle a substance in the food.

As a single example, many adults, particularly among the oriental and negro races, cannot digest lactose (milk sugar) because of their lack of a specific enzyme, lactase. As a result, drinking any noticeable quantity of milk, or eating food which contains milk solids, is likely to cause cramps, bloating and disagreeable effects. For these people, the common practice of fortifying various foods by loading them with milk powder creates a problem.

Allergy. Allergy is an ailment in which a person's system reacts against a usually harmless substance by forming antibodies that attack it. This attack is accompanied by excessive secretion of a body chemical called histamine, and causes a wide variety of symptoms. They include itching, swelling, and inflammation, pain and excessive secretion, and may be severe enough to cause shock, unconsciousness and even death.

Typical allergic ailments include asthma, hay fever, itching, hives, eye irritation and

Fig. 33-1. A good way to avoid indigestion

indigestion. Poison ivy is a very common skin allergy. Allergy may also be implicated in, or provide convincing imitations of, arthritis, headache, hemorrhoids, multiple sclerosis and many other diseases.

Allergic symptoms can be usually be relieved by medical treatment. Antihistamine drugs reduce the amount of histamine in the blood, and stimulants often counteract its effects. The allergy itself may be treated by desensitization shots, but food allergies respond poorly to them. If the allergens can be avoided entirely, the sensitivity may decrease or disappear without treatment.

Allergens can enter the body in many ways, but in this book we are interested only in those that are taken in food or drink.

Food Allergens. Any food, drink, medicine or anything else taken by mouth can be or may contain a food allergen. Usually, however, the allergen is a protein. It may be a natural food substance, one produced by cooking, combination of different substances or by spoilage; or by a synthetic addition such as a spray residue, a preservative or a flavoring. The trouble does not really come from the food or additive, but in the sensitivity that the person develops to it.

Allergic difficulties are the unrecognized basis for many of the limited diets that are urged upon us. For example, a writer may be allergic to an aluminum compound. He finds that food cooked in aluminum pans makes him ill, so he becomes a crusader against use of aluminum utensils. A severe allergy against even one meat may convert a man into an ardent vegetarian.

Diagnosis. Allergens may be very difficult to identify. Something in the air may be blamed on the food, or vice versa. Sometimes they are made either inactive or much stronger by combination with other substances. Doctors' sensitivity tests give important clues, but they are usually less reliable for food than for substances that are contacted or inhaled.

A thoughtful person watching his own diet and symptoms will often be able to find quite accurately what foods disagree with him. But whether he works it out for himself, or has the help of an allergist, his findings should be respected, even though he may not be right every time.

A cook should NEVER deceive a person about the nature of the food. If someone says that he can't eat pork, don't give him pork and swear that it is veal, just to prove that it is all in his mind. He may assure you

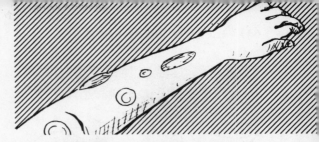

that the veal is delicious and that he feels fine, then go quietly into the bathroom and throw up. If he believes you gave him veal, he might stop eating that too.

For a detailed and sympathetic account of allergies, the reader is referred to Berglund. "IT'S NOT ALL IN YOUR MIND."

POISONS

Avoidance of poisons is a dietary problem that is as old as the gathering of food. There are many fruits, berries, leaves, roots and mushrooms that are poisonous in varying degrees. Portions of garden plants may contain poison. Fish and shellfish taken in certain localities in certain seasons may be dangerous. Spoiled meat and many food mixtures, and improperly canned low acid foods can breed bacteria that create toxins.

But a reasonable amount of knowledge and care is usually enough to keep us out of difficulty with any of these.

There is now a new generation of food poisons — the residues from sprays used on food plants to control insects and fungi. In addition, chemicals added to food during processing as preservatives, stabilizers and flavorings are under examination for possible ill effects.

Built-in Poisons. There are many common plants that are dangerously poisonous, and which became well known in periods where wild food was an important resource. People now are protected by a general suspicion of non-commercial food, or by diligent study that accompanies such food gathering.

There is a very poisonous plant that is too often eaten by mistake, with resulting illness and death. This is the mushroom or toadstool Amanita, which in both the verna and virosa species closely resembles the common commerical mushroom, Agaricus bisporus and the common field mushroom, Agaricus campestris. This problem is discussed on page 267 under MUSHROOMS.

Rhubarb carries a poison, oxalic acid, in its leaves but not in its stems. The taste is bad, even worse than the stems, so that a batch containing leaves is not likely to be eaten even if it is prepared.

If a growing potato tuber loses its ground cover and is partly exposed to sunlight, it will grow a green chlorophyll coat and secrete a poison, solanine. Fortunately, it has a bitter taste which contrasts sharply with the blandness expected of a potato, so it is very seldom that enough is eaten to cause sickness. The chemical is usually present only in the green area.

There are certain fish, particularly in the blowfish family, whose flesh and/or organs are poisonous. There are shellfish on the Pacific coast which are edible in some seasons, and dangerous in others because they eat and concentrate a poisonous plankton.

The mercury content of some seafood worries health officials. However, our diet is so varied that there is little danger to health from this source, even when we eat such foods freely.

Commercially sold food does not often

Fig. 33-3. The deadly Amanita

Fig. 33-4. Food spoils quickly at picnics

include poisonous plants and animals, and local sources can usually provide complete warnings for food gatherers who will take the trouble to ask.

Bacterial Toxins. Food that has been processed — that is, killed, cooked, mixed and/or stored — often offers an excellent growth medium for organisms. Most of them simply cause spoilage with disagreeable taste and smell resulting. Some of them are infectious, and are able to multiply in people who eat the food, making them sick. And a few others manufacture toxins which make the food poisonous.

Clostridium botulinum is a heat resistant bacterium that lives without air and flourishes in low-acid food. It produces a powerful toxin, a teaspoon of which is said to be able to kill a million persons. It is dangerous only in home canned or carelessly canned foods, and is discussed on pages 607 and 610.

Streptococcus bacteria, of the aureus and faecalis species, are common intestinal bacteria that grow vigorously in food and produce a poisonous toxin. A good dose of it results in nausea, cramps, vomiting and diarrhea, usually within 6 hours of eating. This is the common picnic and party food ailment that is often incorrectly called ptomaine poisoning.

Severity of attack varies widely with the amount of the poison and the resistance of

the victim, but it usually lasts only 24 hours. But the embarrassment to the person or persons who prepared the food may last a lifetime.

Most cases of this poisoning occur during the summer, when foods such as cream filled pastry, custard cakes, dairy products, salads and salad dressings and meat mixtures are kept without refrigeration for a few hours. Several hundred milion of the bacteria may be present in a small food particle.

Streptococci are all around us, so you can't keep them out of the food. But you can avoid giving them a running start from gross infections from dirty hands and utensils. See page 648. Keep the food as cool as you can while preparing it, and refrigerate it until used. If you must transport it, pack it with ice in insulated containers, or bury it in blankets. And see that it is eaten as soon as possible after arrival at the festivities.

Chemicals. Many chemicals are used to protect plants while they are growing, and for various purposes during processing. Most of the insecticides and fungicides used on plants are poisonous, and some of the additives are also. Their use is regulated with the purpose of keeping the amount in food below that which would affect the consumer.

There are also many substances that are not poisonous in themselves, at least not in the concentrations used in food, but which might have unfavorable long range effects on people eating them. Their use is under study by the Food and Drug Administration, and any that prove to be harmful are restricted or eliminated from approved lists.

In general, the consumer is quite well protected by regulations restricting the use of chemicals on or in food, and by self-regulation of the food industries. However, mistakes are made, laws are sometimes disregarded and there are people who are abnormally sensitive to certain compounds. In general, it is wise to keep a suspicious attitude toward chemical tampering with food.

Aside from the health aspect, many chemicals that are added to food to improve it have an opposite effect. Much of the commercially prepared food is disagreeable to eat because of over-smoothness, over-whipping and/or over-flavoring. But these defects are obvious, and the products showing them can be avoided.

Spray Residues. Fruit and vegetables are sprayed to control insects and diseases. Most of the sprays are poisons. The before-1940 types made use of arsenic, copper, sulfur and pyrethrum. Of these, only arsenic is seriously poisonous to humans, and our bodies can dispose of small amounts without ill effects.

But now we have a whole new series of synthetic poisons capable of long term buildup in the body. The first of them, DDT, is being outlawed and is not supposed to be used on food plants. But the long range effects of others is still largely unknown, and any prudent person will wish to keep his consumption of them to a minimum.

The amount of spray found on fruits and vegetables, and the danger from it, is limited by regulations concerning time of spraying and material to be used, according to the time before harvest and the probability of the outer contaminated surfaces being eaten or discarded.

The Department of Agriculture is sincerely interested in protecting the consumer, and it has wide and increasing powers to regulate and prohibit the use of poisons on commercial crops. Although it is also the farmers' friend, and wishes to provide them with every reasonable defense against the insect, fungus and virus pests that would make widespread agriculture impossible without poisons, the Department is usually (although not always) successful in keeping the amount of poison you get with your food well below the point

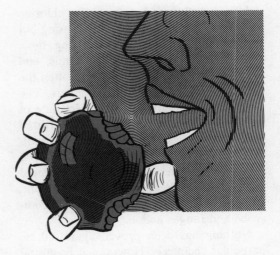

Fig. 33-5. A little fruit skin should do you no harm

where it would damage your health.

Commercial cleaning after harvest removes a great many spray-contaminated surfaces.

A further precaution which you can take yourself is to remove and discard the skin of apples, pears and peaches, and the outer leaves of lettuce and cabbage. Just washing is usually ineffective, as the sprays are made to be sticky, and often sink into and become part of the skin as well.

But if you like skin, it will probably do no harm to eat it in moderate quantities. Berries can't be peeled, and removing grape skins is too much work.

Organic Culture. There are fruits and vegetables that are grown without use of poisonous sprays, and generally without artificial fertilizers. They are sold under the description "organically raised", usually at a premium price.

Quality may be anything from premium down to scarred and misshapen. Only a few people can raise them well. They are seldom available in either frozen or canned form.

Additives. Commercially prepared food usually contains one or more non-food substances, put in as a preservative, thickener, stabilizer or flavoring. Others, like chlorine bleach for flour, are used in processing but apparently disappear before eating time.

The use of additives of all kinds, and particularly the preservatives, are often the subject of attack by health crusaders. The non-food preservatives include benzoate of soda, put in cider and other unsterilized fruit juices to slow the action of alcohol-making yeasts, calcium proponate baked in bread to reduce its tendency to mold and sulfur dioxide as a general anti-oxidant, enzyme inhibitor and reducer of mold, microbe and fungus action.

Nothing has been proved against these particular chemicals. However, it is natural that preservatives should come under particular suspicion as potential poisons to the human system, because most of them are used to interfere with natural deterioration processes, and many of them work by killing organisms, or by slowing their multiplication.

Since all life has certain structures in common, a killer of one kind may well be a poisoner of others. However, unless a chemical can be shown to acumulate in the body, in the manner of DDT or lead, the possibility of damage from tiny doses is quite small.

There is a group of additives that are used to thicken and stabilize canned and prepared food. Some of them, like pectin, are natural substances in wide use; some, like Irish moss and agar, are natural but not used in home kitchens, and many are synthetic.

The last two groups are the subject long range testing programs, and any that show signs of being toxic are quickly removed from the market.

Flavorings. Both natural and synthetic flavorings are used with great freedom in prepared foods. In general, it is assumed that natural flavors are both safe and good, but this is not necessarily so. Prussic (hydrocyanic) acid, one of the deadliest poisons,

can be concentrated from some peach pits and bitter almonds. Nicotine, belladonna and many other poisons are natural substances widely distributed in plants.

However, natural flavorings that are in use at present are all safe.

Synthetic flavorings are also believed to be non-harmful, but are under the same suspicious examination as other additives, and are dropped if found to be dangerous.

Coumarin, a vile-tasting synthetic once widely used in baked goods, was mercifully eliminated. Sodium cyclamate, the best of the non-fattening sweeteners, enjoyed great

Fig. 33-6. Food additives are thoroughly tested

popularity in diet foods until it was taken off the general market because massive doses of it caused cancer in laboratory animals.

Body Resistance. In thinking about poisons and maybe-poisons, both those sprayed on the growing plants and those used for preservatives, appearance or flavor, it should be remembered that the human body has efficient defense mechanisms.

Most foreign substances that it cannot tolerate can be dealt with. Some of them are rejected promptly by throwing up, by diarrhea or through the kidneys, others are chemically changed in the liver or elsewhere into less harmful or less active substances, and some of the original and of the altered chemicals are stored in tissues where their capacity for damage is reduced or stopped. Stored poisons are gradually eliminated from the body by replacement of the cells in which they are lodged.

An example of storage-for-elimination is that arsenic taken into the system in small quantities may be deposited in the hair and fingernails.

Tolerance. Every person has an individual tolerance (called a threshold) for each poison, both in regard to the amount of new poison circulating in the system, and old chemical stored in tissues. If this amount is exceeded, some sort of ill health or illness, which may possibly result in death, will be caused.

When long-lasting poisons are taken in very small doses over a long period of time, as is usual with spray residues on produce, the effect on health will be largely determined by the ability of the body to get rid of it as fast as it comes in. If it cannot, the poison in the system will increase in quantity. If this goes on long enough, it will cause trouble.

The onset of illness from very gradual poisoning is likely to be slow and the cause unknown, so that symptoms may be severe by the time the difficulty is found or guessed. They may continue for a long time after intake of the chemical has stopped, unless means are known to clean the accumulations out of the system.

Lead and DDT are examples of poisons that are not excreted readily, and that therefore may build up inside us enough to cause serious trouble, even if doses are small.

Extent of Damage. Thanks to the resistance of the human system, and vigilance of government agencies and consumer groups, damage to health from the poisonous qualities of chemical sprays and additives seems to be comparatively rare in occurrence. The illness and death that can be justly blamed on them is only a tiny frac-

tion of that formerly caused by cholera, typhoid, tuberculosis and other ailments that technology has so greatly reduced.

However, "comparatively rare" is a term that when used in connection with the large percentage of 200 million people (considering the United States alone) who eat chemically sprayed or processed food, means that tens or perhaps hundreds of thousands of individuals may be suffering from the presence of these chemicals in their systems.

This makes a real health problem that deserves attention, but it is not a cause for hysteria nor even for elaborate precautions in preparing and eating food.

INFECTIONS

Living plants tend to be almost sterile internally, and do not ordinarily support any organisms causing disease in man. But dangerous microorganisms may be present on the outer surfaces.

Animals may be infected with a wide variety of diseases that can be transmitted to humans.

The majority of the infections from food are because of contamination by organisms that were not originally part of it. The bac-

Fig. 33-7. Sanitation is important

teria and viruses concerned may be from fertilizer, air or water, but most often from hands or utensils.

From Excrement. The most common and dangerous source of infection is human fecal matter. Most organisms, good and bad, that live in our bodies find their way into the intestines, where conditions for growing and multiplying are ideal for many of them. The excrement should therefore never be used as fertilizer, nor left exposed where flies can get on it and track it around.

The flush toilet, backed up by adequate septic tank and fields or a sewage disposal system will render it harmless, but inadequate systems may just transfer the infection potential to another location.

The most dangerous part is any trace that may get on hands that later manipulate food or utensils. There is a case history of a woman who was known as Typhoid Mary, because any family that employed her as a cook soon developed typhoid fever.

She was infected with the disease without being made sick by it, and was innocently infecting her employers. But the usual schoolbook report on her is too delicate to mention the fact that if she had

Fig. 33-8. You can chlorinate water

washed her hands thoroughly after wiping herself, she would not have spread the infection.

Urine is not usually a disease carrier, but the whole excretory area may be contaminated. It is therefore essential that any person involved in food preparation wash hands carefully after each use of the toilet.

Typhoid and cholera, the most serious of the diseases of this nature, are now so rare in the United States that they are not a health problem. But there are still many infectious and toxin-secreting organisms that can cause a great deal of unpleasantness if cleanliness is neglected. Streptococcus was mentioned on page 644. Another very common type is the salmonella.

Water-carried. Water can carry many disease organisms. It supplies them with little nourishment, but transports them effectively from their source to the next victims.

Ordinary clean water containing dissolved oxygen tends to gradually kill most organisms that drift with it. It is said that a briskly running stream will purify itself in a few hundred feet. However, this is true of only light contamination, and normal rate of flow. A stream that is polluted with other types of waste, or that is in flood, can carry infections for many miles from a single source.

Public water supplies are usually treated with sufficient chlorine to kill organisms that might have been present in the reservoir or other source, or that might enter leaking pipes from leaking sewers.

Doubtful water can be purified by boiling for 15 minutes, or by adding sodium hypochlorite solution (the common household laundry bleach) in the proportion of 4 drops to a quart of water (or one teaspoon in 5 gallons), and letting it stand 10 minutes. A traveler can use Hallazone pills for the same purpose.

Salmonella. Salmonella is a name for a group of bacteria similar to those that cause

Fig. 33-9. Clamming should be limited to clean water

typhoid, and which are sometimes known as paratyphoid. They live in the intestines of man and many animals, (including rats, mice and some insects) in the ground and in the dust of the air.

In small numbers they seem to be harmless, but if a considerable number are eaten all at once, they multiply in the digestive tract, and in about 3 days produce an illness that may include headache, chills and all the worst digestive symptoms. Recovery time varies from a few hours to a week.

This illness can be prevented by cleanliness, cooking and refrigeration, in the same general manner as the streptococcus poisoning discussed earlier.

Hepatitis. Infectious hepatitis is a virus disease that can be communicated directly from person to person, but is also very frequently acquired by eating shellfish from polluted water, or other food that has been contaminated by sewage. The organism is highly resistant to heat, and many shellfish are eaten raw or only lightly cooked.

The principal precaution against catching it is to eat only shellfish that come from commercial sources or from water that is safely away from sources of pollution. Thorough cooking is a secondary precaution, but the time and heat required to kill the virus have not been established.

Trichinosis. Trichinosis is caused by a nematode that lives in the flesh of a wide variety of animals in a dormant form. When the flesh is eaten, the organism lays eggs in the intestine of the new host. The new generation travels into the flesh, grows up causing pain and various severe side reactions, and then becomes dormant, waiting for another predator.

This organism is killed by heating it to 137° F, or by being held at zero temperature for 30 days. The principal source of infection for humans is pork, and the disease is discussed more fully under that heading, on page 119.

Part Five / THE KITCHEN

34

CLEANING UP

GENERAL COMMENTS

Cleaning up a kitchen and a dining room after a meal may be as big a job as preparing the meal and it seems much bigger because it is not as interesting. The amount of work involved can often be reduced by a clear understanding of what should be done and why.

Among the items to be considered are the characteristics of water and water temperature, the soap, detergent and other cleaning compounds; the tools for wiping, scraping, scrubbing and drying; the types of soil to be removed and the preferred means for each, and finally the desirability of owning and using a dishwasher.

If this looks like too much information on a dull subject it can be skipped. Hot water, soap or detergent, and elbow grease will do the job, and less knowledge may merely mean more work or poorer results.

From a time standpoint, the most efficient way to wash up is to persuade every reasonably competent person within reach to help; or at least as many of them as can be fitted into the kitchen. Any possible loss in resulting breakage or questionable cleanliness may or may not be compensated by the feeling of togetherness that is generated.

There is no doubt that cleaning can do a great deal of damage. There is the obvious danger of breakage of china and glassware by inexperienced, careless and/or high spirited helpers. Porcelain finishes, glassware and painted china may be permanently marred by one use of an abrasive powder. Teflon is surely damaged by abrasives, and probably by scraping and perhaps even by careless stacking. A good automatic dishwasher may take hand-painted patterns off china and warp non-boilable plastics.

The materials that are removed by a cleaning process are called soil. On cooking utensils and dishes they are mostly food remainders, which include a wide variety of substances and conditions.

WATER

Water is the basic material for washing things. It is abundant, cheap, safe and is an excellent solvent for a great variety of substances. But it has a rather high surface tension (see page 653) that prevents it from penetrating, dissolving or even wetting many substances, it does not dissolve nor mix

with oil and grease, and it may carry undesirable substances in solution.

These difficulties are overcome by heating and adding chemical compounds.

Heating. Making water hot improves its
cleaning ability in several ways. It lowers
its surface tension, increases both the speed
of solution and the amount that can be
dissolved off most substances, and enables
it to liquefy and float off many fats. Also,
hot water evaporates quickly so that drying
is speeded.

Effectiveness increases with temperature
to and past the boiling point. Steam is used
industrially as a cleaner. But work around
a kitchen is dangerous enough without adding steam and scalding-hot dish water. A
temperature of 115° F is enough for most
hand dish washing, and 125 is about as hot
as many people's hands can tolerate.

Still hotter water in the pipes can be
cooled to any desired temperature in an
ordinary mixing faucet, but adjusting and
usually readjusting the handles is a nuisance
which it is better to avoid. There is also a
danger of poor adjustment or carelessness
resulting in using the too-hot water directly,
with painful results.

CHEMICALS

Most chemicals used in kitchen cleanup
are dissolved in water to increase its ability
to remove dirt and food remainders.

Soap and Detergent. Soap, made by
treating animal and vegetable fats with lye,
is the oldest of the dissolve-in-water cleaners. It had practically a monopoly until
World War II, but since then has lost most
of the market to synthetic detergents made
from petroleum and other industrial chemicals.

We ordinarily speak of soap (animal-
vegetable base) and detergent (usually petroleum base) as if they were entirely different substances, and this book follows the
custom most of the time. However, the distinction between them is not always clear, so

Fig. 34-1. Some helpers are too high spirited

their manufacturers have coined some new
words.

One of these is surfactant, meaning any
chemical which becomes chiefly active at
the surface of water in which it is dissolved. This term includes soap, the more
active parts of detergents, and a few other
substances.

Soap and detergent increase the cleaning
power of water in a number of ways. These
include lowering surface tension (the wetting action described on page 654) emulsifying and dissolving fats, and dissolving or
loosening and suspending solids.

Solvents. Most household cleaning is
done with such part-dissolving, part-trans-
porting molecules linking water and other
substances. But there are also chemicals
that dissolve certain types of soil directly,
as water dissolves sugar.

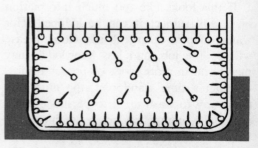

Fig. 34-2. The round ends dissolve in water, the
straight ones in oil

Gasoline, lighter fluid and carbon tetrachloride dissolve grease readily. But they do not mix with water, and would have to be used in large quantities. They have chemical smells, the first two are flammable and explosive and the third is poisonous. They are therefore not used in the kitchen.

Ammonia dissolves many forms of grease readily. But it is a gas at room temperature and has a pungent smell and is extremely irritating to eyes and throat. It is sold as a dilute water solution, or as a minor ingredient in cleaning compounds. Its vapor may be used to soften soil that is hard to get at, as in ovens.

Lye (Caustic Soda). Lye or caustic soda is known specifically as sodium hydroxide, NaOH. It removes grease by changing it to soap so that water dissolves it. It is sold under various trade names such as Drano for use in cleaning plugged drain pipes.

Lye is poisonous. It burns the skin very badly on contact, is a skin irritant even in very weak solutions and destroys fabrics if it is concentrated. It should not be used, ever, as a kitchen cleaner. Some dishwasher detergents contain a little free lye, and are intended for use only in automatic dishwashers, not for hand washing.

The combination of lye with water, fat and some other substances generates heat, which may cause almost explosive boiling and spattering. First aid for lye burns includes flushing it off with acid such as vinegar.

BEHAVIOR OF CHEMICALS

Surface Activity. Many of the useful actions of soap and detergent depend upon the fact that they are made of comparatively long thin molecules, one end of which is attracted to water, so is called water-loving or hydrophilic; while the other end is repelled by water and attracted by oil, and is called hydrophobic.

The water-loving end dissolves in water,

the other end seeks to escape from it, so the molecules migrate to most water surfaces and stay there. In Figure 34-2 they are shown with round heads for the water end and straight tails for the other.

Most glass and metal surfaces carry a layer of combined water and have a moderate attraction for the heads, but air, oil and most kinds of soil attract the tail.

This concentration at the surface provides maximum action from whatever quantity is in solution, and it has important effects on fats and various other substances that form many of these surfaces.

Surface Tension. The molecules at the surface of water are linked together weakly by a natural force called surface tension. It is caused by attraction between molecules, which causes them to pull on each other, so that those on the surface are pulled

Fig. 34-3. Surface tension shapes drops

downward and toward each other, forming a compact surface film.

Drops of water falling through the air, or resting on certain substances, are pulled into ball-like shapes by this force. The smaller the drop, the more its shape is controlled by it.

A tiny drop of water resting on a waxed surface will be a globe, slightly flattened on the bottom, as in Figure 34-3, left. A somewhat larger drop will have a flat top and bottom with curved sides, as in the center. After that size, increase in quantity of water will enlarge the top and bottom flats, without affecting depth of water or shape of sides.

On a smaller scale, surface tension delays or prevents the soaking of water into fine spaces in dust, dirt and other materials, and usually prevents it from making any close contact with waxy or greasy surfaces. It is involved in the refusal of oil and water to mix without special procedures being followed. It is a major drawback in attempting to use plain water for cleaning, particularly if the water is cold.

Soap, detergent and various other substances weaken the attraction that causes surface tension, permitting water to penetrate into very small spaces, and to spread out and cling to surfaces which normally would repel it. It can therefore dissolve and/or soften materials much more readily, because of the tremendously greater area of contact, and the ability to go between dirt and the surface to be cleaned.

The ability of a chemical to weaken water's surface film is called its wetting power.

Surface tension is stated in dynes, a measure of the energy required to move the surface. In contact with air, mercury has the highest tension, about 350. Pure water has 72 and water with dissolved detergent 28.

Tensions existing between two liquids, or between a liquid and a solid, are complicated and variable.

Demonstrations. Wetting power can usually be demonstrated by adding the chemical to water that is held above its normal level by surface tension. This might be a round drop of water on a dry surface, or an overfilled glass or cup in which the water is rounded above the edge. Usually, adding a little detergent will cause the top to flatten or the glass to overflow.

Also, a wad of fine steel wool will float on plain water, but sink suddenly if detergent is added, or slowly if the water is heated, as water penetrates the fine spaces between the wires.

The speed of this reaction can be observed by placing the steel wool at one end of a tub and adding the detergent at the other.

Water-Oil Mixtures. There are certain fluids which will not mix together under normal conditions. Oil and water are the best known example, and their behavior is important in both cooking and cleaning. A salad dressing of just oil and vinegar (vinegar is mostly water) separates cleanly into an upper layer of oil and a lower one of vinegar. If it is stirred together the oil breaks up into rounded drops and masses, which rise to the surface, and recombine as soon as the stirring stops.

If the mixture is beaten vigorously, as with an egg beater, the oil drops become very tiny and take longer to rise, but within a few minutes separation is again complete.

But if you can make the droplets small enough so that each contains only a few molecules, and keep them that tiny, the random motion of the water molecules will prevent them from rising, and the mixture will be almost permanent.

Such a mixture is called an emulsion. It may be produced by special machinery, as when milk is homogenized to reduce the cream (fat) droplets to emulsion size, or by adding some substance with an affinity for both oil and water that will break down the surface tension between them and prevent oil from recombining. Yolk of egg is such a substance, and mayonnaise is a stable oil-yolk-vinegar emulsion.

This quality of preventing recombination is called dispersion.

In soap and particularly in detergent, the

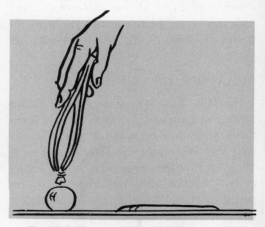

Fig. 34-4. Demonstration of surface tension

tail ends of the molecules have an affinity for fatty substances. An oil droplet surrounded by plain water has a surface tension against the water of about 30 (dynes). When the water contains a detergent, its molecules find the oil, dissolve their tail ends in it, and reduce its surface tension to less than 3.

With the lower tension, any sort of mechanical stirring, beating or scraping will break up the oil globules into smaller and smaller sizes until they are either a true emulsion, or near enough to it so that the oil will remain suspended long enough to go down the drain with the water.

Viscosity. Viscosity is the thickness or flow-resistance of a fluid. Very high viscosity fluids, such as warm asphalt, may appear to be solids for a short time, as their flowing motion is extremely slow. Viscosity almost always decreases with rising temperature, and increases as the temperature is lowered. This effect is very noticeable with some substances, and comparatively slight with others.

The viscosity of water is increased by dissolving detergent in it. This enables it to hold more and bigger particles in suspension, so that they when they are wiped off a dish it will take more time for them to settle back onto it.

There is no clear relationship between viscosity and surface tension. Also, there are chemicals that are very effective in keeping particles in suspension without adding greatly to the viscosity.

Foam (Suds). Foam is made up of many small or mixed-size air bubbles. Such bubbles form in plain water, but high surface tension, low viscosity and rapid evaporation give them such a short life they are hardly noticed.

Most soap and detergent encourage the creation of bubbles when they are dissolved in water. Any movement of the liquid that mixes air into it creates bubbles, which may persist for a long time, partly because molecules of the cleaning agent both give strength to the thin bubble films, and protect the water in them against evaporation.

Suds have little cleaning effect in themselves, but they often indicate the amount of active soap or detergent present in a solution. As the cleaner is used up by combining with dirt or with chemicals in the water, the suds get smaller and weaker.

However, there are detergents that are made up to have very few suds (chiefly for use in clothes washing machines), that you might happen to use for dishes. Then, lack of foam would not indicate a lack of cleaning power.

SOAP

Most soap is made by combining almost any animal or vegetable fat with lye. When cooked together at proper temperatures and concentrations, they yield crude soap and glycerin. Various refining processes and added substances are used to produce the variety of bars and flakes or powders now or recently on the market.

Liquid and special soaps may be made with fat and potassium hydroxide.

Soap is an excellent cleaning agent. Its principal drawback is its reaction with impurities in water to form insoluble compounds which consume soap, and which leave a film on objects being washed, and

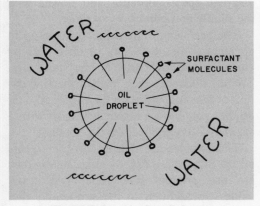

Fig. 34-5. Breaking an oil droplet

Ingredient	Function
Surface-active agent	Reduce surface tension
Phosphate	Buffer, assist suspension, dispersion and emulsification of spoil
Sodium sulfate	Additional electrolyte to aid wetting and dispersion
Methyl cellulose	Prevent re-deposition of soil
Sodium silicate	Prevent metal corrosion
Fatty acids	Stabilize foam
Sodium perborate	Bleaching agent
Perfumes, antioxidants, fluorescent dyes, etc.	Improve appearance and odor of product

Fig. 34-6. Detergent composition

often a heavy deposit on a tub or sink at the waterline.

Hard water, carrying lime (calcium and magnesium carbonate) in solution, is the worst offender, but acids in water may also react with soap.

DETERGENTS

The approximate composition of a typical household flake or powder detergent is shown in Figure 34-6. The principal use of

Fig. 34-7. We had suds in our waterfalls

each ingredient in the compound is indicated. Quantities are not shown because of current conditions of argument and change.

Surface-Active Agents (Surfactants). Surfactants are the most active part of the detergent, and the most expensive.

Surfactants account for most of the distinctive cleaning characteristics of synthetic detergents. They are usually made with sulfuric acid and synthetic chemicals derived from petroleum according to exact procedures. The manufacturer has closer control over his product than he has with soap, which is based on different vegetable fats whose availability and cost varies with crop conditions, and on animal fat which is a semi-waste product that varies in nature and has spectacular ups and downs with the supply and popularity of meat.

The petroleum bases can be made up in an almost infinite variety of chemicals by changing the structure of the molecules. The alkylbenzene that formed the foundation of most detergents until 1965 had over 80,000 possible arrangements, each with a slightly different effect on the product.

The chances are that no two detergents on the market are exactly alike, unless they are one product sold under two brand names. In addition to the surfactants that are possible, the proportioning to other chemicals for different purposes is variable.

It is probable that every detergent you buy is at least adequate for every ordinary cleaning job, and that each of a number of them is superior to all others for some particular use.

The original surfactant base, alkylbenzene sulfonate (ABS), is very resistant to decomposition by bacteria in sewage disposal plants and in the ground. As use became widespread, foam overflowed the plants, and appeared in rivers (most conspicuously at the foot of waterfalls) and in drinking water.

As a result, this compound has been replaced by linear alkyl sulfonate (LAS) to produce a new generation of soft or biodegradable detergents that decompose about as readily as soap, but have the same general cleaning qualities as the older hard varieties. The changeover was a gigantic chemical and engineering job.

Builders. Builders are inorganic salts (for example, sodium tripolyphosphate and soldium sulfate) that both improve the detergent and reduce its cost.

Tripolyphosphate is mildly alkaline and sulfate is neutral, bu they nevertheless serve to neutralize hard water, by combining with the calcium to make soluble compounds that do not interfere with washing. They help to break up solids, and put them (and keep them) in suspension in various ways.

One of the principal differences between heavy-duty and light-duty detergents is the alkalinity of the builder. Heavy duty types are meant for commercial use, and include washing soda, trisodium phosphate and perhaps a trace of lye. All of these chemicals are unkind to the hands.

The use of phosphates in detergents is under attack because they contribute to over-growth of algae in lakes which receive sewage or effluent from sewage plants. They are not removed or neutralized by most present methods of treatment.

A few liquid detergents are phosphate-free, but eliminating phosphorous from all detergents without diminishing their effectiveness may be a task more difficult than the change from hard to soft surfactants.

Softeners. Softeners are chemicals such as borax which combine with calcium and magnesium carbonate and other minerals commonly found in hard water, to produce soluble chemicals which do not interfere with the action of soap and detergent.

Most detergents have enough softening ability in their builders to counteract the hardness in most water. If the water is exceptionally hard, other parts of the mixture are used up in the softening process, so greater amounts of detergent are required. Reduction in phosphate content is likely to affect cleaning efficiency in hard water more than in soft water.

A household water supply can be softened by passing it through a tank of zeolite, a complex crystalline material, or synthetic substitutes for it. It reacts with calcium and magnesium carbonates, changing them to sodium salts which have no hardening effect. The mineral content of the water is not reduced, but it is changed to a type that

Fig. 34-8. Shake before using

neither interferes with washing nor makes deposits in pipes.

The zeolite tank is recharged at intervals by treatment with salt.

This softened water should not be used for drinking by people on low sodium diets. It tends to give an off flavor to coffee and tea.

Other Chemicals. The other chemicals that make up a detergent formula are intended solely for usefulness in washing fabrics, and will not be found in a special dishwashing preparation.

Liquids. Many household detergents are in liquid form. It is natural to assume that these are water solutions of solid material such as is found in flakes, but this is generally not so. A liquid detergent, or at least its most important surfactant part, is generally born liquid, and it may contain only a little more water than its solid cousins.

The advantage of a liquid is that it mixes with and dissolves in water immediately. There is no chance of any of it sinking to the bottom or getting caught in a corner and avoiding its share of the work. Its efficiency, weight for weight, is about the same. Phosphate content is lower, and it may be phosphate-free.

Its disadvantages are manufacturers' problems in producing a clear, attractive liquid that will not cloud up or separate under any of the many conditions it may encounter during transportation, storage and sale, and the more expensive packaging (usually plastic bottles) that is required.

Detergent that separates or becomes cloudy in the bottle usually needs only a good shaking to recombine it. Its cleaning qualities are unlikely to be affected. Most of these liquids now come in non-transparent plastic bottles anyhow, so you can't see them and you don't have to. But shake the bottle occasionally, just in case it needs it.

ABRASIVES

An abrasive is a relatively hard substance used to grind or polish material that is usually softer than itself. In household cleaners, abrasives may be finely ground insoluble material mixed with cleaning powders, or steel wool and various shapes of thin, loose metal or plastic. They are usually not soluble in water. The process of cleaning with them is often called scouring.

In general, a sharp edge of a substance will cut or scratch only substances that are softer than itself. A diamond will scratch any other material, glass will scratch carbon steel but not stainless, steel will scratch copper, copper will scratch plastic and a plastic knife will cut butter. Butter is too near the bottom of the scale to cut anything much.

A soft substance may wear away a hard one. Bare or leather-shod feet may wear deep grooves in stone steps. Razors are sharpened by rubbing (stropping) with leather. But in the kitchen these processes are too slow, and you may safely assume that for abrasive action you must use substances as hard or preferably harder than that which you wish to remove.

Domestic abrasives are usually powder mixed with detergent and a bleaching agent, and may be in the form of either a powder or a paste.

Abrasive can be separated by adding enough water to dissolve the detergent. Any powder that dissolves completely is probably not an abrasive, even if it feels gritty.

Powders and Pastes. Abrasive compounds sold for use in the kitchen are usually so finely ground that the scratches they make are not visible without use of a magnifying glass or a microscope. However, numerous microscopic scratches may quickly spoil the shine or luster of enamel, paint, polished metal, porcelain and Formica, make glass cloudy, take off the non-stick surface of broken-in black iron, and remove Teflon from pans and painted-on designs from dishes.

Fig. 34-9. A pan polisher

The minute scratches make dirt stick more easily and thoroughly the next time. Repeated use will wear completely through surface finishes. On the other hand, abrasives are beneficial to the inside bottom finish of spun aluminum pans, as they cut the ridges down toward a smooth surface.

A good quality abrasive should have all particles practically the same size. If sizes are mixed, the larger pieces make noticeable scratches. For any one material, very small size pieces will do minimum wear-away and scratching damage and produce the best appearance, but require maximum work.

An extremely fine abrasive, such as may be found in metal polish, toothpaste or jewelers' rouge, will wear away a surface very slowly without perceptible scratching, but results take time and patience. They can sometimes be used to smooth off a surface damaged by harsh (coarse) abrasives, and possibly to restore its gloss. However, they do not replace any material, just take some more away from the high spots or ridges.

Use. Abrasive powder or paste makes easier the work of scouring pans and other articles to remove hard crusts of food, removing stains and crusts from sinks, stoves and other appliances, and temporarily

brightening many kinds of surfaces. But the immediate benefit should always be weighed against probable damage to the finish, and the fact that this damage will allow the surface to get dirty faster, and will make the next cleaning more difficult.

Powder abrasives are meant to be made into a paste with water, then rubbed on with a cloth, or occasionally with a brush or even a finger tip. Their effect varies with the relative hardness of the abrasive and the substances being cut; the shape of the powder grains and the pressure used. A small quantity is usually as effective, and often is more effective, than a large quantity.

The wear effect is distributed fairly uniformly over the area being treated, including parts that should be removed and parts that should be left. That is, a bit of charred food on an aluminum pan will be worn away by rubbing with abrasive, but the bare metal around it will be worn away also. Only the metal under the food will be untouched. Repeated cleaning in this way will leave an uneven surface.

The best policy for the beginner is not to use abrasive powder or paste at all for anything. Immediate advantage in faster and brighter cleaning is apt to be too costly in long range damage.

So far as the outer surfaces of sinks and major appliances are concerned, abrasive may be said to be habit forming. One use may so damage the finish that it will lose its brightness more quickly, will be very difficult to restore without more abrasive, which will damage it further so that it will dull even more quickly.

Abrasive-treated surfaces are also more subject too soaking in of substances that cause deep stains that are difficult to remove.

There are some circumstances in which an abrasive is needed, but try everything else first, including a bleach.

Steel wool. Steel wool consists of a tangle of roughly shredded steel wire that is so small in diameter that a pad or handful of it is soft to the touch. There are several grades of fineness, the thickest gauge being known as coarse and the thinnest as very fine or grade 0000.

The pieces of wire are ragged and are irregular in length, shape and surface. The grinding or abrasive action they produce when rubbed against a surface is regulated by the fineness of the wire, the irregularities of its surface, the hardness of the steel and the pressure exerted against it.

Handle it conservatively, particularly in the coarse grades, as it may contain pieces thick and sharp enough to puncture your finger if you push it hard.

Steel wool may be sold and used by itself, or in pads such as Brillo with soap packed in its spaces. Soap may be applied separately when using plain steel wool.

Steel rusts when it is wet and even moist. Pads that include soap hold moisture, and rust more rapidly than the plain wool unless a preventative is mixed in. Rust does not interfere with effectiveness until the wires start to break up, but it makes it messy to use and even to have on hand. It may make difficult-to-remove stains on surfaces where it is left to dry.

Its use does not damage most surfaces as seriously as powdered abrasives do. The wires tend to slide along a smooth hard surface, with little digging or wear, and then catch on projecting dirt, ripping and tearing it as well as wearing down its surface.

The low carbon steel ordinarily used is not as hard as glass or porcelain, so it should not damage them. But it will remove Teflon and Formica, spoil the surface of black iron and wear away aluminum.

Other pads. Brass or copper wire pads are softer and less damaging (and also less effective) than steel wool.

There are also pads of interlocked links of heavy gauge stainless steel wire. These do not rust, and can be cleaned and re-used

Fig. 34-10. You can keep them shining

again and again. They are harder than regular wire, so are capable of scratching harder materials. But the wire is thicker and is smoothly rounded so that they actually do little scratching unless used with heavy pressure.

Plastic or nylon string may be bunched or loosely woven into cleaning pads. The strings should be angular in cross section, to provide many small edges to help with the scraping action as the pad is rubbed against a utensil.

Plastic is soft — about like fingernails — so it cannot scratch anything itself. But it can drag along hard particles such as chips of china, with damaging effects. But if kept clean it is the safest of the cleaning devices. It is not effective on hard materials.

METAL POLISH

A metal polish may consist of soap (or detergent), one or more solvents, a fine abrasive, and wax or other materials to improve appearance. The soap removes ordinary dirt and stains, the solvents dissolve compounds of the metal and sometimes the metal itself, the abrasive removes non-soluble soil and stains, and the other materials leave a pleasing lustre and may give protection against further staining or corrosion.

Polishes are seldom labeled as to contents, but you can usually determine the nature of the important ingredients by using one a few times. Abrasives settle out on long standing to gritty cake or powder. If they are the principal ingredient you may have to work hard to get results with the polish.

Solvents usually work rather quickly and easily. If they attack the metal as well as the dull oxide, sulfide or other surface discoloration, the label may caution you to use it sparingly and to rub it off promptly.

The abrasive, if any, will be of the very finest type and should leave the surface with a bright and apparently smooth surface. On solid metal the wear that it causes may not be important, but it can reduce silver plate or copper plate to plain steel, if used often and vigorously.

A solvent-type cleaner is usually to be preferred. But apply it sparingly and don't let it stand on the metal, unless its action is guaranteed to be limited to the tarnish.

BLEACHES

A bleach is usually a substance that releases either chlorine or oxygen. These gases remove the coloring from a wide variety of natural and artificial substances.

The chlorine type, a solution of sodium hypochlorite in water, is the stronger of the two, and must be used with caution on colored materials.

The best use for either of them is on soaked-in stains rather than on surface soils.

Bleaches act as disinfectants, as the released gases will kill most forms of bacteria, even in fairly weak concentrations. A use in purifying drinking water is mentioned on page 648.

A bleach may take several hours and several applications to remove a stain. But little labor is involved and there is hardly any danger of damaging white surfaces.

TOOLS

A few substances can be rinsed off dishes

Fig. 34-11. A rubber squeegee

with plain water, preferably hot. Many more can be taken off by soapy hot water and hand rubbing. But for convenience and efficiency you need certain tools to assist in cleaning up dishes and utensils.

Precleaners. Some cleaning is done before the article reaches the dishwater. Immediate use of a rubber (not stiff plastic) squeegee, Figure 34-11, to scrape egg mixtures, dough and other materials from mixing bowls or pans both salvages food that would otherwise be wasted, and reduces the amount of cleaning and load on the dishwater.

If no squeegee is available, a little extra work with a spoon may serve the same purpose. For efficiency, hold the utensil so that the material moves downward and outward as it is scraped.

A turner or spatula, or a table fork or knife, may also remove considerable material in advance of washing. Some of the salvage, for example the crust of an angel food that sticks to the pan, is delicious. Older readers may remember spoon-scraping or licking the dasher of an ice cream freezer.

Even if there is no taste or salvage advantage, removal of food in advance of the dishpan keeps the cleaning water cleaner and the cleaning job more pleasant. But this may not be so if the washing is done under running water.

Precleaning has the advantage of removing food when it is soft. Even a few minutes of drying in the air makes some materials much harder, while hours will make almost any of them difficult to remove.

Hardening can be prevented by filling the utensil with water, but in spite of best intentions, this may not be done.

Scrapers. Scraping may be done before and during washing with almost any simple small utensil, or with fingernails. A tablespoon may be preferred for curved surfaces and a small turner for flat ones. Scraping (including the precleaning just dis-

Fig. 34-12. Scraping angles

cussed) takes care of foods that are bulky or sticky enough to clog up a cloth or brush, or hard enough to resist them.

Efficient scraping removes the food with minimum effort, without gouging or scratching the utensil or dish. Both objectives are best served by holding the scraping tool at a slight angle — almost parallel — to the surface to be cleaned, as in Figure 34-12, top. A steeper angle, as in the bottom drawing, is occasionally necessary to get particular spots, but this takes more energy and is more apt to dig into soft or delicate surfaces.

Scraping may be done dry, but it is usually easier under running water or submerged in the dishpan. If there is much resistance, the pan or dish should be held firmly on a solid surface during the work.

A scraper such as a turner or spatula has two outstanding advantages. It seldom clogs, and if it does, it is easily freed of sticking material by scraping with any utensil or edge. And it concentrates its force on projections, which are usually meant to be removed, instead of wasting energy on the pan or dish itself.

Sharp edges are most efficient, but also are most likely to do damage if handled improperly. A single-edge razor blade is excellent for fine work. Plastic scrapers are

very unlikely to damage anything, and therefore can be used with enough vigor to often more than compensate for lack of a hard or sharp edge.

A razor blade sometimes stains a hard white surface grey. A steeper angle may prevent this, but you may have to change to another tool. Such a stain may be difficult to remove.

Brushes. A dish-washing brush should have stiff fiber bristles. Wire brushes are usually too stiff and harsh for use on dishes or cookware, although very fine, closely set brass bristles may be both effective and non-damaging. Your choice is generally between natural bristles of animal hair (usually pig's) or synthetics such as nylon.

Natural bristles may wear away more rapidly, and will soften temporarily if left wet for a while.

The basic brush is a rigid wood back with straight bristles, Figure 34-13, center. It is at its best on flat surfaces, and is poor on concave curves and nearly useless in corners. The loop design, right, is best for all around kitchen use. The bristles are held between a pair of wires twisted tightly together and bent into a loop, so that bristle ends point out in every direction.

This design is equally efficient on flat and curved surfaces, and does a fair job getting into corners.

The bottle brush, left, is a pair of straight wires twisted together to hold bristles in a long-handled spiral cylinder, with an extra tuft at the end. This is a "must" for milk bottles and other deep narrow containers, but cannot be used as well as the others in open work.

Bristle material is too soft to scratch anything, and ends provide a large number of tiny, self-cleaning edges to cut into crusted food particles. The important thing to remember is not to press a brush so hard that the bristles bend until the smooth sides are against the work.

In Figure 34-14 (A) and (B) will give

good results, while (C) does less cleaning than a dishcloth, except at the end of strokes where the curve of the bristles may be reversed to bring the tips into action momentarily.

A brush does its most effective cutting against a raised edge that obstructs its smooth movement across a surface, but it is not as selective or nearly as positive as a scraper. However, since with ordinary bristles it can do no harm, and its exact angle and method of use are not as critical as with a scraper, it is both easy and effective for general loosening of soft to medium hard foods.

If a brush becomes clogged with thick deposits, it can be cleaned by holding it in running or still water and working the bristles back and forth with the fingers.

A plastic-handled brush may include a scraper which can be used instead of the brush whenever desirable.

One disadvantage of brushes with metal cores and handles is that if used with too much pressure or at a wrong angle the metal may come in contact with the article being cleaned, and scratch or gouge it if it is soft.

Dishcloth. The fabric dishcloth is a basic tool for kitchen washup. Any cloth or rag can be used, but the best type is a rough-weave, open-textured absorbent cotton cloth made up for the purpose, usually in 15-inch squares with bright patterns and bound edges. It may be used dry or damp, but it is at its best when in the water or just after being lifted out of it.

Depending on the type of cleaning and the preference of the user, a dishcloth may be used folded, crumpled up, or with a single thickness over a finger or fingers. From a safety-of-fingers standpoint, several thicknesses are preferable for rough cleaning, particularly where projections and sharp edges might be encountered. A well used cloth may have holes in it.

A dishcloth may have to be opened and

Fig. 34-13. Kitchen brushes

rinsed frequently if food remnants are thick and sticky. Overcooked starch can gum up a cloth (or a brush) into an almost hopeless mess.

Scraping before washing eliminates most of this problem. But if it happens, remove the bulk of the glop from the cloth with the side of your finger under running water, and rinse and squeeze with soap and water to remove the remainder.

It is important that a dishcloth be dried out between uses, as otherwise fine food particles remaining in it will decay, with growth of organisms that will give it a bad smell.

After each use, run clean water into it, squeeze or wring it lightly between your hands, and spread it in a single layer over the edge of the sink or in any convenient place, or hang it up. This takes just a few seconds, and should keep it fresh for quite

Fig. 34-14. Effect of pressure on brush bristles

a while. But it should have frequent laundering, also.

Sponge. A sponge can be used for the same general purposes as a dishcloth. It is not as efficient, as its surfaces are too soft and smooth for effective rubbing action. But it will carry a very large amount of water-detergent mixture in its pores, in the larger brick-shaped sizes it is convenient to hold, and it does not get gummed up seriously with sticky foods.

In addition to the brick shapes, there are round and oval sponges, and thin flat ones that resemble small dishcloths.

Most sponges in the stores are the synthetic type, which are cheap enough to be expendable. However, it is still a good idea to avoid rubbing them over sharp or rough spots, as it is very easy to tear pieces out of them, and it does not take many tears to reduce a sponge to rags.

These sponges are almost completely mold-resistant. However, food particles can decay in their pores. They should be well rinsed and squeezed after each use, and put in a place where drying out is possible. They can be laundered.

DISH WASHING METHODS

Dishes and pans may be washed by hand by three general methods: dishpan, running water and spray brush; and also by various combinations of these. If your hands are sensitive to hot water and detergent you should wear rubber or plastic gloves, particularly for the dishpan.

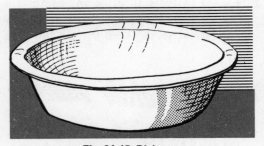

Fig. 34-15. Dishpan

A fourth and popular method, use of an automatic dishwasher, will be discussed in a separate section.

Dishpan. A conventional aluminum or plastic dishpan is round or oval, 15 to 20 inches in longest dimension across the top, 5 or 6 inches deep, with sloped sides. An old fashioned sink would hold two of them.

A modern sink with the drain closed may serve as a dishpan, but this involves extra care in preparation. You don't want to dump a half panful of cold vegetable water into the hot dishwater. Of course, you can always carry it to a bathroom sink or toilet.

Articles should be thoroughly scraped and perhaps lightly rinsed in running water also, then put in a dishpan. This should be nearly filled with hot soapy or "detergenty" water. Each article should be lightly rubbed on all surfaces with brush, dishcloth, sponge or fingers; and rubbed harder where resistance is encountered.

Thoroughness may be checked by both touch and sight. The cleaned piece is then rinsed and put in a drain rack.

Rinsing may be done in a number of ways. If there are two dishpans (or two sinks), the second one is filled with clean hot water, and the washed dishes are placed in it. If there is only one pan, the hot water may be allowed to run slowly from the faucet, and each dish is held under it briefly.

If the sink is equipped with a spray hose, the rack may be filled with unrinsed dishes, then sprayed with hot water. Or, if the dishwater is reasonably clean, rinsing may be omitted.

Dishwater temperature may be between 110 and 125° F, depending on individual heat tolerance. Hotter water washes better, but not enough better to justify discomfort. Since contact with the rinsing water is shorter, it can be about 10° hotter.

Under the Faucet. The easiest way to wash a few lightly soiled dishes is to hold

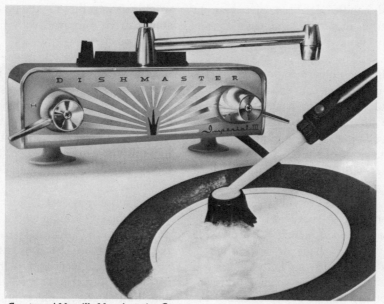

Fig. 34-16. A brush spray unit

them one by one under running hot water, wiping or rubbing with fingers, a dishcloth or equivalents. A cake of soap is kept handy. It is rubbed on difficult or oily spots, or the cloth or brush is rubbed on it.

Rinsing is practically automatic, as it only involves holding the article under the water for a fraction of a second after cleaning is completed.

A question is frequently asked — and often incorrectly answered — about the comparative amounts of water used in under-faucet and dishpan washing. There are two principal factors — the number and type of articles to be washed, and the rate of water flow that you consider desirable.

In general, pans and dishes for an ordinary meal for two, washed under the faucet, will use less than a dishpan of water. You can easily check amounts by putting in a dishpan, or plugging the drain so that all the water is caught, washing your dishes under the faucet and observing whether the pan fills or overflows.

Brush Spray. A spray brush usually has a rubber water tube about two feet long, tapped into a two-valve faucet so that lifting a button or moving a lever shuts off whatever water is going through the faucet, and diverts it through the tube to holes in the center of a ring-shaped brush. When water is turned off at the handles the button returns automatically to the faucet position.

The simplest type carries water only, with temperature adjusted by the HOT and COLD handles. It is useful for removing thick deposits of food before using the dishpan, for light and medium washing that can be done with plain hot water and brushing, and for rinsing.

A more elaborate and far more useful unit is shown in Figure 34-16. It includes a reservoir or tank for a mixture of liquid detergent and water — proportion about one tablespoon to one pint. Its rubber tube is double, one part carrying water diverted from the faucet by a button valve, with detergent mixture in the other.

The detergent tube ends in a valve closed by a spring. Thumb pressure on a button in the brush handle opens the valve, causing detergent to be drawn into the water stream by vacuum in a mixing device called a venturi.

With this combination you can wash and scrub dishes and pans in running water. Since contact of the water with your hands is, or can be made, brief and occasional, you can use hotter water than in a dishpan. Water comes out of the spray holes in the brush center with considerable force, which combines with the friction of the bristles to remove most food remnants easily.

Detergent can be supplied intermittently (it is seldom needed steadily) by pressing the valve button whenever it is wanted. Rinsing is done with the button released.

Certain precautions are needed, however. The rubber tube normally comes out of the right side of the tank, and is used in the right hand. The loop of tube in or above the right side of the sink is likely to catch and overturn bottles, glasses or any tall pieces standing there, so they should be placed in the center or to the left.

A certain amount of care is needed to avoid fouling up the brush, and perhaps transferring grease or sticky stuff from a very dirty dish to a reasonably clean one, whether the later is in the batch being washed, or in tomorrow's.

For example, if you are washing a frypan that is thick with bacon grease, first hold the brush at a slight distance from it, and spray it with full force of your hottest water with occasional jets of detergent, holding the pan at an angle so that it overflows easily. This removes most of the grease.

Then scrub it with the brush with hot water and liberal detergent, dumping the pan whenever the water becomes discolored. In this way you can get the pan clean without fouling the brush.

If you find that the brush is greasy, use it to squirt hot water with detergent into a cup, bowl or other container, and wash the brush out with the same motions you would use in scrubbing the container. Thick stuff can be removed with fingers or another brush.

The main drawback to operation of this device is the possibility of the detergent tube clogging. This is almost always the result of being too generous when putting detergent in the tank. Do not use more than the instructions suggest, and if you have no instructions, keep down to one tablespoon of liquid detergent for a tank of water.

Don't use powdered detergent, even if you dissolve it completely in water before putting it in the tank, as it may separate. If the brush has not been used for a week or more, stir up the mixture with a spoon or with the spray, before pressing the detergent button. Keep the container covered, and if dirt gets in it, get it out.

To open up a clogged tube, first unscrew the brush tube from the handle (you will probably need pliers) and lift off the tank cover. Direct a stream of water through the handle, hold down the detergent button with your thumb and block the water with a finger. This will force water pressure back through the detergent tube and out a vent at the top of the tank. Block the vent with a finger of your other hand.

The water will then be forced through the part of the tube that goes into the bottom of the tank. Allow it to flow for about half a minute. Then turn off the water, and reassemble the unit.

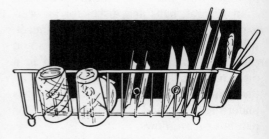

Fig. 34-17. Air-drying on a rack

Aside from this possible nuisance, maintenance is likely to be limited to a new brush at six month to two year intervals, and a new hose every two to five years.

Drying. Dishes may be dried by rubbing lightly with a towel, or by leaving them on a rack until the water evaporates.

Dish towels may be either smooth or (less often) shaggy in finish. Size is often 14 by 24 inches. Colors may be bright and varied. It is important that they be clean.

Drying is easiest and produces the best results when the dishes are still hot from rinsing, either while still dripping or after a few seconds to drain. A common procedure is to hold the dish in a fold of the towel with one hand and rub it with the rest of the towel, held in the other hand. Movement is light and rapid.

The dish should be clean. If it is not, small bits of soil may be removed with the towel or a finger nail, while greater amounts call for re-washing.

Several plates of the same size can be done together. They are held and upper and lower surfaces wiped in the regular way, then the top plate is shifted to the bottom and drying motions are repeated. Care should be exercised to avoid chipping.

Hand drying usually makes dishes bright and clean. It gives you a second chance to catch omissions in washing, prevents spotting from evaporation of drops of hard water and often gives extra lustre to the surfaces.

But it is easier to park the dishes in a rack, not touching each other, and let Nature take its course. Most or all of the water should evaporate in a few minutes if the dishes are hot and the air is dry, or in a few hours on a damp day. The possible disadvantages are lack of time before re-use, spots and streaks if the water is hard, overlooking of poor dishwashing and lack of sparkle.

You can mix up the two methods in several ways. You can towel-dry only the items

Fig. 34-18. When to wash them?

you need in a hurry, or only the glasses and silver that show spots the most, and leave the rest to dry by themselves. Or you can start with air-drying, and use the towel to wipe off spots or a few drops of water as you take them out of the drainer.

Spotting may be avoided by finishing washing by a rinse in a pan of water containing a small amount of a wetting agent (rinse conditioner) that lowers the surface tension of water so that it spreads in a thin even film whose evaporation will leave the minerals in an almost invisible layer. Such a layer can be rubbed off more easily with a towel than spots can.

WHEN

There are different ideas about when dishes and cooking utensils should be washed. A man whose wife is away for a week might figure that the last hour before her return will take care of it. A finicky housekeeper may wash every cup or spoon as soon as it is used. Most of us are somewhere between.

Immediate. In cooking, it is usually efficient to wash up at least some of the mess as you go along. There should be periods during preparation of a meal when no work is immediately necessary, but things in the oven or on the burners must be watched or waited for. Such time may be used to advantage in washing whatever is already soiled.

The amateur cook tends to use two or three times as many pans, dishes and utensils as are needed by the experienced housewife for the same work. This is perfectly all right — until you are used to the job, you have more important things to worry about than dirty dishes. But you are likely to run out of clean items, and even if you do not, you are piling up a depressing task that may reduce appreciation for your cooking.

Washing up as you go along will keep up the supply of clean cookware and dishes, and eliminate any embarrassment that may be caused by using too many.

An important advantage of almost-immediate cleaning is that you catch remnants while they are still soft. That is, except for anything that you may have burned.

Wet Storage. If your cooking schedule does not allow time off for washing, or if you don't want to distract yourself, you should at least attempt to provide for keeping food remnants soft or workable until you or someone gets to scraping and washing them away.

Unwanted grease in frypans or elsewhere should be poured into a can, preferably one kept handy for the purpose. This should be done while it is hot, the hotter the better, as it is thinnest and pours most freely and completely then. BUT remember that hot grease is dangerous, and wide pans are often unsteady. Particularly, don't have any water in the can or you will get anything from rapid boiling to a minor explosion. And don't pour it into plastic or cardboard, as it may melt right through.

Grease seldom gets very hard, but it sticks to brushes and dishcloths, and the less that is present for washing, the better.

Almost everything else can be kept soft and removable by storing under water. It takes only a few seconds to fill bowls and pans with water as you finish with them (except let the pans cool a little first, to avoid possible warping if the water is cold), and it may save many minutes of scrubbing later.

Fig. 34-19. Automatic dishwasher

Utensils may be put in pans or bowls that are soaking. It is important to keep egg beaters or whisks from drying with food on them. They can be cleaned of soft deposits under running water, but dried-on materials may require the most tedious hand work imaginable.

Soaking is also an effective softener of hard crusts and scorched-on deposits, particularly if you add a little detergent to the water.

AUTOMATIC DISHWASHER

This is an important appliance that is too remote from cooking to justify detailed consideration of its several varieties. However, understanding of its basic characteristics is becoming a part of general kitchen knowledge.

Complete processing of dishes may take from 40 to 65 minutes, depending on the model and on the number of washes. Automatic timing is not affected by the size of the load, but the quality of the work may be.

Construction. A dishwasher may be a free-standing unit, or be built into or under a counter, with permanent plumbing connections. Or it may be on wheels, with snap-on hose connections, so that it can be used in one place and stored in another.

Dishes may be loaded into it through a front door onto sliding racks or through a top door into lift or slide racks. It is designed to be water-tight with the door closed, and should be heavily insulated to conserve heat and to muffle a considerable amount of noise.

A typical automatic dishwasher includes a high pressure water pump, a spray mechanism, a waterproof heating unit (700 to 1,000 watts), dispensers for detergent and sometimes for a wetting agent, a sump and strainer, and a drain or pump-out arrangement.

Water Supply. Water is supplied directly from the hot water system. It is supposed to be 140 to 160° F. Some household heaters may have difficulty supplying water that hot. In any case, such temperatures may be uncomfortable and even dangerous for general household use. Washing is done about as well at 120 or 125°, but drying may be inadequate.

A dishwasher may use 8 to 16 gallons of water in processing a batch of dishes.

Pre-cleaning. Articles are usually emptied and scraped before they are put in a dishwasher, and they may be rinsed also. Emptying relieves the washer of dilution and chilling by unnecessary liquids. Scraping reduces the work that it has to do and the amount of debris that must be handled by the strainer. Rinsing removes soft food that might harden before the washer is started.

Both scraping and rinsing keep the wash water cleaner and more effective. They also avoid risk of including toothpicks or fine chicken bones that might go through the strainer and jam the pump.

With any one washer, these precautions are usually more important with a heavy load than with a light one.

There is a difference of opinion about whether burned food or other hard crusts should be removed before washing. If they are pretty will scraped off, the washer should be able to finish them off cleanly. If they are left on, the washer should soften them so that scraping and hand washing become much easier.

You can take your choice, except that anything that is likely to come off in chunks should be removed in advance.

It is said that with a good modern dishwasher, none of these precautions are necessary, as the machines are sufficiently powerful and well-guarded to handle almost anything that you may put in them, and still put out a load of clean dishes.

Loading. Dishes and other pieces are arranged in the tray racks according to their layout and the preferences of the user. A small load should be spread out over the available space, instead of being arranged compactly in a small part of it. Either the instruction book or ordinary judgment should indicate which spaces are best used for what.

Bowls, cups, glasses and pans should have their openings toward the spraying device, and downward to drain.

Fig. 34-20. Stacking in a dishwasher

Fig. 34-21. Water sprays are strong, and multi-directional

The machine may be loaded gradually through the day, and washing done when it is full or at the end of the day. Under other conditions, there will be enough items from each of several meals to justify running it.

Washing and Rinsing. Washing and rinsing are done by high pressure water moving from the pump through fine holes in a revolving wash arm, a spinning tube, or some other device. These sprayers are turned by reaction from the water leaving them. An arm may rotate at 60 revolutions per minute, while a tube may turn 10 times that fast.

Another construction uses high speed impeller blades in the sump in the bottom of the chamber, which force water upward over the load, without use of a spray pump.

Detergent for washing is placed in a container, from which it is washed by the spray. There may be two or even three compartments to provide for separate wash cycles without opening the machine to renew the supply.

The rate of water flow through the system may be as high as 45 gallons a minute, with a basic supply of only 2 or 3 gallons. Food particles and other debris are strained

out of it each time it enters the pump. The water temperature may be maintained or even increased during circulation by the heating unit.

When a wash time is completed, a drain valve opens that permits water to flow out, or to be pumped out. New water is then admitted for rinsing, which is done in the same manner but without detergent. This water is removed in its turn, before the next operation, which may be wash, rinse or dry.

An automatic control may provide for two washes, each followed by a rinse, and then for one to three additional rinses. The first wash-rinse cycle may be skipped by turning the control knob past it when startnig the machine, if there is not enough soil on the dishes to require both washes.

It may be possible to start with a pre-wash rinse. This flushes cool water out of the pipes, removes loose material, and starts the softening of any dried food.

A rinse-hold cycle is used for a part load, which is then left in the machine until washing time.

Deluxe model washers may have a container for a wetting agent (rinse conditioner) that automatically feeds into the water during the last rinse cycle. This prevents spotting of the dishes from evaporation of drops of hard water.

Drying. After the last rinse, dishes are dried by circulation of air. It is heated electrically, and may be circulated by a fan or impeller. Drying usually takes at least half of the whole washing cycle. If you are in a hurry, you can take the most urgent pieces out and do them by hand.

The washer is sometimes run only in the DRY phase in order to warm up dinner dishes. Some of the more sophisticated machines have a special timer setting just for this purpose.

Dishes may be left in the washer after drying until they are needed, or taken out and put away as soon as they have cooled sufficiently for comfortable handling. Until you know the machine well, it is a good idea to look at them critically, to see if they are completely clean.

If they are not, consider what you may have done wrong, before you blame the appliance.

TYPES OF SOILING

It is often helpful to bear in mind the particular characteristics of various food substances, in relation to their reaction and resistance to cleaning processes.

Oil. Cooking and salad oils are usually medium to medium-thin viscosity; easily poured liquids at room temperature. But although the bulk of such an oil can be easily removed from a container by tipping it to pour, a thick film will cling. This gives an oily feeling and appearance, and with long standing, enough may drain from it to build a small puddle in the bottom.

Oil will not mix with water, and it is almost unaffected by it when it is cold. Hot water — the hotter the better — may remove most of the film if assisted by pressure spray or by rubbing. Addition of a small amount of soap or detergent to the hot water or to the wiping cloth or sponge used with it, will permit total removal. Cleanser and cold water may work satisfactorily also, but if hot water is available it should be used.

Wiping out oil may make the cloth or sponge oily, even with detergent and hot water, whenever there is enough oil to get into pores before it meets enough detergent to dissolve or carry it. The cleaning problem is then transferred to the cloth, which must be worked in hot water and cleanser before it is used on other objects.

It is a good idea to do the first cleaning of an oil dish or pan with hot water, detergent and a squeegee, the side of a finger (gloved or ungloved) or with a pressure spray, then finish up with a brush or cloth.

A little waste oil can be poured down the sink drain if there is a sewer connection

Fig. 34-22. Be sure your grease can has a bottom

or a good septic system. If the system is weak or lacking, put the oil in tight-lidded or capped jars or bottles that are being put in the garbage. It should never be poured out on the ground, or into a stream or lake.

Grease. Grease is similar to oil except that it is solid at room temperature, although it may take a long time to solidify after being melted. When melted, it is oil.

Grease occurs in the kitchen not only as a part of the supplies, for example butter, margarine and shortening, but also as a waste product that is trimmed off meat or is melted (rendered) out of it in the course of cooking.

Grease is found in solid masses in fry and broiler pans, and as spatters and smears on oven walls, range tops, splash guards and dishes. When in a roasting pan it may be utilized in making gravy, but if it is not, it must be disposed of.

The first step in grease disposal is availability of a container — preferably a used can — in which hot grease can be poured while it is still liquid. There are two requirements — no holes and no water in the bottom. I once cut both ends out of a hash can, then absent-mindedly tried to use it for hot grease storage. It didn't work.

And water in a can may make the grease come right back out the top, dangerously. A wide can is better than a narrow one, as it provides a larger target with less likelihood of spilling down the sides.

Used grease was formerly very valuable in the kitchen, for shortening and for soap making. In war times it had value at the butcher's. But now it is put in the garbage, with its container capped or right side up with care until it is out of the house, because it might be soft enough to flow. You can discard it as soon as it is cool, or just whenever the can is full.

Broilers and roasting pans usually contain a mixture of watery meat juice and grease. If it is not used for gravy, it may be poured into the grease can, and the juice poured out after it is cooled. Or you may allow the pan to cool, then skim the solid grease and put it into the can or directly into the garbage.

Any substantial amount of grease left in pans or on dishes that are to be washed should be scraped off with a tool or wiped out with a paper towel, or rinsed off with a spray or strong stream of very hot water. A cloth, sponge or brush used directly in grease will probably become clogged or at least smeared with grease, and may be more difficult to wash than the original utensil.

After the rough bulk cleaning, the residue is removed with hot water and detergent in the same manner as oil. Detergent may be sprinkled on it in advance of washing, to loosen hard areas.

Both oil and grease stick to the fingers and other objects, and make smears on the next items which are handled, which may be other pans or dishes, cloths, brush handles or clothing. It is a very good plan to wipe your fingers on a paper towel or a cloth soaked in detergent solution after each time you touch grease or raw meat, to avoid spreading it around.

For the same reason, always wash the outsides and the handles of pans, and the bottoms of plates, when you are doing their working surfaces.

Starch. Starch forms a substantial part of the bulk of many common foods and ingredients, including potato, spaghetti and the rest of the pasta group, corn, flour and tapioca. It has the characteristic of being hard when raw, soft or fluffy when cooked and pasty when overcooked. Starch pastes have extensive industrial use.

Any cooked starch will tend to stick to containers, and when overcooked it will give convincing evidence of its suitability for use in glue. It is a nuisance not only because it sticks to everything, but also because there is likely to be quite a large quantity of it.

As a first step in cleaning up starch, don't overcook the food. Second, remove as much as possible for eating, using spoon, knife or squeegee. Third, fill the emptied container with water to keep it soft. Fourth, when removing starchy remainders use plenty of water and tools that are readily cleaned (knives, spoons and scrapers, not cloth or brushes).

Try to start starch removal with cold or warm water. Hot water might hydrate it more, adding to its paste-like behavior.

Scorches and Burns. The most difficult and often most embarrassing soil to remove is that produced by food that has been allowed to scorch or burn in cooking utensils. Almost any substance will be difficult to remove when mistreated in this way. Burning usually makes the material hard, and is likely to attach it to the pan as if it would never come off.

The preferred first step would be not to burn the food at all. But after the damage has occurred, try to scrape the burnt material off dry, but don't try too hard. Sometimes it will peel or chip quite readily, and most or all of the following steps can be avoided.

But don't keep chipping at it if it is resistant, and don't gouge the surface of the pan. Be very careful, of course, if it is Teflon, but it probably won't be because Teflon tends to prevent the sticking that is the beginning of most scorch-burn damage.

Whatever is left after scraping should be soaked in hot water and detergent for a few

Fig. 34-23. This pan will be hard to clean

minutes, and tried again with a scraper. If it still won't come off, leave it to soak in the solution until the next washup period. A few hours soften all but the most stubborn burns. Repeated removal of softened surface speeds the soaking-in process.

The operation of removing burnt-on soil from iron pans by heat is described in Chapter 36.

Stains. A stain is a discoloration that has soaked below the surface, so that even complete cleaning down to that surface does not remove it. This happens to porous material such as wood and cloth, and also to enamel, paint and even stainless steel.

Stains may be removed by bleaching, and (except for cloth) grinding away the discolored material with an abrasive. The two methods may be combined. Bleaching is the preferred way to work on white enamel. Try laundry bleaches first, then ink eradicator.

Results may be delayed, so do not despair if there is no immediate effect.

Bleaches may discolor (or uncolor) and therefore damage colored surfaces, so they should be used on them with caution.

Damage from abrasives is discussed on pages 658 and 659.

Stainless steel darkens when overheated. It can often be restored to its original appearance by rubbing with soap and steel wool, or by other light scouring. But sometimes the discoloration extends too deep for removal. It does not interfere with cooking performance.

Lime. If the water supply is hard, there is a tendency to build up deposits of rock-like lime (calcium and magnesium carbonates) in pipes, boilers, tea kettles, sink edges and other places where water stands and/or evaporates. Its basic color is white, but it is often tinted by other minerals. It spoils the appearance of visible surfaces, and inside things it adds weight, cuts down on water space and interferes with heat transfer.

Most acids dissolve the lime slowly, removing thin layers and loosening and softening thick ones. The most convenient one in kitchens is vinegar, diluted with three or four times its volume of water. Kettles and other containers are filled with the solution to above the level of the crust.

Surfaces that cannot be conveniently flooded may be treated by covering with cloth or sponge, which is kept moist with the solution. The softening-dissolving may take anywhere from a half hour to a day or more, depending on the type of lime and its thickness.

Thin, exposed deposits can then be removed with a razor blade or other scraper. A tea kettle, which is likely to have the thickest and most inaccessible deposit, you can bang on the bottom with some soft object, and perhaps pour or shake the broken pieces out of the top or the spout.

Kettle deposits can be reduced or perhaps prevented by emptying after each use, so that the lime does not become concentrated by repeated heating of some of the same water.

Lime deposits in pipes and boilers are problems for the plumber, who is likely to advise just leaving them until the parts need replacement because of various complications. These include possibility of blocking pipes with loosened pieces of crust or opening of leaks which had been sealed by the lime.

Water softeners are described briefly on pages 657 and 658.

OVEN

Ovens get dirty in two ways. There is the slow building up of deposits from smoke and splatter on all surfaces, and more or less bulky spills that are chiefly on or near the bottom. Oven heat dries and burns material from both sources into hard

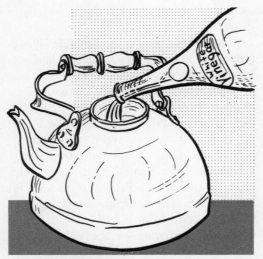

Fig. 34-24. You can dissolve scale out of a kettle

black deposits that adhere firmly to both metal and enamel.

The problem of removal is solved in self-cleaning ovens by providing means to superheat it to 900 to 1,000° F, so that the carbon and other organic deposits will burn and go off as vapor, leaving only a loose ash that can be brushed or vacuumed away. See page 750. However, most ovens now in use do not have this desirable feature.

There are a number of special cleaners for ovens, whose function is to soften deposits so that they can be scraped or even wiped away.

Some of these should be brushed or wiped onto the soiled areas, one or several times, until the material is weak enough to be removed. Others operate by means of vapor, so that the opened container is placed in the oven (cold or warm, according to directions) for a specified time, after which the soil should be loosened.

Most of these special oven cleaners are useful. Some are very effective, others moderately so. But most of them contain free lye or other dangerous chemicals, and you should wear gloves (and, according to some authorities, protective clothing, goggles and a face mask) when using them.

You can obtain part of their effect by wiping a mixture of detergent and warm water over the surfaces several times, and/or allowing a small quantity of ammonia to evaporate from a saucer in the closed oven.

Even if accumulations are softened and loosened, it is quite a job to clean an oven thoroughly. Bottom, sides and top add up to a big surface area. Racks must be cleaned, and possibly gas burners or electric heating element supports.

Racks are always removable, and can be cleaned in the sink. Some ovens have removable liners, many have removable doors. Check your instruction book to see if heating elements may be taken out. Any part is easier to clean out of the oven than in it.

Your oven interior may be enamel, bright

metal or some of each. As with all such surfaces, try to avoid gouging with scrapers and don't use abrasives except as a last resort.

Clean up as much of spilled material as you can, as soon as you can. It keeps on hardening for quite a while, and may smell and smoke when the oven is hot. But a full scale oven cleaning should be done only occasionally, as it is a big job, and will take too much of the fun out of cooking if you do it every time you use the oven.

GARBAGE

Garbage is household waste, most of it from the kitchen. It includes food that is trimmed away during preparation or left uneaten in pans and on plates, food that is spoiled or surplus, containers made of metal, glass, plastic or paper; paper of all kinds and miscellaneous waste.

Garbage items may be classified in a number of different ways for various reasons. When back-yard incineration was generally approved, and even required in many areas, the important distinction was whether they were burnable or non-burnable. Acceptability to drains is another characteristic that is important, chiefly in regard to clogging action.

If you have a garbage disposal unit, grindability of coarse pieces determines how they are handled. Moistness, sogginess or greasiness is important if you put it in paper bags or cardboard boxes. And the question of bad smell, how soon and how much, is of interest.

Burning. The burnable part of garbage is often referred to as trash. Burning of it is now widely disapproved as a contributor to pollution. It is forbidden in many places, including some where it was required some years ago. It can be a significant creator of air pollution in densely settled areas, but has a negligible effect in rural surroundings.

If trash burning is prohibited by law, it should not be done. But if it is permitted,

it can be done in such a way that it will create less smog than the same material would if burned in a commercial incinerator after being crushed with moist garbage in a truck.

Only paper, cardboard, thin plastic and similar materials should be burned. Do not include thick plastic (it is likely to melt into thick lumps, or smoke excessively), newspapers or magazines of more than 8 pages, unless crumpled to allow air to get between the sheets. Cloth is likely to burn slowly and smell badly. Paper food containers (for cream, cottage cheese and such) should be rinsed before discarding, and kept until dry before burning.

All material to be burned should be dry. An open mesh wire basket, with a floor several inches above the ground and a top to prevent big sparks from rising, makes a good incinerator for outdoors. Material should be loosely dumped or piled in it, not packed down.

Lighting a fire in a breeze can be difficult. But if the trash includes a large or medium paper bag, put a scrap of paper in it, and strike a match with both hands inside the bag to light the paper. A wind so strong that it would blow out a match so

Fig. 34-25. A mobile burning basket

Fig. 34-26. Plumbers' snake

protected is too strong for safe burning.

A simple indoor incinerator should also be loaded only with dry and readily burnable trash. Those that have gas or other flames in them can be fed rougher fare, but don't ever put materials in them that cause dark smoke to come out of the chimney.

Compactors. Trash compactors or mashers are electric powered presses that can reduce most solid household wastes to a fraction of its bulk. They are effective with cans, bottles, cardboard, paper and many kinds of scraps.

Materials fed to them may be dry or damp, but not liquid, juice-filled or water-soaked.

Fluids are incompressible. If strongly confined they simply resist pressure, but they usually leak or spurt out of the sides. They can be drained away, or retained if the material is automatically sealed in a plastic bag.

Trash compactors are standard equipment in most industries that have compressible waste. They are just beginning to be available in household sizes.

Possession of both a compactor and disposal unit (described below) should make it possible to reduce the garbage problem to insignificance. Except that a package of compressed garbage may be too heavy for you to lift.

Down the Drain. Liquids, semi-liquids and finely divided solids are washed down the sink drain, and with reasonable good luck, should go on into the sewer or septic system. But liquids that turn to solids, and

solids that are coarse, stringy or sticky, can and often do clog the drain. This happens most readily in the U-shaped trap directly under the sink, but can also occur at ordinary bends or even in straight pipe.

Grease is the principal cause of clogging. It is liquified by cooking or by hot dish water, then is chilled and hardened by contact with the cool walls of the pipe. In hardening, it is likely to seize and hold scraps of other waste, and build up to restrict and then block the flow of water.

Such a block can usually be partly or wholly opened by chemicals, often lye or sulfuric acid, that react with the grease and other material to produce heat and soluble compounds, by following directions on the container.

Both these chemicals can burn exposed skin quickly and badly. They should be handled with great caution, and because of the danger of boiling and splattering, the user should wear protective clothing, including rubber gloves, goggles and a face mask.

If chemicals do not open the drain, you might be able to ream it out with a snake. This is a stiff but flexible steel ribbon that is twisted into the pipe from the sink, or from a point where it can be opened. A snake should be able to follow the curves of the pipe, although patient work may be needed to get it through some spots, and will then open a channel that can be enlarged by flushing with a stream of hot water. This type of snake should be available in hardware stores.

If neither chemical nor snake do the job, either because you don't have them or they don't work, call a plumber.

Clogging of a sink drain can be prevented, or at least made less frequent, by avoiding the flushing of grease or greasy food into the drain. It is said that finely divided non-stringy solids, like coffee grounds, carry grease with them and prevent it from settling down.

Waste Disposers. A food waste disposer is a motor-driven garbage grinder that is fastened directly below the sink, replacing the strainer and the trap. Figure 34-27 shows one of these devices. It has a rotating table fitted with impellers, and surrounded by a shredding sleeve. Garbage gets cut into pieces fine enough to escape into a lower compartment, from which they are flushed into the drain by a steady flow of cold faucet water.

Disposers can (or should be able to) handle almost any food waste except hard seafood shells. They usually cannot grind metal and metal foil, glass, china, leather, cloth, string, feathers, rubber and hard surfaced paper. If poorly built or badly worn, they may not be able to cut fibers such as corn husks, asparagus stems or pineapple tops.

A disposer usually has a top cap that can be used to keep water from draining out of the sink, a guard to stop or slow pieces or fluids being kicked back up by the impellers, a turntable that automatically reverses direction of spin each time it is turned off and on, an inlet connection for dishwasher discharge just below the sink connection and a removable outlet elbow.

A continuous feed disposer can be operated the whole time you are washing dishes. The less convenient batch type has a switch that can be turned on only by putting the sink stopper in closed position, so that you let it finish grinding one batch before you feed it again. Either type should be flushed out after each use by running with just water flowing through it for a minute or more.

Disposers jam occasionally when a piece or accumulation of food gets solidly between an impeller and the grinding ring. Reversing models can usually be freed just by stopping and starting. At other times, you may have to poke around with a broom handle or some other wooden or plastic implement to free it. Food that piles up in the center sometimes needs to be pushed around by a similar tool.

But never work down there with your fingers, as they are too easily ground, or with a utensil, as that can damage both the grinder and itself.

The drain pipes below a disposer seldom clog, because the grease is usually well enough mixed with other foods so that it does not build up deposits. But if it should happen, disconnect the outflow pipe and use chemicals or a snake.

Disposers increase the load on a sewage system, and their installation is prohibited in many communities. Use of one is inadvisable with a cesspool or a just-adequate septic system.

Fig. 34-27. Waste disposal unit

Courtesy of Hobart Manufacturing Co.

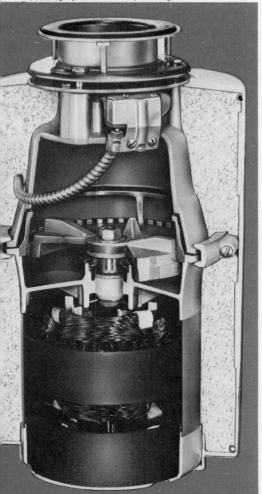

Fig. 34-28. Sink baskets

Smell. Kitchen garbage usually decays rapidly, developing an offensive smell. This smell eventually permeates pails and even sheds in which it is stored, and may be very difficult to eradicate. This problem is made more severe by the decreasing frequency of garbage collection in most areas.

A disposer gets rid of most of the smell-making material. Rinsing cans and other containers before throwing them away will usually take care of the rest.

Another modern way of handling the situation is buy plastic garbage bags, big enough to serve as liners for your garbage pail or pails. Put one in the pail, put garbage in it, and when it is full or has become smelly, fasten the bag with a twist and put it out for collection.

Such bags at present are made of heavy, dark green plastic, are practically air and smell-tight and cost from 6 to 15 cents each, depending on size and weight, and whether they are on sale.

It is also usually possible to handle and store garbage in ordinary paper bags, which are used first for liners in the kitchen pail, by observing some precautions. These precautions may be regarded as an intolerable nuisance by some and as a minor and rewarding task by others.

Most garbage smell is due to decomposition of food substances by bacteria and molds, which can thrive only in the presence of moisture. It is also moisture that soaks and weakens paper bags (a no-cost byproduct of food shopping) so that they are not usually considered adequate for garbage. Both problems can be combatted by keeping your garbage dry.

Most liquid, semi-liquid and soft moist foods, except for oil and grease, can be flushed down the sink drain if quantities are moderate. Trimmings such as vegetable leaves and stems, and fruit peels and cores, are usually not wet unless the processing is done under water.

If they are dry, avoid wetting them. If they are wet, drain them in a sink basket, Figure 34-28, before disposal. Put oil or soft grease in used jars with lids. An occasional soggy mess can be put in a plastic bag, preferably a used one. Cans, jars and cardboard cups should be rinsed to remove most of any food sticking to them.

Garbage treated in this way is usually safe in a brown paper grocery bag (although occasional leakage will occur) and it will be very slow to develop an unpleasant odor. The pails shold be washed thoroughly and then aired whenever they develop a smell.

35
TOOLS AND GADGETS

SMALL TOOLS

There are many small tools that are needed in a kitchen, and many more which make work easier, or more pleasant or efficient. There are also a few that have little practical value. It is not worth while to describe them all in this book, but enough will be mentioned to supply a general indication of types available.

Some of these items can be purchased in almost any hardware or variety store anywhere in the country, others are common in some localities and rare or unknown in other areas, and still others that seem to be rare everywhere. If a particular item is wanted very much and seems to be unobtainable, manufacturers of that or similar tools listed in the Acknowledgements section should be asked for suggestions.

There is a wide range of price and quality in many of these small tools. I mention price first because it is a single, simple standard. Quality may mean a number of different things.

In materials, the standard low and medium cost material is mild steel, the qualities of which will be discussed under KNIVES.

Aluminum is lighter and does not corrode, but it is weaker and cannot be used effectively for cutting. Nickel and chromium plate reduce or prevent rusting of steel and improve its appearance. Stainless steel (see KNIVES for this also) is very strong and is rust proof, and for most purposes is top quality.

Cheap utensils are bare metal, more expensive ones may have plastic or occasionally wood handles, for more comfortable grip and better appearance.

Quality may be a matter of materials used, lasting qualities, fineness of finish, ease of operation, efficiency of work, and/or results obtained. If, for one reason or another, you use a beer can opener only once or twice a year, the best quality for you may be the cheapest 10¢ or give-away model, as it takes the least space, and no opener would ever wear out at that rate.

But if you take pleasure in the appearance and feel of a bright metal opener with thick plastic handle, the quality features can be worth the small extras in cost and storage space.

The following is meant to serve only as a general guide to representative kitchen

Fig. 35-1. Knives

tools, but not to utensils for table use.

KNIVES

A kitchen cannot be operated long without a knife, and for full efficiency it needs a number of sizes, and perhaps of types. Some of these are shown in Figure 35-1. All of these should be good quality for surest results, but even a very cheap knife may give long and good service.

Only hand powered knives will be dis-

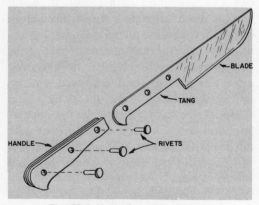

Fig. 35-2. Knife, handle and rivets

cussed here. Electric powered models are described in Chapter 37.

A knife has three principal parts — the blade, the tang, and the handle. The blade, of course, is what does the cutting. The non-cutting part that extends into the handle is the tang. The tang may be a long triangle jammed into the handle and temporarily held into it by a collar, or anything up to a center filler for the whole handle, riveted in place.

The full-tang-and-rivets is the best, a part tang and rivets may be just as good, but unless the glue used in assembling is exceptional, the part tang without rivets is likely to become loose, annoying and even dangerous after a few months or years of use.

Steel. The blade (and tang) may be made of mild or low carbon steel, which is the cheapest kind and the easiest to fabricate, but it does not usually sharpen well nor hold a sharp edge long; high carbon steel, which generally can be made much sharper and will hold an edge longer than mild steel, but which becomes increasingly brittle as carbon percentage and hard tempering is increased; ordinary stainless steel, which is tough and hard, but will not take a very sharp edge, but which holds whatever edge it has very well, and is not easy to stain and does not stain foods; and high carbon stainless steel which has the advantages of regular stainless steel, plus excellent ability to hold an edge.

A distinguishing test between these stainless steels is that only the high-carbon type is attracted by a magnet.

Non-stainless steel rusts easily and should never be left wet or damp for more than a few minutes. The rust makes stains on the flat surfaces, and may spoil the cutting edge quickly. Chromium plating will prevent the stains unless it is scratched, but it is not extended to the edge or is removed from it in the first sharpening, and so does not protect it.

Hardness. Hardness, which is an essential quality of a good cutting edge, is regulated in high carbon steel by tempering. The steel is heated, then cooled quickly, sometimes by placing in water or oil at a particular temperature. If such a knife is heated, it will lose its temper, and will no longer be as good a knife. The chances of retempering it properly in the home are poor.

Heat will also cause chromium plating to curl up and flake off. Never leave a knife in food that is being cooked, and particularly not in any place where it might get heated directly by a burner, as there it will probably lose its edge and possibly its handle too.

Shaping. A knife may be stamped out of a sheet of steel, in which case it will be the same thickness from tang to point, and from edge to back. A beveled knife is cut from a bar that is thicker at one side than the other. This will taper from the back toward the edge, but not from tang to point. This gives extra strength, without thickening the blade at the edge.

A forged knife is hammered into shape by a machine, and is likely to taper down toward both the point and the edge, a shape that gives maximum efficiency. In addition, the forging process usually improves the grain of the steel, enabling it to take and hold a finer edge.

However the blade is prepared, the edge is sharpened by grinding. There are three principal methods, shown in Figure 35-3.

Grinding. The roll grind is for strength, and is used chiefly with heavy-bladed tools that cut partly or entirely by impact, such as cleavers and axes. The flat grind is usable for almost any purpose, and can be made fine or coarse depending on quality of steel and purpose. A flat edge can be produced or sharpened on a flat stone or file, or on a grinding wheel if the knife is held parallel to it.

Hollow grind is the sharpest, and has the most delicate edge in proportion to thickness of blade. It is produced on a grinding wheel if the knife is held across the wheel, and on most mechanical or electric sharpeners.

Standard knives have edges that are straight or smoothly curved. Many special knives are scalloped or toothed. For any one degree of sharpness these shapes will cut better than a standard edge, as variable direction of pressure, or a saw-like or tearing action is added to slicing. The advantage is greatest when the edge is dull. This construction may also be found in some plated tableware and in knives made of materials other than steel.

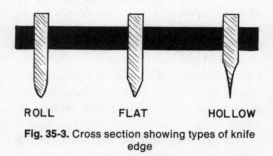

ROLL   FLAT   HOLLOW

Fig. 35-3. Cross section showing types of knife edge

There are two disadvantages, which are important enough to prevent general use. One is that the tearing action tends to pull food apart as it is cut, so that close holding and light pressure are usually necessary. The other is that they are difficult to sharpen, requiring hand work, and take much more skill and patience than a smooth edge.

Sharpeners. There are several knife sharpeners on the market, which will produce a hollow edge on a blade that is drawn through a slot. Results are variable. A good unit in good condition may provide an excellent edge, but it will probably not be as good as that produced by a skillful man with hand tools.

A cheap sharpener with steel cutters in bad condition can peel slivers of good steel off an edge, leaving the knife ragged and perhaps ruined. If you use one of these devices, be sure to inspect the result carefully every time, so that if damage is caused it will be limited.

A good sharpening job can be done on a grinding wheel, either hand cranked or electric powered. The knife is held at right angles to the wheel (parallel to its axle) with the blade and stone in contact at an angle of about 15 degrees, as shown in Figure 35-4. Or try to reproduce the angle of the original edge, part of which is likely to be still in like-new condition near the handle.

Use very light pressure and move the knife back and forth lengthwise so as to get an even result and avoid heating up any one spot. Make a double stroke on one side, then on the other, then inspect it carefully. The freshly cut metal will be shiny, and you can tell where you have cut, and how much. You should have a transparent safety shield over the wheel, or wear glasses, for protection against metal particles.

A knife may also be sharpened by diagonal strokes on a flat stone, at about a 15 degree angle. This does not produce the hollow grind, but a flat edge can do good cutting.

Handles. Knife handles may be made of wood, plastic, or plastic-treated wood. Fine old knives sometimes have bone handles. Any of these materials is likely to be damaged by even brief exposure to full burner heat; some of them deteriorate even in hot dish water. However, trouble with handles is usually in their fastenings to the tang.

There are a number of glues that are theoretically capable of permanently bonding a plastic handle to a steel tang, but in practice it still seems to be necessary to use rivets. They should be countersunk, and ground or polished down so as to be flush with the surface of the handle.

Handles are of many different shapes, choice among which is largely a matter of personal preference. For comfort and good control, a long knife should have a fatter handle than a short one. Handles are also made larger with increasing width of blade.

Use and Abuse. A knife will cut with simple downward pressure if it is sharp and/or the material is readily cut. Butter and many vegetables may be cut in this manner. For slightly harder materials you may rock the knife, so that cutting pressure is applied on smaller areas.

But it is usually more efficient to move the knife back and forth, saw-fashion, while cutting. Much less pressure is required in relation to knife sharpness and food resistance. This may be very important with fresh breads, which may be compressed into unappetizing dough by even moderate pressure, and any article with a filling that may squeeze out of its shell.

On the other hand, stringy meat, soft cake and many other materials may be pulled apart by the sawing motion, particularly if the knife has teeth. You may be able to hold a piece of meat together with your fingers (with due regard to not slicing them too) while cutting it. In any case, light pressure and a sharp edge usually

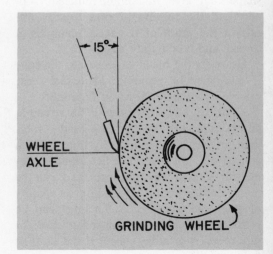

Fig. 35-4. Sharpening on a grinding wheel

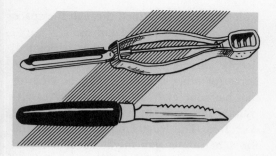

Fig. 35-5. Paring tools

reduces the dragging effect that tears food apart.

Frozen food that is not fully freezer-cold may sometimes be cut by pressure, but responds very slowly, if at all, to back and forth motion unless the knife is saw-toothed. Pressure tends to melt the frost immediately beneath the edge. It can be increased by rocking the blade, and by pressing down on the blade with the other hand, protected by a glove or a pot holder.

This should not be done with a first class knife, as a delicate edge might be blunted.

A short, heavy-bladed knife, such as a hunting knife, may be held vertically and cutting done by pressure on the point. If it is possible to make a few cuts through in line, they should weaken a block so that it can be broken. It is dangerous to use either a thin-bladed or a folding pocket knife in this way, as it might break, or close hard on your fingers.

Accidents and damage may be caused by the block moving sideward under pressure, or by the knife penetrating suddenly and cutting the table top or other surface beneath the work.

Whenever possible, make cuts when the food is firmly held down on a solid surface that will neither damage the edge nor be damaged by it. It takes unusual skill to cut right through an object without at least touching the surface below it. If that surface is metal, enamel, glass, china or any

other hard substance, it will tend to dull the knife edge, the extent of the damage depending on the hardness and abrasiveness of the surface, the pressure on the knife, and the amount of sliding motion. The surface might also be scratched.

Softer substances such as wood, plastic and cloth usually do little damage to the knife edge, but will be scratched or cut. Paper is a soft material, but it is usually abrasive enough to dull edges quite quickly.

The cook may be justified in considering that the edges of ordinary knives and the surface of metal tables and ordinary china are somewhat expendable, so that she can do a lot of cutting on ordinary surfaces, gaining in convenience more than may be lost in wear or damage.

But plastic tops on tables and counters should be treated with great respect, as scratches are easy to make, ugly to look at, and almost impossible to repair.

The best protection for both knife and surface is a wood cutting board. But sometimes scraps will serve, as for example a potato may be sliced on a mat of its own peelings.

Cutting is made easier by holding material so that it cannot move with the knife, and by putting it under tension, so that the cut tends to widen as it is made. If the cut tends to close, cutting will be difficult or impossible.

OTHER CUTTERS

There are a variety of cutting, slicing and peeling utensils that are not ordinarily considered to be knives.

One class has a cutting edge which may be a knife, or knife-like, and a device that limits the depth of cut, and therefore the thickness of the slice or peel that can be formed.

Peeler (Paring Tool). Figure 35-5, top, shows an inexpensive tool that will peel potatoes, apples and many other vegetables and fruits with a minimum of effort

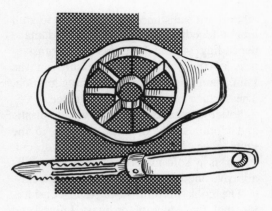

Fig. 35-6. Coring tools

and concentration. The thin end has two sharp blades with curved backs facing each other across a narrow opening.

When this is moved along the surface of a potato (for example) the forward blade rides along the surface, depressing it slightly. The following blade cuts under the skin to a depth slightly greater than that maintained by the front one, which acts as a shoe to prevent deeper cutting.

The rounded end is moderately sharp, and is used for digging eyes out of potatoes, and bad spots and discolorations out of any food being peeled. The triple blades set in the other end are an added tool for lengthwise slicing (Frenching) of string beans,

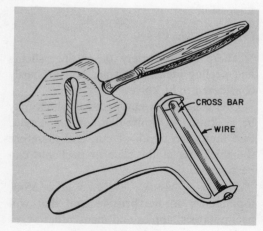

Fig. 35-7. Cheese slicers

which are simply pushed through the space which is crossed by the knives.

Corers. A simple corer has a pointed, deeply curved blade. You push into an apple (or other fruit) at either the stem or the blossom end, so that its curve surrounds the core, then twist it to cut the core free. The length is rather stingy, and for a big apple you might have to repeat the cut from the other end in order to get all the way through.

The corer shown at the bottom in Figures 35-5 and 35-6 has a paring tool on its back.

A combination corer and slicer has cutting blades in a frame. When pushed down into an apple, it will cut out a round core and divide the rest of the fruit into segments.

Either corer may fail to remove all the hard area or seeds. If this is important, check before serving.

Cheese Tools. Figure 35-7, top, shows a Scandinavian cheese slicer and server. The floor of the server has a cross slot with a sharp lowered edge opposite the handle. If you put the server flat on the cheese and pull it toward you, it will cut a thin slice.

The slicer (bottom) cuts with a fine wire. Thickness of cut is regulated by resting the cross bar or heel on the surface of the cheese, then raising the handle for a thick cut or lowering it for a thin one. The wire cuts as the tool is drawn toward you.

This gadget can only handle rather narrow pieces of cheese (the wire in this one is only 3 inches long), and you have to practice quite a bit before you can make a slice with even thickness.

Tomato Slicer. The tomato slicer consists of a set of thin, serrated blades set at 1/4 inch intervals in a light frame. It can be used to slice almost any fruit or vegetable of proper size, and hard boiled eggs also. But its usefulness is limited by the difficulty of holding the object while you cut it.

Fig. 35-8. Slicing a tomato

The piece must be large enough so that you can hold the bottom while you slice part way through, and then hold the top while slicing is completed.

Egg Slicer. The slicer for hard boiled eggs, Figure 10-14, has a number of fine, taut wires set in the top of a hinged frame. The egg, minus its shell, is placed in a hollow in a metal base, which has slots that correspond with the position of the wires. Pulling down the top should cut the egg into a number of thin slices.

The hollow holds the egg, so you don't have to risk your fingers under the cutters.

Occasionally the egg surface is too tough for the wires to penetrate readily. If you apply more pressure there is a chance you will crush the egg or break the slicer. The best procedure is to raise the frame, pick up the egg and rub it on the wires. They will penetrate easily with this sliding motion. Push the frame down, get your fingers out, and complete the slicing.

Slices of hot egg are more apt to crumble than cold ones.

The egg slicer may also be used for tomatoes, (but they may have to be peeled), cucumbers and other foods, but they must be tender specimens.

Pressure Slicer. There are various devices in which a cutting unit moves by pressure (either direct or through levers) along a slide or track, so that the piece of food being cut is forced through a grid of wires or knives. The VEG-O-MATIC in Figure 35-9 is an example.

It has a stationary base, and a vertically movable top. The base is equipped with two rings, in each of which a thin strip of steel is arranged to make parallel knives 3/8 of an inch apart. The rings may be set with the cutters parallel to cut slices either 3/8 or 3/16 inch thick, or at right angles to cut 3/8 inch squares.

Fig. 35-9. Pressure slicer

Courtesy of Popeil Brothers, Inc.

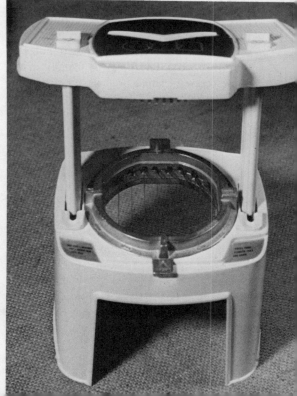

First you assemble the knife discs in the base in the arrangement you wish. Then place a piece of the food (for example, a whole potato or a quarter of a cabbage) on the knives, and lower the top into contact with it. Then ram the top down with a fast, two-handed stroke.

If you try a gentle push it may not pierce the top of the food properly, and may mash more than it cuts.

Rotary Slicer. A rotary slicer consists of a flat steel disc sharpened all the way around the rim and a sliding or hinged rack which supports the food and moves it into contact with the knife-disc. The disc is turned by an electric motor or a crank handle.

An electric driven model will be described in Chapter 37. The hand cranked one works in the same manner, but it is not nearly as efficient. A disc should rotate at high speed with a fair amount of power to do good cutting. It is difficult to turn a crank at the necessary rate at the same time you manipulate the rack and perhaps hold the whole unit down on the table.

Scissors. A pair of scissors consists of two specially shaped knives hinged together. The cutting blades are on one side of the hinge, and the loop type handles on the other side. The hinge is usually a machine screw (a small bolt with a slot in the head), which is held by threads in the blade opposite the screw head, or by a nut.

Courtesy of Ekco Housewares Co.

Fig. 35-10. French fry cutter

The blade edges are cut straight across, or beveled on the outer sides only. Any taper on the inside would cause material to wedge between the blades without being cut. The angle of grinding is such that the edge is thick, and not nearly as sharp as a knife. This is because cutting is done largely by a shearing action which increases power and efficiency, but which also exerts a side pressure that would bend or chip a fine edge.

Edges are somewhat thinner and sharper in light scissors for fine work than in general purpose models, but never become knife-like. The blade is almost always much thicker at the back than at the edge, with

Fig. 35-11. Rotary slicer

Courtesy of General Slicing Machine Co.

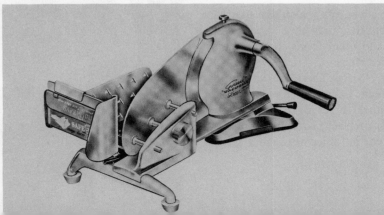

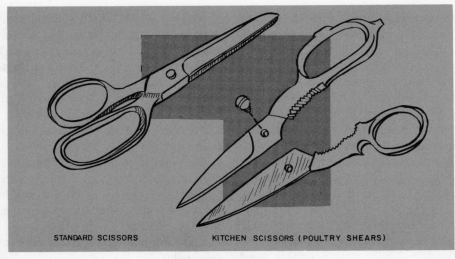

Fig. 35-12. Scissors

STANDARD SCISSORS   KITCHEN SCISSORS (POULTRY SHEARS)

all the taper occurring on the outside surfaces.

The blades are usually slightly curved so that when the scissors are closed they touch only at the hinge and the point. As they are opened, the outer point of contact should travel inward, at the point of the V made by spreading the blades. As the scissors are closed the contact point travels outward again, and all cutting action is performed by it.

The hinge screw should be tight enough to keep the blades in point contact with each other in every position from fully closed to fully open, but should not be tight enough to make the scissors stiff to operate, or to cause excessive wear on the blades. This ideal condition is not often reached, but it is worth trying for.

Tension is adjusted by turning the hinge screw with a small screwdriver. If there is a nut, it may have to be held with pliers. Some scissors hold an adjustment for a long time, but in others the screw tends to turn by itself, either to loosen or tighten. If threads strip, particularly inside a blade, it may not be practical to repair the scissors.

Loose scissors can sometimes be made to do light cutting properly by twisting the finger-held blade as you use it, so that the edge is turned inward to scrape on the other blade.

Scissors have a tendency to twist the object being cut. This is particularly noticeable when the material is thin, flexible and tough, or the scissors are loose or dull. Then it may twist to wedge between the blades, remaining partly uncut and perhaps straining the hinge. Try to keep the work at or near a right angle to the direction of blade movement.

The greatest leverage and strongest cutting action of the scissor is near the hinge. As the object being cut moves away from the hinge you are not able to exert as much force on it, and there is an increased tendency to twist the blades.

Small scissors are easily ruined by attempts to cut objects too large or hard for them. Once blades are bent or a hinge is stretched by abuse, the scissors are unlikely to do first quality work again. Hard material such as metal or glass will damage the edges. You may be able to cut through thin steel wire readily, but it will put a permanent nick in one or both blades.

A tough slippery object may slide away from the hinge as the scissor is closed, so that it does not get gripped to be cut. One blade may have notches or teeth to reduce such sliding.

Every kitchen should have at least one pair of scissors for general use. Poultry or kitchen scissors are excellent. They are heavily built, 8 or 9 inches long overall, with handles longer than the blades, one notched blade and usually a clamp for twisting bottle caps as an extra convenience.

Hacksaw. The hacksaw has a limited but definite use in the kitchen. It consists of a bow frame with a detachable, fine-tooth blade. It will cut very hard materials — bone, china, glass and mild steel.

Its kitchen job is usually cutting hard frozen food, when you have to divide a package right out of the freezer. It is slow, but it will almost always get through it.

The teeth are bent slightly outward on each side of the blade, so that it cuts a slot a little wider than itself, and should not bind as a knife does when the cut is deep. But the material must be held so that it will not bend inward at the top and close the cut.

The real need here is for a saw or a knife with an electrically heated blade. This does not seem to be available, however, and the hacksaw is the next best thing.

The commercial model hacksaw shown in Figure 35-13a is much more effective than the kitchen model in 35-13b. It has the additional advantages of usefulness for odd jobs around the house, and availability of replacement blades in any hardware store.

Chopping Jar. A chopping jar usually consists of a glass jar with a screw top, with a 4-bladed knife inside it. The knife is on the lower end of a vertical shaft that slides up and down in the lid, and has a small pressure handle on the top. A plastic disc or pad in the bottom of the jar separates steel and glass, and cushions the strokes of the knife.

The food to be chopped, which must be firm, crisp and moderately soft, is sliced or chunked if necessary to fit, then put in the jar to fill it not over half way to the top. Screw on the lid.

You push the handle down, usually with your palm, for the cutting stroke. Release it and a spring returns it to the top. Chop rapidly with light strokes, turning the handle slightly but frequently to distribute the cutting action evenly. It will probably be necessary to tilt or shake the jar frequently to bring material within reach of the knives. For this reason, you may prefer holding it in your hand to resting it on a table.

The models I have tested have been quite inefficient. The inside diameter of the jars has been much greater than that of the knife, so that unchopped food has room to accumulate at the edges. It may be a constant nuisance to shake it back into the center, and the size of pieces tends to be very irregular.

The bottom disc is loose, so that it may be pulled up by food that is only slightly sticky, or by shaking the jar to get food into the center. It may stand on edge and

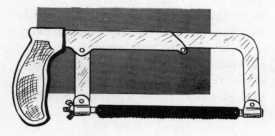

Fig. 35-13a. All-purpose hacksaw

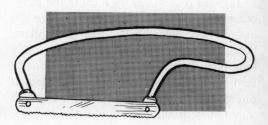

Fig. 35-13b. Kitchen hacksaw

block the knife completely, or simply allow a piece of food to slip under it, so that it rests at an angle.

In either case, the chopper becomes as useless as a denture with a sharp piece of food under it, and must be emptied, the disc put back in place, and the food put back before chopping can be resumed. By that time, you could have done the job with a knife, perhaps several times.

The disc can be fastened down by putting a lump of soft butter or grease under it. But it might pull up anyhow, and you may not want to risk mixing the grease with the food being chopped.

HANDLING DEVICES

Objects used and handled in a kitchen may be hot, cold, heavy, slippery, corrosive, sharp and/or clumsy. Bare hands are the most efficient handling tools ever devised, but they are tender and easily hurt, so they must be protected in many types of work, and stepped up in gripping power in a few.

Gloves. Many people are allergic or otherwise sensitive to soap, detergents, grease, or other substances used in kitchens. Complete protection may be afforded by rubber or plastic gloves, unless the allergy extends to these substances also.

If the only purpose of the gloves is protection against dishwashing chemicals, a common situation, they may be very thin. If protection against moderate heat or slight cuts is desired, they should be somewhat heavier.

Almost complete protection against burns from quick handling of hot pans and even live coals may be obtained by wearing asbestos gloves, but they are thick and clumsy, and interfere with efficient use of the fingers. Thick, padded mittens of pot holder material may also be clumsy, but can be loose enough to slip on and off without effort.

Canvas gloves with leather palms pro-

vide reasonable protection with less bulk and discomfort. Plain cotton gloves are even less bulky, but afford only limited protection.

Asbestos, leather and cotton are all porous and therefore provide no protection against hot water or chemicals in water. For wet work, you get rubber or plastic gloves which are waterproof and chemical-resistant, but which afford almost no heat protection.

Pot Holders. Most people would rather not be encumbered with gloves or mittens while cooking. Bare hands can be given all necessary protection against hot objects (and very cold ones too) by pot holders.

Fig. 35-14. Chopping jar

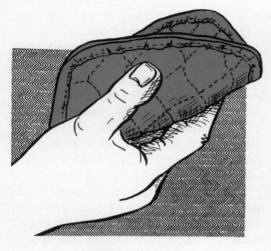

Fig. 35-15. Pot holder

These are squares of thick cloth which are held in the hand when grasping hot (or suspected to be hot) objects. They are of many different materials and designs, and they are all good unless they are wet or have holes through them.

A wet holder conducts heat too rapidly to be safe, one with holes in it may allow you to be badly burned, although in an area no larger than the hole.

Pot holders may be obtained with a small permanent magnet at one corner or in a loop handle, enabling you to hang them on any vertical iron or steel surface by simply putting them in contact. If there is only one magnet, you may have to select the right side for contact. Sometimes a magnet will catch and spill a light metal pan in passing. Other holders have only a loop, calling for a hook or nail for a hanger, and still others have no magnet or handle, and you simply lay them on any convenient surface.

Pot holders are also used for protecting table and counter surfaces from hot pans, and for protection of glass pans from too sudden cooling. First place the holder, then put the pan on it.

Most pot holders are made of cotton. Similarly sized squares can sometimes be obtained in asbestos or glass cloth. These may not be as flexible or as easy to use, but they will not catch fire if carelessly left near a flame although they may get too hot to touch safely. Such a fabric can be put under a pan over a gas burner to reduce heat to a slow simmer, so as to avoid sticking and burning of delicate foods.

Tongs. Tongs are convenient for handling hot food, such as corn on the cob, baked potatoes and asparagus. In an emergency, they can be used to lift or move pan lids, cookie tins and other hot but light objects, but stability may be doubtful.

Tongs are made in many sizes and shapes, three of which are shown in Figure 35-16. Operation may be either hinge or scissor-fashion. The gripping teeth or loops can be at any of several angles, each of which has advantages or disadvantages.

Tongs are perhaps not strictly necessary, as you can cook without them. You may replace them by using bare fingers with a quick, light touch, a combination of a fork and tablespoon, and in many other ways. But they are dignified, non-painful and should reduce dropping of food.

Turners. Turners are flat-bladed tools that are slid under food in pans, in order to

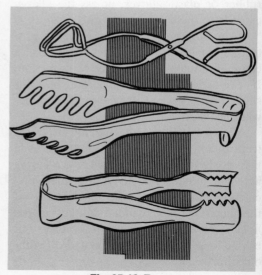

Fig. 35-16. Tongs

pick it up, stir or loosen it. They are made in a great many shapes and sizes, of metal, plastic or plastic-coated metal.

The most efficient type is made of thin steel. The thinness enables it to slip under fragile pieces, and to have a knife-like effect in cutting stuck parts. It also makes it somewhat flexible, to adapt to the direction of thrust and shape of the pan.

It is usual for slots or holes to be cut through the blade, to allow grease or other liquid to drain through, and to increase flexibility.

A spatula is a long, narrow, unslotted turner, usually quite flexible. It is excellent for cutting under items like eggs and patties, but is a little too narrow to carry them easily.

Many turners are coated with Teflon, for use with Teflon treated pans. Unfortunately, this plastic wears off the edge after a few uses, after which it is useful only in providing a non-stick carrying surface on the blade.

Pliers. Pliers are a scissor-like tool with long handles and short jaws. The jaws in the one shown include flat outer sections for gripping thin or small objects, and curved and toothed inner parts for holding and turning larger ones. One jaw can be moved on the hinge pin to change the size of opening, and the angle at which the jaws close. There is a wire cutting attachment next to the hinge.

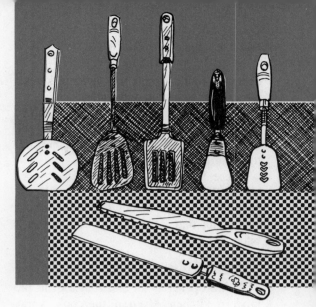

Fig. 35-17. Turners

Pliers are not considered to be kitchen equipment, but they are very useful there in many ways, most of them emergencies. Use them for taking things apart and putting them together, picking up hot objects, pulling oven pans to an edge where they can be gripped with a pot holder; opening soda bottles if you can't find the opener, loosening screw tops that are small enough to grip, straightening bent pieces of metal such as fork tines and pan handles, and picking up objects in narrow spaces where you can't reach.

Pliers develop very high pressure at the jaws, so you may have to be careful not to bend or break objects that you hold with them. In spite of this tight grip, a round

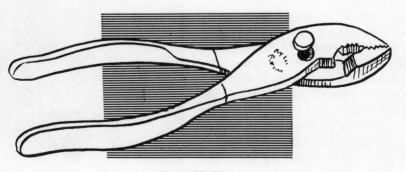

Fig. 35-18. Pliers

691

or nearly round handle may twist inside the jaws if the weight is unbalanced.

It is often wise to pick up with the pliers in one hand, and steady the load with the other hand (with a pot holder if needed) to be sure against upset.

These tools come in many sizes, styles and qualities. A medium size general purpose pair, 6 to 7 inches long, does about everything that is needed in this line in a kitchen.

CAN OPENERS

A can opener is an essential tool in the modern kitchen. Even if the cook works largely from the garden, the produce market

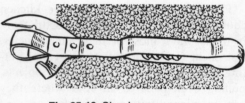

Fig. 35-19. Simple can opener

or the freezer, there are many supplementary and emergency items which are obtained from cans.

There are three widely different types of opener. One, used merely for puncturing the top of the can so that liquid may be poured from it, is discussed below, under the heading Puncture Opener.

Knife-and-Lever. The old fashioned can opener, Figure 35-19, has a short strong-pointed knife, a fulcrum and a handle that acts as a lever. The knife is pushed into the can top near the rim, and is slid horizontally beneath it, then raised by lifting the handle. The fulcrum piece stays in place on top, so that the rear of the knife is pulled upward and forward to make a cut in the metal.

The knife is then pushed forward under the top again, at a slightly different angle to avoid the rim, and is pulled up to make another cut. This sequence is followed un-

Fig. 35-20a. Clamp-handled rotary

til the top is cut more than half way around, so that it can be bent upward, or is cut all the way around so that it can be removed.

This is the most rugged and dependable of the top-removal openers, but it is also the most work to use, and leaves a dangerously jagged edge on both can and top. It is a good idea to keep one hand for emergencies, and hope you will never have to use it. Fortunately, they are inexpensive and are usually made up to include other tools.

The one illustrated includes a bottle cap remover, a puncture opener and a corkscrew, with the last two items folding into the handle when not in use.

Hand Rotary. There are several types of hand-held rotary can openers. The one with plier-like handles shown in Figure 35-20a is simple to use. With these clamp

Fig. 35-20b. Non-clamp rotary can opener

handles apart, you place the knife on the top of the can just inside the rim, with the gear wheel on the outside of the can. Squeeze the clamp handles together, so that the gear will grip the rim from the outside, and the knife will penetrate the top.

Then, keeping a firm grip on the clamps, turn the gear handle so as to rotate the can away from you or move the opener toward you.

The knife should make a smooth, easy cut all around the top just where it meets the rim, but may leave one sharp point where it comes back to the place of starting. If the cut-out top falls into the can, push it down on one side. The other side should rise to a point where you can grasp it.

There is a smaller opener that lacks clamp handles. The knife is forced into the can top by turning the gear handle. You start it by placing the lower flange and gear against the side of the can, with the upper flange resting on the top of the rim. Rotate the knife by lifting its back until the point is against the top of the can, and hold it in this position while you turn the gear handle, top away from you. This will pull the whole opener toward you, causing the knife to cut into the can. Continued turning of the gear handle will cause a smooth cut to be made all the way around.

When the cut is completed (partial, or completely around, as you prefer), turn the gear handle backward to free the opener for removal.

Both these openers will deteriorate with long use, as the knife dulls, the gear teeth wear, and joints get loose. Clamp handles allow satisfactory performance in much poorer condition, as you can apply extra force to make up for deficiencies. Both types are very cheap and do good work. For any considerable amount of can opening, however, a wall-type is preferable.

Wall Rotary. A good wall-type hand-cranked can opener, such as that shown in Figure 35-21, is usually removably fastened to a bracket, which is attached by screws to a door jamb, a trim board or some other vertical flat wood surface. Plaster or plaster board are not strong enough to hold a can opener for very long.

A hinge mounting permits swinging the opener back against the wall when it is not in use. Some can be lifted off the hinge pin, while others have a complete hinge, and are removed by sliding up and off a bracket. Removal is desirable for cleaning and repair.

This unit has a flange and a toothed wheel or gear to hold and turn the can, a circular knife, a crank handle and a clamp handle, and a magnetic lid holder. Gears connect the knife axle to the crank when the clamp handle is down, and an automatic slide device disconnects the gears when the clamp is lifted.

The circular knife is straight-sided toward the rim of the can, and beveled on the other side. This bevel tends to push the knife toward the rim while it is cutting, and aids the clamping effect of the flange, wheel and handle. The knife rotates in the opposite direction from the wheel, and cuts downward into the can top.

To operate this opener you swing it into a convenient position, and lock it there by

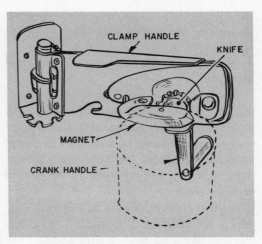

Fig. 35-21. Wall-mounted can opener

lowering it into a socket. Pull the clamp handle all the way out, place the can so that the side is tight against the flange and wheel, then push the clamp handle in a half circle toward the wall, so that it is flat down on the top of the unit. This causes the knife to penetrate the can top, meshes the knife-to-handle gearing, and clamps the can between the knife and the wheel so that you should not need to support it.

However, it is an extra safety precaution to keep a hand on or under the can, in case something slips.

Turning the handle will now rotate the can and the cutting wheel, so that a smooth and almost effortless cut may be made around the top, just inside the rim. When the cut is completed, grasp the can, release it by pulling the clamp handle all the way toward you, and remove the can.

The lid will be held in position by the magnetic head. In removing it, always grasp it by the upper and lower surfaces, not by the edges. These edges are knife-sharp, and any unexpected resistance to pulling will cause them to cut your finger and thumb if they are in contact. By contrast, the flat surfaces should be completely safe.

The wall rotary should be taken off its bracket and thoroughly cleaned in soap (or detergent) and water now and then. It should be lubricated with some type of edible oil before putting back in service.

Electric rotary can openers are discussed on page 743.

Puncture Opener. This device is widely known as a beer can opener. However, it is equally useful for opening fruit drinks and other canned liquids, and is being made unnecessary for beer cans by tab type tops that are designed to be opened without tools.

Several types are shown in Figure 35-22. (A) is the simplest. It is under four inches long, is stamped out of steel about 1/16 inch in thickness, and is so cheap that it is

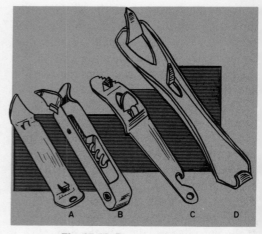

Fig. 35-22. Puncture openers

often given away with a few cans of beer. One end is tapered at the sides to a point. Just before the taper a cut center strip is curved downward to catch the can rim, and the rest is curved up and then down to obtain a good angle for penetration.

To use it, you hook the center projection to the outside of the top of the can rim, push the handle toward the can and raise it. This causes the point to move down to penetrate the can, and the wedge-shaped blade to push down a triangle of the can top. The handle is ordinarily raised all the way to produce a liberal opening for pouring.

A second cut should be made at the opposite side of the top, to allow air to enter so that the liquid will pour smoothly. The air hole requires only penetration of the point; it need not be as large as the pouring hole. This unit's handle includes a bottle opener and a hole by which the opener may be hung on a hook or a nail.

(B) is a more elaborate model, with a plastic and metal handle, a bottle opener, and a foldaway corkscrew. It is about an inch longer, is more substantial, is pleasanter to hold and use; but it is bulkier and is seldom given away. So far as the cutting blade is concerned, it is usually no better quality than the cheaper one.

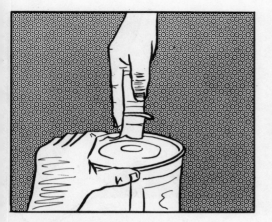

Fig. 35-23. You can open a can with an ordinary knife

The openers labeled (C) and (D) free operators from the drudgery of making two attacks on the can to make the two holes necessary for smooth pouring. (See page 15 for an explanation of smooth and gurgling pouring). Each of them has a second knife that will make a small puncture at the center or toward the opposite side of the can top at the same time the main hole for pouring is made.

(C) operates in the conventional way, being hooked on the near side of the can. Extra thumb pressure over the second point may assist its penetration. (D) hooks on the far side of the can. You start with the handle vertical, and pull it down toward you.

In an emergency, a puncture opener can be used to open a regular can, by making a series of overlapping cuts around it. This is quite a bit of work, and the edges on both can and top are very jagged.

Knife. Any strong knife with a sharp point may be used to open a can, either completely or by puncture. Hold the knife in a vertical or near-vertical position so the sharpest part of the point contacts the can, then push firmly downward. For removal of the lid, make the cut about 1/8 inch in from the rim and parallel to it. Continue the cut with a series of downward slices,

keeping firm pressure against the edge, and changing the angle each time enough to keep it away from the rim.

You can cut completely around, or stop an inch short, pry the free end of the lid up with the knife, and bend it back to a vertical position. The cut will have sharp, down-curved edges, but should not be as jagged as one made by a lever-opener.

To pour juice, make two short cuts connected at an angle, then push down the triangle of metal between them. A small stab hole at the other side of the top is enough to let air in while pouring.

There are objections to using a knife as a can opener — danger of cutting yourself, and possibility of breaking or dulling the knife. A cut — and a severe one — might be caused by the knife slipping under pressure or breaking, or a pocket knife folding unexpectedly.

You can protect yourself by holding the blade on the sides from the back with a heavy pot holder and, with a folding knife, keeping the edge toward you and pulling as you press down.

Breakage or slipping is only likely with a long blade.

Wear on ordinary heavy kitchen knives is usually slight, little greater than from cutting the same length and thickness of newspaper. But a razor blade, or a high grade carving knife with a thin edge, will be ruined by fine pieces breaking out of, and will not cut the steel nearly as well as the thicker, coarser edge.

Opening a can with a knife is not recommended ordinarily, but in consideration of the popularity of electric openers and the occurrence of power failures, it should be kept in mind as a possibility. And it might be the only way to save a picnic.

BOTTLE AND JAR OPENERS

Bottle Opener. Many liquids and foods are preserved in glass bottles or jars with clamp or twist type tops. The most common variety is the soda bottle with a gasketed metal top puckered down at the edges to grip a circular flange at the bottle mouth. This is easily removed by any tool that includes a tooth or hook to catch the pucker of the cap, a fulcrum part to rest on the center of the cap and a few inches of handle for leverage. You catch the tooth under the cap and raise the tool, thus bending and then pulling off the cap.

If you want to use the cap again, pull up part way in several places before raising it all the way off. This will avoid twisting it out of shape, and allow it to re-seal the bottle if put back on it.

Can openers and other small tools often have a bottle opening attachment. For maximum convenience, you can get a heavy duty opener for fastening to a wall or door jamb with screws, which you will never have to look around for, once you learn where it is.

A possible drawback is that the bottle gives you a lot of leverage, and if you carelessly get the opener tooth under the bottle flange instead of the cap, you may break the neck off the bottle. This would not make soda or any thin liquid unsafe to drink, but it might spill it, and will certainly prevent re-use of the bottle.

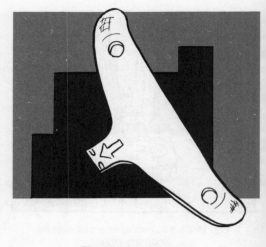

Fig. 35-25. Lid Flipper

In absence of an opener a bottle cap can be removed with pliers or a screwdriver, or by placing its edge on a metal edge and pressing down on its top. There are also a number of kitchen gadgets that have a usable bottle opener somewhere in or on them.

Pry-Off. Glass jars and tumblers may have clamp-type lids, which are removed by lifting or prying from one side.

Jars with clamp tops usually have a ridge below the lid, which can be used as a fulcrum while prying. You can use any piece of flat metal thin enough to fit between the ridge and the lid, thick enough to bend or break with moderate pressure, and long enough to give you leverage. Fingernails are not recommended unless they are very heavy duty.

Figure 35-25 shows a Lid Flipper. The side piece is inserted between ridge and lid, and twisted by means of the handle. If you don't have it, try the back of a table knife, a large coin or a screwdriver (not the drink kind).

These jars are being replaced by twist-tops, and you may never have to struggle with one.

The jelly glass or tumbler with press-on lids does not have a ridge to provide a

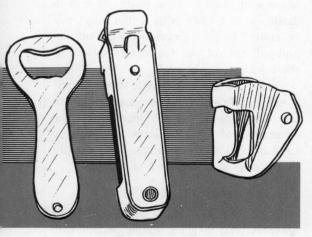

Fig. 35-24. Bottle openers

fulcrum, but is usually a looser fit. You can often remove the lid by holding fingernails tight against the glass and moving up, or you can use a different part of the Lid Flipper. A hook-type bottle opener lifts it easily, but generally bends it out of shape so that it cannot be re-used.

Twist-Off. Twist-type lids are now found on most food jars in the stores, and on many jars for home canning also. They are usually fairly easy to take off, but are sometimes difficult and occasionally impossible. Sticking is usually caused by spilled food or corrosion cementing glass and cap together.

All screw caps for jars and bottles should have right hand thread. You turn them counter-clockwise to loosen. That is, if you place or visualize a watch face up on the cap, your direction of effort should be opposite to the direction in which the hands are moving.

Normal loosening procedure is to hold the cap by one hand, the jar in the other, and twist them in the proper opposite directions. Use your stronger hand (if there is a difference) on the cap as it offers less surface to grip.

The bare dry hand usually has a better grip than cloth, about equal to leather. If the jar is wet it will be slippery, and cloth will grip better than fingers.

There are several approaches to loosening a stuck twist cap which do not require special tools. One is to appeal to the

Fig. 35-26. Jam and jelly jars

strongest-handed person within sound of your voice.

Another is to dip the cap and upper surface of the jar in hot water, or run hot water over them. This causes the fast-heating metal cap to expand away from the slower-to-heat glass, and may dissolve out sugar or other easily soluble or softenable substances causing sticking.

Or you can hammer the top lightly in the center. This may work by cracking the cementing substances with shock or vibration, and/or by changing the shape of the cap, tightening it at the top and loosening it at the bottom of the threads. If the rim of the cap is notched, you can hammer on the ridges to try to force the cap to turn.

There are a few special tools for twist

Fig. 35-27. Lever-type twist opener

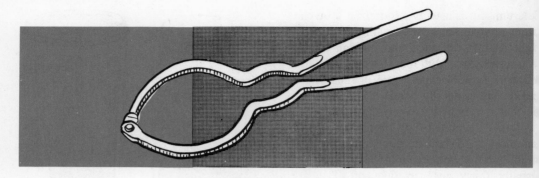

Fig. 35-28. Clamping twist opener

cap removal. One is a thick rubber ring, which you stretch like a rubber band around the cap, then twist the outside. Under most conditions, the rubber gets a better grip than your hand, and its thickness gives you leverage.

Figure 35-27 shows a lever-type twister. There are two pairs of toothed clamps, one of which can be slid on a slotted track. They are placed on opposite sides of the cap. The movable one is tightened and held against the cap by a clamp handle.

Pulling on the slide handle supplies good leverage, and the teeth get an almost unbreakable grip on a notched cap and a good one on, or into, a smooth rim.

The clamp tongs in Figure 35-28 are excellent for caps that have notched rims, but may not grip on smooth ones.

Corkscrew. A corkscrew is a pointed spiral of thick stiff wire with a handle, which is used for pulling corks out of bottles. Such corks were once very widely used, but are now mostly limited to imported wine. A corkscrew may therefore be unused or rarely used in many households, but if it is needed, there is nothing else that can take its place.

A wine bottle cork is often made much larger on the bottom than the top. It is squeezed into the neck under high pressure, and expands below it. A great deal of force may be required to pull such a cork.

Most corkscrews are fold-away acces-sories in can openers such as that in Figure 35-19, or in other small kitchen tools. You place the screw at right angles to the handle and turn it down into the cork, as near its center as possible, until the handle reaches the top of the bottle. If the top of the cork is lower, further turning will pull it up until it is even with the glass.

The bottle is then placed firmly on a counter or table, or preferably on the floor, and is held down with one hand (and perhaps with feet and knees also) while the corkscrew is pulled slowly up with the other hand. With luck, or perhaps skill, the cork will come out of the bottle. Without either, the screw may pull up through the cork, leaving a ragged hole in the center, or the top of the cork may break out.

The basic cause of this misadventure is usually a stuck or defective cork. But it is made more frequent by the fact that most corkscrews are too small in diameter to get a good grip, and that most people pull too rapidly and jerkily.

Sometimes you can get a new grip and finish pulling the cork. More often you have to push it down into the bottle with a small blunt instrument, where it will be a variable problem during pouring. The first glass or two is likely to have small pieces of cork in the wine, which you can remove by fishing with a spoon or by pouring through a sieve.

A deluxe corkscrew, Figure 35-29 left,

has a long screw shaft, an inverted cup that rests on the bottle neck and a pair of levers that can lift the shaft. You hold the levers up while turning the screw into the cork, deeply enough so that the rim of the cup rests on the bottle. Then you push the levers down, lifting the shaft and pulling the cork out of the bottle and up into the cup.

Effort is much less than in straight pulling, and the smoothness greatly reduces the danger of stripping or breaking the cork.

At the right of the illustration you will see a pocket model that is often carried by head waiters and wine stewards. Set the screw and the hinged lever at right angles to the handle, and turn the screw into the cork until the tip of the lever rests on the bottle neck. Then pull the handle up.

This little gadget exerts a smooth, powerful pull. But the screw is small, and may pull out of the cork. Also, the leverage is offside, so that the screw tends to tilt and finish its motion at an angle. You can turn it in deeper after pulling a quarter or half inch, and after a little practice you can press the lever hinge toward the center as you pull, avoiding the tilting.

BEATERS

Preparation of food often involves stirring, beating, whipping, chopping or liquefying processes. There is a variety of uten-

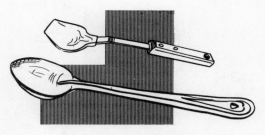

Fig. 35-30. Big spoons

sils, ranging from simple spoons and forks to complicated and expensive devices such as electric-powered mixers and blenders, to do this work.

Spoon. The basic stirring device is a spoon — a teaspoon for a cup or less, a tablespoon (or its undersize relative the oval soup spoon), up to a quart or two, and special stirring spoons such as those in Figure 35-30 for larger quantities or special results. The curved surface of the spoon fits well into the curved inner bottom surfaces of pans and bowls, and does a fair job of scraping along flatter parts. It is hard and strong enough to cut into firm substances, and its solid hollow or bowl can be depended upon to move them.

However, mixing action occurs only where material flows around the edges, and the hollow may become filled with sticky parts of the mixture, so that it needs scraping out from time to time. The spoon can be used easily for transferring parts of the mixture, and for testing samples by taste or otherwise.

Spoons in tableware sizes may be silver, silver plate or stainless steel. Larger ones are steel, either stainless or plated for rust protection; wood, nylon or some other strong plastic.

The steel spoons are used for most purposes, but wood is often superior for mixing dough and other thick material, and for any stirring in aluminum or Teflon vessels. A wooden spoon is thick with rounded edges, and the material is soft. It will not scrape hard material, but gives a special mixing

Fig. 35-29. Corkscrews

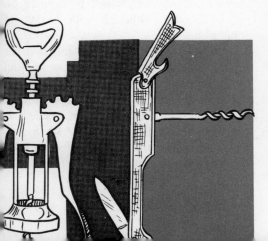

Fig. 35-31. Perforated spoons

effect to soft ones. Big plastic spoons are intermediate between steel and wood in behavior and use.

The perforated mixing spoons in Figure 35-31 are made only in large sizes, and may be of steel or plastic. They retain the good edge contact and most of the regular spoon's ability to move solid materials, and offer a faster mixing effect with less effort. However, they are not as good for transferring food or testing samples.

The concave or bowl side of a spoon is held forward in ordinary stirring. But the back or convex side is good for mashing

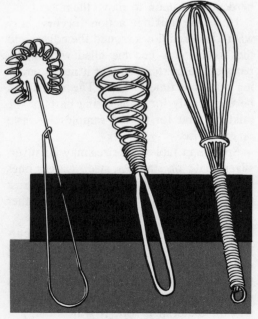

Fig. 35-32. Whisks

or kneading firm substances, as in softening butter or mixing butter and sugar, a process often called creaming.

Handles are often not strong enough for this type of work, however, and will bend next to the bowl. They can usually be straightened one or two times without damage, but repeated bending will weaken and finally break them.

Fork. A table fork is often used for light stirring and mixing. It makes good contact with straight surfaces, but is clumsy on curved ones. It has a firm scraping action, but all substances except quite thick ones slide between the tines. Stirring effort is less, and mixing action is faster and less certain.

A fork may be used for light beating, as in scrambling eggs. Before egg beaters became popular, forks were used for many types of beating, including making stiff meringue out of egg whites.

Whisk. The whisks shown at the sides of Figure 35-32 are good for light to medium stirring and beating. The light coil of wire follows both flat and curved surfaces readily, but it has weak scraping action for hard or sticky substances. The effort required is small to moderate, mixing action is rapid, and lumps tend to break up readily.

Whisks are excellent for stirring and/or light beating of thin substances such as eggs or egg-milk mixtures, but are usually ineffective with fluids that are thick with flour or undissolved sugar. When clogged they can usually be cleaned by tapping on the bowl edge, although with a risk of splattering.

The whisk in the center is designed for mixing in a cup or glass with an up and down motion, compressing and releasing the spring. This movement is combined with whatever rotary stirring is needed. It can also be used for ordinary stirring in pans and bowls, and is more effective than other whisks at getting into corners.

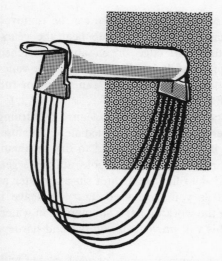

Fig. 35-33. Dough or pastry blender

Dough Blender. A dough or pastry blender consists of about a half-dozen stiff wires, set parallel and curved into a tight loop with a handle across the open or upper side. It is used in mixing fat into dry flour, usually in the process of making pie crust.

The device is held by the handle, and pushed down and pulled up through layers of fat and flour. The wires cut the fat, and the flour enters the slots. Many-times repetition of the process results in the fat being cut up into more or less fine pieces separated from each other by films of flour.

This operation is called cutting-in. It is described on page 451.

Egg Beater. A standard egg beater, Figure 35-34, has two sets of metal vanes turned by a hand crank and gears. There are usually four vanes in a set, but there may be only two. Two shafts are spaced so that the circles of rotation of the vanes overlap. The beater is held in a vertical position by one hand, and the crank turned with the other hand.

The crank gear is large and the vane gears are small, with the result that the vanes turn much faster than the crank. Their high speed combines with the turbu-

lence produced by their overlapping to make the egg beater very efficient at mixing and particularly in mixing in air. Full speed is often not needed, and any desired speed can be obtained by changing the speed of cranking.

The two vane sets rotate in opposite directions, with the result that the vanes move in the same direction where their paths overlap in the center. Movement of the vanes forces fluids to flow through the center, where it is mixed and churned between them. As it comes out some of it flows outward to mix with surrounding material in the bowl, and some gets carried around by the vanes for another trip through the center.

Thin liquids tend to flow out and mix, thick or foamy ones may keep following the vanes. If the beater is held in one place in the bowl in advanced stages of beating egg whites or cream, much of the material will stay out of reach of the vanes. It is necessary to move the beater around in the bowl as you beat, preferably with a slow

Fig. 35-34. Egg beater

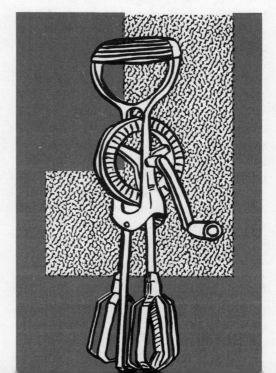

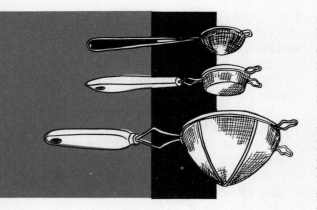

Fig. 35-35. Sieves

rotary motion, or to stop it occasionally and stir the mixture together. These motions also serve to scrape sticky stuff off the bowl sides.

But if you are beating anything white in an aluminum pan, avoid contact with sides and bottom as much as possible, as you may scrape off enough grey oxide to ruin the appearance of the product. The oxide is usually harmless but is unattractive.

Beaters tend to splatter a little, particularly if the liquid is shallow and/or the bowl sides low. Flying droplets are small, but may be numerous so that you should wear old clothes or an apron to avoid damage. And if you beat fast in a saucer or shallow bowl you may cause a large part of the mixture to go over the sides, and perhaps further.

These beaters usually are limited to medium or light fluids. The gearing for high speed means that they have little power, and become very difficult to crank in heavy mixtures. Hard lumps may jam between the two sets of vanes. Construction is usually not very rugged, and vanes may bend or gears strip if the unit is forced to work against heavy resistance caused by thick or lumpy material.

Stiffly beaten material tends to cling to the beater when you are finished. Much of it will fall off if you turn the beater slowly

as you raise it. Still more can be removed by tapping the beater, up near the gears, on the bowl edge or on an outstretched finger. If what is still clinging to the vanes is worth the trouble, you can scrape or rub it off with your finger.

Beaters may be easily cleaned by turning under running water immediately after use. But if material is allowed to dry on them, you may have considerable difficulty getting it all off. If you can't rinse a beater as soon as you have used it, try to leave it with the working parts submerged in water, as this will prevent drying out and hardening.

Vanes may be made of steel, plated with nickel or chromium, or of stainless steel, the last being preferable from every standpoint except that of price.

METAL STRAINERS

The word strainer can be used generally to cover devices that will allow part of a substance to pass through, while holding back larger, coarser or thicker parts of it. Materials used include paper, cloth, powder, porous china and woven or perforated metal. Metal is the material most used in the kitchen.

The three types of metal strainer to be considered here are the sieve, the sifter and the colander. The first and last are often called just strainers. A food mill is a strainer with means to push soft food through the holes.

Sieve. A typical sieve, Figure 35-35, has a working or straining part made of mesh made from rust-resistant steel wire, usually curved into bowl or cup shape. It is reinforced by a frame of heavier wires or bands that are part of or fastened to a handle on one side and to a tab or rest on the other side.

Sizes range from less than a half cup to several quarts, nominal capacity. Holes in the mesh are usually 16 to 28 to the inch, with smaller sizes usually having the finer mesh. But deep fry strainers are very much coarser.

Sieves are used chiefly to strain solid or lump material out of liquids. If tea is made by steeping (soaking) loose tea leaves in hot water, the resulting brew may be poured into cups through a strainer which holds back the leaves.

If the problem is a matter of lumps, they may either be left behind in the sieve to be used elsewhere or discarded, or they may be pressed through it with the back of a spoon.

Sieves are not strong, and only light pressure can be applied.

A sieve is also used for washing food, which is placed in it so that water can be poured through it.

When the liquid that passes through the sieve is to be saved, the sieve is rested on or in a container if possible, or is held over it. If it is in it, resting on its handle and tab, it may occupy most of its space, and will not drain until it is lifted out. A stand to hold a sieve is a convenience for this reason.

Most general purpose sieves have rounded bottoms. Liquid pouring through them may come down from the center, but may just as well come through one or more places toward the sides. For this reason the container should be nearly as large as the sieve if waste and slop is to be avoided.

If this is not possible, the mixed liquid should be poured in a thin stream into the center of the sieve, and material held on the sieve must be kept pushed to the side so that liquid will not run over it past the edges of the container.

Sifter. A sifter is a sieve that is equipped with some means of agitating the contents so as to cause them to go through the sieve. They are used mostly for dry powders, particularly flour, which would bridge over the holes in a sieve instead of going through them if they were not pushed around.

The sifting serves to remove foreign ma-

Fig. 35-36. One-hand flour sifter

terial, break up light cakes or lumps, mix different substances together and aereate or fluff up the product.

The old fashioned flour sifter is a can whose bottom is a rounded sieve. A set of four wire scrapers are mounted on an axle and turned by a crank. They slide or scrape along the upper surface of the sieve, loosening the powder and pressing some of it through the holes.

More flour falls through the holes after each scraper has passed, but it would soon clog them if it were not continually scraped by the blades. This sifter is efficient, trouble free and reasonably easy to clean. But you have to use two hands to operate it, so it has practically disappeared.

Figure 35-36 shows the one-hand one-cup type of sifter that is popular now.

Colander. A colander is a bowl of thin metal with holes punched in it, supported on short legs or a circular stand and fitted with two handles. The holes may be about 1/8 inch in diameter, much larger than those in the coarsest sieve. Construction is stronger, equivalent to that of a light pan. They are made only in medium and large sizes.

A primary use of a colander is washing and draining vegetables. The filled colander is held or placed under the faucet, and the contents swished around so that water can

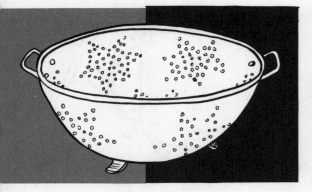

Fig. 35-37. Colander

reach every part, and carry dirt and other materials away through the bottom holes. The colander is often used as a carrier in picking vegetables.

The colander is also useful for separating boiled food from the cooking water. The whole pan can be dumped in. The load is retained, and the juice can be caught in a container under the colander, or allowed to go down the sink drain. This is particularly convenient with small pieces like peas and slippery ones like spaghetti, that may sneak out under a pan lid while pouring off water.

A colander is much easier to wash than a sieve.

Food Mill. A food mill is a strong, colander-like sieve equipped with a device that mashes food that is in it, and forces the liquid or fine parts out through the holes. One type in common use was shown in Figure 27-10. It has an unattached wooden pestle that nestles into its socket-like bottom, and is revolved with a pressing motion around the sides.

The other, not illustrated, has a pair of paddles or dashers that rub along the circular bottom when turned by a crank.

Both do good work. The pestle model is somewhat bulkier and less convenient, but it is smoother in operation, is not subject to jamming and has a longer life expectancy.

THERMOMETERS

Several kinds of thermometers are made for kitchen use, each specialized for one or at most a few functions. They are used for checking temperatures in ovens, refrigerators and freezers; in fat for frying and syrup for candy or preserving and inside meat to tell how well done it is. And there are of course thermometers to tell you the temperature in the room, and outdoors.

The most familiar type of thermometer uses a glass rod with a very fine hollow or tube in it. The hollow expands into a bulb or bulge at the bottom. The bulb and part of the rod is filled with colored liquid, the air is exhausted from the top to make a vacuum, and both ends are sealed. If the bulb is warmed, expansion of the liquid causes it to rise in the tube, while chilling makes it shrink to a lower level.

The tube is mounted on a back plate that is marked in degrees Fahrenheit, Celsius or both. The top of the liquid indicates the temperature.

Another type of thermometer that is now more widely used has a dial marked with various temperatures, and a hand or indi-

Fig. 35-38. Assorted thermometers

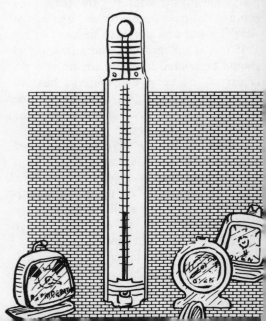

cator that rotates on a center shaft. The hand is turned by gears turned by pressure of confined, expanding fluid against a diaphragm and returned by spring action. Or they may be moved by an expanding coil spring, or by a bar made of two unlike metals that bends when heated.

Thermometers are not perfectly accurate. Even those used in laboratories may have errors up to 2 per cent, plus or minus, and those sold for kitchen use are even less precise. But these errors are usually for the whole operating range, and the manufacturer may calibrate the instrument to be most accurate at the temperature where it is most likely to be used.

For eaxmple, a candy thermometer may be very truthful between 210 and 230° F, but way off at frying and lukewarm heat, if it has that wide a range.

Candy Thermometer. The average candy thermometer is a conspicuous example of unsuitable design. The instructions that are printed on it or that accompany it specify that it be immersed at least 2 inches deep in the liquid, and that it should not touch the bottom of the pan. This calls for a minimum depth of about 2-1/4 inches, and some clamp or device to hold the thermometer clear of the pan bottom.

A study of pan sizes and shapes, and the amounts of candy or syrup that are usually made in the home, indicates that a 2-inch depth of liquid is extremely rare. Sugar solutions have a strong tendency to boil over, and cannot be prepared in a brimful small pan, and family needs seldom call for a 2-inch depth in a large one.

Experiments with a number of brands and models did not show up a single sample that could be relied upon to support itself in a small pan. The clamp was sometimes so loose and sloppy that it would not hold at all, or would release at a touch from a stirring spoon. One held well on a 3-quart pan (7-1/2 inches in diameter) but would spring off the thermometer on any smaller circle. Only one had a bottom guard to prevent the tip from resting on the bottom.

In boiling water, reducing depth from 2 inches to one inch lowered the reading from one to 3 degrees in different instruments. Resting the tip on the bottom would increase the reading by a slight amount.

To the bystander, it would seem that modern technology should make possible the production of a thermometer of this type with an insensitive tip that could be rested on the pan, a sensitive length of 1/2 inch or at the most one inch and a clamp that would hold it securely on the side of any pan.

But until such a model appears, we have to make do with what we can get.

Other Types. A frying thermometer is similar to a candy model, except that it operates in a higher temperature range. A single thermometer is often used for both purposes, but separate ones may be preferred for easier reading and perhaps for greater accuracy.

Meat thermometers have a pointed metal stem, which may be called a probe, and a dial that is usually marked both in degrees Fahrenheit and with names of meats, each of which is supposed to be properly cooked when the indicator points to its name.

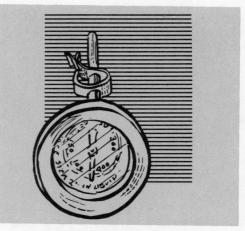

Fig. 35-39. Candy thermometer

The probe should be inserted in solid flesh, as that is what you want to cook. Bone is usually a little hotter and fat a little cooler. The probe can be pushed directly into tender meat, but if there is noticeable resistance, punch a hole first with an ice pick, a skewer or a narrow-bladed knife.

A roast should be taken out when the thermometer reads a few degrees below desired temperature, as the inside temperature continues to rise for 10 to 20 minutes, as it becomes equalized with the hotter outside parts.

An oven thermometer is usually a compact dial type, with a flat base standing it on a grate or pan, and a hook for hanging it to a grate. It is useful as a side check on the thermostat, although it is not likely to be more accurate. But remember, in the first heating from cold, the thermostat will permit the oven to run as much as 50 degrees over its setting.

Refrigerator-freezer thermometers are quite similar to oven models, except that they have a low temperature range instead of a high one.

Testing. You can cook successfully, although less conveniently, without ever using a thermometer. But if you do use one, it should be accurate, or you should know the type and extent of its inaccuracy. The importance of this varies with what you are doing. Candy-making may be affected by a degree one way or the other, while a variation of 25 degrees in oven temperature may not be serious if you check cooking progress occasionally.

There are two temperatures that are fixed and reliable — the freezing and boiling points of plain water. It freezes at 32° F, and a mixture of water and plenty of ice will stay at that temperature. At sea level, water at a rolling boil will be 212°, except for possible variation of a fraction of a degree with barometric pressure.

If you live substantially above sea level, and know your altitude, you can figure your local boiling point from the table in Figure 2-7.

If the range of a thermometer includes either the freezing or the boiling point, and the sensing part of the instrument is submersible, you can measure its error at that point, and add or subtract it from its other readings. For example, if your candy thermometer thinks that water boils at 209°, and you want to cook fudge to 234, take it off when the thermometer says 231. But pay attention to other indications also.

You can also compare thermometers with each other, and with temperatures in ovens or appliances that are regulated by thermostats.

36
PANS AND POTS

MATERIAL

Cooking utensils may be made of a number of materials, including aluminum, cast iron, mild steel, stainless steel, glass or earthenware. Each of these has advantages under certain conditions, and a variety of them is found in most kitchens.

Desirable Qualities. Qualities of materials that are generally (but not always) desirable include good heat conduction, resistance to corrosion, breakage, denting, staining and marring by cleaners; heat resistance, non-stick surface, light weight, long life and low cost.

Heat Conduction. A pan on a surface burner transmits the burner heat to the food. If it is a good heat conductor, it does this with minimum loss of heat and of time. In addition, the good conductor spreads heat rapidly through the whole bottom of the pan, preventing parts immediately over a flame from being tremendously hotter than the rest of the area.

Hot spots cause sticking and burning, while cool spots make cooking slow and irregular.

There are great differences in the thickness of metal in pans. As the floor becomes thicker it conducts the heat a little more slowly to its upper surface, but at the same time it distributes heat much more evenly.

The amount of heat absorbed by a pan from flame, electric coil, or oven heat is affected by whether its outer surface is shiny or dull. A bright surface reflects away part of the heat, and does not heat up as quickly as it would if it were dull, and often does not become as hot.

The rather small loss of efficiency due to brightness is important only in baking (see pages 415 and 721), but if cooking over a burner is done with little or no water in a pan that is partly bright and partly dull, burning is likely to occur over the dull areas.

Dents, warping and irregular thickness of metal will interfere with heat distribution and will probably cause hot spots.

Other Features. Our next five items cannot be entirely separated from each other. By corrosion we mean chemical change such as the rusting of iron and pitting of aluminum, which not only wastes away the material, but spoils the finish and mars its appearance. Staining may also be corrosion, but to such a shallow depth that there is no noticeable loss of material or change in finish. Resistance to denting depends on both the material and its thickness.

Most surfaces are damaged somewhat by scouring with metal pads and particularly with abrasive cleaner powders, but in some the damage is severe and immediately apparent, in others the damage may show slowly or not at all.

Pleasing appearance is a combination of original design and material, and the extent to which it has resisted damage. No well-used utensil will preserve a good appearance without care and cleaning, but the amount of necessary cleaning work will vary greatly with different materials and designs.

It is easier to handle a light pan than a heavy one. The difference may not depend on the material, as a heavy gauge pan of the light metal, aluminum, will weigh much more than one made out of thinner steel.

All cooking utensils can withstand normal cooking temperatures without damage. But if a dry pan is left on a burner, temperature may rise high enough to oxidize aluminum into powder, and to discolor and warp stainless steel. The Pyrex type of glass utensil can stand almost any amount of heat, but not abrupt changes from heat to cold.

Non-stick quality varies among metals. The Teflon plastic, which can be applied to any basic material, is superior to any of the natural finishes. Its nearest competitor is well cared for black iron.

Expected life and cost are items that should be considered together. Some heavy aluminum cookware that was originally almost prohibitively expensive has not deteriorated in over 30 years of active service, while a cheap aluminum pan of thinnest gauge, or one of poorly enameled iron, may be scrapped after a few months.

In general, the cost of cooking utensils that do not include their own heat units is low compared to the overall investment in kitchen equipment, and the daily cost of food. It is therefore usually sound economically to get the best (if you want the best) and to replace it if it becomes worn or damaged.

A damaged pan, that by reason of dents, missing enamel, or being partly bright and partly dull, is likely to cost more in spoiled food than it would cost to replace it, every week that it is kept. In figuring the cost of spoilage, you may reasonably take into account frustration and embarrassment, as well as cost of materials.

ALUMINUM

More than half the surface cooking utensils and oven "tins" used in the United States are made of aluminum. It has the advantages of rapid heat conduction, light weight, resistance to corrosion, pleasing appearance, and reasonably low price.

Aluminum conducts heat faster than any

Fig. 36-1. Dry pans may burn through

other substances except silver and copper. Silver is priced out of competition, and has other serious disadvantages. Copper combines with some foods to produce poisonous or off-color compounds, and therefore should not ever be used for inside surfaces.

Corrosion. Aluminum is highly resistant to corrosion when cold and at ordinary cooking temperatures. However, this resistance is not quite what it seems. Aluminum tarnishes immediately on exposure to air. Its tendency to combine with oxygen is so strong that it is used in explosives and in an automatic welding mixture, thermite. But the oxide that forms so quickly on an exposed surface of metallic aluminum forms a coating over the metal that is microscopically thin, yet is air-tight and waterproof, preventing the corrosion from penetrating.

The oxide is similar in color to aluminum, but is less bright. Although it is one of the hardest minerals that exists, the coating is crystalline and is easily scraped off. Stirring or beating in an aluminum pot may color white food a depressing shade of gray.

The protection afforded by the oxide coating is lost at high temperatures. A dry aluminum pan left on a burner is likely to have holes burned through it. This happens quite quickly to thin sheet, and slowly with heavy castings.

Aluminum is darkened by hard water, eggs, and exposure to any alkali. Acid foods tend to remove the dark appearance. Solutions of salt and of some other minerals may make pits in it, if left in contact for more than a few hours.

Pure aluminum is quite soft. For utensils, it is usually hardened by the addition of a very small amount of copper or a larger proportion of magnesium.

Weight. Most aluminum utensils are made of sheet material pressed into shape. The thinnest gauge used is less than 4/100 inch thick. It is found chiefly in the inexpensive cookware in small sizes. The upper edge should be rolled over for strength and to avoid a sharp edge. Such pans are light, easy to handle and cheap, but they often are unstable because of overbalancing by the handle, and they are easily dented and often warp out of shape. Finish is usually smooth, inside and out.

Heavier aluminum sheet, up to 15/100 inch thick, provides stronger and longer lasting utensils, with better heat distribution and stability. Outside finish is smooth, but the inside is likely to be machined so that there are many fine grooves which may cause food to stick until they are smoothed by wear and scouring. Denting and warping occur.

Cast aluminum makes the heaviest and best aluminum ware. Casting permits making a handle base part of the structure, so that no rivets or other fastenings need appear on the inside of the pan. Outside finish may be grained or mirror-bright, inside may be either smooth or machined. Castings will not dent or bend, but may be broken by a

Fig. 36-2. Foil pans and dishes

heavy blow. They distribute heat more evenly than any other cookware.

Anodizing. Anodized aluminum is prepared by polishing the metal to a satin finish, submerging it in an acid bath, and passing an electric current through the acid, using the aluminum as the positive terminal, or anode. The action of the current and the acid produces a very firm layer of oxide,

Fig. 36-3. Dirt may build up on a pan bottom

which is porous enough in its outer layers to absorb dye.

The metallic sheen of the original metal is largely preserved, and it can be tinted to almost any color. The finish is highly resistant to both wear and discoloration.

Foil. Heavy aluminum foil is shaped into various sizes and kinds of oven and broiler pans, which are cheap enough so that they may reasonably be discarded after one or several uses. They have a bright and pleasing appearance, but are so weak that they must be handled with care.

IRON AND STEEL

Black Iron. Black iron cooking utensils are made of heavy cast iron with a gray or black finish. It is most used for fry pans, occasionally for Dutch ovens, and rarely for saucepans. The frying surface is usually smoothly finished. Foods stick and burn on it readily when it is new, so use plenty of oil or fat (not butter) and keep heat low for the first few times you use it.

It should then develop a smooth, oily finish to which most foods do not stick under normal cooking conditions. There are old time cooks who will not clean their iron fry pans with anything but hot water and a sponge or very soft cloth.

While I do not suggest going to this extreme, I do say that you should never use steel wool or any abrasive cleaning powder on the inside of a valued iron fry pan. Stuck food may be removed by a combination of soaking in soap and water, and scraping with a spatula or dull knife held almost parallel to the surface so that it will not gouge the metal. Use normal amounts of butter or oil in frying, even though it might not stick without it.

There is a tendency for hard carbon to build up on the outside of iron implements, as the color makes it difficult to see whether it is perfectly clean, and any food or grease left on it burns into a hard coat of carbon the next time it is used.

The resulting roughness looks like part of the pan, makes complete cleaning difficult, and encourages leaving more material to build more carbon. When well intrenched, this material cannot be removed by any normal household methods, but only by a grinding wheel (a long, hard job, and very difficult to produce a smooth surface).

The best way to get rid of it is to heat the whole pan to a dull red heat in a self-cleaning oven, a fireplace or an outdoor wood fire, that has burned until there is a good bed of hot embers. After this treatment, any remaining carbon will be dust which can be removed with a stiff brush. The whole pan must be oiled immediately to prevent rust. The cooking surface will lose its non-stick finish, and will have to be broken in again.

Iron is also used as a basis for glazed or enameled finishes. Enamel lasts much better on this rigid metal than on a soft or flexible one, but should still be treated respectfully.

Stainless Steel. Stainless steel is an alloy of steel, nickel and chromium. It does not rust or corrode, is highly resistant to staining, does not discolor food and has a bright silvery color. It is strong and warp-resistant. If it is struck a hard blow it will bend rather than break.

Its drawbacks are slow conduction of heat and comparatively high cost. Also, it

Fig. 36-4. You can shine them for decorations

darkens if it is overheated. The discoloration can sometimes be removed by scouring, but is often permanent.

The outside bottom of a stainless steel pan is sometimes plated with copper or aluminum, to distribute heat more quickly and evenly. The burner heat can spread uniformly through the plating, then upward through the steel. There is another combination, an aluminum pan with an inner lining of stainless steel.

Copper tarnishes readily and easily gets to look messy. It is best to clean it with some special copper brightening compound that dissolves the tarnish. Scouring is less effective, and removes too much of the thin metal.

Polished copper-bottom pans make an excellent display when hung on a wall.

OTHER MATERIALS

Enamel. The enamel used on cooking utensils is always porcelain enamel, which is glass-like surfacing baked on at a temperature of about 1600° F. The base material may be treated iron, steel, aluminum or glass.

The utensil is fully shaped, cleaned in an acid bath, a process called pickling. It is then galvanized (coated with zinc) or Bonderized (dipped into a phosphate solution) in order to prevent rusting.

Two or more coats of enamel may be separately applied and fused onto this prepared metal. The base coat is usually dark blue because of the presence of cobalt or nickel oxide. Other coats may be in any color of the spectrum, but usually the choice of color in the store is very limited, with white and yellow being the most common solid colors at present.

Low priced enamel ware is likely to be a solid color with black trim, or dark with light speckling. High priced ware is likely to have at least two colors, and beautiful patterns may be obtained.

Porcelain enamel is a smooth, glass-like surface that is highly resistant to tarnish and discoloration, does not flavor or discolor food, is easy to clean, and is usually colorful and attractive, offering a pleasant contrast to the metal of other cooking utensils. But it is brittle and easily chipped. Enamel lasts much longer on thick, rigid metal than on thin, dentable sheet.

Spots of metal exposed by chipping may rust, and they are always conspicuous as interruptions in the smooth surface. Pieces of a disintegrating surface are likely to get in food, but in such small amounts that any ill effect is most improbable.

Glass. The problem of making and using cooking implements of glass is that it is naturally very brittle, and most varieties

Courtesy of Corning Glass Works

Fig. 36-5. Glass pans

will crack if unequal heating or cooling causes one part to expand or contract more.

Glass must be made thick for strength against breakage from blows and dropping. As it is a poor conductor of heat, this means that the bottom surface of the floor of a frypan might temporarily be hundreds of degrees hotter than its top surface.

The problem of heat cracking has been met with special types of glass which expand very little when heated. The best known low expansion glass is Pyrex, made by the Corning Glass Works. It has been successfully used for many years in most types of cooking implements, including both oven and on-the-burner types. But there are recent recommendations that a thin wire trivet be used between glass and the surface of an electric burner.

Pyrex will break if dropped on a hard surface, or if exposed to extremes of unbalanced temperature. It must not be put in cold water when it is hot, nor put on a burner or into a hot oven when it is refrigerator-cold. But if used with a little caution and common sense, such glass utensils can be used for many years.

More recently, a no-expansion glass, Pyroceram, has entered the cooking implement field under the trade name of Corning Ware. It can be moved from a freezer to a hot oven, or vice versa, without damage, and can be used on surface burners as well. At present this material is available in milky white glass containers with decorated sides, with only covers of transparent glass.

Glass has a smooth hard surface which does not react to or get damaged by any food. It does not contribute or take away flavor. When clear, it enables you to see what is being cooked.

Glass often seems hard to clean, but this is only because it allows you to see all the dirt clearly. For example, where water is hard you might keep using a metal tea kettle until it had 1/8 of an inch of scale on the bottom, and think nothing of it because you wouldn't see it. A glass kettle starts to look cloudy with 1/200 of an inch of this coating, so you would clean it.

Never scrub glass with powdered abrasives, as they may damage the smooth surface permanently, giving it a cloudy appearance.

Teflon. Teflon is a plastic of the fluoro-carbon resin family which is used for inside lining of cooking utensils. It forms a very excellent non-stick surface. Foods can be cooked in it without fat or water, with only a little risk of sticking or burning. Any food that does stick, or that is left in the pan after serving, can usually be washed out easily.

Teflon is usually applied to aluminum, in the heavier sheet grades for surface burners and the lighter ones for oven use. It can also be used on iron, steel and glass. It is supplied in a number of different colors, of which gray and brown are most popular. All colors except black may change somewhat with overheating or time, but the quality of the surface is not affected.

Teflon is baked onto utensils at a high temperature, and is somewhat more heat resistant than aluminum.

The serious drawback to the use of Teflon is that it is moderately soft, so that it is readily scratched by careless use of turners or stirrers, and is removed by cleaning with abrasives.

Manufacturers recommend that no metal utensils be used in contact with Teflon, so that turners, spatulas and stirring spoons be made of plastic, or coated with Teflon or other plastic. This precaution is not entirely practical, as most plastic turners are too thick for convenient use, and a soft coating wears off a metal edge quickly.

The wearing qualities of Teflon are greatly improved by shaping the surface of the metal underneath it into a forest of micro-scopic projections. The Teflon fills between them and covers their tops thinly. Under rough treatment the surface of the Teflon will be removed, but the metal points will then receive and withstand further scraping, protecting the coating between them.

At this stage, the Teflon still makes up most of the exposed surface, and the non-stick qualities continue to be excellent.

Even without this arrangement, Teflon is

Fig. 36-6. Pan, pot and kettle

much tougher than was originally thought. It will last a long time even if regular metal tools are used, as long as they are handled gently and kept at slight angles so that they will not dig in. But don't try to cut or stab any food while it is cooking on it.

Teflon is as likely to be spoiled in handling and cleaning as in cooking. Rough piling of pans and other objects on top of each other, careless scraping off of food, and any use at all of abrasives such as steel wool or powdered cleaners, will do severe damage.

However, the pan remains usable, and it is only the special advantages of Teflon, and the appearance of the pan, that are endangered.

The manufacturer may recommend that some oil be used on Teflon when it is heated the first time. After that it can be used dry.

But you will probably want to continue to use butter or grease in frying anyhow, as part of the taste of the food depends on the fat in which it is cooked. "Frying" an egg on a dry Teflon pan gives it a special (and good) taste and appearance, but it is really not fried unless oil or fat is involved, and it won't taste fried.

Earthenware. Casserole dishes for use in ovens are sometimes made out of a coarse china covered by an enamel-like glaze. This earthenware does not corrode or show stains. Its poor conducting quality (worse than glass) slows the start of cooking, but keeps food warm or hot long after the oven is turned off.

China is brittle, and will break or chip on impact. It may or may not be broken by abrupt temperature changes.

SAUCEPAN

A discussion of this rather important subject of cooking implements is confused by the fact that they have many different and often overlapping names. This section will supply definitions, descriptions, and discussions of use in order that the reader will understand what is meant by references elsewhere in the book.

However, other people may use many of these terms for different meanings, with just about as much chance of being right.

A saucepan, usually called pan or pot, is a cooking implement designed for cooking foods in water or watery liquids over direct surface burner heat. Strictly speaking, it is a pan if it has one handle, a pot if it has two, and a kettle if it has a single handle hinged to both sides. But roasting pans and some dishpans have two handles. Distinctions are seldom followed carefully in cookbooks and there is no particular reason why they should be.

Saucepan — pot — kettle sizes range from one pint up to 10 or 12 quarts. Small sizes are usually pans, the larger ones are pots. Kettles are limited to very large sizes, and are becoming uncommon.

These utensils are usually lumped together as "pots and pans", but the word pan is much more widely used than pot, and has therefore been given priority in this chapter's title.

For cooking efficiency a saucepan should have a bottom the same diameter as the burner, plus or minus a half inch or an inch. If smaller than the burner it will allow heat to be wasted around it, will tend to get too hot at the upper edge of the liquid, and may expose the handle to too much heat.

Minimum damage from side heat will occur if the sides are straight up and down. However, for convenience in stacking, the sides should flare out so that pans of the same size can be placed inside each other. Many kitchens do not have room to either hang them, or place them separately on shelves.

However, different sizes of straight sided pans can be stacked, with the smaller inside the larger.

Saucepans are not ordinarily exposed to temperatures much over 212° F, unless the water in them boils away unnoticed. This expectation of moderate heat permits them to be made of very light metal. However, they are more satisfactory and last longer if medium or heavy thickness is used.

Handles. The handle of a pan is preferably made of a material that conducts heat slowly, as this reduces its tendency to burn fingers. It should also be resistant to heat, to prevent or reduce damage if the pan is overheated, or the handle is left exposed to flame.

Wood is a slow conductor and has a pleasant feel, but its heat and flame resis-

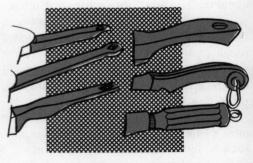

Fig. 36-7. Pan handles

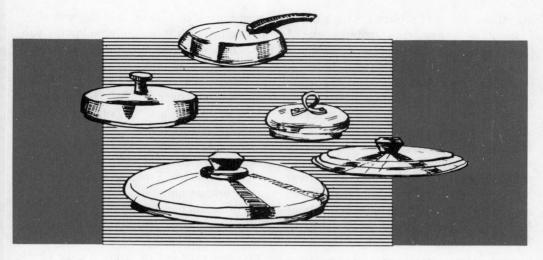

Fig. 36-8. Pan lids

tance are poor. Some of the heat resistant plastics give better results, but you usually do not know whether a particular handle is good plastic or bad plastic.

Metal is dangerous, as it conducts heat rapidly, but it is almost immune to heat damage. Iron is less dangerous than aluminum. Conduction of heat from the pan can be reduced by forming metal in tube or channel shapes, decreasing the quantity of metal in proportion to its surface. But this does not help if the part you touch has been in the direct path of burner heat.

It is a good idea to make a habit of using a pot holder or other protection in handling hot cooking utensils.

Glass pans may have clamp-on metal handles, which are removed for thorough cleaning, or when using the pan as an oven dish.

A handle should not be so heavy that it will tend to tip the empty pan, but this defect is quite likely in small sizes. You can check the balance by tapping the end of the handle lightly downward. If the pan rocks and returns to its proper position it should be all right, but if it tips over it will be troublesome to use.

The outer end of a handle should always be provided with a hole or hook so that the pan can be hung up. Many kitchens that are short of shelf space have an empty wall.

Handle Fastenings. Wooden and plastic handles are not usually fastened directly to the body of a pan, as it becomes too hot. A metal projection from the pan or handle is used to make the actual attachment. It may be extended into a bolt or strip that forms the backbone of the handle.

It is important that this metal and its connecting screws or rivets be kept beneath the surface of the cooler material, so that it will not be touched while grasping the handle.

Cast utensils, and those of glass or clay, may have handles or handle bases made in one piece with the body of the pan. If the pan is pressed into shape, the handle or its base may be welded to it, or fastened through drilled holes by rivets or bolts.

A rivet has a rounded bump at each end, which may interfere slightly with cleaning. It tends to work loose, but very seldom breaks or pulls out. But the looseness can be annoying. You might be able to tighten rivets by holding one end against something hard and solid and hammering the other. Or you can remove it by grinding or chiseling off one end, and replace it with a bolt.

Installing a new rivet requires special (but simple) equipment and skill.

A loose bolt may be tightened, unless it is stripped or badly stretched, in which case you take it out as you would a rivet.

These small bolts are called machine screws. Replacements should be carefully selected. An aluminum pan and handle should have aluminum fasteners, as contact with steel sets up an electric current in the presence of moisture that causes rapid corrosion. Use chromium plated bolts for iron and steel, as ordinary steel rusts,

Fig. 36-9. Double boiler

and brass of cadmium plate may react with food to form mildly poisonous substances.

The bolt (screw) head should be rounded or countersunk and should be inside the pan, so that the harder-to-clean nut and extra threads are on the outside.

Many wooden or plastic handles are hollow, with one or more squared surfaces fitting around or into matching sockets in the pan fastener. They are held in place by a long screw or bolt, that is threaded either into the pan or into a nut at the outer end

If such a handle is carelessly made, has

been burned or is loose, it is likely to allow the bolt to turn inside it, dumping the pan. A handle that feels only slightly loose may let a heavy load turn.

Some such handles can be tightened with a screwdriver or pliers. But it may be necessary to remove the bolt, put on some washers, and replace it.

Lids. Saucepans often need lids, for reasons discussed in the chapter on BOILING. Medium and good quality pans often have fitted or matching lids.

For casual use, any lid big enough not to fall in and small enough not to get unbalanced and fall off the side can be used. You can even get by using a cake or pie pan as a lid.

But a lid should have a handle, preferably of heat-resistant plastic. It should not burn your fingers even when water is boiling in the pan. But test it with a light touch before you pick it up. For metal lid handles always use a pot holder or some other protection.

Double Boiler. A double boiler, Figure 36-9, consists of two pans — a lower one in which water is heated or boiled over a burner, and an upper one in which food is cooked or warmed. They are shaped so that a substantial part of the upper pan is exposed to the steam in the lower.

Fit is fairly tight so that little steam escapes unless the burner is excessively high.

The double boiler is used where gentle heat is wanted. As long as there is water in the bottom, the temperature of the food will not rise above boiling, scorching and burning cannot occur and sticking is unusual. As a further refinement for delicate recipes, the water level is kept below the upper pan, so that heat is carried to it only by steam, rather than by more rapid conduction through water.

The drawback to use of a double boiler is that it is very slow getting started. It takes a long time to get the food hot. After that, cooking may be almost as fast as over direct heat, and it needs little or no attention.

You can get a faster start by heating the two pans separately. While you bring the water in the bottom to a boil, put the food in the top over a high or medium flame, stirring constantly if necessary, until it is thoroughly heated but has not started to boil. Then put the top on the bottom.

There are some delicate recipes with which you should not do this.

Sometimes you can cook a small quantity of a vegetable in the lower part of a double boiler, while you heat cream sauce or some other delicacy in the top. And both the bottom and the top can be used separately as ordinary saucepans.

Steamer. A steamer is any type of covered pan or set of pans that has boiling water in the bottom and a rack, sieve, or perforated pan to hold food out of the water and in the steam. One type is the same as the double boiler just described, except that the upper pan's bottom is full of holes. It cannot be used for sauces or other liquid foods, but is fine for many vegetables.

Since drained vegetables do not swap flavors with each other to any great extent, you can cook or warm several different ones at the same time. You can separate them with foil strips if you wish, but don't wrap them. The steam must be able to circulate through spaces in the food in order for this method of cooking to be efficient.

A steamer can be made out of any reasonably high-sided covered pan by fitting it with a rack which will hold the food to be cooked above boiling water in the bottom.

Steaming time may be about the same as for boiling, but only if a liberal supply of steam surrounds the food. If the food is in a separate container (as for example the perforated double boiler mentioned above) and/or boiling is not vigorous, cooking may be much slower.

Courtesy of Ekco Housewares Co.

Fig. 36-10. Top pan of a steamer

Pressure cookers were discussed under BOILING, starting on page 42.

Waterless Cookers. Pans or pots made of cast aluminum, or of very heavy gauge sheet aluminum, equipped with close-fitting lids, are often called waterless cookers. The combination of thick metal and excellent conduction keeps interior temperatures even, and if started on a slow flame enough water may be distilled from the food to supply steam to continue the cooking. Results obtained are similar to those in a steamer.

The Dutch oven is a waterless type pot used to cook pot roast and some other cuts of meat, as well as vegetables. It used to be a low-sided pan with a high domed cover, but now it is a heavy pot and cover of standard shape.

FRYING PAN

The frying pan, called frypan for short or

Courtesy of Ekco Housewares Co.

Fig. 36-11. Dutch oven, and trivet

Fig. 36-12. Metal frypans

skillet for elegance, is used for cooking food in or on a shallow layer of oil or grease. It is quite different from the deep fat frying kettle.

In the frypan, each piece of food is usually in contact with the pan, or at the most is a few thin layers above it. The pan is therefore typically wide bottomed and low sided. The sides may flare out widely for easy access to the bottom, and for efficiency in heat gathering.

Most frypans are made of metal. It is thicker than in saucepans of equivalent quality, to improve heat distribution between vacant and occupied areas, and to reduce or prevent warping.

There are also glass frypans, such as those in Figure 36-13.

Sides. Frypan sides are usually quite low, from 1 to 2-1/2 inches. The higher models may be called skillets or chicken-fryers.

Sides may be vertical, or flare out to a variable extent. They usually meet the bottom at a sharp angle, which may or may not be rounded in for ease of cleaning, but in chef-style, bottom and sides are blended in a continuous curve.

The angle gives wider floor area in proportion to top diameter, but requires aiming a turner almost straight down to get under the food at the side. This is a nuisance, and is an extra hazard for Teflon. You cannot spill food smoothly over the sides by tilting the pan.

But the chef style, which lacks all these disadvantages, is much less popular, and is often difficult to obtain.

Bottom. The upper surface of the bottom is the important part of a frypan. It should be level, so that grease will not run into hollows and leave the high spots dry. It should have a reasonably non-sticking surface. Grease is supposed to take care of prevention of sticking, but some foods will absorb all the grease you give them, and still be able to stick. And healthy frying of many foods calls for using a minimum of grease.

Add to this the fact that the best of cooks may be careless, either in supplying grease or in watching the progress of the cooking, it is clear that a non-sticking frypan material or finish is desirable.

Aluminum pans that have been spin-molded may have circular grooves in the bottom that make it feel as rough as sandpaper. Such a pan tends to stick badly the first few times it is used. Scouring improves this surface.

Griddle. A griddle is basically a large

Fig. 36-13. Glass frypan

Courtesy of Corning Glass Works

frypan with practically no sides. The surface may be flat with a slight turn-up (1/4 to 3/8 inch) at all edges to retain grease, or it may have arrangements to drain grease off to a side gutter or pocket.

One popular size is 10-1/2 inches square, large enough for 4 slices of French toast or 4 fried eggs (6 if you crowd them a little). This is oversize for most standard electric and all gas burners, so there is a tendency for the center, or whatever part you have over the heat, to be hotter than the outlying parts.

Warping after a few months, even with careful use, is common.

Teflon finish is almost standard on griddles, but they are occasionally made in heavy bare aluminum, or black iron.

Courtesy of Wear-Ever Aluminum, Inc.

Fig. 36-15a. Tea kettle

Fig. 36-14. Griddle

Omelet Pan. The omelet pan is a very special fry pan with a hinge in the middle. The omelet is started in one half, and when you think it is enough done on one side, you fold the other side of the pan over its top and turn it over, thus turning the omelet without the trouble and risk of getting a spatula or other tool under it and trying to turn it all in one piece. Or you can start half the mix in each side, add a filling to one, and turn the other over on top of it.

The omelet pan must be carefully finished to a non-stick surface, and/or greased according to directions, because if you get an omelet stuck down in a half pan with no room to work a spatula along the bot-

tom to it, you have trouble, or perhaps just scrambled eggs.

KETTLES

Frying Kettle. The frying kettle is a deep, straight sided pan or pot of sturdy construction, into which is fitted a removable basket or strainer insert. In some electric ranges there is a burner which can be lowered to provide a well for inserting a special frying kettle.

You fill this implement about 3/4 full of frying fat (not butter or margarine) and heat it to the temperature your cooking requires, for example, 390° F for French fried potatoes. See FRYING, Chapter 3, for more details.

The food is placed in the basket and lowered into the hot fat for the recommended time, then lifted out. The quantity cooked in one batch must be limited so as not to cool the fat too much. A proportion of 1/2 pound of food to 8 cups of fat is usually safe.

Tea Kettle. The tea kettle, or more realistically, water kettle, is designed just to heat water, usually to a boil. It was originally used largely for tea making, but lately seems more devoted to instant coffee and miscellaneous work. It fills the occasional need for boiling water in general cooking,

719

Fig. 36-15b. Glass kettle and coffee pots

and it can make up part of the deficiency when the hot water supply is weak.

Water can be heated just as well in a pan, but it cannot be handled or poured as easily.

These kettles may be made of stainless steel (with or without a copper plated bottom), aluminum or glass. Capacity may be from 1 to 5 quarts. A standard construction shown in Figure 36-15a has a wide bottom, an inward curve or bulge of the sides, a pouring spout, a top opening with a close fitting lid and an overhead plastic handle (bail) on metal supports hinged or rigidly fastened at the front (spout end) and the rear, or at the rear only.

A glass kettle is similar, but uses a glass handle rigidly fastened to the back. Be sure not to place this kettle so that burner heat can get at the handle directly, or at least be doubly sure not to touch it barehanded.

The whistling tea kettle has no opening in the top, and is filled through the spout. The whistle is in a plastic spout closure, which is swung out of the way for filling or pouring by pressing a button on the rigidly fastened handle. When the water reaches a full boil enough steam is generated to make a loud enough whistle to tell you that the water is ready, even if you are in the next room with the TV on.

Since kettles are used only for water they are not ordinarily cleaned inside, and in hard water areas scale will build up. It insulates the bottom so that heating is slower, and eventually may cut down noticeably on capacity.

Buildup of scale can be reduced by emptying the kettle after each use, and starting again with fresh water. This avoids concentrating the minerals.

You can check a kettle with a lid by looking in it. If you see a deposit on the bottom, soak it overnight with a solution of vinegar or other mild acid in water. Use a tablespoon to a cup for routine cleaning, and up to 3 tablespoons for a heavy deposit.

This acid will dissolve light scale, and loosen thicker pieces so that you can scrape or scour them.

You can't inspect the inside of a whistling kettle, but if your water is hard you can be pretty sure it is accumulating scale. Give it a vinegar treatment once a month or at least once in three months.

If it rattles afterward when dry you have loosened heavy pieces of scale. These can sometimes be shaken out the spout, but you may have to dissolve them with a long soak in strong vinegar solution.

OVEN UTENSILS

There are three types of implements generally used for cooking in an oven. There is the light metal tinware used for cookies, biscuits, muffins, cake and bread; heavier metal roasting pans, and casseroles and baking dishes of glass or china.

Since most broiling is done inside an oven or compartment, broiler pans belong under this heading too.

Tinware. Tinware used to be made of thin sheet steel plated with tin on both sides. But tin is becoming scarce, and it

Courtesy of Ekco Housewares Co.

Fig. 36-16. Whistling tea kettle

darkens and may warp on repeated exposure to heat. It has been largely replaced by aluminum. This is usually thinner sheet than would be used on surface burners, as oven utensils are subjected to less heat and banging around. Teflon linings are quite common and satisfactory.

There are also disposable pans made of heavy aluminum foil, often crimped or corrugated for extra strength. They are fragile but cheap.

Old cooks generally say that new shiny tinware cannot provide first quality baking, and it is only after it gets old and dull (broken in) that it is satisfactory. Several range manufacturers and many cookbooks say that good results can be obtained only with shiny pans, and they should be discarded when they get dull.

You can cook successfully with either kind, as long as you understand the difference. Bright pans reflect away heat, so they stay cooler and cook more slowly than dull ones. You can compensate for this by having the oven 25° F hotter for bright than

for dull. But you will probably find that crust against the pan will be thinner and lighter in comparison to the unshielded top crust.

A pan that is partly bright and partly dull is almost sure to cause trouble, overcooking on the dull side or undercooking on the other.

Cookie Sheets. Cookie (cooky) sheets are usually made of aluminum. They are flat, have a size range from about 8 x 8 to 14 x 18 inches. There is a low rim on one or more sides for strength.

They are used for baking cookies, toasting or drying bread in the oven or under the broiler, and supporting custard cups and other objects too small to stand safely on a rack. They should be stacked on edge against a wall when not in use, as they might be bent by piling objects on them.

Cake Pans. Layer cakes are baked in round, shallow pans with vertical sides. Diameter is usually 8 or 9 inches and side height about on inch. These are sometimes equipped with a flat piece of metal hinged

Fig. 36-24. Glass casseroles and coffee pots, decorated

Courtesy of Corning Glass Works

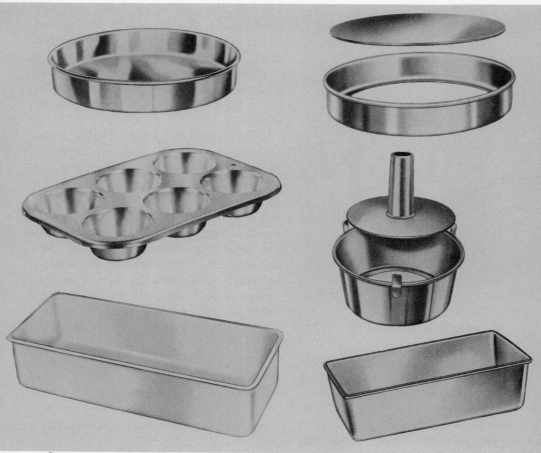

Fig. 36-18. Aluminum ovenware

to the center and following the bottom and edge contour up one side.

When the cake is cooked, this strip is rotated in a full circle, cutting free any spots where the cake might have stuck. Or the bottom may rest on narrow side flanges, without fastening, so that it can be pushed up and the cake cut off it with a long knife.

Loaf pans may be used for either cake or bread. They are rectangular (or occasionally square). For deep loaves, size is often around 9 to 10 inches long, 4-1/2 to 5-1/2 wide and 2-1/2 to 3 inches deep. They are sometimes fitted with glass covers.

Special pans for angel food and sponge cake are ring shaped. One standard bottom diameter is 8-1/4 inches. The sides are high, and slope outward on the outside and inward toward the center, perhaps to make it easier to get the cake out.

The sides are not supposed to be greased, as the cake should be cooled upside down in the pan (see page 437), and it must stick in order not to fall out.

These pans may be made in two or more pieces, so that they can be taken apart for easy removal of the cake. Otherwise it is necessary to cut down all around it with a long knife.

Muffin tins were described on page 421,

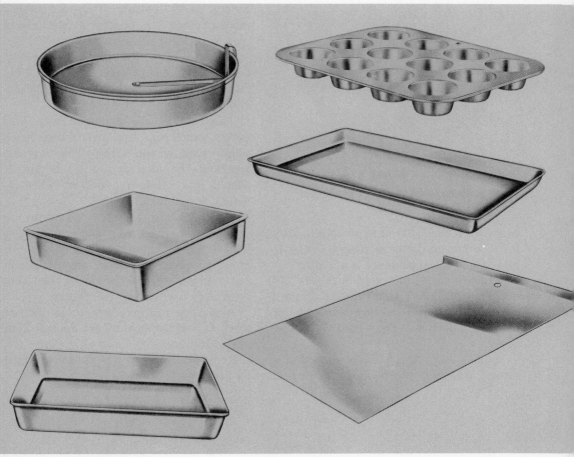

Courtesy of Wear-Ever Aluminum, Inc.

Fig. 36-19. More aluminum ovenware

and pie pans were discussed on page 447.

Casseroles. A casserole is a high sided baking dish. The same word is used for non-dessert mixtures cooked in such dishes, because some of them contain such a variety of ingredients that a truly descriptive name might fill a paragraph. The dish is also standard for baking puddings.

A casserole (the container) is usually made of glass or pottery, but sometimes of enameled iron or other materials. It may be finished crudely or simply, or be beautifully shaped, finished and decorated. It may be lined with Teflon.

The basic shape is usually round, but it may be oval, square or rectangular. Sides may be vertical or slope outward slightly. Corners are rounded for evenness of cooking and ease of cleaning.

There is a close fitting lid which is usually transparent glass. Covering is not needed for some casserole mixes, but is essential for others.

Most casseroles are designed for oven heat only, and must not be put on burners, or exposed to abrupt changes in temperature. But these limitations do not apply to those made of Pyroceram.

A casserole is sometimes sold with a supporting frame in which you can burn a

Fig. 36-20. Glass casserole, solid color

candle or a wick soaked in alcohol to keep the dish hot on the table. This is a convenience, and the appearance is attractive.

Standard casserole capacities are 10 ounces, 1, 1-1/2, 2 and 3 quarts. Custard cups may be considered tiny casseroles, for individual portions. They hold 4, 5 or 6 ounces.

Souffle dishes are specially shaped casseroles, with high, steep sides with vertical fluting on the outside. They are usually made of china or of opaque glass instead of clear glass. One is shown on page 401.

Roasting Pan. Roasting pans are large and heavily built. They are usually oval but may be rectangular. They are made in several sizes, 11 to 16 inches long.

They are usually equipped with high covers, which permit use over a roast much thicker than the pan is deep. The cover can sometimes be used as a separate pan. It should nest inside the bottom when inverted, for storage.

Cookbooks generally tell you not to use your roasting pan cover, and one suggests that its only employment should be for growing flowers. But covers are valuable in controlling color and texture of crust, and preventing oven-soiling by splatter.

A roasting pan may have a low rack or trivet to hold the meat off the floor and out of the drippings.

Roasting and broiling pans are described on pages 64, 71 and 72.

37

ELECTRIC APPLIANCES

There is a large and increasing variety of electric-heat appliances which provide for cooking both specialty and regular items without using a standard range. Some are simple, cheap and moderate in current consumption. A single hot plate, used in the same manner as a top burner on a stove, is an example.

At the other extreme are oven-broiler-rotisserie combinations, that are complex and expensive and can only be plugged into heavy duty circuits. Most appliances have automatic controls.

Some of them are indispensable or nearly so. It is possible to make toast under a broiler or by holding the bread with a fork over a surface burner, but most people would rather do without. And the non-electric waffle iron disappeared many years ago.

But an item such as an electric frying pan merely does more conveniently what could be as well done in a regular frypan, and the convenience in use should be considered together with the inconvenience of storing it or working around it when it is not being used.

There is also a wide range of electric-power appliances that reduce the labor of beating, mixing, grinding, cutting and blending food.

Selection. There are at least five questions to ask yourself before going out to purchase an electric appliance. They are: Do you want it? Do you need it? Will you use it? Have you room for it? And is it worth its cost to you? This cost may be that of the appliance, plus the rewiring involved in installing a heavy enough circuit so you can use it.

If enough of these questions rate a "yes" answer, you next have to decide on the quality, complexity and price. In some items there is little difference among various models except perhaps in quality. But if you want an electric beater mixer, you have a range between a simple motor driven egg beater for less than $15.00 and a deluxe rotating-bowl model with enough attachments to make you think of a machine shop, for over $100.00.

There are certain basic requirements. Any electrically operated or connected appliance should carry the Underwriters' Laboratories Seal of Approval, which may

725

Fig. 37-1. A mark of approval

be written out or abbreviated into the letters UL in a circle, as in Figure 37-1. This may be stamped into the metal, or be on an attached label.

A label on the cord means only that the cord has been approved, not the appliance. If an advertisement for an appliance states that the cord is UL approved, you may assume that the appliance itself is not.

The UL seal indicates that the Laboratories, a nonprofit organization, has approved the design of the appliance and makes occasional tests of production models. Their interest is primarily in safety, and any unit not carrying the seal may be

Fig. 37-2. Your wiring may be overloaded

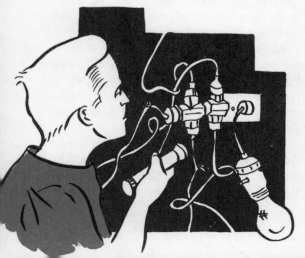

suspected of being very dangerous to use.

The electric outlets into which you will or might connect the appliance must have heavy enough wiring to supply it. The rating in watts should be on a plate on the unit. If it is given in amperes instead, multiply by the voltage. That is, a four ampere rating of 120 volts means 480 watts. An ordinary house circuit may be designed for 1200 to 1800 watts (10 to 15 amperes).

Do not figure that the appliance will be the only user of current on the circuit, as lights and other appliances may be connected also. Another point is that motors use up to twice their rated amperage when starting.

Because of increased demands for light, and multiplication of appliances, many homes already have overloaded circuits. One more unit may be the last straw. It is a good idea to have an electrican check the situation.

ELECTRICITY

A general understanding of the behavior of electric current is useful in understanding and using appliances.

All matter is composed of atoms. Each atom is made up of electrically charged particles. In its center are heavy, positively charged protons, around which move much lighter electrons, each carrying a negative charge. Complete atoms have the same number of protons and electrons. Their charges cancel out, so the atom is neutral. electrically.

Some of the electrons can be detached by magnetic or chemical forces, so that they move into other atoms, displacing electrons from them. An atom which loses an electron has a positive charge, one which gains an electron has a negative charge. Movement of electrons makes up electric current. If it is through the air, it makes a visible spark.

A substance that allows electrons to move through it freely is a good conductor of electricity, while one that resists and stops their movement is a non-conductor or insulator. But even the best of conductors offer some resistance at ordinary temperatures, and most insulators will allow passage of some electrons.

Current. Electrical current is the flow of electrons through a conductor. Its behavior can be compared to flow of water through a pipe.

To begin with, there is no current in either case if there is no movement. But there is a difference in that electrical current must make a complete circuit back to the spot where it started.

Pressure is needed to make the flow. In water it is supplied by a pump or by gravity, and it is measured in pounds per square inch. In electricity the pressure, called electromotive force, is supplied by a generator or a battery, and is measured in volts.

Water flow may be measured in gallons per minute, cubic feet per second, or similar quantity-time standards. The corresponding measure for electricity is the ampere. This is a rather small amount of current, but it represents a flow of over 6.2 billion electrons a second.

The separate measures for force and volume must be considered together in estimating the work that can be performed. To find the power or energy of an electrical current, the volume of flow (amperes) is multiplied by the pressure (volts) to produce a power measurement in watts.

One ampere times one volt makes one watt. A watt-hour is a one-watt current flowing for an hour. A kilowatt hour, which is the unit of measurement on our utility bills, is 1000 watt-hours.

Resistance. Flow of electricity is impeded by the resistance of the conductor, so that voltage is lower at the working end of the line than at the supply end. The lost energy is turned into heat. This is a useful effect in a heating appliance, but a wasteful and sometimes destructive factor in wiring.

Resistance in a wire varies with its material, its length, its cross section (thickness) and its temperature.

Copper and aluminum are the best conductors among metals cheap enough to use for the purpose. Copper is a somewhat better conductor than aluminum, and is preferred for wire as it is more flexible. Iron has 5 to 7 times as much resistance as copper. Sulfur, the poorest conductor among the elements, has billions of times more resistance than copper.

Air is a fairly good insulator, and water is a fairly good conductor, particularly if salt or other minerals are dissolved in it. Most wiring systems depend on being partly

---

Ampere = volume of current
Volt = pressure of current
1 Watt = 1 ampere × 1 volt
1 Kilowatt = 1000 watts
1 Megawatt = 1000 kilowatts

Fig. 37-3. Measurements of electricity

insulated by air. If they are wet the current is likely to follow the outside of insulation and parts, instead of staying in the wires and connectors where it belongs.

Such a wet system may prevent an appliance from operating, may damage it and may be very dangerous to you.

Resistance increases in direct proportion to the length of a line. A 10-foot extension cord has twice the resistance of one 5 feet long. But it decreases in proportion to increases in the cross section area (thickness).

The #16 wires in the cord to a 1200-watt frypan are large enough to supply it with current without noticeable drop in voltage. But if you should disobey directions, and connect it through an ordinary extension cord with smaller (# 18) wires, the extension would probably not deliver the full voltage, and would heat up and possibly burn out.

Resistance in metals increases as their temperature rises. As an overloaded wire gets hot it is less able to handle the load and gets hotter still. This is an important factor in the melting of undersize wire and poor connections, and burning of insulation.

Resistance is to flow or amperage and is ordinarily not affected by increase in voltage. Long lines are therefore operated at the highest practical voltage, to decrease the proportion of loss in transmission. But working units such as light bulbs and heating coils burn out if voltage is increased beyond their designed capacity.

Alternating Current. Electricity is used in two forms, direct and alternating. In direct, (DC) the electrons always flow in one direction through the circuit, from negative to positive. In alternating (AC) the direction of flow is reversed many times a second. The frequency of reversing is called its cycle.

Household and industrial current is usually 60 cycle, that is, it changes direction 60 times during every second.

The speed of electricity is so great that 1/60th of a second provides ample time for each pulse to come from a power plant hundreds of miles away, do work in your appliance, and return to the power plant, before the next pulse starts in the reverse direction through the circuit.

Direct current is used whenever a battery is the power source, as in a car, and it is generated, or converted from an alternating current source, for many special purposes.

The great advantage of alternating current is that its voltage can be easily increased or decreased in a simple machine called a transformer. Very high voltage, sometimes up to 650,000, is used in transmission lines. This is stepped down to 3000 to 15,000 in distribution lines, and to a dual voltage, about 120-240, for household use.

Circuit. The path of electrical current from the power house through household appliances and back to the power house is a circuit. Also, any closed path it takes, for example from a fuse box through a toaster and back, is also called a circuit. In a flashlight, the current's path from battery through bulb and back to battery is a complete circuit.

In a battery or DC circuit, the wiring to the working part is called live, and the return wiring or connection is called the ground. The live part will make sparks if you tamper with it, the ground will not.

In an AC circuit, the current is going two ways because of the alternation, so both wires are live. But a third or neutral wire is supplied when heavy current must be handled and this may be called a ground.

The flow of current through a circuit is limited to the amount that can pass through its point of greatest resistance. In a house circuit this may be a fuse which contains a wire or strip that will heat to the melting point, breaking the circuit and stopping flow of current, at some specific amperage.

Threaded fuses, with capacities of 10 to 30 amperes, have glass tops that usually allow you to see whether they are intact, or melted (blown). There are usually several of them in one fuse box. You should keep

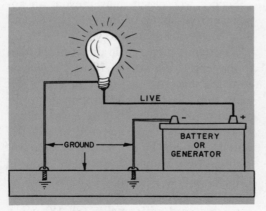

Fig. 37-4. Simple electric circuit

spares on hand. They are safe to change if your hands and the floor are dry.

There are also cylindrical fuses, with capacities of 30 amperes and more, which are held by two spring clamps. The fusible strip is not visible, so you have to guess or use a test lamp to determine its condition. If any bulb or appliance in a circuit is on, a test lamp will light if its wires are placed at opposite ends of a blown cylinder fuse, and will not light if the fuse is intact.

Wear rubber gloves or use pliers with insulated handles in changing these fuses. Their center part is non-conducting, but your fingers must be very close to the clamps.

A circuit breaker can be used instead of a fuse. It is a switch that opens automatically with an overload. It may keep closing and opening, with a buzzing or clattering sound, as long as the overload exists. Or it may simply stay open until you close it by pressing a button. Breakers are much more convenient than fuses.

Short Circuits. The part of an electrical circuit that includes an appliance is designed to have work done by the current, which is confined to certain pathways. If it can evade or break out of such pathways to take a short cut back to its place of origin, it creates a new or short circuit. This deprives the appliance of part or all of its power.

Worse, the uncontrolled crossover will usually permit the passage of much more current than the circuit is designed to supply, causing overheating and blowing of the fuse or opening of the breaker. And if the new circuit is through a person, the effect can be anything from startling to fatal.

Very often, the defect in the confinement of the current allows it to enter the frame or body of the appliance. If this is not grounded by a connection to a neutral wire or an underground metal pipe, all of its metal becomes part of a live circuit, although usually no current passes through it.

If you touch it, you will become part of the circuit too. The effect on you will depend on the character of the defect in the wiring, the intimacy of your contact with the appliance and how well you are grounded.

If the defect allows passage of only a slight current, your fingers are dry and touch the metal lightly and you are wearing rubber soled shoes and are standing on a dry floor, you will feel only a slight tingling.

If the defect is serious, and you have wet feet, or are partly grounded by having dry fingers on a radiator or a faucet handle, you will get a severe jolt. Under this condition, if both hands were wet you would get a very severe shock which could be fatal.

If you get even a little shock from an appliance, you should repair or discard it, as it can be very dangerous. You cannot depend on your hands always being dry, or that you are not grounded in some way.

Increase in voltage makes short circuits both more likely and more dangerous.

Major appliances such as ranges have their frames grounded. An increasing number of smaller units are supplied with a 3-wire cord. The third wire connects the frame to the neutral wire in your house system, through a special wall or baseboard receptacle. You can put an adapter plug in an ordinary receptacle, connecting it by means

Fig. 37-5. Fuses

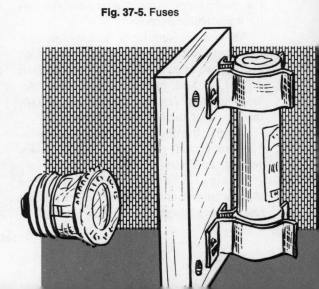

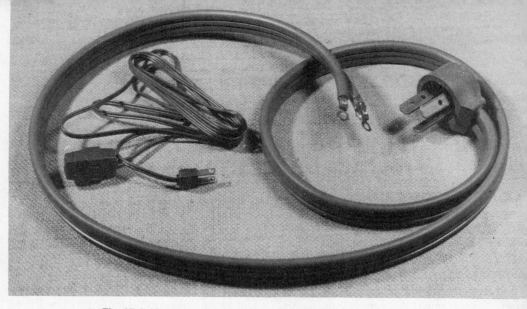

Fig. 37-6. Heavy 3-wire range cord, and light-duty extension cord

of a small wire to a fastening screw for the receptacle cover.

A grounded appliance can become dangerous only under very unusual conditions. But you may not know that it is defective, and the short can use considerable current before it becomes bad enough to warn you by blowing a fuse.

The presence of a grounded appliance increases the danger from an ungrounded one, as it applies an extra surface to which you might be grounded while handling it.

CONSTRUCTION

Most electric appliances for the kitchen are made up of various arrangements of a few basic types of unit, plus special items for a particular purpose.

All cookers require a heating element (resistance unit) to turn electric current into heat. There must be means to turn this heat on and off, and, in all but the simplest devices, ways to regulate its intensity and/or the time that the food is exposed to it.

Mixing, beating and cutting devices require motors, together with the necessary controls and wiring.

Heating Elements. Heating elements usually consist of wires made of metal that resists the passage of electricity through it.

Some of the electrical force at the wall socket is lost in such wires by being changed into heat, which may be anything from gentle warmth to white-heat, depending on the metal used, the thickness of the wire and the supply of electricity.

Such metal must be able to resist corrosion at high temperatures, and is usually some special alloy such as nichrome (nickel-chromium) steel.

The temperature of the wire is raised by increasing the amperage and lowered by reducing it. The total heat or cooking effect produced by the element depends both on its temperature, and the area (surface area of the wire or its casing) that is involved.

The wires are sometimes straight but are more often spiral, to permit packing more wire and therefore more heat-producing material in a given space. Tight spirals provide more heat than flat or loose spirals, for any one thickness of wire and length of unit. See Figure 37-7.

Wires may be stretched through air between insulated posts, or held in grooves or on backings of porcelain, mica or other insulating material.

A bare wire in a turned-on heating element is hot enough to give you a bad burn. But it is also a live wire, which if touched could give a severe and perhaps fatal shock. It can also transmit such a shock through a metal pan or utensil. It can remain live even if the unit is switched off and cold, for reasons given below.

There are also insulated heating wires. A closely packed spiral may be packed in magnesium oxide insulation, and encased in a protective sheath of round or flattened iron tubing. There may be one, two or three wires in a tube, which can be curved into any convenient pattern.

This insulated construction is standard in ranges, and is found in some lighter appliances. It is more expensive, and slower to heat and to cool than bare wire, but it is much, much safer.

Motors. Electric motors are used in appliances wherever power is needed to rotate, push, pull or otherwise move working parts. Such motors usually operate by magnetic attraction or repulsion between current flowing in a rotating armature and magnets in a stationary case. The principle and construction of motors are too complicated for discussion here.

Most appliance motors operate on 120 volt alternating current from the house wiring. They are timed by the 60-times-a-second reversal of current flow, and are so accurate in turning speed that they operate clocks practically without error. But if they are required to turn loads that are too great for them, or if voltage drops below their requirement, they will slow down, overheat and will be damaged if the condition is not corrected promptly.

Do not use an electric motor when the lights are dim. It is good practice to disconnect refrigerators and freezers under such conditions, but the avoidance of motor damage might be outweighed by danger of forgetting to reconnect them when power is restored.

Battery-operated appliances use DC current. They merely slow down and eventually stop when the battery gets weak, or a

poor connection develops, but they do not suffer damage from use in this condition. But they cannot be used for very long, as a battery gives up very soon after its voltage drops noticeably. It is good to have a spare battery or set of batteries on hand, or to use re-chargeable batteries and have a charger ready.

Battery-operated appliances are often too weak to do their job properly even with full-strength batteries. Such units may fail to operate when their power is reduced only slightly.

Submersion. Appliances usually need washing after they are used. But if they contain electrical wiring, soaking in dishwater can be damaging and dangerous. Water, specially chemical-laden water, is a much better conductor than air, and it can remain

Fig. 37-7. Straight and spiral wires

in small places for a very long time without evaporating.

Electricity following moisture may take a short cut (short circuit) permitting it to go through the appliance without doing any work, or worse yet, travel into the frame of the unit and then to or through anyone who touches it.

So you can't really wash and soak most of these appliances. Just give them delicate sponge baths, making sure no water oozes into their works. But there are submersible models, that are sealed so that water cannot get into their vulnerable parts.

If an appliance label says that it is submersible, you can wash it almost like any other equipment. Except, don't soak it for more than 15 minutes or so. Seals are not

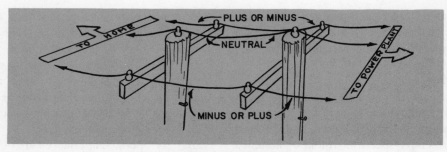

Fig. 37-8. Three-wire power supply

always perfect, and given enough time, they may leak.

Many units put the delicate thermostat in a removable plug, which you pull out when you disconnect the current. The heating unit itself is sealed so that the pan or whatever can be washed in the dishpan. The thermostat plug can only be wiped, but you would usually have to be very sloppy to get food on it.

CONTROLS

Simple Switches. The very simplest appliances may not have switches. To start one you plug the wire into an electric outlet, to stop it you pull the plug out. But most of them have at least switches by which they may be turned on and off.

Most appliance switches are of the single pole type, in which only one of the two leading (lead-in) wires is disconnected in the OFF position. As a result, parts of the appliance may be "live" and capable of delivering a serious shock even when it is turned off.

Referring to Figure 37-8, ordinary 60 cycle alterating current, which is standard for homes, is brought in by a three wire system. One wire serves to complete the circuit back to the power house, and can be said to be dead, neutral, or grounded. For many purposes it could be replaced by a connection to a metal pipe that is in contact with damp ground.

One of the pair of live wires is charged at plus 120 or 130 volts while the other is at minus the same amount. The 120 or 130 volt circuits used for lights and for small appliances are connected to one of the live wires and to the ground wire.

When you plug the appliance cord into an outlet, one wire in the cord will be charged and one will be grounded. You do not know which one, and as a matter of operation it does not matter. A switch interrupts the circuit and turns off the appliance just as effectively by opening the ground wire as the live one.

However, from a safety viewpoint there is a big difference. On the average the switch will open only the ground wire 50 per cent of the time. This leaves the heating element and/or other parts of the internal wiring live, and capable of striking back if you

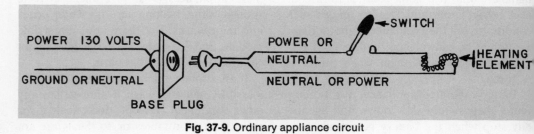

Fig. 37-9. Ordinary appliance circuit

meddle with them. The most common cause of trouble is clumsy attempts to retrieve a slice of bread caught in a toaster.

Even with the switch off, touching the heating element with the tine of a fork may permit a 120 volt charge to travel up the fork, perhaps into the toaster frame and probably into the person holding the fork.

For this reason, NEVER fool around in any way with the insides of an electric appliance unless you unplug it first. If you unplug it and go away, check to make sure it is still disconnected when you come back, as some Helpful Harry with tidy instincts may have reconnected it.

Some of the newer appliances are equipped with dipole switches, which disconnect both sides of the circuit when they are open. They are in the minority, however, and you should not count on one being present.

Regulating Switches. A switch may offer 2, 3 or many more settings for a heating element, or speed choices for a motor. This is done by regulating the amount of current that can pass through the switch, by resistance units and other methods. Most of them are operated by turning a dial.

One type is known as a step control, because it can be used in only a limited number of settings, which in a heat unit may be OFF, LOW, MEDIUM and HIGH. In motor regulation, steps may indicate relative motor speed, or an action to be expected at that speed, as STIR, BLEND or WHIP.

The stepless or infinitely variable control is active through its full revolution, and will increase or decrease current by amounts as tiny as are desired. This permits regulation to exactly suit the job, but loses the convenience of known results from known settings. There may be clicks or slight resistance at certain positions to offset this disadvantage, however.

Timers. Two types of timer are used in the kitchen. One talks about what should be done, the other does it.

The first kind is a short-period alarm

Fig. 37-10. Don't poke metal in the toaster

clock. It may be built in or plugged in an appliance or range, or be an entirely separate unit. It can be part of a clock that tells time, or one that only counts minutes and hours to zero from a starting point, as on page 6.

In either case, if you want to be reminded when it is time to check the roast, turn the steak or even to phone the office, you set it for the time you want. At or near the proper moment it will ring a bell or start to buzz. A buzzer, which is usually found only in electric powered units, is safer as you should hear it sooner or later. You might fail to

Fig. 37-11. Regulating switch for thermostat

notice the short ring of a bell, even though the sound is usually much louder.

The action timer is usually a built-in electric clock, which may or may not tell time. It has one (or more rarely two) hands which can be set for time intervals by turning a knob, usually much too small for a convenient grip. It is wired into an electrical switch or circuit in such a way that it will cut off the flow of current at the end of the set time. It may or may not start buzzing also.

The most usual application of this timer is turning off the heat in an oven at the end of a cooking period. Or it may turn the heat down to a keep warm or holding temperature, instead of shutting it off completely.

A timer may also be constructed to turn current on. Electric ranges so equipped can be set to turn on at a certain future time, and then turn off (or way down) after a cooking interval. But of course you have to do some arranging to take advantage of this automatic service. The food must be in the oven, the temperature control must be where you want it and the oven control must be set at AUTOMATIC.

These timers in ranges operate through electrical circuits, even with gas heat. Such a circuit usually includes an outlet in which you can plug an electric coffee pot or other light cooking unit, so that it can be controlled by the same clock.

Thermostats. A thermostat is a device that operates a switch or a valve automatically in response to a change in temperature.

A hydraulic thermostat has a thin liquid-filled tube with a bulge or bulb at one end and a movable diaphragm at the other. The bulb is mounted at the point where control is needed, for example on the inner side of an oven compartment, and the diaphragm is connected to an electric switch or heat regulator, or a gas control valve.

Expansion of the fluid in the bulb when

Fig. 37-12. Two-burner hot plate

it is heated causes it to move through the tube and press against the diaphragm, pressing it outward so that it operates the control. Cooling and contraction will allow fluid to re-enter the bulb, allowing the diaphragm to move inward by atmospheric pressure or spring action, thus re-setting the switch or valve.

A thermostat may also be made of two strips of metal with different expansion rates, fastened tightly together. Heating will cause the combined strip to curve away from the side with greatest expansion.

This movement is used to make or break electrical contact, or is magnified with gears and levers to operate more complex devices. There are many other arrangements that can be used in thermostatic controls.

A thermostat may have a simple on and off action, allowing full supply of heat or none. The alternation of on and off positions is called its cycle, or cycling. It is necessary to have the turn-on temperature at least several degrees below the turn-off temperature to avoid an excessively rapid cycle.

Increasing the interval slows the cycle, so that a burner will turn on and off less often, but if the interval is too great the temperature in the oven or pan will fluctuate too much for good results.

Cycling may be largely avoided by a throttling type thermostat, which will start to cut down the heat gradually as its turn-off point is approached, turn it off when it is reached, then gradually restore it as temperature drops toward a full-on requirement. A throttling device is more difficult and expensive to make and to service than an on-off unit.

Most thermostats in the kitchen are adjustable, usually according to markings on the dial by which you turn on the unit. Settings may be given in temperatures, in purpose (simmer, boil, fry, etc.) or in both ways.

An oven thermostat is likely to have a special mechanism that allows the oven to overheat 25 to 50 degrees during its first cycle. This supplies extra heat to warm the enclosure without too much or too quick dropping in the oven temperature.

Thermostats may be greatly affected by details of placement and of heat distribution, so that they may not give expected results even when perfectly accurate. In addition, they may be inaccurate in themselves. The combination of these possibilities makes it advisable to test them occasionally.

An oven might be tested with a thermometer, but a question might arise as to which side of a disagreement was wrong. Browning of sensitive baked goods, such as cookies, against experience or a good recipe, or other comparisons, may be used.

Signal Light. Signal lights are not exactly controls, but they supply important data for control.

Many appliances are equipped with a small light, usually red, that indicates that current is on. Some are lighted whenever the unit is plugged in, some only when a heating element is switched on, and others indicate that the unit is fully hot and that current has been switched off by a thermostat.

There may be a light for each burner or unit, or only one for the whole appliance.

Such a light, or lights, can be very useful, but only after you have learned their meaning.

HOT PLATES

Hot plates are portable electric surface cookers. There are a few very light, very simple and rather unsafe models with a single small heating unit, that are chiefly used by travelers who wish to do water heating or very light cooking in hotels and rooming houses.

The two-burner models for kitchen and family use all have at least OFF-ON switches, and usually offer a choice of LOW, MEDIUM and HIGH heat. One burner may have greater heat capacity then the other. With both burners fully on, current consumption is about 15 amperes (1800 watts), which means that one can be used on a standard house circuit if it has no load. But there is only about half to 2/3 the heating capacity of two standard electric range burners.

Cheaper models may have bare heating wires, wound into spirals and recessed into a porcelain backing which supports the pan being heated. Sometimes during moving such wires get shaken or forced out of the grooves. Never use one that is in this condition, as the wire will be live when current is on, and will go into the body and metal handle of a pan placed on it.

In better units, range-type insulated elements are standard.

Hot plates may be used for cooking or heating food outside the kitchen, for keeping buffet food hot (although most models seem to be too hot for this) and for emergency use if the range is out of order.

TOASTERS

Well Toaster. The two-slice automatic well toaster is now practically standard for kitchen use. A large family may use a four-slice model built on the same principle.

There are usually four vertical heating elements. The two wells or slots include fixed wires that keep the bread upright, and a movable floor with two positions: UP, for putting bread in and taking it out, and DOWN for toasting. The floor is controlled by a handle or handles at one end of the toaster, and by a timer or a thermostat which can be regulated to produce various degrees of toasting, from LIGHT to DARK.

If there is a thermostat, it may operate on only one well, which should be marked.

There should be a sliding tray in the bottom for convenience in removing crumbs.

Most surfaces are uninsulated metal, which may get very hot. In many models there is danger of touching live wiring, so the toaster should be disconnected before a de-crumbing operation.

To make toast, you set the adjustment for the color you want, place bread in the wells and push down the handle. It locks in bottom position and automatically turns on the current (an automatic toaster is normally left plugged in all the time). After an interval, the timer or thermostat will release the platform, and it will be pushed or snapped up by springs so that the toast can be easily removed with the fingers.

Once in a while an over-enthusiastic snap-up will throw toast up in the air, but this is unusual.

Means are provided to raise the rack for inspection of progress, at any time. In some models you simply raise the same handle with which you pushed it down. Others have a separate release button.

Well toasters are designed to operate with standard slices of bread, which are about 4 x 4 inches, either regular thickness (1/2 inch) or thin (3/8 inch). Slices of French or other bread that are too small to be lifted within reach are a problem. They can usually be dumped out by turning the toaster upside down, but you will need thick gloves, as the toaster walls get very hot. And unless you are more conscientious than most about cleaning the crumb tray, you are likely to get an embarrassing pile of crumbs along with the toast.

Another procedure is to make sure the lift is up, then spear the toast with a plastic fork, or some other nonmetallic utensil, and lift it up. There are two objections to using a metal fork. One is that it might touch a live wire with spectacular results. The other is that it might damage delicate parts.

If you must use metal, disconnect the toaster and be very careful.

Timers and Thermostats. The timer in a toaster must be adjustable, as prefer-ence in color of toast varies, as does the speed of browning of different types of bread. Fresh bread is slower to toast than stale bread, and browning time is also affected by the type of flour, presence or absence of raisins, refrigerator or freezer chill, and other factors. More time is needed when the toaster starts cold than when it is hot.

These factors, and differences in the basic speed of the toaster itself, cause toasting time to vary from 50 seconds to over 3 minutes. LIGHT setting on the adjustment is for minimum time.

Many of the irregularities in toast color that occur with timers may be avoided by use of a toaster with a thermostat. There is usually a close relationship between surface temperature and color. Such a toaster might not need any adjustment to change from using room-temperature bread to slices fresh out of the freezer, although the toasting time could be twice as long. Nor would it

Courtesy of National Presto Industries

Fig. 37-13. Two-slice automatic toaster

necessarily need a change of adjustment with bread of different freshness.

However, the thermostat will need to be adjusted for the way in which the bread surface reflects heat, which is a difficult quality to judge from inspection.

One bread might reflect heat so effectively that it would trip the thermostat before the bread started to brown; a bread with poorer reflecting qualities might dry out or burn on the same thermostat adjustment. There are no rules for anticipating these differences, except your experience with the breads that you use.

With either system, if the toast is too dark, you might be able to lighten it by holding it vertically and scraping the surface with a knife. This will take care of lightening the color, but it may still be too dry. Deeply burned edges may be cut off.

If the toast is too light you can try again. A timer should then usually be adjusted to LIGHT, or the toast should be watched and brought up for inspection every few seconds. The thermostat type should be turned toward DARK. Sometimes a thermostat will be stubborn about rejecting a particular slice of bread untoasted, but you can usually keep it at work by holding down the handle.

Slow toasting tends to produce a dry hot product, greater speed leaves it moister and less hot inside for the same surface color.

Serving. Whenever possible, toast should be served immediately, hot out of the toaster. If this is not possible, wrap it lightly in cloth or put it in a warm place.

Hot toast should not be placed on a cold surface. This will cause moisture to condense in its under side, making it soggy. Cloth, paper or any support that allows air circulation reduces this effect.

Some people like toast so pale that it is barely warmed, others prefer it dark and crisp. It may be eaten dry, with butter or margarine, and/or with jelly, jam, peanut butter or other spreads.

Fig. 37-14. Electric broiler

BROILER

An electric broiler may be used instead of a broiler in a range because of greater convenience, less heating of the kitchen or preference for cooking outside of the kitchen. In addition, many of them have a spit-roasting or rotisserie attachment, which is less commonly found in a range.

There are two basic types, open and cabinet. The open ones serve simply as broilers and rotisseries, while the cabinet models are enclosed like an oven, are equipped with thermostats, and can be used for a limited amount of baking.

There is a variety of sizes and shapes in both types, with weight from 5 to 28 pounds, and current requirement 9 to 15 amperes (1100 to 1800 watts). They are from 1-1/2 to 2 feet long, and 6 to 13 inches in their other two dimensions. Some have carrying handles and some do not.

The low current requirement permits using them in a standard modern house circuit, if nothing else is turned on. Heating can be expected to be slower than in a range, with its much heavier heating units and insulated walls.

Some of these appliances have the heating element over the food, some under it. The smaller cabinets may provide for either way — you just turn them upside down. There is a pan or tray to catch drippings, which may be part of the burner mounting, or separate.

The walls and particularly the top of a cabinet may get very hot. This may be turned to advantage by building a griddle into the top.

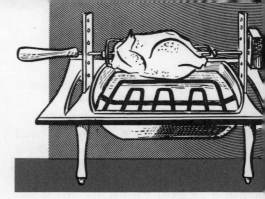

Fig. 37-15. Rotisserie

Rotisserie. The broiler may be bought principally to obtain the rotisserie. This usually consists of a horizontal metal bar centrally located under or over the heating element. It is rotated slowly by an electric motor, and can be adjusted upward or downward to vary its exposure to heat.

The object to be cooked is usually impaled on the bar, and fastened to it by a pair of sliding forks. Or a rack may be placed on the bar, and a pair of objects tied to it, one on each side. A whole chicken or other bird would be spitted (impaled) on the bar, a cut-up chicken, steaks, or chops would be put on the rack.

It might be necessary to tie down chicken legs to prevent them from getting too near the heat, and to keep them in balance.

A rotating object causes vibration and even pounding if it has more weight on one side of the axle than another. An effort should be made to get a proper balance with the first insertion. If action is rough, it should be adjusted until the turning is reasonably smooth. In most cases of unbalance, slowing the rate of rotation reduces the vibration.

Rotation of food under a broiler permits much deeper penetration of the cooking effect in proportion to surface changes than is obtained by broiling on a flat rack. The meat is also self-basting, as melted grease will creep along the surface, pulled down by gravity but raised by rotation, for some time before dripping off. However, the cook must still be careful that no parts are dried out or burned by being exposed to more than their share of heat, and perhaps by being placed so that the moving grease does not reach them.

Rotisseries are frequently used outdoors, if there is electric current in the area. This is all right in dry weather, but the insulation on the wiring is seldom designed to withstand moisture. A damp day, a sudden shower, or being left outdoors in the dew might easily produce short circuits that would make the cooker dangerous to people as well as to fuses.

ROASTER

A roaster or oven such as the one in Figure 37-16 is as satisfactory as a range oven in quality of roasting. These units may be obtained in various sizes and with a range of equipment although they seem to be declining in popularity. Basically, there is a frame or tub of metal, insulated, with heating elements in the walls and floor, and a smooth, sealed inner surface. A large pan fits snugly inside it, and has overlapped edges to prevent spill from getting between it and the oven walls.

The snug-fitting hinged or lift-off top is usually of light aluminum, and includes a glass window. One or more racks may be placed in the pan.

There may be an overhead broiler attachment also, which may be arranged so that it cannot be turned on at the same time as the oven units. Current requirement may be very large.

Fig. 37-16. Portable oven

The roaster itself cannot safely be placed in water, and it is too heavy to carry to the sink anyhow. The liner pan can be removed and washed. It may be possible to turn this pan over and use it for a lid, and the roaster tub for a pan, to increase the height to allow for a large turkey.

This roaster must be used with the cover in place, as it serves the purpose of the door in a regular oven. This does not prevent satisfactory browning and development of excellent flavor.

FRYERS

Frypan. The electric frypan can be one of the most useful of the extra cookers. It offers a large frying area with thermostatic control, can be used as a saucepan and easily kept down to simmering temperature if desired, warms coffee cake and leftovers quickly and easily and can even do a little roasting and baking. It can be used for cooking at the table, Japanese style.

Most of these pans have a cooking area about 10 inches square, sides 1-1/2 to 2 inches high, and domed lids giving a clearance from the floor of 4-1/4 to 5-1/2 inches. The lid may be arranged so that it can be propped up in one or more positions. Current consumption is between 1000 and 1500 watts.

These pans are made of aluminum. Many of them have a non-stick surface, but others are plain aluminum, or have a stainless steel lining. There are usually two handles. Thermostats are almost always the plug-in type, on the electric wire. When this is pulled out, the pan is submersible and can be washed in the sink.

Coffee cake or rolls being heated should not rest on the floor of the pan, as the bottom might harden or burn before the inner parts were warm. You should rest them on a trivet, or on a foil plate that has been slightly bent or crumpled so that it touches the pan in only a few spots.

An electric griddle is a frypan with very low sides. It does not have a cover, and lacks the wide range of usefulness of the full frypan.

Waffle Iron. The waffler, also called waffle baker and waffle iron, is one of the first of the electric appliances. It was described earlier, under WAFFLES, page 445.

A waffle baker may also be fixed for changing over to a griddle. The smooth griddle surfaces may be the backs of the waffle-pattern grids, so that you release a catch, take them out, and turn them over. Or you may remove grids which are backed up by griddle surfaces. This arrangement

Courtesy of Mirro Aluminum Co.

Fig. 37-17. Electric frypan

usually makes a better griddle than a waffle baker, because of uneven transmission of heat to the waffle surface.

A griddle in a waffle baker frame is ideal for producing a certain kind of toasted cheese sandwich, and other items that profit by being heated and squeezed at the same time. If the surfaces can come close enough together, you can get evenly cooked flat bacon, if you like flat bacon, and if there is a way of disposing of the grease.

Fryer-Cooker. The fryer-cooker, Figure 3-10, is primarily designed to keep a large supply of fat or oil at a proper temperature

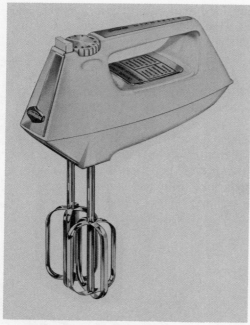

Fig. 37-18. Hand-held electric beater

for deep frying. It is comparatively wide and low for two good reasons, stability (a flood of near boiling oil on the kitchen personnel and floor represents COMPLETE disaster) and efficient cooking (with a heavy load, fat varies more in temperature from top to bottom than from side to side). This appliance can also be used for blanching vegetables in water before freezing, making stews and soups, and as an oven (range or Dutch).

A thermostatic control sets temperature up to 450° F.

The frying basket, colander-type or a coarse sieve, is used to lower food into the fat and salvage it again. It should have a device to hold it up out of the fat for draining. The handle is detachable, to allow putting the lid on.

There may be a spout that can be used for draining fat from the cooker, if it is not plugged with crumbs. This operation is best performed when the fat is warm. If it is hot

it is dangerous, if it is cold it is slow moving and will not drain completely. Draining is done into a storage container, and it is important to find a two-level area (stove top and chair?) that will support both units during the operation. If there is no spout, you pick the cooker up and pour carefully.

It is very important that a deep fryer of this type be stable against overturning, that there is a working place for it where it will not be in any danger of being upset, and that the bottom be sufficiently insulated so that it will not cause heat damage to counter tops. It is much safer and more convenient than deep frying in a pot on a stove burner.

Thermostatic control is a convenience for anyone, but it is particularly important for people inexperienced in deep fat frying. It allows at least a close approximation of recipe-recommended temperature, without tedious turning up and down of heat, and testing with a thermometer. However, it is still important to have a frying thermometer, to check on real or imagined errors in the thermostat.

The frying operation itself is discussed in Chapter 3.

BEATERS, MIXERS AND BLENDERS

Food preparation often involves mixing,

Fig. 37-19. A beater and its work

smoothing, aerating and pulverizing foods. Basic tools are the egg beater and whisk, plus spoons of various sizes, and forks. But many of these jobs involve a considerable amount of time and effort, so that assistance by electric power may be very welcome.

It must be remembered, however, that many of these appliances are not made to do really heavy jobs and a stiff mix may force you back to hand work, unless you want to tamper with the recipe to get a thinner mix, or risk burning out a motor.

All home electric mixing devices have motors that use alternating current. Such a motor is designed to run at a fixed speed, and if forced below this speed by overloads it will overheat and burn out, requiring expensive repair. You can change the speed by a variable control, but whatever rate it is set at, it must actually turn.

There are few appliances that do not require storage and/or shelf space. This is often a stronger argument than cost against their purchase. And the ones that can perform the greatest variety of jobs best are the biggest. This is particularly true in the mixer family.

Beater. A simple electric beater, such as that shown in Figure 37-18, substitutes an electric motor for the hand crank. It may or may not have more power than a hand beater, but it is capable of much higher sustained speed. It should have a speed adjustment so that it can be used for slow mixing. The slow speeds produce better results in many jobs, and cause less splattering.

Beware of high speeds in shallow bowls, particularly if the sides have a flat slope. The mixture might fly away from the beater with enough force to completely redecorate the kitchen.

There is no supporting frame for the vanes. Each set of four is attached to a shaft, which is pushed up inside the motor frame for use, and pulled out for cleaning.

Courtesy of Sunbeam Appliance Co.

Fig. 37-20. Heavy duty electric mixer

The detents that holds the shafts may get tired after long use, so that you might have to rest the bottoms on your hand to keep them in until you can rest them on the bowl bottom.

These small electric beaters are used for the same purposes and in much the same manner as hand beaters. They need a little more storage space, and take a few extra seconds to assemble and plug in, but they can operate more rapidly and require only the effort of holding upright. But be careful not to beat a mix heavy enough to slow one down, as such overload may cause the motor to overheat and burn out.

It is desirable for an electric beater to have a heel stand, so that it can be set aside temporarily without putting the vanes on or in anything. An attachment for hanging it on a hook for storage might be handy.

If small children are or might be in the kitchen, the beater should be unplugged when it is not actually being used, as the switch is easy to manipulate and the vanes can easily damage fingers.

Mixer. The unit shown in Figure 37-20 consists of a heavy duty electric mixer with variable speed control, mounted in a stand which also supports a bowl on a power-rotated turntable. The turntable is off-center, so that the beater is near one side of the bowl, and the rotation of the bowl causes the same effect as moving the beater in a circle around the edges.

Beaters are shaped to work closely against the edges of special bowls, to minimize hand scraping during work.

This stirring-while-beating effect, and the usually strong construction and powerful motor of the beater allows the effortless and largely unattended mixing and/or beating of quite heavy mixtures, such as cake batter and mashed potatoes. However, each of them has its limits, and these may be quite low in some of the cheaper models. If the beaters seem to turn more slowly than they should for their speed setting, or if the mechanism is unusually noisy, the mixture may be too thick.

The easiest check is to put a hand on the motor case. It should be warm, but if it is hot, turn it off immediately. Most mixtures can be considerably thinned without noticeable damage to the product by adding one or two tablespoons of milk. This helps with mashed potatoes, but for them the most important item is boiling the potatoes until soft before trying to mash them.

There are also mixers in which the bowl is stationary and the beater head revolves in a small circle, for the same effect. In others the bowl is rotated by the action of the beater in the mixture, instead of by direct power. There may be one, two or rarely three different sizes of bowl which can be used.

As with all beaters, best results are usually obtained if the mixture is at least half an inch deep, but not much above the top of the curve of the vanes. Shallower depths waste energy and cause splatter, deeper ones may allow the mix to work up into the beater, or to splatter or overflow the side of the bowl.

A great variety of attachments are available, which are attached and used with varying degrees of simplicity and difficulty. They include slicers, grinders, blenders, sharpeners, juice extractors and drink mixers. The mixer head may be permanently hinged to the stand, or removable for use as a portable beater.

Mixers are bulky and fairly expensive. If you have frequent use for one and the place to put it conveniently, it is worth while. Some people believe that cooking is impossible without it. But it deserves good care. It should be wiped clean after every use, the beaters taken out and washed, and a plastic cover put over when it is not in use. If the instructions call for oiling it, oil it in just the way they say.

But above all, don't work it so hard that it slows down and heats up.

Blender. A blender might be described as an upside down, high speed mixer.

A motor, with control switches, is located

Fig. 37-21. Electric blender

Courtesy of Sunbeam Appliance Co.

in the base. It turns a two-piece vertical shaft that extends through the bottom of a container, and turns a beater consisting of 4 short, sharp knives.

The container is usually glass and has a cover to prevent food from splashing out. The bottom may be (and should be) removable. The top may be two-piece, with a small inner cap or measuring cup which allows adding materials during beating, without losing the splash protection at the edges.

A number of beater speeds are provided through push buttons or a rotating switch. Top speed is very high, 8,000 to 10,000 revolutions a minute. This speed and the sharpness enables it to chop, grind, shred or liquefy a great variety of materials, some of which are quite hard or tough.

In general, low speeds are used for soft materials and for powders to be mixed with water or other fluids, medium speed for grinding coffee, chopping nuts and making crumbs; and high speed for heavy sauces, batters and grinding very hard material.

The space in which the knives work is small, so that coarse or resistant material may arch over them. This can be prevented by cutting food in fairly small pieces, no dimension over one inch for vegetables or 1/2 inch for cheese, by adding water to force circulation of the pieces, and by pushing the material down and to the center whenever necessary with a narrow-bladed rubber spatula.

Any liquid required by the recipe should be put in first, to reduce possible sticking of solids to the bottom.

Action is usually very fast, and is completed in seconds rather than minutes. Directions usually do not specify time, but call for stopping when the correct texture or appearance is reached.

The removable bottom is convenient in getting out thick and sticky materials, and for cleaning the container and beater after use. But it is important to screw the locking cap on firmly, and not to twist the con-

Fig. 37-22. Electric can opener

tainer when settling it in place or removing it.

If the bottom is fixed in place, the easiest cleaning method is to run the beater on high speed for a few seconds with water and detergent in the container.

CAN OPENER

The electric can opener operates in the same general way as the wall rotary described on page 693. Bringing the clamp handle all the way down not only forces the drive gear against it and the cutting wheel into it, but also closes a switch so that a motor turns the gear.

The opened can is removed downwardly after fully releasing the clamp handle. A table model may not have clearance for a large can unless it is placed at the edge of the table.

This electric type requires a little less effort than one with a hand crank. The present cost is around $8.00 to $20.00, and a

Courtesy of Sunbeam Appliance Co.

Fig. 37-23. Electric knife

good one may last as long as the kitchen without any servicing other than cleaning. But some are unsatisfactory because of poor clamping or penetration, excessive noise, lack of power rotation of the cutting wheel and/or difficulty in cleaning.

In one model the noise is such that the neighbors can count the cans you are opening and estimate their size.

Even the best electric opener should be backed up by a hand-operated unit, in case of power failure.

An electric opener may be a complete unit, even including a built-in knife sharpener, or it may be just an accessory on a multiple-use power tool.

KNIVES

Electric. An electric or reciprocating knife usually consists of a pair of flat, coarse-toothed saw blades in close side-to-side contact, which are alternately moved rapidly forward and backward a short distance. The teeth of the two blades are always moving in opposite directions except for the moment when they are stopped at the end of their stroke.

Any material that is soft enough for the teeth to penetrate will be cut rapidly and smoothly. The action might be compared to that of a row of tiny scissors.

You apply very little pressure and do not use any sliding or sawing motion when cutting with an electric knife. Do not expect to cut anything hard, as the teeth must dig in to get a grip. It is possible to cut very thin, straight slices even in meat that has a tendency to fall apart.

However, it is not a tool that necessarily does a good job on the first trial. Consider-

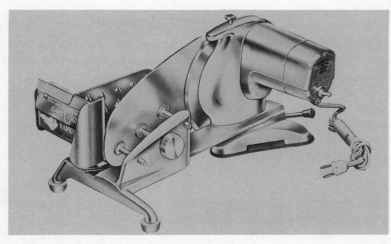

Courtesy of General Slicing Machine Co.

Fig. 37-24. Electric rotary slicer

able practice may be required before you can take full advantage of its abilities.

At present, most of these units use house current, which is supplied through a wire that enters the back of the handle, and which may be somewhat inconvenient because of weight and tangles.

Battery power disposes of the cord but involves the weight of the batteries, and the possibility of power loss or failure in the middle of a carving job.

Rotary. The motor driven rotary slicer is useful when large quantities of boneless meat or other even-textured foods are to be sliced.

The unit in Figure 37-24 consists of a flat, sharp-rimmed steel disc which is turned by an electric motor, and a sliding or hinged rack or table which supports the food and moves it into contact with the knife-disc.

There is an adjustable stop that regulates the thickness of the slices, which usually can be made very thin, and which will at any rate all be the same. On each backward movement of the rack after cutting a slice, the rack is moved sideward to bring the freshly cut side of the meat against the stop. It is of course important to hold the meat in such a way that fingers cannot get within range of the knife.

There are non-electric models in which the knife is turned by a hand crank, but they are not as satisfactory, as the average person may find difficulty in turning the disc fast enough and with sufficient force to do a clean slicing job. A disc is not a particularly efficient knife, except at high speeds.

You have to have quite a bit of meat to cut before it pays to find a slicer in the closet, set it up, clean it and put it away. The meat must be free of bones, and solid enough not to be torn apart by the rotation of the knife.

Unless you do a lot of meat slicing, or are particularly inept with a carving knife, a slicer may not be worth either its cost or its storage space to you. But it does beautiful work.

38
RANGES (STOVES)

GENERAL DESCRIPTION

A range, which is more frequently called a stove, is a major appliance that is responsible for most (and often all) the cooking that is done in a kitchen. It has surface heat units plus one or more ovens. It is almost always heated by electricity or gas. It may be a free-standing unit complete in itself, built-in with other appliances and cabinets or divided so that the burners are in one place and the oven(s) in another.

Operation of the various styles is basically similar.

A free-standing range, Figure 38-1, has a flat upper cooking surface, under which is an oven, and perhaps a storage drawer also. There are several widths, from 19 to 42 inches, but usually one standard height, 36 inches, and a single front-to-back depth of 25 inches. These uniform measurements facilitate kitchen planning.

A rear panel, called a backsplash or guard, reduces or prevents grease from spattering on the wall behind the range, and serves as a mounting for controls and indicators.

A deluxe range with upper and lower ovens is shown in Figure 38-2. The upper oven can be used without stooping, and its supporting back plate assures that the wall will not be spattered. The cooking surface, which is now in the middle, is sometimes arranged to slide forward when in use, so that it will not be too thoroughly roofed over by the upper oven.

Construction and Finish. The frame of the range is usually made of steel pieces welded together. The outside surfaces are made up of double panels of sheet steel, separated by a layer of rock wool or fiber glass insulation. Outside finish is usually enamel of either the porcelain or synthetic type, but is occasionally stainless steel or other metal for some parts.

The enamels are offered in white and in an increasing variety of colors.

Traditionally, oven linings have been porcelain enamel in dark colors and/or speckled patterns to make staining less conspicuous. Now they are often chromium plated or coated with Teflon. Both finishes provide good appearance and easier cleaning, and reflection of heat from the bright chromium adds a small amount to oven efficiency.

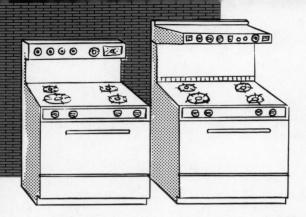

Fig. 38-1. Single-oven ranges, right hand one with warming shelf

Linings may be either solidly fastened or removable for cleaning.

Catalytic linings are discussed below under Self-Cleaning Ovens.

Leveling. The range is supported at the four corners on short legs, some or all of which include a leveling screw, which is a threaded adjustment which raises or lowers its corner of the appliance when it is turned.

Weight must be taken off a leg in order to adjust it. A range is heavy, 135 to 350 pounds, and offers a poor grip for lifting. It can be pried up by a bar, but care is needed to avoid injuring its light metal covering and the floor tile. If it is possible to tilt by lifting with fingers only, or by pushing against the top, this should be done.

If legs are not adjustable, a tapered wood shingle makes an excellent shim. The projecting part can be cut or broken off when the job is finished.

A carpenter's level is the best tool for leveling up a range. Lay it on the bare cooktop if possible, and if not, across the top of burners. Place it diagonally, then adjust a leg at either end of it until its bubble is centered. Then do the other diagonal in the same way, then re-check the first one.

Finish by checking front to back, and side to side, and also see if the oven grate is level. If there are discrepancies, you can make compromises, or call a service man.

It is very important for proper baking and for shallow frying that the range be level.

Cooking Surface (Cooktop). According to practice in the industry (manufacture and service), the surface heat units are supposed to be called burners on a gas range and units or elements on an electric. However, it makes talking and writing about cookery much easier to follow the general custom of calling both of them burners.

A modern range usually has four burners. This is not adequate for relaxed preparation of a complicated meal, but it seems to have been agreed upon as the most satisfactory arrangement. Manufacturers sometimes offer their wide models with 5 or 6 burners, but they do not seem to find the popularity that they deserve.

Burners may be arranged in many ways. When burners are close together, a pan handle is likely to get too much heat from

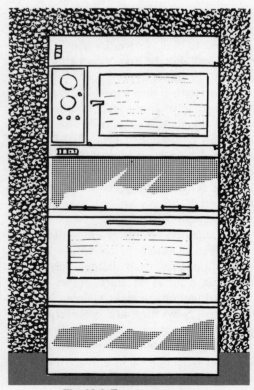

Fig. 38-2. Two-oven range

the adjoining one, or be left projecting dangerously over the side of the range. But this problem may be preferred to using valuable space just to separate them.

Arrangement is more critical with gas than with electric stoves, as their raised grates cause severe tipping to any pan or bowl that is not fully on the top or on a grate. Electrics are or should be less uneven, and their units provide a reasonably stable parking area when they are cold.

It is usual to have two "sizes" of burner, one or two extra strong and the others standard. These may be the same apparent size in gas, but the more powerful ones are bigger in the electrics.

A cooking (frying) well or a griddle may replace one or two of the burners.

The cooktop usually has slightly raised edges, which make spills less likely to go over them. This is a very desirable feature, specially at the sides, where it might be very difficult to clean in the narrow gap between the stove and the next appliance. The cooktop can usually be raised to clean up material that has spilled through burner holes into cups or a pan.

Most cooktops are part of ranges, but they are also manufactured and sold separately, for installation as part of countertops.

Oven. An oven is a heatable box, in which food can be cooked from all sides by hot air and radiated and reflected heat. The whole box, except for the floor in gas ovens, is heavily insulated for efficiency, to prevent overheating the kitchen and for safety of people and appliances near it. However, it is desirable to allow some cool air to enter at the bottom and some hot air to leave through a vent at the top, as this circulation tends to prevent the formation of different temperature layers of air inside it, and is needed to renew the oxygen supply to gas burners.

Gas burners are usually placed under the floor, rather than in the oven itself. The

Fig. 38-3. A stove should be level

burner compartment may then serve as a broiler, or an additional burner for broiling may be put in the top of the oven. Electric elements are placed inside the oven, and are usually both in the bottom and the top.

Heat is built up and maintained in the oven by radiation from the heated units or

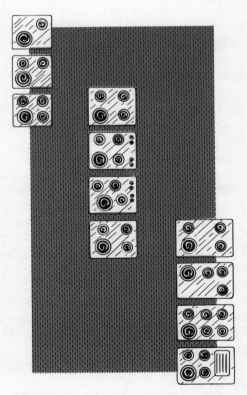

Fig. 38-4. There are many arrangements for burners

floor, by upward movement of heated air and by reflection of heat from all inner surfaces.

Interference with any part of this heat system will change the characteristics of the oven. Bottom radiation is often seriously reduced by allowing spilled material to accumulate on the floor and around lower elements, or by putting foil or cookie tins in the bottom to catch spill. Too-large or too-crowded-together baking pans, or a clogged vent, interfere with air circulation.

Accumulated grime interferes with the reflective ability of the lining.

An oven is usually 18 inches deep, and may be from 16 to 24 inches wide and 13 to 15 high. It contains one or more flat racks, made of thick stiff wire rather widely spaced, which rest on brackets or corrugations on the walls. They slide in and out, should include stops to prevent pulling them all the way out accidentally, and should be movable upward and downward into several positions.

Door. The door is usually hinged at the bottom, so that it can serve as a loading shelf when swung down to a horizontal position. It should be counterbalanced and/or equipped with stops so that it will stay partly open when desired.

Such opening may be to check progress of cooking, to keep down air heat during broiling, to change air circulation during tricky baking or just to heat the kitchen.

The door should be removable, usually by lifting straight up off the hinges while it is open. You can then wash the door in the sink, and get closer to the oven to clean inside it.

A window in the door permits you to observe progress of cooking without opening it. There should be a light inside the oven.

Self-Cleaning Oven. Cooking causes grease, grime and spilled food to deposit and build up on oven walls and other interior parts. It becomes hardened by heat,

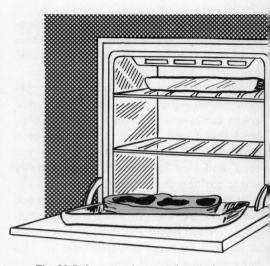

Fig. 38-5. An open door can be used as a temporary shelf

and is usually difficult and messy to remove. Methods are mentioned on page 674.

The self-cleaning-by-heat oven can be raised to a temperature of 800 to 1000° F, which is hot enough to incinerate all food remainders. The organic part is distilled or burned off as vapor, leaving only a film of loose dust behind. This should be wiped out with a damp cloth.

Special construction is needed to obtain such a high temperature. Insulation is very heavy, so that the oven is somewhat smaller than in standard construction in the same size range. The upper air vent may be fitted with a cooling device or a smoke eliminator. The door has a special gasket, to give it an almost air tight fit. There may be an additional heating element or elements.

Special controls are needed, which vary among different models. There is a special switch or switch position to start the cleaning operation, which should have its own signal light. There is an oven lock which prevents opening the door when the switch is in cleaning position and the oven has passed a certain temperature, often around 500° F.

This lock avoids the danger of a flameup if an opened door allowed a burst of fresh air to reach the superheated soil. Once started, the cleaning is automatically timed, and will go through heating, holding and cooling periods without attention. The timer is adjustable in some models, and fixed in others. The job takes 2 or 3 hours.

In a 2-oven range, both may be self-cleaning, or one may have this feature and the other have removable linings, which can be placed in the first one.

Self-cleaning does not permit you to be sloppy without penalty. A very dirty oven and a leaking door gasket may produce an uncomfortable amount of smoke.

Your wire shelf racks will lose their shiny finish if left in during cleaning. And some models might not give themselves a thorough cleaning job everywhere. And you do have to wipe away the ash when the cleaning is finished.

It is useful to have a smoke hood, or some forced ventilation system for the kitchen, if you are going to do heavy cleaning this way.

Cost of cleaning is low, ranging from 9 to 18 cents in different models, with electricity figured at 3 cents a kilowatt hour. The extra cost of purchase is partly compensated by the generally superior quality of the ranges carrying this feature, almost double-fast oven heating for ordinary cooking and thick insulation that prevents oven heat from being wasted in the kitchen.

Perhaps the most serious drawback is the addition of another complication to oven control boards, many of which were already a little too intricate for many cooks.

Another self-cleaning arrangement is to include catalytic material in oven linings, that gradually disintegrates thin layers of food. Action starts somewhere above 300° F, but is most effective at 400 or higher.

Such linings may be only on the sides and back, or may be complete except for the door.

Vents and Hoods. The upper vent for an electric oven, if there is one, usually opens under a surface unit. The gas oven vent is likely to be in or around the back-splash. In either case it is likely to handle a considerable volume of air when the oven is hot.

This air carries both the variable amount of dirt and fumes present in the kitchen air, and extra amounts coming from cooking in the oven. It will carry very heavy contamination during broiling and high temperature roasting, particularly if food is allowed to burn.

The vent should have a filter to partly clean the air coming out of it. If it does not, and it is easily accessible, you can provide a makeshift filter by packing the opening loosely with medium steel wool which has been dipped in hot cooking oil and then drained thoroughly.

Vapor from ovens and from top burner cooking tends to make a kitchen dull and dirty; rapidly if cooking is careless and slowly if it is conservative.

Fig. 38-6. Self-contained smoke hood

Courtesy of Tappan Co.

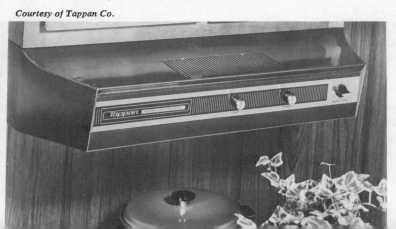

Such vapor and dirt, and a large percentage of cooking smells, can be eliminated by installing and using a smoke hood. This is a hood or canopy over the cooking area, in which there is a suction fan that pulls the air through filters. It may then be circulated back into the room, or discharged outdoors through a pipe.

Filters may be made of fiberglass, aluminum or other heat resistant material. They are removable and washable, and should have a long life. If discharge is into the room, there should be an additional activated charcoal filter to take outdoors. This is replaced when it gets used up.

If hood filters are not properly maintained, their passages, fans and other parts will become coated with grease. This is a fire hazard and will probably smell. Cleaning them can be a major undertaking, out of proportion to the small nuisance of cleaning filters.

A hood is not cheap, the fan is likely to be noisy, and it is a responsibility to keep it clean. However, it can easily be worth all that if it saves one redecorating job in the kitchen.

Broiler. Any compartment or support where food can be placed underneath or over a burner can serve as a broiler. In a gas range it is usually a compartment below the oven. In an electric it is the oven itself, preferably with only the top burner turned on.

Food to be broiled may be placed in a shallow pan, or on a rack or perforated tray over a drippings pan. A rack without a pan might be fine for cooking food, but it would allow fat and juices to make a hopeless mess of the bottom of the compartment.

Shallow pans, that hold drippings around the food, are well suited to a number of items, including such widely different ones as fish and candied sweet potatoes. However, the modern housewife is expected to do almost all her broiling on an arrangement similar to that in Figure 4-9.

A wide drip pan is supported by brackets on the sides of the broiler drawer, compartment or oven. It can be placed up near the burner, or down away from it. A tray in the pan has slots that permit grease to drain into the pan, but are not large or numerous enough to encourage the drippings below it to catch fire. This is an important point, discussed on page 71.

The speed and quality of broiling is affected by the intensity of the heat and by the distance between it and the surface of the food. In days before thermostats, the cook could regulate a gas broiler flame by turning its control valve.

Now that the valve handle can often be turned only to temperatures and not to flame size, broiling may have to be done at maximum flame and heat. Then the only way to regulate the cooking is to move the food upward or downward. The same situation is found in most electric broilers.

This is inefficient, and is reminiscent of the Indian's comment, "White man make big fire and stay far away, Indian make little

Fig. 38-7. Small fire, close

fire and stay close." The cook is often forced to move a hot broiler pan up or down, the compartment may need the door opened because of excessive heat and even the kitchen gets too hot.

Broiling under these conditions is likely to produce a maximum amount of disturbance, but its excellence of flavor and texture cannot be obtained by any other cooking method.

Some ranges do offer controllable size or temperature in a broiling unit, and this flexibility is very much in their favor.

A rotisserie, also known as a spit-broiler or spit-roaster, is offered as an option with some deluxe ranges. This accessory is discussed on page 738.

Thermostat. Thermostats were described on page 734. Range ovens usually have the hydraulic type, in which heat causes liquid to expand in a bulb, go through a tube and move a switch.

An oven thermostat usually has an overrun device, that permits heat to rise 10 to 20 per cent above its setting during the first heating of a cold oven. This is to allow for the walls not being fully heated, so that temperature will drop much more rapidly after the burner goes off, than it will in later cycles.

An oven thermostat may also be operated by a probe. This is inserted into a roast, and the desired internal temperature is set on a dial. When this point is reached inside the meat, the oven will be turned off, or turned down to a keep-warm setting.

Timers. Timers were discussed on page 6, under ORGANIZATION.

Oven timers are of the action type. In electric ranges they turn it on and off, in gas they usually only turn it off. In some models of each they may permit it to keep going on a low or keep-warm temperature, by changing a thermostat setting.

A common arrangement on electrics is to have two clocks that have hour hands only. One of them, usually on the left, is set for the time that the oven should turn on, the other for the time it should turn off, the interval between them being the cooking time. Then the control must be activated by pushing a button or turning a knob, according to the make and model.

When the timer has completed its work it should be put out of action, again by proper treatment of some button or knob. If you forget this, you may find your ordinary cooking mysteriously (and perhaps disastrously) interrupted.

The oven should always be turned off on its own control while not in use. And of course it must be turned on and to the temperature you want whenever the timer is supposed to operate it.

GAS RANGES

Gas ranges are available in many different makes, styles and qualities. Selection among them must be made on a basis of money available and personal preferences.

There are two organizations which oversee standards of quality for the industry. If a range conforms to stringent standards of safety, durability and performance, the manufacturer can put on it seals of approval from the American Gas Association and/or the Gas Appliance Manufacturers Association.

These seals are worth looking for on a new range.

Gas. Most cooking gas is now either natural gas piped from wells, or "bottled" butane or propane made by refining the natural substance. There is another type of gas, manufactured from coal as a byproduct of making coke, which was once the principal domestic gas but which is now seldom used in homes.

The heat content of gas is measured in British Thermal Units, abbreviated as BTU. One BTU is the amount of heat required to raise one pint (or pound) of water 1° F. For example, it would take 140 BTUs to bring a pint of water at 72° up to boiling.

Type of gas	Heat Content, BTUs per cubic foot
Butane	3175
Propane	2500
Natural	1050
Manufactured	525

Courtesy of Countywide Gas Service

Fig. 38-8. Heat content of cooking gas

A decitherm is a larger measure which equals 10,000 BTUs.

Figure 38-8 shows the content of four kinds of gas, in BTUs per cubic foot. Because of the differences in heating ability and other characteristics, it is necessary to make alterations in burners if the supply is changed from one gas to another.

Maximum flame temperature for either natural or bottled gas that has been mixed with the correct proportion of air is said to be about 3600° F. Because of imperfect proportioning and mixing, and other factors, actual flames usually have a lower temperature.

Bottled Gas Supply. Bottled gas is usually supplied to homes in one of two ways. It may be delivered in individual cylinders, holding about 850 cubic feet (at 60° F at atmospheric pressure, which is 2,165,000 BTUs) or be carried in small tank trucks and pumped into a fixed tank through a meter.

Cylinders are installed in pairs. One is connected to the line to the stove, the other is shut off. When the first tank is emptied, it is shut off and the other one is connected. The shift between tanks may be done manually by turning valves, or automatically by a pressure-balancing mechanism.

The automatic device may raise a signal to indicate that the change has been made, and the provident householder should order a filled cylinder immediately.

With the meter system, the responsibility is the supplier's. However, the size of the tank and the frequency of filling it are based on the average consumption of gas. If this should be greatly increased at any time, because of guests, experiments, leaks or other reasons, the supplier should be notified. He can then make a special trip if it seems to be indicated.

In both types of supply there is a pressure regulating valve that maintains full pressure at the stove until almost the last bit of gas is used. Then the burners simply go out. This is a common but not very serious annoyance with a pair of tanks with hand valves. It is uncommon with automatic controls or metered pumping, but can be disastrous to a meal.

Propane is the standard bottled gas in northern areas, as it has the lowest boiling point, −45° F. Butane has a boiling point of about −32°, and is used in southern areas where this does not create a problem.

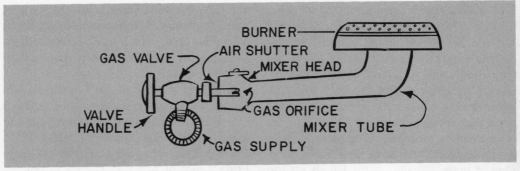

Fig. 38-9. Gas burner construction

Pumped-in gas may be billed on the basis of gallons (bottled gas is liquid at the 100-pound pressure used). Propane contains about 91,500 BTUs per gallon, at 60° F.

Burners. Figure 38-9 shows a cross section of a top burner. Gas under pressure is admitted through a control valve, then goes through a small jet opening called an orifice into a mixing chamber or tube. Its high speed pulls air into the chamber through adjustable ports, and moves the resulting mixture of gas and air through a tube into the burner. It emerges through a series of holes and combines with additional air as it burns.

Air should mix with the gas in proper quantity to provide just enough oxygen to combine with all the burnable substances, chiefly hydrogen and carbon. A proper mixture provides a clean, steady flame, sharply divided into inner and outer zones of different shades of blue.

If there is not enough air in the mixture the flames will be yellow at the tips; if no air is being admitted into the mixing chamber the flames will be almost all yellow, like a match or candle flame. The yellow flame will be much longer than the blue one, not nearly as hot, and will make a black, hard-to-remove deposit of soot on pan bottoms.

Too much air will produce flames that are more intense in color and smaller. They will tend to dance away from the burner, and are likely to either go out or flash back to the orifice, burning with a roaring sound and heating the tube and burner instead of the pan. Shut off the gas immediately if this happens.

The control valve can be opened to any point on its range, from just barely enough gas to maintain a low flame to full high. Unfortunately, the motion is not always smooth. Some valves stick or bind slightly, causing jerky turning and occasional difficulty in regulating the flame exactly.

Sometimes the valve is fitted with three or more detents that cause it to click and

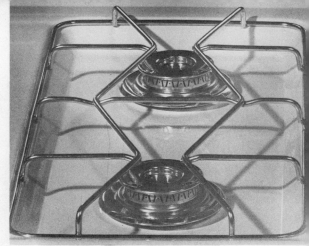

Courtesy of Caloric Corp.

Fig. 38-10. Burners and grate

hold lightly in position. These permit you to obtain and repeat certain sizes of flame, without special care or adjustment.

Adjustment. Gas mixture is usually adjusted by a service man, but if he is not available you may be able to do it yourself. The first and biggest problem is to locate the air ports into the mixing chamber. Their size is usually controlled by a rotating shutter locked by a screw.

Get in such a position that you can loosen and move the shutter and watch the burner flame. With the burner turned high, loosen the screw and move the shutter until the tips of the flames are yellow. Then reduce the opening slowly until the color just disappears.

Next turn the gas down slowly toward the smallest flame, watching for yellow tips. If they appear, and do not disappear in a few seconds, reduce the air further until the

Fig. 38-11. Removable cooktop

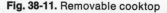

Courtesy of Caloric Corp.

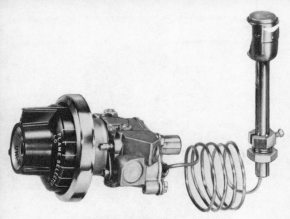

Fig. 38-12. Thermostatic top burner

tips are blue again. When you can turn the flames up and down through their full range without yellow appearing for more than a moment, lock the adjustment.

If the burner holes are partly clogged (almost always the result of food boiling over the sides of pans) the flames will be uneven in length, and may not be present at some of the burner ports. Try poking the holes clean with a toothpick.

If this does not fix it, take the burner out of the range, soak it in hot water and detergent, and clean it with a stiff brush, possibly assisted by a piece of wire, a toothpick or a thin nail.

Cleaning is easy with the thin caps used on modern burners, but more difficult with the heavy castings formerly used.

The burner and tube assembly is not connected to the gas system when the valve is turned off. It is usually possible to lift them out without using tools, after taking off grates and tinware and raising the cooktop.

However, burners may be clamped or bolted down when the range is shipped from the factory. If the installer forgot to remove these tie-downs, you will have to do it to get the burner out.

Pulsation of a flame or flashing back to the orifice may be caused by improper seating of part of the burner, a bent burner ring or some other mechanical defect.

Some stoves have non-adjustable mixing chambers. Gas sprays from a nozzle across an open air space into a tube. These are supposed to provide an accurate mixture without adjustments. If trouble does develop, you need a service call.

Burner Accessories. A gas burner must have a grate above it to support pans in or above the flame. There is usually a ring shaped bowl or aeration plate under the burner, and a spill tray below that.

The grates usually consist of rings holding slender fingers which support the cooking utensil. They are usually made of enameled cast iron, which is brittle enough so that you had better not drop one, or of stainless steel. The enamel is generally black or dark, and the steel darkens with use.

The grate rests in sockets in the cooktop, or top plate of the stove. Set it in place, then turn it until it clicks into the sockets. The grate should not shift or rock, and is supposed to be able to support a carefully centered object only 2-1/4 inches in diameter.

Its upper surface is about one inch above the cooktop. This allows flame and heat to spread under and around a wide pan without subjecting the top enamel to excessive heat.

The spill ring is set below and outside the burner. It looks good, and it may regulate the rising of free air around the burner. It seldom has capacity to hold much spill, or at least not more than enough to make it necessary to take it out and wash it. It may be protected by a disposable ring of foil.

There should be a sliding tray or trays under the burners, flat with edges turned up just enough so that a cup or two of liquid might be held in it. It slides out the front, or is reached by raising the cooktop. It should be checked now and then, even if you are not aware of having dirtied it.

There are also two-burner grates of similar construction that rest in depressions in the cooktop, and can be removed and replaced by simple lifting. These are usually stainless steel.

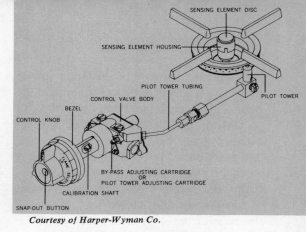

Courtesy of Harper-Wyman Co.

Fig. 38-13. Details, thermostatic burner

Thermostatic Burner (Uni-Matic). A thermostatically controlled top burner is offered as an option or as standard equipment on some ranges. It is designed to enable you to set a control knob at a desired temperature, and have a pan on the burner stay at or near it without further attention.

The thermostat is instructed by a small disc called a sensor or sensing plate, which is supported above the grate level at the center by a light spring. This presses against the bottom of a pan placed on the burner grate. Changes in disc temperature cause the thermostat to open and close the gas valve.

Figures 38-12 and 38-13 show such a unit. The control is marked with temperatures ranging from 140 up to 400°, and for low, medium and high flame.

You first put the pan of food on the grate. Then turn the control knob to HIGH, and leave it there until the burner ignites. If you don't want a high flame, turn the knob clockwise until the flame height suits you. Then push the knob down, and turn it counterclockwise to the temperature that you want.

The control should allow for the fact that the lower surface of the pan bottom is a little hotter than its upper surface where the food is cooked. This difference is greater with a thick iron pan than with a thin aluminum one. Some instruction books tell you to always use a thick aluminum pan. In any case, select a pan with a smooth clean bottom, and make sure that the sensor is clean, so that it can make a good contact.

When the pan reaches the set temperature, the thermostat will turn the gas down so the flame will be low, or go out. When the pan cools below the temperature setting the gas valve will be opened, and the flame will rise to the height at which you set it originally.

A high flame and/or a low temperature setting will cause the flame to go up and down frequently during cooking. A low flame might never reach a high temperature setting, so that the burner would be on continuously, and the only function of the thermostat would be to reassure you against possible over-heating.

Most satisfactory results may be obtained by keeping a flame that would just shut down occasionally.

The accuracy of a thermostat is always open to question. This one can be roughly checked by boiling water. If it is set at 212 to 215°, it should shut off when it has brought water to a strong boil. If it does not, adjust its temperature until it does shut off, and notice how near to (or far away from) 212° it is.

This unit acts as an ordinary burner if the control knob is not pushed down.

Using the Burners. For efficiency, the bottom of a pan should be about the same diameter as the burner flame. If the pan is smaller, heat will be wasted around the sides, the sides will get overheated, often causing browning or burning at the top line of the food, and the handle is likely to get too hot. All these difficulties can be reduced by turning down the flame.

A pan that is much too large for the burner tends to be heated too much in the center and not enough at the sides. Confined and reflected heat under it might damage enamel and chrome.

Pans should be placed so that their handles will not get overheated. A small pan on a big burner should be off center so that flame and heat will not come up around the base of the handle. And don't turn the pan so that the handle gets heat from another active burner. You can get a very quick and nasty burn from a hot metal handle. A wood or plastic handle won't burn you so badly, but it might go up in flames itself.

Also, pan handles should not project over the edge of the stove where they might be hit by passersby. It is best not to have the range next to a passageway, as it increases danger of upsetting pans by collision. You may not have enough space to avoid all these dangers, but do the best you can.

Try to get a habit of using a light touch on a pan handle, or any object on or near

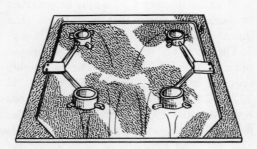

Fig. 38-14. Pilot tubes

a stove, as it might be very hot. The light touch will give you a small burn or none, where a he-man grip could cause real damage to your fingers. This applies not only to pans still on the stove, but also to others you might have moved away from it a few moments before.

It is good policy to leave cooked food on turned-off gas burners (which lose much of their heat in a few seconds), and to return empty pans to turned-off burners for cooling, after a double check to make sure that they are off.

Many kitchen surfaces are plastic that may be permanently marred by a hot pan, and a pan might warp if it is put on a cold or wet surface when it is hot.

PILOTS

Cooktop Pilot. Most ranges are equipped with one or more small, constantly burning pilots to light the burners automatically whenever they are turned on. The pilot is a small flame, with a gas consumption sometimes as low as 80 to 100 BTUs an hour. Pilots do not have mixing chambers, so the color is yellow.

There may be a pilot for each burner (rare), for each pair of burners or one for all four. A small flash tube runs from alongside the pilot flame to a lighter port in the burner. When gas-air mixture is admitted to the burner, some of it is directed by the lighter port through the tube, at the end of which it is ignited by the pilot.

The flame flashes back through the tube and lights the burner. Gas-air coming out of the lighter port then burns before it reaches the flash tube, so that it is just one of the many burner flames.

This is a delicate mechanism, and its proper operation depends on a number of factors. The first of these is flame size, which is controlled by a screw adjustment near the base of the pilot. A small or low flame is economical of gas and produces little heat, but it may not light the burner promptly or dependably, and it may even be blown out by the puff made by the mixture igniting in the flash tube. Or it might go out by itself.

Irregularities in gas supply, popping of a burner or stove cleaning are all threats to a weak pilot.

A too-high flame wastes gas, may heat parts of the cooktop too much and is likely to smoke. Correct height may be 1/4 to 1/2 inch.

If the flash tube is even slightly out of position, or if there is dirt in either the lighter port or the tube, gas-air may not go through it in sufficient quantity to ignite promptly, or perhaps at all.

In some ranges the burners will not light

properly unless they are turned on full. With less volume they either fail to light, or pop back into the mixing chamber.

According to American Gas Association standards a burner should light within 4 seconds of the gas reaching it, which means 5 or 6 seconds after it is turned on. This is a long time. A properly tuned up pilot-burner team should light in about 2 seconds, but you probably don't have a grievance unless it takes longer than the standard.

Minor difficulties in the flash tube might be overcome by bringing the open hand down briskly over the unlit burner about one second after turning it on. This raises pressure in the burner momentarily, increasing the flow of gas in the tube.

Manual Control. Some years ago a different type of pilot was available. A single pilot flame of rugged size was connected to 4 burners by flash tubes. Depressing a button greatly increased the flow of gas to the pilot, causing its flame to spread through the tubes to all burners. It was operated by turning a burner valve with one hand, and pushing down the pilot button with the other.

This mechanism was quick, dependable, and free of service difficulties. However, the American housewife apparently did not care for the drudgery or perhaps the responsibility of pushing the button, so it was scrapped in favor of full automatic arrangements.

Solid State. At the opposite extreme, there are now "solid state" mechanisms that light burners automatically, without the presence of a pilot flame. But they may take a very long time, and depend on the house electric current for operation.

Oven Pilot. A pilot light for an oven has a more responsible job than one for top burners. An unlighted pilot in the open does not build up an explosive gas mixture in a closed room for a long time, nor ever if ventilation is good. A top burner might be turned on and unlighted for some time

before creating a hazard, but in the confined space in an oven the danger point could be reached quickly.

If the oven thermostat has a full-on full-off cycle, the pilot may have to light the burner dozens of times during the cooking of a single meal. Also, you can usually see at a glance whether a top burner is lighted, but you need to open the door and put your head almost on the floor to see an oven burner.

The oven pilot is therefore designed with built-in safety features.

There is a thermostat over the pilot. If its flame goes out, the thermostat shuts off the gas supply to the oven burner, and in some models, to the pilot also. This pre-

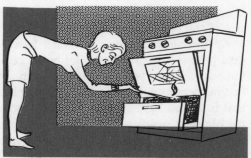

Fig. 38-15. A long fireplace match is convenient for lighting a pilot

vents leakage of gas into the oven and the air. It also prevents the oven from heating.

When you turn on the oven, be sure to listen. If you do not hear the burner go on after its normal interval, you will probably have to relight the pilot.

If its flow of gas does not shut off automatically, there will be gas in the oven, which you can smell. First make sure the burner is shut off. Fan the gas out by opening and closing the doors to both oven and broiler compartments repeatedly, then leave them open for a few minutes and fan again. If the smell is almost gone it should be safe, but if you want to be extra careful, stand to one side and put a lighted match in the burner compartment.

Then light another match and light the pilot. It is a very good idea to know in advance where it is. Otherwise, find it with a flashlight.

If the thermostat also shuts off gas to the pilot, you don't have to worry about gas in the oven, but you have other problems. There should be a button, probably painted red, somewhere among your controls that you can press to allow gas to bypass the thermostat and enter the pilot. You press it for a few seconds, then light the pilot while you still hold it.

If the bypass is not there, or you can't find it, you have to heat the thermostat by holding a candle or some other flame at the pilot, until the valve opens, and it lights.

If this happens even once, and cannot be blamed on a cutoff of the gas supply, the size of the pilot flame should be increased.

An increasing number of ovens have a dual pilot system. A small pilot burns continuously. When you turn on the oven, at first burner gas flows only into a larger pilot that is ignited by the small one. Heat from the big pilot opens a valve that allows gas to flow into the burner, which is lit by the two pilots.

This method permits the use of a small, economical pilot flame for steady use, and a large hot flame for sure lighting of the burner. It takes several seconds to go through the process, so don't hold your breath until the burner lights. You may also find that the burner does not shut off for several seconds after you turn it off.

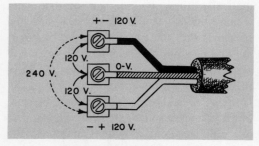

Fig. 38-16. Voltage in a range

ELECTRIC RANGE

Electric ranges are similar to gas ranges in general size and in layout of frame, cabinet, oven or ovens and cooktop, and the same general results are obtained in cooking. However, entirely different mechanisms are used for producing and regulating the heat.

Current. The standard American range uses 60 cycle alternating current from a three wire system, with a nominal voltage rating of 115-230 or 120-240.

The range is connected to the house wiring by a heavy 3-wire cord called a pigtail or a range cord. The three terminals inside the range are called blocks. One is energized at plus-minus 120 volts, one at minus-plus 120 volts and the third is grounded or neutral and has zero voltage.

Inside the range, 240 volts are obtained by connections across the minus and plus blocks, and 120 volts by circuits between the zero block and either of the others. See Figure 38-16.

The framework of the range is grounded, usually to the zero-volt wire, so that any leakage of current into it, due to failure of insulation or other causes, is drained away without it becoming dangerously charged.

An electric range requires a large capacity meter box and main switch, and heavy wiring to the connecting plug. Maximum current demand (that is, with everything turned on) ranges from 10 kilowatts (43 amperes) for a kitchenette range to 20 kilowatts (87 amperes) for an elaborate model.

However, in many localities, ranges are assigned a de-rated amperage for the load represented by the number of units likely to be turned on at one time. This is a smaller figure than that of maximum load, and often permits range installation with a 50 ampere box.

In any case, re-wiring an old house for a new electric range may cost more than the range itself. But the fringe benefit of getting

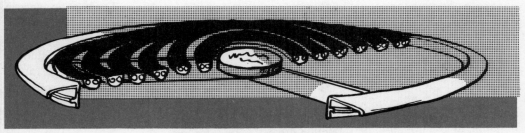

Fig. 38-17. Cutaway of electric unit

an adequate house electrical system might be worth more than the total cost.

Heating Elements (Units or Burners). Electric ranges obtain heat from the passage of current through wire made of alloys such as nichrome (nickel-chromium) steel which offer resistance to passage of electric current and are not easily damaged by heat and corrosion.

The electrical energy consumed in overcoming resistance is turned into heat. The amount of this heat can be regulated by changing the voltage. Higher voltage provides more intense heat, that is, a higher temperature.

Cooking effect depends both on the temperature, and the area heated.

In modern ranges the heating element wire is wound in close spirals, packed in magnesium oxide insulation and encased in a protective sheath of round or flattened iron tubing. One, two or three wires may be in a single tube. The tubes are curved into flat spirals with their flat sides up for surface burners, and in any convenient shape for ovens and broilers.

An assembly of heating element or elements, insulation, tubing and connectors is called a unit, element or burner.

Surface units are fairly well standardized at 6-inch or regular and 8-inch or giant sizes. The 6-inch units may use 1000 to 1650 watts, with a usual value around 1200. Eight-inch have a range from 1900 to 2200 at present. They are occasionally equipped with a quick heat arrangement, which can double the wattage (and heat

output) for a brief period. For comparison, 1000 watts is roughly equivalent to 3400 BTUs.

Modern top units usually have a stepless control that permits varying the heat by any desired amount. The majority of ranges in service, however, offer five distinct heat settings, which may be called SIMMER, LOW, MEDIUM LOW, MEDIUM HIGH and HIGH.

Each uses about half as much current as the next higher one. This works out so that the lowest setting of a two-element unit with 5 heats uses about 1/16 of the wattage of the HIGH position.

A surface burner may take 1-1/2 to 2 minutes to reach its maximum steady temperature. It heats fastest on HIGH. There should be enough heat to start cooking after about 30 seconds. After turning off, a burner may stay hot enough to keep water boiling for several minutes.

Any food spilled on a hot electric coil is promptly incinerated to powder or a film. There is no danger of plugging up burner holes or doing similar damage if food is allowed to boil over.

There are various arrangements for holding and cleaning spill that goes under the burners. There will probably be a bright metal reflector cup, and a tray below that. The cup can be lined with foil only if you can keep it well away from the heating element, to avoid any possibility of leakage of current.

The burner unit should be easily removable, by lifting it clear of its supports and then pulling it out of its socket. In replac-

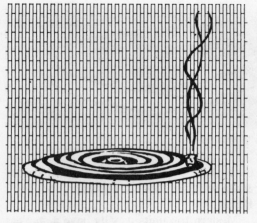

Fig. 38-18. Electric elements are self-cleaning

ing it, be careful that it is thoroughly plugged in, and resting correctly in the supports. Otherwise, it may be off level and wobbly, and might even have a poor electrical connection.

A great many special burners are offered on electrics. They are not all found in every model nor necessarily in every year. There is a thermostatically controlled burner, similar in principle, use, advantages and disadvantages to the similar unit on the gas stove. There are very convenient burners of adjustable size — you can cut off electricity to the outer parts of a large burner when using a small diameter pan.

There is (or has been recently) a deep well cooker for deep fat frying, or for steaming. It involves a special cooking pot that can be pushed down into one section of the stove, so that its top is flush with the surface and a burner is under it.

The burner may be adjustable in position, so that it can be raised to the surface for use with ordinary pans. Since this takes space inside, it is suited to a wide range where it takes drawer instead of oven space.

Another special unit, for wide ranges only, is a flat griddle occupying the space of two burners, which is convenient for pancakes or for any large scale shallow-fry operations.

Ceramic Cooktop. There is an electric range cooktop that has four heating elements set flush with the bottom of Pyroceram sheets that give an entirely smooth and practically stainproof top to the range. All units are thermostatically controlled. A yellow color appears in the ceramic when it is heated.

This top can serve as a counter when not being used as a stove.

Oven. The heating units for an electric oven are in the oven compartment itself, rather than under it as in most gas ovens. There are usually two elements, one at the floor and the other at the top. Either may draw current of 2000 to 4000 watts.

In some models the top unit is used for broiling only, the bottom for baking and roasting only, but they may both be on while heating a cold oven, or one may turn down instead of off.

There is almost always a thermostatic control. There may also be a timer, which will turn heat on at a set time, and turn if off, or down to a keep-warm basis, after an interval.

An electric oven heats much more rapidly than most gas ovens, a reversal of conditions in the top burners. This is largely because electric units can be directly in the compartment being heated, and 2 can be used at once.

Self-cleaning electric ovens may heat even more rapidly than standard ones, rising from room temperature to 350° F in as little as 4 minutes, as against 7 or 8 for a standard type.

COMPARISON

The choice between an electric and a gas range may be difficult to make. Costs are generally comparable, but there is one factor that may make the electric more expensive. It may require installation of a bigger fuse box and heavier wiring, which might cost more than the stove itself. Gas connection to a main might or might not be costly, but individual tanks are usually installed free or at a nominal charge.

Gas provides quicker heat at the burners but slower heat in the oven. The difference is noticeable, but rarely has any important effect on the time it takes to prepare a meal.

Heat regulating problems are very different. The majority of electric ranges now in use have a limited number of cooktop heat settings. With these, it often happens that one setting is too hot for a delicate bit of cooking, and the next lower one is too cool, leading to the necessity of making frequent adjustments.

On the other hand, once you get used to an electric burner, you know what results you will get from a particular setting, and can pretty well depend on getting them each time. The new stepless controls eliminate the problem, and may have clicks or indicators to keep the advantage of a known setting. The gas control valve is stepless, and usually clickless, but it may be cranky and difficult to turn just the amount you want.

The temperature of electric units varies from about 200 to 300° F at the low setting to 1500 or more when fully on. The theoretical temperature of a gas flame is 3500°, and while your own flame may be considerably short of this, it is still extremely hot. Turning an electric element lower reduces its temperature, while the turned-down gas flame is still just as hot as when on full, but the volume of heat is reduced.

Since a pan radiates heat away and food absorbs it, this has the same effect in general cooking. But if you are trying to make a cream sauce while you do six other things, or you just want to keep a panful of something hot, you are likely to find low heat more relaxing than small heat.

You can make an approximate comparison of operation costs by figuring that a kilowatt hour of electricity will produce about 3400 BTUs of heat. A gas supplier will either bill you in decitherms (see page

Courtesy of Corning Glass Works

Fig. 38-19. Ceramic cooktop, cut away to show a heating element

754) or supply you with the BTU content content of the gallons or cubic feet for which he does charge you.

A gas oven will usually heat the kitchen more than electric will, because of the larger volume of air required to support burning of the gas. This might be good or bad, depending on the house temperature.

An electric is subject to partial or complete failure of individual heating units, and may be expected to require more servicing than a gas range.

The pilot light is the most unsatisfactory feature of the gas stove, and the electric

Fig. 38-20. Overhauls may be required

has no comparable disadvantage. Each pilot must be lit constantly, whether you are using the stove or not, as long as you might want to use it. A small, efficient pilot will produce about 100 BTUs of heat an hour, at a cost of less than 50 cents a month. A small waste and a small cost, but it can be annoying.

Also, pilots are temperamental. You should train yourself to listen after turning on a gas jet until you hear the soft plop that indicates lighting.

In general, gas is a more reliable heat source than electricity. Blocking or rupture of a gas main is very unusual, and bottled gas will run out only as a result of gross carelessness by householder or supplier.

But electrical failure is always a definite possibility, for reasons ranging from a fuse-blowing short circuit in the home to errors in the design and operation of an interstate distribution system. Possession of a camp-type gasoline or propane stove, with a moderate supply of fuel, is only partial insurance against this. It will not save an elaborate dinner, but it can provide simple hot food.

On the other hand, the presence of a gas system in a house carries a very slight but definite danger of asphyxiation or explosion. Electricity is dangerous also, but it is always in a house whether you cook with it or not.

None of the conveniences, inconveniences and hazards listed in this section are as important as personal preference.

39

REFRIGERATION

REFRIGERATION

Refrigeration is usually a mechanical process of cooling an enclosed area by transferring some of its heat to the outside of the enclosure. This description covers most refrigerators, freezers and air conditioners. Cooling may also be done by absorption of heat by controlled melting of ice or evaporation of water, and of course by exposing to some naturally cool or cold temperature of water, air or underground storage areas.

Refrigerators and freezers are frequently made as a combination in a single cabinet or box, with an insulated division and separate outside doors. While both parts are designed for cold storage of food, the details of their use are so different that they will be discussed separately.

REFRIGERATOR

The refrigerator is a basic unit of kitchen equipment. It is used chiefly for chilling of food, and for short-term preservation of perishable items. It is also used extensively in making ice cubes, but this function is being taken over by freezers.

The box or cabinet is almost always free-standing, with a door on vertical hinges, which are usually on the right, but can be obtained on the left. There is a steel frame, an outer shell of enameled sheet metal and an inner shell of metal or plastic. The space between shells is packed with insulation, except for spaces for the machinery.

The whole cabinet may be a refrigerator (except for a small freezing unit box), but it is now more usual to have 2/3 to 5/6 of the space for refrigeration, and the balance for a separate freezing compartment. The freezer section may be across the top, at the bottom or one side, with the first arrangement most used at present.

The door is insulated, and has a gasket to prevent air leakage. Latches are seldom used, having been replaced by magnetic strips at the contact edge of a hollow gasket. These hold the door shut, gently but firmly, and provide for a nearly perfect air seal by pulling the gasket itself firmly against the metal of the cabinet.

Cooling Cycle. Figure 39-3 shows the layout of a refrigerator mechanism that was standard before the appearance of frost-free models. Its effectiveness depends on the absorption of heat by an evaporating

Fig. 39-1. Refrigerator with freezing compartment

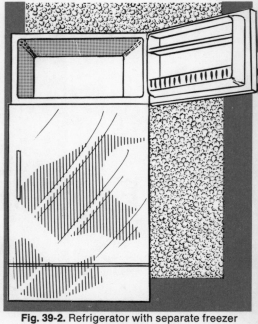

Fig. 39-2. Refrigerator with separate freezer section

liquid, the concentration of heat with a rise in temperature when vapor (or any gas) is compressed and the tendency of heat to flow from warm objects or fluids into cooler ones.

The system is partly filled with a liquid that has a low boiling point. It is called a refrigerant, and is usually a synthetic substance designed specially for this use. Freon was the first of this type, and is the best known. Its boiling point is around 21° F. It is neither bad-smelling nor poisonous, so that it does not create a major nuisance or hazard if it leaks out of the system.

Liquid refrigerant under pressure sprays through a restricting valve (nozzle) into tubes in a freezing unit or evaporator in the refrigerator cabinet, near the top. It turns into gas or vapor, absorbing heat from the passage walls, chilling them below the freezing point of water. The vapor flows (or is sucked) into a compressor or pump, which compresses it.

Compression concentrates the heat which was taken from the freezing unit, making the gas hot. It is forced through tubes of a condenser that is like an automobile radiator, and is cooled by air that circulates or is blown against the outside of the tubes by a fan. Being cooled and under pressure, it turns back to liquid. It is then sprayed into the freezing unit passages again.

The pump and fan are driven by an electric motor or motors, usually through belts.

The frost-free refrigerator, which will be discussed on page 772, has the same cycle, but the freezing unit is located in an air passage in the wall of the cabinet.

Air Circulation. A refrigerator is well insulated, but heat nevertheless works into it through its walls and door. When you open the door, cold air flows out of the bottom of the cabinet and warm air from the room enters the top.

Whenever the door is closed, the warmest air rises to the top of the cabinet (it is lighter than cold air) and loses some of its heat to the freezing unit. It is then cold and therefore heavy, and moves to the bottom, displacing warmer air that moves up to-

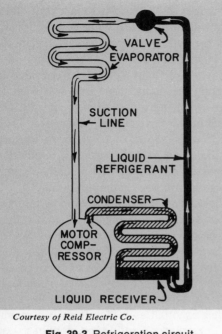

Courtesy of Reid Electric Co.

Fig. 39-3. Refrigeration circuit

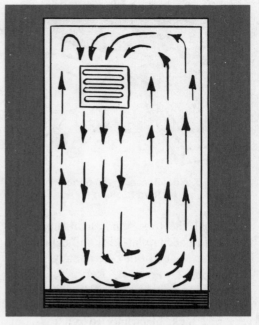

Fig. 39-4. Air circulation in cabinet with freezing
compartment

gether with air warmed by heat leakage
through the walls.

This circulation continues as long as the
freezing unit is cold and the cabinet walls
are slightly warmed.

Air circulation normally keeps the temperature fairly even throughout the interior,
but its effectiveness varies with design and
with load. Door shelves are usually warmer
than interior shelves, and locations close to
the freezing unit and on the bottom of the
cabinet are inclined to be colder than other
areas.

Freezing (Cooling) Unit. In the conventional or non-frost-free refrigerator, the
freezing or cooling unit is a box like affair
located near the top of the inside of the
cabinet. Liquefied refrigerant evaporates in
tubes in its walls and floor, absorbing heat
so as to create a below-freezing temperature. There may be a plate across the back
and a door on the front.

Circulation of air on the outside surfaces
provides for cooling the whole refrigerator.
Lack of circulation inside causes interior

temperature to remain below freezing, so
that this compartment can be used for temporary storage of frozen food, and for making ice cubes and some frozen desserts. It
is usually not cold enough for long term
storage.

Condenser. The condenser is located
at the back or in the bottom of the cabinet.

In back mounting, the tubes are on the
inside of a wide piece of thin metal mounted
vertically a few inches behind the back outer wall of the cabinet. The refrigerant in
the tubes warms the air in this restricted
space, causing it to rise. This sets up a
chimney-like circulation that does not need
a fan, and that cools the tubes and their
support sheet.

This rear cooling increases the depth of
the refrigerator. It is necessary to have a
few inches clearance above the top, to allow
air movement.

In bottom mounting, the tubes are in the
base of the cabinet. A fan blows air around
them whenever the compressor is operating. This method is efficient and takes little

Fig. 39-5. A condenser in the bottom may be hard to clean

space, but the tubes and their supporting fins tend to accumulate dirt and debris, and should be cleaned out occasionally.

Cost of Operation. Refrigerators are usually long lasting and relatively trouble free pieces of equipment. Unless you have very bad luck, electricity to run the compressor is likely to make up most of your operation expense.

The amount of current used varies with the efficiency of the mechanism, the quality of insulation, accuracy of door fit, setting of the controls, temperature of the room and specially with the frequency and duration of door opening. You might expect to use from 80 to 150 kilowatts a month, costing from $2.40 to $4.50 at a rate of 3 cents a kilowatt, for combination refrigerator freezers rated at 16 or 17 cubic feet.

INTERNAL ARRANGEMENTS

Temperature. Temperature of the air in the cabinet is regulated by an adjustable thermostat, usually located on the side or back. It may be adjustable from 32 to 50° F, or for a smaller range.

The thermostat may be made of strips of metal that expand at different rates, so that when fastened together they will bend one way when heated and the other way when cooled. Or it may be a metal bulb filled with gas or fluid which expands when warmed so as to move a lever against a spring.

In either case, expansion in the thermo-

stat causes it to close a switch that starts the refrigerator motor, while contraction allows the switch to open so that the motor and cooling action stop.

There are many factors to consider in selecting the temperature that you want to keep, which may vary somewhat with the model of the refrigerator. In general, 33 to 36° F will keep most foods fresh longest, but there is a risk of freezing if circulation is poor or the control is irregular. Settings as high as 40° are commonly used.

Closed compartments may have temperatures substantially higher or lower than that on the open shelves.

Capacity. The capacity of refrigerators is rated in cubic feet. Most of those on the market have a net refrigerated volume in the 10 to 18 cubic foot range, but there are models as small as 3 feet. This is a manufacturers' nominal rating, possibly based on putting the unit and its door on their backs and filling them with water.

The actual usable space, after allowing for shelves, trays and trimming, might be 15 to 25 per cent less.

A cubic foot of water weighs about 62-1/2 pounds. Most foods are fairly close to water in weight-for-volume (specific gravity), but because of space in and around packages, and need for accessibility, you may not be able to put in more than 20 pounds of food for each cubic foot of actual space.

Most kitchens have far too little refrigerated space for convenience and efficiency. A large family, or one that entertains frequently, can usually make good use of two standard models. This may be for capacity to cram in perishable food, to take advantage of bargains and/or reduce the frequency of routine trips to stores for staples such as milk, and to make any given stock of food more accessible by spreading it over more shelf space.

The cost of refrigerator shelf area is comparable to that of custom built kitchen cab-

768

inets, and the range of usefulness is far greater. You have the option of using it for cooling, or shutting it off and using it for ordinary storage. However, some extra space is occupied by the insulation and machinery.

Shelves. Refrigerators are supplied with a varying number of shelves, some or all of which may slide in and out for convenience in getting at food stored at the back; and which may be moved up and down for varying headroom requirements, or removed completely. Adjustable and removable shelves are a great convenience, and no refrigerator is likely to be entirely satisfactory without them.

Shelves are always (or almost always) made of parallel rods or wires in frames. There may be one or more cross rods on the bottom for reinforcement. This open construction is necessary to permit proper circulation of air. Extensive covering of shelves with foil, cookie tins or other material will prevent proper balance of temperature.

When the full set of shelves is both adjustable vertically, and removable, the householder must decide on their arrangement for himself. Generally, delivery is made with one shelf too many for ordinary purposes. You will probably do better with reduced shelf space than with inadequate headroom. Close shelf spacing makes it impossible to place many ordinary jars or cans on shelves, and makes it quite difficult to reach articles stored toward the back.

Access to the back is improved by a sliding shelf, as you can pull half to two-thirds of its depth out into the open. There should be a stop to prevent it from coming all the way out. Check for this with an empty shelf, before loading it. Or a set of shelves may be hinged to swing out for access or inspection.

The modern refrigerator has increased its usable space greatly by putting shelves in the door. This doubles the "front space"

Fig. 39-6. Variable height in shelf spacing is efficient

where it is most convenient to put articles. But very heavy loads in the door should be avoided, as they might strain the hinges.

Compartments. A refrigerator may have separate compartments for meat (meat keeper), vegetables-and-fruit (crisper), butter, cheese and freezing.

Meat and vegetable sections are usually drawers that are closely fitted and may have gaskets to almost eliminate air circulation. The U.S. Department of Agriculture recommends that meat be kept at 30 to 35° F, most vegetables at 40 or a little higher, and general refrigerator space at 37.

Exact shadings of temperature are difficult to obtain, but in the frost-free models they can be approached by distribution of cooling areas and insulation.

Lack of air circulation in these drawers prevents drying of food.

Butter and cheese compartments are usually in the door, and are separated from the rest of the refrigerator space by a light door or flap. Heat working slowly through the door from outside, and trapped behind the flap, may keep such compartments 10 to 15° warmer than the cabinet interior. This is excellent for butter, as it is difficult to use when it is very cold, and it keeps well at 50° or even higher.

Some cheese is benefited by cool instead of cold storage, other varieties are not.

Dryness. The air in a refrigerator is dried by the deposit of its moisture on the freezing or cooling unit. But when the door is opened, warm, slightly moist air from the room enters it, becomes chilled, loses its capacity to hold moisture, and becomes damp. The humidity in the refrigerator therefore varies widely. In normal use it tends to be rather dry on the average, and food stored in it should be covered or protected to avoid loss of moisture.

Frost free models have more drying effect than those that accumulate frost, because of actual removal of the moisture and forced circulation of air. Humidity may sometimes be as low as that found in a dessert in summer.

Covering to prevent evaporation also confines smells, so that they are less likely to mix with each other and get in the wrong foods.

FROST

In a standard refrigerator, the cooling unit is kept at a temperature that is below freezing. It is always colder than the air around it, so moisture tends to condense on its surface, as it does on an iced drink glass on a hot day.

But since this surface is below the freezing point, the moisture condenses as ice crystals, which build one on another to form a steadily thickening deposit of frost which soon hardens into ice. This frost or ice acts as an insulator that decreases the efficiency of the unit, requiring it to run longer to cool the air around it.

It is therefore necessary to remove the frost occasionally.

Manual Defrosting. In a standard refrigerator, you defrost by turning the control to OFF, or by pulling the plug, then allowing the ice to melt. You put a wide shallow pan under the cooling unit to catch the water, or perhaps you merely remove food from a pan that is already there. Unless you are very short of time, you keep the refrigerator door closed.

Within a few hours the ice will start to melt and water will drip into the pan. Shortly afterward, the ice will start to loosen, so that it can be pulled off in pieces. If they are allowed to remain, some of them will melt and drip where they are, but others will splash into the pan or bounce into other areas.

The drip pan is usually designed to hold the melt from 1/8 to 1/4 inch of frost. The average refrigerator is not defrosted until deposits are much deeper than that. The result is that the pan must be emptied several times, to avoid overflow that would need to be mopped off the floor of the cabinet, and which might water-spoil food.

Fig. 39-7. A frost-free model may be desert-dry inside

You empty the tray by sliding it out from its supports and carrying it to the sink. Its area is quite large in proportion to its depth, and it requires a steady pair of hands to move it without slopping water into the refrigerator and onto the floor. If it is full to the brim it is almost sure to spill.

If you think it is too full to handle safely, pull it out just far enough so that you can get at it, then dip water out of it with a cup into another container until the level is down far enough. A little water will drip during this bailing, but not nearly as much as would be likely to pour out of a full pan.

Pieces of ice can be parked in the pan, or carried away. Never use tools to remove them, as you may puncture or collapse cooling tubes.

You can hurry the job in a number of ways. Remove the ice trays, empty them and replace full of hot water. But you may have to wait for partial defrosting before you can get them out. Ice cubes will keep a while in a plastic bag in a couple of paper bags.

Ice will melt faster if you leave the door open, but food will spoil faster also. You can remove the food, pack it in a picnic cooler or in blankets, and use a heater in the manner described for freezer defrosting, page 774.

When all the ice is off the freezing unit, both inside and outside, dry it with a soft cloth, replace the ice trays filled with fresh water, empty and dry the drip pan, and turn on the control or plug in the wire.

One defrosting seldom does measurable damage to food in the refrigerator, as the melting ice keeps it cold. If there should be frozen food in the freezing unit, it is likely to thaw. It should be taken out during the process and wrapped thoroughly, or better yet, eaten promptly.

Automatic Defrosting. A refrigerator may be automatically defrosted every day (usually at night) by a timing device that

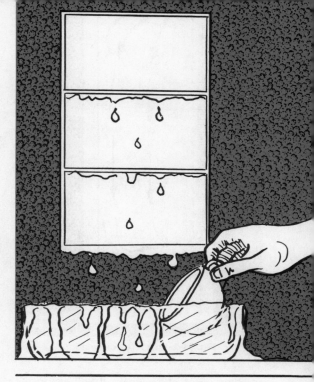

Fig. 38-8. A full water pan may call for dipping

shuts it off for the necessary length of time. The timer may be built into the control switch, or be a separate unit in the electric cord. It is usually adjustable both for the length of the defrosting period and the time at which it will occur. It will go off schedule if there is a power failure.

When defrosting is done daily there is usually only a very thin layer of ice to be removed. When melted it drips into a pan under the unit, and usually evaporates by the next thawing period. But after evaporation, it is usually re-deposited as frost, along with other moisture that evaporates from food or enters when the door is open.

It is therefore likely that this cycle will have to deal with increasingly heavy deposits of frost, unless you interrupt it occasionally by emptying the pan first thing in the morning.

If a refrigerator is designed for automatic defrosting, it may have a drain tube for the pan that will take the water outside the cabinet, and drip it on the condenser or

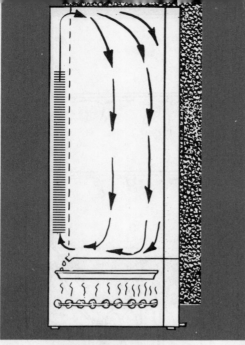

Fig. 38-9. Frost-free circulation

freezer. The cold unit may then be a plate or coil located in the wall or base of the cabinet, connected by air ducts to the bottom and top of the food compartment.

Whenever the compressor is running, a small fan moves air across the cooling surface and circulates it through the refrigerator. While the compressor is shut off by the thermostat, the temperature of this isolated cooling unit rises above freezing before restarting. Any frost on it melts and runs down into a pan which is kept warm by the compressor so that the water evaporates quickly.

The moisture goes out into the room instead of back to the cooling unit. The temperature inside the cabinet should not rise enough to do any harm during this cycle, as it occurs during normal OFF periods.

A more elaborate system, used only in freezers at present, defrosts the cooling coil by means of an electric heater which turns on automatically once a night while the compressor is off. Defrosting is accomplished in a few minutes without increase in food storage temperature. The water evaporates from a pan warmed by the compressor.

A frost free refrigerator should not be packed solidly with food on any shelf, as this may interrupt air circulation and allow some spots to get well below freezing, while others are warm. All food kept in it for more than an hour or two should be carefully covered or wrapped to prevent evaporation, as its air is likely to be very dry.

in some other place where it will evaporate into the kitchen air. This eliminates, the buildup problem entirely.

Automatic defrosting is a convenience, and it improves the mechanical efficiency of the refrigerator. However, it diminishes its efficiency for cold storage of food, which is basically what you have it for. The warming of its interior that occurs once a day diminishes the life of perishable foods noticeably.

For example, in one unit milk would stay sweet for more than a week without defrosting, but for only five days when it was done automatically.

If the cooling mechanism were made reversible, so that it could put heat into the freezing unit for a short period, defrosting could be done quickly and with little or no damage to food. Heat pumps that both heat and cool houses function in this way. However, there is an easier solution to the problem of refrigerator frost.

Frost Free. A refrigerator does not need a freezing compartment if there is a freezer (deep freezer) in a separate section of the same cabinet, or if it is designed to be sold and used with an accompanying

FREEZER

Home freezers, often called deep freezers, work on the same principle as refrigerators, but are kept much colder, preferably around zero, in order to freeze food rapidly and to preserve frozen food for long periods. Cabinet insulation is thicker, and a more powerful cooling mechanism is used in proportion to size. Consumption of electricity may be somewhat lower.

Methods of freezing, and of storing food in freezers, were discussed in Chapter 30, FREEZING AND DRYING.

Cabinets. Three types of cabinet are used: upright, combination and chest.

The upright or standup looks like a refrigerator. New ones are usually a frost free design with circulated air. Others have cooling tubes in or under the shelves, which are not movable. The door is held closed magnetically, or with a latch.

In combinations, the freezer is a small upright, built above, below or beside a larger refrigerator in the same cabinet.

The chest freezer has its door in the top, and has cooling tubes in the walls and perhaps in the floor. It is usually fitted with wire baskets, by means of which upper layers of food can be easily removed for access to lower layers.

Uprights are more convenient, but less efficient since cold air pours out of them every time the door is opened, letting in a corresponding amount of warmer air from the room. They take less floor space, but usually hold less food in proportion to size,

as they cannot be packed as solidly as a chest. Articles are more likely to be lost, forgotten and buried in a chest, particularly if it lacks vertical dividers in the lower part.

Defrosting. While new freezers are usually frost free, most of those that are in use tend to accumulate heavy ice on cooling tubes, shelves and food packages. This frost diminishes mechanical efficiency, and disguises and fastens down food so that it becomes difficult to use. And there can be so much of it that its removal is a major job.

The first step is to turn off the current, preferably by disconnecting the wall plug. That way you can be sure that is OFF.

It is best to take out all the food. Put a thick layer of newspaper on a table or on the floor, and pile the frozen articles on it as compactly as possible. This is a good time to do a little quick sorting, to refresh your memory as to what you have. But if they are coated with frost, leave it on them. Put a blanket or two over them, and tuck one under the edge packages to keep out drafts.

Then connect an electric heater, and

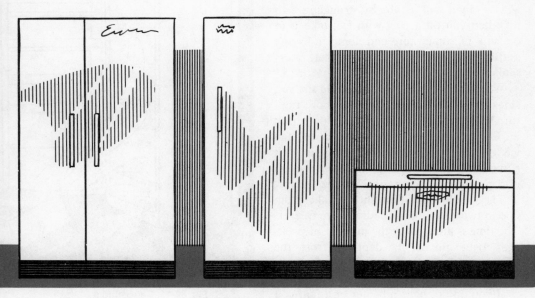

Fig. 38-10. Freezer cabinets

place it to heat the empty cabinet. One that includes a fan will do the best job. But you can get by with radiant heat, or with just a fan circulating room air, if you must.

An upright is heated from the floor or a chair in front of its open door. But you will probably have to put the heater (or the fan) inside a chest, and reverse its position occasionally.

Provide yourself with a couple of shallow pans or trays for ice, a bowl or deep pan for water, a plastic scraper and some rags. Your freezer may have a sump in the bottom to catch water, and a hose to drain it into a container. Otherwise, the upright usually has no place to catch water, but the rags will soak it up if you leave them in the bottom, across the doorway. The chest holds water well, but it may be a minor problem to bail and mop it out.

As the ice starts to become soft and loose, scrape and pry the pieces loose with the plastic scraper. Do not use any other tool, and be gentle with this one, as the Freon refrigerant may run very close to the surface in concealed tubing. Ice around exposed tubing may be hard to get off, but you should leave it until it comes off easily, as you might kink a tube by struggling with it. When you fill a tray with ice, take it to the sink or somewhere and dump it. Wring out the rags into the bowl as they get water-soaked.

When the ice is all off, dry off the shelves, sides and bottom with towels or more rags, turn on the current, and put the food back in. On this trip you should knock off any ice on the outside of the packages if it comes off easily, but don't make it enough of a project to delay repacking the freezer.

The whole operation should take from one to two hours for a medium size freezer. The time is affected by the number of packages to be moved, the depth of frost, the efficiency of the heater, and how fast you work.

If you do not have a heater or a fan, you can leave the freezer door open until the ice is loose and melting, a process which may take only an hour or two for a cabinet freezer in a hot room. In a chest it will be very slow, and is not practical if you must leave food out during the work. Thawing time can be greatly shortened by putting pans of hot water, or even bricks heated in the oven, in the freezer.

ICE CUBES

A secondary but often important function of refrigerators and freezers is the production of ice cubes. They are seldom (or perhaps never) really cubical, but the name is convenient. Ice cubes are primarily for cold drinks, but may be used in making ice cream, packing picnic food and for various other purposes.

Trays. Cubes are ordinarily made in low rectangular pans (trays) that hold about a pint of water and make about 18 cubes.

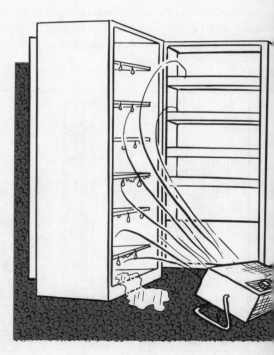

Fig. 38-11. Defrosting a freezer

Dividers determine the size and number of pieces. In addition to these somewhat standardized pans, there are narrow plastic ones with a single row of cubes, individual or one-cube cups, often supplied with a rack to support a number of them, mini-cube trays and special molded shapes.

Cubes may be made in the freezing compartment of a standard refrigerator, or in any freezer where there is enough level space for a tray. Time is highly variable, according to the temperature and circulation in the freezing space, contact of the tray with the floor, the material of the floor, whether it contains cooling tubes, and the number of trays or cubes done at one time.

Cubes in one hour from room temperature water is very good performance. A freezer should not take over 2 or 3 hours, while a freezer compartment inside a refrigerator may take 2 to 24.

Removal. Trays that are placed on open racks or on top of packages of frozen food seldom cause any difficulty in being lifted and removed. But those placed on a flat metal floor may stick to it when frozen, particularly if you spilled water in putting them in.

Such pans are pried loose by inserting a key or cam under the overhanging top edge of the tray, then turning it. Never hammer them, or pry them with sharp tools, unless you are very sure that the floor does not contain any tubes carrying refrigerant.

Most metal trays have mechanical devices that loosen the cubes when a lever is moved. They vary greatly in ease of operation and effectiveness. If the tray has been in for a long time it may be so covered with frost that the lever cannot be moved.

Plastic trays will often release many or even all of their cubes if they are held in both hands and twisted back and forth. Narrow, single row trays are easier than double rows. Such trays are likely to get tired eventually, and break.

Loosening by either lever or twisting can

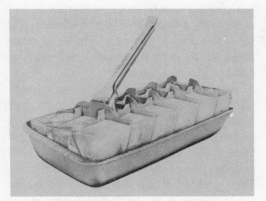

Fig. 38-12. Ice cubes in their tray

be made much easier by holding the tray under hot running water briefly, mostly upside down, or allowing it to stand at room temperature for 10 or 20 minutes. This will also loosen cubes in simple trays and other containers.

Crushing. Ice cubes are often crushed before use. Smaller pieces increase the speed of chilling, and are easier to manage.

Crushed ice is used in cocktail shakers, under seafood cocktails and other chilled specialties, and in making ice cream.

Courtesy of Sunbeam Appliance Co.

Fig. 38-13. Electric ice crushing attachment

Crushing may be done by tamping a bag of ice with a hammer (see ICE CREAM), by squeezing cubes one at a time in a small press, or by a rotary chipper that may be hand or electric powered.

Automatic Ice-Maker. Most new freezers can be equipped with an automatic ice-maker. This device will make ice cubes (sometimes doughnut-shaped) until it has filled a bin, which may hold from 3 to 10 pounds (an ice tray makes about one pound) Then it stops. When the ice is reduced by use or evaporation, it will make some more.

This device makes unnecessary the small but sloppy and annoying job of emptying and refilling trays, and is insurance against being caught without ice. But its cost, including connection to a cold water line, can be justified only by using a considerable quantity. If the cubes stand a long time they may combine in one big lump. It fills quite a bit of space.

Anyhow, don't throw away your trays. Most of the automatics are very slow, taking 4 to 8 hours to make each pound of ice. If you empty the bin you will have to do some waiting, unless you use trays on the side.

With any way of making ice, it may be advisable to keep a few pounds of cubes in the freezer, sealed in a plastic bag, for emergencies.

APPENDIX

A Guide to Spices

The material below, and on following pages to 785, has been reproduced by permission from "A GUIDE TO SPICES — How To Buy Them — How To Store Them — How To Use Them," presented by The National Restaurant Association in Cooperation with The American Spice Trade Association.

TIPS ON THE ART OF SEASONING

In most cases spices and herbs should be used to aid and enhance the natural flavors of foods, *not obscure them.* The overall impression should be one of savoriness without any particularly dominant spice apparent. Exceptions to this would be foods such as curry or chili or gingerbread where the character of the dish depends on its spice.

HOW MUCH?

Since the pungency of each spice differs and its effect on different foods varies, it is not possible to offer a blanket rule for the amount to use. Following recipes that have been well tested is the surest practice. Where no recipe is available, start with about 1/4 teaspoon of spice to each pound of meat or pint of sauce or soup. Make this 1/8 teaspoon in the case of red pepper (or cayenne) and garlic powder. You will probably find these starter quantities should be increased in many instances, but it is easier to add than subtract.

WHEN TO ADD?

Ground spices are ready to give up their flavors quickly. When used in a medium to long cooking dish, they should not be added until *near the end of the cooking period.* Otherwise, they should be added about the same time as the salt. In uncooked dishes, such as salad dressings and fruit juices, the spiced liquid should be left standing for several hours to develop good flavor. In the case of salad dressings particularly, add the spices to the vinegar and leave this to stand before adding the oil. If it is not possible to let it stand, the liquid should be brought to a boil and cooked, thus letting the heat bring out the flavor.

Whole spices are especially useful in long cooking dishes. They should be added at the beginning of cooking. It is a good idea to place them in a small cheesecloth or muslin bag so that they may be easily removed when the desired flavor level is obtained. This also avoids any chance of pieces of whole spice remaining in the finished dish. Seeds such as poppy and sesame should be toasted before they are used. Whole (or "leaf") herbs should be crumbled finely just before they are used, to release best flavor.

HOW TO BUY

Strength, quality of flavor and good color are the most important considerations in buying spices. Any good, quality jobber or supply house will have high quality spices to offer. A jobber, backed by a quality spice packaging house will be able to supply consistently fresh, well flavored seasonings. To judge quality, examine the spice first for rich, fresh color (particularly important in the herbs and paprika); then bring it slowly up to the nostrils. Its pungence should rise up to meet you. It should be strong and fresh (excepting, of course, the few non-aromatic or faintly perfumed items such as mustard seed, sesame seed, poppy seed, etc.).

BEWARE OF IMITATIONS

If a restaurant stresses good food it cannot afford to use something like imitation black pepper, mace or nutmeg. These products are cheap because they are made by spraying a little oil of the spice on a large amount of carrier (usually ground soya, buckwheat, cottonseed hulls or other waste grains). In the long run, however, they are very expensive because they do not do the flavoring job that is required of true pepper, mace or nutmeg. The real spices are not only vastly superior in flavor, they go farther and are more stable.

HOW TO STORE SPICES

For best results, spices should be stored in as cool and dry a place as possible. Heat robs their flavors and dampness will cake them. Be sure also that containers are tightly closed after every use so that their valuable volatile oils are not lost. In very hot climates, it may be practical to place capsicum spices (paprika and red pepper) in the refrigerator to guard against infestation.

HOW LONG WILL THEY KEEP?

Under good conditions (see above) spices will retain aroma and flavor for a long period. The whole spices will keep longer than ground spices. The herbs tend to lose flavor a little faster than such items as pepper, ginger, cinnamon, cloves, etc. As a result, many users prefer to buy herbs in the whole (or "leaf") form in which state they store better. A restaurant, however, should never have to test spice storage life because seasonings should be purchased in reasonable quantities and re-ordered frequently.

LET SPICES SAVE TIME AND LABOR

Among the newer developments in the spice industry are dehydrated vegetable seasonings, including various forms of onion, garlic, sweet peppers, celery, mint, parsley and mixed vegetables. These are labor savers when a recipe calls for the seasoning quality of any of these vegetables. If the recipe includes much liquid (i.e. stews and sauces) and the flakes are to remain in the liquid for several minutes before the dish is served, it may not be necessary even to rehydrate them. In the case of instant minced onion and parsley flakes, they will rehydrate sufficiently in about five minutes. For sweet pepper flakes, celery flakes and mixed vegetable flakes, you should allow about 20 minutes for rehydration (either before or during cooking). If, as in the case of a salad or garnish, rehydration is indicated, use equal parts of flakes and water for onion and parsley. For celery and sweet pepper, use twice the amount of water as flakes and when rehydrated, strain off the excess water. *One part of instant minced onion or parsley flakes is equal to about four parts of the raw product in seasoning strength.* One part of celery or sweet pepper flakes is equivalent to about *two parts of the raw vegetable.*

The Spice Shelf

Careful measuring is the best way to produce consistently good seasoning results.

In the following section you will find a listing of the products that are available, along with some how-to-use tips. Note that at the end of each listing there is a section called "Available". This indicates what forms of the spice are commonly offered today. Not all spices and herbs are sold in both whole and ground forms whereas some come in a number of designations, i.e. "cracked", "rubbed", "minced", etc., each made to fill some specific cooking need. Poppy and sesame seeds, for example, are never sold in ground form because they have such a high oil content. Attention to this can give you better results from your spice purchasing.

ALLSPICE
(Pimenta officinalis)
Origin and Description: *Jamaica, Mexico, Central* and *South America.* Allspice is a pea-sized fruit which grows in small clusters on a tree. Picked green, they are shrivelled brown berries after curing. As its name implies, allspice is reminiscent of several spices—cinnamon, nutmeg and cloves.
Uses: Whole—pickling meats, gravies, boiling fish. Ground—baking, puddings, relishes, fruit preserves. Try adding a dash to tomato sauce.
Available: *"Whole Allspice"* *"Ground Allspice"*

ANISE (Pimpinella anisum)
Origin and Description: *Spain* and *Mexico.* Anise is a dried greenish-brown seed of a foot-high annual shrub. It is much used in flavoring licorice.
Uses: Good in cookies, candies, sweet pickles and as beverage flavoring. Sprinkle on coffee cakes, sweet rolls. For anise cookies, just add ¼ teaspoon ground anise to cookie batter.
Available: *"Anise seed"*

APPLE PIE SPICE
(See section on "Blends")

BASIL (Ocimum basilicum)
Origin and Description: *U.S.* and *North Mediterranean* area. Also known as "Sweet Basil," Basil is the cleaned and dried leaves and tender stems. Its aromatic flavor has a pleasing leafy note.
Uses: An important seasoning in tomato paste and tomato dishes. Use in cooked peas, squash and snap beans. Famed for use in turtle soup. Sprinkle chopped basil leaves over lamb chops before cooking.
Available: *"Basil Leaves"*

BARBECUE SPICE
(See section on "Blends")

BAY LEAVES (Lauris nobilis)
Origin and Description: *Turkey, Greece, Yugoslavia* and *Portugal.* Bay leaves are the dried leaves of an evergreen tree. These smooth oblong leaves are deep green on the upper surface and paler beneath. The flavor is sweet and herbaceous with a delicate floral spice note.
Uses: For pickling, stews, spice sauces and soups. Excellent for fish or chowder. Good with variety of meats, such as fricassee of kidney, heart or oxtail. Add bay leaf, with whole peppercorns, to tomato sauce for boiled cod.
Available: *"Bay Leaves"*

CARAWAY SEED
(Carum carvi)
Origin and Description: Mostly from: *Netherlands.* The biennial plant grows two or three feet high and the seeds are somewhat curved, tapering toward both ends. The flavor is a combination of Dill and Anise with a slight fruitiness. Caraway is the important ingredient in the cordial Kummel.
Uses: Widely used in baking, especially rye bread. Good in sauerkraut, new cabbage, noodles and soft cheese spreads. Sprinkle over French Fried potatoes; on pork, liver, kidneys before cooking. Sprinkle canned asparagus with caraway before heating.
Available: *"Caraway Seed"*

CARDAMOM SEED
(Elettaria cardamomum)
Origin and Description: *Guatemala, India, Ceylon.* Tiny brown seeds which grow enclosed in a white or green pod varying from ¼ to 1 inch in length. The flavor is sweet and spicy with a camphoraceous note.

779

Courtesy of National Restaurant Association
Courtesy of American Spice Trade Association

Uses: Whole—(in pod) used in Mixed Pickling Spice. Seed—(removed from pod) flavors demitasse. Ground—flavors Danish pastry, bun breads, coffee cakes. Improves flavor of Grape Jelly. Sprinkle ground cardamom on iced melon for breakfast or dessert.
Available: *"Whole Cardamom"* *"Ground Cardamom Seed"*

CAYENNE PEPPER
(See "Red Pepper")

Celery Seed

CELERY SEED
(Apium graveolens)

Origin and Description: *India* and *France.* Celery seed is a minute, olive-brown seed obtained from the celery plant. *Celery Salt* is made by combining celery seed with salt. Celery Seed has been described as having a parsley-nutmeg flavor.
Uses: Excellent in pickling, salads, fish, salad dressings, and vegetables. For a different flavor, add celery seed to braised lettuce (about ½ teaspoon to a head lettuce). Ground celery excellent in tomato juice cocktail.
Available: *"Celery Seed"* - *"Celery Salt"*

CELERY FLAKES

Origin and Description: *United States.* Dehydrated, flaked leaves and stalks of vegetable celery.
Uses: Soups, stews, sauces, stuffings.
Available: *"Celery Flakes"*

CHILI POWDER
(See section on "Blends")

CINNAMON (Cinnamomum cassia)

Origin and Description: *Indonesia* and *Indo-China.* Cinnamon comes from the bark of an aromatic evergreen tree. Almost all cinnamon sold in the U.S. is of cassia cinnamon variety (the spice trade often refers to it merely as "cassia"). This has the reddish brown color and pungently sweet aroma and flavor we expect in cinnamon. We also import a small amount of Cinnamomum Zeylanicum (Ceylon cinnamon) which is more buff colored and milder flavored.
Uses: Whole—pickling, preserving, flavoring puddings, stewed fruits. Serve with clove-stuck lemon slices in hot tea. Used in hot wine drinks. Ground—baked goods, often in combination with allspice, nutmeg and cloves. The principal mincemeat spice. Combine with mashed sweet potatoes and with sugar for cinnamon toast. Dust on fried bananas.
Available: *"Stick Cinnamon"* *"Ground Cinnamon"*

CINNAMON SUGAR
(See section on "Blends")

CLOVES
(Caryothyllus aromaticus)

Origin and Description: From *Zanzibar and Madagascar.* Cloves are the fruit (dried flower buds) of a tree belonging to the evergreen family and are dark brown and dusky red in color. The flavor is characterized by a sweet, pungent spiciness.
Uses: Whole—for pork and ham roasts, pickling of fruits, spiced sweet syrups. Ground — baked goods, chocolate puddings, stews

Cloves

vegetables. For a tastier meat stew add a small onion studded with 2 or 3 whole cloves.
Available: *"Whole Cloves"* *"Ground Cloves"*

Coriander Seed

CORIANDER
(Coriandrum sativum)

Origin and Description: Mostly from *Morocco* and *Yugoslavia.* Coriander is the dried fruit of a small plant. It is nearly globular and about ⅛ inch long. Externally, the seed is a weak orange-yellow to a moderate yellow-brown, often with a purplish red blush. In flavor it has a sweet dry, musty spice character tending toward lavender.

Uses: Whole—in mixed pickles, gingerbread batter, cookies, cakes, biscuits, poultry stuffings, mixed green salads. Ground—in sausage making, to flavor buns. Rub ground coriander on fresh pork before roasting.
Available: *"Coriander Seed"* - *"Ground Coriander"*

CRAB BOIL
(See Section on "Blends")

CUMIN (Cuminum cyminum)

Origin and description: *Iran, French Morocco* and *Spain.* Cumin is a small dried fruit, oblong in shape, and resembles caraway seeds. The flavor is penetrating. Sometimes known as "Cominos" seed.
Uses: An important ingredient in curry and chili powder. Available whole and ground. Good in

soups, cheese, pies, stuffed eggs. For canapes, mix chutney with snappy cheese and garnish with cumin seed.
Available: *"Cumin Seed"* - *"Ground Cumin Seed"*

CURRY POWDER
(See Section on "Blends")

DILL SEED
(Anethum graveolens)

Origin and Description: Mostly from *India.* Dill is the small dark seed of the dill plant. It is brown, broadly oval in outline and rounded at both ends. The flavor is clean, aromatic with a green weedy note.
Uses: Used for pickling, in cooking sauerkraut, salads, soups, fish and meat sauces, gravies, spiced vinegars, green apple pie. Sprinkle dill seed on potato salad, cooked macaroni or when cooking sauerkraut.
Available: *"Dill Seed"*

Fennel Seed

FENNEL (Foeniculum vulgare)

Origin and Description: *India* and *Rumania.* Fennel is a small seed-like fruit with an agreeable odor and aromatic sweet taste somewhat like Anise.
Uses: Popular in sweet pickles and Italian sausage. Used in boiled fish, pastries, candies and liqueurs. Add a dash to apple pie for an unusually good flavor.
Available: *"Fennel Seed*

GARLIC (Dehydrated)
(Allium sativum)

Origin and Description: Most of the garlic used in dehydrated products is grown in the U.S. This is the most strongly flavored of the plants in the allium family and is used in a wide range of dishes. Very pungent.
Uses: Very convenient way of adding garlic flavor to foods.

Available: *"Instant Garlic Powder* - *"Garlic Salt"* -- *"Instant Minced Garlic"*

Ginger

GINGER (Zingiber Officinale)

Origin and Description: *Jamaica, India* and *West Africa.* Ginger is the rhizome (root) of a tuberous plant. Externally it is a weak, yellow-orange, internally a yellow brown. The flavor is warm and fragrant, with a pungent spiciness.
Uses: Whole — chutneys, Conserves, pickling. Stew with dried fruits, applesauce. Ground—gingerbread, cakes, pumpkin pie, Indian pudding, canned fruits, pot roasts and other meats. Rub chicken inside and out with mixture of ginger and butter before roasting.
Available: *"Whole Ginger"* - *"Ground Ginger".*

HERB SEASONING
(See section on "Blends")

ITALIAN SEASONING
(See section on "Blends")

MACE (Cortex myristicae)
fragrantis)

Origin and Description: *East* and *West Indies.* Mace is the fleshy growth between the nutmeg shell and the outer husk, orange-red in color. Flavor resembles nutmeg.
Uses: Whole (called "Blade") — excellent in fish sauces, pickling, preserving. Add a chopped blade to gingerbread batter. Good in stewed cherries. Ground—essential in fine pound cakes, contributes a golden tone and exotic flavor to all yellow cakes. Valuable in all chocolate dishes. Use 1 teaspoon ground mace to 1 pint of whipped cream, cuts, oiliness, increases delicacy.
Available: *"Ground Mace"*

MARJORAM
(Maioren hortensis)

Origin and Description: *France, Chile* and *Peru.* Marjoram is an herb of the mint family. It has a peculiar, sweet-minty herbaceous type flavor.
Use: Leaf—delicious combined with other herbs in stews, soups, sausage, p o u l t r y seasonings. Good in fish and sauce recipes. Sprinkle over lamb while cooking for an excellent flavor touch.
Available: *"Marjoram Leaves"* -

MINT FLAKES
(Mentha spicata or Mentha piperita)

Origin and Description: *U.S.* and *Europe.* Dehydrated, flaked leaves of spearmint or peppermint. Strong, sweet flavor.
Uses: Mint Flakes are used for flavoring soups, stews, beverages, jellies, fish, sauces, etc.

Mint

MIXED PICKLING SPICE
(See section on "Blends")

MIXED VEGETABLE FLAKES

Origin and Description: *United States.* Mixture of dehydrated, flaked vegetables, usually composed of celery. green peppers, carrots.

Uses: Convenient means of seasoning soups, stews, sauces, stuffings.

Mustard

MUSTARD
(White—Sinapis alba; Brown—Brassica juncea)

Origin and Description: *U.S., Canada, Denmark,* the *United Kingdom* and *The Netherlands.* Both varieties are herbs, widely cultivated. Mustard is a small seed, the brown or black being dark brown spheroidal seeds, while the yellow or white are subglobular seeds. The yellow or white is the m i l d e r flavored whereas the brown or black is the pungent variety from which the mustard typically served in Chinese restaurants is made.

Uses: Whole—used to garnish salads, pickled meats, fish and hamburgers. Powdered—meats, sauces, gravies. Add ½ teaspoon powdered mustard for each two cups of cheese sauce for macaroni.

Available: *"Mustard Seed"* - *"Powdered Mustard".*

NUTMEG (Myristica fragrans)

Origin and Description: *East West Indies.* Nutmeg is the kernel of the nutmeg fruit; it grows on a somewhat bushy tree which reaches a height of 40 feet. The fruit of the nutmeg tree is variable in shape—either globular, oval or pear-shaped. The fleshy husk, grooved on one side, splits, releasing the deep-brown aromatic nutmeg. (An orange-red network of fleshy growth between the nut and outer husk is known as Mace). Nutmeg flavor is described as sweet, spicy type.

Uses: Whole—to be grated as needed. Ground—used in baked goods, sauces, puddings. Topping for eggnog, custards, whipped cream. Good on cauliflower, spinach. Sprinkle on fried bananas, on bananas and berries with cream. Best spice for flavoring doughnuts. A pinch of nutmeg adds flavor to the crust for meat pie.

Available: *"Whole Nutmegs"* *"Ground Nutmeg".*

ONIONS (Dehydrated)
(Allium capa)

Origin and Description: Made in U.S. Dehydrated and processed onions. Now sold in several forms corresponding to the various sizes of onion cuts normally used in seasoning, i.e., slices, chopped, minced, etc. Convenient, labor savers wherever onion flavor is desired.

Uses: Soups. chowders, stews, salads, dressings, sauces steaks, hamburgers, etc.

Available: *"Instant Chopped Onion"* - *"Instant Onion Powder"* - *"Granulated Onion"* *"Sliced Onion"* - *"Onion Salt"* *"Onion Flakes"*

OREGANO
(Lippia graveolans and Origanum species)

Origin and Description: *Greece, Italy* and *Mexico.* Known also as Origanum and Mexican Sage.

Uses: Good flavoring for any tomato dish, hence, used in Pizza and other Italian specialties.

Available: *"Oregano Leaves"* *"Ground Oregano"*

Paprika

PAPRIKA (Capsicum annum)

Origin and Description: *Spain, Central Europe* and the *United States.* A sweet red pepper, ground after seeds and stems have been removed. Most paprika sold in U.S. is mild and sweet in flavor, slightly aromatic and prized for brilliant red color. A type which has a slight pungency is also available.

Uses: Used as colorful red garnish for any pale foods. Important ingredient in Chicken Paprika and Hungarian Goulash. Used on fish, shell-fish, salad dressings, vegetables, meats. gravies, canapes. For an excellent canape mix paprika with cream cheese and celery seed and serve on crackers.

Available: *"Paprika"*

PARSLEY FLAKES
(Petroselinum sativum)

Origin and Description: Made in U.S. Dehydrated, flaked parsley leaf and stem material.

Uses: Seasoning and garnish. Flavors soups, salads, meat, fish, sauces and vegetable dishes. For Spiced Potato Cakes made from leftover mashed potatoes, or to reheated mashed potatoes, try adding some p a r s l e y flakes, onion salt and paprika.

PEPPER BLACK & WHITE
(Piper nigrum)

Origin and Description: *India, Borneo* and *Indonesia.* Small dried berry of vine. Whole pepper is known as peppercorn. Pepper is the world's most popular spice. White pepper is black

Courtesy of National Restaurant Association
Courtesy of American Spice Trade Association

peppercorn with the outer black cover removed. Use fresh pepper; buy small quantities and replace often! Flavor is warm, pungent, aromatic.

Uses: Adds a spicy tang to almost all foods. A "must" in the kitchen and on the table. Whole (Black & White)—used in pickling, soups and meats. Ground (Black or White) meats, sauces, gravies, many vegetables, soups, salads, eggs, etc. For curing Virginia-style hams. Dash fresh black pepper in tossed green salad. White pepper particularly useful in light colored sauces, soups, vegetables where dark specs are not wanted.

Available: *"Whole Black Pepper"* - *"Ground Black Pepper"* - *"Coarse Ground Black Pepper"* - *"Whole White Pepper"* - *"Ground White Pepper"*.

PEPPER FLAKES
(See Sweet Pepper Flakes)

POPPY (Papaver somniferum)

Origin and Description: *Netherlands.* Tiny seeds of poppy plant; about 900,000 to the pound. Best is blue-colored seed from Holland. Has a crunchy nut-like flavor.

Uses: Excellent as topping for breads, rolls, cookies. Also delicious in salads and noodles. Filling for pastries. Add poppy seeds to buttered noodles and mix thoroughly.

Available: *"Poppy Seed"*.

Poppy Seed

POULTRY SEASONING
(See section on "Blends")

RED PEPPER (Capsicum)

Origin and Description: *U.S., Mexico, Africa, Japan, Turkey,* etc., depending on type. The pungent red peppers. There are dozens of types varying in degree of heat. A product sold as "Cayenne" or "Red Pepper" may contain several varieties in order to obtain desired strength. There are no heat standards for "Cayenne", "Red Pepper", etc., so it is better to consult your supplier as to the relative strength of his various products.

Uses: Whole—Pickles, relishes, hot sauces. Crushed—sauces, pickles, highly spiced meats, a prime ingredient for many Italian specialty dishes, including certain sausages. Ground—with discretion in meats, sauces, fish, egg dishes. A touch of Ground Red Pepper (or Cayenne) plus ¼ teaspoon paprika added to 2 or 3 tablespoons butter makes excellent sauce for vegetables.

Available: *"Whole Red Pepper"* - *"Crushed Red Pepper"* - *"Ground Red Pepper"* - *"Cayenne"*.

ROSEMARY
(Rosmarinus officinalis)

Origin and Description: *France, Spain and Portugal.* A spikey herb; looks like curved pine needle and is sweet and fresh-tasting.

Uses: Used in lamb dishes, in soups and stews. Sprinkle on beef before roasting. Flavors fish and meat stocks. Add a dash of rosemary to boiled potatoes in the early stages of cooking.

Available: *"Rosemary Leaves"*.

SEASONED or FLAVOR SALT
(See section on "Blends")

SAFFRON (Crocus sativus)

Origin and Description: *Spain.* The World's most expensive spice, yet a little goes a long way. Takes 224,000 stigma of a crocus-like flower to make a pound. Flavor is distinctive and agreeable in character, but its ability to give food an appetizing yellow color is equally prized.

Rosemary

Uses: In baked goods. Most highly esteemed in *"Arroz Con Pollo"*, the rice-chicken dish of Spain. To add golden color and delicious flavor to rice, boil pinch of saffron in water for a moment before adding rice.

Available: *"Saffron"*.

SAGE (Salvia officinalis)

Origin and Description: Choicest comes from *Yugoslavia;* also grown in *Greece.* Sage is a perennial shrub about 2 feet high. Flavor is camphoraceous, with a minty spiciness.

Uses: Particularly good with pork and pork products. Used in sausages, meat stuffings, baked fish and poultry. Excellent in salad greens.

Available: *"Sage Leaves"* - *"Rubbed Sage"* (finer consistency than Leaves) *"Ground Sage"*.

SAVORY (Satureia hortensis)

Origin and Description: *France* and *Spain.* Herb of the mint family, grown in many climates. Flavor is delicately sweet and herbaceous resembling thyme.

Uses: Combined with other herbs, makes an excellent flavoring for meats, meat dressings, chicken, fish sauces. A pinch of savory gives a lift to scrambled eggs.

Available: *"Savory Leaves"* - *"Ground Savory"*.

SEAFOOD SEASONING
(See section on "Blends")

SHRIMP SPICE
(See section on "Blends")

SESAME (Sesamum indicum)
Origin and Description: *Central America, Egypt, and U.S.* Sesame is a small, honey-colored seed with gentle, nut-like flavor and high oil content.

Uses: A rich toasted-nut flavor when baked on rolls, breads and buns. Principal ingredient in Oriental candy, halvah. Add to lightly c o o k e d cold. spinach which has been blended with soy sauce. Turn out of custard cup and top with grated raw beets or carrots.

Available: *"Sesame Seed"* (it is a good idea to specify hulled also, since restaurants would not be satisfied with "u n h u l l e d" Sesame).

SWEET PEPPER FLAKES
Origin and Description: Made in U.S. Dehydrated, flaked sweet green or red peppers, or a mixture of both green and red (the red being sweet, not hot).

Uses: A convenient way of adding green or red pepper flavor to sauces, salads, vegetables, casseroles, when a fine diced pepper is called for.

Sweet Pepper

TARRAGON
(Artemisia dracunculus)
Origin and Description: *France* and *Spain*. Tarragon is a small perennial plant which forms tall stalks about one and one-half yards high. Minty, herbaceous and Anise-like in flavor.

Uses: Used in sauces, salads, chicken, meats, egg and tomato dishes. The important flavoring of tarragon vinegar. Just before taking broiled chicken out of oven, season and sprinkle with finely minced tarragon and serve with pan gravy.

Available: *'Tarragon Leaves"*.

THYME (Thymus vulgaris)
Origin and Description: *France* and *Spain*. Thyme is a low shrub about a foot high. The leaves and stems of this garden herb have a strong distinctive flavor.

Uses: Used in stews, soups and poultry stuffings. Excellent in clam and fish chowders, sauces, croquettes, chipped beef, fricassees. Thyme and fresh tomatoes go together like hand and glove. Sprinkle thyme over sliced tomatoes in bed of lettuce, use vinegar and olive oil dressing, with salt and pepper.

Available: *"Thyme L e a v e s"* - *"Ground Thyme"*.

TURMERIC (Curcuma longa)
Origin and Description: *India, Haiti, Jamaica* and *Peru*. Root of the ginger family, orange-yellow in color. Important ingredient of curry powder. Flavor has a mild ginger-pepper note.

Uses: Used as flavoring and coloring in prepared mustard, and is used in combination with mustard as flavoring f o r meats, dressings and salads. Used in pickling, Chow-Chow and other relishes. Try a little turmeric in creamed eggs, fish, seafood.

Available: *"Ground Turmeric"*.

BLENDS
Many mixtures, or blends, of spices have been developed by spice manufacturers to make the art of seasoning a quick and easy task. In some cases a specific blend may be unique with the company that produces it; in others, the blend may be one that has been adopted by most spice packagers. The following are the blends that are now sold by most spice firms and thus would be available to restaurants throughout the country:

APPLE PIE SPICE
A ground blend of the sweet baking spices, with a predomi-

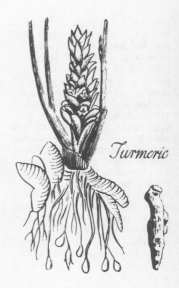

Turmeric

nance of cinnamon. Cloves, nutmeg or mace, allspice, and ginger are typical inclusions also. Good for all fruit pies and pastries.

BARBECUE SPICE
A ground blend of many spices such as chili peppers, cumin, garlic, cloves, paprika, salt and sugar. Designed to be the basic seasoning for a barbecue sauce, but good also in salad dressing, meat casserole, hash brown potatoes, eggs and cheese dishes.

CHILI POWDER
A ground blend of chili peppers, oregano, cumin seed, garlic, salt and sometimes such spices as cloves, red pepper and

Oregano

Courtesy of National Restaurant Association
Courtesy of American Spice Trade Association

allspice. Basic seasoning for Mexican-style cooking, including chili con carne. Good in shell fish and oyster cocktail sauces, boiled and scrambled eggs, gravy and stew seasoning. Try it in ground meat or hamburgers.

CINNAMON SUGAR

There are few if any times in cooking and baking when cinnamon isn't accompanied by sugar and this skillful blend of the two thus becomes a very convenient product. It is especially useful for cinnamon toast and as a quick topping for many other sweet goods.

CRAB BOIL OR SHRIMP SPICE

These products are similar or identical (depending on the manufacturer) both being mixtures of several whole spices that are to be added to the water when boiling seafood. Typically, they include whole peppercorns, bay leaves, red peppers, mustard seeds, ginger and other spices in whole form.

Cumin Seed

CURRY POWDER

A ground blend of as many as 16 to 20 spices, designed to give the characteristic flavor of Indian curry cookery. Ginger, turmeric, fenugreek seed, cloves, cinnamon, cumin seed, black pepper and red pepper are typical with others being used according to the manufacturer's individual formula. Used in curry sauces, for curry eggs, vege-

Basil

tables, fish and meat. Try a dash in French dressing, scalloped tomatoes, clam and fish chowders and split pea soup.

HERB SEASONING

This is a savory blend of herbs, particularly suited to salads and salad dressings. Actually, the blend varies somewhat according to the brand, but the end uses are essentially the same. Note that the term "herb" specifically refers to the milder flavored leafy products (i.e. marjoram, oregano, basil, chervil, etc.) as opposed to the stronger flavored tropical spices (i.e. pepper, cloves, cinnamon, etc.)

ITALIAN SEASONING

Italian dishes have become so popular in this country that cooks asked for a simple way to achieve the characteristic flavoring of this cuisine. While no one blend could accomplish this completely, it is well known that such seasonings as oregano, basil, red pepper and rosemary are certainly typical of many Italian

Garlic

creations—particularly the popular pastas and pizza. Italian Seasoning characteristically contains these and possibly garlic powder and others.

MIXED PICKLING SPICE

A mixture of several whole spices, usually including mustard seed, bay leaves, black and white peppercorns, dill seed, red peppers, ginger, cinnamon, mace, allspice, coriander seed, etc. Useful for pickling and preserving meats and to season vegetables, relishes, and sauces. Also good in stews and soups.

POULTRY SEASONING

A ground blend of sage, thyme, marjoram and savory and sometimes rosemary and other spices. For poultry, veal, pork and fish stuffings. Good with paprika for meat loaf. For a delightful combination, add to biscuit batter to serve with poultry.

Savory

PUMPKIN PIE SPICE

A ground blend of cinnamon, cloves and ginger. Designed particularly for pumpkin pie, it is good also in spice cookies, gingerbread and breakfast buns. French fry slices of raw pumpkin and dust lightly with pumpkin pie spice for a delicious "something new".

SEAFOOD SEASONING

A ground blend of approximately the same spices as used in Crab Boil and Shrimp Spice with the addition of salt. Especially good in seafood sauces because the ground seasoning blends into the sauce completely.

Courtesy of National Restaurant Association
Courtesy of American Spice Trade Association

Can Name	Can Dimensions²	Approx. Net Wt.³	Net Contents Liquid Product⁴	Some Products for Which Ordinarily Used
2z Mushroom	200 × 204	3¼ oz.	3¼ fl. oz.	Mushrooms
5z Baby food	202 × 214	4¾ oz.	4¼ fl. oz.	Baby foods, chocolate syrup
6z	202 × 308	6 oz.	5¼ fl. oz.	Tomato paste, tomato sauce, juices
6½z	202 × 314	6 oz.	6 fl. oz.	Frozen concentrates, juices
Evaporated milk	206 × 208	6 oz.	6 fl. oz.	Evaporated milk
Meat spread	208 × 109	3 oz.	2¾ fl. oz.	Meat spreads
......	208 × 208	½ lb.	4¾ fl. oz.	Meat products
4z Pimiento	211 × 200	4¾ oz.	4 fl. oz.	Pimientos, chopped olives
......	211 × 208	7 oz.	5½ fl. oz.	Cranberry sauce
4z Mushroom	211 × 212	6¾ oz.	6½ fl. oz.	Mushrooms
8z Short	211 × 300	7¾ oz.	7 fl. oz.	Baked beans, tomato sauce, shrimp, specialties
8z Tall	211 × 304	8½ oz.	7¾ fl. oz.	Vegetables and fruits, juices, specialties
No. 1 Picnic	211 × 400	10½ oz.	9½ fl. oz.	Vegetables, some fruit juices, soups, meat, fish, specialties
Beer	211 × 413	......	12 fl. oz.	Beer and carbonated beverages
Half-quart beer	211 × 604	......	16 fl. oz.	Beer
16z Domed	211 × 604	......	8 fl. oz.	Whipped cream, toppings
No. 211 cylinder	211 × 414	13 oz.	12 fl. oz.	Fruit juices, nectars, tomato juice
Evaporated milk	215 × 315	......	14½ fl. oz.	Evaporated milk
4z Flat pimiento	300 × 108	4 oz.	3¾ fl. oz.	Pimientos
......	300 × 308	11½ oz.	11¼ fl. oz.	Pork and beans
Chocolate syrup	300 × 315½	1 lb.	13 fl. oz.	Chocolate syrup
......	300 × 402	14½ oz.	13 fl. oz.	Infant formulas
No. 300	300 × 407	14½ oz.	13½ fl. oz.	Vegetables, some fruits, juices, soups, meat, fish, pet foods, specialties
......	300 × 409	1 lb.	14 fl. oz.	Meat products
No. 300 cylinder	300 × 509	1 lb. 3 oz.	1 pt. 1 fl. oz.	Soups, pork and beans, specialties
¼ lb. Flat	301 × 106	3¾ oz.	3½ fl. oz.	Salmon
No. 1 Tall	301 × 411	1 lb.	15 fl. oz.	Fruits, some vegetables, juices, fish, specialties
No. 303	303 × 406	1 lb.	15 fl. oz.	Most commonly used size for vegetables, fruits, juices, soups, specialties
No. ½	307 × 113	7 oz.	5¾ fl. oz.	Tuna
½ lb. Flat	307 × 200¼	7¾ oz.	6½ fl. oz.	Salmon
No. 1 Flat	307 × 203	9 oz.	8 fl. oz.	Pineapple
......	307 × 208	......	9 fl. oz.	Sausage, fish flakes, coffee

Courtesy of American Can Co.

Can sizes

Can Name	Can Dimensions²	Approx. Net Wt.³	Net Contents Liquid Product⁴	Some Products for Which Ordinarily Used
No. 2 Squat⁵	307 x 302	½ lb.	.....	Nuts
12z Vacuum	307 x 306	12 oz.	13 fl. oz.	Vacuum packed corn
No. 95	307 x 400	1 lb. 1 oz.	1 pt.	Breads, sea foods
No. 2	307 x 409	1 lb. 4 oz.	1 pt. 2 fl. oz.	Vegetables, fruits, juices, soups, specialties
Jumbo	307 x 510	1 lb. 9 oz.	1 pt. 7 fl. oz.	Pork and beans, mushrooms
32z (Quart)	307 x 710	2 lb. 2 oz.	1 qt.	Fruit juices and drinks
No. 1¼	401 x 207.5	14½ oz.	12½ fl. oz.	Pineapple
Shortening⁵	401 x 307.5	1 lb.	.....	Shortening
No. 2½	401 x 411	1 lb. 13 oz.	1 pt. 10 fl. oz.	Fruits, some vegetables and juices, meat products
......	401 x 509	2 lb. 3 oz.	1 qt.	Frozen concentrates
......	401 x 602	2 lb. 6 oz.	36¾ fl. oz.	Spaghetti, beans in tomato sauce
......	404 x 309	1 lb. 8 oz.	22 fl. oz.	Meat products
No. 3 Cylinder	404 x 700	3 lb. 2 oz.	1 qt. 14 fl. oz.	Fruit and vegetable juices
Vacuum Coffee⁵	502 x 308	1 lb.	......	Coffee
Vacuum Coffee⁵	502 x 607	2 lb.	......	Coffee
Shortening⁵	502 x 514	3 lb.	......	Shortening
No. 10	603 x 700	6 lb. 10 oz.	3 qt.	Institutional size for vegetables, fruits, juices, meat, and fish products, soups, specialties
......	603 x 812	8 lb. 4 oz.	1 gal.	Soft drink syrups
12z Oblong⁵	314 x 202 x 303	12 oz.	......	Meat products
Pullman Base⁵	402 x 310 x 608	3 lb.	......	Meat products
Pullman Base⁵	402 x 310 x 1208	6 lb.	......	Meat products
Pullman Base⁵	414 x 410 x 1100	8 lb.	......	Meat products
Miniature Base Ham⁵	512 x 400 x 211	1 lb. 8 oz.	......	Ham, pear-shaped
#1 Base Ham⁵	710 x 506 x 300	3 lb.	......	Ham, pear-shaped
#1 Base Ham⁵	710 x 506 x 312	4 lb.	......	Ham, pear-shaped
#2 Base Ham⁵	904 x 606 x 308	5 lb. 3 oz.	......	Ham, pear-shaped
#4 Base Ham⁵	1010 x 709 x 412	10 lb. 3 oz.	......	Ham, pear-shaped
¼ Drawn	405 x 301 x 0145	3¼ oz.	......	Sardines
No. 1 Oval	607 x 406 x 108	15 oz.	......	Sardines, sea foods

² In inches and sixteenths of inches. Dimensions vary slightly within manufacturing tolerances. Diameter is listed first, followed by height.

³ The net weights of various foods in the same size can will vary with the density of the product. The weights cited are for foods of average density, except where the container is largely used for one specific class of product.

⁴ The volume figures cited are average commercial fills.

⁵ Key-opened cans.

Courtesy of American Can Co.

Can sizes, continued

GLOSSARY

This GLOSSARY lists many terms used in cooking and in the text, but makes no effort to cover all of them. Definitions have been selected or made up to cover only their more common and reasonable kitchen-and-dining-room meanings.

Figures following definitions indicate pages on which a detailed discussion of the subject commences. Additional references will be found in the INDEX.

A

Air Cell. A bubble of air between the shell membranes at the thick end of an egg. 173

Allspice. Spice made from the berry of the pimento tree. Chiefly used in spiced cakes and pies. 779

American Cheese. Cheddar cheese. 219

Angel (Food) *Cake.* White, sponge-like cake containing flour and egg whites, without shortening. Usually baked in ring pan.

Anti-Oxidant. A substance that reduces or stops the combination of oxygen with food substances. 589

Appetizer. Food or drink served in small portions before a meal.

Apple. The widely grown fruit of a tree of the rose family, equally prized raw and cooked. 289

Apple Butter. Spiced, fine-textured apple sauce.

Apple Sauce. Apples cooked until mushy, sweetened and usually strained. 549

Aromatic. Having a pungent and agreeable odor.

Arrowroot. A starch obtained from root-stalks of a tropical plant of the same name. Used as a thickener. 355

Aspic. Jelled unsweetened juice of cooked food. 499

Au Gratin. Sprinkled with bread crumbs and/or melted cheese, and browned.

Avoirdupois. Standard system of weights in United States and Britain, in which 16 ounces equal one pound. 7

B

Bacon. The cured sides of the hog. 125

Bake. To cook by dry heat, usually in an oven. 63

Baking Powder. A chemical powder formed of a mixture of baking soda and an acid salt, which releases carbon dioxide when moistened, with or without heating. 408

Baking Soda. Sodium bicarbonate, $NaCO_3$ a powder that releases carbon dioxide when combined with acid. 409

Barbecue. An outdoor cooking party, a grill or other apparatus for outdoor cooking or meat grilled with a highly seasoned sauce. 85

Basil. Fresh or dried leaves of aromatic herbs of the mint family. 779

Baste. To pour or brush drippings or other liquids over food to add flavor and reduce drying 69

Baster. A bulb-and-tube syringe used for sucking up drippings and distributing them on food. 69

Batter. A liquid or semi-liquid dough. 414

Bay Leaf. An aromatic herb used to season meat and vegetable dishes. Also called laurel leaf. 779

Bean. Oval seeds, and seed pods, of various leguminous plants. The seeds usually are rich in protein. 241

Beat. To stir vigorously so as to blend thoroughly and/or make smoother, lighter or fluffier. If done with a spoon or a whisk the motion is partly vertical, to take in air with each stroke. 18

Bicarbonate of Soda. Baking soda, NaCO₃. **409**

Biscuit. Tender flaky bread made with chemical leavening and usually baked in small cakes. **420**

Biscuit Ware. Thick, soft pottery. The term originally referred only to unglazed pieces, but is now used for glazed-surface thick china also.

Bisque. Thick creamy soup, usually including shredded shellfish.

Blanch. To cook briefly in boiling water to destroy enzymes or to loosen fruit or vegetable skins. **582**

Blanc-Mange. Cornstarch pudding.

Blend. To combine two or more foods completely. Also, to process in a blender. **22, 743**

Blender. A high speed electric-powered beater having short sharp blades. **742**

Body. Fullness or richness of flavor and/or texture of a food.

Boil. To heat a liquid so that bubbles of its vapor break its surface.

To cook food in boiling water. **33**

Blossom End. The end or side of a fruit opposite the point of attachment of the stem.

Boil Down. To boil a liquid mixture to reduce its volume, concentrate its flavor and/or thicken it.

Bone. A part of an animal's skeleton. To remove bones from meat.

Bottle. A glass container with its neck narrower than its body.

Botulism. Food poisoning from a toxin produced by a bacillus living in low-acid foods in the absence of air. **610**

Bouillon. A clear strained soup or soup stock.

Braise. To cook by searing in fat, then simmering in a little water or water and fat in a covered pan. **57**

Bread. In a broad sense, any cooked mixture consisting mostly of moistened flour or meal.

In a narrow sense, loaves made by baking yeast-leavened dough. **417** To coat food with bread or cracker crumbs. **53**

Brightware (Tinware). Metal cooking utensils for use in ovens. **720**

Brine. Salty water, sometimes with vinegar, sugar, molasses and/or saltpeter, used in pickling, curing or preserving food. **333**

Brisket. A cut of beef, or possibly other meat, from the area of the breastbone and the five lower ribs. Usually made into corned beef.

Broil. To cook by direct exposure across an air gap to flame or other heat source. **69**

Broiler. Any device for broiling. **70**

A young chicken suitable for broiling, weight 2 to 2½ pounds, cut into at least two pieces. **140**

Brown. To cook food until one or more surfaces are brown.

Brown Rice. Unpolished rice. **318**

Brown Sugar. Sugar that is unrefined or partly refined. **342**

Brunch. A late morning meal that combines breakfast and lunch.

Butt. The thicker end of a cut of meat.

Butter. A 4 to 1 mixture of milk fat and water, that is a high quality spread, shortening and flavoring. May be salted. **212**

To spread butter on a food or a pan.

Buttermilk. Sour skimmed milk left after churning butter, or skimmed milk soured by selected bacteria. **205**

C

C. Abbreviation for Celsius or Centigrade.

Cacao. A tropical tree.

Seeds of the cacao tree, used in making chocolate and cocoa.

Cake Flour. Low protein white flour made from soft wheat. **405**

Calcium. A mineral required by the body, chiefly for bone building. **633**

Calorie. A heat energy unit used in measurement of food values.

Can. A sealed metal food container. **605**

To sterilize food by heating it inside cans or sealable glass jars. **608**

Canadian Bacon. Bacon made from pork loin.

Candy. Food consisting mostly of sugar, usually made up of small pieces or flat bars and eaten between meals. **559**

To encrust food with sugar.

Cane Sugar. White sugar or sucrose. Identical with beet sugar. **341**

Cantaloupe. A muskmelon with ribbed rind and orange flesh, usually small. **312**

Capon. A castrated rooster, which is larger and heavier than other chickens.

Carafe. A glass container with a rounded base, used to hold and serve beverages.

Caramel. White sugar that has been heated until it is light brown. **343**

Chewy candy.

Caramelize. To turn brown as an effect of heat; particularly in regard to sugar. **343**

Caraway Seeds. Small, aromatic seeds of the caraway plant. Used as a flavoring or garnish with bread, cheese and other foods. **779**

Carbohydrate. Any of a group of food compounds of carbon, hydrogen and oxygen, such as starch and sugar. **630**

Carbonated Water. Water, usually flavored, containing dissolved carbon dioxide under pressure.

Carbon Steel (High Carbon Steel). Steel that contains a considerable quantity of dissolved carbon. It is harder and can be kept sharper than low carbon (mild) steel. **680**

Carotene. A yellow pigment in fruits and vegetables that is changed to Vitamin A in our bodies. **225**

Casserole. A deep, heavy baking dish, usually with a close-fitting cover. **723**

A non-dessert food mixture cooked in a casserole dish. **395**

Catalyst. A substance that causes or speeds up a chemical reaction, without being altered by the reaction. **632**

Catsup (Ketchup.) A highly seasoned thick sauce, usually with a tomato base.

Caviar. The salted roe of sturgeon or other fish. An expensive delicacy.

Cayenne (Red) *Pepper.* Ground red pepper with a hot, biting flavor. **783**

Celery Salt. A mixture of salt and ground celery seeds, used for providing a celery flavor.

Cellulose. A tough, indigestable but non-toxic carbohydrate found in many plants. It supplies roughage in the diet.

Cereal. Any edible, starchy grain produced by members of the grass family. **317**

Breakfast food made from grain. **323**

Chafing Dish. A utensil used for warming, cooking or keeping-hot food at the table, by means of a small flame or electric unit.

Cheddar. A firm white or yellow cheese made from cow's milk. Some varieties are known as American cheese. Used for most cheese purposes. **219**

Cheese. A solid or semi-solid milk product usually made from partially dried, processed milk curd. **218**

Cheese Cake. A rich soft cake having cream cheese or cottage cheese as a principal ingredient.

Chicken. The most important domestic fowl for meat and egg production. **135**

Chili Pepper. A hot pepper that may be ground into cayenne pepper, or pickled and served as a relish.

Chili Powder. A blend of spices including chili pepper, oregano, cumin and garlic. **784**

China. A ceramic made of baked clay, used in most tableware.

Dishes made or usually made of china.

Chipped beef. Thinly sliced beef, dried and salted.

Chive. An onion-like herb whose grass-like leaves are chopped and used as flavoring and garnish.

Chlorine. A chemically active gas used in water purification and in bleaches.

Chocolate. Roasted cacao beans ground into a fine powder and pressed into cakes, usually in combination with sugar. **338**

Chop. A small cut of meat from the rib or loin part of the animal.

To cut into small pieces in a random manner. **21**

Chowder. A thick soup, usually containing clams or fish, with potatoes and salt pork. **484**

Churn. To agitate rather slowly so as to cause clotting and separation, usually in making butter out of cream. **213**

Cider. Unpasteurized apple juice.

Cinnamon. An aromatic spice consisting of bark of twigs of a tropical evergreen tree, or powder made from the bark. Principal use is in baked goods and desserts. **780**

Citric Acid. The principal factor in the acid or sour taste in citrus fruits. Also found in many other kinds of fruit.

Clarify. To remove cloudiness from a liquid by filtering, by freezing, or by precipitating particles by adding egg shells and/or whites or other materials.

Cob. The thick, hard, inedible stem that forms the base for corn kernels. **254**

Cobbler. A deep dish fruit pie, with a single crust which is usually made of biscuit dough. **553**

Cocktail. A mixed alcoholic drink, chilled and served in a small glass.

An appetizer, usually fruit, fruit juice or seafood.

Cocoa. A powdered chocolate from which about half the fat has been removed. **339**

Coffee Cake. Usually yeast bread, slightly sweetened, often combined with nuts and spices, and/or topped with thin icing, nuts or crumbs. **424**

Colander. A perforated metal vessel standing on legs. **703**

Condensed Milk. Cow's milk, concentrated by evaporation of water, protected from spoilage by addition of 42 to 44 per cent of sugar, then sealed in cans. **207**

Condiment. Seasoning served at the table.

Conch. A very large sub-tropical snail, tasty but often tough.

Confection. Candy, or a small quantity of food or decoration made mostly of sugar.

Confectioner's Sugar. Finely powdered sugar, often mixed with a little cornstarch to reduce clumping. **342**

Consommé. A clear soup, stock or dilute extract made from meat or poultry.

Converted Rice. Rice that has been partly cooked before removal of husks. The process retains vitamins and minerals, but increases cooking time.

Cook. To prepare food for eating by the action of heat.

Cookie (Cooky). Small, thin cakes, usually crisp in texture. **442**

Cookie Sheet. A wide flat pan of thin metal, with one or more turned-up edges. **721**

Cool-Rise Bread. Bread made from special yeast dough that has been raised or proofed in a refrigerator. **408**

Coral. Roe of the female lobster.

Corer. A curved knife designed to remove fruit cores. **684**

Corkscrew. A pointed metal spiral used for pulling corks out of bottles. **698**

Corn. In the United States, a grain whose seeds or kernels grow on a large cob. **254**

To preserve food in brine. **103**

Corn Meal (Cornmeal). Meal or coarse flour made by grinding corn kernels. **321**

Corned beef. Beef that has soaked in brine. **103**

Corn Starch (Cornstarch). A finely powdered starch extracted from corn. **355**

Corn Syrup. A syrup, consisting mostly of glucose and water, made from corn. **376**

Cottage Cheese. Soft, white cheese made from milk curd with little processing and no ripening. **220**

Cottage Pudding. A dessert made of plain cake, usually yellow, and a sweet sauce.

Cps. Abbreviation for cups.

Crab. An edible crustacean. **165**

Cracker. A thin crisp wafer made from flour dough, usually unsweetened.

Cranberry. A red, acid berry that grows in marshes.

Cream. Milk that contains 18 per cent or more of milk fat. **198**

To mix or crush to a soft or creamy consistency. **20**

Cream Cheese. A white, unripened cheese made from cream. **221**

Cream Sauce. White sauce, or white sauce enriched with cream. **198**

Cream of Tartar. A white powder that has an acid reaction. **408**

Crisp. To be fresh and firm. Opposite of wilted.

To rinse leaves in cold water, or to chill them while wet, to make firm and crisp. **488**

To toast bread or crackers until they are dry or brittle. **54**

Croquette. A cone, ball or cake of minced food, coated with batter or crumbs, and fried. **389**

Cruet. A small glass bottle used for vinegar or oil. **368**

Cruller. A long doughnut, formed by twisting two strands of the dough together.

Crust. Any outer surface of a food that is harder than the interior. **68**

Pastry layers forming the top and bottom of a pie. **447**

Crustacean. A class of active aquatic animals, including lobsters and crabs, that have hard outer shells and many legs. **163**

Cube. To cut into small (¼ to ½-inch) more or less cubical pieces. **237**

To tenderize meat by slicing or imprinting a square pattern of cuts into its surface. **106**

Cucumber. A small cylindrical green fruit related to the squashes, usually eaten raw in salad. **262**

Cup. A small open container with a handle.

A measurement that equals ½ pint or 8 fluid ounces.

Cup Cake. A small cake, making an individual serving, which is usually baked in a muffin tin.

Curd. The semi-solid part of soured milk. It is rich in protein, and is the basis of most cheese. **197**

Any food resembling milk curd.

Curdle. To separate a thick liquid into a thin liquid and particles or masses of curd. **211**

Cure. To preserve and to change flavor of a food by soaking, injecting or surface application of salt, flavorings and preservatives, or inoculating with organisms.

Currant. An acid berry related to the gooseberry.

A variety of small seedless raisin. **309**

Curry. A powdered mixture of spices, usually including cayenne, coriander, cumin and tumeric. **785**

Any dish that is strongly seasoned with curry powder.

Custard. A Cooked mixture of egg, milk and sugar, which may be solid or liquid. 527

Cut In. To combine solid shortening with flour and other powders by repeated cuts through both substances. 451

To produce a lumpy or grainy mixture. 451

Cutlet. A thin cut of meat, usually veal and usually from the leg. 117

D

Dash. A very small amount, usually one to 3 drops, of a strong flavoring.

Deep Dish Pie. A fruit pie made in a moderately deep dish, with only a top crust. 464

Deep Fat. Hot fat that is deep enough to cover or float food being cooked in it.

Deep Fry. To fry in deep fat. 58

De-Grease. To remove fat from soup or other liquids. 482

Dehydrate. To remove moisture from food, usually to preserve it. 600

Deliquesce. To become liquid by absorption of moisture from the air.

Demitasse. A very small coffee cup.

Strong black coffee served in a demitasse cup after dinner.

Dessert. Any food that is usually served at the end of a meal. It is usually sweet, but cheese and fruit are considered to be desserts if served at dessert time. 527

Detent. A checking device that will hold a handle in a particular position against moving under light pressure, but permit it to move under heavier pressure.

Devil. To prepare minced food with strong seasoning.

Dextrose (Glucose). A not-very-sweet sugar manufactured by plants from carbon dioxide and water, and by animals from starch and other sugars. 341

Dice. To cut into small more or less cubical pieces, ⅛ to ¼ inch. Result is finer than cubed food, and coarser than minced. 237

Dip. A thick, sour or seasoned sauce in which crackers, vegetable sticks or other food bits are dipped while eating as appetizers. 221

Dot. To distribute small bits of a topping over food.

Double Boiler. A set of two pans used for cooking delicate mixtures. The upper one, fitting snugly into the lower, contains food. The lower contains boiling or simmering water. 716

Dough. A firm or elastic mixture of flour and liquid, usually including a leavening agent, salt, sugar, water, milk, eggs, seasoning and/or other materials. 411

Doughnut. A deep fried cake, usually ring-shaped. 443

Dps. Abbreviation for drops.

Draw. To disembowel (eviscerate) poultry or fish. 139, 155

To steep.

To clarify butter. 216

Drawn butter. Butter that has been clarified or seasoned.

A sauce of melted butter and water or stock, thickened with flour.

Dredge. To coat food by dipping it in flour, crumbs or sugar. 53

Dress. To clean fish or fowl for cooking, by removing feathers, scales and innards.

Dressing. Sauce for salad. 368

Stuffing for poultry. 141

Dried (Dry) *Milk.* Milk, usually skimmed, that has been dehydrated and powdered. 209

Drippings. Juice and melted fat that accumulate in a pan below meat or fish during roasting or broiling. 362

Drop Cookie. A cookie formed by dropping a spoonful of soft batter onto a baking sheet. 442

Dry-Fry. To fry with little or no fat.

Often called pan-broiling. 57

Dumpling. A piece of dough cooked in soup, stew or drippings.

A piece of fruit cooked in a wrapping of biscuit dough. 557

Dust. To sprinkle lightly with a powder such as flour or sugar.

Dutch Oven. A heavy pot with a close-fitting lid. 717

E

Earthenware. Utensils of porous baked clay that are made waterproof by a glazed surface.

Eel. A snake-shaped, scaleless fish.

Egg. In cooking, usually the ovoid (egg-shaped) reproductive body produced by the female chicken. 171

Eggbeater. A hand cranked rotary beater, having two sets of vanes with overlapping rotation in opposite directions. 701

Egg Slicer. A frame fitted with parallel cutting wires, hinged to a slotted base. 685

Electronic (Microwave) *Cooking.* Cooking of food by penetrating it with high frequency radio waves. 73

Emulsifier. A substance that retards or prevents separation of an oil-and-water mixture. **369**

Emulsion. A stable mixture of two or more liquids that ordinarily separate from each other. **369**

Enamelware. Pans and utensils made of iron, steel or pottery covered with a glass-like layer of baked enamel. **711**

Endosperm. The starchy part of grain kernels. **404**

English muffin. A flat, round, tough bread patty cooked on a griddle. **423**

Entrée. In the United States, the main or meat course of a meal.

Enzyme. An organic substance that can cause or assist a specific chemical reaction. An organic catalyst. **566**

Evaporated Milk. Unsweetened sterilized canned milk from which 60 per cent of the water has been removed. **206**

Extract. A substance, usually fluid, containing the concentrated flavor of a food. **337**

A solution in alcohol of a flavor. **337**

F

F. Abbreviation for Fahrenheit.

Fat. Any edible compound made up of glycerol and certain (fatty) acids, occurring in both plant and animal tissues. **101**

Fell. A membrane just below the skin of an animal, particularly on a lamb leg. **128**

Fermentation. Chemical change in food caused by yeast or bacteria. **407**

Filet Mignon. A boneless steak cut from the narrow end of the beef tenderloin.

Fillet. A strip of fish or meat that has been separated from bones. **157**

Flaky. Crisp, tender and easily crumbled into thin flat particles or small sheets.

Flan. The Spanish name for baked custard, usually with caramel sauce.

Flank. The sides of an animal between the ribs and the hips.

Float. A milk or carbonated beverage with ice cream floating in it. **522**

Floating Island. A dessert consisting of mounds of sweetened meringue floating on stirred mustard. **529**

Flounder. Any of a group of flatfish, that are cooked as fillets, or whole.

Flour. Finely powdered grain, usually wheat kernels. **403**

To apply a light coat of flour to a damp food or a greased pan.

Floweret. A small section of the surface of a head of cauliflower or broccoli, with its supporting stem.

Fold. Light mixing together of liquids of different textures, usually with a slow, vertical stirring motion. **19**

Food Mill. A strong container having numerous small holes through which food may be forced by rotary motion of a blade or roller. **704**

Fowl. Any bird.

A domesticated bird raised for food.

An elderly chicken.

Frankfurter (Hot Dog). A very popular reddish sausage made of beef, or of beef and pork, with seasoning. **380**

Freeze. Reduce temperature of food until its liquids become solid.

Freeze-Dry. To dehydrate a food by freezing it, then causing its moisture to change directly from ice to vapor. **603**

Freezer Burn. Hardening of surfaces of frozen food because of drying. **595**

French Fries. Deep fried potato strips. **276**

French Fry. To cook in deep fat.

French Toast. Bread dipped in eggs and milk, then fried. **531**

Fresh Ham. Uncured ham. **121**

Fricassee. A stew, usually chicken. **146**

Fritter. A small fried cake made of batter that surrounds or is mixed with pieces of food. **557**

Frizzle. To fry or heat until crisp.

Frost. To put icing on a cake. **440**

To chill glasses so that a layer of frost builds on them when exposed to air.

The deposit of ice crystals that forms on refrigeration units. **770**

Fructose (Levulose). A sugar found in fruit. It is somewhat sweeter than cane sugar (sucrose). **341**

Fruit. Any developed ovary of a seed plant.

In cookery, members of this class that have soft or fleshy pulp, are eaten when ripe or nearly ripe, and that are usually served as dessert instead of as a vegetable. **289**

Fruit Cake. A cake made with a little batter and a lot of dried or candied fruit, nuts and flavoring.

Fry. To cook or brown in or with hot liquid fat. **49**

An informal meal featuring a fried food, a fish *fry*.

Fryer. A chicken weighing 1½ to 3 pounds.

Fungus. A non-flowering plant that contains no chlorophyll, and grows only on organic matter, which may be living or dead. Molds and mushrooms are fungi (funguses).

G

Game. Any wild animal, bird or fish ordinarily obtained by hunting or fishing for sport.

Garlic. The strongly flavored, foul-smelling bulb of a plant of the onion family, widely used as a seasoning. **335**

Garlic Salt. A mixture of ground garlic and table salt.

Garnish. Bits of food added to a dish chiefly for appearance.

Gelatin. An animal protein that can cause water to set into a jelly. **349**

A flavored dessert or salad jelly made with gelatin. **497, 535**

Gelatinization. Absorption of water into molecules in sufficient quantity to cause a fluid to thicken or solidify. **349**

Giblets. Edible entrails of a fowl, usually the liver, gizzard and heart. **140**

Ginger. A pungent, biting spice. **781**

Gingerbread. A dark cake or cookie flavored with molasses and ginger.

Glaze. Any substance used to give a glossy surface or coat to food, and the coating itself.

A protective coating of ice. **595**

Glucose (Dextrose). A sugar, less sweet than cane sugar, present in many fruits and vegetables, and the principal ingredient of corn syrup. **341**

Gluten. The group of proteins in grain, especially in wheat. **404**

Goose. A large, web-footed bird with dark meat, both wild and domesticated. **149**

Goulash. Beef stew served on noodles.

Gourmet. A discriminating person who appreciates good cooking and eating. **330**

Granulated Sugar. White (cane or beet) sugar in the form of small grains. This is the form that is meant by the unmodified word "sugar" in recipes. **341**

Grape. A smooth-skinned edible berry growing in clusters. **308**

Grapefruit. A large yellow citrus fruit, with pale yellow or pink flesh. **302**

Grater. A sheet of metal having sharp-edged perforations that cut food into shreds or fine particles. **21**

Gravy. Juices and melted fat exuded by meat while cooking, with or without separation and/or thickening. **146**

Grease. Soft fat.

To put grease or oil on a pan or other surface to prevent sticking.

Green (String) *Bean.* Varieties of bean cultivated for their narrow, green, edible pods. **241**

Green Pepper. The unripe fruit of the sweet pepper. **272**

Greens. The edible leaves and small stems of a variety of plants, when cooked as vegetables. **264**

Griddle. A flat, nearly rimless frypan. **719**

Griddlecake (Pancake) (Hot Cake). A flat, thin, tender cake or bread often served as a breakfast dish with butter and syrup. **444**

Grill. A grating or other support for food cooked over hot coals. **85**

An electric broiler. **737**

To cook on a grill. **90**

Grinder. A device that reduces food to fine pieces or powder, usually by means of rotating cutters.

Grit Cells. Clusters of hard cells found in the flesh of pears. **294**

Grits. Coarsely or finely ground hominy. **321**

Gumbo. A soup thickened with okra, or the okra itself.

H

Half-and-half. A Mixture of milk and cream that contains 10 or 12 per cent butterfat. It may be made of equal parts of whole milk and light cream.

Half shell, on the. A bivalve mollusk (clam or oyster) served raw in one half of it shell.

Ham. The thigh of an animal, especially a hog, when used for food. **121**

When unmodified, usually the cured thigh of a hog, or a cut made from it. **123**

Hamburger. Ground or chopped beef. **115**

A patty of such meat, or a sandwich made with it. **475**

Hang. To suspend meat or game from a hook for aging, for the purpose of tenderizing and developing flavor.

Hard sauce. An uncooked dessert sauce, made of confectioner's or powdered sugar with butter or cream, with or without flavoring. **375**

Hash. Chopped cooked meat, usually combined with potatoes and gravy. **381**

Head Lettuce. Lettuce that grows in a ball or head. The principal varieties are iceberg and Boston. **488**

Heavy Cream (Whipping Cream). Cream containing 35 to 40 per cent butterfat. **199**

Herb. Any soft plant whose leaves or other parts are used for seasoning.

High. Slightly spoiled and smelly, but pleasing to many tastes. Used in reference to meat, particularly game.

Hollandaise. A rich sauce made with egg yolks, butter, acid and seasoning. **360**

Home Fries. Cooked potatoes, sliced or chopped and shallow-fried until brown. Onions and seasoning may be added. **276**

Hominy. Shelled corn kernels, and meal (grits) made from them. **321**

Homogenizing. Breaking down fat particles in a water-liquid to such small sizes that they do not separate from it. **201**

Honey. A thick, very sweet liquid made by bees from flower nectar. **375**

Hors d'oeuvre. Small pieces of tasty food served before a meal or with cocktails.

Hydrogenation. A process of solidifying oil by adding hydrogen to its molecules. **631**

Hygroscopic. Having a tendency to absorb moisture from air. **332**

I

Ice. A frozen food made with sugar and fruit juice or water and flavoring. **545**

To apply icing to a cake. **440**

Ice Cream. A frozen dessert containing sweetened milk, cream or custard. **537**

Icing. A sugar mixture used to cover, sweeten and decorate cakes. **437**

Infusion. A solution obtained by dissolving only parts of a solid, for example, the flavorful substances from tea leaves.

Ingredient. Any substance that is made part of a mixture.

Instant Coffee. A dried coffee concentrate that is readily soluble in water. **516**

J

Jam. A cooked mixture of sugar and crushed fruit or berries. **626**

Jell (Gel). Congealing of a liquid into a weak solid or jelly.

Jelly. A weak, quivery solid made by of water-liquids and gelatin or pectin. **349, 619**

Jigger (shot glass). A small measuring glass for liquor, holding about 1½ ounces.

Juicer. Any device that separates juice from fruit. **300**

Julienne. Cut into long, very thin strips.

Junket. A dessert made with milk and sugar, jelled with rennet. **533**

K

Kebob. A cube of meat, usually lamb, marinated, then broiled on a skewer.

Ketchup (Catsup). A thick, highly seasoned tomato sauce.

Kidney. Urine-secreting organs, that are tasty and tender when from young animals. **132**

Kidney Bean. Mature, kidney-shaped brown-red beans.

Any bean seed with a kidney shape.

King Crab. The largest variety of edible crab, found in the northern Pacific.

Kiss. A small baked meringue.

Knead. To mix thick soft material, usually dough, by pushing, pulling, pressing and turning. **413**

Knife. A utensil consisting of a sharp-edged blade set in a handle. **680**

Kohlrabi. A member of the cabbage family raised chiefly for a thick, tender bulge in the stem. **265**

Kuchen. Sweetened yeast dough, used chiefly in coffee cake. **424**

L

Ladyfinger. A small, narrow sponge cake.

Lamb. A young sheep, usually less than twelve months old. **128**

Lard. Pork fat processed so as to be smooth, soft and white.

Lasagne. Broad, flat or ruffled noodles, or a casserole made with such noodles. **398**

Leaven. To lighten dough or batter by organic or chemical production of gas bubbles inside it. **406**

Leavening. A material that will lighten a mixture by producing gas bubbles. Yeast and baking powder are leavenings. **406, 408**

Leek. A mild-flavored member of the onion family. **266**

Legume. A family of plants with protein-rich seeds. It includes beans, peas and peanuts.

Lemon. A small yellow citrus fruit valued chiefly for its very acid juice. **303**

Lettuce. Plants with crisp green leaves that are eaten raw in salads. **487**

Lime. A small green citrus fruit, usually very acid, that is used in flavoring. **304**

A mineral deposit left by hard water. **673**

Liqueur. Any of a number of sweet, strong

alcoholic beverages, usually taken in very small amounts after dinner.

Liquor. Any distilled alcoholic beverage.

A liquid in which food has been cooked.

Liver. An organ of vertebrates that is highly nourishing and is often prized as food. 131

Lobster. Large ten-legged marine crustaceans having the front legs modified into claws. 163

Loin. The sides and back of an animal, between (but not including) the ribs and the hipbone.

M

Macaroni. A general name for pasta. 324
Pasta in the form of tubes, often in short pieces bent into "elbows". 328

Macaroon. A small chewy cookie containing almonds or coconut.

Madrilene. Tomato-flavored consomme.

Malt. Barley, or sometimes other grain, soaked until it sprouts, then dried.

Maize. The European name for corn.

Maple Sugar. A very sweet sugar made from the sap of the sugar maple tree. 343

Maple Syrup. A highly valued sweet syrup made from sugar maple sap, or from maple sugar. 377

Marbling. Fine, closely spaced veins or pockets of fat in meat. 102

Margarin (Margarine). A substitute for butter which has similar fat content and is used in the same manner in cooking and as a spread. 216

Marinade. A liquid, usually acid and seasoned, in which food is soaked for flavor and, in the case of meat, for tenderizing. 371

Marinate. To soak food in an acid liquid.

Marmalade. A preserve, usually semiliquid, and usually made from citrus rind and pulp.

Marron. The French word for chestnut. In America, usually a chestnut preserved in sweet syrup.

Marrow. Soft tissue found in the cavities in bones.

Mayonnaise. A thick, smooth sauce or salad dressing made principally with eggs, oil, acid (lemon or vinegar) and seasoning. 370

MDAR (Minimum Daily Adult Requirement). The calculated amount of a vitamin or mineral needed daily by an adult for maintenance of good health. 633

Meal. Ground cereal, particularly corn. It is coarser than flour. 321

Bone or other substances ground to meal-like fineness or texture.

Mealy. Dry, powdery, finely granular, sometimes over-soft.

Meat. The edible flesh of any animal, including birds or crustaceans, but seldom fish.

In a narrower sense, the flesh of domesticated mammals.

Meat Thermometer. A thermometer with a probe with a sensitive tip that can register internal temperature of a roast or other meat while it is cooking. 705

Meat Pie. A meat stew with a single upper pie crust. 392

Melba Toast. Very thin (1/4-inch) dry toast.

Melon. Large to very large, mildly sweet fruits of members of the gourd family. 312

Meringue. Stiffly beaten egg whites, with or without sugar, either raw or cooked as kisses or topping for pie or dessert. 189

Microwave (Electronic) Cooking. Fast cooking by means of high frequency waves that are absorbed by water, causing production of heat. 73

Milk. A whitish opaque, highly nourishing fluid produced by mammals for nourishing of their young.

Usually, cow's milk. 193

Milk Shake. A frothy beverage made by beating up milk, sugar and flavoring, often including ice cream. 522

Milk Toast. Toasted bread soaked in milk, with or without sweetening and seasoning.

Mince. To cut or chop into very small pieces.

Mineral. Non-organic compound containing an element or elements necessary for nutrition. 633

Minute Steak. A thin, small beef steak that is usually dry-fried.

Mixer. Electric kitchen appliance equipped with one or two revolving beaters. 741

Mocha. A mixture of coffee and chocolate flavors.

Originally, a high quality Arabian coffee.

Molasses. A syrup byproduct of sugar refining that is used for flavoring. 376

Mold. Small fungus plants, commonly in groups having a furry appearance.

A dish or pan of distinctive shape, used for forming jelly or other food, which is taken out (unmolded) before serving. 497

Mollusk. A large family of invertebrates, most of which have shells and live in the water. It includes oysters, clams, scallops, snails and squids.

Monosodium Glutamate. A white powder that is added to foods to accentuate their flavors. **345**

Mousse. A dessert consisting of whipped cream with beaten egg whites or gelatin, with sugar and flavoring. May be chilled or frozen. **545**

Muffin. A small, cup-shaped bread, usually light in texture and slightly sweetened. **421**

Mushroom. An umbrella shaped fungus.

Muskmelon. Any melon having a hollow interior partly filled with seeds. **312**

Mussel. An edible bivalve mollusk with a blue or purple shell.

Mustard. A pungent yellow-brown condiment sold in paste or powder form.

Mutton. The flesh of sheep at least one year old.

Mycelium. Root-like feeding strands of fungus.

N

Noodle. A pasta made with added eggs, usually shaped into fine or wide ribbons. **328**

Nut. A dry fruit whose flesh is enclosed in a hard shell.

The edible kernel (flesh) of such a fruit. **314**

O

Offal (Variety Meats). Organs of animals that are or may be used for food. **130**

Oil. Liquid fat.

Okra (Gumbo). A green seed pod used as a vegetable and as a thickener. **267**

Olive. A small, firm, oily fruit that is pickled. Used as a relish, and for flavor and decoration.

Olive Oil. Salad or cooking oil extracted from olives.

Omelet. Usually an egg-milk mixture cooked with little or no stirring. **186**

Onion. An edible bulb with a pungent odor and taste, used as a flavoring and as a vegetable. **268**

Open-faced. Without a top covering, as a sandwich having only one (bottom) slice of bread. **478**

Orange. A citrus fruit with moderate size, round shape, orange color and sweet or near-sweet taste. Highly valued for juice. **301**

Organic Food. Food grown and processed without chemical (non-organic) fertilizers, insecticides, preservatives or flavorings. **645**

Osmosis. The movement of water through a membrane, from a weak solution into a more concentrated one. **39**

Oyster. A highly valued bivalve mollusk, eaten either raw or cooked. **167**

Oyster Plant (Salsify). An edible root, shaped like a carrot with an oyster-like flavor. **280**

P

Pan Broil (Dry-Fry). To fry with little or no fat.

Pancake (Griddle Cake) (Hot Cake). A flat, thin tender cake fried on a lightly greased hot griddle. **444**

Pandowdy. A dessert made of a layer of sliced apples or other fruit, covered with biscuit batter and baked. **553**

Pan-Fry. To fry in a fry pan, usually with shallow fat. **56**

Pan Gravy. Unthickened gravy whose principal ingredient is drippings from roasting meat. **363**

Papain. A meat-tenderizing enzyme obtained from papaya fruit. **107**

Papaya. A large, tasty, melon-like fruit of a small tropical tree.

Paprika. A usually mild red pepper powder, used more for decoration than for flavor. **782**

Parboil. To partially cook food in boiling water. Similar to blanching, but cooking time is usually longer. **36**

Pare. To peel thinly. **232**

Parmesan. A hard Italian cheese, chiefly used in grated form as a flavoring. **221**

Parsley. A herb with lacy, aromatic leaves, used chiefly as a garnish. When chopped or dried it is used for flavoring.

Parsnip. A white edible root, mild and slightly sweet, with a distinctive flavor. **270**

Pasta. A general name for the various shapes of food such as macaroni, spaghetti and lasagne, made from unleavened semolina wheat dough. **324**

Pasteurize. To heat sufficiently to destroy undesirable organisms, without sterilizing the food. **201**

Pastry. Baked goods made with a flour-and-fat dough, usually having a flaky texture. Pie crust is the best known form.

Loosely, any small, sweet baked food.

Pastry Blender. A number of parallel stiff wire loops set in a handle, used chiefly in mixing flour and fat for pastry. **701**

Pastry Brush. A small, fine soft brush used

to apply glazing material to surfaces of baked goods.

Pastry Cloth. A dense, heavy cloth that is dusted with flour and used for a non-stick base for rolling out pastry dough. 455

Pastry Shell (Pie Shell). A baked, empty lower pie crust. 458

Patty. A small, flat, usually rounded cake of chopped food.

Pea. Small, round seeds of a leguminous plant of the same name. 270

Peach. An edible fruit with a pit, a loose fuzzy skin and sweet yellow (or rarely, white) flesh. 296

Peanut. A legume whose pods develop underground. The edible seeds are nut-like after roasting. 315

Pear. A sweet tender fruit closely related to the apple. 294

Pecan. A relative of the hickory nut with a thin shell and large tender meat.

Pectin. A substance found in fruit that can cause liquid to jell if sugar and acid are present. 351

Peel. To remove the skin or outer layer of fruits or vegetables. 232

Fruit skin after removal.

Pepper, Black. A popular spice, used both as whole berries (peppercorns) and as powder. 335

Pepper Mill. A small grinder used for making pepper powder out of peppercorns at the table. 335

Persimmon. A soft, juicy, seedless, tomato-colored fruit that has a rich sweet flavor when fully ripe, but is astringent and bitter before then. It is very sloppy to eat.

Percolator. A coffee pot in which boiling forces water upward through a tube, so that it filters back through a basket of ground coffee. 509

pH. A symbol for the acidity of a solution. A pH of 7 in neutral, lower figures show increasing acidity, higher ones indicate alkalinity. 607

Pickle. To preserve in seasoned vinegar.

Any food preserved by pickling.

Pie. Food baked or served in a pastry shell or crust. Usually a dessert, less often a meat stew. 447

Pie Crust. Pastry rolled into thin sheets and used for pan lining and/or topping for a pie. 448

Pimento (Pimiento). A mild, sweet red pepper.

The tropical tree and berry from which allspice is made.

Pineapple. A large, cone-shaped, edible tropical fruit. 306

Pizza. An open face pie, having cheese, tomato and other foods in a thin layer on a bread crust.

Pkg. Abbreviation for package.

Plantain. A large, unsweet cooking banana. 241

Plum. A soft fruit of variable sweetness having a hard pit. 290

Poach. To simmer.

In reference to eggs, to cook in water after removal from shells. 181

Popcorn. A variety of corn in which the kernels explode into white soft masses when they are heated. 321

Popover. A very light hollow muffin, made without any leavening except eggs. 423

Porcelain. A dense, smooth-surfaced china.

Porcelain Enamel (Baked Enamel). A glassy surface coating fused to metal or other bases by heat. 711

Pork. The edible flesh of the pig. 118

Pot. Any cooking vessel except a frypan.

A two-handled cooking vessel. 714

Pot Cheese. A variety of cottage cheese.

Pot Roast. A roast, usually a non-tender cut of beef, cooked slowly in a covered pot with little liquid. 113

Potable. Suitable for drinking.

Potato. Edible root tubers with white flesh. 273

Potato Chips. Very thin potato slices fried until light brown and crisp, then salted.

Poultry. Domesticated birds used as food. 135

Preheat. To heat an oven or a pan to cooking temperature before putting food into it.

Preserve. To process food so that it can be stored for long periods.

Fruit preserved in syrup.

Pressure Cooker. A strong cooking pan with a gasketed, air-tight lid, and a pressure valve or indicator. 585

Proofing. Causing or allowing the expansion of raw dough by the action of yeast. 413

Protein. Complex organic substances containing nitrogen. 630

Prune. Dried plum. 298

Pt. Abbreviation for pint.

Pudding. A sweet dessert that is too soft to stand in cut slices. 530

Non-sweet food mixtures with a pudding consistency.

Puffball. Edible fungi that are round in shape.

Pullet. A hen chicken less than one year old.

Pulp. Soft, moist, weak mass of matter, such as the flesh of very ripe fruit.

Food that has been processed until it is structureless.

Pumpkin. A very large edible fruit of a vine of the gourd family, that can be used in the same manner as winter squash. 283

Purée. A smooth, thick mushy food pulp, usually obtained by sieving or electric-blending. 484

Pyrex. Trade name of the Corning Glass Works for a type of heat-resistant glass.

Q

Qt. Abbreviation for quart

Quahog. A hard-shelled round clam of the Atlantic coast.

Quick Bread. Breads such as biscuits and muffins that are leavened without yeast. 414

R

Radish. The pungent, edible root of a quick-growing member of the mustard family. 280

Raisin. Dried grape. 308

Rancid. Rank taste and smell of spoiled (usually oxidized) fat. 569

Raspberry. A sweet, edible berry that is hollow or thimble-shaped. 311

Recipe. A list of ingredients for a mixture or a product, together with directions for combining, cooking and/or other processing. 4

Reconstitute. To restore a concentrated food to its original water content and bulk. 601

Rehydration. Restoration of moisture to a dried food. 601

Render. To heat meat or bones to separate the fat by melting.

Rennet. A preparation made from stomachs of young calves, used in jellying milk. 532

Rice. The seed of a water-loving grain. 318

To press food through a ricer.

Ricer. A kitchen utensil consisting of a perforated basket and a hand operated plunger that pushes soft food through the holes.

Rind. A skin or outer covering that may be removed as inedible or undesirable.

Ripen. To mature toward most desirable eating condition.

Roast. To cook meat in an oven. 63

Meat cooked in an oven.

Rock Salt. A coarse salt used to freeze ice cream and de-ice sidewalks. 333

Rock Lobster. Spiny or warm-water lobster. 165

Roe. The eggs of female fish. 156

Sometimes the milt or sperm of male fish. 156

Roll. A small bread shape. 419

Any food rolled up before cooking.

Romaine. A lettuce with long, rather stiff leaves. 488

Rotary Beater (Egg Beater). A hand or electric beater with two sets of vanes that rotate in overlapping paths. 701, 740

Rottisserie. A device that causes a large piece of food to rotate while being broiled. 738

Round. The part of a beef hind leg between the rump and the shank.

Roux. A mixture of equal quantities flour and fat, used as a base for white sauce. 357

Rump. The hip portion of an animal.

S

Saccharin. A non-fattening sugar substitute with great sweetening power, but having a bitter aftertaste for many people. 345

Salad Dressing. Any sauce used on salad, but usually one containing vinegar. 368

Salad Green. Any green leaf that is eaten in salad. 487

Salmon. Fish which have pink or red flesh, and live in the sea but breed in fresh water.

Salsify (Oyster Plant). A root that has an oyster-like flavor. 280

Salt. Usually, sodium chloride, an abundant mineral that is refined from sea water, or mined. 331

Salt Cellar. A very small open container of salt, now replaced by salt shakers, a change that may be regretted in humid weather. 333

Salt Pork. A fatty back or middle portion of a pig, preserved in brine.

Sandwich. A combination of bread and other food — usually two slices of bread with filling between. 471

Sandy. Having an unwanted gritty texture. 560

Sauce. A liquid or semi-liquid accompaniment to a food. Exception — hand sauce is solid. 357

Saucepan. A moderately deep pan with a projecting handle. 714

Sauerkraut. Shredded, salted cabbage fermented in its own juice.

Sausage. Finely chopped meat, often pork, seasoned and stuffed into casings. 379

Sauté. Pan fry, usually briefly with little fat.

Scald. To heat a liquid to a little below its boiling point.

To dip in hot water to loosen skin or to blanch.

Scallion. An immature onion. Both the small bulb and the leaves are eaten raw.

Scallop. A bivalve mollusk whose large shell muscle is the part used as food. 167

To bake in a casserole, usually with crumbs on top.

Scouring. Vigorous cleaning of a surface, usually by rubbing with abrasives. 659

Scrambled Eggs. Eggs that are stirred or beaten together before cooking, usually with milk or water, and are stirred while frying. 184

Sear. To brown the surface of meat by resting it briefly on a hot pan. 113

Season. To alter the flavor of food by adding salt and condiments.

To age meat by hanging it in a cool place.

Seasoning. Ingredients added to food for flavor rather than nourishment. 329

Semolina. A fine wheat meal, coarser than flour, used in manufacture of macaroni products. 325

Shaved. A brittle substance cut into thin slices that crumble.

Shellfish. Any aquatic animal having a shell. 163

Sherbet. A fruit ice or a thin ice cream. 545

Shirred Eggs. Opened eggs cooked in an oven or under a broiler.

Shish Kebab. Small pieces of lamb or other meat broiled on skewers with small onions and tomato pieces.

Shortcake. A dessert made with biscuit or sponge cake, raw berries or peaches, and whipped cream. 555

Shortening. Fat used in baked goods. 411

Shortness. A rich, crumbly or flaky texture in baked goods created by a liberal proportion of fat. 411

Shred. To cut, shave or grate into fine, slender strips. 237

Shrimp. A small and very popular crustacean. 163

Sieve. A utensil made of wire mesh in a bowl shape, fastened into a wire frame. 702

Sift. To pass food through a sieve or a sifter. 406

Sifter. A sieve equipped with scrapers that help food to pass through its holes. 703

Simmer. To cook in water that is below the boiling point. 40

Sirloin. The rear portion of a loin, usually of beef.

Skewer. A long pin, usually metal, on which food is broiled.

A pin used to fasten pieces or sections of food together during cooking.

Skillet. A frypan with high sides, or a gourmet's name for any frypan.

Skim. To remove floating matter from a liquid surface.

Skim Milk (Skimmed Milk). Milk from which all cream has been removed. 196

Slc. Abbreviation for slice.

Slcs. Abbreviation for slices.

Sliver. To cut into long thin pieces.

Slurry. A thin paste produced by mixing a solid (usually powdered) with a liquid.

Smoking. Curing meat, poultry and fish by exposure to wood smoke. 103

Soda. Baking soda (bicarbonate). 409

A soft drink containing carbonated water.

Sodium Bicarbonate. Baking soda, $NaHCO_3$, a white crystalline powder that is the basic ingredient in most chemical leavening compounds. 409

Soft Ball. The stage in candy making when a drop of syrup cooled in water will shape to a soft ball between the fingers. Syrup temperature is then about 234°F. 562

Soft Drink. A drink containing no alcohol.

Soft (Weak) *Flour.* Flour with a low protein (gluten) content. 405

Softener. A substance or device that changes or removes chemicals in hard water. 657

Souffle. A casserole mixture containing a quantity of stiffly beaten egg whites, which rises during cooking. 401

Souffle Dish. A casserole dish with sides that are vertical and are fluted on the outside. 724

Soup. Liquid or partly liquid food made by water cooking of meat, fish and/or vegetables. 481

Spaghetti. Pasta shaped into solid strands, 325

Spare Ribs. A cut of pork including only lower ribs and the meat between them.

Spatula. A turner with a flat narrow blade which is usually flexible. 691

Spice. Any of a number of flavorful, aromatic and/or pungent vegetable substances, mostly tropical, used to season food. 334

Spider. A long-handled iron frying pan.

Spiny Lobster (Rock Lobster). Warm-water lobsters having meaty tails but lacking large claws. 165

Spit. A pointed rod, heavier than a skewer, on which food may be turned and roasted.

Sponge Cake. A light cake made without shortening. 436

Spore. The seed body of a fungus.

A phase of certain bacteria, in which they are dry, hard and resistant to heat.

Squash. The fleshy fruit of trailing vines, eaten as vegetables. 281

Stabilizer. A substance that delays or prevents separation of parts of a mixture. 369

Starch. A carbohydrate found in most plants. It is valuable as a staple food and as a thickening agent. 351, 404

Steam. To cook by direct exposure to steam in a covered pan. 41

Steamer. A double pan, the upper one having a perforated bottom. 717

Steak. A slice of meat, usually beef, and ¾ to 1½ inches thick. 114

Steel. The metal from which knives, major kitchen appliances and many utensils are made. 679

Steep. To soak in hot water to extract flavor. 520

Stew. To simmer or boil gently for a long time. Usually meat or a meat mixture, but may be fruit.

A mixture of meat, potatoes and vegetables that has been stewed. 391

Stir. To move a spoon or other tool through a liquid or loose substance with a generally circular motion. 17

Stock. A liquid base for soups and gravies made by simmering meat or fish remnants, then skimming and straining.

Stone-ground. Slowly and coarsely ground between old fashioned millstones.

Strain. To pass foods through a strainer, sieve or cloth to remove oversize pieces or impurities.

Strainer. Any device that will pass liquids or fine particles and hold back coarse pieces. Usually a sieve or a colander, but not a sifter or a food mill. 702

Strawberry. A large, flavorful berry. 309

String Bean (Green Bean). Beans grown for their slender green pods, which are eaten when immature. 241

Stuff. In cookery, to fill a cavity or heap a hollow with soft, seasoned material.

Stuffing. A seasoned mixture, usually mostly bread crumbs, used to fill the cavity of a fowl, fish or vegetable before roasting or baking. 141

Sublime. To change from a solid state to vapor, without liquefying. 594

Succotash. A mixture of kernel corn and lima beans, preferably cooked together. 244

Sucrose. The sugar extracted from sugar cane and sugar beets. It is our standard white sugar. 341

Sugar. Any of a number of water-soluble carbohydrates important in life systems of plants and animals.

In cookery, white granulated sugar consisting of sucrose obtained from sugar beets and sugar cane. 341

Sugar Beet. A rather unsweet, turnip-like beet root that is an important source of white sugar.

Sugar Cane. A tall, perennial, tropical grass that stores sucrose sugar in its stalks.

Sugar Maple. The northeastern maple tree from whose sap maple sugar and syrup are obtained.

Surface Tension. In a liquid, inward attraction of the molecules that tends to hold its surface together. 653

Surfactant. A substance that reduces the surface tension of water and increases its dissolving power. 652, 656

Sweetbreads. Thymus glands (neck or throat sweetbreads) or pancreas glands (stomach sweetbreads) of young animals. 132

Sweet Butter. Butter to which no salt has been added. 215

Sweet Corn. Corn that is intended to be eaten in the milk stage as a vegetable, rather than allowed to mature for grain. 254

Sweet Milk. Whole milk that is fresh and unsoured.

Sweet Pepper. A mild flavored pepper used as a vegetable, either when immature and green or mature and red. 272

Sweet Potato. The fleshy, tuberous root of a vine in the morning glory family. It has yellow or orange flesh, is sweet, and is usually baked or boiled. 278

Syrup (Sirup). A sweet, more or less thick liquid used to sweeten and embellish desserts and pancakes, and for preserving fruit. 375

T

Table Salt. Salt (sodium chloride) that has been highly purified and finely ground. Tiny amounts of other substances may be added to reduce caking. **331**

Tannin. Bitter, astringent vegetable compounds widely found in foods, particularly tea. **519**

Tapioca. A starchy substance obtained from cassava root, used chiefly as a thickening agent, or as a principal ingredient in desserts. **534**

Tart. A taste that is sharp or sour, but not disagreeable.

A very small pie (one portion), often having only bottom crust.

Tb. Abbreviation for tablespoon.

Tartar (tartare) *Sauce.* A sauce served with sea food, made with mayonnaise and a wide choice of other ingredients. **361**

Tartrate. A compound of tartaric acid, usually cream of tartar; or a baking powder containing cream of tartar. **408**

Tea. A drink made from the leaves of the tea plant. **518**

A tropical plant with aromatic leaves.

An afternoon meal.

Teflon. The trade name for a fluorocarbon resin, used as a coating on the inside surfaces of pans, which has remarkable non-stick qualities. **713**

Tenderizer. A substance such as papain that softens or weakens meat fibers to make it easier to cut or chew. **106**

Thicken. To increase the thickness (viscosity) of a liquid by adding thickening agents, or by boiling away part of its water.

Thickener (Thickening Agent). A substance that can make a liquid thicker, usually by absorbing water molecules into a loose soft structure. Starch, gelatin and pectin are the principal thickeners for home use. **349**

Tinware. Light pans for use in the oven. Formerly tin-plated steel, they are now usually aluminum. **415, 720**

Toast. To brown, crisp and/or dry by direct heat. **735**

Toasted bread.

Tomato. A large, soft juicy fruit, red or yellow in color, that is used both raw and cooked, as a salad ingredient, a vegetable and a flavoring. **283**

Tomato Paste. A thick, concentrated tomato purée.

Topping. Any food that is placed in a thin layer on top of another food, for flavor or decoration. **441**

Toss. To turn or mix food by flipping the pan, or by chiefly up-and-down motions of a fork and spoon.

Tossed Salad. A salad containing greens, chopped vegetables and dressing, that is mixed at the table. **490**

Trivet. A low stand that can hold meat out of the juices in a roasting pan, or support hot dishes at the table.

Trichinosis. A disease caused by nematodes that are found in pork. They can be killed by thorough cooking or prolonged freezing. **121**

Truss. To tie the legs and wings of a bird close to the body before roasting. **142**

Tsp. Abbreviation for teaspoon.

Tube Pan. A ring-shaped pan with sloped sides and core, that can be rested upside down on brackets. It is used for baking sponge and angel food cakes. **722**

Tuna Fish. The canned meat of large marine fishes related to the mackerel, which is a staple American food.

Turkey. A very large bird, served chiefly as a roast on holidays and at big meals. **148**

Turner. A kitchen tool with a wide, usually somewhat flexible blade that is used for turning and removing pan-fried food. **690**

Twist. A strip of paper or plastic, usually containing a fine wire, which can be twisted around the neck of a bag to seal it. **574**

U

Unmold. To remove a food, usually jelly, from a mold or other container in one piece. **498**

Upside-down cake. A cake which is baked over a layer of fruit and is turned upside down when served. **553**

Utensil. A tool, implement or container used in the kitchen.

V

Vanilla. A popular flavor obtained from the pods (beans) of a tropical vine. Most used here in the form of an alcohol extract. **337**

Variety Meats. Edible organs of animals. **130**

Veal. The flesh of calves, which are beef animals less than a year old. **116**

Vegetable. Any edible plant part that is not a fruit regularly served for dessert. 223

Vegetable Oil. Any edible oil obtained from plant seeds or fruits.

Venturi. A mixing device in which a narrow high pressure spray of gas or liquid pulls another substance with it through a larger exit passage.

Vermicelli. Pasta made into very slender rods, thinner than spaghetti. 326

Vinegar. Dilute acetic acid, obtained by secondary fermentation of fruit juice or by distillation of fermenting grain. 336

Viscera. The internal organs of any animal.

Viscosity. The thickness or resistance to flow of a liquid. 655

Vitamin. A complex organic compound that acts as a catalyst in body processes. 632

W

Waffle. A crisp flat cake, baked in a double griddle that marks it with a deep pattern, usually squares. 445

Walnut. Usually the English walnut, which is large with a wrinkled shell. Meats are sweet and easily removed.

Watermelon. A melon that has seeds sparsely distributed through its flesh. It may be very large. 313

Waxy Maize. A special variety of corn whose starch will not form a gel or jelly. 356

Wet Peaks (Soft Peaks). The condition of meringue when it clings to a beater as it is raised, and is left standing in a peak. 410

Wetting Power. The ability of a chemical to reduce the surface tension of water, and to soak into fine spaces. 654

Wheat Germ. The embryo of a wheat grain. 317

Whey. A clear liquid that separates from the curd when milk is curdled. 197

Whip. To beat vigorously in such a manner as to introduce air into a mixture. 18

A light, frothy dessert.

Whipped Butter. Butter that contains about 25% air, making it bulkier and softer. 214

Whipping Cream. May refer to any cream with enough butterfat (usually 30% or more) to be suitable for whipping, or may mean only heavy cream, with about 40% fat. 199

White Cake. Cake made without egg yolks. 434

White Flour. Flour made from wheat grains that have been stripped of bran and germ. The unmodified word "flour" in a recipe means white flour. 354, 403

White Pepper. Ground pepper, prepared from peppercorns whose black skins have been removed. 335

White Rice. Rice from which hulls and bran have been removed. This is what is meant by the unmodified word "rice" in a recipe. 318

White Sauce (Cream Sauce). A basic sauce made of flour, butter and milk. 357

Whole Milk. Milk from which nothing has been removed. The unmodified word "milk" in a recipe always means whole, sweet milk. 193

Whole Wheat. Descriptive of flour or baked goods made from the entire wheat kernel. 406

Wild Rice. A rice-like grain that grows in shallow northern lakes, is very expensive and is considered a delicacy.

Wine. Fermented juice of grapes or berries, but non-grape wine must carry the name of the berry used.

Y

Yam. A root vegetable similar to the sweet potato, but with flesh that is usually deeper in color and more moist. 278

Yeast. A microsonic one-celled organism chiefly noted for its ability to change sugar to carbon dioxide and alcohol. The carbon dioxide leavens bread, the alcohol is the important factor in wine-making. 406

Yogurt. A thick, smooth, sour milk produced by action of special strains of bacteria. 205

Yolk. The yellow part of an egg. 172

Yorkshire Pudding. A popover that is supposed to be baked in a pan with beef drippings.

Z

Zucchini. A green summer squash. 281

INDEX

This INDEX covers the text, the illustrations, and the Appendix.

Boldface type is used to emphasize the more important references in a group. Chapter and book titles are in small capitals.

When there is a question about whether a compound word such as "cornstarch" is one word or two, it has been divided and treated as two.

In an index of this size, it is not possible to entirely avoid omissions and errors. Lack of a reference therefore does not necessarily mean that the desired information is not in the book. It might be listed under related subjects, or in the Table of Contents.